P9-CEV-332

OZ CLARKE'S WINE ATLAS

OZ CLARKE'S

WINE ATLAS

WINES & WINE REGIONS OF THE WORLD

PANORAMIC MAPS PAINTED BY KEITH & SUE GAGE

LITTLE, BROWN AND COMPANY

BOSTON NEW YORK TORONTO LONDON

First Edition

ISBN 0-316-14697-8
Library of Congress Catalog Card Number 95-76295
A CIP catalogue for this book is available from the British Library

Created and designed by Websters International Publishers
Axe and Bottle Court, 70 Newcomen Street, London SE1 1YT

10 9 8 7 6 5 4 3 2 1

Published simultaneously in the United States of America by Little, Brown and Company (Inc.), in Great Britain by Little, Brown and Company (UK), and in Canada by Little, Brown & Company (Canada) Limited

Colour separations by Columbia Offset, Singapore

Printed in Italy by Officine Grafiche De Agostini, Novara

Page 1: Vineyards in the Cantabrian foothills in Rioja Alavesa, northern Spain; pages 2–3: Detail from the panoramic map of Napa Valley, Sonoma Valley and Carneros, northern California

Project Editor Fiona Holman
Project Art Director Jason Vrakas
Art Editor Victor-Manuel Ibañez
Senior Sub-Editor Celia Woolfrey
Designers Adelle Morris, David Brown
Assistant Editors Julia Colbourne, Sara Harper, Pauline Savage
Additional Editorial Assistance and Research Phil Cooper, Annie Hubert, Jennifer Mussett, Lyn Parry, Kim Parsons, Jane Shaw
Desktop Publishing Jonathan Harley
Index Naomi Good
Production Charles James
Associate Editors Susy Atkins, David Gleave, Dave Hughes, Richard Mayson, Richard Neill, Margaret Rand, Simon Woods
Consultant Geologist Professor Jake Hancock

Pictorial Cartography Keith and Sue Gage of Contour Designs, assisted by Joe Wilkes, Linda Leggate, Katy McFarlane, Sue Cowell, Doreen King
Pictorial Map Editor Wink Lorch
Schematic Maps compiled by Andrew Thompson
Schematic Maps European Map Graphics
Illustrations Aziz Khan, James Robins, Coral Mula
Studio Photography Stephen Marwood

Further acknowledgments are on page 320

UNDERSTANDING THE MAPS

There are two styles of map in this Atlas – the handpainted panoramic vineyard maps, which are the main feature, and the more conventional regional and country maps.

- **The panoramic maps** These are detailed artists' renderings of the world's great vineyard areas. In many areas, the vineyards have never been mapped before. In every case we have checked locations with local organizations and/or individual winemakers, but total accuracy is almost impossible as plantings are changing all the time. In some New World areas massive planting is taking place, while in some outlying European areas vineyards are being grubbed up. As well as vineyards, general landscape features, such as forests, rivers and mountains, have been painted as accurately as possible. All the panoramic maps have an element of perspective and this inevitably introduces slight distortion; a vineyard or village in the north, at the top of a map, will appear smaller than one in the foreground. Scale bars indicate distances covered from east to west. However, because of the effect of perspective, total distances are given from north to south. Map colours are appropriate for late summer, just before the grape harvest. The vineyards have been painted bright green, with surrounding land often yellow or brown as other crops have usually been harvested by this time. Field boundaries and vine row directions are mainly notional.

Where annotation is shown, it is minimal so as not to spoil the effect. More detail is given on the key maps that accompany the most detailed maps. Wineries are located at the main installation, not necessarily the tasting or visitors' centre. 'Top Vineyards, Châteaux and Wineries' shown are the author's personal selection.

- **Other wine maps** Wine regions shown on these maps are official growing areas (the panoramic maps show planted vineyard areas). To the best of our knowledge, boundaries are correct at the time of going to press. If you have more up-to-date information we would be delighted to hear from you.

CONTENTS

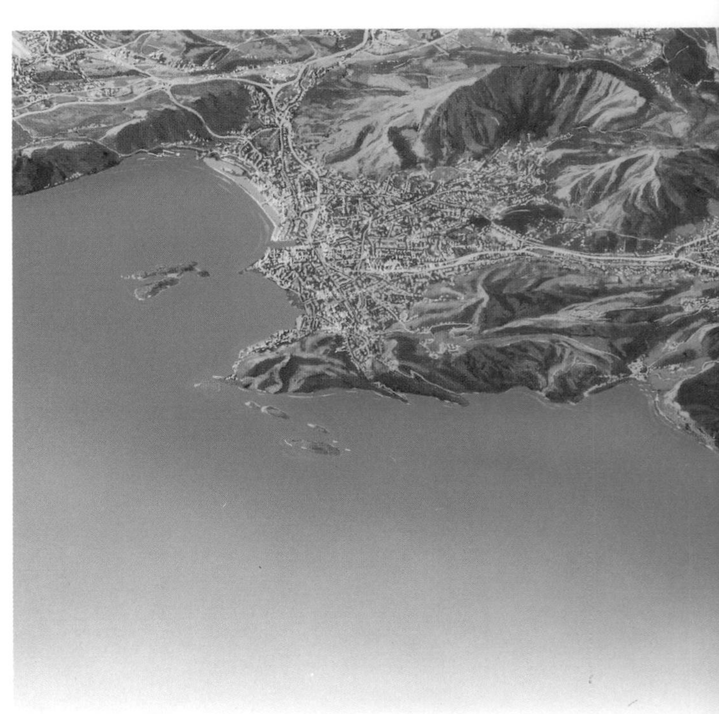

A small chapel separates the Schönhell and Würzgarten vineyards in the village of Hallgarten, Rheingau.

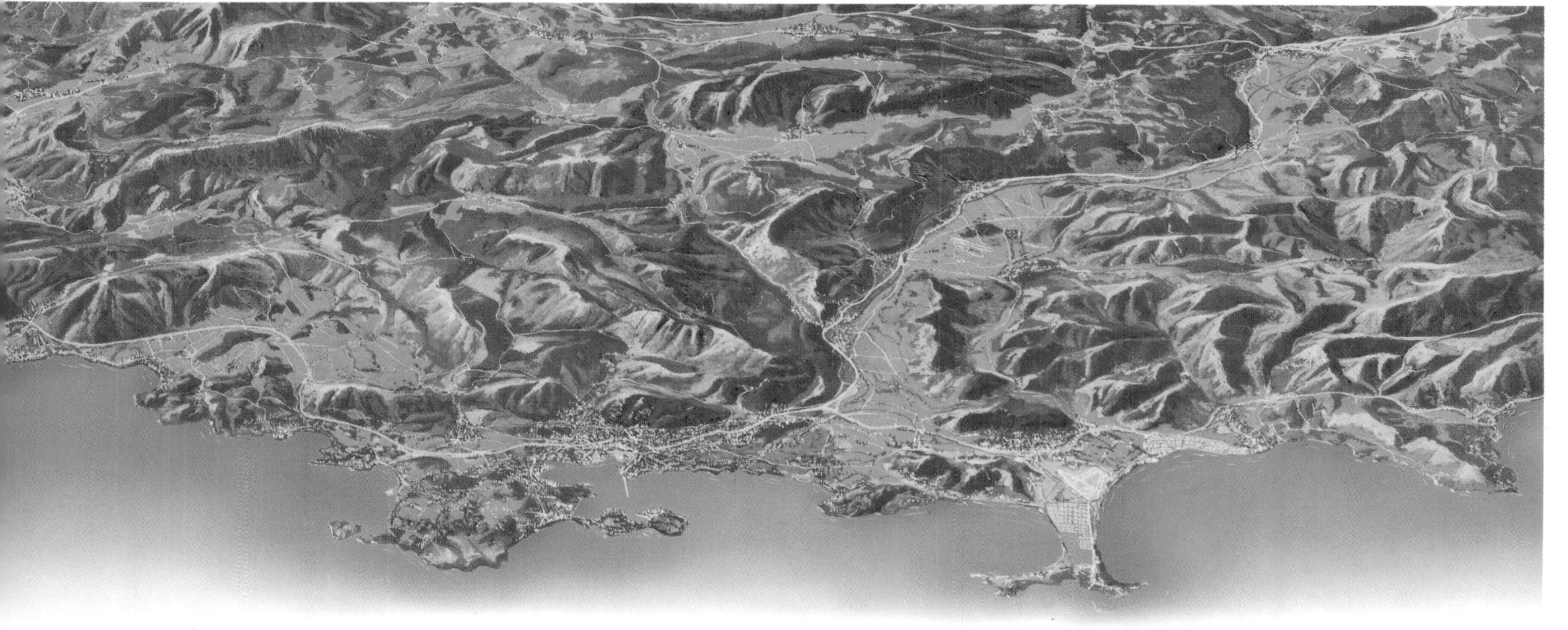

Detail from the panoramic map of Provence, southern France.

Detail from the panoramic map of the Brunello di Montalcino wine area in southern Tuscany, famed for its dark Sangiovese wines.

Harvesting Airén grapes in La Mancha on Spain's vast, windswept central plateau.

The high-altitude Delatite vineyards, up on the northern slopes of the Great Dividing Range in Victoria, produce aromatic dry whites and fruity reds.

INTRODUCTION

Mountains, here the Massif du Canigou, form a spectacular backdrop to many of the Roussillon vineyards in southern France.

THESE DAYS, WHEN I VISIT A WINE REGION, I no longer say, show me the wineries, show me their shining new stainless steel tanks, show me their fragrant new French oak barrels. No. I say, show me the land. Show me the vines and where they grow. It's not that I haven't always been interested in the vineyards – I've spent a substantial amount of time ever since I was a student poking about in them in every corner of the globe. It's just that the emphasis has changed: we are now in the second phase of a great revolution in wine. The first phase was to do with the winery. Dramatic progress in understanding fermentation and how to extract the best possible flavour and character from the grapes was paralleled by an explosion in high-quality winery equipment across the world. A global invasion of so-called 'flying winemakers' followed – highly proficient winemakers (usually Antipodean) who would impose a modern regime wherever they landed, and who generally have managed to transform mediocrity into quality even in the most backward and inhospitable of locales. This has led to a situation whereby the world now has more decent, clean affordable wine to drink than ever before.

So it's time for the second phase. Every good winemaker in every country in the world knows that the final limiting factor on wine quality is the quality of the grapes. And every winemaker knows that some regions grow better grapes than others, some areas within those regions are more suitable, some small patches of the very same field are better than others – and some growers care more about their work and will always produce the finest fruit.

This second phase of the wine revolution is rooted firmly in the vineyard. And that is why you are now far more likely to find me out there among the vines rather than seated at the tasting table. If I am in Côte-Rôtie, I want to climb to the highest point on the slope from whose grapes the juice always runs blackest and sweetest. I want to stand with my face held up to the sun, imagining how it creeps into view at dawn and fades with the evening shadows. I want to feel the poor stony soil crumble beneath my feet and touch the twisted, tortured trunk of the vine which each year struggles to survive on this barren slope and ripen its tiny crop. If I'm in Margaux, I want to tread the warm, well-drained gravel outcrops and then step off into the sullen clay swamps nearby and know why the gravel-grown grapes are precious and the clay-clogged ones are not. I want to see the Andes water gushing down off the mountains into the fertile vineyards of Chile's Maipo Valley. I want to feel the howling mists chill me to the bone in California's Carneros, and then feel the warm winds of New Zealand's Marlborough tugging at my hair. I want it all to make sense.

And I hope this Atlas will help. I was convinced I wanted to write it as soon as I saw the prototype. It was a map of Chablis, the one on the front of the jacket. I saw the town, the little valleys, I saw which hills were high, which were low, which faced the sun, and which were protected from the wind. I had never seen a map before that made me exult in the sense of place like this one. Suddenly it was blindingly obvious why the Grand Cru wines were riper, fatter, more intense, why the Premier Cru wines were better than basic Chablis. I had walked through all the vineyards, but this new perspective was shattering. It was as though I was hovering in a helicopter directly above the vines, able to dip down and swoop in and out of every tiny twist in the slope, through every gully, round every outcrop of rock. The roads and railways I had travelled, the rivers and hilltops I'd used for reference – all were set out before me.

So what we have tried to achieve in these brilliant maps is a grand aerial tour of the world's vineyards. Focussing minutely on areas where there are particularly exciting features dictating the character of the wine, but also taking a broader regional view to put the world's great vineyards into context. And in my writing, I have tried to achieve a distillation of all that

Vines snake across the low Carneros hills, one of California's top, cool-climate wine areas.

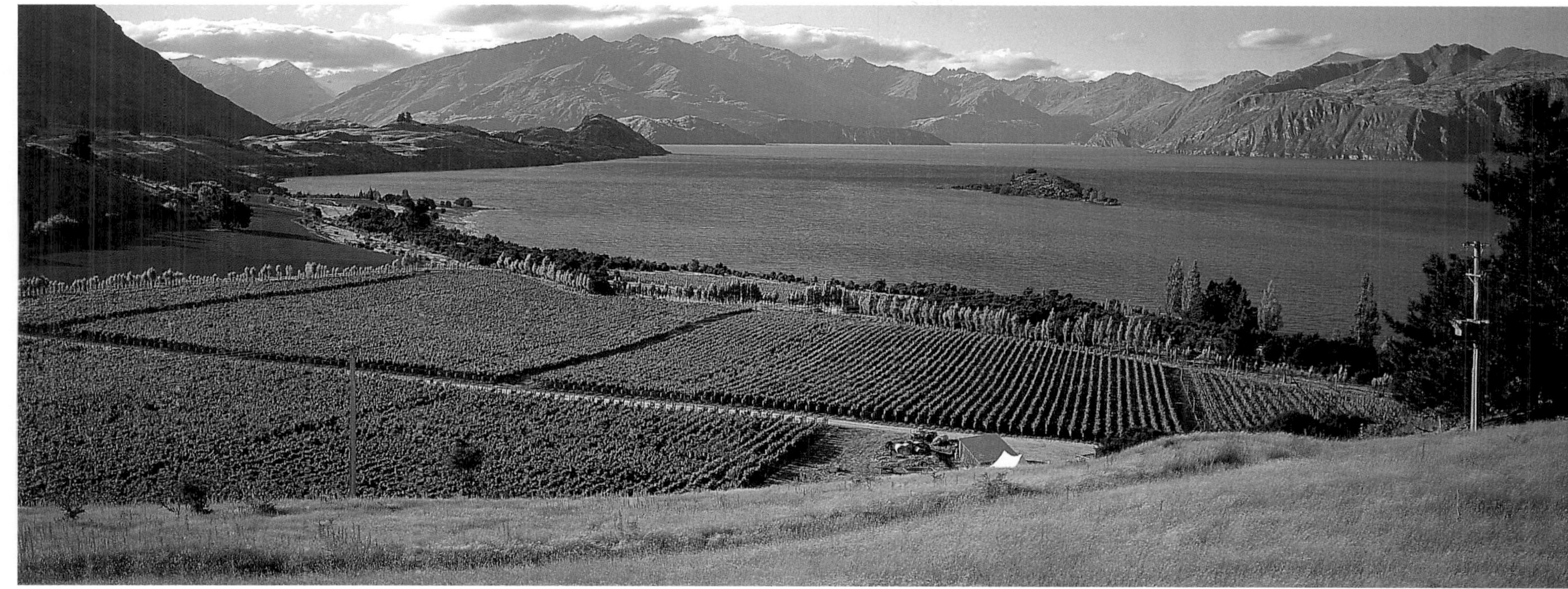

The Rippon Vineyard enjoys a glorious setting on the slopes of Lake Wanaka in Central Otago on South Island, one of New Zealand's exciting new wine regions.

travelling I have done since student days. Some villages and their vines seem unchanged since then and may still be unchanged a hundred years from now. Has anything much really changed in the quiet communities of Burgundy's Côte d'Or, in the hamlets high up in Portugal's Douro Valley towards the Spanish border, in the friendless huddles of huts on Spain's bleak La Mancha plain? In other places, there were no vines at all when I first passed through, yet now they stretch as far as the eye can see. The North Fork of Long Island, New York, was all potatoes when I first went there. A 100-hectare (250-acre) vineyard now carpets the English North Downs near Dorking, making my childhood memories of pastureland and copses of tall, dark trees seem ever so long ago. Some places seem to have slipped into poverty and decline. Others have a Klondike air as the gaze of fashion turns upon them and their wines, and every available scrap of land is planted up with vines. I just hope that when the dust settles in Coonawarra or Hawke's Bay, the right vines will have been planted on the right soils by the right people. And in this age when change has come faster than ever before in the world of wine, it is equally certain that within the decade some of those now in decline will be fired by a new confidence and popularity; others now considered so chic will be struggling in the tough real world as their first flush of fame dissolves; and yet others, at this moment mere pastureland or rocky mountainside, will become flourishing vineyards producing wines whose flavours may be entirely different to anything yet achieved on this planet.

And through all this will run the constant theme: the relationship between the land and its climate, the grape varieties planted, and the commitment of the winemakers concerned.

These elements have always been intrinsically connected, yet frequently the relationship has been an insincere one because the history of wine is littered with examples of human endeavour failing to match the quality of a site. To say that a piece of land is a great vineyard site is only to say that it has the potential to produce great wine, so long as the right grapes are planted and the desire for greatness burns brightly in the breasts of the growers. Even today I doubt whether half the long-established great vineyard sites of the world are being farmed in such a way as to maximize quality. Even now, our shelves are littered with wines from supposedly great vineyard sites in Germany, Italy, France and Spain that do no credit to the producers and bring shame on the great names they bear.

But just as the massive advances in wine-making technology made available excellent wine from areas that had never before excelled, so the dramatic progress made in vineyard management and the manipulation of the vine, enabling it to perform well in less than perfect mesoclimates, has made the definition of a great site today far more wide-reaching than ever before. Wine styles that were lauded a generation ago may not be appreciated now; wines that are lapped up with enthusiasm these days have flavours that weren't possible a generation ago. Things are moving so fast that a rearguard action is being fought by those fearful of change. It is a misguided battle. It is leading to much pointless and sterile argument about modern styles of wine versus traditional styles, about wines that supposedly taste of their birthplace – their *terroir*, to use the French term – as against wines that merely taste of the grape.

These arguments lead nowhere. If modern 'technological' wine is derided then equally we must discount the efforts of the technologically impressive quality leaders in Bordeaux, Burgundy, Piedmont, the Douro and the Mosel. As for *terroir* – virtually any wine of any quality tastes of where it was grown, in that the soil, the climate and the weather conditions have all influenced the composition of the grape. That so many talented new winemakers can make great wines from grapes grown in areas previously unregarded or entirely new to the vine is a cause for rejoicing not recrimination. This Atlas celebrates the new as much as the old, the iconoclastic as much as the traditional, the courageous and crazy as much as the conservative and complacent. It is an Atlas of yesterday and today for today and tomorrow.

An Atlas is a book of images. With my words I have tried to flesh out these images, to give the extra dimension of personal experience and opinion. But in the end, it is the breathtaking majesty of the maps that matters, their thrilling demonstration of the whole landscape in which wine is created. Add to these maps some photographs of such allure that I want to pack my bags and head off whenever I open the pages, and we have the heart of this book.

In this Atlas I've tried to show the world of wine in all its natural, timeless beauty. A vineyard evolves. It is not about political wrangling, about special interest pleading protectionist legislation. It is about a piece of soil, the sun, the wind and the rain, and the happy chance of men and women wanting to love that place, cherish it and, through their vines and the wines they make, bring it to its fullest expression. Wherever those vineyards are, whether they are great or small, famous or unknown, I dedicate this book to them and to those who care for them.

THE WORLD OF WINE

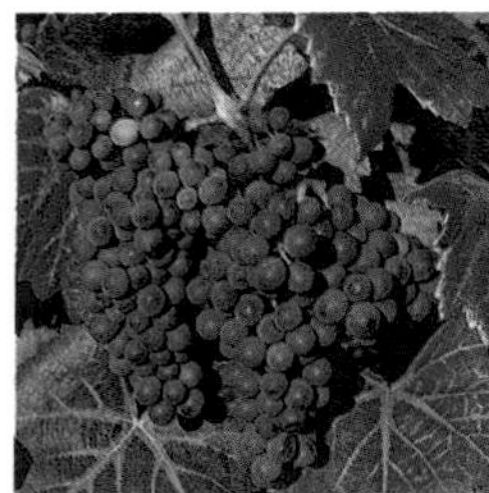

A COUPLE OF THOUSANDS YEARS AGO, this map of the world of wine would have looked very different. The densest concentration of vineyards and the highest consumption of wine would have been in the Middle East and the Eastern Mediterranean, and Greece and Italy would have contributed quite a bit too. But the rest of Western Europe would hardly have registered at all – and the rest of the world hadn't been discovered yet!

The adoption of Islam by most Middle Eastern and North African countries, with its prohibition of alcohol, has meant that, though vineyards there still survive and flourish, hardly any of them produce grapes for wine – consumption is neglible now in the countries that first discovered wine – and the centre of wine production has shifted to Western Europe, in particular to the countries of Italy, France and Spain where an entire gastronomic culture has built up centred on wine and where there are thousands of individual wines. Some of these are traditional classics of international reknown but many others are of local interest only. And as pioneers from Europe settled in far-flung corners of the globe, they took with them the European wine-drinking culture. There are now significant contributions to the world of wine from many of thes newer wine regions, especially California and other regions of North America and, in the southern hemisphere, South Africa, Australia and New Zealand.

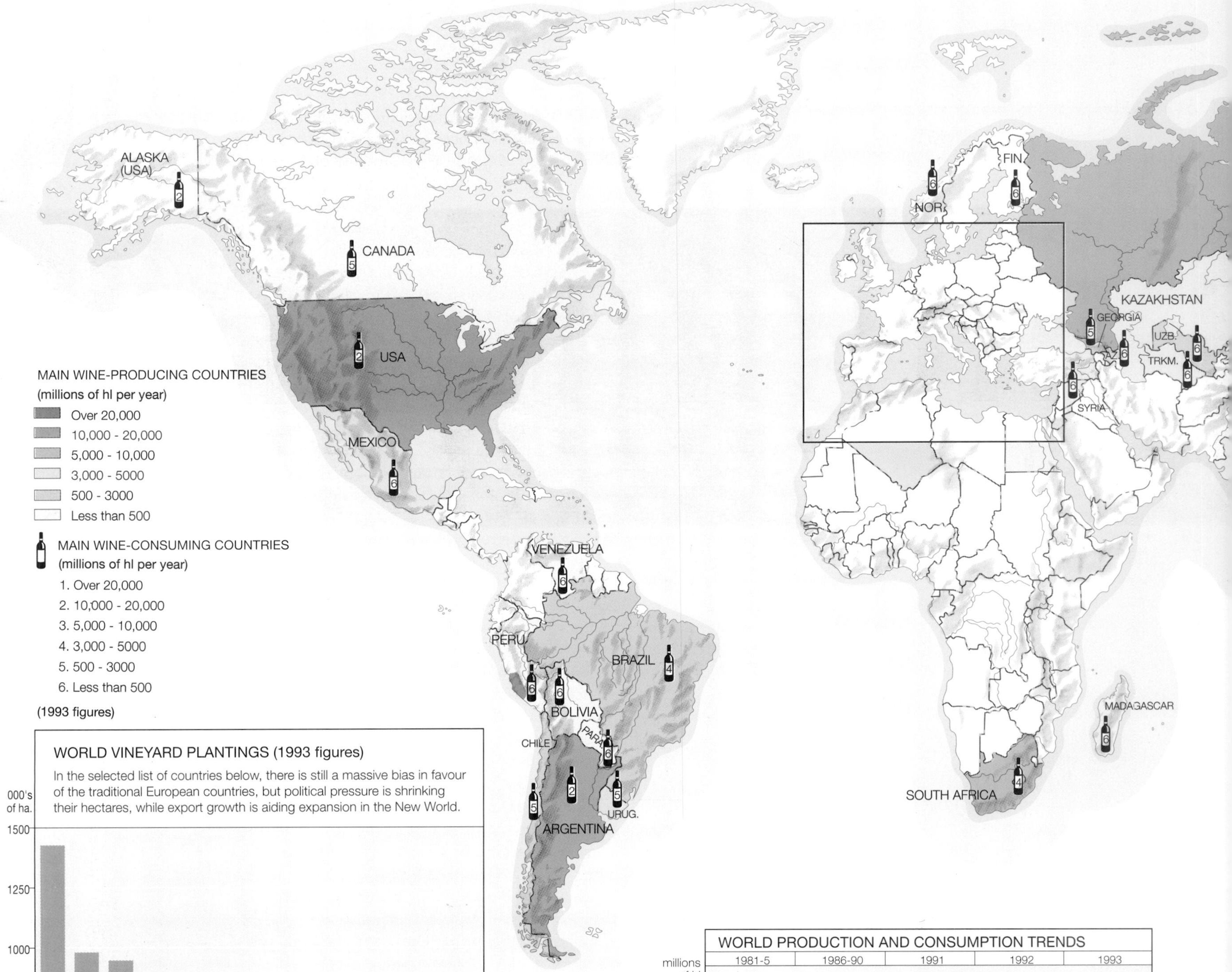

ALASKA (USA) 2
CANADA 5
USA 2
MEXICO 6
VENEZUELA 6
PERU 6
BRAZIL 4
BOLIVIA 6
CHILE 5
PARA. 6
URUG. 5
ARGENTINA 2
NOR 6
FIN 6
KAZAKHSTAN
GEORGIA 5
UZB. 6
TRKM. 6
SYRIA 6
MADAGASCAR 6
SOUTH AFRICA 4

MAIN WINE-PRODUCING COUNTRIES
(millions of hl per year)

- Over 20,000
- 10,000 - 20,000
- 5,000 - 10,000
- 3,000 - 5000
- 500 - 3000
- Less than 500

MAIN WINE-CONSUMING COUNTRIES
(millions of hl per year)

1. Over 20,000
2. 10,000 - 20,000
3. 5,000 - 10,000
4. 3,000 - 5000
5. 500 - 3000
6. Less than 500

(1993 figures)

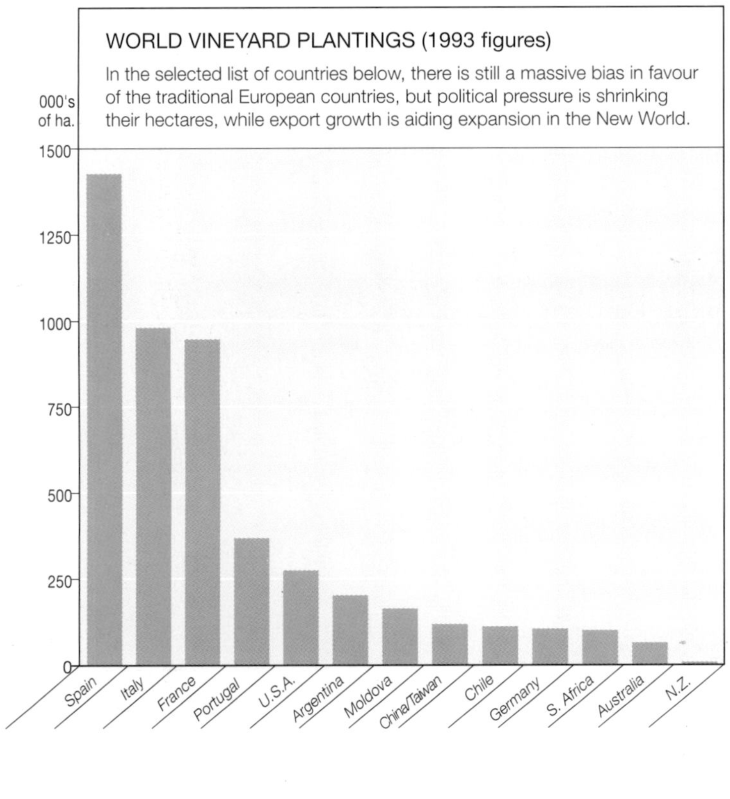

WORLD VINEYARD PLANTINGS (1993 figures)

In the selected list of countries below, there is still a massive bias in favour of the traditional European countries, but political pressure is shrinking their hectares, while export growth is aiding expansion in the New World.

000's of ha.
1500
1250
1000
750
500
250
0

Spain, Italy, France, Portugal, U.S.A., Argentina, Moldova, China/Taiwan, Chile, Germany, S. Africa, Australia, N.Z.

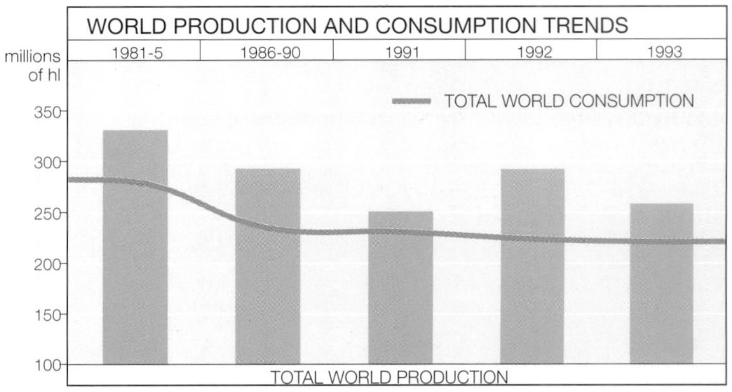

WORLD PRODUCTION AND CONSUMPTION TRENDS

millions of hl
1981-5, 1986-90, 1991, 1992, 1993
TOTAL WORLD CONSUMPTION
350
300
250
200
150
100
TOTAL WORLD PRODUCTION

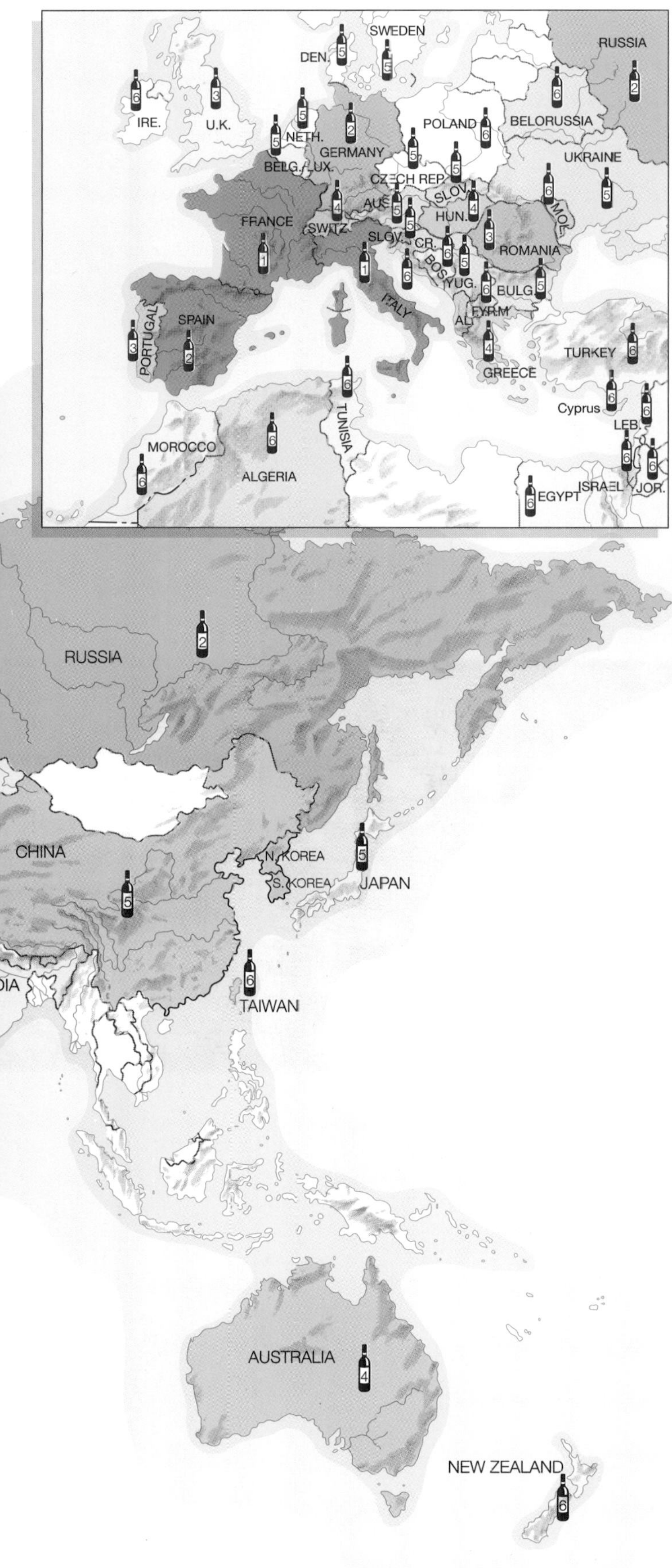

WINE PRODUCTION AND CONSUMPTION

Our map of the world shows where wine is made and where it is drunk. The countries in the darkest colour are those producing the most wine – Italy and France, followed by Spain. Although these three countries still top the world league, in recent years they have undergone steep declines, both in their total vineyard plantings and in the amount of wine produced.

Italy's vineyards have shrunk from 1,215,000 hectares (3,002,224 acres) in the early 1980s to 950,000 hectares (2,347,418 acres acres) now – and the figure is still falling. Interestingly, production has only fallen by 14 per cent over the same period, reflecting increased efficiency in the vineyards. Indeed, there is no major wine-producing country in the world registering an increase in vineyards, and the global figure has fallen 15 per cent from 9,823,000 hectares (24,272,300 acres) in the early 1980s to 8,281,000 (20,462,070) in 1993. But note the figure for China/Taiwan: vineyards have increased here since the early 1980s from 34,000 hectares (84,013 acres) to 168,000 hectares (415,122 acres) in 1993 and production has risen from 1,502,000 to 3,500,000 hectolitres in 1993. Global wine production in the same period has fallen by 22.3 per cent from 333,568,000 to 259,269,000 hectolitres in 1993.

Consumption has also fallen worldwide, particularly in the traditional European wine nations, France, Italy and Spain. Only Portugal of the leading producers seems to be holding firm. What is happening is that wine as the everyday beverage is being replaced, especially by young people, with cola or beer, yet increasingly wine of higher quality is being consumed – although in lower quantities.

Some of the most telling figures demonstrating how the balance of wine is shifting can be seen in the export figures. Taking the early 1980s as our starting point, Italy's exports are well down, France's fairly stable and Spain's well up. Eastern European figures appear depressed because of the collapse of the USSR, their largest customer. But look at the figures for Chile – up from 131,000 to 866,000 hectolitres in 1993; look at South Africa – risen from 68,000 to 250,000 hectolitres. And look at New Zealand – from 3000 in the early 1980s to 86,000 hectolitres in 1993 and still rising. And Australia, from 84,000 to 1,029,000 hectolitres in 1993. That's some change.

If we had to look forward a generation, I suspect we would see quite serious shrinkage among the vineyards of Western Europe, and a decline in wine consumption in traditional wine-producing countries. But we would see a significant increase in vineyards in South America, South Africa and the Antipodes, probably accompanied by increased consumption in South Africa and the Antipodes. And we'd also see a massive increase in production and consumption in China. As some cultures grow tired of the wine tradition, others will discover it. As some societies switch to producing different crops, other societies will plant vineyards with a fury. And as some countries export less, others will dramatically increase the amount they sell abroad.

PRODUCTION AND EXPORTS

= PRODUCTION 1 million hl

= EXPORTS 1 million hl

(1993 figures)

millions of hl

60
50
40
30
20
10
0

N. Z.
Bulgaria
Chile
Moldova
China/Taiwan
Portugal
Australia
S. Africa
Germany
Argentina
U.S.A.
Spain
France
Italy

INCREASING IMPORTANCE OF EXPORT MARKETS

This graph on the right shows how, with falling domestic consumption, export markets are becoming ever more important to world production. Most countries' vineyards developed originally to supply the needs of their own populations. The big exporters of wine tend to be the big producers – Italy and France jostle for top position, with Spain not far behind.

The surge in southern hemisphere production is export-led – for example, New Zealand doubled its exports between 1990 and 1995 alone. The really big exporters in terms of percentage of production are not Italy and France, but Germany, Portugal and Bulgaria who all make wines geared specifically to export markets. Germany exports cheap table wines, Portugal exports masses of port, and Bulgaria sends over all that Cabernet Sauvignon.

THE VINE & ITS ENVIRONMENT

WHEN DID YOU LAST SEE A WILD VINE? The answer, quite possibly, is that you've never seen a wild one. Not really wild. The nearest is probably the kind that respectfully shades the courtyards of Mediterranean cafés. Which is a bit like comparing a dowager's poodle to a dingo.

Wild vines rampage over everything in their path in their determination to find sunlight. They produce leaves and fruit many yards away from their trunks; and if you made wine from their grapes it would be thin, dilute stuff, short on flavour and high on acidity – because the vine doesn't exist to produce wine. It exists to produce grapes and reproduce itself. So when man decides to intervene and turn the vine from its original purpose, he has a fair bit of work on his hands.

The grower must consider every last detail of the vine's environment: the draining capability of the soil and the minerals present in it, the angle of the slope to the sun, the amount of sunshine and rainfall in that particular spot, the strength of the wind and the likelihood of frost. If he is French he will refer to the whole package – climate, soil and exposure – as *terroir*. Every *terroir* is unique, he will say, and the individuality of each is the basis of wine law in his country, so it must be right. His New World counterpart will say that this is nonsense. There are mesoclimates, which are the climatic conditions affecting a whole vineyard, yes, and there are micro-climates, which are the conditions pertaining to the individual vine, but what really matters at the end of the day is how you make the wine. He's saying that all the greatest sites and conditions in the world don't count for a tuppenny damn if you don't make the wine correctly. Of course, they're both right – and both wrong.

The traditional view is that the finest wines come from marginal climates – places where it is almost, but not quite, too cold to ripen those particular grapes. It is where the vine has to struggle to ripen its grapes that the best flavours are found. Long, cool ripening seasons give subtle flavours with a good balance of fruit, alcohol and acidity. In a hot climate like Australia, growers can seek out higher altitudes or places cooled by maritime breezes to provide the sort of temperatures more suitable for growing vines.

That's one reason why hills are important to viticulture; another is that slopes offer better exposure to the sun. They also give better drainage, and like all the factors involved in viticulture, they offer the grower a multitude of choices. At the top of the slope it will be cooler – fine in a hot climate but perhaps too cold in a cool one. Go too far down, though, and you run the risk of frost, since cold air collects in the valley floor and the more fertile soil at the bottom of a slope makes it more difficult to ripen your crop. Then there is the question of which way the slope faces: in the northern hemisphere due south is marvellous, but east-facing slopes will catch the morning sun, west-facing slopes the warm afternoon sun. And while shelter from the wind will make a vineyard warmer, a breeze dries the grapes after a shower so that they don't rot.

And there is the vexed question of soil – vexed because not all agree on its importance. How much does it contribute to the flavour and style of the wine? Riesling, for example, seems to take far more of its flavour from the soil than does Chardonnay. There's no hard-and-fast rule; it depends on the soil, and it depends on the vine.

The vine's environment is so complex and finely balanced that to alter one part of it affects everything else. Pruning, drainage, soil type, and exactly the right amount of sun and rain at the appropriate times are all vital to its development.

CASE STUDY OF A VINEYARD

St-Estèphe is in the north of the Haut-Médoc, and the deep, undulating gravel beds that mark out the best parts of the region are getting a bit sparser here. As a result there are only five Classed Growth châteaux in the commune, and vineyards here are far more likely to make Cru Bourgeois wine than Grand Cru Classé. One of these châteaux, Cos d'Estournel, is in the south of St-Estèphe, and faces Château Lafite (in Pauillac) across the tiny Jalle de Breuil stream that divides the two communes. The land immediately around the stream is low-lying and not planted with vines; but then the ground rises, the gravel takes over again and there is Cos d'Estournel, the best property of the commune.

You can see the slope in the photograph of Cos d'Estournel's vineyards. You can see how dense the gravel is; it's quite warm, heat-retaining soil, and as a result some 60 per cent of the vineyard is planted with Cabernet Sauvignon. It drains well, but there is enough sand in it to ensure that it holds some humidity in the summer to protect the vines from drought. And while the photograph doesn't show the Gironde (it is just over a mile away), the estuary affects the climate of the whole region, softening the extremes of winter and summer. And look how closely the vines are packed in. Growing them cheek by jowl this way reduces yields and increases concentration. It's all part of making the vine work hard for its living.

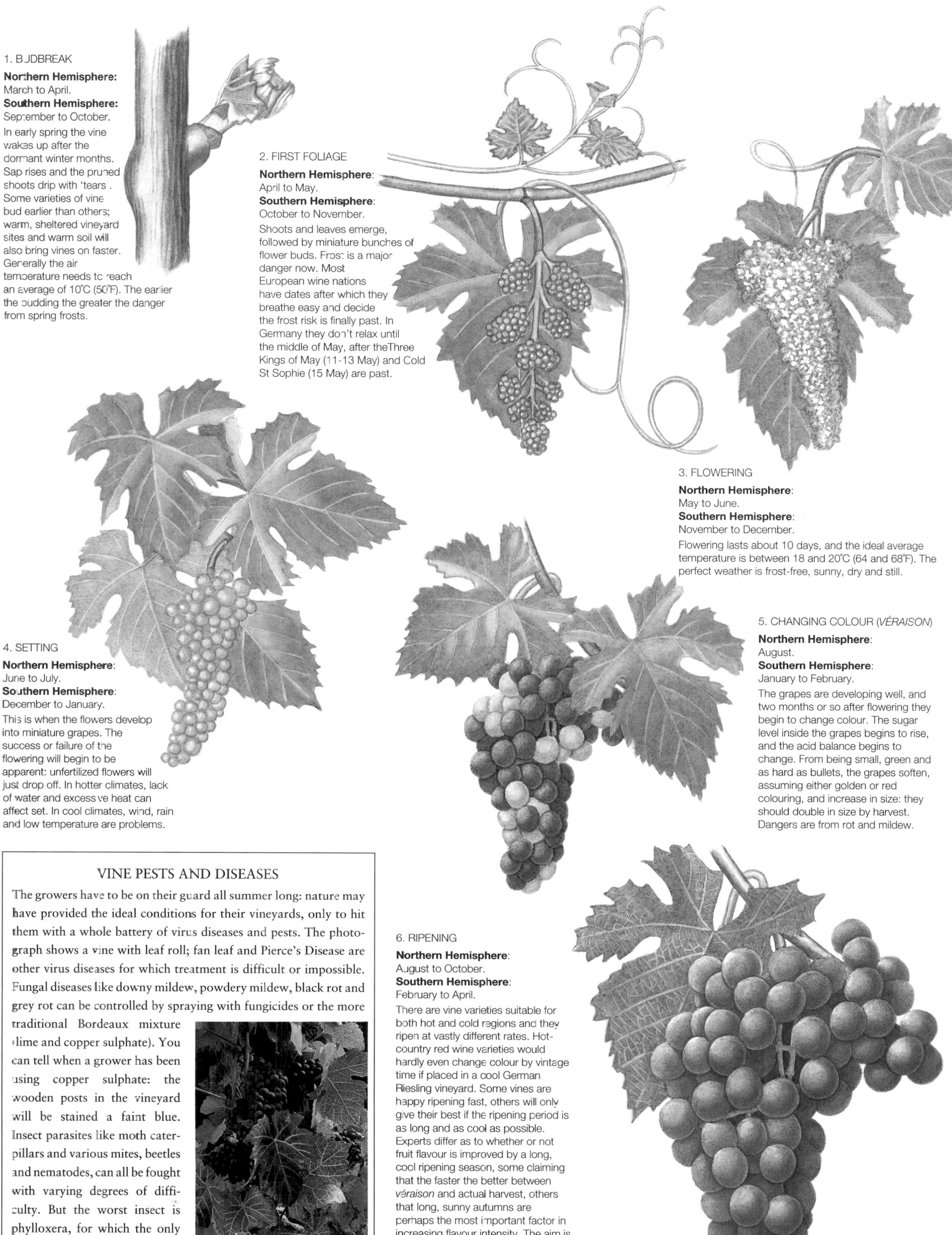

1. BUDBREAK

Northern Hemisphere: March to April.
Southern Hemisphere: September to October.

In early spring the vine wakes up after the dormant winter months. Sap rises and the pruned shoots drip with 'tears'. Some varieties of vine bud earlier than others; warm, sheltered vineyard sites and warm soil will also bring vines on faster. Generally the air temperature needs to reach an average of 10°C (50°F). The earlier the budding the greater the danger from spring frosts.

2. FIRST FOLIAGE

Northern Hemisphere: April to May.
Southern Hemisphere: October to November.

Shoots and leaves emerge, followed by miniature bunches of flower buds. Frost is a major danger now. Most European wine nations have dates after which they breathe easy and decide the frost risk is finally past. In Germany they don't relax until the middle of May, after theThree Kings of May (11-13 May) and Cold St Sophie (15 May) are past.

3. FLOWERING

Northern Hemisphere: May to June.
Southern Hemisphere: November to December.

Flowering lasts about 10 days, and the ideal average temperature is between 18 and 20°C (64 and 68°F). The perfect weather is frost-free, sunny, dry and still.

4. SETTING

Northern Hemisphere: June to July.
Southern Hemisphere: December to January.

This is when the flowers develop into miniature grapes. The success or failure of the flowering will begin to be apparent: unfertilized flowers will just drop off. In hotter climates, lack of water and excessive heat can affect set. In cool climates, wind, rain and low temperature are problems.

5. CHANGING COLOUR (*VÉRAISON*)

Northern Hemisphere: August.
Southern Hemisphere: January to February.

The grapes are developing well, and two months or so after flowering they begin to change colour. The sugar level inside the grapes begins to rise, and the acid balance begins to change. From being small, green and as hard as bullets, the grapes soften, assuming either golden or red colouring, and increase in size: they should double in size by harvest. Dangers are from rot and mildew.

VINE PESTS AND DISEASES

The growers have to be on their guard all summer long: nature may have provided the ideal conditions for their vineyards, only to hit them with a whole battery of virus diseases and pests. The photograph shows a vine with leaf roll; fan leaf and Pierce's Disease are other virus diseases for which treatment is difficult or impossible. Fungal diseases like downy mildew, powdery mildew, black rot and grey rot can be controlled by spraying with fungicides or the more traditional Bordeaux mixture (lime and copper sulphate). You can tell when a grower has been using copper sulphate: the wooden posts in the vineyard will be stained a faint blue. Insect parasites like moth caterpillars and various mites, beetles and nematodes, can all be fought with varying degrees of difficulty. But the worst insect is phylloxera, for which the only answer is to graft the vines on to resistant rootstock.

6. RIPENING

Northern Hemisphere: August to October.
Southern Hemisphere: February to April.

There are vine varieties suitable for both hot and cold regions and they ripen at vastly different rates. Hot-country red wine varieties would hardly even change colour by vintage time if placed in a cool German Riesling vineyard. Some vines are happy ripening fast, others will only give their best if the ripening period is as long and as cool as possible. Experts differ as to whether or not fruit flavour is improved by a long, cool ripening season, some claiming that the faster the better between *véraison* and actual harvest, others that long, sunny autumns are perhaps the most important factor in increasing flavour intensity. The aim is to build sufficient sugar in the grape, while keeping acidity in balance, and, for reds, getting the right amount of tannin and colour.

WORLD CLIMATE & VINEYARDS

IF IT WEREN'T FOR THE GULF STREAM current warming up the west coast of France, we'd have no Classed Growth Médoc reds. If it weren't for the sea fogs cooling down the west coast of California we'd have no Napa Valley Cabernets. If it weren't for the cold Benguela current from the Antarctic soothing the fevered brow of the Western Cape, South Africa would be far too hot to make exciting table wines. And thank goodness for the rain-shadows of Washington State in the USA, of Marlborough in New Zealand and Alsace in France that create a long, dry autumn which lets fruit hang confidently on the vine and ripen magnificently against all the odds. Thank goodness, too, for the tempering effects of Lakes Ontario and Erie on the Canada/USA border. Without these huge lakes, there'd be no Ontario wine industry and no grapes would ripen in Ohio or upstate New York.

But on the other hand – damn those late spring frosts that appear out of the calm April night skies and decimate the crop in Chablis, damn the drought that creeps up unnoticed in Australia's New South Wales, stressing the hardiest vines almost beyond endurance. Damn the cyclonic storms of autumn that sweep in on Gisborne and Hawke's Bay in New Zealand and dump a month's rain in an hour on vines so tantalizingly, agonizingly close to perfect ripeness. And for that matter – damn the damp grey clouds that sit like sullen duennas over the South Downs of England from spring to autumn, spoiling the chances of decent cricket and a decent wine vintage. It's the world's climate in all its variety. One of the things that becomes ever more evident as the debate on global warming rages, is that all the climates of the world are interlinked, and whatever happens in one place will set off chain reactions that will affect conditions right round the world.

Right the way through the Atlas I'll be talking about climate conditions and how they affect individual vineyards. The elements of climate that are most relevant to viticulture are temperatures – obviously you need a certain level to ripen grapes; variability of day and night temperatures; continentality, or the difference between winter and summer temperatures; actual sunlight; rainfall and an area's relative humidity; and wind. The best vineyard sites have traditionally been fairly cool ones, with a measure of summer rainfall and long, dry autumns, or those with Mediterranean climatic conditions, with winter rainfall, relatively high temperatures and ideally, moderating maritime breezes. In the Old World grape growers have slowly discovered the best conditions over the centuries. In the New World, every year brings the discovery of new and exciting sites for vines.

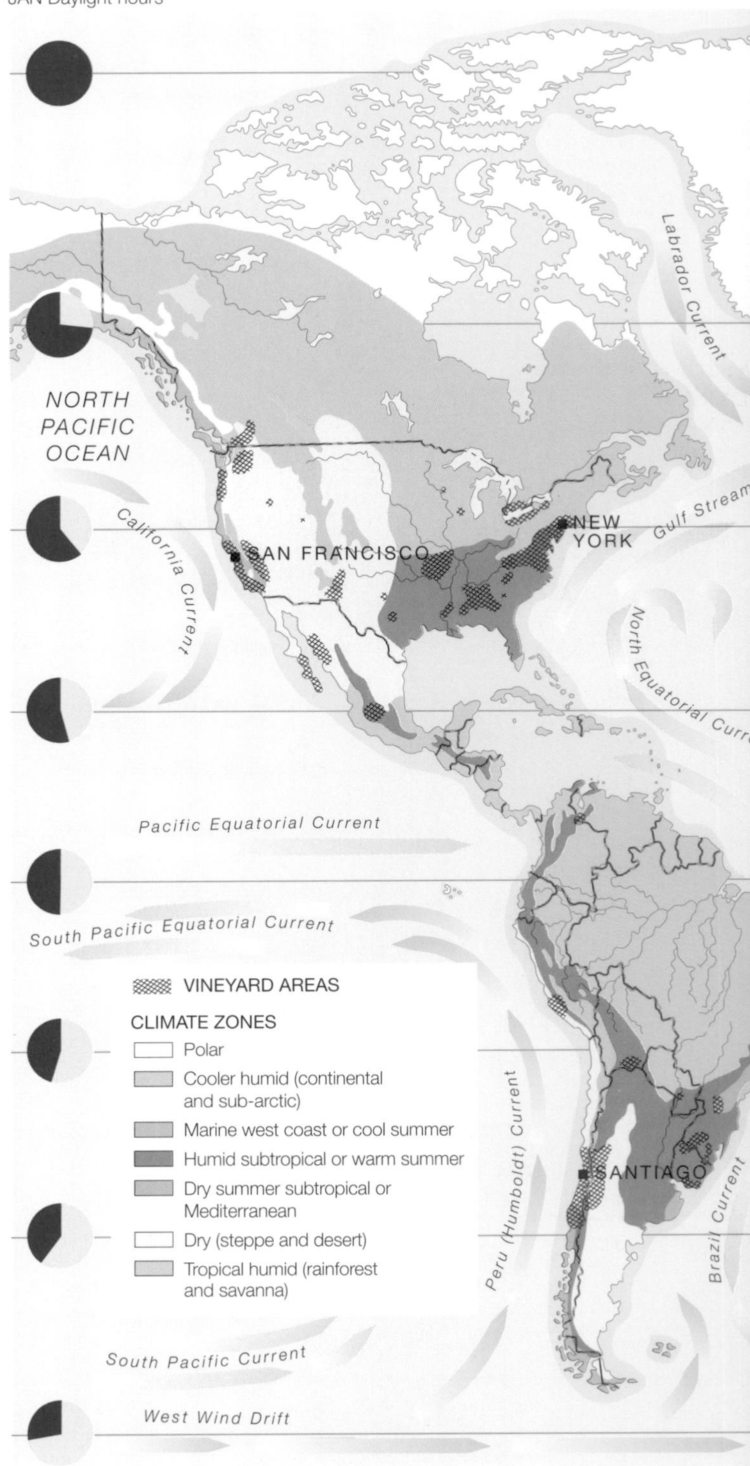

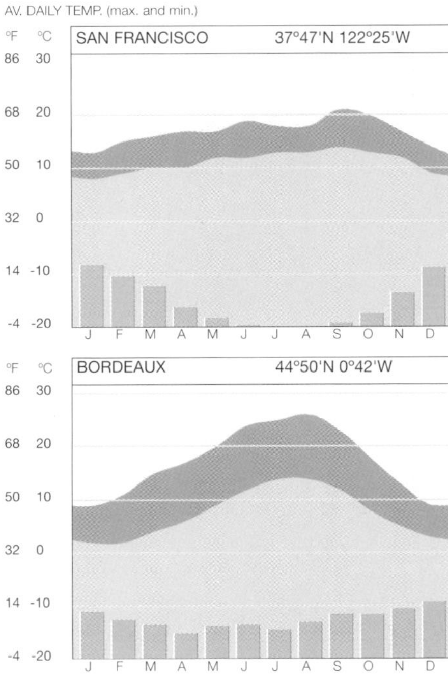

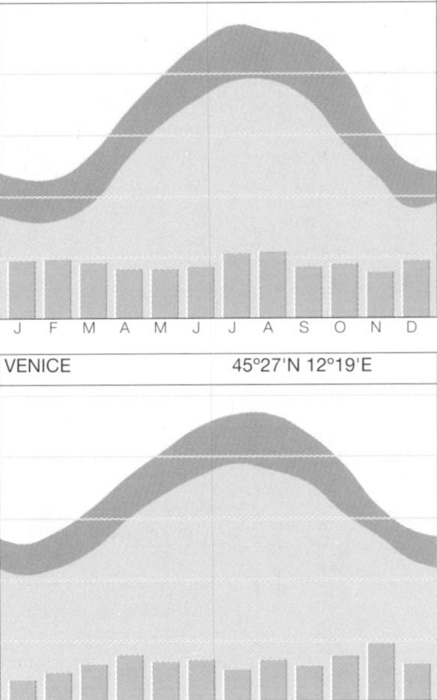

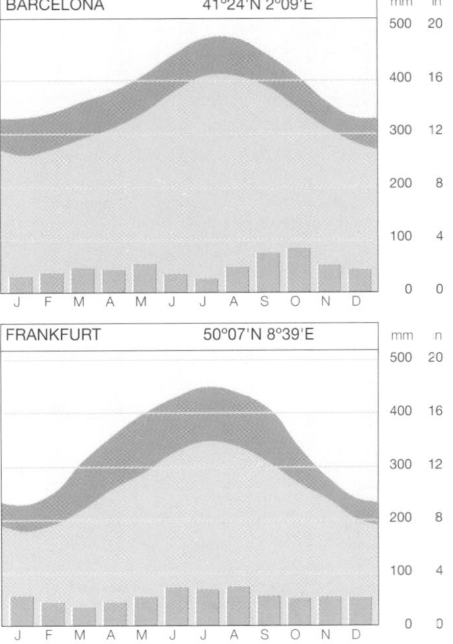

NORTHERN HEMISPHERE

It's not just the amount of rainfall that matters; it's the pattern of it. Bordeaux gets most of its rain during the winter months, with enough from April to August to keep the vine growing well. Less rain in August and September would be better for vines: not for nothing is one of the standard anti-mildew sprays known as Bordeaux mixture. In San Francisco the reverse is true: lack of summer rain means that irrigation is necessary to save the vine from stress. But perhaps the most striking contrast is between San Francisco, with its temperate maritime climate, and the extremes of New York. Even the continental climate of Frankfurt doesn't soar and plummet with such rapidity.

SOUTHERN HEMISPHERE

The striking feature about the rainfall in these southern hemisphere cities is how little of it there is. An Adelaide summer gets far less than a Barcelona summer. Santiago, Cape Town and Perth all manage some properly rainy winter months, but the all-important growing season is extremely dry. No wonder they need to use irrigation in their vineyards.

And then it's so hot in most of these cities. An Adelaide winter is considerably warmer than a winter in Bordeaux, never mind Frankfurt. It demonstrates precisely why the need in Australia is for high-altitude vineyard sites: they've just got to beat those high temperatures somehow.

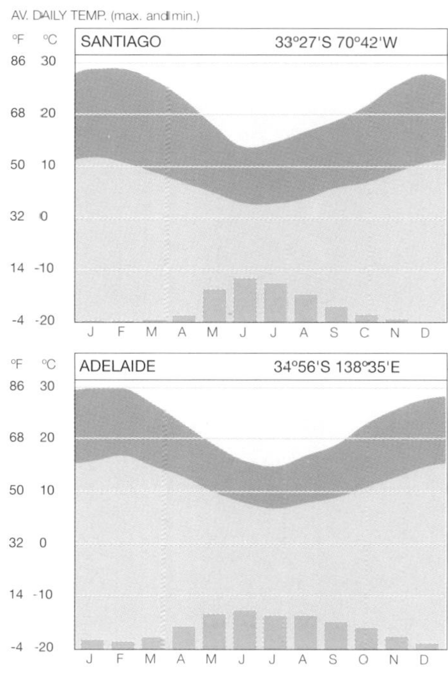

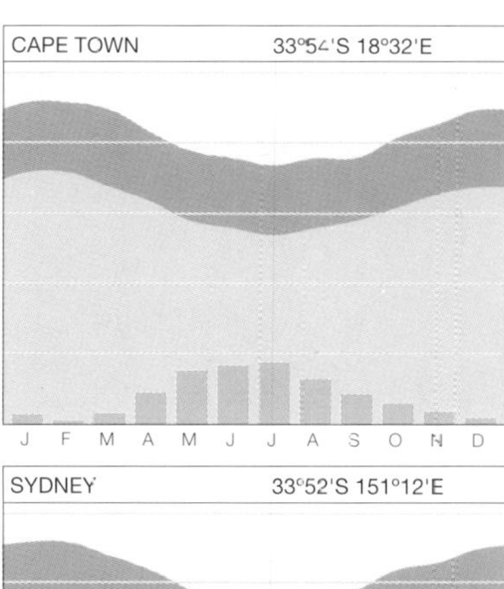

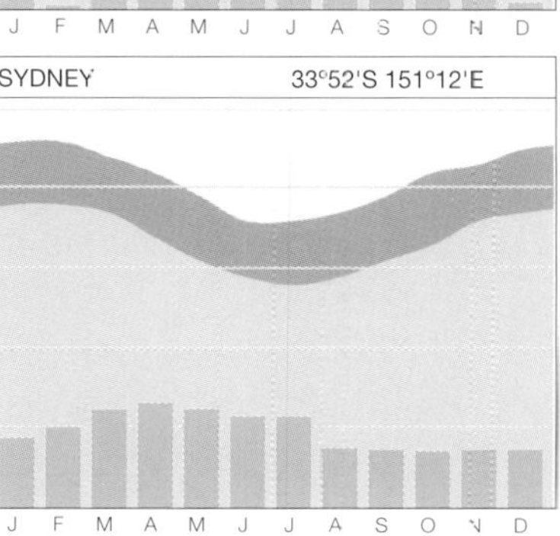

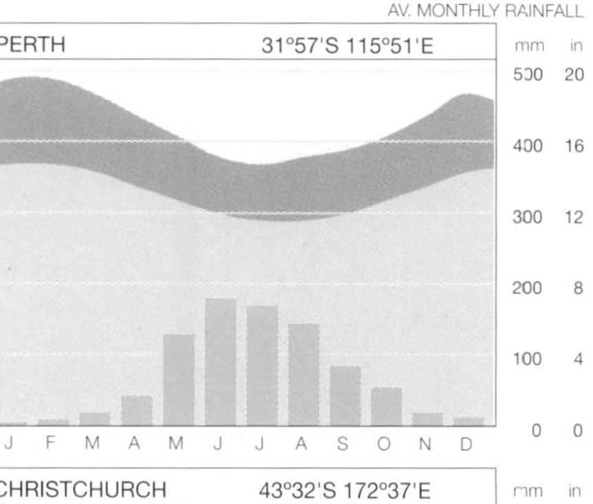

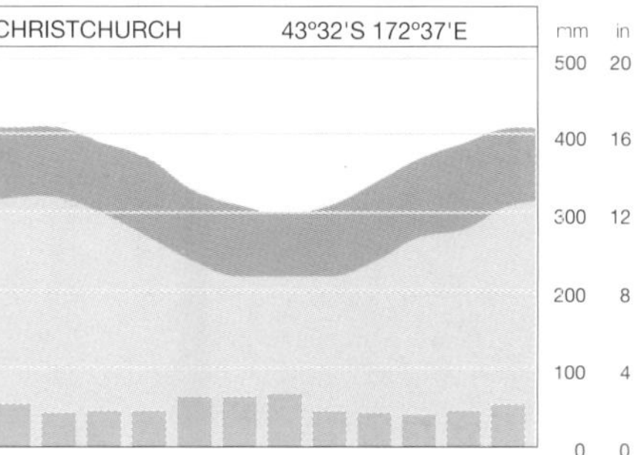

SITING THE VINEYARD

SO I'M A GROWER – I can choose the exact vines I want. I can survey the whole region to find the soil type that suits them. I can get all my meteorological data together, telling me precisely whether I've got a cool, warm or hot climate to contend with, and I can adjust my methods and aspirations accordingly. There's only one thing that's almost guaranteed to upset my most detailed calculations – the weather. The blasted, wretched, fickle, heartless weather. That's why, from budbreak to harvest, you can spot a winemaker by his furrowed brow and narrowed eyes. He's got stuck like that, from perpetually trying to see what's coming over the horizon.

Since I can't control the weather, I have to rely on a system of checks and balances to soften its extremes. In a cool climate, the problems are ones of frost, rain, wind and early autumns. An east-, south- or west-facing slope can help. There are ways in which the grower can deflect frost, as well. But nothing is ever perfect, and each advantage quite often has an associated snag. For example, a supposedly ideal south-facing slope may be the warmest of all, great for ripening the grapes in a cool climate. But it will also be where the snow melts first. In a harsh winter, snow actually keeps the ground relatively warm, and the sites which lose their protective covering of snow too early can then be exposed to damaging frost.

But planting vineyards on a slope has few disadvantages – except that they are more difficult, and therefore more expensive, to work. If I want to get twice as much sunlight onto my vines I have to plant them on a 26° (58 per cent) slope that faces the sun rather than on the flat. Conversely, if I am in a very hot climate, I can plant on an equivalent slope facing away from the sun, and get 50 per cent less sunlight. But if my slopes are so steep that I am forced to terrace them, then all my vines are effectively planted on flat land. In Portugal's Douro Valley, this isn't a problem – there's plenty of sunshine to go round – but in Germany, where every half hour of warming sunshine counts, terraces are increasingly a thing of the past.

Woods near vineyards are also to be reckoned with. A good, thick wood can shelter vines from cold winds, but can also shade them from warming sunshine. A large expanse of

SOLVING THE CLIMATE PROBLEM
This anti-frost wind machine (right) *which works by preventing cold air from settling among the vines is expensive and only feasible in large tracts of vineyards, as here in Stags Leap in the Napa Valley. Sprinkling the shoots with water, which then freezes and protects the vines against still lower temperatures, is also effective.*
The Napa Valley suffers from drought as well as frost, so irrigation will help these young vines (far right) *to establish themselves.*

CHOOSING A SITE

SEA
Cold coastal currents can often cause temperature inversions which lead to fogs, as in San Francisco.

COAST
The area next to the coast will get more rain due to moisture-laden maritime breezes.

RIVERS AND LAKES
Water stores heat, so raising the temperature of the surrounding area, as well as reflecting sunshine onto nearby slopes.

TOWN
A group of buildings warms the air and helps keep the valley frost-free.

IDEAL VINEYARD SITE

ASPECT TO SUN
Because of the inclination of the earth, south-facing slopes in the northern hemisphere and north-facing slopes in the southern hemisphere will obtain more direct sunshine than others.

SLOPE ANGLE
An adequate slope is needed to get the best angle of incidence with the sunshine and to encourage good air circulation which prevents frosts and fogs.

SHELTER
Wooded hills provide shelter for the vines from winds.

water at the foot of a slope – a broad river or lake – can reflect light back onto the vines. Conveniently, this effect is most marked when the sun is low (in the spring and autumn), extending the growing season by a crucial few extra weeks. However, in a hot climate I may want to avoid that because all my efforts are directed to seeking lower temperatures and preventing drought. But water doesn't just reflect heat: as the sun heats up the earth, very useful cooling breezes come off the water. As for the sea, well, the Gulf Stream warms the whole of France's west coast – and that includes Bordeaux – while the Pacific acts as a massive air conditioner in California, Chile, Australia and New Zealand, pushing cold air far inland to regions that otherwise would be way too hot.

IDEAL VINEYARD SITES

Do the photographs below show ideal vineyard sites? No, they do not, but because of the ingenuity of vine growers and the quality of their wine we have come to regard them as such. The Doctor vineyard at Bernkastel on the Mosel is cold, windswept, and situated almost as far north as any grape variety will ripen. And so growers have sought the spots where the landscape will help them out: on the steep slope with its slaty soil, above the river. Both the river and the soil act as a heat store, reflecting much-needed warmth back onto the vines. And then there are the vines themselves: Riesling, which is resistant to cold and is one of the few varieties that will ripen in this location. If you planted Nebbiolo or Syrah, all the disadvantages of the site would become clear.

Montana's Brancott Estate in Marlborough, New Zealand, looks as different as could be from Bernkasteler Doctor, but that doesn't make it ideal: there's a shortage of water for irrigation and a risk of frosts. You couldn't just grow any old vine here. Again, it's a question of finding the final piece in the jigsaw and slotting it in to produce, in this case, brilliant Sauvignon Blanc; Cabernet Sauvignon, though, won't ripen. It's sunny but cool here, and as summer turns into autumn the sunshine just goes on and on, giving the sort of long, slow ripening that packs flavour into the wines.

TWO CONTRASTING VINEYARDS
Far left: *The steep Doctor vineyard clings to the slopes above the town of Bernkastel on the banks of the Mosel river in Germany. This tiny vineyard (only 3.26 hectares/8 acres), much of it at a gradient of 60 to 70%, has been established for hundreds of years.*
Left: *In contrast, Montana's Brancott Estate in Marlborough, New Zealand, is a great flat swathe of over 200 hectares (500 acres) of vines and was created out of nothing as recently as the 1970s.*

The Importance of Soil

Hang on a minute, while I divide myself in two. Right. Done it. Now, let me introduce myselves. On the one hand I'm a New World grower – let's say I come from California. I don't think soil is that important. Sure, it holds the vine upright, and sure, I've got friends in places like the Rutherford Bench who swear that it works magic, but to me it's the climate that matters. I don't really go for all this European stuff about the soil affecting the taste of the wine. How could it?

On the other hand I'm an Old World grower – perhaps I come from Alsace. I have Riesling and Gewürztraminer growing in several Grand Cru sites, and the wines taste different from each vineyard. The climate is the same in all of them; the only thing that's different is the soil. I can't understand my New World colleagues who say that soil doesn't affect the taste of a wine. How could it not?

Okay, I'm taking up two extreme positions here. But you see, both are right. And to begin to show why, both of me will chorus: what matters most about soil is drainage.

How dull. But how fundamental. You see, a well-drained soil is a warm soil, and a wet soil is a cold soil. It's the temperature of the soil, much more than that of the air, that decides when a vine is going to start budding in the spring – and that's one of the factors that decides what vines can be planted where. The temperature of the soil also influences the acidity of the wine: cold soils give more acidic wines, since heat burns off acidity.

A well-drained soil is basically one with bigger particles. There are four basic categories of particle sizes in soil: coarse sand, fine sand, silt and clay. Gravel and stones, of course, are the biggest of all; water pours through quickly, but essential nutrients will not be held in the soil, and it may need to be well-fertilized before it bears fruit. At the other end of the scale, if the particles are 0.002mm or less in diameter then the soil is clay. Think how tightly clay holds water – indeed, it can hold it so tightly that the vine can't get at it. A well-drained, warm gravel soil can actually have more water available to the vine than a wet clay one. So in areas of heavy rain (Bordeaux, for example), a well-drained gravel soil has obvious advantages over a non-draining clay one. Until there's a drought, I hear you say. Well, even then a gravel soil can sometimes be better. In poor soils (and stony soil, with big particles, is poor soil) the vine's roots have to plunge deeper so that in a hot, dry summer they are more likely to be able to find moisture; in clay soils the roots are found mostly within the first few feet of soil.

But I'd hate to give you the idea that one type of soil is automatically better than another for wine; soils that heat up quickly in the spring also get colder in the winter, and are more affected by frost; in hot climates they can reflect too much heat on to the grapes, and burn them. Small amounts of organic matter in the soil, be it gravel or clay, can also help to even out water availability. And a cold clay soil can not only be beneficial in holding back an early-ripening vine like Merlot, but it can give the wine more structure and solidity, too.

Then there's the question of pH. Alkaline soils, with a pH of seven or more, tend to be young soils. They are high in calcium, from shells left behind when the sea receded, and they tend to produce wines high in acidity. Champagne's soil is like this. There's a lot of alkaline soil all over Europe. But the New World, particularly Australia, has older soils and the pH may be pretty neutral, though old rocky soils can be acidic. The soil of California's Napa Valley is generally more acidic than the young alluvial gravel of Bordeaux. The wines of Bordeaux are naturally more acidic than those of Napa. There's absolutely nothing wrong with having completely different soils to Bordeaux, Burgundy, Champagne and all the other star performers of the Old World, unless you slavishly set out to make identical wines. Some of the New World producers did exactly this to start with, presuming that if their Chardonnay didn't taste like Burgundy and their Cabernet like Bordeaux it was somehow inferior. Thank goodness that phase has passed and

DIFFERENT SOILS FOR DIFFERENT VINES

There is no single soil type that is ideal for wine. And to prove it, many different soils have proved themselves perfect for particular grape varieties in particular climates. So acidic granite produces great Syrah in Hermitage and the best Gamay in Beaujolais; limestone seems to suit Chardonnay in many places, including Champagne, Chablis and the Côte d'Or; and the rich grey-blue marl of Barolo retains water and is cold – ideal for the longer, slower ripening of Nebbiolo in a warm climate. Schist can give rich, spicy reds in the Rhône's Côte-Rôtie and Portugal's Douro Valley. Clay soil reduces bouquet but gives structure to a wine, so in Alsace it is favoured for the broader, more aromatic grape varieties like Gewürztraminer, rather than for the more subtle Riesling. In Germany's Mosel Valley, steep slate slopes impart a haunting beauty to Riesling wines. However, the warm, black basalt soils of Forst and Deidesheim in the Pfalz provide Rieslings that are far more exotic and fleshy.

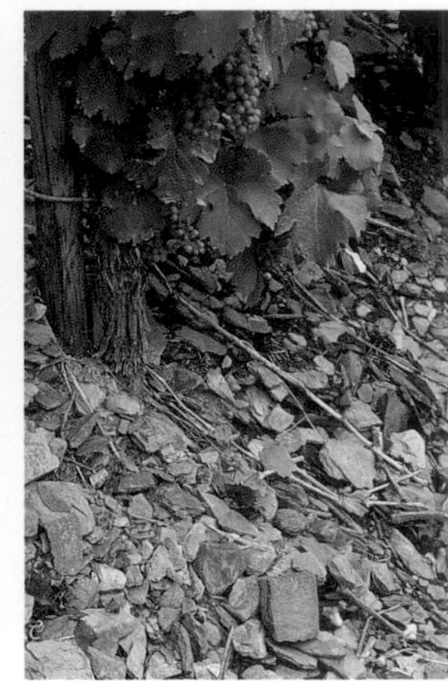

Clockwise, from top left: *1. Clay is not considered the best soil for growing vines. The small flat clay particles fit together closely keeping water locked between them, and the soil water will stagnate. One of the only advantages of a clay soil is that in a hot region, such as here in the Napa Valley in California where there is a lot of both clay and silt, it can hold enough water to sustain the vine all the way through a long, dry summer.*
2. Chalk soil has the remarkable ability to retain water well, but has sufficient cracks to let excess water drain away easily. So it is valuable both in hot Jerez in southern Andalucía (as here) and in chilly Champagne.
3. The dark slate soil of the Mosel Valley absorbs heat and helps the Riesling to ripen in a cool climate. In a hot climate it could reduce acidity but that's not necessary here.
4. When the vines of Ch. d'Angludet in Margaux are dormant the gravel soils are revealed. Gravel, with plenty of natural voids, allows water to drain through quickly, so preventing the vines standing in waterlogged soil.

producers can search our their special patches of land with entirely different characteristics and so massively enlarge the range of wines in the world today.

Soil is formed by the long, continuous process of the breaking down and weathering of the bedrock, so the characteristics of the bedrock are the underlying key to the qualities of the soil above. Limestone, including chalk, produces soils which have large proportions of calcium, with high alkalinity. Sandstone produces sandy soils, and very hard rocks such as granite have thin soils because of the resistance of the rock to weathering.

So can the soil affect the flavour of the wine? Yes, it can affect the acidity and the tannin (both via the pH of the soil). Stonier soils give lighter, more perfumed wines; richer soils with more clay give more solid wines. But what about particular 'mineral' flavours? Elsewhere in this Atlas I talk about the specific smoky tang that Riesling acquires on slate soil. It's not imagination: I could pick it out for you, blind. And, although it is true that only a minute percentage of the ions from the minerals and trace elements assimilated by the vine from the soil will find their way into the finished wine, it is also true that the same grape grown by my Alsace self on different soils will taste different. At least, it will if I keep the yields down. Because that's an important point when considering the influence of soil on wine: it is most noticeable when yields are low, and where the climate is marginal. Indeed, a great vineyard site is one where all the parts of *terroir* (soil, exposure, climate) combine to iron out the vagaries of a marginal climate, and thus produce the best possible wines year in, year out.

But to get back to my Californian self: suppose I've got more or less neutral soil that doesn't have any particular character to impart to the wine? (Not all soils in California are like this, of course.) Well, then, lucky old me. I can grow a wide range of vines, in theory; and what does best where will be decided by the climate, not the soil. So you see, we really are both right. Well, we can agree to differ, anyway.

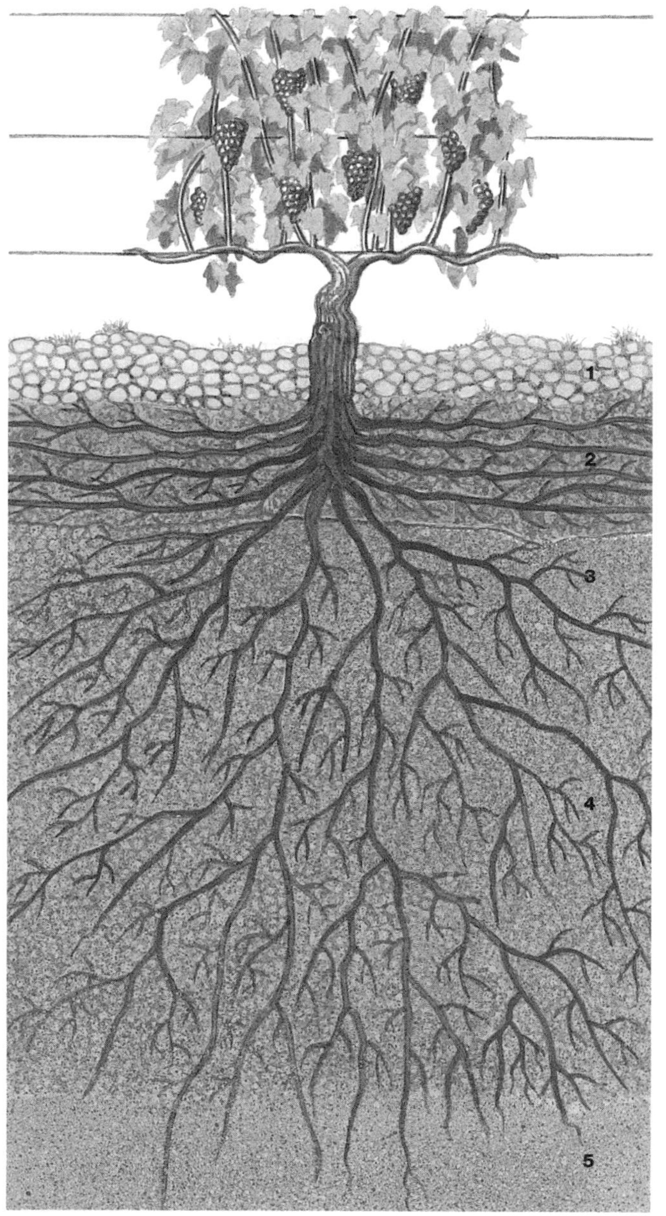

BELOW THE VINE

1. STONES

Pebbles and stones on the surface help to retain heat within the topsoil and reflect sunlight back onto the vine.

2. TOPSOIL

This is the main root zone, 15-30cm (6–12in) thick in most soil. Topsoil is formed from weathered bedrock, organic matter from decaying plants and animals, and fertilizers.

3. SUBSOIL

This is pure, weathered bedrock which lays the foundations for the all-important tap roots which stabilize the vine.

4. BEDROCK or PARENT MATERIAL

The bedrock is the underlying geology. Since soil is formed from broken-down and weathered rock, the bedrock has a great influence on the soil characteristics. The bedrock can be used by roots only if it is well-pored or fissured.

5. WATER TABLE

The water table is the level beneath which the rock is saturated with ground water and, provided it is not stagnant, can provide a good water source for a vine if it is only a few yards from the surface.

GLOSSARY OF COMMON VINEYARD SOILS

Acid soil A soil with a low pH value. These soils tend to occur mostly in wetter climates where high rainfall leaches the calcium out of the soil. The rootstock and vine variety can be chosen for their sympathy with various soil pH.

Alkaline soil A soil with a high pH value, usually due to the presence of calcium (see Calcareous soil) or salt.

Alluvial deposits (alluvium) Materials deposited from rivers, usually gravels, sands and silts, such as are found in the Graves area of Bordeaux and Marlborough in New Zealand, usually associated with free-draining soils.

Calcareous soil A soil with a high calcium content which comes from a limestone geology. Chalk is a form of limestone. It has a high pH (alkaline) and usually has good aeration, drainage and structure. Many vines do well on calcium-rich soils, particularly the Chardonnay grape as in Chablis and parts of the Côte d'Or.

Chalk A form of limestone with a characteristic white or pale colour and alkaline pH (see Limestone and Calcareous soil). It has proved particularly good for vines growing in cooler and wetter climates such as the Champagne region of France.

Clay The smallest size of soil particle. Soils rich in clay particles are usually cold and acidic with poor drainage and can have a tendancy to waterlog.

Colluvial deposits (colluvium) Weathered rock and soil debris which have slid down slopes and been deposited at a lower level.

Gravel The French word for gravel, *graves*, has given its name to the Graves area of Bordeaux. Pebbles covering the ground, usually of alluvial origin, retain heat and are freely drained.

Granite An igneous rock in which the crystals are large enough to be distinguished without a microscope. Granite sometimes forms hard rock masses which reflect the heat of the sun, for example, the hill of Hermitage.

Limestone A sedimentary rock made of calcite (calcium carbonate), typically pale in colour and with a high pH. Chalk is a form of limestone. See Calcareous soil.

Loam A soil composed of equal proportions of clay, silt and sand particles. Usually a well-balanced and fertile soil.

Loess Wind-blown silt which covers the topsoil.

Marl A sedimentary mixture of clay and limestone, some with more clay than limestone, some with more limestone than clay.

Organic matter Humus from living organisms, usually plants and fallen leaves, and manure.

pH A soil's acidity or alkalinity.

Sand Large, granular soil particles which consist of weathered rock and quartz. A soil consisting of large proportions of sand will be warm and freely drained, but will be poor in nutrients and rather acidic.

Scree The slope of debris at the bottom of a cliff which has fallen due to erosion and weathering. It consists of various-sized fragments of rock and is usually steep.

Silt Larger than clay and smaller than sand, silt holds water well and is relatively fertile, as seen in the Napa Valley.

Slate A hard rock formed from shales and clays put under pressure. Its heat-retaining qualities provide an excellent environment for vines, sometimes passing on metallic flavours, as in for example the Bernkastel wines from the Mosel Valley in Germany.

Terra rossa A red soil formed when the calcium is leached out of limestone, leaving a clay coloured red from dehydrated iron compounds. It is associated with Mediterranean climates (wet winters and very dry summers) which enable the leaching and hydrating processes to occur, but its most famous manifestation is at Coonawarra in Australia.

THE MODERN VINEYARD

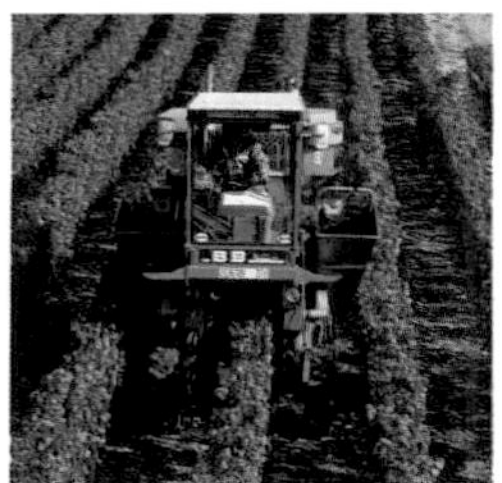

THIS IS THE MOMENT OF DECISION for the grape grower. He has picked the most favourable spot the landscape has to offer; he has analysed the soil and observed the climate. He has decided which vine varieties will cope best with both. Now he must plant. But before he can put a single vine in the soil, there is one more thing he must do. Virtually all the vines these days are grafted on to phylloxera-resistant rootstock, to protect them from one of the most devastating of all vine pests. But because the rootstock comes from a different vine species, it throws another element into the equation. He must choose a rootstock that is compatible with the soil, the climate and with his vines: some rootstocks are more vigorous than others, some are more resistant to drought or cold and so on. So his choice of rootstock will affect the style and quality of his wine.

Then he must decide how densely to plant his vines. Higher density planting reduces the yield per vine, which is crucial for quality in a cool climate – around 5000 vines per hectare (2000 per acre), and occasionally as many as 10,000 (4000), are common in Europe. Vines spaced more widely develop bigger root systems, which is useful where drought is a problem; Californian and Australian growers often settle for 1100 to 1600 vines per hectare (450 to 650 per acre).

Pruning, training and canopy management are all directed towards making the vine produce the optimum-sized crop (as many grapes as it can bring to full ripeness in a particular climate and soil). In a cool climate on poor soil, for example, the vine can ripen fewer grapes than in a warm climate on deep, rich soil, so you should prune harder to reduce the number of fruiting buds. Then you train the vine in order to make it bear its bunches of grapes where you want them: partially exposed to the sun so that they'll ripen; with good air circulation so that they won't rot; high enough off the ground to avoid frost, or low enough to benefit from the heat stored in the soil.

VINE MANAGEMENT

This is now accepted as fundamental to the eventual quality of the wine. The aim is to nurture a healthy plant which will deliver a crop of healthy grapes at whatever quantity and quality level the grower desires, by choosing a highly productive or a less productive clone, and planting it on a vigorous or less vigorous rootstock. To create competition and reduce crop levels, the vines can be closely planted. On non-vigorous soils, for example, the Médoc gravel banks, a simple training system will suffice. On fertile, productive soils, for example, most New Zealand sites, training the vine through different trellising and pruning methods can transform the quality of the fruit.

Double Guyot *This simple system is the most common one used in Bordeaux and involves training two canes along a wire, one to each side of the vine. The number of buds left on each cane after pruning will dictate the probable size of the crop.*

Scott Henry *Developed by an Oregon vineyard owner this system is popular in the New World as it increases yields and ripeness. By training the canopy vertically, the fruit is exposed more effectively to sunlight and air circulation and the canopy available for photosynthesis is increased.*

1. Winter pruning is the grower's main way of controlling the yield. Here at Château Léoville-Barton in St-Julien a worker is removing most of the previous year's growth, to leave just a few buds – a small enough quantity for the vine to cope with bringing to full ripeness.

5. Many sorts of fertilizer can be used in spring to improve the soil. This mustard looks pretty when it flowers in the spring, but its real function is to be ploughed in later in the year as organic fertilizer. This is California's Napa Valley, with Mount St Helena in the background.

9. Irrigation is essential in many hot, dry New World vineyards. It is especially important when establishing young vines like these ones at Cowra in New South Wales. The drip irrigation system is widely used nowadays – the amount of water can be controlled carefully as each vine has its own water supply.

13. Preparations for the harvest must be made in good time. All the equipment must be spotlessly clean, and barrels like these at Covey Run Vintners in Washington State must be rinsed out and disinfected ready for the new vintage while the grapes are still ripening out in the vineyard.

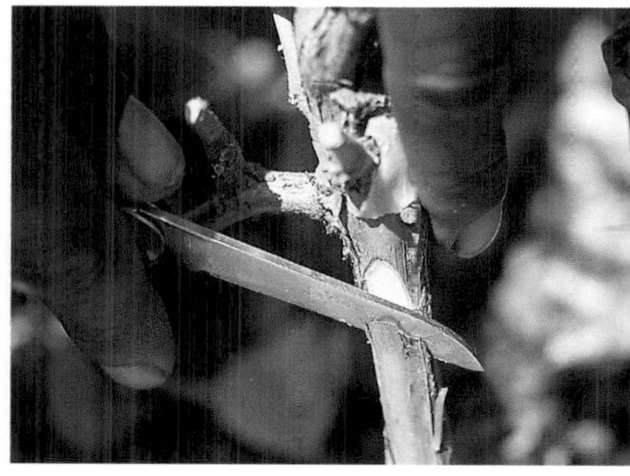

2. Chip budding is the quickest way of transforming an inferior vine variety into a better one. Make an incision in the existing vine, as here, and graft into it a bud of the new variety, and in a year you have a crop of the new variety's grapes.

3. Virtually all vines are grafted on to phylloxera-resistant rootstock, to protect them from one of the most devastating of all vine pests. You can see the callus that has formed around the graft. These young vines are now ready to plant.

4. When the ground is warm enough and the risk of frost is reduced, new rootstocks can be planted out and new vineyards prepared for vines. Even ancient regions like Montepulciano in Tuscany can create new vineyard sites from pastureland.

6. All sorts of pests afflict the vineyard, as spring advances. Milk cartons around the rootstock in Rex Hill Vineyards in Oregon stop animals nibbling the tender new growth as well as protecting it from being scorched by the sun.

7. Tying up foliage is a task that continues throughout the growing season. Left to itself the vine would create too much shade and humidity for grapes to ripen and stay healthy. These are Barbera vines near Casorzo, in Piedmont, Italy.

8. Mildew is a constant threat in all but the driest vineyards. These young vines at Manakau Harbour in South Auckland, New Zealand, will need to be sprayed again after the next spell of rain and again after that, knowing Auckland.

10. Summer pruning (here being done by machine in Fronton, near Toulouse) is the removal of excess foliage that would otherwise shade the grapes. The vine must, however, retain enough leaves to be able to ripen its crop.

11. A great deal of research is being done into trellising methods. Here at Petaluma in South Australia the canopy is held aloft by catch wires to give maximum exposure of the grapes to the sun, essential in a cool climate.

12. Once the grapes begin to ripen a new enemy appears: birds. Anti-bird netting is the answer, even if it means that these harvesters at Breaky Bottom in Sussex, England have to get underneath it in order to pick the grapes.

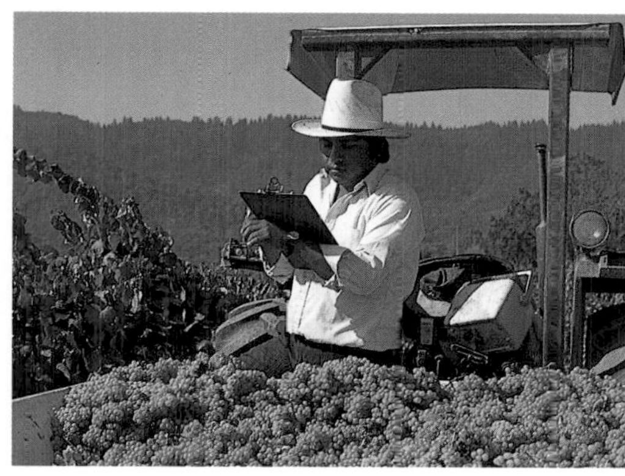

14. The big moment. The grapes are harvested and transported to the winery to be pressed and transformed into wine. These Chardonnay grapes for the Robert Mondavi winery in California are from an independent contract grower.

15. The growing season ends late for some grape growers. To make Eiswein they must leave the grapes on the vines for perhaps another two months after the normal harvest date, protecting the grapes against rain and birds in that time.

16. After the grapes have all been picked, winter pruning starts again. The branches that will produce next year's crop must then be tied down (this is at Trittenheim in the Mosel, Germany) ready for next year's growth.

GRAPES OF THE WORLD

THERE ARE THOUSANDS AND THOUSANDS of grape varieties in the world. So why is it that when you go out to buy a bottle of wine you sometimes seem to be faced with a choice of only Chardonnay or Cabernet Sauvignon? How come those thousands sometimes seem to have been narrowed down to two by both winemakers and retailers?

There are several answers. Most varieties are used either for dessert grapes or for raisins, or are rarely grown, or are the wrong species for wine-making. And of the 1000 or so varieties that are at all significant for wine, only about 30 have international relevance – which does of course leave a great many obscure, but possibly excellent, local varieties to be discovered by the adventurous drinker.

Virtually all of those 1000 varieties are of the same species, *Vitis vinifera*. This is the species most people mean when they talk about wine vines. And yet *vinifera* is only one branch of the vine family; there are dozens of others, growing in diverse climates all over the world, from the *Vitis amurensis* of Siberia to the *Vitis cariboa* of the tropics. They all produce grapes; indeed the first settlers in America made their first wines from native species. These wines, usually made from *Vitis labrusca*, *Vitis riparia*, or *Vitis berlandieri*, had a flavour usually described as foxy, although a cross between hawthorn blossom and nail varnish might be more accurate. You can still taste such wines in some parts of North America, on the island of Madeira or in remote parts of Austria. They can sometimes be OK – but you can see why *vinifera* won the day.

A few years ago Chardonnay was thought of as being a Burgundian or Champagne speciality; now it's grown in almost every wine region with aspirations. But such movements of vines are not new – merely faster than they used to be. Vine cuttings have been transported vast distances over the centuries by crusaders, traders and missionaries. It was missionaries who took cuttings from Spain to the Americas. The Syrah of the Rhône and Australia (where it is called Shiraz) is believed to have come from Shiraz in Persia. And many of the vines we think of as being Italian are, in fact, Greek in origin.

And why would people bother to do this – take cuttings of a favourite variety to a country that probably already had plenty of vines of its own? Because it has always been recognized that the single most important factor in the flavour of a wine is grape variety. Every grape has its own flavour, though most need particular climatic conditions to bring out their flavour to best advantage. Cabernet Sauvignon grown in too cold a climate will produce a thin, grassy wine; in too hot a climate it risks being baked and raisiny. But when the worldwide movement of vines has produced a chance combination of right vine, right climate and right soil, that's when classic wine styles have been established.

CABERNET FRANC

To think of this merely as Cabernet Sauvignon's less important sibling is to do it a disservice. It produces good, but not great wines as a varietal (although it is the main grape by quite a long way in Ch. Cheval Blanc, which is about as great as red wine can get). But its value as a blending grape in Bordeaux is enormous, because it is less tannic and acidic than Cabernet Sauvignon on its own. It's an early ripener, so also does well in the cool Loire.

CABERNET SAUVIGNON

This became the world's most famous red grape because Bordeaux was the world's most famous red wine, and right around the world, when local producers decided to improve their quality, they looked to Bordeaux for inspiration. Simple really. Luckily Cabernet Sauvignon is up to the challenge and seems to relish travelling almost as much as nestling among the pale gravel banks of its spiritual home in Bordeaux's Médoc region. Thick-skinned, slow to ripen yet rot-resistant if caught by autumn rains, it has a God-given ability to provide deep colour, reasonable tannin, a universally recognizable flavour of blackcurrants, black cherry and plum virtually anywhere it is grown (except the coolest and the very hottest sites). In every wine-making continent, Cabernet Sauvignon has become a byword for full-flavoured, reliable red wine.

CHARDONNAY

The world's favourite white grape is adaptable enough to make everything from light, dry sparkling wine to sweet, botrytized dessert wine, but its dry, oak-aged incarnation, based on the great wines of Burgundy's Côte d'Or, is the style best known to consumers. This is the one found from Chile to China, and from California to New South Wales. Clearly, then, the vine is happy in a wide range of soils and climates, though being an early ripener it also buds early, which can be a problem in such frost-prone regions as Champagne and Chablis. Otherwise, it is resistant to cold and yields well virtually anywhere it is grown.

The wine has such an affinity with new oak, which adds rich, spicy butteriness to the wine, that it can be easy to forget what its actual varietal flavour is. Unoaked, cool-climate Chardonnay is pale, appley and acidic; these flavours gradually soften towards melon and peach as the climate warms. Simple Chardonnays are made to be drunk young, and certainly most New World examples should not be aged for more than a few years, if that. In Burgundy, however, it makes one of the most long-lived of all white wines.

CHENIN BLANC

This versatile white grape is capable of producing wines that are dry or sweet, still or sparkling, for instant consumption or for cellaring for a decade or more. However, it has yet to reach great heights away from France's Loire Valley. Here, on chalky soils and in distinctly cool climates, it can produce some of the most individual wines to be found anywhere in the world: in both dry and sweet styles, highly acidic when young, wines that can, indeed should, be put away for years. In New Zealand and Western Australia, some delicious dry examples are surfacing, but in South Africa

Chardonnay

Cabernet Sauvignon

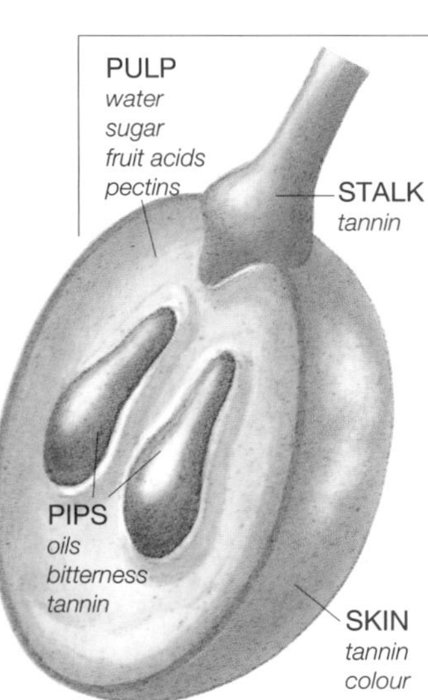

COMPOSITION OF A GRAPE

When it comes to imparting flavour to its wine, the actual juice of the grape rarely has very much to offer. Muscat juice is sweet and perfumed – that's why we eat Muscat grapes as well as make wine from them – but most of the great wine grapes of the world are no fun to eat. At best a ripe grape has a sugary, neutral-flavoured and colourless pulp. Some of the character for a wine comes from its skin. As the grape ripens, the skin matures; its tannins become less aggressive, its colour deepens and all the perfume and flavour components build up in the skin. The trick is to try to ripen the grape so that sugar, acid, tannin, colour and flavour are all in balance at the time of harvesting. Both the pips and the stalks are very bitter and modern winemakers usually de-stalk the grapes and avoid crushing the pips.

(where it is called Steen), Argentina and California, few producers attempt anything more adventurous than cheap, off-dry whites.

GEWÜRZTRAMINER
The name means 'spicy Traminer' and that spice is a smell of roses and lychees, sometimes mangoes, often with a dab of cold cream – the sort of nose that, as you might guess, needs plenty of acidity on the palate to back it up. But Gewürztraminer can be all too low in acidity, and only in cool climates can its tendency to high sugar levels be kept in balance. At its best in Alsace, followed by New Zealand and Italy's Alto Adige, it buds early and is susceptible to frosts. But if it survives these and is affected by noble rot in a warm autumn, superb sweet wines can result.

GRENACHE NOIR
We don't see much varietal Grenache about and yet it covers mile after mile of vineyards in Spain (where it's called Garnacha Tinta), the south of France, California and parts of Australia. The reason is that this is a blending grape *par excellence*: in Rioja and Navarra in Spain, its burly fruit fills out the rather more restrained Tempranillo grape; throughout southern France, but especially in southern Rhône, its high strength, juicy, peppery character is a crucial part of many blends, in particular Châteauneuf-du-Pape. California and Australia, too, are fast rediscovering its heady charms.

Gewürztraminer

Merlot

Nebbiolo

Pinot Noir

MALBEC
Certainly this vine is accorded little honour in its homeland of Bordeaux, but elsewhere Malbec is beginning to gather a following. In Bordeaux its job was primarily to soften the tough Cabernet Sauvignon. In the drier, hotter vineyards of Cahors, Malbec (here known as Cot or Auxerrois) can produce deep, damsony wine that becomes dark and tobacco-scented with age. And that's exactly the character that is now attracting attention in Argentina, Chile and South Australia.

MERLOT
This red grape, with its rich, plummy fruit, its fondness for oak-aging and its tendency to mature in bottle relatively quickly, is a natural partner for Cabernet Sauvignon. The two are the basis of the Bordeaux blend, and in fact Merlot is by far the more widely planted of the two in Bordeaux, ripening earlier and giving bigger crops. All around the world where the Bordeaux red wine model has been copied, Merlot has been planted, yet not always successfully – it can ripen almost too quickly in hot climates and give too much crop in fertile soils. On its own, it produces vast amounts of lighter wine in north-eastern Italy, increasingly exciting, juicy reds in southern France, Hungary, California and Chile, and is a vital grape in Washington and New York States, and in New Zealand.

MÜLLER-THURGAU
This grape gets into this list only because of the spectacular number of vineyard regions it has colonized, despite only being created as a cross between Riesling and Silvaner in 1883. It was intended to provide Riesling-like quality with high yield, no disease and early ripening. Well, pigs may fly one day, too. It is now, unfortunately, one of Germany's most widely planted grape varieties, and while capable of mild, floral wines, it more commonly provides the base wines for the lifeless Liebfraumilchs, Piesporters and Niersteiners that despoil Germany's reputation abroad. It has since spread to England, Austria, Central Europe and northern Italy with occasionally pleasing results, but is probably at its best in New Zealand.

MUSCAT BLANC À PETITS GRAINS
This is the aristocrat of the Muscat family, a low-yielding vine prone to mutation that produces intensely grapy wines of more delicacy and elegance than any of its cousins. It also comes in all colours from white to brownish red, and can make fortifieds the colour of burnt toffee, but it is seldom sufficiently red to make a proper red wine.

Muscat Blanc à Petits Grains is scattered throughout France (especially in the *vins doux naturels* of Roussillon and the Rhône, and the fragrant, dry wine of Alsace), and Italy, where it creates Asti and scented wines in the Alto Adige. In Greece and Australia it makes intense, fortified wines.

NEBBIOLO
I always hear a shrug of resignation in this name. Why? Because it comes from the Italian word for fog, *nebbia*. I imagine those north-western Italian winemakers of centuries back shaking their heads over their late-ripening vine and indulgently naming it after the fog that was invariably around when they came to pick in late October. Today, growers plant it high up the slopes, so that it can make the most of the autumn sunshine. And it can make the most sensational wines. Barolo and Barbaresco are the stars: strange and unyielding yet wonderfully fragrant, tannic yet pale, bullish but perfumed with violets.

PINOT GRIS
Some of Europe's most exotic, hedonistic white wines ooze from this grape in Alsace, Germany and Hungary. Yet cross the Alps and you'll find northern Italy producing oceans of light, innocuous and rather pricey dry whites without the unctuous honey and raisin richness that is so exciting further north. It's all to do with yields and attitude: the Italians view white wine as a palate cleanser; the northern Europeans see it as their chance for vinous glory and coax every ounce of character they can from grapes like Pinot Gris. High in extract and sugar yet low in acidity, it shouldn't age, but it does – brilliantly. You'll find a few patches of it in Burgundy, a good deal in Romania and Oregon and the odd vine in New Zealand.

PINOT NOIR
If you're a grower, this is the most tantalizing of all vines – and the most disobliging, the most unforgiving and yet the most rewarding. This red variety likes a cool climate, because it buds and ripens early, while in too hot a region it just produces solid, baked-tasting or flabby wines. So why plant it? Because when you get it just right – as the best growers in Burgundy's Côte d'Or often do – the wines are sensual, fragrant, silky yet slightly savage, not so much

intellectually impressive as unforgettably pleasurable. It is now planted worldwide but until recently has strongly resisted growers' attempts to create great flavours. Now exciting and decidedly non-Burgundian reds are appearing from California and Oregon, Chile, South Africa, Australia and New Zealand – not many, but enough to show the way. Switzerland, Germany and Italy prefer to stick with milder interpretations. And if it doesn't ripen, it can be turned into fizz, as usually happens in Champagne.

Riesling

Sauvignon Blanc

Sémillon

Syrah/Shiraz

RIESLING
This marvellous grape deserves a better deal. Producer of some of the most heavenly, aristocratic and elegant of wines, grown under tortuous conditions, it is nonetheless disdained and dismissed throughout most of the world. Yet in the Mosel and Rhine Valleys of Germany, stunning results are achieved by growers prepared to limit yield and caress the grapes to ripeness. Water-white wines as fleeting as gossamer share honours with sweet wines of such intensity as to strike the most babble-mouthed drinker dumb. This cold-resistant, late-ripening vine is also a superb performer elsewhere. Austria produces wonderful Riesling, and both Italy and Eastern Europe could and sometimes do. East and west coasts of North America produce good examples, while in Australia and New Zealand it produces totally un-European yet world-class flavours, both sweet and dry.

SANGIOVESE
The workhorse red grape of Tuscany, Sangiovese, also plays a part further south in Italy as well as north in Emilia-Romagna, where it produces oceans of lighter red wine for the trenchermen of Bologna. However, Tuscany is Sangiovese's heartland and, in various clonal manifestations, it is the main grape of Chianti and Vino Nobile di Montepulciano, and the sole grape of Brunello di Montalcino. With its thick skin and excess of pips it can make raw, lean wine if picked before it is fully ripe, and only the best vineyard sites regularly excel with it. Blended with Cabernet, it can make a fascinating bitter cherry and chocolate red of considerable style. Elsewhere, California has had increasing success.

SAUVIGNON BLANC
Ask any wine drinker for the homeland of Sauvignon Blanc and there's a very fair chance they'll say New Zealand. Yet there wasn't a single Sauvignon vine in New Zealand as recently as 1970. It's just that the wonderfully tangy, aggressive flavours of New Zealand Sauvignon have completely outpaced those of its original source, the Loire Valley and Bordeaux in France. New World winemakers took Sancerre in the Loire Valley as a role model for bone dry, unoaked white wines, but they were rarely too successful until New Zealand showed them how to do it. Now dry, green-tasting Sauvignon is made all over Europe, the Americas and the Antipodes. Fermented and aged in oak, it is totally different – toasty, nutty and long-lasting. Bordeaux is the home of this style, but the method has spread worldwide.

SÉMILLON
Thin-skinned, prone to rot and without any particular aroma, Sémillon is not, on the face of it, a white grape destined for international fame. Yet plant it in Sauternes, let botrytis get to it, blend it with some Sauvignon Blanc and you have one of the great sweet wines of the world. On its own it can be too low in acidity, though Australia has made a speciality of varietal Sémillon. Yields must be kept low or the resulting wine will be flabby and dilute.

SYRAH/SHIRAZ
Heat is what this red vine likes: give it a hot, dry climate, poor soil, and it'll be as happy as a sandboy. Syrah also needs decent weather for flowering as it is prone to *coulure*, or poor fruit-set, when bunches of smaller berries drop off. It loves the northern Rhône: those impossible slopes, that granite soil, those serious growers that keep its yields down – perfect. Australia also provides hot, dry conditions and Shiraz responds magnificently. It has only recently become trendy, but California and South Africa are already producing excellent examples and I've seen exciting wines from Argentina, Italy, New Zealand and even Switzerland.

TEMPRANILLO
I really don't know where Spain would be without the Tempranillo grape. All the major red wine regions rely on it to a greater or lesser extent, and yet it performs very differently in the various regions and adopts different names too. Rioja is its heartland, where, so long as it isn't overcropped (sadly, it usually is), it gives fruit, perfume and ageability to the reds. In neighbouring Navarra, it plays second fiddle to Garnacha. It is fairly important, but less exciting, as Ull de Llebre in Penedés, yet extremely dark, rich and fragrant as Tinto Fino in the low-yielding vineyards of Ribera del Duero, and as Cencibel in the La Mancha and Valdepeñas regions. Elsewhere in Spain it's known as Tinto Madrid or Tinto de Toro, while in Portugal it's Aragonez or Tinto Roriz.

VIOGNIER
Funny. Even just a few years ago, there was hardly a wine lover in the world who'd ever heard of Viognier. And now it's got the aura of a supermodel: as flouncing, pouting, petulant, perfumed, riding it's popularity for all it's worth before someone says, hang on, is it really that good? Well, yes and no. As the grape of Condrieu and Château-Grillet it can produce wines of heady mayflower perfume and unctuous peach and crème fraîche flavours – when it's not overcropped. Nowadays it usually is, in which case better value examples are springing up all over the south of France, and California and Australia are also getting in on the act.

ZINFANDEL
The USA imported the first cuttings of this versatile red vine from Europe in the nineteenth century – they were probably relatives of southern Italy's Primitivo variety. But 'Zin' has become a Californian speciality, being used for everything from red, white and 'blush' wines, that range from dry to a sweet, late-harvest style, to port-style wines. Its best expression, however, is as a richly fruity red wine, full of blackberry or plum flavour and for this it needs a relatively cool climate, and not too much irrigation, since yields can be high. Sugar levels can go sky-high, too, and result in a baked, port-like taste. The most concentrated flavours of dark blackberry fruit and pepper come from old vines. Mexico, Chile, South Africa and Australia are also producing good results.

Wine Styles

Winemakers throughout the world have tended to look to Europe's classic styles for inspiration but they are now developing their own new classic styles, which, though based on the originals, are unmistakably, gloriously different.

RED WINES

CABERNET SAUVIGNON BLENDS/BORDEAUX

These are based on the great red wine of the Médoc in Bordeaux. At their best, they exude much of the blackcurrant fruit, cedar, mint and cigar-box perfume of the original, together with its tannic grip. Although they rarely achieve the finesse, they often more than compensate with more fruit, power and ripeness. Cabernet is almost always blended with Merlot and Cabernet Franc in Bordeaux, but California, Chile, Australia, New Zealand, South Africa, Italy, Spain and Eastern Europe often make Cabernet unblended. However, most are now experimenting with Merlot, Cabernet Franc and Malbec, while some countries add local varieties – Tempranillo in Spain, Sangiovese in Italy and Shiraz in Australia.

BEAUJOLAIS

Winemakers the world over have been inspired by the light, gluggable Beaujolais wines, released as Beaujolais Nouveau each November. At its best, this is the ultimate, easy-going red and producers worldwide recognize the fact. California makes Nouveau-style wines from Zinfandel and Gamay, and there are similar wines from Italy and Spain both made by the same carbonic maceration technique as Beaujolais. Carbonic maceration is widely used in the Rhône and the Midi to soften the unprepossessing fruit of certain local vines, in particular Carignan, and to bring out the best in Syrah.

PINOT NOIR/BURGUNDY

This is the most temperamental of grapes, both to grow and to vinify. In the right hands it's the most seductive and sensual of all red wines – fragrant, often delicate, redolent of strawberry, cherry and plum. But get it even slightly wrong and you end up with a glassful of overboiled jam. It's also a reluctant traveller, and not many regions can coax it out of the sulks. California is doing nicely, particularly Carneros and Santa Barbara, and Oregon is promising though patchy. Australia, New Zealand, South Africa, Chile and even Spain have good examples.

SYRAH/RHÔNE

The originals here are the beefy, brawny yet fruit-packed styles of Hermitage and Côte-Rôtie in the northern Rhône. Savage, spicy, sensual, rich in loganberry fruit, flecked with licorice, smoke and coated in chocolate – that's Rhône Syrah at its best. Australian Shiraz is the same grape, and these two styles have now set an example, being tentatively but excitingly followed in California, Argentina and South Africa. France's Midi is now bursting with brilliant examples – expect to see more and more warm-climate regions jumping on the bandwagon.

WHITE WINES

CHARDONNAY/BURGUNDY

Chardonnay could, with some justification, be called the most popular grape variety in the world, not because of its total plantings, which are relatively small, but for its massive annual percentage increases in every area that aspires to quality. The original style comes in tiny quantities from a few small villages in Burgundy's Côte d'Or. Villages like Meursault and Puligny-Montrachet have perfected a style of dry white, usually fermented and aged in barrel, that manages to offer a richness owing nothing to sugar, a fatness that is never bloated or coarse, a perfume like the drifting smoke from a spice caravan's evening feast. Every major wine-producing country has fashioned its own version of this great wine style, in particular the USA on both seaboards, Australia and New Zealand. Chile, Argentina, South Africa, the south of France and Spain are also producing fine examples. A lighter, non-oaked or barely oaked style is almost becoming a byword for dry white wine in Eastern Europe, Italy, and southern France – indeed almost anywhere the grape will grow.

SAUVIGNON BLANC

If Chardonnay has come to be a shorthand description of a round, ripe, soft, dry style of white wine, then Sauvignon has come to stand for the palate-slapping, tongue-tingling, in-your-face tangy green flavours epitomized by New Zealand Sauvignon Blanc. Yet New Zealand Sauvignon isn't the original – it's a copy inspired by Sancerre's cool, dry wines from Sauvignon grapes grown in France's Loire Valley. But for once the copy is actually better than the original, and producers in search of that zingy gooseberry, asparagus, nettles and lime attack use Marlborough in New Zealand as their benchmark. Other countries haven't found it easy to duplicate the sheer exuberant sharp-edged intensity of fruit, but Chile, South Africa and Australia are getting there. Pessac-Léognan in Bordeaux is the classic oak-aged style and the USA, Australia and New Zealand also do it well.

RIESLING/RHINE AND MOSEL

The classic Riesling flavours – steely yet flowery in youth, honeyed and petrolly in maturity – are still best achieved in the Rhine and Mosel areas of Germany. However France's Alsace and Austria's Wachau also make fuller and drier versions. Australia's Rieslings are fatter and less delicate, yet they age beautifully, while New Zealand's are gorgeously floral and perfumed. The Pacific North-West and New York State in the USA also make good examples.

SWEET WINES

The classic sweet wines are made from grapes affected by noble rot – *Botrytis cinerea* – during warm, humid autumns. This fungus concentrates the sugar in the grapes and intensely sweet wines result. The great European examples come from Sauternes in Bordeaux, Coteaux du Layon in the Loire Valley, the Rhine and Mosel in Germany, the Neusiedlersee in Austria and Tokay in Hungary. Canada, Germany and Austria make remarkably sweet Icewines from frozen grapes.

SPARKLING WINES

It wasn't until California, New Zealand and Australia began to imitate Champagne methods that the great fizz producers of north-eastern France had any serious rivals. The world has since benefited, as Champagne's own quality has improved, and more New World producers increasingly achieve similar standards by using cool-climate fruit, and by understanding better how to referment the wine inside its own bottle.

FORTIFIED WINES

The idea of fortifying a wine with brandy or neutral spirit started because of the need to stabilize the wines of Portugal and Spain for export to northern Europe. From such humble beginnings these wines are now port and sherry respectively, and, along with Madeira and Marsala, are the great fortified styles of Europe. However, southern France, Spain and Italy have long arrested the fermentation of wines – particularly Muscats – to preserve sweetness. Cyprus and the Crimea also have a long tradition, and the fortified Muscats and Tokays of Australia and the Muscats of South Africa are world class.

For Icewine, grapes are left to freeze on the vine, and the ice crystals separated from the concentrated juice during pressing.

Some of the finest sweet wines are due to the fungus Botrytis cinerea *which desiccates the grape, leaving it rich in sugar.*

From Grape to Glass

There are as many different ways of making wine as there are winemakers – or perhaps as there are grape varieties, mesoclimates and markets. There are refinements and adjustments to be made at every stage of the basic diagram we show here. Are you picking in hot weather, for example? Then you may need to cool the grapes before crushing. Do you want to extract more flavour from white grapes? Then try macerating the skins and juice together before fermentation. Are you out to make the very finest wine possible? Then you will ferment the grapes from each plot of vineyard separately and age the resulting wines separately until you decide which lots to blend into your final wine. You will understand that the contents of each oak barrel will taste subtly different to those of its neighbours, and you will put your final wine together with rigorous selectivity. Or do you want to make a sound commercial blend that will appeal to a wide audience at a low price? Then your efforts will initially go into ensuring hygiene, and controlling the temperature of the fermentation; into keeping the new wine from excess contact with the air; into using only healthy grapes at optimum ripeness in the first place, perhaps adding oak chips for a bit of spice. But one fact holds true for all winemakers, no matter what level of quality they are aiming at: the final wine can only be as good as the grapes, and the best winemaker in the world can only retain that quality. That's why the years of work that must be put in before a single grape is picked – choosing, siting and planting a vineyard – are so important.

A word about rosé. It is perfectly possible to make pink wine by blending red with white, although in the EU Champagne is the only rosé allowed to be made this way. The other methods both involve macerating red wines on their skins for just long enough for the juice to be coloured. When you have got the right colour you can then press the grapes and proceed to ferment the juice as for white wine (opposite), or you can simply run out as much pink juice as you want and ferment the rest on the skins as red wine. This latter method, known in France as *saignée* (because the vats of red are 'bled') is a way of making good full-flavoured rosé and at the same time giving the red wine more colour and concentration.

► Nearly all grapes are crushed and destemmed before fermentation. The stalks contain more bitter tannin than most winemakers want, though some will add a percentage of the stalks back into the fermentation vat to increase tannin.
Before the invention of sophisticated machinery the best method of crushing grapes without releasing the aggressive tannins in stalks and pips was by treading. In the Douro Valley many wine producers continue to follow this tradition and most of the very best quality port wines will be made from grapes trodden by foot. Whatever the method, once the process is completed sulphur will usually be added to kill wild yeasts and prevent oxidation.

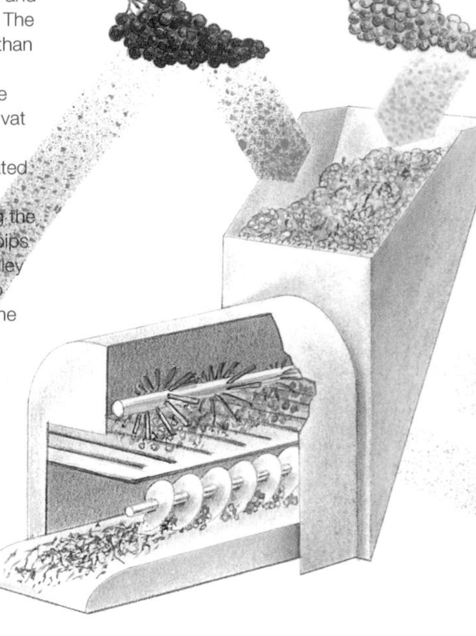

► Some red wines undergo carbonic maceration, a process used in Beaujolais to produce juicy, aromatic reds, and also adopted elsewhere. Whole bunches of grapes are put into a sealed vat which is filled with carbon dioxide. Intracellular enzymatic fermentation takes place, producing highly coloured, low-tannin juice, while normal fermentation takes place among the broken grapes and juice at the bottom of the vat. After about a week the juice is run off the skins and the remaining whole grapes are pressed. A normal yeast fermentation of both components then continues without the skins. If done carefully the wines will be fresh and flavoursome but if not they may develop an unpleasant 'bubblegum' aroma.

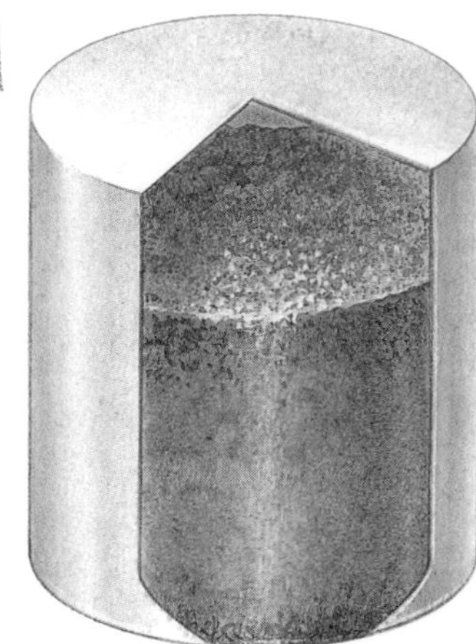

Fortified Wine

These wines require different techniques again. Fortified wines are wines that have been strengthened by the addition of alcohol in the form of high-strength, neutral spirit or brandy. This may be done during fermentation, in order to stop the wine fermenting any further. Port is made this way. When the juice has reached around six per cent of alcohol naturally, grape spirit is added and all the unfermented sugar remains in the wine, making it very sweet.

In the case of sherry, which is all naturally bone dry, the fermentation is allowed to finish and the brandy is added later, before the wine begins its lengthy aging in solera. Madeira, too, is allowed to finish its fermentation before being fortified.

The *vins doux naturels* of the south of France are made in a similar way to port, with the fermentation being arrested by the addition of brandy; much less brandy is added than is the case with port, and the result is a much more delicate wine. The process of fortification is not just intended to increase alcoholic strength but is also an essential integral ingredient in helping to create different and distinctive wines.

Sparkling Wine

All sparkling wine is made by keeping carbon dioxide gas dissolved in the wine under pressure. Then, when the pressure is released, you get a glorious rush of bubbles. In the Champagne method the gas is a by-product of a second fermentation. In the next best method, the second fermentation is in bottle, but once it is complete, the bottles are emptied into a large tank (still under pressure, so as not to lose the fizz), and the wine is rebottled leaving the lees behind. This is what labels mean when they say 'fermented in the bottle' rather than 'fermented in this bottle'. The *cuve close* method, generally considered less good again, involves doing all the second fermentation in tank, under pressure. The cheapest way of all is to pump carbon dioxide into still wine: this is known as the *pompe bicyclette* method. There is also the Russian Continuous method, a system devised in Russia but used elsewhere, notably Portugal. Still base wine is pumped through a system of tanks. As it passes through it ferments again, is aged and filtered and emerges as finished wine. It is sparkling wine production on an industrial scale: it's fresh and clean, but no, it's not Krug.

▼ White wines are fermented without their skins, so the grapes are first pressed and the skins discarded (sometimes bunches are pressed whole). The gentler the pressing, the better and more elegant the flavours will be: harsh pressing forces too many bitter or coarse compounds from the skin and pips. Solids are removed from the juice (known as must) before fermentation by settling, centrifuging or filtration.
The best winemakers often like to ferment must that is as clear and clean as possible. In contrast the red wine-to-be, a pale sticky soup of skins, pips and juice, goes into vat to begin fermentation. Cultivated yeasts may be added, or the yeasts in the winery may be allowed to work on their own. Red wine can be fermented in different sorts of vats: big open containers are still common.

SWEET WINE. Usually the yeast will go on working until all the sugar in the must has been converted to alcohol, and the wine will taste dry. But if the must is intensely sweet (as with Sauternes or Tokay) then the yeasts might give up of their own accord at a certain level of alcohol, leaving a high level of residual sugar in the wine. They cannot work in too alcoholic an environment. The winemaker may also take the decision for them, and stop the fermentation when the wine has reached the balance of alcohol and residual sugar required, by adding sulphur dioxide to kill the yeasts, or by centrifuging to remove them. In Germany in order to add sweetness it is possible to add unfermented grape juice or Süssreserve to dry wine. Another way of making sweet wine is by adding grape spirit to arrest fermentation. This is the method used for port.

▼ After pressing, the white must is fermented. Nowadays specially cultivated yeasts are preferred in order to ensure successful fermentation. In the past winemakers had to rely on natural yeasts already present on grape skins or in the winery. Acidity can be corrected if necessary with tartaric and/or malic acids. White wine, like red, can be fermented in varying materials, from new oak barriques to glass fibre, cement or stainless steel. The containers should be spotlessly clean. Modern stainless steel vats allow easy temperature control and low temperature fermentation of white wines, which retains all their freshness and aroma. In some areas the wine is left in contact with the yeast (or lees) after fermentation to soften and mellow.

► As the fermentation progresses, colour leaches from the skins into the red grape must. To encourage this, the skins, which rise to the top of the vat and form a thick 'cap', need to be constantly broken up and prodded down (traditionally with large wooden poles) into the must. Alternatively the wine needs to be continually pumped over the cap. Some wineries use rotary vinifying drums to the same effect.

Many red wines, including all those intended for long aging, are left to macerate on the skins for some days or weeks after fermentation is complete to extract tannin from the pips and skins.
When the winemaker is satisfied, the wine will be run off the skins, and the residue put through a press. This must be carefully judged or else the finished wine will never soften sufficiently to be enjoyed.

◄ Some varieties, Chardonnay for example, are fermented and matured in oak barrels, and are left on their lees to gain texture and flavour. Others, such as Riesling, do not benefit from oak aging.
It is a mistake to believe that time spent in barrel will enhance any wine irrespective of quality or origin. As many winemakers have found to their cost, it is not a remedy to cure poor wine. To get the best results top-quality base wine must be used.

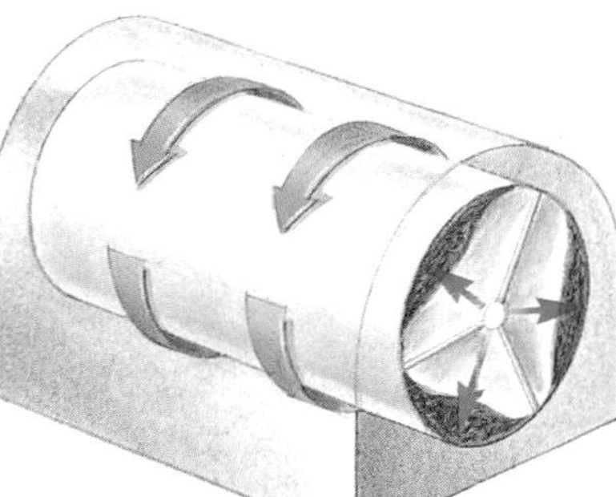

◄ The wine pressed from the skins will be tougher and more tannic than the free-run wine. It will be aged separately, and a little may be added to the final blend to give it more guts.
The most traditional and gentle of the many presses is the basket press, where pneumatic power or human muscle eases the wine from the skins. Steel presses often contain a rubber bladder which, when inflated, presses the skins against the sides and allows the wine to run clear. Excessive pressure will release bitter-tasting compounds into the wine from skins and pips but this is easily avoided by a careful winemaker

MALOLACTIC FERMENTATION is a process that has only come to be understood properly this century. It tends to happen naturally, when the cellars warm up in the spring, and the new wine begins to work once again. This is due to naturally present bacteria which metabolize the harsh, appley-tasting malic acid in the wine into softer-tasting lactic acid. Nowadays it is common for red wines to undergo the malolactic. The one place it must not be allowed to happen is in bottle, where it will produce a slight fizz and distinctly 'off' smell. In hot climates where acidity is at a premium, the winemaker may choose to prevent this second fermentation in white wines. This can be done by filtration. For white Burgundy it is generally considered desirable and in California it can add richness and complexity to the wine.

▼ Red wines are often aged in oak barrels. New oak imparts extra tannin and rich vanilla aromas; older barrels will not add much flavour but will have a gentle oxidative effect which can add complexity though diminish fruit. Barrels made from French oak are particularly appreciated.

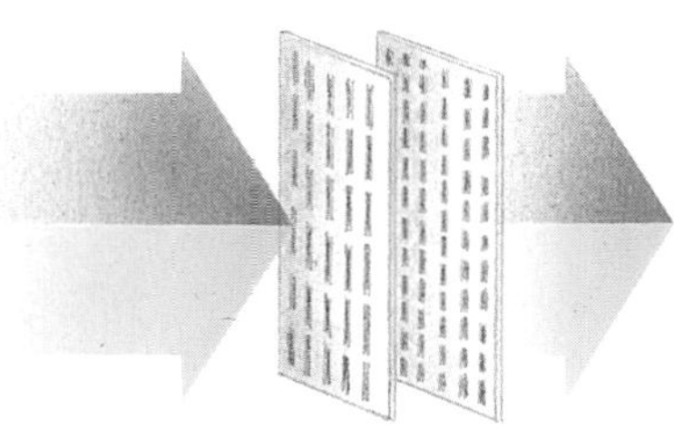

► As the wine begins to settle, solids and yeast cells will fall to the bottom of the barrel, and every few months the wine will be racked off these lees and into a clean barrel.
At this stage the wine is blended, fined – using egg white, bentonite or other substances to remove finer particles – and stabilized to the level required, in preparation for bottling.

▲ Nowadays white wines generally go through a membrane filter so they can be guaranteed yeast- and bacteria-free. But filtration (and centrifuging, another option open to the winemaker) does remove some of the flavour, and so the very finest wines are often not filtered.
Although some red wines are only racked and not fined or filtered, most undergo a coarse filtration process before bottling.
The object is a clear, bright wine with no cloudiness.
Sometimes, usually the result of sudden cold, clear tartrate crystals may appear in bottles of wine, but they are harmless. These bottles should be stood upright to allow the crystals to collect at the bottom before the wine is carefully poured.

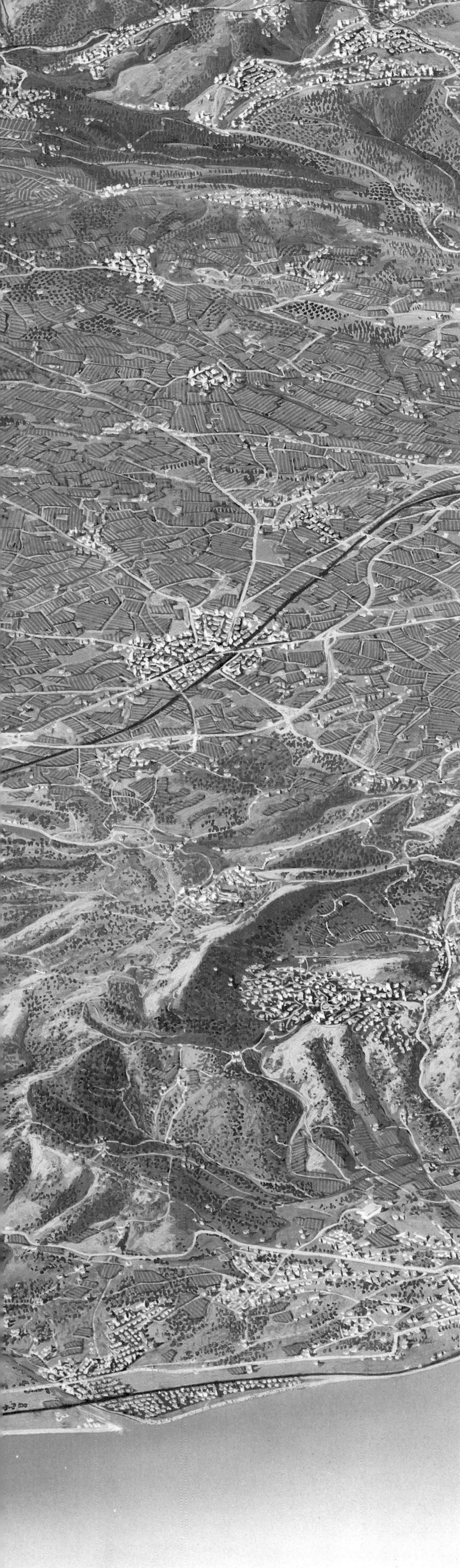

WINES & WINE REGIONS OF THE WORLD

LIST OF PANORAMIC MAPS

Left: the heart of the Penedés vineyards in north-east Spain.

FRANCE

WE'VE HAD OUR TIFFS. I've stormed off and formed fleeting, flirtatious liaisons with other nations round the world. But true love is true love. I've always come back to France. Other countries can do *some* things better but when it comes to wine, no country can do so many things as well as France. My love of France, my respect for her natural genius in wine is deepened, not diminished, by contact with her rivals in Europe and elsewhere. The more I learn about wine in Chile, Australia, California, Italy, Spain or New Zealand, the more I appreciate France.

But then, France is lucky. Her geographical situation is ideally suited to most of the grape varieties that make great table wine and her geological make-up has provided numerous sites perfectly suited to the measured ripening of these varieties. This combination provides a wide array of areas that achieve a precise balance between too much heat and too little, between too much rain and too little. The result is that the great varieties like Cabernet Sauvignon, Pinot Noir, Syrah, Chardonnay and Sauvignon Blanc – plus a host of others – will generally creep towards ripeness rather than rush headlong and, just as with an apple or a peach, slowly ripened fruit gives the most delicious flavour, the balance between sugar and acidity and perfume is most perfectly achieved.

Nowadays, modern vineyard technology can mimic such conditions up to a point in warmer areas, and perfect cellar and winemaking conditions could be created at the Equator or the North Pole. But such developments are only a generation old. France's other priceless natural asset has always been perfect wine-*making* conditions. For 2000 years before the advent of refrigeration techniques, most major wine areas were sufficiently cool by vintage time for the wines to ferment in a controlled way without artificial help. Such other great wine nations as Italy and Spain, the United States and Australia had few areas that could rely on such luck.

And France has been making wine for 2000 years and more. And almost from the start her wines were not merely for the domestic market. The Romans enthusiastically imported them. Later, as the great northern trading nations rose to prominence, France was their natural trading partner. France was the crossroads of Europe when they ventured south. For all this time, France has been making wine for the rest of the world, not just for herself, and as the rest of the world sets out gamely to copy her achievements, the old original still stands supreme.

The impressive Château de Monbazillac in south-west France has been producing a sweet wine in the style of Sauternes for many centuries.

The Wine Regions of France

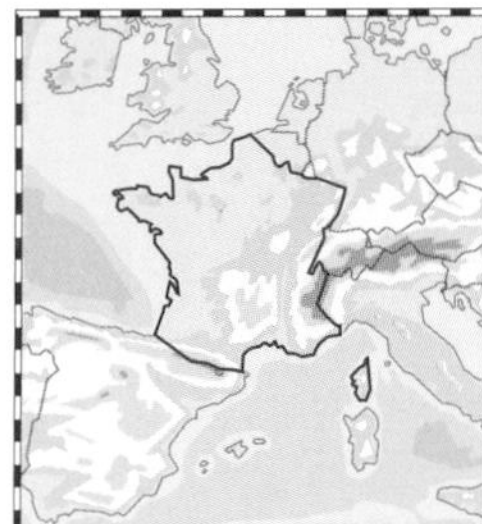

We're standing on the brow of the Montagne de Reims in the Champagne region of northern France. The pale springtime sun hardly takes the edge off the damp westerly gale scudding in over the soggy plains. We're just about at the northern limit beyond which the classic grape varieties will not ripen, but it feels as though we're way past it. Back in town we descend, windswept, into the cool chalky cellars dreaming of a good log fire and a hot toddy. No such luck. We have the 'clear wines', the *vins clairs*, to taste. They cut into our gums with the raw attack of a hacksaw scything through a crab-apple. Undrinkable. Yet when the local magicians have been to work, this reedy, rasping liquid will be transformed into Champagne, the classic sparkling wine of the world. No riper grapes, no less sour wine, no warmer, more protected slopes would do.

So let's flee to the other end of France to the parched terraces teetering above the Mediterranean at Banyuls, just yards from the Spanish border. Let's go at vintage time and protect ourselves from the searing heat as the sun and scorching wind shrivel the Grenache grapes half-way to raisins on the vine. Back in the warmish cellars we taste the thick, sweet juice crushed off these ripened grapes, then we taste the wines of one year old, two years, five years, ten, getting deeper, more treacly, more chocolate-rich, more prune and damson dark. Banyuls Grand Cru. The nearest thing France produces to vintage port. Some would say it's better. No less ripe grapes, no less luscious wine, no cooler, less protected sites would do.

These are the two extremes of France. In between, almost every conceivable type of wine is made, from the driest to the richest of whites, from rosés as ethereal as sweet pea's bloom to ones as ruddy as a butcher's cheeks, from reds to toss back from the jug, carefree as minstrels, to reds as serious and solemn as temples. All of these I'll try to show you in the following pages. We've got maps for all the significant areas in France, and detailed maps of the most exciting and important. The object of the maps is to make the vineyards come alive, to put them in the context of the valleys and mountainsides they inhabit, of the towns they surround and the rivers they front.

France's vineyards are roughly divided into three. On the Atlantic coast, from the Loire Valley, down through Bordeaux and on to the western Pyrenees, the climate is maritime. The presence of the Gulf Stream moderates the climate but rain carried in on the westerly winds is a continual problem. In the Loire Valley, mesoclimate and well-drained soils are crucial to the chances of decent wine. In Bordeaux, though the Landes pine forests draw off much rain, free-draining gravel beds are necessary for the great Cabernet Sauvignon to ripen. This influence spreads up the Dordogne, Lot, Garonne and Tarn rivers, gradually diminishing until the Mediterranean influence takes over east of Toulouse. The grape varieties, the styles of wine, the food, the lifestyle and the landscape all change.

The vine grows naturally and easily right around the warm, inland Mediterranean Sea. The summers are hot and dry, the winters are mild. Close to the sea, the breezes ameliorate the sun's heat without interfering with the ripening of the grapes. Otherwise, the heat is tempered by planting vines up towards the mountain ranges that crowd in on the coastal plains and by regular westerly and northern winds. Vast quantities of ordinary wines are made out of grapes like the red Carignan and Cinsaut and the white Macabeo and Ugni Blanc. When the vine grows this easily, the winemaker must tame its vigour if he or she wants quality. Old vines and infertile stony soils reduce the yields, and then some magnificent wines ensue. The *vins doux naturels,* from Banyuls in the Pyrenees to Beaumes-de-Venise and Rasteau in the Rhône Valley are heady and sweet. The Languedoc-Roussillon region is undergoing a revolution based on old, dark, savage reds from the varieties of the South, as well as bright, exciting, modern reds and whites from the international varieties led by Cabernet, Merlot, Syrah and Chardonnay. Provence is still nervously nibbling at the revolution on her doorstep, but the reds and whites of the Rhône Valley are roaring and prancing with a self-belief in their stupendous qualities that is a joy to behold.

Above Lyon, the climate changes again. It becomes more continental as the Mediterranean influence wanes, and to the west, in the upper reaches of the Loire, the Atlantic influence flickers and dies. The winters become harsher, the summers hotter. Vineyards can stretch much further north on this eastern side of France, but they don't find it easy to ripen their grapes. Frequently autumn storms herald the end of summer a crucial week or so before the vintage is ready, so mesoclimates are all-important here. In Burgundy sheltered south-east-facing slopes protected from the wet westerly winds and angled to every ray of sun are at a premium. The scattered mountain sites of Savoie and Jura hack out their small warm mesoclimates from the forest and the rock. Alsace squeezes up against the Vosges mountains whose peaks and forests to the west provide a rain-shadow, making the region one of the sunniest and driest parts of France. And then there's Champagne. A few unlikely but ideal sites allow the Pinot and Chardonnay grapes to ripen just enough to make the magical drink that is Champagne.

THE CLASSIFICATION SYSTEM FOR FRENCH WINE

The French have the most far-reaching system of wine quality control. The key factors are the 'origin' of the wine, its historic method of production and the use of the correct grapes.

QUALITY CATEGORIES

Wine is divided into two groups – quality wine (AC and VDQS) and table wine (*vin de pays* and *vin de table*).

- **Appellation d'Origine Contrôlée (AC, AOC)** This has covered the main wine regions of France and is slowly being extended. The seven most important requirements are as follows: *Land* Suitable vineyard land is minutely defined. *Grape* Only those grape varieties traditionally regarded as suitable can be used. *Degree of alcohol* Wines must reach a minimum (or maximum) degree of natural alcohol. *Yield* A basic permitted yield is set for each AC, but the figure may be altered each year. *Vineyard practice* AC wines must follow rules about pruning methods and density of planting. *Wine-making practice* Each AC wine has its own regulations. Typically, chaptalization – adding sugar during fermentation to increase alcoholic strength – is accepted in the north, but not in the south. *Tasting and analysis* Since 1974 wines must pass a tasting panel. *Varietal labelling* There is a move by the AC authorities to restrict the use of the grape variety's name on the label of AC wines except where this is a long-established practice. They argue that the uniqueness of French wines lies in their *terroir* and not in the grape. While we ponder this, expect the *vins de pays* – which can and do use varietal names on their labels – to increase their market share.
- **Vin Délimité de Qualité Supérieure (VDQS)** This group is, in general, slightly less reliable in quality and is being phased out. No more *vins de pays* are being upgraded to VDQS and occasionally existing ones are upgraded to AC.
- **Vin de Pays** This category gives a regional definition to basic blending wines. The rules are similar to AC, but allow more flexibility for yields and grape varieties. Quality can be stunning, and expect fruit, value and competent wine-making.
- **Vin de Table** 'Table wine' is the title for the rest. No quality control except for basic public health regulations. *Vins de pays* are available for about the same price and offer a far better drink.

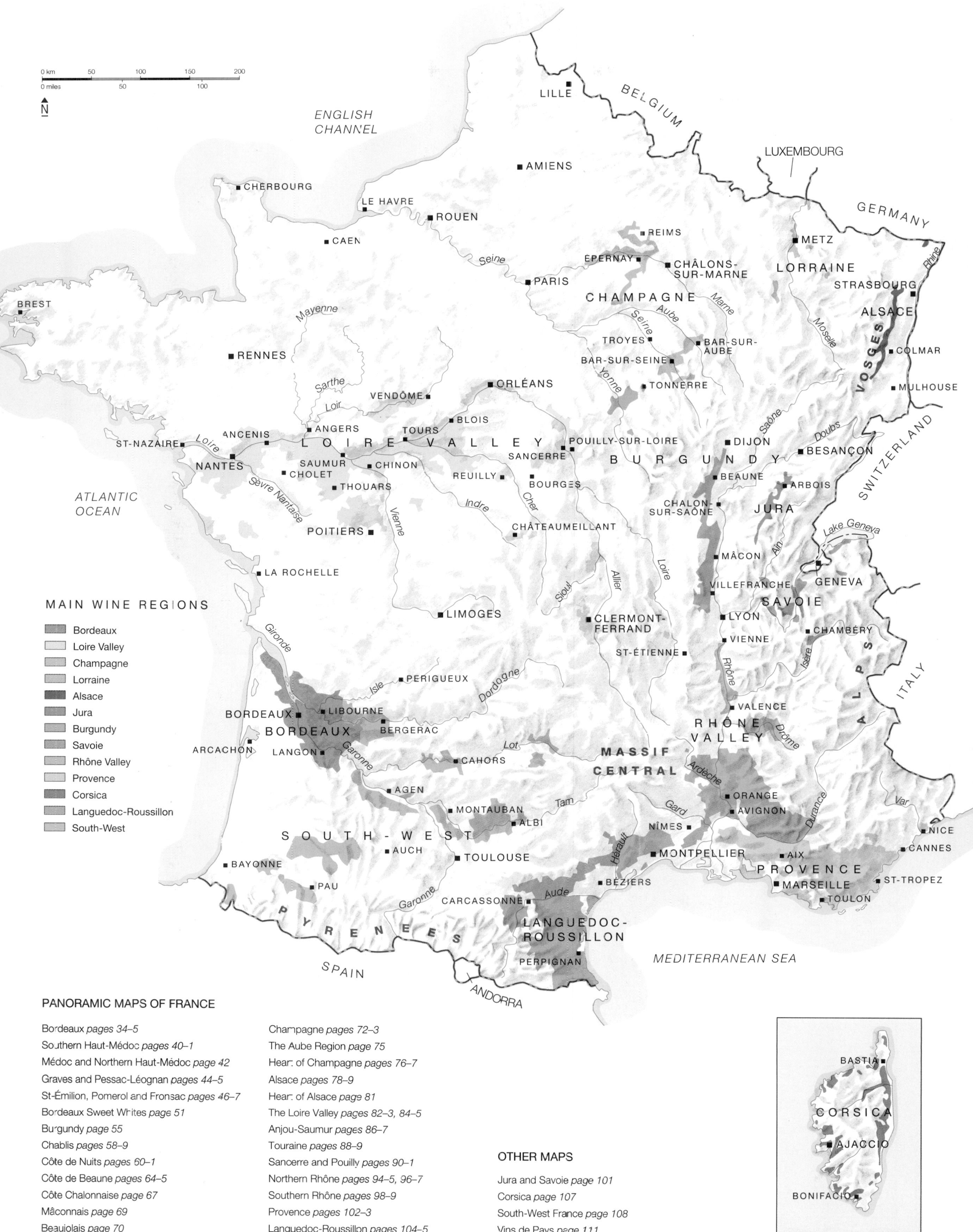

MAIN WINE REGIONS

- Bordeaux
- Loire Valley
- Champagne
- Lorraine
- Alsace
- Jura
- Burgundy
- Savoie
- Rhône Valley
- Provence
- Corsica
- Languedoc-Roussillon
- South-West

PANORAMIC MAPS OF FRANCE

OTHER MAPS

BORDEAUX

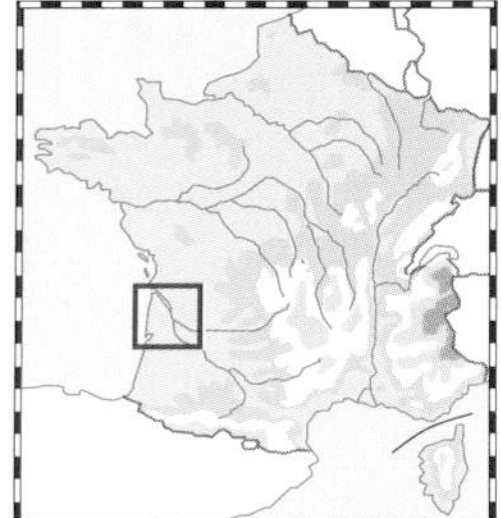

I CAN'T HELP IT. I love Bordeaux. It isn't the most friendly of wine regions. It isn't the most beautiful. Its wines can be pig-headed and difficult to understand when they are young, and positively harsh when they're still in barrel. But you know what they say about your first time. Bordeaux was my first time. My first ever wine visit, my first ever vineyards.

And Bordeaux was my first wine-tasting. And Bordeaux was my first great wine. First, first, first. I suppose it's not so strange for someone brought up in England. When I was at university, great wine was red, and great red wine was Bordeaux. Of course, we tried other wines from time to time, especially when money ran short, but if we were being treated to dinner by our richers and betters, we felt short-changed if the red wines weren't Bordeaux. Every wine-tasting session would always end up as a tortuous yet passionate discussion of the minutiae of different Bordeaux properties and vintages as we lapped up every scrap of knowledge we could. So it was only natural that one summer vacation I would optimistically jump into my Mini and, armed with a precious introduction to Peter Sichel at Château d'Angludet in Margaux, head off to what I hoped would be wine drinkers' nirvana.

Bordeaux is as much a story of politics and history as it is a story of wine. Look at the map. To the left I had expected great rolling hills and dales all covered in vines. Jovial bucolic cellar masters and their swains ever keen to swap a tale and share a jar. Villages and towns bustling with the busy activities of wine. I should have gone anywhere but Bordeaux.

At first I found no vineyards at all. Bordeaux was a splendid, haughtily magnificent place – well, the centre was; the rest was sprawling suburbia and endless industrial estates. And as I drove out towards Margaux, the little villages seemed sullenly asleep and the land damp, low-browed and devoid of vines. I did find the vines; of course I did once I got to Margaux; I did find friendly if not exactly gregarious people, and across these broad, undulating acres, I did find some amazing châteaux – the grand houses at the centre of many estates – but the Médoc with the best will in

0 km 2 4 6 8
0 miles 2 4

AC WINE AREAS

1. Médoc
2. Haut-Médoc
3. St-Estèphe
4. Pauillac
5. St-Julien
6. Listrac-Médoc
7. Moulis
8. Margaux
9. Pessac-Léognan
10. Graves
11. Cérons
12. Barsac
13. Sauternes
14. Côtes de Bordeaux-St-Macaire
15. Bordeaux Haut-Benauge or Entre-Deux-Mers Haut-Benauge
16. Ste-Croix-du-Mont
17. Loupiac
18. Cadillac or Premières Côtes de Bordeaux
19. Entre-Deux-Mers
20. Graves de Vayres
21. Premières Côtes de Bordeaux
22. Côtes de Bourg
23. Côtes de Blaye and Premières Côtes de Blaye
24. Fronsac
25. Côtes Canon-Fronsac or Canon-Fronsac
26. Pomerol
27. Lalande-de-Pomerol
28. St-Émilion
29. St-Émilion satellites (Lussac, Montagne, St-Georges, Puisseguin)
30. Côtes de Castillon
31. Bordeaux-Côtes de Francs
32. Ste-Foy-Bordeaux

BORDEAUX/BORDEAUX SUPÉRIEUR AC

OTHER AC BOUNDARIES

VINEYARDS

TOTAL DISTANCE NORTH TO SOUTH 144KM (89½ MILES)

N

0 km 2 4 6 8
0 miles 2 4

the world isn't exactly a sylvan paradise. Once those vines start, that's all you get where the soil's at all suitable – vines. I found a few hills and dales around St-Émilion but even there it is mostly just a carpet of vines. The Graves isn't quite so wall-to-wall because half the best vineyards are now buried under suburban houses and an airport.

No great scenery, just vines, vines, vines. And that is the key to why Bordeaux, by the end of the twentieth century, can claim the title of the World's Greatest Wine Region.

Look at the map again. Although there are numerous places in France, the rest of Europe, America and the southern hemisphere that can boast brilliant wines, most are produced in tiny quantities in little mesoclimates dotted about the place. Bordeaux has great swathes of land suited to different sorts of wine and around 200 properties producing perhaps 100,000 bottles of wine each that veers between the good and the brilliant almost every year. That's an awful lot of wine. There are several hundred more properties on slightly less favoured land whose wine can be still very good. Altogether there are about 4000 properties that bottle their own wine and another 15,000 or more growers that don't, making a grand total of between 800 and 900 million bottles of wine. Every year.

CLIMATE AND SOIL

Most of the area on the map grows vines to a greater or lesser extent, but it is only certain favoured localities that regularly achieve exceptional quality. The sea to the west gives some clues. The Gulf Stream draws in warm tropical currents up this western shore of France, crucially ameliorating temperatures near the coast. Yet the Bay of Biscay is also notoriously stormy. Only the vast stretches of Landes pine forest to the west break the salt-laden westerly winds and suck down much of the rainfall that could otherwise ruin a vintage. The consequence is a pattern of generally hot summers and long, mild autumns still only just warm enough to fully ripen the local grape varieties. But there's a fair amount of rainfall too.

Here's where the gravel and the limestone slopes come in. The Garonne, the Dordogne, and the Isle rivers have, over the millennia, deposited deep gravel terraces in the broad ridges that characterize the Médoc and many parts of Pessac-Léognan and Pomerol. Gravel is virtually free-draining. When excess rain does fall, it drops straight through the gravel. The limestone slopes of St-Émilion, Bourg, Blaye and the Premières Côtes de Bordeaux achieve this to a lesser degree.

Vines put down deep roots in gravel and limestone as they search for scant supplies of nutrients. In a climate only just

WHERE THE VINEYARDS ARE *This map shows the greatest fine wine area of the world in all its glory. Although there are vineyards on virtually every segment of the map, with the exception of the great pine forests of the Landes that spread their protective shield along the Bay of Biscay to the west, the best vineyards are those situated close to the rivers Garonne and Dordogne, and the Gironde estuary. The important Garonne vineyards start around Langon, with the Graves region which follows the left bank up to Bordeaux. Sauternes and Barsac are clustered round the river Ciron, while the best vineyards to the south of the city are Pessac-Léognan. The Médoc runs like a tongue of land northwards from the city, with the best vineyards between Macau and St-Estèphe, close to the Gironde. Across the estuary, at Bourg and Blaye, are vineyards more famous in Roman times, and following the Dordogne east towards Libourne, Fronsac has also enjoyed greater renown. However Pomerol, next to Libourne, and St-Émilion have never been more famous. Lesser vineyards spread out from St-Émilion, and the area between the Dordogne and the Garonne – Entre-Deux-Mers – is a source of much decent red and white wine.*

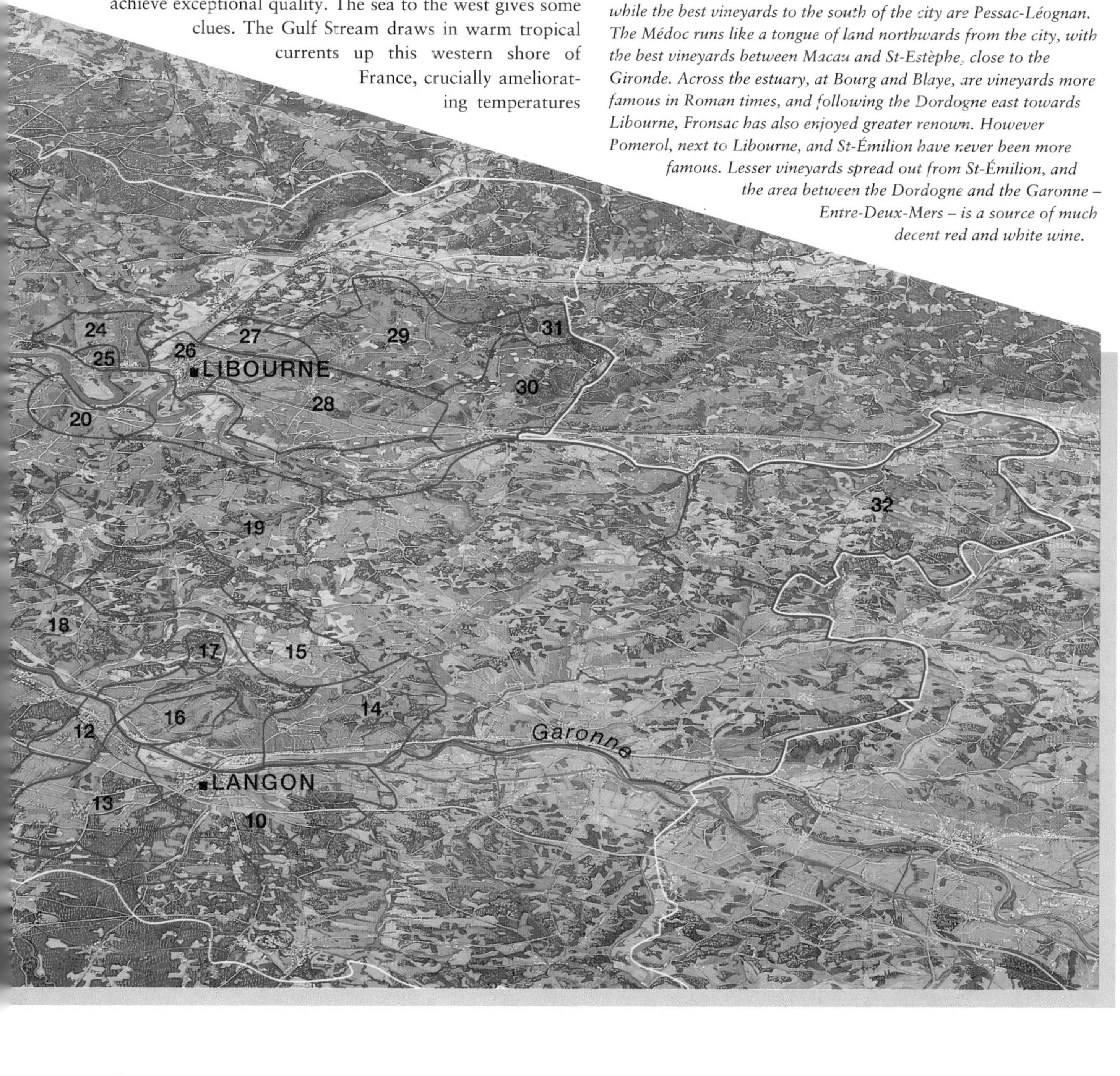

The fortress-like tower of Château Latour overlooks the Gironde estuary.

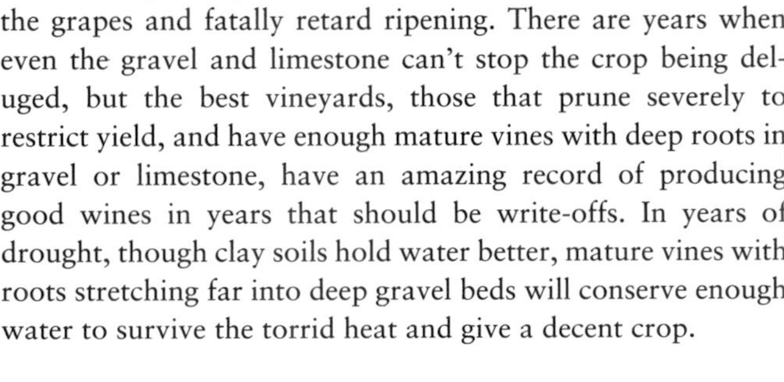

warm enough to ripen the crop, an excess of water would bloat the grapes and fatally retard ripening. There are years when even the gravel and limestone can't stop the crop being deluged, but the best vineyards, those that prune severely to restrict yield, and have enough mature vines with deep roots in gravel or limestone, have an amazing record of producing good wines in years that should be write-offs. In years of drought, though clay soils hold water better, mature vines with roots stretching far into deep gravel beds will conserve enough water to survive the torrid heat and give a decent crop.

GRAPE VARIETIES

Most of the greatest wines of France rely upon a single grape variety for their personality and quality. Hardly any wines of Bordeaux do. There can be as many as five different varieties used for red wines, and few good properties use less than three. White wines come from five main grape varieties and almost all properties use at least two. But this is a model of simplicity compared to the early nineteenth century when over 30 red and almost as many white varieties were planted in the region.

The taste is only one part of the reason for planting several different varieties. Simple farming practicality is at least as important. Although the Gironde estuary and the Dordogne and Garonne rivers contribute stability of day and night temperature, spring frosts do still occur. And though the Gulf Stream broadly acts as a warm water heater for the entire coastal region round Bordeaux, maritime climates are very fickle, and June is often plagued by clouds and damp weather. Though Bordeaux generally enjoys the warm hazy autumns typical of a mild maritime climate, the Bay of Biscay can still send over torrential rainstorms in the months of September and October for several days at a time.

Spring frost can kill young buds on the vine, so all the Bordeaux varieties bud at different times. A farmer might thus lose some of his crop, but not all. Good weather at the flowering period is crucial because that is when the size of the crop is decided. Bordeaux varieties flower at different times: a few days of rain might decimate the potential Merlot harvest while leaving the Cabernet crop unaffected. And the Bordeaux varieties ripen at different times. Rain might catch the Merlot and Cabernet Franc crop but afterwards the sun often returns and it can bring the slower-maturing Cabernet Sauvignon or Petit Verdot to super-ripeness.

But of course taste does matter and each variety not only contributes its own flavour but also complements the flavours of the others to produce the inimitable Bordeaux style. And each variety does more or less well on different types of soil and in different climatic conditions. Part of the skill for a Bordeaux proprietor is knowing which patch of land to plant with which variety, and then working out how much of each will make up the best final blend. In an area like the Haut-Médoc, where, in the best vineyards, the old timers say the soil 'changes with every step', it all helps explain why seemingly identical neighbouring properties produce wines that are always fascinatingly different.

Cabernet Sauvignon is the most famous red variety, contributing a powerful colour, a sinewy structure of tannin and a dark, brooding fruit that takes years to open out to blackcurrant, black cherry, cedar and cigars. It doesn't like damp clay and only performs to its potential on deep, well-drained gravel. It is the king of the Haut-Médoc's top vineyards, important in Pessac-Léognan, but much less important in the cooler clays of St-Émilion and Pomerol.

Merlot is the king in St-Émilion and Pomerol, and indeed is the most widely planted variety in Bordeaux. It thrives in rich but cool, damp clay, it gives high yields yet ripens early and produces succulent juicy wines of high alcohol and good colour. In Pessac-Léognan and the Médoc it is planted on less well-drained soils and softens and fattens the austere beauty of Cabernet Sauvignon.

The lesser red varieties are the perfumed yet light-bodied Cabernet Franc, used as a seasoning in the Médoc but important in St-Émilion and Pomerol particularly on limestone soil; Malbec, a juicy richly flavoured grape now in decline; and Petit Verdot, an excellent late ripener, full of perfume, colour and tannin, but notoriously tricky to grow.

Sémillon is the most important white grape variety, and is particularly important in Graves and Sauternes. The wine it gives is a bit flat and waxy on its own but gains marvellous complexity when blended with Sauvignon Blanc and aged for a year or two. In Sauternes its susceptibility to noble rot makes it the favourite grape of sweet wine makers.

Sauvignon Blanc is a trendy grape, and is increasingly grown in white areas, but in Bordeaux by itself it rarely achieves the exciting flavours it can attain in the Loire or New Zealand. Blended with Sémillon, it adds a mouthwatering tang and an acid backbone that can work tremendously well. Muscadelle is an aromatic grape that can add a spiciness to dry whites, and a grapy richness to sweet whites. Colombard adds

THE SOIL OF THE MÉDOC

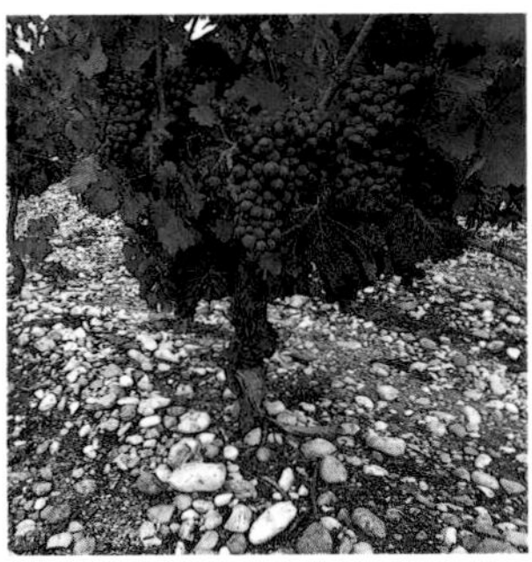

This is a Cabernet Sauvignon vine in the Médoc. The diagram shows an example of how the layers of soil give the vine's roots depth and moisture without over-feeding them.The soil is well-drained which prevents the vine roots from suffering 'wet feet'.

1 consists of pebbles, which help to keep the plant warm, but offer very little in the way of nourishment.

2 is composed of marl, a limy-clay, which is highly fertile and retains moisture well. This gives the plant an extra boost of minerals and moisture, but the layer is thin enough not to provide a drainage problem.

3 is compacted sand which the smaller roots cannot penetrate. The major roots go down into the next layer.

4 is a thick layer of gravelly sand with organic matter which holds water and nutrients in a form which the root can easily absorb. Most of the plant's nutrients come from this layer.

5 is composed of compacted sand, which, again, is difficult to penetrate.

6 consists of well-defined layers of red and yellow sand which cannot retain moisture.

7 consists of small ellipses of grey sand. These retain a certain amount of moisture which the roots exploit.

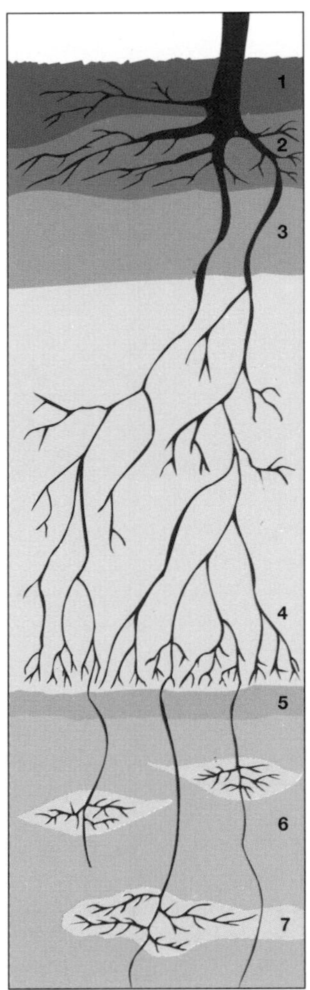

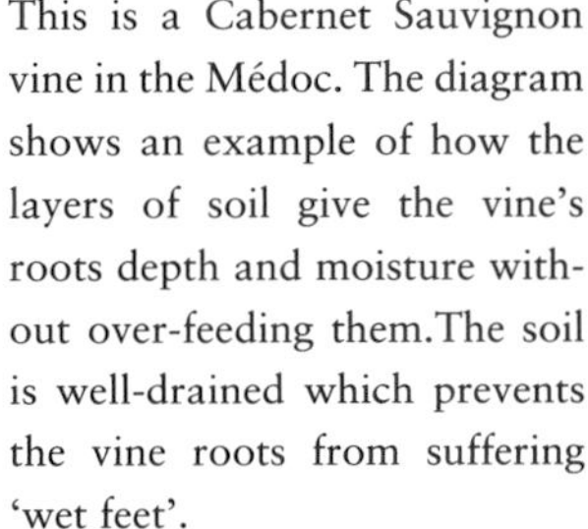

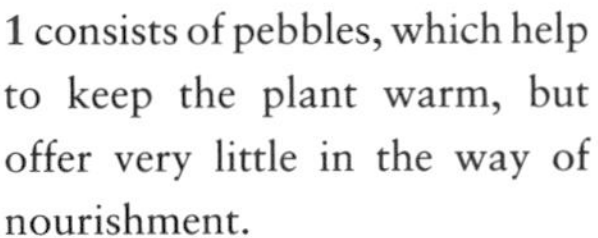

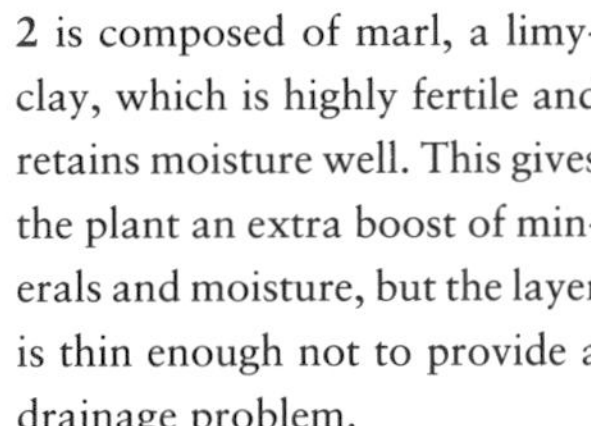

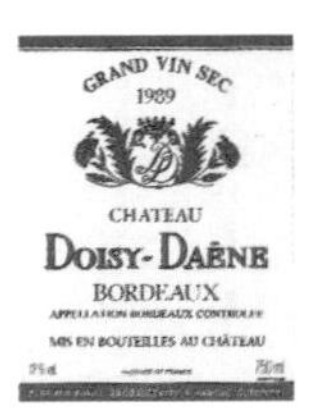

a crucial green fruity zest to whites especially in the Bourg and Blaye areas. Ugni Blanc is Cognac's distilling grape, and though still grown in Bordeaux, produces pretty thin stuff.

WINE-MAKING IN BORDEAUX

The styles of wines these grapes produce depend upon the amounts of each in the blend, the siting of the vineyard, and the ambitions and talents of the producer. Splendid sites are in a minority, as are ambitious producers. Over 80 per cent of growers do not bottle their own wine, simply selling the grapes, the juice or the wine to merchant houses, or to the co-operatives, whose members amount for about one-third of the total Bordeaux production.

Consequently, basic Bordeaux Rouge or Bordeaux Blanc will generally be a light, simple wine from the less-favoured hinterland of Bordeaux, wines of both colours usually exhibiting the lean though often appetizing characteristics of grapes that struggle to ripen in the cool conditions. Sometimes the white has this greenness masked by sugar.

Even in these lesser areas, however, an ambitious proprietor can do a great deal to improve his or her wine. Modern trellising and pruning systems are dramatically improving the quality of grapes in the Entre-Deux-Mers. Severe pruning and then rigid selection of only the best grapes means that even a property in a basic *appellation* can cream off any superior juice and bottle it separately. Replacement of old wooden and cement vats with stainless steel allows a proprietor to maximize whatever fruit and freshness his wine possesses. And the use of new oak barrels for fermenting whites and/or aging wines of either colour dramatically deepens and intensifies the flavour of the wine. Throughout the hinterland proprietors are now striving to improve their wines by these methods. In the top areas such methods are commonplace, and so they should be, because the great Bordeaux wines are expensive and we should expect the proprietor to have done his best on our behalf.

THE CHÂTEAU SYSTEM

The word 'château' is a grand sounding title. Its literal translation is 'castle', and if you have visions of turrets and high fortified walls, keeps and portcullis gates guarding the moat – well, that's all right. There are a few châteaux like that in Bordeaux, but very few. The idea of a 'château' coming to represent a particular wine grew up in the eighteenth century when the wealthy businessmen and parliamentarians of Bordeaux began to hanker for magnificent estates at which to relax and indulge in a bit of showing off. The Médoc was the area most of those grandees chose to explore and there are several stunning properties right the way north through the vineyard areas, but understandably, the most impressive are generally found closer to the city itself.

Almost all these properties developed vineyards too, and by 1855 a hierarchy had sufficiently developed for a famous classification to be made that still largely holds good today. What also began to occur was the adoption of the title 'château' for an estate's wines, even when there was no imposing building deserving the name.

In recent years the use of the word 'château' has spread through Bordeaux as a mark of supposed superiority and individuality. A property in a famous area like, say, Pauillac or St-Émilion can still get a good price for its wine even when sold anonymously in bulk. In the lesser *appellations*, or in the vast tracts of land that can only claim a Bordeaux or Bordeaux Supérieur *appellation*, the price for bulk wine is likely to be miserable. Any proprietor determined to improve his wine and thus his selling price will find that calling his estate 'Château Something' is the first step in adding value to his wine, however uncastle-like his farmhouse may be.

Many famous châteaux in Bordeaux have names which record the historical links between France and England. Château Palmer is named after a British soldier who fought in the Napoleonic Wars. It produces some of the best wine in Bordeaux.

APPELLATIONS AND CLASSIFICATIONS

There are three levels of AC in Bordeaux as well as numerous classifications which have sprung up in the last 180 years or so.

- **General regional AC** 'Bordeaux' is the basic catch-all AC covering red, white, rosé and sparkling wines from the Gironde *département*. With a higher minimum level of alcohol the wine can use the AC Bordeaux Supérieur.
- **Specific regional ACs** These are the next step up the ladder and cover large areas, for instance Entre-Deux-Mers for whites, and Haut-Médoc for reds. They often apply to one colour of wine only.
- **Village ACs** Within a few of the regional ACs the most renowned villages have their own *appellations*, e.g. St-Estèphe, Pauillac, St-Julien, Margaux, Listrac and Moulis in the Haut-Médoc, Pessac-Léognan in the Graves, and Barsac and Sauternes.
- **The 1855 Classification** The famous 1855 Classification of Gironde wines was conceived for the Exposition Universelle in Paris to cover Bordeaux red and white wines. It was simply a list drawn up in a couple of days based on the prices wines were obtaining on the current market and intended for a single event: it was never meant to be a permanent guide. Apart from Château Haut-Brion in the Graves, all the red wines are from the Médoc (see page 38) while the sweet whites of Sauternes and Barsac were separately classified (see page 50). It continues to be a remarkably accurate guide to the wines of the Haut-Médoc and the only change to the list since 1855 has been the promotion of Château Mouton-Rothschild from Second to First Growth in 1973. It is difficult to understand why it is still so accurate since the classification applied to the château name, not to the vineyards it owned, and some of these vineyards are now completely different from those of 1855. A Classed Growth château can annex land from a non-classified estate, and hey presto, that land is suddenly Classed Growth land. However, if a non-classified château buys land from a Classed Growth, that land loses its right to Classed Growth status. Nowadays the better properties receive the highest prices, regardless of their classification.
- **Other classifications** Graves had to wait until 1953 for its reds and 1959 for its whites (see page 45). Pomerol has no classification, although St-Émilion does – and it is revised every ten years to take account both of improving properties and of declining ones (see page 49). Finally the Crus Bourgeois of the Médoc and Haut-Médoc is a grouping of over 200 properties below the Classed Growth level and last classified in 1978.

One of the world's priciest wines in the typical high-shouldered Bordeaux bottle.

THE MÉDOC & HAUT-MÉDOC

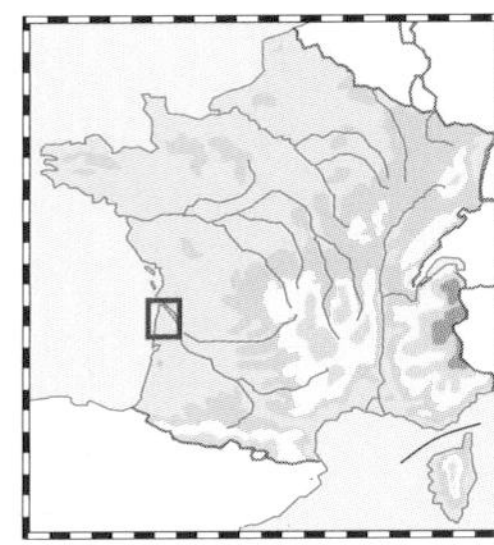

RED GRAPES
Cabernet Sauvignon is the main variety, performing brilliantly on the warm gravelly Médoc soils. Lesser varieties are the softer perfumed Cabernet Franc, Merlot planted on cooler, less well-drained soils, Malbec (in the Bas-Médoc) and the rarely used Petit Verdot.

CLIMATE
The soothing influence of the Gulf Stream sweeping along the Atlantic coast produces long, warm summers and cool, wet winters. The Landes pine forests act as a natural windbreak, sheltering the vineyards. Heavy rains can be a problem at vintage time.

SOIL
The topsoil is mostly free-draining gravel mixed with sand, the subsoil is gravel with sand plus some limestone and clay. The best vineyards are on the gravel outcrops.

ASPECT
Generally low-lying and flat with the main relief provided by gravel ridges and low plateaux, especially in the Haut-Médoc. Most, though not all, of the top vineyards are on very gentle rises facing east and south-east towards the Gironde estuary.

THE BEST PLACE to get a good look at the Médoc is from the middle of a traffic jam. I'd recommend about 9am or 5.30pm on a nice bright spring day, sitting patiently on the lofty span of the Pont d'Aquitaine which sweeps across the Garonne river north of the city of Bordeaux.

And look north, as far as the eye can see – out there are the great vineyards of Margaux and Cantenac; further on – from this height they should still be visible – are St-Julien, Pauillac and even St-Estèphe. Ah, bliss, please God keep the traffic snarled up a while longer while I pause to dream.

I'm afraid dreams are your best bet. You are getting by far the best view of the land that is the Médoc, home to many of the greatest red wines in the world. But there's not much to see even from the bridge. There are the industrial estates, the sprawling suburbs, the scrubby-looking trees and the mud flats glumly following the Garonne's shores round towards Macau and Margaux. But the vineyards? Don't great vineyards need slopes and hills and precious perfect exposures to the sun? It's difficult to believe that in this flat, marshy-looking pudding of a place these unique pre-conditions exist, but they do.

The highest spot in the Médoc – all 80km (50 miles) long of it – is only 43m (140ft) above sea level. That's at the village of Listrac-Médoc, not even one of the best places. Look it up on the map below. Can you spot this Mount Everest of the Médoc? Me neither. And all the best vineyards are between 4m (13ft) above sea level (parts of Château Montrose in St-Estèphe and other good properties in Pauillac, St-Julien and Margaux creep down this close to the slimy edge of the Gironde estuary) and 29m (95ft) (Pauillac's Château Lynch-Moussas outstretches Château Pontet-Canet to reach these giddy heights). Amazingly, this pathetic 25m (80ft) spread is enough to provide growing conditions for Cabernet Sauvignon, Cabernet Franc, Merlot and Petit Verdot vines that the entire wine world envies and would give anything to possess.

Right. Let's get off this bridge – if we can – and head up towards Margaux. But keep your eyes peeled for two things – drainage ditches, and those times when you suddenly realize that the land is almost imperceptibly rising up a metre or two. You might also look right to check whether you can see the glistening waters of the Gironde because the saying is that all the best vineyards in the Médoc are in sight of the estuary. And thinking about this, I realize there's hardly a single top vineyard without a view of the water.

Those drainage ditches are crucial because, before Dutch engineers arrived in the seventeenth century, the Médoc was a desolate, dangerous, flood-prone swamp. The Dutch, being, I suppose, world experts on matters of drainage, dug the great channels that still slant across the Médoc to the Gironde and created dry land where bog existed before. The slight rises in the land show where gravel ridges, washed down from the Massif Central and Pyrenees millennia ago, provide islands of warm free-draining soil rising out of the clay. Remember that the Médoc is not a particularly warm place, and the Cabernet Sauvignon, the main grape, takes a long time to ripen. It *has* to have these deep gravel beds if it is going to do well in most years. Indeed in parts of Margaux, the fine gravel is mixed with white pebbles which, they say, helps the ripening process by reflecting the light on to the grapes.

THE 1855 CLASSIFICATION OF RED WINES

This is the original 1855 list brought up to date to take account of name changes and divisions of property as well as the promotion of Château Mouton-Rothschild 1973. In the list below the château name is followed by the commune.

- **Premiers Crus (First Growths)** Lafite-Rothschild, Pauillac; Latour, Pauillac; Margaux, Margaux; Haut-Brion, Pessac/Graves; Mouton-Rothschild, Pauillac (since 1973).
- **Deuxièmes Crus (Second Growths)** Brane-Cantenac, Cantenac; Cos d'Estournel, St-Estèphe; Ducru-Beaucaillou, St-Julien; Durfort-Vivens, Margaux; Gruaud-Larose, St-Julien; Lascombes, Margaux; Léoville-Barton, St-Julien; Léoville-Las-Cases, St-Julien; Léoville-Poyferré, St-Julien; Montrose, St-Estèphe; Pichon-Longueville (Baron), Pauillac; Pichon-Longueville-Comtesse-de-Lalande, Pauillac; Rauzan-Gassies, Margaux; Rausan-Ségla, Margaux.
- **Troisièmes Crus (Third Growths)** Boyd-Cantenac, Cantenac; Cantenac-Brown, Cantenac; Calon-Ségur, St-Estèphe; Desmirail, Margaux; Ferrière, Margaux; Giscours, Labarde; d'Issan, Cantenac; Kirwan, Cantenac; Lagrange, St-Julien; la Lagune, Ludon; Langoa-Barton, St-Julien; Malescot-St-Exupéry, Margaux; Marquis d'Alesme-Becker, Margaux; Palmer, Cantenac.
- **Quatrièmes Crus (Fourth Growths)** Beychevelle, St-Julien; Branaire-Ducru, St-Julien; Duhart-Milon-Rothschild, Pauillac; Lafon-Rochet, St-Estèphe; Marquis-de-Terme, Margaux; Pouget, Cantenac; Prieuré-Lichine, Cantenac; St-Pierre, St-Julien; Talbot, St-Julien; la Tour-Carnet, St-Laurent.
- **Cinquièmes Crus (Fifth Growths)** Batailley, Pauillac; Belgrave, St-Laurent; de Camensac, St-Laurent; Cantemerle, Macau; Clerc-Milon, Pauillac; Cos-Labory, St-Estèphe; Croizet-Bages, Pauillac; Dauzac, Labarde; Grand-Puy-Ducasse, Pauillac; Grand-Puy-Lacoste, Pauillac; Haut-Bages-Libéral, Pauillac; Haut-Batailley, Pauillac; Lynch-Bages, Pauillac; Lynch-Moussas, Pauillac; Mouton-Baronne-Philippe, Pauillac; Pédesclaux, Pauillac; Pontet-Canet, Pauillac; du Tertre, Arsac.

I'm taking the D2 road up from Bordeaux because I never fail to thrill when the woodland sweeps aside and a broad, very gentle slope to my right displays the excellent Château la Lagune. Almost immediately I plunge into more woods, but deep in a glade to my left is the fairytale keep of Château Cantemerle whose gravel crest spreads out beyond the trees.

MARGAUX

A moment more and we're in the *appellation* area of Margaux, but not in its heart. There is a fair bit of sand and clay in many of the vineyards at Labarde and at Cantenac, but there are some fine properties, particularly on the south-west-facing slope round Château Brane-Cantenac. However, this is one of the thankfully few areas where the validity of the 1855 classification as a guide to the quality of the wines is questionable, because the patently fine vineyard sites do not regularly produce patently fine flavours. It's no good having lovely vineyards if you don't put heart and soul – and, I fear, bank balance – into the creation of great wine. Indeed, if I wanted to find the most interesting and quality-orientated producers in this southern stretch of Margaux, I would look away from these favoured banks to the less naturally blessed plots of land. Château Siran, right down near the Gironde in Labarde, doesn't look a very promising site for fine wine, yet this cool, reserved, but ultimately classically perfumed red is regularly of Classed Growth standard.

There is only one Classed Growth in the backwoods, behind Cantenac: the Fifth Growth Château du Tertre, sitting on a knoll of gravelly soil just north of the little village of Arsac. Though the wine doesn't immediately show its charming side, with a little maturity du Tertre opens out into a delightful blend of blackcurrant fruit and violet perfume far more consistently than do many of the properties with higher classifications and supposedly better sites nearer the Gironde river. Châteaux Monbrison and d'Angludet aren't classified at all. Yet, due to the determination of their respective proprietors, the wines they produce, from supposedly inferior soil, can easily outclass many Classed Growth Margaux wines. It is possible that Margaux has even more potentially great vineyard land than Pauillac of St-Julien. We won't know for sure until we have a similarly determined and talented group of proprietors and winemakers running the châteaux.

Altogether there are five villages in the Margaux *appellation* totalling 1165 hectares (2879 acres) and including a grand total of 21 Classed Growths, but the greatest Margaux vineyards begin around the village of Issan, and continue on to the little town of Margaux itself. We're on a broad plateau here, gently sloping east to the river, and the ground seems white with pebbles and even the gravelly soil is frequently a pale sickly grey. But that's excellent for the vines. The soil offering very few nutrients, the vines send their taproots deep below the surface. As a result the wines of Margaux are rarely massive – though Châteaux Rausan-Ségla and Margaux can be deep and chewy – yet they develop a haunting scent of violets and a pure perfume of blackcurrants that is as dry as those sun-bleached pebbles yet seems as sweet as jam.

The Margaux vineyards continue north to Soussans, yet they become darker, the clay more evident and suddenly we

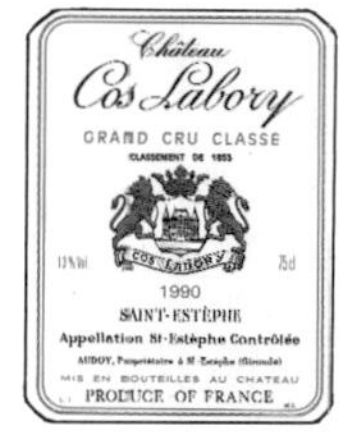

Cos d'Estournel is perfectly situated on a south-facing gravel bank and produces some of the best wines in St-Estèphe. Its exotic, oriental-looking cellar building is one of the architectural highlights of the Médoc.

AC WINE AREAS AND MAIN CHÂTEAUX

1. Ch. Clarke
2. Ch. Maucaillou
3. Ch. Poujeaux
4. Ch. Chasse-Spleen
5. Ch. Lascombes
6. Ch. Margaux
7. Ch. Rausan-Ségla
8. Ch. Palmer
9. Ch. d'Issan
10. Ch. du Tertre
11. Ch. d'Angludet
12. Ch. Giscours
13. Ch. Siran
14. Ch. Cantemerle
15. Ch. la Lagune

MARGAUX = AC WINE AREAS

AC BOUNDARIES

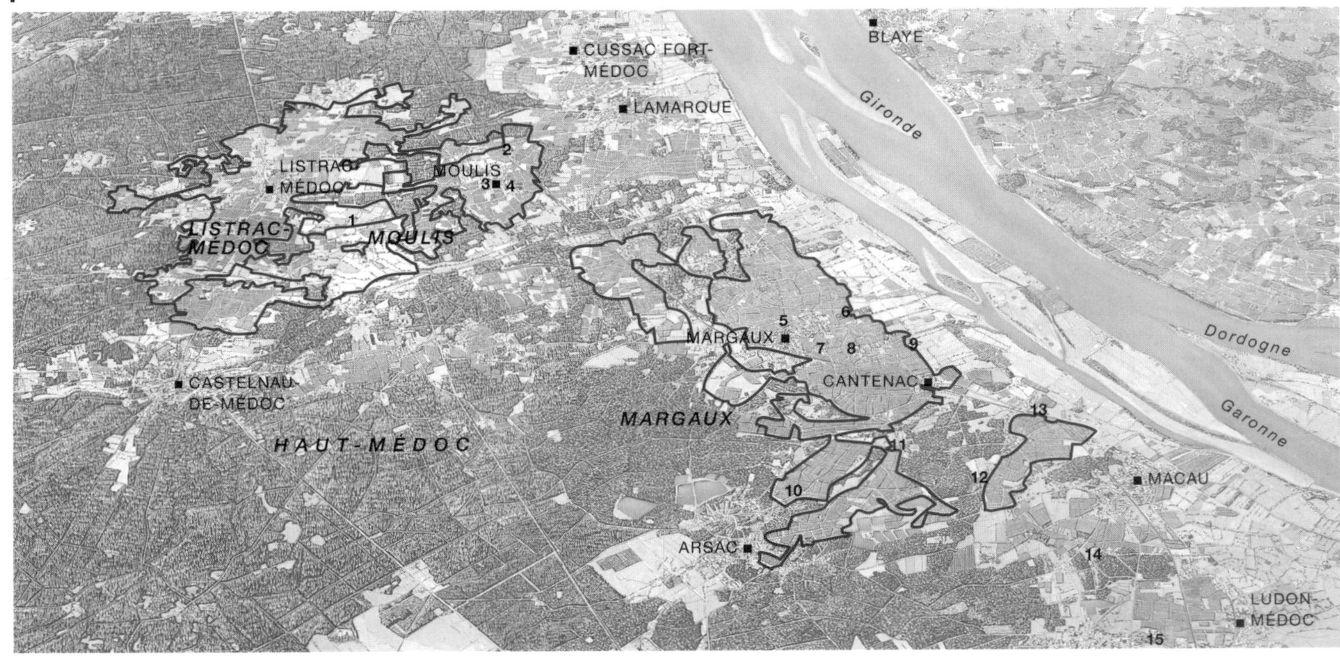

0 km 1 2
0 miles 1

0 km 1 2
0 miles 1

dive into marshy woodland and they've gone. A matter of 5m (16ft) or so difference in height and we lose all that gravel and are left with damp cold clay. We're now in a kind of no-man's-land until we reach St-Julien about 12km (8 miles) ahead. There are vineyards here, around Lamarque and Cussac, the best being accorded the *appellation* Haut-Médoc, but they lack the brilliance of Margaux, crucially because the vineyards lack the depth of gravel and the drainage.

MOULIS AND LISTRAC

There are, however, two small *appellations* just west of Arcins that do have gravel and can produce excellent wine – Moulis and Listrac-Médoc. Neither of these villages has any Classed Growth properties, but looking at the excellent vineyard sites of Moulis in particular, you could be excused for thinking that the growers there were a little unlucky. Above all, over near the railway, around the village of Grand-Poujeaux there are some splendid deep gravel ridges which would definitely have qualified for honours if they were within the boundaries of such major villages as Margaux or St-Julien. Never mind; it allows us as wine drinkers that rare experience in Bordeaux – relatively bargain-priced wine of classic quality. The leader of this group of gravel-based wines is Château Chasse-Spleen – splendidly dark and sturdy but beautifully ripe at its core. Other high grade wines also come from such châteaux as Maucaillou and Poujeaux.

Moulis is the better of these with a fine ridge of gravel running through its midst. Listrac-Médoc has the gravel, too, but is a crucial mile or so further away from the mild influence of the Gironde, and is another 20m (65ft) higher. Higher vineyards are cooler vineyards and in a marginal climate like the Médoc, even 20m (65ft) makes a difference.

Whereas the Moulis wines are generally marked by an attractive precociousness, a soft-centred fruit and smooth-edged structure, Listrac wines are always sterner, more jut-jawed, less easy to love. The quality is there all right, but the style is rather old-fashioned and reserved. Even a supremely well-equipped and well-financed property like Château Clarke that strains every sinew to make a spicy, ripe-fruited oak-scented 'modern' classic, is often ultimately defeated by nature, its wine demanding the traditional decade of aging most Listracs have always needed to shine.

ST-JULIEN

You have to change gear when you cross the wet meadows and the drainage channel beneath Château Beychevelle and enter the St-Julien AC. You change down a gear to navigate the left turn and upward sweep of the road as suddenly the vineyards surge into existence once more. But you change gear up in wine terms, up into the highest gear in the red wine world because St-Julien and its neighbour Pauillac have more great red wine packed tight within their boundaries than any other patch of land on earth. The St-Julien *appellation* is only 820 hectares (2026 acres) but has 11 Classed Growths; Pauillac has 1049 hectares (2592 acres) and ten Classed Growths, including three First Growths. Here the Cabernet Sauvignon, aided and abetted by the Merlot, the Cabernet Franc and the Petit Verdot, exploits the deep gravel banks and the mellow maritime climate to produce grapes of an intensity and, above all, a balance between fruit and tannin, perfume and acid, that you simply don't find elsewhere. Add to this some of the world's highest prices for wine, which in itself is no good thing, but when the profit is re-invested in an almost obsessive care of the vineyard, superior winery equipment and row upon row of

SOUTHERN HAUT-MÉDOC — VINEYARDS — N

TOTAL DISTANCE NORTH TO SOUTH 18KM (11 MILES)

WHERE THE VINEYARDS ARE *The map tells part of the tale of the Médoc immediately. The wide Gironde estuary provides a warming influence to the east, the pine forests to the west protect the region from salt-laden winds coming off the Bay of Biscay and draw off much of the rain from the clouds in wet weather. But the other part of the Médoc's story, the soil, isn't so apparent. All the best vineyards in the Médoc are on gravelly soil. Where there are concentrations of vineyards, as there are around the little town of Margaux, this is because the banks of warm gravelly soil crucial for the ripening of the Cabernet Sauvignon dominate the landscape. Where the vineyards are piecemeal, the gravel will have been largely displaced by damp clay. Such vineyards as there are on this soil will generally depend on the earlier-ripening Merlot.*

Macau and Ludon in the south have good vineyards, but the real fireworks start at Labarde, one of five villages making up the Margaux AC. The best vineyards are concentrated around Cantenac and Margaux itself. North of Soussans, the vineyards become scrappier as the gravel banks largely disappear until re-emerging at Château Beychevelle in the St-Julien AC (see page 42). Haut-Médoc is the highest AC these vineyards can claim. West of Arcins there are two small but high quality ACs – Moulis and Listrac. There are no Classed Growths here, but there are several châteaux of high enough quality, especially on the gravel ridge around the village of Grand Poujeaux. The islands in the estuary have vineyards, but they aren't much good and only qualify for the basic Bordeaux AC. I know. I've picked their grapes. I couldn't wait to get back to dry land.

fragrant new oak barrels in which to age the wine, well, your pockets have to be deep, but you buy not only superb quality but enviable consistency too.

Château Beychevelle looks merely attractive from the roadway. Seen from the gardens and lawns that run down towards the Gironde, it is a stunning piece of eighteenth-century architecture. The villages of Margaux, St-Julien and Pauillac may consist largely of featureless vine monoculture, but the numerous enchanting and occasionally magnificent châteaux buildings do add a certain air of romance and sophistication.

And I'm all for that, because otherwise, I'm afraid we're back to the same basics as in Margaux further south – drainage and gravel. These impoverished soils really make the vine reach deep into the earth for nutrients, and, despite modern fertilizers and certain vine clones bred for high yield making their presence felt, such infertile soil naturally keeps the volume of the harvest down. We're in a cool climate here, remember. Gravel is a warm, well-drained soil and a small crop ripens more quickly when those autumn rain clouds start to build up out in the Bay of Biscay.

That drainage channel we drove over close to Château Beychevelle is very important, because there is a whole ridge of vineyards running westwards towards St-Laurent whose soils are a little heavier than is usual for St-Julien, and yet whose angle to the south and slope down to the drainage channel help to produce excellent wines. Châteaux Gruaud-Larose and Branaire-Ducru are the most significant of the properties here.

However, for the true genius of St-Julien – of wines of only middling weight that develop a haunting cigar, cedar and blackcurrant fragrance as they age – we need to go back to the slopes near the Gironde where three gravel outcrops push their way eastwards and downwards towards the estuary. Château Ducru-Beaucaillou and the three Léoville properties occupy these slopes. Great wines all.

PAUILLAC

You can't tell where you leave St-Julien and enter Pauillac, the vines are so continuous. Well, yes you can – there's another little stream helping to drain famous vineyards like Châteaux Latour and Pichon-Longueville-Comtesse-de-Lalande. Where the road crosses the stream, there's the boundary. And there is a change in wine style; the Cabernet Sauvignon becomes even more dominant in Pauillac, the wines are darker and take longer to mature and yet have a more piercing blackcurrant fruit that mingles with the cedar and cigar box fragrance.

MÉDOC AND NORTHERN HAUT-MÉDOC

VINEYARDS

TOTAL DISTANCE NORTH TO SOUTH 25KM (15½ MILES)

N

0 km 1 2
0 miles 1

WHERE THE VINEYARDS ARE *This is the most concentrated area of fine red wine in Bordeaux. Gravel banks begin at Château Beychevelle, at the bottom of the map, and are most impressive close to the waterfront in the St-Julien and Pauillac ACs, where the best properties get the full benefit of the warm estuary and the best drainage.*

Pauillac ends very abruptly at Château Lafite-Rothschild. A drainage channel and meadow create an interlude, but then there's another low bank and we are in St-Estèphe, the largest of the Médoc ACs. Three of St-Estèphe's five Classed Growths are found here but generally this AC has more clay than gravel, so few of the wines achieve the brilliance of Pauillac.

From Blanquefort to St-Seurin wines not covered by the main village ACs are allowed the title Haut-Médoc. The vineyards become patchy as suitable land is more difficult to find. North of St-Seurin are the vineyards of the Médoc AC, occasionally good but rarely thrilling.

0 km 1 2
0 miles 1

Certainly the extra Cabernet Sauvignon will deepen the colour of the wine. But that extra percentage of Cabernet is only possible because Pauillac has the deepest gravel beds in the whole Médoc, stretched out across two broad plateaux to the south and north of the town of Pauillac. And there's some iron in the gravel and a good deal of iron pan as subsoil. No one's ever proved it, but a lot of traditionalists reckon iron in the soil gives extra depth to a red wine.

You certainly get your depth in Pauillac. Pauillac has three of the 1855 Classification's five First Growths, each playing a different brilliant variation on the same blackcurrant and cedarwood theme, as well as a host of other excellent properties. Once again, the saying that the best vineyards all have a view of the river holds sway, because the buffeting of tides and currents that piled up the crucial gravel banks has obviously left the deepest ridges close to the estuary. But these ridges go a long way back in Pauillac and standing on tip-toe you can still just about see the vines from properties like Pontet-Canet and Grand-Puy-Lacoste. In fact these two properties give some of the purest expressions of blackcurrant juice and cedar perfume of any châteaux in Pauillac. Every signpost in St-Julien and Pauillac bears yet another name dripping with the magic of memorable vintages. How much longer can this parade of excellence go on?

Not much longer, I'm afraid. Cruising north past Château Lafite-Rothschild, past its tall stand of proud poplars and its unusually steep, well-drained vineyards, there's one more drainage stream ahead of us, and one long slope running along its north bank.

ST-ESTÈPHE

Here we're in St-Estèphe, and despite the quality of these frontline St-Estèphe vineyards like Châteaux Cos d'Estournel and Lafon-Rochet facing Pauillac over the Jalle de Breuil stream, from now on, the gravel begins to fade and clay begins to clog your shoes. We're further north and ripening is slower here than in, say, Margaux. There's much more of the earlier-ripening Merlot planted to try to provide fleshy flavour from the clay soils. And despite the size of the St-Estèphe *appellation*, at 1142 hectares (2822 acres) only a whisker smaller than Margaux, a mere five properties were classified in 1855. The best wines are very good, full, structured and well-flavoured, but if you sometimes wonder whether they don't lack a little scent, whether they don't carry with them the vaguest hint of the clay beneath the vines, you're not wrong.

HAUT-MÉDOC

St-Estèphe marks the northern end of the great Médoc villages. Yet from the very gates of Bordeaux at Blanquefort, right up to St-Seurin-de-Cadourne, about a mile north of St-Estèphe, there are patches of land outside the main villages where a decent aspect, some good drainage and sometimes some gravel occur.

Château Loudenne in the Bas-Médoc is one of several Bordeaux properties which have been in English hands for generations.

Often these vineyards are interspersed with woodland a mile or so west of the main villages, and almost all of these can carry the Haut-Médoc AC. There are even five Classed Growths within the Haut-Médoc AC, but, these apart, few wines exhibit the sheer excitement of the riverfront gravel bed wines. Good proprietors make good wine. For great wine, you need a bit more help from the Almighty.

MÉDOC

North of St-Seurin lies the Bas-Médoc, the Lower Médoc, though its wine *appellation* is simple Médoc to spare the locals' egos. It's a flat, rather wan landscape covering 3500 hectares (8650 acres), right up to the tip of the Médoc peninsula, though in effect the vineyards peter out north of Valeyrac. There is much sodden evidence of the marsh the whole area was before the Dutch started draining the area in the eighteenth century. I find the landscape relaxing, but it is not ideal wine country, though there are a few gravel outcrops and a certain amount of sandy clay. Between them they manage to produce a good deal of decent sturdy red, and just occasionally, as at Châteaux Potensac, la Tour-Haut-Caussan, or la Tour-de-By, something really good.

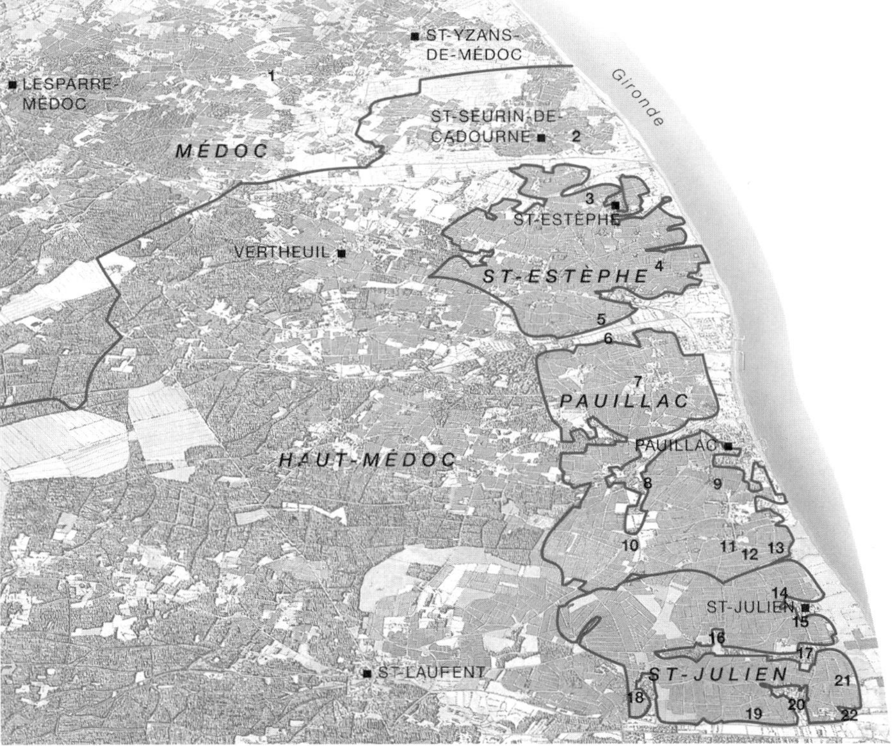

AC WINE AREAS AND MAIN CHÂTEAUX

1. Ch. Potensac
2. Ch. Sociando-Mallet
3. Ch. Calon-Ségur
4. Ch. Montrose
5. Ch. Cos d'Estournel
6. Ch. Lafite-Rothschild
7. Ch. Mouton-Rothschild
8. Ch. Grand-Puy-Lacoste
9. Ch. Lynch-Bages
10. Ch. Batailley
11. Ch. Pichon-Longueville
12. Ch. Pichon-Longueville-Comtesse-de-Lalande
13. Ch. Latour
14. Ch. Léoville-Las-Cases
15. Ch. Léoville-Poyferré
16. Ch. Talbot
17. Ch. Léoville-Barton
18. Ch. Lagrange
19. Ch. Gruaud-Larose
20. Ch. St-Pierre
21. Ch. Ducru-Beaucaillou
22. Ch. Beychevelle

PAUILLAC = AC WINE AREAS — AC BOUNDARIES

Graves & Pessac-Léognan

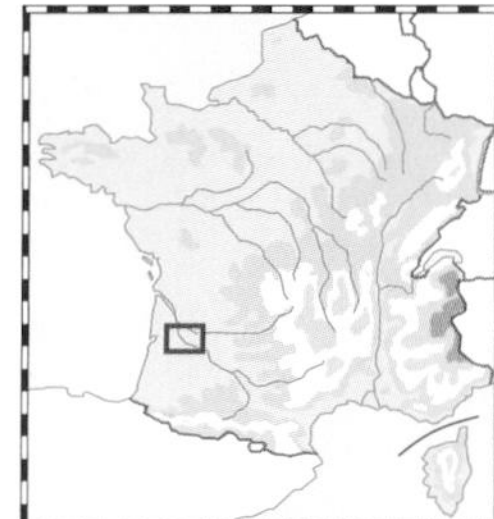

I WONDER HOW MANY of the famous old Graves vineyards I've walked over – and never knew it. How many have I driven over, how many have I taken the train through, spent the night in – even landed an aeroplane in – and never known. Dozens, I reckon, because the majority of the famous Graves vineyards of a century or so ago have long since been eaten up by the sprawling expansion of the city of Bordeaux, and the development of the airport complex.

At the beginning of the twentieth century there were 168 wine properties in the three major communes closest to the city of Bordeaux – Talence, Pessac and Mérignac. Now there are only nine. Mérignac had 22 properties in the nineteenth century. That was before the international airport, the hotels and the industrial parks. Now there is just one Mérignac property left gamely holding back the tidal waves of progress.

Well, you can't have it both ways. The Graves region was the centre of fine wine production in Bordeaux for hundreds of years because it reached right to the very outskirts of the city. In the days when transport was both difficult and dangerous, this proximity to the town was of crucial importance. Bordeaux became rich and powerful by establishing itself as the chief supplier of French wine to northern Europe, and later to America. So the city naturally gets bigger. Remove a few vineyards, build a few houses, cut down some more forest, plant some more vineyards. It was a natural progression.

What the city builders didn't know – or didn't care about – was that the unique gravelly soil that gives the Graves region its name doesn't stretch out to infinity. It is only present in the zone closest to the heart of Bordeaux. Look at Talence and Pessac on the map. They've got the best soil in the Graves but there's hardly room for a row of vines among the crowded rows of suburban villas. Look at the town of Léognan. At last, signs of a few vineyards appear. A mere couple of miles further south, and the gravel starts to disintegrate into sand and clay. Good wines abound in these southern reaches of the Graves, all the way down to Langon, but no great ones.

The Graves region technically begins to the north of Bordeaux, at the Jalle de Blanquefort, the southern boundary of the Médoc. It then continues round and through the city for 56km (35 miles) before ending just to the south of Langon. The vines now cover about 4400 hectares (10,870 acres) as against more than 10,000 hectares (24,700 acres) a hundred years ago. Of these, 1005 hectares (2480 acres) are in the Pessac-Léognan AC, 368 hectares (910 acres) can be used for the production of the rare semi-sweet Graves Supérieures, and the rest are AC Graves. Since 1987 the traditional superiority of the soil immediately to the south and west of the city has been rewarded with a separate *appellation* Pessac-Léognan, which covers ten communes. All the 13 Graves Classed Growths are inside the Pessac-Léognan borders.

It is here in Pessac-Léognan that the deep ancient gravel banks predominate, washed down over the millennia from the Pyrenees, and the excellent quality of the reds such soil can produce is no new phenomenon: Samuel Pepys was noting in his diary in 1663 that he had come across 'a sort of French wine called Ho Bryan that hath a good and most particular taste that I ever met with'. I'm not sure about the grammar, but the gist of this tasting note is that he'd found a wine called Haut-Brion that was an absolute smasher. Haut-Brion is today the leading Pessac-Léognan château and one of Bordeaux's greatest wines. In 1663 it provided the first example of a single property's name being recommended in the English language and it is reasonable to assume it was the best Bordeaux wine being produced at that time.

0 km 1 2
0 miles 1

NORTHERN GRAVES AND PESSAC-LÉOGNAN

VINEYARDS

TOTAL DISTANCE NORTH TO SOUTH 25KM (15½ MILES)

N

0 km 1 2
0 miles 1

RED WINES

In those days the wine of Graves and Pessac-Léognan would almost certainly have been red. The protective pine forests to the west, the warming Garonne river to the east and the pale, well-drained gravel soil, as well as the fact that the Graves vineyards are in any case the most southerly in Bordeaux – all these factors would have helped the grapes to ripen earlier than in the Médoc to the north or in St-Émilion to the north-east. In those days most Bordeaux reds were pale and thin; vineyards that could produce ripe grapes were much prized. Even today, Pessac-Léognan has a reputation for producing good red wines in less good years because of its ability to ripen Cabernet Sauvignon and Merlot grapes that little bit earlier before the autumn winds sweep in off the Bay of Biscay. In the genuinely hot Bordeaux years like 1982, 1989 and 1990 the vines are likely to suffer from that rare phenomenon in a cool area like Bordeaux: heat stress. For classic Graves flavours – a mellow earthiness, a soft-edged yet cool plum and blackcurrant fruit and, as the wine matures, a thrilling tobacco-cedar scent – cooler vintages like 1981 and 1988 are the ones to seek out.

WHITE WINES

Forty per cent of the vineyard area is planted to whites – Sémillon and Sauvignon and, here and there, a little Muscadelle to add a hint of exotic spice if necessary. With the exception of minute amounts of brilliant wine from properties like Châteaux Haut-Brion, Laville-Haut-Brion and Domaine de Chevalier, white Graves was a byword for decades for flat, sulphurous, off-dry, soupy liquids as a result of antediluvian wine-making. Even the majority of the Classed Growths produced dull, mediocre wine. However, the explosion of demand for good white wine during the 1980s, and the consequent spiralling of price for such wines as white Burgundies and white Loire Sauvignons, persuaded the more forward-looking growers to make a bit more effort. After all, Sémillon and Sauvignon Blanc are both good grape varieties and complement each other brilliantly, and both the gravelly Pessac-Léognan soil and the sandier southern Graves soil are suitable for high quality white wine production. All that was needed was the will to improve, the know-how and some investment and during the 1980s, led by Domaine de Chevalier and Châteaux de Fieuzal and la Louvière, almost all important properties modernized their wineries, and most began using new oak to ferment and to age their wines. Although Graves and Pessac-Léognan are best known for red wines, the modern white equivalents are easily of the same quality, and are now without doubt some of France's most exciting modern wines.

THE 1959 CLASSIFICATION OF THE GRAVES

The Graves classification came out first in 1953 but for red wines only. White wines were added in 1959. The châteaux names below are followed by the commune:

Bouscaut, Cadaujac (red and white); Carbonnieux, Léognan (red and white); Domaine de Chevalier, Léognan (red and white); Couhins, Villenave d'Ornon (white); Couhins-Lurton, Villenave d'Ornon (white); de Fieuzal, Léognan (red); Haut-Bailly, Léognan (red); Haut-Brion, Pessac (red); Laville-Haut-Brion, Talence (white); Malartic-Lagravière, Léognan (red and white); la Mission-Haut-Brion, Talence (red); Olivier, Léognan (red and white); Pape-Clément, Pessac (red); Smith-Haut-Lafitte, Martillac (red); la Tour-Haut-Brion, Talence (red); la Tour-Martillac, Martillac (red and white).

RED GRAPES

The main variety is Cabernet Sauvignon backed up by Cabernet Franc, a rather higher percentage of Merlot than in the Médoc further north, and some Malbec.

WHITE GRAPES

Sémillon and Sauvignon Blanc dominate, with occasionally a little Muscadelle.

CLIMATE

The most southerly vineyards in Bordeaux are slightly warmer and wetter than the Médoc, leading to earlier ripening for most varieties.

SOIL

In the north of the region, nearest Bordeaux, the topsoil is typically gravelly, giving way to sand and clay mixed with limestone further south.

ASPECT

Outside the vast urban sprawl of Bordeaux the landscape is one of rolling low hills and numerous small valleys. It is generally higher than the Médoc, providing gentle slopes with good aspect to the sun. This, with the higher overall temperature, aids early ripening of the grapes.

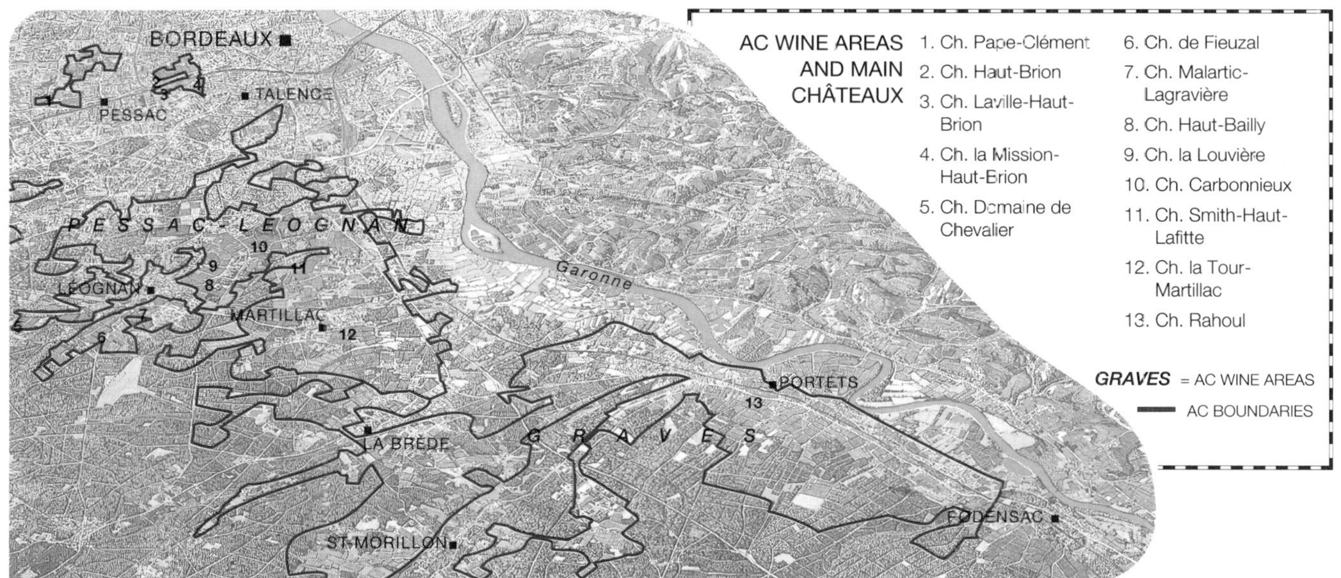

WHERE THE VINEYARDS ARE *I'm always surprised when I visit the Pessac-Léognan and Graves regions at how few vineyards there are in such illustrious names in the wine world. Lots of suburban villas, lots of pine forests, quite a few meadows and a few orchards, but surprisingly few big chunks of vineyard land. Is it me, I wonder? Am I looking in the wrong places? Well, this map reveals in graphic detail the fact that this famous vineyard area, which was the original source of the Bordeaux wines that were shipped to northern Europe from the twelfth century onwards, really doesn't have all that many vineyards. The vines cover only 4400 hectares (10,870 acres), as against more than 10,000 hectares (24,700 acres) a hundred years ago. Many of the vines that have disappeared in the last century were in the area at the top left of the map, an area now covered with the houses of the city of Bordeaux itself. The most important surviving estates in the suburbs of Bordeaux are Château Pape-Clément in Pessac and Châteaux Haut-Brion and la Mission-Haut-Brion in Talence, and these are tiny sploshes of green surrounded by houses on all sides.*

The other highly important area of Pessac-Léognan is distributed between the small villages of Léognan, Cadaujac and Martillac. South of here the less gravelly, sandier soils spread down the left bank of the Garonne, past the sweet wine enclave of Cérons and the large ACs of Sauternes and Barsac, finally petering out just south of Langon. The vineyards on the opposite bank of the Garonne are those of the Premières Côtes de Bordeaux.

An exciting new wave Pessac Léognan dry white in the classic Bordeaux bottle.

St-Émilion, Pomerol & Fronsac

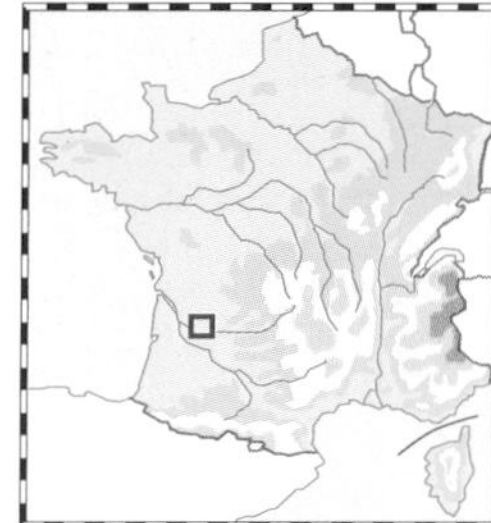

RED GRAPES
Merlot does best on the cooler, heavier clays of St-Émilion and Pomerol, with greater or lesser amounts of Cabernet Franc and Cabernet Sauvignon on gravel outcrops. There is some Malbec in Fronsac.

CLIMATE
The maritime influence begins to moderate, producing warmer summers and cooler winters. It is drier than the Médoc with frequent, sometimes severe frosts.

SOIL
A complex pattern shows gravel deposits, sand and clay mixed with limestone. The top vineyards are either on the *côtes* around St-Émilion or on the gravel outcrops of Pomerol/Figeac.

ASPECT
Generally flat, especially in Pomerol, the land rises steeply in the *côtes* south and south-west of St-Émilion. Elsewhere the slopes are at best moderately undulating.

St-Émilion wine and customs are promoted by the ancient organization La Jurade.

WHAT A DIFFERENCE 31km (19 miles) makes. I head east from Bordeaux, on the N89, away from the prosperous, cosmopolitan city, and by the time I cross the Dordogne river into the Libournais wine region, I am in a totally different world.

The main town, Libourne, has none of the majesty and grandeur of Bordeaux, no quays telling of an illustrious trading past. Although Libourne does have a quay, with wine merchants' offices huddled together beneath some willow trees at the edge of the Dordogne, it is a toytown affair compared to Bordeaux. Libourne's narrow streets and folksy market square could be in any of a hundred towns in France.

The vineyards, too, have none of the charming sylvan air of so many of the properties in Pessac-Léognan, carefully carved from the encroaching woodland all about, nor the proud self-confidence of the great vineyard estates of the Médoc. The Libournais is packed with vines: indeed, there is room for little else, so much so that in this region you get few of the copses and meadows that provide a welcome break from vineyards in the Médoc. But, unlike the Médoc, this is down-to-earth vine-growing, with nothing vainglorious or indulgent. St-Émilion has 5200 hectares (12,850 acres) of vines, yet these are divided between more than 1000 growers. Pomerol has a mere 729 hectares (1801 acres), and the average holding is only 4 hectares (10 acres). A successful Médoc property is likely to average 40 hectares (100 acres). So we're going to look in vain for the startling architectural follies that bring the dull Médoc landscape to life. With a few exceptions, a sturdy no-nonsense farmhouse is all we'll get in the Libournais; anything else is a waste of precious vineyard space.

But there are redeeming features in this region. Founded in the eleventh century (though originally settled in Roman times) the town of St-Émilion is a jumble of rust-red roofed houses, squeezed into a cleft in the limestone plateau looking out over the flat Dordogne Valley. The coarsely cobbled streets are narrow and steep and the whole town has been declared an ancient monument to preserve it for posterity.

And then there are the flavours. I'm almost tempted to say and then there is the flavour, because the joy of almost all the great wines of Pomerol and St-Émilion lies in the dominance of one single grape – the Merlot. The red wines of Bordeaux are famous for their unapproachability in youth and their great longevity. That reputation has been built by the grandees of the Médoc, where Cabernet reigns supreme. Cabernet Sauvignon wines are tough and aggressive when young, but Merlot wines exhibit a juicy, almost jam-sweet richness just about from the moment the grapes hit the vat. Bordeaux without tears? You want Pomerol or St-Émilion. Their best wines will age just as long as the best Médocs, it's simply that they're so attractive young that most of them never get the chance.

There is some Cabernet Sauvignon planted in the Libournais – perhaps 15 per cent – but the lack of warm gravel soils in most of the Libournais means that it rarely ripens properly despite the climate being rather warmer and more continental than in the Médoc. Château Figeac in St-Émilion and Château Vieux-Château-Certan in Pomerol are two exceptions that manage to ripen it well. In Pomerol and St-Émilion the Cabernet Franc gives far better results than Cabernet Sauvignon, especially where there is a decent amount of limestone in the soil and subsoil. Fronsac traditionally uses some of the soft-centred, deep-coloured Malbec to round out its wines.

Though vines have been grown here since Roman times, the emergence of St-Émilion as one of Bordeaux's star turns is fairly recent and Pomerol's soaring reputation is a good deal more recent still. History and geography have conspired against both areas. The majority of Bordeaux's export trade has always been carried on from Bordeaux itself. Those 31km (19 miles) may seem trivial now, but until the 1820s there were no bridges across the Garonne and Dordogne rivers between Bordeaux and Libourne. Few Bordeaux merchants felt the need to make the short but tiresome journey to the Libournais when they had the Graves and the Médoc on their doorstep. A band of Libourne merchants did grow up to ship the local wines, but they were generally regarded with disdain and Libournais wines were accorded little respect and low prices.

When the Paris–Bordeaux railway opened in 1853, with a station in Libourne, this helped to free the local producers from the thrall of Bordeaux's merchants, and ever since, one of the mainstays of Libourne's trade has been the network of consumers built up in northern France, Belgium and Holland who happily soak up whatever wine is available, undeterred by the fact that not a single Libournais wine was included in Bordeaux's 1855 Classification.

CLASSIFICATIONS
St-Émilion is divided into two *appellations*: basic St-Émilion AC and St-Émilion Grand Cru AC. The latter now has its own classification system (see page 49), which includes a mechanism for promoting and demoting wines during an intended revision every decade, making it potentially one of the best systems of its kind. The classification comprises two categories: Premier Grand Cru Classé, divided into Groups A and B, and Grand Cru Classé. At present, despite the demotion of seven Grands Crus Classés in the 1986 revision, there are too many tiny properties in the Grand Cru Classé and Grand Cru sections which would hardly reach the level of Cru Bourgeois in the Médoc. More demotions are needed, but a few promotions are in order too.

Pomerol has no classification system, and doesn't seem to need one, since the wines of this commune are now the most expensive in Bordeaux. This is a remarkable achievement. Pomerol was only officially delimited as an AC in 1928 and I've read books published after World War Two that sniffily described Pomerol as merely a subdivision of neighbouring St-Émilion. Those guys had clearly never tasted a bottle.

0 km 1 2
0 miles 1

WHERE THE VINEYARDS ARE *The Libournais is a red wine region covering the area north of the Dordogne river. Libourne became important as the shipping port for all the wines produced on the banks of the Dordogne. Although it never achieved the stature of Bordeaux, Libourne is still the base for the major companies shipping Fronsac, Pomerol and St-Émilion wines.*

The slopes and hills to the west of Libourne are those of Fronsac and Canon-Fronsac. This attractive region was the obvious location for the Libourne business community to build their estates, and until the nineteenth century the Fronsac wines were regarded as the leading lights in the area. The area east of Libourne is now more important. Pomerol and St-Émilion also produce wines of much higher quality.

From the air Pomerol seems like one carpet of vines without any notable features. But below the surface there is a fascinating array of soil types producing different characteristics in the wines, and excellent quality overall. South of the town of St-Émilion, a cleft slices into the plateau and provides slopes for many of St-Émilion's finest wines on its south and east-facing aspects. This is the Côtes area of St-Émilion. Other good vineyards lie just north of the town and on the plateau between St-Émilion and Pomerol. To the south are extensive but uninspiring vineyards on low-lying land spreading towards the Dordogne. Much better are the hilly vineyards of Lalande-de-Pomerol and the St-Émilion satellites north of the tiny Barbanne river.

AC WINE AREAS AND MAIN CHÂTEAUX

A. Fronsac
B. Canon-Fronsac
C. Pomerol
D. Lalande-de-Pomerol
E. St-Émilion
F. Montagne-St-Émilion
G. Lussac-St-Émilion
H. Puisseguin-St Émilion

1. Ch. de Sales
2. Ch. Latour-à-Pomerol
3. Ch. Trotanoy
4. Ch. Petit-Village
5. Ch. Vieux-Château-Certan
6. Ch. Pétrus
7. Ch. Lafleur
8. Ch. la Fleur-Pétrus
9. Ch. Gazin
10. Ch. Cheval Blanc
11. Ch. Figeac
12. Ch. l'Angélus
13. Ch. Canon
14. Ch. Ausone
15. Ch. Magdelaine
16. Ch. Belair
17. Ch. Canon-la-Gaffelière
18. Ch. Pavie
19. Ch. Troplong-Mondot
20. Ch. Balestard-la-Tonnelle

AC BOUNDARIES

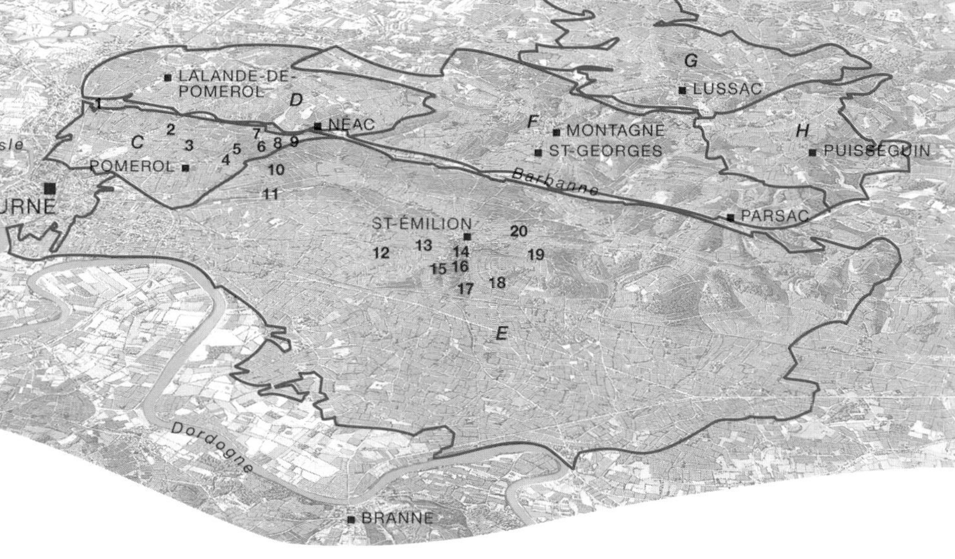

A leading Pomerol wine protected from light by the dark green Bordeaux bottle.

The intensively farmed Libournais is an exclusively red wine region. There are a few white wines made over towards Bergerac, east of St-Émilion, but what concerns us are the totally red wine regions of Fronsac, Pomerol and St-Émilion, and their satellites, along the northern banks of the Dordogne.

ST-ÉMILION

There aren't many vineyards where you can stumble upon well-preserved Roman archaeological remains, but you're quite likely to in the *côtes* vineyards clinging to the steep slopes directly to the south of the town of St-Émilion. Much of St-Émilion's wine is still stored in caves which were dug into the limestone rock in Roman times.

There is no doubt that wine was being made in St-Émilion by the Romans, and one can trace its modern history as far back as 1289 when Edward I, King of England and Duke of Gascony, specified boundaries for St-Émilion, encompassing eight communes in all, that are virtually unchanged today. With the exception of a few vineyards on flat, alluvial-rich river land near Libourne, the 5200 hectares (12,850 acres) of St-Émilion still adhere to the old historic boundaries.

Though obviously affected by the proximity of the Bay of Biscay, St-Émilion's climate is more continental than that of the Médoc to its north-west. Although there are more extreme temperature drops at night in St-Émilion, warmer daytime temperatures and fewer summer-to-autumn rains in most years mean an early harvest in most vintages.

The only areas of warm gravel soil in the region are the small St-Émilion *graves* zone next to Pomerol, and some gravel residue down by the Dordogne. The lack of it elsewhere retards ripening, and explains the present-day dominance of the Merlot grape in St-Émilion. Merlot is an early-ripener and is quite at home in cool, damp, fertile clays. Even where the soils are warmer and better-drained, Cabernet Franc is the preferred variety rather than Cabernet Sauvignon.

One major reason for the growers' enthusiasm for Cabernet Franc, or Bouchet as they call it locally, is the pervasive presence of limestone in many of the best St-Émilion vineyards. Just as Cabernet Franc thrives in the Loire valley on very limey soils, so do Merlot and Cabernet Franc on the plateau that surrounds the town of St-Émilion, and the steep slopes that fall away towards the Dordogne river plain. Nearly all the best wines come from these slopes of the plateau directly south and south-west of the town of St-Émilion.

The ground slowly drops away to the north and west of the town and the unspectacular land produces attractively soft but not memorable wines. The soils here are called *sables anciens* or 'ancient sands'. Vines grown in sand usually produce wines with loose-knit gentle flavours, and that's what you get here.

But hold on. Just before we come to the border with the Pomerol AC on the D245, there's a dip for a stream, after which the ground seems to rise in a series of waves towards the north. Just for a moment, the deep gravel topsoil which is so important in most of Bordeaux rears its head. These *graves* soils only cover around 60 hectares (150 acres) out of the whole AC but two of the most magnificent of all St-Émilions – Château Figeac and Château Cheval Blanc – are here and pack these vineyards with more Cabernet Sauvignon and Cabernet Franc than Merlot. The results are stunning.

ST-ÉMILION SATELLITES

Four *appellations* are based north of the Barbanne river, which acts as the northern boundary for St-Émilion and Pomerol. These *appellations* used to sell their wines simply as St-Émilion, but since 1936 they have only been allowed to hyphenate St-Émilion to their names. These are Montagne, St-Georges (part of the commune of Montagne), Lussac and Puisseguin. The wines are similar to St-Émilion, fairly soft though a bit earthy sometimes, and they never quite gain the perfume and sheer hedonistic richness of a really good St-Émilion.

POMEROL

There isn't much to see in Pomerol apart from fields, vines and a tall church spire. Bordeaux often seems determined to prove that the dullest-looking vineyards can produce the most memorable flavours. In which case Pomerol, only 12km (7½ miles) square, squeezed into the virtually flat land to the north and east of Libourne, is a *tour de force*. But let's look below ground. Luckily, in this very small area, with only 729 hectares (1801 acres) of vineyards, we'll find a surprising diversity of soil types which contribute to the fascinating array of flavours the wines offer. As for grapes, the juicy Merlot is king here in Pomerol. These are among the most luscious, heady and sensuous red wines in the world and, though Cabernet Franc and the odd few rows of Cabernet Sauvignon help out, Merlot bestrides Pomerol in brilliant braggart fashion. Every grape must have its perfect vineyard site. For Merlot, it's Pomerol.

The easy equation is clay and Merlot. Merlot loves clay soil, and there is a lot of clay in Pomerol. Given that the climate is basically the same as that of St-Émilion – relatively warm in Bordeaux terms – the Merlot shoots to super-ripeness in most vintages. At the heart of Pomerol lies the great Château Pétrus with its thick clay soil, mixed up with a bit of sand and a thick but broken crust of iron pan. Around it lies a plateau which is a mere 35m (115ft) high – a mix of cloggy clay with gravel and chunks of rusty hardpan, stretching for nearly 2km (1 mile) from Château Trotanoy in the west, to Château Cheval Blanc over the border in St-Émilion. Just about all the greatest

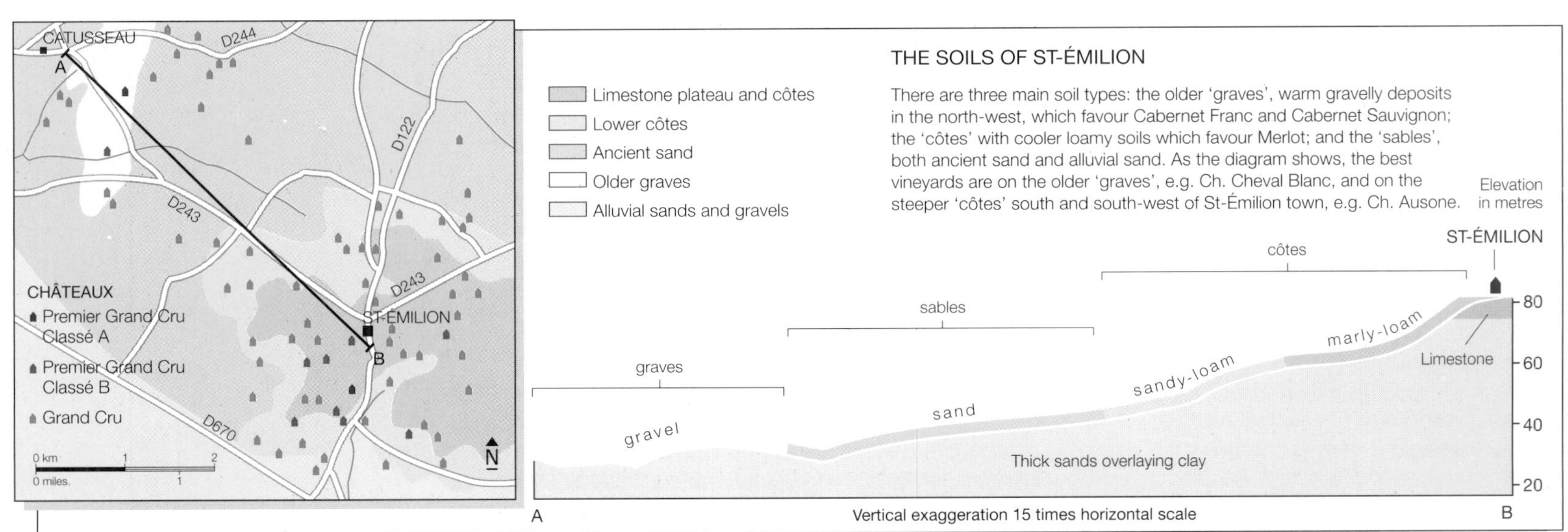

Pomerols come from this tightly packed patch of land. This is the centre of the *appellation*, but there's more to Pomerol. Gravel now begins to play a bigger part than clay as the vineyards spread out from the centre, and the wines lose the heart-thumping richness of the greatest Pomerols, yet they continue to blow kisses of soft-centred pleasure across the stern brow of Bordeaux. When the vineyards reach the town of Libourne, and stretch across its northern suburbs, the gravel becomes sandier, then sand and sandy clay take over. These vineyards produce nice wines still, but they are predictably enjoyable rather than swirling with exotic abandon.

LALANDE-DE-POMEROL

North of Pomerol, over the Barbanne river, is the *appellation* of Lalande-de-Pomerol with its 900 hectares (2225 acres) of vines. In general, the sandy gravel soils produce attractive, slightly leaner versions of the Pomerol style, but the commune of Néac, whose wines used to be sold under its own name, has a plateau of good gravelly soil producing wine of a very decent Pomerol flavour and weight.

FRONSAC AND CANON-FRONSAC

Fronsac is a delightful little region of tumbling hills and gullies bordered by the Dordogne and the Isle rivers immediately to the west of Libourne. This rolling countryside comes as something of a relief after the flat monoculture of Pomerol and most of St-Émilion, and it rates as my top picnic spot in the Libournais. But the wines, which were more highly regarded than those of St-Émilion until the middle of the nineteenth century, resolutely fail to shine. The vineyards are good – particularly the south-facing limestone bluffs of the Canon-Fronsac subdivision – and there has been a lot of investment recently in the area, and Merlot, Cabernet Franc and Malbec are all suited to the terrain. And yet, and yet... The wines have some of the plummy richness of Pomerol, some of its mineral backbone too, and develop a little Médoc-like cedar perfume with maturity, but they still fail to find their own personality.

THE 1986 CLASSIFICATION OF ST-ÉMILION

St-Émilion was first classified in 1954 and allowed for a revision every 10 years, when it would be possible to promote or demote châteaux according to their performance. The 1986 classification also reduced the St-Émilion ACs from four to two – St-Émilion Grand Cru AC and simple St-Émilion AC.

- **Premiers Grands Crus Classés (First Great Growths)**

A Ausone, Cheval Blanc.

B Beauséjour-Duffau-Lagarrosse, Belair, Canon, Clos Fourtet, Figeac, la Gaffelière, Magdelaine, Pavie, Trottevieille.

- **Grands Crus Classés (Great Classed Growths)** l'Angélus, l'Arrosée, Balestard-la-Tonnelle, Beauséjour-Bécot, Bellevue, Bergat, Berliquet, Cadet-Piola, Canon-la-Gaffelière, Cap de Mourlin, le Châtelet, Chauvin, Clos des Jacobins, Clos la Madeleine, Clos de l'Oratoire, Clos St-Martin, la Clotte, la Clusière, Corbin, Corbin-Michotte, Couvent des Jacobins, Croque-Michotte, Curé-Bon-la-Madeleine, Dassault, la Dominique, Faurie de Souchard, Fonplégade, Fonroque, Franc-Mayne, Grand-Barrail-Lamarzelle-Figeac, Grand-Corbin, Grand-Corbin-Despagne, Grand-Mayne, Grand-Pontet, Guadet-St-Julien, Haut-Corbin, Haut-Sarpe, Laniote, Larcis-Ducasse, Lamarzelle, Larmande, Laroze, Matras, Mauvézin, Moulin-du-Cadet, Pavie-Decesse, Pavie-Macquin, Pavillon-Cadet, Petit-Faurie-de-Soutard, le Prieuré, Ripeau, St-Georges-Côte-Pavie, Sansonnet, la Serre, Soutard, Tertre-Daugay, la Tour-du-Pin-Figeac (Giraud-Belivier), la Tour-du-Pin-Figeac (Moueix), la Tour-Figeac, Trimoulet, Troplong-Mondot, Villemaurine, Yon-Figeac.

THE WORLD'S GREATEST RED WINE

Vision. Passion. Money. And a good pair of Wellington boots. That's what you need to make the greatest red wine in the world. A decent vineyard would help, of course, packed with a brilliant, unique soil and subsoil, but that's where the boots come in. Château Pétrus occupies a tiny buttonhole of land at the heart of Pomerol that is just about the thickest, most squidgy clay I've ever had the temerity to tread upon. Rule number one on visiting Pétrus: don't wear a decent pair of shoes because you'll never be able to clean the clay off.

On the surface, this clay is mixed with some sand, but as the soil gets deeper it turns into cake-like clay before becoming entangled with a rock called *crasse de fer* – a resolute, tough layer of rusty hardpan, nuggets of which have crumbled off over the millennia. Does it give a mineral quality to the wine? Swathed deep in the lush velvet embrace that old Merlot vines can impart, I think there *is* a streak of mineral cool brilliantly counterbalancing the kasbah scent and round-hipped sensuous fruit of Pétrus.

The Pétrus vineyards are a mere 11.5 hectares (28½ acres), and were originally only 7 hectares (17 acres). But as early as 1878 it won a gold medal at the Paris Exhibition, the first Pomerol wine estate to do so. Pétrus's modern fame is the result of the happy coincidence of two visionaries – the late Madame Loubat, who owned the property until her death in 1961 and the merchant Jean-Pierre Moueix, the creator of the reputation of today's Pomerol. She knew her wine was Bordeaux's finest, he believed her and made it his life's quest to prove it to the world.

He succeeded brilliantly and carried the whole of Pomerol upward with Pétrus. His son Christian now manages the property and is the impassioned carrier of the Pétrus flame. He keeps the yields as low as possible partly by thinning his valuable crop every July; he has even introduced a gravel ditch drainage system that allows such dense clays to ooze away the moisture they don't need. He supervises the replanting of 1 hectare (2½ acres) of vines every eight or nine years, keeping the average age to 40 years, and preserving for as long as possible the 75-year-old vines that bleed their tiny amounts of concentrated nectar into the final blend.

If the weather is wet at vintage time he supervises the helicopter which hovers low over the vines in order to drive off the extra moisture that would dilute his precious juice. He puts the entire Moueix picking team of 180 people into the vineyards at a moment's notice – and only in the afternoon when any dew has evaporated. They clear the entire vineyard in only two or three afternoons, allowing him to pick at optimum ripeness and to minimize the risk of bad weather. But above all, he has inherited his father's vision, and his father's love for this tiny fragment of blue-tinted messy mud that produces the greatest red wine in the world. The Wellington boots he bought himself.

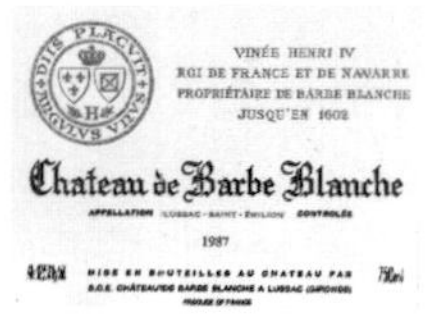

Bordeaux Sweet Wines

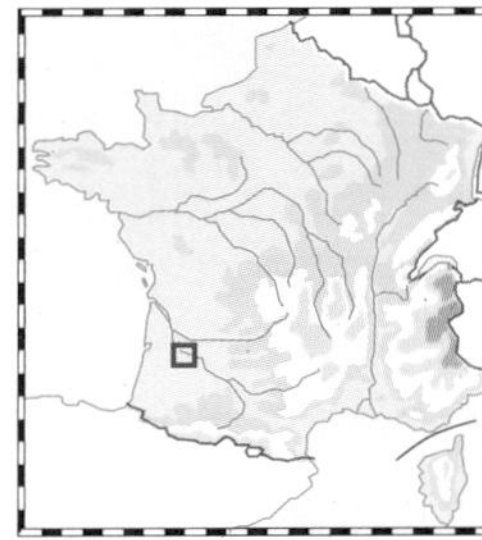

 **WHITE GRAPES**
Sémillon, the variety most prone to noble rot, is blended with much lesser amounts of Sauvignon Blanc, and sometimes a little Muscadelle.

 **CLIMATE**
This is milder and wetter than Graves. The crucial factor for the growing of grapes for sweet wine is the combination of early morning autumnal mists rising off the Garonne and the Ciron rivers and plentiful sunshine later in the day – humidity and warmth being ideal conditions for promoting noble rot.

 **SOIL**
The common theme here is clay with varying mixtures of gravel, sand and limestone. Both Sémillon and Sauvignon Blanc vines can do well in all these conditions.

ASPECT
The landscape ranges from moderately hilly around Sauternes, Bommes and Fargues to lower, more gentle slopes towards the river in Barsac and Preignac.

It's a fruit farmer's nightmare. Here I am, desperately trying to ripen my grapes in the supposedly warm days of an early autumn in the southerly reaches of the Bordeaux area – and every morning this great cloud of mist rises off the surface of local river and creeps up the slopes of my vineyard. How can my grapes ripen in the morning sun when they're shrouded in chilly mist? How can I keep them free of disease when they're blanketed with damp fog every morning?

Well, at least by the end of the morning the sun has blazed its way through the mist and burnt it all away. Heat now courses through my vineyards – but it's hardly an improvement because the hotter the day becomes, the more the humidity left over from the fog makes the air as sticky and clammy as a Turkish bath. Trying to avoid not breathing out all over the vines is a virtual impossibility.

Which, in this case, is the whole point of the exercise. I'm talking about the vineyards of Sauternes and Barsac here. They make some of the greatest sweet wine in the world. And the only way they can get their grapes sufficiently full of sugar is to encourage them to rot on the vine. But this isn't any old kind of rot: it's a very particular version called noble rot, or *pourriture noble*. And the Sauternes and Barsac regions are two of the few places in the world where it is a natural occurrence.

If you look on the map, you'll see the little river Ciron sneaking past Sauternes and Bommes, then turning to the north-east as its little valley widens out and fills with vines, until it finally hits the major river Garonne between Barsac and Preignac. The crucial point is that the Ciron is a fairly short river that rises from deep springs in the nearby Landes. It is ice-cold. The Garonne is considerably warmer, especially by the end of the summer, and the collision of two water flows of very different temperatures is what creates the mist, particularly in early morning, which then drifts back up the Ciron Valley and spreads out through the vines. However, this mist just by itself is no good. Why Barsac and Sauternes are so special is that by the time those mists become daily occurrences in the autumn, the Sémillon and Sauvignon (and occasionally Muscadelle) grapes in the vineyards should be fully ripe, and turning plump and golden. If the grapes are unripe or unhealthy due to poor weather conditions, noble rot will not develop, although the closely related black rot, sour rot and grey rot will all develop and simply destroy the grape as they would any fruit.

NOBLE ROT

Noble rot is different. Instead of devouring the skin and souring the flesh inside, the noble rot spores latch on to the skin and gradually weaken it as the grape moves from ripeness to overripeness. The skin becomes a kind of translucent browny gold but the grape is still plump and handsome. Not for long. If the warm humid weather continues, the skin is so weakened by the noble rot that it begins to shrivel. The water content in the grape dramatically reduces while the sugar, glycerine and acidity content is concentrated by dehydration.

A noble-rotted grape looks horrible – wizened, shrivelled. It feels horrible too. Pick one and it will dissolve into a slimy mess between your fingers, the skin so weakened it can hardly contain the flesh. But persevere. Put that nasty gooey pulp into your mouth, and instead of the sourness most rotten fruit displays this is intensely, memorably, syrupy sweet, sweeter than any grape could possibly be if left to ripen in the normal way.

That's the magic of noble rot. This sugar level may be twice the level achieved through natural ripening. When the thick golden juice ferments into wine, the yeasts cannot work at alcohol levels much higher than 13 to 14 degrees. But that grape may have been picked with potential alcohol levels of 20 to 25 degrees. As the yeasts slow down and become comatose in their own giddy creation of alcohol all that remaining sugar stays put in the wine – as natural sweetness. There are great sweet wines like port and Liqueur Muscat made by adding brandy to a fermenting wine to stun the yeasts into inactivity, but infection by noble rot is the classic method to produce totally natural sugar levels high enough to create such superbly liquorous sweet wine.

Without attack by noble rot, the great sweet wines of Sauternes and Barsac would not exist. The trouble is, noble rot does not attack all the grapes on a bunch at the same time, and sometimes doesn't attack them at all, even in a particularly suitable mesoclimate like that of Sauternes and Barsac.

There are three stages of noble rot. The first is the 'speckled grape' phase when the grape is fully ripe and begins to exhibit speckles on its golden skin. Then there is a 'full rotted stage' when the colour quickly changes to purple brown and the grape seems to collapse in on itself. You can make good sweet wine from grapes that reach this stage. However if you hang on a few days longer, and if the autumn weather stays dry and warm, the grapes reach the third stage – 'roasted or preserved' – when they are totally shrivelled and covered in fungus. The concentration of sugar and chemical changes in the juice at this stage are what give the dramatic flavour of great Sauternes.

The best producers are after these 'roasted' berries. The pickers are told to go through the vines picking off 'roasted' berries, if necessary one by one. This is time-consuming and very expensive. They have to go through the vineyards again and again as the individual grapes rot. There may be as many as ten of these *tries* as they are called, and the whole process of picking can drag on for more than two months. At the end of

Clear bottles are used for sweet Bordeaux such as the legendary Château d'Yquem.

THE 1855 CLASSIFICATION OF SAUTERNES

This is the original list but brought up to date to take account of name changes and divisions of property. The château name is followed by the commune:

- **Grand Premier Cru (Great First Growth)** d'Yquem, Sauternes.
- **Premiers Crus (First Growths)** Climens, Barsac; Coutet, Barsac; Clos Haut-Peyraguey, Bommes; Guiraud, Sauternes; Lafaurie-Peyraguey, Bommes; Rabaud-Promis, Bommes; de Rayne-Vigneau, Bommes; Rieussec, Fargues; Sigalas-Rabaud, Bommes; Suduiraut, Preignac; la Tour-Blanche, Bommes.
- **Deuxièmes Crus (Second Growths)** d'Arche, Sauternes; Broustet, Barsac; Caillou, Barsac; Doisy-Daëne, Barsac; Doisy-Dubroca, Barsac; Doisy-Védrines, Barsac; Filhot, Sauternes; Lamothe-Despujols, Sauternes; Lamothe-Guignard, Sauternes; de Malle, Preignac; de Myrat, Barsac; Nairac, Barsac; Romer-du-Hayot, Fargues; Suau, Barsac.

WHERE THE VINEYARDS ARE *The heart of sweet wine-making in France is the strip of land that runs along both sides of the river Ciron in the centre of the map. About 2000 hectares (4940 acres) of vineyard in five communes produce Sauternes, and Barsac, the area to the north of the Ciron, can call its wine Barsac or Sauternes. The mesoclimate that creates noble rot is more important than the soil, which alternates between gravel and sand and clay. Barsac is relatively flat, and relies upon its proximity to the Ciron and the Garonne for the noble rot conditions to develop. The wines are particularly fragrant but are rarely as luscious as those of the other villages. Preignac, to the south, is also fairly flat, but its major property – Château Suduiraut – is on a small hillock right next to Sauternes' greatest property, Château d'Yquem.*

All the top properties in Bommes, Fargues and Sauternes itself are spread over little hillsides. They get the benefit of noble rot in the autumn and better conditions to produce ultra-ripe grapes. The result is wines of a more intense, luscious character.

Also on the map are the other areas of sweet wine production in Bordeaux: Cérons, Cadillac, Loupiac and Ste-Croix-du-Mont.

it all, a property like Château d'Yquem will produce perhaps one glass of wine from each vine. A top red Bordeaux property would get nearer a bottle a vine. No wonder Yquem is one of the most expensive wines in the world. It deserves to be.

The Sémillon grape is the most important sweet wine grape, since its skin is prone to rot in any case and its wine has a propensity towards lanolin and waxy fatness when it ages. Add the lusciousness of noble rotted residual sugar and the result is smooth, rich and exotic. The Sauvignon Blanc does not rot so easily, but most vineyards have perhaps 20 per cent Sauvignon because it imparts an acidity and crispness that gives an exciting lift to the unctuous Sémillon. Muscadelle is occasionally used to add a natural honeyed texture. However, it is more likely to be found in outlying vineyards, further from the Ciron, where noble rot does not develop so well and some extra richness is much needed.

Noble rot only develops on a regular basis in Barsac and Sauternes. Cérons, north of Barsac, traditionally makes a mildly sweet wine, though without real lusciousness. However, most producers in Cérons now make dry wines that they sell as AC Graves. On the far bank of the Garonne there are three villages within the larger Premières Côtes de Bordeaux AC that make sweet wine – Cadillac, Loupiac and Ste-Croix-du-Mont. In really warm years like 1990 they can make excellent rich wines, but noble rot develops only patchily here and the sweetness is more likely to come from shrivelling by the sun. In most years the wines are mildly sweet at best.

AC WINE AREAS AND MAIN CHÂTEAUX

1. Ch. Nairac
2. Ch. Broustet
3. Ch. Climens
4. Ch. Doisy-Daëne
5. Ch. Coutet
6. Ch. Doisy-Védrines
7. Ch. St-Amand
8. Ch. Gilette
9. Ch. Bastor-Lamontagne
10. Ch. Rabaud-Promis
11. Ch. Suduiraut
12. Ch. Lafaurie-Peyraguey
13. Ch. d'Yquem
14. Ch. Guiraud
15. Ch. Rieussec
16. Ch. de Fargues

SAUTERNES = AC WINE AREAS — AC BOUNDARIES

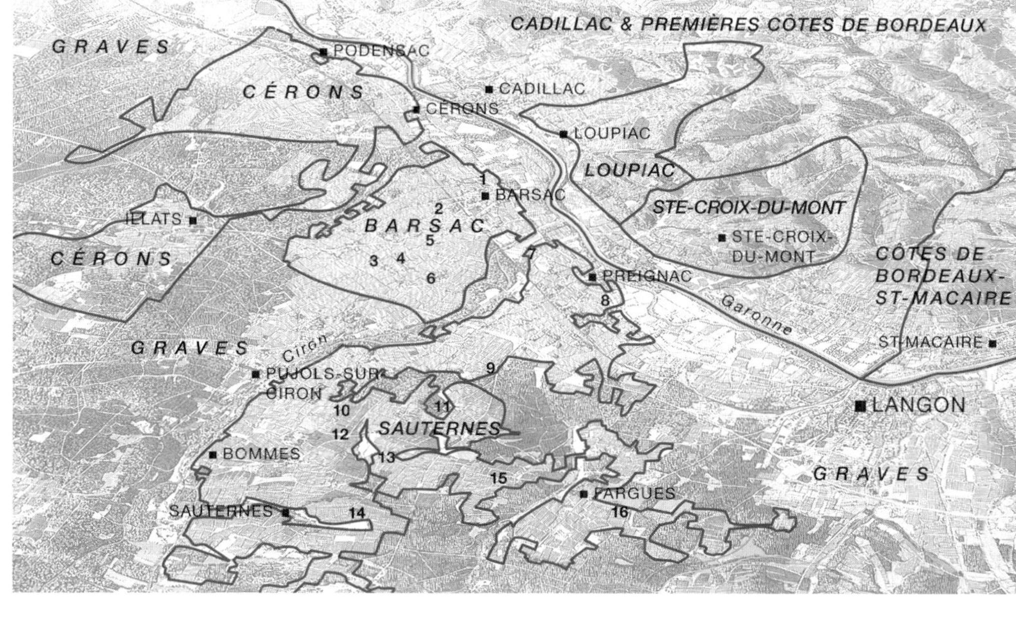

0 km 1 2
0 miles 1

SAUTERNES AND OTHER SWEET WHITE WINE REGIONS

VINEYARDS

TOTAL DISTANCE NORTH TO SOUTH 18KM (11 MILES) N

0 km 1 2
0 miles 1

Rest of Bordeaux

The Côtes de Blaye has some ancient vineyards but its wines are rarely special.

Some of the outlying vineyard areas of Bordeaux were famous centuries ago when the Médoc was just a marsh. And there are other areas, with little reputation so far, which will be shining stars within a generation, given a little luck and a good deal of effort and investment. The trouble is, when you lose a reputation, or when you fail to adapt to the changing tide of fashion, it's difficult to make up the lost ground. Stand on the high ground above the town of Blaye on the right bank of the Gironde estuary and you're standing among vineyards that were established by the Romans and highly regarded by the English when they were masters of Aquitaine. But Blaye wines are little regarded today. Take the ferry from Blaye across the Gironde to Lamarque, between the world-famous *appellations* of Margaux and St-Julien, and there you can stroll between the vines of the superstars of twentieth-century Bordeaux, estates that didn't exist when the wines of Blaye were famous.

PREMIÈRES CÔTES DE BLAYE, CÔTES DE BLAYE

Blaye is now rather a forlorn region. It is a pleasant enough place with its uplands facing the Gironde, mixing vineyards with meadows and orchards, but it doesn't take an Einstein to realize that the vine plays a subsidiary role to other agricultural pursuits. Out of about 60,000 hectares (148,000 acres) of agricultural land, only 4200 hectares (10,380 acres) are planted with vines. Of these, 3500 hectares (8650 acres) are red, and the Merlot grape dominates with 60 per cent. This makes sense. Even if the Romans liked to sit on the quayside at Blaye watching the sun set in the west, they should have noticed that the wind got up rather too frequently and that it blew straight into their faces rather cold and wet. Consequently many of the best sites are on fairly steep slopes, soaking up whatever sun there is and drawing off the drizzle when necessary. There's not much gravel, so there's not much Cabernet Sauvignon. The clay and limestone soils can ripen Merlot, though without distinction, the reds having a rather listless, jammy quality. Most of them use the *appellation* Premières Côtes de Blaye. Sauvignon is the dominant white grape at 45 per cent but rarely performs well without being beefed up with Colombard, which occupies 30 per cent of the white acreage. Whites are generally sold as Côtes de Blaye. A shining exception to the generally drab quality is the imaginative, indeed inspired, estate of Haut-Bertinerie. They have 75 per cent Cabernet Sauvignon in their red – but then they've installed the revolutionary rapid-ripening 'Lyre' training system in their vineyards. Blaye needs more like Haut-Bertinerie.

CÔTES DE BOURG

Bourg is a smaller area directly upstream of Blaye on the right bank of the Dordogne where it flows into the Gironde. The steep sandstone slopes and plateau with occasional patches of gravel are much more intensely cultivated with vines than the Blaye region just to the north, with 3600 hectares (8895 acres) of reds and just 50 hectares (125 acres) of white. I often taste the rather brusque reds and think, well, yes, there is something there, a dark dry fruit, a hint of blackcurrant tumbled in rough earth that tells me – yes, Bourg reds could be splendid if the will and investment were there. But stainless steel tanks, new oak barrels and reductions in the yields of your vines all cost a lot of money. If there is no guarantee of return, who can make such investment? The good quality co-operative at Tauriac does its best, but Bourg, like Blaye, needs a star to rise from its ancient vineyards.

With the warmest, driest mesoclimate in the area, the Côtes de Francs is one of the rising stars of Bordeaux's lesser regions.

BORDEAUX–CÔTES DE FRANCS

Côtes de Francs has got the star every small, unsung *appellation* needs. In fact it has three stars, and more could well follow. It is a tiny area tacked on to the eastern end of the St-Émilion satellite *appellations*. Indeed, the growers used to sell their wines as St-Émilion. Although the region gained its own *appellation* in 1967, there were just a few scattered vineyards and a fairly moribund co-operative to make use of it. No one knew why it deserved special attention.

Not quite true. The owners of Château Vieux-Château-Certan, one of the greatest of all the Pomerol estates, could see why. They bought Château Puygueraud and Château Claverie. And the owners of Château Cheval Blanc, one of the greatest St-Émilions, and Château l'Angélus, another exciting St-Émilion, they could see why. And so they bought the ancient Château de Francs. The limestone and clay soil is good for growing vines. The mesoclimate is reckoned to be both the driest and the warmest in all Bordeaux, and the hillside slopes are all angled towards the sun, as well as being the highest in the Gironde *département*. These prescient families had the resources to invest in this unknown quantity regardless of Côtes de Francs' lack of reputation. Their wines are now showing wonderful fruit and character, and will soon outshine many of the more famous St-Émilions just a mile or two to the west. And they already outshine the wines of Côtes de Castillon, Côtes de Francs' direct neighbour to the south. The wines are almost all red, and Merlot is the dominant grape, but there are a few white vines as well.

CÔTES DE CASTILLON

Côtes de Castillon wines are all red, and many people say they are as good as those of the Côtes de Francs, but they aren't. A lot of the vineyards are on flatter, clay-rich soil near the river Dordogne and despite their good coarse fruit, the wines rarely lose that clay-clod quality. It's amazing how a certain earthiness relentlessly hounds the fruit in wines from those Bordeaux vineyards that are dominated by clay, with the exception of the rare, great sites of Pomerol and St-Émilion. Even so, the Merlot is the grape you have to have for clay, and over 50 per cent of the plantings are Merlot, with the easy-ripening Cabernet Franc making up the bulk of the rest.

When you move away from the Dordogne, northwards, you are quickly into a world of quite steep slopes, often woodland, sometimes pasture, but just as likely to be covered with a sweep of vines. There's more limestone in the clays here, and there's a fairly good limestone subsoil too. Merlot and Cabernet Franc enjoy that, and the increase in quality as you move up into the woods is easy to see. It's no coincidence that the two best Castillon wines – Château Pitray and Château Belcier – are located well back from the river. So far back, in fact, that Belcier is allowed to declare itself as Côtes de Francs if it wants to – and I think it should.

ENTRE-DEUX-MERS

Cross over the Dordogne at the little town of Castillon-la-Bataille, remembering just for a brief moment that it was here that the English finally lost control of Aquitaine to the French in 1453, and within a mile or two we're in what is Bordeaux's most charming rural area – the Entre-Deux-Mers. The name means 'between two seas' and refers to the two rivers – the Dordogne and the Garonne – that make an 80-km (50-mile) long wedge from the borders of the Gironde *département* as they head north-west, getting closer and closer till they finally join and together become the Gironde estuary just north of the city of Bordeaux.

This is a landscape of charming little villages, friendly *prix-fixe* family restaurants full of good humour and rough-and-ready food. The roads dip and twist through forest, pasture and orchard, streams with nowhere much to go glint in the sun and tease and taunt you to bring your *charcuterie* and flagon of wine to the water's edge and dally the day away.

And there's lots of wine to choose from. The Entre-Deux-Mers is the great well from which most simple red and white Bordeaux is drawn. Most of it is sold under the Bordeaux or Bordeaux Supérieur title, and the most important producers are the co-operative cellars spread through the region. Some of the white wine uses the Entre-Deux-Mers *appellation*, and there are other small, unexceptional *appellations* adjoining the Entre-Deux-Mers. Graves de Vayres in the north-west which faces Fronsac across the Dordogne is, as its name implies, a gravelly outcrop in a zone where gravel is pretty rare. With 300 hectares (740 acres) of red and 200 hectares (495 acres) of white you'd expect something a bit out of the ordinary, but in fact most of the wine is simply pleasant AC Bordeaux. Ste-Foy-Bordeaux has 100 hectares (247 acres) of red and white vines in the north-east, while St-Macaire and Haut-Benauge are minor zones primarily for white wines in the south of Entre-Deux-Mers. Most growers in these *appellations* are quite happy to declare their wine as simple AC Bordeaux.

PREMIÈRES CÔTES DE BORDEAUX

To the south-west of the Entre-Deux-Mers, bordering the Garonne, there is a recognizable and definable leap in quality. Here in the Premières Côtes de Bordeaux *appellation* which stretches in a long, narrow strip from the city of Bordeaux in the north to Langon in the south, the land rises to a majestic limestone escarpment high above the Garonne. The plateau and the flowing slopes are thick with vines, and the views across the river to the Graves and Sauternes *appellations* are some of the most magical in all Bordeaux.

This is an area beginning to rediscover its glorious past. Along with the Graves, these vineyards provided much of the wine that first made Bordeaux famous in the Middle Ages. Although thought of recently as an *appellation* making semi-sweet wines, all the action is in red and dry white (though as yet the white can only be labelled Bordeaux). It may be because the views are heavenly or it may be that the vineyard sites are excellent, but there is now a lot of investment here, in modern wine-making equipment and imaginative wine-making. The reds are marked by an unusually juicy, come-hither character for Bordeaux, while the dry whites leave an extra intensity increasingly emphasized by oak-barrel maturation.

It's not inconceivable that the steeply sloping vineyards around the villages of Cadillac, Loupiac and Ste-Croix-du-Mont (all enclaves in the Premières Côtes – see also page 51), whose *appellations* are for sweet wines, will gradually convert to dry white and red. It depends so much on fashion. A few good Sauternes vintages, a bit of razzmatazz for dessert wines, and the growers can make a living. When sweet wines go out of vogue they can make a better living out of dry.

A classy label on the bottle can lift the image of a simple Bordeaux AC wine.

The Entre-Deux-Mers is best-known for dry whites. It makes lots of good red and white which is generally sold as simple AC Bordeaux.

BURGUNDY

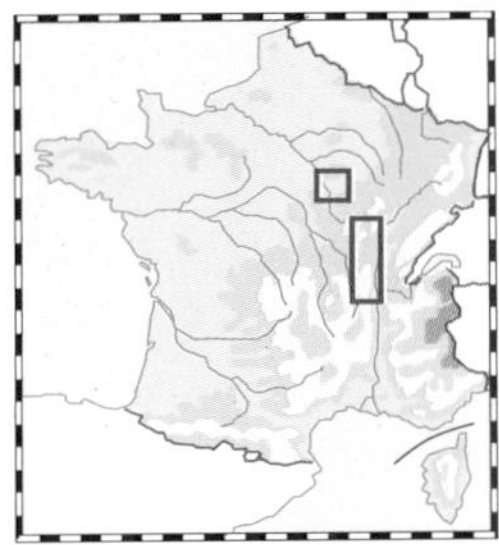

BURGUNDY. I LUXURIATE IN THAT NAME. I feel it roll around my mouth and my mind like an exotic mixed metaphor of glittering crusted jewels, ermine capes, the thunder of trumpets and the perfumed velvet sensuality of rich red wine. And it has been all those things, because Burgundy is not just the name of a wine. Between the fourteenth and sixteenth centuries, Burgundy was a Grand Duchy, spreading up eastern France, encompassing Belgium, to the shores of the North Sea. Its power and wealth rivalled that of the throne of France itself. Burgundy *was* the pomp and circumstance of jewels and ermine and trumpet voluntaries, as well as the flowering of arts and architecture and the subtle but pervasive influence of some of France's greatest monastic establishments.

These may have faded, but one part of Burgundy's glorious history remains: its remarkable ability to provide the soul and the stomach with the sustenance of great food and great wine. Look at the map opposite, at the town of Mâcon, right in the centre. To the east of Mâcon lie the rich farmlands of the Saône valley packed with vegetables and fruit, but most famous for the chickens of Bresse. To the west of Mâcon as the hills of the Morvan rise up towards the central plateau of France, the small town of Charolle has given its name to the local Charollais cattle that provide France's finest beef.

And between these two extremes of mountain and plain, as the ridges slope down towards the flat valley floor, vineyards, providing every sort of wine for the feast, from the gurgling reds of Beaujolais in the south to the intense, beetle-browed giants of the Côte de Nuits reds in the north, from the round, supple Chardonnays of the southern Mâconnais to the steely-eyed austerity of Chablis in the far north. The Mâconnais and the Chalonnais also provide excellent fizz. Only sweet wines are lacking, though the sweet blackcurrant liqueur Crème de Cassis of Nuits-St-Georges goes some way to redeeming this.

GRAPE VARIETIES

Pinot Noir has had more exasperated expletives hurled at it than just about all other great grapes put together. It is a tantalizingly difficult grape to grow successfully, its juice is tantalizingly difficult to ferment and mature to just the right level, but, ah, when it works, there's no grape like it.

The Côte d'Or is its heartland, although some is grown in the Yonne, and a fair amount in the Mâconnais and Chalonnais. It's a very ancient vine, and prone to mutation. It buds early and ripens early, but is an erratic yielder and is prone to rot. If this all sounds as if it's too much trouble, you'd be right – were it not capable of the most astonishing marriage of scent and succulence, savagery and charm when grown by an expert in one of Burgundy's best sites.

Of the other red varieties, Gamay makes deliciously juicy wines in Beaujolais, less good ones in the Mâconnais, and is a marginal producer in the Côte d'Or. César and Tressot are two old Yonne varieties.

The traditional Burgundy bottle has sloping 'shoulders' and olive green glass.

Chardonnay is grown with such success round the world that it is easy to forget that Burgundy is where it made its reputation. It can, in the right circumstances, still produce its greatest wine here, particularly on the limestone slopes of the Côte de Beaune. However, it performs reliably well all over Burgundy. It buds early, making it prone to frost in Chablis, but it ripens early too and is a consistent yielder of generally ripe grapes. This allows it to produce lean but balanced wines in Chablis, marvellously full yet savoury and refreshing wines in the Côte d'Or, chalkier yet attractive wines in the Côte Chalonnaise and plumper, milder wines in the Mâconnais.

Of the other whites Aligoté is quite widely grown, especially in the northern Côte Chalonnaise, and produces a sharp lemony wine, sometimes with a soft smell of buttermilk. Pinot Blanc and Pinot Gris are occasionally found.

THE YONNE REGION

The Chablis or Yonne region is, in fact, about 160km (100 miles) north of Beaune and it used to be at the centre of a vast vineyard area supplying Paris with basic *vin ordinaire*. The Yonne was one of several regions east of Paris which churned out oceans of what must have been very thin, mean reds and whites to slake the thirst of Parisians. None of the areas was very suitable for vine-growing, and when the railways came and made possible the transport of enormous amounts of cheap wine from the Mediterranean coast, demand for these raw northern brews disappeared. Only the very best survived, and the most famous of these is Chablis, centred round the little town of Chablis and some surrounding villages, where suitable mesoclimates and limestone and clay soil allow the Chardonnay grape to creep to ripeness and create highly individual wine. Elsewhere in the Yonne other grapes, mostly red Pinot Noir and white Chardonnay and Aligoté, are grown in outlying areas mainly south-east of Auxerre, but are only accorded the Bourgogne *appellation*, the best of them like Irancy and Epineuil also using their village name on the label. Many of their grapes now go to make very good Crémant de Bourgogne sparkling wine. The village of St-Bris even has a VDQS for its Sauvignon Blanc.

CÔTE D'OR

Dijon, right at the top of the map, is at the northern end of the world-famous Côte d'Or, and from here, right the way south to Lyon, there is an almost unbroken vista of vines, comprising the Burgundy region. However, because we are fairly far north here, the southern warmth only begins to dominate around Mâcon, so mesoclimates of vineyards facing towards whatever sun there is are crucial for ripening grapes. The Côte d'Or, which is divided into the Côte de Nuits between Dijon and a point just south of Nuits-St-Georges, and the Côte de Beaune, continuing southwards past Beaune to a point just west of

WHERE THE VINEYARDS ARE *The Burgundy region relies crucially upon the slopes of the mountains in the west to provide suitable vineyard land. The Saône Valley to the east is rich, fertile agricultural land and as such is not fit for fine wine production. You can see vineyards down by the river Saône, but they produce regional Bourgogne AC at best, and more generally* vin de pays. *The mountains rising to the west are the beginnings of the Massif Central that runs like a broad backbone down the centre of France. These hills and dales are generally too high and too exposed to westerly winds and rain to be warm enough to ripen grapes.*

The ridge below which the slopes drop away to the plain provides ideal protection from wind and angles the land towards the south and east to gain maximum warmth from the sun. Between Dijon and Chagny in the north lies the narrow but high quality sliver of vineyards known as the Côte d'Or. Burgundy's greatest reds and whites are produced here.

West of Chalon-sur-Saône the local climates become less protected and the Côte Chalonnaise reflects this with vineyards appearing only sporadically in the best sites. However passing Tournus to Mâcon, Villefranche and Lyon the warmer south allows the vineyards to spread away from the protective hills, though the finest Mâconnais whites and Beaujolais reds still come from the steep slopes to the west of the vineyards between Mâcon and Villefranche.

The inset map shows the Yonne region, a northern outpost of Burgundy, whose best known wine is Chablis.

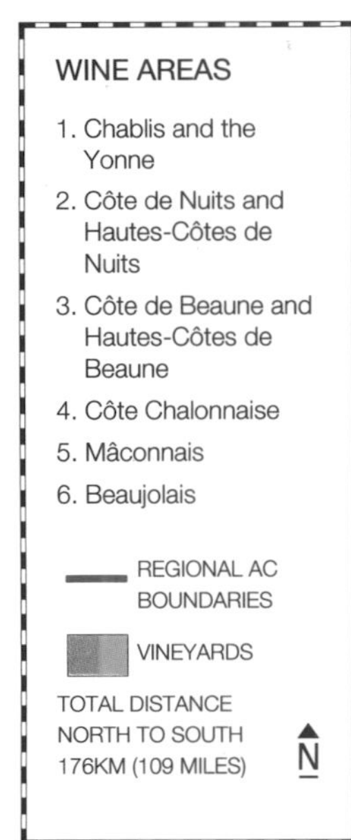

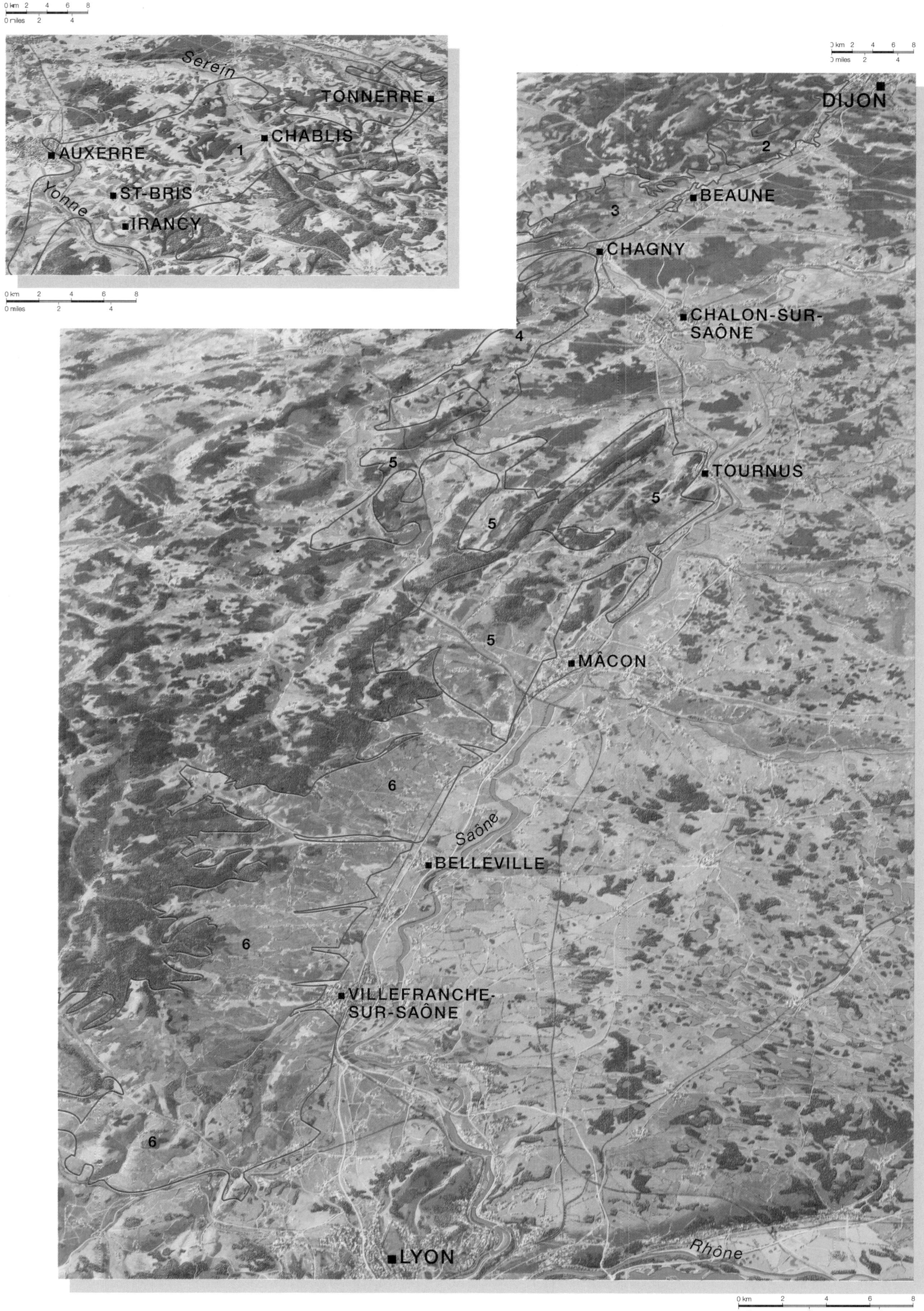
0 km 2 4 6 8
0 miles 2 4
Serein
TONNERRE
CHABLIS
AUXERRE
1
Yonne
ST-BRIS
IRANCY
DIJON
2
BEAUNE
3
CHAGNY
CHALON-SUR-SAÔNE
4
5
TOURNUS
5
5
5
MÂCON
6
Saône
BELLEVILLE
6
VILLEFRANCHE-SUR-SAÔNE
6
LYON
Rhône

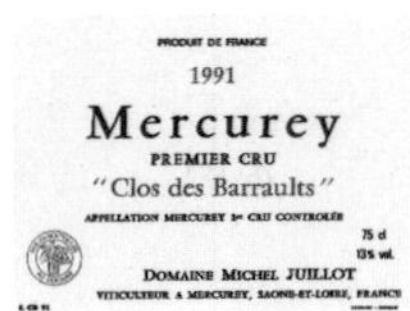

Chagny, consists of east- to south-east-facing, well-drained slopes on alkaline ground, mixing rich marls and pebbly limestone for the best results. The map shows the hills stretching away to the west, and the tiny strip of vines hugging the ridge – these hills provide crucial protection from the prevailing westerly wind, as well as drawing off a lot of the moisture from the clouds before they reach the Côte d'Or. Pinot Noir dominates the Côte de Nuits, while Chardonnay and Pinot Noir share the Côte de Beaune. Scattered vineyards just to the west of the Côte d'Or, in the area called the Hautes-Côtes, can make good, light wine in warm years.

CÔTE CHALONNAISE

South of Chagny and west of Chalon-sur-Saône, the protective ridge of mountains breaks down somewhat, and this region, the Côte Chalonnaise, is more sparsely planted with vines, the vineyards generally nestling into south- and south-east-facing mesoclimates and leaving the more exposed land free for grazing and orchards. Chalonnais reds and whites can be good, but their less perfect vineyard conditions shows in the wines' relative leanness. Traditionally, much of this wine was transformed into sparkling wine, Crémant de Bourgogne, but increased demand for red Pinot Noir and white Chardonnay still wines has encouraged producers to make more efforts to ripen their grapes, and investment by some of the region's leading producers in new oak barrels for making the wine has also greatly improved standards.

MÂCONNAIS

South-west of Tournus and west of Mâcon, the vineyards begin to spread out. This is the Mâconnais, increasingly a white Chardonnay region, though Gamay and Pinot Noir are also grown for red wines. The best vineyards are still those closest to the ridge of hills in the west, and famous wines like Pouilly-Fuissé are dependent on steep slopes and well-drained limestone soils for their quality. The flatter land that spreads out towards the Saône is mirrored by softer, less defined wines, usually selling under the title Mâcon Blanc, or Mâcon Blanc-Villages. They are, in general, a very mild interpretation of Chardonnay character, but a new generation of young growers is beginning to show what the area could achieve with more effort. In the south of France, in Eastern Europe and obviously in the New World, winemakers are producing excellent, tasty, fairly priced Chardonnays from land that supposedly lacks the advantage of Burgundian *terroir*. The new wave of growers are starting to realize that a Burgundian birthright is a big plus in the wine world, but that the world doesn't owe them a living just because of it. As it is, however, the production today is largely in the hands of highly efficient co-operative groups intent on supplying decent, but not spectacular, wine.

BEAUJOLAIS

The Mâconnais region blends imperceptibly into Beaujolais just south of the Pouilly-Fuissé *appellation*. Here almost all the wines are red (there is just a little rosé and occasional Beaujolais Blanc from the Chardonnay) and the grape is the Gamay. Once again the western slopes play their part, providing good southerly and easterly aspects, protection from wind and good drainage. The soils on the slopes to the north-west and west of Belleville are granite-based and provide the generally unregarded Gamay grape with a rare chance to shine. These slopes harbour the 'Ten Crus' – the communes that produce the best Beaujolais wine, and use their own name on the label rather than that of Beaujolais. Intermingled with the Crus, and spreading southward, are the communes that make Beaujolais-Villages, while the broader, clay-dominated vineyards reaching down to Lyon provide simple quaffing Beaujolais in vast quantities.

The vineyards at Savigny-lès-Beaune are partly protected by the thick swathe of forest which crowns the upper slopes along much of the Côte de Beaune.

MERCHANTS, GROWERS AND CO-OPERATIVES

Burgundy's vineyards are some of the oldest in France, established by the Romans, if not by the Gauls before them, nurtured through the centuries by the monasteries, and subsequently by the great power of the Duchy of Burgundy itself. Once large homogeneous estates, Burgundian vineyard holdings are nowadays incredibly fragmented due to the Napoleonic laws which decreed that every inheritance be equally divided between all offspring. Yet the reputation of the wine from the main villages and vineyards continued to grow. To cope with an increasingly erratic supply, a merchant class grew up, based primarily in the town of Beaune, but also in Nuits-St-Georges, whose job was to seek out sufficient small parcels of the well-known vineyard names to make up into saleable and marketable quantities. These merchants would buy from numerous growers and blend the wines and bottle them in their cellars. Honest merchants made up good wines, dishonest merchants didn't. But however good the blending, in a region like Burgundy where nuance of flavour should be everything, those nuances were lost. In the Mâconnais and Beaujolais smallholders were more likely to band together into co-operatives. These might well then sell on their blends to merchants, but several in the Mâconnais, like Viré, Lugny, Igé and Clessé, have established strong reputations of their own.

Burgundy's reputation for much of the twentieth century has been created and maintained by these *négoçiant*, or merchant houses, and most of the 'Meursault' or 'Beaune' or 'Nuits-St-Georges' you find will be from a merchant. But in the Côte d'Or, a region that has made more efforts than any other to define precisely why its different parcels of land are special, it is worth seeking out individual growers' wines. A lazy grower will still produce poor wine, but a committed grower will give you an expression of himself and the soil he works that is rare and precious in the modern world.

Fuissé in the Mâconnais is one of the villages responsible for Pouilly-Fuissé which, in committed hands, can be a truly great and characterful dry white wine.

CRÉMANT DE BOURGOGNE

To say that the vineyards of Burgundy are ideally suited for the production of sparkling wine is only true up to a point. Their prime objective is the production of still wines – some of the world's most perfumed reds and some of the most majestic and complex whites from the best vineyards in the centre and north, and pleasantly rounded, fruity reds and gentle whites from the southern vineyards. But Burgundy is a marginal vine-growing area. The weather is unpredictable, and frequently the wine produced is too thin and unripe to make enjoyable drinking on its own. In the old days such wines would often be bolstered by the addition of heavy wines from the Mediterranean. But a much better use for light, unripe wine is to make it into fizz.

The Côte Chalonnaise, especially Rully with its exposed limestone slopes, used to be the centre for Crémant de Bourgogne and Nuits-St-Georges boasted several well-known brands. But the best producers are now in the Auxerrois region of the Yonne where excellent white and rosé is produced, particularly at the Caves de Bailly, and in the Mâconnais where co-ops like Lugny and Viré use much of their Chardonnay and Pinot Noir grapes to produce excellent Champagne-method sparkling wine.

But there is a difference between here and Champagne: marginal Burgundy may be, but it's not as marginal as Champagne. The base wine is always just that little bit riper and rounder than the tooth-scouringly acid base wine of Champagne, and so when the wine, complete with sparkle, is finally poured it will taste just that little bit riper and rounder than Champagne. This can be a good thing, but somehow it also means that Crémant de Bourgogne never hits the heights of Champagne. It's a good, reliable sparkler, but it's not one to put away for a special occasion. Drink it for fun instead.

APPELLATIONS AND CLASSIFICATIONS

There are five basic levels of AC in Burgundy.

- **General regional ACs** 'Bourgogne' is the basic catch-all AC covering red, white, rosé and sparkling wines which do not qualify for one of the higher ACs. This category includes Bourgogne Passe-Tout-Grains, a mix of Pinot Noir with the inferior Gamay, and Bourgogne Grand Ordinaire which doesn't really deserve an AC at all.
- **Specific regional ACs** These are a half-way house between general regional *appellations* and single village ACs, for example, Chablis or Beaujolais.
- **Village ACs** These apply to the wine of a single village and there is a growing move to include vineyard names on the label, even if they're not of the top rank, for example, Meursault 'le Cromin'. The majority of village wines are still blends of several vineyards within the village. The Bourgogne Hautes-Côtes de Nuits and Hautes-Côtes de Beaune ACs apply to certain villages in the hills to the west of the main Côte d'Or vineyards. Côte de Beaune-Villages and Côte de Nuits-Villages apply to villages, blended or separate, in their respective parts of the Côte d'Or.
- **Premiers Crus (First Growths)** Despite the name, these are the second best vineyard sites in Burgundy. Even so they include some of the region's finest wines. The village name on the label will be followed by the vineyard name, for example Gevrey-Chambertin 'Combe-aux-Moines'.
- **Grands Crus (Great Growths)** These are Burgundy's tiptop vineyards and are found only in Chablis and the Côte d'Or. They are so carefully and jealously delineated that every single row of vines is separately assessed. The reds are mostly in the Côte de Nuits and the whites are only in Chablis and the Côte de Beaune. A Grand Cru vineyard name can stand alone on the label without the name of the village, for example, Chambertin from the village of Gevrey-Chambertin. Indeed, many of the Côte d'Or villages have hyphenated their own name to the name of their most famous vineyard. Grand Cru and Premier Cru classifications apply only to the vineyard and the potential for quality such a site posseses. The human element is not counted, and while a good grower can maximize a site's potential, a bad grower or winemaker can equally ruin a Premier Cru or Grand Cru through lousy viticulture or lousy wine-making.

One of the Nuits-St-Georges red wines, bottled at the domaine by the grower.

Chablis

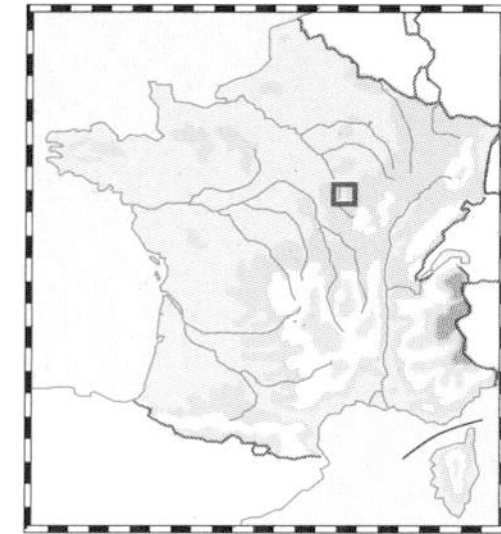

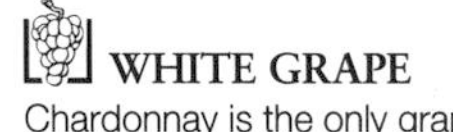

WHITE GRAPE
Chardonnay is the only grape allowed for Chablis.

CLIMATE
The maritime influence lessens as you go east and the winters become longer and colder, the summers warmer and drier. Hail storms and spring frosts are the greatest hazards to vines in this northerly region.

SOIL
The soil is a mixture of marly limestone and clay with two main types: Kimmeridgian and Portlandian.

ASPECT
The exposure and angle of the slope are critical in this northern region. The best vineyard sites are on the south-east- and south-west-facing slopes of hills along the banks of the Serein.

It's so cold! As I scramble up the damp slopes of the Grand Cru vineyards looming above the little river Serein, the freezing air worms its way under my coat and seems to settle very precisely inside my joints. I stumble down the stairs to the producers' cellars and an eternal truth is revealed: if hot air rises, cold air descends. From the mist-wreathed woodland above the vineyard slopes, to the grey charmless tarmac of the town streets, the cold finally tumbles down the stairway like a cloud of invisible ice, into the cellars where the wine is fermented and matured. Ah, the rigours of Chablis in early spring.

This cold, this chill austerity in the climate, in the vineyards, in the little town and its maturation cellars too, gives Chablis its uniqueness. Its glinting, cold green, mineral attack allows Chablis a special hauteur in a modern wine world caught in a feeding frenzy for the heady flavour of ripeness and warmth. This niche is one that the growers and producers of Chablis would do well not to desert in the face of these hot-blooded flavours of Chardonnay from warmer climes.

Chablis' vineyards are right at the limit beyond which the Chardonnay grape will not ripen. The Kimmeridgian limestone clay – a soil with fossilized oyster shells – present in all the traditional Chablis vineyard sites, gives a very particular character to the wines. Modern moves to increase Chablis' vineyard area, to increase yields in the vineyards – never a quality option in areas where the vine struggles to ripen – and to maximize the use of the malolactic fermentation to produce a soft, easy dry white wine merely serve to dilute Chablis' personality. No wonder the price is often no different from a supposedly inferior Mâcon-Villages; the flavours become virtually interchangeable, why should one pay more?

Let's look at the heart of Chablis to see why it became famous in the first place. The *appellation* initially intrigued me because it is the first vineyard area you come across as you roar down the Autoroute du Soleil from Paris. But Chablis gives little indication in its wines or geography of being anything to do with the warm south. It comprises a small, chilly, isolated jumble of vineyards in the frost-prone valley of the river Serein about 160km (100 miles) north of Beaune, the wine capital of Burgundy's Côte d'Or.

This northern outpost of the Burgundy region is virtually all that is left of the extensive Yonne vineyards that used to supply the bulk of Paris' everyday wine, before the railways brought warmer and more suitable wine regions within easy reach. I've never read a complimentary word about those old Yonne wines, which must have been weak in the extreme, but Chablis survived – just – because the grape it grows is the great Chardonnay of white Burgundy fame. Huddled along the banks of the tiny river Serein, angled towards the south-west and protected from the harsh winds of this semi-continental climate, there are a few slopes of Kimmeridgian limestone that can, in a good summer, produce sublime dry white wine. Its fame was such that the name Chablis has been used indiscriminately throughout the world to describe dry (or not so dry) white wines, made from whatever kind of grape the country in question was adept at producing. True Chablis is a dry white wine that only comes from these vineyards, and only uses the Chardonnay grape.

There has been a considerable expansion of vineyards in recent years, and the area now stands at about 4000 hectares (9880 acres) of vine. This is a tenfold increase since the 1950s, and it goes without saying that most of the expansion has come on less suitable sites including land made up of the less perfectly balanced Portlandian clay.

GRANDS CRUS AND PREMIERS CRUS

However, despite the general expansion, the Grands Crus have remained virtually unchanged and command a long, steep, south-west-facing slope of vines rising up at between 150 and 250m (500 and 820ft) from the river Serein opposite the town of Chablis. If we remember that this is a cold, inhospitable

THE CHABLIS VINEYARDS

Chablis' only Grand Cru vineyards sit lower down the south-west-facing slopes opposite the town where more sunshine means better ripening. The soil of the Grand Cru vineyards is rich in lime which enables the Chardonnay grapes to remain acid while ripening thoroughly.

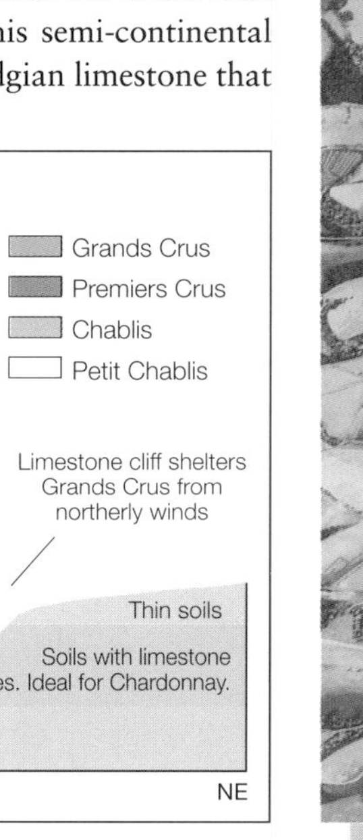

WHERE THE VINEYARDS ARE *Bang in the middle of this map is the little town of Chablis, with the best vineyards, the Grands Crus, clustered on nearby slopes. These vineyards are ideally positioned on south-facing slopes, though the river Serein's warming influence in summer can be balanced by a serious predisposition to creating lethal frost pockets in springtime. The best Premiers Crus are Montée de Tonnerre and Mont de Milieu south-east of the Grands Crus, Fourchaume to the north and Montmains to the south-west, though none of these vineyards is quite so well sited as the Grands Crus, and the wines are correspondingly lighter. The further you get from the protective entrance of the Serein Valley, the more haphazard the mesoclimates become, and the more scattered the vineyards, until the typical northern French landscape of cereal fields, forest and grazing land takes over once again.*

0 km 1 2
0 miles 1

region in which to grow grapes, the mesoclimates created by aspect to the sun and the warming influence of the river and the town are all-important. Frost has always been a far greater problem in Chablis than elsewhere in Burgundy and the Grands Crus were always the worst hit, for the narrow Serein Valley tends to trap cold air masses. Various protection methods are now used to combat the worst effects of the frost but in the 1950s the viability of these great vineyards was being called into question. In 1956 Les Clos, which produces the nuttiest, most honeyed of all the Grands Crus, was being used as a ski slope.

There are seven different Grand Cru vineyard sites covering 100 hectares (247 acres), all contiguous, but all subtly different. Their true characters only become evident with a judicious marriage of low yields in the vineyards and a few years' aging in the bottle. The modern tendency to use new oak barrels for both fermenting and aging the wines can produce delicious results but usually blurs the distinctions between each site.

There has been a massive expansion of Premier Cru vineyard sites with the result that the words 'Premier Cru' on a Chablis label no longer guarantee a wine much superior to a basic Chablis. However, there are some excellent Premier Cru sites, usually not quite so steep as the Grands Crus, and often with a more south to south-east aspect, thereby missing the best of the warm afternoon sun. Those on the east bank of the river Serein are thought of as best though there are fine Premier Cru vineyards directly south-west of the town.

CHABLIS AND PETIT CHABLIS

Simple Chablis is made further away from the town of Chablis itself, its quality depending upon the mesoclimate and the determination of the grower. Petit Chablis – the lower form of Chablis from the least suitable sites – used to be fairly common, but most Petit Chablis sites have now been upgraded to Chablis, though they rarely deserve it.

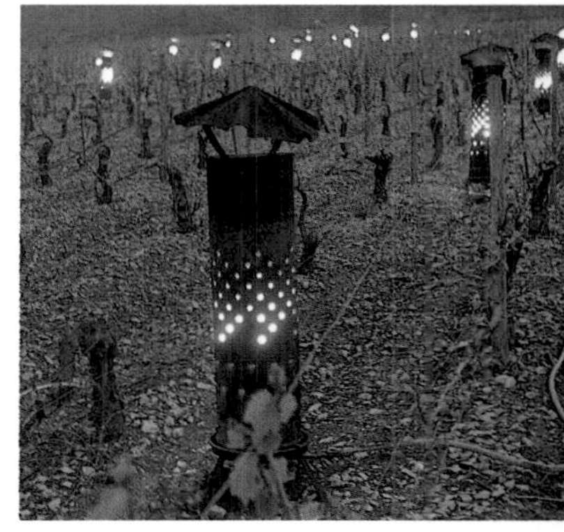

'Smudge pots' (charcoal or oil burners) are one of many methods to stop spring frosts from killing the young vines.

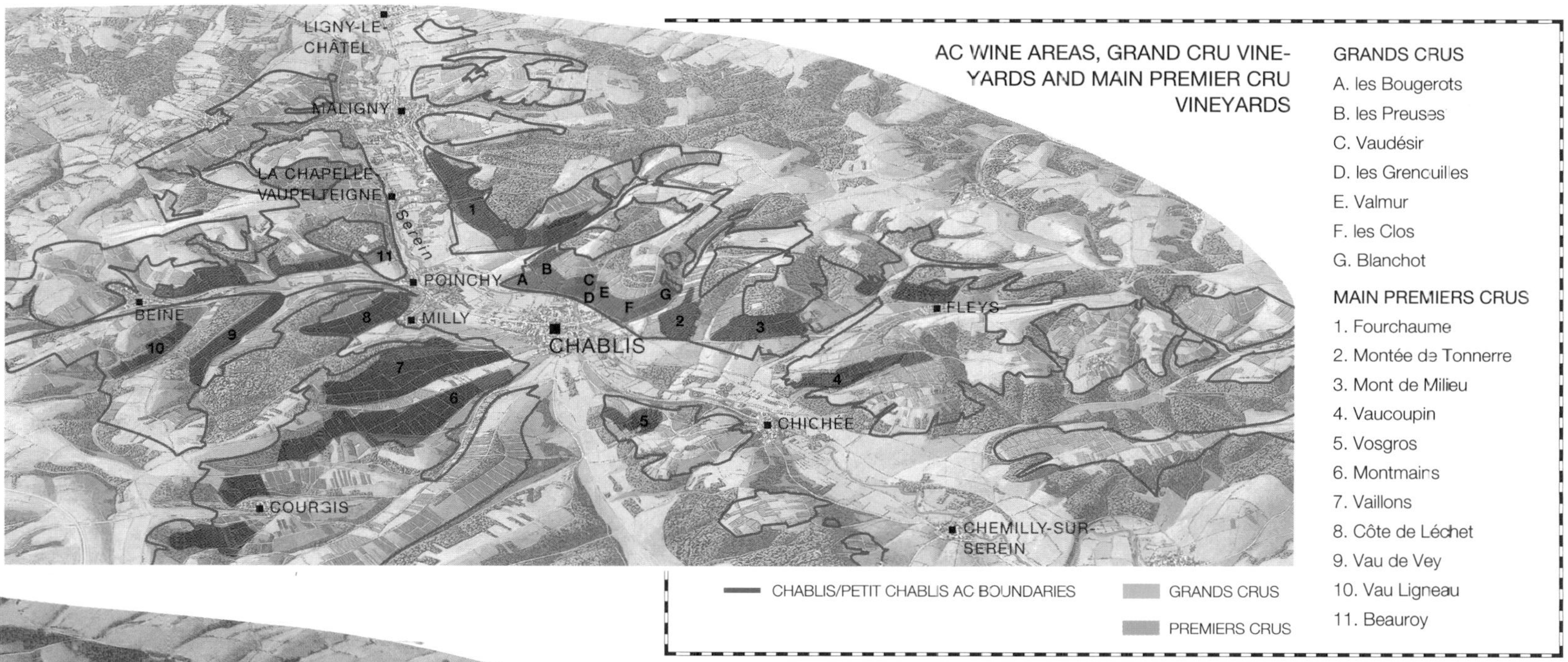
AC WINE AREAS, GRAND CRU VINEYARDS AND MAIN PREMIER CRU VINEYARDS
LIGNY-LE-CHÂTEL
MALIGNY
LA CHAPELLE-VAUPELTEIGNE
Serein
POINCHY
BEINE
MILLY
CHABLIS
FLEYS
CHICHÉE
COURGIS
CHEMILLY-SUR-SEREIN
GRANDS CRUS
A. les Bougerots
B. les Preuses
C. Vaudésir
D. les Grenouilles
E. Valmur
F. les Clos
G. Blanchot
MAIN PREMIERS CRUS
1. Fourchaume
2. Montée de Tonnerre
3. Mont de Milieu
4. Vaucoupin
5. Vosgros
6. Montmains
7. Vaillons
8. Côte de Léchet
9. Vau de Vey
10. Vau Ligneau
11. Beauroy
CHABLIS/PETIT CHABLIS AC BOUNDARIES
GRANDS CRUS
PREMIERS CRUS

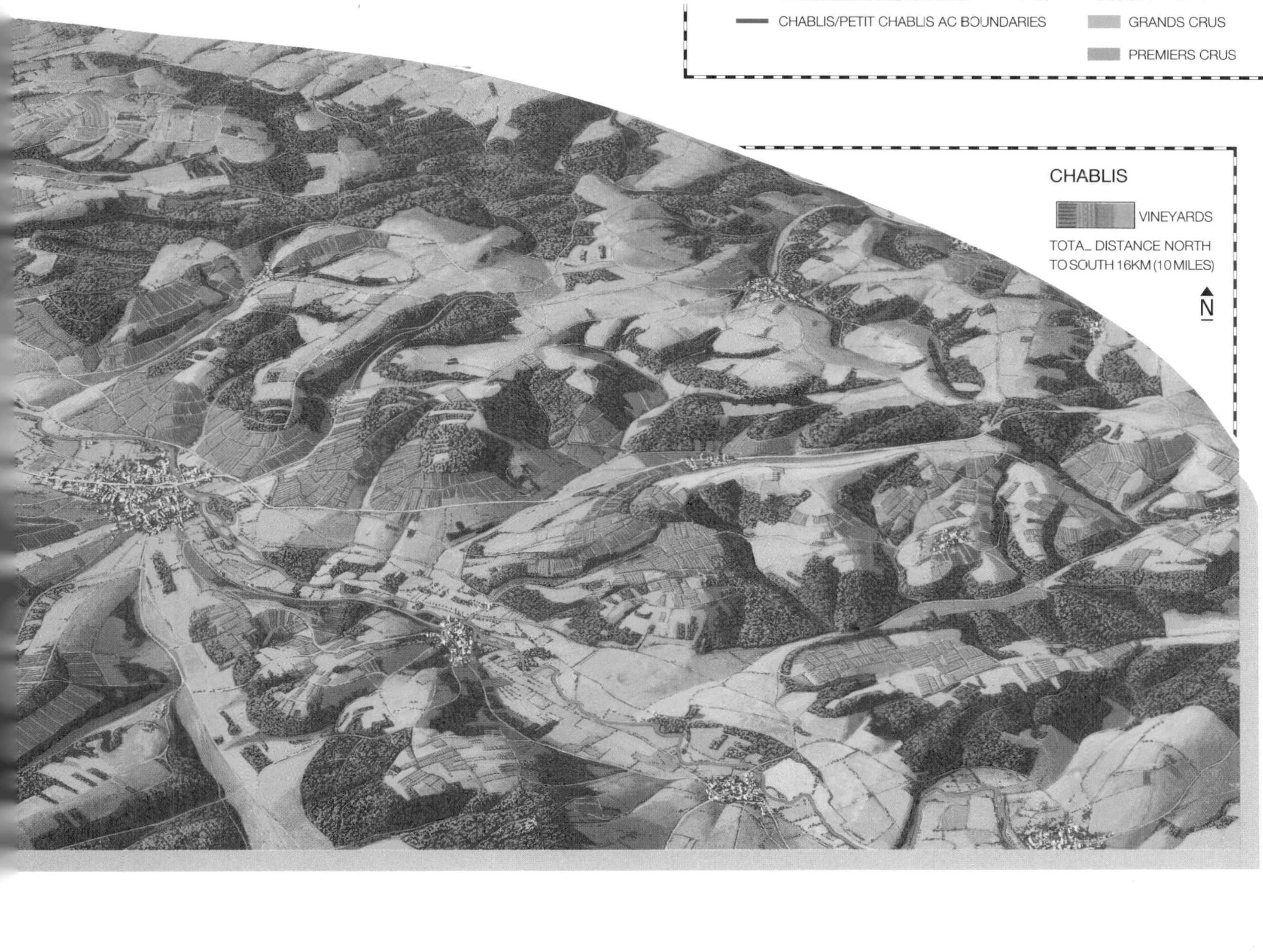
CHABLIS
VINEYARDS
TOTAL DISTANCE NORTH TO SOUTH 16KM (10 MILES)
N

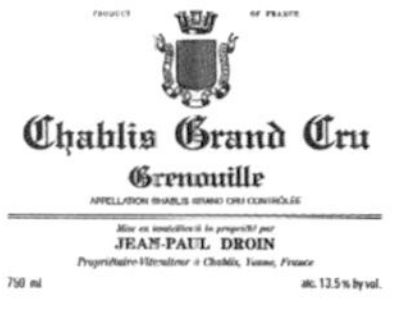
Chablis Grand Cru
Grenouille
JEAN-PAUL DROIN

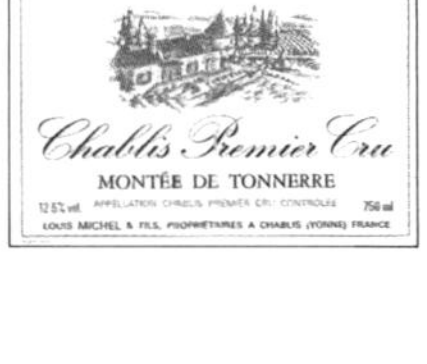
Chablis Premier Cru
MONTÉE DE TONNERRE

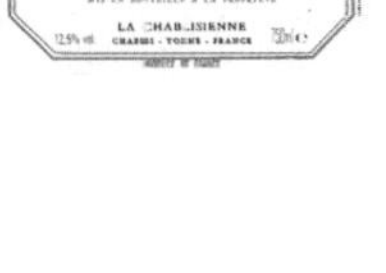
La Chablisienne
CHABLIS

Côte de Nuits

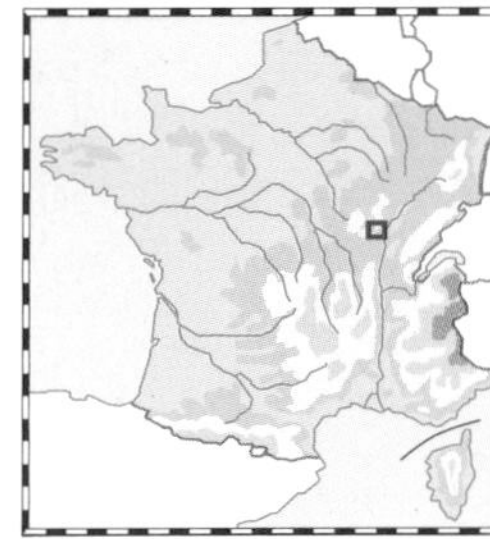

My favourite place in the Côte de Nuits, one of the world's greatest vineyard regions, isn't the most famous. It's in the village of Prémeaux, just to the south of the town of Nuits-St-Georges. Here you can step off the N74 road into the vines right below the marvellous Clos Arlot vineyard. At this point, the Côte de Nuits is little more than 90m (295ft) across, one side to the other. Admittedly this is the narrowest part, but the point is that the Côte de Nuits, which includes many of the most famous red wine names in the world, is a mere sliver of land snaking its way in and out of an east-facing escarpment that marks the eastern edge of the Morvan hills. The Côte lies between 250 and 350m (820 and 1150ft) above sea level. The escarpment is limestone, and continues down the slope to the plain. On this slope, over the millennia, soil has been created through a mixture of eroded limestone, pebbles and clays. An outcrop of rich dark marlstone is particularly in evidence in the middle of the slope at around the 275m (900ft) mark. All the greatest vineyards are situated within 25m (80ft), more or less, of this mark and face mainly east or south-east.

PINOT NOIR'S HOMELAND

The really top vineyards are planted with red Pinot Noir. Indeed the whole Côte de Nuits is overwhelmingly a red wine slope, with just a little rosé being made at Marsannay in the north, and a few bottles of rare white being made at Morey-St-Denis, Nuits-St-Georges and, most famous, the Musigny vineyard at Chambolle-Musigny. Otherwise Pinot Noir rules. White grapes prefer the impoverished, easy-draining limestone soils, and in the Côte de Beaune to the south there are various instances of limestone dominating the slopes. But here in the Côte de Nuits, limestone merely seems to temper the rich marl soil and reduce its fertility. Over-fertile soil never produces great wine, but this mixture seems just right.

CÔTE DE NUITS CLASSIFICATIONS

The great vineyards start in the village of Gevrey-Chambertin and form an almost unbroken line through Morey-St-Denis, Chambolle-Musigny, Vougeot to Vosne-Romanée. Nuits-St-Georges vineyards are also very good, though none are placed in the very top rank. Over the centuries the best sites have consistently ripened earlier than those too high up the slope or on flatter ground at the bottom. So a minutely accurate system of vineyard classification has evolved. The Grands Crus are so carefully and jealously delineated that every single row of vines is separately assessed. The same goes for the second rank of vineyards – the Premiers Crus. There are numerous instances of certain rows of vines being excluded from the higher *appellation* and condemned to the third tier – the village *appellation*. Even so, the village *AC* is still only applied to decent land – which almost always lies between the N74 and the escarpment to the west. Some vineyards, in the north at Brochon and

RED GRAPES
Pinot Noir is the only grape allowed in non-generic wines.

WHITE GRAPES
Among the few Côte de Nuits whites Chardonnay is the main grape with occasionally some Pinot Blanc.

CLIMATE
This is sunnier in the growing season than Bordeaux but the autumns are cool and the winters long and cold. Spring frosts and hail can cause problems. The Hautes-Côtes are less protected from the prevailing westerly winds and can get heavy rain.

SOIL
The Côte d'Or is basically a limestone ridge where weathering has produced a stony scree-like limestone and clay topsoil, especially on middle slopes, which provides the best drainage for the vines.

ASPECT
The top vineyards are situated on the middle slopes at 250–300m (820–985ft) where the steeper gradients as well as the soil structure facilitate drainage. The south- or south-east-facing aspect of the best sites also enhances exposure to the sun and therefore ripening in these northern vineyards.

WHERE THE VINEYARDS ARE *There are a lot of vineyards on this map. But the ones that really matter, the world-famous red wine vineyards of the Côte de Nuits, are few in number and precisely delineated. The Côte de Nuits begins where the hills rise up south of Dijon. The N74 road runs due south and, with a few exceptions in Gevrey-Chambertin, Morey-St-Denis and Nuits-St-Georges, marks the eastern boundary of good vineyard land. All the best vineyards occupy a thin band of this east-facing escarpment between Gevrey-Chambertin and Nuits-St-Georges. Here the aspect to the sun, the drainage afforded by the slopes and the protection provided from wind and rain by the hills to the west, all combine to create what many consider to be the Pinot Noir grape's spiritual home. The vineyards to the west, in the mountains, are the Hautes-Côtes de Nuits. They are higher and less well protected than the uplands of the Côte de Nuits. The wines made here are generally pleasant but are often on the light side.*

CÔTE DE NUITS AND HAUTES-CÔTES DE NUITS

VINEYARDS

TOTAL DISTANCE NORTH TO SOUTH 28KM (17½ MILES)

N

0 km 1 2
0 miles 1

Fixin, and in the south, between Premeaux-Prissey and Corgoloin, use the collective *appellation* Côte de Nuits-Villages. Relatively unsuitable land, such as the flatter vineyards to the east of the N74, better suited to cattle and vegetables, is relegated to regional or generic *appellations* – Bourgogne, Bourgogne Passe-Tout-Grains and Bourgogne Grand Ordinaire – a good deal more Ordinary than Grand.

But the good Côte de Nuits Burgundies are very grand indeed. Red wines from a cool area like Burgundy should be delicate, not monumental, but that relatively rich soil, sloped east and south-east, can, when the summer is warm and the grape grower careful to limit his yield, produce wines of disturbing, heady brilliance. These can often be dark and brooding when young, especially those from Gevrey-Chambertin, but may break out into glorious exotic scents as they age, in particular at Vosne-Romanée and Chambolle-Musigny, finally maturing into a state of delectable decay, when all the savagery, sweetness and scent melds into a dark, sweet autumn richness of quite astonishing beauty. From the best growers, the nuances of flavour detectable in wines from vines only yards apart offer a marriage between the hedonistic and the intellectual that hardly any other wines ever manage. From a bad grower or merchant, there are few bigger, nor more expensive, disappointments than a thin, lifeless wine masquerading under these great names.

The fragmented nature of vineyard ownership in Burgundy means the harvest is still mostly done by hand.

VILLAGES OF THE CÔTE DE NUITS

If you look at the top of the map, you can hardly spot a vine. There *used* to be loads of vineyards to the south-west, but Dijon's suburban sprawl has swallowed them up. In any case, they were mostly planted with Gamay to make cheap quaffing wine for Dijon, not classy Burgundy. Chenôve still has a few vines on the slope just north of Marsannay, but Marsannay is the first serious village. It used to be famous for rosé, but is now an increasingly useful supplier of good, perfumed though lightweight reds. The slopes at Couchey, Fixin and Brochon might look pretty suitable for vines: they grow Pinot Noir, but little of great excitement ever comes to light. Fixin's heavy clay soils can give good reds in a hot year.

The real fireworks start at Gevrey-Chambertin. Here the rich marl soil comes properly into play, with red clays peppered with stones, and outbreaks of rich subsoil through a thin layer of topsoil on the higher sites. The narrow east- and south-east-facing slope under its protective forest brow continues almost unbroken between Gevrey-Chambertin and Nuits-St-Georges. Here the Pinot Noir really shows what it can do.

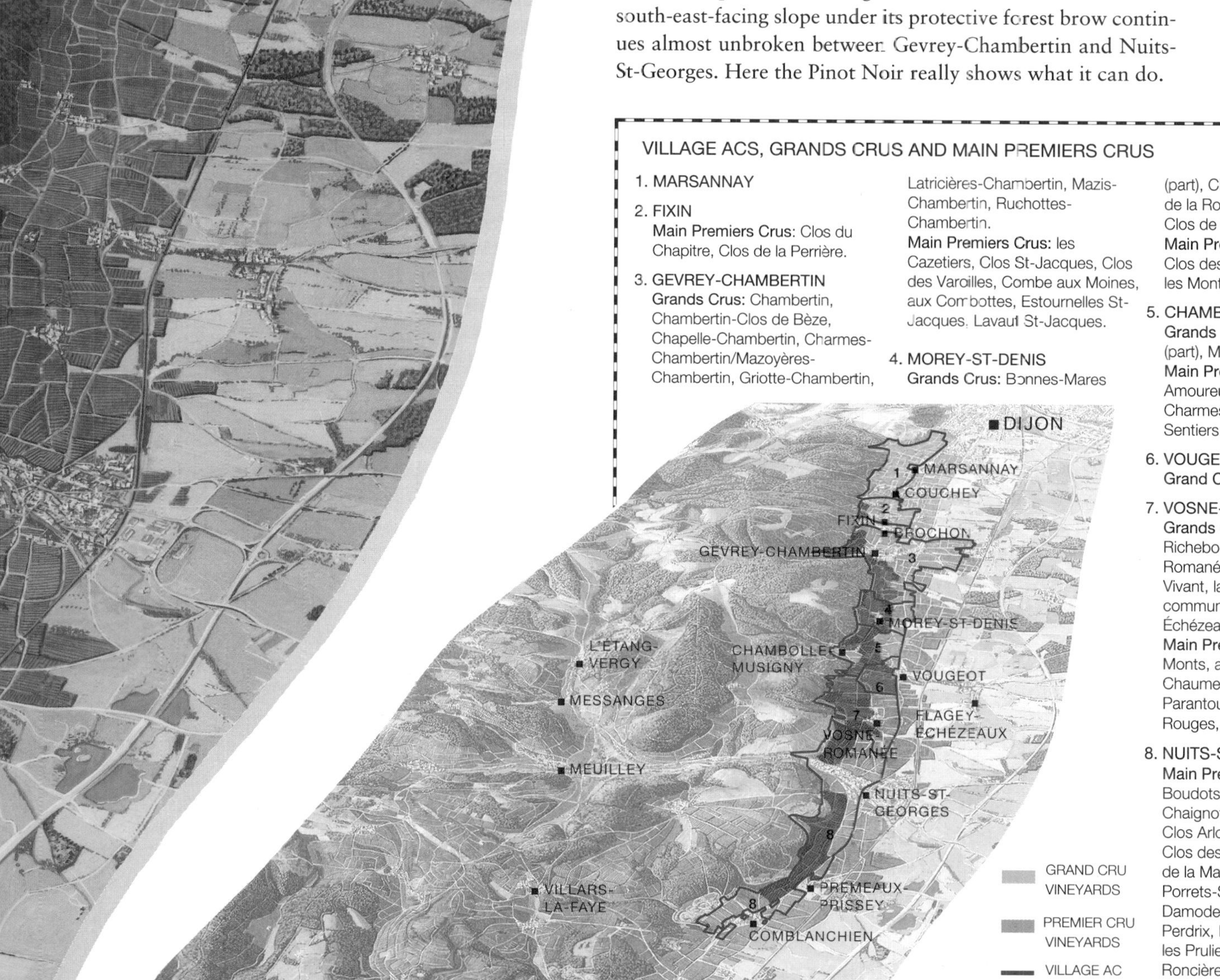

VILLAGE ACS, GRANDS CRUS AND MAIN PREMIERS CRUS

1. MARSANNAY
2. FIXIN
   Main Premiers Crus: Clos du Chapitre, Clos de la Perrière.
3. GEVREY-CHAMBERTIN
   Grands Crus: Chambertin, Chambertin-Clos de Bèze, Chapelle-Chambertin, Charmes-Chambertin/Mazoyères-Chambertin, Griotte-Chambertin, Latricières-Chambertin, Mazis-Chambertin, Ruchottes-Chambertin.
   Main Premiers Crus: les Cazetiers, Clos St-Jacques, Clos des Varoilles, Combe aux Moines, aux Combottes, Estournelles St-Jacques, Lavaut St-Jacques.
4. MOREY-ST-DENIS
   Grands Crus: Bonnes-Mares (part), Clos des Lambrays, Clos de la Roche, Clos St-Denis, Clos de Tart.
   Main Premiers Crus: la Bussière, Clos des Ormes, les Millandes, les Monts Luisants, les Ruchots.
5. CHAMBOLLE-MUSIGNY
   Grands Crus: Bonnes-Mares (part), Musigny.
   Main Premiers Crus: les Amoureuses, les Baudes, les Charmes, les Cras, les Fuées, les Sentiers.
6. VOUGEOT
   Grand Cru: Clos de Vougeot.
7. VOSNE-ROMANÉE
   Grands Crus: Grande-Rue, Richebourg, la Romanée, la Romanée-Conti, Romanée-St-Vivant, la Tâche, and (in the commune of Flagey-Echézeaux) Échézeaux, Grands-Échézeaux.
   Main Premiers Crus: les Beaux Monts, aux Brûlées, les Chaumes, Clos des Réas, Cros Parantoux, aux Malconsorts, les Rouges, les Suchots.
8. NUITS-ST-GEORGES
   Main Premiers Crus aux Boudots, les Cailles, aux Chaignots, Clos des Argillières, Clos Arlot, Clos des Corvées, Clos des Forêts-St-Georges, Clos de la Maréchale, Clos des Porrets-St-Georges, les Damodes, aux Murgers, aux Perdrix, les Porrets-St-Georges, les Pruliers, la Richemone, Roncière, les St-Georges, aux Thorey, les Vaucrains.

The château of Clos de Vougeot is now home to the Chevaliers du Tastevin, an organization which celebrates and promotes the traditions of Burgundian wine.

Those village names, by the way. Over the centuries, the best Côte d'Or villages found that they had one vineyard above all whose wines people sought. The village of Gevrey had Chambertin, the village of Chambolle had Musigny, and so on. So, to grab a little reflected glory from their greatest vineyard – and a little more profit from allying their less exciting wine with that of the star performer – wine producers hyphenated the vineyard name to that of the village for their wines.

So. Back to Gevrey-Chambertin. This village distinguishes itself with nine Grands Crus – the most of any Côte d'Or commune – safely protected from the wet westerlies by the Montagne de la Combe Grizard. The lesser vineyards spread down to and, unusually, across the N74, where a pebbly subsoil is supposed to provide enough drainage. Maybe. The potential of riches at every level in Gevrey is high but the variations among producers is dramatic. It's a problem of popularity. Chambertin, which can be so sensuously savage at its best, is one of France's most famous reds. Wines with Chambertin in their title are not difficult to sell.

Morey-St-Denis is a good deal less famous, but the vineyards are just as good. There are five Grands Crus, on slightly steeper slopes with a little more limestone in evidence and, indeed, one steep, infertile site – Monts Luisants – that is famous for a beefy white. The reds, led by Clos de la Roche, have a sweet, red, fruity depth and a chocolaty softness.

Chambolle-Musigny is set into a little gully in the hillside, and this loss of protection for the vines means the Grand Cru, Bonnes-Mares, ends north of the village. The other Grand Cru, Musigny, doesn't commence till the south-east-facing slope begins again near Vougeot. At its best, Chambolle-Musigny can be hauntingly perfumed.

The chief wine of Vougeot is the 50-hectare (125-acre) walled Grand Cru, Clos de Vougeot. This runs right down to the N74, on to considerably lower and more alluvial soil than any other Grand Cru. Add to this 70 different proprietors all eager to exploit the famous name, and you have a recipe for some decidedly rum bottles of Clos de Vougeot. At its best, though, it is fleshy and rich.

Directly above the fine, higher vines of Vougeot are those of Grands Crus, Échézeaux and Grands-Échézeaux. Their parent village, Flagey, is in fact down on the plain, and they are considered to be part of Vosne-Romanée. Lucky them, because the other six Vosne Grands Crus, especially la Tâche and la Romanée-Conti, are the most famous and expensive of all Burgundies. Intoxicating in their spice and heady scent, thrilling in their depth of dark fruit, they really do lead the way. The red clays spattered with pebbles undoubtedly put the other Vosne Grands Crus and Premiers Crus on a special level.

Nuits-St-Georges might seem hard done by to be Vosne's neighbour – you have no Grands Crus. Instead it has 38 Premiers Crus. In the valley to the west the protective curtain is broken, and many of the vineyards are on flat alluvial soil. But south of Nuits down to Premeaux, the slopes steepen, narrow, and veer back towards the south-east. Here great wines are made, Grands Crus in all but name.

THE HAUTES-CÔTES DE NUITS

Up in the hills behind the Côte de Nuits slopes, planted in carefully selected sites, are the vines of the Hautes-Côtes de Nuits *appellation.* In warm years, the Hautes-Côtes de Nuits vineyards with the best aspect and drainage can make light, pleasant, mostly red, wine from Pinot Noir. But the word 'high' is important. We're far north here for a major red wine area. Red grapes usually need more heat to ripen than white – and the higher you get above sea level, the cooler the sun's rays become and the more exposed you are to wind and rain.

Côte de Beaune

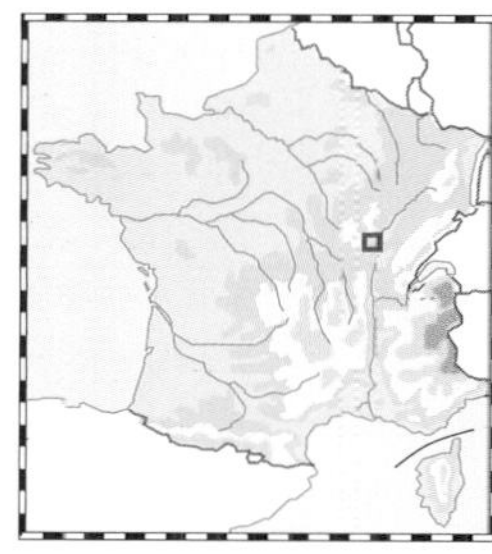

I'm not a great respecter of traditions and reputations just for the sake of them. In the world of wine, I often think that there are more ill-deserved reputations and baseless traditions than the other way round. But I have to say, the first time I trekked up the narrow lane from the main road (the N6) at the village of Chassagne-Montrachet, patted the crumbling stone wall on the left rather gingerly with my hand, and then sneaked into the vineyard of le Montrachet, my heart was thumping with excitement.

Le Montrachet is quite possibly the greatest white wine vineyard in the world. But why? I tasted the grapes from its vines, then crossed the lane to taste the grapes of Bâtard-Montrachet – another of the great Grand Cru vineyards – only 9m (30ft) lower down. They were different. Le Montrachet's grapes seemed to have more intensity, more vibrant personality before they'd even been picked off the vine. I clambered over the wall above le Montrachet to the adjacent Chevalier-Montrachet vineyard. It's a matter of a couple of yards, but the stony soil of Chevalier gives more austere grapes, which in turn gives leaner, haughtier, yet still superlative wine.

Since then, on other occasions I've scratched away at the soil of le Montrachet, and know that it is stonier and less rich than that of its neighbours, except for the ultra-stony Chevalier-Montrachet. I've noticed how the slope is just that little bit steeper as it gently changes angle from an easterly to a south-easterly aspect. I've felt my face warmed by early morning sun, in the midst of its vines. I've sweltered under blazing midday sun; and in high summer, late into the evening, as the surrounding vineyards are cooling down the shade, I've felt the sun's rays still streaking towards me across le Montrachet's tiny clump of vines, as it sinks into a dip in the hills.

Mesoclimate. The perfect conjunction of soil, angle of slope, and aspect to the sun, providing just that bit more chance for these northern grapes to ripen to perfection. In every commune on the Côte d'Or, the endlessly changing geological and climatic conditions create little plots of vineyard, some only a few hectares broad, that give wines of more power, personality or finesse than those of their neighbours. This is what makes the Côte d'Or so fascinating, yet so exhausting a region to get to know.

Whereas the most famous wines of the Côte de Nuits, directly to the north of the Côte de Beaune, are all red, most of the world-renowned wines of the Côte de Beaune are white. And that's down to those mesoclimates again. In fact, 75 per cent of the Côte de Beaune wines are red. The fertile, red-tinged soils, and periodically, the marl that is such a feature of the Côte de Nuits, occupy the majority of the slopes, and in these cases Pinot Noir predominates. But the slopes here are less extreme, and the red Côte de Beaune wines, even from the one red Grand Cru vineyard of Corton, right next to the Côte de Nuits, have a rounder charm and less savage power than those of the Côte de Nuits itself. Wines from Aloxe-Corton, Beaune, Volnay and, in a rougher way, Pommard, are all marked by perfume rather than by power.

The whites at their best, however – from Chardonnay grapes planted where limestone dominates the darker clays – are marked by virtually every characteristic you could ask of a dry white wine. I say dry, because there is no sugar left in wines like Corton-Charlemagne, Meursault, Puligny-Montrachet, Chassagne-Montrachet, or the host of others that the different villages make. Yet the honey and butter lusciousness, the cream, the wafted scent of grilled nuts still warm from the fire, the cinnamon and nutmeg spice that ripples through the orchard fruits – all these flavours, plus the taut backbone of mineral, of herb, of smoke from a forest glade, are there. I can remember bottles like these drunk 20 years ago as clearly as if my glass were being refilled in front of me this very minute.

What is equally exciting is that, if you seek out good producers, you really can taste the difference in wines which come from neighbouring patches of vines. The Burgundian system of delineating each vineyard plot with distinctive characteristics is the most comprehensive in the world. Meursault-Perrières does have stonier soil than its neighbour Meursault-Charmes; the wine is tauter, it promises more, and will perhaps give more sublime satisfaction in time. That's how it should be. And fairly frequently, that's how it is.

CÔTE DE BEAUNE CLASSIFICATIONS

As in the Côte de Nuits, the top vineyard sites are given the status of Grand Cru, but the procession of Grands Crus at around the 275m (900ft) mark isn't repeated in the Côte de Beaune, and there are only two groups of Grands Crus – one in the north, at Aloxe-Corton, and one in the south straddling Puligny-Montrachet and Chassagne-Montrachet. Apart from

RED GRAPES

Pinot Noir is the only permitted grape in non-generic wines.

WHITE GRAPES

Chardonnay is the main grape with some Pinot Blanc.

CLIMATE

The slopes are gentler here, providing less shelter from the westerly winds, so rainfall is higher than further north and heavy rain can be a problem. The temperatures are marginally milder than in the Côte de Nuits.

SOIL

The soil structure is basically similar to the Côte de Nuits, but with limestone outcrops more in evidence and these are often where the best vineyards, such as le Montrachet, are sited.

ASPECT

These are lower slopes and more gentle gradients than in the Côte de Nuits but the south- to south-east-facing aspect of many vineyards is even more critical here.

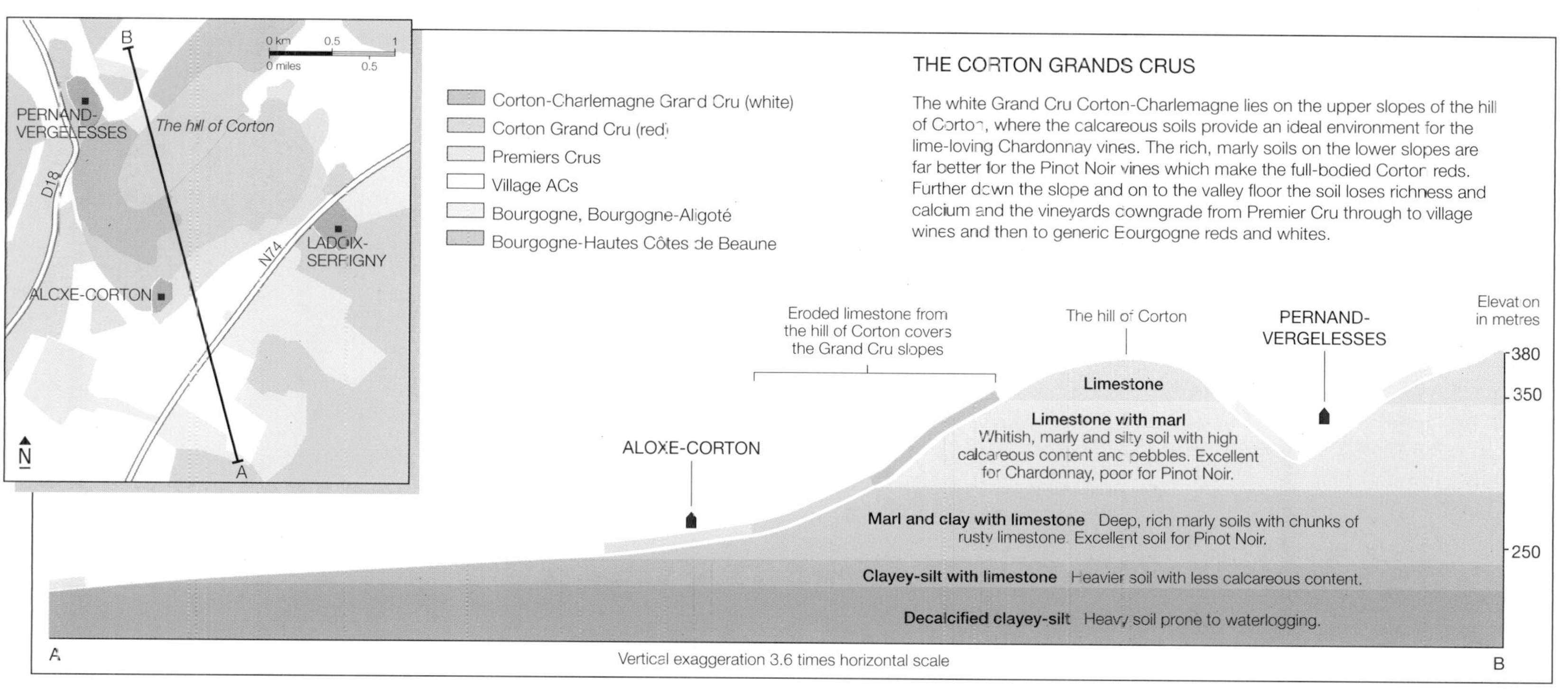

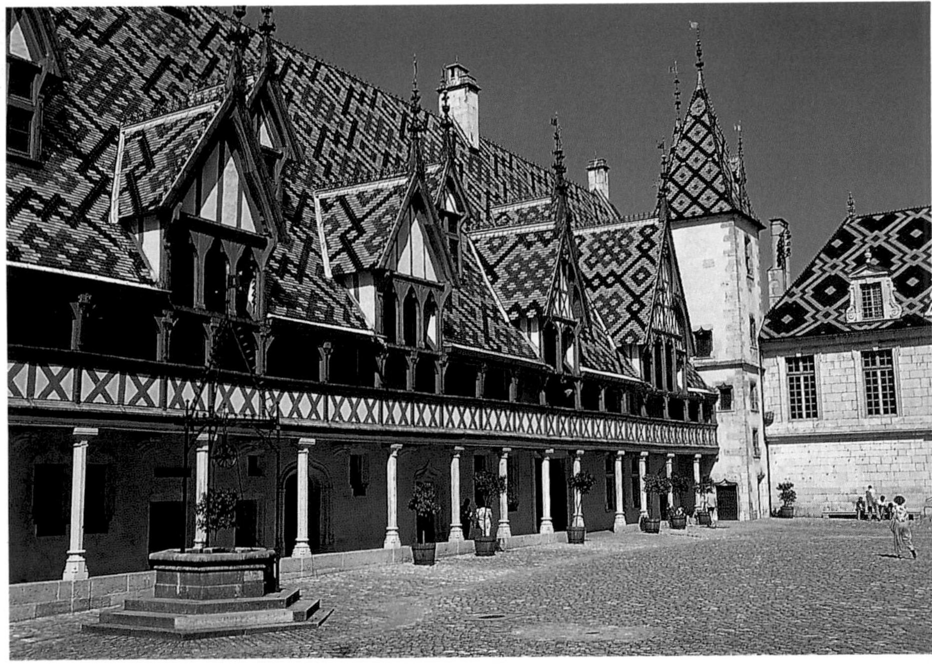

The flamboyant fifteenth-century Gothic Hôtel-Dieu is headquarters to the Hospices de Beaune, a charity famous for its November wine auctions.

these two, the best vineyards for both red and white wine are Premiers Crus. The same detailed examination of every row of vines takes place to determine the status of a plot of land, because in this cool area, the slightest nuance can make the difference between great and merely good wine. An almost imperceptible dip in the field, a scarcely registered change in slope angle or exposure to the sun, a brief streak of clay running across a limestone ridge – all these tiny details combine to form the great imponderable the French call *terroir*. And of all the French areas to take *terroir* seriously, the Côte d'Or, with its detailed classification, is the most passionate.

Below these levels are the village *appellations*, and though many of these are on flatter, alluvial land, the quality is still pretty good. Sixteen villages can use the title Côte de Beaune-Villages for their reds, rather than their own village name, but these days this option is rarely exercised except by merchants keen to make up a blend. Côte de Beaune is a tiny red and white *appellation* from a slope west of Beaune. The least good vineyards only qualify for the Bourgogne, Bourgogne Passe-Touts-Grains, or Bourgogne Grand Ordinaire ACs.

VILLAGES OF THE CÔTE DE BEAUNE

The Côte de Beaune really begins with the great hill of Corton, and three villages share its slopes – Ladoix, Aloxe-Corton and Pernand-Vergelesses. This impressive, proud crescent of vines swings right round from east to west with the pale, weathered limestone soils of Corton and Corton-Charlemagne producing white wine right up to the forest fringe at 350m (1150ft). The lower slopes produce round, succulent red Corton; in general the east-facing slopes are best for red, the west-facing for white.

Savigny is tucked into the valley just north-west of Beaune with less protected and, indeed, occasionally north-facing vineyards, producing generally lean wine. However, the slopes return in fine steep form at Beaune, and excellent red and white Premiers Crus reach down towards the town itself. Pommard and Volnay have steep, uneven slopes climbing up into the scrub-covered hills. They jig in and out, creating numerous different aspects to the sun, affording less constant protection for the vines than those of the Côte de Nuits as the grapes struggle to ripen. This means that the mesoclimate becomes particularly important, especially for the demanding Pinot Noir which dominates Pommard and Volnay. These are often jealously delimited by wall enclosures. Any white wines in Volnay will be sold as Meursault.

The heart of the Côte de Beaune lies between Meursault and Chassagne-Montrachet. Here, between 240 and 300m (790 and 985ft), with a few fine vineyards as high as 350m (1150ft) round the hamlet of Blagny, the Chardonnay revels in the spare stony soils and the limestone outcrops jutting to within inches of the surface, delights in the dips and curves of the east- to south-east-facing slopes and produces a fascinating array of brilliant flavours. All are minutely but recognizably different, and every one, when created by a serious producer, a triumphant vindication of the notion of *terroir*. At Chassagne-Montrachet the soils become heavier again, spreading south-west to Santenay and then trailing away further west to Maranges, and more red than white is grown once again.

HAUTES-CÔTES DE BEAUNE

You can see numerous vineyards in the hills behind the Côte de Beaune. These are included in the *appellation* Hautes-Côtes de Beaune. It's a heavenly part of Burgundy, with twisting country lanes, ancient avenues of trees, and a tranquillity conducive to relaxing with the very best of Burgundies. But these slopes are a crucial 50 to 100m (165 to 330ft) higher than those of the Côte de Beaune, are less perfectly angled to the sun and less protected from wind and rain. They produce pleasant light reds and whites when the weather's warm – just right for a picnic in one of the high meadows.

CÔTE DE BEAUNE AND HAUTES-CÔTES DE BEAUNE

TOTAL DISTANCE NORTH TO SOUTH 25KM (15½ MILES)

VINEYARDS

N

0 km 1 2

0 miles 1

VILLAGE ACS, GRANDS CRUS AND MAIN PREMIERS CRUS

1. LADOIX
   Grands Crus: Corton (part), Corton-Charlemagne (part).
2. PERNAND-VERGELESSES
   Grands Crus: Corton (part), Corton-Charlemagne (part).
   Main Premiers Crus: les Basses Vergelesses, Île des Hautes Vergelesses.
3. ALOXE-CORTON
   Grands Crus: Corton (part), Corton-Charlemagne (part).
   Main Premiers Crus: les Chaillots, les Maréchaudes.
4. CHOREY-LÈS-BEAUNE
5. SAVIGNY-LÈS-BEAUNE
   Main Premiers Crus: aux Guettes, les Jarrons, les Lavières, aux Serpentières, aux Vergelesses.
6. BEAUNE
   Main Premiers Crus: les Avaux, les Boucherottes, les Bressandes, les Cent Vignes, Champs Pimont, le Clos des Mouches, le Clos de la Mousse, Clos du Roi, les Épenottes, les Fèves, les Grèves, les Marconnets, les Teurons, les Toussaints, les Vignes Franches.
7. POMMARD
   Main Premiers Crus: les Arvelets, les Boucherottes, Clos Blanc, Clos de la Commeraine, les Épenots, les Pézerolles, les Rugiens.
8. VOLNAY
   Main Premiers Crus: les Angles, Bousse d'Or, en Champans, Clos des Chênes, Clos des Ducs, les Santenots, Taille Pieds.
9. MONTHÉLIE
   Main Premiers Crus: les Champs Fulliot, les Duresses, sur la Velle.
10. MEURSAULT
    Main Premiers Crus: les Charmes, les Perrières, les Genevrières, les Gouttes d'Or, le Poruzot. Red wines can also be sold as Volnay or Blagny.
11. AUXEY-DURESSES
    Main Premiers Crus: Climat du Val, Clos du Val, les Duresses.
12. ST-ROMAIN
13. PULIGNY-MONTRACHET
    Grands Crus: Bâtard-Montrachet (part), Bienvenues-Bâtard-Montrachet, Chevalier-Montrachet, le Montrachet (part).
    Main Premiers Crus: le Cailleret, le Champ Canet, Clavoillon, les Combettes, les Folatières, la Garenne, les Pucelles, les Referts, la Truffière.
14. ST-AUBIN
    Main Premiers Crus: le Charmois, la Chatenière, en Rémilly.
15. CHASSAGNE-MONTRACHET
    Grands Crus: Bâtard-Montrachet (part), Criots-Bâtard-Montrachet, le Montrachet (part).
    Main Premiers Crus: les Baudines, la Boudriotte, en Cailleret, les Champs Gains, les Chaumées, les Chenevottes, Clos St-Jean, les Embrazées, les Grandes Ruchottes, les Macherelles, la Maltroie, Morgeot, la Romanée, les Vergers Vigne Blanche.
16. SANTENAY
    Main Premiers Crus: Beauregard, le Clos des Mouches, le Clos de Tavannes, la Comme, Grand Clos Rousseau, les Gravières, la Maladière, Passetemps.
17. MARANGES

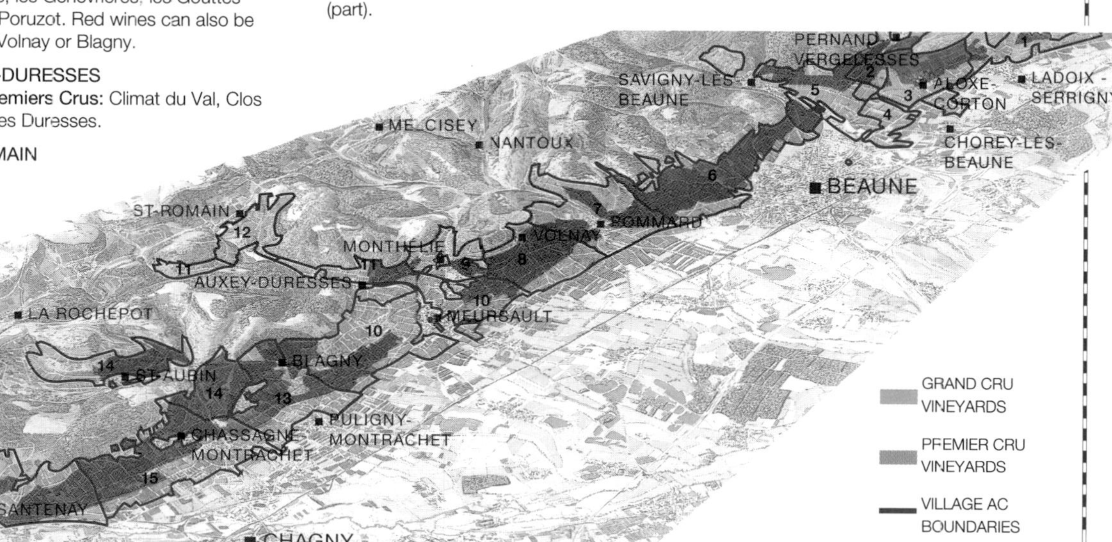

WHERE THE VINEYARDS ARE

The Côte de Beaune is much less of a single strip of land directly beneath an escarpment than the Côte de Nuits. In the Côte de Beaune there are several large re-entrants into the hills which harbour major vineyard sites; the vineyards themselves slope much more gently and expansively towards the plain, and the soil structures are far less homogeneous, veering between austere barren limestone and rich marly limestone. With the exception of Volnay, whose delicate red wines are produced largely on light, stony soils, it is the heavier soils that produce red wines. The lighter, limestone-based soil produces the peerless whites such as at Meursault, Puligny and Chassagne. The hill of Corton at the top of the map is unusual in that it has two Grands Crus, one for red and one for white wine. The historic town of Beaune is regarded as the wine capital of Burgundy. Excellent villages like St-Aubin, St-Romain, Auxey-Duresses and Monthélie are less well-known and less popular. The vineyards right up in the hills to the west are the Hautes-Côtes de Beaune.

Côte Chalonnaise

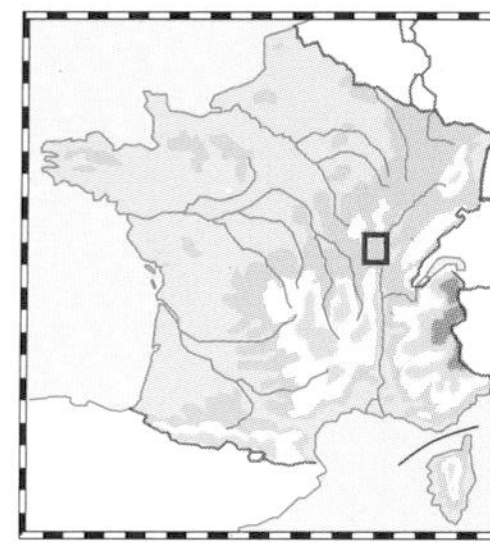

RED GRAPES
The main grape is Pinot Noir.

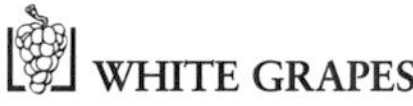
WHITE GRAPES
The main grape is Chardonnay with some Aligoté at Bouzeron.

CLIMATE
It is less sheltered from westerly winds here than in the Côte d'Or, but though it is cooler the Côte Chalonnaise can also be drier. Getting enough sun to ripen the grapes is the main problem.

SOIL
The soils here are based on limestone or a mixture of limestone and clay.

ASPECT
In this scattering of low hills, a good aspect is vital for ripening, and the best sites are on south-, south-east- and east-facing slopes at about 220–350m (720–1150ft).

I KNOW ALL ABOUT the prevailing westerly winds in the Côte Chalonnaise. A few years ago, in high summer, I was nosing about the Burgundian vineyards trying to work out what was what, and ended up at dusk with no hotel booking. How exciting, I thought. A night under the stars, warmed by the balmy August zephyrs. I hardly bothered with a blanket but plonked myself down on the broad ridge of vineyards, just south of Bouzeron, my head lain gently against a venerable Aligoté trunk and drifted off to sleep with a little smile of contentment playing over my lips.

Then the wind got up. Wow. Balmy August zephyrs? Atlantic gale more like, as I stumbled freezing back to the car and spent a miserable remainder of the night waiting for an early, and chilly dawn, slotted imaginatively between the driving wheel, the gear stick and hand brake.

It made me appreciate just what a crucial job the high hills in Burgundy do in protecting their thin ribbon of vineyards against the prevailing westerly winds. In the Côte d'Or, the range of hills is relatively unbroken from Dijon in the north to Santenay in the south. But then they trail unconvincingly away to the west, and what takes their place around the town of Chagny is a hotchpotch of hillocks and hummocks, disjointed, disorganized, offering only occasional shelter from the wind and occasional sloping land angled towards the sun.

This is the Côte Chalonnaise. A jumbled collection of microclimates, growing the same grapes as the Côte d'Or to the north, occasionally making wines of similar quality, but rarely with their richness, their roundness, or their perfume. A poor relation? Yes. But before you start feeling sorry for the Chalonnais winemakers consider what they are a poor relation to. The greatest Pinot Noir and Chardonnay vineyards in France, possibly in the world? A poor relation to these doesn't sound so bad, and it isn't.

Even so, you do have to choose your vineyard site carefully in the Côte Chalonnaise. All the best sites are on limestone-dominated slopes which are slanted, sometimes steeply slanted, to between south-east and south-west to catch every available ray of sun. The vines are generally planted at between 220 and 350m (720 and 1150ft) above sea level. This is much the same as in the Côte d'Or, but, with the shining exception of the top section of the famous hill of Corton, no exciting Côte d'Or vineyards are placed above 300m (985ft). The leanness that characterizes many Chalonnais reds and whites is easily explained by this relatively high altitude, the less-than-perfect wind protection, and the lack of gently angled, continuously south-east-facing slopes.

Gently sloping Chalonnais vineyards and stony soil usually produce lean wine.

BOUZERON

The leanness doesn't matter at Bouzeron, the most northerly Chalonnais commune, because Bouzeron has made its reputation with a lemon-sharp, peppery, yet buttermilk-scented dry white from the Aligoté. There is some Chardonnay and Pinot Noir sold simply as Bourgogne, but Aligoté de Bouzeron is the main wine here. Wine from old vines, marked *vieilles vignes*, generally has a little more Chardonnay-like richness to it.

RULLY

Just round the Montagne de la Folie from Bouzeron is Rully, whose reputation has traditionally been as a sparkling wine producer, but which now deserves better. The rather light, lean wines from some fairly steep limestone slopes do have the delicacy and acidity much prized by fizz-makers, but a better understanding of vineyard practice and wine-making, and a bit of self-confidence have been injected into the area by merchant houses like Rodet. These have brought forth light but cherry-scented Pinot Noir reds, and lean-limbed but tasty Chardonnays, especially when oak barrels are used for aging. Some of the better vineyards have Premier Cru status, but it doesn't mean that much.

MERCUREY

Mercurey to the south is the largest Chalonnais village *appellation*, over 90 per cent of it being red wine from the Pinot Noir. Again, we're not talking about really big-boned wines here – the leanness still comes through – but there is a considerable difference in perfume and style between the lighter wines from the limestone slopes and the chunkier ones from the clay vineyards. The whites have rarely been special, but as with Rully, efforts by leading growers, as well as the main merchant houses like Faiveley and Rodet have greatly improved the whites and added more flesh to the reds. There are a fair number of Premier Cru vineyards, the best south-facing slopes located to the north of the town.

GIVRY

Givry has an impressive ring of south-east-facing vines rising to the west of the town. Although the soil here begins to shift away from the friable limestone of the north towards a more fertile mix of clay and sandy limestone, Givry's best sites give a red wine of reasonable depth and considerable flavour in warm years. After a few years' aging, these wines can develop an almost sweet strawberry and cherry fruit. Those sheltered slopes do pay off. There is a little white from Chardonnay, none of it exciting.

MONTAGNY

Several miles south, again on steep slopes and in the clefts of little valleys, the all-white Montagny *appellation* is at last producing interesting Chardonnay wines from what is clearly excellent vineyard land. Montagny whites used to be bone dry and stony-flavoured and not much fun to drink. Now, with better vinification and the judicious use of oak barrels, they can be excellent, dry, yet softly toasty whites. Premier Cru on a Montagny label simply means the wine has reached a higher minimum alcohol level. Daft.

The most important producer of Montagny is the go-ahead co-operative at Buxy. Not only has the co-operative created high quality white from Montagny where only potential existed before, but it has transformed the quality of basic Chalonnais reds and whites. These used to be sold simply as Bourgogne but, in 1990, after considerable lobbying from Buxy, a new Bourgogne-Côte Chalonnaise *appellation* was created. The southern Chalonnais continues to develop and will produce exciting wines in the future.

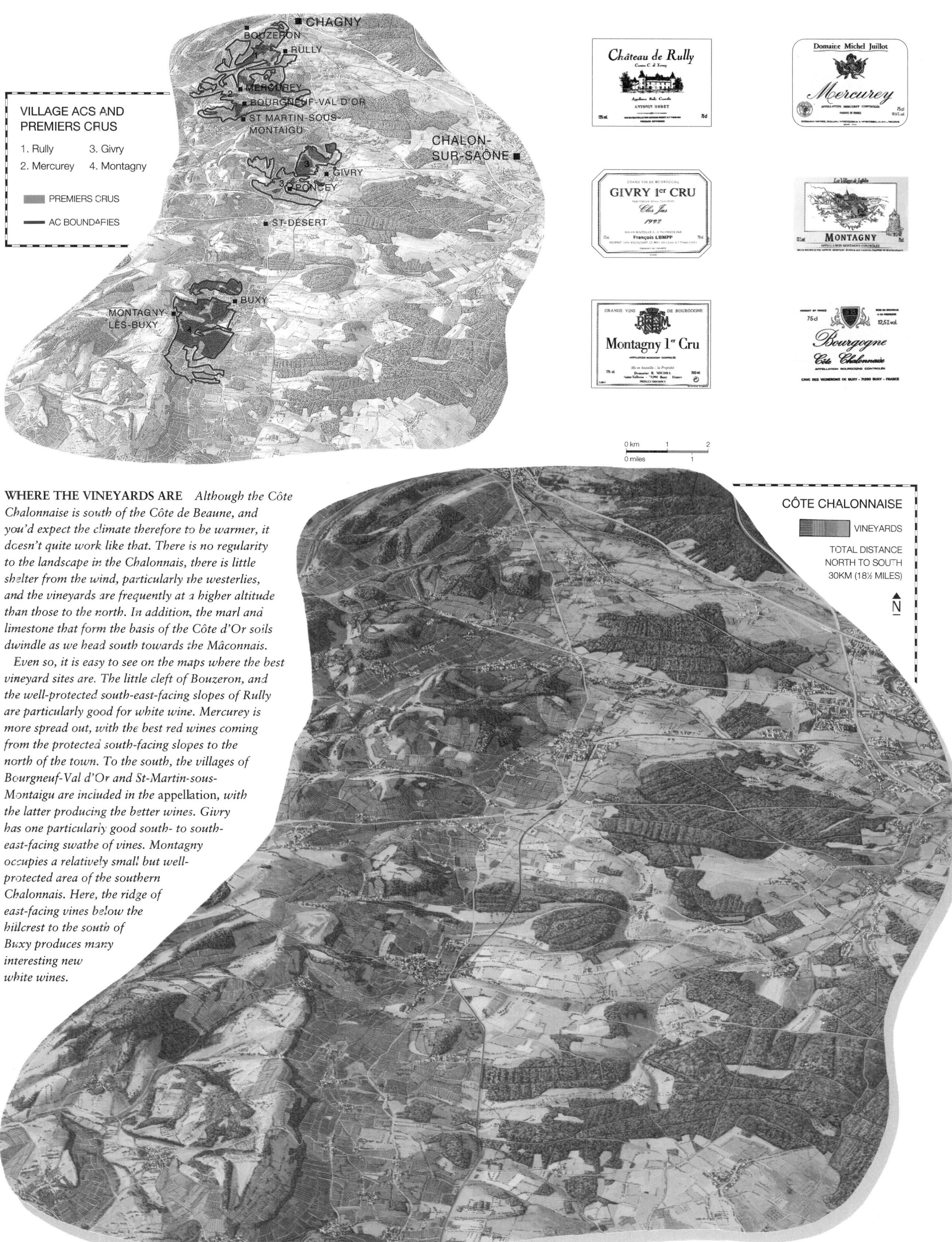

WHERE THE VINEYARDS ARE *Although the Côte Chalonnaise is south of the Côte de Beaune, and you'd expect the climate therefore to be warmer, it doesn't quite work like that. There is no regularity to the landscape in the Chalonnais, there is little shelter from the wind, particularly the westerlies, and the vineyards are frequently at a higher altitude than those to the north. In addition, the marl and limestone that form the basis of the Côte d'Or soils dwindle as we head south towards the Mâconnais.*

Even so, it is easy to see on the maps where the best vineyard sites are. The little cleft of Bouzeron, and the well-protected south-east-facing slopes of Rully are particularly good for white wine. Mercurey is more spread out, with the best red wines coming from the protected south-facing slopes to the north of the town. To the south, the villages of Bourgneuf-Val d'Or and St-Martin-sous-Montaigu are included in the appellation, *with the latter producing the better wines. Givry has one particularly good south- to south-east-facing swathe of vines. Montagny occupies a relatively small but well-protected area of the southern Chalonnais. Here, the ridge of east-facing vines below the hillcrest to the south of Buxy produces many interesting new white wines.*

MÂCONNAIS

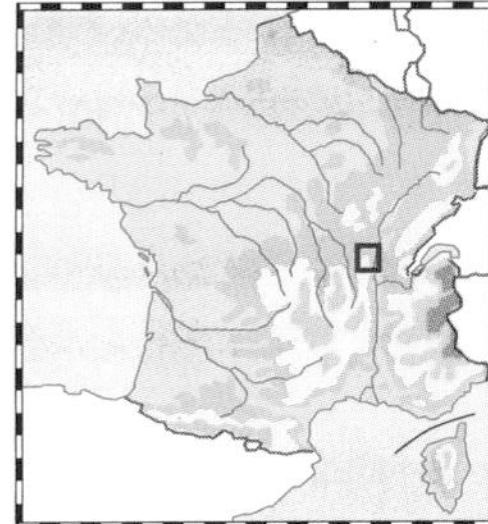

RED GRAPES
Gamay is the main variety, followed by Pinot Noir.

WHITE GRAPES
Chardonnay is the main grape, with small amounts of Aligoté.

CLIMATE
The Mediterranean influence begins to be felt in higher temperatures and occasional storms. The overall annual rainfall is higher than in the Côte d'Or to the north. Spring frosts can be a problem.

SOIL
There are two basic types of soil: limestone, favoured by the white vines, and a mixture of clay and sand, favoured by the red.

ASPECT
This is a region of low hills cut by a series of transverse valleys which usefully create south-, south-east- and south-west-facing slopes with good exposure to the sun.

YOU CAN APPROACH the Mâconnais at 270km (170 miles) per hour – on the TGV train from Paris that drops its dazed travellers at Mâcon station before surging onward to Lyon and the Mediterranean. Or you can approach the Mâconnais at half the speed, or slightly less if you're a law-abiding citizen, on the Autoroute du Soleil. Or you can approach it at whatever ambling, easy-going pace that the farmers' droning tractors, the smallholders' wheezing Deux Chevaux and the odd roaming sheep, cow and goat will let you – by the country roads that twist and turn through the charming rural backwaters at the southern end of the Côte Chalonnaise, gradually dropping down to the blander, broader spaces of the Mâconnais.

I'd take the time to meander, if I were you. The Mâconnais stretches north to south for about 50km (30 miles) from the southernmost tip of the Côte Chalonnaise to the border with the Beaujolais region at St-Vérand. It isn't the most startling of landscapes, being mainly a continual vista of gently rolling hills and dales. Vines share the land with other crops and with Charollais cattle. The wines aren't the most startling of wines either. But something does happen here, amid the orchards, the meadows and the rather four-square spreads of vineyard land.

The air that can seem so damp and chill right the way through northern France, and most poignantly so in Burgundy's Côte d'Or, seems warmer here, friendlier, more benign. The fogs here seem more like wisps of white cotton, rather than the palls of grey misery further north. The sun spreads itself more broadly in a sky that is wider and coloured increasingly with the azure of the South stretching into infinity. And the houses – these are what finally tell you you're leaving the North behind. The angular, defensive rooftops and storm-coloured slates give way to the warm, rounded terracotta tiles of Provence. The roofs become almost flat, and open porches and verandahs or *galeries* face southwards towards the sun. The heart-warming South begins here in the Mâconnais.

But does the Mâconnais produce wines worthy of its position at the portals of the South? It definitely could – in a few instances, it does – but in general, Mâconnais wines suffer from what is, I suppose, an understandable identity crisis.

GRAPE VARIETIES

Until quite recently, most of the 6000 hectares (14,825 acres) of Mâconnais vineyards produced red wine, mainly from Gamay, but with some Pinot Noir being grown. There has not been one single famous Mâcon red wine in living memory. Most of the Gamays are earthy and rough, with acidity dominating their meagre fruit. From the villages of Igé in the centre of the region and Mancey in the north, occasional full-bodied reds emerge. Local wine producers absorb much of the Pinot Noir to make sparkling Crémant de Bourgogne, and now less than a third of the Mâconnais vines are red.

Not surprisingly, and reflecting the explosion of worldwide interest, the Chardonnay grape now occupies two-thirds of the Mâconnais vineyards (there is just a little Aligoté too). Indeed, there is a village called Chardonnay here, near Tournus in the north of the region, that tradition claims as the birthplace of the Chardonnay vine. There is no reason why this shouldn't be true as Chardonnay is the traditional white grape round here. But you would have hoped that the Mâconnais, so proud of having sired the most famous white grape in the world, would make a bit more effort to show what wonderful flavours the grape can produce.

THE POUILLY APPELLATIONS

Certainly the Mâconnais region has some of the best Chardonnay vineyards in France – those that produce Pouilly-Fuissé. This wine has become rather too famous for its own good, primarily because of its phenomenal success on the American market, and this has had the usual consequences of overproduction, and scary price hikes.

Yet the beautifully angled vineyards that carpet the lower slopes of the magnificent rock of Solutré and its near twin the rock of Vergisson in the south of the region are of a superb quality. A few growers here produce delectable examples of Chardonnay under the Pouilly-Fuissé banner, with the round, oatmealy softness of a Meursault fattened out and honeyed by the warmer southern sun. Yet most Pouilly-Fuissé is made by co-operatives and sold under merchants' labels. When produced in such circumstances it is rarely worth wasting your effort twisting the corkscrew.

Pouilly-Fuissé comes from five villages – Chaintré (the least good), Solutré, Vergisson, Pouilly and Fuissé. The nearby villages of Loché and Vinzelles, between Pouilly-Fuissé and Mâcon, have attached Pouilly to their names to share a bit of the glory, but, though their wines can be pleasant, the vineyards are flatter and more fertile and thus are less capable of growing the best Chardonnay grapes.

ST-VÉRAN

A more recent Mâcon *appellation* is St-Véran which lies right on the border with the Beaujolais region. Vineyards in the southern part of the *appellation* around the villages of St-Vérand, Chânes, Chasselas, Leynes and St-Amour-Bellevue

THE SOLUTRÉ

If I were to be in the Mâconnais on Midsummer's Day, I'd head for the massive jut-jawed rock of Solutré that rears out of the vineyards round Pouilly-Fuissé like a shark's snout breaking through the billowing green waves. The local inhabitants celebrate the longest day of the year by lighting a great bonfire of old vines and pruned branches, in honour of the Gauls' victorious battle for independence that took place near here in AD511.

Standing at the base of this magnificent rock, and looking up its near-vertical face, you can see why, in this gently rolling landscape, with the broad Saône plain to the east, the Gauls chose this natural fortress. Then look down, at your feet, and think back another 15,000 years. Here, in 1866, a massive deposit of Stone Age remains was discovered at the base of the rock. Among the remains was a metre-thick layer of about 1000 horse skeletons. It seems the prehistoric inhabitants of Solutré herded wild horses up the gentle eastern slope, then stampeded them over the cliff at the western end. Then they ate them.

0 km 1 2 3 4
0 miles 1 2

SOUTHERN MÂCONNAIS
VINEYARDS
N
TOTAL DISTANCE NORTH TO SOUTH 13KM (8 MILES)

can produce either white St-Véran, which has mopped up most of what used to be called Beaujolais Blanc, or red St-Amour, one of the top Beaujolais Crus, and it is not uncommon to find producers here who make both wines. There is another section of St-Véran vineyards north of Pouilly-Fuissé, on the outskirts of the villages of Davayé and Prissé.

The quality of St-Véran is fairly good – the wine is light (it is comparatively rare to find St-Véran wines fermented in oak, unlike Pouilly-Fuissé). There are also hints of muskiness and tropical fruit, despite the wine's dryness. If you want to check out the discreet charm of the Mâconnais, St-Véran is a good place to start.

WHERE THE VINEYARDS ARE *The map shows the intensively planted southern section of the Mâconnais that contains all the most famous vineyards. The most famous are those of Pouilly-Fuissé, directly west of Mâcon. The map shows how beautifully angled the vineyards are to the south-east, below the rocks of Vergisson and Solutré. Further south the St-Véran vineyards, around the village of St-Vérand, catch all the afternoon sun with their south-westerly exposure. The village of St-Amour-Bellevue marks the northern end of the Beaujolais region. St-Véran vineyards are also found to the north-east of Pouilly-Fuissé with considerable quantities coming from the communes of Davayé and Prissé. The next best wines in the Mâconnais come from the 43 communes allowed to attach their name to Mâcon Blanc-Villages.*

MÂCON BLANC

The wine most commonly found in the Mâconnais is Mâcon Blanc-Villages, though there is also a simple Mâcon Blanc *appellation*. Altogether 72 communes produce this wine, and 43 can add their own name – as in Mâcon-Lugny, Mâcon-Viré or Mâcon-Pierreclos. Production is dominated by one of France's most efficient networks of co-operative cellars, who are responsible for 60 per cent of all Mâconnais wine. Their organizational clout has brought about much of the region's prosperity. The standard of wine the co-operatives produce is generally decent to boot, but to really understand the potential of these pleasant vineyards set amid meadows, copses and glades, you must try the wines of the small but growing band of individual proprietors. They are fiercely committed to raising standards by opposing machine harvesting and high yields, and their Chardonnay wines show how good the Mâconnais could be. Interestingly, the co-operatives produce some of France's best sparkling wine, as Crémant de Bourgogne.

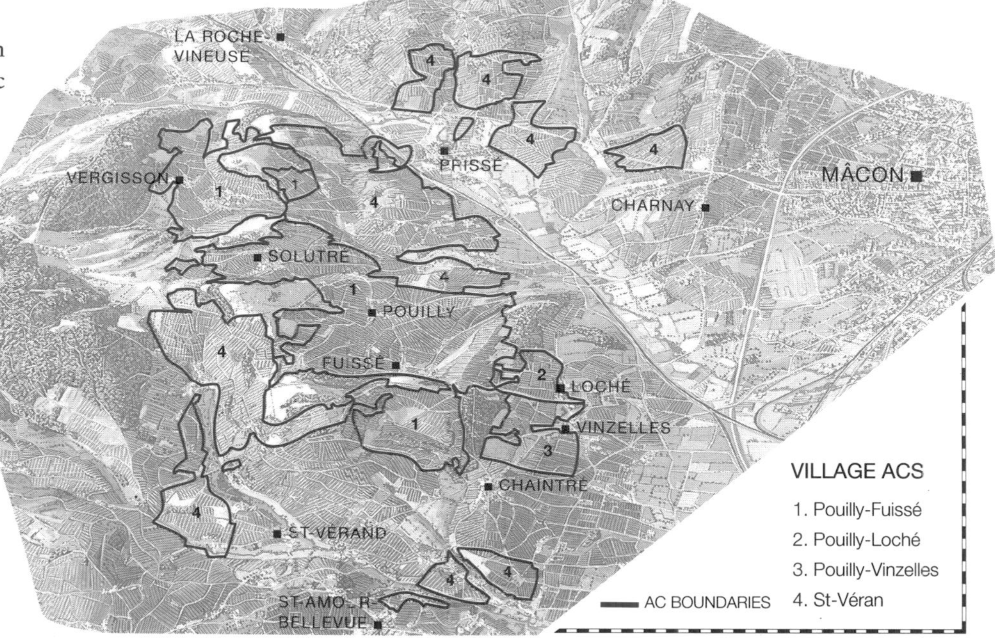

BEAUJOLAIS

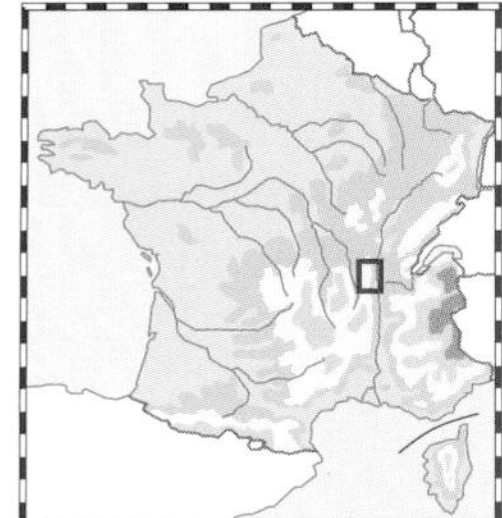

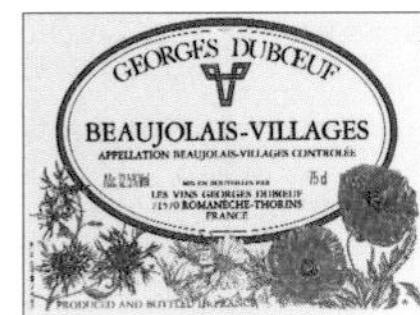

I LIKE TO THINK OF BEAUJOLAIS as a state of mind rather than a place, dependent on contours, kilometres and references on the map. In my mind this is a magical haven of hills, of a bucolic way of life far removed from the drab conformity of our city existences. That doesn't need a map of time and place, just a vaguely remembered sketch of the head and heart.

I would still rather take the map below and say, do you see how that track rises from Chiroubles up to the forest rim above the village – well, scramble up there, and you can picnic in blissful solitude. Or do you want the best view out over the fat, prosperous Saône Valley and on, to the snowy peaks of the Alps? Or would you like the most succulent frogs' legs in France, and juicy-pink entrecôtes, washed down with fragrant Côte de Brouilly straight from the jug? Follow me.

Yes, I like to pretend that Beaujolais is all about the magical dream-time hills, the romantic peasant life. But it isn't. And perhaps it never was, because in those days of yore, in the days immortalized by Chevalier in his famous novel *Clochemerle*, the Beaujolais region was a beautiful, but poverty-stricken land. Its job was to provide the basic jug wine of Lyon, France's second city. The Lyonnais had monumental thirsts, but were used to paying little for their daily tipple.

BEAUJOLAIS NOUVEAU

Beaujolais is now one of France's most prosperous wine regions, but that prosperity only arrived with the advent of the marketing man's dream wine – Beaujolais Nouveau. What a stroke of genius. Beaujolais has been drunk as young as possible in Lyon since the vineyards were first planted. But first the Parisians caught on to the idea, in the 1950s, then the British joined them in the 1970s, then the Americans, then the Japanese – the world. By the 1980s Beaujolais Nouveau had been relentlessly sold and oversold as the concept of the first wine of the year's harvest released on the third Thursday in November – gushing, purple-pink wine hardly old enough to have forgotten the flavour of the grape upon the vine.

Beaujolais Nouveau has been the creator of the current prosperity of the Beaujolais region, and it mops up 30 per cent – 60 million bottles – of all the wines produced in the area. But its success has saturated Beaujolais' reputation to such an extent that it is easy to lose sight of the fact that we're talking about an important wine region here. This comprises 22,000 hectares (54,000 acres) of vineyards, producing a good 40 per cent of Burgundy's total volume of wine.

Traditionally Beaujolais has always been included as part of the Burgundy wine region even though the geology and climate are different. The wine is different too. The dominant grape here, and the only one used for Beaujolais, is Gamay, barred from all but the most basic wines in the rest of Burgundy because of the raw, rough flavours it generally produces.

But in Beaujolais the soils are different, and here – maybe only here – the Gamay can produce bright, juicy-ripe glugging wine difficult to beat for sheer uncomplicated pleasure. This should be particularly so in the gently rolling, southerly vineyards nearest Lyon, where the rich clay and limestone soils grow the light, easy reds sold simply as Beaujolais or Beaujolais Nouveau. But yields are far higher than they used to be, and consequently many of the wines lack the fruit and perfume that made Beaujolais famous in the first place.

THE BEAUJOLAIS METHOD OF FERMENTATION

If we think of Beaujolais Nouveau as merely some modern marketing man's creation, we've got it all wrong. Nowadays the razzmatazz of Beaujolais Nouveau Day in November can

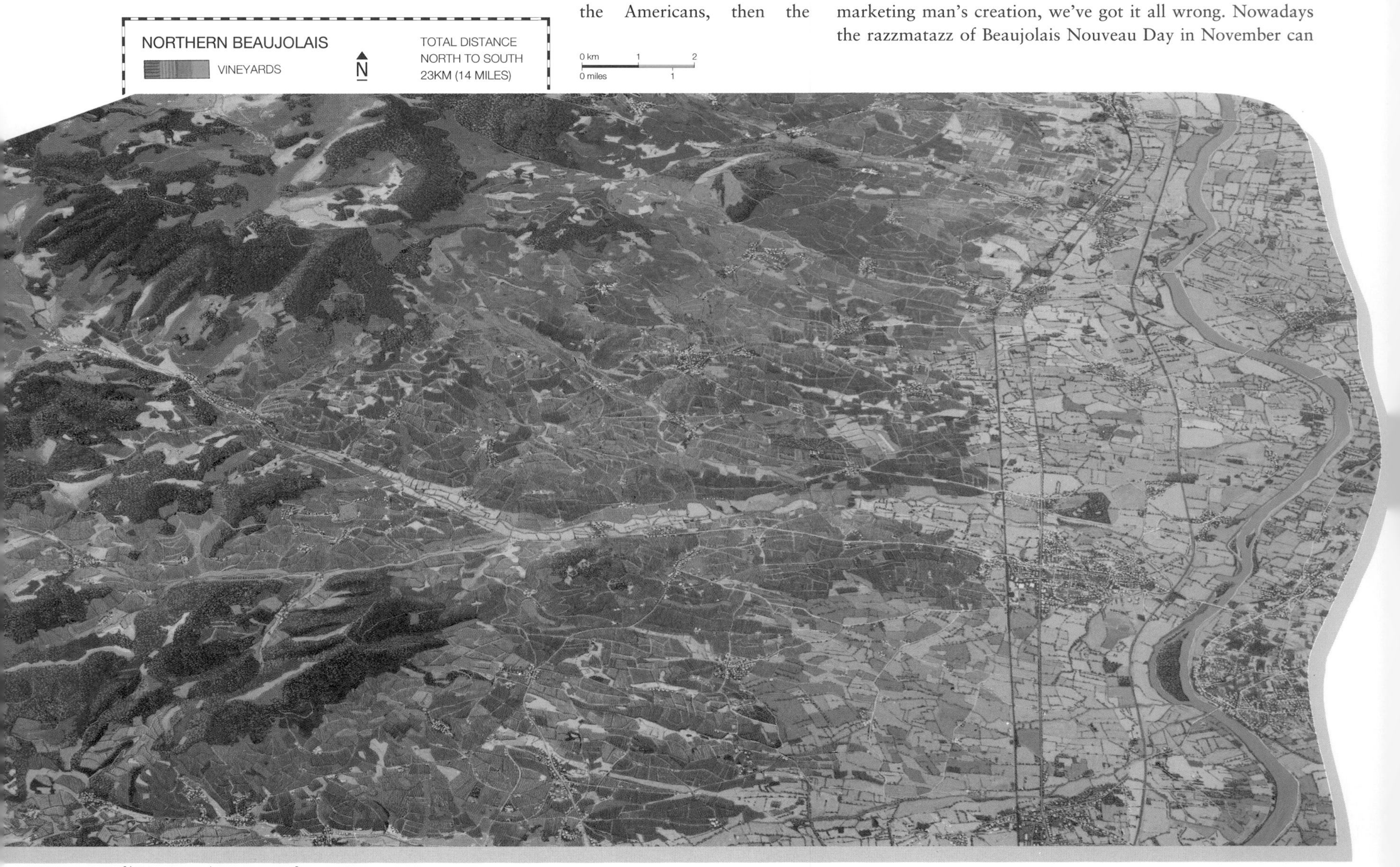

NORTHERN BEAUJOLAIS

VINEYARDS

N

TOTAL DISTANCE NORTH TO SOUTH 23KM (14 MILES)

0 km 1 2
0 miles 1

0 km 1 2
0 miles 1

often obscure little details like whether we actually like the taste of the wine or not. But the release of the first wine of the vintage has always been a cause for celebration and merry-making throughout the wine regions of the world. Far from being a modern phenomenon, the Nouveau celebrations take us right back to the heart of tradition!

However, not all red wines are suitable for the Nouveau treatment. Luckily Beaujolais' Gamay grape naturally has a bright strawberry and peach flavour that is accentuated when vinified by the Beaujolais method.

Grapes are harvested by hand, and then, instead of being crushed, the whole bunches are piled into a vat. Those at the bottom of the vat break, the juice seeps out and begins to ferment as usual, warming the vat and giving off carbon dioxide that rises like a blanket to the top of the vat.

This encourages the whole, unbroken grapes to begin to ferment inside their skins. Since the colouring and flavouring components in the skin are next to the flesh, this 'whole grape fermentation' or carbonic maceration extracts these elements, yet doesn't extract much of the bitter tannin that is near the surface of the skin. After four to seven days the grapes split open, spilling their dark, fruity, but not bitter, juice into the vat. This mixes with the traditionally fermented juice at the bottom of the vat to create a red wine strong on perfume and colour but low in tannin. This juice is drawn off and the rest of grapes are pressed. This pressing will certainly give rather more tannin, but thanks to carbonic maceration, colour and fruit perfumes will still dominate. This method, or variations on it, is used with varying degrees of success by all the other Nouveau makers around the world.

THE BEAUJOLAIS CRUS

The northern part of Beaujolais – which is covered by the map below – contains the potentially superior vineyards. The most important of these vineyards are the ten Beaujolais Crus, or 'growths', which account for 25 per cent of all Beaujolais, and which each have their own *appellation contrôlée*. These Cru vineyards are reckoned to produce wine with an identifiable character, and most have a granite subsoil which is rarely associated with fine wine (Hermitage in the Rhône valley, south of Lyon, being a notable exception).

St-Amour is the most northerly commune, actually sharing its vineyards with the Mâconnais St-Véran *appellation*. Going south, then come Juliénas, Chénas and Moulin-à-Vent, all capable of producing well-structured wine. The perfumed wines of Fleurie and Chiroubles come next, followed by Morgon, whose best wines develop a delightful cherry perfume. Régnié, the newest Cru, has yet to prove itself better than a good Villages, but Brouilly, the largest Beaujolais Cru, and Côte de Brouilly can produce delightful wines.

BEAUJOLAIS-VILLAGES

Thirty-nine other communes, mostly in the north of the region between Vaux-en-Beaujolais and St-Amour-Bellevue on the border with the Mâconnais region, qualify for Beaujolais-Villages status. This *appellation* is for wines that are better than basic Beaujolais but supposedly less fine than the Crus. But then, what do we mean by fine?

To be frank, in the Beaujolais region, we're not after the qualities of longevity and complexity that may characterize the greatest reds from Bordeaux, Burgundy or the Rhône. The uncomplicated cherub-cheeked, red-fruit ripeness and spicy blossom perfumes of the best ordinary Beaujolais is still what we want. But we want those red fruits to be riper, those perfumes to be more heady, and the wine's soft-centred, smooth consistency to leave lingering trails in the memory long after the flavour fades. These are the blessings of youth.

There is hardly a Brouilly, a St-Amour or a Chiroubles that should be aged for even as long as a couple of years. An occasional bottle of Moulin-à-Vent, Juliénas, Fleurie or, particularly, Morgon does begin to resemble a rather charming mild-mannered Côte de Beaune Burgundy, after five to ten years' age, but these are the exceptions.

As in the rest of Beaujolais, yields are generally too high even in these top vineyards, and a grape like the Gamay can only aspire to class if yields are kept low.

RED GRAPE
Gamay is the only variety allowed for Beaujolais, accounting for 98 per cent of the whole region's red grapes.

WHITE GRAPE
A tiny amount of Chardonnay and other varieties is used for the very little white wine made here.

CLIMATE
Warmer and sunnier than northern Burgundy, the region is partly protected by the Monts du Beaujolais from prevailing westerly winds.

SOIL
The most important aspect is the granite subsoil which influences all the northern zone and on which Gamay thrives. Further south nearer Lyon, the soil is richer, primarily clays and limestone, and is less suited to Gamay.

ASPECT
The vineyards lie between 150 and 500m (500 and 1640ft) and face all directions. Fleurie and Moulin-à-Vent have many south-east-facing vineyards which are protected by the hills to the north-west.

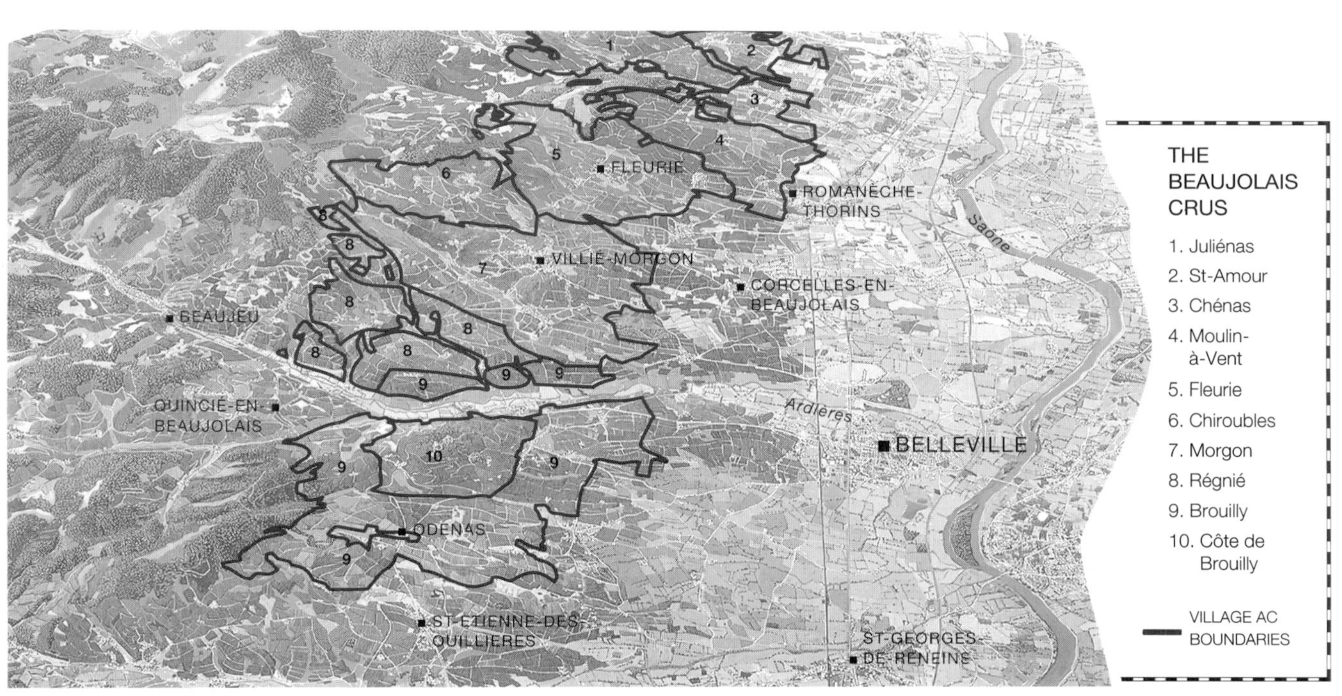

WHERE THE VINEYARDS ARE *This map shows the northern part of the Beaujolais region, yet covers all the most important vineyard sites: these are the ten Beaujolais Crus and most of the 39 communes making Beaujolais-Villages. To the west of the railway line in the rolling hills with vineyards facing in all directions, it's a virtual monoculture of vines, while in the east the flat land of the Saône valley is almost entirely farmland.*

As you head westwards the flatter, reasonably fertile but less well-drained soils make straightforward Beaujolais; the gentler slopes make Beaujolais-Villages; while on the steeper, inhospitable granite outcrops from the Monts de Beaujolais, where the Gamay grape performs at its best, all the top Beaujolais Cru vineyards are situated; until, at heights of around 400m (1310ft), ripening becomes a problem, even this far south, and the vineyards revert to Beaujolais-Villages once more.

CHAMPAGNE

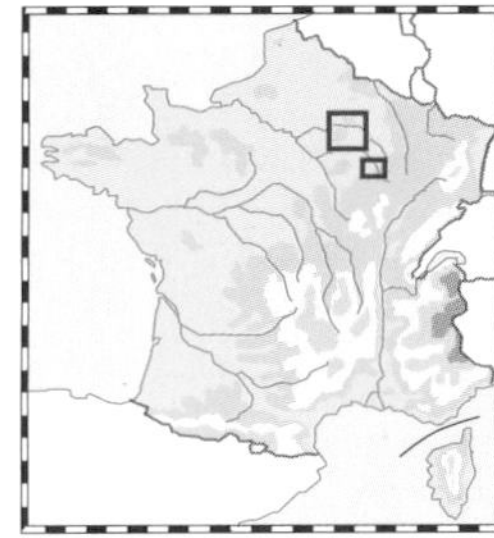

 **RED GRAPES**
Pinot Noir and Pinot Meunier account for three-quarters of all Champagne grapes.

 **WHITE GRAPE**
Chardonnay accounts for about one-quarter of the vineyards.

 **CLIMATE**
Cold, wet, continental climate but the northerly latitude gives more daylight hours in the growing season than Provence. Rain and late spring frosts are the main enemies.

 **SOIL**
Shallow topsoil as little as 15cm (6in) in places covering subsoil largely of chalk up to 200m (650ft) thick.

ASPECT
Mainly east- and south-east-facing vineyards, lying between 100 and 200m (330 and 650ft) high, and protected by thickly wooded hilltops.

Vineyards in the Marne Valley are on south-facing slopes to catch all available sunlight.

THEY WEREN'T PAYING THE AREA round Reims and Épernay north-east of Paris any compliments when they called it Champagne. They weren't thinking of glittering first night parties, of dandies and dancing girls, the hectic celebrations of a Grand Prix winner or the tingling joyful tension of a lover with warm words in his mind and brave deeds in his heart.

The word 'Champagne' comes from the Latin *campania* meaning 'open, flat countryside', and I sometimes feel this is a positive understatement as I urge the car onwards. Driving through the pale, lonely plains to the east of Reims, the sea of corn enlivened by an occasional steepling grain silo, I feel more as if I were in the depths of the Oklahoma prairie than trying to make a dinner date in the heart of one of the world's greatest wine regions. As I plough through the flat sugar-beet fields of the Pas de Calais, still saturated by squalls from the English Channel, past the giant slag heaps of long-dead coal mines and once more out on to the chalky windswept plains to the north of Reims, I don't scent the slightest possibility of any vines ever ripening under such inhospitable conditions.

And they don't. This whole expanse of north-eastern France is a desolate, underpopulated province of broad cornfields and dark forbidding forests, which experienced some of the fiercest fighting in World Wars One and Two. And in what many historians reckon may have been the bloodiest battle ever to take place, Attila the Hun was finally turned back east of Reims near Châlons-sur-Marne. It is simply too cold, too windy, too rainy for growing grapes in this region.

CLIMATE AND SOIL

But in this flat landscape there is one brief eruption of low hills – a grouping of cliffs, slopes and valleys of ancient chalk. These hills *do* provide just the amount of protection and privileged mesoclimate that the grape vine needs. Take a look at the map. The Montagne de Reims is one of these. The Côte des Blancs is another. The cleft where the Marne river pushes its way westward towards Paris is a third. And little pockets like the Côte de Sézanne and the Aube (see page 75) further south can also provide suitable conditions for ripening the vine. Just.

Yet this knife-edge between ripeness and unripeness is what gives the wine of Champagne its peculiar suitability to form the base for a sparkling wine. And the cold autumns and icy winters that grip the whole region in joyless embrace are what, by chance, created the now famous bubbles in the first place.

High acidity is crucial in the base wine for a good fizz. If you can lengthen the ripening time of the fruit as much as possible so that it only creeps to maturity in the golden days of autumn, you are going to retain high acidity, yet have physically mature grapes. The flavours these give are infinitely superior to those obtained from grapes grown in warmer climates simply picked early. All you then get is green, raw unripeness. You can't make great wine out of that.

In the few favoured vine-growing mesoclimates of Champagne, the annual mean temperature is about 10.5°C (51°F), a half degree above what is generally regarded as the minimum required to ripen any high-quality grape variety, although training the vines close to the ground will increase the temperature somewhat. The number of hours of sunshine in the growing season are actually as high in Champagne as in the considerably warmer vineyards of Alsace. But whereas Alsace, sheltered behind the Vosges mountains, has much higher temperatures and less rain due to its continental climate, Champagne's days are cooled by the damp Atlantic breezes that sweep in unhindered from the west.

And those winds often bring rain – and at the wrong time too. Although the total annual rainfall is lower than in regions like Bordeaux, Burgundy and the Loire, nearly 60 per cent of it falls in the summer and early autumn, with July and August being particularly hard hit when the rain causes mildew and rot among the ripening grapes. But this is where the importance of the right soil comes in. With the exception of the southerly Aube, Champagne's vines are planted on a thick chalk subsoil. The topsoil differs within the region – the Montagne de Reims has a kind of brown coal lignite and some gravel, the Vallée de la Marne has far more sand, and the Côte des Blancs has clay – but this topsoil is frequently so thin that the chalk keeps breaking through.

The chalk is porous and fissured, holding enough water to nourish the vine but not drown it. The vine roots burrow into the soft, almost spongy, stone thus anchoring the plant against climatic extremes above ground. Since the chalk is so close to the surface, it is relatively warm, and indeed, may even reflect sunlight back on to the vine, aiding the grapes' final struggle for ripeness as autumn drifts towards winter.

FROM STILL WINE TO SPARKLING

This rather sombre scenario means that truly ripe, sun-filled flavours simply aren't part of the Champagne repertoire, although historically the region's reputation was based on still *red* wines. These must have been pretty feeble and thin and I'm glad I didn't have to rely on them for washing down my Sunday roast. But highly acidic grapes, picked just as winter set

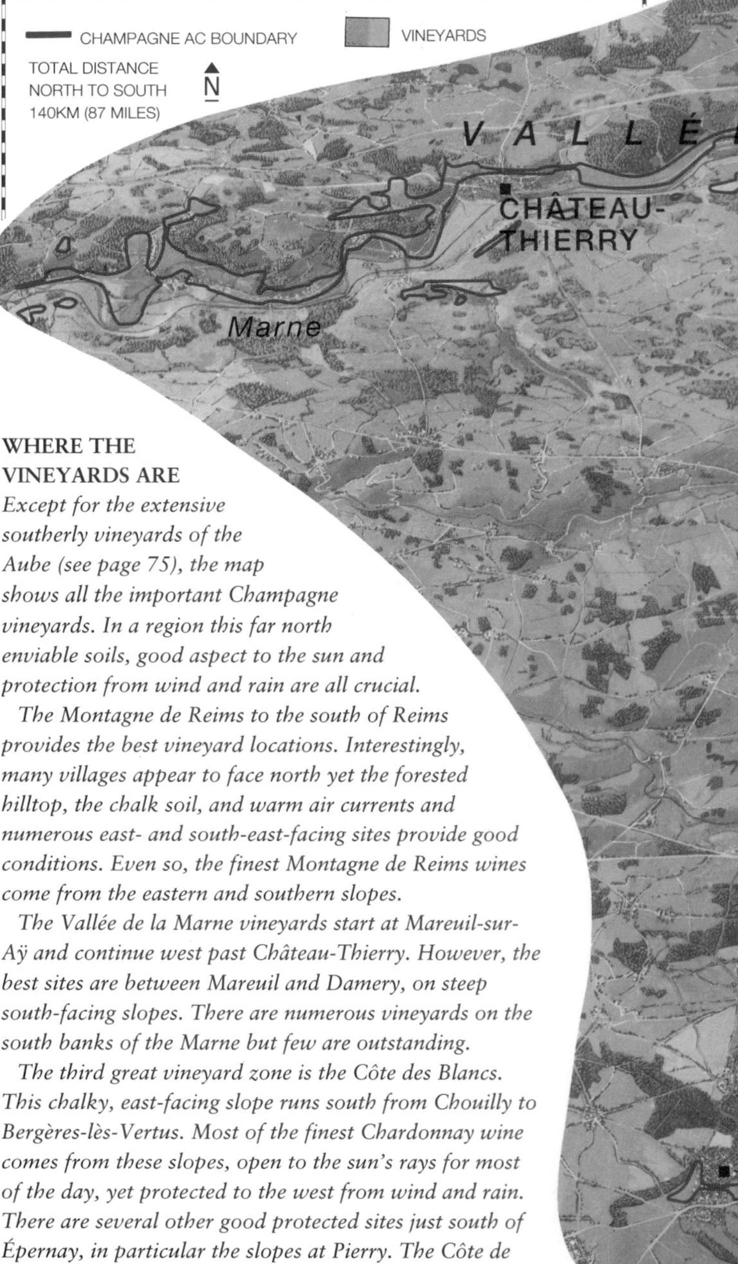

WHERE THE VINEYARDS ARE

Except for the extensive southerly vineyards of the Aube (see page 75), the map shows all the important Champagne vineyards. In a region this far north enviable soils, good aspect to the sun and protection from wind and rain are all crucial.

The Montagne de Reims to the south of Reims provides the best vineyard locations. Interestingly, many villages appear to face north yet the forested hilltop, the chalk soil, and warm air currents and numerous east- and south-east-facing sites provide good conditions. Even so, the finest Montagne de Reims wines come from the eastern and southern slopes.

The Vallée de la Marne vineyards start at Mareuil-sur-Aÿ and continue west past Château-Thierry. However, the best sites are between Mareuil and Damery, on steep south-facing slopes. There are numerous vineyards on the south banks of the Marne but few are outstanding.

The third great vineyard zone is the Côte des Blancs. This chalky, east-facing slope runs south from Chouilly to Bergères-lès-Vertus. Most of the finest Chardonnay wine comes from these slopes, open to the sun's rays for most of the day, yet protected to the west from wind and rain. There are several other good protected sites just south of Épernay, in particular the slopes at Pierry. The Côte de Sézanne, with its chalky, east-facing slopes and forested hilltops also provides classic Champagne conditions.

in, would have fermented slowly and inefficiently. As the freezing winter air filled the wine cellars, the yeasts would simply have become too cold to go on with their job: they'd have packed it in and gone into hibernation. In the days before central heating they'd have lain dormant until the following spring had warmed the cellars up and – hey presto – they'd have finished off their fermentation with a final brisk burst of bubbles to emerge as still wines.

The English and the Parisians used to buy a lot of Champagne wine. Since young wine was prized more than old wine until modern times, it would be shipped to them in barrel during the winter. Come the spring, it would begin bubbling again. Traditionally much effort was put into ridding the wines of their bubble, but in England, in the carefree period after the Restoration of Charles II in 1660, and in the self-indulgent, pleasure-mad days in France that followed Louis XIV's death in 1715, a vogue developed for frivolous sparkling wines that may have upset the connoisseurs of those times, but has ensured Champagne's fame ever since.

In the seventeenth century no-one understood exactly why the fizziness came and went. The English managed to preserve the bubbles rather longer into the summer because they had developed particularly strong glass bottles and they used cork rather than rags soaked in oil as a stopper. Bottles would still burst, but not half as often as did the weaker French bottles. It fell to one of Champagne's legendary figures – Dom Pérignon, who was in charge of the cellars at Hautvillers Abbey between 1670 and 1715 – to introduce strong bottles and corks, to work out how to control the fizz and then how to start the fizz going again in a still wine.

The reputation of Champagne is based on this last achievement. By adding a little yeast and sugar to a still wine and then

Champagne bottles are made of thicker glass than usual to withstand the pressure.

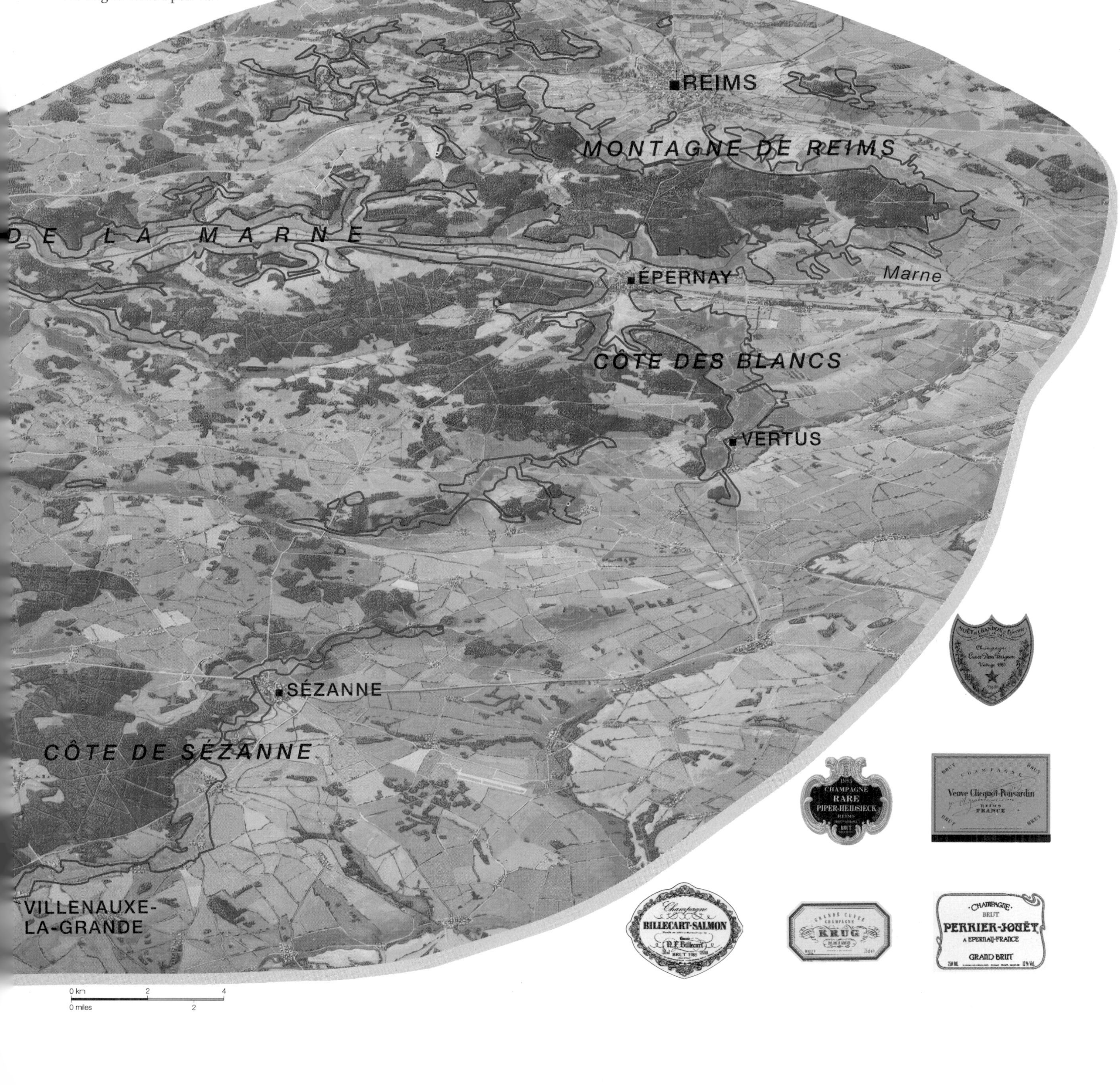

corking the bottle tightly, wine re-ferments in the bottle and the bubbles dissolve, waiting to burst forth when the bottle is opened. This is the traditional 'Champagne method' of making sparkling wine and is used across the world for top class bubbly. Others have since improved upon Dom Pérignon's methods for creating a reliable sparkling wine, but he was perhaps more important for formulating other principles that are now accepted as fundamental to quality in Champagne. Above all, he saw the need to restrict yields to achieve ripeness, and to blend the wines of different vineyards and communes together to produce the best end result.

THE CLASSIFICATION OF CHAMPAGNE VINEYARDS

In the marginal climate of Champagne, there are few vineyard sites that can produce an attractive, multi-faceted wine most years. However, the three grape varieties used for Champagne, each grown on different sites, can contribute a more rounded flavour to a final blend. Older 'reserve' wines held back from the previous year may also be added in for extra flavour.

As a result, Champagne is usually a blend of different wines, frequently from all over the region, and most of it is sold as non-vintage. A vintage is 'declared' only in especially good years, and the wines made from a selection of the best grapes. The so-called 'de luxe' *cuvées* are also blends from different vineyards, unless they come from a single grower.

Merchant houses – the most important are based in Reims, Épernay and Aÿ – and co-operatives handle the bulk of Champagne production, and they buy grapes from the growers at prices determined by a tribunal of officials, growers and producers each year.

Prices are fixed by a system known as the *échelle des crus*, or 'ladder of growths'. Villages, rather than individual vineyards, are classified according to quality on a scale ranging from 100 per cent down to 80 per cent. There are 17 villages accorded the title Grand Cru, and these receive 100 per cent of the agreed grape price per kilo. The 41 villages accorded Premier Cru status receive between 90 and 99 per cent of the agreed price. All the other less-favoured villages receive between 80 and 89 per cent of the agreed price per kilo.

GRAPE VARIETIES

Not only are some vineyards better than others, but they are also better suited to particular grape varieties. Three grape varieties are grown in Champagne – two black varieties, Pinot Noir and Pinot Meunier, and one white, Chardonnay. Just south of the city of Reims, are the vineyards of the Montagne de Reims, which boasts vines on its northern, eastern and southern slopes. Pinot Noir dominates these vineyards, and much of the backbone for the Champagne blends come from these grapes and from those grown in the Aube region. Altogether the Pinot Noir grape variety covers about 35 per cent of the total vineyard area.

Chardonnay dominates the chalky, east-facing slopes of the Côte des Blancs south of Épernay. The other particularly successful areas for Chardonnay are the village of Villers-Marmery at the eastern end of the Montagne de Reims, and the Côte de Sézanne to the south. Chardonnay from the northern sites adds zest and lively, lean fruit to the Champagne blend, while that from the less chalky Côte de Sézanne is likely to add a creamy, honeyed roundness. Chardonnay covers about 27 per cent of the total vineyard area.

Pinot Meunier is the Champagne workhorse, covering about 38 per cent of the vineyards. In general it is planted in the lower-lying vineyards because it buds late, thus avoiding the worst of the frost. Most villages grow some Pinot Meunier, with the exception of the top Côte des Blancs communes, and Bouzy in the Montagne de Reims. Pinot Meunier is particularly prevalent west of Épernay in the Vallée de la Marne where the valley vineyards are susceptible to frost. Blended with the two varieties it can add a pleasant, mildly perfumed quality that softens the more austere, slow-developing characteristics of Pinot Noir and Chardonnay.

THE CHALK OF CHAMPAGNE

There is a thick, billowing seam of chalk that runs across northern France to Calais and across southern England. This is the subsoil for the Champagne vineyards. There are two main sorts: micraster, found on the lower slopes and the plain, and belemnite, found in all the best vineyards and on the upper slopes. Chalk has a perfect balance between porosity and water retention and is able to nourish vines equally well in dry or wet years. Its brilliant whiteness helps the soil's ability to reflect sunlight back on to the vines, and chalk retains heat well, vital factors in such a northerly vineyard region. Chalk is also alkaline, which in turn produces grapes with high acid levels – perfect for sparkling wine. In addition, the region's *caves* or cellars, dug deep into the chalk, mainly in the towns of Reims and Épernay, are cold and damp, providing an ideal environment for storing bottles while the Champagne inside undergoes its second fermentation. This is because the slower the yeasts set to work, the smaller the bubble and the more persistent the fizz in the finished wine.

The cru vineyards The best vineyards are found on the chalk slopes covered with downwash material from the upper slopes. The high proportion of calcium in the chalk prevents the vines from taking up iron and this is compensated for by the annual use of fertilizers.

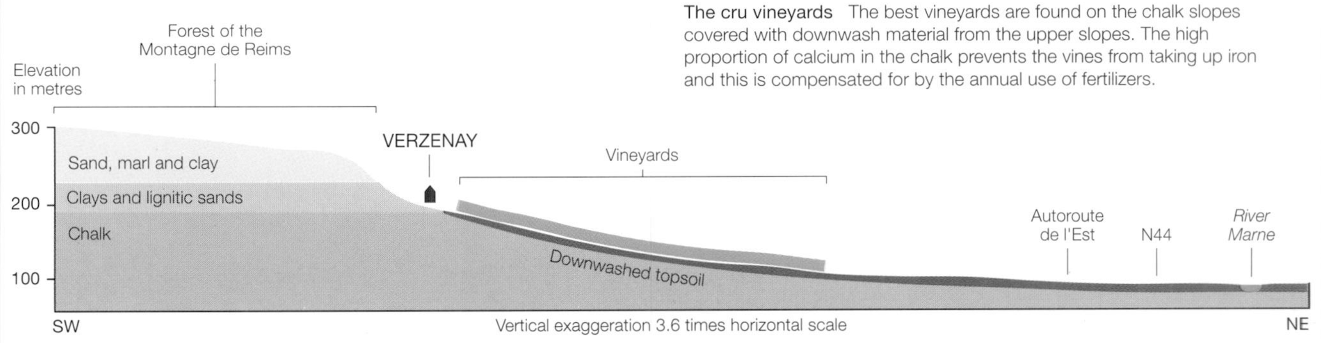

THE AUBE REGION

The Aube's problem traditionally has been that it is situated in the Champagne region but not quite, and in the Burgundy region, well almost. At least now the new stretch of the A26 autoroute between Reims and Dijon slices between the two main Aube towns of Bar-sur-Aube and Bar-sur-Seine so that we can see the region's dual personality for ourselves.

As it happens, Chablis in the Burgundy region is a lot closer to Bar-sur-Seine than any of the main Champagne vineyards, but the Burgundians rejected the Aube growers, some of whom then petitioned to be included in the Champagne *appellation*. The Aube growers as a whole only got themselves included in the Champagne *appellation* after several years of violent resistance to their claims by the Marne growers. Until 1927 they had to be content with the demeaning title of 'Champagne of the Second Zone'. In other words, inferior.

This attitude has lasted right through to the present day, but is increasingly untenable. Many of the more snobbish *grande marque* Champagne houses still talk as if the Aube did not exist and hardly any of them will admit to using Aube wines for their brands. Yet most of them *do* use a proportion of Aube grapes to add a bit of life to their non-vintage blends.

In fact, the Aube is one of the most important sources of full-flavoured, ripe Pinot Noir grapes in all Champagne. There are now well over 6000 hectares (14,825 acres) of vineyards in the Aube, out of a total in the Champagne region as a whole of just under 30,000 hectares (74,000 acres). Some 80 per cent of those Aube grapes are Pinot Noir.

Despite past schisms, the links between Burgundy and the Aube are close. The vineyards around Épernay at the heart of the Champagne region are a good 110km (70 miles) north of the Aube, while Chablis is only 40km (25 miles) to the south-west. The Aube soils are the same as those of Chablis, the best sites having Kimmeridgian limestone clay subsoils, and there's a good splattering of Portlandian limestone, Chablis' other soil, as well. Even the weather has more in common with Chablis than with Champagne. Greater maximum heat in the Aube is balanced by more extreme cold and the general effect is of riper, rounder, slightly raspberryish, yet earthy fruit.

This slightly red-fruit flavour is especially marked in a local oddity, the Rosé des Riceys. This is a still rosé wine, aged in cask, and made only in the warmest years. Although the cask-aging drives out any richness, there is a core of curious sweetness as though you'd left a punnet of raspberries to wither and shrivel in a hot desert wind. Annual production of this wine is as little as 7500 bottles.

Although a few growers bottle their own wine, most Aube sparkling wines either head north for blending with the Champagnes or are sold by the large co-operative, the Union Auboise at Bar-sur-Seine, whose Devaux blend of Champagne puts many a smarter *grande marque* to shame.

The Aube is further south than the main Champagne vineyards and its warmer climate makes it an important source of Pinot Noir grapes.

WHERE THE VINEYARDS ARE *The Aube is closer to the Chablis region of Burgundy than to the main Champagne vineyards to the north. While the principal Champagne vineyard region is affected by breezes coming from the Atlantic, the Aube has a more continental climate and in particular is prone to frost. The landscape resembles the outlying areas of Chablis more than the main Champagne areas themselves. Most of the land is broad and rolling but there are also low, wooded hills with relatively steep slopes and, where the aspect is broadly to the south, patches of vines among pasture and other crops. The best examples are to the east of Bar-sur-Seine, along the valley, and beneath the forest between Polisy and Les Riceys. North-east of Bar-sur-Seine, in this cool part of France, the land flattens out and becomes far too exposed for grapes to ripen.*

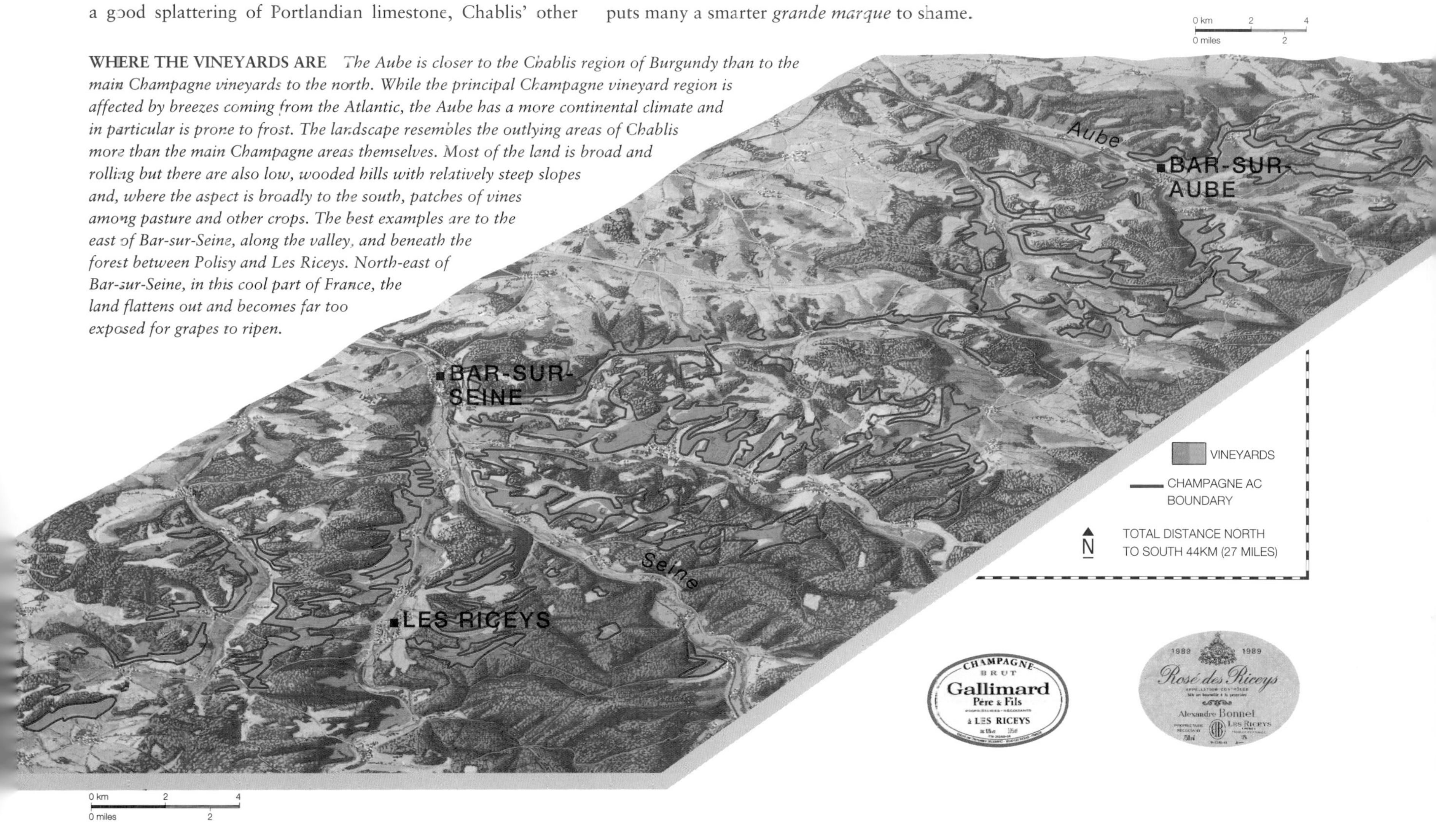

0 km 2 4
0 miles 2

Aube
BAR-SUR-AUBE
BAR-SUR-SEINE
Seine
LES RICEYS

VINEYARDS
CHAMPAGNE AC BOUNDARY
N
TOTAL DISTANCE NORTH TO SOUTH 44KM (27 MILES)

CHAMPAGNE BRUT Gallimard Père & Fils LES RICEYS

1989 Rosé des Riceys Alexandre Bonnel Les Riceys

0 km 2 4
0 miles 2

Heart of Champagne

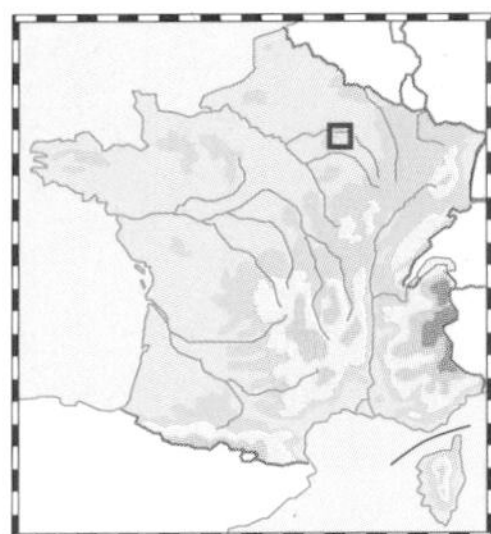

Before we go any further, let's remind ourselves of the one factor that dominates all others in Champagne. The cold. In all my trips to Champagne, whatever the time of year, there's hardly a day when I haven't felt some cool dampness underfoot as I first step into the vineyard of a morning. It's a rare evening when I haven't been glad I'm wearing a jacket as the sun sets behind a forested hill and leaves me in its mildly chilly shade. And come vintage time, since I often spend a day or two in the region as the grapes are coming in, pondering the close of one more summer, I have hardly ever squeezed a Chardonnay or a Pinot Noir berry off the vine and exalted in its sweetness and aroma. They're just not ripe enough.

In this part of France we're just about at the limit beyond which you can't even pretend to ripen grape varieties like Chardonnay or Pinot Noir, even in the hottest of years. Only the most perfectly suited locations are going to manage it at the best of times. Fortunately in the Champagne region, there is a whole cluster of just such places.

There are three main zones at the heart of Champagne and each is best suited to a different grape variety, producing quite different styles of wines. Remember, in the majority of cases, it is the blending of wines from the various vineyards across the region that creates the finest Champagne. There *are* some excellent single-vineyard Champagnes, but the sum of the parts in Champagne is almost always a great deal better than anything the individual components can manage by themselves.

MONTAGNE DE REIMS

Nowhere is this more true than in the wines of the Montagne de Reims. Look at the map. Reims is the city at the top, and the group of forested hills just to its south constitute the Montagne de Reims. In a cold, far northern area like Champagne, surely only the most protected southerly sites will ripen the grapes properly? But remarkably, some of the darkest-coloured, hardest-to-ripen Pinot Noir grapes, and some of the longest-lived wine in the Champagne region come from vineyards that are on the *north* side of the Montagne de Reims.

How is it that villages such as Mailly-Champagne, Chigny-les-Roses and Verzenay, located on these nothern slopes, are able to produce such deep, sturdy wine? Various reasons are traditionally given, many of them based on the possible warming effect of the nearby city of Reims, and the supposed thermal blanket of warm air that protects the vines in winter and aids ripening in summer.

But I don't think that that fully explains matters. Most of the good vineyards don't actually *face* north, and those that do ripen on average only eight days later than those that don't. Directly south of Reims – where the vines would have to face due north – there *aren't* any vines. They do appear on slopes to the south-west, on what is known as the 'petite Montagne', but the good vineyards of Écueil, Sacy and Villedommange are facing virtually due *east*, with some slopes even inclined towards the south.

South-east of Reims, between Rilly-la-Montagne and Mailly-Champagne, many of the vines *do* face north, but, unlike elsewhere on the Montagne, most of these vines are on the almost flat lower slopes and they get a fair share of the cool but long summer's day sun. However, these villages are renowned for making austere, gaunt, slow-maturing Pinot Noir wines. With the exception of the remarkable Vilmart wines from Rilly, I've never found them that enjoyable on their

Remuage – *where bottles are turned and tapped daily to dislodge sediment – is traditionally done by hand.*

WHERE THE VINEYARDS ARE *In a cool northern area like Champagne, it's as important to look at the land that isn't covered with vines as that which is. All the flat land you can see here is arable land. It couldn't support grapes because it doesn't catch enough of the sun's heat, and hasn't enough protection from wind and rain. This protection is provided primarily by the wooded hilltops which dominate the landscape south of Reims, and to the south and west of Épernay. The vineyards only rarely venture out into the plain. Remarkably, some of the better vineyards on the northern face of the Montagne de Reims between Rilly-la-Montagne and Mailly-Champagne are on flattish northern slopes. There has been an expansion eastwards from the Côte des Blancs on to flat land, but the quality of grapes doesn't compare with those from the east-facing slopes between Cramant and Vertus.*

However, all the best Champagne grapes are grown on sites first planted hundreds of years ago, and the map shows us why these plots of land were chosen. The eastern and southern parts of the Montagne de Reims are well protected by the forested hilltops, and round Ambonnay and Bouzy there is a natural south-facing amphitheatre, ideal for ripening the predominantly Pinot Noir vines. Between Avenay and Damery the Marne Valley has steep, south-facing chalky slopes protected from wind and rain and ideally placed to soak up the sun. South of Épernay there are good sites at Pierry, Mancy and Grauves, but the real class act is the magnificent east-facing chalk slope of the Côte des Blancs, protected, well-drained and angled towards the sun – just what a northern vineyard needs.

0 km 1 2
0 miles 1

own, yet their reputation comes largely because this sturdy, lean backbone provides a crutch to support softer, blander wines in many Champagne Houses' blends.

The best Montagne de Reims villages lie between Verzenay and Bouzy. Here the slopes curve round from north to south. They benefit from the protection of the forested hilltop but the best sites also have an eastern-to-southern aspect. Three other important factors come into play. These are exposure to morning sun from the east, a chalk soil that both reflects heat and stores it as the sun's direct rays disappear to the west, and the protection from westerly winds and rain offered by the Montagne de Reims. Such a combination allows villages like Bouzy in particular, with its warm, south-facing amphitheatre of vines, and Verzenay to a lesser extent, to produce deep-flavoured Pinot Noir wines against the odds.

VALLÉE DE LA MARNE

The Marne Valley begins where the Montagne de Reims' southern slopes sidle down to join the river between Avenay and Mareuil-sur-Aÿ. Meandering west for the first 10km (6 miles) or so, between Mareuil and Damery, you come to a magnificent sweep of vineyards, dipping and diving in and out of the hilly slopes, but above all maintaining a marvellous south-facing aspect for the carpet of vines that swoops down from the hills above Épernay to the broad valley floor.

This area, in particular the slopes around Aÿ, can produce beautiful Pinot Noir wines, but west of Damery, towards Paris, the valley gets narrower and wetter, and the chalk becomes a thin strip rather than a broad band, with sandy clays increasingly taking over, and most of the *appellation* area is planted on this sedimental layer. Neither the Pinot Noir nor the Chardonnay grape will ripen under these conditions, but the less pernickerty Pinot Meunier will, and so this variety dominates the plantings in this area.

Vines grow on both sides of the Marne Valley, with the northern banks being superior. Yet there are exceptions. The little village of Leuvrigny, on the south bank, provides Pinot Meunier grapes for Krug, Deutz and Roederer – three quality-conscious Champagne houses. And in the hinterland south of the river, good, broad-flavoured Champagne pops up in villages like le Breuil, or, closer to Épernay, in the underrated villages of Pierry and Grauves. These are virtually part of the Côte des Blancs, the third great Champagne zone.

Pierry, in particular, has perfect south-west-facing vineyard slopes. Their drawback is that they are mostly planted with Pinot Meunier when they are good enough to do great things with Chardonnay and Pinot Noir.

CÔTE DES BLANCS

It's much easier to understand what's special about the Côte des Blancs – a long, east- and south-east-facing slope of chalky soil. This stretches from the Butte de Saran in the north just outside Épernay to below the town of Vertus in the south. For about 15km (9 miles) there's nothing but vines, and the vast majority of these are Chardonnay.

Chardonnay doesn't find it easy to ripen in Champagne. But Chardonnay loves chalky soil and long warm days without too much rain. The Côte des Blancs provides both of these requirements better than anywhere else in the region, and the result is the most regularly high-yielding of all the Champagne zones, but also the most reliably attractive wines.

Many of the wines are sold unblended as Blanc de Blancs Champagne, which is made only from Chardonnay grapes, but grapes from the villages of Cramant, Avize, le Mesnil-sur-Oger and Vertus also provide many Champagne blends with a fragrance and fresh, lemony zing that is absolutely crucial. If the wine is young and the bubbles dance and twirl around your mouth, that will be the Côte des Blancs talking. And if the wine is old and a soft, toasty foam creams and coils around your tongue, that will be the Côte des Blancs talking too.

N

THE HEART OF CHAMPAGNE

VINEYARDS

TOTAL DISTANCE NORTH TO SOUTH 40KM (25 MILES)

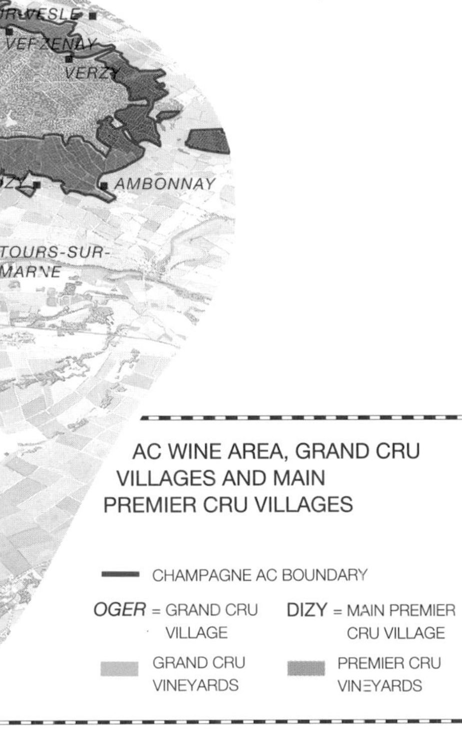

ALSACE

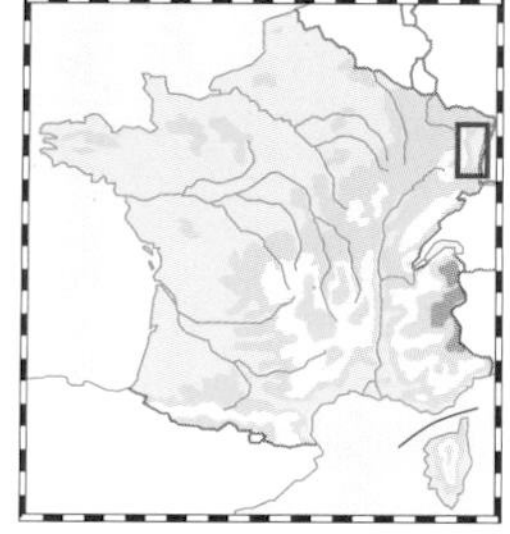

RED GRAPES
Pinot Noir is the only red grape, occupying about 7.5 per cent of the plantings.

WHITE GRAPES
Riesling is the most widely planted, followed by Pinot Blanc, Gewürztraminer and Sylvaner in almost equal amounts. Pinot Gris and Muscat trail far behind, with negligible amounts of Chasselas used in Edelzwicker, and Chardonnay in Crémant.

CLIMATE
Despite the northerly latitude, the region benefits from plentiful sun and low rainfall caused by its location in the rain shadow created by the Vosges mountains.

SOIL
The region divides into three main zones – mountain, mid-slopes, and foothills and plains. The best sites are on the middle slopes which are limestone based with marly clay and sandstone topsoils.

ASPECT
The vineyards are sited between 170 and 420m (560 and 1380ft) with the best sites on the well-drained, sheltered steep middle slopes.

YOU ONLY HAVE TO STAND in the middle of the steeply sloping vineyards to the west of Colmar to realize there's something special about Alsace. Over to the west the dark clouds pile ominously above the mountains; yet here, where the Riesling and Gewürztraminer vines climb gamely up towards the wooded brows of the Vosges eastern foothills, the sky is as clear and blue as dreams, the sunshine is warm and mellow, the air is pure and sweet with the perfume of flowers and alive with the twittering chatter of insects. In these vineyards, grapes for some of the most heady and exotic wines in Europe can ripen in the summer sun .

The vineyards of Alsace sit in a rain shadow created by the Vosges mountains which rise high above the Rhine Valley. Most of the rain brought by the westerly winds is shed over these mountains and forests. By the time the clouds reach the vineyards they have just enough rain left to cast a few refreshing showers on the vines and then evaporate into the warm air. Alsace is almost as far north as vineyards can go in France – only Champagne is marginally further north. Yet that rain-shadow allows Colmar to be the second driest spot in France, beaten only by Perpignan, down on the Spanish border. Perpignan broils under torrid skies. Not so Alsace. Perpignan excels at producing rough-and-ready hot-climate reds, whereas Alsace, because of the cooler northern temperatures, allied to day after day of clear skies, can provide the ripeness – and therefore the higher alcoholic strength – of the warm south and also the perfume and fragrance of the cool north.

The enigma goes much further than mere climatic conditions. Politically Alsace is caught between two inimical philosophies. The Rhine is southern Germany's great waterway. Nowadays it forms a natural frontier as it runs northwards from Basel on the Swiss border but, in less peaceful times, the river, and the flat farmland on both of its banks, formed an obvious battleground whenever the French and Germans went to war. The frontier then was seen as the Vosges mountains to the west, on whose eastern foothills all Alsace's vineyards are planted. Prussia gained control of Alsace in 1870, France won the region back in 1918; by 1940 Alsace was once again under German occupation, before finally reverting to France in 1945.

After several generations of confused national identity, the region has settled into a reasonably

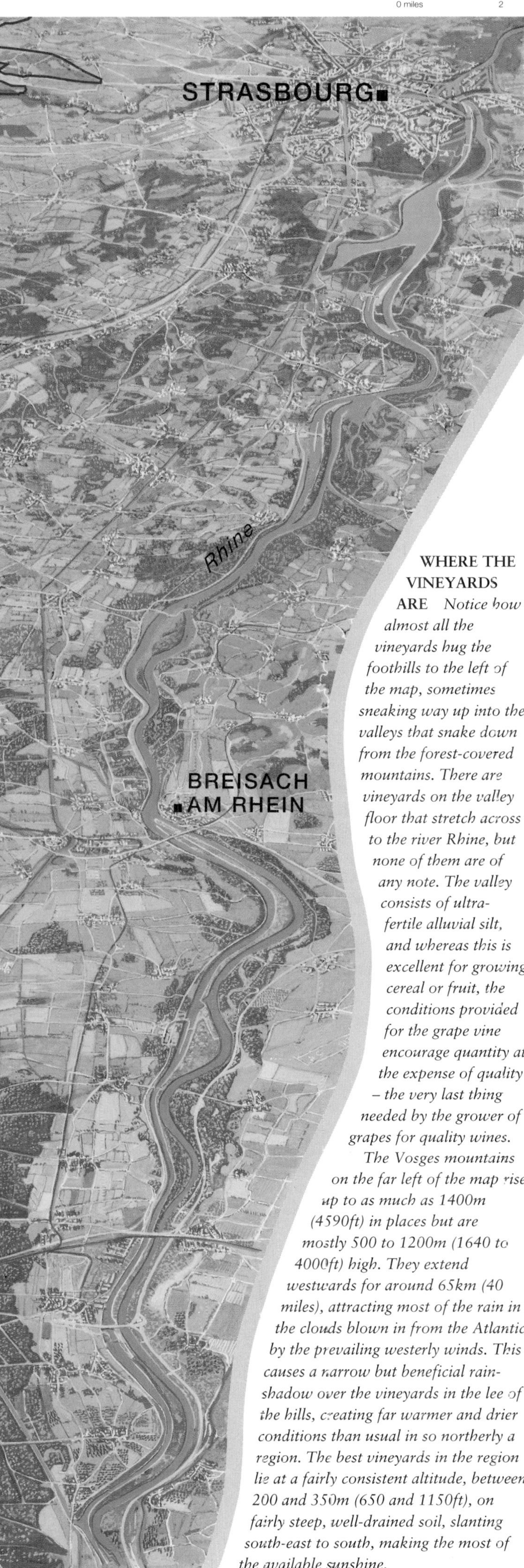

WHERE THE VINEYARDS ARE *Notice how almost all the vineyards hug the foothills to the left of the map, sometimes sneaking way up into the valleys that snake down from the forest-covered mountains. There are vineyards on the valley floor that stretch across to the river Rhine, but none of them are of any note. The valley consists of ultra-fertile alluvial silt, and whereas this is excellent for growing cereal or fruit, the conditions provided for the grape vine encourage quantity at the expense of quality – the very last thing needed by the grower of grapes for quality wines.*

The Vosges mountains on the far left of the map rise up to as much as 1400m (4590ft) in places but are mostly 500 to 1200m (1640 to 4000ft) high. They extend westwards for around 65km (40 miles), attracting most of the rain in the clouds blown in from the Atlantic by the prevailing westerly winds. This causes a narrow but beneficial rain-shadow over the vineyards in the lee of the hills, creating far warmer and drier conditions than usual in so northerly a region. The best vineyards in the region lie at a fairly consistent altitude, between 200 and 350m (650 and 1150ft), on fairly steep, well-drained soil, slanting south-east to south, making the most of the available sunshine.

contented dual personality. The Alsatian people maintain proudly, even ferociously, that they are as French as any Frenchman can be. Yet most of the names of their villages are German and the villages themselves look as though they've stepped off the set of some German operetta; most family surnames are German (though their Christian names are frequently French), and indeed the local Alsace dialect has far more in common with German than French.

GRAPE VARIETIES

The grape varieties that make Alsatian wine are, for the large part, German too. Her two most famous grapes – Riesling and Gewürztraminer – though enthusiastically planted in Germany and much of Central Europe, are conspicuous by their absence in any of France's other *appellation controlées*. Sylvaner doesn't appear elsewhere in France, Pinot Gris and Pinot Blanc are tolerated at best in a very subordinate role in Burgundy. Only the red Pinot Noir, Burgundy's best red grape, and the white Muscat, planted in the fortified wine *appellations* around the Mediterranean, are granted genuine legitimacy in France. In Germany, however, Riesling, Gewürztraminer, Pinot Blanc (known as Weissburgunder) and Pinot Gris (known as Ruländer or Grauburgunder) and even Sylvaner, in the Franken and Rheinhessen regions, are regarded as producing most of that country's greatest wines.

WINE STYLES

The dual personality of Alsace is reflected by the wines too. Alsace's French grape varieties take on a Germanic perfume, while the German grapes proudly distance themselves from the flavours one would find over the border in Germany itself.

The difference is most marked with the Riesling. Although there is now a vogue for bone-dry Riesling in Germany, it is difficult to ripen the grapes sufficiently and the most exciting German Rieslings have residual sugar left in them. Alsace's best Rieslings, on the other hand, are fat and round in the mouth, yet marvellously dry, streaked with cold lime pith acidity yet thick with glycerine ripeness.

The two countries' other wines are also quite distinctive. Germany's Gewürztraminer is generally made with a certain fat sweetness and perfume. Alsace goes for the perfume of roses and the ripeness of lychee and mango, yet generally manages to keep the wine bone dry. Germany's Pinot Gris or Ruländer is attractively honeyed but sweetish, while Alsace's is impressively broad and honeyed but remains intriguingly dry. However, Alsace Pinot Noir leans towards the fragrant floral scents of German Pinot Noir (Spätburgunder) rather than the meatiness of Burgundy, and Alsace Muscats have a light, dry grapy perfume rather than the heady but weighty hothouse flavours preferred in the Muscats from France's far south.

> **APPELLATIONS AND CLASSIFICATIONS**
>
> - **Alsace AC** This is the general Alsace AC which covers the whole region and appears on all labels. Any of the permitted grape varieties may be used.
> - **Crémant d'Alsace AC** This AC is for sparkling wine produced over the whole region and made in the traditional method usually from Pinot Blanc or Riesling.
> - **Alsace Grand Cru AC** This AC covers certain special vineyards (see page 80).
> - **Vendange Tardive** A late-harvested wine made from very ripe grapes of the varieties Gewürztraminer, Riesling, Pinot Gris and occasionally Muscat.
> - **Sélection de Grains Nobles** A higher category than Vendange Tardive made from even riper grapes of the same varieties.

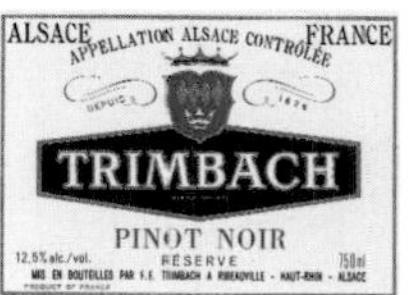

Known as flûtes, Alsace bottles are distinctively tall and slender.

HEART OF ALSACE

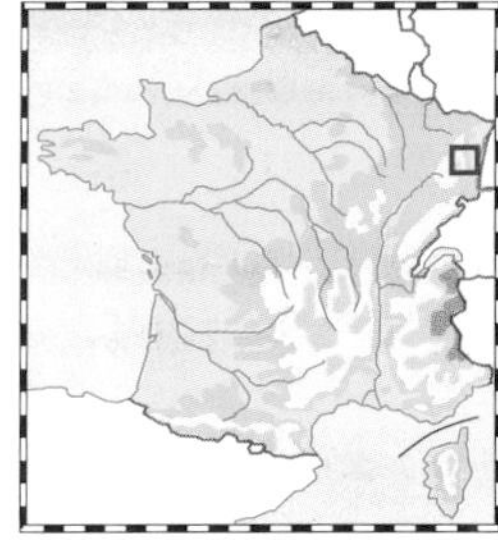

THOUGH ALSACE'S WINE REGION stretches north to the border with Germany at Wissembourg and south almost to Mulhouse, a distance of about 110km (70 miles), virtually all the finest wines come from a central section of vineyards in the Haut-Rhin *département* west of Colmar, a miraculously preserved medieval market town which is rightly called the Wine Capital of Alsace. Good wines are made in the north of Alsace, in the Bas-Rhin *département*, but they rarely have the ripeness or intensity of those from the vineyards of the Haut-Rhin, which lie further south.

The vineyards that twist in and out of the folds in the Vosges eastern foothills are dotted with magical little villages that make you rub your eyes in disbelief at their unspoilt charm. And they're not some kind of Walt Disney copy – these are real working villages. Those tilting gabled houses are inhabited by the people who tend the vines and make the wine, those rickety wooden doors do lead down to cellars that have housed the vats and barrels for hundreds of years.

The vineyards on these slopes also date way back, as the Romans had planted most of the lower foothills with vines by the second century. There are specific vineyards like Goldert in the village of Gueberschwihr and Mambourg in Sigolsheim, whose documented reputation stretches back to the eighth century, when Alsace was ruled by the Franks, and these ancient vineyards now form the core of the present Grand Cru system of wine classification in Alsace.

GRANDS CRUS

Grand Cru means 'great growth' and is intended to apply to particular patches of land that have traditionally produced the finest grapes. A similar system in Burgundy has produced famous names like le Montrachet and Chambertin which have, for centuries, enjoyed global renown. However, hardly any of the Alsace Grand Cru names are known except to a few devoted fans, and it wasn't until 1983 that a provisional list of Grand Cru sites was produced. Alsace's turbulent history has much to do with this, since it takes a fair bit of time to build the reputation of a Cru, and in the critical nineteenth and twentieth centuries, when areas like Burgundy and Bordeaux were advancing their fame, Alsace was concentrating on expanding its vineyards into the flat, over-fertile soils of the plain nearer the Rhine in order to produce cheap wines.

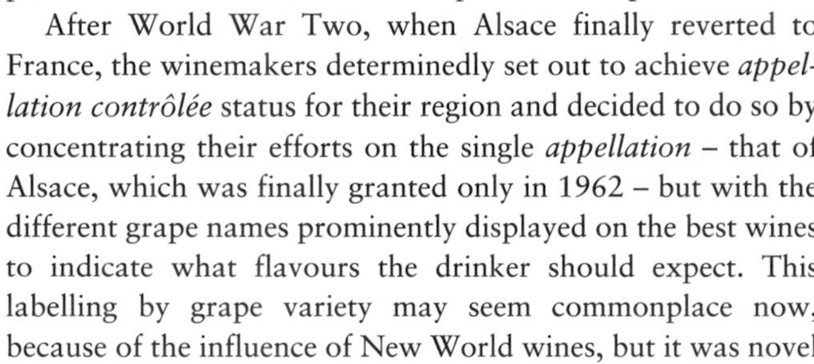

After World War Two, when Alsace finally reverted to France, the winemakers determinedly set out to achieve *appellation contrôlée* status for their region and decided to do so by concentrating their efforts on the single *appellation* – that of Alsace, which was finally granted only in 1962 – but with the different grape names prominently displayed on the best wines to indicate what flavours the drinker should expect. This labelling by grape variety may seem commonplace now, because of the influence of New World wines, but it was novel in France, where more and more precise delineation of the origin of a wine was at the heart of the *appellation* system.

The people with the power to market and promote Alsace as a wine region of quality were the big merchant houses, and since their objective was to produce large quantities of wine at various but consistent levels of quality, they needed to blend from numerous different vineyards and hardly ever named the actual vineyard site, preferring to promote their own names as brands. This worked well enough, but when export markets like Britain and the United States became increasingly interested in single-vineyard wines from the top European wine regions during the 1980s, conflict between the merchants, the growers, and indeed the co-operatives became inevitable. Despite owning large tracts of Grand Cru vineyards, the leading merchant houses of Beyer, Trimbach and Hugel are most unwilling even now to put vineyard names on their wines and, indeed, they do not market Grand Cru wines, preferring to emphasize their companies' reputation instead.

Their position is understandable and not solely self-interested, because houses like Hugel have been most influential in promoting the quality classifications of Vendange Tardive for wines from super-ripe grapes, and Sélection de Grains Nobles for wines from grapes which have been affected by noble rot. However, the concept of superior vineyard sites is crucial in marginal vineyard regions where only the most favourable mesoclimates can truly excel. Good drainage and a good aspect to the sun are vital in any vineyard area at the limits of the vine's ability to ripen.

At present there are 50 Grand Cru sites covering 12 per cent of Alsace vineyards, which seems rather a lot. However, with lower permitted yields than those enjoyed by simple Alsace wines, and the use of only four noble grapes allowed – Riesling, Gewürztraminer, Pinot Gris and Muscat (and these must be unblended) – as yet the Grand Cru vineyards only produce four per cent of the region's wines.

There is no doubt that many of the best sites, exploited by the best growers, do produce unique personalities in the wine that dominate varietal character, especially in Rieslings. Those Grands Crus that genuinely deserve a special reputation, and whose vines are tended with care and respect, will eventually establish top reputations for themselves and be able to charge top prices. But there are still numerous wines sporting Grand Cru labels that offer nothing special. But then, the same is true in Burgundy. The Grand Cru classification is important, but the person who grows the grapes and makes the wines is always going to be the most important quality factor. It is almost always better to buy a supposedly less exalted wine from a committed, talented producer, than to pay extra money solely for the name of the vineyard. The vineyards' inherent quality merely offers the winemaker the chance to make great wine. It doesn't guarantee it.

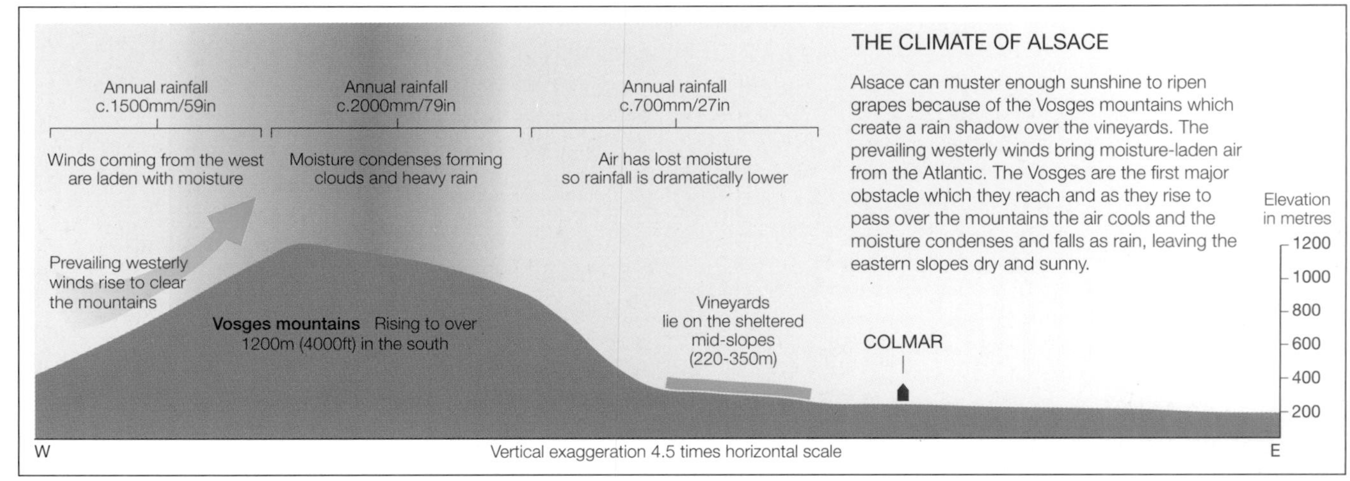

WHERE THE VINEYARDS ARE *There is not a single top-quality Alsace vineyard that doesn't rely on the protection of the Vosges mountains. The reason that most of the very best Alsace vineyards are in the central block of foothills between Bergheim and Gueberschwihr is that the Vosges mountains are at their highest and broadest at this point. Further north, the mountains are substantially lower, and do not provide such an efficient rain-shadow. Good wines are made in the northerly Bas-Rhin region of Alsace, but they rarely have the ripeness or intensity of those from the vineyards of the Haut-Rhin shown here. The map clearly demonstrates how the vines sweep up towards the wooded hilltops, yet peter out towards the flat valley floor. If you look at the location of the Grands Crus shown on this map, all of them are either in the lee of the hills or else, as in the case of Froehn and Mambourg, on large outcrops of steeply sloping land away from the foothills. The excellent drainage provided by the steepness of the slopes and the favourable aspect to the sun provided by the south- to south-east-facing angle of the slopes are crucial, particularly in a vineyard area such as Alsace, which is at the limits of the vine's ability to ripen. Every last minute of sunshine is vital.*

To qualify for the Grand Cru AC, a vineyard can only be planted with Riesling, Gewürztraminer, Pinot Gris or Muscat, but some of today's Grand Cru vineyards first made their reputation with other varieties. Sonnenglanz in Beblenheim was renowned for Sylvaner and Wintzenheim's Hengst used to be famous for Chasselas and Pinot-Auxerrois.

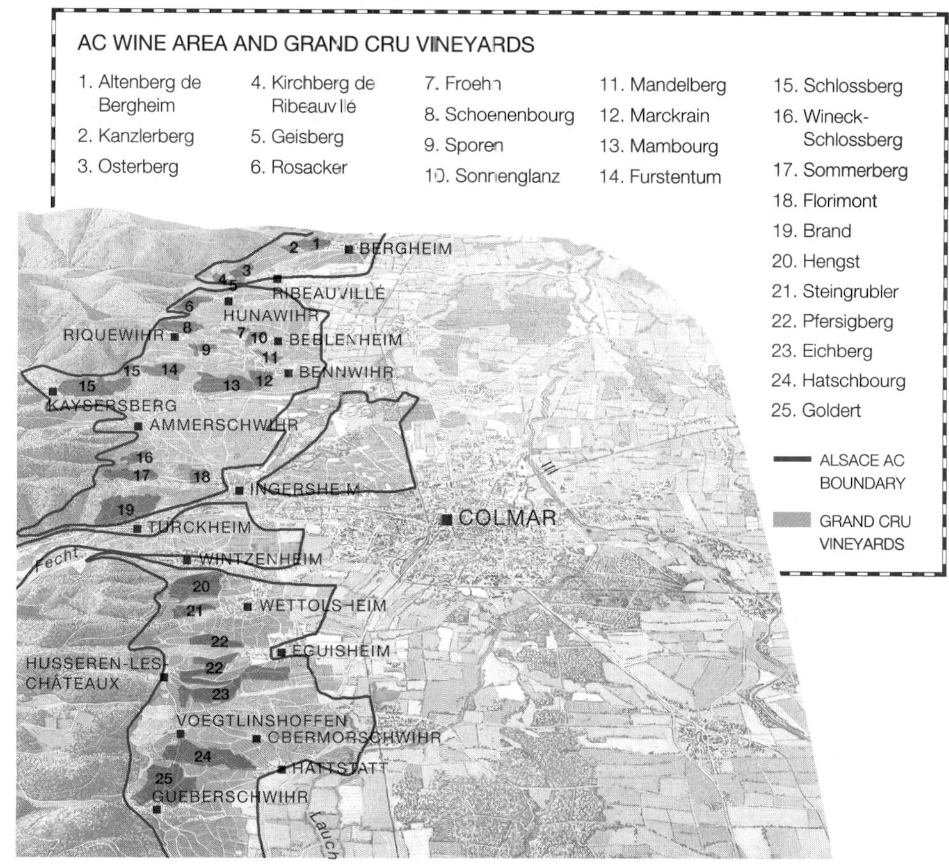

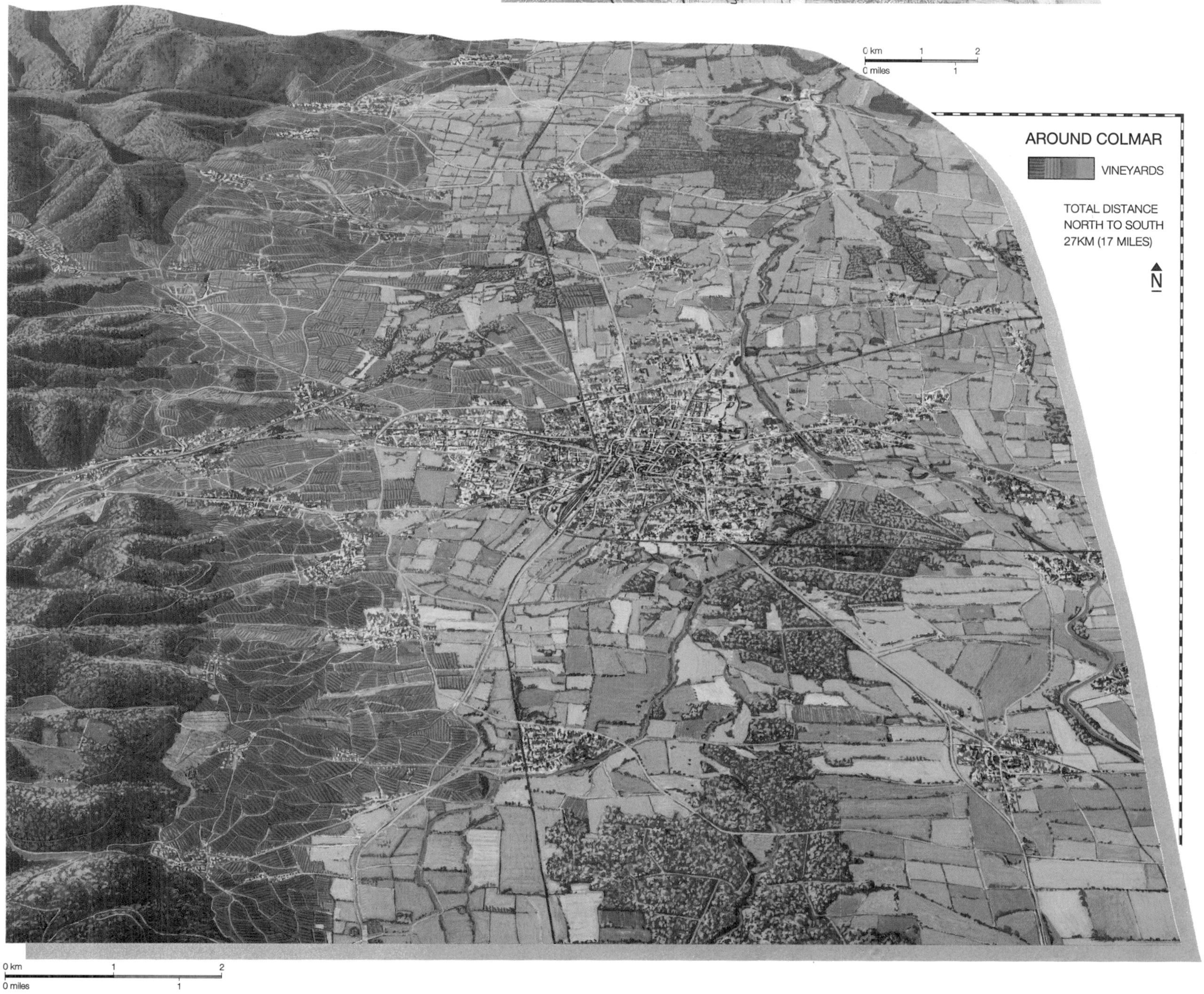

0 km 1 2
0 miles 1

AROUND COLMAR

VINEYARDS

TOTAL DISTANCE NORTH TO SOUTH 27KM (17 MILES)

N

0 km 1 2
0 miles 1

The Loire Valley

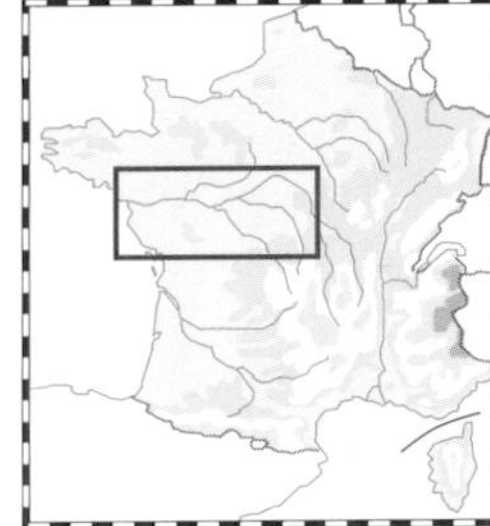

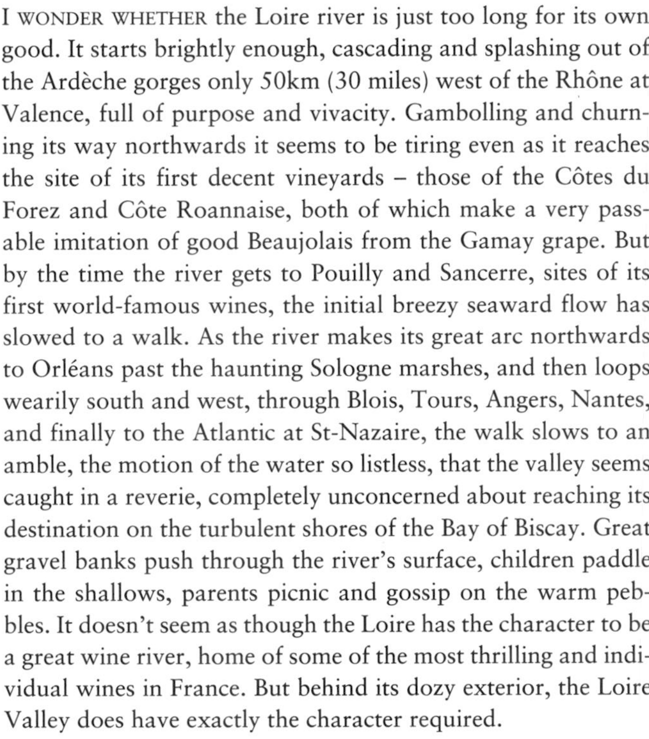

I wonder whether the Loire river is just too long for its own good. It starts brightly enough, cascading and splashing out of the Ardèche gorges only 50km (30 miles) west of the Rhône at Valence, full of purpose and vivacity. Gambolling and churning its way northwards it seems to be tiring even as it reaches the site of its first decent vineyards – those of the Côtes du Forez and Côte Roannaise, both of which make a very passable imitation of good Beaujolais from the Gamay grape. But by the time the river gets to Pouilly and Sancerre, sites of its first world-famous wines, the initial breezy seaward flow has slowed to a walk. As the river makes its great arc northwards to Orléans past the haunting Sologne marshes, and then loops wearily south and west, through Blois, Tours, Angers, Nantes, and finally to the Atlantic at St-Nazaire, the walk slows to an amble, the motion of the water so listless, that the valley seems caught in a reverie, completely unconcerned about reaching its destination on the turbulent shores of the Bay of Biscay. Great gravel banks push through the river's surface, children paddle in the shallows, parents picnic and gossip on the warm pebbles. It doesn't seem as though the Loire has the character to be a great wine river, home of some of the most thrilling and individual wines in France. But behind its dozy exterior, the Loire Valley does have exactly the character required.

NANTAIS

Since the river's flow is so mild, let's begin by looking at the vineyards at its western seaward end, and then push our way upstream aided by the brisk westerly winds, to Sancerre and Pouilly, several hundred miles away. Well, I have to admit these wines of the Nantais, as the western section is called, are indeed the mildest, the least memorable of the entire river. But they are some of the most famous, for this is the home of Muscadet and the four Muscadet *appellations*, which between them now constitute the second highest volume of French wine production after Bordeaux Rouge.

Muscadet is famous because it is so irreproachably, ultra-gluggably anonymous. At best it has a quenching freshness, a hint of lemon and pepper, a hint of apricot, and if you're lucky, a hint of cream. But we're talking about hints here – the one thing Muscadet never does is taste of a good deal of anything. And that is the basis for its success. Muscadet isn't the name of an area: it's the local name for the Burgundian grape variety of Melon de Bourgogne. Because this was the only variety in the Nantes region to survive the devastating frosts of 1709–10, it was enthusiastically adopted by the local growers. For over two centuries the Muscadet, and its more acidic neighbour the Gros Plant, did an excellent job of providing cheap, light white wine to accompany the superb local seafood.

But Parisians eat seafood too – from autumn to spring there are oyster stalls all over Paris' *boulevards* – and they adopted Muscadet as their seafood wine. During the 1970s and 1980s the export markets, in particular Great Britain, started drinking it as a kind of first step French dry white.

Given the stale, lifeless quality of much cheap Muscadet, it would be easy to say that this mirrored the sluggish brown estuarial waters of the river as it oozes through St-Nazaire. But Muscadet need not be a poor drink – it is only exploitation of an easily remembered name by greedy merchants that makes it so. Good Muscadet, especially from the delightful jumbled rolling countryside of the Sèvre-et-Maine area to the south-east of Nantes can be an absolute charmer: relatively neutral in taste, but with a streak of grapefruit and pepper assertiveness and a mild creaminess too. Because of the innate neutrality of the grape, the best examples are left on their yeast lees, and are undisturbed before being bottled directly off the lees – thereby capturing a little of the yeasty creaminess and also some of the

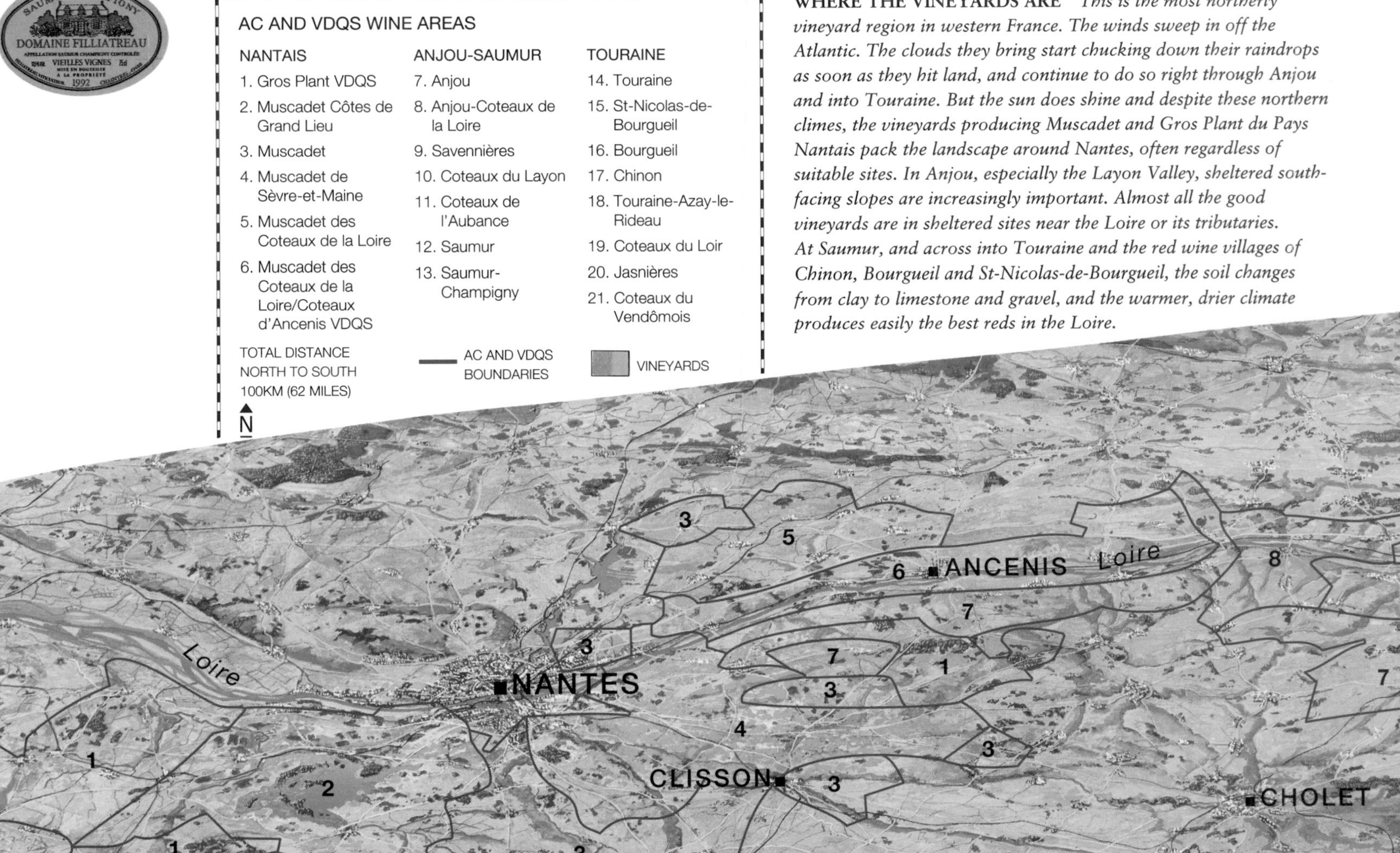

WHERE THE VINEYARDS ARE *This is the most northerly vineyard region in western France. The winds sweep in off the Atlantic. The clouds they bring start chucking down their raindrops as soon as they hit land, and continue to do so right through Anjou and into Touraine. But the sun does shine and despite these northern climes, the vineyards producing Muscadet and Gros Plant du Pays Nantais pack the landscape around Nantes, often regardless of suitable sites. In Anjou, especially the Layon Valley, sheltered south-facing slopes are increasingly important. Almost all the good vineyards are in sheltered sites near the Loire or its tributaries. At Saumur, and across into Touraine and the red wine villages of Chinon, Bourgueil and St-Nicolas-de-Bourgueil, the soil changes from clay to limestone and gravel, and the warmer, drier climate produces easily the best reds in the Loire.*

natural carbon dioxide in the wine. These wines are labelled *sur lie* and their blend of freshness, neutrality and soft texture do make them the perfect seafood wine. The tangy, acid Gros Plant du Pays Nantais, from the flat vineyards whipped by the salty ocean gales to the south-west of Nantes, can equal Muscadet as the perfect accompaniment to seafood. And if I had to choose one city in France in which to enjoy brilliant seafood, Nantes would take some beating.

ANJOU-SAUMUR

We need to head upstream – past Ancenis, where, surprisingly, the Alsace grape Pinot Gris makes a little, vaguely sweet wine under the title Malvoisie – before we really begin to discover the fascinating variety that belies the river's somnambulent appearance. This brings us to Anjou, with its plantations of the thoroughly difficult, exasperating, but sometimes majestically rewarding Chenin Blanc grape variety.

Much of Anjou isn't ideal for the vine – remember that the Loire Valley is as far north as the vine can ripen on the west coast of France, and most of Anjou is planted with cereal crops and vegetables, which are able to withstand the wind and rain better than any grape vines can. Those vines planted away from the various river valleys on exposed land are unlikely to produce anything but the most basic wine, generally a pale pink or the palest of pale whites. This explains why much of the cheap Anjou Rosé to be found sulking among the pink wines on every merchant's shelf is so poor – the grapes are grown on these exposed sites that would be better suited to cabbages, and they just never ripen.

But there are sheltered spots, usually facing towards the south-west, ideally planted on limestone or slate soils, that can produce some absolute corkers.

Most brilliant of these, and most unexpected, are the sweet wines that peek out from the folds of the river banks along the Layon Valley, and to a lesser extent, the Aubance Valley, both of which are formed by southern tributaries of the Loire river. The climatic feature that allows the Chenin Blanc to ripen at all along the cool Loire Valley is a generally warm early autumn that, with luck, pushes the late-ripening Chenin Blanc to a decent level of maturity. But the crucial factor which occurs on the banks of these little tributaries is the humidity that rises from the streams in warm autumns. This causes noble rot to develop in the grapes, which, as in Sauternes, naturally concentrates their sweetness to a remarkable degree. It doesn't happen often, but when it does, these luscious wines can be utterly magical.

This is a typical, gently sloping Loire vineyard. The land nearest the river is too fertile for vines.

Generally, however, the Chenin Blanc makes medium or dry wines in Anjou. The most famous of these is the dry Savennières, perched on the north side of the Loire just to the west of Angers, a gaunt, austere wine with the distant beauty of an ice maiden. Most of the rest of Anjou's whites come from vineyards spread across the fields south of the Loire, and nowadays benefit enormously from the legal inclusion of both Chardonnay and Sauvignon Blanc in the blend for Anjou Blanc, as well as greatly improved modern wine-making.

But for those grapes that fail to ripen properly, there may still be a haven: in the eastern part of Anjou bordering on Touraine, is Saumur, one of France's chief production centres for sparkling wine. The soils around Saumur are more chalky than in the rest of Anjou, and this encourages a certain leanness in the wines. This, combined with cool ripening conditions, often produces just the sort of acid base wine that sparkling wine manufacturers like.

Red wines are less successful in most of Anjou because the predominantly clay soils don't ripen the grapes sufficiently, but there are pockets of decent Gamay and Cabernet – the best

The classic Muscadet bottle has tapering, straight 'shoulders'.

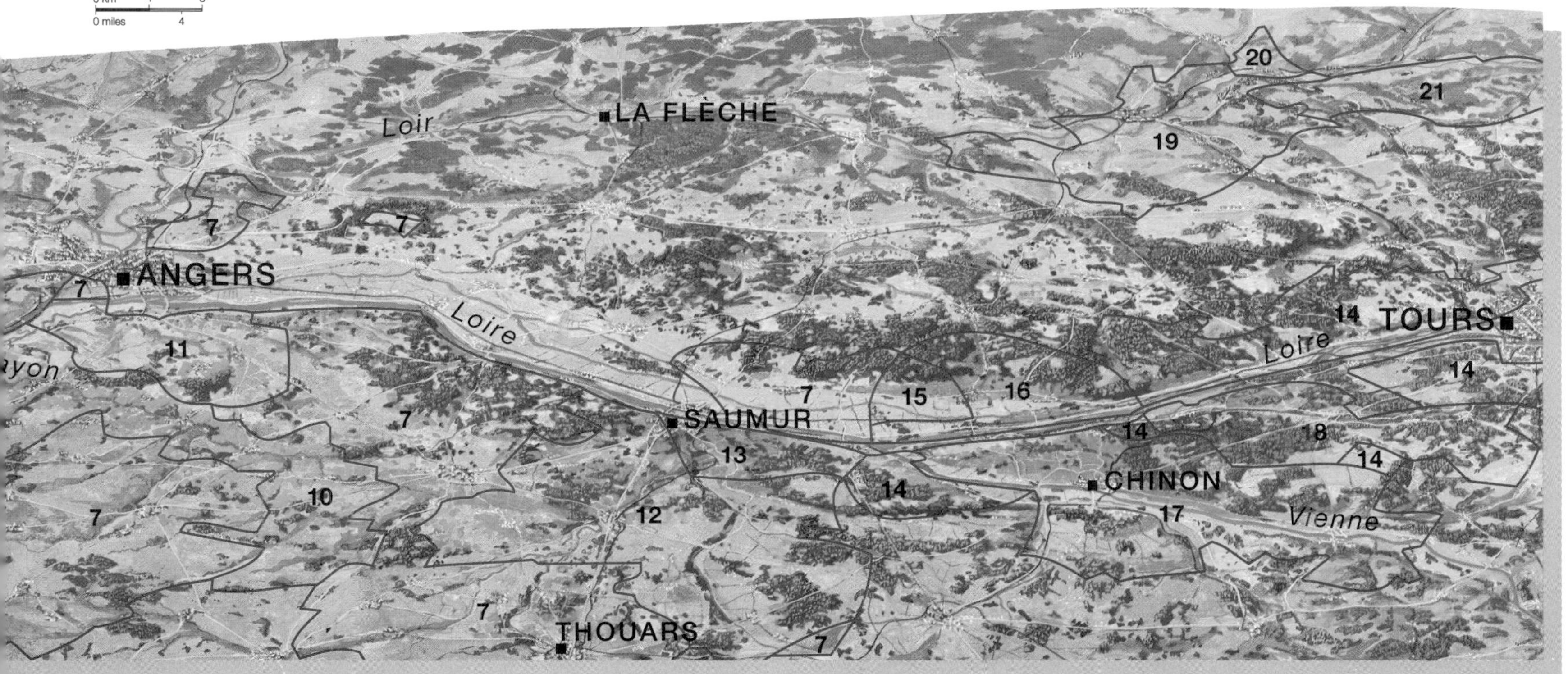

The Loire Valley was the playground of the Valois kings and the French court during the fifteenth and sixteenth centuries. Château de Chenonceau, on the river Cher, is just one of many outstanding Renaissance palaces built during the golden age of French culture.

WHERE THE VINEYARDS ARE *As we move east along the Loire Valley and into the centre of France, the climate becomes increasingly continental. The summer days get warmer and drier, but the nights are colder, and the winters can be bitter. All this is relative: we are still in a region at the northern limits of the ability to ripen grape varieties like Chenin Blanc, Sauvignon Blanc and Cabernet Franc, the chief varieties found in Touraine and the Central Loire vineyards.*

The two best wine areas of Touraine are the red areas of Chinon, and those of Bourgueil to the west of Tours and Vouvray. Tours itself is a beautiful town, and indeed the Touraine area between Chinon and Blois, with its ancient castles and market towns, merits at least as much attention as the wines.

As the river valley moves northward towards Orléans, the landscape is increasingly dominated by dense forests and the vineyards become fewer and further apart. The so-called 'centre of France' is one of the main regions for supplying oak for barrels, and stretches a good 240km (150 miles) or so south of the Loire, to Limoges in the south-west and the Allier Valley in the south-east. Sancerre and Pouilly are the last really important wine areas going upstream, but around Bourges there are three rather small but good areas – Menetou-Salon, Reuilly and Quincy.

Even higher up, towards the source of the Loire in the Ardèche hills, the Côte Roannaise and the Côtes du Forez produce some attractive, fresh, Gamay reds.

Cabernet vineyards can claim an Anjou-Villages *appellation* – and the Saumur-Champigny vineyards, to the south-east of the town, can make delightful fragrant light reds.

TOURAINE

The best Loire reds come from Touraine, a few miles to the east where the breezes seem to soften and the air to mellow. Touraine *appellations* St-Nicolas-de-Bourgueil, Bourgueil and Chinon use the Cabernet Franc grape to create gorgeously refreshing, tangy reds – wonderful young, but also capable of staying fresh for decades.

However, I have to admit that when I'm in Touraine, I find it difficult to concentrate on the wines, because there are more spectacular castles here than anywhere else in France. These bear testament to the Valois kings who, from the fifteenth century onwards, used Touraine for rest and relaxation. Many châteaux are open to visitors, and, though I'm not much of a one for ancient monuments, I have seen a few of these beauties, Chenonceaux, Amboise and Azay-le-Rideau among them.

And in any case, the only other famous wine in Touraine is Vouvray. Cheap Vouvray is a peculiarly nasty sulphurous brew of no virtue whatsoever. But the *appellation* is currently undergoing a revival. From a committed producer the dry, medium, sweet, or fizzy white wines of Vouvray can be a revelation, each of them fit for sipping on the balustrades of some of the most grandiose châteaux.

Vineyards are spread sparsely through the rest of Touraine, and as we follow the Loire up past Blois to Orléans, they become almost non-existent. Given that Orléans is the vinegar capital of France, this may be no bad thing, and it certainly makes one wonder what the local wines used to be like. Yet a tiny wine industry *does* survive here, and the wine is rather good. There's one excellent producer of Chardonnay (here called the Auvernat), namely the Clos de St-Fiacre estate. This is also the domain of several producers of a pleasant, pale, smoky pink wine called Gris Meunier – from the Pinot Meunier grape of Champagne fame! The strangest things do crop up along the Loire Valley.

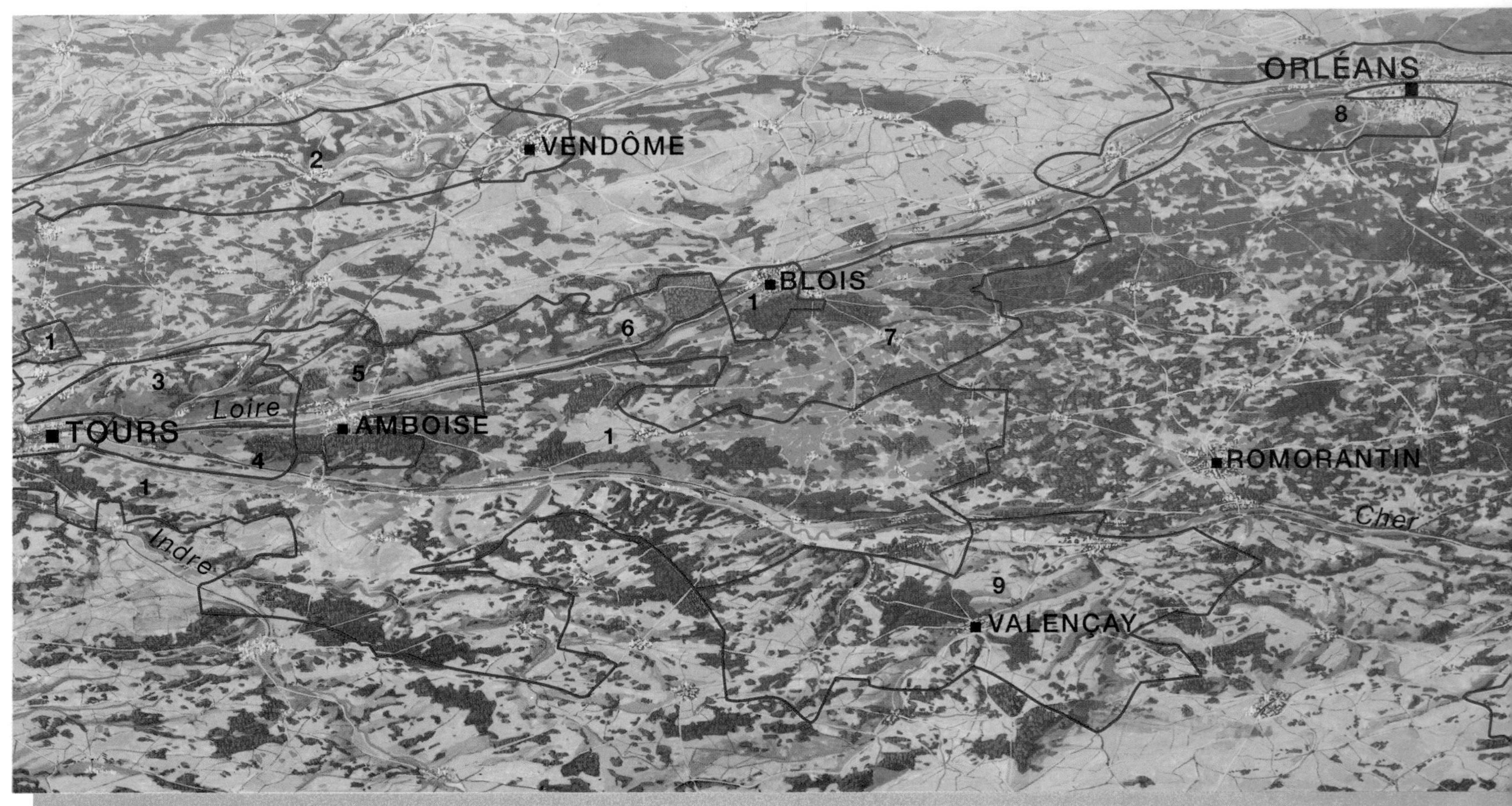

CENTRAL VINEYARDS

As the Loire turns to head south past the minor wine towns of Gien and Cosne, to the mainstream *appellations* of Sancerre and Pouilly-Blanc-Fumé – regarded by many as the quintessential Sauvignon Blanc styles – we come across a few plots of Chasselas. This is basically an eating grape, though it is used for wine in Alsace, Germany and Switzerland – and indeed it was grown for the dining-tables of Paris in the nineteenth century. Chasselas makes wine of just about no discernible character and yet here, in the fancy vineyards of Pouilly, in a world crying out for good Sauvignon Blanc, you still find the odd plot of Chasselas. Weird, but most of Pouilly is more than capable of looking after itself, making high-quality, high-priced Sauvignon. Sancerre across the river also concentrates on Sauvignon whites, but also makes a little rosé and is enjoying a barely explicable vogue for its red Pinot Noir. Red? Well, reddish. Just occasionally, it's an ethereal wine of delicate perfume. Rather more often, it isn't.

If I wanted red *or* rosé, I'd head south-west to Menetou-Salon, and for rosé only, further west still past the historic town of Bourges, to Reuilly. But these two villages, along with Reuilly's neighbour Quincy, are, like Sancerre, much better at making good, snappy Sauvignon whites, filled with the aroma of gooseberries and green grass.

UPPER LOIRE

We could continue up the river, eyes peeled for any signs of life beneath its placid surface, for another 160km (100 miles) and more until, past Roanne, in the Loire gorge, it finally shows fitful signs of life. But if we do, we won't find too many vines trailing down to the water's edge. There's no wine of much great consequence produced between Pouilly and Roanne. Even then, the Côte Roannaise red and the occasional rosé are only renowned by association: the famous Troisgros restaurant at Roanne often serves the first, bright, Gamay red as its house wine. Past the Loire gorge, the Côtes du Forez red is similar in style, but doesn't have a world-famous local chef to trumpet its charms.

THE SPARKLING WINES OF THE LOIRE

It would be easy to look upon the Loire Valley sparkling wine industry simply as a mechanism for soaking up large amounts of otherwise undrinkable local wines, since most of the best sparklers are made from a very acid base wine. But this wouldn't be fair, any more than it would be fair to describe Champagne in those terms. Although in a warm year the late-ripening Chenin Blanc can make excellent still wine, in the all-too-frequent cool years this high acid variety simply doesn't get ripe enough. So a cool year provides the perfect material for sparkling wines.

The best sparkling wines are made by the Champagne method, i.e. with a second fermentation in the bottle, and tend to come from cool vineyards of limestone-dominated soils and subsoils. Both Saumur and Vouvray, which produce the two most important sparkling wine *appellations* in the region, are predominantly limestone areas.

Vouvray and its neighbouring *appellation* of Montlouis use only Chenin Blanc for their fizz and, if you give the bottles a few years to soften, they attain a delicious nutty, honeyed quality, yet retain the zing of Chenin acidity. Saumur Mousseux is usually based on Chenin but may include other varieties like Chardonnay, Sauvignon and Cabernet Franc. Saumur Mousseux made from 100 per cent Chenin is often too lean, so the addition of Cabernet and Chardonnay in particular, adds a very welcome softness.

A new *appellation* – Crémant de Loire, covering Anjou and Touraine – stipulates lower vineyard yields and requires 150kg (330lb) of grapes to make one hectolitre of juice, rather than the 130kg (286½lb) permitted for Saumur. This lower yield means the grapes are not pressed so savagely and so the bitter elements present in the skins and pips are not extracted. The *appellation* also stipulates a longer aging period before release, giving a gentler foaming mousse and attractive hints of yeast and honey. The wines are generally superior to Saumur, but the title sounds rather generic and catch-all, and so it hasn't had the success it deserves.

Very occasionally you may find a Cabernet-based fizzy red, grassy and full of fruit, ideal for picnic glugging.

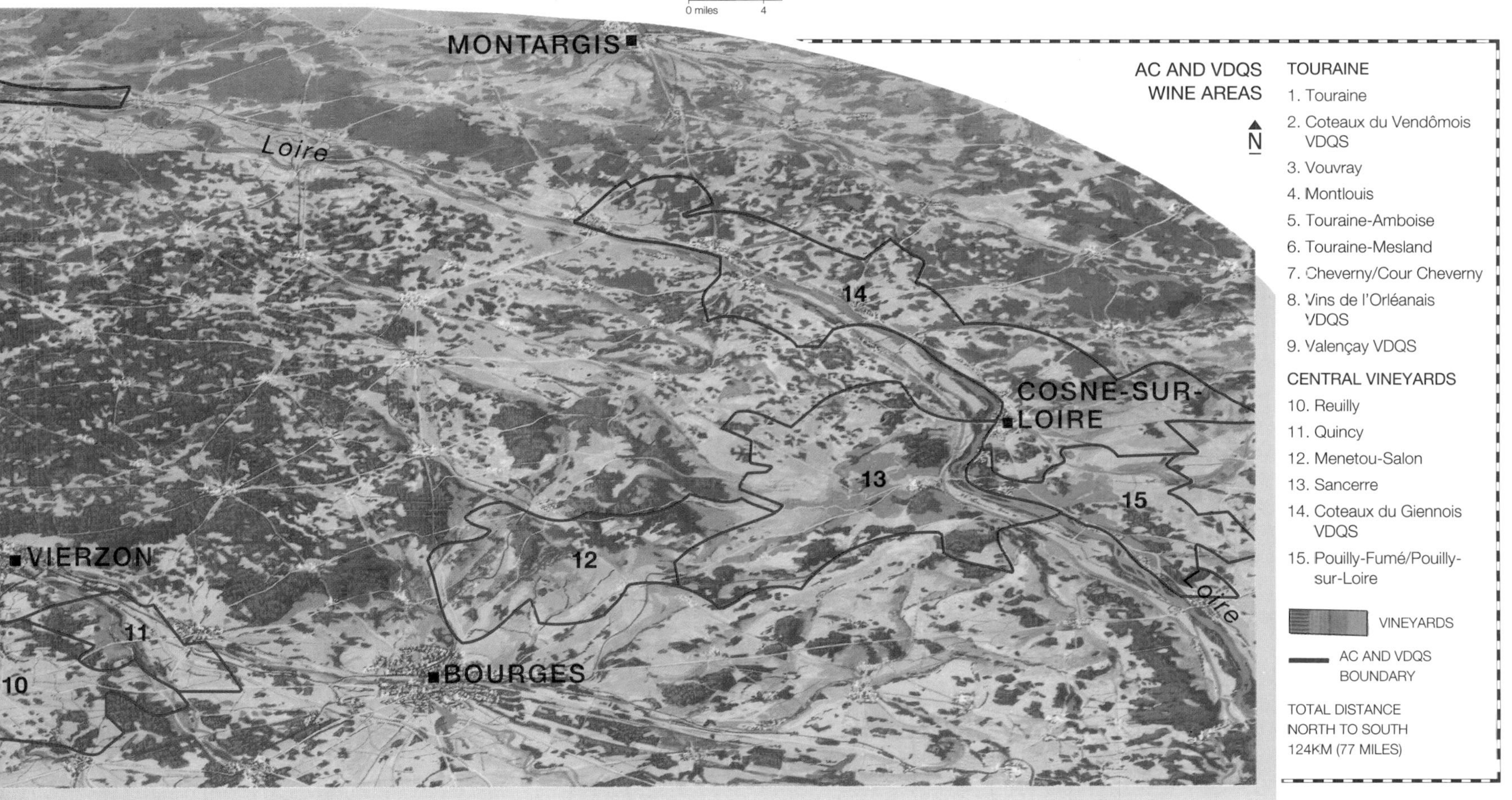

Anjou-Saumur

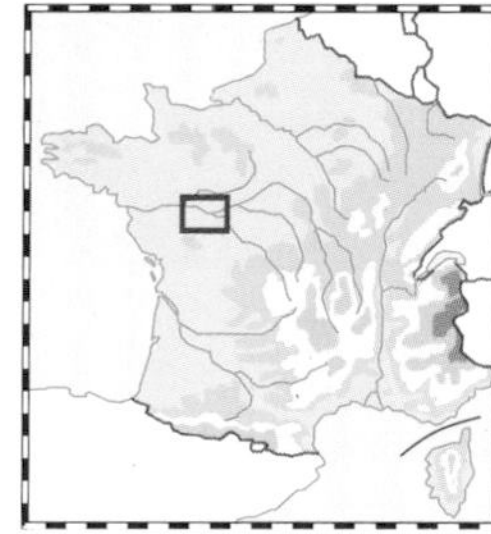

RED GRAPES
Groslot is used for rosé and lesser reds, Cabernets Franc and Sauvignon for the better wines. Gamay is also widely planted, and there is some Malbec, called Cot here.

WHITE GRAPES
Chenin Blanc is the main grape, with increasing amounts of Chardonnay and Sauvignon Blanc.

CLIMATE
A mild maritime climate moderated by the influence of the Gulf Stream produces warm summers and mild autumns and winters. Ripening can be a problem.

SOIL
In Anjou the soil is predominantly dark slate and clay with areas of more permeable shale and gravel which favour the Cabernet grapes. Much of Saumur is limestone characterized by pale outcrops of a chalky freestone known as *tuffeau blanc*.

ASPECT
In this area of low hills specific aspect to the sun is vital for ripening. The best sites are on the steeper slopes and face south-west, south or south-east.

AT LAST ANJOU HAS GOT ITSELF a decent wine in which to incorporate its name – Anjou-Villages, red wine from a relatively recent grouping of 46 different Anjou villages deemed to have better than average vineyard sites. Only Cabernet Franc and Cabernet Sauvignon varieties may be used for Anjou-Villages and, with the lucky coincidence of the excellent 1988, 89 and 90 vintages providing ripe, juicy, dark grapes to get the new *appellation* started, there's every sign that it will be a success.

These hinterland villages need all the help they can get. They are centred on Brissac-Quincé and spread across the indeterminate rolling agricultural land running from west of Angers across to Saumur. The sweet wines of the Layon Valley, the small, high-class, dry white *appellation* of Savennières, west of Angers, and the sparkling and red wines of Saumur are among the several enclaves of high-quality wine in Anjou. Despite these, the image of the province has been relentlessly dragged down for decades by the mediocrity of most Anjou Rosé and the over-sulphured, off-dry Anjou Blanc.

Well, self-help is at hand. The drift away from rosé wines by the drinking public forced the Anjou winemakers to rethink. Many of the vineyards in Anjou are too exposed and the soil is too cool and moist for them to be able to produce anything special, and, apart from ripping up their vineyards, growers there have little choice but to continue with the uninspired Groslot red grape for rosé, or the unsuitable late-ripening Chenin for whites. Initially it was thought that rosé drinkers would trade up to a superior Cabernet d'Anjou Rosé. They didn't: they traded out of rosé altogether, mostly to white – but not to Anjou Blanc!

The trouble is, much of Anjou isn't particularly suited to grape-growing – the great open spaces full of cereals and sunflowers and vegetables bear witness to that. But modern winemaking methods can and do help. The Beaujolais method of fermentation – carbonic maceration – is increasingly employed for the widely planted Gamay grape, and it makes a fairly rustic, but juicy, purplish red if the grapes are ripe. For the Cabernet-based wines the problem is how to get enough colour and flavour from grapes that rarely ripen fully in Anjou without risking bitter, tannic harshness from unripe skins and pips. The local producers have developed a method of fermenting in sealed vats and bubbling nitrogen through the liquid: this method quickly extracts enough flavour and colour yet doesn't exaggerate the tannins. Similarly white Anjou producers are using stainless steel, cold fermentation and a period of skin contact (allowing the grapes to steep in their juice before fermentation), thus improving the wine's fruit and balance. Add in a permitted 20 per cent of Chardonnay or Sauvignon with the Chenin, and Anjou Blanc is now often attractively dry, rather than unattractively sweetish.

WHERE THE VINEYARDS ARE *The border between Anjou and the Muscadet region of Nantais is only just to the west of the map and these wild, open acres enjoy the mixed blessing of a maritime climate. They do avoid the extremes of temperature of a continental climate and, in general, enjoy a reasonably balmy autumn, but they also get the damp, westerly winds which drive inland from the Bay of Biscay. A certain amount of Coteaux de la Loire is grown in these vineyards, but it's hard work. Then see how dramatically things change where the Layon river joins the Loire at Chalonnes.*

On the Loire's north bank, suddenly there are sufficient plateaux to protect vineyards beneath them – and Savennières immediately benefits from this protection. The Layon meanders in to join the Loire from the south-east. Its northern banks have ridges of hills and forests to protect the vines and allow the long autumn ripening which the grapes need to make great sweet wine. The land becomes wooded and undulating from here, right across to Saumur. This creates a myriad of mesoclimates where even a late ripener like Chenin Blanc has a chance to build up sugar. At Saumur we are into the chalky freestone subsoil which also dominates Touraine, and gives excellent conditions for white grapes.

SAVENNIÈRES

The one dry Anjou white which has always been revered, if not exactly fêted, is Savennières. The vineyards don't amount to more than 60 hectares (150 acres), looking out over the islands and channels of the wide Loire towards the mouth of the Layon river, but they can produce the Loire's best dry whites. When this *appellation* was granted in 1952 the permitted yield was set artificially low, and the minimum alcohol level extremely high, because the wine was then generally sweet, and good sweet French wines always have very low permitted yields and high minimum alcohol levels. However Savennières is nowadays almost always dry, and the restrictions are a mixed blessing. On the slate and clay soils, high alcohol is only

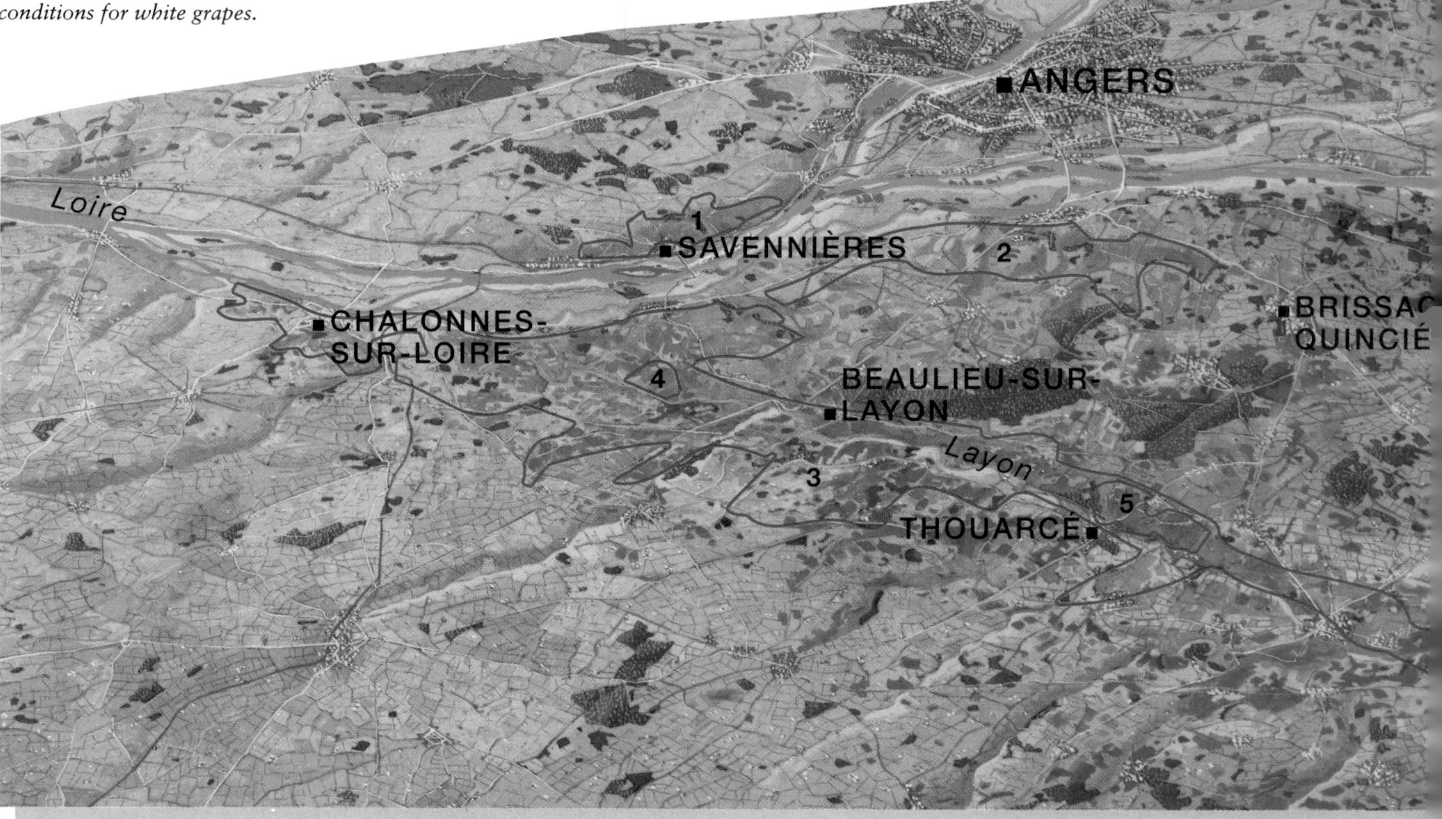

CLOS DE LA Coulée de Serrant 1991

possible most years because of the low yield, and it is this rare, high ripeness level from the tricky Chenin grape that gives Savennières wine the ability to age and improve for a generation or more. There are two small Grands Crus – la Roche-aux-Moines and Coulée-de-Serrant, whose steep slopes and excellent exposure to the sun further intensify the taut, but fathoms-deep, flavour of these wines.

SWEET WINES OF THE LAYON VALLEY

Across from Savennières the Layon river joins the Loire, and it is along its northern banks that the Chenin grape produces some of the finest sweet wines in France. Even so, it is a struggle to achieve the necessary overripeness, and only the most favoured sites manage it on a regular basis. Great sweet wines can only be made when the grapes are attacked by the noble rot fungus which intensifies the sugar so that it becomes a syrupy goo. Long, warm autumn days and early morning mists provide perfect conditions for noble rot to develop.

For the last few miles before the two rivers join, the influence of both causes morning mists along the Layon. In particular at Quarts de Chaume and Bonnezeaux, a perfect sheltered south to south-west exposure allows grapes every chance to ripen, then rot. Even so, noble rot doesn't happen uniformly. Often the pickers have to comb the vines again and again, picking the grapes that have nobly rotted, sometimes grape by grape, and leaving the rest to develop the welcome fungus.

Coteaux du Layon covers 25 communes in the Layon Valley. Coteaux du Layon-Villages covers six of the best seven villages between Faye d'Anjou and St-Aubin de Luigné. Coteaux du Layon-Chaume applies to the best village in the valley. Quarts de Chaume and Bonnezeaux are the two Grands Crus with perfect conditions and slopes for when the autumn weather holds. Both the Coteaux de l'Aubance and the Coteaux de la Loire make reasonable sweetish white wines.

SAUMUR

Interestingly, there is an occasional, rare sweet Chenin called Coteaux de Saumur produced at the eastern end of Anjou, but Saumur is far more important for its sparkling wine and its Cabernet reds. The soil changes as you head south-east from Angers to Saumur. The dark clay and slate of Angers has been replaced mostly by limestone, especially a layer of chalky freestone called *tuffeau blanc*. This freestone layer is over 50m (165ft) thick in places, and not only provides a completely different subsoil for vines, in particular along the south bank of the Loire where the red grape vineyards are situated, but it also offers the perfect medium for wine cellars.

Champagne in north-eastern France is built on chalk, its vines grow on chalk, its wines mature in underground chalk cellars. It is nearly the same in Saumur, where there are reckoned to be 1000km (620 miles) of underground passages and cellars. Sparkling Saumur is based on Chenin grapes, but Chardonnay and Sauvignon are permitted up to 20 per cent as they are in the rare still Saumur Blanc. Red grapes are permitted up to 60 per cent for the white sparkler and 100 per cent for the rosé. Still Saumur Rouge is based on Cabernet Franc, though Cabernet Sauvignon and the rare Pineau d'Aunis are permitted. On Saumur's chalky soils the Cabernet Franc grape does best, producing light but often attractively grassy reds, and, in the small Saumur-Champigny area, especially on the freestone plateaux south-east of the town, this is often married to a keen, mouth-watering blackcurrant and raspberry fruit.

Many consider the Chenin grape reaches its dry white wine potential in Savennières.

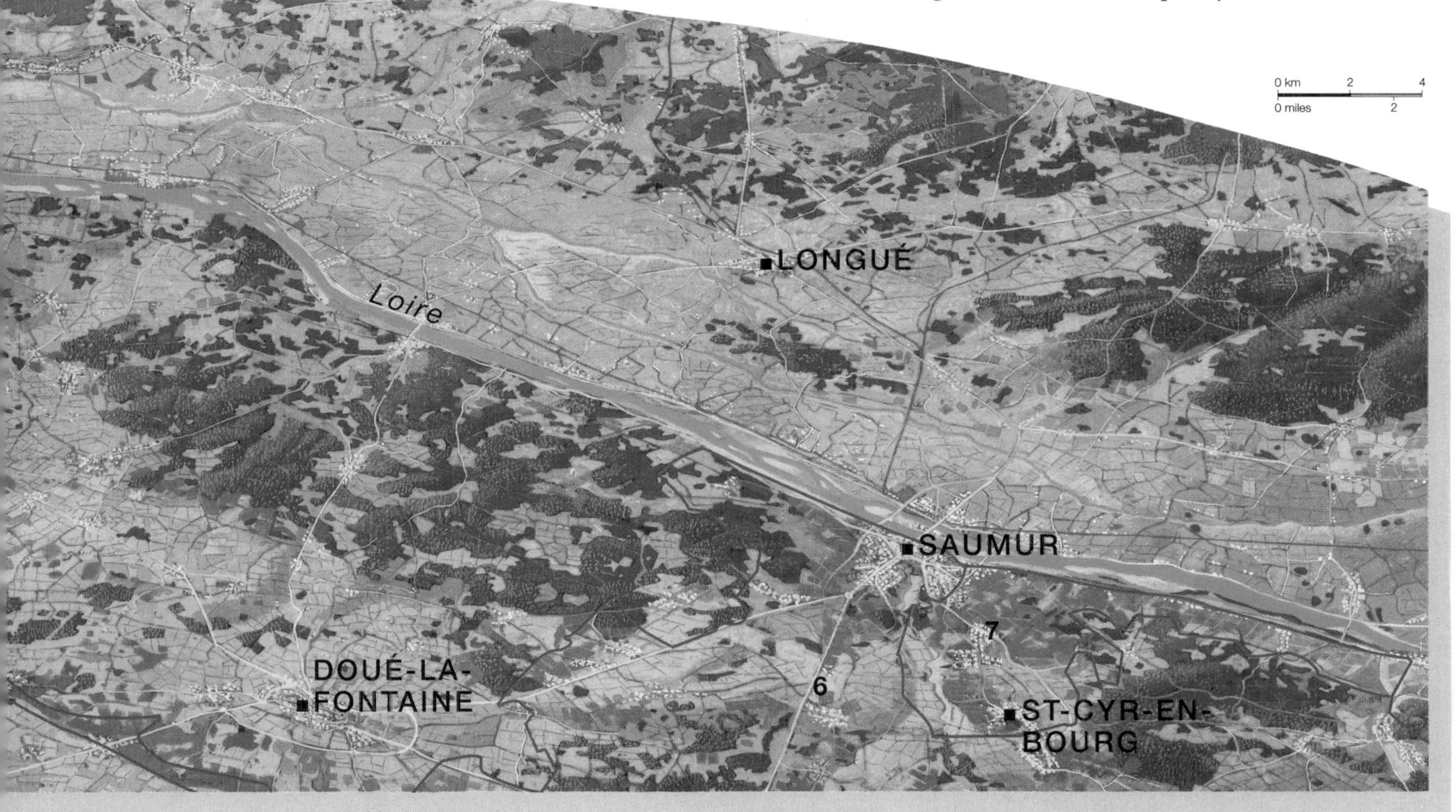

AC WINE AREAS

1. Savennières (including Coulée-de-Serrant and la Roche-aux-Moines)
2. Coteaux de l'Aubance
3. Coteaux du Layon
4. Quarts de Chaume
5. Bonnezeaux
6. Saumur
7. Saumur-Champigny

VINEYARDS

AC BOUNDARIES

TOTAL DISTANCE NORTH TO SOUTH 40KM (25 MILES)

N

Touraine

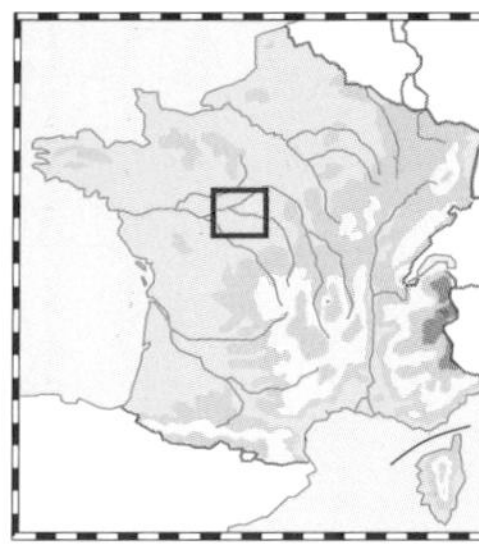

RED GRAPES
Gamay accounts for two-thirds of Touraine red wines, though the quality grape is Cabernet Franc. Other lesser varieties are Cabernet Sauvignon, Malbec (Cot) and Pineau d'Aunis.

WHITE GRAPES
Chenin Blanc dominates, with Chardonnay and Sauvignon Blanc both fairly widely planted.

CLIMATE
The climate is similar to Anjou-Saumur but with rather lower rainfall. Early autumn is usually sunny, favouring late-ripening varieties such as Chenin Blanc.

SOIL
The flatland near the river is mostly sandy alluvial flood-plain with outcrops of sandy gravel; the slopes and plateaux are mostly limestone and chalky freestone (*tuffeau blanc*) with some clay.

ASPECT
The vineyards are at 40 to 100m (130 to 330ft), usually on south-facing slopes.

THIS IS ABOUT THE ONLY TIME in this book I'm going to give lumps of granite and slabs of brick and mortar precedence over the flavour of the wines or the contours of the vineyard sites, because Touraine, with its array of peerless châteaux, is different. Why were these Renaissance masterpieces built along the banks of the Loire, and its tributaries the Cher, the Indre and the Vienne, which join the main river to the west of Tours? What were they used for and by whom?

Proximity to Paris, and climate, provide the keys. As the Loire flows down from Orléans to Tours and Saumur, its vast forests are full of game for hunting, and its fertile river valley land is ideally suited to the production of fruit and vegetables. It was this natural abundance of the land, and the mild, benign climate that made this middle section of the Loire the obvious choice for the Court of France to use as a playground, a place to build holiday homes – well, holiday castles, this being the Court – and to relax from the rigours of ruling.

The legacy is some truly magnificent châteaux – from a whole hatful I will pick just a few. The dream-like Azay-le-Rideau – where Balzac found inspiration for several of his novels – is set serenely on an island in the middle of the Indre river. Part of Chenonceaux, a château of an extraordinary haughty grandeur, actually straddles the river Cher. Chambord, east of Blois, is the largest of all the châteaux, with 440 rooms and 365 fireplaces – one for each day of the year. Chinon, on the Vienne river, towers above the pretty gabled town where Rabelais learned to drink deep and long, where Richard the Lionheart died, and where Joan of Arc first pumped some courage into the veins of her King, Charles VII of France.

Most of Touraine is so suitable for vegetables, flowers, cereals – and virtually anything else you could want to plant – that the vine, accustomed to thriving in infertile conditions, is often conspicuous by its absence. The cattle fatten contentedly on lush river meadows, the forests are still thick with game. In early summer the whole region seems to blaze with flowers. By late summer the trees are weighed down with France's best pears and apples, cherries, nuts and plums. And early autumn – well, early autumn generally sees a wonderfully calming warmth bathing the valley. It's too late to have any effect on vegetables or fruit, but it is what makes fine wine possible in these vineyards of France's north-west.

The Chenin Blanc, the Loire's native white grape, is late-ripening, and desperately needs the late autumn of this region to get past its initial thin, sour state. Chardonnay and Sauvignon Blanc both ripen more easily and are quite widely planted. The reds also need the extra warmth of autumn, and are primarily made from the Bordeaux grapes – Cabernet Franc, Cabernet Sauvignon and Malbec (or Cot as it is called here). The Gamay grape variety, though more used to the hot summer weather of Beaujolais in southern Burgundy, is equally important in Touraine's reds.

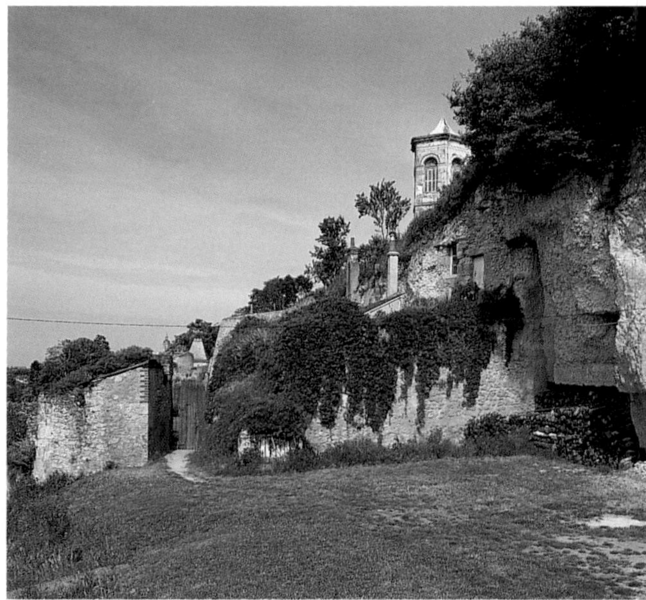

Vouvray is one of the largest Loire appellations *and vines have been planted here since the fourth century. Gaston Huet's vineyard, pictured here, lies on a chalky freestone subsoil and has subterranean cellars which have been hewn out of the cliff face.*

WINE AREAS

Our map covers the heart of Touraine, and its most famous wines. These comprise Vouvray, to the east of Tours, and the group of red wines – Chinon, Bourgueil and St-Nicolas-de-Bourgueil – which lie to the west.

Touraine has a general *appellation* for reds, whites, pinks and sparklers that covers the less-favoured vineyard areas. Three superior villages – Mesland, Amboise and Azay-le-Rideau – can tack their own name on to the Touraine AC.

South-east of Blois, the strange Romorantin grape makes fairly hairy wine at Cour-Cheverny. North of Tours on the Loir (sic) river, Jasnières makes unforgiving, but occasionally rewarding, stone-dry whites from the Chenin.

VOUVRAY AND MONTLOUIS

However, to see just how good the Chenin grape can be, we need to come back to the Loire, to the vineyards of Vouvray that lie above the low chalky cliffs lining the north bank of the river. Using only Chenin Blanc, Vouvray comes in a welter of styles, and the sparkling version is the best of the Loire fizzes.

The still wines can be searingly dry, pushing anyone's sensitive gums to the limit when young, but undergoing a magical transformation over 20 to 30 years. Vouvray can also be sumptuously rich, developing increasingly more nuances of flavour for half a century or more. Or it can be anywhere between: the mildly sweet *demi-sec* (when made carefully by a committed producer) is a heavenly balance between high acid, mellow quince and honeysuckle fruit.

A word of caution: cheap, anonymous Vouvray *demi-sec* is likely to be poor stuff. If you do want a similar style to Vouvray but at a lower price, Montlouis, south-east of Vouvray, is more likely to provide good examples. Vouvray's

0 km 2 4
0 miles 3

AC WINE AREAS

1. St-Nicolas-de-Bourgueil
2. Bourgueil
3. Chinon
4. Montlouis
5. Vouvray

VINEYARDS

AC BOUNDARIES

TOTAL DISTANCE NORTH TO SOUTH 50KM (30 MILES)

N

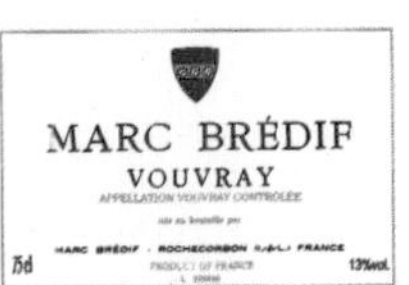

wide variety of styles is due to soil and to climate. Those low cliffs are of an unusual chalky limestone, with a topsoil made of a mix of clay and gravel, and sometimes flint. This limestone base means the wines retain acid even in the hottest years. When the autumn is late – and sometimes this season can continue into November – great sweet wines are possible either through dehydration of the grapes by heat (as in 1989), or by noble rot (as in 1990).

In less warm years, *demi-sec* is the more popular style. When the autumn fails, only the dry version is possible, but most wines will end up being made into fizz.

CHINON, BOURGUEIL & ST-NICOLAS-DE-BOURGUEIL

The Loire's best reds (as well as a little rosé and white) come from the trio of villages at the western end of the map, where the Vienne river slides in from the south-east to join the Loire. The reds of Chinon, Bourgueil and St-Nicolas-de-Bourgueil are remarkable wines, because so much of their character seems to lie in a fresh, joyous raspberry fruit, and a summer scent of warm earth and stone, and yet they can age as well as all but the best wines from Bordeaux.

Again, climate and soil give some clues. The Cabernet Franc, the dominant grape here, doesn't need as much warmth to ripen as the Cabernet Sauvignon (though a few producers use a little of this too). Consequently the mild summer is sufficient to produce a pleasant, light-bodied, red fruit character. When the autumn is good, the wines dramatically deepen in colour and strength, yet never lose their gorgeous soft-centred raspberry and sweet earth perfume, sometimes heightened by a haunting scent of violets.

This whole area has less rain than its neighbours, but Bourgueil in particular has a warm, dry mesoclimate because its best vineyards are protected from cold, wet, northerly winds by a 120m- (400-ft) high wooded plateau.

The deepest, darkest wines are from the *coteaux* slopes of chalky freestone and limestone clay soil that run up towards the plateau. Below these, good wines come from gravelly soils,

WHERE THE VINEYARDS ARE *This map shows the heart of the Loire, where the best red wines are produced, as well as excellent whites, dry or sweet, and fine fizz. The reds come from the western end, where the river Vienne joins the Loire from the south-east. The area between the river, St-Nicolas-de-Bourgueil and Bourgueil is mostly flat, alluvial flood-plain, but there are a few outcrops of sandy gravel producing light Bourgueil reds. However, all the best Bourgueil comes from the vineyards you can see beneath the wooded brow of hillside to the north. This plateau protects the vines and provides Bourgueil with a particularly dry mesoclimate. The lower slopes here are relatively gravelly, the higher slopes, especially those to the north-east of Bourgueil above Restigné, are limestone clays over chalky freestone and produce the deeper, darker reds.*

Chinon's best reds come from the slopes directly to the east of the town where clay and gravel mix with limestone, and from the more chalky slopes to the north and west. There are also sandy soils along the banks of the river Vienne planted with vines that yield light reds and rosés. The vineyards of Vouvray mostly lie on plateaux above the chalky cliffs between Tours and Noizay. The similar wines of Montlouis mostly grow east of the city along a gently sloping, sandy clay plateau above reasonably chalky subsoil that inclines southwards towards the river Cher.

while there are outcrops of sandy gravel on the Loire banks that give light, easy-drinking flavours. Often the best results come from blending the wines from the different soils, since Bourgueil from the *coteaux* alone can be rather aggressive and joyless on its own, requiring years of maturity to show its underlying fruit and perfume.

St-Nicolas-de-Bourgueil can be divided into two main vineyard types: those planted on gravel terraces, and others planted on limestone slopes. Generally the wines are a blend of both. They can use either their own name or that of Bourgueil.

Chinon's reds are generally more perfumed and approachable from a young age, but they, too, are often best when the wines from clay and gravel soils are mixed with wine from the limestone slopes. However, their precocious charm doesn't stop the best of them aging at least as well as a pretty good-quality Médoc from Bordeaux.

SANCERRE & POUILLY

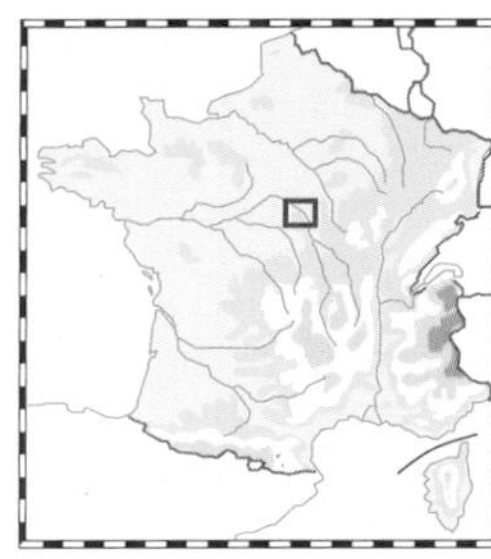

RED GRAPES
Pinot Noir is the main red grape with some Pinot Gris used in Reuilly for rosé.

WHITE GRAPES
Sauvignon Blanc is king here, occupying the best sites throughout the region. There is some Chasselas on inferior sites in Pouilly.

CLIMATE
As the maritime influences wane, summers are longer and warmer, winters cooler and drier. Frost can be a problem early in the year. Shelter from the prevailing north-east wind is important.

SOIL
The soil here is limestone-based with the shallow, pebbly, Kimmeridgian formations of Sancerre producing the best vineyards. Flinty deposits in Sancerre and Pouilly are supposed to affect the wine's flavour.

ASPECT
The hills rise to around 350m (1150ft). Deep crevices in the slopes produce favourable south and south-westerly aspects.

I'M ALWAYS HEARTILY GLAD to see the great mound of Sancerre looming up in front of me on the banks of the Loire. At last. A landmark in the featureless centre of France, a reference point I can relate to. I've approached Sancerre from all directions, but usually from the empty, disorientating acres of waterways and marshland which make up the Sologne, the setting for Alain-Fournier's wonderful novel, *Le Grand Meaulnes*.

This area, more than any other, conveys the sense of isolation that pervades France's lonely heart. And then up looms the hill of Sancerre: beautiful buildings, ramparts, a town square full of bustle and bars and restaurants – and a view. After so much flat land, a view across the low valleys, the exposed ridges of chalk, or up the lazy course of the Loire river as it sidles past from the south – any kind of view – and then I'm back into the square for a seat in the sun and a glass of cold, crisp white wine. Sancerre.

Of all the French whites that I order in bars or restaurants round the world, Sancerre is still the one I choose most often. Although the price of Sancerre has risen and its quality has just as frequently dipped as excessive popularity has taken its toll, it still represents for me the epitome of the thirst-quenching, tangy, tingly fresh, dry white wine.

In fact there is a family of five white wines (six, if we include the rare Coteaux du Giennois from a few miles downstream) that use the Sauvignon Blanc grape to excellent effect. This little patch of France also produces red and rosé wines, but it is the palate-teasing white from the Sauvignon Blanc that made the region famous, and that still produces its best wines by far.

WINE AREAS

Sancerre is the biggest and most important of these *appellations*, covering 14 communes on the west bank of the Loire, the best of which are clustered beneath the steep slopes close to the town of Sancerre itself. Pouilly-Fumé is a white-only *appellation* on the Loire's east bank, a couple of miles upstream from Sancerre. Its wines are of equal quality but sometimes they have slightly more weight, a little more coffee-bean smokiness, and a little less gooseberry crunch.

Menetou-Salon makes red, white and rosé from ten different communes in the charmingly haphazard countryside between Sancerre and Bourges. Its whites, from the Sauvignon grape, are of a similar standard to Sancerre and are always cheaper. Quincy is a small *appellation* on sandy gravel just west of Bourges, producing white Sauvignon wines with a marked, but attractive, gooseberry aggression. A couple of miles further west is the even smaller Reuilly, which produces good whites on its chalky soil, adequate reds, and surprisingly good pale rosés from Pinot Gris. One of the local growers rejoices in the name of Olivier Cromwell, but there are no other outward signs of anti-royalist feeling.

All of these smaller *appellations* are now benefiting from the rise in popularity of Sancerre and Pouilly-Fumé. However, this rise is extremely recent. Until the 1950s, these were country wines no-one had ever heard of. Luckily, a merry band of Parisian journalists and restaurant-owners, enjoying a few jaunts from the capital, took to these sharp, tangy whites gulped down with their lunch on the banks of the Loire. Sancerre and Pouilly-Fumé consequently became chic first in Paris, and then throughout the world.

Yet Sancerre and Pouilly weren't even white wine areas to start with. The present fad for pink and red Sancerre mirrors the situation before the phylloxera bug destroyed the vineyards in the late nineteenth century. Because of the area's proximity to Paris, the fields were intensively farmed and mostly packed with high-yielding, low-quality, red vines whose vast volumes of hooch disappeared down a million uncritical Parisian throats. A further 2000 hectares (5000 acres) or so made reasonable red from Pinot Noir. After the phylloxera scourge, Sauvignon Blanc was chosen as the grape variety to replant both because it was a high yielder, and because it was easier to graft onto phylloxera-resistant rootstocks.

Pinot Noir, for the reds, was generally replanted only in the less suitable, exposed, north-facing plots in Sancerre, and not at all in Pouilly. There are now about 1600

WHERE THE VINEYARDS ARE *Look at that tiny town of Sancerre, perched on its hill, and surrounded by a tight little clutch of slopes and valleys as the limestone rears briefly but dramatically out of the dull, flat farmland of the centre of France. The steep south-facing slopes of these hills are crammed with vineyards. Then look across the river Loire and down a mile or two towards Pouilly. From a landscape of bland cereal fields and meadows, suddenly there is a rash of vineyards. These two vineyard areas make similar wine which is seen by many as the most perfect example of the tangy, grassy-gooseberry dry styles that are the hallmark of good Sauvignon Blanc the world over.*

They are both only this good because of the soil type and the mesoclimate. The open spaces of this part of France would usually not be warm enough to ripen Sauvignon, or Pinot Noir which Sancerre uses for rosé and red. Limestone is the basis for the soil, though Pouilly around St-Andelain and St-Satur north of Sancerre have a good deal of flint that is supposed to influence the flavour of the wine. You should be able to recognize a good Pouilly Fumé, indeed, by its whiff of smoky, flinty aroma. Pouilly's vineyards slope gently south and south-west and are warmed by the Loire. Sancerre's best vineyards, in Bué, Chavignol, Verdigny and Menétréol, cling to those crevices cut into the limestone hills that offer protection from wind and rain and full exposure to the sun. Chavignol is also famous for a goats' cheese called Crottin.

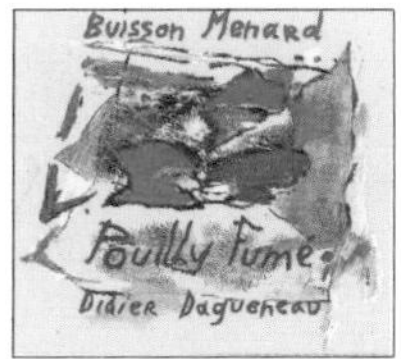

hectares (4000 acres) planted in Sancerre, and about 600 hectares (1500 acres) in Pouilly. Though one or two Sancerre producers now give over some of their good land to Pinot Noir, nearly all the best sites are planted with Sauvignon Blanc. I'm sure this is correct. Sancerre Pinot Noir can achieve a delightful, rather wispy cherry fragrance but rarely more; Sancerre and Pouilly Sauvignon Blanc, on the other hand, can mix hedgerow and meadow scents with memorable intensity. They can reek of freshly roasted beans in a coffee merchant's shop on a cold December morning. They can have a thrilling cut grass, blackcurrant leaves and gooseberry attack that taunts your taste buds. They can, but over-popularity has not helped their quality.

In Sancerre, the best wines come from the villages near Sancerre town, usually from the steep south-facing slopes. Shelter from the wind and exposure to the sun is all-important, often more so than the different types of soil, while cereal crops are grown on land which is too exposed for the vine. Even so, soil does matter – the more limestone the better, in general, and the Kimmeridgian limestones and clay that produce the best Chablis reappear here and give very perfumed wine. There are also patches of limestony gravel, and a few scattered outcrops with flints. In Pouilly the vineyards cover less land but are more dense and compact. The same limestone-dominated clays constitute most of the vineyard land, but there is also a patch of flinty, silex soil near St-Andelain which is sometimes said to be responsible for weightier, correspondingly more minerally wines.

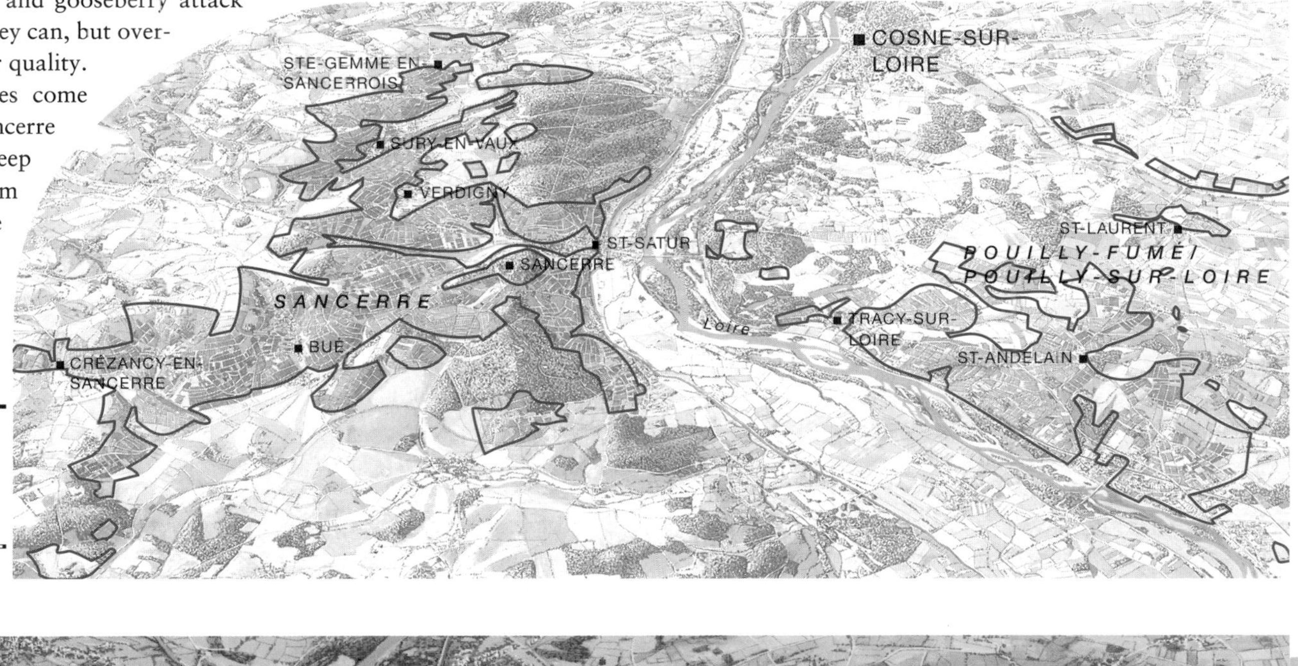

The Rhône Valley

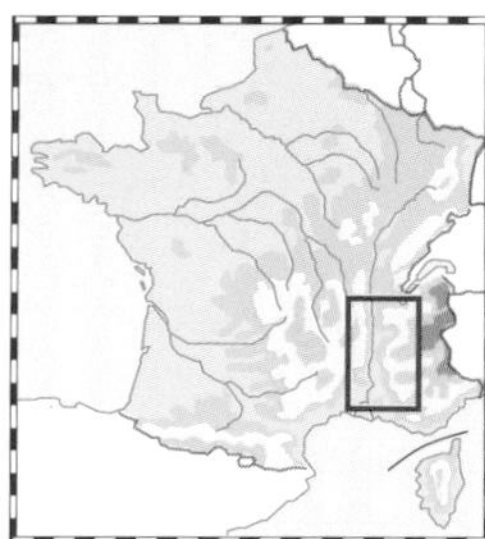

One of my favourite places in France is directly after the cacophonous, frightening, fume-filled tunnel that burrows through the centre of Lyon and emerges in a tumult of overheated, angry drivers and conflicting road signs next to the main railway station. It's a seedy, grubby, mistrustful part of town. So why do I like it so? Just a second. Patience, please. I like it because here I turn right, down the Rhône Valley. This is where I turn away from the last of the glum north and travel towards the broad open skies, the balmy evening air, and the glittering Mediterranean. For me, this urban wasteland is the divide, after which I head into the sweet embrace of the South.

All that tells you precisely nothing about the vineyards of the Rhône Valley, but bear with me. I had to get it off my chest, because the Rhône is as much an emotional destination for me as it is a geographical one, and so it has been for every northern traveller, ever since we began making the long trek south to the welcoming Mediterranean world. This is the artery running down the centre of France, a surging flood sweeping us towards all the pleasures of the South. Anyone who spends long winter hours wrapped up tight against the chilly damp, anyone who searches the leaden summer skies longingly for a glimpse of golden sunshine, will know what I mean.

The Rhône river powers its way through Lyon with the urgency of an express train, churning through the deep channels it has cut itself against the eastern crust of the Massif Central, south of Vienne, before it sweeps out into the parched open spaces south of the hill of Hermitage at Tain. Taking a more languid course, it still gathers awesome power, only half-controlled by the engineering skills of man, and spreads itself across the increasingly arid red landscape past Avignon. It finally ripples out like a fan, its eastern estuary beckoning me past Marseille and Toulon to Provence. Its numerous western streams create a haunting delta of marshes and lagoons backed by the wild hills and valleys of Languedoc, of Minervois and Corbières and the distant Pyrenees. The Rhône, with its great peacock tail of Provence and Languedoc, is one of the parts of France I've come to love most recently, but I think, perhaps, one that I love most of all.

The Rhône river rises way up in the Swiss Alps, and vines are grown along its banks almost continuously from here down to the confluence with the river Durance, just north of the marshy Rhône delta. Along its upper reaches, the Rhône spawns some of the most featherlight, wispy white wines of Europe, as well as some surprisingly beefy reds and whites on the steep, sun-trapped slopes of the Valais. But after melting into the broad, calm waters of Lake Geneva, it re-emerges on the other side of the French border ready for the dash to the Mediterranean. Its first wines on this side, still Alpine and snow-white in character, are those of Savoie and Bugey.

The steep, sun-baked amphitheatre of vines at Cornas. In many areas of France hillside terraces are being abandoned because they are so difficult to work.

NORTHERN RHÔNE

Some 48km (30 miles) of industrial suburbs lie to the south of the city of Lyon, and little to tax the winedrinkers' taste buds occurs until after the town of Vienne. As the autoroute swoops serenely across to the east bank, cast a brief glance, well...this could get tricky at 120km/h (75 mph). I'll keep it personal. *I* always cast a brief glance southwards down the river. The east-facing slopes you'll see are as steep as any in the grape-growing world, and they sport a patchwork of vines that looks as though they must be tacked or glued to the rock. Surely no human being could work this near-cliff-face? Surely no vines could establish a toe-hold on the scree and slate that shifts and slithers on these scarps? But a band of dedicated winemakers does tend such vertiginous slopes as these, and the vines that manage to establish a root system produce wines that are as great as any in France.

These steep slopes are the heart and soul of what we call the northern Rhône, a stretch of the river between the towns of Vienne and Valence, whose great vineyard sites are all characterized by the steepness of their crystalline, rocky hillsides and by the particular grape varieties they use. Life isn't easy here, and the struggle and commitment required to make great wine is mirrored in the passionate flavour of the reds and the wild, heady perfumes of the whites.

Above all, the Syrah grape finds perfect expression here. Syrah vines may have been planted here as long ago as 600BC, if local traditions concerning the hill of Hermitage are to be believed. If so, the savagery of the Syrah's wines, allied to perfumes that seem to have their beginnings in an altogether different, less predictable time, are a fitting and impressive testament. Côte-Rôtie, Hermitage and Cornas are the greatest reds of the northern Rhône, but St-Joseph and Crozes-Hermitage are also capable of fine wines.

The most immediately thrilling of northern Rhône whites are those of the Viognier grape, from the rocky terraces of Condrieu and Château-Grillet. At their best these wines are as overwhelmingly perfumed as a hothouse in summer, but a breathtaking freshness as open and welcome as mayblossom wafting on a spring day's breeze breaks through the aroma of peach and apricot. The Viognier used to be one of the world's rarest grapes. New plantations in Condrieu, however, and in various places throughout southern France, have increased the volumes of its wine by more than a hundredfold.

The Marsanne and Roussanne are not such eye-catching performers, but they provide the white wine of Hermitage, Crozes-Hermitage, St-Joseph and St-Péray. Usually a little flat and broad to start with, they can develop impressive layer upon layer of rich, viscous flavours if you have the patience to wait. St-Péray marks a natural break in the Rhône. Until this point, most of the fine wine has been produced on east- and south-facing slopes of granite marking the edge of the Massif Central. From now on, as the Rhône Valley spreads broad and wide, the emphasis changes.

SOUTHERN RHÔNE

In the southern Rhône, it is the eastern bank that hosts all the fine wines and, with the exception of Châteauneuf-du-Pape, all the truly exciting flavours come from the vineyards in the lee of Mont Ventoux and the Dentelles de Montmirail.

But the natural break isn't just in the wines: it's in the air you breathe, the scorched feel of the soil under your feet, and in the stark difference in vegetation as pear, apricot and cherry

Côtes du Lubéron in the Vaucluse marks the southern Rhône's boundary with Provence. This tranquil, remote area is dominated by co-operatives and produces light, easy-drinking wines.

orchards and vegetable gardens give way to olive and peach groves, lavender and melon fields, and herb-strewn outcrops of rock, bleached as white as a desert corpse's bones.

The sun doesn't necessarily shine for longer periods here, but the whole character of this wide river basin is open and exposed. And once the Mistral starts, the word 'exposed' takes on an entirely new meaning. The Mistral is the fierce north-westerly gale that rakes the people and the crops of the southern Rhône for up to 300 days a year. On the remaining days, don't be surprised to find the Scirocco blowing from the south. The vines are mostly trained close to the ground in little bushes, to defend them against the wind and also to soak up extra warmth from the stony soil. The Mistral is reckoned to send a fair number of people mad each year, but in compensation it does wonders in drying out the crops after a rainfall; rot is rarely a problem down here.

While the northern Rhône specializes in small amounts of high-quality reds and whites, the southern Rhône's chief job is to churn out vast quantities of predominantly red Côtes du Rhône. The Rhône region is, along with Bordeaux and Burgundy, one of three major producers of AC wine, and 85 per cent of this is basic Côtes du Rhône, almost all of it from the south, between the towns of Montélimar and Avignon.

However, there are highlights, too. The little *appellation* of Clairette de Die, way up the Drôme tributary, makes delightful fizz. There are some unctuously sweet fortified wines, led by Muscat de Beaumes-de-Venise, and there are some truly grand table wines, led by the fabulous reds of Châteauneuf-du-Pape. These are followed by those of Gigondas, Lirac and the best Côtes du Rhône-Villages like Cairanne, and sometimes supported by decent rosé in Tavel and Lirac, and bright-eyed whites in Châteauneuf-du-Pape.

The dominant grape is the fleshy, alcoholic red Grenache. However, most wines in the southern Rhône are blends. Châteauneuf-du-Pape allows 13 different varieties, and most reds will add at least Syrah, Cinsaut or Mourvèdre to their blends. Grenache Blanc, Bourboulenc and Marsanne are the most important white varieties.

VINS DOUX NATURELS

Rasteau and Beaumes-de-Venise are the names of two leading communes producing Côtes du Rhône-Villages red wine. But if you're after a slug of gutsy, dry red wine, check that label closely. Beaumes-de-Venise is actually more famous for a golden sweet wine than for its red. Rasteau is more infamous for a sweet red wine than for a dry one. In the torrid heart of the southern Rhône valley, after a day spent toiling through the vineyards and the wine villages, I find the latter distinctly unappealing, yet the former, nicely chilled and served outside in the welcome shade of a plane tree, is one of the most delectable sweet wines on earth.

These two oddballs in the heart of sturdy red wine country are called *vins doux naturels* – which translates as natural sweet wines. Unnatural is more like how I'd describe them, because they are made by whacking in a hefty dose of almost 100 per cent alcohol spirit when the fermentation is only partially completed. This 'muting' as it's called stops the fermentation in its tracks and all the remaining unfermented grape sugar is left in the wine as sweetness.

At Rasteau they use the red wine grape Grenache and although the resulting wine – either in its peppery, jammy but relatively fruity young style, or its tired, oxidized *rancio* style – *seems* to be a throwback to some antediluvian wine culture, sweet Rasteau has only been made since 1932. It has never achieved a more than strictly local following and is now in entirely merited decline. Latest figures show that production is now only a quarter of what it was at the beginning of the 1980s.

Muscat de Beaumes-de-Venise has been made as a sweet wine since the beginning of the nineteenth century, but it has only been a fortified wine since World War Two. The excellent Muscat à Petits Grains, in both white and black forms, is the variety of Muscat grape used. This rich, syrupy fruit has a heady orchard and floral aroma; the winemakers' objective, often triumphantly achieved, is to marry these flavours with a very subtle alcoholic kick, despite the muting taking the strength to 21.5 degrees. As an apéritif or dessert wine, in a sorbet or served with one, Muscat de Beaumes-de-Venise is a delight.

This is one of the most deliciously juicy of all simple Côtes du Rhône reds.

NORTHERN RHÔNE

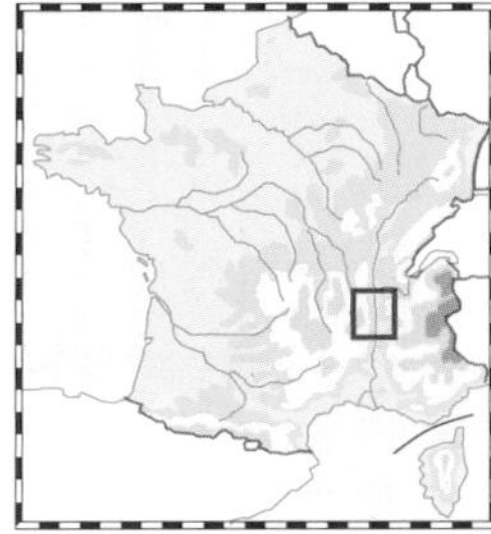

RED GRAPES
Syrah is the predominant grape.

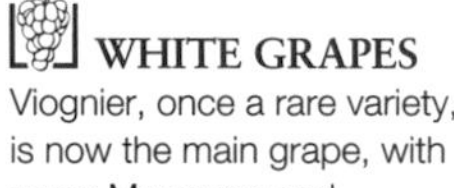

WHITE GRAPES
Viognier, once a rare variety, is now the main grape, with some Marsanne and Roussanne grown too.

CLIMATE
The continental climate with its Mediterranean influence brings burning sun and violent Mistral winds. The Mistral increases the effect of cold in springtime but is useful in drying out a wet harvest. Hail can be a problem.

SOIL
The slopes are crystalline and rocky, with a very fine topsoil of decomposed mica-schist or granite, and a subsoil of granite. Topsoil washed down the hillside by heavy rain over the growing season is carried back up and replaced within the terraces.

ASPECT
Steep, well-drained, south- to south-east-facing terraces etched into the hillsides provide difficult conditions for winemakers, though more alluvial land is now being brought into production. The region's main vineyards cover the slopes along the banks of the Rhône between the towns of Vienne and Valence.

FROM CÔTE-RÔTIE AT AMPUIS way south to Cornas and St-Péray 60km (37 miles) south opposite Valence, the Rhône river has hurled its bulk against the crystalline and granite cliffs of the Massif Central and created a dipping, weaving pattern of dauntingly steep slopes. Where these face south to south-east, they provide brilliant sites for vineyards, but require superhuman effort to exploit them to the full. There have been long periods in history when the terraces of Côte-Rôtie, Condrieu, St-Joseph and Cornas have lain dank and overgrown, deserted by dispirited *vignerons* after a lifetime of toil that gained them no respect. Each of these great vineyard sites has faced extinction because the human toll exacted was too great and the material reward too scant.

One of the most heartening movements of the 1980s and 1990s has been the recognition of the great vineyards of the northern Rhône. Nature has provided great sites, but more than anywhere else in France, these have demanded tremendous sacrifice and commitment from the men and women who work their soil. Until the 1980s, few wine lovers knew of these treasures and even fewer would pay a fair price for them. But during the 1980s and the early 1990s the prices more than tripled, and now a top Côte-Rôtie will outstrip all but the most expensive red Bordeaux, while a Condrieu will equal the price of a top Premier Cru Meursault.

For the products of the finest steep terraced slopes, with their low yields and astonishing concentrated flavours, this is just reward. But take a look at the map. See those steep cliffs at Ampuis, at Condrieu, and at Château-Grillet? These are subject to the special local climates that can make great wine. Then see the broad rolling uplands above the slopes. Here you'll find dairy farms and orchards full of cherries, pears and plums. Fertile, agricultural land such as this is never great vineyard land. Unfortunately you can now find brand new vineyards there too. There is no way these plateaux can produce a great red wine like Côte-Rôtie or a great white like Condrieu, yet they are still allowed the *appellation*.

Perhaps one shouldn't be too harsh, after generations have toiled here for almost nothing. But if the insipid wines of these young, windswept plateau vines is allowed to dilute the quality of the great wines from the steep slopes, then everyone – consumer and producer – will eventually suffer.

Fashion is rightly fêting these northern Rhône wines now, but there are plantations of the red Syrah grape all over southern France and, increasingly, in the New World, as well as enormous new plantations of the white Viognier grape in the Ardèche and in the Rhône and Languedoc further south. It is only by being better than this new competition that we will pay a premium for Côte-Rôtie, Condrieu, Château-Grillet, St-Joseph and the other top northern Rhône wines.

These wines rely on just two grapes for their remarkable flavours and they equal any varieties in France or elsewhere in the world for quality. The red grape is the Syrah, clearly as fine a variety as the Cabernet Sauvignon of Bordeaux, or Burgundy's Pinot Noir, but until recently quite unforgivably overlooked as a grape of international stature. The Viognier is the quality white grape of the northern Rhône, making delicious apricotty wine, but it has the two major drawbacks of being not only a poor yielder but also prone to disease.

CÔTE-RÔTIE, CONDRIEU AND CHÂTEAU-GRILLET

I can't seriously believe that anyone stood at the bottom of what is now the Côte-Rôtie and said – ooh, that looks nice, let's have a few vines up there. The slopes of Côte-Rôtie get as steep as 55 degrees. I'm not joking. I've still got the scars. They soar off into the sky above Ampuis like the death-defying first drop of a ski jump. Except this ski jump is a garbled mass of single vines tethered to a quartet of posts bound together to look like an Indian tepee; and it's criss-crossed with terraces made of dry stone, or even hewn out of the stark face of the rock itself, shoring up the scant soil that gives these vines the bare minimum of nourishment they need.

Vines may have been grown at Côte-Rôtie for as many as 24 centuries, and certainly 2000 years ago one of the Roman travel writers described the steep slopes on both sides of the Rhône as being covered with vines. But I doubt that this was the prime objective. I suspect the farmers at Ampuis simply got fed up with their vines being swamped yet again by the capricious Rhône in full flood. And so they chipped a few terraces higher up into the mica-schist hillsides, and a few years later everyone kept turning up at their place for a snifter before Sunday lunch.

Why? Because straight away this wine – from slopes much more exposed to the sun, better protected from fierce north Mistral winds and able to benefit from the warmth of the river through reflection of light and hot air rising – tasted infinitely more exciting than the flat old river bank stuff they'd had to put up with before.

So generation after generation of *vignerons* scrambled their way higher and higher up this half-vertical cliff-face, hacking away at the rock, risking dreadful vertigo attacks as they gazed down on the rooftops and river beneath them, assuredly developing arthritis in their embattled limbs long before their time. And all because the flavours of the wine were steeped in spice and perfume, the ruby-red fruit was as rich as nectar and a flagon or two inflamed their brains with passion and fantasy.

Syrah thrives on the steep, sun-baked slopes of Côte-Rôtie, and anywhere else in the northern Rhône as far down as Cornas in the south where it can find well-exposed, granite slopes. From such sites the wines will be dark, complex and

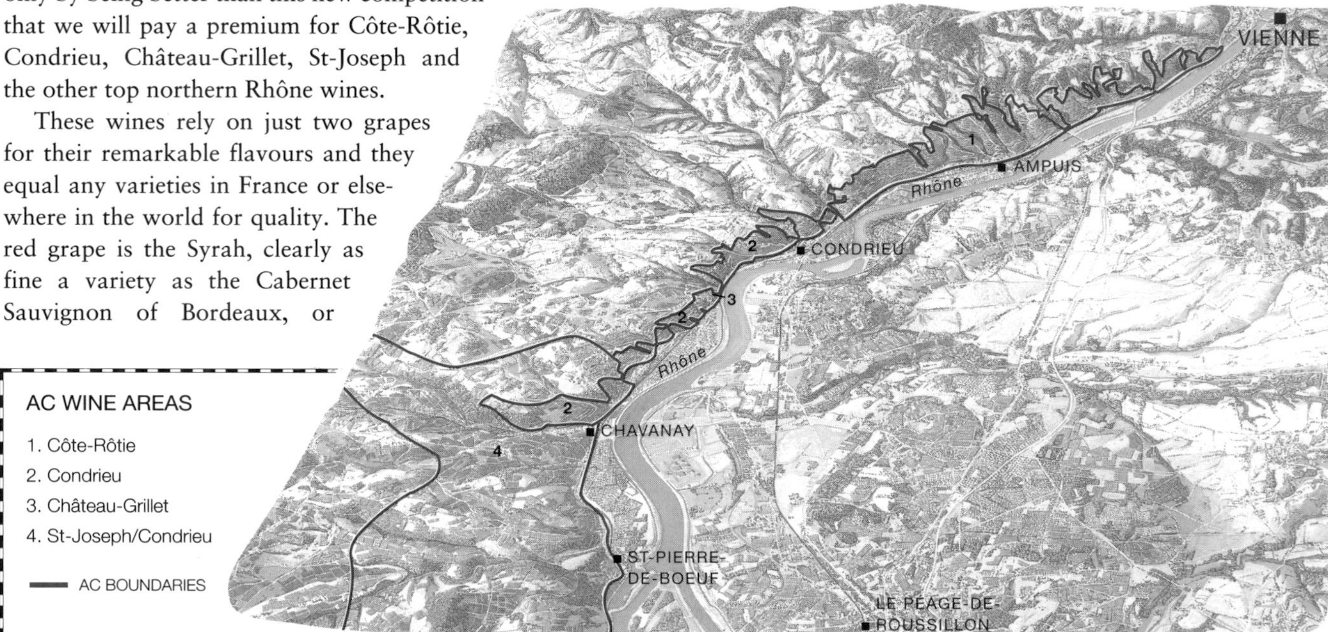

capable of 20 years or more aging in a good vintage. However, there has been an expansion of vineyards on the flat land near the river, which in the past had been planted not with vines but with fruit trees. This development has affected the northern part of the St-Joseph *appellation* in particular, and you can see an example of new vineyards on alluvial land as the river bends away north of the village of St-Pierre-de-Boeuf. The wines from such sites are neither as thrilling nor as impressive as those from the slopes, but the Syrah is such a good variety that the results can still be enjoyably fruity and perfumed.

The white Viognier is used for the Condrieu and Château-Grillet *appellations,* and is also grown in Côte-Rôtie where it can be blended with Syrah. Viognier is a difficult vine to grow, taking far longer than usual to produce high-quality grapes and then being very erratic in yield, but the unctuous texture of its wine, like apricots coated in *crème fraîche*, and the heady mayblossom perfume, make it all worthwhile.

Château-Grillet, one of France's smallest *appellations* with only 3.8 hectares (9½ acres) of vines, is rare and overpriced and has long not lived up to its reputation. However, recent vintages do show improvement, thank goodness.

HERMITAGE

No one's absolutely sure, but as you stand at the base of the hill of Hermitage, wedged in between the railway line and the rapidly ascending vineyard slopes in front of you, you just may be gazing up at the oldest vineyard in the Rhône Valley. There is a strong local belief that the Phocaeans, travellers from southern Greece in ancient times, who worked their way up the Rhône from Marseille, were carrying vines with them. The vine, it seems, would have been the Syrah. The towering hill of Hermitage clearly impressed them, and the locals say that somewhere round 600BC a few Phocaeans stopped off and planted a vineyard there. Which would make Hermitage not only the oldest vineyard in the Rhône Valley, but almost certainly the oldest vineyard in France.

I hope the story's true, because Hermitage deserves the accolade. It's a magnificent vineyard site and when Virgil wrote a couple of thousand years ago that 'vines love an open hill', he couldn't have found a better one than the hill of Hermitage. It is capable of producing majestic reds and intriguing whites, which are able to stand the test of time as well as any other French wines. The red wines manage to combine a rough-hewn, animal power with a sweetness of fruit and wildness of perfume. This may be less academically correct than great Bordeaux and less sensually explicit than great Burgundy, but it catches you unawares and spins you in a dizzy pirouette in a way that no other red wine can. White

The small appellation *of Cornas produces massive, full-bodied, almost black red wine from the Syrah grape.*

WHERE THE VINEYARDS ARE *This map shows why the wines of the northern Rhône are so magnificent and yet so rare. Just look at how steep those slopes are on the north and west banks of the river. But what beautiful exposure to the sun, what marvellous drainage on those granite slopes and what free circulating air to avoid the development of rot and fungal diseases. And when the fierce Mistral wind blows from the north, the worst of the gales won't catch the vines on the best slopes. Even so, such slopes are extremely difficult to cultivate and the yields are restricted. Côte-Rôtie covers only 160 hectares (395 acres), the best grapes coming from the steep slopes around Ampuis. Recent plantings on the plateau land behind produce markedly inferior wine. (That the flat land has been planted at all is a sign of the growing popularity of the wine.) Condrieu has expanded tenfold since 1965, and too much of that expansion has been on exposed, upland fields that can produce pleasant white Viognier wine, but not something deserving the price and renown of Condrieu. Château-Grillet occupies a sheltered little amphitheatre of vines just outside the village of Vérin.*

CÔTE-RÔTIE TO ST-JOSEPH

VINEYARDS

TOTAL DISTANCE NORTH TO SOUTH 20KM (12½ MILES)

N

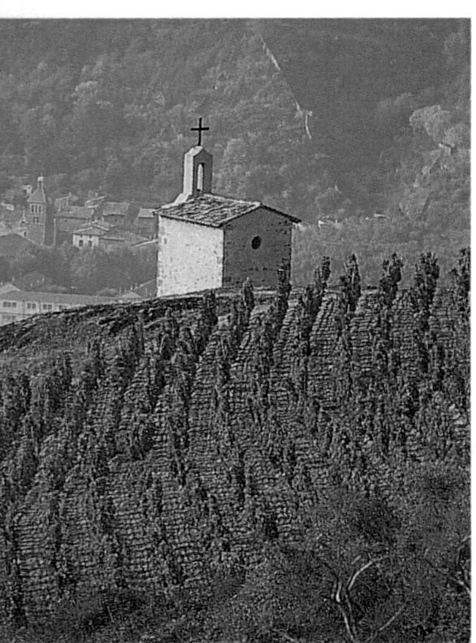

The steep granite hill of Hermitage has excellent exposure to the sun and is possibly the oldest vineyard in France.

Hermitage lacks the immediate charm and fragrance of all France's other great white wines, and may seem fat and sulky almost before it's bottled, but its pudgy sullenness is surely no candidate for making old bones.

I don't think many Rhône winemakers can explain it either, but good white Hermitage, often made solely from the Marsanne grape, but generally with a little Roussanne added, seems to get a second, third, and even a fourth wind, and appears to get younger as its red brother gets older. A leaner, fresher, flinty mineral tone may develop in the white, but it never loses its rich, ripe core of honey, nuts and buns, streaked with spice and topped with crystal sugar.

The Hermitage hill only has 126 hectares (311 acres) of vines, and on the map you can see how wonderfully exposed to the sun these are. The locals say the sun always sets last on these granite slopes of Hermitage, but it's obvious that the sun rises there first as well! The generally granite soils and the numerous terrace walls heat up in the warmth of the sun's rays, and help promote the ripening of the grapes. The drainage is clearly excellent and the Mistral wind will blow away any excess moisture in any case – yes, Virgil would have liked Hermitage!

Over two-thirds of the Hermitage vines are red Syrah, but the rest are white grapes, largely Marsanne with a small amount of Roussanne. The burliest, most virile red wines seem to come from the most forbidding granite plots.

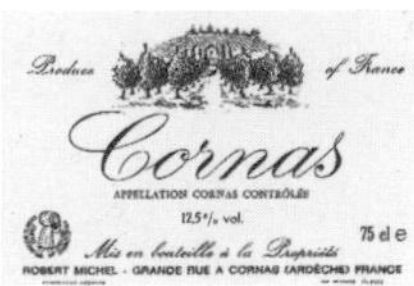

CROZES-HERMITAGE

All round the Hermitage hill, to the north, east and south, is the large *appellation* of Crozes-Hermitage. This is increasingly one of the Rhône's most satisfying red wines (although there is also some white) because the smoky, dark-fruited character of the Syrah is well to the fore, and the wines are ready for drinking when still quite young. Traditionally the best Crozes wine was held to come from the hilly slopes around Gervans to the north and Mercurol to the east of Hermitage, but les Chassis to the south, near la Roche de Glun, has proved their equal in quality despite its flat terrain; this is because its soils are particularly stony and the vines give meagre yields. The current 1200 hectares (2965 acres) of Crozes vineyards can be expected to expand substantially over the coming years.

ST-JOSEPH

The St-Joseph *appellation*, on the other hand, has suffered from its expansion. It was originally based on one single hillside – the south-east-facing terraces you can see between Tournon and Mauves. The first expansion was on to the steep terraced hillsides of six communes on the west bank of the Rhône between Glun and Vion, totalling less than 100 hectares (247 acres) of fine vineyard land. In 1969 the *appellation* was expanded again to include 25 communes beginning opposite Valence in the south, and running a good 65km (40 miles) north, right up to Condrieu. Most of the new vines were planted on the Rhône's flat, fertile banks, and the reputation of the wonderfully perfumed, fruity reds and the weighty, ripe whites from the original granite slopes was sadly eroded by the newcomers. The *appellation* exploded to as many as 640 hectares (1581 acres), and could have grown to 7000 hectares (17,300 acres) before sanity prevailed in the early 1990s, when further vineyard expansion was curbed. Now the terraces above Mauves, Tournon and St-Jean-de-Mouzols are being restored, and with them will come the restoration of St-Joseph's reputation as one of France's most delightful rich, fruity, perfumed and approachable reds.

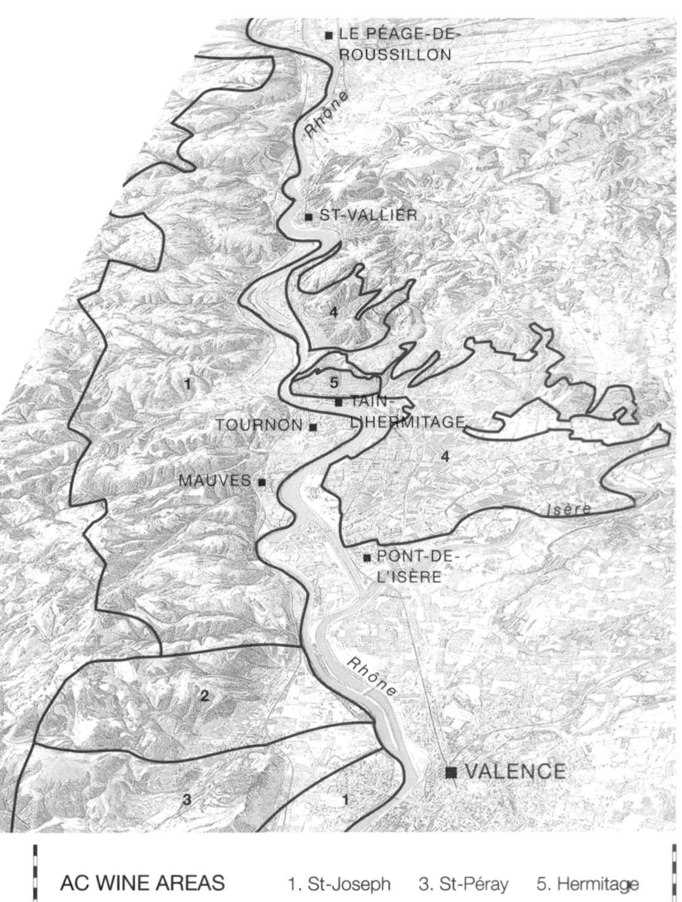

WHERE THE VINEYARDS ARE *Right at the heart of the map is the hill of Hermitage. Towering over the little town of Tain, it may not appear awe-inspiring from this angle, but I can assure you that from the bottom of the vineyard slopes it most certainly is. The hills immediately to the north and east of Hermitage are in the Crozes-Hermitage* appellation. *To the north, Gervans' granite slopes produce good reds, and the sandy slopes at Mercurol to the east are good for whites. However, much expansion and mechanization of vineyards is taking place on the flatter lands to the south. Traditionalists abhor this, but the resulting wines, though lighter, can be good.*

The heart of the St-Joseph appellation *is the terraced cliff-face between Mauves and Tournon, but there are 25 communes allowed to make St-Joseph on the Rhône's west bank. Wherever terraces are used, the wines should be exciting, unlike the wine from bulges of flat alluvial land where the river curves. Much of this has been planted with vines for St-Joseph too, and the wines deserve no more than Côtes du Rhône status.*

At the bottom of the map is the sun-soaked amphitheatre of Cornas where the black-blooded Syrah excels in producing monumental tarry reds. Below Cornas are the beautifully exposed slopes of St-Péray, wasted on producing mediocre still and sparkling whites. It's my guess that we would see some outstanding red wines from here if Syrah were ever planted.

CORNAS AND ST-PÉRAY

Cornas should be immune from expansion fever. The name Cornas means 'burnt earth' and applies to the steep amphitheatre of Syrah vines that cups the little village of Cornas in its suntrap palm. That almost claustrophobic shell of south-east-facing vines, protected even from the destructive Mistral winds, is a cauldron of heat in summertime. The Cornas vineyards produce the blackest, most torrid red wine in the Rhône, perhaps in the whole of France, its dark, essential flavours wrested from deep inside the earth.

Yet even here expansion looms. The use of higher-yielding Syrah clones unable to produce the dense black tarry liquid that marks out great Cornas, and the gradual increase of low-lying plantings of vines to a present total of 70 hectares (172 acres) do threaten Cornas' role as provider of France's most famously old-fashioned red. Luckily there's a long way to go yet, as I still haven't come across a Cornas light enough for me to see through.

Directly south of Cornas you can see another range of beautifully exposed slopes. They look as though they would continue to paint the brilliant tapestry of dark, heady Rhône reds from the great Syrah grape, yet in fact they are planted with white Roussanne and Marsanne, and 80 per cent of their wine is sparkling. St-Péray is a curiosity, certainly, whose wines, still or sparkling, are not exciting enough to ensure their survival, although Wagner apparently ordered a hundred bottles of the stuff to help him break through a writer's block in the middle of composing *Parsifal*. It's a matter of opinion whether or not the St-Péray did the trick.

Already, houses for people commuting to the nearby towns are being built among the vines to capitalize on the magnificent view of the river valley. Now, if they were allowed to plant Syrah on these splendid slopes, I'd almost support a move to expand the Cornas *appellation*!

SOUTHERN RHÔNE

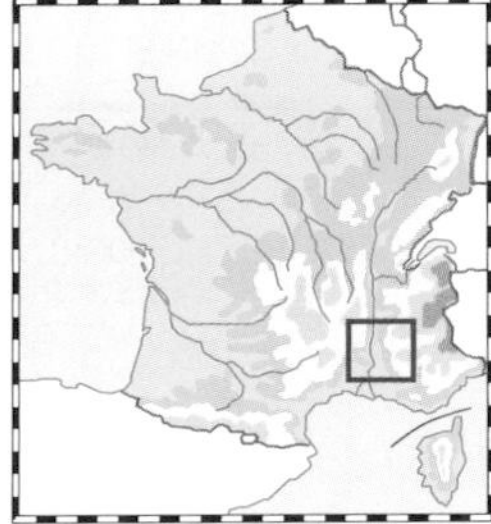

IN THE NORTHERN RHÔNE you need to look upwards if you want to understand the unique qualities of the best vineyards, soaring towards the sky at crazy angles. But in the southern Rhône, you need to look down at your feet. The best vineyards of the south are virtually flat, but covered with stones so closely packed that there is no soil in sight. In the southern Rhône's one truly great vineyard zone, Châteauneuf-du-Pape, it is almost as difficult to keep your balance as it is on the intimidating slopes of Côte-Rôtie. The reason is not steepness, though. It's due to the smooth, slippery stones, often as hot to the touch as an oven door, which slither and slide beneath your feet at every step. In the southern Rhône these white and rust-coloured stones act as a natural storage heater and rain-water sieve. They allow the low-yielding vines of Châteauneuf-du-Pape to give a wine that is as heady and alcoholic as any in France, yet which is packed with perfume and fruit richness.

GRAPE VARIETIES

The south is far more dominated than the north by red wines, and these are almost always blends. The Grenache grape, which doesn't figure at all in the north, is the dominant variety, and this is usually blended with Cinsaut and Syrah, and maybe Carignan and Mourvèdre as well. Châteauneuf-du-Pape can be a blend of 13 different grape varieties altogether, eight red and five white. Three of the red varieties – Counoise, Vaccarèse and Muscardin – are virtually extinct elsewhere, but have excitingly unusual personalities whose potential heights are only just beginning to be explored. It is as if the great southern reds scoop their flavours off the herb-covered hillsides and the hot stony tracks, pluck them from the broiling sky and then boil them together like candy. Grenache Blanc and Clairette are the chief white varieties.

WINE AREAS

Between Valence, in the northern Rhône, and Montélimar, the nougat capital of the world, there is a gap of 44km (27 miles) in which there is hardly a vine. From Montélimar southwards, however, the vine increasingly becomes the dominant crop which is grown on all types of terrain, but for the over-fertile alluvial flatlands down near the river Rhône itself.

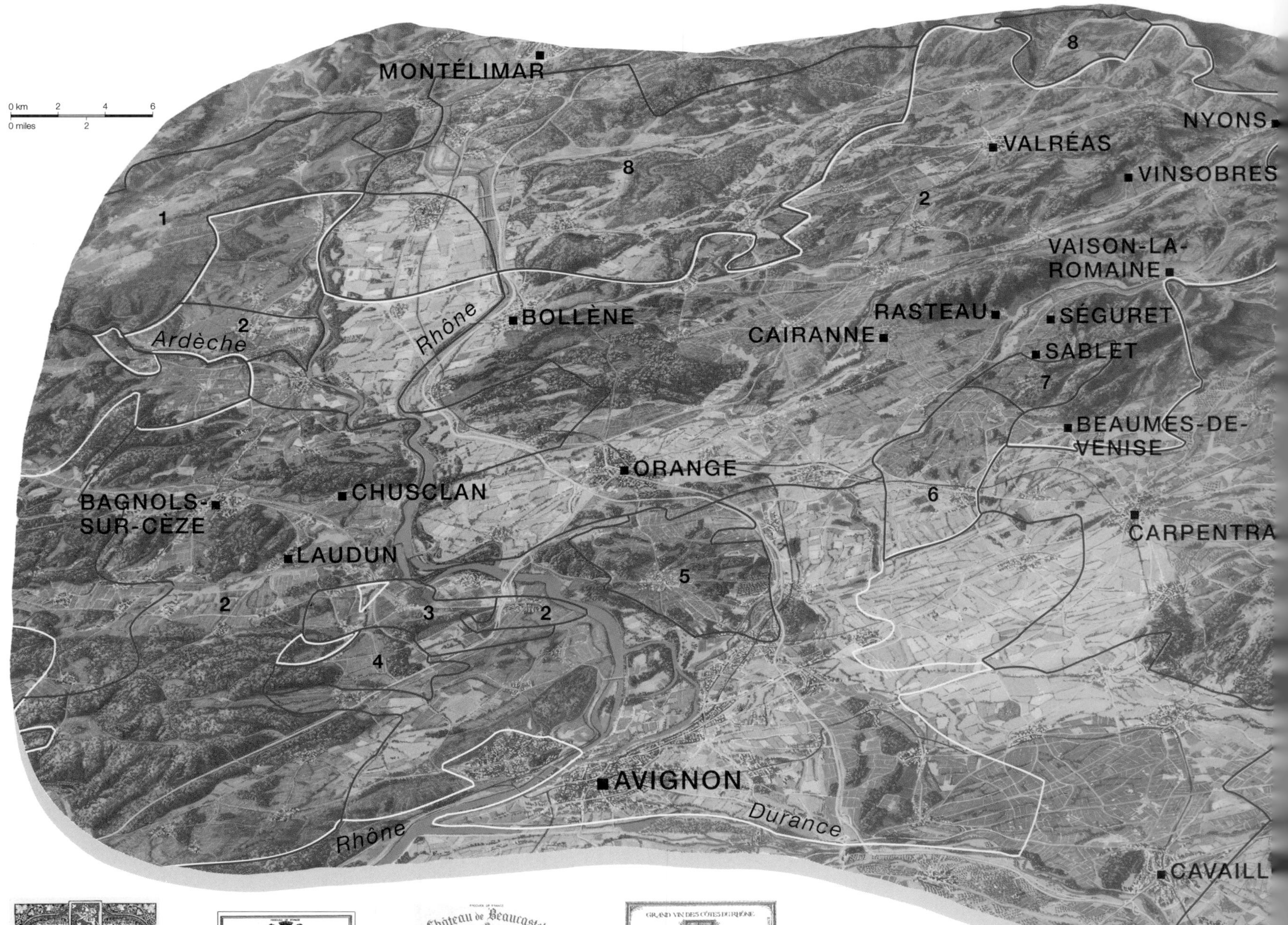

The sun beats down so relentlessly during a typical southern Rhône summer that extra exposure to its rays seems pointless. However, there are some sloping vineyards – the best ones being in villages like Gigondas, Vacqueyras and Cairanne in the eastern foothills. The best vineyards in Châteauneuf-du-Pape are on raised plateau land – and such conditions do add to these villages' ability to super-ripen their grapes. The types of soil in these major villages are also varied, and they affect the ability of different varieties to ripen. The Mistral wind is combated by wind-breaks and by training the compact vines low in bush form, although more modern training on to wires is becoming common in lesser *appellations*, to allow mechanization.

CÔTES DU RHÔNE AND CÔTES DU RHÔNE-VILLAGES

Côtes du Rhône is the blanket *appellation* covering vines from Vienne in the north to Avignon in the south. Eighty-five per cent of all the wine made between these two points is simple Côtes du Rhône and most of it comes from the sprawling vineyards that straddle the Rhône from St-Marcel-d'Ardèche and Bollène to south of Tavel. It is overwhelmingly red and, along with basic Bordeaux and Beaujolais, is France's favourite red quaffer. Generally it is a decent drink, but occasionally a good single estate can up the tempo a bit.

Côtes du Rhône-Villages supposedly applies to the wines of superior communes that don't have the oomph to gain their own *appellations*. The idea is that the best will graduate to their own *appellations*, but so far only two – Gigondas and Vacqueyras – have done so. This leaves 16 communes that can add their own name to 'Côtes du Rhône-Villages' on the label. There are another 54 communes that grow Villages wine, but that may not use their own commune name on the label. The Villages growers must accept a tighter control over their choice of grape varieties, yields per hectare and minimum alcohol levels. In the top Villages this is probably worthwhile; but in the more anonymous communes, growers frequently choose to stick with straight Côtes du Rhône regulations and accept the lower price for fewer restrictions and a higher yield.

Grenache is the chief red variety and provides a rich, heady heart to the wine. For this you'll need dry, stony soil and a little inclination to the sun, as in the best Villages on the eastern slopes. The Syrah grape can overripen in many parts of the southern Rhône, but find it some moister, cooler soil and it will add a gorgeous dark-fruited, serious depth to the flightiest of reds. Most of the top Villages like Cairanne have good chunks of moist clay soil gently sloping towards the plain. The late-ripening Mourvèdre adds a crucial, almost rasping, herb-leaf perfume and wild berry fruit to the more corpulent Grenache. Rich clay soil in a warm, protected spot will suit it just fine.

COTEAUX DU TRICASTIN

The first vineyards south of Montélimar are some of the most recent in the valley, those of Côteaux du Tricastin. There had been vines here in the nineteenth century, but a quick look at the weather and soil will show why the growers had given up.

RED GRAPES

Grenache is the most important of the many red varieties, followed by Syrah and Cinsaut, then Carignan and Mourvèdre, but there are many minor varieties.

WHITE GRAPES

Whites are far less important than reds: the main grapes are Clairette, Muscat and Grenache Blanc.

CLIMATE

The region enjoys a true Mediterranean climate: hot dry summers and warm wet winters. The planting of wind-breaks helps mitigate the force of the Mistral blowing chill blasts down the valley from the Alps.

SOIL

This huge area has a wide variety of soil types, ranging from the heavy clays of the upper slopes of Gigondas to the stony alluvial deposits of the plains around Châteauneuf-du-Pape.

ASPECT

On the lowlands this far south ripening is not a problem, and many of the best vineyards are on the flat land of the valley floor.

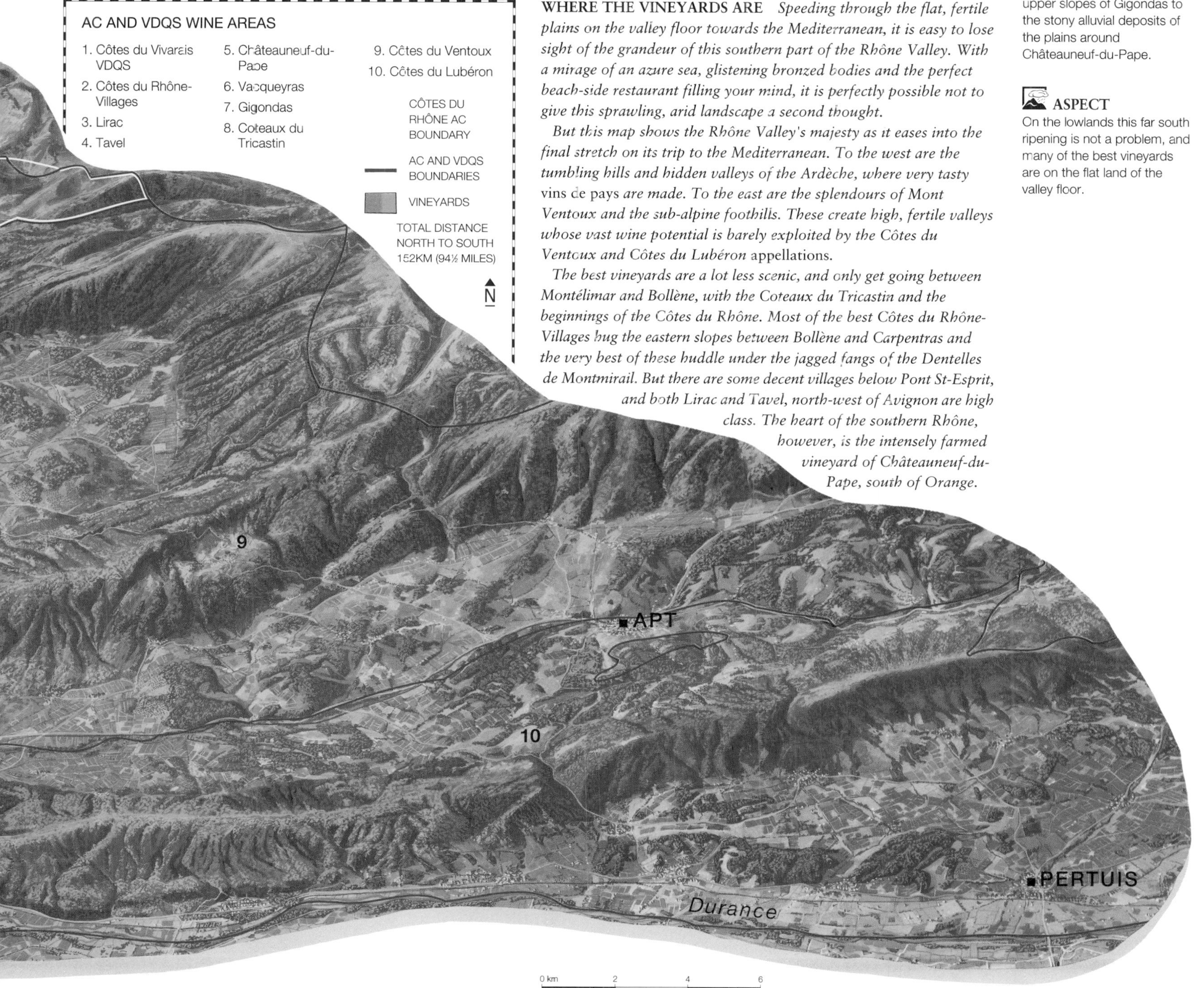

WHERE THE VINEYARDS ARE *Speeding through the flat, fertile plains on the valley floor towards the Mediterranean, it is easy to lose sight of the grandeur of this southern part of the Rhône Valley. With a mirage of an azure sea, glistening bronzed bodies and the perfect beach-side restaurant filling your mind, it is perfectly possible not to give this sprawling, arid landscape a second thought.*

But this map shows the Rhône Valley's majesty as it eases into the final stretch on its trip to the Mediterranean. To the west are the tumbling hills and hidden valleys of the Ardèche, where very tasty vins de pays *are made. To the east are the splendours of Mont Ventoux and the sub-alpine foothills. These create high, fertile valleys whose vast wine potential is barely exploited by the Côtes du Ventoux and Côtes du Lubéron* appellations.

The best vineyards are a lot less scenic, and only get going between Montélimar and Bollène, with the Coteaux du Tricastin and the beginnings of the Côtes du Rhône. Most of the best Côtes du Rhône-Villages hug the eastern slopes between Bollène and Carpentras and the very best of these huddle under the jagged fangs of the Dentelles de Montmirail. But there are some decent villages below Pont St-Esprit, and both Lirac and Tavel, north-west of Avignon are high class. The heart of the southern Rhône, however, is the intensely farmed vineyard of Châteauneuf-du-Pape, south of Orange.

Decent Châteauneuf-du-Pape uses bottles embossed with a papal coat of arms.

The Mistral wind is reckoned to be at its most furious here, reaching speeds of over 100km/h (60mph). The soil is rather like that of Châteauneuf-du-Pape – covered in round flat stones – but Châteauneuf-du-Pape was a famous wine whose renown made it worthwhile to cultivate such barren land. No-one had heard of Tricastin wine, though its black truffles were famous, so these vineyards were abandoned.

In the 1960s, the Algerian War of Independence sent a flood of farmers, who were used to working under tough conditions, back to France. The French government was eager to offer them land and a chance to earn a living, and one of the areas that was singled out lay between Montélimar and Bollène. These settlers have done a remarkable job hewing vineyards out of this unpromising land, and making strong ripe reds with real fruit intensity and little tannin. There is a lot of Syrah planted here and it is often sold as a 100 per cent varietal – it's very good, and cheap considering its quality.

South of the Coteaux du Tricastin, the vineyards rapidly take over large parts of the landscape, but there is a very definite hierarchy governing their quality levels. At the top end of the scale are the communes that have managed to create a track record of better than average wines over the years. These have their own *appellations contrôlées*, and are led by the world-famous Châteauneuf-du-Pape.

VACQUEYRAS AND GIGONDAS

Vacqueyras and Gigondas, on the slopes of the Dentelles de Montmirail, possess particularly suitable local climates and soils, and have their own *appellations* thanks to the efforts of enough growers determined to maximize their grapes' quality. Vacqueyras' soil is particularly stony and produces a correspondingly dark, thick-textured wine. Gigondas' wine is rough-hewn red, but has a sweet core and a muscularity that manages to be inviting rather than daunting. The raw richness is largely due to Grenache, grown on high steep slopes of yellow clay, or slightly lower slopes of heat-retaining stones.

CHÂTEAUNEUF-DU-PAPE

Of all the southern Rhône reds, this is the one which oozes richness and succulent juicy fruit, but which wraps its perfumed sweetness in the heady, open-air fragrance of hillside herbs and baking southern sun. The Grenache is the main grape, capable of ripening to 15 degrees and more in hot years, and there are 12 other permitted grape varieties, seven red and five white, that can be used in red Châteauneuf. Few properties actually use more than four or five in their blends. A little white Châteauneuf is made and is increasingly good.

The headiest, most exotic wines come from vineyards on the stone-smothered plateau just north of the town of Châteauneuf-du-Pape. Immediately east of the town are more vineyards larded with these round flat stones, but further east towards Courthézon and Bédarrides the stones give way to more sand and clay, while in the south the land is generally more gravelly.

TAVEL AND LIRAC

Directly over the river Rhône, on the west bank, are two *appellations* that languish somewhat in Châteauneuf's shadow. Tavel's proud producers would claim they don't languish at all, producing what they claim is France's best, and often highest priced, rosé. I would add, the most alcoholic one too, because these pale but heady, dry, rather fruitless, wines are pretty hefty. They are based on Grenache, but up to nine varieties in total are allowed. Strangely, Tavel rosés do gain depth of flavour after a few years. It's almost as though they wanted to be red wines, and resent their juice being whipped off the colour- and flavour-laden grape skins after a mere 24 hours or so. Perhaps they do.

Many of the vineyards are covered in the same heat-retentive stones as at Châteauneuf-du-Pape, and the arid, infertile surrounding hills look like red wine country. But the subsoils here are basically sand and limestone and, especially on the hillsides to the west of Tavel and the Vallongue plateau to the north, the high alcoholic degree allied to the lightness of body imparted by the limestone soils do, I suppose, favour the production of rosé at least as much as red.

Lirac also has much soil that seems broadly similar to Châteauneuf's, comprising big, bleached stones which carpet many of the vineyards; some of the best vines here are grown on wide, stark plateaux. And Lirac's red wines often try to catch a little of Châteauneuf's grandeur and fame. But, despite a good ripe fruit style and an attractive herb-and-hilltop perfume, they have never really caught the public eye. That's a pity. There are some excellent reds here, and some rosés and whites which aren't bad either.

There are several other wine areas bordering the Rhône that are mostly of minor importance – so far. The potential is enormous, but no-one has ever demanded anything of the myriad of growers there other than the production of large amounts of cheap hooch. Co-operatives dominate production, usually without much regard for quality.

But look on the map at that magnificent natural amphitheatre east of Carpentras, and at the impressive south-facing ridge above the town of Apt. This whole area is known as the Côtes du Ventoux. The mountain ridge south of Apt, running parallel to the Durance river, is the Côtes du Lubéron. The Ardèche mountains are to the west of the river Rhône, full of unsung but good vineyards, and south-west of Montélimar is the Côtes du Vivarais.

But there's one outpost that is already fulfilling its potential – a hidden patchwork of vines way up the Drôme Valley, east of Valence. These produce the heavenly scented sparkling wine from Muscat and Clairette called Clairette de Die Tradition.

CHÂTEAUNEUF

Châteauneuf-du-Pape was the first AC specifically to forbid the landing of flying saucers inside the commune boundaries, back in 1954! The ruling, quirky as it may seem, was tacked on to the six articles formulated by Baron Le Roy of Château Fortia in 1923 which had the objective of protecting the integrity of the vineyard and its wines. This stated the criteria that had to be followed for Châteauneuf-du-Pape. A delineated area, specific grape varieties, training and pruning regulations, a minimum alcohol level, a discarding of 5% of the crop at harvest time, no rosé wine, and a tasting test were among the regulations. These still stand today, but, more importantly, they were taken as the starting point for the entire French *appellation* system that came into being in 1935.

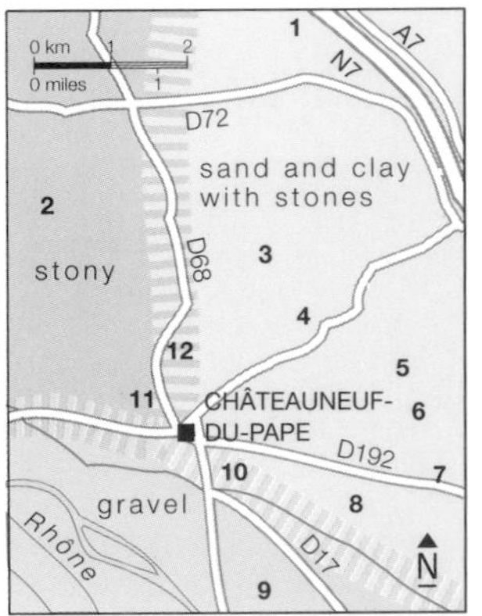

Wine Estates 1. Beaucastel 2. Mont-Redon 3. Rayas 4. Nalys 5. Font du Loup 6. Vieux Télégraphe 7. Font de Michelle 8. la Nerthe 9. Chante-Perdrix 10. Fortia 11. Clos des Papes 12. Bosquet des Papes

Jura & Savoie

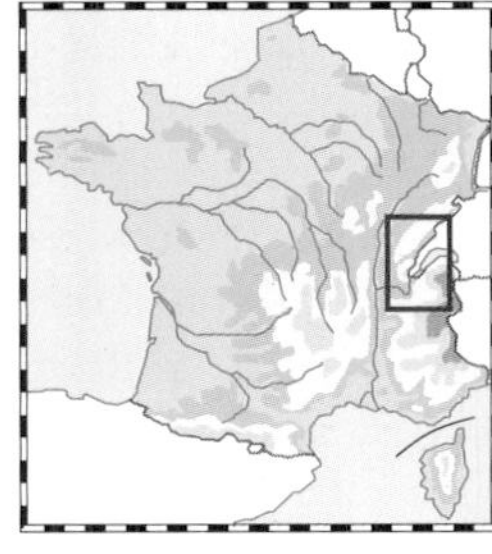

MOUNTAIN PEOPLE ARE DIFFERENT. Isolation breeds an individuality markedly different from that of plains dwellers. It is a hostile, unpredictable environment where life is a continual battle only partly compensated for by the thrill of a mountain peak glimpsed wreathed in cloud when the sun breaks briefly through, by the music of falling water cascading over rocks, by the lonely echo of a night-bird's song rising up the valley. Both the Jura and Savoie reflect this individuality, but in different ways.

JURA

The Jura mountains run up the eastern side of France and act as a natural border with Switzerland. On the Swiss side the thickly wooded slopes fall dramatically down to the calm prosperity encircling Lake Geneva. The French side, staring rather balefully out west across the Saône Valley to the glories of Burgundy, is a mixture of high meadowland, dense forest, astonishing gorges and sudden splashes of tranquil vineyard.

But few of the wines are tranquil. The native Jura grapes are the surly, thick-witted red Trousseau, the indeterminate and pallid semi-red Poulsard and the vicious yet fascinating white Savagnin which is supposed to be related to the Traminer of Alsace – but I don't see the slightest resemblance, especially when it is used to make *vin jaune* or 'yellow wine'.

If the red and pink wines of Jura are merely sullen, this yellow wine is a freakish oddball. The wine has to be aged for six years in cask and during this time a yeast film develops on the wine in exactly the same way as in Jerez's production of *fino* sherry. The result is a wine with a raging, sour woody brilliance.

Château-Chalon is the centre of *vin jaune* and l'Étoile is also important, though it is produced all over the Jura in small quantities. However, there are signs that the Burgundian influence from over the valley is making headway. There is an increasing amount of Pinot Noir grown and it makes an attractive pale red. Chardonnay makes light dry whites so long as it isn't made in casks that have previously held Savagnin, and the local sparkling wine is particularly good.

SAVOIE

Like Jura, Savoie also has about 1500 hectares (3700 acres) of vines and the Burgundian grapes also do well here, but the native grapes and the character of their wines couldn't be more different from those of Jura. Chasselas wine, from near Lake Geneva, is so ethereal as to be almost transparent – in flavour as well as looks. The Jacquère and Altesse or Roussette varieties make wine that is also almost water-white but they pack a tangy angelica and grapefruit pith punch like the glow of green and blue in the heart of a glacier. And Mondeuse is a red grape of formidable dark loganberry and woodsmoke strength when it can find a decent site to ripen in. Which is easier said than done: Savoie is dairy land. The vines get pushed up the rapidly steepening mountain slopes until it gets too cool or too vertical to ripen a grape. But the result is some exceptional wine, most of it quaffed by thirsty skiers every winter.

Crépy is a feather-light Chasselas white from the shores of Lake Geneva and is chiefly memorable for its attractive yeasty prickle of carbon dioxide that the best examples possess. The Seyssel *appellation*, however, does better. The Rhône tumbles and churns through the attractive town, and here, the Jacquère and Roussette produce pale but thirst-quenching fizz. Roussette also makes tart but fine still whites.

Down towards Lake Bourget the Burgundian grapes, Gamay and Pinot Noir, ripen reasonably well, helped by the influence of France's largest lake in moderating the capricious mountain climate. But for me, the core of Savoie is near Chambéry, where the high peaks of the Alps jut out rudely into the valley, and then swing round to follow the Isère Valley up towards the skiing centre of Albertville. Here the Cru villages of Apremont, Abymes, Montmélian, Chignin and Cruet, among others, produce marvellous dry whites from Jacquère and Roussanne, threatening to be insubstantial and pale, then overpowering your palate with the sharp, tingling excitement of the high mountain slopes. On south-facing slopes Mondeuse can give rich reds of black-blooded intensity.

BUGEY

To the west of Lake Bourget is the small Bugey region. Well, not so small any more. In one of those strange quirks of fortune Bugey has become trendy, and these scattered patches of vines now total 500 hectares (1235 acres) set among the woods and hills below le Grand Colombier. All the Savoie varieties are grown here but it is the pale yet surprisingly intense Chardonnay that works best.

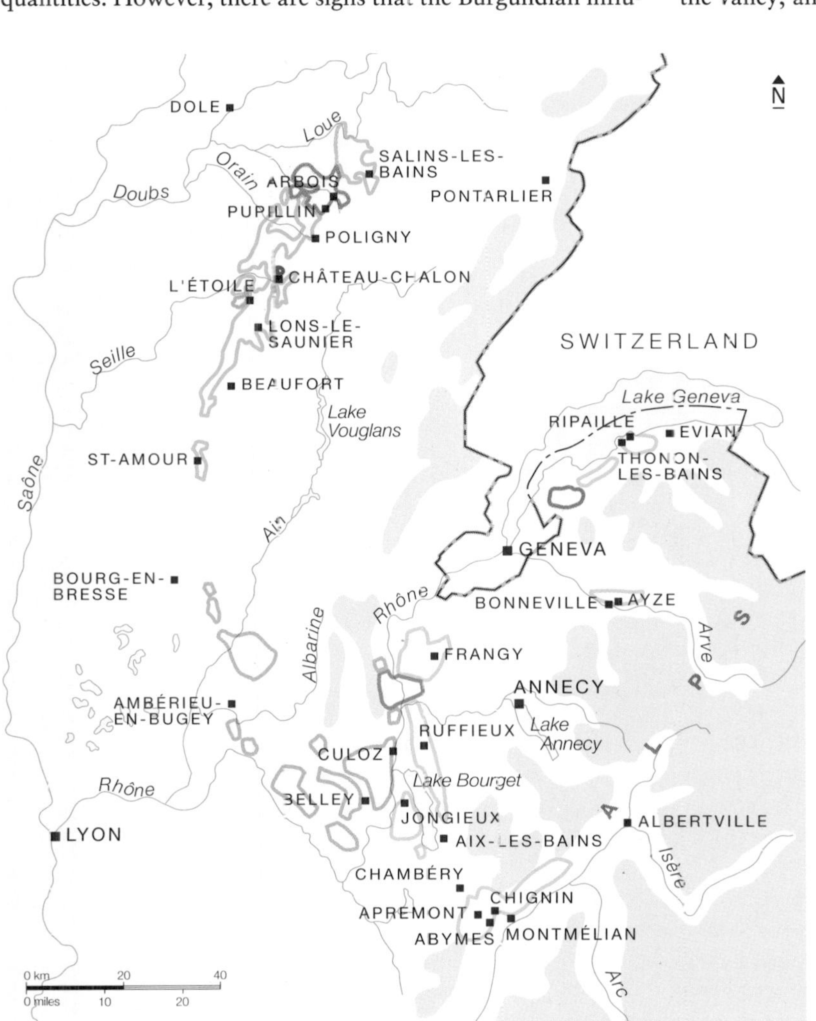

RED GRAPES

Poulsard and Trousseau are the main Jura grapes. A little Pinot Noir may be blended with either. Mondeuse is the most important Savoyard variety. Gamay and Pinot Noir are also common. There is also Gamay in Bugey.

WHITE GRAPES

Savagnin is the main Jura grape, often blended with Chardonnay for wines other than *jaune*. There are increasing amounts of non-blended Chardonnay and some Pinot Blanc. Jacquère and Roussanne (locally called Bergeron) predominate in Savoie, followed by Chasselas, Chardonnay, Roussette and others.

CLIMATE

This is basically a continental climate though with high rainfall and temperatures sharply decreasing with altitude. The severity is moderated by the main lakes.

SOIL

In the Côtes du Jura the soil is mostly dark marly clay on the lower slopes with limestone higher up. In Bugey limestone and marly limestone predominate. Savoie vines are grown mostly on limestone-rich soils which are alluvial in origin.

ASPECT

In the Côtes du Jura the vines are grown on the lower slopes at 250–500m (820–1640ft) often on south-west-facing sites; in Bugey, where it is steeper, they are more widely scattered in the foothills. The vineyards in Savoie are also scattered on the lower slopes, often south- or south-east-facing with good aspect to the sun.

Provence

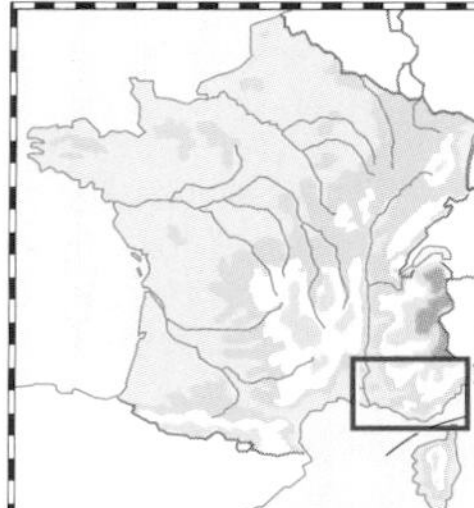

It is difficult to discuss Provence in simple unemotional wine terms. The Ancient Greeks planted vines here in the sixth century BC and the Romans produced wine supposedly fine enough to export to Rome. But if this exotic, irresistible corner of France, stretching from the swooping slopes of the Montagne du Lubéron east of Avignon, from the chill, clear-scented meadows of the alpine pastures far up the Var Valley north of Nice, down through tumbling hills and forests and gorges filled with pine trees, straggling herbs and olive groves, down to the azure and silver sea – if the inhabitants of this enchanted land thought that wine quality mattered, wouldn't they have done something about it by now?

Well, some people are doing something. There are single estates sprouting in les Baux-de-Provence, around Aix-en-Provence, and among the myriad uninspired producers in the Côtes de Provence *appellation* often hewn out of rock and *garrigue* to create new and fascinating flavours where nothing existed before. The old-established *appellations* of Bellet, Bandol and Cassis on the Mediterranean and of Palette near Aix-en-Provence have each got tiny enclaves of ancient individuality amid great swathes of gutless land turning out shabby rosés, fruitless whites and hard, scorched reds not remotely redolent of the lavender, thyme and rosemary that surrounds the vines. Nevertheless, an easy-minded, pleasure-dazzled market of revellers, keen on expenditure and indulgence and devil-take-the-critical-faculties makes it terribly easy for producers to forego the sacrifice and commitment needed to produce the great wine that is certainly possible here. And, yes, I've lazed under a sunshade at midday, gazing out over the broiling sea, quaffing my icy whites and pinks, guzzling my *bouillabaisse*, my *aïoli monstre*, my *rouget* and my *loup* – and, yes, I've been as happy as can be and the devil take my critical faculties too. But vines are crucially important in Provence because most of the land won't support a great deal else. Almost half the cultivated land in Provence is vines, with those other hardy performers, olives and almonds, taking a substantial percentage of the rest. So, accepting that a large amount of Provence wine is simply overpriced holiday hooch, let's see where things are better than this.

GRAPE VARIETIES

In general, pinks and reds come from the usual southern varieties of Grenache, Cinsaut and Carignan. Mourvèdre makes a big contribution at Bandol. Syrah and Cabernet Sauvignon are vital further inland, especially round Aix, while strange ancient grapes like Fuella in Bellet, Tibouren in Bandol and Manosquen in Palette add a certain spice. The whites are dominated by the southern varieties Ugni Blanc and Clairette, with some Bourboulenc and Rolle. Clumps of Sémillon, Sauvignon, Roussanne and Chardonnay also make an appearance.

In such a vast area there are wide differences in soil, but in general the soils are poor and infertile, though there is some

WHERE THE VINEYARDS ARE *This map doesn't include the beaches of St-Tropez, Cannes and Nice – they're further to the east, as is the wine village of Bellet, in the hills behind Nice. But Provence is a vast region and this shows all its glory of sea coast, mountains and valleys. The hills between Arles and Cavaillon shelter the stark vineyards of les Baux-de-Provence, while Palette is directly east of Aix, surrounded by the vineyards of Coteaux d'Aix-en-Provence. These are followed by the Coteaux Varois, while along the Durance Valley lie the Côtes du Lubéron and Coteaux de Pierrevert. The Côtes de Provence vineyards have three main areas: the northern plateau beginning at Toulon to Draguignan, the coastal vineyards below the Massif des Maures from Toulon to St-Raphaël (both continue off the map) and the coastal area from Toulon to la Ciotat. They intertwine with Bandol, but Cassis is just to the west towards Marseille.*

clay in the inland vineyards and some limestone too. Shale and quartz are common nearer the sea. However, Cassis and Bandol have a good deal of clay and limestone and Bandol has gravel too. In the west of Provence the desolate moonscape of les Baux-de-Provence has vineyards planted amid the rubble of bauxite, and only a substructure of water-retentive limestone allows the vine to survive.

The climate differs too, but sun and wind are everywhere in the equation. The Mistral blows right through Provence, and though it barely troubles Bellet in the east, it whips through the low bush vines of Bandol and Cassis, and at les Baux-de-Provence the vines are trained north to south to minimize its force, while Palette rings its north-facing vineyard with pines. Yet with the fierce southern sun, the Mistral is crucial for cooling the grapes; at Bandol it is abetted by sea breezes too, and both these winds keep the vines remarkably free of rot. In fact, rot is rarely a problem in Provence because there is a serious shortage of rain, but if it does fall, it is frequently in the form of thunderous deluges in spring and autumn. With grapes near full ripeness, a good gust of warm dry wind does wonders in keeping disease at bay.

It isn't surprising that in such torrid conditions, red wines perform best. Les Baux-de-Provence has concentrated on reds based on Syrah and Cabernet Sauvignon, sometimes with a little Grenache. That would be thought of as an Australian combination today, but the idea came from a Dr Guyot, one of France's top wine experts in the 1860s. Domaine de Trévallon makes one of the most original and exciting reds in France from 60 per cent Cabernet and 40 per cent Syrah.

Coteaux d'Aix-en-Provence has a considerable reputation for red wines, but is dominated by under-achievers. I prefer the strange, pine-needle gauntness of Palette or the fascinating, herbs and animal power of Bandol. Based largely on the Mourvèdre grape, this is a prospering *appellation* whose wines seem to improve every year as the vines age and Mourvèdre increases its domination. There are good Côtes de Provence reds, usually from estates which have taken the bull by the horns and included grapes like Syrah and Cabernet, regardless of what the local appellation committees say.

Les Baux-de-Provence and Bandol produce the best pinks, Cassis and Palette, in their very different ways, the best white wines with a couple of good Côtes de Provence using Rolle and Bourboulenc. But, I don't know – as the sun rises higher in the sky and the shade of the restaurant beckons, so long as the wine is ice cold, just about anything will do.

The parched, desolate landscape of les Baux-de-Provence is where some of the best rosé and red wines in the South of France are made.

RED GRAPES
Typical southern varieties such as Grenache, Carignan and Cinsaut are most important with significant amounts of Mourvèdre, Syrah and Cabernet Sauvignon.

WHITE GRAPES
The main grapes are Ugni Blanc and Clairette followed by Sémillon, Grenache Blanc, Sauvignon Blanc and Bourboulenc among others.

CLIMATE
The climate is classic Mediterranean – hot dry summers, warm wet winters with blasts from the Mistral helping to dry the grapes after the occasional deluge.

SOIL
A complex soil pattern includes stony limestone, sandstone, clay, shale and gravel underlying the plantings in different areas.

ASPECT
A diverse terrain has vines growing on slopes, foothills and lowland especially where sheltered to the north by ridges and plateaux.

Languedoc-Roussillon

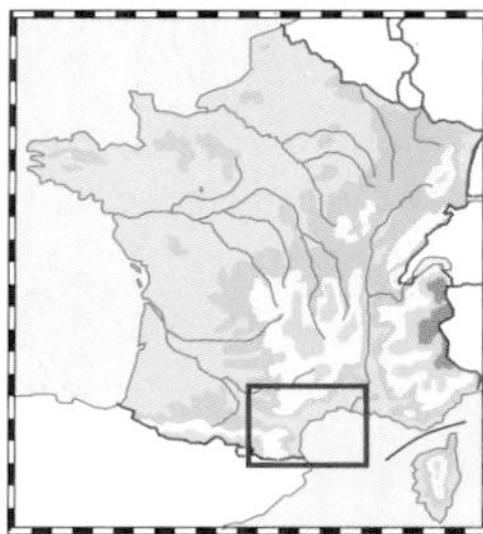

Languedoc-Roussillon is the most complete wine region in France. It is also the most abused. And it is the largest – occupying an area nearly six times as big as the vineyards of Australia, for instance, and 55 times as big as those of New Zealand; in all it provides one-third of France's vineyard acreage, and yet does not have one single world-famous wine style to show for it. It is one of the most old-fashioned, hidebound, reactionary parts of the French wine scene, and at the same time it is France's most exuberantly modern, most outward-looking, most international. Contradictions are at the heart of Languedoc-Roussillon. Let's look at a few of them.

I'm standing picking away at a strange, pinkish soil flecked with slivers of stone, crumbly, hardly able to prevent itself from disintegrating into dust. This is one of the most idiosyncratic and most perfect vineyard soils in France. It's in a tiny valley west of Montpellier in the Hérault. It has no *appellation contrôlée*. When Aimé Guibert bought the property in 1971 there had never been a vine planted there. Now, just over 20 years later, his Mas de Daumas Gassac reds and whites are regarded as two of the greatest wines in France. They still have no *appellation contrôlée*.

Aimé Guibert remains the leading light, but every year sees more passionate, imaginative winemakers arrive in the South of France determined to create great wine their own way, outside the traditional strictures of the grand *appellations* where innovation is generally stifled and rules are strictly to be obeyed. Most of these innovators are French, but not all.

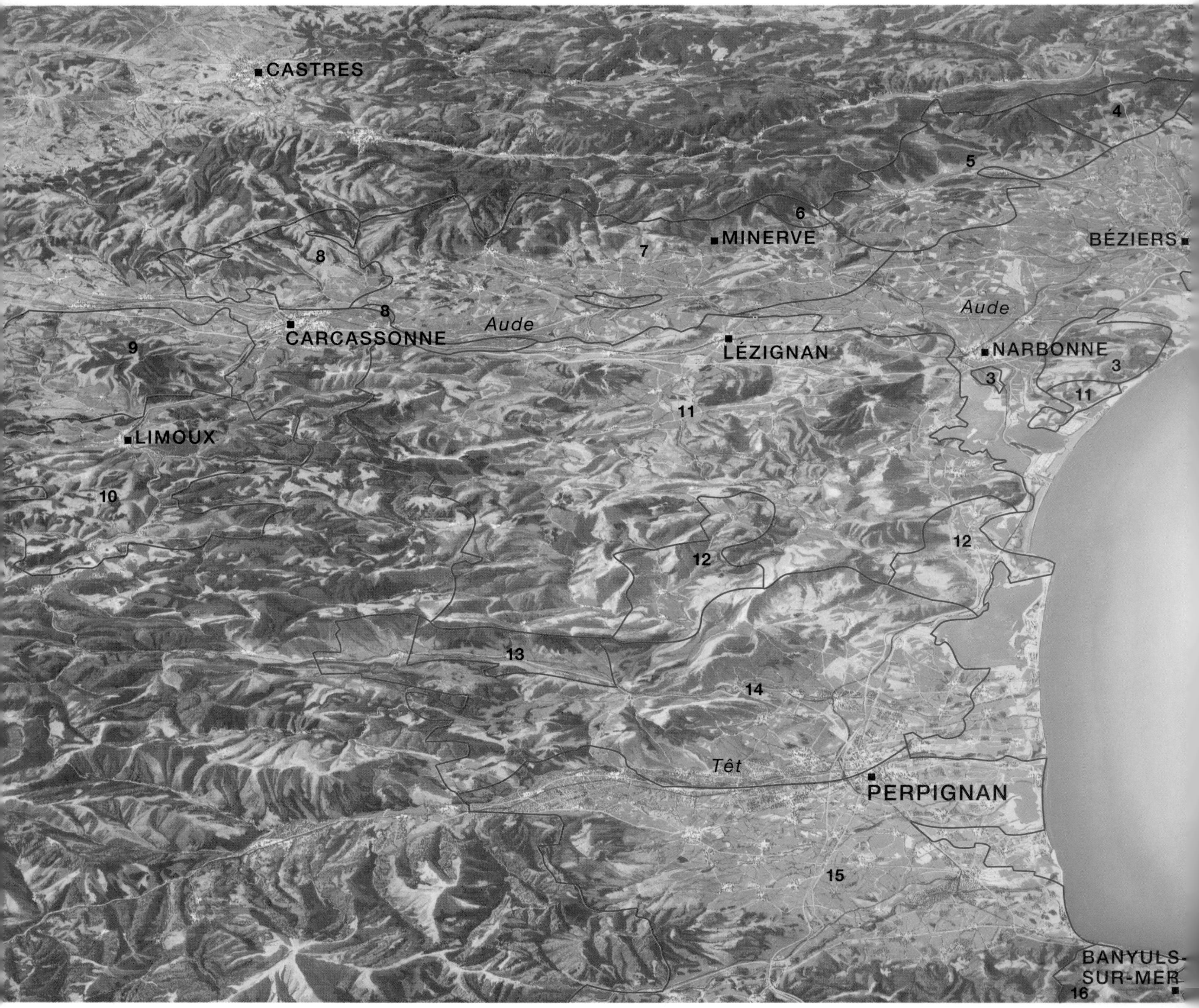

If we head south-west across country, every second village we come to will have a co-operative winery. If we find one in ten where the wine is not stale and flat I should be surprised, but 15 years ago we would not have found one in 50. Still, it's not a co-op we're after. It's a few sheds stuck on the side of the road at Lieuran, north of Beziers. 'G'day, mate' pipes up the tousle-headed winemaker. Australian? He sure is. John Weeks has got an entirely functional state-of-the-art winery packed into these uninspiring sheds at Domaine Virginie and not a vine in sight. He buys in all the grapes he needs and he's turning out delicious crisp, scented dry whites and balanced fruity reds, following the Australian maxim that if you plonk an Aussie down anywhere in the world, with a clean tank and a cooling system, he'll make you good wine. As his compatriot James Herrick, proprietor of 100 hectares (247 acres) west of Narbonne of newly-planted Chardonnay vines – where they'd never heard of Chardonnay before – would add, show an Australian a patch of land, anywhere, and if it's any good they'll grow you a decent crop of Chardonnay.

Is it local, though, or international? Well, the idea is international. But the *laissez-faire* attitude that characterizes the non-AC areas of Languedoc-Roussillon mirrors Australia. So does the hot sun, the dry earth and a reputation that owes nothing to the past but everything to the present and the future. What is 'local' when nothing but mediocrity or worse had ever characterized the vineyards whose grapes Weeks now turns into lovely wine? Put him into any one of those lacklustre, fly-blown co-ops back along the road towards the Gassac Valley and he would transform their wines. Would the flavours still be local? I don't see why not.

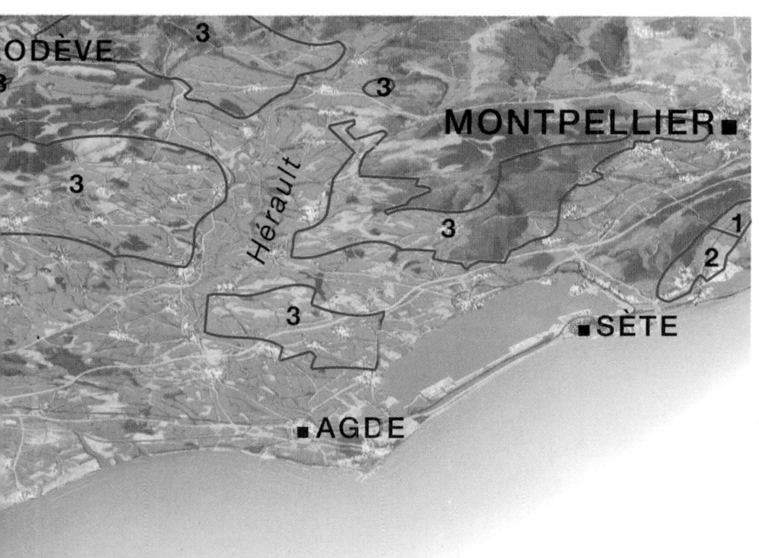

WHERE THE VINEYARDS ARE *Just about the only place on this map where there are no vines is along the ridge of mountain to the north. The higher you go, the cooler it is. But these mountains protect the vineyards from the northerly winds during the day, and at night, the warm air that has risen from the lowlands is pushed back downhill by the mountain air, dramatically cooling the foothills vineyards and ensuring balanced flavours in the fruit. Sea breezes temper the heat close to the coast, but the Mediterranean influence is basically very warm. Further west, this influence lessens and the climate cools and dampens as more temperate Atlantic influences take over. Most of the vineyards higher above sea level are on infertile, stony soil and are best suited to low yields of intensely flavoured black grapes. The lowlands areas are showing themselves highly suitable for the production of fresh whites and light reds.*

AC, VDQS AND VDN WINE AREAS

1. Muscat de Mireval VDN
2. Frontignan VDN, Muscat de Frontignan VDN
3. Coteaux du Languedoc, Clairette du Languedoc
4. Faugères
5. St-Chinian
6. Muscat de St-Jean-de-Minervois VDN
7. Minervois
8. Côtes de Cabardès VDQS
9. Côtes de la Malepère VDQS
10. Blanquette de Limoux, Crémant de Limoux, Limoux
11. Corbières
12. Fitou, Rivesaltes VDN, Muscat de Rivesaltes VDN
13. Côtes du Roussillon-Villages, Maury VDN
14. Côtes du Roussillon-Villages, Rivesaltes VDN, Muscat de Rivesaltes VDN
15. Côtes du Roussillon, Rivesaltes VDN, Muscat de Rivesaltes VDN
16. Collioure, Banyuls VDN

AC, VDQS AND VDN BOUNDARIES

VINEYARDS

TOTAL DISTANCE NORTH TO SOUTH 144KM (89½ MILES)

N

This is one side of what is so exciting in Languedoc-Roussillon. Innovation, excitement, lack of restrictions transforming lead into gold. But there is another side. The side of some of the most ancient wines in France, some of the most ancient and distinctive styles, relying on ancient grape varieties like Carignan, Grenache, Syrah, or Mauzac rather than Cabernet or Chardonnay.

If we go north from Lieuran to Faugères, the road rises away from the plain towards the looming mountains of the Cévennes. The land is bleak but beautiful as we cut across through empty, twisting country lanes curling round the low slopes of the mountain range, the soil is barren, smothered in rock and stone, and only olive trees and vines survive. But there are vineyards that go back to the ninth century at least, when monasteries planted these hills with vines knowing that only poor soil gives great wine. Good soil gives good fruit and vegetables. At Faugères, at St-Chinian, across the base of the towering Montagne Noire to Minèrve, capital of the Minervois where the heretic Cathars were besieged during the Albigensian Crusade in 1210, but where vineyards had been established more than 1000 years before by the Romans, on and on, across the wide Aude Valley into the giddy mountain passes of the Corbières, last holdout of the Cathars, but planted with vines by the Romans too. These are great vineyards that have suffered centuries of neglect but that may justly be thought of as the true cradle of French viticulture.

Nowadays there is a ferocious, proud revival going on in these upland vineyards, and in many other parts of Minervois, and in Coteaux du Languedoc zones like la Clape, the rocky scrub-strewn mountain south of Narbonne that once used to guard its harbour mouth in the days when Narbonne was the First City of Roman Gaul. The wines are generally red, often still based on the Carignan grape, but old Carignan vines in poor stony soil can give excellent wine, especially when abetted by Grenache, Syrah, Cinsaut and Mourvèdre.

There are other great historic wines too. Limoux, high up in the Aude Valley south-west of Carcassonne, claims that its sparkling wine Blanquette de Limoux or Crémant de Limoux – based on the Mauzac grape – is the oldest fizz in the world. Certainly their wines were well-known in 1388 and the locals have set the date of their discovery of how to make it sparkle at 1531, more than a century before Champagne claims to have discovered it.

FORTIFIED WINES

Frontignan, on the shores of the salt lagoons near Montpellier, was known for its sweet Muscat wine in Pliny the Younger's time, and Arnaud de Villeneuve, a doctor at Montpellier, discovered how to make fortified wine here in the late thirteenth century. This discovery spread round Languedoc-Roussillon to Rivesaltes and on down to the Pyrenees at Banyuls where they applied it to the Grenache grape, baked to super-ripeness on the terraced hillsides overlooking the Mediterranean. At Banyuls they don't just fortify this heady purple juice, they age it and purposely oxidize it in large old oak barrels, or sometimes in smaller barrels left out in the elements for at least 30 months. The result is a strange, exotic, dark, treacle-chocolate wine, unlike any other to be found in France. And this is what

Imaginative winemakers are transforming the wines in the Coteaux du Languedoc.

RED GRAPES
There is a huge variety of grapes: traditional (eg Carignan, Grenache, Cinsaut, Syrah) and new for this area (Cabernet, Merlot).

WHITE GRAPES
Whites are less important but include Grenache Blanc, Mauzac, Clairette, Muscat (for VDN), Bourboulenc.

CLIMATE
The summers are hot and dry, winters cool and wet, temperatures decreasing with increasing altitude. The chilly Mistral from the north, and mild sea breezes help cool the vines, and some varieties such as Carignan are drought-resistant.

SOIL
This huge area displays a great diversity of soil types, some highly localized. Broadly they encompass the marly limestone and shale of the hills overlaid with clay in the best sites, red pebbly lateritic soil, gravelly alluvial terraces among others.

ASPECT
The rugged landscape provides numerous and varied sites for vine-growing, the broadly west-east orientation of the valleys combining protection from the north with good southern aspects.

Muscats like these are to be drunk when as young and grapy as possible.

I mean by Languedoc-Roussillon being the most complete region in France – it makes every conceivable sort of wine, and it makes them all increasingly well.

Looking at the landscape on the previous page, it isn't difficult to imagine the whole region having a mass of different climatic and geological conditions, suitable for very different sorts of wine. It was the sheer ease of cultivation, and reliability of weather, that caused the great rolling plain stretching along from Montpellier to Narbonne to become the provider of France's cheap wine from the early 1800s onwards. It is this reliable weather and ease of cultivation that now makes these plains the heartland of the new Vin de Pays d'Oc movement that is making *vins de cépage* – varietal wines – such a new force in French wine. And their most important contribution is to show that modern vineyard and winery methods can make delicious white wines here – something never before achieved.

Yet this is not just prairie; the land dips and rises endlessly, providing a myriad of different soils and mesoclimates. Now, their potential is being explored. Previously, no-one had bothered. And there are a number of increasingly good *appellation contrôlées*. The best are for red wines – Costières de Nîmes, east of Montpellier; several of the top Coteaux du Languedoc Crus like la Clape, St-Chinian and Faugères, as well as Minervois and Corbières. There is a group of good fortified *vins doux naturels* ACs led by Muscat de Frontignan, and one or two lonely white *appellations* like Picpoul de Pinet. The sun is never a problem – and the ever-present wind moderates the heat, the sea breezes being fairly humid and mild, the north winds, which sweep over the Montagne Noire, hard and dry. As we rise up towards this impressive southern bulwark of the Massif Central, the protected sites and the impoverished soil broil the red grapes to a dark but sweet-hearted super-ripeness that, mixed in with the ever-present perfume of bay leaf, Angostura bitters and wild aromas of the hills, makes good modern St-Chinian, Faugères or Minervois thrilling stuff.

Corbières and Fitou are sheltered by their mountain range, as the foothills of the Pyrenees south of the Aude slowly rise to lofty peaks on the Spanish border. Near the Mediterranean, the general effect is hot, but once past Carcassonne, as the Mediterranean influence gives way to the Atlantic, increasingly cool conditions produce truly delicate reds and whites from grapes like Chardonnay, Cabernet and Merlot.

The last great plain before Spain is that of the Agly river. The sun is that bit hotter here, and the relentless Tramontana wind sears the vines. The late-ripening Carignan, helped by the widespread employment of carbonic maceration to extract colour and flavour but not tannin from the grapes and by a leavening of Cinsaut, Syrah and Grenache, produces sturdy Côtes du Roussillon and, largely in the foothills of Corbières, Côtes du Roussillon-Villages. Rivesaltes makes good Grenache *vin doux naturel*, but better Muscat, while way down on the Spanish border, Grenache reigns supreme in the sweet fortified wine of Banyuls. Collioure uses the usual southern red grapes but is finding, above all, that low-yielding, sun-soaked terraces, with their awesome sea view and brow-cooling breeze, just could be one of the great sites for that most tricky but tempestuous of all the southern varieties – the Mourvèdre.

VINS DOUX NATURELS

There are two main styles of *vins doux naturels* – the whites based on Muscat à Petits Grains or Muscat d'Alexandrie and the reds based on Grenache. Each of these naturally achieves very high sugar levels in the hot Mediterranean sun. But the object with the Muscat wines is to preserve their aroma and fruit, so they are sometimes given skin contact before a cool fermentation and, ideally, an early bottling and youthful drinking. Frontignan is the most famous, Mireval and Lunel fairly obscure, St-Jean-de-Minervois rare but good and Muscat de Rivesaltes the most up-to-date and attractive.

To make the Grenache wines of Rivesaltes, Maury and Banyuls, alcohol to 'mute' the wines is added either to free-run juice or to the skins and wine together, and the wines are then kept for between 2 and 10 or more years in casks or vats, sometimes parked outside, sometimes left not quite full if the traditional oxidized *rancio* style is being sought. Young, fresh aromas are not the point here: deep, dark, disturbing richness is.

The Côtes du Roussillon is mainly known for its red wines but you will also find some exotic vins doux naturels *here made from the Grenache grape.*

Corsica

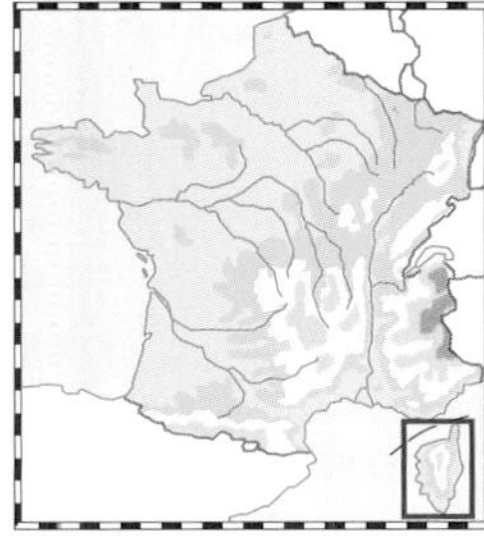

The Ancient Greeks called Corsica the Beautiful Island and, my goodness, I can see why. It's a heavenly place. Well, most of it is. On my first visit the aeroplane gliding down the west coast of the island gave me one of the most stunning views of golden-ochre, sun-baked craggy peaks, teasing mystical, steep-sided valleys disappearing into the rock, coves of dazzlingly pure sand and brilliant azure sea speckled with the white sails of boats at play. My thirst was building by the second and my eyes scoured the parched terrain for those tell-tale patches of soft, lush green that, even in the most arid of landscapes, denote a vineyard in leaf. I didn't see a vine. Not one. Even as I circled out into the Bay of Ajaccio and swooped round, down and on to the airport tarmac at Ajaccio. I knew the Ajaccio region had some of the island's best-regarded vineyards. I knew that Corsica had once been packed with vines and critics even now often say that the island has the perfect climate, with an average rainfall the same as Paris – that is, very high for the Mediterranean – and with the continual presence of the mountains and the sea moderating the heat of the blazing sun.

MODERNIZATION AND TRADITION

Yet critics also say less kindly things. They often did say, and still do, that splendid grapes are rarely turned into fine wine on this lovely island. That first night, in my hotel, having finally located a few vines hidden away to the north of Ajaccio, I tried the red, the rosé and the white wines. I didn't finish a glass of any of them. Then I tried a couple of better-known single-estate wines. Rustic, rough, with a searing volatility. I switched to Campari and soda and remained on it for the rest of my stay. My first general tasting of Corsican wines in London was marked by a melancholy acceptance that, although there seemed to be some interesting fruit flavours lurking in there somewhere, the standard of wine-making – excepting that of the Peraldi estate in Ajaccio – was dire.

But things are slowly getting better, both in the traditional low-yielding, difficult-to-find vineyards of the north, west and south, and in the extremely obvious large mechanized plantations on the flat prairie-land in the east of the island. These two regions are attempting to do very different things, and both are now having some success.

The reclaimed swampy plains of the east had been exploited by French settlers returning from Algeria in the 1960s. By 1973 they had planted 32,000 hectares (79,000 acres) of vines. Today 90 per cent of those new plantations have been grubbed up and only about 10,000 hectares (24,700 acres) remain in all of Corsica. Most of these settlers had attempted merely to produce rough hooch from the usual southern French cluster of grapes – Grenache, Cinsaut, Carignan and Alicante Bouschet. There is no demand any more for that kind of wine and the eastern vineyards that are successful nowadays are those, particularly around the Étang de Diane, that are creating good *vin de pays* from grapes like Chardonnay, Syrah and Cabernet.

However, Corsica's tradition is based on less well-known grapes – the native red Nielluccio (related to Tuscany's Sangiovese), the red Sciacarello and the white Vermentino, all Italian varieties and reminding us that Corsica was Italian for 700 years before France gained control in 1769. Corsica only received its first *appellation contrôlée* in 1968 – it was for Patrimonio, followed by Ajaccio in 1971 – and the majority of Corsican wine still either does not qualify for, or does not seek, *appellation contrôlée* status. But there is now a strong movement on the island to implement the regulations of the overall Vin de Corse *appellation*, and in particular the progressive raising of the minimum percentage required of these three local grape varieties in the wines. This must be the right move for all the traditional vineyards. Yields are low, conditions are difficult, so individuality is the only way to justify what are always going to be higher prices than those for wines produced in mainland southern France.

WINE AREAS

Patrimonio in the north is especially good at producing full-bodied, herb-scented reds dominated by Nielluccio grown on clay and limestone soils as well as some rich exotic, Muscat du Cap Corse. Ajaccio to the west has granite soils that suit the Sciacarello, but Peraldi at least also produces fine Vermentino.

Of the various Vin de Corse *appellations*, Coteaux du Cap Corse in the north has slaty soils which suit the Vermentino, and strong winds and low rainfall which encourage the production of some lovely sweet Muscat. Calvi in the north-west produces good herb-scented rosé and decent gutsy red in reasonable quantities for the local tourist trade. In the south, the poor sandy or granite soils in Sartène, Figari and Porto-Vecchio are all potentially good for the native varieties. Yet most of those who tried to revitalize these areas were after higher yields and quicker profits than such soils can give. The commonest sight now is of vineyards grubbed up and forlorn rather than filled with flourishing bushes laden with juicy Nielluccio, Sciacarello and Vermentino grapes.

Nevertheless the potential in the vineyards is still there. What is now required is a new wave of adventurous investors who are in it for the long haul, and who are intent upon coaxing these ancient idiosyncratic grape varieties into producing good modern, yet authentically Corsican wines.

RED GRAPES

The local varieties are Nielluccio and Sciacarello. Other 'southern' varieties such as Grenache, Carignan and others are also used.

WHITE GRAPES

Vermentino is frequently blended with Ugni Blanc. There is some sweet Muscat.

CLIMATE

A full-blown Mediterranean climate with long dry summers and warm wet winters. Irregular but welcome summer rainfall is brought by the Libeccio and Sirocco winds.

SOIL

The soil types are varied, with slaty soils predominant in the north and gravelly sand and granitic soils in the west and south of the island.

ASPECT

The vineyards are mostly on the lower slopes and the plains. The annual number of hours of sunshine is one of the highest in France so ripening is not a problem and aspect to the sun is not critical here.

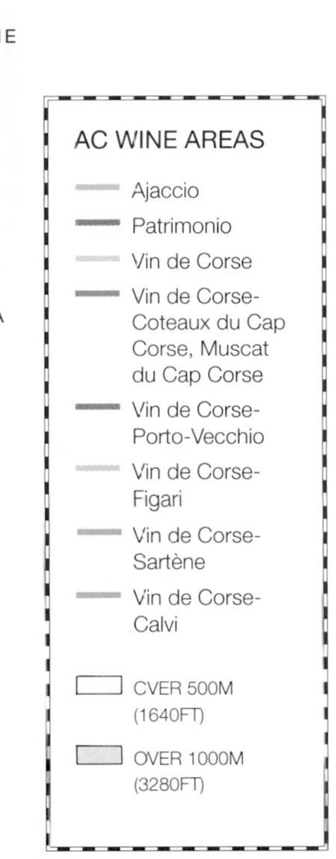

South-West France

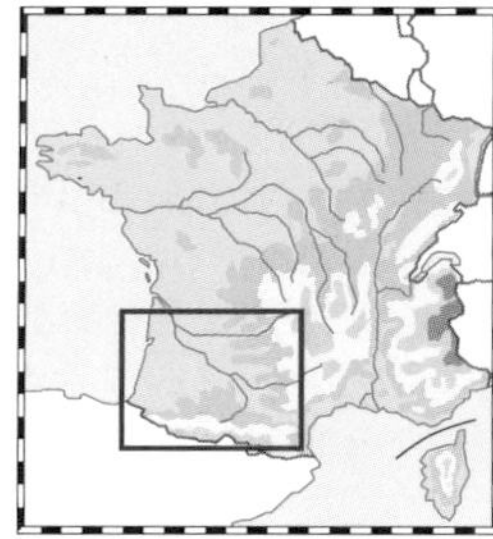

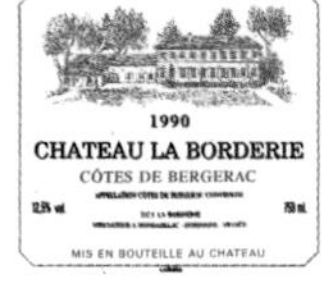

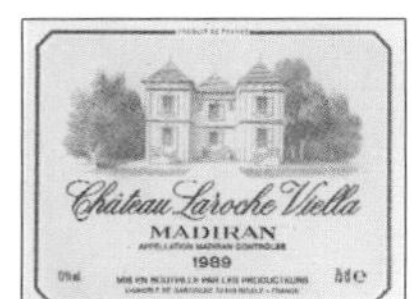

THE SOUTH-WEST OF FRANCE looks so easy to understand. There you have this great king that is Bordeaux lording it grandly over the whole region, its copious robes spilling beneficently outwards from the Gironde. Vassal states like Bergerac, Côtes de Duras, Côtes du Marmandais and Buzet crouch gratefully at the hem, imitating Bordeaux's styles, using the same grape varieties and generally producing good wines, but not so good that they'll disturb the equanimity of the lord-and-master Bordeaux.

That's how it seems. But it's much more complicated than that. Not only do areas like Bergerac and the Marmandais have interesting features of their own, but Buzet is already overlapping with an entirely different culture in the brandy-producing region of Armagnac. Cahors may base its wines on the Bordeaux grape Malbec – but as though in defiance of its long isolation up the winding Lot river, Cahors crafts from it a magnificent, most un-Bordeaux-like wine. Most un-anything-like, in fact. As the hills and valleys roll and coil away from Bordeaux, the Atlantic influence starts to be matched by that of the Mediterranean. And we enter a bewildering, fascinating but introspective world of ancient vineyards, ancient grape varieties and thrilling wine styles that the newly imaginative world of wine is only just discovering.

BERGERAC AND THE DORDOGNE

You wouldn't even know you'd left the Bordeaux region as you take the D936 through the Bordeaux town of Castillon-la-Bataille. The prosperous flat valley of the Dordogne is still a benign rural marriage of maize, meadowland and vines. But at the stroke of a bureaucrat's pen, things have changed. As you cross the *département* border between Gironde and Dordogne the Cabernet and Merlot, the Sauvignon and Sémillon grapes, grown in virtually identical conditions, will no longer be AC Bordeaux but rather AC Bergerac or AC Montravel.

You wouldn't really know you'd left Bordeaux when you taste most of the Dordogne wines either. The soils are similar, generally tending towards the sandy clay types with some lime-

AC AND VDQS WINE AREAS

- Bergerac, Côtes de Bergerac
- Bergerac sub-regions
  1. Côtes de Montravel
  2. Haut-Montravel
  3. Montravel
  4. Saussignac
  5. Monbazillac
  6. Pécharmant
  7. Rosette
- Côtes de Duras
- Côtes du Marmandais
- Cahors
- Vins d'Entraygues et du Fel VDQS
- Vins d'Estaing VDQS
- Vin de Marcillac
- Gaillac
- Côtes du Frontonnais
- Vins de Lavilledieu VDQS
- Côtes du Brulhois VDQS
- Buzet
- Côtes de St-Mont VDQS
- Madiran, Pacherenc du Vic Bilh
- Jurançon
- Tursan VDQS
- Béarn, Béarn-Bellocq
- Irouléguy
- OVER 500M (1640 FT)
- OVER 1000M (3280 FT)

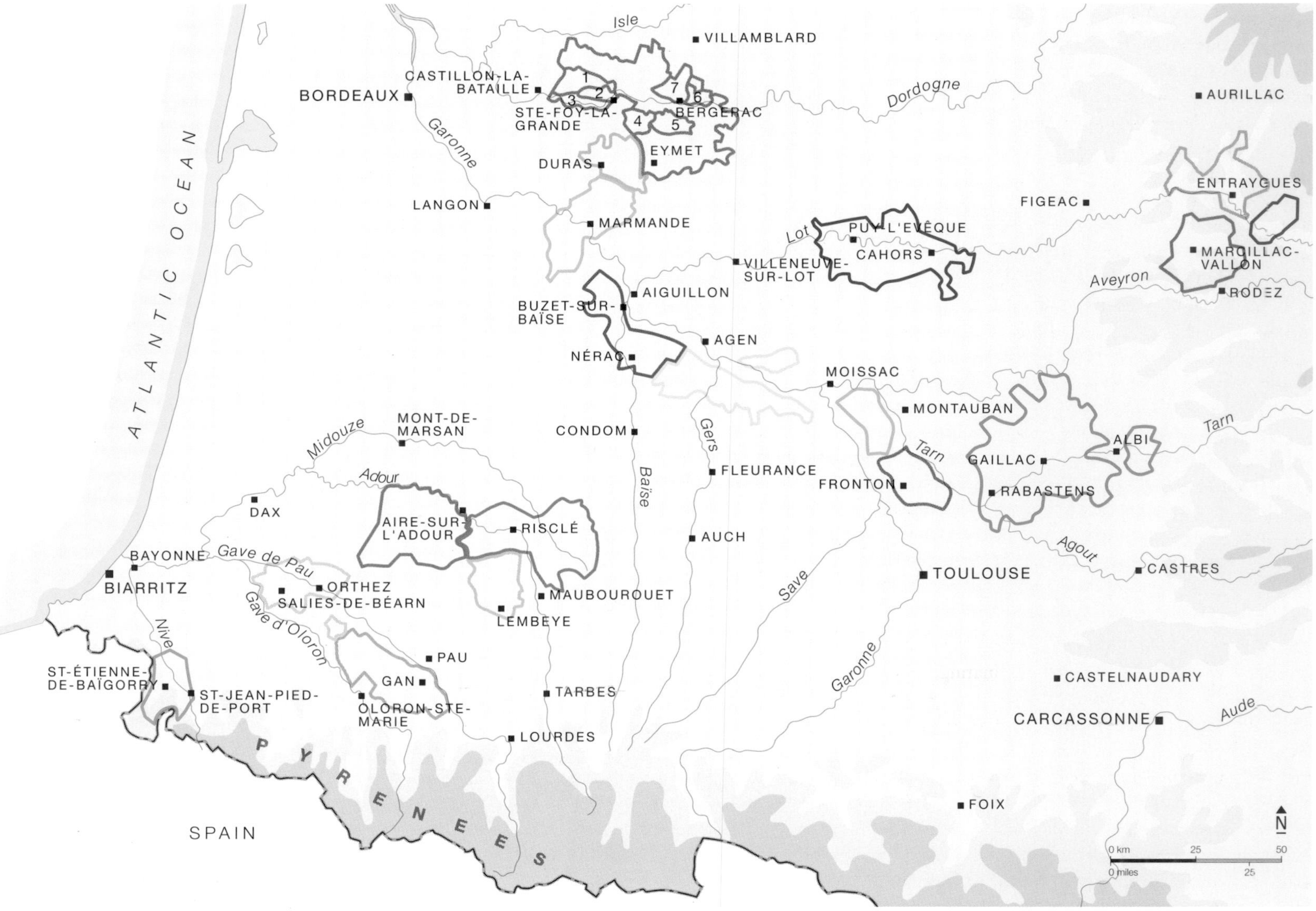

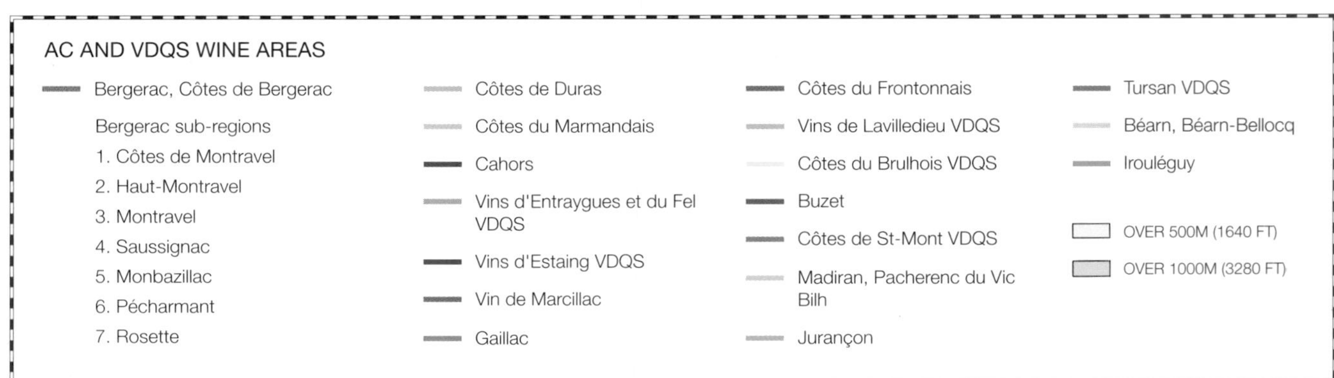

stone outcrops. Sunshine and heat are fairly similar, though rainfall is usually lower. The *appellations* can actually all get a bit confusing, but most of the dry reds and whites will end up calling themselves Bergerac or Côtes de Bergerac, whatever title they are technically allowed to use. At the western end, on the north bank of the Dordogne, the dry whites can call themselves Montravel, the semi-sweets and the fairly sweets can call themselves Côtes de Montravel and Haut-Montravel respectively. South-east of Ste-Foy-la-Grande, sweet wines can be called Saussignac but are generally called Côtes de Bergerac Moelleux, and north-west of the town of Bergerac, Rosette semi-sweet whites hardly ever appear under their own name. The *appellation* Bergerac wines themselves, produced in 93 different communes along the Dordogne, are mostly virtually indistinguishable from their Bordeaux counterparts.

Two sub-regions within Bergerac that outshine the rest and do usually use their own names are Pécharmant and Monbazillac. Pécharmant's vineyards are on a plateau mostly tilted towards the south where a mixture of chalky and gravelly clays sit above an impermeable iron hardpan. These red wines are usually Bergerac's best: deep, dark but full of fruit and capable of aging. Monbazillac's vineyards, however, frequently face north, sloping down to the river valley, losing some heat, but gaining the effects of mists from the river which encourage noble rot and the production of sweet white wine. Most Monbazillac is mildly sweet at best, but there is an increasing number of growers prepared to make the sacrifice necessary for truly sweet wine when the grapes ripen sufficiently.

GARONNE AND TARN WINES

Next to Bergerac lies the Côtes de Duras *appellation*, and, straddling the Garonne Valley further south, the Côtes du Marmandais. These wines are basically Bordeaux in all but name, though in the latter, the presence of the local variety Abouriou in small amounts can add an extra dimension to the red. Buzet, too, on the south banks of the Garonne and intertwined with the Armagnac brandy region, uses the Bordeaux grapes to good effect, with its reds surprisingly good.

But we have to push further up the Garonne, towards Toulouse, then branch east up the river Tarn to find an area that has truly broken away from Bordeaux's influence – the Côtes du Frontonnais, with its marvellous Negrette grape. The Negrette likes the hot Toulouse weather and the deep gravel beds the vineyards occupy and produces a succulent, soft-centred red, velvet smooth and darkly sweet with liquorice and strawberries. It's often blended with grapes like Cabernet Franc and Syrah, but I like as much Negrette as I can get.

Gaillac, further up the Tarn, is a large area, dominated by giant co-operatives, with tremendous potential so far only partly realized. Six white grape varieties are used for a broad swathe of styles, from dry to sweet, from still to hinting at bubbles to fully foaming. Eight different red varieties contribute to wines that are often at their brisk best when peppery and young but are sometimes made to age impressively.

THE LOT RIVER

The Cahors AC, 80km (50 miles) north-west of Gaillac, concentrates on one single wine – a fascinating, tobacco-scented, green apple-streaked yet plum and prune-rich red made largely from the Malbec grape, here called the Cot or Auxerrois. Famous for 'black wine' which was much in demand for blending with pale Bordeaux reds during the years of English supremacy in Aquitaine – and for a good while after too – the region was devastated by phylloxera in the nineteenth century, and it was not until the 1970s that a determined band of local growers, along with a good co-operative, rediscovered its former glories. Now, with vineyards planted on the high stony limestone plateau or *causses*, and the sand and gravel alluvial terraces lower down in the Lot Valley, and a climate caught between the influences of the Atlantic and the Mediterranean, with the Lot river twisting and turning like a demented serpent to create endless mesoclimates, Cahors is producing some of the most individual wines in the South-West.

Further along the Lot and north of Rodez in the Aveyron are three obscure wine areas. Marcillac, with its strong, dry reds mainly from the Fer, is the best known.

THE PYRENEAN FOOTHILLS

Travelling south to the Armagnac area on the south banks of the Garonne, and further on into the foothills of the Pyrenees we come to Madiran, another red wine that would describe itself as one of the South-West's best. Vine-growing in this area was virtually defunct after World War Two, but now there are about 1400 hectares (3459 acres) of vineyards. The Tannat grape is the chief variety, famed for its tough, rugged style – and most Madiran needs quite a while to come into focus, and many examples never achieve it. A little white with the *appellation* Pacherenc du Vic-Bilh, usually dry, occasionally sweet, is also made, from a blend of four south-western grapes with the emphasis on the flinty, pear-skin-scented Ruffiac. Just to the north of Madiran, Côtes de St-Mont uses the same grape varieties to make attractive snappy reds and pleasant whites. The Tursan VDQS makes wines similar to Côtes de St-Mont.

Further up into the Pyrenees foothills are Béarn, a fairly uninspired region, and Jurançon. Jurançon uses the excellent Petit Manseng and the good Gros Manseng and Courbu varieties. Most of the wine is dry and white, but the numerous protected mesoclimates in these valleys, where the vineyards lie at an average altitude of 300m (985ft), allow the grapes to bake in the sun. The low-yielding Petit Manseng often can shrivel on the vines, concentrating its juice and producing luscious sweet wine dripping with honey and nuts, cinnamon and ginger but always refreshingly cut with a slash of lemon acidity.

And if you go on, higher and higher into the cloud-covered chilly mountain valleys right to the border of Spain you'll find the tiny *appellation* outpost of Irouléguy, whose strange gritty mountain red from vineyards on the sheltered valley slopes marks a final, defiant flourish of French tradition before the entirely different world of the Iberian peninsula takes over on the far side of the snowy peaks.

Co-operatives in the Côtes de Duras offer good Bordeaux-style reds and whites at distinctly reasonable prices.

RED GRAPES

The main grapes are the 'Bordeaux' varieties: Cabernets Sauvignon and Franc, Merlot and Malbec with local specials notably Tannat and Negrette.

WHITE GRAPES

Sémillon and Sauvignon predominate in the north, with Petit Manseng, Gros Manseng and other local varieties in the south.

CLIMATE

The climate is similar to Bordeaux with strong Atlantic influences, though with slightly higher temperatures and lower rainfall especially as you go south and east.

SOIL

The great variety of soils include the sandstone and marly limestone of the Bergerac and Tarn regions, Kimmeridgian limestone in Cahors, alluvial sand and gravel in the South-West.

ASPECT

Protection from Atlantic gusts can be important here favouring south-, east- and south-east-facing sites.

Vins de Pays

Some of France's most exuberantly modern wine is being made by vin de pays *producers.*

It's difficult nowadays to realize quite how poor a vast amount of French wine used to be as recently as the 1970s. Wine for the most part in France was not anything exciting or unusual, it was simply the beverage you drank with your meals. Lunch, certainly, dinner, certainly, and in many rural and industrial communities, with your breakfast too, or on your way to work. What was necessary was that it should be cheap, it should have some sort of alcoholic strength to give you a bit of energy and a bit of a lift, and that it should aid your digestion. That it should taste good hardly ever entered the equation, because it hardly ever did.

And it hardly ever had a name except maybe for a fanciful brand name dreamed up by someone in a merchant's office who knew nothing of where the wine came from or which grape varieties contributed. *Pinard,* the French called it, or *onze degrés*, or *gros rouge*. *Pinard* is not politely translatable, *onze degrés* simply meant eleven degrees, its alcoholic strength, and *gros rouge* just means the big red, the rough red, neither adjectives being applied in a complimentary manner.

All of France contributed to this faceless lake of wine but by far the most important area was the Midi, the four *départements* of Gard, Hérault, Aude and Pyrénées-Orientales that make up Languedoc-Roussillon. This area had enjoyed almost uninterrupted prosperity since the Industrial Revolution of the 1820s spawned a workforce millions strong, thirsty and uncritical. *Pinard* had been their drink. During the 1950s they were still drinking it in vast quantities. The average annual per capita consumption of wine hovered round 170 litres.

DECLINING CONSUMPTION

In 1956 the annual wine consumption figure fell for the first time. By 1968 the figure had drifted down to 150 litres per head and to 112 litres by 1983. In 1992, a mere 66 litres of wine per capita were drunk in France. These figures show a major crisis for French wine producers. But whereas almost all the French areas apart from the South had traditions of quality enshrined by *appellation contrôlée* regulations and could afford to let the marginal vineyards waste away or be turned over to other crops, the Midi was a virtual monoculture of the vine, based solely on quantity, not quality. You didn't buy Midi wine by name, you bought it by alcoholic degree. Nearly all the wine available was red; useful, when the new generation of drinkers was demanding white. *Appellations contrôlées* in the Midi of the 1960s were as rare as snowflakes in July.

Throughout the 1960s it became increasingly clear that the continuing decline of French wine consumption was brewing up a major political and economic catastrophe for the Midi. It seemed that people were drinking less but better wine, so those with some kind of geographical or historical individuality were increasingly in demand. The Midi's only reputation had been for anonymous mediocrity so there was no geographical or traditional individuality you could attempt to improve. But if you could *give* them their own geographical identity, if you could formulate a set of regulations loose enough to encourage wine producers without any experience of quality to give them a try, yet tight enough in certain cases so as genuinely to improve the wine's flavour – and if money could be provided to support such a scheme – then disaster might be averted.

With decrees in 1964 and 1968, but particularly with more detailed regulations in 1973 and 1979, a framework of *vin de pays* was established to try to achieve this. *Vin de pays* means 'country wine' – a nice, attractive name implying something local, even parochial – and it was exactly the right choice of name. French wine quality classification has always based itself on delimiting geographically precise vineyard areas. The top rung is the Controlled Appellation of Origin. The second rung is the Delimited Wine of Superior Quality. The *vin de pays* became the third rung, with very loose geographical strictures – any reasonable vineyard land in a set area could use it – but quite strict regulations for production, taking *vin de pays* way above *vin de table* in quality.

There are three types of *vin de pays*. Regional is where a group of *départements* bands together under one name. There are four, the most important being Vin de Pays d'Oc, covering Languedoc-Roussillon. There are 39 departmental *vins de pays* – each one covering an entire *département*. And there are 96 zonal *vins de pays* covering more precise regions inside a *département*. That makes a total of 139 *vins de pays,* of which 60 are in the four *départements* of Languedoc-Roussillon.

In regions where there are also *appellations contrôlées*, the allowed yields are higher and the minimum alcohol lower than for *appellation* wines. Yet *vin de pays* requirements are far higher than for basic *vin de table*. This is crucial in all those swathes of the Midi that had never until recently produced anything but *vin de table*. Yields are between 80 and 90 hectolitres per hectare and minimum alcohol usually 10 degrees whereas a *vin de table* producer might get 200 hectolitres per hectare, and was technically supposed to achieve 8.5 degrees alcohol.

Choice of grape varieties here is crucial. The *vin de table* villains are varieties like Aramon, Alicante Bouschet and Carignan. Of these, only Carignan is allowed for *vin de pays,* while a whole variety of good quality grapes not permitted in local *appellations contrôlées* are allowed for *vins de pays*. In the South this has meant the introduction of grapes like Cabernet, Merlot, Pinot Noir, Chardonnay, Sauvignon and Viognier. This has allowed growers to benefit from the current trend to label wine by grape variety, a practice being stamped on by the *appellation contrôlée* authorities.

When you add to this various tasting and analytical tests as well as tight controls of two of the most common wine faults – excessive volatile acidity and sulphur – the change round is little short of remarkable. There are still bad *vins de pays* as there are bad *appellation contrôlée* wines, but considering that most of the vineyards producing *vin de pays* had no right to produce anything but *vin de table* before, it's pretty impressive.

The other achievement of *vins de pays* has been to encourage imaginative wine-making in areas like the Loire Valley where the local *appellations* were inflexible and wedded to wine styles that simply weren't selling and, once again, in the South. Many producers find the Midi *appellations contrôlées* too restrictive and therefore choose to apply *vin de pays* rules to their vineyards even if they are classed inside an *appellation*. Often the *vins de pays* they make actually sell for more than the local *appellation* wine. Or else there are inspired winemakers like Aimé Guibert at Mas de Daumas Gassac who creates classic wines where nothing existed before using whatever grape varieties come into his head, and several that don't.

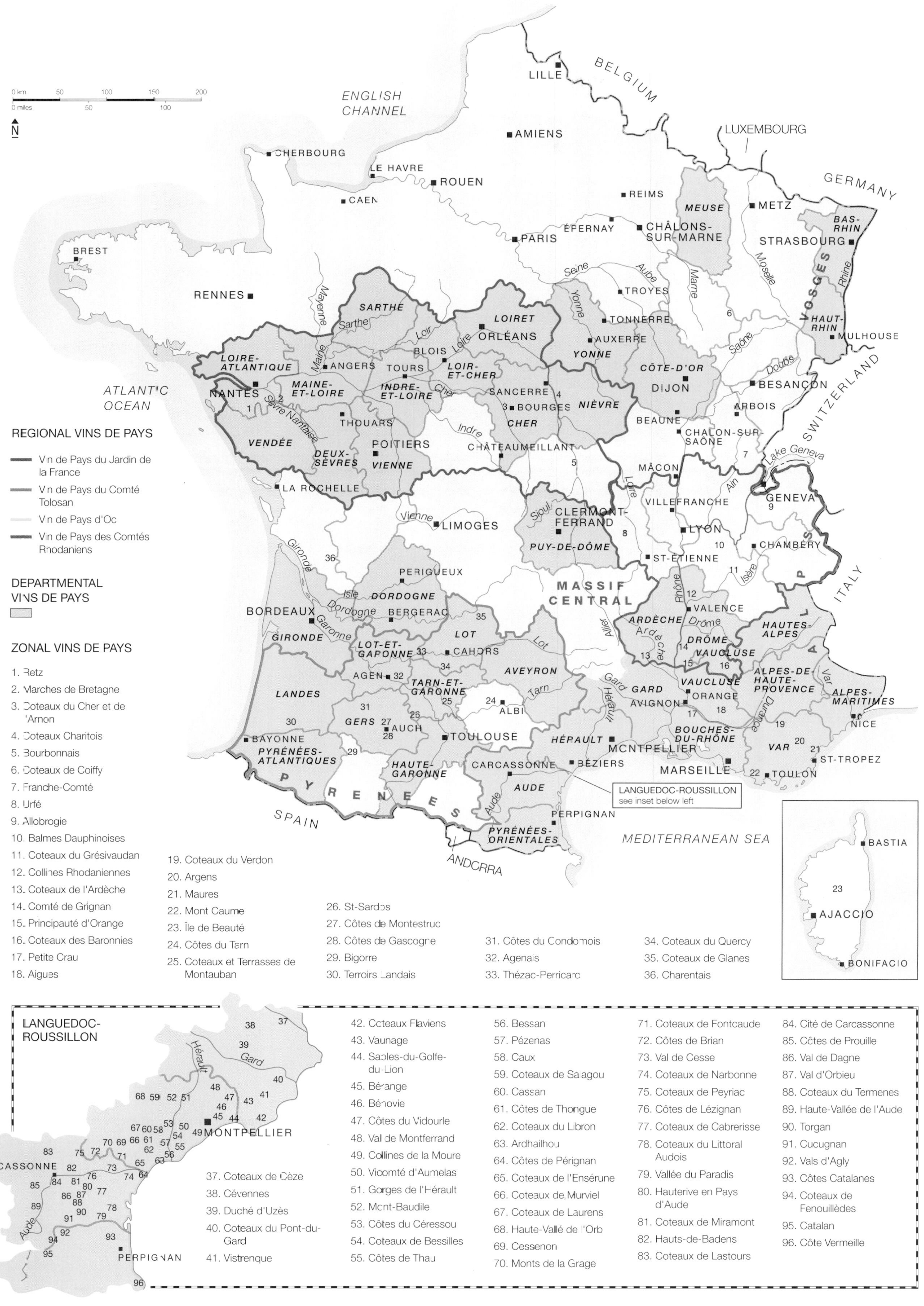

ENGLISH CHANNEL
ATLANTIC OCEAN
MEDITERRANEAN SEA
BELGIUM
LUXEMBOURG
GERMANY
SWITZERLAND
ITALY
SPAIN
ANDORRA
MASSIF CENTRAL
LANGUEDOC-ROUSSILLON see inset below left
REGIONAL VINS DE PAYS
Vin de Pays du Jardin de la France
Vin de Pays du Comté Tolosan
Vin de Pays d'Oc
Vin de Pays des Comtés Rhodaniens
DEPARTMENTAL VINS DE PAYS
ZONAL VINS DE PAYS
1. Retz
2. Marches de Bretagne
3. Coteaux du Cher et de l'Arnon
4. Coteaux Charitois
5. Bourbonnais
6. Coteaux de Coiffy
7. Franche-Comté
8. Urfé
9. Allobrogie
10. Balmes Dauphinoises
11. Coteaux du Grésivaudan
12. Collines Rhodaniennes
13. Coteaux de l'Ardèche
14. Comté de Grignan
15. Principauté d'Orange
16. Coteaux des Baronnies
17. Petite Crau
18. Aigues
19. Coteaux du Verdon
20. Argens
21. Maures
22. Mont Caume
23. Île de Beauté
24. Côtes du Tarn
25. Coteaux et Terrasses de Montauban
26. St-Sardos
27. Côtes de Montestruc
28. Côtes de Gascogne
29. Bigorre
30. Terroirs Landais
31. Côtes du Condomois
32. Agenais
33. Thézac-Perricard
34. Coteaux du Quercy
35. Coteaux de Glanes
36. Charentais
LANGUEDOC-ROUSSILLON
37. Coteaux de Cèze
38. Cévennes
39. Duché d'Uzès
40. Coteaux du Pont-du-Gard
41. Vistrenque
42. Coteaux Flaviens
43. Vaunage
44. Sables-du-Golfe-du-Lion
45. Bérange
46. Bénovie
47. Côtes du Vidourle
48. Val de Montferrand
49. Collines de la Moure
50. Vicomté d'Aumelas
51. Gorges de l'Hérault
52. Mont-Baudile
53. Côtes du Céressou
54. Coteaux de Bessilles
55. Côtes de Thau
56. Bessan
57. Pézenas
58. Caux
59. Coteaux de Salagou
60. Cassan
61. Côtes de Thongue
62. Coteaux du Libron
63. Ardhailhou
64. Côtes de Pérignan
65. Coteaux de l'Ensérune
66. Coteaux de Murviel
67. Coteaux de Laurens
68. Haute-Vallé de l'Orb
69. Cessenon
70. Monts de la Grage
71. Coteaux de Fontcaude
72. Côtes de Brian
73. Val de Cesse
74. Coteaux de Narbonne
75. Coteaux de Peyriac
76. Côtes de Lézignan
77. Coteaux de Cabrerisse
78. Coteaux du Littoral Audois
79. Vallée du Paradis
80. Hauterive en Pays d'Aude
81. Coteaux de Miramont
82. Hauts-de-Badens
83. Coteaux de Lastours
84. Cité de Carcassonne
85. Côtes de Prouille
86. Val de Dagne
87. Val d'Orbieu
88. Coteaux du Termenes
89. Haute-Vallée de l'Aude
90. Torgan
91. Cucugnan
92. Vals d'Agly
93. Côtes Catalanes
94. Coteaux de Fenouillèdes
95. Catalan
96. Côte Vermeille

TREIS MOSEL SEKT

GERMANY

IF EVER THERE WERE A COUNTRY whose vinous treasures need cosseting and cherishing, whose ability to thrill and excite depends upon an annual dance along the knife edge between languorous autumn sunshine and destructive autumn rains, it is Germany. No country's growers must take greater risks than those of Germany to create the brilliant wines upon which her reputation relies. No vineyard sites need to be more carefully chosen for maximum exposure to sun and minimum exposure to wind, frost and rain than those of Germany. And in no country are the most famous names betrayed more shamefully by vineyards having no right whatsoever to be associated with them than in Germany.

Central Germany is pretty well as far north as you can go and still have a reasonable chance of ripening any of the classic grapes. Even in good years it is only rarely possible to achieve alcohol levels that would be regarded as fully ripe in warmer countries. But the genius of the Riesling grape is that, if you allow it to ripen slowly through long, cool summers, and are lucky enough to have a balmy autumn, it is capable of a sublime balance between fruit acidity and fruit sweetness that is unique in the world – even at ridiculously low alcohol levels and scarily high levels of acid. Add a little noble rot and the result is even more remarkable.

Yet this is only possible on special sites. These should be as lovingly delineated and protected as are far less special sites elsewhere throughout Europe. Instead, such action is officially disapproved of as being elitist, while Germany's international reputation has been ruined by a misguided attempt at popularism in providing large amounts of innocuous, cheap wine. Lying at the very limits of the grape's ability to ripen, Germany is the last place that should be providing oceans of cheap wine. It's such a shame, because a whole generation of wine lovers is growing up unaware of the glories of German wine, and the German wine law doesn't help. On the label there is no obvious difference between Piesporter Goldtröpfchen – one of the great natural vineyard sites in Europe – and Piesporter Michelsberg, a general name covering any wine from numerous inferior villages in the locality. Bernkastel is a great wine village with some superb sites, yet wine from the whole of the Middle Mosel can call itself Bereich Bernkastel. What may have began as an attempt to simplify and modernize traditional practice has now become one of the chief instruments whereby Germany's fine wine reputation is defiled.

At Treis on the chilly Mosel the vineyards rise smoothly high above the town. A few decades ago these slopes would all have been cut into small terraces; now the only terraces left are in the churchyard.

The Wine Regions of Germany

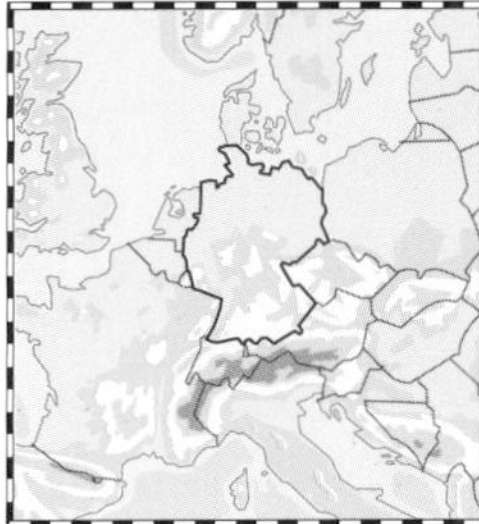

In an ideal world the names on this map of Germany would echo with romance for all wine lovers. 'We're just popping to the Saar for the weekend,' people would boast to each other. 'We try to go every year. We'll fit in an afternoon on the Ruwer, and say hello to the Bernkasteler Doctor as well.' Sounds absurd? It's what Europeans say about Burgundy. You can see them in their cars, driving along the main road through the Côte d'Or, and they can't believe that at last they're seeing road signs to places they've only seen before on labels.

But in fact sightseeing is every bit as crucial to understanding German wine as it is to understanding what makes one Burgundy taste different to another. Maybe even more so, since Germany is cold, and is situated as far north as grapes will ripen. Wine-making is only possible in many parts of Germany when four elements come together: site, climate, soil and grape. And the greatest of these is site.

First of all, nearly all the vineyards are in the southern half of the country. The best vines are often grown where no other crops will flourish: on slopes too steep for cows, or where the soil is too poor or shallow over the underlying rock for wheat to put down roots. But steep slopes have great advantages for vines. They offer shelter from the wind, particularly if they are crowned by woods or if there is a mountain range behind. Then again, they get stronger sunlight: on flat ground the sun's rays strike at an angle; on steeply sloping land they strike perpendicularly. (A great simplification, of course, but that is the principle.) That means fewer shadows and greater heat.

In order to maximize sunshine and warmth, in Germany the slopes must be south-, west- or east-facing. Facing east means that the vines get the morning sun; those facing west get the afternoon sun, and this can be an advantage if fog is common, since it will usually have burnt off by the afternoon. And the best kind of slope of all is in a river valley.

Rivers are crucial to vine-growing in Germany. Nearly all the great wine areas are close to rivers and their tributaries: vines follow the progress of the Mosel and the Rhine, the Main and the Neckar and (to a lesser extent) the Elbe, Saale and Unstrut. The reason is that an expanse of water has the effect of moderating extremes of temperature. They help to ward off frosts and they give humidity in hot, dry summers; and the water surface reflects heat and light back on to the banks, particularly if they are steep.

Not all of Germany is too cold for grapes. A look at the map reveals that most wine areas are in the south. But there is an east-west division of climate, as well as a north-south one, with the climate becoming far more strongly continental as you travel east. Sachsen, Saale-Unstrut, Württemberg, Franken and parts of Baden are affected by this, and have a greater danger of early and late frosts.

To the casual visitor the climate may not appear to vary much from Bonn down to Basel. It's not really that far, after all. But in Germany grape-growing is on the margin, and every half degree counts. In the Pfalz, which is accounted a relatively warm region, the mean annual temperature is 10.1°C (50°F); in the Mosel, always considered distinctly cool, it is 9.8°C (49½°F). You'd hardly notice the difference much of the time. But the Pfalz also has an extra 138 hours of sunshine in the growing season, and produces wines that are rich and fat, whereas the wines of the Mosel are lean and delicate.

Soils in Germany are very varied. Some regions are famous for having a particular soil that gives its character to the wine – Mosel slate, for example – but grapes are grown on limestone, sandstone, marl, loess and many other types. Generally the valleys have richer, alluvial soil and produce richer wines; the slopes, where the soil is poorer, produce more elegant wines. What they have in common is the Riesling grape.

This is the final clue to wine-making in Germany. Great German wines don't have to be Riesling – Silvaner, Scheurebe, the Pinot family and occasionally others can all be first-class – but the Riesling does have an uncanny ability to take advantage of all that German vineyards have to offer, and turn the minuses into pluses at the same time. It thrives on a wide range of soils and reflects the character of the soil in its flavour far more than most grapes (certainly far more than Chardonnay, which tends always to taste of itself). It is late ripening, so given a long, warm autumn and a south-facing slope, it will go on gathering complexity until well into October. It is resistant to cold. Even more remarkably, it can produce good wines at low levels of ripeness as well as when it is so overripe that the berries are brown and shrivelled.

THE CLASSIFICATION SYSTEM FOR GERMAN WINE

German wine law classifies all aspects of a wine: its ripeness, its sweetness and its origin. It does not, however, grade vineyards in order of quality. German wine law is based on the premise that in a cool climate, the ripeness of the grapes is all. The quality categories are based on the amount of sugar present in the grape juice, or must. This is measured in degrees Oechsle, which are a way of comparing the specific gravity of must with that of water. Water has a specific gravity of 1000, so grape juice with a specific gravity of 1100 has 100° Oechsle. Each quality category has a minimum required Oechsle degree, which may vary from region to region.

Quality categories

- **Deutscher Tafelwein** Basic table wine from 4 main regions.
- **Landwein** Similar to France's *vin de pays* but has not taken off in the same way. It can come from any of 17 regions.
- **Qualitätswein bestimmter Anbaugebiete (QbA)** Quality wine from designated regions. These wines are permitted to add sugar to the juice when natural ripeness has not produced enough and yields are high. The wines are usually pretty ordinary.
- **Qualitätswein mit Prädikat (QmP)** Quality wine with special attributes. This is divided into 6 categories of ascending levels of ripeness: *Kabinett* Made from ripe grapes. Most are light, and may have as little as 7 per cent alcohol. *Spätlese* Made from late-picked grapes. *Auslese* Made from selected bunches of late-picked grapes. Some Auslesen are made from botrytis-affected grapes and are sweet. A few are made dry. *Beerenauslese* Made from individually selected berries affected by noble rot. The wine will be very sweet. *Trockenbeerenauslese* Made from individually selected berries that are shrivelled with overripeness. The wines are intensely sweet and very rare. *Eiswein* Made from sound grapes, picked and pressed while naturally frozen.
- **Qualitätswein garantierten Ursprungslage (QbU)** This new category guarantees that 100 per cent of the grapes and Süssreserve (if used) come from the area stated on the label.
- **Einzellage** A single vineyard. Most are at least 2.2 hectares (5½ acres) in size, and many were enlarged under the 1971 wine law to meet the minimum size requirement laid down in that law. Most, but not all, of the finest wines will come from an Einzellage.
- **Grosslage** A group of Einzellagen. Grosslagen can cover large areas of indifferent land, and often take their name from their most famous vineyard. It is impossible to tell from looking at the label whether the name stated is an Einzellage or Grosslage.
- **Bereich** The next largest area. Sometimes a Bereich reflects the character of the wine of a district, sometimes it is drawn on political boundaries. A Bereich wine is likely to be unexciting.
- **Anbaugebiet** A wine region, like Pfalz or Mosel-Saar-Ruwer.

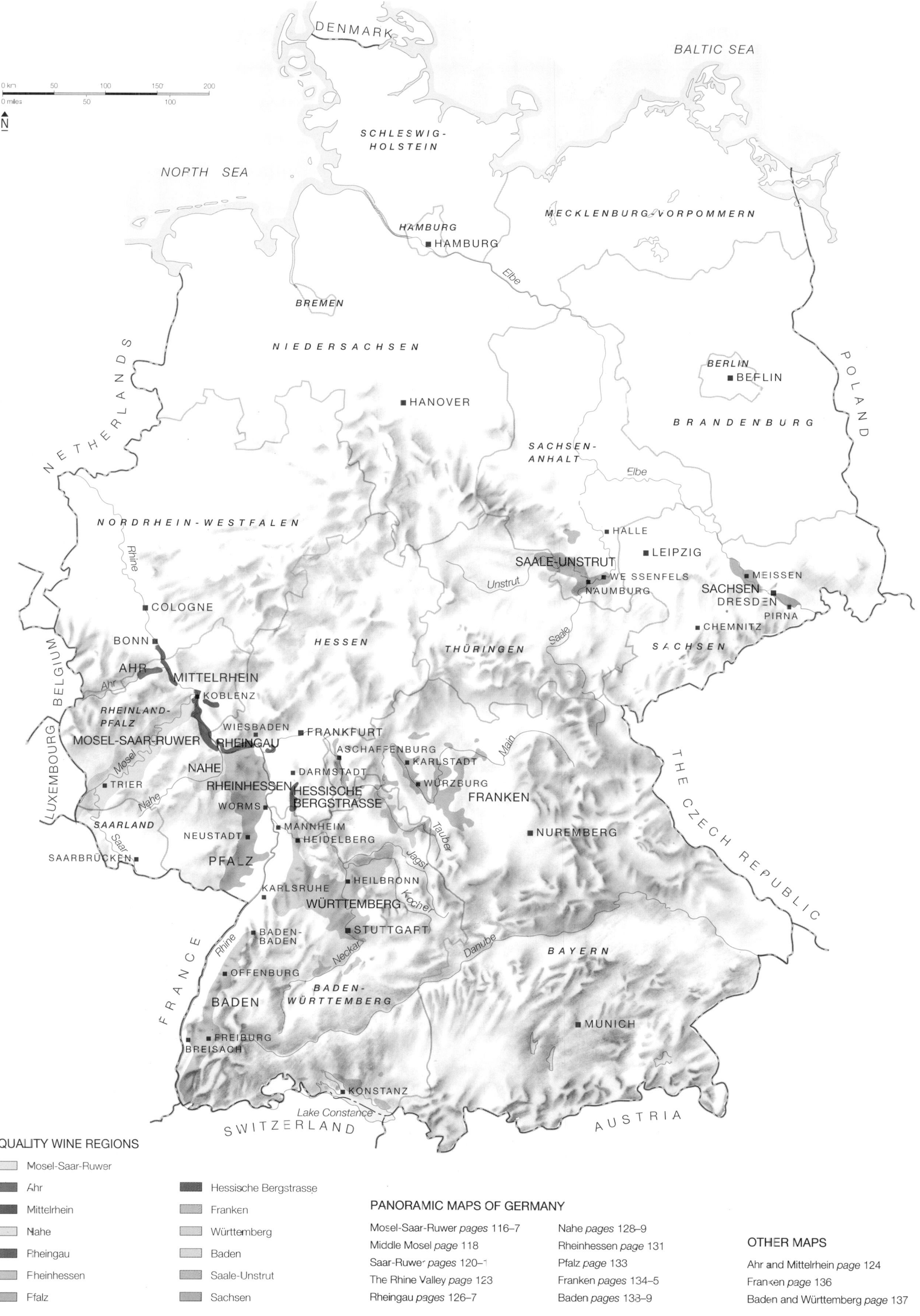
0 km 50 100 150 200
0 miles 50 100
N
DENMARK
BALTIC SEA
NORTH SEA
SCHLESWIG-HOLSTEIN
MECKLENBURG-VORPOMMERN
HAMBURG
HAMBURG
Elbe
BREMEN
NIEDERSACHSEN
BERLIN
BERLIN
BRANDENBURG
POLAND
HANOVER
NETHERLANDS
SACHSEN-ANHALT
Elbe
NORDRHEIN-WESTFALEN
Rhine
HALLE
LEIPZIG
SAALE-UNSTRUT
Unstrut
WEISSENFELS
NAUMBURG
MEISSEN
SACHSEN
DRESDEN
PIRNA
COLOGNE
CHEMNITZ
BONN
HESSEN
THÜRINGEN
Saale
SACHSEN
AHR
Ahr
MITTELRHEIN
KOBLENZ
BELGIUM
RHEINLAND-PFALZ
WIESBADEN
FRANKFURT
MOSEL-SAAR-RUWER
RHEINGAU
ASCHAFFENBURG
KARLSTADT
Main
Mosel
NAHE
DARMSTADT
WÜRZBURG
TRIER
RHEINHESSEN
HESSISCHE BERGSTRASSE
FRANKEN
Nahe
WORMS
LUXEMBOURG
SAARLAND
MANNHEIM
NUREMBERG
NEUSTADT
HEIDELBERG
Tauber
Saar
SAARBRÜCKEN
PFALZ
Jagst
HEILBRONN
KARLSRUHE
Kocher
WÜRTTEMBERG
BADEN-BADEN
STUTTGART
Rhine
Neckar
Danube
BAYERN
THE CZECH REPUBLIC
OFFENBURG
BADEN-WÜRTTEMBERG
FRANCE
BADEN
MUNICH
FREIBURG
BREISACH
KONSTANZ
Lake Constance
SWITZERLAND
AUSTRIA
QUALITY WINE REGIONS
Mosel-Saar-Ruwer
Ahr
Mittelrhein
Nahe
Rheingau
Rheinhessen
Pfalz
Hessische Bergstrasse
Franken
Württemberg
Baden
Saale-Unstrut
Sachsen
PANORAMIC MAPS OF GERMANY
Mosel-Saar-Ruwer pages 116–7
Middle Mosel page 118
Saar-Ruwer pages 120–1
The Rhine Valley page 123
Rheingau pages 126–7
Nahe pages 128–9
Rheinhessen page 131
Pfalz page 133
Franken pages 134–5
Baden pages 138–9
OTHER MAPS
Ahr and Mittelrhein page 124
Franken page 136
Baden and Württemberg page 137

Mosel-Saar-Ruwer

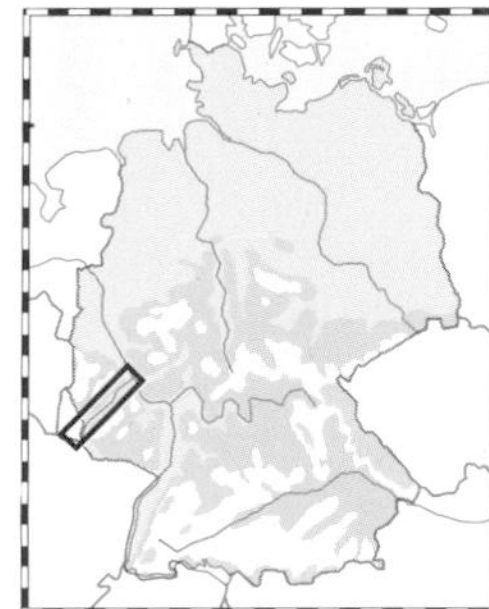

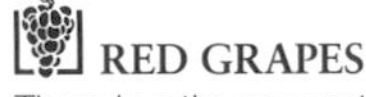

RED GRAPES
There is a tiny amount of Spätburgunder.

WHITE GRAPES
All the great Mosel wines come from Riesling. Müller-Thurgau is the other important grape.

CLIMATE
The Mosel is damp and cool but there are sheltering hills and dams along the river have improved the mesoclimates. The Saar and the Ruwer are cooler.

SOIL
Different types of slate predominate in all areas apart from the Upper Mosel, which has sandstone, shelly limestone and red marl.

ASPECT
The Mosel has many south, south-east and south-west-facing vineyards. The Saar flows north and has fewer ideal sites; the Ruwer's vineyards face mostly west-south-west. Vines are planted at 100–350m (330–1150ft).

YOU KNOW THAT FEELING. You look out of the window in the morning on to clear blue skies. The trees are impossibly green, and the river below the town is glittering in the sunshine. You throw on jeans and a T-shirt and hurry out – and within seconds you're hurrying in again. You want a sweater, two sweaters. This is May in the Mosel, and it's cold.

Then you leave the town and cross the river – and you take off one of the sweaters. You're in the vineyards now, on the lowest slopes where the river reflects all that early morning sunshine straight back on to the vines. It's dazzlingly bright. It's not warm, precisely, but it's warmer, and you can see the town across the river, still in shadow. The vines around you are soaking up all the sun they can get, and you feel guilty about your shadow, spoiling the morning for at least three vines. You scramble up the slopes – and I mean scramble. It's so forbiddingly high and steep here that you wonder if Mosellaners are born with different legs to the rest of us. Each vine is tied to its own 2.5m (8ft) pole, and has its branches pulled back and down to spread the leaves to the sun; you can hang on to these poles as you climb, if you like, because they're embedded in solid rock. And at the top of the slope you're glad of that second sweater again. Not only is it cooler here, but the wind is beginning to whistle round your ears.

This is the essence of the Mosel. Most of it is not that far north, but it is cool and on the margin of where grapes will ripen. In the best stretch, though, the Middle Mosel, the river obligingly meanders in all directions and over the ages has carved out steep slopes that face south, south-east or south-west, and are also sheltered from cold winds. These warm spots are responsible for the fame of the entire river. Overall it's a pretty homogeneous region. Talking about the whole German part of the Mosel – it rises in France as the Moselle 250km (155 miles) south of the German border – together with its two vine-growing tributaries, the Saar and the Ruwer, in one breath really does make sense. There are 12,750 hectares (31,500 acres) of vineyards in all and the similarities of the wines – lightness, delicacy, raciness – are far greater than their differences.

The Mosel enters Germany from France just south of Perl and for almost 40km (25 miles) it runs north along the border with Luxembourg. Here in the Upper Mosel the slopes are gentle, and look out over a river much narrower than it becomes later on – and thus less able to throw the sun's warmth back on to the vines. The Mosel has an average width of only 7.5m (24½ft) though where locks have been built since 1951 the water is broader and the mesoclimate improved. The slopes in the Upper Mosel are even a different colour: they're composed of sandstone, shelly limestone and red marl, softer and warmer in colour than the harsh, dark grey slate that takes over further downstream. The Elbling has been the main grape here since Roman times: it accounts for nine per cent of the Mosel-Saar-Ruwer vineyards, and quite a lot of them are here, producing dry, brisk, acidic wines that seldom manage higher quality than QbA and are a godsend to the Sekt industry. Riesling usually won't ripen here. But the Kerner gives high yields and is one of the reasons (along with the 23 per cent of Müller-Thurgau and 8 per cent of Kerner, 1 or 2 per cent each of Bacchus, Optima, Ortega and Spätburgunder) why the Riesling, which covers 54 per cent of Mosel-Saar-

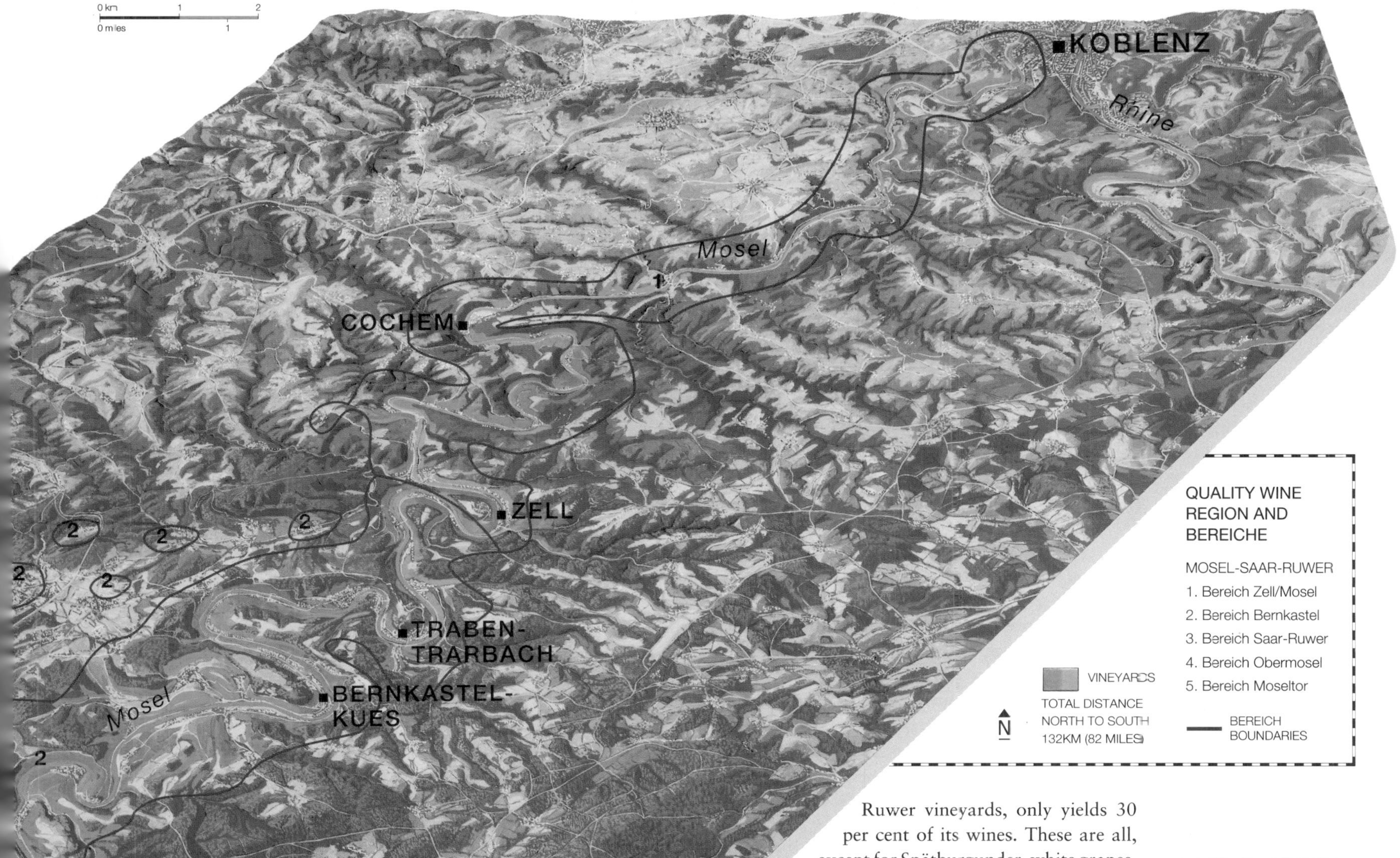

0 km 1 2
0 miles 1

KOBLENZ
Rhine
Mosel
1
COCHEM
ZELL
2
TRABEN-TRARBACH
BERNKASTEL-KUES
Mosel

QUALITY WINE REGION AND BEREICHE

MOSEL-SAAR-RUWER
1. Bereich Zell/Mosel
2. Bereich Bernkastel
3. Bereich Saar-Ruwer
4. Bereich Obermosel
5. Bereich Moseltor

VINEYARDS

TOTAL DISTANCE NORTH TO SOUTH 132KM (82 MILES)

N

BEREICH BOUNDARIES

Ruwer vineyards, only yields 30 per cent of its wines. These are all, except for Spätburgunder, white grapes. Red grapes don't ripen here: it's simply too cold. This coolness is recognized in law, since Mosel-Saar-Ruwer wines require lower Oechsle readings at all QmP levels except Trockenbeerenauslese than do the wines of warmer regions like the Rheingau. Mosel-Saar-Ruwer Riesling Kabinett can have an Oechsle reading of 67 degrees, for example, compared to 73 degrees in the Rheingau. This does not mean that Mosel wines are worse – instead they are lighter, lower in alcohol and with a fragility that is deceptive, since they can last for years.

The Saar and the Ruwer join the Mosel fairly early on in its journey; the Bereiche in these parts are Moseltor and Obermosel for the south, Saar-Ruwer for these two rivers, Bereich Bernkastel for the whole of the Middle Mosel and Bereich Zell for the Untermosel, or Lower Mosel. This last is the most northerly part of the river, from just south of Zell itself right up to Koblenz. The Hunsrück hills press in close to the river, leaving little room to live, never mind cultivate vines. Even so, there are some excellent vineyard sites in the Lower Mosel – steep, terraced slopes of sandy rocks that are even harder than the Devonian slate of the Middle Mosel, but still prone to erosion. Winnigen near Koblenz is one village that would be famous if it were further upstream; Kobern-Gondorf is another. Generally the Upper Mosel is just that bit cooler and windier than the Middle Mosel, though the best sites stand comparison with almost any. What they lack, however, is the sort of famous growers and merchant houses that would spread their fame outside the immediate region. The Mosel-Saar-Ruwer as a whole tends to be a region of small vineyard holdings with only a few growers owning more than 3 to 4 hectares (7½ to 10 acres), and most producers in the Upper Mosel sell their wine at the cellar door.

WHERE THE VINEYARDS ARE

I sometimes think it's a wonder that the Mosel ever reaches its confluence with the Rhine at all. The river has so many twists and turns on the way, trying first one direction and then another, and all because it keeps bumping into rock. The Mosel, over the millennia of its existence, has nudged and eased its way between walls of solid slate, and in doing so it has revealed some of the most diverse and perfect mesoclimates for the vine to be found in any wine region. Look at the way the vineyards hug the river and at the great amphitheatres of vines around Bernkastel-Kues: if there's a sun-trap along these banks, it will be thick with vines. And then look at the way the vineyards occasionally sprawl away from the water, on to flatter land or north-facing slopes. Are those vines going to be as good? The simple answer is, no, they're not. Six thousand hectares (14,825 acres) of these unsuitable vineyards were planted in the late 1960s and 1970s with inferior grapes such as Müller-Thurgau.

Ürdener Prälat
Riesling Spätlese
DR. LOOSEN

Light, flowery Riesling in a slender green bottle is the essence of the Mosel.

MIDDLE MOSEL

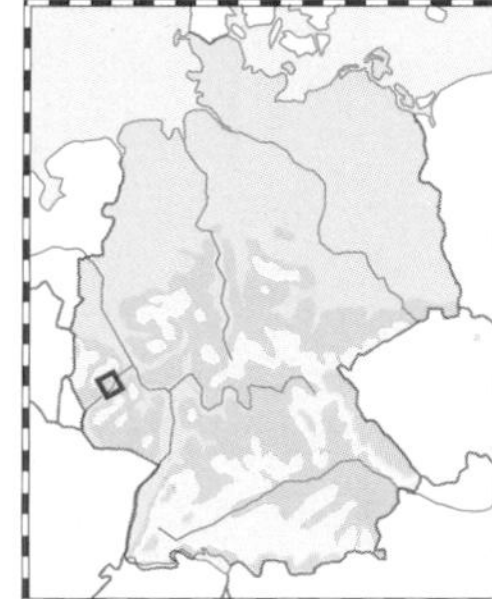

THE SUNDIALS GIVE THE CLUE. In the Middle Mosel there are a good handful of them, with the most famous at Wehlen, Zeltingen and Brauneberg, and they're right in the middle of the vines. The vineyards take their name – Sonnenuhr – from these intruders that squat in their midst. And what can you guess about a vineyard that has a sundial in it? It gets a lot of sun and what's good for sundials is good for vines. And because that sun is so precious in this northerly latitude the towns and villages lie across the river on the shady side (and if they didn't, nobody would be able to see the sundial).

The tortuous bends of the Mosel specialize in producing such ideal sites. The vineyards rise to 200m (650ft) above the river, and beech and fir forests take over on the hilltops, where the altitude means that the temperature is too low and there is too great a danger of frost. The forests provide homes for wild boar, though, and boar are particularly partial to grapes: one grower douses his fences in Lancôme's Magie Noire to keep them away.

The river is wider here than at any other point (and broadened even more by the locks built since 1951) and that means more sunlight and warmth reflected back on to the vines, and more botrytis, too, since it means more early-morning fogs. Sometimes, as at Wehlen, the town owns land on both sides of the river and the town itself huddles on the north-facing bank. In other towns, as in the twin Bernkastel-Kues, a bridge links the two parts and the famous Bernkasteler Doctor vines begin right outside the town as soon as the sun can skim the gables of Bernkastel.

What's less ideal is when a town's north-facing slopes are also planted, and when an Einzellage name includes not only the south-facing slopes but also the much chillier north-facing ones, and even the flat ground by the river. These places were only planted with vines, mainly Müller-Thurgau, in the late 1960s and 1970s. Fruit trees were the original crop, and German wine would be in a better state today if they still

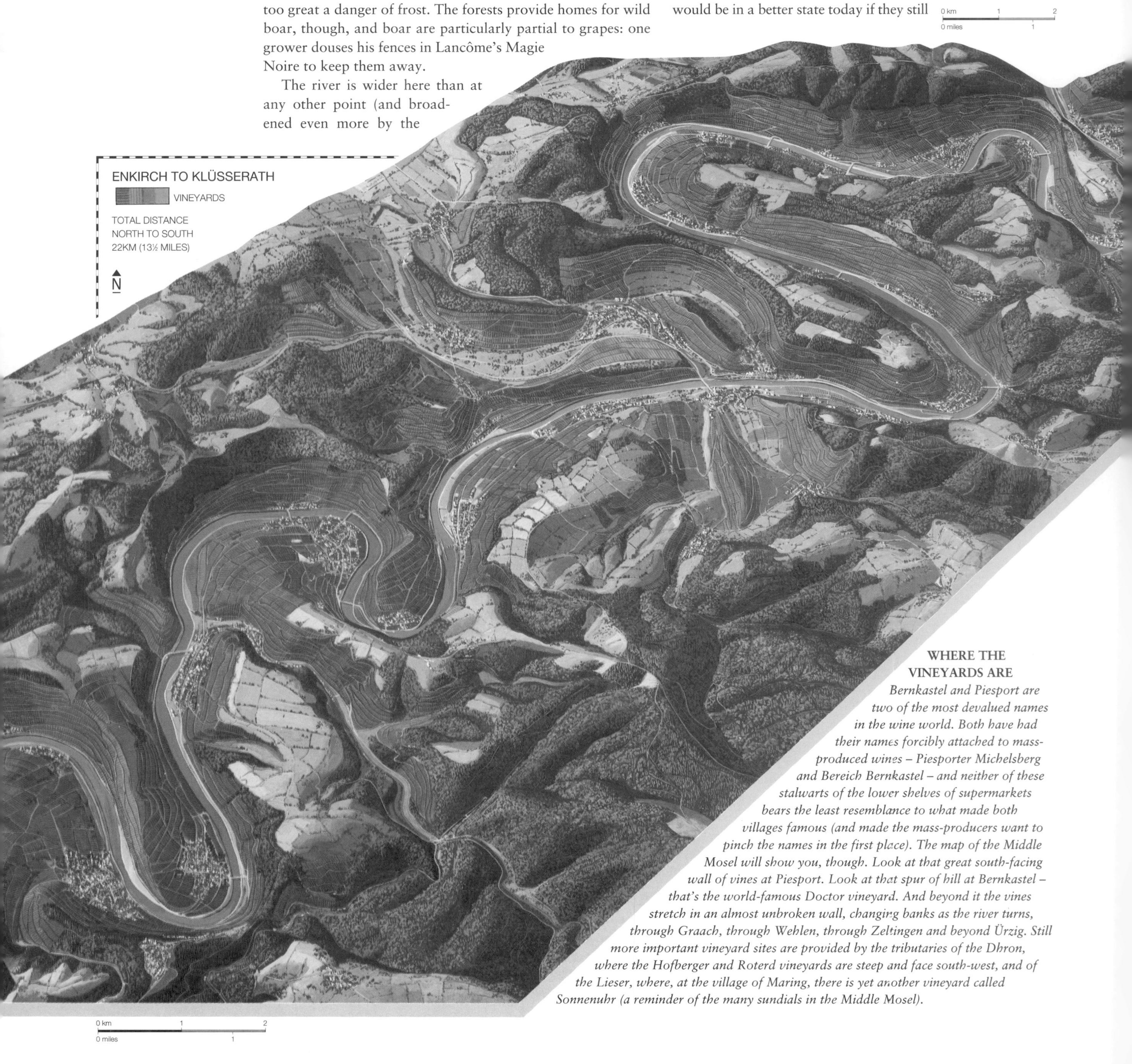

0 km 1 2
0 miles 1

ENKIRCH TO KLÜSSERATH

VINEYARDS

TOTAL DISTANCE NORTH TO SOUTH 22KM (13½ MILES)

N

WHERE THE VINEYARDS ARE

Bernkastel and Piesport are two of the most devalued names in the wine world. Both have had their names forcibly attached to mass-produced wines – Piesporter Michelsberg and Bereich Bernkastel – and neither of these stalwarts of the lower shelves of supermarkets bears the least resemblance to what made both villages famous (and made the mass-producers want to pinch the names in the first place). The map of the Middle Mosel will show you, though. Look at that great south-facing wall of vines at Piesport. Look at that spur of hill at Bernkastel – that's the world-famous Doctor vineyard. And beyond it the vines stretch in an almost unbroken wall, changing banks as the river turns, through Graach, through Wehlen, through Zeltingen and beyond Ürzig. Still more important vineyard sites are provided by the tributaries of the Dhron, where the Hofberger and Roterd vineyards are steep and face south-west, and of the Lieser, where, at the village of Maring, there is yet another vineyard called Sonnenuhr (a reminder of the many sundials in the Middle Mosel).

0 km 1 2
0 miles 1

were there. Müller-Thurgau covers 23 per cent of the Mosel-Saar-Ruwer vineyards – less than in most German regions, but yields are far higher than the 30 to 40 hectolitres per hectare a top grower might take from old Riesling vines on the old, sloping terraces of, say, Zeltingen. Where the terraces have been smoothed out by the Flurbereinigung programme of reshaping the vineyards, the vines are often younger and yields are higher, perhaps 90 hectolitres per hectare – though even Riesling will go up to 120 hectolitres per hectare if it is allowed.

For the best growers, and in the best villages, the names of Middle Mosel and Riesling are synonymous. There's less agreement on what precisely constitutes the Middle Mosel: the most conservative view has it beginning upriver at Trittenheim and continuing as far as Ürzig. But there are excellent sites both upriver and downriver of these points, for example the Bruderschaft site behind the village of Klüsserath. Downriver of Kinheim the soil becomes less slaty and the steep sites are fewer and further apart. The Bereich Bernkastel continues for a few miles beyond Enkirch before meeting the Lower Mosel and the Bereich Zell at Briedel.

At Trittenheim it begins to be clear what the Mosel can do. For a start, the river carves out a magnificent oxbow bend, one of several in the Middle Mosel, and the town has settled itself in the centre, facing its best and most famous site, the Apotheke with its terrifically steep terraces across the river.

MOSEL SLATE

The keys to the Middle Mosel are not just warmth and exposure. These enable the sun to ripen the grapes, but it is the soil that flavours them. The soil in the Middle Mosel is Devonian slate, dark and heat-absorbing, dry and instantly-draining, and decomposes into a thin topsoil that in the past was constantly replenished by the simple method of pulling chunks from the hillsides, breaking them up and scattering the shards among the vines. Nowadays this method is too expensive, but because of slate's low pH it may be necessary to fertilize the soil with lime every couple of years. Stand on these slopes and you'll feel them soft and flaky under your feet. The sun glints on the slate fragments and they slide as you move, rolling and bouncing down between the vines. Slate gives a particularly smoky taste to Riesling grown on it, a tang that, once tasted, will never be forgotten. And when it rains, as it does a lot in the Mosel, the rain pours straight through the soil like water through a sieve. More absorbent soil would try to hold the water, and in so doing would be washed straight down the slope. Since Bernkastel gets roughly twice as much rain as Geisenheim in the Rheingau (and appreciably more than Trier further upstream) it's just as well that it's able to deal with it.

Even on the brightest winter's day the Mosel (here at Fiesport) looks sombre.

WINE STYLES

Where the topsoils are thinnest the wines are more elegant; where they are deeper the wines are fuller. Ürzig gives rich, spicy wine, particularly from its Würzgarten (spice garden) site, and excels in dry years; so does Graach, where the slate has a subsoil of clay or loam, and thus some water pockets. Erden has lighter soil and prefers wet years; Wehlen's best vineyards are the ones at the bottom of the slope, where the temperature is two degrees Centigrade warmer than at the top, and where the river fogs can protect against frost; Bernkastel gives archetypal smoky wines, concentrated and rich. But rich is a relative term in the Mosel. It's a region of Kabinett and Spätlesen wines, and Auslesen only in good years. A Mosel Beerenauslese is a rare bird, and even when the grapes are ripe and nobly-rotten enough, it won't have the lusciousness of a Rheingau version. It's a paradox of the Middle Mosel, that such a forbidding-looking place should yield such delicate wines – but wines with a steel core.

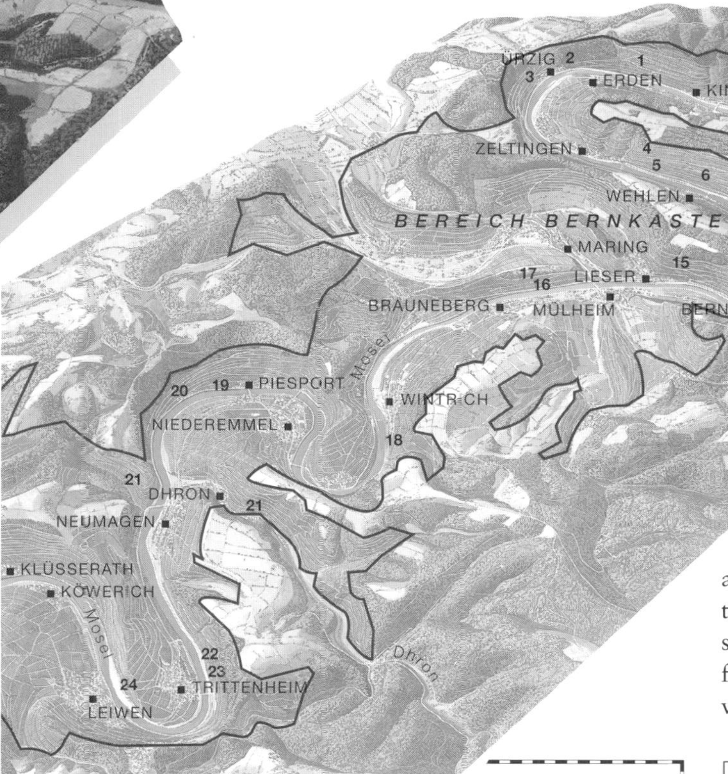

TOP VINEYARDS

1. Erdener Treppchen
2. Erdener Prälat
3. Ürziger Würzgarten
4. Zeltinger Schlossberg
5. Zeltinger Sonnenuhr
6. Wehlener Sonnenuhr
7. Josephshöfer
8. Graacher Himmelreich
9. Graacher Domprobst
10. Bernkasteler Bratenhöfchen
11. Bernkasteler Lay
12. Bernkasteler Graben
13. Bernkasteler Alte Badstube am Doktorberg
14. Bernkasteler Doctor
15. Lieserer Niederberg-Helden
16. Brauneberger Juffer-Sonnenuhr
17. Brauneberger Juffer
18. Wintricher Ohligsberg
19. Piesporter Domherr
20. Piesporter Goldtröpfchen
21. Dhroner Hofberger
22. Trittenheimer Apotheke
23. Trittenheimer Leiterchen
24. Trittenheimer Felsenkopf

— BEREICH BOUNDARIES

BERNKASTELER DOCTOR

Elevation in metres: 350, 300, 250, 200, 150, 100

Wind protection from the wooded Doktorberg hill

Ideal aspect and gradient to maximize sunshine

Frost protection for the vineyards from the town and river

BERNKASTEL

Doctor vineyards

River Mosel

Thick Devonian slate soil retains heat and imparts a distinctive taste to Riesling wine.

SW — Vertical exaggeration 2 times horizontal scale — NE

In the early 1980s there was a lengthy court battle about defining the boundaries of the Doctor vineyards. The vineyard owners brought in a team of experts to specify the physical distinctions of the Doctor slope to prove that it is only in these 3.26 hectares (8 acres) that the famous Doctor Rieslings can be made. The boundaries were determined in 1984, on the basis of the unique *terroir*. The south to south-west aspect and a gradient as steep as 65% in parts maximize sunshine, vital in such a northern latitude (50°) where the sun is relatively low in the sky. The ideal altitude of 120-200m (393-656ft) is low enough to avoid exposure to chilling winds but too high for frost.

Saar-Ruwer

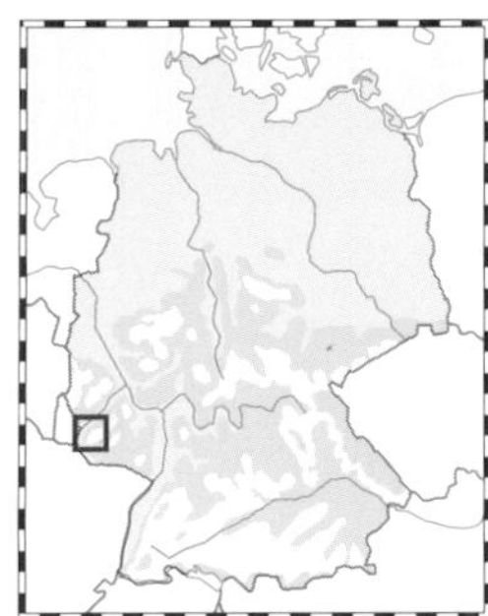

Here, near Wiltingen on the Saar, even the water is slate-grey. The vines are trained on wires, but each plant has its own stake for protection against the wind.

THESE TWO TRIBUTARIES OF THE MOSEL, flowing northwards to join the larger river either side of the Roman city of Trier, are altogether cooler and less promising than much of the Mosel. Thank goodness for that, their growers must say. Being less promising has meant that they escaped the drive to mass production that afflicted even the Mosel in the late 1960s and 1970s. In 1953 the Saar had 842 hectares (2080 acres) planted with vines; by 1971 that had increased to 1044 hectares (2580 acres), and by 1993 had risen only slightly to 1260 hectares (3113 acres). In the Ruwer the land under vine amounted to 304 hectares (751 acres), but instead of showing a steady, if slow increase, it has risen, fallen, risen and fallen again. In 1970 it reached a peak of 330 hectares (815 acres), but by 1993 had dropped to 250 hectares (620 acres).

The reason for this lack of planting mania is quite simple: these are not regions where a grower can make a quick buck. It takes the hardy Riesling vine to withstand the cold winds that blow far more strongly here than along the Mosel, and it takes an old-fashioned mentality on the part of the grower to put up with the low yields – lower than just about anywhere on the Mosel. These vary from grower to grower and from site to site, of course, and (to be honest) yields that pass for low in Germany would rarely be considered so in other top European regions. But in 1993 the average yield in the Bereich Saar-Ruwer was 97.9 hectolitres per hectare; in the Bereich Bernkastel it was 100.9 hectolitres per hectare and in the Bereich Obermosel it was a massive 159.2 hectolitres per hectare. In the altogether bigger vintage of 1992, the Bereich Saar-Ruwer made an average of 150.4 hectolitres per hectare; the Bereich Obermosel made 270.4 hectolitres per hectare. But in the best estates in the Saar-Ruwer, 80 or 85 hectolitres per hectare in a large vintage is the maximum.

Then there is the question of the slow, slow maturation of the wines in bottle. Saar and Ruwer wines are high in acidity, and in a cool year when the Riesling barely ripens they can be low in fruit. But in long warm summers, when the sugar levels rise to meet the acidity, a Saar or Ruwer Riesling can be among the most exciting wines in Germany. But it will take its time. That razor-like acidity will need taming in bottle for several years before it is softened.

THE SAAR

Although they both flow in approximately the same direction and are not far apart, the two rivers produce wines different in character. The wines of the Saar probably show the greatest variation, both in vintage and in geological terms. The Saar can boast soils ranging from loam, quartzite and volcanic to hard and soft slate. But even though the winds are more severe than those of the Middle Mosel, the Saar doesn't look as harsh to the eye. The vineyards don't wall the river in with the determination of those around Bernkastel on the Mosel; there is more pasture and forest, and the land tends to be gathered into large estates whose rambling manor houses sit among their woods and fields with a less mercantile air than do the solid riverside houses of the Mosel owners. But the Saar growers in their manor houses seem to be remarkably impervious to draughts; on a day when tourists are basking outside the bars of Bernkastel, a visitor will need a coat in the Saar. Here, where the Saar, and the Ruwer even more so, are not broad enough to have much tempering effect on the climate, the crucial questions of wine always come down to the weather.

For a small area the Saar's roster of excellent vineyard sites is astonishing – Scharzhofberg in Wiltingen, Ayler Kupp and Herrenberger, Ockfener Bockstein, Serriger Schloss Saarstein (off our map to the south) and several others. This is even more so when only three or four times in a decade do they really produce wines to convert the sceptical.

THE RUWER

If the Saar is a backwater, the Ruwer is so small that you could overlook it completely. Rising in the Hunsrück hills it's hardly more than a stream, yet its gently rounded hills offer some superb west-south-west-facing sites. Like the Saar, it's Riesling country, and again like the Saar, it needs a good year for its style of piercing acidity to come into its own. But its wines, even when young, are less intimidating than those of its neighbour. In the Ruwer the slate is reddish in colour and is more decomposed into a friable soil than the rocky splinters of the Middle Mosel; it contributes to some superb vineyard sites. There is the Maximin Grünhaus estate at Mertesdorf and the Karthäuserhofberg estate at Eitelsbach – both, coincidentally, old monastic properties – and at Kasel there is the Nies'chen vineyard, with its perfect south-south-west exposure. The Avelsbacher Altenberg is in the valley of a tributary of the Ruwer: a tiny stream that joins an only just less tiny stream.

WINE STYLES

The Riesling vines have to be planted on the slopes, because the grapes wouldn't ripen on flatter land here. Only the slopes can catch every bit of available sunshine. Even so, the proportion of QbA wine made here is far higher than in the Middle Mosel: only about 20 per cent of the crop reaches Spätlese or Auslese level. A Beerenauslese here would be a freak, but Eiswein is quite often a possibility. It is perhaps Kabinett wines that best express the taut delicacy of the wines from these valleys. In the trio of wonderful years which blessed Germany from 1988 to 1990, there was actually more wine of Prädikat level made in the Saar-Ruwer than there was ordinary Qualitätswein. Low yields and low levels of ripeness, plus high production costs (many vines are still trained on individual stakes, which require skilled labour), mean that only Riesling will fetch the high prices needed to keep at least some of the draughts out of the manor houses.

The growers, of course, are doing what they can to lower production costs – for example, new vineyards tend to be trained on wires, which are easier to work. Vines being planted nowadays are also often planted further apart to enable narrow, compact vineyard tractors to trundle between the rows.

However, Riesling still remains far and away the principal grape in both regions. In the Ruwer it accounts for 85 per cent of the land under vine; in the Saar 65 per cent. The second most popular grape in both cases is Müller-Thurgau – which of course accounts for the apparently high average yields. Only a few other grapes have made any impact at all here. Kerner has 69 hectares (170 acres) devoted to it in the whole Bereich and Bacchus has 28 hectares (69 acres). There is a little Optima, Ortega and Weissburgunder, and a few growers are experimenting with other grapes such as Ehrenfelser, Reichensteiner, Rieslaner and Ruländer. But these have perhaps only a single hectare (2½ acres) given over to them in the whole Bereich. More remarkably for such a northerly latitude, there are 12 hectares (30 acres) of red Spätburgunder.

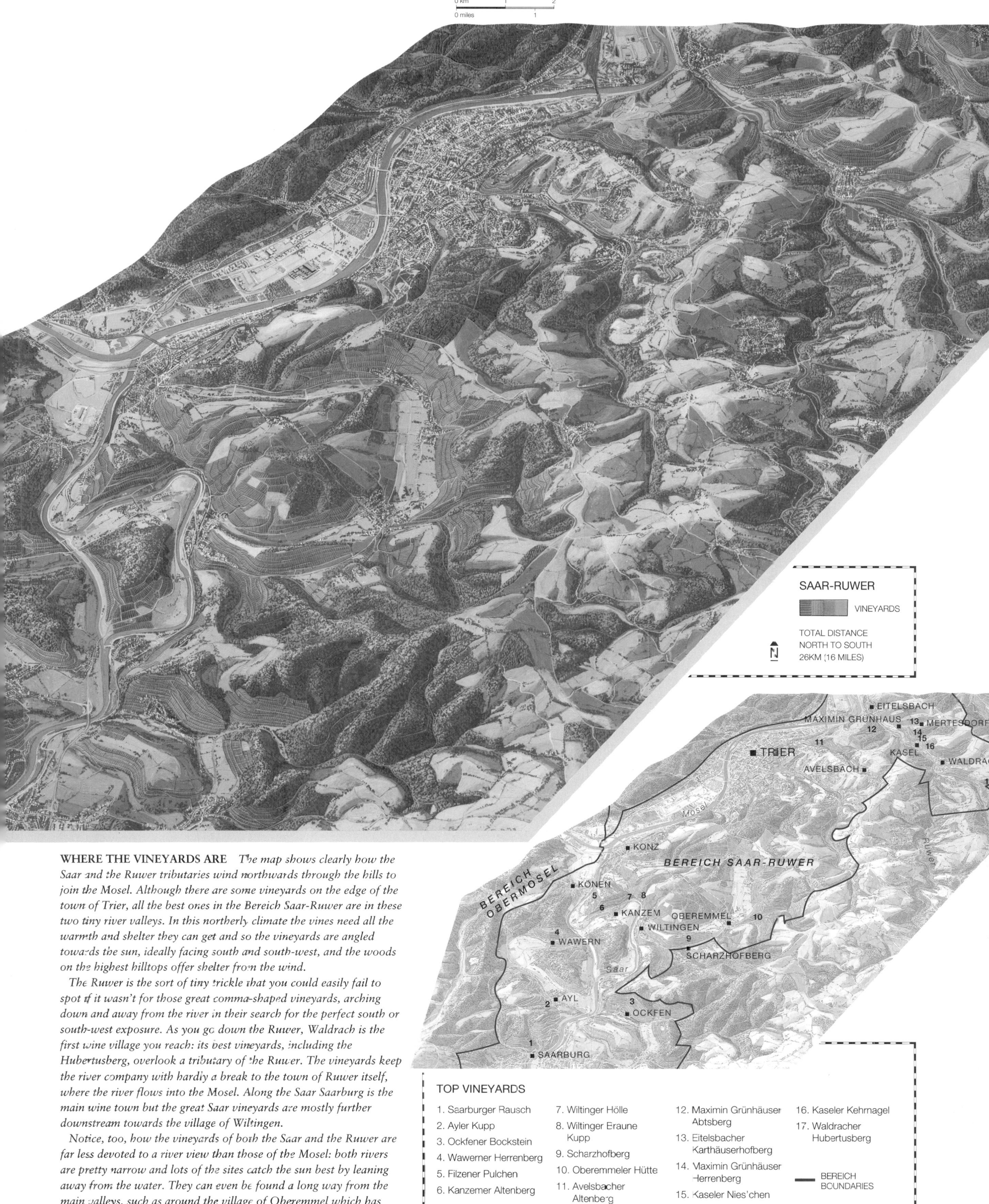

WHERE THE VINEYARDS ARE *The map shows clearly how the Saar and the Ruwer tributaries wind northwards through the hills to join the Mosel. Although there are some vineyards on the edge of the town of Trier, all the best ones in the Bereich Saar-Ruwer are in these two tiny river valleys. In this northerly climate the vines need all the warmth and shelter they can get and so the vineyards are angled towards the sun, ideally facing south and south-west, and the woods on the highest hilltops offer shelter from the wind.*

The Ruwer is the sort of tiny trickle that you could easily fail to spot if it wasn't for those great comma-shaped vineyards, arching down and away from the river in their search for the perfect south or south-west exposure. As you go down the Ruwer, Waldrach is the first wine village you reach: its best vineyards, including the Hubertusberg, overlook a tributary of the Ruwer. The vineyards keep the river company with hardly a break to the town of Ruwer itself, where the river flows into the Mosel. Along the Saar Saarburg is the main wine town but the great Saar vineyards are mostly further downstream towards the village of Wiltingen.

Notice, too, how the vineyards of both the Saar and the Ruwer are far less devoted to a river view than those of the Mosel: both rivers are pretty narrow and lots of the sites catch the sun best by leaning away from the water. They can even be found a long way from the main valleys, such as around the village of Oberemmel which has great sweeps of vines on three sides.

The Rhine Valley

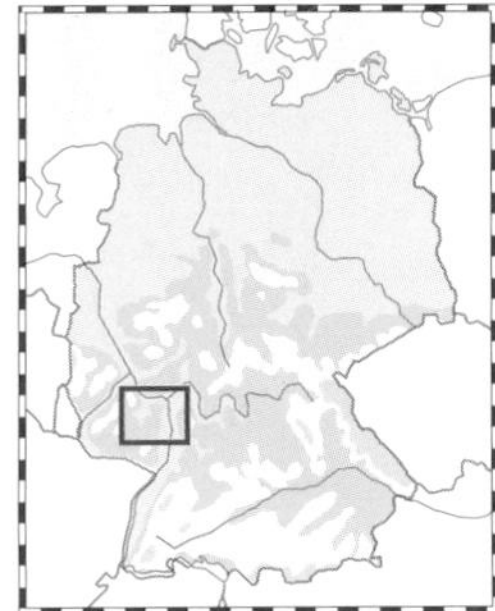

The Rhine is one of the most European of rivers. It rises in Switzerland and flows west along the northern border with Germany. At Basel it leaves Switzerland behind and turns north to form the border between France and Germany for some 170km (105 miles) before setting off through the heartland of Germany. But despite the river's links with Switzerland and France, Rhine wine is universally understood as being German. And if you wanted to get to grips with the nature of German wine, you could do a great deal worse than take a trip up the river from Basel to Bonn.

In fact, to understand German wine at all you have to look at Germany's river systems: it is the rivers that make viticulture an industry in this cool climate and not just a hobby. German vineyards – or at least their more northerly outposts – are as far north as grapes will ripen. Even given that the Riesling is a grape that can resist the cold better than most; even given the long autumns that enable it to go on ripening well into October; in spite of all this, the growing of fine grapes in Germany would be a matter of chance, of reliance on the vagaries of the climate, if the rivers were not there to even up the odds a little. What the rivers do is temper the extremes of climate. They keep frosts at bay and, by reflecting sunlight and warmth, give the vines on their banks an added advantage. In addition, over the millennia they have carved deep gorges out of the rock through which they pass. Those steep banks, when planted with vines, catch all the available sunlight.

Above: German Rhine wine often comes in brown hock bottles. Below: The Mittelrhein is a region of dramatic riverside scenery with perching castles, rugged, rocky slopes and steeply terraced vineyards.

All Germany's wine regions are based, to a greater or lesser extent, on rivers. The Rhine is the main one, but it has a number of tributaries which are also important: the Mosel, the Nahe and the Main are the principal ones. They join the Rhine further north; in the south the Rhine is on its own.

In the far south of the Rhine Valley (south of this map, and stretching up to meet it from the Swiss border) are the vineyards of Baden, one of the few places in Germany where you can wander alongside a vineyard and pull cherries or apricots from the trees – at least, you can provided the owner doesn't see you. Baden is the warmest wine region in Germany. (The EU puts in it Region B, along with Champagne and the Loire, instead of in Region A with chilly Luxembourg like the rest of Germany) and it likes to show its prowess by making dry wines. Unlike the Trocken wines of further north, these wines have the body and ripeness not to taste like battery acid. Baden faces Alsace across the Rhine and uses many similar grapes such as the Pinot family, Riesling and Gewürztraminer. But the most common variety is the less distinguished Müller-Thurgau. At Baden-Baden the Baden vineyards stop for a bit, and then continue on our right as we go northwards – and on our left, on the other side of the Rhine, the Pfalz begins.

THE PFALZ

The Pfalz is really a northerly continuation of Alsace. The south of the Pfalz has never been considered to be as good quality as the north, and taken overall it still isn't. It is a region of small-scale growers, and one of the main sources of Liebfraumilch. But it is also home to some growers of ambition and great imagination – and some of the most exciting wines in Germany are emerging from these flat vineyards. But not until we climb, panting, on to this map can we begin to see why the Pfalz is so famous. We'll take a walk westwards over the wide agricultural plain, towards the wine-making villages north of Neustadt. It's quite a long way from the river – so far that the Rhine can't really be given any credit for the quality of their vineyards. Instead it's the Haardt mountains, a continuation of Alsace's Vosges mountains, in the foothills of which the Pfalz vineyards shelter, that make a warm climate even warmer. There's more Riesling here than there was in Baden, though Müller-Thurgau is still the most popular variety.

RHEINHESSEN

And as we wander away from the hills, heading north-east across the gentle slopes of the Rheinhessen, the Riesling all but disappears. Instead there's Müller-Thurgau and Silvaner, plus Kerner and Scheurebe and a few other varieties – and watch out as you cross the roads, or you'll be mown down by the tankers of simple, grapy, mass-produced wine on their way to the Liebfraumilch cellars. Only when we reach the riverside towns of Oppenheim, Nierstein and Nackenheim and we find ourselves overshadowed by the rust-red hills of the Rheinterrasse are we again in serious wine country. The soil here is sandstone and decomposed red slate, and the hills rear high enough to offer good south-east exposure across the Rhine – not that all the growers take full advantage of this.

RHEINGAU

We'll cross the river here, over to the right bank, and take a bus through the dreary sprawl of Wiesbaden. We're now in the Rheingau, and if we wanted we could follow the Main river upstream past Frankfurt and into the Franken vineyards; but the Rheingau, packed with many of Germany's greatest wine names, is hard to resist.

This, traditionally, is the culmination of the Rhine. The vineyards are crammed in on the foothills of the Taunus mountains, between the river and the forest. As you go west from Wiesbaden the slopes get higher and steeper; the river reflects all the available warmth back on to the Riesling (because it is virtually all Riesling here) and the wines are some of the weightiest, fieriest, most complex examples to be found.

MITTELRHEIN AND AHR

West of Bingen the Rhine resumes its northward course. There are fewer vineyards here in the Mittelrhein than there were 50 years ago; fewer even than ten years ago. The best vineyard sites are often tucked away in the side valleys, and the Sekt industry, with its need for light, lean wines, relies heavily on grapes from this region.

At Koblenz the Mosel joins the Rhine, and after that there's only one more wine region to go before reaching Bonn. The tiny Ahr Valley, though, can spring surprises. Most of its wine is red, or at least pink; it used to be mainly sweetish, though dry wines are more in vogue now. At Bonn the Rhine vineyards stop. The local drink north of here is beer: the hop can ripen where even the hardy Riesling fears to tread.

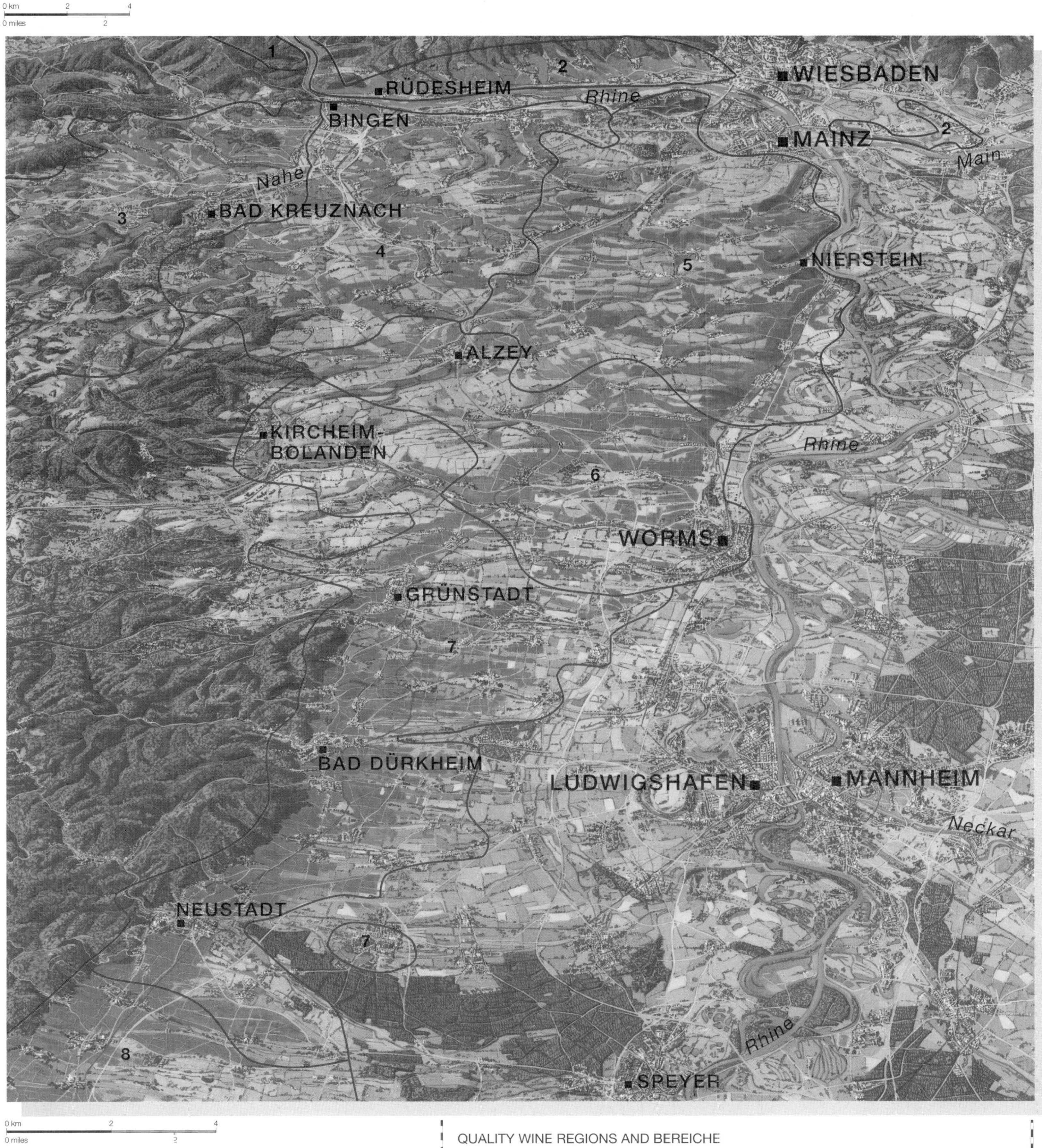

QUALITY WINE REGIONS AND BEREICHE

MITTELRHEIN
1. Bereich Loreley

RHEINGAU
2. Bereich Johannisberg

NAHE
3. Bereich Nahetal

RHEINHESSEN
4. Bereich Bingen
5. Bereich Nierstein
6. Bereich Wonnegau

PFALZ
7. Bereich Mittelhaardt/ Deutsche Weinstrasse
8. Bereich Südliche Weinstrasse

BEREICH BOUNDARIES

VINEYARDS

N

TOTAL DISTANCE NORTH TO SOUTH 89KM (55 MILES)

WHERE THE VINEYARDS ARE *This is a bird's eye view of the greatest of Germany's wine regions, with the exception of the Mosel-Saar-Ruwer; and it also contains some of the most commonplace. The latter sprawl flatly across the centre of the map; the great ones are tucked into the corners, where you could easily miss them if you didn't know what you were looking for.*

On the lower lefthand side of the map are the Haardt mountains; the vineyards on their eastern foothills, sloping down to the plain, are the best parts of the Pfalz. Go north from there, to where the river Nahe winds up to meet the Rhine at Bingen: the scale of the map can just show the height of the Traiser Rotenfels vineyard at Bad Kreuznach. And just north of the Rhine, where it heads westwards at Wiesbaden, and the wooded Taunus mountains take us off the map, that 32km- (20-mile) long strip of vineyards along the Rhine between the forest and the river is the main stretch of the Rheingau.

In contrast, look at the rich farmland enclosed within the great bend of the river at Mainz. With one small exception, the Rheinterrasse between Mainz and Worms, this produces soft, sweetish wine often sold in bulk. The vine shouldn't be allowed to take life too easily: this map shows the difference.

The Rhine with its tributaries, the Nahe, Main and Neckar, is the artery of German wine; indeed before the advent of motorways it was the main artery of Germany itself. Even today it carries a heavy industrial traffic of barges, as well as pleasure-boats; and clustered on its banks at irregular intervals are villages with some of the most famous names in German wine.

AHR & MITTELRHEIN

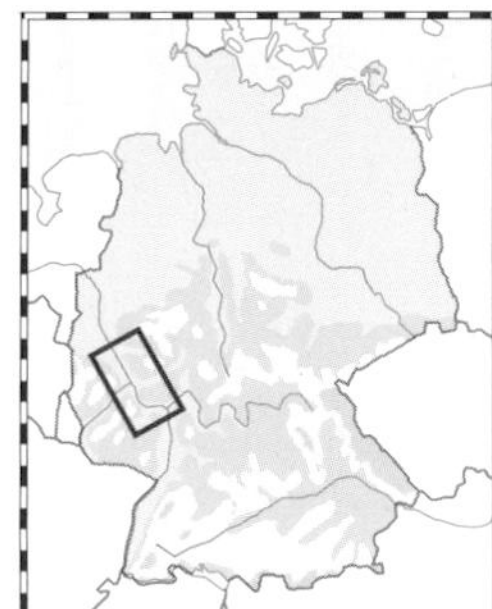

RED GRAPES
Just over half the plantings in the Ahr are Spätburgunder with one-fifth Blauer Portugieser. The Mittelrhein has a little Spätburgunder.

WHITE GRAPES
Riesling and Müller-Thurgau are the main white grapes in the Ahr. Mittelrhein vines are mostly Riesling and there is some Müller-Thurgau, Kerner as well as tiny amounts of other varieties.

CLIMATE
The climate is cool and northerly, but the Eifel hills to the north-west give shelter in the Ahr and steep valley sides offer shelter in the Mittelrhein.

SOIL
There is mainly loess in the Lower Ahr and Devonian slate in the Upper Ahr. The Mittelrhein has mostly quartzite and slate on clay. There is some volcanic soil in the north.

ASPECT
In the Ahr most vines are on river valley slopes, on both the north and south banks, and are often terraced. Mittelrhein vines are on steep valley sides.

WE WANT DIFFERENT THINGS from wines at different times. Sometimes we want a serious wine to sit over with friends, or something rich and complex for a special occasion. Sometimes we want something for gulping with pasta. And sometimes, particularly when we're on holiday, we want something local that we will see nowhere else, and we want to drink it as the sun sets over the hills and while the winemaker serves us some home-made sausage for supper.

Luckily, enough people in Bonn and Koblenz find themselves in this last mood pretty often, often enough to ensure the survival (so far) of the vineyards of the Ahr and Mittelrhein. They are both tourist areas kept alive by people drinking the wines on the spot. Nothing much leaves either region except for the leanest and most acidic wine of the Mittelrhein, which is in great demand by the Sekt houses. Happily both regions are wild and rugged and stunningly beautiful: the Rhine here is dotted with castles, the villages are old and often unspoilt and the air is full of legends of the Lorelei and of Siegfried. You'd feel cheated if the local wine wasn't pretty unusual.

AHR

In the Ahr, the wine is so unusual that it's red. To make red wine in what was, before re-unification, Germany's most northerly wine region, seems odd to say the least. Geography is the secret. Certainly, these are not big, beefy reds of the type one expects from, say, Spain or Italy, but until recently German taste was never along those lines. When German consumers ask for red wine, what they want is something with plenty of raspberry or cherry fruit and perhaps some residual sugar; the national taste for sweetish reds has only recently begun to give way to more international styles.

The Ahr is well suited to producing such wines. It flows eastwards to join the Rhine south of Bonn. If it flowed in a straight line that might be perfect: it would mean a wall of south-facing vines. As it is the river takes a more convoluted path, flowing sometimes south to north and sometimes in any direction you care to name. Vines grow on both banks: some of the vineyards face south, some east, some west. And the soil, at least in the Upper Ahr, is the same Devonian slate that holds the heat in the Middle Mosel. The equation is also the same: steep slopes plus slate soil plus warmth reflected off the river equals good wine. The difference is that in the Ahr the Spätburgunder gets the best spots. This is mostly because red wines are the Ahr's speciality: if a region has a speciality it doesn't change it lightly. The sites that are good for Spätburgunder would also be good for Riesling; but red wine has rarity value in Germany, and Riesling doesn't. Accordingly Spätburgunder accounts for just over half the vines in the Ahr; Blauer Portugieser has another fifth, and Riesling has a mere 10.7 per cent. The Spätburgunders tend to be light but tasty. Some are made into Weissherbst, a pale rosé, but even the real reds aren't that dark. The reds made from the Portugieser tend to be even more neutral – in fact the Portugieser used to be more widely planted than the Spätburgunder but the trend towards dry reds is driving it out of the region.

The biggest Spätburgunders come from the lower reaches of the Ahr, where the heat-retaining loess topsoil gives softer wines. Heppingen and Heimersheim produce notable examples. Further upstream the Devonian slate gives more structure, but the wines are lighter. Overall 93 per cent of vineyards in the Ahr are 20 per cent steep or more, and are often terraced: only four per cent are flat. Yet in spite of all its advantages the vineyard area has been shrinking. I say 'has been' because in the mid-1970s the Ahr had 482 hectares (1191 acres) under vine, and by 1992 this had shrunk to 478 hectares (1181 acres). However by 1993 it had risen to 522 hectares (1290 acres). Thirstier tourists? A general feeling of optimism? Whatever the reason, it's good news.

MITTELRHEIN

The Mittelrhein must be dead envious. Here on the banks of the Rhine between just north of Bingen and Bonn, Riesling is the grape they most want to grow. It covers 74 per cent of these high, inaccessible, perching vineyards, and at its best the wine can be very good. But the Mittelrhein has few of the advantages of the Ahr. For one thing, it is overshadowed by the fame of the nearby Rheingau. For another, the river here flows north-west or north, and often only where there are side valleys – at Bacharach, Oberwesel and Niederheimbach – are there really good south-facing slopes. Bacharach has good east-facing slopes, and Leubsdorf and Hammerstein, with their west- and south-west-facing sites, are also sheltered and warm. The little tributary of the Lahn, where it flows north-west before joining the Rhine, also provides some good sites.

In the southern part, between Boppard and Bacharach, things are easier. There is slate soil and plenty of warmth and mist near the river encourage the growth of noble rot. On the Bopparder Hamm Beerenauslesen are by no means unusual.

Nevertheless, vine-growing is a declining industry in the Mittelrhein. At the end of World War Two there were 1200 hectares (2965 acres) of vineyards planted on these impossibly steep slopes overlooking the river. In 1992 there were 700 hectares (1730 acres), now there are 687 hectares (1698 acres). The terraces are falling into disuse; the younger generation prefers to desert wine-making and seek easier work in the cities. It is dying from the north, in the less favoured areas of the Mittelrhein, where the wines are leaner, more attentuated and more acidic. However, the tourists keep coming, drawn by the legendary beauty of this part of the Rhine Valley. As in the Ahr, they want a drink when they get there and the vineyard area will presumably shrink to a level at which tourism and the Sekt industry can keep it going.

QUALITY WINE REGIONS AND BEREICHE

AHR
Bereich Walporzheim/Ahrtal

MITTELRHEIN
Bereich Siebengebirge
Bereich Loreley

OVER 200M (656FT)
OVER 500M (1640FT)

RHEINGAU

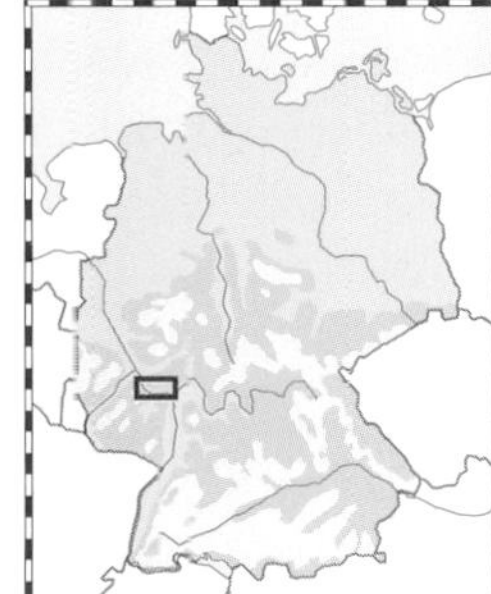

THE ROMANS WERE HERE. So, later, were the Cistercians. So, later still, was Queen Victoria, though she only stayed for lunch. Thomas Jefferson came as well, but unlike Queen Victoria he didn't get a vineyard named after him. The reason that the region attracted so many visitors down the centuries was because good wine could be made here. The reason they kept on coming was because great wine was being made, year after year, in the vineyards above and between a string of villages bordering one particular stretch of the Rhine.

That's one of the things I love about wine: the sheer unlikelihood of the right conditions being thrown together by nature, and then stumbled upon by man. And then that knowledge being handed down from generation to generation, regardless of the whims of bureaucrats or accountants. I don't know what an accountant would say about the Rheingau today. Probably that the yields are too low, the wine takes too long to mature, and isn't there some nice fertile flat land across the river? Why not plant that with something high-yielding and commercial, like Müller-Thurgau?

But the Rheingau is a land of slopes, and it is a land of Riesling. The slopes, except in parts of Rüdesheim where the Rhine narrows as it turns northwards again, aren't as steep as they are in the Middle Mosel, and there's not quite as much Riesling – 82 per cent of 3128 hectares (7729 acres) of vineyards. Just over eight per cent of the vines in the Rheingau are Spätburgunder and this is mostly found in just one commune, Assmannshausen, the first village after the Rhine has turned north again. Just three per cent of the vines is the accountant's delight, Müller-Thurgau. But grapes and slopes don't, on their own, produce great wine regions. The answer to what makes the Rheingau special is very simple: solid rock.

The Rhine flows more or less north-west through southern Germany until suddenly at Wiesbaden it comes up against the Taunus mountains. The river finds its route to the north blocked so it swings westwards, and only 32km (20 miles) later at Rüdesheim is it able to turn north again. The heart of the Rheingau is here, along the stretch of the river that flows west with the vines planted on the south-facing slopes of the Taunus overlooking the river.

LOCAL CLIMATES AND WINE STYLES

It was the Cistercians, settled in the monastery at Kloster Eberbach, who in the twelfth and thirteenth centuries cleared much of the forest from these slopes above the Rhine. No vineyard is higher than 300m (985ft): and this altitude is only reached by the nearby Hendelberg vineyard in Hallgarten. This is about as high as you can get before the wind and the cold become too much for the grapes to ripen properly. But the steeper, higher vineyards do benefit from more sunlight than the lower ones. The Rheingau is fairly cool for viticulture, but the Taunus mountains keep the north and east winds off the vineyards, and the Rhine, about 800m (½ mile) wide here, reflects the sun back on to the vines. The river also encourages the formation of mists which, on warm autumn days, foster the development of *Botrytis cinerea*: nobly rotten sweet wines therefore tend to come from the lower vineyards. Some growers reckon that the middle part of the slope has the best of all possible worlds. It is still within range of the moderating effect of the Rhine – the very top vineyards can miss out on this – but there is no danger, as there is at the foot of the slopes, of too much humidity (which can encourage rot of the wrong sort) or of the vines getting waterlogged in a wet year.

But if the nobly rotten wines come from the lower vineyards, so, paradoxically, do Eisweins, although the conditions that produce them are very different. For Eiswein, mists and noble rot are a distraction: what is needed are healthy grapes with no rot, plus frost. Lots and lots of frost – and the lower-lying vineyards here are the most susceptible to frost. The State Domaine at Eltville has indeed made a practice of making Eiswein every year, though for most producers it is a rarer treat. It is an expensive one, too: many growers admit that in spite of the high prices they can charge for Eiswein, since it is extremely fashionable in Germany, they still don't expect to make a profit from it. They make Eiswein for the fun of it.

The lower slopes, too, yield the heaviest, richest wines; the upper slopes give more delicacy and elegance. Partly this is to do with temperature, and partly it is to do with soil, since the richer soils tend to be further down the slope. At the top of the slopes the soils are more eroded and weathered; there is quartzite and weathered slate here. In the middle there is marl, and at the bottom there is loam, loess, marl and sandy gravel. But with the Rheingau able to boast some 286 different soils (according to one estimate), all suitable for Riesling, generalizations are difficult. And in spite of the fact that the Riesling grape tends to reflect the soil in its flavour, the wines of the Rheingau do possess a striking consistency.

WINE VILLAGES

The Rheingau begins just east of Wiesbaden with the large village of Hochheim, which is not on the Rhine at all. Instead it sits on the right bank of the Main river just before its confluence with the Rhine, and although it has lent an abbreviation of its name – hock – to the English language as a name for all Rhine wine, it is by no means the most typical of Rheingau villages. For a start, Hochheim does not benefit from the shelter of the Taunus mountains. Its vineyard slopes are gentle, and it has limestone in its soil as well as the more usual Rheingau sand and loess. Its wines are earthy and rich. This is where Queen Victoria stopped for a picnic to watch the harvesters at work, one fine day in 1850, and where a vineyard owner with a sharp eye for publicity asked if he could name a vineyard after her: the 5-hectare (12-acre) Königin Victoriaberg which faces south over the Main.

The curve of the river is occupied by Wiesbaden on one side and Mainz on the other and the two cities form a rather unlovely interruption to the landscape. But once out of Wiesbaden's suburbs it's a straight run westwards past some of the most famous names in German wine.

RED GRAPES

There is 8 per cent of Spätburgunder, mainly at Assmannshausen.

WHITE GRAPES

Rheingau Riesling has been famous for centuries and accounts for 82 per cent of the vineyards. There are small amounts of Müller-Thurgau and other varieties.

CLIMATE

The relatively cool climate benefits from the proximity of the Rhine which reflects heat back onto the vineyards.

SOIL

The Rheingau has a wide range of soils, partly depending on the altitude. The higher sites have cuartzite and weathered slate; the mid slopes include patches of marl; and the lower sites have loam, loess, marl and sandy gravel. There is blue phyllite slate at Assmannshausen and Lorch.

ASPECT

The vineyards face south (south-west in Lorch and Assmannshausen) and are sheltered by the Taunus mountains.

Schloss Johannisberg perched high above its sloping vineyards is just one of many ancient aristocratic wine estates in the Rheingau.

The Taunus range begins quietly, with shallow slopes above Walluf and Eltville, which is the home of the important State Domaine. But the great vineyards appear almost immediately, scattered with little apparent rhyme or reason at different altitudes: Wallufer Walkenberg and Eltviller Sonnenberg are just above their respective towns, but Kiedricher Gräfenberg is right up high, and the suntrap of Erbacher Marcobrunn, a fine vineyard if ever there was one and producing some of the Rheingau's most full-bodied Rieslings, is way down by the river. Oestricher Doosberg is low down but Schloss Vollrads is quite high. Schloss Johannisberg is situated about midway up the slope and Oestricher Winkel and Winkeler Jesuitengarten are so close to the river it's a wonder they're not standing in water.

The town of Johannisberg, with its historic Schloss Johannisberg wine estate, has long been so famous, incidentally, that it has not only given its name to that by which Riesling is known in much of the USA – Johannisberg Riesling – but has also had its name rudely taken for the single Bereich, the Bereich Johannisberg, that covers the whole Rheingau.

By Geisenheim, home of a famous wine research institute that has devoted itself, among other tasks, to researching new grape crosses that can stand up to Germany's uncompromising climate, the slopes are distinctly steep. They continue to steepen all the way past Rüdesheim, while the river narrows and gathers itself for one final push northwards. Here the Taunus mountains push in close to the river, forcing the vineyards onto steep terraces. These steepest vineyards take the name of Berg as a prefix: Berg Roseneck, Berg Rottland, Berg Schlossberg and Berg Kaisersteinfels. Above them all towers the Rüdesheimer Berg itself. Here some of the richest, ripest wines in all the Rheingau are made. These hot vineyards that face south across the Rhine to Bingen are also very well drained, making for low yields of around 50 hectolitres per hectare – in very hot years the vines can suffer from drought and the acidity levels can plunge too low. Then it's the slightly cooler spots that produce the outstanding wine.

The Rüdesheim hill is slate, but this is not the same Devonian slate of the Mosel. Nevertheless, it gives its inimitable smoky taste to these wines.

After Rüdesheim the wines become lighter and slatier, sometimes with a flinty taste. This is where the river swings north again and we leave behind the remarkable south-facing stretch of vineyards that have lasted all the way from Wiesbaden. In Assmannshausen Spätburgunder is the speciality. Local palates (and purses) rate it highly. The State Domaine at Eltville produces red Auslesen and upwards from here, from west- or south-west-facing vineyards that overlook the Hunsrück mountains across the river. Red Auslesen may be very much a local taste, but at least they prove that Spätburgunder does get properly ripe this far north.

The last village of the Rheingau is Lorch, where the wines (white again) begin to take on something of the lean acidity of the Mittelrhein that faces this part of the Rheingau across the river. The Rheingau straggles up the right bank for a few more miles past Lorchhausen.

GREAT WINE ESTATES

There is still one other reason why the Rheingau is so famous throughout the world, and it has nothing to do with geography and climate – at least, not directly. It is the presence of large, rich aristocratic estates, lying almost shoulder to shoulder along this stretch of the Rhine that has long been both an acknowledgment of the quality of the region and an incitement to even greater quality.

It is true that there are around a thousand vine-growing families in the Rheingau, dividing a total of 3128 hectares (7729 acres) of vineyards between them, but the region is also home to big estates like Schloss Johannisberg, Schloss Schönborn, Schloss Reinhartshausen (the property of the Prince of Prussia) and others, many of them dating back to the Middle Ages or even earlier. It is a harsh fact of wine history that while nature can provide the sites, it generally takes fortune to bring fame in its wake.

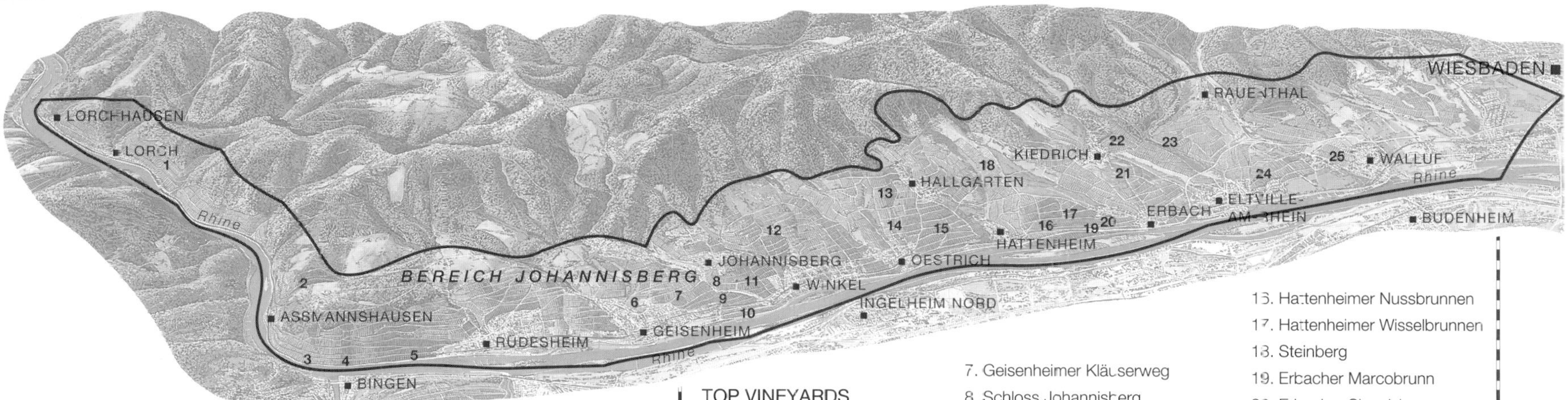

LORCH TO WIESBADEN

TOTAL DISTANCE NORTH TO SOUTH 7KM (4 MILES) VINEYARDS

TOP VINEYARDS

1. Lorcher Kapellenberg
2. Assmannshäuser Höllenberg
3. Rüdesheimer Berg Schlossberg
4. Rüdesheimer Berg Roseneck
5. Rüdesheimer Berg Rottland
6. Geisenheimer Rothenberg
7. Geisenheimer Kläuserweg
8. Schloss Johannisberg
9. Johannisberger Klaus
10. Winkeler Jesuitengarten
11. Winkeler Hasensprung
12. Schloss Vollrads
13. Hallgartener Schönhell
14. Oestricher Lenchen
15. Oestricher Doosberg
16. Hattenheimer Nussbrunnen
17. Hattenheimer Wisselbrunnen
18. Steinberg
19. Erbacher Marcobrunn
20. Erbacher Siegelsberg
21. Kiedricher Sandgrub
22. Kiedricher Gräfenberg
23. Rauenthaler Baiken
24. Eltviller Sonnenberg
25. Wallufer Walkenberg

BEREICH BOUNDARIES

WHERE THE VINEYARDS ARE *The map shows the heart of the Rheingau west of Wiesbaden. The Rhine here is broad and dotted with islands. Occasionally an island might be planted with vines, but the river is the southern boundary of the Rheingau. The vines that creep up to the edge of the south bank near Bingen are in the Rheinhessen; and the few that just sneak on to the map in the far south-western corner, on the left bank of the river Nahe, are in the Nahe region.*

The Rheingau itself is a monoculture. As soon as the urban sprawl west of Wiesbaden comes to an end the vines begin, gradually colonizing every likely slope. And only 3 or 4km (2 miles) away from the river the Taunus mountains begin in earnest, rearing high above the vineyards. Up here it is too cold for the vine; and so instead, the mountains perform the task of sheltering the lower slopes.

This list of top Rheingau vineyards located on the map is not comprehensive, but certainly all these should be included if there is ever a legal recognition of top sites in Germany. If this were to happen (at the moment the German government seems as devoted to lowering the reputation of German wine as to raising it) it would result in a top echelon of vineyards similar to the Grands Crus of Burgundy. Just as is the case in Burgundy, not all of every vineyard is of equal quality. Just 17.9 hectares (44 acres) of Lorcher Kapellenberg is reckoned to be top-ranking out of a total area of 56.9 hectares (141 acres) and of Winkeler Hasensprung's 103.8 hectares (256 acres) only 19.9 hectares (49 acres) is considered to be first class; conversely, all 5.2 hectares (13 acres) of Erbacher Marcobrunn make the grade. Other vineyards judged to be excellent through and through are Johannisberger Klaus and Hattenheimer Nussbrunnen.

THE RHEINGAU SOILS

Riesling is the predominant grape variety in the Rheingau region, producing particularly excellent wines on the higher slopes where the soil is well-drained. These wines such as those from the famous Schloss Johannisberg can take on a slaty taste from the soil. The lower slopes produce fuller-bodied Rieslings from the slightly heavier calcareous soils.

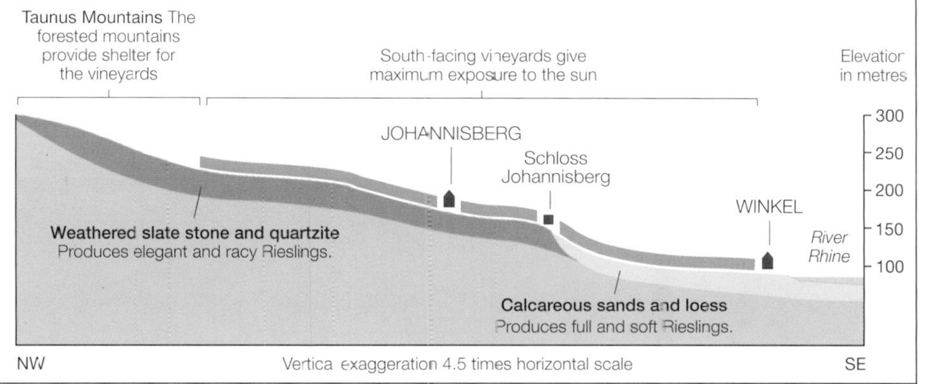

NAHE

I'M ALWAYS PUZZLED BY THE NAHE. Some of the greatest German wines I've ever drunk have come from this tributary of the Rhine. They can be as complex and rich as the best of the Rheingau, with an added flash of mineral fieriness, as though the metals mined along these river banks have somehow got into the wine. The Nahe has vineyard sites as unlikely in their steepness, and growers as good, as anywhere in Germany. So why do people forget about it?

I think it suffers from an identity crisis. The most famous German wine regions can be summarized in a few words: the Mosel is slate and floral delicacy, the Rheingau is rich and complex, Baden is reds and the Pinot family, the Rheinhessen, all too often, is cheap bulk wine. Try and sum up the Nahe and all you can do is refer to other places. The wine is a bit like the Rheingau, but it's a bit like the Mosel, as well. Its most widely planted grape is the undistinguished Müller-Thurgau, with 25 per cent of the vineyard surface; Riesling comes close behind with 24.5 per cent, and the other half is made up of grapes like Silvaner and Kerner. In addition Riesling wasn't planted there at all until the nineteenth century, and until the 1930s most Nahe wine was sold under the generic heading of Rhine wine. A lot of the wine was shipped to the Rhine and Mosel for blending, as well; in short, not much was bottled under its own regional name.

Most of the Nahe vineyards are scattered, and there are no great stretches of vines, with famous vineyard name succeeding famous name for mile on mile as there is in the Middle Mosel or in the heart of the Rheingau. Most of the vineyards are on quite gentle slopes, with only about a quarter of them managing real drama – the most spectacular wine scenery in the Nahe is around the villages of Traisen, with its dramatic Rotenfels precipice, and Schlossböckelheim. Perhaps it's not surprising that the fame of some of the Nahe's growers far outruns that of the region itself. As a result, some of the village names along the river can be obscure to all but the most specialized of specialists.

The Nahe rises in the Hunsrück hills and flows more or less north-east to join the Rhine at Bingen. There are patches of vineyards here and there, not just along the Nahe itself but along and around some of its tributaries, like the Guldenbach, the Gräfenbach, the Appelbach, the Glan, the Alsenz and the Gaulsbach. The Nahe is quite a widely spread area: some 4695 hectares (11,600 acres) of vineyards in all, most of which follow river valleys to some extent. The climate is warm and sunny, and the vineyards are generally well sheltered. It's an area of mixed farming, too, so the vine isn't God the way

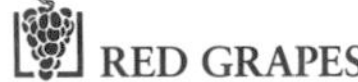

RED GRAPES
There are tiny amounts of Spätburgunder, Portugieser and Dornfelder.

WHITE GRAPES
Most Nahe wines are white – mainly from Müller-Thurgau and Riesling. Silvaner and Kerner are other varieties.

CLIMATE
The Nahe is temperate and sunny. The vineyards are protected by the Soonwald forest and the Hunsrück hills to the north-west but still get adequate rain.

SOIL
The region has many soil types: in the Middle and Upper Nahe there is porphyry, basalt, quartzite and coloured sandstone – the best for Riesling – and others. In the lower reaches soils include quartzite and slate.

ASPECT
Vines grow at 100–300m (330–985ft) and there are many protected south-facing sites on river valley slopes.

it is in the Rheingau just across the Rhine. Nevertheless, it is the banks of the Nahe that one must follow if one is to see how the character of the region develops.

WINE VILLAGES

In the uppermost reaches of the river, from the vineyards around Monzingen, the wines are at their lightest and most delicate. They quickly put on muscle as they go downstream, and they keep their balance while getting weightier, tenser and more taut – and suddenly, at Schlossböckelheim, they are as great as the very best in Germany. From here right up to Bad Kreuznach is the heart of the Nahe. This is where its spicy, minerally, fiery character is to be found, but as is so often the case, it's quite a small heart. For about 8km (5 miles) of river the wines are potentially great; on either side of this stretch of the Nahe they are merely very good.

The Kupfergrube vineyard at Schlossböckelheim used to be a copper mine – it yielded ore until the beginning of this century – and it must have taken a leap of the imagination on the part of the then director of the important State Domaine of Niederhausen-Schlossböckelheim to see it as anything other than a sheer rockface of scrub and stone. Convict labour did the work of clearing the scrub and building the 100 per cent steep slopes out of the rocky hillside before a single vine could be planted. But the south-west exposure was always too good to waste on a mere mine, and the complex, heat-retaining soil – colourful, volcanic porphyry – produces long-lived Rieslings.

Porphyry and many other igneous rocks continue in the soil through Oberhausen and beyond, and the vineyards curve with the river, facing south-west, south or south-east, and sometimes crossing over to the south bank. It is, however, the north bank that supplies the suntraps and Schlossböckelheim, Niederhausen and Norheim have some wonderful Riesling sites. At Traisen the rock turns to sandstone. The red sandstone of the Traiser Rotenfels rears higher, it is said, than any other cliff in Europe north of the Alps and at its foot you will find a 2-hectare (5-acre) ledge of 95 per cent steep earth and scree: the leavings of the Rotenfels over the years, if you like, which is the Traiser Bastei vineyard. With the river Nahe at its foot and the immense 185m (600ft) Rotenfels cliff towering above it, the Traiser Bastei vineyard is as perfect a suntrap for vines as can be found anywhere. Naturally, it is thickly planted with Riesling and yields are very low, sometimes as low as 14 hectolitres per hectare.

Noble rot occurs in these warm vineyards, though not every year. Auslesen are not uncommon, Beerenauslesen and above rather rarer: they're not here for the taking as they can sometimes be in the Rheingau.

At Kreuznach we pass into the Lower Nahe where many of the vineyards are along the tributaries to the west of the Nahe itself. The villages of Guldental, Wallhausen, Roxheim and Weinsheim, in particular, have good sites.

Bad Kreuznach can muster some excellent vineyards, in particular the curve of the Kahlenberg, Krötenpfuhl and Brückes sites above the town. From here downstream to the confluence with the Rhine, though, the hills broaden and become more gentle and the wines, too, broaden and become fuller and fatter and more like those of the Pfalz.

One Bereich, the Bereich Nahetal, now covers the whole region, which is a recent innovation. There used to be two Bereiche, one for the Upper Nahe and one for the Lower, and this did at least reflect the real differences in the wine. It's hard to see the advantage of this unification.

Here, at Schlossböckelheim, it is the most sheltered slopes with the exposure to the sun that are planted with vines.

WHERE THE VINEYARDS ARE *This map shows the finest part of the Nahe. The Rhine is up at the top, with the Rheingau vineyards along the north bank. The Nahe vineyards, west of Bingen on the south bank, do their best to imitate the perfect southerly exposure of those Rheingau slopes in the river bend, but they don't have the advantage of a broad expanse of water to reflect heat back on to them.*

Going up the Nahe from Bingen, you can see how the vineyards seek out south-facing slopes along the small tributaries. Look at the ideal southerly exposure of Burg Layen Schlossberg or the south-west-facing expanses of Wallhäuser Felseneck or Johannisberg. The tributaries play a vital part in the Nahe; without them this smallish region would be tiny indeed. Only after Bad Kreuznach do the vines begin seriously to follow the Nahe itself – and from there until Schlossböckelheim they are virtually inseparable.

The little village of Traisen tucks itself just behind Norheim; it's not actually on the river at all. That way its best sites, the Bastei and the Rotenfels, have a clear river view: you can see on the map how dramatic they are, and how they rear high above the water. At Norheim the Dellchen and Kafels vineyards face south-west and catch the afternoon sun; at Niederhausen the Felsensteyer site faces south-east and warms up early in the morning sun. And further up the Nahe at Schlossböckelheim you can see the 14 hectares (35 acres) of the Kupfergrube vineyard, facing south-south-east and tremendously steep. It's sheltered by the woods above and around it, and wines from the Kupfergrube are among the most expensive of the region.

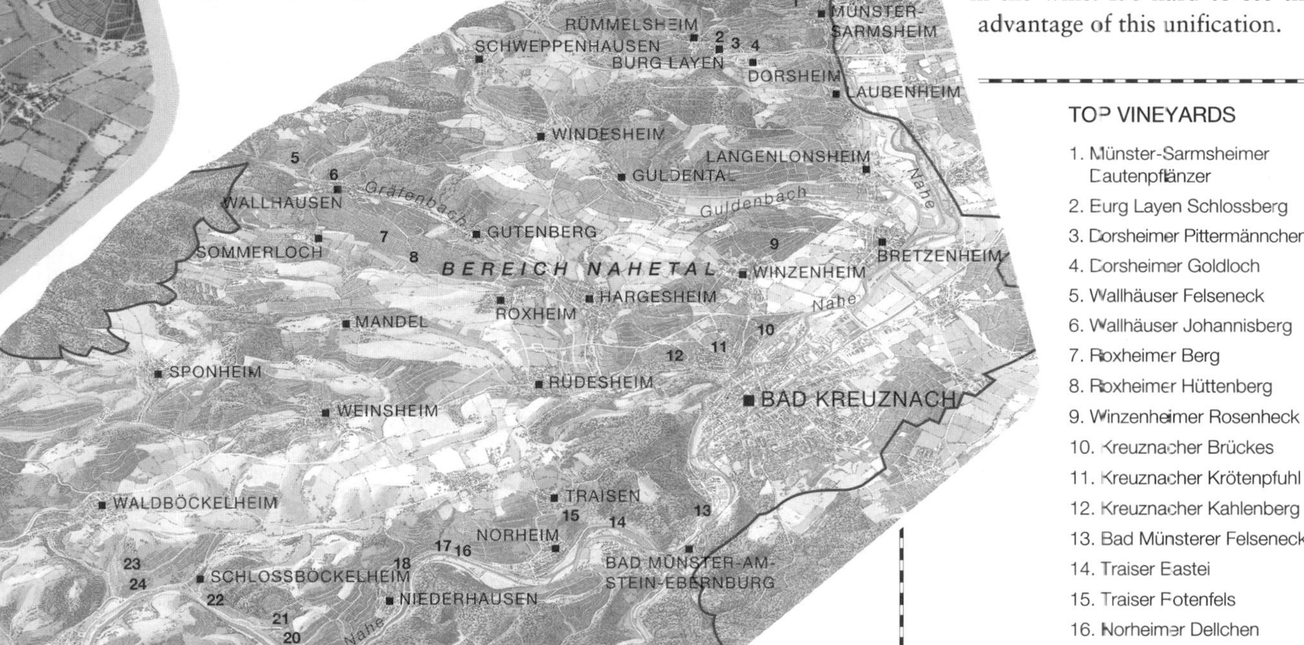

TOP VINEYARDS

1. Münster-Sarmsheimer Dautenpflänzer
2. Burg Layen Schlossberg
3. Dorsheimer Pittermännchen
4. Dorsheimer Goldloch
5. Wallhäuser Felseneck
6. Wallhäuser Johannisberg
7. Roxheimer Berg
8. Roxheimer Hüttenberg
9. Winzenheimer Rosenheck
10. Kreuznacher Brückes
11. Kreuznacher Krötenpfuhl
12. Kreuznacher Kahlenberg
13. Bad Münsterer Felseneck
14. Traiser Bastei
15. Traiser Rotenfels
16. Norheimer Dellchen
17. Norheimer Kafels
18. Niederhäuser Felsensteyer
19. Niederhäuser Hermannshöhle
20. Niederhäuser Hermannsberg
21. Schlossböckelheimer Kupfergrube
22. Schlossböckelheimer Felsenberg
23. Schlossböckelheimer Königsfels
24. Schlossböckelheimer In den Felsen

BEREICH BOUNDARIES

RHEINHESSEN

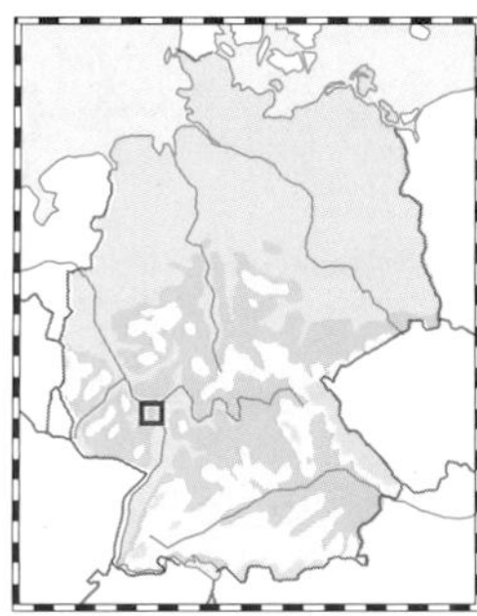

RED GRAPES
There is 6 per cent of Portugieser with a little Dornfelder and Spätburgunder.

WHITE GRAPES
Müller-Thurgau dominates with 22 per cent of the vines; Silvaner has 13 per cent followed by Kerner, Riesling, Scheurebe and Bacchus in almost equal amounts.

CLIMATE
A temperate climate with dry autumns common. The Taunus mountains and the Odenwald forest to the north give some shelter, as do the Hunsrück hills and Pfalzer Wald to the west. The Rheinterrasse sites are particularly sheltered.

SOIL
A wide variety of fertile soils, mainly loess but also limestone, sandy marl, quartzite, porphyry-sand and silty clay.

ASPECT
The Rheinterrasse faces east or south-east with vines up to 150m (500ft); in hillier parts of the hinterland they may go up to 300m (985ft), but the rest of the region is relatively flat.

WHENEVER I GO TO THE RHEINHESSEN I'm made aware that this is a region being pulled in two directions. On the one hand there is good quality: low yields, vines that are generally Riesling or the excellent Silvaner, steep sites and careful viticulture, meticulous wine-making and a top grower's name on the label. On the other hand there are the bulk blends: usually Müller-Thurgau and Kerner, from flattish vineyards that produce Germany's equivalent of the wine lake and, every harvest, a convoy of lorries to deliver the wine made from over-produced, bloated grapes to a merchant house. Merchant houses are vital in the Rheinhessen. Not that they need to be based there; all they have to do is buy wine in bulk from growers or co-operatives, and blend to the style of their particular brand. Sixty per cent of Rheinhessen wines are sold this way.

Now, this is not to decry every branded wine, because there are some good ones in the Rheinhessen. There are even some good Liebfraumilch brands (they're generally the big international ones that cost more). But I always reckon the test of a good restaurant is whether the locals eat there. And to compare the Rheinhessen to a restaurant, do the Germans drink Liebfraumilch? No, they do not.

This ambivalence in the Rheinhessen is partly a result of its geography, but it's been spurred on (at least in the downwards direction) by the relentless demand for ever-cheaper wine from a region warm enough and easily worked enough to be able to produce it. Mechanical harvesters are feasible on these gentle slopes; production costs can be very low. And will the wine bear the name of an Einzellage? No, it will not. It will have a Bereich name, or quite likely just a brand name, one of those cosy, mock-heritage names that is supposed to suggest that the wine has been hand-made by 100-year-old monks.

RHEINTERRASSE

The Rheinterrasse, Rheinhessen's best known area, is a string of villages along the west bank of the Rhine, south of Mainz. From the north, they are Bodenheim, Nackenheim, Nierstein, Oppenheim, Dienheim, Ludwigshöhe, Guntersblum, Alsheim and Mettenheim. These villages benefit from the fact that the land rises along this stretch of the bank and provides sloping vineyards that overlook the river to the east and south-east, and also from the reddish soil. The soils are very sandy even though some of the rock is actually a sandy clay and they produce some of the Rheinhessen's best wines. Oppenheim also benefits from the northern end of a ridge of limestone that runs north from Alsheim. Vines are grown here at up to 150m (500ft) above sea level, and the slopes are seldom more than 30 per cent steep.

Rieslings from the Rheinterrasse (and this is the only real Riesling area in the Rheinhessen) can be as minerally and complex as the best of the Rheingau, though there is always a little extra breadth to them, an extra touch of softness. In dry years Oppenheim, with its more gently sloping vineyards and greater access to moisture, is the best bet; Nierstein gains concentration in wetter years.

OTHER WINE AREAS

After the Rheinterrasse the other quality area in the Rheinhessen is south-east of Bingen, in the north-west corner of the region, where the river Nahe meets the Rhine. Not that the vineyards overlook either river: instead they face south, on slopes of red quartzite that give the wines smoky depth and good definition. In nearby Ingelheim facing the Rheingau the Riesling and Silvaner give way to Spätburgunder, though the red wines that result are light and raspberryish rather than dark and sturdy. It was from his palace here that Charlemagne is reputed to have looked across at the slopes of Johannisberg in what is now the Rheingau, and noted the slopes where the snow melted first. He then ordered vines to be planted there.

Rheinhessen's hinterland is not devoid of good wines. But the inland hills are cooler than the river valleys, the soil is not so quickly warmed by the sun, and good wines tend to be more the result of an individual grower's determination than an obvious gift of nature. Some good hillsides are to be found in the west, which the locals regard, rather optimistically, as their version of Switzerland. Vines can be found up to 300m (985ft) here. The central part of the Rheinhessen is known as Hügelland or hill country and is where the three Bereiche (Bingen in the north-west, Nierstein in the north-east and Wonnegau west of Worms) meet.

GRAPE VARIETIES

Müller-Thurgau is the workhorse grape of the Rheinhessen; it covers 22 per cent of the vineyards. Next comes Silvaner (potentially high quality, often made dry, but with a falling share – 13.3 per cent – of the land under vine) and the aromatic Kerner. Riesling, in fact, covers just 8.1 per cent of the Rheinhessen's 26,137 hectares (64,584 acres), but tends to dominate the better sites. Some of the newer crosses, like Bacchus, as well as Kerner and Scheurebe, are immensely popular with the Rheinhessen growers, most of whom have only a few hectares of vines and sell their grapes to the co-operatives. They are then blended into Liebfraumilch or an inexpensive Grosslage blend, and over half the total production of Liebfraumilch comes from the Rheinhessen. Most of the rest comes from the Pfalz; the Nahe and the Rheingau are the other permitted areas for Liebfraumilch but make

TOP VINEYARDS

1. Laubenheimer Johannisberg
2. Laubenheimer Edelmann
3. Laubenheimer Klosterberg
4. Bodenheimer Hoch
5. Bodenheimer Silberberg
6. Gau-Bischofsheimer Herrnberg
7. Nackenheimer Rothenberg
8. Niersteiner Pettenthal
9. Niersteiner Brudersberg
10. Niersteiner Hipping
11. Niersteiner Kranzberg
12. Niersteiner Glöck
13. Niersteiner Ölberg
14. Niersteiner Heiligenbaum
15. Niersteiner Orbel
16. Oppenheimer Herrenberg
17. Oppenheimer Sackträger
18. Oppenheimer Kreuz
19. Dienheimer Tafelstein
20. Ludwigshöher Teufelskopf
21. Guntersblümer Bornpfad
22. Guntersblümer Himmelthal

BEREICH BOUNDARIES

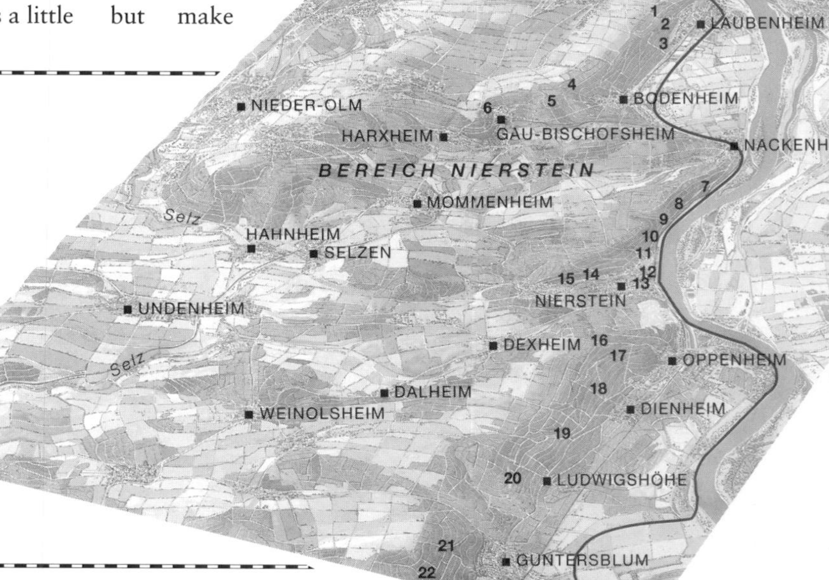

only a tiny percentage between them. It is noticeable that the Rheinhessen only makes 11.2 per cent of its wines dry, compared to 41.7 per cent in the Rheingau, 29.6 per cent in the Nahe and 52.9 per cent in little Hessische Bergstrasse. This means that the wines are not being produced primarily for a German audience: Germans just love dry wines these days. And since the Rheinhessen is Germany's largest wine region, that's an awful lot of sweetish, watery wine being made.

LIEBFRAUMILCH

The Gothic church Liebfrauenkirche, from which Liebfraumilch takes its name, is in Worms, in the very south of the region. Wine from its own vineyard adjacent to the church now takes the name of Liebfrauenstift-Kirchenstück, while the wine to which it has given its name need only be 'of pleasant character', of QbA quality, of between 18 and 40 grams per litre residual sugar, and made from at least 70 per cent of any of the following: Müller-Thurgau, Kerner, Silvaner or Riesling. In other words there is no requirement for it to contain any classic grape varieties at all. It comes from all three of Rheinhessen's Bereiche, since the boundaries do not follow any particular geographical logic.

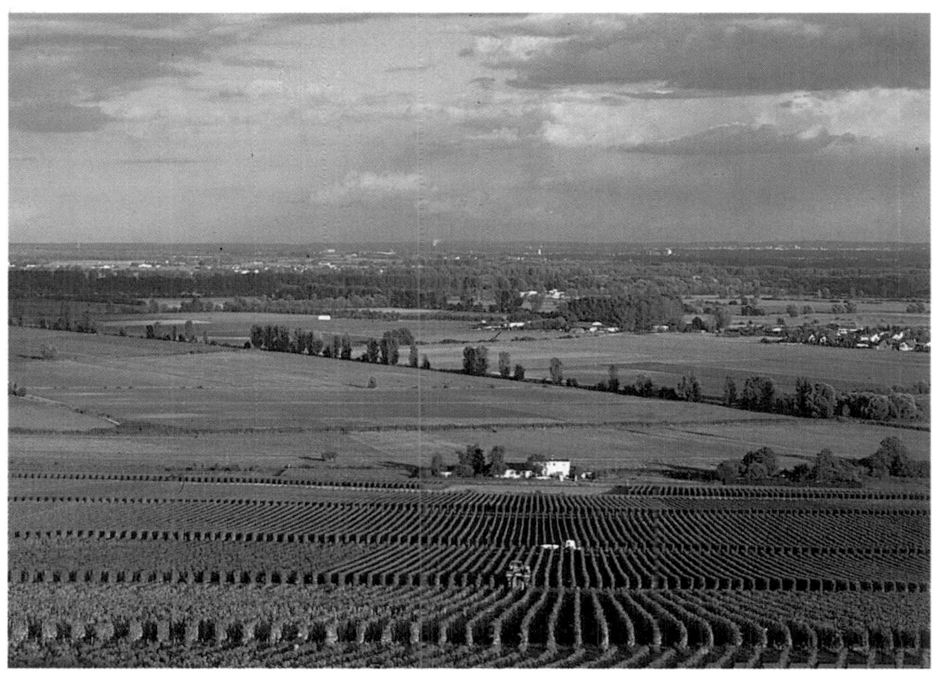

Vines at Gau-Bischofsheim overlook the endless Rheinhessen plain.

WHERE THE VINEYARDS ARE *It all looks rather idyllic on the map. Once south of the urban sprawl of Mainz, the Rheinhessen becomes gentle and bucolic. There are fields of maize and other cereals; there are woods and small villages, and the broad Rhine ambles northwards along the eastern edge. Even the Rheinterrasse, probably the Rheinhessen's best known area, doesn't look all that dramatic, compared to some wine landscapes.*

The villages facing the Rhine along the Rheinterrasse benefit from sloping land facing east and south-east over the river and soils on which Riesling thrives. Nierstein, the centre of the Rheinterrasse, has some wonderful vineyard sites. It is famous also because of the abuse of its reputation: Nierstein has had to give its name to the Bereich covering vineyards in the east of Rheinhessen. The Bereich accounts for about one-third of the region's wines and almost all of them unmemorable while the growers in Nierstein itself struggle to maintain their high reputation.

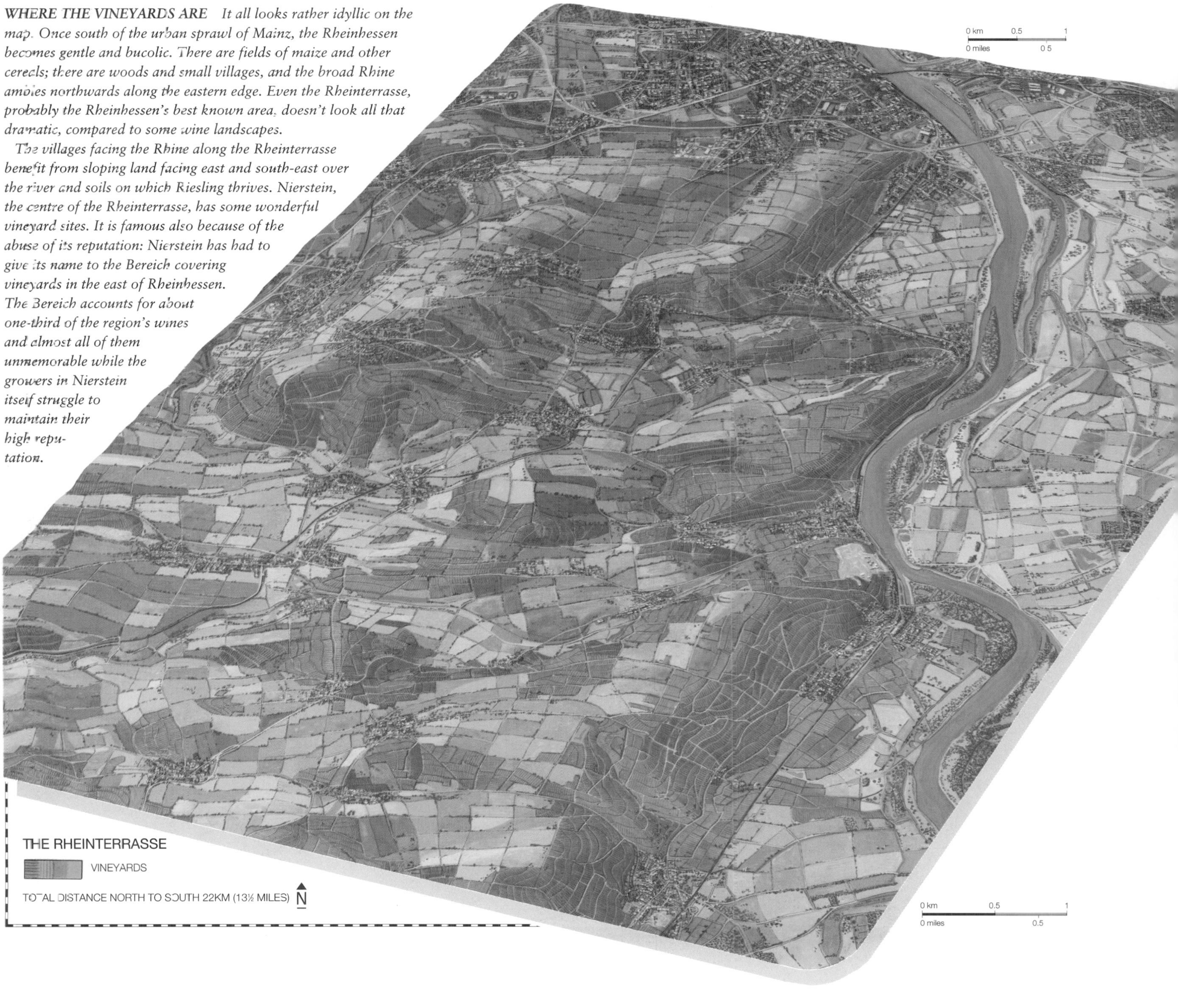

0 km 0.5 1
0 miles 0.5

THE RHEINTERRASSE

VINEYARDS

TOTAL DISTANCE NORTH TO SOUTH 22KM (13½ MILES) N

0 km 0.5 1
0 miles 0.5

PFALZ

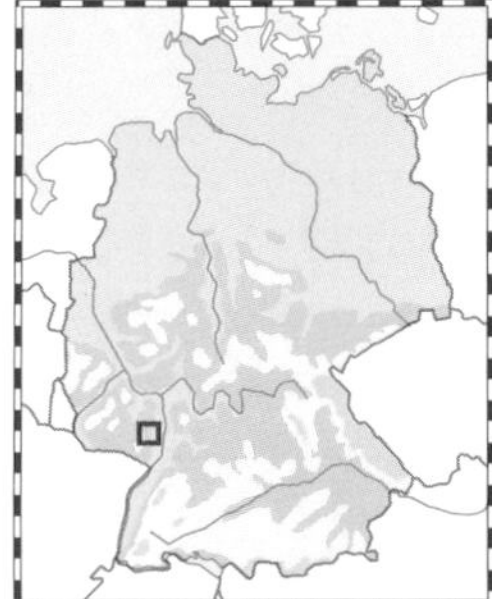

DIE PFALZ – IT EVEN SOUNDS RICH and ripe and spicy. If you had to guess, you might say it was a land of fertile soil and good living, of rich food and rich wine to match. And you'd be right. In fact, if you were to imagine something along the lines of Alsace you'd also be right, because if you were to head due south off this map after a little while you'd find yourself crossing the border into France. The hills would be the same, and so would the river, flowing northwards at some distance from the vine-growing hills. Many of the grapes would be the same, and many of the growers would have Germanic names, but the language, and the flavours, would be different.

The Haardt mountains, which shelter the Pfalz vineyards and rise up to the west of them, are simply a northerly continuation of the Vosges. The soils are as mixed as they are in Alsace and the villages are just as picturesque, full of full-size gingerbread houses. Yet something happens to the wines as you cross from France into Germany. Even though nowadays they are being made largely dry, they are still indefinably German, just as Alsace wines, though made from Germanic varieties, are indefinably French. If anyone doubted that the character of the winemaker is crucial in wine-making, that short trip from Pfalz to Alsace should convince them.

The Pfalz is divided into two Bereiche, the Mittelhaardt/Deutsche Weinstrasse north of Neustadt and the Südliche Weinstrasse to the south. Traditionally the best wines have come from the north – indeed, traditionally the only good wines came from the north, even though the establishment in 1991 of a single Bereich to cover the whole of the north ignores the fact that the far north, north of Kallstadt, does not yield the same quality as the best villages.

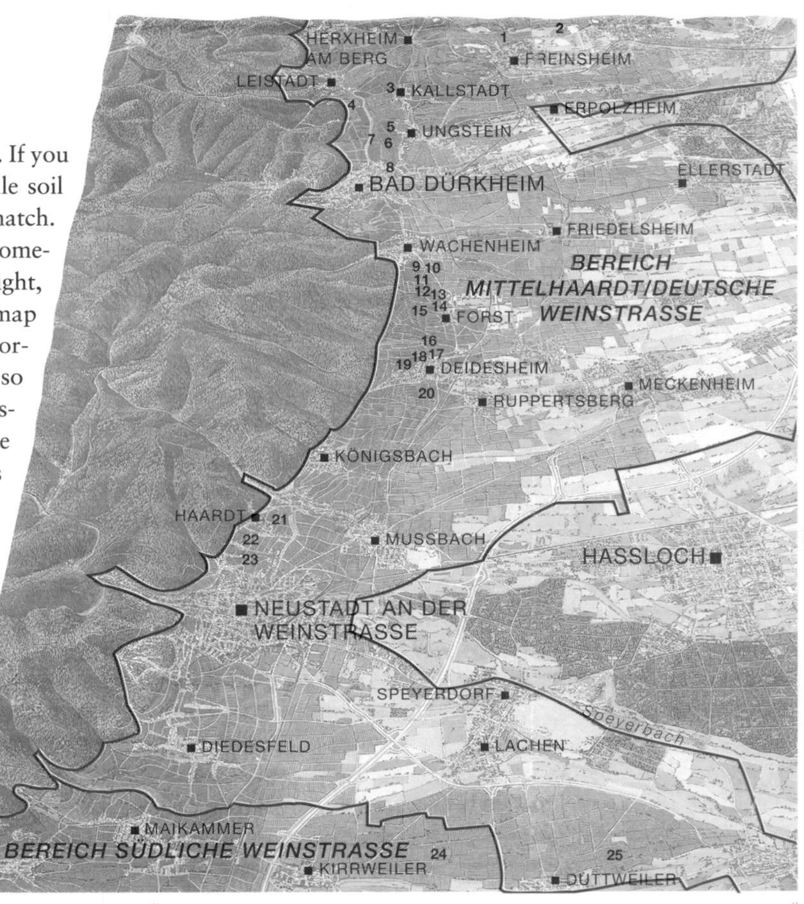

TOP VINEYARDS

1. Freinsheimer Musikantenbuckel
2. Freinsheimer Goldberg
3. Kallstädter Saumagen
4. Kallstädter Annaberg
5. Ungsteiner Weilberg
6. Ungsteiner Herrenberg
7. Dürkheimer Spielberg
8. Dürkheimer Michelsberg
9. Wachenheimer Rechbächel
10. Wachenheimer Goldbächel
11. Wachenheimer Gerümpel
12. Forster Pechstein
13. Forster Jesuitengarten
14. Forster Kirchenstück
15. Forster Ungeheuer
16. Deidesheimer Kalkofen
17. Deidesheimer Grainhübel
18. Deidesheimer Hohenmorgen
19. Deidesheimer Leinhöhle
20. Ruppertsberger Reiterpfad
21. Haardter Herzog
22. Haardter Herrenletten
23. Haardter Bürgergarten
24. Kirrweiler Mandelberg
25. Duttweiler Kalkberg

— BEFEICH BOUNDARIES

SÜDLICHE WEINSTRASSE

The Südliche Weinstrasse was long thought of as being the home of broad, fat, overcropped wines that quickly flopped over into blowsiness. It still is the source of a good part of the production of Liebfraumilch. More than half comes from the Rheinhessen; and what these two areas have in common is flattish, easily worked vineyards and a large proportion of high-yielding grapes like Müller-Thurgau and Kerner. But something has been happening in these quiet, rural villages in southern Pfalz which is gaining a reputation for being one of the most exciting regions in Germany. There are ambitious growers prepared to jettison their heritage of bulk wine and make themselves a name for quality.

It is even more fertile here than further north. Yields can be high, and are often too high, from these heavy, lime-rich soils. When it comes to grapes, think spiciness. There is not much Riesling, therefore, but Morio-Muskat, Pinot Gris (alias Grauburgunder) and, particularly in the far south, Gewürztraminer. Pinot Blanc and Silvaner, too, take on more spice here than they do elsewhere, and Müller-Thurgau can be a veritable pot-pourri. The best growers, of course, only take fairly low yields from their grapes, ferment them dry, and then often break an unwritten rule of German wine-making and age their Pinot family wines in new oak. But then they've already broken another unwritten German rule by producing serious wines from flat or almost flat vineyards.

The reason that gentle slopes (or no slopes at all) can be persuaded to give fine wines here is partly to do with the climate. It is very dry and sunny, and only a little less warm than Baden to the south. Steep slopes are vital in cool regions like the Mosel if late-ripening varieties like Riesling are to have a chance of ripening; here in the southern Pfalz it's not such a battle. The Südliche Weinstrasse is an area of small farmers who are only part-time vine-growers (the average vineyard holding for the whole Pfalz is less than 1 hectare/2½ acres); the Mittelhaardt is where the big wine estates are found.

THE MITTELHAARDT/DEUTSCHE WEINSTRASSE

Even though this is the part of the Pfalz where the best quality wine is made, results are still mixed: the vineyards sprawl over the sandy river plain, and there's plenty of bulk wine made up here as well, but the Pfalz's star turn is the string of villages from Neustadt north to Wachenheim.

Neustadt is not particularly hilly – in fact it's not all that steep anywhere in the Pfalz. The vineyards continue on sandy-soiled slopes through Ruppertsberg, suddenly steepening at Deidesheim. The vines are planted up to 250m (820ft) on these slopes, and they're sheltered by the hills; here the Rhine is really too far away across the plain to make a great difference to the wines. We're in Riesling country now, although in few places in the Pfalz does Riesling take over to the exclusion of all other grapes as it does in the Middle Mosel or Rheingau. It only accounts for 20 per cent of the total vineyard, in fact, although the proportion is creeping up; Müller-Thurgau accounts for 21 per cent, and that figure is slipping.

At Forst the soil is varied by an outcrop of black basalt which makes already warm soil even warmer; not surprisingly, growers in vineyards that do not benefit naturally from this

 RED GRAPES

Portugieser accounts for 10 per cent. Dornfelder and Spätburgunder also do well although still only planted in tiny amounts.

 WHITE GRAPES

Mainly a white wine region, the Pfalz has important plantings of Riesling, even though Müller-Thurgau outnumbers it slightly. Kerner and Silvaner are other important varieties.

CLIMATE

This is Germany's sunniest and driest wine region and it is almost as warm as Baden.

SOIL

The soils are very varied, including loam, weathered sandstone (especially near the Haardt mountains), shelly limestone, granite, porphyry and slate. The Südliche Weinstrasse has heavier, more fertile soils than the northern Mittelhaardt.

ASPECT

Vines are planted either on the plain or on the gentle east-facing slopes of the Haardt mountains up to 250m (820ft).

The village of St Martin is in the heart of the hilliest part of the Pfalz.

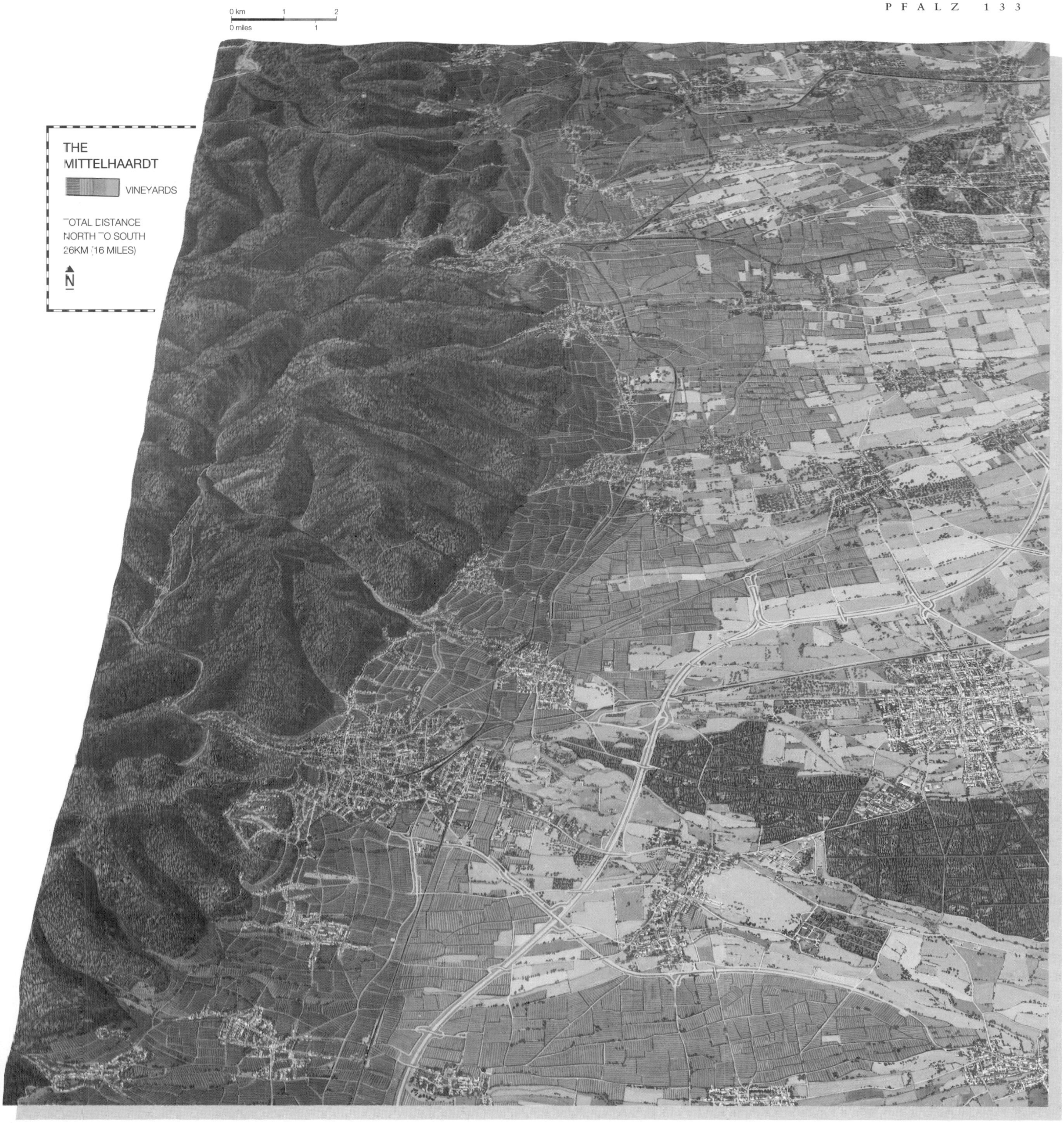

0 km 1 2
0 miles 1

THE MITTELHAARDT

VINEYARDS

TOTAL DISTANCE NORTH TO SOUTH 26KM (16 MILES)

N

basalt have got into the habit of importing it, to the particular benefit of the Mariengarten and Kirchenstück vineyards, and those in Deidesheim.

Most of the great vineyards here and in Wachenheim are 100 per cent Riesling, but at Bad Dürkheim, except in the best sites, red grapes are in favour, particularly Spätburgunder. It is perhaps surprising that red grapes are not grown more widely in the Pfalz – but then they would not be suited to bulk production, and the top villages have made their reputations with other varieties. The reputation of the whole region is of fairly recent date. Until the end of World War Two Pfalz wine was generally bottled elsewhere, and a lot was blended with wine from the Mosel, which has a certain logic to it if you care nothing for regional character. The Pfalz has been steadily reinventing itself ever since.

WHERE THE VINEYARDS ARE *You could easily confuse this map of the Pfalz with that of Alsace. There's that same narrow, sheltered strip of vineyards, the same spilling of vines on to the plain towards the Rhine, and the mountains, crowned with forest, can be clearly seen stretching away to the west. In fact, these Haardt mountains on the Pfalz map are a northerly continuation of Alsace's Vosges mountains.*

Even though the southern Pfalz proves time and time again that flat or flattish vineyards can make excellent wine, there is a clear distinction in the Mittelhaardt, the area shown on the map, between the plain and the hills. Here, the plain, with its intensive farming and higher yields, is the home of bulk wine. Kerner and Müller-Thurgau predominate, and the Riesling is concentrated on the east-facing slopes north of Neustadt. At Deidesheim you can see how the slope suddenly gets steeper. But Forst probably has the most famous Pfalz site of all: the Jesuitengarten.

0 km 1 2
0 miles 1

FRANKEN

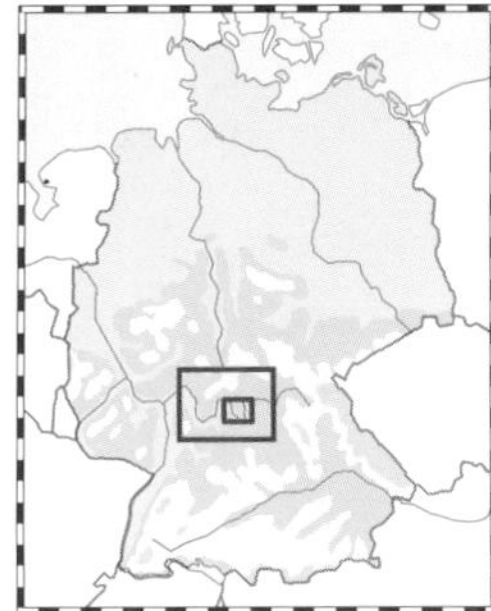

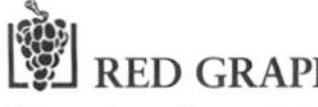

RED GRAPES
There is a tiny amount of Spätburgunder.

WHITE GRAPES
Silvaner is at its best in Franken, even though Müller-Thurgau accounts for almost half the vineyards. Other important varieties include Bacchus and Kerner. There is a little Riesling, Scheurebe, Perle, Ortega and Traminer.

CLIMATE
Franken has a continental climate, with a short growing season, cold winters and warm summers.

SOIL
The soils are very varied, with heavy, weathered red marl in the Steigerwald, clay/ limestone and loess in the Maindreieck and weathered coloured sandstone and light loam in the Mainviereck.

ASPECT
Most vines are planted on south-facing slopes, usually in river valleys. Many vineyards are steep, going up to 60 per cent in some places.

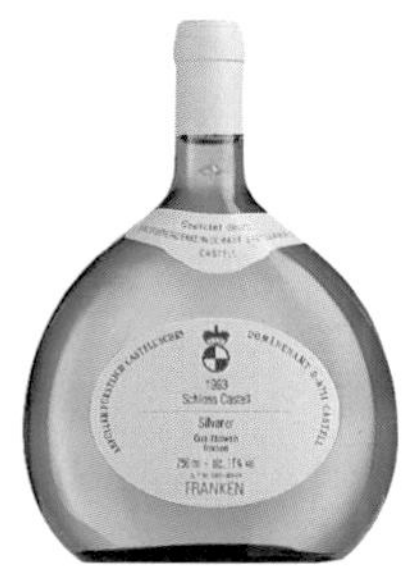

The traditional flask-shaped Bocksbeutel is used for Franken wines.

THERE'S SOMETHING ABOUT FRANKEN WINE. It gives me the most terrible thirst. I have done my best in snooping about the cellars of Würzburg, and those of the little villages around the city but I have to admit, after an hour or two of impressive but relentlessly dry Silvaners and Müller-Thurgaus, only occasionally relieved by something perfumed and rich, I am panting for a beer. And Würzburg does have more than its share of cellars where the beer foams from the barrel and the platters are piled high with sausages and piles of gritty bread.

It's easy to forget that much of Germany finds it a struggle to make wines suited to the traditionally robust German fare. That's how Franken wines got their reputation – the earthy Silvaner grape, not generally renowned for producing wine of much personality in its own right, comes into its own here, giving wines of far weightier texture than most of Germany's other 'dry' wines. And that's why it's so difficult to find Franken wines outside Germany – the Germans pay high prices for every bottle they can get.

There's also another reason – the climate. Apart from the even more easterly regions of Saale-Unstrut and Sachsen, it is the only vine-growing region of Germany to have a properly continental climate of cold, cold winters and warm summers. But it also has a short growing season, and spring and autumn are unpredictable. Early spring can be warm, encouraging the vines to bud early; the weather can then turn, and a hard frost can destroy the crop. In February 1985, for example, temperatures of -25°C (-13°F) for several nights running killed 2.5 million vines in Franken, with the southern part and Maindreieck the worst affected areas. Autumns can be long and warm, making sweet wines a possibility, or they can be cold and wet. As a result yields can fluctuate here more than anywhere else in Germany – and only the biggest estates can rely on having enough wine to export, year after year.

Franken lies 80km (50 miles) east of the Rheingau and is centred on the river Main. The vineyards are scattered, and sometimes are so far apart that the bureaucrats haven't even bothered to assign Grosslagen to them. As a result Bereich names are much used – Bereich Mainviereck is in the west, where the Main roughly describes two sides of a square (the name means 'Main square'); Bereich Maindreieck ('Main triangle'), where the river becomes two sides of a triangle, is in the centre; and in the east is Bereich Steigerwald.

The soils are in fact very varied in Franken: there's a fair bit of marl and sandstone and some loam, gypsum and clay. There are some top vineyard sites, too: including the steep, south-south-west-facing Casteller Schlossberg, Rödelseer Küchenmeister, or, in Iphofen, the Julius-Echter-Berg vineyard, again steep, and with excellent south-south-west exposure.

GRAPE VARIETIES

Silvaner and, to a lesser extent, Riesling, are the star grapes. Riesling is not greatly favoured in Franken: it's too late a ripener for the region's short growing season. But Silvaner attains heights it reaches nowhere else. 'Earthy' is the word usually used to describe it; it's minerally, too, and high in acidity and extract. Made dry (and Franken's wines are always dry, except when noble rot makes one of its rare visits), it is an ideal food wine. Overall in Franken, Müller-Thurgau is the most common variety. It can be good here – certainly more distinguished than in most of Germany – but it's still not as good as Silvaner, so it's a pity that so much land was planted with it in the 1960s and 1970s at the expense of Silvaner.

Silvaner accounts for 19 per cent of Franken's 5962 hectares (14,732 acres), but after that it's largely a litany of new grape crosses like Bacchus and Kerner. They don't do badly here, but frankly they're never likely to be as interesting as a good Silvaner. The first, Müller-Thurgau, was bred in

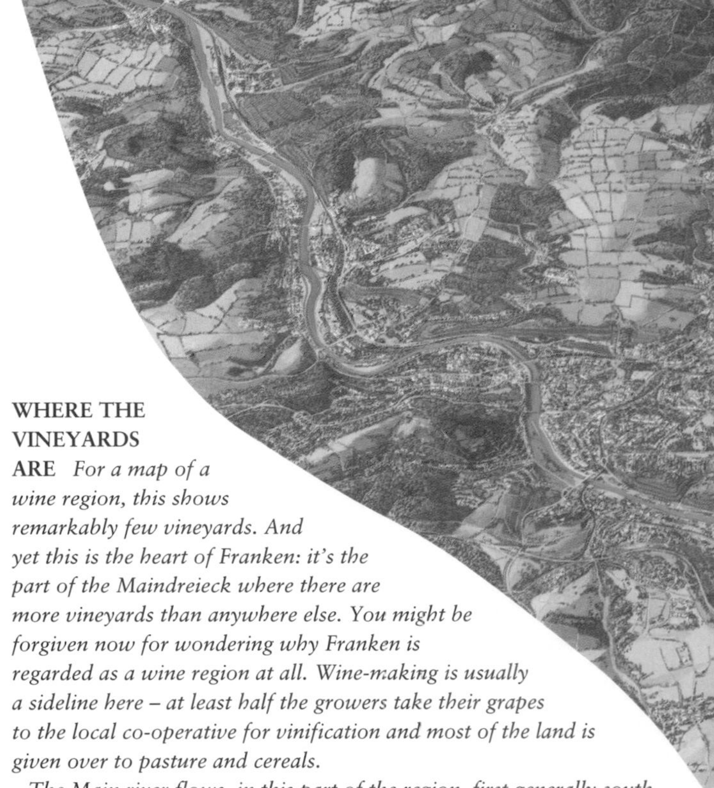

WHERE THE VINEYARDS ARE *For a map of a wine region, this shows remarkably few vineyards. And yet this is the heart of Franken: it's the part of the Maindreieck where there are more vineyards than anywhere else. You might be forgiven now for wondering why Franken is regarded as a wine region at all. Wine-making is usually a sideline here – at least half the growers take their grapes to the local co-operative for vinification and most of the land is given over to pasture and cereals.*

The Main river flows, in this part of the region, first generally south and then generally north-west through Würzburg. Just south of the city there is a south-west-facing wall of vines: these are the Randersacker vineyards rising above the river. Go a little further north, and just as the city of Würzburg peters out there is another straight, south-facing cliff. This is the Stein vineyard which has just about everything a vineyard could ask from nature. The river and the city both keep it warm, and the water reflects sun and heat back on to the vines. As a result temperatures here in the summer can reach 40°C (104°F), and Auslesen wines and above are not uncommon.

1882 but the drive to produce ever more of them is new. They spring, via their various parents, from the Geisenheim Viticultural Institute in the Rheingau. The idea behind all of them is much the same: the Riesling has many advantages, among them its resistance to the cold of Germany's winters. But it yields relatively meanly and ripens late in the year – just when the cold can be setting in and there is a risk of it not ripening at all. The ideal vine would have all the advantages of Riesling – plus the sheer breed of its wines – but would ripen earlier and yield more generously. The new varieties that pass Geisenheim's stringent tests and appear in the vineyards are, of course, only a minute proportion of all the crosses that are bred and tried out. Most of them have Riesling not too far back in their ancestry. The most successful include Scheurebe (Riesling x Silvaner – the same as Müller-Thurgau, but a different crossing) which makes excellent, rich, botrytized wines with good acidity and pink grapefruit and pepper flavours.

Other crosses are Bacchus (Silvaner x Riesling) whose wines are rather soft but can reach good sugar levels; Kerner (Riesling x Trollinger), which has the advantage of being early-ripening. Quite well balanced, its wine has a whiff of Muscat. Perle (Gewürztraminer x Müller-Thurgau) and Ortega (Müller -Thurgau x Siegerrebe) are also aromatic. None of them is exciting, except for Scheurebe. But if you are a Franken grower selling your grapes to a co-operative and your big problem is early, cold winters, you can see the attraction of using crosses.

BEREICH MAINDREIECK

In the Maindreieck the soil turns to limestone. Some 70 per cent of Franken wine comes from this central area, on what is if not quite the doorstep of the city of Würzburg, then certainly

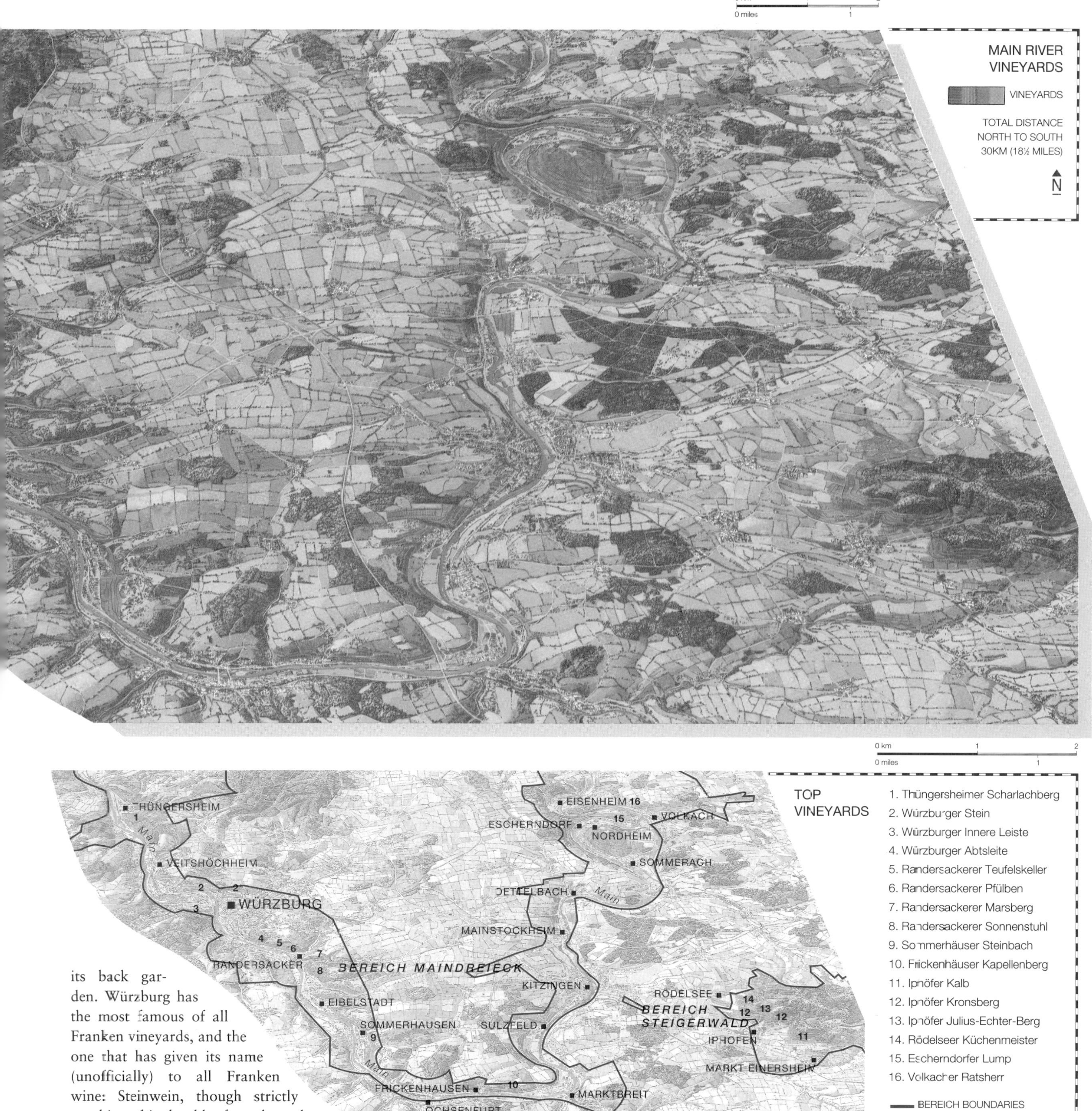

its back garden. Würzburg has the most famous of all Franken vineyards, and the one that has given its name (unofficially) to all Franken wine: Steinwein, though strictly speaking, this should refer only to the wine of the Stein vineyard, a great cliff of heat-retaining limestone that looks southwards over the city. Look for Silvaner from here, or Riesling, for the full Würzburger Stein Experience.

Würzburg has more to offer than wine, however (more than beer, too), and it is undoubtedly one of the loveliest cities in Germany. The magnificent eighteenth-century Residenz of the Prince-Bishops who ruled Franken boasts a fresco by Tiepolo, among other treasures.

There are more vines around Würzburg than anywhere else in Franken. Go to the villages north and south of the city: on both sides of the river Main, where slope and exposure allow, vines are planted. Further upriver, at Escherndorf there is another top Silvaner spot, the very steep, south-facing Lump site, where marly clay overlays limestone.

BEREICH STEIGERWALD

This is the easternmost Bereich and the scattered vineyards lie away from the Main, on the western slopes of the Steigerwald. The climate here is more continental than in the rest of Franken and the deep, rich soils produce full-flavoured, fruity wines with a vigorous acidity. The best wine villages in the Steigerwald are Iphofen, Rödelsee and Castell, all on heavier,

The orderly Stein vineyard, in the city of Würzburg, has given its name to Franken wine as a whole.

marly clay. Castell, on the slopes of the Steigerwald, is the home of Franken's finest wine estate, the Fürstlich Castell'sches Domänenamt, which makes excellent Müller-Thurgau and Silvaner as well as wonderfully concentrated Rieslaner in top years.

BEREICH MAINVIERECK

The smallest and least ambitious of Franken's three regions is the Bereich Mainviereck. It's the furthest west and has the fewest vineyards, scattered at intervals along the Main as it wends its way through Wertheim as far as Aschaffenburg. There are a few along the north bank of the river Rück, a tributary of the Main north of Klingenberg, and around Hörstein near the Hessen border. It's mostly Riesling here, though there's some Spätburgunder south of Aschaffenburg. The soils are largely sandstone and loam, the former used particularly for Spätburgunder. Red vines can be found along the Main south of Rück, too, in Erlenbach, Klingenberg, Miltenberg, Grossheubach and Bürgstadt. And the wines? Not bad – but they're not the most thrilling in Franken.

But if all this sounds as though wine-making in Franken is difficult, as though the growers only do it to make themselves suffer – think again. The vineyard area has increased by more than 50 per cent since the early 1980s – in 1981 Franken had just 3847 hectares (9506 acres). The region may suffer from cold winters – that's why the vineyards tend to huddle around the river, or in the shelter of woods, so they can gain whatever protection is going – but it also has hot summers and these allow it to do what few parts of Germany can do, which is make dry wines. Dry wines are extremely fashionable now in Germany, and personally I'd rather have a dry Silvaner from here than a dry Riesling from the Mosel, with its lower extract and lean structure. So, it seems, would a lot of Germans.

THREE GREAT WINE ESTATES

Franken's great wine estates have, since the Middle Ages, included charitable institutions similar to (though, in one case, bigger than) the Hospices de Beaune in Burgundy. Their principal was the same: the poor and needy could be provided for out of the income from wine.

The Bürgerspital zum Heiligen Geist is the oldest, having been founded in 1319 to provide for the old people of Würzburg. Johannes von Steren was the founder, at a time when Franken's vineyards were far more extensive than they are now. In the Middle Ages, in fact, Franken was Germany's biggest wine region, with 40,000 hectares (99,000 acres) of vineyards at its peak.

The decline began in the sixteenth century, roughly at the time that Würzburg's other great charitable institution, the Juliusspital, was founded in 1576. This was a religious establishment, set up by the Prince-Bishop Julius Echter von Mespelbrunn. As you might expect from a Prince-Bishop, it was on a lavish scale. Both it and the lay Bürgerspital were endowed with prime vineyard sites and both acquired more over the years, so that now the Bürgerspital owns 140 hectares (346 acres), including the biggest chunk of the Stein vineyard, and the Juliusspital owns 160 hectares (395 acres), which makes it the third largest wine estate in Germany and bigger than the Hospices de Beaune. It owns part of the Stein and part also of Escherndorfer Lump and Iphöfer Julius-Echter-Berg, among others.

The other great Franken estate has the unromantic name of the Staatlicher Hofkeller – which sounds dull until you realize that its premises are in the cellars of the Residenz (Tiepolo didn't paint any ceilings that far down, sadly) and that this was the winery of the Prince-Bishops of Würzburg. In 1803, with the invasion of Napoleon and the subsequent secularization of church land, it was taken over by the Bavarian state, and now owns 173 hectares (427 acres) of vineyards.

The Juliusspital, however, managed to avoid being handed over to the state, and both it and the Bürgerspital survive. Yet vine-growing in Franken continued to decline. The increasing popularity of tea and coffee, competition from Bavarian beer, the industrial revolution, poor weather in the nineteenth century – all these played their part. And then as now, Franken's lack of a market for its wines outside its borders told on it. Indeed, Franken's wine trade as a whole was poorly developed: in the eighteenth century there were even police rules against selling wine, ostensibly to prevent Würzburg from running out. The vinous disasters of the nineteenth century – oidium, mildew, phylloxera – completed the process of decline. Now Franken's vineyards are flourishing again, though at a lower level – and they still keep the wine for themselves.

Baden-Württemberg

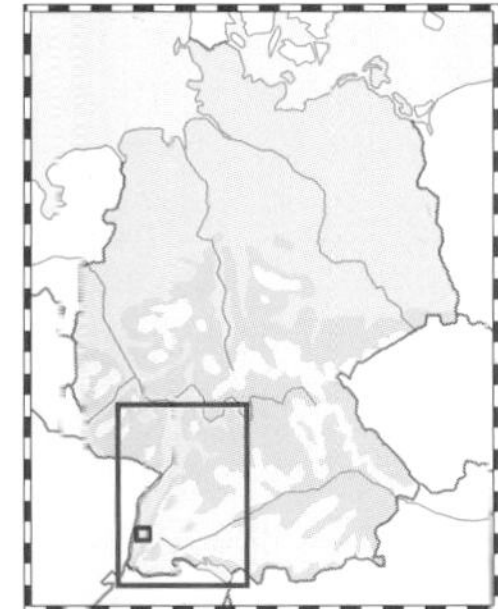

Baden and Württemberg are the odd ones out among the German wine regions. They make wines different in character from the rest of the country and different even from each other. They are both remarkably diffuse in terms of styles and grapes, and Baden even has a wine area that is really not Baden at all, but lies within Franken. But here they are, yoked together into the state of Baden-Württemberg, and while Baden's wines are trying to make an impact on foreign markets, the growers of Württemberg don't bother as the local inhabitants drink every drop they make.

BADEN

Everybody thinks of Baden as being a long, narrow strip of vineyards stretching for 130km (80 miles) between the spa town of Baden-Baden down the Rhine Valley to Basel in Switzerland. That's certainly the main part as 80 per cent of its wines come from here. But wines labelled Baden also come from the Bereich Tauberfranken, tucked in between the south of Franken and the north of Württemberg and only belonging to Baden at all because a political boundary says it does. South-west of that there's another chunk of Baden vineyards, this time wedged in south of Hessische Bergstrasse and west of Württemberg. And then right down in the south-east, south of the Danube, there's a little enclave of Baden vines on the banks of Lake Constance. Even the bureaucrats recognize that although these four are all counted as Baden this doesn't make them the same. Accordingly, the five Bereiche in the main strip alongside the Rhine – that is, from the south, Markgräflerland, Tuniberg, Kaiserstuhl, Breisgau and Ortenau – have different, and generally higher, minimum must weights for each category of wine (Kabinett, Spätlese and so on) than do the others. Yet all of Baden is classified, in EU terms, as being in Region B (along with such places as the Loire and Champagne) instead of in the cooler region A along with the rest of Germany.

Well, it certainly is warmer here in Baden. The climate is generally continental, with cold winters and warm summers. The five Bereiche that make up the principal part of Baden are tucked in between the Rhine and the foothills of the Black Forest; they are effectively the mirror image of the Alsace vineyards just over the border. But the climate isn't quite as good as it is in Alsace. It's a little cooler and a little damper, though the vines are sheltered by the forest that crowns the hills.

The Markgräflerland is where Swiss viticulture shades into German. The speciality of the gentle, fertile district is the Gutedel, alias Chasselas, which makes a crisp, somewhat neutral wine that is usually pretty unremarkable. It is not until near the beautiful medieval city of Freiburg that the typical style of Baden wine – dry, full, winey rather than flowery, and relatively low in acidity – begins to emerge.

It reaches its peak in the twin areas of Kaiserstuhl and Tuniberg. Most of Baden is given over to mixed farming, with the average vineyard holding only 0.6 hectares (1½ acres), but in the Kaiserstuhl there is hardly any other crop to be seen. The Kaiserstuhl is the stump of a three million-year-old volcano, covered with wind-blown loess, and its southern slopes, in particular the village of Ihringen, are Germany's warmest.

There is Riesling to be found here, as there is in most of Baden, but Riesling is not usually what Baden does best. This is the part of Germany where the Pinot family shines, with depth and weight that is akin to the wines of Alsace across the river. Grauburgunder or Pinot Gris, Weissburgunder or Pinot Blanc, and Spätburgunder or Pinot Noir all ripen well here – it's one of the few parts of Germany able to make red wines that are properly red. But not even the Kaiserstuhl, with its warm temperatures, makes much botrytized wine. It's too dry here for the fungus to flourish – and besides, the wines don't always have the high acidity needed to support it.

The Tuniberg is smaller than the Kaiserstuhl, and only 304m (997ft) high compared to the latter's 576m (1890ft). Almost every inch of it is covered with vines, but the soil is limestone rather than volcanic and it is slightly cooler and

QUALITY WINE REGIONS AND BEREICHE

BADEN	WÜRTTEMBERG
Bereich Tauberfranken	Bereich Kocher-Jagst-Tauber
Bereich Badische Bergstrasse/Kraichgau	Bereich Württembergisch Unterland
Bereich Ortenau	Bereich Remstal-Stuttgart
Bereich Breisgau	Bereich Oberer Neckar
Bereich Kaiserstuhl	Bereich Württembergischer Bodensee
Bereich Tuniberg	Bereich Bayerischer Bodensee
Bereich Markgräflerland	
Bereich Bodensee	OVER 500M (1640FT)
	OVER 1000M (3280FT)

RED GRAPES
Baden has nearly 75 per cent of Germany's Spätburgunder. Trollinger is Württemberg's main red grape.

WHITE GRAPES
Müller-Thurgau leads a long list of white varieties in Baden, followed by Grauburgunder, Gutedel and Riesling and others. Riesling is Württemberg's main white grape, followed by Kerner and Müller-Thurgau.

CLIMATE
Baden is Germany's warmest wine region. Many of the vineyards are sheltered by the Odenwald mountains and the Black Forest. Württemberg is warm, and sheltered by river valleys and the Swabian Alps.

SOIL
Baden has mostly rich and fertile soils. There is gravel near the Bodensee, and limestone, clay, marl, loam, granite, loess, sandy marl elsewhere, plus volcanic soil on the Kaiserstuhl. Württemberg's soils are usually deep and well-drained. There is red marl, clay, loess, loam and shelly limestone.

ASPECT
Most Baden vineyards, except the Kaiserstuhl and Tuniberg, are on level or gently sloping land. In Württemberg they are on the gentle slopes of river valleys.

damper than its big brother, although like the Kaiserstuhl it has a topsoil of loess.

Loess is the rule in the Bereich Breisgau, as well, which runs up the Rhine Valley north of Freiburg, hugging the slopes of the Black Forest. There is slightly more rainfall here, and slightly higher acidity in the wines. As elsewhere in Baden, the slopes were reorganized and re-terraced in the 1960s and 1970s under the Flurbereinigung programme, and the vineyard area overall has doubled. Output also soared, until the Baden growers decided that enough was enough and that yields would simply have to be restricted. From the 1984 vintage onwards, accordingly, they have been set at no more than 90 hectolitres per hectare; still fairly generous, but a definite improvement. There is an emphasis in Baden on organic viticulture, too, that tends to lower yields even further. Baden's yields are among the lowest in Germany. (This sort of collective decision is made easier by the fact that some 90 per cent of wine in Baden is made by the co-operatives, with individual estates a rarity.)

The Bereich Ortenau is home of some of Baden's best Rieslings, particularly on the granite hills east of Offenburg. Durbach is the archetype: Riesling from here (they call the grape Klingelberger locally) is dry and minerally. There are little valleys running eastwards into the Black Forest, too; south-facing sites here regularly yield wines of Spätlesen and Auslesen quality. Rosé (or Weissherbst) wines are something of a speciality in much of Baden and Ortenau produces good ones, usually from Spätburgunder.

The vineyards die away abruptly at Baden-Baden. At Pforzheim they begin again: this is the Bereich Badische Bergstrasse/Kraichgau, which runs all the way north to Heidelberg. The vineyards are dotted here and there, taking their turn with wheat and other crops in the landscape, and occasionally finding good south or south-west exposure on the banks of the Neckar.

In the Bereich Tauberfranken, the wines are Franconian in character, sappy and dry; they are grown along the little Tauber river, which joins the river Main at Wertheim.

Finally, the Seewein (or 'lake wine') of the Boden See (Lake Constance) is made almost entirely from Müller-Thurgau, or Spätburgunder which is frequently vinified as a rosé. The broad expanse of the lake modifies the cool climate, reflecting summer warmth back on to vines that, at up to 570m (1870ft) above sea level, are the highest north of the Alps.

The convoluted slopes of the Kaiserstuhl have been carved into terraces to take advantage of every favourable aspect.

WÜRTTEMBERG

In Württemberg nearly half the vineyards are planted with red grapes and Trollinger is the most widely planted. Sometimes red grapes may be mixed with white to make Schillerwein, named after the poet and a Württemberg speciality. Schwarzriesling, alias Pinot Meunier, is also popular, as is Kerner among white grapes, though its favourite white is the Riesling. The wines can be good but they are also expensive due to insatiable local demand. The bulk is sold in litre bottles for drinking immediately, so most of the demand is for wine that is sound, fresh, dry and appealing, but not too complex or challenging. Reds may still be slightly sweet.

Württemberg is better suited than most German regions to making red wines. Its climate is more extreme than Baden's, with colder winters but sunnier summers, and red grapes ripen well. Soils tend to be marl and limestone; here it is shelter, and good exposure to the sun, that determine where the vine can be grown and where it can't. Württemberg is a sprawling region and even in the central area, Bereich Württembergischer Unterland, where three-quarters of the vineyards are situated, they are scattered.

River valleys are the key to wine-making here. Some of the vineyards follow the river Neckar as it zigzags northwards to join the Rhine at Mannheim; others hug the narrower valleys of the Tauber, Jagst and Kocher, all tributaries of the Neckar. There are side valleys, too, planted with vines where a suitable spot presents itself, so the vine may be pushed far into Swabia to the east or the foothills of the Black Forest to the west.

Württemberg's other smaller Bereiche are the Oberer Neckar in the south, with only 60 hectares (150 acres) under vine; the Württembergischer and Bayerischer Bodensee, 6 hectares (15 acres) nudging the Bodensee outpost of Baden, and Remstal-Stuttgart, which includes 40 hectares (100 acres) of vines in the city itself.

FLURBEREINIGUNG

Flurbereinigung, or the remodelling of vineyards, is possibly the most radical and ambitious project to take effect in the vineyards of Germany since the Romans planted them in the first place. It is done only at the express wish of every village, with every grower, part-time or not, having an equal vote. If the vote is yes, then all the vines are uprooted, all the centuries-old terraces are bulldozed and the boundaries that separate plot from plot are temporarily eradicated. The bulldozers smooth their way over the slopes and new, larger terraces are created; new access roads are built and tarmacked, and drainage is improved. The land is then reallocated. The process started in the nineteenth century, was given a boost in the 1920s by the replanting that became necessary with phylloxera, speeded up in the 1950s and by the 1970s was at work almost everywhere. Flurbereinigung means four years without a profitable crop, so the costs are high, though subsidies are available from the government. Up to 15 per cent of the land is lost to new roads, but labour costs fall by up to 25 per cent, and yields can rise dramatically. Over half Germany's vineyards have now been remodelled, and 80 per cent in Baden, which has embraced the programme particularly enthusiastically.

THE KAISERSTUHL

 VINEYARDS
 N

TOTAL DISTANCE NORTH TO SOUTH 18KM (11 MILES)

WHERE THE VINEYARDS ARE *Three million years ago the Kaiserstuhl was an active volcano. Then, gradually, it died. Over the millennia the elements wore it down, inch by inch, a bit here, a bit there, until it was ready to be domesticated. Terraces were built, and vines planted; they thrived on the rich, volcanic soil, and now the Kaiserstuhl supports vines on every suitable slope. The villages are clustered down in the valleys, and the forest has the hilltops to itself, but otherwise this horseshoe-shaped volcanic rock, 576m (1890ft) high, is entirely given over to viticulture. It's monoculture of a sort seldom seen in Baden. And why not? There's plenty of flat land all around the Kaiserstuhl for cereals and cattle.*

Look how perfect the exposure is on these south- and south-west-facing slopes. The mesoclimate here is dry, and the river is just about close enough to help to moderate extremes of temperature. The grapes don't roast here, but they do develop richness and complexity during a long, long growing season. Even so, it gets pretty warm. Summer days when the thermometer reaches a Mediterranean 30°C (86°F) or more are common, and Ihringen, tucked into the southern slopes, is accounted the warmest village in Germany.

The Tuniberg, in comparison, looks like small fry. The hill reaches 304m (997ft), which means that this limestone outcrop (that it is here is pure coincidence; the Tuniberg does not have volcanic origins) can be entirely planted with vines and no point is too high and cool to be left to forest. The vineyards on both hills have been completely rebuilt as part of the Flurbereinigung programme; and new terraces have been constructed to replace the old. In all 80 per cent of Baden's vineyards have been reorganized this way.

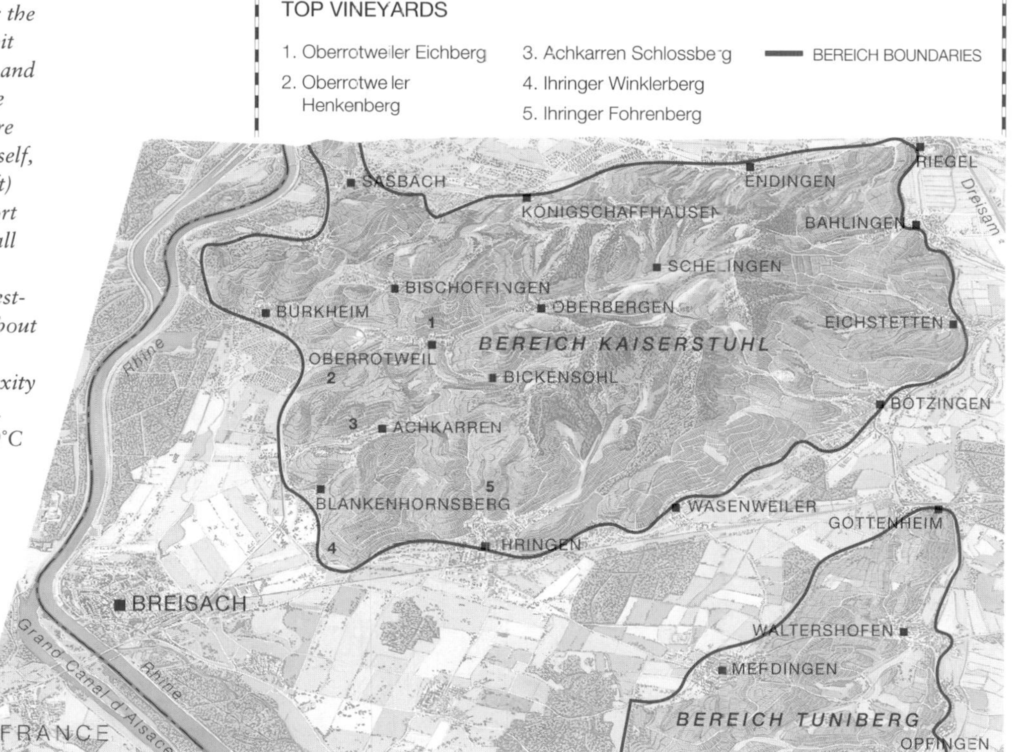

0 km 1 2
0 miles 1

Hessische Bergstrasse

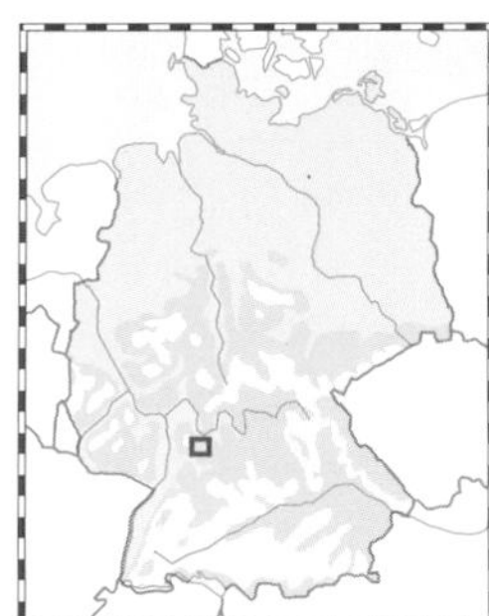

RED GRAPES
There is a tiny amount of Spätburgunder.

WHITE GRAPES
Riesling accounts for over half the plantings. Müller-Thurgau, Silvaner and Grauburgunder are the other important grapes.

CLIMATE
The climate is mild.

SOIL
There are various weathered light soils, including loess, gravel, gneiss and basalt.

ASPECT
Vines are planted on the south-facing slopes of east–west valleys as well as on the west-facing slopes. The Odenwald shelters the vines from the east wind.

BERGSTRASSE: THE MOUNTAIN WAY. What picture does the name conjure up? Sunday hikers in shorts and boots and backpacks, threading their way along the crest of a hill. Or going back a century or more, travellers from the university city of Heidelberg in the south, wending their way north to Darmstadt and on to Frankfurt. Going back still further, monks journeying to and from their monastery at Lorsch, south-west of Bensheim, and their vineyards; and before that, Roman centurions, since this road, the Strata Montana, was built by the same Romans who planted the vineyards and indeed brought the vine to Germany.

The Bergstrasse continues south of Heidelberg as well, but nowadays lies within Baden – and is accordingly known as the Badische Bergstrasse. The part of the Bergstrasse vineyards that fall into the state of Hessen have their very own region, the Hessische Bergstrasse.

Until reunification and the two wine regions of the former GDR came to join the party, Hessische Bergstrasse had the distinction of being Germany's smallest wine region. It was probably also its least-known outside the country; in fact it is likely only due to the fact that hiking is thirsty work that the vineyards thrive as much as they do. But the hikers continue to come, and they need refreshment; and the reason they come is that Hessische Bergstrasse is particularly pretty. It is planted with fruit trees, which are interspersed with vines along its main 16-km (10-mile) stretch. Vines and fruit trees compete all along the slopes of the Odenwald which runs along the crest of the hills and in the spring the profusion of blossom brings out the tourists.

The Rhine, flowing north through a flat, fertile valley, is to the west of the region. To the east is the Odenwald, and the vine is planted on the south-west-facing slopes of the foothills, and also on the south-facing slopes of the small side valleys. Logically Hessische Bergstrasse is a northerly extension of Baden, but the Flurbereinigung programme that has transformed Baden's vineyards over the past three decades from labour-intensive terracing to more manageable gentler slopes workable by tractors has hardly touched the region. Here there are still small terraces laboriously cut into the hillsides, each terrace supporting a few rows of vines, and needing enormous and expensive upkeep. This is the way all German vineyards used to look, a generation or more ago.

GRAPE VARIETIES

There are two Bereiche in the region: Starkenburg, which encloses the 16-km (10-mile) stretch of hillside that is the main part of Hessische Bergstrasse, and Umstadt, a more isolated area east of Darmstadt and north of the main vineyards. In the latter, Müller-Thurgau, Silvaner and Riesling are grown; in the main part of the vineyards Riesling dominates, taking up some 54 per cent of the planted land. It gets the best, warmest, most sheltered sites and can reach Spätlese and Auslese level and even occasionally beyond, but it is usually on the delicate side. It has good fruit, and has similarities to Rheingau Riesling, though with a more rustic streak. These Rieslings could never be mistaken for the structured richness of the Rheingau, the lean elegance of the Mosel or the broad fatness of the Pfalz. But there is certainly good quality and good value to be found here. The less-regarded Müller-Thurgau, which accounts for 15 per cent of the land under vine, is simple, everyday wine, fresh and attractive.

Numerous other vines are planted in small quantities: there is about 7 per cent of Silvaner and 6 per cent of Grauburgunder or Pinot Gris; Kerner has 3 per cent of the vineyard, Ehrenfelser, a new crossing, has 3 per cent and the grapefruit-scented Scheurebe has 2 per cent. Traminer has just 1 per cent. There is a small amount of Spätburgunder or Pinot Noir, though not nearly as much as there is in Baden to the south of Hessische Bergstrasse, and it makes light wines that are really more curiosities than serious reds.

The woods help to shelter the vineyards on the hills of Heppenheim.

Yields, generally speaking, are fairly low – on a par with the Nahe and the Rheingau as opposed to the enormous number of hectolitres per hectare from the Rheinhessen and the Pfalz. They are lower, too, than in Baden to the south, where the climate is warmer and the soil more fertile.

WINE VILLAGES

There are some very good vineyard sites, though none of them are famous beyond the region's boundaries. At Heppenheim there are the Centgericht and the Steinkopf vineyards, the former owned in its entirety by the Staatsweingut Bergstrasse or State Domaine. It is particularly good for Riesling Kabinett Trocken or Halbtrocken. Bensheim is the other leading commune, and the village of Schönberg has the Herrnwingert vineyard, also owned by the State Domaine. The Streichling vineyard in Bensheim, south-facing and sloping, is also good.

Apart from the State Domaine there are few other individual cellars. With around 1000 growers owning just 400 hectares (1000 acres) of vines, vineyard holdings are often tiny, and most of the wine is made by the co-operative in Heppenheim. Some of the growers mix vines with other crops and are full-time farmers; others tends their vines at weekends and commute to computer screens during the week.

CLIMATE AND SOIL

The Riesling thrives here because of the mild climate and the long growing season. Hessische Bergstrasse notches up more hours of summer sunshine than the warm Pfalz across the Rhine, and it's nearly as warm as Baden to the south. Hence all the fruit trees. Hessische Bergstrasse isn't known as the spring garden of Germany for nothing. It's also a region of late-harvest wines. It doesn't make much over Spätlese level, but they can be good, both rich and balanced. And it's using the advantages of its warm climate to make more and more Halbtrocken and Trocken wines – more Trocken than Halbtrocken, in fact.

The soils vary, but are generally fairly light. Indeed it is these light soils that help to keep the yields down. North of Bensheim there is decomposed granite stretching north to Zwingenberg; Heppenheim has loess and yellow sandstone, and elsewhere there is mostly sand or light loam. Hessische Bergstrasse's problem is that there is pressure on the land from housing. It is a region that seems likely to shrink (in terms of wine production) until it reaches a level at which tourism will support it. That level may have been reached; I hope so.

SAALE-UNSTRUT & SACHSEN

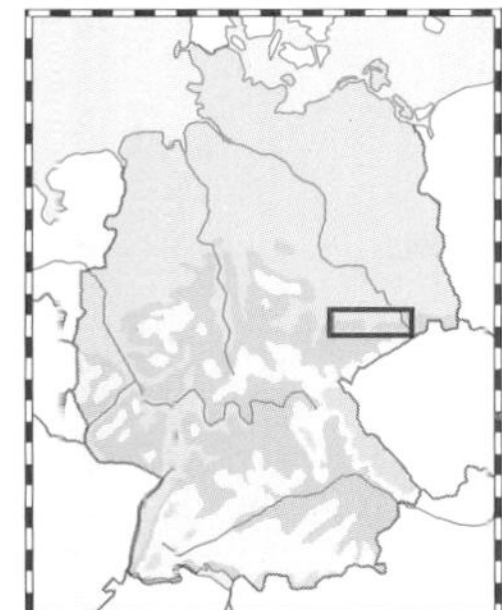

REMEMBER WHEN THE WALL came down? In the weeks that followed all the talk was of factories and output and GDP and inflation and how the GDR (East Germany) was in a far worse state than anyone had supposed. The Easterners, we gathered, all wanted to drink Coca-Cola. But what else did they drink? Did they make wine? I'd never really thought about it. I'd heard that there were a few vineyards way over the eastern horizon, but there'd always been quite enough to occupy me on the Rhine and the Mosel, without venturing into regions that made wine nobody could buy anyway. And now here they were, two small orphaned wine regions, blinking painfully in the harsh light of the Western market.

The GDR had imported a lot of wine from other parts of Eastern Europe, and no wonder. Saale-Unstrut has a mere 390 hectares (964 acres) under vine and Sachsen has just 300 hectares (740 acres); compare that with the Rheinhessen, which has 26,137 hectares (64,584 acres). They clearly weren't equipped to quench the thirst of their countrymen. In fact, not many of their countrymen ever got to drink much of their own local wine anyway. East German wine was either a privilege for Party bosses, or it was useful for trading, in situations where money alone wouldn't get you the car spares or whatever it was you needed. What the wine tasted like wasn't tremendously important, especially since there was nothing good coming into the country to compare it with.

Com 1990, these two tiny regions found themselves pretty well overnight under the umbrella of the 1971 German wine law. The West sent them experts on viticulture, experts on wine-making, experts on this, that and the other. The Easterners learnt quickly. At first their main aim was to produce as much as possible, as fast as possible. Now there are signs that they're beginning to think – hang on, perhaps that's not quite right. Maybe if we make our wine better, then the tourists will buy it. Maybe that's the way forward.

They're right, of course. Yields are tiny in both regions: between 30 and 40 hectolitres per hectare, partly because the vines were planted far apart; partly because the vine clones were poor, and imported from Hungary and Czechoslovakia since the GDR had no vine nurseries of its own; and partly because of the weather. It's not a reflection of high quality, unlike in Burgundy, for example, where low yields are an indication of a producer doing everything in the pursuit of quality.

CLIMATE AND SOIL

The weather can be harsh in these regions, but it's only because it's so extreme that viticulture is possible at all. Summers are hot and sunny and bring plenty of extract to the wines to balance their high acidity; conversely, winters are long and cold. Saale-Unstrut is the most northerly wine region of Germany, and Sachsen is not far behind; in Saale-Unstrut late frosts, hitting the vines roughly four years in every ten, cut the crop by 20 to 70 per cent. In Sachsen the cold is even harsher, and spring frosts, a threat until well into June, can reduce the harvest by up to 90 per cent.

In both regions, then, it is only the most sunny and sheltered sites that have any chance of ripening grapes. South-facing slopes in river valleys are generally the only option: the rivers Saale and Unstrut provide these, generally south-east-facing along the Saale and south-west-facing along the Unstrut. Freyburg, on the Unstrut, is the main focus for vineyards; steep, south- or west-facing limestone slopes offer the vine some of the best opportunities to be had in the whole region. In Sachsen it's the southern reaches of the Elbe that are the focus, with the greatest concentration of vineyards being around the city of Meissen. Tourists to here and to Dresden are likely to be Sachsen's main market in the near future.

The main difference between the regions is soil. Saale-Unstrut's vineyards are planted on limestone and occasionally on sandstone; the former gives more structured wines. Sachsen's are on granite subsoil, which gives milder, softer wines. Topsoils here are of loam, loess, sandstone or porphyry with sand on low-lying sites by rivers. There is plenty of sandstone here, but on the whole it is not planted with vines.

GRAPE VARIETES

In both regions the best and warmest sites are planted with Riesling, although autumns are really too early and cold for this late-ripening grape to show at its best. The early-ripening and reliable Müller-Thurgau is the main grape, and gains some structure from the low yields (which even with better management and better clones probably won't go much above 50 or 60 hectolitres per hectare). There's some good Silvaner in Saale-Unstrut, and small amounts of Weissburgunder, Traminer and Gutedel. There's a very little Portugieser, too, for red wines, but nobody expects any great colour or ripeness. Sachsen has all the last three, and in rather greater quantity. In Saale-Unstrut the wines are usually vinified dry; Sachsen makes a softer, lighter style which may well appeal to the tourists – of which Sachsen is likely to be the main beneficiary.

VITICULTURE

The sloping vineyards are terraced, but had been allowed to fall into disrepair under the GDR. Now the stone walls supporting the terraces are being repaired and the aim is to retain them: there is, so far, no move to smooth them out in the manner of the rest of Germany. The Freyburger Schlufterburg in Saale-Unstrut is being turned into a model vineyard, under the advice of the Geisenheim Viticultural Institute. The idea is that the terraces will be a tourist attraction and part of the character of the region. (Both regions already have tourist wine routes organized.) Another reason might be that a Flurbereinigung programme to reorganize the vineyards would be horrendously expensive and just not feasible at the moment. Replanting is going ahead and the vineyard area is increasing, though it is unlikely to reach anything like the level of the Middle Ages, when 5000 to 6000 hectares (12,355 to 14,255 acres) were planted in Sachsen alone.

RED GRAPES
Portugieser accounts for only 3 per cent of the vines.

WHITE GRAPES
Müller-Thurgau is the main grape, accounting for over one-third of the vines. Other varieties include Silvaner, Riesling, Weissburgunder, Traminer and Gutedel.

CLIMATE
This is a continental climate, with cold winters, hot summers and a danger of late spring frosts.

SOIL
Saale-Unstrut has limestone and red sandstone on the slopes and deeper fertile soils in the valleys. In Sachsen there is loam, loess, granite and weathered porphyry.

ASPECT
In Saale-Unstrut vines are planted up to 200m (650ft), along the banks of the Saale and Unstrut rivers and on hills near Freyburg. Most of Sachsen's vines are on south-east-facing slopes along the Elbe river valley.

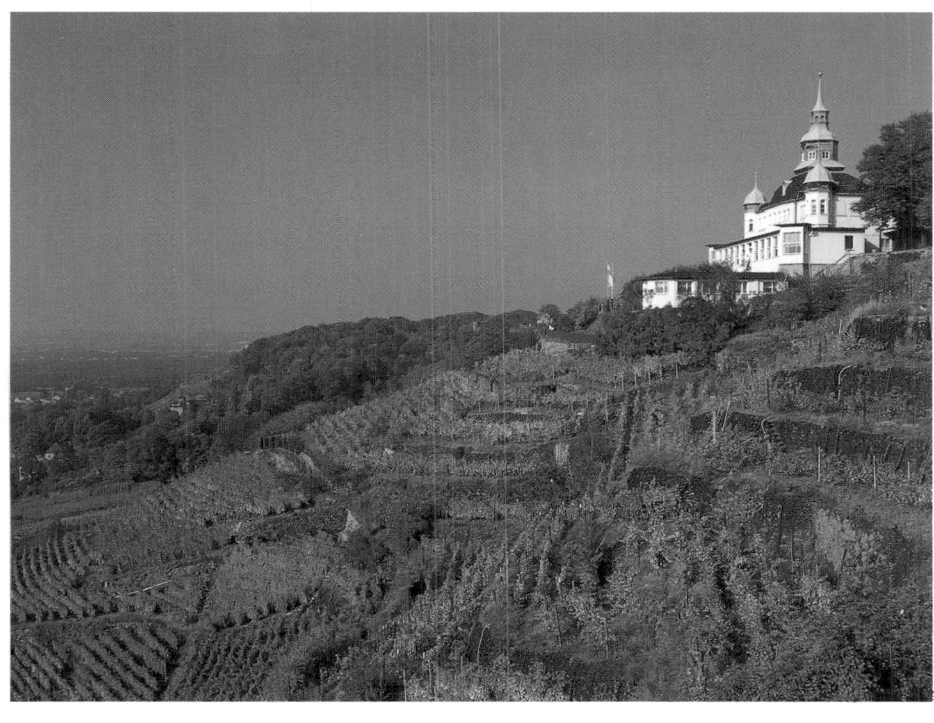

Sachsen's vineyards, seen here at Radebeul between Meissen and Dresden, are still planted on steep terraces.

SWITZERLAND

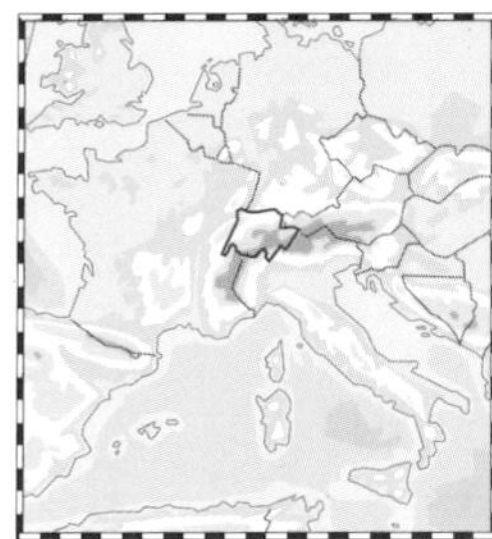

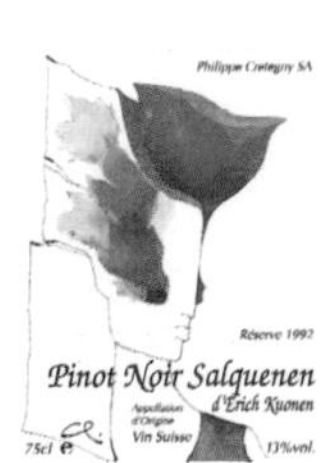

This rosé comes in the Bordeaux-shaped bottle popular in Switzerland.

SWITZERLAND AND SKIING? Yes. Switzerland and cheese? Sure. Switzerland and glorious Alpine peaks glistening with fresh-fallen snow, Switzerland and steep-sided valleys, waterfalls and mountain streams cascading into deep glacial lakes, Switzerland and yodelling if you must – but how many of us think of Switzerland and wine? Go into any neighbourhood shop and I challenge you to find a single bottle of Swiss wine.

There are two reasons. The Swiss do in fact make rather a lot of wine, but they drink even more than they make, and there's hardly ever any available for export. And if there were, the prices, for what are usually at best pleasant light wines for drinking young, would shock most non-Swiss into abstention.

But that shouldn't surprise us. Everybody knows that Switzerland is an expensive country. You don't go there if you want a cheap holiday. The cost of manual labour is 20 to 30 per cent more than in neighbouring countries, and the cost of producing wine can be four times as high as in France, because of the steepness of the slopes and the expense of maintaining the terraces. The vineyards are also small: the average holding is less than half a hectare (1 acre). But while the wine often has charm, while it may have individuality and go well with food, it's not great wine. The most serious wines are probably the Petite Arvines of the Valais, which can age in bottle for a good few years, but most Swiss wine is best drunk young. French-speaking Switzerland probably makes better Chasselas than most places (not many other places make it, actually) but Chasselas is never going to be earth-shaking. Italian-speaking Switzerland makes good Merlot – but then so does Italy – and German-speaking Switzerland concentrates on Pinot Noir (or Blauburgunder) and Müller-Thurgau (which, since Dr Müller was Swiss and produced his grape cross in the Swiss canton of Thurgau, the Swiss surprisingly call Riesling-Sylvaner).

So Swiss wines are probably best not exposed to the international market place, geared as it is to heavily oaked Chardonnay from the New World. But if you happen to be in Switzerland – well, now, that's different of course.

Most of the wine comes from French-speaking Switzerland – 11,000 (27,000) of the country's 14,800 hectares (36,600 acres) of vineyards are here, compared to 3000 hectares (7500 acres) in German-speaking Switzerland and only 800 hectares (2000 acres) in Italian-speaking Switzerland. On the map the vineyards tend to be squeezed round the edges and in the corners, with only a few isolated patches in the more mountainous centre of the country. And with the exception of some of the scattered vineyards in the German-speaking cantons, all Swiss vineyards depend on the beneficial influence of water for their existence. That water may be a river, such as the Rhône which runs through the Valais and the southern Vaud; quite often it's a lake and there are lots of these in Switzerland. But a large body of water to moderate extremes of temperature and reflect the ample sunshine back on to the vines is vital here, particularly where the vines grow at altitudes of 350m (1150ft) or more. That's already higher than most vines in Europe – but here it's nothing.

The other climatic factor affecting Swiss viticulture is the wind – and usually it's benevolent. In the southern part of the country the Foehn wind blows up the valleys from the south, warming and drying the grapes. Neuchâtel and Geneva are subject to a north wind, which is less good news, and in Zürich and points north of here the prevailing wind is westerly and the vineyards need to be planted on sheltered slopes.

In such a mountainous country shelter is not hard to come by. Every

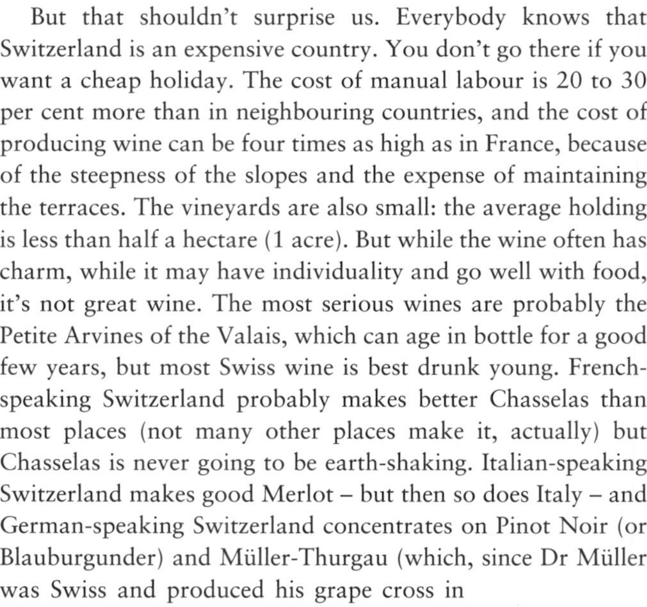

Valais *pages 144–5*

vineyard region has its protecting range. In Geneva, where the vineyards are relatively flat, there is a whole collection of them: the Jura, the Mont-de-Sion, the Salève, the Voirons and the Vuache, which send the rain clouds off into France. Neuchâtel has the Jura and the Valais has the Alps.

WINE REGIONS

Of all the Swiss wine cantons, the Valais is the most important and it also has the greatest variety of grapes (see page 144). The Vaud, in terms of area under vine, comes next. Four-fifths of the Vaud's wine is white, nearly all of it Chasselas which, since this grape reflects the soil on which it is grown, changes in character according to whether it is planted on the scree of Chablais, the moraine of Lavaux and La Côte or the puddingstone of Dézaley in Lavaux, where the wine is more structured.

The high altitude vineyards of Côtes-de-l'Orbe, Bonvillars and Vully are influenced by the Rhine basin and by Lake Neuchâtel. La Côte, on the banks of Lake Geneva, is planted half with red (Gamay and Pinot Noir) and half with white grapes. Swiss red wines used to be low in acidity and high in yield but now steps are being taken to reverse that situation. The vines are also being planted in cooler sites so that the grapes gain more acidity. But the wines still nearly always tend to be light in colour and body. A few producers are experimenting with aging their reds in new oak, but the majority of the wines – even those from the warm Valais – just don't have the gutsiness needed for this sort of treatment.

Reds are on the increase in the canton of Geneva, where they're mostly Gamay. Chasselas is still in the majority, though. This is calm, rolling, fertile land, in most of which the vineyards are scattered among fields of other crops. In Neuchâtel we're still in Chasselas country: it covers 56 per cent of the vineyards, growing on soil that is mostly limey, with alluvial soil lower down the slopes. It's dry and sunny, though not quite as sunny and not quite as dry as the Valais. When it does make a red wine it makes it from Pinot Noir, of which it has its own clone, called Cortaillod.

Neuchâtel was the first canton to limit yields. They have now been restricted all over the country by a Federal Decree of June 1992 – and not before time. A prevailing fault of Swiss wines was the flabbiness and wateriness that result from overproduction, and matters reached a head in 1982 and 1983, when there was a surplus and the wine just didn't sell. The legal limit is now 1.4 kilograms of grapes per square metre for white grapes, and 1.2 kg/m² for reds, which is still quite high. Even 1 kg/m² is equivalent to 75 hectolitres per hectare – pretty high for cool-climate vineyards. Individual cantons may also impose their own, tighter rules if they so wish.

Fribourg, with vineyards at Broye and Vully, has varying amounts of sandstone in the soil; again, the vineyards are lake-influenced. And the canton of Jura has only recently rectified its record of being the only French-speaking canton with no vineyards at all, by planting just 5 hectares (12 acres). In Bern, ostensibly French-speaking, quite a lot of the population sticks to German – but they're happy to grow Chasselas (which they call Gutedel in German) if they want. The canton includes the vineyards of Lake Thun, looking rather lonely all by themselves in the middle of Switzerland, but they don't do so badly. They're south-facing, the vines grow up to 600m (1970ft) and Switzerland's favourite warm wind, the Foehn, keeps the chill off. Lake Thun, however, does grow the vines of German-speaking Switzerland: Riesling-Sylvaner and Pinot Noir.

In the 17 German-speaking wine cantons of east Switzerland, there's not a lot else except vineyards. We're much further north here, almost at the limit of vine cultivation, and the climate is cooler and often wetter. The average minimum annual temperature is 9°C (48°F), which is as low as you can happily go for viticulture, and spring as well as winter frosts can be a problem. But the vines are grown at up to 600m (1970ft) in parts of Graubünden, and the growers seek out sheltered south-facing sites. The soil varies: there is chalky limestone in the Jura foothills, sandstone in the middle and limestone, moraine and schist elsewhere, with alluvial cones in parts of Graubünden. The cool climate here, though, doesn't stop them growing red wine. Seventy per cent of the vines are red, mainly Pinot Noir. Whites are mostly Riesling-Sylvaner.

In the Italian-speaking canton of Ticino, the architecture is increasingly Italian the further south you go. Here, south of the Alps, the climate is more influenced by the Mediterranean. That means lots of sun and plenty of rain, too, and even the rain has an Italian temperament: it arrives in short, violent storms. The region south of Mount Ceneri, the Sottoceneri, is the commercial centre for viticulture (with Merlot as its flagship wine); north of here vines may still be grown on the sort of pergolas you see in the Alto Adige, but most of the wines never go further than the owner's dining table.

THE CLASSIFICATION SYSTEM FOR SWISS WINE

Switzerland has a plethora of federal and cantonal regulations, and uses three different languages. Its wines fall into three basic categories.

- **Wines from an individual canton or region within a canton** These may bear a place name, a combination of place and grape name, or a generic name (for example, Fendant).
- **Wines from an area larger than a canton** These take a broader indication of origin (for example, Romand, for wines from the Suisse-Romande).
- **Table wines** These wines are usually sold by the litre, and labelled as Red or White.

OTHER CANTONAL REGULATIONS

In the Valais, a distinction is drawn between Controlled Appellation of Origin and Appellation of Origin, with the former being stricter; in Geneva, as well as these two categories there are Grand Cru and Premier Cru wine, which are more precisely delimited and have to meet stricter requirements. In the German-speaking cantons there is a seal of quality – Winzer-Wy, or Vintner's wine – awarded by a tasting panel, and Ticino labels its best Merlots with the VITI seal.

Early-morning mist over Lake Geneva at Dézaley. Switzerland's vineyards are dependent on such large expanses of water to moderate the temperature.

VALAIS

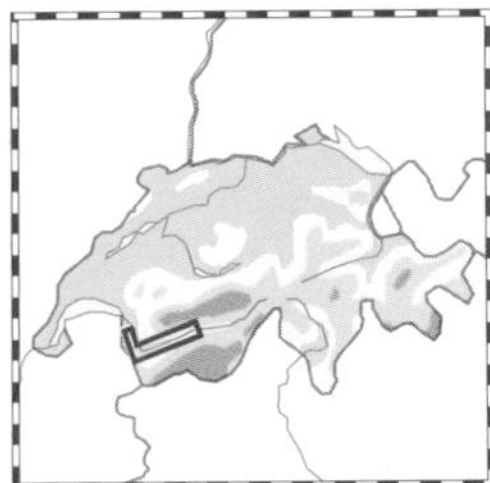

FOR A WINE ENTHUSIAST, the train from Geneva to the Simplon Pass into Italy has to be one of the greatest journeys in the world. Heading out along the idyllic north shore of Lake Geneva to Lausanne, the Vaud vineyards crowd in on the track. Turning east and south past Vevey and Montreux on to Yvorne and Martigny, the tranquil beauty of the lake is matched by the increasing grandeur of the mountains and the strips of vineyards reaching down into the valley floor.

At Martigny the railway track does a right-angle turn to the left, and, stretching up to Sion and Sierre, are the south-east-facing slopes of the Bernese Alps. Glue your face to the left-hand windows of the train. I don't know anywhere else where the monoculture of the vine is more beautiful or more startling. Vines seem to climb vertically up the spectacular mountain faces, tiny villages perch on plateaux cut off from every other manifestation of life except their vines, and even in the height of summer, the great mountain peaks glow with luminous snow as this Alpine suntrap bakes its perfectly exposed vines to a quite remarkable degree of ripeness.

Past Sierre, the vines need to seek nooks and crannies to ripen fully and at Visp, just before the Simplon tunnel, a little narrow gauge railway trails off up to Zermatt past the death-defying terraces of Visperterminen, possibly the highest vines in Europe at 1100m (3600ft).

But you have to step off the train and actually trek up the mountainsides themselves to understand fully quite how remarkable these vineyards are. And it's only by braving the elements in person that the unique character of the Valais vineyards makes sense. The sun and the steep angle of the vineyard slopes you can gauge from the train. The wind, you can't. And however perfect those slopes, they still wouldn't be able to ripen grapes at these altitudes without the wind. This wind is called the Foehn – and it is Switzerland's godsend. It blows up the valleys from the Mediterranean south, and it blows east–west along the Rhône Valley, crucially raising the temperature, and helping the grapes to ripen. The Rhône also does its bit: vines only grow successfully in Switzerland where there's a large expanse of water to moderate the temperature and reflect heat back on to the vines, and the Rhône does that admirably.

GRAPE VARIETIES AND WINE STYLES

This Rhône is, of course, the same Rhône that produces massive, tannic Syrah reds a long way downstream in France. Here, though, 58 per cent of the wines are white, from Chasselas (here called Fendant), Sylvaner, Marsanne (alias Ermitage), Pinot Gris (alias Malvoisie), Arvine, Amigne, Muscat, Riesling and a few others, including increasing plantations of Chardonnay.

The reds are principally from Pinot Noir and Gamay, often blended into that Valais speciality, Dôle, which must be 80 per cent from these two grapes. Less ripe blends can be sold as Goron. Pinot Noir is also sometimes bottled on its own. Sometimes it's perfumed and good, and generally speaking the Valais' reds are, the fullest-bodied in Switzerland, though red wine is not, to me, what Switzerland's about, even when it's made from Syrah. Yes, there is some Syrah here, if only a tiny amount.

ST-LÉONARD
SION
CONTHEY
VÉTROZ
CHAMOSON
Rhône
LEYTRON
RIDDES

RIDDES TO LEUK
VINEYARDS
N
TOTAL DISTANCE NORTH TO SOUTH 12KM (7½ MILES)

0 km 1 2
0 miles 1

GOÛT DU CONSEIL
MONT D'OR VALAIS
DOMAINE DU MONT D'OR S.A., SION

1991
SION
VARONE
SION

Fendant
SOLEIL DU VALAIS
VARONE
SION

NOUVEAU SIERRE
FENDANT
SIERRE VALAIS

Some of these vines – Petite Arvine, for example – are found nowhere else in Switzerland. They thrive here in the Valais because this long gorge, where the Rhône flows approximately south-west for about 50km (30 miles) and then north-west into the more isolated vineyards of the Bas Valais, is one of the sunniest parts of the country, with 2100 hours of sunshine per year. Most of the vineyards are on the right bank, facing south and catching all the sun. It's dry, too, with between 400 and 700mm (16 and 28in) of rain per year – in fact, since the soils are light and well-drained it's sometimes rather too dry for comfort, and irrigation has to be used. The *vignerons* used to have little canals called *bisses* cut into the hillsides to carry melted snow down to the vines, but now you're more likely to see the draped hoses of drip irrigation.

You might think that getting any water up or down these mountains would be a feat of engineering, but the Swiss, to judge from their vineyards, are good at engineering. Some of these slopes have gradients of as much as 85 per cent, and there's no way you can cultivate anything except ivy on a slope that steep. So the mountains are terraced, with the neatest stone walls I've seen anywhere. Even the supporting walls tower high above your head: the Swiss have taken mountains and they've fortified them. Now, if that's not devotion to the vine I'd like to know what is. It also requires an enormous communal effort. There are 5231 hectares (12,925 acres) of vines in the Valais, and 22,700 owners; that's not many vines each. Only about 700 owners bottle their own wine; the rest take their grapes to the co-operatives or sell to the merchant houses, and the wines are sold mostly by grape name or by style. Village names, with the exception of a few like Sion don't feature all that much.

Sion is famous for its Fendant (or Chasselas), a variety which, rather like the Riesling, reflects the character of its soil in its flavour. Sion has schist; elsewhere in the Valais there is limestone in a long stretch from Leuk in the east to Saillon in the west, with the greatest concentrations of limestone at Leuk and Sierre. West of Saillon, at Fully and Martigny, there is hardly any limestone, which makes these prime areas for Gamay. And at Saillon and the villages to the east, Leytron, Chamoson and Ardon, there is gravel. The growers have put it there themselves as it retains the heat admirably and reduces water evaporation. Chamoson also has the largest alluvial cone of the region which provides good conditions for Sylvaner, here called Johannisberg.

Leuk, set in a position where it catches all the sun, makes good Dôle; Salquenen also makes good reds. Val d'Anniviers, facing Sierre, is the home of a local speciality, Vin des Glaciers, made originally from the now all-but-extinct Rèze grape, but nowadays usually from Arvine and others. It's aged at high altitude in a modified solera system.

The stretch of vineyard between Leuk in the east and Martigny in the west is the main part of the Valais. Eighty-five per cent of the vineyards are here, and they're nearly all on the north bank. Only in isolated spots on the south bank is the mesoclimate right for vines. Charrat, just before the river bends and heads north for Lake Geneva, has good Gamay.

But there are two other parts of the Valais besides this main stretch of vineyards. There is the Bas Valais, the stretch of the river leading to Lake Geneva, where the vines face mostly west or south-west. But even including the vineyards in Martigny and Entremont, the region can only boast 217 hectares (536 acres) of vines – just 4 per cent of the total.

Then there are the scattered vineyards east of Leuk, the Haut-Valais – and they really are *haut*. There are only 150 hectares (370 acres) of vines here, but they include the Visperterminen vineyard.

RED GRAPES
Pinot Noir is found throughout the Valais. Gamay is the other main variety.

WHITE GRAPES
Nearly half the vineyards are given over to Chasselas, with Sylvaner being restricted to the best vineyards. There are small amounts of other varieties, including the indigenous Amigne, Arvine, Humagne Blanc and Rèze.

CLIMATE
The Valais is Switzerland's sunniest wine region. It is always windy, and the Foehn wind helps to raise the temperature. Rainfall is low.

SOIL
The soil is generally light and well-drained and warms up rapidly. There is limestone, gravel, schist, as well as various alluvial cones along the Rhône.

ASPECT
Vines grow as high as 1100m (3600ft), at Visperterminen; elsewhere they grow to 750m (2460ft), mostly on south-facing slopes overlooking the Rhône. The slopes are usually terraced and irrigated.

WHERE THE VINEYARDS ARE *The map shows the main part of the Valais, the broad expanse of south-facing vineyards on the north bank from Riddes to Leuk. They're dwarfed by the mountains: altitudes that sound fantastically high when compared to other vineyards elsewhere in the world look pitifully low compared to peaks that are snow-covered all the year round. But look how the vineyards creep just a little bit higher into the warmer side valleys and how the flatter land on the valley floor has only a few vineyards. Instead there are orchards – the Swiss are fond of fruit brandy to polish off a meal.*

On the south bank of the Rhône, and further west, where the river takes an abrupt turn for the north-west, there are a few vineyards, but these are found in small pockets rather than in a continuous band – a reflection of their less good exposure. But look how all the vineyard land twists in and out, ducking round an outcrop here, nudging the water's edge there and then drawing back as the sun and the shadows and the changing soil alter the balance for the vine. Deciding which vines to plant in which spots in an area like this has taken centuries.

The vineyards of the Valais – here at Chamoson – are among the highest in Europe. They get plenty of sun and the wines can be quite high in alcohol.

Austria

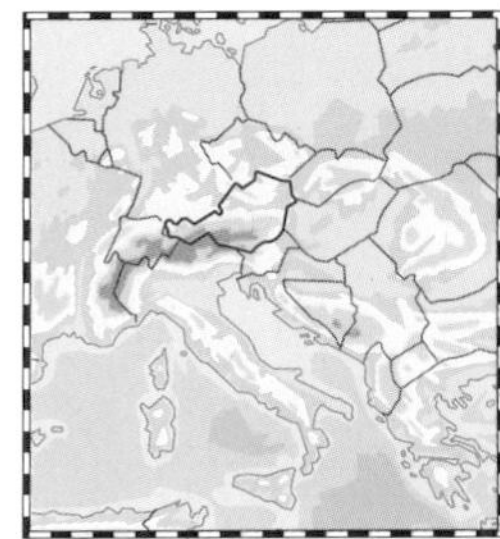

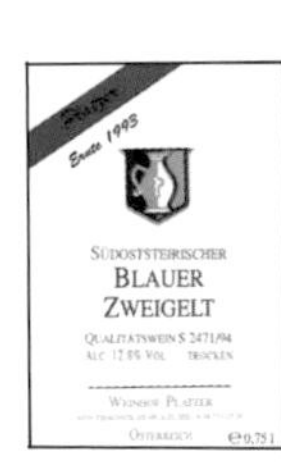

THERE ARE DAYS WHEN I think I might turn vegetarian. Funnily enough, those days always occur when I'm in Austria – when I've been there 24 hours, to be precise. It's the result of a day spent tasting wine in growers' cellars while the grower's wife urges me to spread more lard on my bread; of lunch in a country Buschenschenke, or inn, where a vast plate of ham and sausage and black pudding is put before me; of more bread and lard during the afternoon; of supper in another Buschenschenke where another plate of sausage is preceded, not by peanuts, but by a plate-sized slice of rye bread spread thickly with smoked lard. And it's the prospect of several more days of the same diet. So I drink the wine – it's the nearest thing to fresh fruit I'm likely to get.

The Austrians, you see, are a hospitable people. Besides which, the Buschenschenken in which you can eat sausage and cheese and drink wine are crucial to the wine economy. Austrian wine would take a very different shape without them. A Buschenschenke is a family-owned country inn, in which the food and the wine are all home-produced. The ones I'm talking about are in the east of the country, since that's where the vineyards are – the Austrian vineyards have a climate influenced, in the main, by the warm, dry climate of the Pannonian plain, to the east. Further west it's too mountainous and the climate too extreme.

A lot of wine-making families own Buschenschenken: in Styria (Steiermark), for example, there are 4000 growers, which includes (for tax purposes) mothers, fathers, grandparents and children, and 800 Buschenschenken. They sell to tourists, since Styrian wine is particularly fashionable, and the tourists expect each inn to be able to offer a full range of wines. As a result nearly all Austrian growers grow as many different grape varieties as they can. They may only have 10 hectares (25 acres), but at the very least they'll grow Grüner Veltliner, Weissburgunder, Welschriesling, Traminer, Müller-Thurgau, Rhine Riesling, Sauvignon Blanc, Blauburgunder and Blaufränkisch, because that's what their customers want to drink. That said, there are regional specialities.

WINE REGIONS

In the northern part of Burgenland, the Neusiedl lake makes great sweet wines possible: south Burgenland makes decent reds; Niederösterreich (Lower Austria) makes the best Grüner Veltliner (this grape is an Austrian speciality) and Styria makes high acid, low alcohol wines for which, as I've said, people will drive miles. Vienna (Wien) has a wine region to itself and is a bit of a Jack-of-all-trades, with whole villages on the outskirts of the city apparently dedicated to serving wine to tourists.

It is the climate that makes Austrian viticulture feasible, and where the wine rises above everyday quality, it is because of a better mesoclimate. So favourable is the climate in eastern Austria, indeed, that vineyards are scattered everywhere, rising up on odd south-facing slopes while maize or pumpkins or orchards occupy the lower ground. There is none of the feeling of battling against the elements that one gets in parts of Germany – and accordingly there is no skeleton of moderating rivers to be found underlying the wine map. The Danube runs east to west through Lower Austria, but only in the Wachau is the river genuinely necessary to the vine.

The Wachau lies at the western end of Lower Austria. Here the banks of the Danube rise into cliffs of rock and scrub, and the landscape is as beautiful and uncompromising as any in the Mosel. Some of Austria's finest dry whites come from these vineyards overlooking the river, just as her finest sweet whites come from the lush, low-lying, foggy Neusiedlersee in Burgenland. This is the other place where water plays a major part in Austrian wine – the large, shallow Neusiedl lake encourages the botrytis fungus to attack the grapes with an avidity that is seen nowhere else in Europe.

Most of the rest of vinous Austria is gently hilly or flattish. The hilliest region is Styria, down on the border with Slovenia, where the vines grow between 350 and 600m (1150 and 970ft) on the Alpine foothills to avoid the frost in the valleys. In spite of the high rainfall, 900–1000mm (35–40 in) a year, drought can be a problem on the well-drained sandy or stony soils, as

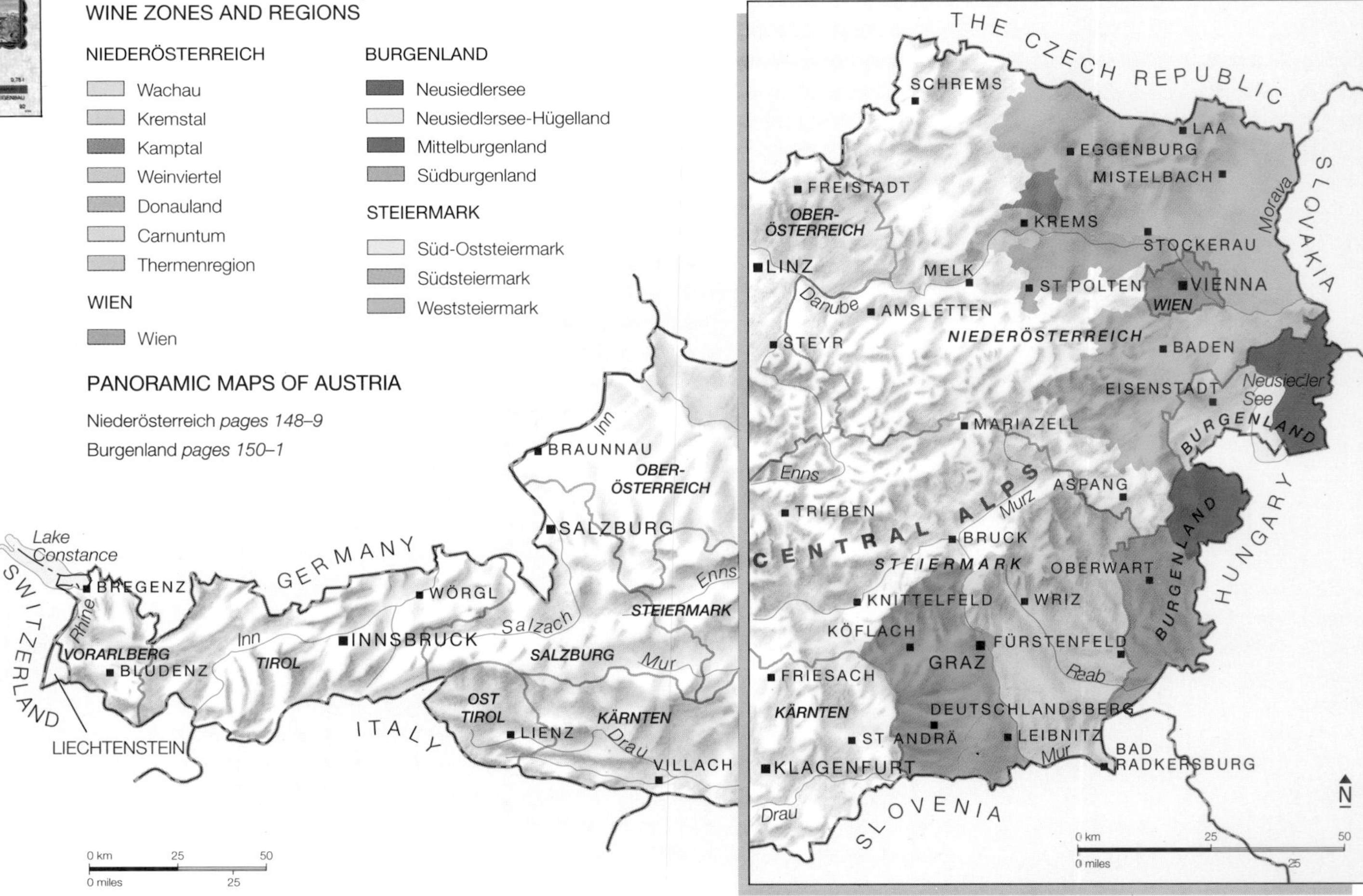

can erosion. Finding the right sheltered, south-facing site is the key in Styria – but even so, the wines always have a lean, green streak to them. Even the botrytis-affected wines (and they may get botrytis as many as six years out of ten) don't taste as rich and as fat as those of Burgenland.

The fashion, though, is for the dry wines. Austria as a whole makes dry wines rather than sweet or semi-sweet, and the Austrian taste for dryness and acidity really took off with the Austrian wine scandal of 1985, when a small number of growers in Burgenland were caught adding the chemical diethylene glycol to their sweet wines to make them taste even richer. The Austrians want to put the scandal behind them now, and rightly so, but it has been of great importance in changing national tastes in subsequent years. The current, very strict, wine law is another legacy of the scandal.

Styria, down on the border with Slovenia, is divided into West, South and South-East Styria, of which the South-East is the largest in area and has 1000 hectares (2500 acres) under vine; the hills are lower here and the climate less extreme than elsewhere in Styria. South Styria looks the smallest area on the map, but has 1900 hectares (4700 acres) of vines, mainly around Leibnitz and down to the Slovenian border. The specialities are Chardonnay (here called Morillon), Sauvignon Blanc and Gelber Muskateller. West Styria has a mere 250 hectares (620 acres), nearly all given over to a fearsome rosé called Schilcher, made from the Blauer Wildbacher grape and notable for its tooth-piercing acidity. The slate soil and the climate, with its hot days and cold nights, are the key to making Schilcher – that and the hordes of tourists who will buy a grower's entire stock within four months of the harvest.

Vienna's vineyards are concentrated to the west of the city, though there are also some within the city itself. But it is the suburbs of Grinzing, Nussberg and Heiligenstadt that flourish on the proceeds of the vine. It's a short journey for the Viennese and the tourist buses to these vine-covered courtyards where the accordionist plays until late into the evening – and you might even get some vegetables with your pork.

THE CLASSIFICATION SYSTEM FOR AUSTRIAN WINE

Austria's wine categories are basically similar to those of Germany, although different, usually higher, must weights (the amount of original sugar in freshly picked grapes) are required for each category in acknowledgment of the more favourable climate. Must weights in Austria are measured in degrees KMW, or Klosterneuburger Mostwaage and each quality category of wines sets a minimum number of KMW: as a rule of thumb, KMW multiplied by five give the Oechsle measurement.

- **Tafelwein** Basic table wine of at least 13 degrees KMW.
- **Landwein** Country wine from a specific region, with at least 14 degrees KMW.
- **Qualitätswein** Quality wine from a single region; it may be chaptalized. The minimum KMW is 15 degrees and the maximum is 19 for whites and 20 for reds.
- **Kabinett** This is not a Prädikat category, unlike Kabinett in Germany. The wine may not be chaptalized, and must have a minimum KMW of 17 degrees.
- **Prädikatswein** These categories may not be chaptalized and may not have Süssreserve added to sweeten them. *Spätlese* Made from fully ripe grapes with at least 19 KMW. *Auslese* Made from fully ripe grapes with a minimum KMW of 21. *Eiswein* Made from grapes picked and pressed when frozen, with a minimum KMW of 25 degrees. *Beerenauslese* Made from overripe or nobly rotten grapes with a minimum KMW of 25. *Ausbruch* An Austrian category for wine made from overripe, nobly rotten or shrivelled grapes with a minimum KMW of 27 degrees. *Trockenbeerenauslese* Made from overripe, nobly rotten or shrivelled grapes with a minimum 30 degrees KMW.
- **Sweetness categories** These new regulations date from 1993. *Extra dry* Has up to 4 grams per litre residual sugar. *Dry* Up to 9 grams per litre residual sugar if the acidity is not more than 2 grams per litre less than the sugar level. *Medium dry* Between 9 and 12 grams per litre residual sugar. *Medium* Between 12 and 45 grams per litre residual sugar. *Sweet* Over 45 grams per litre residual sugar.

Austrian wine bottles come in many different shapes, but Burgundian bottles are increasingly popular.

The region of South Styria, with its hills, vineyards and poplars, is often referred to as Austria's Tuscany.

NIEDERÖSTERREICH

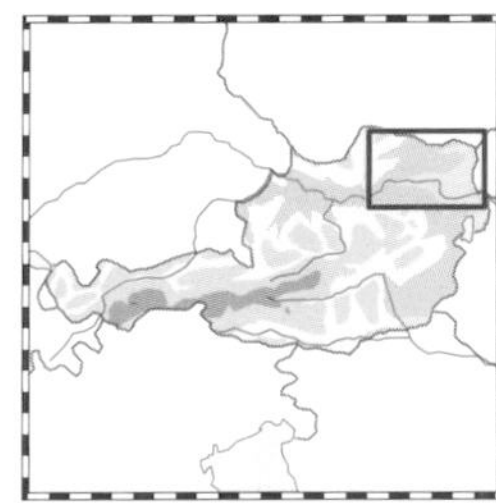

RED GRAPES
Blauer Portugieser is the most popular red grape. There is some Zweigelt and small amounts of Blauburgunder (Pinot Noir) and Merlot among other varieties.

WHITE GRAPES
Niederösterreich produces the best Grüner Veltliner in Austria, and nearly half the vineyards are planted with it. Other grapes include Müller-Thurgau, Welschriesling and Riesling.

CLIMATE
The climate is generally dry, but Lower Austria is a large area and there is great variation. Most parts are fairly warm; the eastern Weinviertel can be cooler and damper.

SOIL
Granite subsoil is common, particularly in the Wachau. Topsoils include stony schist, limestone, gravel, loess in Krems and occasionally loam.

ASPECT
Most Lower Austrian vineyards are on plains or gently rolling hills. In the Wachau the Danube Valley is the focus, with the banks getting steeper west of Krems.

NIEDERÖSTERREICH (LOWER AUSTRIA), situated on the fertile Danube plain, is one of the loveliest parts of Austria. It is a land of hills crowned with vast baroque monasteries and tunnelled with troglodyte wine cellars, of terraced slopes and fertile fields, of picturesque villages and, of course, the broad Danube: calm, powerful and yes, blue.

The map shows the focus of the whole area: a stretch of the Danube where four wine regions gather along its banks. In the west, on both sides of the river, is the Wachau, home of Austria's finest dry white wines. Next to it, also on both banks of the Danube, is the new region of Kremstal. Kamptal is centred on the river Kamp and the important wine town of Langenlois while Donauland stretches away to the east along the Danube as far as Vienna. All these regions make dry whites, and the Wachau makes the best Rieslings in Austria.

These Rieslings both are and are not like German Rieslings. Coming from a relatively warm climate, the wines are dry, full of extract, and minerally rather than flowery. They age well, although the Austrian taste is for young wine and they seldom get the chance. The grapes grow in conditions as demanding as those of any German vineyard: about half the Wachau is terraced, and the vines have to work hard for their living on shallow, stony soil that is often only 50cm (1½ft) deep; underneath there is granite. The Wachau receives about 450mm (18in) of rain a year, but the summers are very dry, and the only concessions the vine gets is irrigation, though if the growers have any sense, not too much.

The eastern end of the Wachau makes broader wines, but only where the soil is shallow and poor is Riesling planted, on slopes up to 300m (985ft). On the flatter land and the sandy soil nearer the river, Grüner Veltliner is grown and, if in the right hands and providing yields are kept to around 40 hectolitres per hectare, the wines can be quite serious, with good structure and even the ability to age for a few years. There is Weissburgunder here, too, and Müller-Thurgau, but it's the Riesling that gets the prime south-facing sites.

The terraces must be a nightmare to work. Some growers say they're three times more work than the flat vineyards, others that they're as much as five times more; either way, they're a lot more expensive, and the flatter vineyards, as mechanization increases, are getting cheaper and cheaper to work.

I could go on forever about the Wachau and its wines, but I won't, because next door to it is Kremstal, and the wines here are pretty good, too. Lower Austria generally is the home of Austria's best Grüner Veltliner (it's too warm in Burgenland and too cold elsewhere in the country) and Kremstal produces Grüner Veltliners as good as those of the Wachau, again providing the yields are kept low. The climatic influence is from the south-east – the great Pannonian plain stretches across into Hungary, where it is warm and dry – and Krems gets less than 500mm (20in) of rain per year.

The town of Krems is the wine capital of these parts, and the town of Stein, next door, can boast some of the best vineyard sites in all Austria. There is the Steiner Hund vineyard, steep and terraced and ideal for Riesling, and there are the vineyards on the hills overlooking Stein and the little town of Und. Then there is the Krems Valley, winding down from the north-west; and to the east of Krems there is a great swathe of vineyards around Rohrendorf on sandier soil.

The wine centre of Kamptal is Langenlois, which before 1986 had a whole wine region named after it. Now its fame rests mostly on the high-quality grapes coming from the great curve of south-facing vineyards that arches around the town. Here there is Grüner Veltliner, Ruländer, Chardonnay, Weissburgunder, Blauburgunder, Merlot and both Cabernets – the usual Austrian cocktail of varieties, plus some good growers to make the most of it all.

Donauland, or 'Danubeland', is the western half of what used to be until 1986 the region of Donauland-Carnuntum; the other part, Carnuntum, lies south-east of Vienna and runs up to the Leitha Hills, which separate it from Burgenland. The climate here is warm and dry and, especially near the Burgenland border, fairly similar to that of Burgenland itself. Donauland looks to the town and old monastery of Klosterneuburg as its capital: the monastery is the largest single vineyard owner in Austria, and the town is the home of Austria's first viticultural institute and the inventor of Klosterneuburger Mostwaage or KMW, the Austrian system for measuring must weight.

South of Carnuntum and Vienna is Thermenregion, a region of spas and hot springs. It's sunnier and drier here than in Vienna, and as warm as you'd expect from a place with its own inbuilt central heating. But it is windy here, and it's this wind that prevents much noble rot settling on the grapes. So its wine capital, Gumpoldskirchen, developed its own speciality: semi-sweet wines made from a blend of two local grapes, Rotgipfler and Zierfandler, and it was precisely this style of wine that went out of fashion overnight when the Austrian wine scandal broke in 1985. The growers turned to dry wines, often made from Welschriesling, but now there are signs that the traditional style could make a comeback. The Zierfandler is planted on the higher slopes of the hills, where it develops plenty

of acidity, and the Rotgipfler lower down. Red wines are the speciality in the south of Thermenregion and the best ones come from vineyards planted on the stony soils of the villages of Tattendorf and Teesdorf.

The biggest region of Lower Austria, the Weinviertel, also produces good reds, particularly on the granite soil around Retz near the Slovakian border, where there is less rain than in any other Austrian wine region. In the north-east of the Weinviertel the climate is damper and the vineyards here are a source of good Grüner Veltliner. In some of these villages there are wonderfully pretty *Kellergassen*, tiny pedimented cellars built in a row into the hillside, along narrow lanes running between high banks.

Anyone on a vineyard tour of Austria really should try to get an invitation to one of these cellars, if only to get a glimpse of a wine-making tradition that goes back centuries. The lanes can be rural, and grown with trees and ferns; and at regular intervals there are front doors, like a scene out of a child's fairy tale. Inside, the narrow cellars run deep into the hills, and each one is wide enough for only one row of barrels on each side and a pathway down the middle. As you go further into the hill the temperature drops dramatically, and your breath condenses in the air; and in these emerald or scarlet-hooped black barrels is the entire harvest of one small-scale grower.

He may take some samples of wine for you to try, using either a pipette or just a length of hosepipe. The wine will be cold and fresh, high in acidity and with all the character of the grower. There'll be Grüner Veltliner and Müller-Thurgau and Welschriesling and three or four others, and just when your teeth are beginning to chatter and you've lost all feeling in your feet, he'll lead you back outside where it's warm and sunny.

Most of the grapes for Austria's Sekt industry come from east of the Weinviertel, though the Sekt companies have their offices in or near Vienna. Austrians tend to have a sweeter tooth for sparkling wines than for still, and most Austrian Sekt tastes heavy and over-sweetened to a foreign palate. Some is made by the Champagne method but even so, none of it is terribly attractive.

Above Unterloiben in the Wachau the vines are grown on steep terraces overlooking the Danube.

WHERE THE VINEYARDS ARE *This map shows why the Wachau is Niederösterreich's leading quality region. To the west of Krems the banks of the Danube begin to rise into steep hills, and by Dürnstein (where Richard the Lionheart was imprisoned: the castle ruins are still there today) they are high, rugged and arid. The vineyards here, facing south or south-west across the river, get all the sun they could want, and the Danube does its bit by reflecting all that warmth back on to the slopes. The great rocky outcrops and stony soils found around here hold the heat, too. The warm days and cool nights mean that the grapes retain their acidity and have lots of flavour, as well as getting nicely ripe. The town of Dürnstein is a bit of a tourist trap, but pretty nonetheless – and it's worth a visit just for the view.*

There are lots of little tributaries flowing into the Danube through these hills. The Krems and the Kamp rivers offer good sites along their banks, but really it's the Danube itself that is the focus of viticulture in this part of Lower Austria. East of Krems is a flatter area of mixed farming. Here the vineyards spread away from the river, both north and south, clustering around the villages.

South of the Danube the vineyards spread over gently rolling hills, alternating with other forms of agriculture.

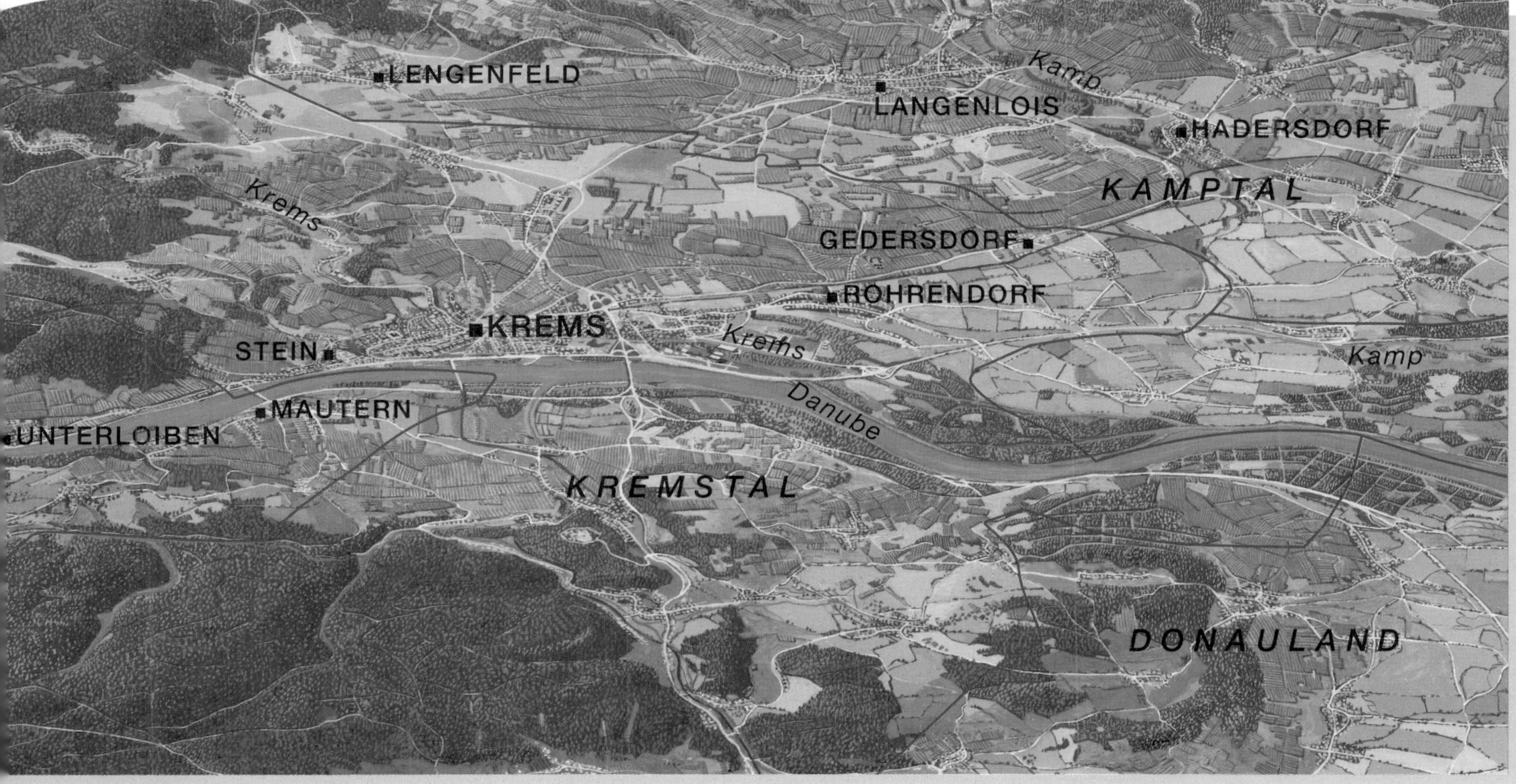

BURGENLAND

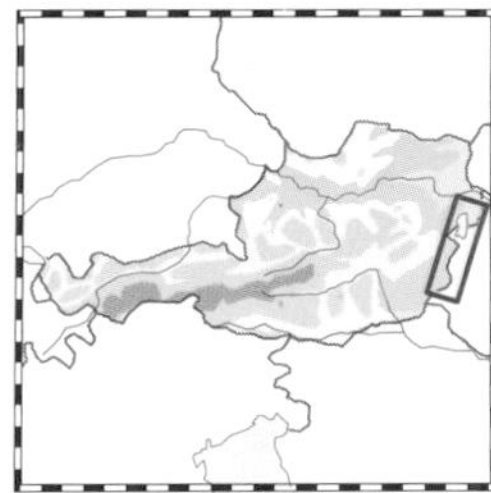

FOR LOVERS OF LUSCIOUSLY SWEET botrytis-affected wine, the marshy, reedy corner of Austria that is mapped here is one of the most remarkable places on earth. Nowhere else, except in Hungary's Tokajhegyalja, does *Botrytis cinerea* attack the grapes so reliably every year; nowhere else is it so easy to make great sweet wines. In Germany and France growers watch their grapes anxiously for the first signs of the fungus that will shrivel and brown the grapes and impart its distinctive flavour to the wines. In the vineyards bordering the Neusiedl lake they don't need to worry: they know the noble rot will arrive – it always does. As a result their nobly rotten sweet wines are far less expensive than those from other regions; perhaps because of this (and certainly partly because of the Austrian 1985 wine scandal in which some of the wines from here were implicated) the wines are not always prized highly abroad. More fool us.

The Burgenland is on the border with Hungary, and has had the sort of chequered history that often affects border areas. Until 1921 it was part of Hungary, and joined Austria just in time for the economic hardship of the 1920s and 1930s. After the end of World War Two the Burgenland was part of the Russian zone of occupation, and it was only when the Russians left in 1956 that the way was clear for investment in the vineyards. So while fine sweet wines have been made around the Neusiedler See since the sixteenth century, it is only in recent decades that they have been made in such large quantities. The southern shores of the lake, indeed, are still part of Hungary and form part of the Sopron wine region. But unlike the Austrian vineyards around the lake, these Hungarian vineyards are largely planted with red varieties, both Cabernets, Merlot and Pinot Noir.

The eastern shore of the lake, a broad, shallow expanse of water that imparts humidity to the area, has an even shorter history of viticulture. This was a largely forgotten part of the country, given over to cattle farming until the late 1950s, when the local Chamber of Commerce suggested to farmers that they plant bulk vines like Grüner Veltliner and Müller-Thurgau for basic blending wine. Neither grape is remotely suited to this hot, humid, flat region where grapes ripen early and can lack acidity unless care is taken in the wine-making process; it has only been with the planting of aromatic varieties like Traminer, and traditional Burgenland vines like Welschriesling and Weissburgunder, that fine wines have emerged.

The soil on both sides of the lake is sandy, since the lake itself once covered an even larger area than its current 152 square kilometres (59 square miles). Away from the immediate lake area the soil is loam, which tends not to heat up quite as fast, and there is limestone in the foothills to the west of the lake. The eastern side of the lake is even warmer than the

WHERE THE VINEYARDS ARE *It's difficult to see the Neusiedler See from a distance: the land is so flat that the reed beds hide the shimmer of the water. Only the brightly coloured sails of the pleasure boats mark where the water is deep enough to sail. At its deepest point the lake only reaches about 2m (6ft) – the shallow water heats up quickly and, since this is the hottest part of Austria, the water temperature can be 30°C (86°F) in late summer. The whole of the western side of the lake is more undulating. It is thickly planted with vines towards the south, but where the Leitha Hills rise up in the north the vines climb a little way up the slopes.*

The eastern side is flat all the way into the vast Hungarian plain. The Seewinkel is an area dotted with hundreds of ponds and small lakes; some of these dry up in the summer, but there are enough to make this a remarkably humid area. This humidity combines with the warmth that has given the Podersdorf region the nickname of Hölle (hell) to make Podersdorf, Illmitz and Apetlon centres of sweet wine production. Further north, around Gols, dry whites and reds are made: look how the little lakes of the Seewinkel don't reach that far.

The same is true of the west side of the Neusiedl lake: sweet wines are made only where humidity can reach the vines. Beyond a narrow strip running alongside the lake, the vineyards produce dry whites and reds, which have greater acidity (since the nights are cooler) as the vines rise up the slopes of the Leitha Hills. The centre for sweet wines here is Rust, a picturesque village crammed with tourist coaches in the summer and nesting storks in the spring.

RED GRAPES
Blaufränkisch, with 12 per cent of the vineyard, is the single most widely planted variety. There are small amounts of Zweigelt and other varieties.

WHITE GRAPES
The Austrian speciality, Grüner Veltliner, has 19 per cent of the land under vine. Weissburgunder, Neuburger and Furmint are much used for Ausbruch wines.

CLIMATE
This is the warmest and driest wine region in Austria. The average annual temperature in the Neusiedlersee at Illmitz is 10.9°C (51½°F).

SOIL
The soil is very varied, with sand around the Neusiedler See and loam further away. There is limestone in the Leitha Hills and the Rosalein Hills to the west of the lake. Elsewhere there is gravel and deep loam.

ASPECT
The region is generally flat. Neusiedlersee-Hügelland is gently undulating, with good south and south-east facing slopes, and there are occasional ranges of hills in Mittelburgenland. In the north-east of Südburgenland the Eisenberg faces east and south-east over the plain.

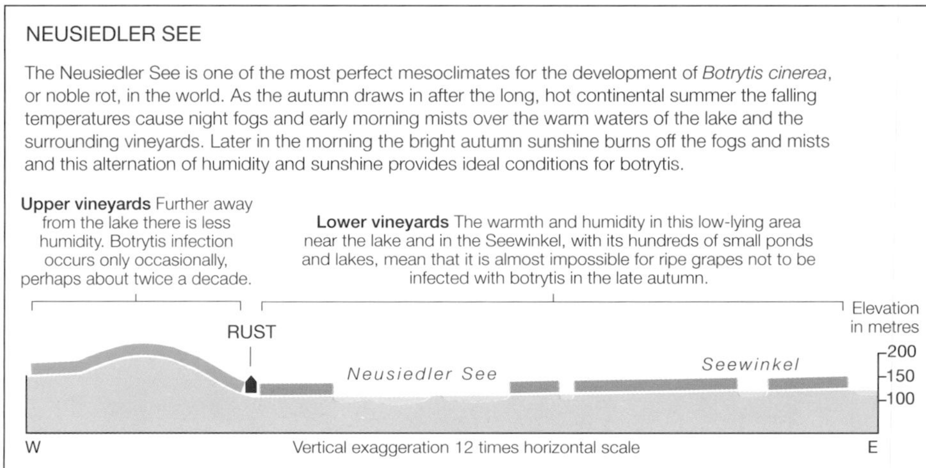

NEUSIEDLER SEE

The Neusiedler See is one of the most perfect mesoclimates for the development of *Botrytis cinerea*, or noble rot, in the world. As the autumn draws in after the long, hot continental summer the falling temperatures cause night fogs and early morning mists over the warm waters of the lake and the surrounding vineyards. Later in the morning the bright autumn sunshine burns off the fogs and mists and this alternation of humidity and sunshine provides ideal conditions for botrytis.

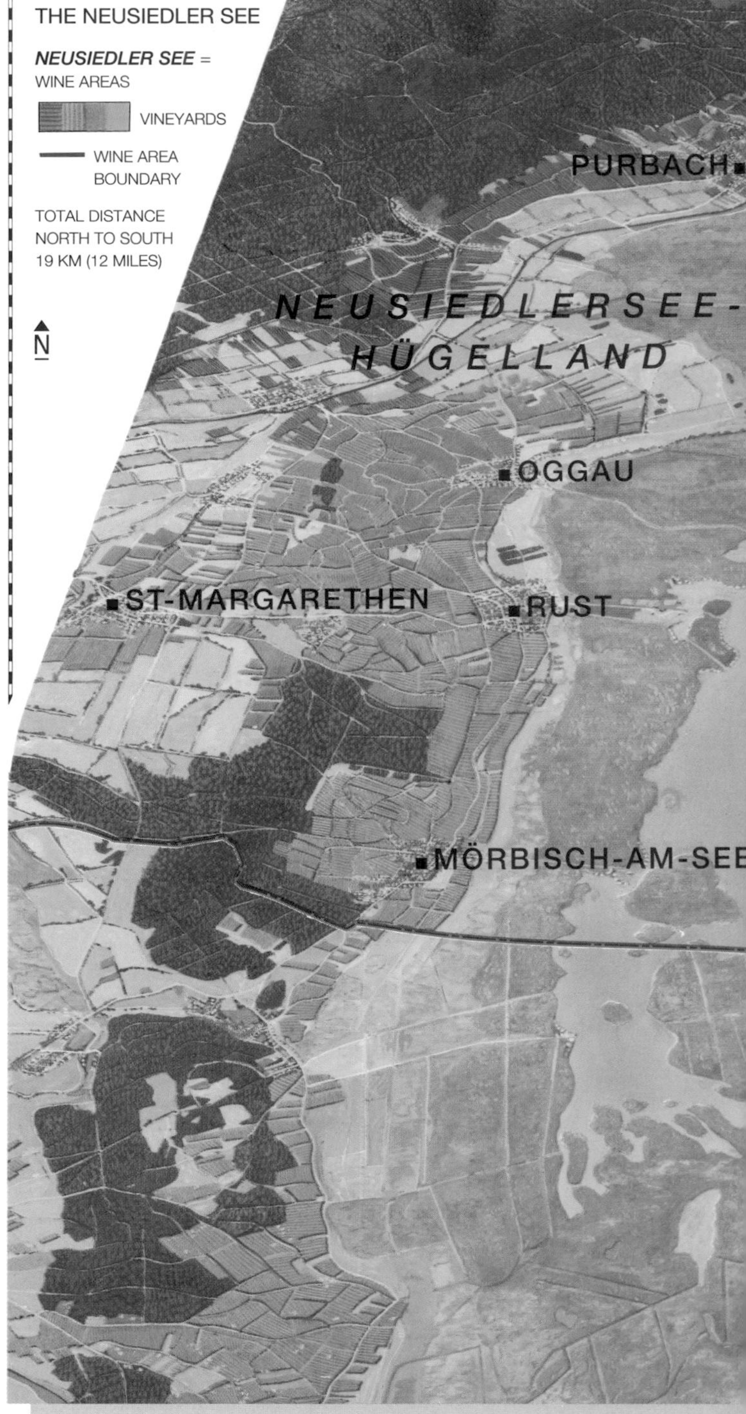

western; the grapes ripen here some two weeks earlier, and in late September 1989, when the grapes were still green on the western side, the first grapes for Trockenbeerenauslesen wines were picked on the eastern side. Yields on the eastern side are fairly high, at around 60 or 70 hectolitres per hectare, though nobly rotten grapes are more likely to give half that figure.

However, Burgenland is not all sweet wines. The region extends in a knobbly strip south-west of the lake along the Hungarian border through the flat Mittelburgenland down to Südburgenland and the border with Slovenia.

The Mittelburgenland is red wine country. Ninety-five per cent of the grapes are red, and most of them are Blaufränkisch, often from high-yielding vineyards and the wines are somewhat sweet and jammy. The more enterprising growers follow an international path of dry wines, sometimes aged in new oak, and often given extra backbone with some Cabernet Sauvignon. Yields from such growers are around the 50 hectolitres per hectare mark; others can take much more. The majority of wines are bottled by co-operatives or (much less so these days) merchants, but more and more growers, particularly in the best villages – Horitschon, Neckenmarkt and on the often gravelly soil of Deutschkreuz – are taking the bit between their teeth and bottling their own wine.

Südburgenland is an altogether quieter place. It is a region of summer rain and relatively late ripening, and of mixed farming except in the best spots. These are the villages of Deutsch-Schützen and Eisenberg just to the north; this latter, as its name suggests, is a hill which faces east over the Hungarian plain. The village of Rechnitz, too, produces good whites. The grapes are mainly Zweigelt and Blaufränkish for reds and Welschriesling and Müller-Thurgau for whites – plus such rarities as Concord, Noah, Otello, Hinkton, Seibel and Ripatella. These last are only rarities in Austria; in the US they are commonplace, since these are the names of native American vines of the sort bred for rootstocks of European vines. Only in a few places in Europe are these vines grown for wine. Madeira is one such (though not for Madeira wine); darkest Südburgenland is another, where the wine is known as Uhudler. Don't expect to find it in your local shop, though: it's not precisely legal, and it's certainly not exported. I rather wish it were – it has a long and by no means disproven reputation as an aphrodisiac.

The square-shouldered bottle is often used for Burgenland's ultra-sweet wines.

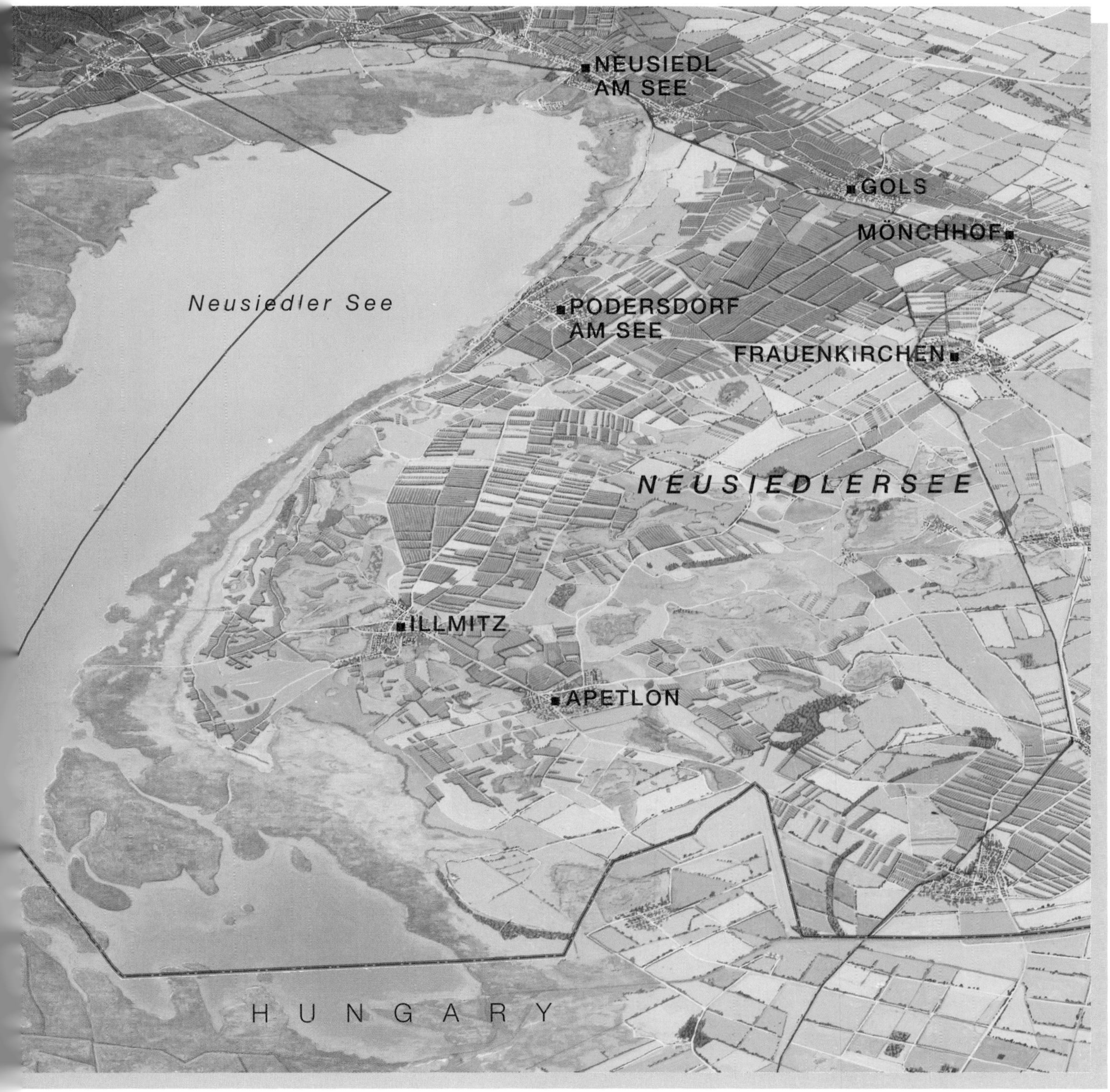

0 km 1 2
0 miles 1

NEUSIEDL AM SEE
GOLS
MÖNCHHOF
Neusiedler See
PODERSDORF AM SEE
FRAUENKIRCHEN
NEUSIEDLERSEE
ILLMITZ
APETLON
HUNGARY

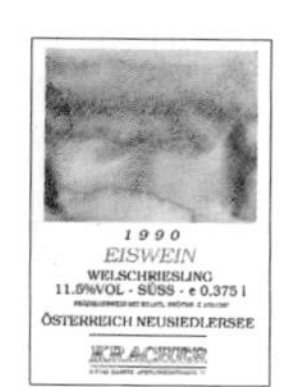

ITALY

Italy. Oh, what an exasperating country. No other nation can so easily fill my eyes with tears at the sheer beauty of its human achievements, yet no other country makes steam shoot from my ears in fury at the wholesale squandering of nature's gifts. But, I wonder, is it possible to have it any other way?

There are countries where you can easily understand the potential and range of their wines, good or bad. Reliable, conformist, unlikely to let you down. Unlikely to thrill you either. Italy's not a bit like that. Some of her most famous vineyards produce some of her worst wines. Some of her greatest wines had no legal standing at all until 1995. The DOC system (the *Denominazione di Origine Controllata*), set up in 1963 to try to make sense of the anarchy that was Italian wine, has spent as much time enshrining mediocrity and protecting incompetence as it has promoting and preserving quality and regional character. In an area such as Tuscany, where great wine names like Chianti and Vino Nobile di Montepulciano had come to be meaningless, the region's innovative, quality-conscious producers were forced to go outside the law rather than submit to regulations that had nothing to do with excellence and everything to do with political expediency. Around Naples, the source of some of the greatest wines of the Ancient World, hardly anyone these days bothers to register their vineyards for DOC. In any case, it's too easy to sell whatever wine they make – regardless of its quality or provenance.

And yet, and yet. From the northern terraces in the snowy embrace of the Tyrolean Alps to the southern islands that are mere specks on the horizon within hailing distance of Africa, Italy has more continuous vineyard land than any other country. The world's biggest producer, making one-fifth of all the world's wine; the world's biggest consumer of wine; and its biggest exporter, sending abroad nearly one-quarter of the total wine exported from every country in the world! The Apennine backbone running down the centre of the country means that increasing sunshine can always be countered with altitude. The Ligurian, Tyrrhenian, Ionian and Adriatic seas provide maritime influences to calm and soothe all the wine regions except those of the far north. And most of the grape varieties are Italian originals.

The modern new wave of wine across the world has been based largely on French role models and French grape varieties. But there will come a time when new directions are needed, new flavours are required. It'll take some genius to disentangle them all, but Italy, with her maverick mentality, her challenging wine styles, and her jungle of different grape varieties, will be the place to look.

Young Merlot vines on the Grattamacco estate, in the hills above Castagneto Carducci on the Tuscan coast, illustrate the move in Tuscany towards experimenting with international grape varieties to make some exciting wines.

The Wine Regions of Italy

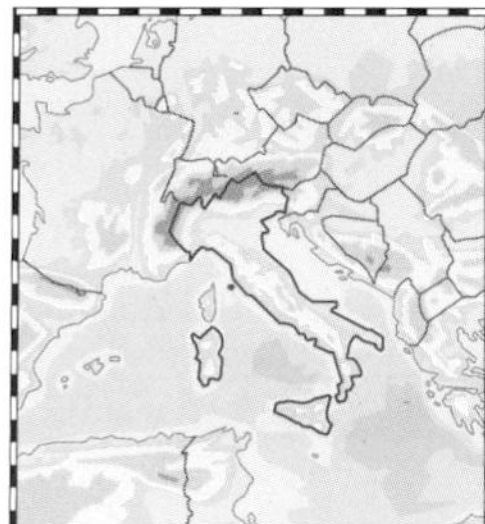

Vines and Italy seem to go together. Indeed, given the amount of wine that Italy produces, a visitor arriving in the country for the first time might easily expect every imaginable nook and cranny to be planted with vineyards. But how wrong that person would be. True, there are vast tracts of vines in Italy, but these tend to be concentrated in a few regions: Piedmont in the north-west, Veneto and Friuli in the north-east, Tuscany and Emilia-Romagna in central Italy, Puglia in the south and the islands of Sicily and Sardinia. And with such a broad geographical spread, there is obviously great vintage variation, not only throughout the peninsula but also within each region.

It is easy to forget just how long Italy is, stretching from the cool, alpine slopes of the Aosta Valley right down to the tiny island of Pantelleria which almost touches the African shores off Tunisia – in Milan you are, in fact, closer to London than to Palermo, the capital of Sicily. Italy is ideally suited to the cultivation of the vine. Eighty per cent of the country is hilly or mountainous and in the alpine foothills of the north and along the Apennines that curve their way south to the very tip of the Italian mainland, there are many beautifully exposed hillsides on which the vine can bask. And the altitude of these slopes often serves to moderate the differences in temperature from one end of the country to the other. During the summer, the vineyards around Bolzano in the Alto Adige can be hotter than those in Chianti or even the deep south.

This illustrates rule number one of Italian wine: do not generalize. If you do fall into the trap, you are bound to come up against an exception to the general rule. In addition to the affect of altitude, the region's proximity to water can confound logical expectations of what the climate should or shouldn't be in a certain area. The Adriatic and Tyrrhenian seas cool the country's eastern and western flanks, while inland lakes such as Garda in the north-west or Trasimeno in Umbria create local climates that greatly influence the style of wine produced. And then there are the rivers that criss-cross the country's wine zones, from the Tanaro in Piedmont, that acts as a geological boundary between the Roero and Langhe hills, through the Po that bissects northern and central Italy, to the Adige in the north-east, and Tuscany's Arno and Lazio's Tiber. In some cases, these rivers serve to moderate the climate, but with others, most notably the Po, they provide fertile valleys in which the vine performs like an athlete on steroids.

Given the great climatic and topographical diversity, it is hardly surprising that Italy has such a wide range of native grape varieties, most of which are suited only to their local growing conditions. The Nebbiolo, for instance, only seems to flourish in Piedmont, and nowhere better than on the limestone rich soil of the Langhe hills; the Moscato grape, though grown throughout the peninsula, excels in the white, chalky soils around Canelli in Piedmont's Monferrato hills.

Further east, around Verona, the white Garganega and red Corvina flourish in the Dolomite foothills, while in the hills along the Slovenian border, international varieties like Pinot Grigio and Sauvignon do battle for supremacy with natives like Tocai Friulano and Ribolla. On the eastern coast, in the Marche and Abruzzo, the Montepulciano grape holds sway, but attempts to transport it across the Apennines to Tuscany have been thwarted by the cooler climate there. Sangiovese, however, produces meagre wines on the eastern coast, but in Tuscany rises to great heights in Chianti, Montalcino and Montepulciano. It is planted throughout the peninsula, as are Barbera and the white Trebbiano, the latter being Italy's most widely planted grape variety, accounting for 12 per cent of all the vineyards. But while Barbera and Sangiovese can produce great wines in the right sites, Trebbiano is prized only for its resistance to disease and prodigious yields.

Moving south, we come across varieties first brought to the peninsula 3000 years ago by the Greeks, the Uva di Troia, Negroamaro, Aglianico, Gaglioppo and Greco di Tufo and, not surprisingly, these all perform brilliantly in the southern heat. When northern varieties like Sangiovese and Trebbiano are planted in the south they ripen as early as August, and as a result produce wines of ineffable neutrality, but the native southern grapes, more accustomed to the hot summers, have a much longer growing season, which allows the grapes time to develop interesting and complex perfumes.

The islands, too, have their own varieties. In Sicily the Nero d'Avola is unrivalled, while in Sardinia, evidence of Spanish domination in the Middle Ages is still to be found in grape varieties like the red Cannonau (Spain's Garnacha) and Carignano (Cariñena) and the white Vermentino (said to be Malvasia). Here, as elsewhere in Italy, the importance of matching these grape varieties with suitable terrain and climate cannot be underestimated.

THE CLASSIFICATION SYSTEM FOR ITALIAN WINE

Italy's wine laws evolved out of the chaos of the 1950s and in 1963 the Italian government set up a system of *denominazione di origine*, or denomination of origin, which was based loosely on the French *appellation contrôlée* system. Until recently only about 10 per cent of the enormous Italian wine harvest was regulated by wine laws. This is now set to change as the reforms passed in 1992, known as the Goria law, gradually begin to take effect and incorporate more wines into the various categories.

QUALITY CATEGORIES

Wine is divided into two categories – quality wine (DOCG and DOC) and table wine (IGT and VdT).

- **Denominazione di Origine Controllata e Garantita (DOCG)** This top tier of Italian wine started off as a tighter form of DOC, as a way of recognizing the finest Italian wines. There were more stringent restrictions on grape types and yields and the wine had to be analyzed and tasted by a special panel before being granted its coveted seal. Although set up in 1963 the first DOCG was not granted until 1980 and even by the mid-1990s only 15 wines had been granted DOCG status. In its revised form it will recognize any specific DOC wine which follows a strict quality discipline in good years, as well as giving due recognition to particularly good vineyard sites.
- **Denominazione di Origine Controllata (DOC)** This level applies to wines made from specified grape varieties, grown in specified zones and aged by prescribed methods. To a certain extent the DOC rules serve to preserve existing traditions (traditions established during the years after World War Two with more of an eye to quantity than quality) at the expense of progress, and do not always guarantee good quality. Nearly all the traditionally well-known wines are DOC, and more get added to the list each year.
- **Indicazione Geografica Tipica (IGT)** This is a new level of table wine, designed as an Italian version of the successful French *vin de pays* category. The wines can use a geographical description on the label followed by a varietal name.
- **Vino da Tavola (VdT)** This is the most basic classification and no geographical or varietal distinctions can be made on the label. Perversely, because some individual producers have become disillusioned with the wine laws which restrict their originality and initiative, some of Italy's greatest wines carry the humble *vino da tavola* designation. In future, these wines are certain to be incorporated fully into the system and given due recognition.

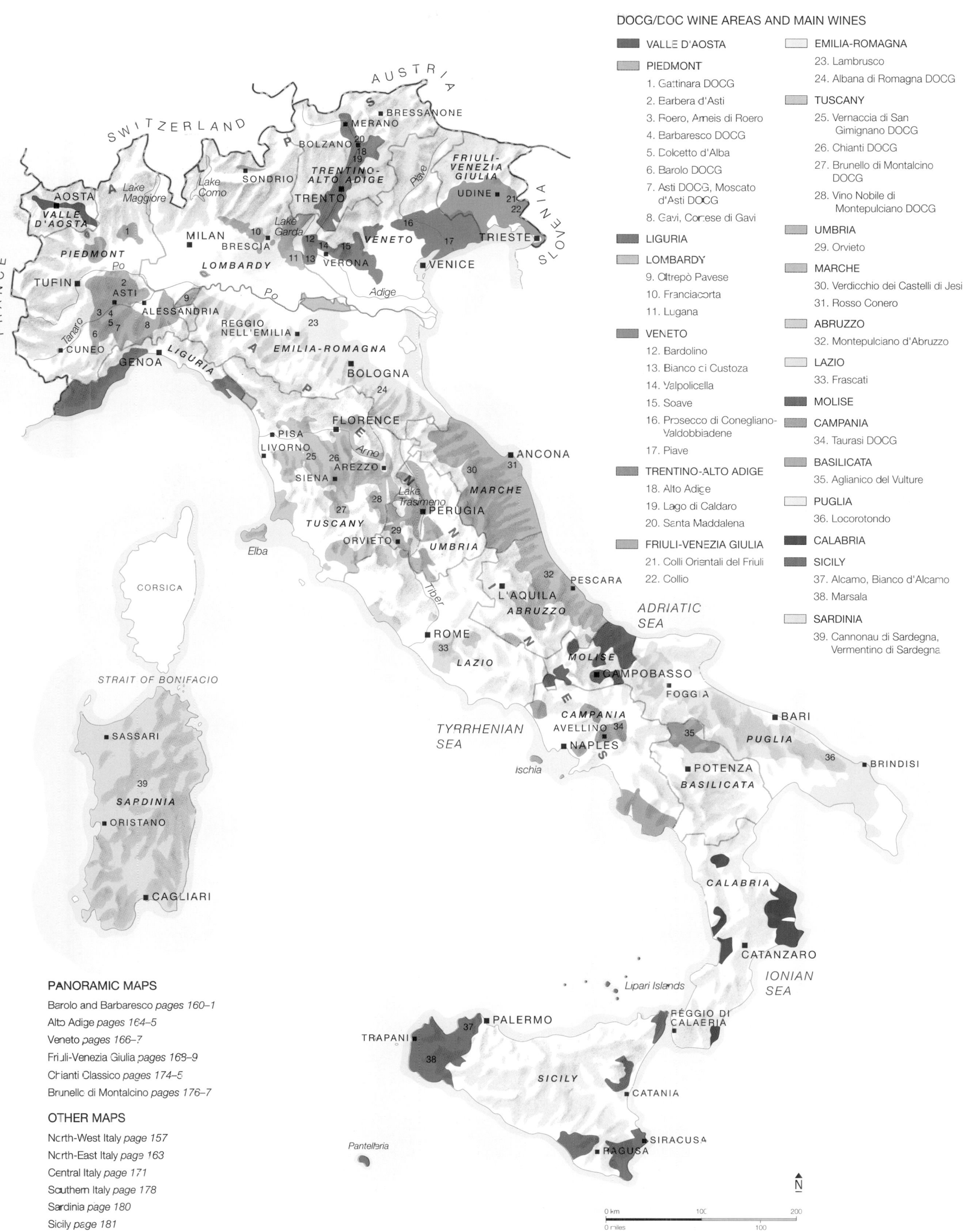
DOCG/DOC WINE AREAS AND MAIN WINES
VALLE D'AOSTA
PIEDMONT
1. Gattinara DOCG
2. Barbera d'Asti
3. Roero, Arneis di Roero
4. Barbaresco DOCG
5. Dolcetto d'Alba
6. Barolo DOCG
7. Asti DOCG, Moscato d'Asti DOCG
8. Gavi, Cortese di Gavi
LIGURIA
LOMBARDY
9. Oltrepò Pavese
10. Franciacorta
11. Lugana
VENETO
12. Bardolino
13. Bianco di Custoza
14. Valpolicella
15. Soave
16. Prosecco di Conegliano-Valdobbiadene
17. Piave
TRENTINO-ALTO ADIGE
18. Alto Adige
19. Lago di Caldaro
20. Santa Maddalena
FRIULI-VENEZIA GIULIA
21. Colli Orientali del Friuli
22. Collio
EMILIA-ROMAGNA
23. Lambrusco
24. Albana di Romagna DOCG
TUSCANY
25. Vernaccia di San Gimignano DOCG
26. Chianti DOCG
27. Brunello di Montalcino DOCG
28. Vino Nobile di Montepulciano DOCG
UMBRIA
29. Orvieto
MARCHE
30. Verdicchio dei Castelli di Jesi
31. Rosso Conero
ABRUZZO
32. Montepulciano d'Abruzzo
LAZIO
33. Frascati
MOLISE
CAMPANIA
34. Taurasi DOCG
BASILICATA
35. Aglianico del Vulture
PUGLIA
36. Locorotondo
CALABRIA
SICILY
37. Alcamo, Bianco d'Alcamo
38. Marsala
SARDINIA
39. Cannonau di Sardegna, Vermentino di Sardegna
PANORAMIC MAPS
Barolo and Barbaresco pages 160–1
Alto Adige pages 164–5
Veneto pages 166–7
Friuli-Venezia Giulia pages 168–9
Chianti Classico pages 174–5
Brunello di Montalcino pages 176–7
OTHER MAPS
North-West Italy page 157
North-East Italy page 163
Central Italy page 171
Southern Italy page 178
Sardinia page 180
Sicily page 181
AUSTRIA
SWITZERLAND
FRANCE
SLOVENIA
AOSTA
VALLE D'AOSTA
PIEDMONT
TURIN
ASTI
ALESSANDRIA
CUNEO
GENOA
LIGURIA
MILAN
BRESCIA
LOMBARDY
SONDRIO
Lake Maggiore
Lake Como
Lake Garda
MERANO
BRESSANONE
BOLZANO
TRENTINO-ALTO ADIGE
TRENTO
VERONA
VENETO
VENICE
FRIULI-VENEZIA GIULIA
UDINE
TRIESTE
Piave
Adige
Po
Tanaro
REGGIO NELL'EMILIA
EMILIA-ROMAGNA
BOLOGNA
FLORENCE
PISA
LIVORNO
Arno
AREZZO
SIENA
TUSCANY
Lake Trasimeno
PERUGIA
ORVIETO
UMBRIA
ANCONA
MARCHE
Elba
CORSICA
PESCARA
L'AQUILA
ABRUZZO
Tiber
ROME
LAZIO
ADRIATIC SEA
MOLISE
CAMPOBASSO
FOGGIA
CAMPANIA
AVELLINO
NAPLES
TYRRHENIAN SEA
Ischia
BARI
PUGLIA
BRINDISI
POTENZA
BASILICATA
STRAIT OF BONIFACIO
SASSARI
SARDINIA
ORISTANO
CAGLIARI
CALABRIA
CATANZARO
IONIAN SEA
Lipari Islands
PALERMO
TRAPANI
REGGIO DI CALABRIA
SICILY
CATANIA
SIRACUSA
RAGUSA
Pantelleria
N
0 km 100 200
0 miles 100

North-West Italy

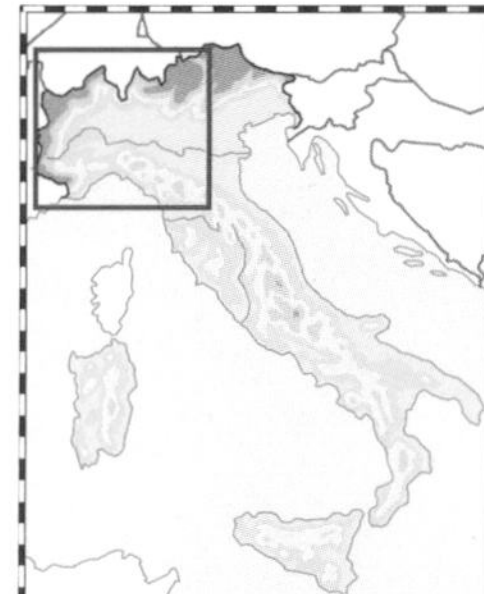

The adrenalin invariably surges through my veins as I leave behind the winding road, snaking its way down Mont Blanc's slopes to join the new road that runs through the Aosta Valley to Turin and the rest of Italy. Such excitement is, in part, the reaction of a sun-starved northern European arriving in the luminous landscapes of Italy, but there is also, for the wine lover, the added attraction of Italy's greatest wine zone just over an hour's drive away in Piedmont's Langhe hills around the city of Alba.

The corrugated, sub-alpine hills and the clay and limestone soils of the Langhe provide the perfect environment for the cultivation of the vine, and the growers' dedication results in some of the most exciting wines in Italy. But it's a relatively recent phenomenon for the thought of the Langhe to set my tastebuds tingling in anticipation. Once my gums would have trembled at the prospect of tasting the sort of hard wines that Barolo and Barbaresco used to be. But today I find myself increasingly drawn to the new style of delicately balanced wines emerging from this region, wines which, far from betraying their ancient reputation for power and thrilling hauteur, are transforming, then rebuilding it in a most remarkable way. None of the arrogance of old Barolo and Barbaresco has been lost; there's no hail-fellow-well-met open-handed New World bonhomie about these wines. Yet there is a core of sweet fruit and beguiling perfume coiled within the surly exterior that used to be destroyed by long years of aging in ancient wood, yet which now bursts through the tannic shield with a firework display of blackberries and tar, wild mountain strawberries and the bright, sweet fragrance of rose petals.

But the Langhe hills form a small island of quality in a sea of mediocrity. For though north-west Italy, and Piedmont in particular, has a reputation for producing some of the best wines in Italy, quality seldom matches expectations. Piedmont, for instance, has the highest number of DOCs of any region in Italy (more than 40), yet outside the Langhe, with a few exceptions in the neighbouring Monferrato hills, there is little that can compete on the international stage. And away from Piedmont, on the vertiginous cliffs of Liguria, in the craggy hills of Aosta or on the Lombardy plain, you tend to find wines that are fine in a local restaurant but which are disappointing when drunk back at home.

North-west Italy should produce better wine, for it has all the necessary natural attributes. Mountains – the Alps to the north and west, the Apennines to the south – form a protective semi-circle, and separate Italy from France and Switzerland. They also act as a natural border between Piedmont (its name is derived from the fact that it lies at the foot of the mountains) and the coastal region of Liguria to the south. Rivers like the Po, Tanaro and Bormida irrigate the lush, low-lying valleys that produce some of Italy's best fruit, while hills like the Langhe and Monferrato, and the alpine foothills of Lombardy, provide the vine with ideal growing conditions.

The Po, Italy's longest river, rises in the Alps near the French border before cutting a broad swathe through the plains of Piedmont, Lombardy and the Veneto, dividing as it goes northern, alpine Italy from Emilia-Romagna and central Italy. The broad, fertile Po Valley, unsuitable for viticulture (though its very fertility has tempted many a greedy and foolish grape grower), is bordered to the north by an outcrop of limestone and dolomite (calcium magnesium carbonate) that forms the foothills of Lombardy's Alps. These extend into the Veneto, where they play host to the Classico zones of Valpolicella and Soave, but in Lombardy are largely responsible for the wines of Franciacorta.

While the Alps act as a protective helmet for Italy's head, the Apennines – curving eastwards along the southern border of Piedmont before turning south – act as the spine. And, as with the Alps, their presence has a profound influence on the peninsula's viticulture. In south-west Lombardy, the foothills of the Apennines sustain the vine in the Oltrepò Pavese DOC zone, while to the south, vines cling to the steep Ligurian slopes that tumble headlong into the Mediterranean, producing wines like Cinqueterre and Vermentino that quench the thirst of numerous tourists.

Steeply terraced vineyards surround the village of Manarola in the ruggedly beautiful Cinqueterre region of Liguria, once accessible only by sea.

Italy has few landlocked regions, yet in the north-west of the country only Liguria can boast contact with the sea. Such proximity to the water gives to this slight, crescent-shaped region a more moderate climate than that of Piedmont, Lombardy and the mountainous Aosta to the north. Inland, the winters are bitterly cold, the summers long and hot and the autumns generally fine until thick fogs descend for days on end in early October. If the fogs hold off, or are counterbalanced by sunny afternoons, then the prospects for a fine vintage are greatly increased.

PIEDMONT

In Piedmont, Italy's largest region, the Langhe and Monferrato hills (together accounting for over 90 per cent of the region's wine production) are often wreathed in thick swirls of fog. Known as *nebbia* in Italian, the fog has given its name to one of Piedmont's – indeed Italy's – greatest grape varieties: Nebbiolo. This fickle variety, the sole component of Barolo and Barbaresco, ripens late, and is quite often struggling to reach maturity when the fogs cover the valleys and the lower slopes. When Nebbiolo wins the battle, the results are splendid; when the fog wins, the growers are left with a rather insipid, green and rasping red wine that leaves tasters grimacing and wondering what all the fuss is about.

But Piedmont has more weapons in its armoury than just the noble Nebbiolo. Other red grapes like Barbera and Dolcetto produce greater volumes of wine. Barbera is a prodigious variety that appears to flourish wherever it is planted, and it has the great virtue of ripening easily to produce a rich, black-fruited wine that is high in acid and mercifully low in tannin. Dolcetto is at its best as a vibrant purple-red wine, packed with plummy fruit and wild-eyed spice, unsophisticated, undemanding, and marvellously easy to knock back in flagons. Since the best land is usually given over to Nebbiolo, we rarely see great examples of these two grapes.

Though noted for its red wines, Piedmont also produces large volumes of white wine, primarily from the Moscato grape grown in the Monferrato hills. Its heavenly scent, all peaches and elderflowers, is found in the best of Asti and

MAIN DOCG/DOC WINE AREAS

VALLE D'AOSTA
- Valle d'Aosta

PIEDMONT
- Carema
- Gattinara DOCG
- Ghemme
- Erbaluce di Caluso, Caluso Passito
- Barbera d'Asti
- Roero, Arneis di Roero
- Barbaresco DOCG
- Barolo DOCG
- Dolcetto d'Alba
- Asti DOCG, Moscato d'Asti DOCG
- Brachetto d'Acqui
- Gavi, Cortese di Gavi

LOMBARDY
- Oltrepò Pavese
- Franciacorta
- Lugana
- Riviera del Garda Bresciano
- Valtellina

LIGURIA
- Rossese di Dolceacqua
- Cinqueterre

OVER 300M (984FT)

OVER 600M (1968FT)

EZIO VOYAT

ROSSO "LE MURAGLIE"

Moscato d'Asti, and it makes it a perfect antidote to the Langhe's brooding reds. Less reliable, but marvellously scented with a fruit that veers between pears and white peaches are still wines from the Arneis and Favorita varieties.

OTHER REGIONS

The rest of north-west Italy's wines are dwarfed by the colossus of Piedmont. Liguria's wine, which accounts for less than a half of 1 per cent of Italian production, is consumed mainly by the summer tourists, and generally suffers the fate that easy popularity and a thirsty tourist trade always brings to a region – carelessly mediocre quality and sky-high prices. But the potential for quality in Liguria is good. The overriding sensation I've got from good examples of wines like Ormeasco, Rossese, Pigato and Vermentino is of the fat, round, ripe body so often missing in Italian wines, allied to some fascinating flavours. This all makes sense, because the vines are mostly grown on warm mountain slopes with a strong maritime influence. There aren't that many good examples, but they are worth seeking out.

Aosta has the same problem – a thirsty tourist trade from the ski resorts willing to hoover anything down at high prices. However, it's a high, cool alpine valley, where ripening the grape is by no means easy. I've had quite good, herb-scented Gamays and Nebbiolos, and a couple of rather good Moscatos, but whereas I would go out of my way to find Ligurian wines, I think I'll just drink Aostan wines when I'm stopping off *en route*.

Only Lombardy, with about 17,000 hectares (42,000 acres) of vineyards, can even attempt to challenge Piedmont, more than double in size with its 35,000 hectares (86,500 acres). Unfortunately, much of what is produced in areas like the Oltrepo Pavese in the south-west of Lombardy (generally sound but uninspiring varietals), and in the Valtellina in the mountainous northern section of the province (where Nebbiolo makes a rare foray outside Piedmont), is second rate, and is in any case soaked up by Milan, Italy's industrial centre and the nearest large city. There is little incentive for producers to improve while local demand remains high, so for real quality we must turn back to Piedmont.

Springtime near Monforte d'Alba in the Langhe hills. The vineyards here produce some of Italy's finest wines, including the robust Barolo.

Piedmont

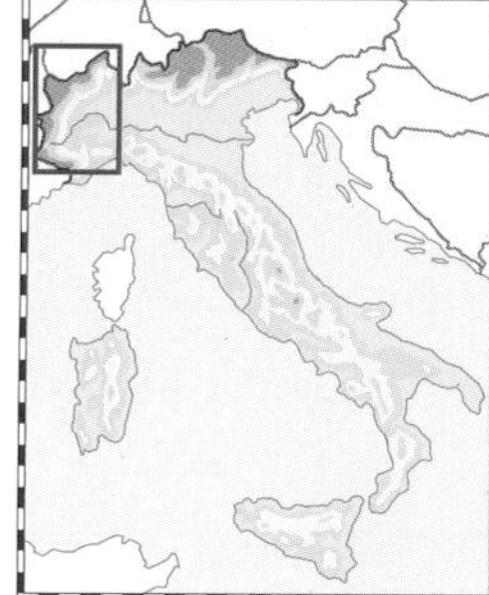

If, like me, your first experience of Piedmont is the great city of Turin, then you might be excused for wondering where the vineyards are in this, the greatest of all Italian wine regions. The heart of Turin is beautiful – in the discreet, industrious style that set the Piedmontese apart from their fellow Italians – but as you move away from the centre, Turin becomes an urban jungle set in the centre of a flat, monotonous terrain.

This land-locked region is supposed to have cold, bright winters and hot, bright summers, but the people who write the textbooks have never been there at the same time as me. In summer, when I have visited, the heavy, clammy warmth reduces any distant view to a haze, while in autumn or winter, a thick, eery fog can suddenly descend and limit visibility to about five yards. On a clear spring or winter day, however, the Alps are visible to the north and west, but anyone in search of vineyards is left wondering in which direction they might lie.

An intelligent move would be to head west, towards the mountains and the border with France, working on the assumption that the foothills would offer plenty of sites ideally suited to the cultivation of the vine. But it's not quite as simple as that. The mountains of eastern Savoy are surprisingly lacking in vineyards, and the hills to the south-west are equally bare. A foolhardy soul who struck out east towards Vercelli would soon find themselves ankle deep in paddy-fields, for this part of the Po Valley grows most of the rice for the risottos that are found on menus throughout the country.

If you head north from the paddy-fields, you do stumble upon some vineyards, for unlike the alpine foothills to the west, those to the north are lightly carpeted with vines. These northern foothills rise up from the unremitting flatness of the Po Valley, and provide superb south-facing slopes for vines.

South-east Piedmont, here at Montemagno, near Asti, is one of the most intensely cultivated vineyard areas of northern Italy.

SÉSIA VALLEY

To the north of Vercelli's paddy-fields lies the Sésia Valley, cutting its course between the industrial town of Biella and the moneyed resorts of Lake Maggiore. The Nebbiolo grape – Piedmont's and perhaps Italy's greatest red variety – has reigned supreme in the glacial soil of the hills that flank the Sésia river for centuries now, but its fabled past sits uneasily with the current reality. Of the million or so bottles of wine produced annually in the seven DOC zones in this area, only Gattinara, a recent DOCG, can make even a feeble claim to rank among the region's most noted wines. The other zones – Lessona, Bramaterra, Boca, Ghemme, Sizzano and Fara – dine out, like an aging film star, on the fact that they were once more famous than the new kids on the block, Barolo and Barbaresco. But that was a long, long time ago.

DORA BALTEA VALLEY

To the west of the Sésia lies the Dora Baltea, another river valley carved by the glaciers that swept down from the Alps during the last Ice Age to sculpt the face of northern Italy. Here, on the border between Piedmont and the Valle d'Aosta, is some of the steepest vineyard terrain in Europe. These mountain terraces form the Carema DOC zone, comprising about 40 hectares (100 acres) of Nebbiolo planted wherever the sheer granite face gives way to a patch of arable land. It is only in the longest, hottest summers that wines worthy of consideration are produced, but even then they are more prized for their delicate perfumes than for their structure.

To the south of the town of Carema, as the hills soften and the flatlands of the Po Valley once again come into view, the Nebbiolo's dominance is momentarily relaxed. Here, around the town of Caluso, a small amount of both dry and acidic, and rich, golden, sweet white wine is produced from the Erbaluce grape. After such a circular journey from Turin, through about 10 per cent of Piedmont's wine production, a glass of white wine is a welcome sight.

Suitably refreshed, it is time for the intrepid traveller to head off in search of the remaining 90 per cent of Piedmont's

vineyards. Since all other directions have been tried with only limited success, there's nothing for it but to head south-east. At first, the vineyards of Chieri and Castelnuovo Don Bosco seem nothing more than fool's gold, but after a while, as we move into the hills around the town of Asti, it is obvious that we have struck a rich, apparently endless, seam of the real thing.

MONFERRATO HILLS

As the Po and the Tanaro rivers head towards their confluence just north of the city of Alessandria, they embrace the steep, calcareous Monferrato hills. The southern, eastern and western slopes are covered with vineyards as far as the eye can see and the vines are trained low. Most of them are Moscato, for this is Asti country, and local vine growers have enjoyed rocketing sales of this sparkling wine – known these days simply as Asti rather than Asti Spumante. Indeed prices for Moscato Bianco grapes are sometimes the highest of any variety in Italy. Anyone who thinks Asti is an innocuous frothy fizz to keep troublesome maiden aunts quiet should buy a bottle from a good producer, or perhaps a bottle of the sweeter, semi-sparkling Moscato d'Asti, search out a shaded bower on a blisteringly hot afternoon, pour themselves a cool glass of this lovely wine and quietly contemplate how lucky they are to be alive. I mean it – the wine is that good.

The local red wine comes from the Barbera grape which, around Nizza Monferrato and Castel Boglione, is planted on the best vineyard sites and produces red wines of intense colour, soft tannins and, usually, mouthwatering acidity. Between them, Barbera and Moscato account for about 80 per cent of the wine produced in the Monferrato hills. But that's not the whole story. Piedmont is such a land of paradoxes and surprises. Barbera can make pretty serious wine if it wants to – full, burly, broad-shouldered stuff. But what about Freisa, Brachetto, Malvasia, or Ruché? These are four red varieties that make wine as care-free and happy-go-lucky as any in the world – as though they are determined to undermine the solemnity of many of Piedmont's reds. Freisa generally makes fizzy and lighter reds and has a delightful raspberry scent. Brachetto fairly bubbles with a joyous Muscat candyfloss and rose scent. Malvasia can also sparkle coyly and fill the room with the perfume of roses, while Ruché is still, pale red and delightfully grapy.

In comparison, the gushing purple-proud Dolcetto and the pale, rather herb-harsh Grignolino seem almost serious. The same producers who have ridden the Moscato wave have cautiously set their sights on Chardonnay, but with only limited success. They should persevere, however, for the other native white grape, the Cortese, seldom produces anything other than an acidic, neutral white, even in Gavi, its most successful spot in the south-east corner of the Monferrato hills. But it does say something about the shortage of so-called 'serious' dry whites in this red wine hunting ground that its frankly neutral wines have become excessively chic and expensive despite their lack of any discernible character.

LANGHE AND ROERO HILLS

This lack of decent dry whites has affected the Roero hills just north of Alba on the Tanaro river's left bank. Both the Arneis and the Favorita have suddenly sprung to prominence after generations of neglect, because, in the right hands, they can produce lighter, orchard-scented whites for a local market that is starved of them. The good examples are outnumbered by the bad. In any case, the light, sandy Roero soils are just as suited to Nebbiolo, but in a much lighter, more perfumed style than over the river in Barbaresco and Barolo. Given careful treatment, wine from this Nebbiolo d'Alba, or Roero as it can be called, is thirst-quenching and delightful.

In winter, snow-covered mountains provide a contrast to the bleak Barolo vineyards.

On the opposite side of the Tanaro Valley, south of the towns of Asti and Alba, lie the Langhe hills. Though smaller than the Monferrato hills in terms of territory and quantity of wine produced, the Langhe are far more important with regard to quality. Thanks largely to the renown of Barolo and Barbaresco, the hillside plots of clay and limestone are Italy's most expensive vineyard land. Though excellent Dolcetto and Barbera is to be found in the Langhe, the best sites are reserved for the Nebbiolo, which here rises to the full height of its remarkable powers.

Like any maestro, the Nebbiolo grape is a sensitive creature. Within the almost 1200 hectares (3000 acres) of vineyard that make up the Barolo zone are many minor variations in soil, altitude and exposure, each of which coaxes out a different facet of Nebbiolo's character. On the lighter chalky soils of the commune of La Morra in the north-west of the zone, for instance, the Nebbiolo displays the gentler, more graceful side of its nature, while on the heavier soils of Serralunga d'Alba in the south-east, rich in iron and limestone, its dark, brooding and explosively powerful character is more often to the fore. The same subtleties exists in the Barbaresco zone, where just under 500 hectares (1235 acres) of Nebbiolo are planted. Such a complex character, in such diverse zones, deserves further study (see page 160).

ALBA AND TRUFFLES

Any town that can boast two wines of such renown as Barolo and Barbaresco is fortunate indeed. Alba, however, is not content with just its wine. This small town of about 30,000 inhabitants is also noted for its food – which ranks with Italy's best – and the legendary white truffle found in the countryside around. This small white fungus is dug up near the roots of oak trees by specially trained dogs that cost almost as much as a plot of vines in the Langhe. Early morning hunts are followed by discreet trafficking in Alba's truffle market.

In October and November, the restaurants and hotels are packed, booked months in advance by those keen to undertake a culinary pilgrimage here. Each restaurant tends to have its own suppliers, and there are subtle yet noticeable variations in quality between truffles. Truffle can be grated over raw meat, risotto, pasta or in some cases, scrambled eggs. At its best, the truffle's memorable perfume is perfectly complemented by the equally evocative aromas of the best Barolos and Barbarescos, although the modern wines have more fruit and floral aroma and less mushroomy smell.

RED GRAPES
Piedmont boasts a number of distinctive red varieties including Barbera and Dolcetto and the famous Nebbiolo of Barolo and Barbaresco. Grignolino has a dedicated following and Freisa is returning to favour.

WHITE GRAPES
Moscato is most widely known, but Cortese and Arneis are more fashionable. Erbaluce is declining as Chardonnay increases.

CLIMATE
The continental climate has long cold winters, slightly moderated by the influence of rivers. Summers are warm, although hail can be a problem, while autumn is plagued by fog.

SOIL
Subsoils are generally calcareous marl with some areas of glacial moraine. Topsoils are clay, sand and gravel, and can be very fertile.

ASPECT
Nearly half of Piedmont is mountainous with vineyards frequently planted on high, steep slopes and terraces carefully angled to take best advantage of exposure.

Barolo & Barbaresco

RED GRAPES
Nebbiolo rules supreme in both Barolo and Barbaresco but it needs careful siting. Dolcetto and Barbera are more accommodating.

WHITE GRAPES
Although considered chiefly a red wine area, Moscato, Chardonnay and Sauvignon Blanc also thrive here.

CLIMATE
The continental climate is tempered by air currents flowing along the Tanaro Valley, bringing slightly cooler summer temperatures and allowing formation of autumn fog which causes Nebbiolo's slow ripening.

SOIL
The soil is generally fertile with calcareous bluish-grey marl in the west, and an iron-rich sand and limestone conglomerate in the east.

ASPECT
Most vineyards here face south-west to south-east on steep to very steep hills. The Barolo vineyards, at 250 to 450m (820 to 1500ft) are higher than the Barbaresco ones, which lie at between 200 and 350m (650 and 1150ft).

I used to think that Burgundy was exasperatingly difficult until I first visited Barolo and Barbaresco. Before that, and despite the urging of friendly Italophiles, I had failed to find the magic they purported to divine in a glass of Barolo. All I found was a hard, tannic wine, its fruit eviscerated by long aging in large, old oak casks.

Throughout the 1980s, I searched on numerous occasions for the complexity and greatness that was said to reside in the Nebbiolo grape. More often than not, though, I ended up in need of a dentist, my teeth and gums suffering from the full-frontal assault of tannin and acidity. As the decade progressed, however, things changed. My doubts, and Nebbiolo's wall of tannin, seemed to crumble at the same rate. In 1986, the 1982s were released, and for the first time I glimpsed something of the magic of the Nebbiolo grape. By the time the 85s came my way in 1989, I was convinced that the producers in Barolo and Barbaresco were finally managing to bottle the wine in time to capture Nebbiolo's delicate perfumes of roses, liquorice, violets, mint, cherries and game.

But as the wines improved, the differences between the various producers became more marked. Previously the stylistic variations had been masked by tannin and oxidation. Now I began to find that the new approach in the vineyards brought lower yields with better ripeness and riper tannins. In the cellar, the extraction of better tannins meant less aging in barrel and more in bottle, which in turn ensured greater freshness, releasing the many beautiful notes Nebbiolo is capable of sounding.

Soon afterwards, I visited Alba for the first time, keen to discover the source of these striking notes. First stop was Barolo. Alba lies on the banks of the Tanaro river, and the first slopes of the Langhe hills rise up from the narrow plain just to the south of the town. The road out of Alba is straight enough, but once you reach the small town of Gallo d'Alba, the road begins to twist and climb. It then splits into three, heading off towards Serralunga d'Alba, Castiglione Falletto and Monforte d'Alba, or La Morra and Barolo.

Being a moderate soul, I took the middle road and began climbing towards Castiglione Falletto. I got a sore neck, and almost drove into the ditch on several occasions, as I tried to get my bearings and distinguish the south- and south-west-facing slopes. Those vineyards with the finest exposure are planted with Nebbiolo. Those with an easterly or south-east aspect are planted with varieties like Dolcetto and Barbera, or with white grapes like Chardonnay.

As the road evens out, you get a spectacular view of the whole of Barolo. To your right are the La Morra and Barolo vineyards, while to your left are those of Serralunga. Snow-capped mountains loom behind the hilltop town of La Morra, and the lighter, whiter chalky soil of the vineyards that stretches below seems to reflect the snow.

The soil in the western part of Barolo is a Tortonian calcareous marl, while in Serralunga in the east, there is Helvetian marl with higher levels of lime and iron. Because of the Nebbiolo's sensitivity to soil, the wines from the former tend to be lighter and more fragrant than the powerful, tannic wines which characterize Serralunga. The spur which runs through Castiglione Falletto to the southerly vineyards in the commune of Monforte d'Alba produces wines that combine the power of Serralunga with some of the grace of La Morra and Barolo.

Barolo's 1190 hectares (2940 acres) are split between just over 1200 growers. Such fragmentation of the vineyards results in as many different approaches to wine-making as there are plots of land, producing a complex and confusing mosaic of wines. Old-timers remember when Nebbiolo, the last grape to be harvested in the Langhe, would be left in its fermentation vat, in contact with its skins, until after Christmas. The resulting wines would be so tough that they required aging in large *botti* (casks) for anything up to ten years before the tannins had softened sufficiently for the wine to be bottled. By that time, however, the wine would have oxidized. 'People used to compliment a wine by saying it smells just like Marsala,' recalls one old producer.

In the 1960s, changes took place in the cellars of Barolo and Barbaresco as younger producers like Renato Ratti, Angelo Gaja and Aldo Conterno travelled to France's wine regions and glimpsed a different approach to wine-making. Cleaner, fresher and softer wines were the aim, though disputes raged about how to achieve them. Some proposed little contact with the skins and even less with oak; others proposed substituting small oak barriques for the large *botti*; others simply advised reducing yields and cleaning up their act in the cellar.

This debate led to the grouping of top producers into traditionalist and modernist camps. The complexity of the zones and of Nebbiolo itself, as well as the approach of different growers, however, defies such a simplistic solution. And in Barbaresco, where lower vineyards and a closer proximity to the Tanaro results in a warmer mesoclimate and, therefore, an earlier harvest, the wines are in any case different in character.

BAROLO'S TERRA BIANCA

Barolo's famous terra bianca, or white earth, is a milky calcareous marl bearing reflective and alkaline qualities. To the west of the town of Barolo, near the impressively sited Castello della Volta, the younger Tortonian soil is bluish in colour from magnesium and manganese, which stimulate growth and flavour, producing elegant, early drinking wines. The land to the east has the older Helvetian soil, more beige-yellow in colour from rust, producing powerful, long-lasting reds. Between these, running north-east from the town, is the Cannubi ridge (*connubio* means marriage or union), with the perfect combination of soil producing wines with the finest characteristics of both areas, the strength and staying power of the east mixed with the finesse and delicacy of the west. Owning vines here is a mark of prestige.

Vineyards producing elegant and perfumed reds
Cannubi vineyards – both elegant and strong wines
Vineyards producing powerful, long-lasting reds
CASTELLO DELLA VOLTA
BAROLO
'CRU' BUSSIA SOPRANA
Talloria dell'Annunziata
Bussia
Elevation in metres
400
300
200
younger Tortonian soil
older Helvetian soil
NW
Vertical exaggération 2.4 times horizontal scale
SE

If the overall quality of the wines coming out of cellars in Barolo and Barbaresco today are anything to go by, then the debate has been healthy. Not only are the wines much better than they were 10 or 15 years ago, but the growers have established themselves as a great force in the region. In the past, merchants would buy wines from numerous growers and blend them together, in a similar fashion to a Champagne *négociant*, to produce a wine that represented a house style. The power of Serralunga would be softened by the grace of La Morra in a fine example of this generic style of Barolo.

The improvements that have taken place in the vineyard and the cellar have led to a new emphasis on the wines of individual communes, and within these communes, single vineyards. Specific terms such as *Bric* (hilltop), *Sori* (slope), and *Vigna* (vineyard) have begun to appear on the labels – with a grape like Nebbiolo, provenance cannot be overstated.

The future appears bright for the producers of Barolo and Barbaresco. Living standards have improved from a decade or so ago and growers are diversifying into non-Italian varieties, for example, Cabernet Sauvignon, Syrah, Sauvignon Blanc and Chardonnay. But success has brought conservatism. Many of the younger growers seem to think there is only one way to make a good Barolo: early picking and short maceration followed by aging in barrique.

It would be a shame if this resulted in a lack of diversity, since Barolo and Barbaresco have everything else going for them, and I can only hope there is no slowing down of the kind of experimentation which in the past couple of decades has improved these wines beyond all recognition.

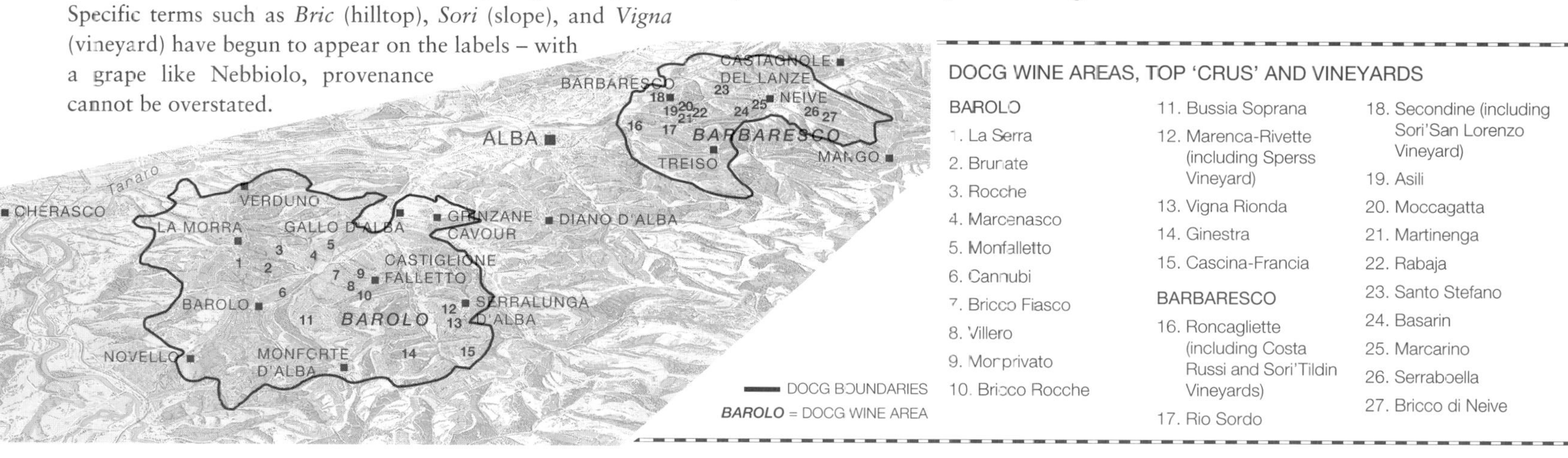

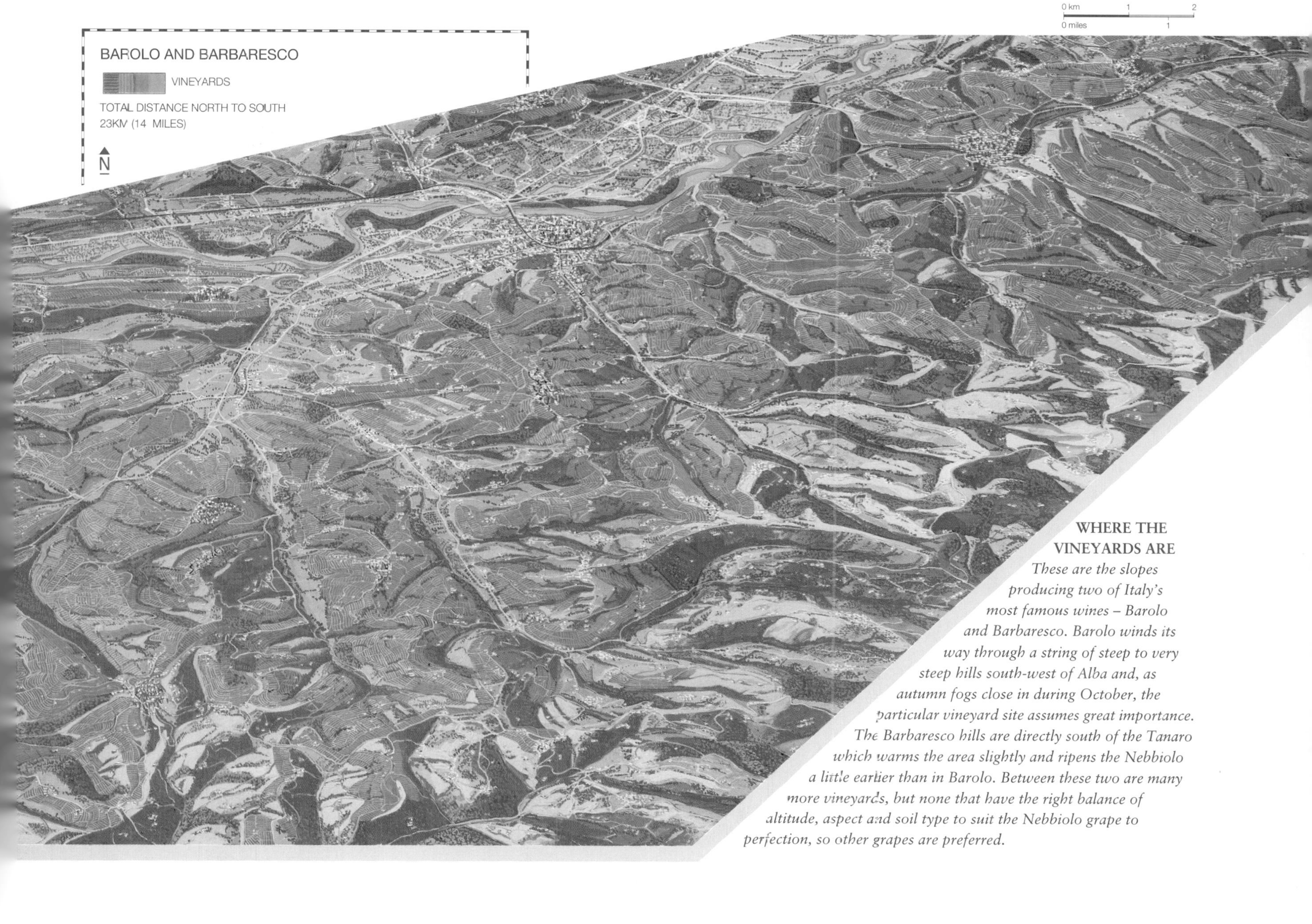

0 km 1 2
0 miles 1

BAROLO AND BARBARESCO

VINEYARDS

TOTAL DISTANCE NORTH TO SOUTH 23KM (14 MILES)

N

WHERE THE VINEYARDS ARE
These are the slopes producing two of Italy's most famous wines – Barolo and Barbaresco. Barolo winds its way through a string of steep to very steep hills south-west of Alba and, as autumn fogs close in during October, the particular vineyard site assumes great importance. The Barbaresco hills are directly south of the Tanaro which warms the area slightly and ripens the Nebbiolo a little earlier than in Barolo. Between these two are many more vineyards, but none that have the right balance of altitude, aspect and soil type to suit the Nebbiolo grape to perfection, so other grapes are preferred.

North-East Italy

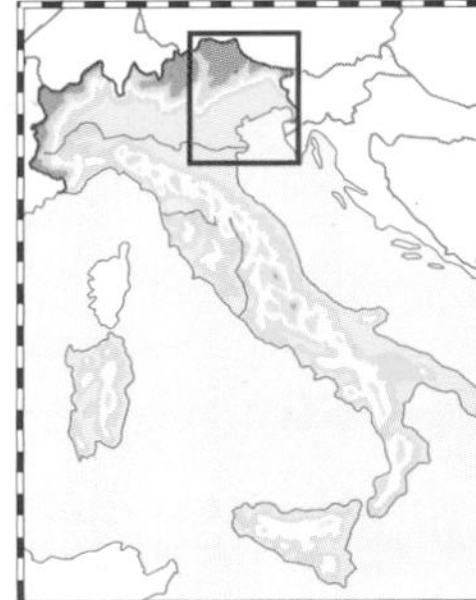

Soave, Valpolicella, Pinot Grigio. Each of these wines, virtually synonymous with Italian wine as a whole, is produced in north-east Italy – yet this is perhaps the least Italian of all parts of the country. To the north is Austria, to the east Slovenia, and both have contributed to the diversity of culture, peoples, food and wine that exists in north-east Italy. Names of winemakers like Gravner and Haas hardly evoke images of pasta and Chianti, yet both are as Italian as Pavarotti and Fellini.

North-east Italy is a region that has been at the crossroads of Europe since at least Roman times. Merchants, scholars and soldiers coming from the north or east would pass through this part of the country on their way to Rome, Florence or Milan, as would the great traders of Venice, the city that controlled much of the world's commerce in the fourteenth and fifteenth centuries. Each of these visitors left a legacy that we are enjoying today. The Malvasia grape of Friuli was undoubtedly brought back from Greece by Venetian merchants, as perhaps was Ribolla, which today can still be found in the Peloponnese. And the French varieties so prevalent here, Chardonnay, Cabernet and Merlot, owe their presence not to the fact that they fell off a passing bandwagon in the past decade but that they were brought back from France by horse and cart in the wake of the Napoleonic invasion almost two centuries ago.

Even earlier than that, other 'foreign' varieties were being planted in what is today part of north-east Italy – before the early part of the twentieth century, both Friuli-Venezia Giulia and the Alto Adige were part of the Austro-Hungarian Empire. The hills of Friuli were filled with varieties like Riesling, Müller-Thurgau and, later, Sauvignon Blanc and the Pinots Blanc and Noir (called Pinot Bianco and Nero in Italy). Wines made from these grapes were particularly highly regarded by the Habsburg court. Such a ready market for their wares gave the grape growers of Friuli an incentive to produce quality, but this was removed when the region joined Italy in 1919.

The quality of the wines from the north-east shot back to its previous peak when, in the 1960s and 1970s, increasing wealth among the people of prosperous cities like Milan and Venice created a clamouring market for the varietals from the hills of Collio and the Colli Orientali. The same factors – climate, soil and grape variety – that produced the wines enjoyed by the Habsburg monarchs successfully came back into play.

Alto Adige – or Süd-Tirol as most of the inhabitants prefer to call their region – wasn't at all happy to be detached from Austria in 1919 as part of the peace treaty. They were even less happy as the determined attempt to Italianize their towns and villages by Mussolini meant great train-loads of immigrants from further south in Italy being dumped on their doorsteps. Place names were Italianized and the Tirolean German that had been spoken for hundreds of years was banned.

Nowadays this mountain province seems a charming and contented place, but there is even still a simmering undercurrent of Tirolean nationalism, and the majority of the people still prefer to speak German, and follow Austrian customs. One benefit of being detached from Austria could perhaps be seen in Alto Adige's tourist industry as German, Swiss and Austrian holidaymakers crowd through the Brenner Pass and fill the locals' coffers with gold. But one side-effect of this is that the majority of Alto Adige's vineyards are for red grapes in an area that would seem brilliantly suited to high-quality whites. It's those tourists again. With traditions of very light, mild reds in their own countries, they have encouraged the wholesale plantation of the Vernatsch or Schiava grape to produce enormous volumes of semi-red wine of completely forgettable quality. But the white wines are gaining ground and, though often derided in Italy itself as having too much flavour and perfume, are proving well-suited to palates elsewhere in Europe and America.

North-east Italy is protected from cool north winds by the Julian pre-Alps to the north. From the hills just outside Gorizia the snow-capped peaks of this protective barrier can be seen standing guard on the border with Austria. In the east, the tree-covered hills were once bisected by the southern reaches of the Iron Curtain, while to the south lies the Adriatic, its gentle waters providing a moderating influence on the continental

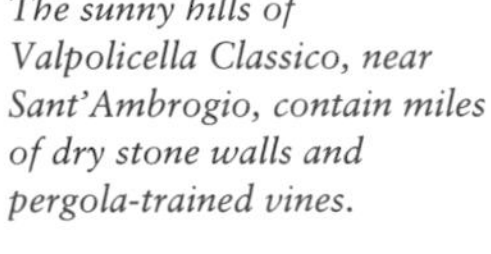

The sunny hills of Valpolicella Classico, near Sant'Ambrogio, contain miles of dry stone walls and pergola-trained vines.

climate that would otherwise prevail here. The hills of Gorizia and Collio are the source of the best wines in this region: rich and perfumed varietals like Pinot Grigio, Tocai Friulano and Pinot Bianco that often stake competing claims to the title of Italy's best dry white wine – and rightly so. Moving further west, away from the hills and onto the plains, the soil becomes more fertile, the vines more prodigious and the wines increasingly insipid. This trend continues and reaches its lowest point in the Piave Valley. The Piave, one of the two great rivers in the north-east (the other is the Adige), flows from the Alps through an alluvial plain in the eastern Veneto into the Adriatic north of Venice. Its fertile plain produces a great deal of the bulk wine used to pad out the blends of the Veronese merchants to the west.

THE VENETO

Bordered to the south by the Po river and to the west by Lake Garda, the Veneto accounts for about 10 per cent of Italy's wine, ranging from the gushing torrents of Piave to the intense trickles that emerge from the hills of Valpolicella. As well as Valpolicella, perplexingly one of Italy's best-known red wines, the region is also home to Soave, Bardolino, Breganze, Bianco di Custoza and huge amounts of Pinot Grigio (see page 166).

The best wines of the Veneto, including the Classico (or hilly) areas of Soave and Valpolicella, come from the chain of hills that rises from the northern rim of the Po Valley. The valley itself is the home of most of the basic stuff that makes the region such an important player in the wine mass-market. The heat here in summer is unbearable, the temperatures often rising higher than those in the low-lying Salento peninsula 900 km (560 miles) to the south. It is only as you move into the hills that relief from the heat is granted, not only for people but also for vines. The cooler night time temperatures up in the hills is one of the factors behind the finer wines produced here.

In the hills on the western shores of Lake Garda, the shimmering leaves of olive trees provide a rare Mediterranean touch to this northerly region. While the rest of north-east Italy labours under the hot summers and cold winters that characterize a continental climate, the proximity of Lake Garda moderates the winter temperatures here to such an extent as to make this the northernmost point in Europe where the olive is cultivated.

FRIULI-VENEZIA GIULIA

The vineyards of Friuli-Venezia Giulia may be a great deal closer to the Mediterranean, with many of the vines planted on low land running down towards the Adriatic and the Gulf of Trieste, but they don't feel balmy too often. With the Julian and the Carnic pre-Alps directly to the north there is a continual seesaw of air currents between the cold, wet mountains and the sea that keeps the region mild and damp by Italian standards, with fairly continual breezes (see page 168).

TRENTINO-ALTO ADIGE

The Mediterranean influence quickly recedes once past the northern shores of Lake Garda. The same glacier that carved the lake also cut an almighty swathe through the Dolomites to the north. The result – the Adige river and its valley – is for the most part cast in shadow by the steep, granite walls of the mountains. This fertile valley runs south from the border with Austria, taking in Alto Adige and Trentino. For political purposes, the region is known as Trentino-Alto Adige, but the two have little in common. A strong Germanic influence remains in Alto Adige but grapes like Riesling, Silvaner and Müller-Thurgau are slowly giving way to Chardonnay and Pinot Grigio, though Schiava (Vernatsch to the locals) remains the most widely planted variety – thanks to an Austrian affinity for light, innocuous reds that this variety excels in producing.

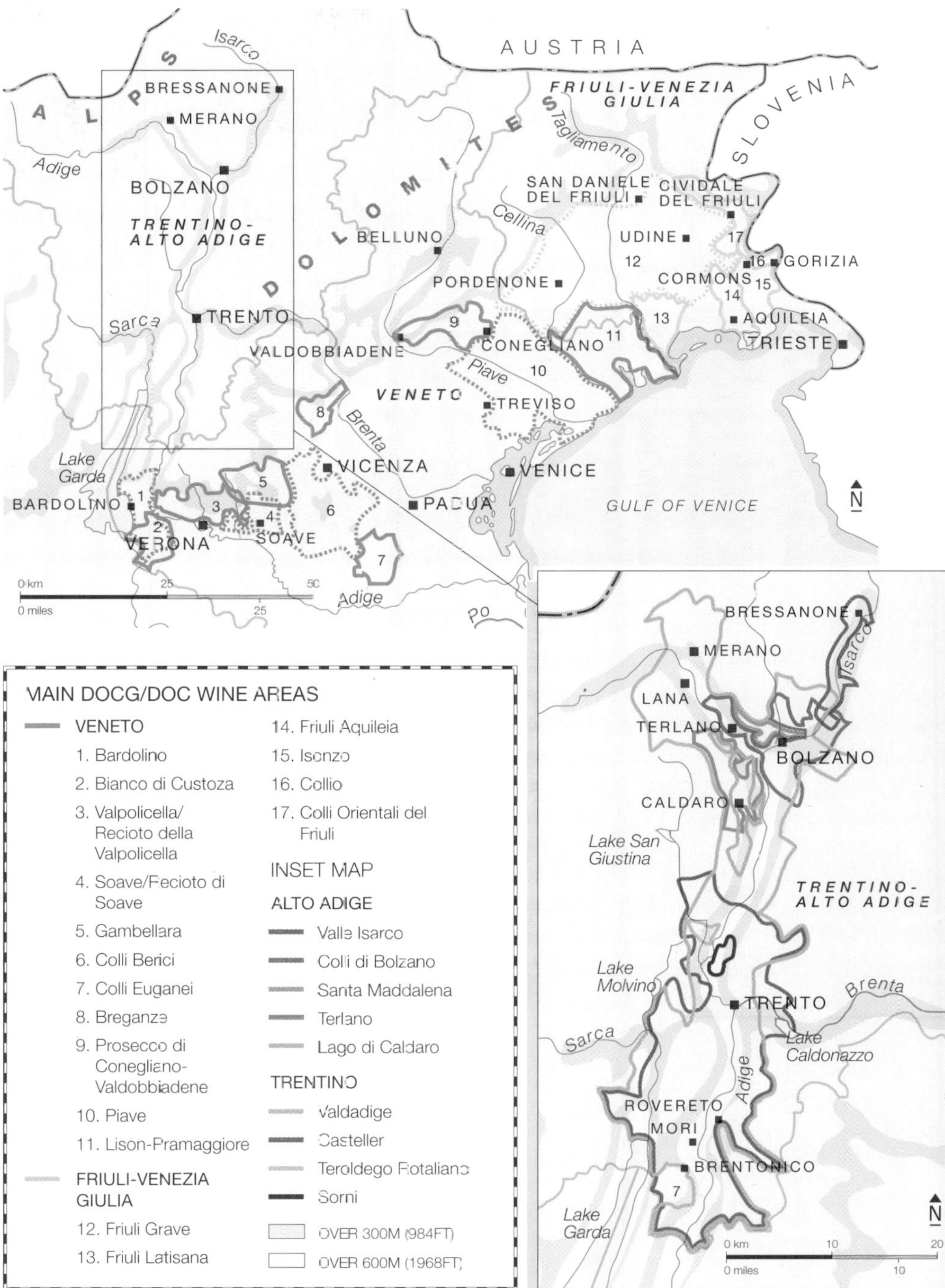

The snow-dusted Dolomites often serve to convince people that this is an area to which the term 'cool-climate viticulture' must be applied. Anybody checking the temperature chart in an Italian newspaper in July will know that this need not be the case: Bolzano is often the hottest place in the whole country. As elsewhere in Italy, altitude here can play an important role in moderating extreme temperatures, but, unfortunately, too many of the vineyards here are on the valley floor. One reason why Trentino wines have often seemed flat and dull is that so many of their vineyards are on fertile valley floor land: most of the valley floor in Alto Adige is given over to apples.

At their best, the wines of the Süd-Tirol are fragrant and intense, but often lack the weight that the same varietals display in other parts of Italy, a factor local producers attribute to their northern European approach to viticulture. If by northern European they mean a desire to produce more litres of wine per vine than nature would normally intend, as is the habit in so many of Germany's vineyards, then I'd have to agree. But the great German vineyards produce wines of superb intensity. It's the same in Alto Adige and Trentino: where there's a will to excel, the vineyards and the grape varieties are all there waiting to be pushed to the limit (see page 164 for more detail).

TRENTINO-ALTO ADIGE

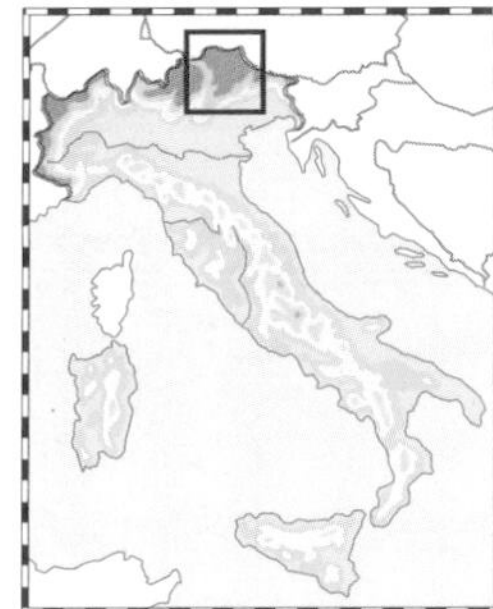

RED GRAPES
The most significant local varieties are Vernatsch (Schiava), Lagrein, Teroldego and Marzemino. Cabernet Sauvignon is making ground as Cabernet Franc, Merlot and Pinot Noir begin to decline in popularity.

WHITE GRAPES
Although native Traminer and Nosiola remain locally important, Chardonnay and Pinot Grigio continue their relentless march. Müller-Thurgau, Sauvignon Blanc and Moscato also produce wines of good quality.

CLIMATE
The north has a continental Alpine climate with great temperature fluctuations. Summers can be very hot, especially on the valley floor. Trentino is less extreme though slightly warmer overall.

SOIL
Soils of sub-regions vary, but generally they are infertile, light and well-draining. The subsoil is limestone with alluvial deposits of gravel, sand or clay.

ASPECT
The mountainous terrain means that most vineyards are found in river valleys where they are often planted on steep terraces.

IN A PERFECT WORLD the most beautiful wines would come from the most beautiful vineyards. In which case, Italy's reputation for wine would probably soar over that of any other nation because she has more heavenly vineyard sites than any other country I can think of. There's a reasonable chance that, if sheer scenic splendour were relevant, the Trentino-Alto Adige region would be looked upon as the greatest wine region in the world. The Dolomites and the southern Alps exert such a glorious heart-stopping influence that I don't believe there is a single bad view in the entire province. Certainly I can't think of one vineyard that isn't a scenic delight, either because it's nestling beneath the steep peaks, or because it's clinging improbably to scraps of land halfway up the giddy slopes.

In such circumstances, it's easy to bask in the midday sun on the shores of the Lake Caldaro, or perch precariously among the vine pergolas of Santa Maddelena so high above the roofs of Bolzano that the hubbub and roar of this busy city is lost in the still mountain air, and think – I don't care what the wine tastes like, I'm just glad to be alive. If it's easy for the visitor, it's even easier for the grower. Such is the tourist trade, especially in Alto Adige, the northern half of the region, and so thirsty are the visitors who throng south from Austria, Germany and Switzerland, that few producers ever feel the need to strike out for excellence. They can make more money the easy way – by maximizing their yields and selling the pleasant but light and dilute wines for healthy sums to the tourists. Tourism does great things for the prosperity of a region, but it rarely does much for the quality of the wine.

Yet Trentino-Alto Aldige has all the prerequisites of a great wine region. Well, two wine regions really, because Trentino and Alto Adige should not really be linked at all, since they have very different histories and personalities. Trentino runs north from Lake Garda to the Dolomites above the town of Trento. It is historically linked with northern Italy, in particular the ancient republic of Venice and before that the Etruscans.

Alto Adige is a very different matter. The boundary between the two is very precise, as the Adige Valley closes in like a pincer at Salorno, the high mountain walls warning off intruders from the south. North of here, the majority of the inhabitants do not use the title Alto Adige – they call their homeland Süd-Tirol (South Tyrol), because until 1919 when it was traded to Italy as part of the spoils of World War One,

0 km 1 2
0 miles 1

Süd-Tirol belonged to the Austro-Hungarian Empire, and to this day it is bilingual with a strong inclination towards the German. All the towns have both Italian and German names. Travelling round the region you're not imagining things if you think that German features rather more prominently on road signs than Italian. Was that really someone wearing Lederhosen and a Tyrolean hat I just saw? It almost certainly was. And dumplings, smoked pork belly and sauerkraut are indeed what you see on the menu. It may not seem quite right sitting here reading this atlas, but I tell you, it does seem right in Bolzano or Merano or on the shores of Lake Caldaro. And what is more, with such food, the light fluffy reds of the region are exactly the right wines. All the wines are labelled in Italian and German too but since most of the wine trade is with German speakers from the north, many of the bottles sport German titles in far bigger letters than their Italian ones.

And the Alto Adige wine tradition is strongly Germanic. The most widely planted grape is the Schiava or Vernatsch that produces a soft, mild, light red that can be absolutely delightful from a good grower but is normally sold off in large bottles as the most innocuous of red table wine. White grapes like Riesling, Silvaner, Müller-Thurgau and Traminer – named after the local town Tramin (or Termeno) – abound. There is also the French Pinot family, red and white, as well as Chardonnay and Cabernet, and the excellent local Lagrein. But as you can see, this is a wine region with a culture in no way related to the Italy of further south, except that yields are relentlessly high, and co-operatives and merchants dominate production. Alto Adige was the very first Italian area to react to the wave of modern ideas and techniques that swept the world in the 1970s and 1980s. Blessed with an endless variety of infertile, well-drained, south-facing mountain slopes, some of Italy's longest sunshine hours, yet altitudes that stretch from 250 to 1000m (820 to 3280ft) generally leading to warm days and chilly nights during the ripening season, it seemed that Alto Adige, with its aromatic white grape varieties, and Trentino, a little warmer and lower and ideally suited to international varieties like Chardonnay, Pinot Bianco and Merlot, were set to lead the Italian Renaissance.

Yet it never quite happened. Friuli, to the north-east of Venice, took over the characterful white wine mantle – you have to remember that most Italians don't like their white wines to have much flavour, which could be one reason for the false dawn in Trentino-Alto Adige. Although it had seemed that the protected south-facing suntraps in the hills and the warm gravel banks on the valley floor would produce thrilling reds, few materialized and Tuscany and Piedmont easily saw off any challenge to their authority by the end of the 1980s. Alto Adige's finer reds were frequently from its own Lagrein grape, while many of the most interesting Trentino reds come from her local Marzemino and Teroldego varieties. It's lovely to see indigenous varieties surviving, but the potential is there for so much more. Apart from a few gorgeous sweet wines from the Muscat grape in Alto Adige and from the Nosiola in Trentino, the only area of activity in which the region has made as much of its potential as it should is in high-quality sparkling wines. Certainly, conditions are ideal – both in the vineyard, and for the winemaker, during the long cold winters when the wines can slowly mature. Trentino fizz is some of the best in Italy. But in table wines, despite the sporadic signs of determination on the part of producers like De Tarczal, Foradori and Pojer & Sandri in Trentino, and Lageder, Grai, Tiefenbrunner and Walch in Alto Adige, the ease of catering to the tourist market still generally beats going the extra mile for excellence.

The steep slopes of Santa Maddalena above Bolzano produce light but tasty reds from the Schiava grape.

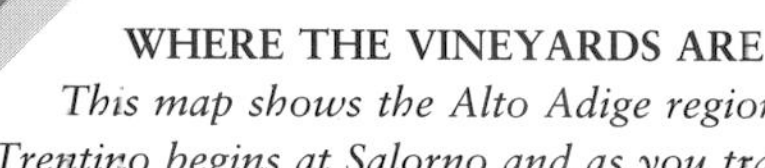

WHERE THE VINEYARDS ARE

This map shows the Alto Adige region: Trentino begins at Salorno and as you travel south, the mountains become less commanding and the fertile valley floor is planted more frequently with high-yielding vines. But in the Alto Adige, one of the points of pride is that the valley floors are given over to fruit crops, primarily apples, while the slopes are dominated by vines. The southern part of this map shows this well: vineyards cram the western slopes between Termeno and Salorno and seek out the sunny nooks and plateaux to the east above Salorno as far as Ora, and down on the flat fertile plain are packed some of the most important apple orchards in the EU. The ancient pergola system of vine-training makes for picturesque vineyards here but gives high yields of grapes that are not always fully ripened. More modern, quality-conscious training systems are slowly being introduced, but it shows how wonderfully suited the area is to the vine that the best wines can still be so good. Delicious snappy light whites are grown at the top of the Isarco Valley near the Brenner Pass. The sunbaked slopes above Bolzano produce fragrant Santa Maddelena reds; and the Adige Valley up towards Terlano and Merano produces masses of lighter red, while the mountainsides reaching down to Salorno can produce exciting whites.

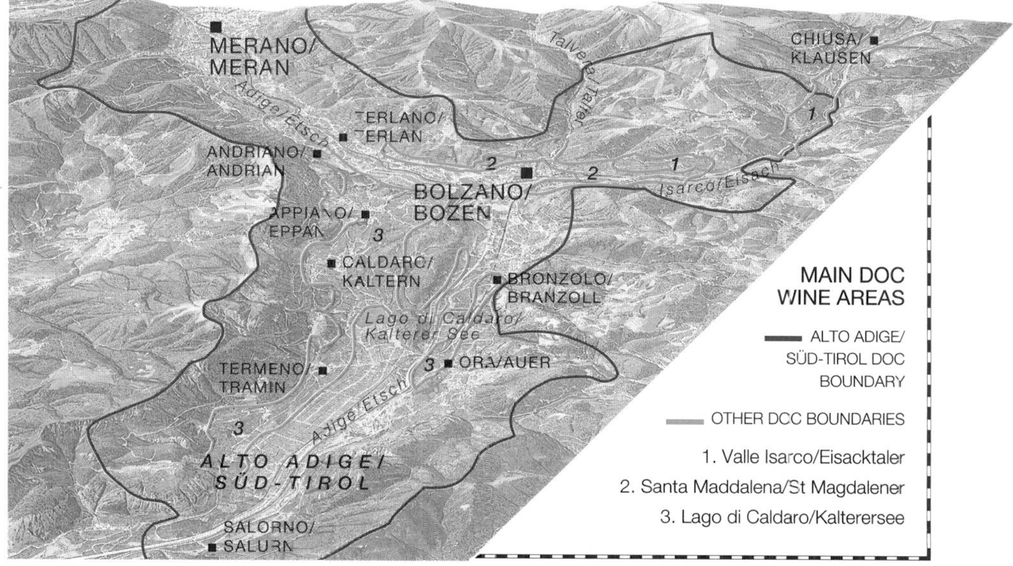

VENETO

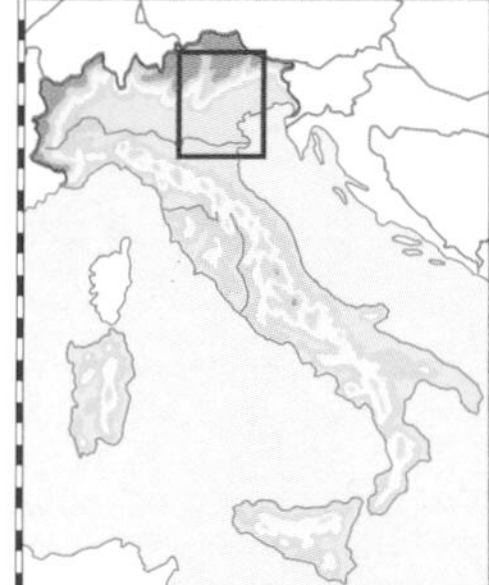

IT IS LIKELY THAT one of your first experiences of Italian wine was a bottle of Veneto wine. It could have been Soave, Bardolino or Valpolicella, or Bianco, Rosso, Merlot or Tocai del Veneto, or even a Pinot Grigio, Chardonnay or Cabernet. For not only does the Veneto produce a vast array of wines, but it also churns out a huge volume, from vineyards all over the region, from the shores of Lake Garda in the west to the Piave Valley in the east, from the alpine foothills in the north that stretch as far as Trentino to the dull, monotonous flatlands of the Po Valley to the south. Quality varies from anonymous whites and weedy reds to the few outstanding wines produced in the Valpolicella and Soave Classico zones in the hills that flank Verona.

Although greater Italian reds are found in Tuscany and Piedmont, no other region can produce such a range of styles at a consistently decent average level of quality and charge relatively little for them. The styles of wine, from native grapes in the west like red Corvina and white Garganega to international stars like Chardonnay and Pinot Grigio, Cabernet and Merlot, are generally soft, accessible and reassuringly international, while the consistent quality comes from the presence of one of Italy's wine schools at Conegliano, in north-east Veneto. The school has trained a generation of winemakers who have marched forth to transform the region's bountiful crop into clean, faultless wine. And, even if coupled with anonymity, this consistency has been popular with consumers.

Names like Valpolicella and Soave are world famous and, initially viewed as good-value wines in the 1960s, they soon helped forge for Italian wine the cheap and cheerful image it has come to acquire. Despite this image, the Classico vineyards of both zones, up in the alpine foothills that spring suddenly from the northern lip of the vast Po Valley, remain the finest in the region, both in terms of current quality and future potential. Both Classico zones must be distinguished from the wines of the plains which can only use the straight Valpolicella and Soave names. On the plains the soil is richer in gravel, and as a result, irrigation is more widely used and therefore yields are higher. The wines are consequently more dilute than those from the stony, limestone hills of the Classico zones.

In Soave Classico, the Garganega grape reigns supreme. Traditionally supplemented with Trebbiano di Soave to add perfume to the wines, it is now blended with Chardonnay or Sauvignon by the best producers in all but a few cases. From producers like Pieropan (one of the few still to use Trebbiano di Soave), Anselmi, Pra and Suavia, these wines have an attractive purity of fruit and understated perfumes, and are never better than when drunk with fresh seafood.

The quality of Soave has increased more rapidly than that of Valpolicella Classico in recent years, though the potential for quality in the latter zone far outstrips that in Soave. The steep slopes of the Valpolicella Classico zone, the climate of which is tempered by its proximity to Lake Garda, are ideally suited to the Corvina grape. Unfortunately, bad practices that became established in the post-war years resulted in the Corvina being diluted by the Molinara and Rondinella grapes. The high percentage of Molinara used and the fact that the vines are traditionally trained high in a pergola form that can, in many cases, lead to excessive yields and a further dilution of quality are why many people think of Valpolicella as a light red wine. When the Corvina vine is properly trained, however, the wine has good colour, richness and finesse.

In sites where the proportion of Corvina is high, or where good viticulture is practised, the wines have much more depth and intensity, and can rival a good Chianti for concentration.

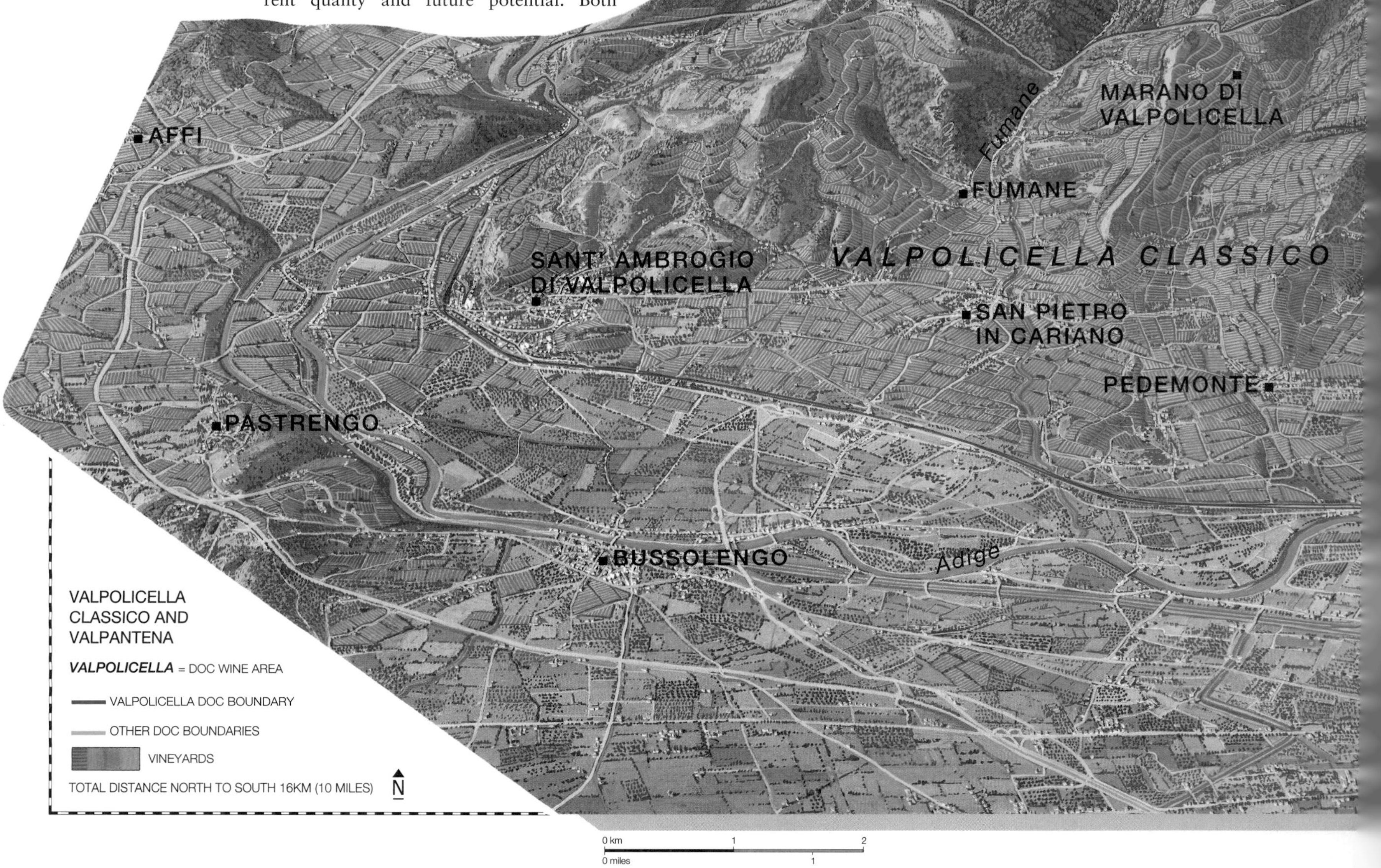

Traditionally, such concentration was achieved by refermenting the young wines on the skins of the dried grapes used in the production of Amarone and Recioto. These refermented wines, known as *ripasso*, had better alcohol and weight than the younger wines, but were often coarser, for the technique is rather like making a cup of tea with a used tea bag: all the goodness has been extracted first time around.

The great wines of Valpolicella, however, are the dry Amarone and sweet Recioto. The grapes (primarily Corvina) are picked early and laid out on mats to dry until the February following the vintage. This drying process concentrates sugars, acids and flavours, and the resulting wines, rich, intense and alcoholic, are, at their best, unique in the world of wine.

To the west of Valpolicella, across the Adige in the western corner of Veneto, the glacial shores of Lake Garda are carpeted with vines. The red grapes, a similar mix to those in Valpolicella, are used here to make Bardolino which is lighter in style than its more illustrious neighbour, thanks to the glacial soil. The white wine of the zone is Bianco di Custoza which is a surprisingly characterful blend of Garganega, Tocai, Trebbiano and Cortese grapes.

To the east of Valpolicella, the same range of alpine foothills plays host to the Breganze DOC. North of Vicenza, it incorporates a diverse range of varietals including Tocai, Pinot Grigio, Pinot Bianco, Vespaiolo, Merlot, Cabernet and Pinot Nero. Further east, the Prosecco grape crowds out all other competitors on the hills around Conegliano, where it produces a decent enough fizz that charms the tired palates of Venice. To the south of Vicenza, the volcanic hills are home to the Colli Berici and Colli Euganei DOC zones, where a similarly wide range of varietals is used to give wines which have, at their best, more intensity than Breganze manages to achieve.

In the far eastern reaches of the Veneto, the hills give way to the broader plains of the Piave Valley which produces a seemingly endless source of Merlot and Cabernet. Beyond Piave, astride the border with Friuli, the Lison-Pramaggiore zone has an affinity for Cabernet, Merlot, Tocai and Pinot Grigio, which are reliable if rarely distinguished wines.

RED GRAPES
Corvina, Molinara and Rondinella are used for Valpolicella and Bardolino. Merlot and Cabernet are popular in the Veneto.

WHITE GRAPES
Garganega is grown everywhere but is best known in Soave. Trebbiano is widely used for blending, and Prosecco makes sparkling wines of great popularity.

CLIMATE
The influence of Lake Garda and protection of the alpine foothills combine to produce a generally mild climate, but the plains can be hot in summer.

SOIL
Around Lake Garda is a mixture of moraine, sandy gravel and clay. Further east there is calcareous clay and limestone. Piave has sand and clay over gravel with finer loam near the Adriatic.

ASPECT
The best vineyards are on hillsides as the plains are too fertile for good quality wine production.

WHERE THE VINEYARDS ARE *The best Valpolicella vineyards are in the steep hills north of Verona in the Classico and Valpantena zones. The altitude in these hills ranges from 100 to 400m (330 to 1300ft) above sea level and the soil is full of limestone pebbles. The Classico zone consists of three main valleys: Negrar, Marano and Fumane. All the valleys are open to the north and act as funnels for the cool wind that blows off the Lessini mountains to the north. Fumane is the most open of the three valleys, and as a result it receives more light, which helps the grapes to achieve greater ripeness, and gives wines that are more robust in style. Marano is the most closed valley, but because far fewer of its vineyards have southerly exposures, the wines are lighter and finer, and tend to have a higher level of acidity. Negrar has some of the best vineyard sites (Jago and Moron) in the whole Classico zone, but a higher percentage of Molinara in the vineyards here tends to obscure the true quality of the sites which, at their best, produce fine, powerful wines that age wonderfully. To the west, Sant'Ambrogio is classified as a semi-valley, its vineyards more exposed to the moderating effect of nearby Lake Garda (just off the left of the map) than to the northerly winds.*

To the east, the Valpantena is the only valley that has similar climatic and soil conditions to those in the Classico zone. The cool breeze blowing down the valley helps to produce supremely elegant wines, the best of which has always been Bertani's, whose estate at Grezzana has some outstanding vineyards.

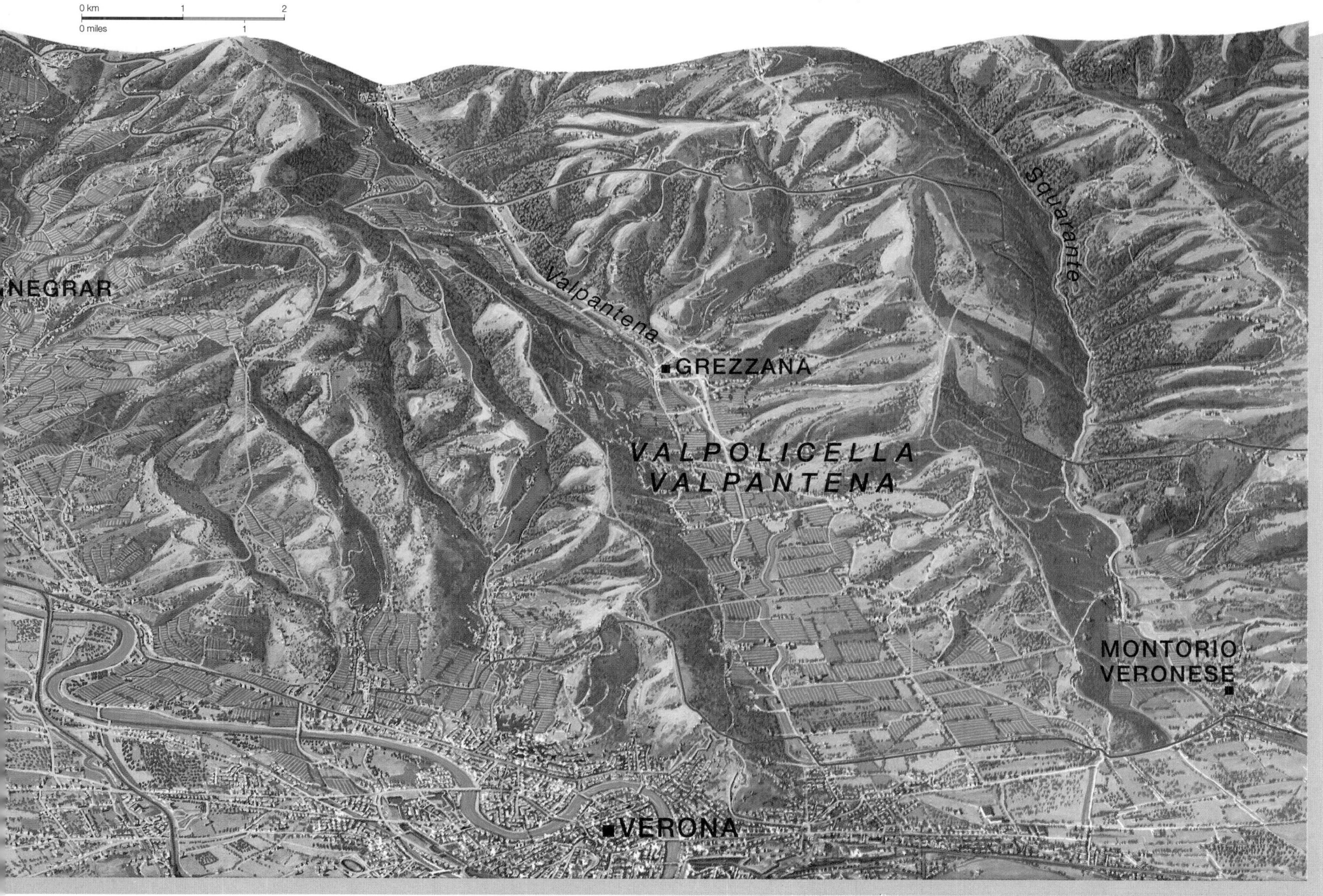

Friuli-Venezia Giulia

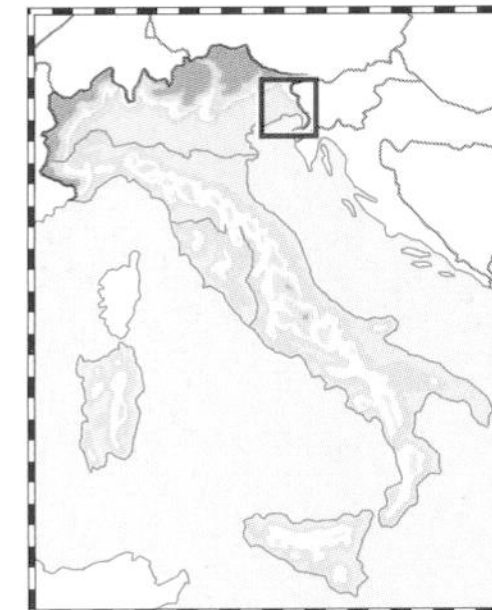

Tucked into the north-eastern corner of the country, stretching from the plains of the eastern Veneto to the borders with Austria and Slovenia, Friuli is a relative newcomer to united Italy as it was, until 1919, part of the Austro-Hungarian Empire. Perhaps because of this, the locals view themselves as hard-working, constant northerners who are different from their more fickle, flighty neighbours elsewhere in Italy.

There is a certain truth in this as far as making wine goes. Over the past couple of decades, Friuli white wines (which account for approximately two-thirds of DOC production in the region) have become a byword for modernity and consistency. Forty per cent of all wine produced here is entitled to DOC status (the national average is 10 per cent). Thanks to its Austro-Hungarian legacy and its proximity to Eastern Europe, Friuli has a wide range of both imported and native grape varieties. And, as an added bonus, it has some outstanding vineyard sites, mainly in the Collio and Colli Orientali hills.

Friuli's northern borders are defined by the Julian and Carnic pre-Alps, which make up just over 40 per cent of the total land area. These inhospitable peaks hold no prospects for the vine, although, as well as forming a stunning backdrop to the vineyards, they do trap the cool wind, the Bora, that blows off the Gulf of Trieste. The Bora blows from the south across the rest of Friuli, which is comprised largely of the Venetian Plain and the gentle hills along the Slovenian border which are home to the Collio and Colli Orientali zones. The cool Tramontana wind that blows off the mountains from the north also moderates the climate. These two zones, though geographically identical, are divided by provincial boundaries. The sandstone and marl hills are flecked with limestone, the soil being nicely friable, well-drained and easy to work. Terraces, known as *ronchi*, have been carved into the hills in order to pander to the vine's temperamental nature and to facilitate work in the vineyards.

The numerous cultural influences to which Friuli has been subjected over the centuries have resulted in a multitude of primarily white grape varieties of German, French, Italian and Eastern Europe origins. Riesling and Traminer perform well – though, rather like a beetroot-red northerner on a sun-drenched beach, they seem to hanker for the cooler reaches of their German homeland. Pinot Grigio, Pinot Bianco, Chardonnay and Sauvignon have had no such problem adapting – reflecting, perhaps, the greater similarities that exist between growing conditions in France and northern Italy. The native Ribolla Gialla is currently enjoying something of a revival, though its

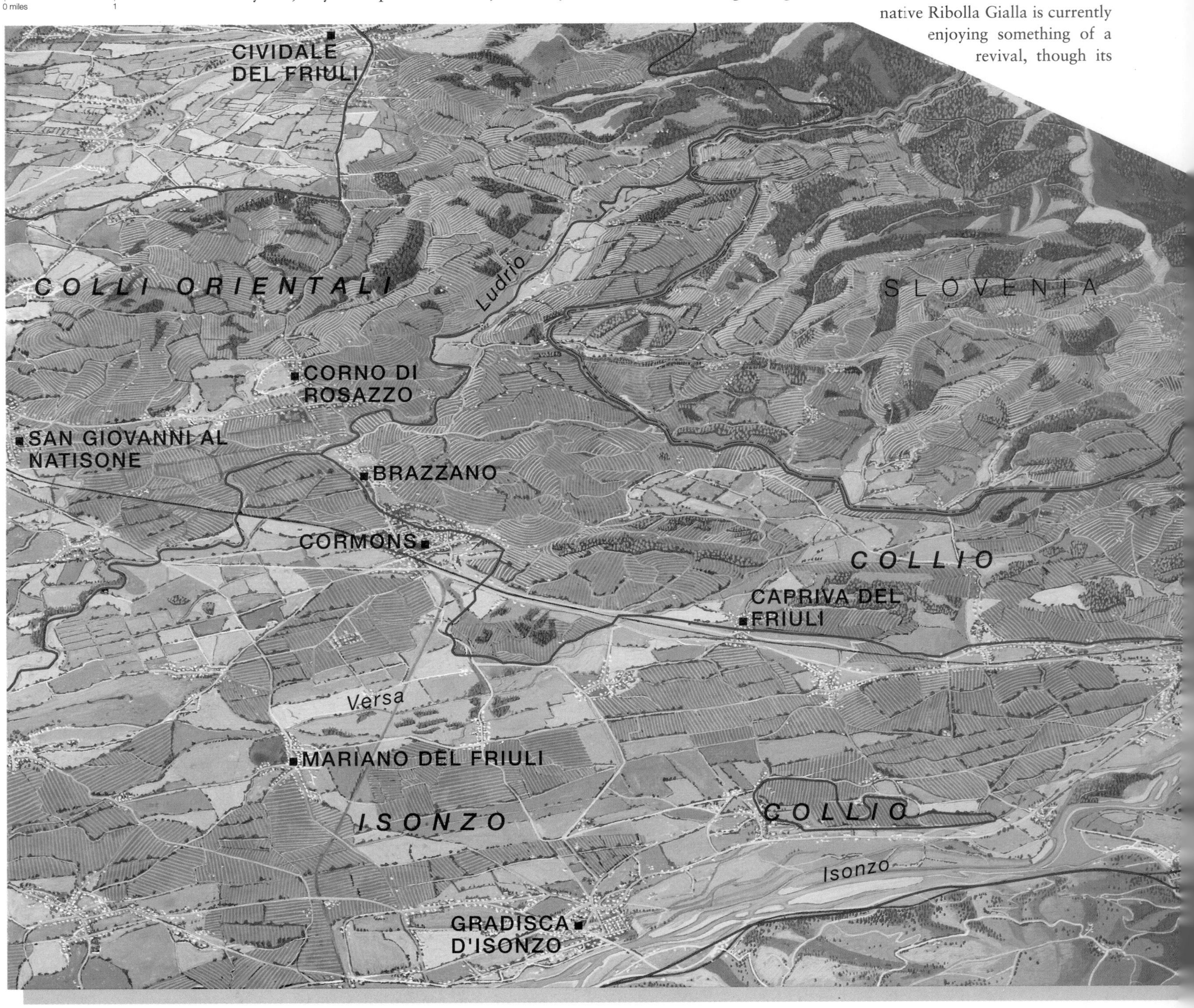

0 km 1 2
0 miles 1

CIVIDALE DEL FRIULI
COLLI ORIENTALI
Ludrio
SLOVENIA
CORNO DI ROSAZZO
SAN GIOVANNI AL NATISONE
BRAZZANO
CORMONS
COLLIO
CAPRIVA DEL FRIULI
Versa
MARIANO DEL FRIULI
ISONZO
COLLIO
Isonzo
GRADISCA D'ISONZO

0 km 1 2
0 miles 1

waxy nature and tangy acidity do not endear it to palates with a greater affection for the richer, rounder styles of Australian and Californian wines, while the Tocai Friulano can produce some of Friuli's most interesting dry whites.

Other natives include Picolit and Verduzzo, both of which are highly regarded locally for the quality of their sweet wines, but the quality is such that it does not transfer successfully to the international stage. Of the reds, Refosco dal Peduncolo Rosso can, at its best, be as much of a mouthful to drink as it is to pronounce, while Schioppettino produces lighter wines. Neither, however, produces wines of the stature of the whites.

In Collio and Colli Orientali producers like Mario Schiopetto and Vittorio Puiatti began producing fresh, modern varietals in the 1960s when the rest of the peninsula was still churning out wines that bore a greater resemblance to poor-quality sherry. Others, like Jermann, Gravner, Livio and Marco Felluga, Abbazia di Rosazzo and Radikon followed, making this a rare area in Italy where small growers and merchants outnumbered the large merchants and co-operatives. Their success was immediate, though, it must be said, easy, while the rest of Italy lagged behind. These largely unoaked whites very firmly emphasized the primary fruit aromas of the varietal and were supported by a viscous richness on the palate derived from the warm growing conditions and low yields. Such wines were immeasurably more characterful than those made from Trebbiano or other grapes elsewhere in Italy. As a result, Friuli in general, and Collio and Colli Orientali in particular, acquired this great reputation for quality, something which was reflected in the prices the wines fetched. Despite (or perhaps because of) these prices, the wines soon came to be seen as rather one-dimensional and in an attempt to add complexity, growers like Gravner began experimenting with oak and a partial malolactic fermentation.

As you move onto the plains, the quality and price both descend, and the differences between the zones become far less pronounced. In the far west, the Friuli

Here at Oslavia, north of Gorizia, the Collio vineyards lie close to the Slovenian border.

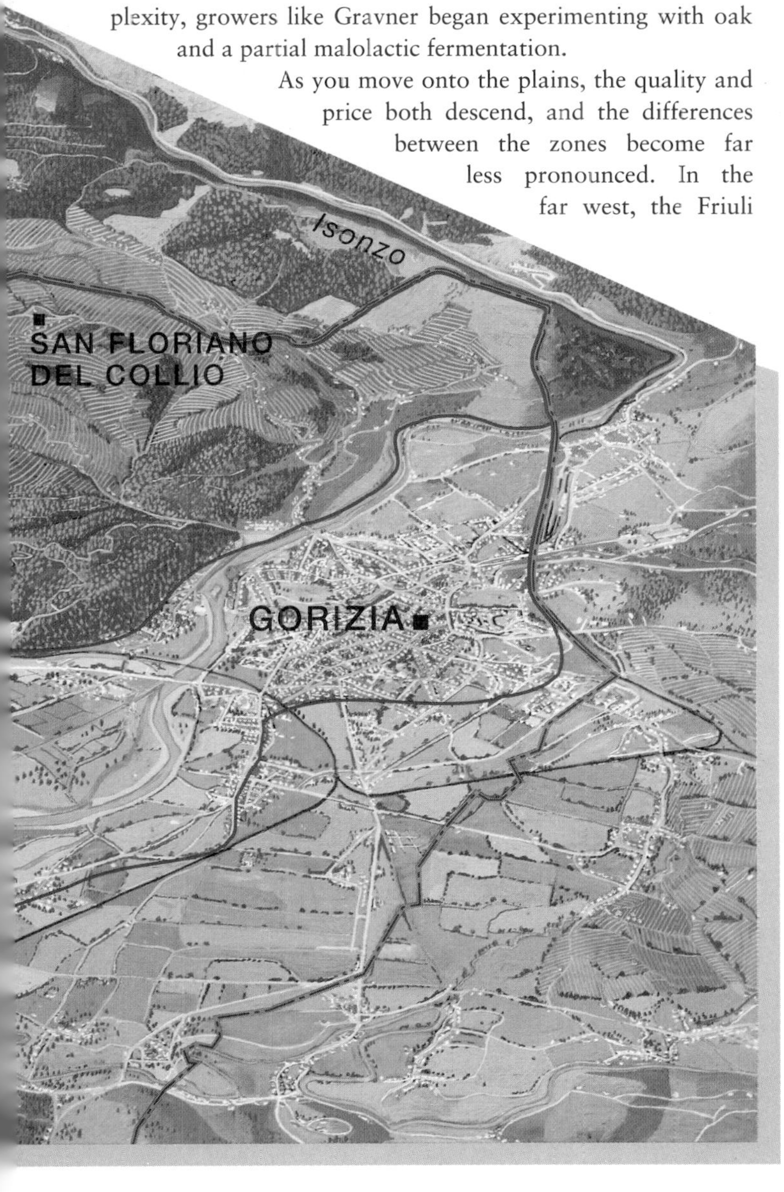

Grave zone, produces more red than white wine. The soil on this large alluvial plain consists mainly of gravel, which results in reds of decent weight and colour. A great deal is sold in bulk, though there are some attractively herbal Merlots and some rather weedy Cabernets. As elsewhere in north-east Italy, Pinot Grigio and Chardonnay are on the increase.

Red wines also predominate between Grave and the Adriatic, in the Latisana zone. Here, however, the soil is more fertile, and the wines lack the weight that the best in Grave can attain, though they are usually eminently drinkable. A similar drinkability prevails east of Latisana in the Aquileia zone, but in Isonzo, situated between Aquileia and Collio, more intensity creeps into the wines as the hills begin rolling towards Gorizia.

In all areas, the grape mix is similar to that in Collio and Colli Orientali. This predilection for the varietal has proved a very useful marketing tool, but the lack of diversity has been an even greater impediment to international success. Greater diversity of style rather than solely of varietal will be the key for producers in Friuli.

WHERE THE VINEYARDS ARE *Thanks to modern technology, excellent raw materials and some fine vineyard sites, Collio and Colli Orientali are considered to be Italy's best white wine zones. Two-thirds of Collio's best sites are said to be in Slovenia and, as a result, many grapes are transported across what used to be the border with the Iron Curtain. In Collio, north of Gorizia along the border with Slovenia, the chalky vineyards on the lower-lying hills, 100 to 150m (330 to 500ft) above sea level, give wines of great intensity, especially around San Floriano and Oslavia. To the west, between Gorizia and Cormons and especially on the slopes west of Capriva, the wines combine richness and perfume. It is here that many of the best producers (among them, Schiopetto, Jermann and Puiatti) are situated. South of Cormons the soil consists of more gravel than limestone, and we move into the Isonzo zone. The climate, though, is similar to Collio's and some producers, notably Stelio Gallo and Francesco Pecorari, are showing that the wines can have similar stuffing, if slightly less refinement than the best Collio can offer – but only if the approach to viticulture is equally rigorous. North of Cormons, the slightly cooler climate gives Collio wines with more delicate aromas. Colli Orientali is merely a north-easterly extension of Collio and virtually all its best vineyards are along the border of the two zones, around Rosazzo.*

Isonzo
SAN FLORIANO DEL COLLIO
GORIZIA

CIVIDALE DEL FRIULI TO GORIZIA
COLLIO = DOC WINE AREA
DOC BOUNDARIES
VINEYARDS
TOTAL DISTANCE NORTH TO SOUTH 24KM (15 MILES)
N

RED GRAPES
Red varieties are no longer predominant in the region but Merlot still counts for one-third of vineyard plantings. Cabernet Franc is losing ground to Cabernet Sauvignon, and Refosco is also in decline.

WHITE GRAPES
Tocai Friulano remains the most planted white grape but Chardonnay, Pinot Bianco, Pinot Grigio and Sauvignon are on the increase. Picolit and Verduzzo are two ancient Friuli varieties.

CLIMATE
To the north, the Carnic Alps have the heaviest rainfall in Italy but generally the Friulian climate is mild and fine. The coastal plains can be hot and dry in the summer.

SOIL
Hillside vineyards are often planted on crumbly marl and sandstone. Elsewhere soils range from clay, sand, and gravel to the alluvial deposits of the Isonzo river, and famous limestone formations of the Carso.

ASPECT
The best vineyards lie on choice slopes between the Alps to the north and the Venetian plain to the south and west.

Central Italy

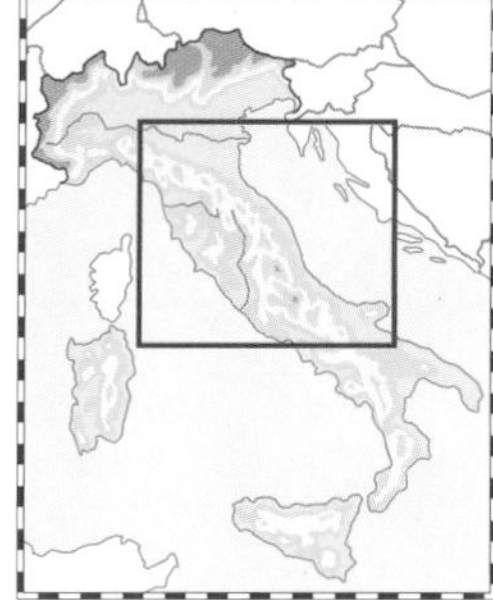

The disparate collection of regions lumped together as central Italy separates the sub-alpine landscapes of the north from the ancient hills and plains of the southern part of the country. Bisected by the Apennines, central Italy begins on the southern bank of the Po river and stretches to an imaginary line, running from the Gargano Massif to the Gulf of Gaeta, that separates Lazio from Campania and Molise from Puglia.

In vinous terms, there is a thin thread of cohesion that links the wines of central Italy. Grapes like the ubiquitous Trebbiano, Sangiovese, Montepulciano and Lambrusco dominate the vineyards, but only in a few places do they result in knolls of quality in a turbulent sea of quantity. Some grapes – notably Trebbiano and Sangiovese – straddle the Apennines but appear in distinctly different guises on the eastern and western flanks, but most others, in typically Italian fashion, are local heroes rather than national figures. Tuscany, because of its great wealth of wines, is covered separately on page 172.

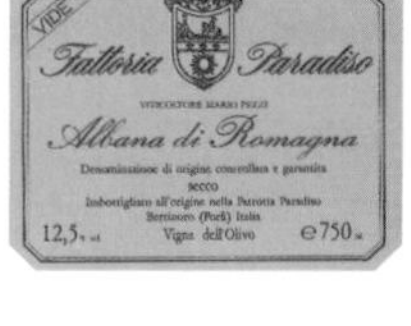

The climate in central Italy varies greatly, depending upon the proximity to the Adriatic Sea which hugs the eastern coast or the Tyrrhenian Sea which defines the western coast. Within these confines, climatic differences can be attributed to altitude or latitude, since more than 500km (300 miles) separate Piacenza in the north-west corner of Emilia-Romagna from the border with Puglia. In general, the vineyards on the eastern coast benefit from the benign influence of the Adriatic. The further inland you go, the higher you climb into the Apennines, where the winters are colder and the summer heat less tempered by the cool maritime breezes. In the western half – Tuscany excepted – there is a less even coastal strip, with the vertebrae of the Apennine spine acting more as a home to vines than any verdant Mediterranean paradise.

EMILIA-ROMAGNA

The broad Po river acts as the northern border of central Italy. The lush, fertile plains of the Po Valley are among the most intensively farmed land in Italy. Most of this is orchard, but the land around Modena, Reggio nell'Emilia and Bologna is carpeted with red Lambrusco vines. The vast Lambrusco production – which is dominated by several enormous co-operatives – is not all destined for large, screw-top bottles: there are, if you happen to be in the region, any number of bottles that contain the genuine article. Whether from the DOC zones of Grasparossa di Castelvetro, Salamino di Santa Croce, Reggiano or Sorbara, real Lambrusco is a frothing, purple drink with high acidity and a touch of sweetness that perfectly complements the rich cooking of Emilia.

The vineyards near Panzano in Tuscany's Chianti Classico zone are some of the best in central Italy.

The rest of Emilia-Romagna's wine tends to come from the Apennine foothills that cut across the southern part of the region. To the west, the Piacenza hills form the basis for the Colli Piacentini DOC, while those around Parma and Bologna are known respectively as the Colli di Parma and Colli Bolognesi. In each of these zones, up to ten different varietals or blends are designated separately under the DOC umbrella. In general, quality from grapes such as Trebbiano, Barbera, Malvasia and even Chardonnay, Sauvignon and Cabernet, is sound rather than exciting.

To the east of Bologna, the Romagnan hills are the nucleus for the Sangiovese, Trebbiano and Albana di Romagna zones. The latter is Emilia-Romagna's only DOCG zone, where the eponymous grape produces a decent dry and an excellent sweet white wine, while the former two are notable only for their lack of distinction. Neither is worth a detour, so the thirsty traveller is well advised to continue south to the Marche.

MARCHE

After Romagna's rather insipid Trebbiano and Sangiovese, the wines of the Marche are a welcome relief. Though an awful lot of it is, in fact, made from the self-same grapes, the discerning drinker can seek out some excellent Verdicchio and Montepulciano. The former, undoubtedly one of Italy's best native white grape varieties, has had to overcome the reputation it acquired when it was bought more for its amphora- shaped bottle than for the intrinsic merit of the wine. The best Verdicchio – from producers like Bucci, Garofoli and Umani Ronchi – has a richness and viscosity that is seldom found in Italian white wines. This richness is matched by the reds from Montepulciano, most notably Rosso Conero. Produced on the Adriatic coast in the shadow of Mount Conero, this wine at its best shows the generosity that the Montepulciano grape can – when properly cultivated – lend to wines.

ABRUZZO AND MOLISE

Unfortunately, much of the wine in Abruzzo is symptomatic of poorly grown Montepulciano. This great grape, which can make wines of irresistible dark chocolate flavours, and which is traditionally trained low in the *alberello* or bush system (*gobelet* in France), was twisted into ill-conceived configurations by wayward bureaucrats in the 1960s, when it was recommended that the vine be trained high in a pergola or *tendone* system. Such stupidity has conspired to rob the Montepulciano of its stuffing, and has resulted, at best, in light, cheap, quaffing wines. The Trebbiano grape is the sole white variety planted in Abruzzo and even in the best of hands, its indomitable neutrality makes temperance an appealing prospect.

Continuing south into Molise, where over half the land is mountainous, most viticulture is concentrated on the coastal strip, where hot summer temperatures are moderated by cool sea breezes. The only important DOC, Biferno (reds from Montepulciano and whites from Trebbiano), accounts for less than a quarter of 1 per cent of the region's total production. With the odd exception, the rest is consumed locally or sent north for blending. One producer, di Majo Norante, has shown that quality can be achieved in Molise from white grapes like Greco, but their wines are dogged by inconsistency.

LAZIO

Though the temptation here is to push further south into Puglia, we must complete our journey through central Italy by wending our way across the Apennine mountains into the southern part of Lazio. The mountains form the eastern

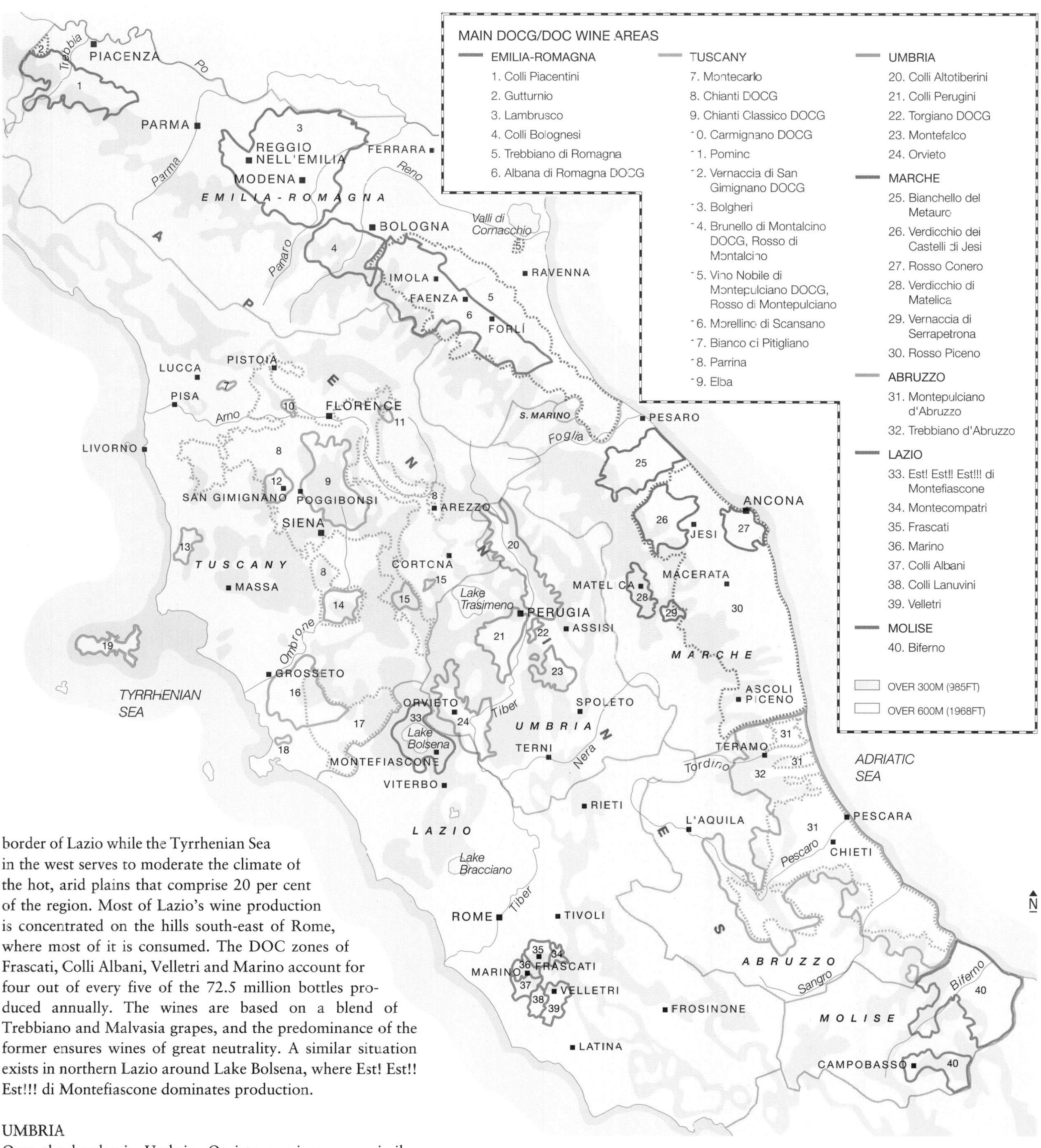

border of Lazio while the Tyrrhenian Sea in the west serves to moderate the climate of the hot, arid plains that comprise 20 per cent of the region. Most of Lazio's wine production is concentrated on the hills south-east of Rome, where most of it is consumed. The DOC zones of Frascati, Colli Albani, Velletri and Marino account for four out of every five of the 72.5 million bottles produced annually. The wines are based on a blend of Trebbiano and Malvasia grapes, and the predominance of the former ensures wines of great neutrality. A similar situation exists in northern Lazio around Lake Bolsena, where Est! Est!! Est!!! di Montefiascone dominates production.

UMBRIA

Over the border in Umbria, Orvieto survives on a similar blend, made more bearable as the percentage of grapes like Grechetto increases. Nearly all of Umbria consists of hills or mountains, ensuring that the vine has many a felicitous spot in which to flourish. The higher altitude of the 'green heart of Italy' compensates for the land-locked nature of the region, a fact that would normally render it too hot for viticulture. Grechetto is the most characterful native white variety, producing wines of good depth and breadth in the Colli Martani DOC which borders Montefalco to the west. Its red counterpart, Sagrantino, is one of Italy's great red grape varieties, but it is only found around the town of Montefalco, where the new Sagrantino di Montefalco DOCG is located. It produces deep-coloured, tannic wines of great intensity and length. As small barrels become a more regular part of the production process, we can expect Sagrantino to soften in style.

Umbria's other noted red is Torgiano. This Sangiovese-based red is the monopoly of the Lungarotti family, pioneers in Umbrian viticulture. But whereas 20 years ago they were ahead of the game, the intervening period has seen them creep forward while others have raced ahead. Not surprisingly, Torgiano seems less exciting as a result, though the oak-aged Riserva retains a certain appeal.

Tuscany

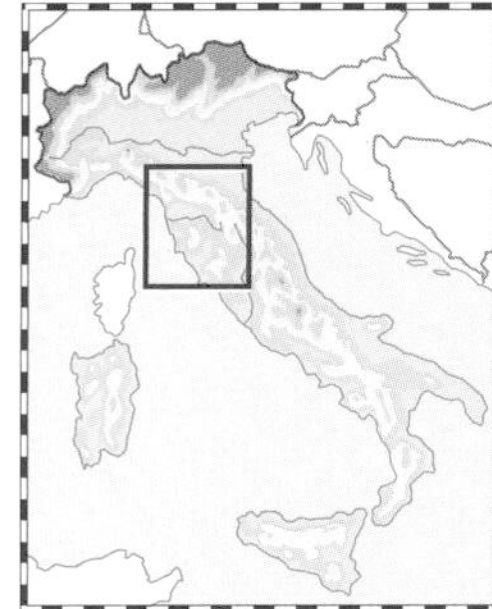

RED GRAPES

The chief grape of Tuscany is the Sangiovese, also known as Brunello, Prugnolo Gentile, and Sangioveto. Canaiolo Nero and Mammolo are other local varieties now being joined by Cabernet Sauvignon and Merlot.

WHITE GRAPES

Vernaccia produces the best white wine but high-yielding Trebbiano is much more common. International varieties are led by Chardonnay, Pinot Bianco and Sauvignon Blanc.

CLIMATE

The temperate climate of the central hills is in complete contrast to the river basins which trap summer heat and damp, and the drier, hotter coastal regions. Hail can be a threat to fruiting vines.

SOIL

The soil is generally calcareous, with tufa and some sandy clay. The flaky marl called *galestro* is highly desirable, and features in Montalcino and the Chianti Classico zone. Near Pitigliano the soils are volcanic.

ASPECT

The best vineyards are carefully sited on slopes and steep hills, often interspersed with olive groves and woodland.

How impossible it is to look at Tuscan wine objectively. For anyone born and brought up in Western culture, imbued as it is with the Renaissance, for anyone who has ever looked at those Renaissance landscapes, all blue hills forming a backdrop to a Madonna or a Medici – well, Tuscan wine is what they drank. Every time I pick up a glass of Vernaccia I expect it to meet Michelangelo's description of a wine that 'kisses, licks, bites, thrusts and stings', rather than the dim, dull brew of today. But then I'm a bit of a romantic. You might have noticed.

And the other thing about Tuscany is how much like its pictures it looks. You know the sort of thing – cypresses, rounded green hills, old farmhouses with carved stone doorways and cool, dark interiors, the brilliance of the sun, the vast blue distances. It is a place where civilization seems unimaginably old, and intensely alive. Everything is done with grace and beauty.

It affected me, the first time I actually went to look at vineyards there, as it affects everybody. You can't go to Tuscany without wanting to be more like the Tuscans: you crave that easy knack of producing the most delicious meal imaginable from the simplest ingredients; of pouring local wine harvested less than a year ago from slopes that your hostess can point out to you, just across the valley – there, do you see? Where the last of the evening sun is catching the vines and where the grey-green olive trees further round the hill are already in shadow.

So no, I can't be objective about Tuscan wine. I become disproportionately angry when the Tuscans get it wrong, and irrationally ecstatic when they get it right. And whenever I go there I imagine myself in a painting – although reason tells me the landscape is very different now to what it was like then, and in fact is probably better cared for than it has been for years.

But first, the basics. To the west of Tuscany is the Mediterranean, in which basks the island of Elba with its echoes of Napoleon. To the east lie the Apennines, arching round to the north; while to the south there's Lazio, Rome and the Mezzogiorno. The land lies flat near the coast, as if to let the Mediterranean climate as far inland as possible, but most of Tuscany is hilly. Not necessarily seriously hilly, although you'll find white grapes cultivated up to 210m (700ft) and reds up to 165m (550ft), but often just gently rolling. The hills are essential for viticulture because summers here can be long and hot, and hills that rise high enough to temper the heat or catch a cooling breeze can make all the difference between a baked, flat white wine and one with finesse and elegance. For reds, slopes provide the concentration of heat that the sun-loving Sangiovese grape needs to ripen. So it's the hills that provide the mesoclimates that serious winemakers want.

And serious winemakers love Tuscany. You don't have to be a Tuscan to make good wine here. You can be a rich immigrant from Rome, Lombardy, Milan, or from anywhere; the main thing, from the point of view of the hardheaded locals, is that you're investing – and it's your sort that has done a lot to redress the desolation that spread throughout the region in the 1950s. The land was farmed then by a system of sharecropping, by which the peasants who worked the land divided the harvest with those who owned it. This meant riches for the landowners and poverty for the peasants, and the frosts of 1956, which left dead olive groves and vines in its wake, were the final straw. The peasants fled the land for jobs in factories. And when Tuscany's vineyards were replanted, largely between 1965 and 1975, it was with quantity rather than quality in mind. That seemed to be where the market lay: people craved light, fresh, zippy reds, sold as often as not in straw-covered *fiaschi*. But nowadays the trend is in the opposite direction – Chianti even has a programme called Chianti 2000, aimed at planting the best clones in the most appropriate places.

Tuscany's main grape is the Sangiovese. To put it in perspective, 72 per cent of the region's wine is red, and if it's red it's probably at least 75 per cent Sangiovese. The rest of the blend may be any of several grapes: Cabernet Sauvignon, Cabernet Franc, Merlot, Canaiolo Nero, Mammolo, Colorino, Ciliegiolo, or white grapes like Trebbiano, Vermentino, Canaiolo Bianco or Malvasia. (You might think that adding white grapes to a wine that is supposed to be red can do little for its colour or extract. You would of course be right: the best producers don't do it, even if the law says they should.) Some 14 clones of Sangiovese are well-known, and some even have their own names, like the Brunello of Montalcino or the Prugnolo Gentile of Montepulciano. These two are among the best, and one reason why the Sangiovese-based wines of these two places have managed to establish such a reputation for themselves. Other clones, often those planted in the 1960s and 1970s, can be lacking in colour, extract, flavour and just about everything else, and favoured only for the huge crops they give. But being planted with inferior vines does not, unfortunately, prevent a region or a wine from being awarded DOC status. Tuscany has a high proportion of DOC wines and a third of its production is DOC or DOCG.

The whites in Tuscany are mainly from the Trebbiano, in whole or in part, but for all that this is one of Italy's main quality wine regions, vines do not dominate the landscape. Even prestigious Montalcino is half given over to forest, and there is more land planted with olive groves there than with vines. Tuscany is still a region of mixed farming. Wine is a part of everyday life here and the vine, accordingly, knows its place.

It is the ready availability of sun-drenched slopes that makes Sangiovese the most popular planting in Tuscany. The

further north you go the lower down the slopes you find the best Sangiovese: as low as 50 to 200m (165 to 650ft) in northerly Carmignano and from 250 to 600m (820 to 1970ft) in Montepulciano in the south. Other grape varieties, even Pinot Noir, may be planted at higher altitudes where it gets too cold for Sangiovese. Marl soil high in calcium seems to suit the vine best, but there are big variations, with more sand in Montepulciano. What gives the wines their finesse, though, is the difference between the warm daytime temperatures and the cool nights. Most noticeable in the north, in Montalcino and Chianti, this difference evens out towards the south, and the wines of Montepulciano are accordingly richer, beefier and higher in alcohol.

SUPER-TUSCANS

It all started in 1974. Tignanello and Sassicaia were the first so-called 'super-Tuscan' wines, and wineries piled on to the band-wagon faster than you could count. The idea was to thwart the more restrictive aspects of Italian wine law by producing wines that flaunted their *vino da tavola* status – and their extremely high prices. Tignanello comes from the Chianti Classico zone but is nearly all Sangiovese; Sassicaia, from Bolgheri near the coast, is a blend of Cabernet Sauvignon and Cabernet Franc. Both are aged in small oak barrels, a move that, to its detractors, smacked of distinctly un-Italian activities. The wines that followed were sometimes entirely Sangiovese and sometimes from both Cabernets, and quite often a blend of all three. The idea spread out of Tuscany to Piedmont and elsewhere in Italy, and white wines took it up, particularly Chardonnay and Sauvignon Blanc. But with the passing of the Goria Law in 1992 the necessity of a Vino da Tavola tag disappeared. The Super-Tuscans can now, if they want, come under the wing of a law suddenly flexible enough to cover them, and prepared to hand out DOCs and DOCGs like medals. Sassicaia, ever the first, became DOC (under the name of Bolgheri Sassicaia) with the 1994 vintage. Others may follow.

VIN SANTO

When you step from the blazing sun into the cool of a Tuscan farmhouse, this is what, according to tradition, you should be offered. Literally 'holy wine', *vin santo* is made by everyone with some spare Trebbiano grapes and room under the rafters in which to dry them on straw mats. Malvasia actually makes better *vin santo*, so naturally the DOC regulations (not all *vin santo* is DOC) say that Trebbiano must be the main grape. This is Italy, after all, where the other great tradition is that the law is an ass. The grapes are left to shrivel until they are crushed, usually sometime between November and March (the longer they are left, the more concentrated the sugars will be and the sweeter the wine). They are then aged in small barrels for at least three years and sometimes for more than ten.

There are two DOCs, which overlap geographically and leave much of Tuscany out – and *vin santo* is made everywhere, whether DOC or not. The DOC of Colli dell' Etruria Centrale covers the Chianti region; Val d'Arbia includes Radda, Monteriggioni and land east as far as Brunello di Montalcino. All can be very sweet, bone dry or anything in between. Quality varies just as widely.

The Altesino vineyards in the Montalcino hills benefit from the area's warm, dry climate.

Chianti

The name Chianti is synonymous with Italian wine. It embodies its glorious and frustrating confusion and, while seldom rising to great heights of quality, when partnered with a plate of pasta it is difficult to beat. Chianti evokes images as diverse as straw flasks, cypress-clad hills, peasants and aristocrats. It is, in short, the Everyman of Italian wine. This is quite a claim for something that began humbly, several millenia ago, in the wooded and isolated hills south of Florence. The wine first came to prominence about 800 years ago. At this time, Florence was the banking capital of the world. Its bankers – the Medici, Strozzi, Corsini, Albizi and Frescobaldi families, among others – funded the wayward campaigns of most of the despotic tyrants of medieval Europe, and became rich in the process. This wealth spilled out of the city into the countryside, where the great villas and estates that now lure tourists to these verdant hills in summer were developed into agricultural properties. Because of the rocky soil, only the olive tree and the vine flourished, yet its products were greatly appreciated in affluent Florentine society.

This wealthy market provided the impetus to the development of Chianti as a quality wine zone. By the beginning of the fifteenth century, Chianti's name was already established and, as has happened the world over when a certain area attains fame, others tried to pass off their usually inferior products as the real thing. This led, in 1716, to the Grand Duke of Tuscany mapping out the borders of the zone in an attempt to prevent fraud. While delimiting the area, the Grand Duke also pushed the borders north from their original area towards Greve and Panzano. Such elasticity, however, did little to staunch the flow of ersatz Chianti, a flow that increased towards the end of the nineteenth century when Chianti enjoyed a boom thanks to the shortage of wine created by phylloxera. By this time, virtually every red wine in Tuscany, no matter what its provenance or history – and some, like those from Rufina, Carmignano and Montepulciano, had histories every bit as rich and noble – was being sold under the name of Chianti.

There were many at the time who argued that some form of legal definition was required to protect – or even define – the name of Chianti, but this was generally ignored in the rush for sales. It was only several decades later, during the slump that inevitably followed the boom, that people began to think along these lines. This resulted in the Dalmasso commission being set up to inquire into Chianti, and as a result of its report in 1932, new boundaries were established. Chianti the geographical area became, in reality, a generic term for Tuscan red wine.

The original zone was doubled in size to take in the lower-lying, clay-clogged hills closer to Florence, and was renamed Chianti Classico. This new name distinguished it from the six new Chianti zones that were created by appending to the name a broad geographical designation. In most cases, this was simply a matter of mopping up all the vineyards in a particular province like Florence or Siena that weren't already covered by another zone. It is an idiotic basis upon which to define a wine, yet it was confirmed by the DOC laws of 1967, reaffirmed when the DOCG was introduced in 1984 and remains in practice to this day.

In the province of Siena, for instance, any grapes grown outside the Sienese part of Classico, or beyond the borders of the Montepulciano and Montalcino zones, are entitled to the name Chianti Colli Senesi. Never mind that the zone covers as wide a variety of soils and mesoclimates as you could hope to find, it's just that the area fits neatly into the politically defined borders of the province of Siena. Similarly in Florence, all area under vine not covered by Rufina, Pomino, Carmignano,

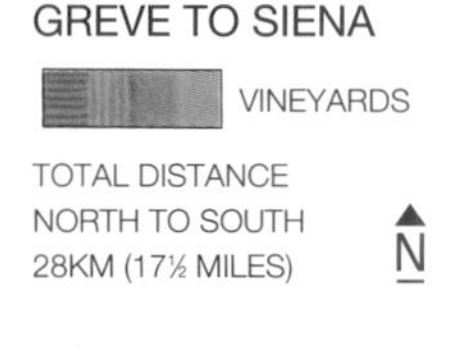

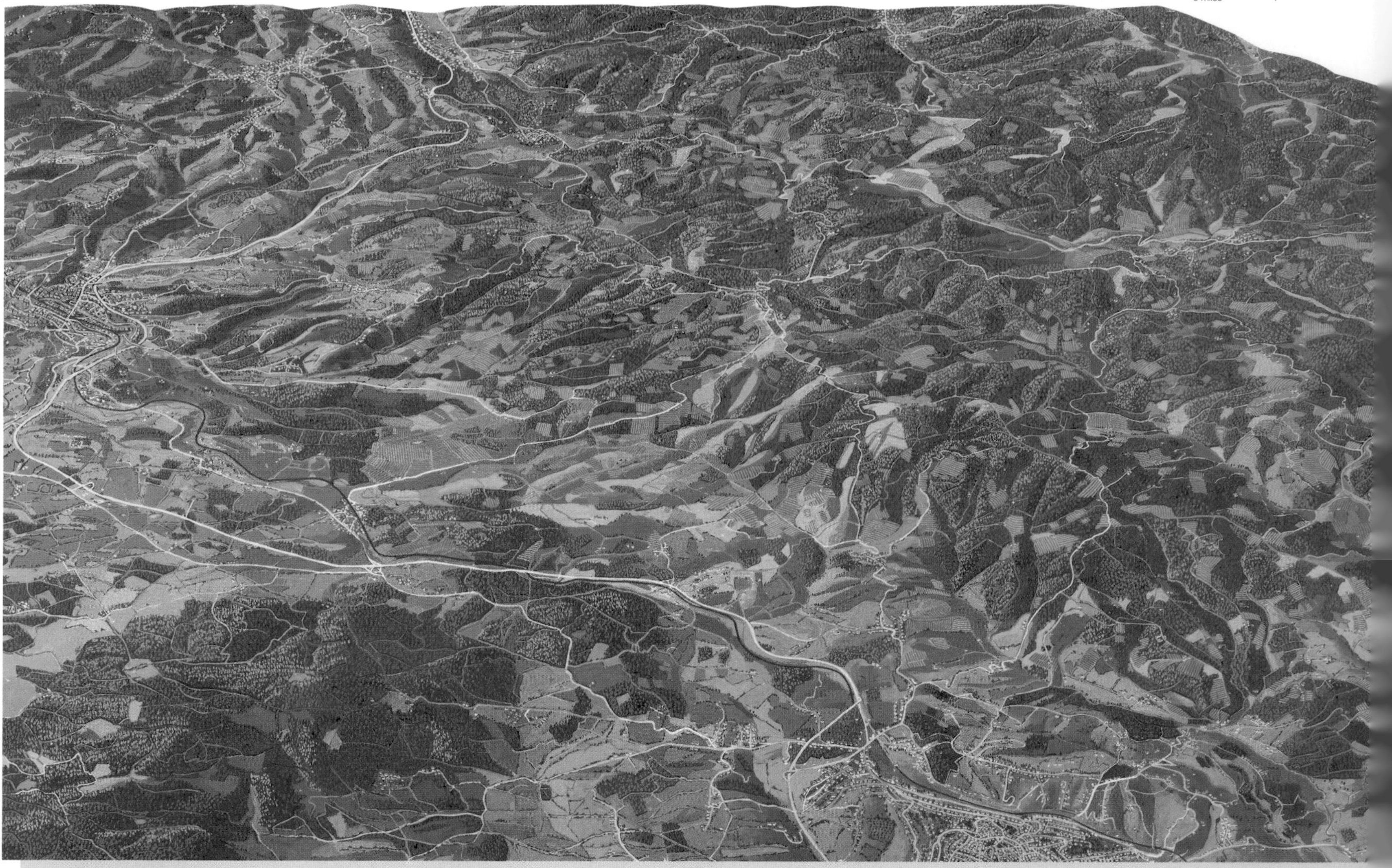

Montalbano and Classico is delimited as the Colli Fiorentini, despite the fact that this takes in two such diverse zones as the Val d'Arno and the Val d'Elsa.

Now whether you believe in the sanctity of the *terroir* or not, it is manifestly stupid that wines produced in such distinct zones as these should bear the same name. Indeed, the whole system of French AC – and, by extension, DOC – was developed to aid and protect the consumer in their choice of wine. By extending the name of Chianti over vast tracts of Tuscany, from the green rolling hills of central Classico to the arid Sienese slopes, from the cool reaches of Rufina to the low-lying vineyards of the Colline Pisane, the Italian authorities have succeeded not only in confusing the adventurous wine drinker, but also in robbing the growers of their individual identities.

There are something like 7000 growers in the seven Chianti zones, and it is likely, given the diversity of soil, altitude, climate and, to a lesser extent, varietal composition, that there are as many different styles of wine. The soil varies from stony *galestro* in the heart of Chianti Classico, a shaly clay that, along with limestone, provides the best home for the Sangiovese grape, to clay in the Colli Senesi (the second largest, in terms of production, of the seven zones) and the Colli Aretini and lighter, sandier soils towards the coast. Even within Classico, altitude varies between 150 and 550m (500 and 1800ft), differences which result in great variations in temperature. The vineyards in the central Classico hills are cooler than those down on the coast because of their altitude, something which in turn gives finer, more perfumed wines.

Proximity to forests, valleys or rivers throws another complicating variable into the equation. Those vineyards on the western flank of Classico, for instance, produce fuller wines than do their neighbours several miles nearer the central part of the zone, largely because of the warmth generated by the Val d'Elsa. In the Rufina zone, on the other hand, the cool breeze funnelled down the Sieve Valley from the Apennines sets this tiny area apart from its neighbours, creating a unique mesoclimate and a distinctive style of wine.

THE SANGIOVESE GRAPE

Through all the variations in climate, soil and altitude within the Chianti zone there would appear to be one constant factor: the Sangiovese grape. The grape forms the mainstay of Chianti, being used on its own in some of the best wines, or blended with native varieties like Canaiolo and Colorino, or international ones like Merlot and Cabernet, in others.

In lesser wines, white grapes like Trebbiano and Malvasia still find their way into the blend, tawdry tattered remnants of the lean times in Tuscany, when they were used to boost production and render the wine lighter and ready for drinking at an earlier stage. As vineyards are replanted, however, their numbers are diminished, at least among the quality producers.

Consistency, however, is not the Sangiovese's strong point. As well as needing low yields to produce grapes of quality, it is extremely sensitive to soil and climate, so alters its guise to suit the surroundings of its environment. In the Colli Aretini, the sandy clay soils yield wines with good colour and robust, generous fruit that is best drunk young. These are plumper, pasta wines compared to the sleek, lean, aristocratic and intense characters produced further north in Rufina, where the clay and limestone soils and cooler climate have carved another figure for the Sangiovese. In the best parts of the Colli Senesi, around the town of Sinalunga, the Sangiovese changes into a burly, muscular beast that intimidates the thin, rather insubstantial weaklings from Pisa and Montalbano.

RED GRAPES

The most important grape is Sangiovese (locally also called Sangioveto). Canaiolo Nero and Mammolo are also sometimes used in Chianti as well as increasing amounts of Cabernet and Merlot.

WHITE GRAPES

Trebbiano is widely planted but decreasing in importance. Malvasia del Chianti is also in decline as Chardonnay and Sauvignon Blanc become more fashionable in varietal wines.

CLIMATE

The central hills of the Chianti Classico zone are cooler and more temperate than the coast. Hail is sometimes a problem in summer and the occasional frost can be quite severe and damaging.

SOIL

Stony calcareous soils are varied by parcels of limestone, sand, clay and schist. In the heart of Chianti Classico the shaly clay known as *galestro* gives wine with particularly good body.

ASPECT

The region is characterized by sloping vineyard plots among woods and groves of olives. Altitude plays a key role in determining the style and quality of Chianti produced.

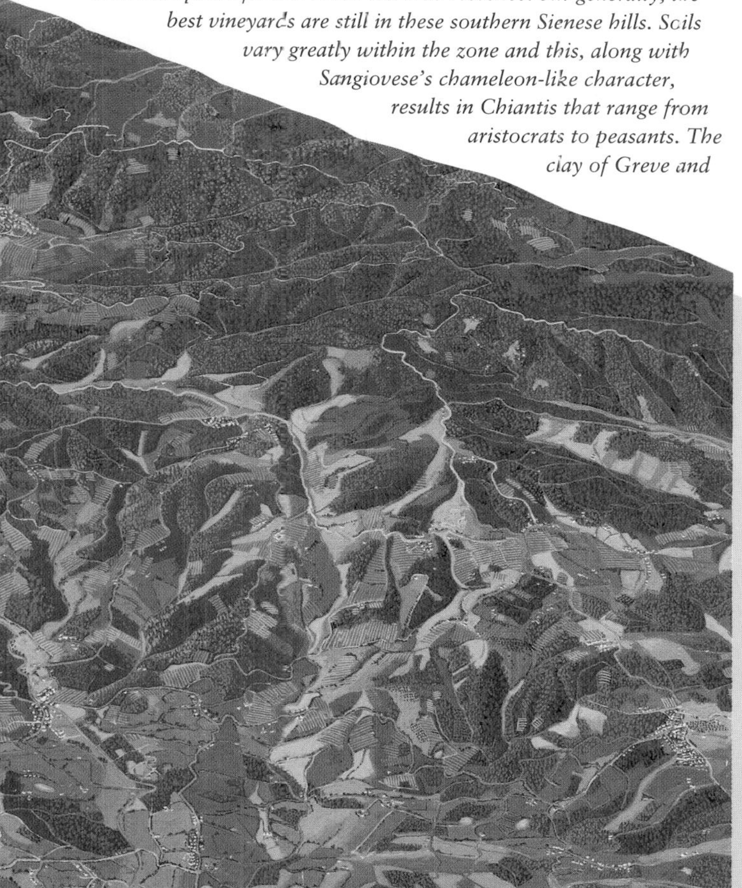

WHERE THE VINEYARDS ARE *This map shows the southern half of the Chianti Classico zone and the three communes – Radda, Castellina and Gaiole – that comprised historic Chianti, the area noted for the quality of its red wines since at least the thirteenth century. In 1932 the zone was extended to take in the lower-lying hills that spread further north towards Florence. but generally, the best vineyards are still in these southern Sienese hills. Soils vary greatly within the zone and this, along with Sangiovese's chameleon-like character, results in Chiantis that range from aristocrats to peasants. The clay of Greve and the northern part of the zone gives way, in Panzano, to* galestro*, a friable, shaly clay that, along with the limestone* alberese *which begins to appear also at this point, provides the ideal growing conditions for the Sangiovese grape. Both* galestro *and* alberese *dominate the vineyards of Radda and Gaiole and in the south, around Castelnuovo Berardenga, the potent mixture of tufaceous rock and* galestro *gives some of the greatest wines of Chianti at estates like Castell'in Villa and Felsina Berardenga. Yields from these sites are invariably low. In the past decade, in the search for quality, many estates, including Fontodi, Rampolla and Isole e Olena, have replanted their higher vineyards which had been abandoned in the 1960s and 1970s in favour of lower-lying, more easily worked sites.*

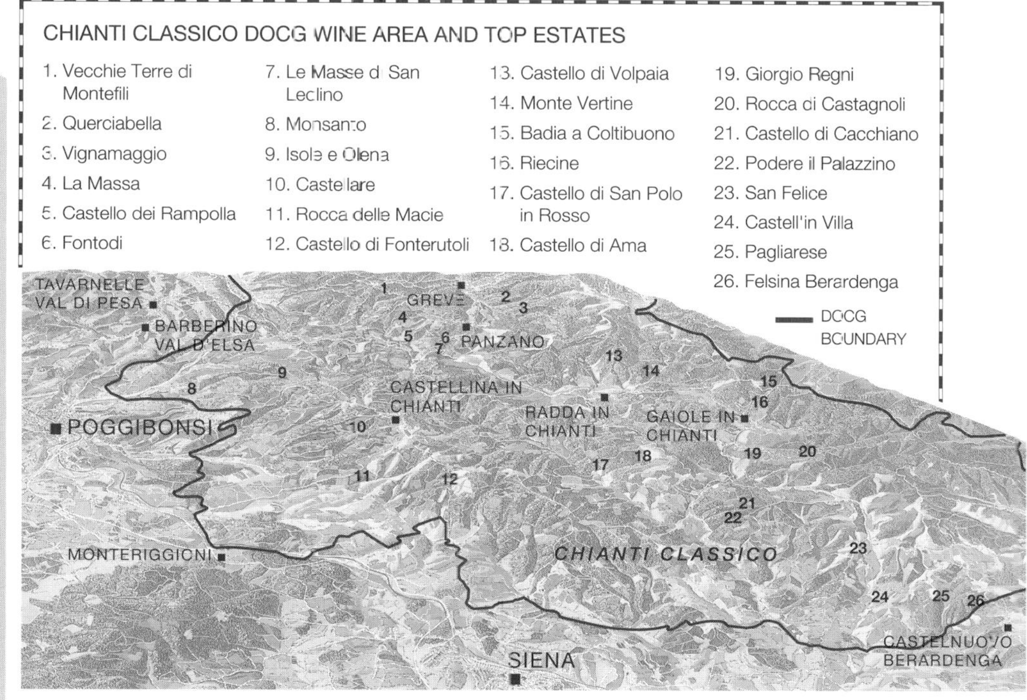

BRUNELLO DI MONTALCINO

RED GRAPES
Brunello is another name for the Sangiovese of Chianti. Some producers have also made experimental plantings of Cabernet.

WHITE GRAPES
Moscato Bianco is grown to produce Moscadello di Montalcino. Chardonnay and Sauvignon Blanc are also beginning to be planted.

CLIMATE
The temperate hill climate benefits from the influence of the Tyrrhenian Sea, while nearby Mount Amiata offers protection from storms.

SOIL
The best vineyards are planted on the prized *galestro* (shaly clay). Elsewhere in Montalcino sandy clay is often combined with limestone.

ASPECT
The longest-lived wines come from the relatively cooler, higher vineyards found on the four major slopes which dominate Montalcino. Further plantings have recently been made on lower-lying terrain.

The cool terraces of Montalcino are surrounded by arid, patchwork plains.

LEAVING BEHIND THE WOODED HILLS of Chianti and the ancient towers of Siena, and heading south towards Buonconvento, Mount Amiata and Rome, I could be forgiven for thinking that I have seen the last of Tuscany's vines. The hills of the Val d'Orcia are parched brown, the heavy, clay soil proving more suitable to the cereal crops that sway in the gentle, southerly breeze than to the vine. The horizon is open, with only a few gentle hills occasionally providing some relief from an otherwise unbroken vista. There are none of the nooks and crannies created by the undulating hills of Chianti, where the vine stretches around a hill like a languorous cat in search of the last rays of warning sunlight; here the vines would wither under the relentless sun.

Then, just past Buonconvento, I turn to my right, and as the road winds uphill, clay gives way to *galestro*, vines replace wheat and, at 600m (1970ft) altitude, I arrive in Montalcino, the town famed for its Brunello, Italy's longest-lived, and some would say, greatest wine. This is a town that lives on and for wine. On the main street, there is a wonderful bar, the Fiaschetteria, serving any number of Brunellos by the glass. Along with other shops in the town, the Fiaschetteria also sells a comprehensive selection of wines. Since extended aeration used to be regarded as vital for drawing the aromas of Brunello out of their cavernous, dark depths, you could well strike lucky with some sullen old brute finally cracking a smile after a couple of days open behind the bar. With modern Brunellos, I'd want one opened on the day I drank it.

The renown now enjoyed by Brunello is a rather recent development. Indeed, it was only in the 1960s that whispers reached the outside world of wines of incredible longevity from the cellars of one producer in Montalcino called Biondi-Santi. The legendary 1891, tasted by few but lauded by all, managed to put first Biondi-Santi and then Montalcino on the map. A legend was created, and as with all legendary wines, the prices of Biondi-Santi wines climbed higher than Mount Olympus. Some producers, able to sell their wines at half the price (still double what the better bottles of Chianti fetched), were happy to let Biondi-Santi make all the running. Others, keen to leap onto this bandwagon, planted vineyards, increasing the area under vine from less than 100 hectares (247 acres) in 1968 (soon after the Biondi-Santi-drafted DOC regulations came into force) to just over 900 hectares (2225 acres) today.

Despite this growth, the legend lives on, thanks to careful management by the producers but there is no doubt that Montalcino is a zone with a great vocation for viticulture. Rising from the sea of clay, it is ringed by a protective wall of valleys – the Ombrone to the west, the Orcia to the south and east – and mountains, with the forbidding face of Mount Amiata standing guard on Montalcino's southern flank. These protect the vineyards from intemperate weather and help make the Brunello zone the most arid of all Tuscany's wine areas, with about 500mm (20in) of rainfall a year. But the hot, arid nature of the region is relieved by cooling breezes blowing off the sea, a luxury given to neither Chianti nor Montepulciano.

The dry, hot climate brings the grapes to maturity quicker than in Chianti or Montepulciano. In years like 1993, the producers in Montalcino had their grapes safely in the fermenting vats while their colleagues to the north were still struggling to complete the harvest amid the onset of autumn rains. In overly hot years, however, the wines of Montalcino can be brutish in character, and lacking any of the gentler tones found in the best Chiantis.

Perhaps because of their stature, the wines of Montalcino traditionally have been aged in large, old oak barrels for a protracted period in order to temper their ferocious tannins. A compulsory aging period of four years was inserted into the DOC law in 1966, reduced to three and a half years recently. This lengthy period may have been fine a generation or so ago, when tastes were different, but today it too often results in all the freshness the wines ever had perishing under the onslaught of wood. True, Biondi-Santi's great old wines (made as recently as 1964) were able to withstand this aging, and their high acidity also enabled them to age well in bottle. But what about the lighter years, when elegance is prized above structure? Three and a half years in oak would put paid to whatever elegance the wine initially may have had. The argument continues, with most producers resorting to subterfuge of one sort or another in order to preserve their wine's character before consigning it to bottle. Greater liberty would be greeted positively by all. Indeed, it would make sense for there is now a great diversity of differing Montalcino wine styles.

WINE STYLES

Brunello's original claim to greatness was based on the longevity of the wine (and an inflated price), and the so-called classic style of Montalcino, as exemplified by Biondi-Santi, is still made by producers based in the north of the zone where the soil is *galestro*-rich and the vineyards are relatively high, at between 400 and 500m (1300 and 1640ft) above sea level.

On new wine estates in the north-west and north-east of the zone, producers like Castiglion del Bosco, Caparzo and Altesino, have planted vineyards on clay soils not previously cultivated with the vine. Though the wines from these vineyards are good, they often need to be given a bit of polish by the addition of a little something from vineyards around Sant' Angelo in the south of the zone or from the *galestro*-rich vineyards around Montosoli to the north of the town of Montalcino. Though its soil is similar to that in the classic area, Montosoli's vineyards are lower

WHERE THE VINEYARDS ARE *As the Montalcino zone has expanded, areas not previously cultivated have come under vine, and Montalcino is now producing a much greater diversity of wine styles from its vineyards than ever before. What might be termed the classic style of Biondi-Santi lives on, not only at the family's Il Greppo farm but also among other producers in the north of the zone around the town of Montalcino. Here the soil has more* galestro *than clay, and this, combined with the higher altitude, results in wines that have a higher acidity and a leaner, steelier fruit than those from the south. This style is best exemplified by Costanti's Colle al Matrichese estate and, when they are good, Biondi-Santi.*

In the south around Sant'Angelo, a completely different style of wine is produced. There is more clay and limestone in the soil, and the greater warmth generated by the nearby Val d'Orcia gives fuller, richer wines with a lower acidity that tend to be fleshier and more accessible when young while ceding none of their aging ability. Producers like Il Poggione, Talenti, Argiano, Col d'Orcia, La Chiesa di Santa Restituta and Banfi are here, a collection of talent that challenges the old guard to the north.

MONTALCINO

 VINEYARDS

TOTAL DISTANCE NORTH TO SOUTH 19KM (12 MILES)

N

lying than those of Costanti and Biondi-Santi, and therefore produce fuller, richer wines.

This great diversity of wine styles from the different areas of Montalcino illustrates once again the limitless number of masks the old trouper Sangiovese has at its disposal. As part of the myth management process, producers in Montalcino, led by Biondi-Santi, propagated the theory that their particular clone of Sangiovese, called Brunello, was distinctive from, and superior to the inferior clones to be found elsewhere in Tuscany. Independent research showed that there were numerous clones of Sangiovese in their vineyards, so they adopted a new position by claiming that Brunello was merely a local name for the Tuscan grape stemming from the fact that, in the hot, arid Montalcino summers, the grapes often acquired a brownish hue at ripening, hence Brunello, or 'little brown one'. One authority has even claimed, after finding the name Brunello mentioned in a fourteenth-century manuscript, that it is a geographical name, and therefore unique to Montalcino.

Either way, the sole use of Sangiovese to make their wines did make the producers of Montalcino unique in Tuscany. But now that others in Chianti and beyond are adopting the same approach, and improving the quality of their raw materials, the Montalcino producers will have to fight to retain their preeminent position. This they seem already to be doing. Realizing that selling their wines at high prices brings with it a certain responsibility with regard to quality, as far back as 1984 they set up a 'junior' DOC called Rosso di Montalcino. This younger brother to the Brunello DOCG has proved particularly successful, not only in maintaining the generally high standard of quality in the zone but also in giving a new, modern and extremely attractive red wine to widen the choice in Tuscany, and in providing producers with much needed cash at a stage when any revenue from Brunello is still several years away. They do seem to have all the luck in Montalcino.

0 km 1 2
0 miles 1

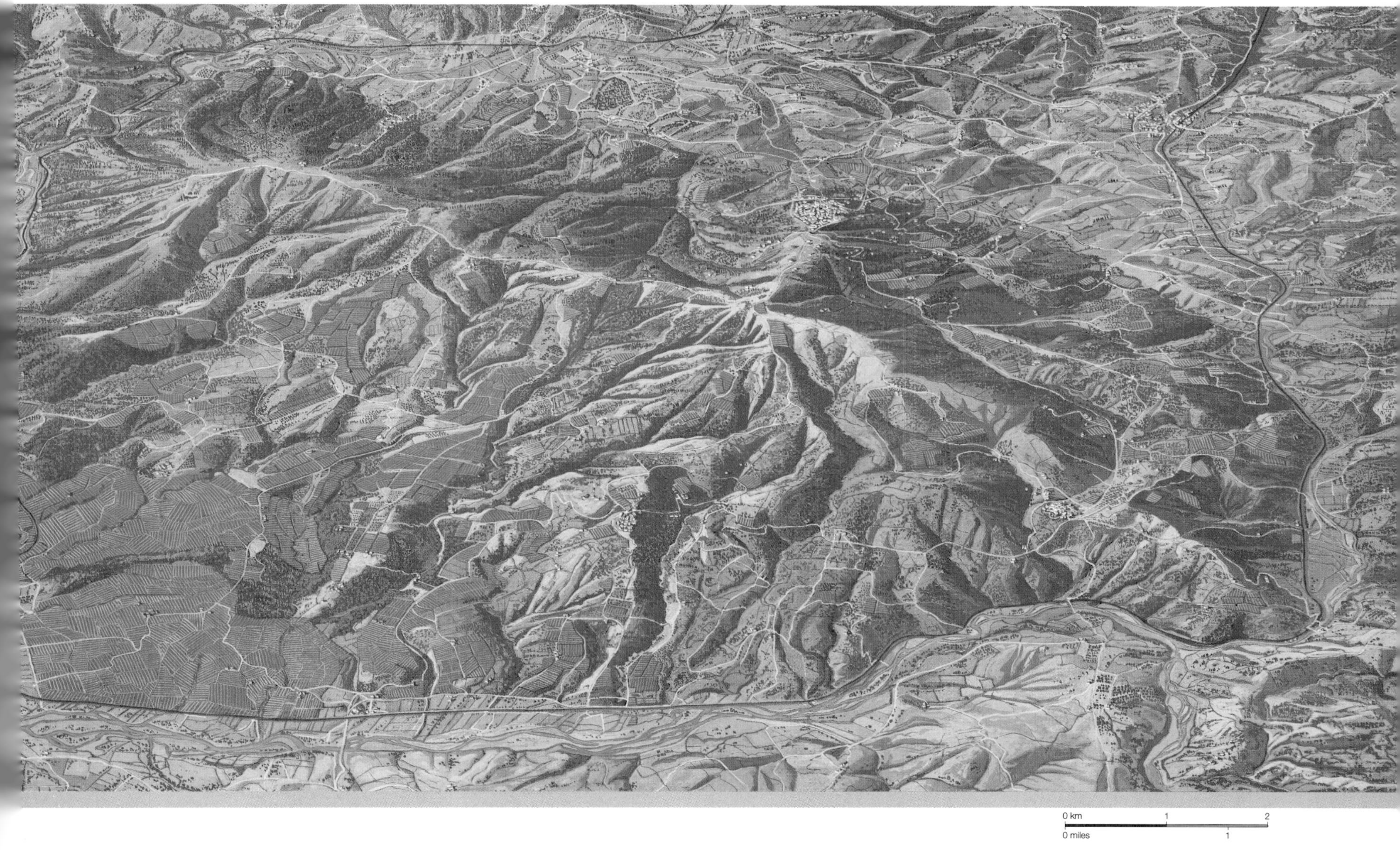

Southern Italy

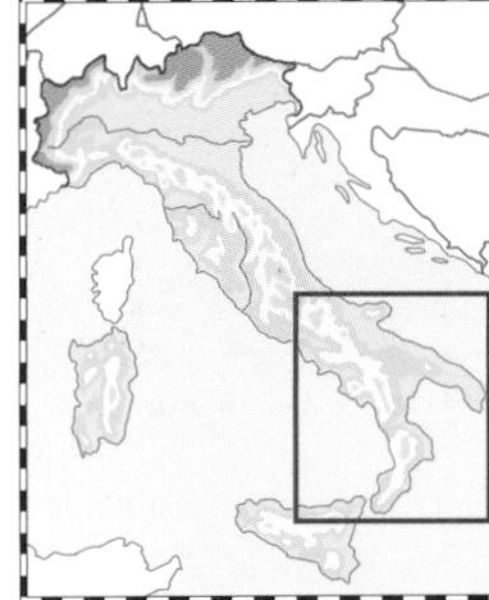

RED GRAPES
Local grapes, such as Negroamaro, Primitivo, Uva di Troia and Aglianico still feature.

WHITE GRAPES
Native varieties include Greco di Tufo, Fiano, Falanghina and Greco di Bianco.

CLIMATE
The plains can be bakingly hot and arid but in the Apennines the climate is almost alpine.

SOIL
Soils vary from calcareous, alluvial and volcanic to clay, sand and marl.

ASPECT
Altitude is important in determining vineyard sites and methods of vine-training.

Southern Italy is the spiritual home of Italian wine. The vine's first foothold on the peninsula was said to have been in the south, where it thrived as it had never done before in any other Mediterranean habitat. Indeed, such was its affinity for the hills and plains of southern Italy – whether the lower slopes of Mount Vulture in Basilicata, Puglia's Salento plains or Calabria's Cirò – that the Greeks called their new colony Enotria Tellus, or 'The Land of Vines'.

An eerie sense of history pervades southern wines, both in the vineyard and in the cellar. The vines tend to be trained low in the *alberello* system, a configuration said to have been imported by the Greeks; and the generous and exotic flavours of figs and spices found in grapes like Negroamaro, Gaglioppo and Aglianico evoke the vine's Mediterranean origins to a much greater extent than the cooler, northern Italian wine flavours ever can, reflecting a tangible sense of an unbroken tradition stretching back 3000 years and beyond.

The Phoenicians, Greeks, Romans, Normans and Bourbons have all been seduced by the Mezzogiorno, Italy's south. It is a land of incomparable light, unbearable heat, unencumbered plenty, immovable indolence and unbelievable corruption, a land showered by the gods with opportunities squandered by man. To people from the north – whether from Italy or Europe – it is a foreign land, full of scents of musk, sensuality and seduction. The industriousness that pervades the cultures of northern Europe is lacking here, where life under the searing sun is taken at a more relaxed pace. Such a languid approach to life is often confused with lassitude, yet it is, along with a diet of fresh vegetables and pasta, responsible for giving southern Italians the longest life expectancy of any Europeans.

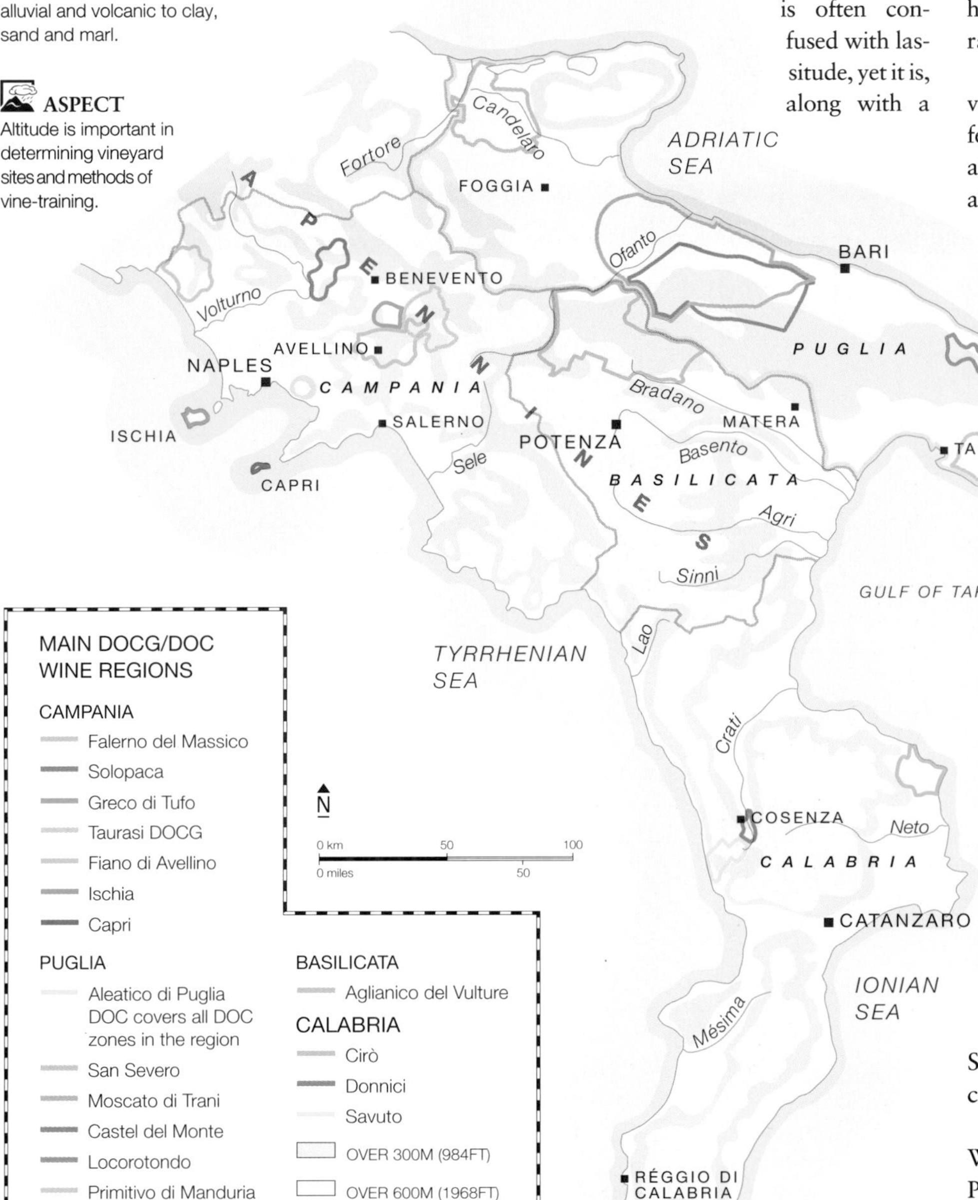

Yet the rich inheritance of native grape varieties is now the South's greatest strength. Few other wine regions can boast such individual varieties as Negroamaro, Uva di Troia, Montepulciano, Aglianico, Gaglioppo, Primitivo, Piedirosso, Moscato, Greco di Tufo, Fiano, Falanghina and Mantonico.

Unfortunately this lackadaisical, if healthy, approach to living has meant that the southern vineyards were easy prey to the focussed, aggressive northerners. Historically, the Bourbon aristocracy based in Naples had supported local quality wines, but Italy's unification saw northern merchants invade the south, intent upon sourcing dark, ripe reds to bolster their pale northern brews, and many ancient, heady, exotic wines disappeared into blending vats in Verona, Florence and Alba. In addition, the traditional, low-yielding, bush-trained vines were often replaced over the next century by high-yielding, wire-trellised ones, and the great southern grapes by the unsuitable Trebbiano and Sangiovese from further north. Those grapes from high-trained Trebbiano and Sangiovese vines produce little worth drinking. Not only are yields too high, but the northern varieties ripen too quickly in the south losing in the process all the flavours they might have shown if grown in a cooler climate. On the other hand, those growers who retained their bush-trained vines are, with modern wine-making technology, now in a position to capitalize on the superior nature of their raw materials. If such indigenous wealth can be harnessed to modern technology and an international outlook, then the heady perfumes of the south will smile indulgently on their rather less well-endowed cousins from the north.

These varieties, as the Greeks noted, are ideally suited to the varied terrain and climate of the south. Altitude, topographical features and proximity to the sea can all exert profound moderating influences on latitude and result in mesoclimates considerably cooler than one would imagine in such a southern environment. On the slopes of Basilicata's Mount Vulture, for instance, Aglianico vines planted at 500 to 600m (1640 to 1970ft) high are, in late October, among the last in Italy to be harvested. Such a long growing season results in wines which, with their elegant and complex flavours, belie their southern origins. In Campania's Irpinian foothills, altitude similarly influences Taurasi (also from Aglianico) and whites like Greco di Tufo.

In other areas, however, it is proximity to the sea that tips the scales in favour of quality wine production. In Calabria's Cirò zone, for instance, the cool breezes blowing off the Ionian Sea refresh the low-lying Gaglioppo vines, extending their growing season and resulting in the wonderful flavours of liquorice, figs and cumin found in the best wines. Similarly, in Puglia, on the flat Salento peninsula that comprises the stiletto heel of Italy's boot, the winds blowing between the Adriatic and Ionian seas alleviate what would otherwise be desert conditions and produce the ideal climate for strapping reds – Salice Salentino, Copertino and Brindisi, among others – that can be some of Italy's best wines.

WINE REGIONS

Puglia is the South's most important wine region. Stretching almost 400km (250 miles) into the Adriatic, the mostly flat

Most of Calabria is covered by rugged mountainous terrain which gets blasted to a barren beauty during the bakingly hot summers. One of the few crops the scrubby land can support is vines, as here at Frascineto in the DOC zone of Pollino.

landscape means that Puglia produces 17 per cent of all Italian wine. Much of this bulk comes from the northern part of the region, where high-trained Sangiovese and Trebbiano vines in the San Severo zone account for about 30 per cent of Puglia's total DOC production. In central Puglia, the Uva di Troia grape forms the base for the Castel del Monte, Rosso Barletta and Rosso Canosa DOCs, all of which have yet to realize their full potential. Quality remains patchy, and though I've been saying this for a few years now, the promise for the future is great.

Further to the south, in the Salento peninsula, the bush-trained Negroamaro grape reigns supreme. Because it produces, as its name suggests, wines that are dark and bitter, the Malvasia Nera is used to soften its rough edges and make the wines more supple and aromatic. This successful partnership works well in DOCs like Salice Salentino, Copertino, Squinzano, Leverano and Brindisi, where flavours of game, chocolate and prunes give way to a generous body and a velvety texture. And thanks to this partnership and some inspired wine-making, this once backwards part of Puglia now leads the south in the production of quality wines.

In theory, this accolade should go to Aglianico del Vulture, Basilicata's only DOC. The Aglianico grape is one of Italy's finest red varieties, and the long growing season in the hills south of Melfi provides it with an ideal stage on which to perform. But while the script is a classic, the performance tends to be amateurish. The young wines often have a thrillingly vibrant flavour, but by the time they are bottled, they are dull and flaccid. Only producers such as D'Angelo and Paternoster score the odd hit.

Calabria forms the toe of the Italian boot, kicking out into the Ionian and Tyrrhenian seas and only missing Sicily by the 3km (2 miles) that are the Straits of Messina. With the exception of its 780km- (485 miles) long coastline, the whole of the region is wild and mountainous. But although such a terrain should provide many ideal vineyard sites – and in Greek times Calabria was noted for the quality of its wines – little quality wine is produced today.

Over 90 per cent of Calabria's DOC wine comes from the Cirò zone, situated on the Ionian coast. The reds from the Gaglioppo grape tend to have less colour but more tannin than those from Puglia's Negroamaro, but display a similar broad range of exotic flavours. In recent years the great advance here has been the introduction of temperature control in wine-making, resulting in wines with fresher, more defined flavours. The white wines of Cirò, made from the Greco grape, have benefited to an even greater extent, though they are less distinctive than their red counterparts.

To the north of Calabria is Campania, bordered to the east by Basilicata and northern Puglia, to the north by Lazio and to the west by the Tyrrhenian Sea. Campania is better known for the beautiful Bay of Naples and Mount Vesuvius than for the intrinsic quality of its wines, but in the Apennine foothills that slope gently from the inland mountainous peaks to the flat shoreline there exists great potential. The grapes – reds like Aglianico and Piedirosso, and whites like Greco and Falanghina – are in place, and the cool hills of northern and central Campania provide ideal conditions for them to flourish. Despite the efforts of producers such as Mastroberardino (a classic example of a one-eyed king in the kingdom of the blind), Campania remains even less developed than Puglia when its lush green hills should be producing some of Italy's best wines. As with the rest of the south, far too many opportunities are being squandered.

SARDINIA

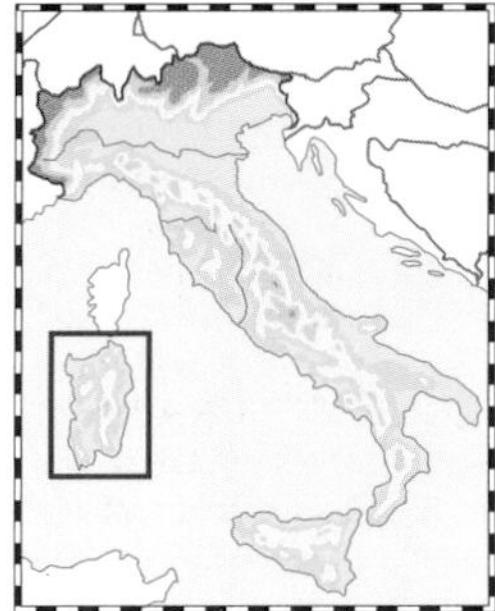

RED GRAPES
Cannonau, Monica and Carignano are the most important traditional varieties.

WHITE GRAPES
Torbato produces the best wine but Nuragus accounts for a third of vineyard plantings. Other significant varieties are Vermentino, Vernaccia di Oristano and Malvasia Sarda.

CLIMATE
Sardinia has ample sunshine. The south and west are exposed to hot winds from Africa. Drought can be a problem away from the influence of the mountains.

SOIL
Most of Sardinia comprises granite and volcanic rock. The remainder includes calcareous deposits, alluvial sand, gravel and clay.

ASPECT
The better wines come from the hills, but many new vineyards are in flat, dry regions.

CONSIDERING THAT IT IS the second largest island in the Mediterranean, Sardinia remains curiously unknown to the outsider. It is also remarkable, given its great strategic importance, that while it was often subjected to long periods of foreign domination, the island was never really conquered. The feeling of strangeness often experienced by travellers on Sardinia is emphasized by the continuing use of the native Sardo language which is an amalgam of Spanish, Catalan and Arabic built on a Latin foundation. Equally mysterious, especially to the foreign tourists who descend on the island every summer from the maritime nations of northern Europe with their ancient fishing traditions, is that the people of Sardinia resolutely eschewed the lure of the sea and its wealth and remained hill and mountain dwellers until very recently. The root of this conundrum must reach back into antiquity as do the odd stone towers called *nuraghi* which dot the landscape of the island for no known purpose.

Nowadays the island is beginning to gain a reputation for its gloriously rugged coastline and shimmering sea, in places almost the colour of lapis lazuli. The fine sandy beaches of the lovely Costa Smeralda peninsula have already been discovered by the rich and famous, but elsewhere you can still find secluded bays of unsurpassed beauty.

Not many tourists venture into Sardinia's wild, mountainous interior where most of the inhabitants can only scrape a living by tending their sheep. These mountains, hills and plateaux which make up 85 per cent of the island would be well-suited to quality wine-making, but the majority of Sardinia's vineyards are planted by growers who choose the easy option offered by the Campidano plain between Cagliari and Oristano, or else the flatlands near Alghero. As vines need to struggle to produce their best fruit it is evident that this lazy approach has contributed significantly to the flow of unexciting and even downright poor wine which has borne down like a tidal wave from the co-operative cellars. In the north the terrain varies between wooded hills with an equitable climate where grapes grown on granite-based soil can produce appealing, well-balanced red and white wines, to the plain of Alghero where the hot and dry conditions mean that extra care needs to be taken to prevent the vines from producing too high a yield or the grapes from overripening.

The vineyards to the west of the island also improve in quality with altitude. Malvasia di Bosa comes from steep volcanic hill sites, whereas the grapes for Vernaccia di Oristano benefit from the rich alluvial sand and gravel of the Tirso Valley, where the hot, dry climate enables the grapes to reach optimum ripeness. The east of the island is heavily influenced by the Gennargentu mountains where the vineyards benefit from cooling north-easterly winds. Up in the coastal hills the climate becomes somewhat hotter and drier, and the mixed granite soil generally only renders comparatively low yields.

The fertile soils of the south, allied with hot, dry conditions, best suit fuller, strapping reds like Cannonau. Ordinary table wines made here tend to be very ordinary.

GRAPE VARIETIES AND WINE STYLES

The strong sense of separation from the rest of Italy is reflected in the grape varieties which are grown on Sardinia. Although several are indigenous, some of the most important come from Spain, fostered by the Aragonese who arrived on the island in the thirteenth century. The majority of these varieties have confirmed the popular wisdom that the hot maritime climate is best suited to the production of big strong aperitif and dessert wines. Here Sardinia has one of its few points in common with Sicily.

Nevertheless, as times and tastes have changed, there has been growing pressure from export markets for light table wines. The co-operatives, which account for 60 per cent of Sardinia's production, recognized a passing bandwagon, jumped on it with ill-considered haste, and started pumping out rivers of anonymous white, ideal for the European wine lake! Now the pendulum is starting to swing back and a number of fresh, dry yet fruity whites are being made from Nuragus and Vermentino. The finest white, however, comes from the rare Torbato grape grown chiefly around Alghero.

Putting new trends aside, the most distinctive wines continue to be those traditional oddities for which Sardinia was once best known. Vernaccia di Oristano develops a light film of flor yeast in cask, similar to that of sherry production, which prevents spoilage while imparting a distinctive spiced and nutty character. Its history dates back to at least the sixteenth century when it was widely appreciated throughout Italy, and it can come either fortified or not. Nasco, made from the grape of the same name, is another rare delight which also can be fortified and comes in dry, medium-dry or sweet styles.

Malvasia di Bosa, too, can be vinified in different ways according to tradition and the foibles of the winemaker. It may either be found as a sweet or dry aperitif or else as a fortified wine. Sometimes, like Vernaccia di Oristano, a film of flor yeast might be allowed to develop in cask for added flavour and complexity. Malvasia di Cagliari can likewise be made sweet and fortified but is generally considered best as a delicate dry aperitif. The red grape variety, Cannonau, though usually now made as a dry table wine, can make a glorious, sweet, mouth-filling dessert wine of real quality, and often it is likened to port.

Apart from these fascinating Sardinian specialities, most wine from the island is fairly run-of-the-mill. Some of it will be made under the rules of the four regional DOCs, but much of the best everyday table wine is non-DOC.

SICILY

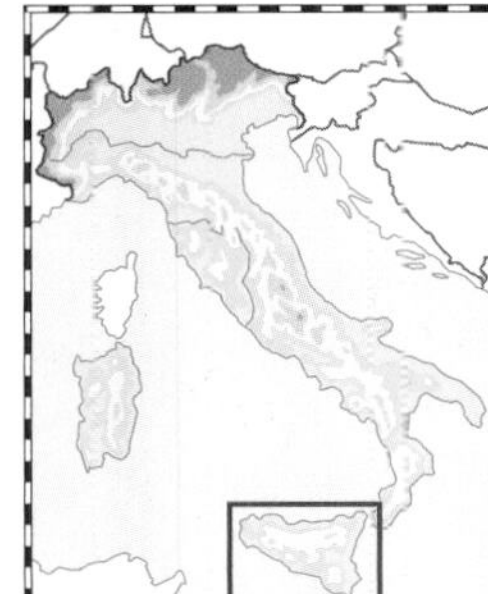

WHEN I THINK OF SICILY I am immediately transported back to the incredibly haunting ancient Greek temple and theatre at Segesta, or else I can see again the gloriously inspiring medieval mosaics in the cathedral of Monreale up above Palermo. My first ever job offer was as a baritone with Opera Massima in Palermo. They don't know how lucky they are that I turned to wine. Stop someone in the street, however, and ask what they associate with Sicily and nine out of ten will probably reply the Mafia. Sadly, the only time that this beautiful island gets a mention in the newspapers is when another vicious gangland atrocity has been committed. How much better it would be to balance this by reporting on the magnificent scenery, fine beaches and remarkable art and architecture which you can find all over Sicily.

The traditions of wine-making on the island stretch back, with only a few interruptions, to antiquity, and reached previously unimagined heights in the late eighteenth century when the English first created Marsala. With the decline in popularity of fortified wines, Sicily began to be side-tracked. Now its fortunes are looking up again as it becomes a source of table wines of a genuinely individual style.

The north of Sicily is dominated by the tail end of the Apennines which sweep down through the entire length of Italy. The south of the island, in contrast, consists mainly of arid, scrubby hills where irrigation is essential. The main geographical feature in the east is the brooding presence of the volcano Mount Etna, so it is not surprising that much of the island's soil is volcanic in nature. The hills of the north are cool, with good rainfall but also sufficient sun to ensure ideal conditions for grapes to ripen. The south and east are less well-favoured, lying in the path of hot winds blowing directly from North Africa. Paradoxically, the coolest vineyards, planted on the slopes of Etna, overlook Catania, one of the hottest cities in Italy. The centre of Sicily provides first-class conditions for viticulture through a felicitous combination of cool, high altitudes and mixed volcanic, clay and limestone soils. In the west lies the greatest expanse of vineyards, not only in Sicily, but in all Italy. Here the hot, dry climate and generally arid conditions lead to highly concentrated wines ideal for Marsala.

GRAPE VARIETIES AND WINE STYLES

The reputation of Sicily as a wine supplier was built upon its sweet dessert and fortified wines and these continue to show the greatest depth, style and complexity. Best known until it declined in popularity and quality was Marsala, now once more achieving great heights after a courageous and successful overhaul of its rules of production. You should attempt to overcome your preconceived notion of Marsala as a wine fit only for sauce in some local Italian restaurant, and try instead a dry or *vergine* version. It will come as a revelation. Marsala can be made from different grapes and can come in various styles and levels of sweetness. These include Grillo, Catarratto, Inzolia and Damaschino. The first of these is thought to have migrated to Sicily only in the nineteenth century, but the remaining three have been grown on the island since early times.

The sweet tradition is further reflected in a fascinating range of luscious wines made either from Moscato or Malvasia. The most northerly of these comes from the Aeolian Islands, or Isole Lipari, and is called Malvasia delle Lipari. It is naturally sweet, with an exquisite bouquet. On the other side of Sicily lies the sun-baked volcanic island of Pantelleria. Here the rich, intense Moscato wine is made from dried and concentrated grapes of a variety of the Moscato known locally as Zibibbo. In between these two geographic extremes come Moscato di Noto and Moscato di Siracusa, but sadly these extraordinary sweet wines are made only in tiny quantities in some years, if at all.

Table wines are often poor and dilute, and thoroughly lacking in any recommendable character. In a region where 90 per cent of the output comes from co-operatives it is usually the private producers who achieve the best quality. On a positive note it is very refreshing to find that Sicilians remain largely faithful to their traditional vine types and do not try to ape the rest of Italy and elsewhere by rushing to plant international grape varieties. The down side is that only two and a half per cent of Sicilian wine qualifies for DOC. The best that does includes Cerasuolo di Vittoria. This deep, cherry-coloured red is made mainly from Frappato and Calabrese grapes and comes from the south of Sicily, just west of Ragusa. It is joined by Bianco d'Alcamo, which occasionally can be made to show real class, though more often it is watery and anonymous. The grape used is Catarratto, with a little Grecanico and Trebbiano. Faro, further north, is undistinguished, while Etna in its white and red versions, if not *rosato*, can be decent when handled by a dedicated and careful winemaker.

The combination of numerous co-operatives, political corruption, and lack of quality means that the two wine names most widely known outside Sicily are Corvo from the independent Duca di Salaparuta, and Regaleali. The first of these now accounts for around ten million bottles a year of reliable and, in their top selections, excellent wine made from local grapes from vineyards all over Sicily. The second is the creation of Count Tasca d'Almerita whose family makes wines of world-class standard. These two pioneering companies faultlessly demonstrate that Sicily can turn out the kind of wine which the world now increasingly demands.

RED GRAPES
The best red variety is Nero d'Avola (Calabrese), followed by Nerello. Others are Frappato di Vittoria and Perricone (Pignatello).

WHITE GRAPES
Forty per cent of Sicily's vineyards are planted with Catarratto Bianco. Trebbiano Toscano is also widespread. Inzolia and Carricante thrive, but Grecanico is declining and Zibibbo is often grown as a table grape.

CLIMATE
Rainfall is scarce throughout much of the island, and the south is particularly arid. The north and east are cooler and less prone to drought.

SOIL
Near Etna the soils naturally are volcanic. Elsewhere they range from chalky clay to limestone.

ASPECT
Many vineyards are irrigated and planted very densely. The best are found on the cooler slopes in the north and east. The most extensive vineyard area in Italy is on the plain and low hills surrounding Trapani.

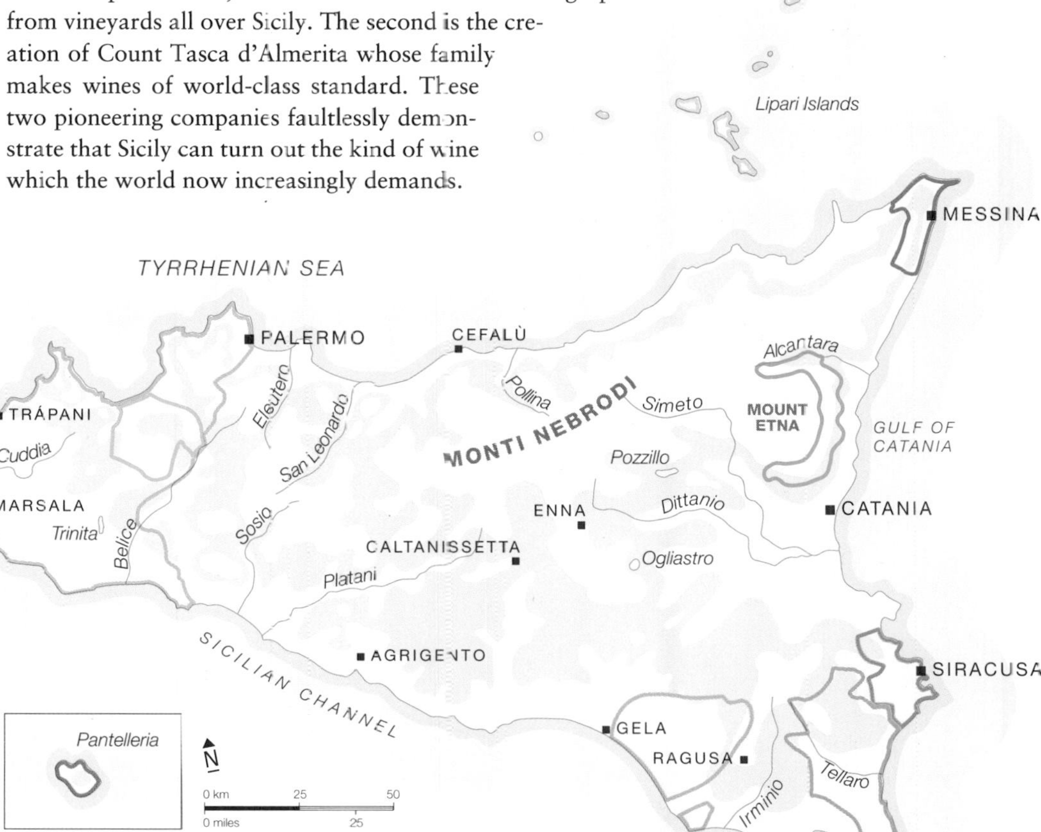

SPAIN

I WAS BEGINNING TO WONDER whether we'd have to wait for ever, but, thank goodness, there are now unmistakable signs that the country that has more land devoted to vines than any other nation, and yet has relentlessly underperformed for generations, is at last beginning to show what it can do. With the exception of a few well-known areas like Rioja, Penedés and Jerez, Spain had little reputation on the international stage. But now it's all change as a new, vibrant Spain begins to muscle into the limelight, demanding attention for a potent brew of indigenous styles that are being recreated with the benefit of modern technology, and international styles that are surfacing with an unmistakable aura of Spain.

Spain is basically a great deal hotter and drier than its more famous wine neighbour France, so the variation in local climates is less and the range of grapes that find conditions ideal is limited. It has taken her a long while to appreciate the need to search out mesoclimates influenced by altitude and by maritime cooling conditions. And it has taken her some time to realize that hot-climate grapes like Garnacha, Cariñena, Tempranillo, Verdejo and Airén can produce delicious flavours if approached with up-to-the-minute New World technology and attitudes.

The lush, hilly North-West is heavily influenced by cool, damp Atlantic conditions and the fragrant whites and tangy, juicy reds are marvellously individual. Further south along the Duero river are some of Spain's most exciting reds and whites.

Andalucía in the South-West doesn't have much to offer in terms of table wines, but the fortified wines of Jerez and Montilla-Moriles can be among the world's greatest. Málaga's fame has faded since the nineteenth century, but occasional bottles still show how exciting her wines can be. The large area of the Levante stretching between Alicante and Valencia and the vast plateau of La Mancha and Valdepeñas inland to the south of Madrid used to be synonymous with cheap, coarse flavours that filled the flagons of forgettable international brands owned by brewers and distillers. Yet the enormous potential for low-priced, attractive wine is at last being realized as the giant wine companies modernize their wineries and their techniques.

The North-East has traditionally been thought of as the quality wine capital of Spain, with famous reds and whites from Rioja and Penedés, and Cava sparklers. But here, too, the winds of change are blowing, and areas like Navarra, Somontano, Campo de Borja and Costers del Segre are making thrilling contributions to the new, exciting Spain.

The Garnacha vine is Spain's most widely planted red variety and thrives in the hot, dry, windy climate of Cariñena, one of Aragón's four wine regions.

The Wine Regions of Spain

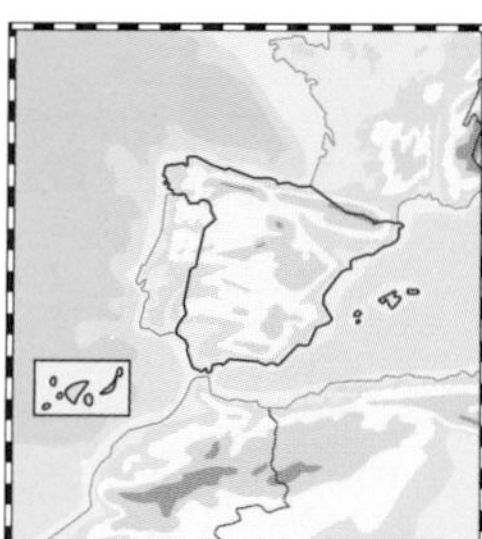

However much the New World entices and enraptures the dedicated follower of wine fashion, Spain somehow manages to hang on to its reputation as one of the most exotic countries to grow the grape. How has it done this? There was a period in the 1980s when much of Spain's wine was desperately mediocre, and we turned right round and headed east to Central Europe for reliable wine bargains. But across the Iberian peninsula in the 1990s, the arrival of shiny new equipment, the replanting of vineyards with better varieties as well as disease-free vines and the use of highly trained enologists, some of them from abroad, all helped to revive enthusiasm on the part of Spanish wine-makers. And all the time we were grumbling about the quality of most of her wines, the vinous tradition and heritage of Spanish wine-making never quite lost its magic.

We can't really put this down to Spain's rich treasure trove of native grape varieties (Tempranillo, under a variety of local pseudonyms, and Albariño are the best of the bunch), or an assortment of unique wine styles – only sherry, maybe red Rioja and Galicia are truly original. But there is the varied landscape of the wine regions: the broad Duero Valley; the dramatic, rocky foothills of the cool Pyrenees; the lush hillside pastures of Galicia; the scorching, stony, central plains of La Mancha; or the baked white plains of Jerez in Andalucía. It seems that however much the landscape and climate alter, there are always vineyards – indeed, Spain has the world's largest acreage under vine. It is not, however, its largest wine producer. Spain is a mainly arid country, where vines are usually only planted on land which isn't fertile enough to grow other crops, and its comparative low yields and many out-of-date wine-making practices have kept its total volume down.

Spain's most important geographical features are the huge central plateau or *meseta* which occupies the heartland of the country and high mountain ranges rising steeply from the coast around this plateau – the Pyrenees, the Cantabrian mountains, and the sierras Guadarrama, Morena and Nevada are the main ones. Not surprisingly in a large country of such diverse scenery, the climate varies from the cooler uplands to the coastal Mediterranean and Atlantic belts sandwiched between the sea and the mountains and, inland in the high *meseta*, arid semi-desert with its extremes of temperature.

Variety is the key to Spain's wine regions and starting in the north-east, important vineyard areas are found within Navarra, Aragón and Catalonia. The large region of Navarra is an increasingly important producer of acclaimed reds and *rosados*, and Aragón's little Somontano DO is a picturesque, verdant spot in the Pyrenean foothills where wine-making is progressing at a cracking pace. Further to the south-east in Aragón, Cariñena sits sweltering in the sun. Over to the east in Catalonia, the vineyards are divided between small, demarcated areas: Alella's sea-facing vineyards produce good white wine, while craggy Priorato is responsible for some of the heftiest reds in the world, and wine-making in Penedés is way ahead of the rest of Spain. Nestling up to Navarra is La Rioja, with its world-famous Rioja wine from the upper Ebro Valley.

The north-west of the country is known as 'green Spain' because of its Atlantic climate and high level of rainfall. Perched above the Portuguese border in Galicia are the wetter regions of Rías Baixas, producer of some of Spain's most fragrant whites from Albariño and Ribeiro, a pretty, hilly place with rapidly improving wines. On the north Atlantic coast in the País Vasco are the small DOs of Getaria and Bizkaia, where the traditional wine of the Basque seaboard, Chacolí, is produced. In Castilla y León, through which the Duero river makes its way to Portugal, is the flat region of Toro, best for its red wines, and Rueda, producer of fresh whites. Just beyond this is the tiny Cigales DO, where the *rosado* flows fresh and plentiful, and the up-and-coming Ribera del Duero, literally, 'the bank of the Douro', a high pine-strewn, undulating wine region of increasing renown and popularity.

Down in central Spain, the land is as hot and baked as you will find anywhere in Europe. Castilla-La Mancha stretches out to form a huge, arid plateau of windmills and vines, alternately whipped by cold winters and scorched by impossibly hot summers. It is dry and mostly inhospitable, but here lie more than half of Spain's vineyards. La Mancha also includes the DO of Valdepeñas in its southern extreme, increasingly known for highly drinkable red wine.

Over to the east of La Mancha is Utiel-Requena with its *rosados*, and Valencia, famous for its grapy dessert wine, Moscatel de Valencia. Much of Spain's south-eastern corner has no vines, but turn the corner into the far south coastal districts and you stumble into Málaga, its famous fortified sticky wines produced from vineyards on hot inland plots. Just above it is Montilla-Moriles, another sunbaked area where white soil and Pedro Ximénez grapes create sherry look-alikes.

The real thing is, of course, produced further west in Jerez and Manzanilla where vast, gently sloping vineyards cover areas of chalky soil known as *albariza*. Jerez's neighbour to the north-west, Condado de Huelva, used to sell its fruit to the sherry producers; now it is turning its attention to light white wines. And, finally, there is wine produced on the happy holiday islands. In Mallorca, Binissalem is the main Balearic wine area while the wine producers in the Canaries have recently gained DO status in four areas.

THE CLASSIFICATION SYSTEM FOR SPANISH WINE

Spanish wine law is administered by the Instituto Nacional de Denominaciones de Origen (INDO) and run by local Consejos Reguladores. Rioja was the first region to set up a Consejo Regulador in 1926, followed by Jerez and Málaga. Legislation revolves around a DO (*denominacion de origen)* system which was revised when Spain joined the EU in 1986. Like all EU countries Spain's wine is divided into two levels, quality wine (Vino de Calidad Producido en Región Demarcada or VCPRD) and table wine (Vino de Mesa).

QUALITY WINES

- **Denominacion de Origen (DO)** Roughly equivalent to French ACs, these are the best-known, classic wines of Spain and there are now over 40 DOs. Each DO has its own Consejo which, together with the local government and INDO, decides on such issues of quality control as yields and grape varieties.
- **Denominacion de Origen Calificada (DOC)** This new super-category came into being in 1991 with the award of a DOC to Rioja. It is reserved for wines which have a long tradition of high quality. Regulations are more stringent and include rigorous tasting. Rioja remains the only DOC to date.

TABLE WINES

- **Vino de la Tierra (VdlT)** This is wine from a specially demarcated region which does not have a DO at present but which has a character that is identifiable as local to its region. At least 60 per cent of the wine must come from the stated region. This category roughly corresponds to the French *vin de pays*.
- **Vino Comarcal (VC)** This is the next stage down in quality. There are 28 areas at the moment and they have no great pretension to quality. Producers may put a vintage on the label.
- **Vino de Mesa (VdM)** This is wine made from grapes from unclassified vineyards, or wine which has been declassified by blending from different classified regions. The label has no vintage.

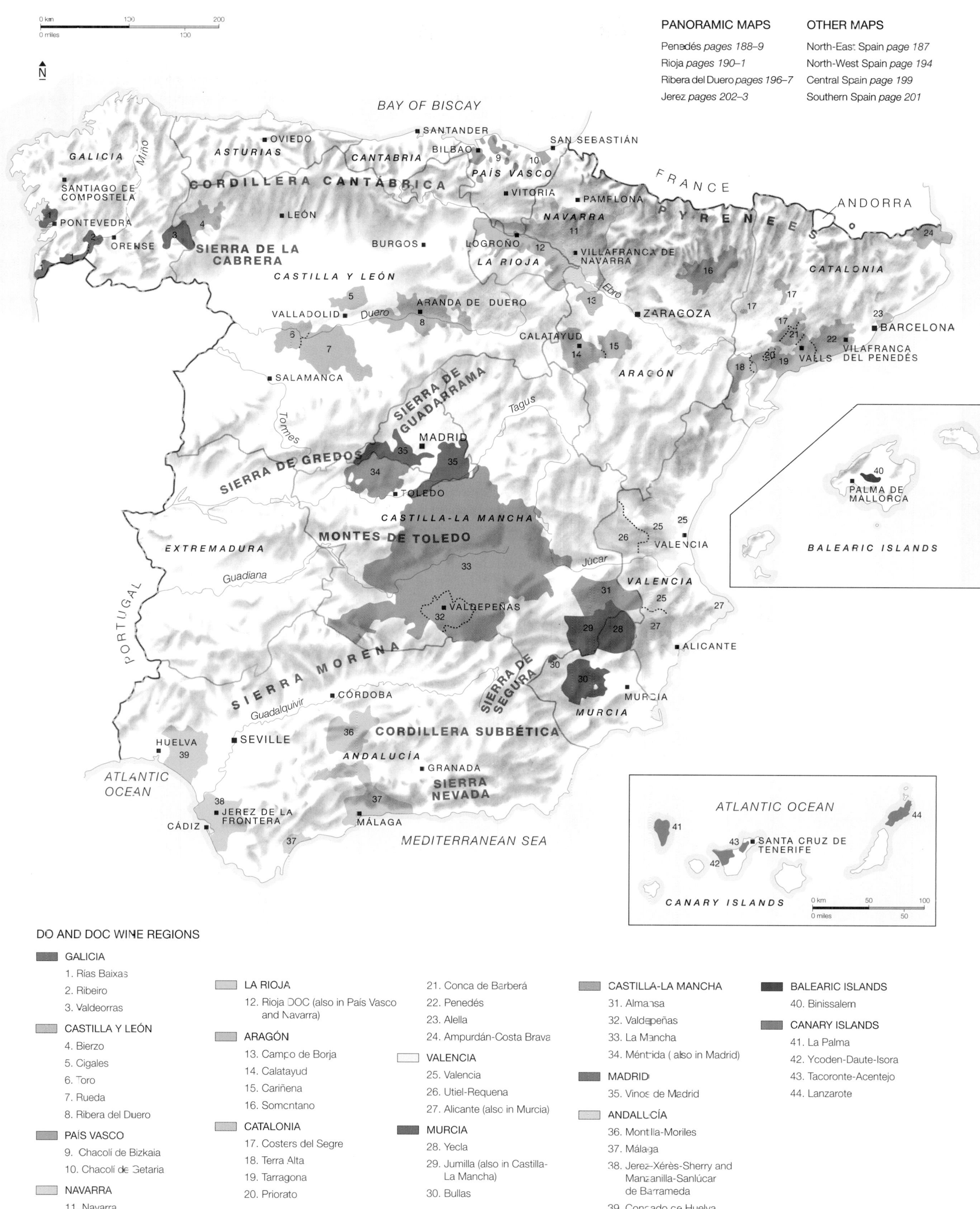
0 km 100 200
0 miles 100
N
PANORAMIC MAPS
Penedés pages 188–9
Rioja pages 190–1
Ribera del Duero pages 196–7
Jerez pages 202–3
OTHER MAPS
North-East Spain page 187
North-West Spain page 194
Central Spain page 199
Southern Spain page 201
BAY OF BISCAY
OVIEDO
SANTANDER
SAN SEBASTIÁN
GALICIA
ASTURIAS
CANTABRIA
BILBAO
PAÍS VASCO
Miño
CORDILLERA CANTÁBRICA
VITORIA
PAMPLONA
FRANCE
ANDORRA
SANTIAGO DE COMPOSTELA
LEÓN
NAVARRA
PYRENEES
PONTEVEDRA
ORENSE
SIERRA DE LA CABRERA
BURGOS
LOGROÑO
VILLAFRANCA DE NAVARRA
LA RIOJA
CATALONIA
CASTILLA Y LEÓN
Ebro
VALLADOLID
Duero
ARANDA DE DUERO
ZARAGOZA
BARCELONA
CALATAYUD
VILAFRANCA DEL PENEDÈS
VALLS
ARAGÓN
SALAMANCA
SIERRA DE GUADARRAMA
Tagus
Tormes
MADRID
SIERRA DE GREDOS
TOLEDO
PALMA DE MALLORCA
BALEARIC ISLANDS
CASTILLA-LA MANCHA
VALENCIA
MONTES DE TOLEDO
EXTREMADURA
Júcar
Guadiana
VALENCIA
PORTUGAL
VALDEPEÑAS
ALICANTE
SIERRA MORENA
SIERRA DE SEGURA
CÓRDOBA
MURCIA
Guadalquivir
MURCIA
HUELVA
SEVILLE
CORDILLERA SUBBÉTICA
ANDALUCÍA
GRANADA
ATLANTIC OCEAN
SIERRA NEVADA
JEREZ DE LA FRONTERA
CÁDIZ
MÁLAGA
MEDITERRANEAN SEA
ATLANTIC OCEAN
SANTA CRUZ DE TENERIFE
CANARY ISLANDS
0 km 50 100
0 miles 50
DO AND DOC WINE REGIONS
GALICIA
1. Rías Baixas
2. Ribeiro
3. Valdeorras
CASTILLA Y LEÓN
4. Bierzo
5. Cigales
6. Toro
7. Rueda
8. Ribera del Duero
PAÍS VASCO
9. Chacolí de Bizkaia
10. Chacolí de Getaria
NAVARRA
11. Navarra
LA RIOJA
12. Rioja DOC (also in País Vasco and Navarra)
ARAGÓN
13. Campo de Borja
14. Calatayud
15. Cariñena
16. Somontano
CATALONIA
17. Costers del Segre
18. Terra Alta
19. Tarragona
20. Priorato
21. Conca de Barberá
22. Penedés
23. Alella
24. Ampurdán-Costa Brava
VALENCIA
25. Valencia
26. Utiel-Requena
27. Alicante (also in Murcia)
MURCIA
28. Yecla
29. Jumilla (also in Castilla-La Mancha)
30. Bullas
CASTILLA-LA MANCHA
31. Almansa
32. Valdepeñas
33. La Mancha
34. Méntrida (also in Madrid)
MADRID
35. Vinos de Madrid
ANDALUCÍA
36. Montilla-Moriles
37. Málaga
38. Jerez-Xérès-Sherry and Manzanilla-Sanlúcar de Barrameda
39. Condado de Huelva
BALEARIC ISLANDS
40. Binissalem
CANARY ISLANDS
41. La Palma
42. Ycoden-Daute-Isora
43. Tacoronte-Acentejo
44. Lanzarote

North-East Spain

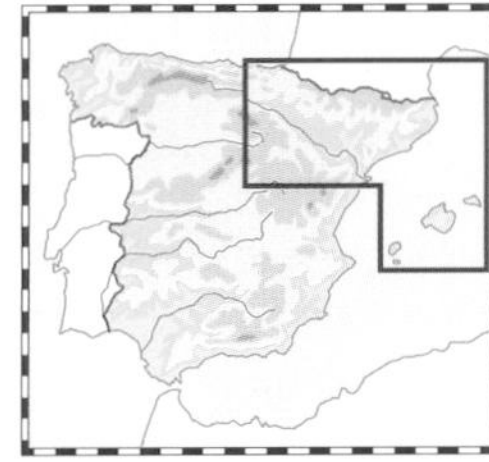

RED GRAPES
Tempranillo, Garnacha Tinta, Cariñena, Monastrell, Moristel and Graciano are the main ones. Cabernet Sauvignon and Merlot are also grown.

WHITE GRAPES
Macabeo (Viura), Garnacha Blanca, Xarel-lo, Parellada, Malvasía are the principal varieties, with some Chardonnay.

CLIMATE
This varies, from the damp northern Basque coastline to the pleasant moderate conditions of Rioja and the Catalan coastline, to the semi-arid parts of southern Aragón and inland Catalonia.

SOIL
These are very varied, from the reddish-brown limestone of Navarra and Cariñena to the calcareous clay of parts of Rioja and Penedés chalk.

ASPECT
Vineyards are found on flat plateau land, coastal hills and high inland terraces.

I MUST HAVE WANDERED THROUGH north-eastern Spain more than most parts of Europe. Our first ever family holiday abroad was on the Costa Brava and the first time I escaped from the family for my own holiday I ended up very excited and nervous in Barcelona railway station late at night *en route* for Tarragona and Tangier. I was all of 16. My parents thought I was on a cosy campsite in Normandy. I wish. A year or two later, I had my first, not entirely pleasurable taste of Chacolí in San Sebastián – I *was* on a campsite this time. Usually anything tastes good on a campsite. This didn't. My first experience of Rioja must have been a bit more successful because I don't really remember bedding down for the night in a ravine near Cenicero where I almost got run over by a train just before dawn. That's always a sign that the local wine was good and you drank deep.

Since then, though I've usually been in a bit more of a rush, I have made time to traverse the Pyrenees – west to east, not north to south – in and out of France and Spain, along tiny mountain roads, touching on Navarra and Huesca, but every time the broad, flat prairies of the Ebro Valley get too oppressive, I'd hightail it back to the hills. And I have struck out into the lean and mournful hinterland west of Barcelona, beyond Lleida and Zaragoza, greeting its infrequent and forgettable towns with quite unreasonable enthusiasm, and in passing marvelling at what prescient force drove the Raventós family to establish the Raimat estate in this remote saltbrush purgatory.

Raimat have carved their impressive estate out of some of the least promising land in Spain, but the north-east in general is well-endowed with widely differing conditions. You couldn't get much more different than the straggly dribs and drabs of vines that half-ripen in the damp, cool hills near San Sebastián and suck their moisture directly off the Bay of Biscay. Their thin Chacolí wine has a strictly local following. Just south of these Basque vines the Cantabrian mountains soar, and soak up most of the rest of the moisture that rolls in from the Bay of Biscay. They act as vital protection for Rioja's and Navarra's vineyards, without which grapes like Tempranillo and Garnacha would never ripen. The Pyrenees which act as the border with France aren't so much a protective range, since the ice-cold winds that whip southwards through the valleys originate in their chilly peaks. But they do provide water, not rain but irrigation water from the many rivers that hurtle out of the foothills before joining the Ebro and heading east for the Mediterranean. Without them, much of Aragón and western Catalonia would be near-desert. Indeed, it's surprising how close you get to the Mediterranean before the landscape relaxes and the hills become less jagged and withdrawn. It's a fairly narrow coastal strip from the French border down through Barcelona to the mouth of the Ebro below Tarragona, but the Catalans characteristically make use of every inch of land they've got.

Vineyards near Laguardia show the yellow calcareous soil of Rioja Alavesa.

PAÍS VASCO

Where better to start for a tour around north-east Spain than in the country's tiniest DOs, those of Chacolí de Getaria and Chacolí de Bizkaia, in the Basque country of País Vasco. Here, on Spain's Cantabrian coast, the climate is exceedingly damp – about 1600mm (63in) of rain falls each year. It's also pretty cool, but that doesn't stop the locals farming a small number of vines of the local grape, Ondarribi Zuri from which they make the traditional cider-like Basque white wine usually quaffed locally with fresh Atlantic seafood. A small amount of red wine is also made, from Ondarribi Beltza. In this damp region where fungal diseases quickly take hold, the vines are traditionally grown on overhead trellises. The arrival of new technology in the late 1980s, followed by the swift ejection of much old wood from the wineries, was rewarded in 1990 with DO status. Down in the south of the region, in the province of Alava, are the finest Basque vineyards: the Rioja Alavesa sub-region has some of the best Rioja vineyards of all (see page 190).

NAVARRA

This large region used to be best known for its *rosado* wine from the Garnacha grape but Navarra's progress over the past decade has been an example to the rest of Spain. New technology, plus better vineyard management out on Navarra's soft, deep, fertile soils, has begun to coax excellent results out of traditional red Garnacha and, increasingly, from Tempranillo and Cabernet Sauvignon (see page 192). The officially funded experimental winery, Evena, at Olite is one of the most important in Europe, and its influence has been enormous. Navarra seems determined to emerge from under the shadow of its even-more-famous neighbour to the south, Rioja.

LA RIOJA

The region of La Rioja has only one classified wine, Rioja, but it is to date the only one in Spain to be awarded a new super-category, the Rioja DOC, higher than a simpler DO. Rioja's three sub-regions span a segment of the upper Ebro Valley between Haro and Alfaro, with Rioja's capital Logroño marking its centrepoint. I deal with Rioja in more detail on page 190.

South of the Cantabrian mountains, the climate feels more Mediterranean and Rioja is sunny enough to merit its high number of second homes for those who live in the large industrialized cities of Bilbao and San Sebastián north of the mountains. But it remains a surprisingly peaceful part of world, and even Logroño is relatively unspoilt considering it sits in the centre of one of the world's best-known wine regions.

ARAGÓN

The former kingdom of Aragón covers a wide sweep of land below the central Pyrenees, with the long Ebro river running south-eastwards through the region. Around the edges of the wide, flat Ebro Valley are the vineyards. Aragón used to churn out uninspiring wines, but standards are improving generally (see page 192). Directly below Rioja lies Campo de Borja and here as in Rioja, the Ebro plays an important part in forming

the landscape. In Campo de Borja, and also in Cariñena further south, the climate is distinctly continental – in other words, the summers are baking hot and the winters potentially very cold. Add to that a dry wind from the north and you've got some pretty tough conditions for the vine, and wines made from red Garnacha here are cranked up full on the alcohol front. Calatayud, cut off from the Ebro Valley by several small mountain ranges, is a little more humid than Cariñena.

However, Aragón's most interesting DO is north from here across the Ebro. Somontano is a pretty, verdant spot in the Pyrenean foothills. Little mountain streams and a high rainfall keep this area green and fertile, and its mild continental climate in the protective shadow of the Pyrenees helps it make exciting wines, some from the traditional local red grape Moristel, and some from international varieties such as Cabernet Sauvignon, Merlot and Chardonnay.

CAVA

Catalonia's Champagne-method sparkling wines were colloquially called *Champaña* but after a few legal tussles with the Champagne producers of northern France, the Spanish agreed in 1970 to change the name to Cava, meaning 'cellar' in Catalan. The first Cava was made in the town of San Sadurní de Noya in the heart of Penedés by José Raventós of the firm, Codorníu. Raventós had visited Champagne in 1872 and he returned to Spain determined to use the local grapes – Macabeo, Parellada and Xarel-lo – to make a similar sparkling wine. The same varieties are still used today: Macabeo is rather neutral-tasting, though sharpish, making it a good base for sparkling wine; Xarel-lo provides an earthy flavour and higher alcohol; while Parellada is finer and flowery. Chardonnay was authorized in 1986 and plantings are rapidly increasing since Spanish Chardonnay fizz can have lovely fruit and flowery-buttery flavours, as well as a softer character than Champagne.

Cava differs from all the rest of Spain's DOs in that it's not confined to one geographical area and the grapes can be sourced from 159 specified villages all over northern Spain, although most of them are from Penedés in Catalonia.

CATALONIA

The thriving city of Barcelona and its hinterland has made Catalonia one of Spain's most prosperous regions and an independence of spirit and a strong cultural tradition is symbolized by the existence of an official second language, Catalan. The cluster of wine regions along the coastal belt show Catalonia, with its warm Mediterranean climate, to be an important part of Spain's wine story (see page 188). Much of its wine prosperity is based on Cava, and Penedés, as well as being the heart of Cava production, is also Catalonia's most modern DO.

South-west of Penedés, Terra Alta and Priorato mark out the high ground and are ruggedly beautiful places, but the wines from here are still quite rough and alcoholic. The scattered Costers del Segre DO, in the arid west of Catalonia, is famous for the Raimat estate and not much else; the cool, high-altitude Conca de Barberá produces a lot of aromatic white grapes for Cava as well as increasingly good international varieties, and Tarragona, the largest Catalan DO, churns out some fairly basic wine, mostly white. North of Barcelona lies the Alella DO which produces some good fresh white wines, and right in the north is Ampurdán-Costa Brava.

BALEARIC ISLANDS

The tourists on the Costa Brava aren't the only ones who frolic close to a wine industry. Mallorca also has a wine region, Binissalem DO, which lies north of Palma de Mallorca and east of El Pla, the island's rolling central plateau. To the north the Sierra de Alfabia shelter the vineyards from the wet northerly winds. Hot summers, mild winters and limestone in the light soils all add up to good conditions for vines and the grapes can become extremely ripe. In the nineteenth century, sweet Malvasía wine from Binissalem was popular; nowadays the native varieties, Manto Negro and Callet produce dry reds, while Moll (or Prensal) is used for the light whites.

Rioja is usually a blend of several grape varieties from all over the region.

CATALONIA

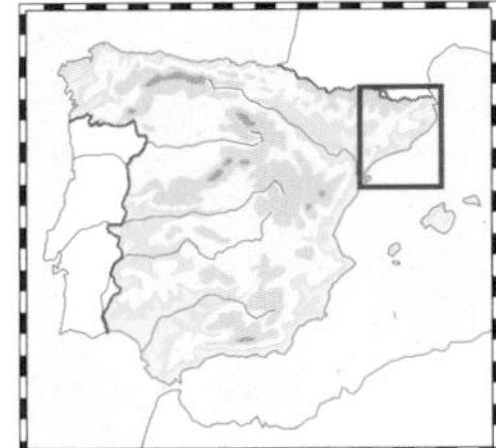

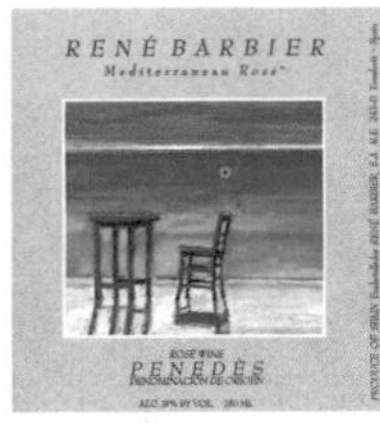

IT'S ALMOST LIKE CROSSING the border into another country. With its separate language (Catalan) much in evidence, its thriving capital city of Barcelona and an independence of spirit unmatched anywhere else in Spain, Catalonia, tucked up into the north-east corner of Spain, is like a little kingdom of its own. That fiercely proud nature is never more in evidence than among the winemakers of the region. Catalonia has always been a prosperous place, and Cava, Spain's Champagne-method sparkling wine, and the mould-breaking Penedés winemaker, Miguel Torres Jnr, have contributed to that wealth.

Catalonia has a great deal of rugged mountain landscape. As well as the Pyrenees which dominates the north of the region, there are mountains hemming in the Mediterranean coast all the way south. The coastal zone, where many of the vineyards are situated, some even within sight of the glistening sea, enjoys a mild Mediterranean climate but as you travel inland towards the border with Aragón, the climate becomes more continental, with hotter summers and colder winters.

PENEDÉS

The Penedés DO completely dominates wine-making in this part of Spain, and provides not only the widest variety of wine styles but also the most innovative leadership in wine in the whole of Spain. More than thirty years ago Penedés was no better known than any other of the Catalan wine areas, but that was before Miguel Torres returned from wine-making studies in France in 1961 to work at the family bodega of Torres at Vilafranca del Penedés in the heart of the region. Since then he has introduced a whole host of international grape varieties into the extensive Torres vineyards – not just Cabernet Sauvignon and Chardonnay but also Riesling, Gewürztraminer, Muscat d'Alsace, Sauvignon Blanc and Pinot Noir – as well as using vine-trellising systems, higher planting densities, organic methods and mechanical pruning quite unknown in Spain at the time. As well as his pioneering methods in the vineyard, Torres has experimented in the bodega – single-variety wines, blending local Parellada and Tempranillo with international varieties, earlier bottling of red wines and temperature-controlled stainless steel fermentation are just a few examples. The Torres influence is not confined just to Penedés – in neighbouring Conca de Barberá their Milmanda vineyard is used to make superb, rich, barrel-fermented Chardonnay of the same name. Miguel Torres has also masterminded vineyards in Chile and California and the Torres name has become known worldwide. The whole of Penedés now basks in his reflected glory and where Torres has led, other winemakers in the region have followed.

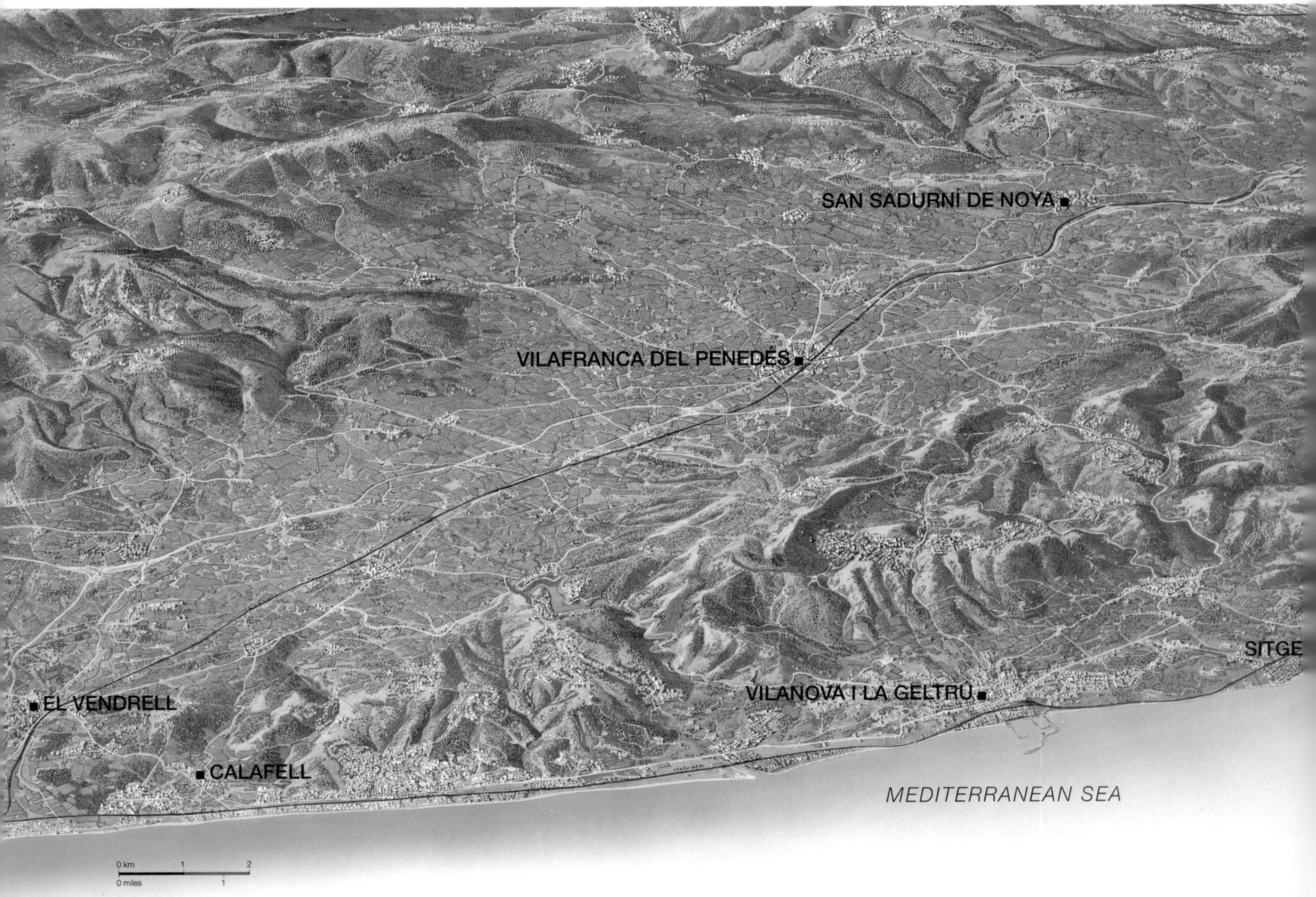

Vineyard conditions differ greatly between the hot, flat coastal strip and the cooler, upland hills. The most aromatic grapes come from the Penedés Superior 40km (25 miles) inland and many of the grapes from these Torres-owned, higher-altitude vineyards are making some of Spain's most progressive wines. About 90 per cent of Penedés wine is white, mainly from Xarel-lo, Macabeo and Parellada (the best for quality), and Chardonnay has been allowed since 1986. The whites can be fresh and lightly aromatic but most of them will never be

great wine. As a result of the Cava boom, red wine has been rather neglected in Penedés. The reds can be rather thin, although the Torres wines from Cabernet Sauvignon and its blends with Tempranillo are some of the exceptions.

Penedés is the most important region for Cava production. In 1898 José Raventós started building his cellar at San Sadurní de Noya where he made the first Cava, Codorniú, and Cava companies now own one-fifth of the Penedés vineyards. Not all the grapes for Cava come from Penedés, but a lot of them do, and many of the big name producers are based at San Sadurní de Noya, where a number of them make still wine as well as sparkling. Wine-making in Penedés revolves around two regional centres, San Sadurní de Noya and Vilafranca del Penedés – go there and you'll see signs for bodegas in every nook and cranny surrounding the residential areas of both towns. The wealth and technical expertise generated by the prosperous Cava industry have kept Penedés way ahead of the rest of Catalonia, but Penedés' problem is that it is so well known for Cava, and Torres is so famous as a brand, that the region itself lacks identity. Nonetheless, this is one of the most modern DOs in the whole of Spain.

OTHER CATALAN WINE AREAS

The most important development in Catalonia outside Penedés is at Lleida, in the parched wastelands between Barcelona and Zaragoza. Here the Raimat winery, owned by the Raventós family of the giant Codorníu group, rises from the scrub. It was the force behind the granting of a DO in 1988 to several patches of vineyard in the area, now called Costers del Segre. Raimat owns over 1200 hectares (3000 acres) here, one-third of the total DO plantings, which are (unusually) irrigated, and include Chardonnay, Cabernet Sauvignon, Tempranillo, Pinot Noir and Merlot. None of the region's traditional white wines were previously up to much but Raimat's wines, both still (especially the Chardonnay, Cabernet Sauvignon and Tempranillo) and sparkling, have been consistently good to excellent.

Right up in the north of Catalonia the tiny Ampurdán-Costa Brava DO hugs the border with France, squeezed in by the Mediterranean and the Pyrenees. Here the mountains come almost down to the sea and the lower foothills are covered in vines. But it isn't all a holiday-making idyll along this beautiful rocky coastline – you'll notice the vines here are firmly tied to stakes, standing up bravely against a dreaded wind locally known as *tramontana*, which can blow up to 140km (90 miles) per hour from the north, and for days on end. The wines here are mostly reds from Garnacha and Cariñena and the whites come from Macabeo and Xarel-lo. Nevertheless, along with many other areas of Catalonia, new international grape varieties, such as Cabernet Sauvignon, Merlot and Chardonnay, are creeping into the vineyards. This is an area dominated by co-operatives using grapes from small, family vineyards. The area is also well-known for producing good-quality corks.

Further south in Catalonia the wine regions cluster together around Barcelona and Tarragona. Down by the coast near Barcelona is Alella, which is rapidly becoming a victim of expanding urbanization. As the city grows, so the poor Alella vineyards, which are capable of producing rather tasty fresh white wines, disappear under new buildings. The DO was extended in 1989 to include land at higher altitude so that now Alella runs from the coast inland to the foothills of the Cordillera Catalana. The new areas are cooler because they are higher, and are based on a limestone bedrock in the shelter of the mountains. Down on the coast the vines are mainly Garnacha Blanca – in the new, higher vineyards you'll find Pansa Blanca (Xarel-lo), and quite a bit of Chardonnay now, with which Alella is getting to grips successfully.

For spectacular mountainous scenery head for Priorato and Terra Alta, relatively inaccessible inland areas to the south of Catalonia. Weave round their precipitous twisting roads, and you're sure to emerge green and shaky for the experience – but it's worth it. These are among the most dramatically situated vineyards in Europe. Rugged mountains form a backdrop to the terraced vineyards cut into the steep hillsides and interspersed with almond and olive trees. Priorato has a special soil known as *llicorella* which glints with mica particles – its heat-retaining qualities help create monstrously powerful and alcoholic red wines. Terra Alta, literally 'high land', had little contact with the rest of the country until the beginning of the twentieth century. The southernmost DO in Catalonia, it is chequered with green oases nestling in between the mountains. Light reds, *rosados* and whites are produced by the better bodegas here.

Elsewhere in Catalonia, the DOs fan out towards the Tarragona plain. The large DO of Tarragona sprawls around the city of the same name to a radius of 30km (18 miles). The land rises gently from the sea and is peppered with vineyards producing unremarkable table wines and a few fortifieds. Conca de Barberá sits in a natural basin protected by the rolling Tallat, Prades and Montsant mountain ranges. The area produces vast numbers of hazelnuts and almonds, as well as much of the base wine for Cava. It is also the home of Torres' Milmanda vineyard and such is the clout of Penedés nowadays that Conca de Barberá is rumoured to be merging with the Penedés Superior sub-region.

MARTORELL

WHERE THE VINEYARDS ARE *The map shows the heart of Penedés, around the towns of San Sadurní de Noya, the thriving centre of Cava production, and Vilafranca del Penedés, where Torres have their ultra-modern vinification plant.*

The vineyards are arranged in three tiers, moving up in steps from the coastline, and these provide a wide range of growing conditions. The strip of coastal vineyards is known as the Bajo Penedés. The vineyards here are planted traditonally with Moscatel but hardy red varieties that can cope with the blazing summer sun are taking over. Across the ridge of hills in the broad valley around Vilafranca del Penedés is the Medio Penedés, where 80 per cent of the Penedés vineyards are found. It's still fairly hot here but a mixture of varieties (mainly Xarel-lo and Macabeo for Cava but also some red ones) benefit from the cooler, higher altitude, between 250m (820ft) and 500m (1640ft) above sea level. Further inland and higher still, up to 800m (2600ft), is the Penedés Superior with a climate almost as cool as Bordeaux. When you climb higher there's not much in the way of villages but the scattered vineyards are highly prized. Here are found the high-quality white grapes, mostly aromatic Parellada for Cava, but also experimental plantings of Gewürztraminer, Riesling and Muscat, which are revolutionizing Penedés white wines.

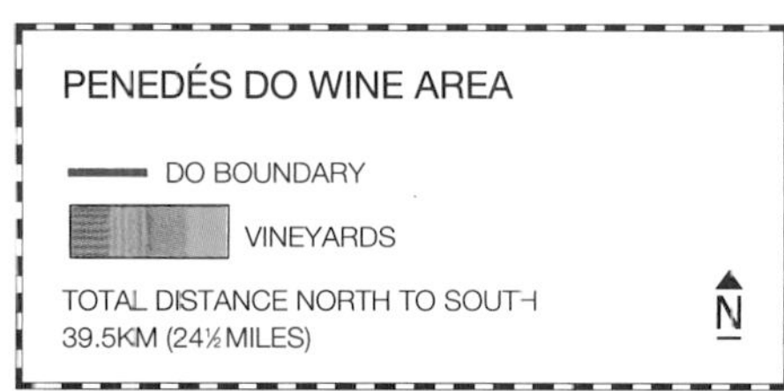

The high-altitude Penedés Superior is the scene of much new planting.

RED GRAPES
Garnacha Tinta, Cariñena, Monastrell, Tempranillo (locally called Ull de Llebre) are the main traditional grapes, with increasing amounts of Cabernet Sauvignon, Merlot and even Pinot Noir.

WHITE GRAPES
Macabeo, Garnacha Blanca, Xarel-lo, Parellada are the chief varieties, with decreasing amounts of Malvasía. New wave whites use Riesling, Muscat, Chardonnay, Gewürztraminer and Sauvignon Blanc.

CLIMATE
Coastal Catalonia enjoys a Mediterranean climate and it becomes drier and more extreme further inland.

SOIL
This varies, depending on whether you are in the rugged mountainous areas or nearer the coast. There is some limestone in the northern coastal regions. The Penedés lowlands have sand while the highlands have clay. Quartzite and slate make up a special soil called *llicorella* in rocky Priorato.

ASPECT
There are low-lying vineyards on the coast at between sea level and 200m (650ft), while inland the vines can be set into terraces on the sides of steep foothills, up to 800m (2600ft) in Priorato and Terra Alta, or on alluvial river valley floors, as in Tarragona.

Rioja

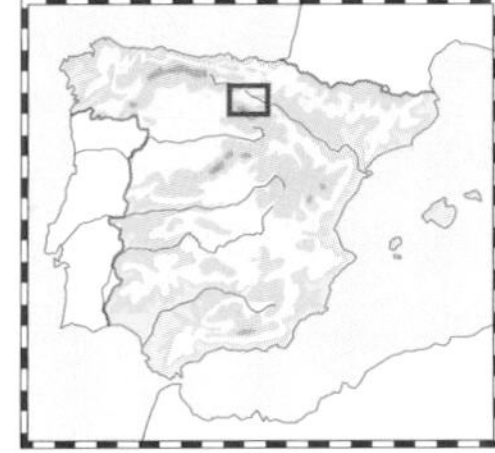

RED GRAPES
Tempranillo is the most important variety, followed by Garnacha Tinta and a little Mazuelo and Graciano. There is some experimental Cabernet Sauvignon.

WHITE GRAPES
Viura (Macabeo) is the main white grape. There is a tiny amount of Malvasía and Garnacha Blanca.

CLIMATE
The Sierra de Cantabria protects most of the vineyards from the Atlantic weather, and for the most part, Rioja is sunny and temperate. Rioja Baja, to the south-east, has a Mediterranean climate and is hotter and more arid.

SOIL
Rioja Alavesa has yellow calcareous clay soils, as do parts of Rioja Alta. Rioja Alta and Rioja Baja are mainly alluvial silt, with ferruginous clay on the higher ground.

ASPECT
Vines are planted on relatively high ground in the Alavesa and Alta sub-regions, usually between 400 and 800m (1300 and 2600ft). In the Baja the ground slopes down to nearer 300m (985ft) and the vines are planted on the flat, fertile valley floor.

I THINK WE SOMETIMES forget what life was like before Rioja. Even I have to keep reminding myself. But I can remember the wonderful flavour of strawberry and blackcurrant swathed in soft, buttery vanilla of the first Rioja reds I tasted. So soft, so easy, so enjoyable. Red wine wasn't supposed to be this simple to understand, this irresistible. In the days before the New World wine revolution taught us that it was OK to have fun with fine wine, Rioja was quietly preparing the way. The French cottoned on to Rioja as a source of reasonable red wine when their own diseased vineyards began to die off in the nineteenth century, and it is still the feather in Spain's wine-making cap, despite some pressure from Ribera del Duero.

Rioja was originally the name for the basin of land formed by the small Oja river, which flows into the Tirón near Haro. The Tirón eventually joins the large Ebro river, and it is a chunk of the much larger Ebro Valley that Rioja has come to stand for – the part that lies 100km (60 miles) south of the Atlantic and bounded by mountains on the north and south.

It would be nice and easy if the autonomous region of La Rioja corresponded to the wine-making region classified Rioja DOC, but this would be too simple, of course. Parts of La Rioja have no vines in them at all, while the Rioja DOC veers off across the regional boundary into both País Vasco and Navarra and, to a lesser degree, Burgos. The Rioja DOC is divided into three sub-regions: Rioja Alavesa lies north of the Ebro and is entirely within the province of Alava in País Vasco; Rioja Alta is in the west and lies entirely within the province of La Rioja. Rioja Baja is the third sub-region and lies to the east of Logroño, taking in land on both sides of the Ebro, as well as the Navarra enclaves. Logroño, Rioja's capital city with a population of 120,000, lies just west of the point where the three sub-regions meet, roughly halfway along the 120-km (75-mile) west-to-east stretch of the Rioja DOC.

Although Rioja is relatively close to the sea, the mountain ranges that surround it along the northern edge, especially the Sierra de Cantabria, shelter the vineyards from the cold winds of the Atlantic, so that it's quite usual to be standing in warm sunshine among the vines, while in the distance, clouds gather threateningly over the mountain tops.

RIOJA ALAVESA AND RIOJA ALTA

The Rioja Alavesa vineyards start among the foothills of the Sierra de Cantabria and stretch down to the steep north bank of the Ebro river. The vines descend in terraces, starting at 800m (2600ft) above sea level, and finishing near the north bank of the Ebro at just below 400m (1300ft).

Cross the river and you are in Rioja Alta, which follows the south bank of the Ebro, apart from a small enclave of land on the north bank. The two sub-regions aren't radically different from each other, and the boundary between them simply follows political provincial boundaries rather than soil types which would make more sense from a wine point of view. In these Riojan highlands, where soils vary every time you place one foot in front of the other, mesoclimate counts for much more than whether you happen to be in Alta or Alavesa.

We're still on fairly high ground, especially in the south of Rioja Alta, where the land creeps up to 700m (2300ft) above sea level again. Despite the mountains' protective embrace, cool breezes do creep in from the Atlantic here, moderating the temperature in the summer, and helping to create frosty winters. Generally speaking, the further east you go, nearer to Logroño, the warmer and drier the climate. The average annual temperature in Haro is 12.8°C (55°F), while in Logroño it's just over 13°C (55.4°F) and further east in Alfaro at the extreme end of the DOC, it leaps up to 13.9°C (57°F).

Some the region's most delicately scented and elegant red wines come from the yellow calcareous clay soils of Rioja Alavesa, which also extend into Rioja Alta. The more varied soils of Rioja Alta, which include patches of ferruginous clay and alluvial silt, tend to produce firmer, leaner wines. Both

WHERE THE VINEYARDS ARE *The map shows the western half of the Rioja DOC, the Rioja Alavesa and Rioja Alta sub-regions – the flatter, more arid Rioja Baja begins further east of Logroño. The Alavesa vineyards are north of the Ebro river, and extend from the foothills of the Cantabrian mountains down to the river. The Rioja Alta vineyards lie to the south of the river with one small enclave north-east of Briones on the other side of the Ebro. The whole DOC is closely concentrated on the Ebro Valley, the Sierra de Cantabria forming a dramatic backdrop along the northern edge and protecting the vineyards from the Atlantic weather to the north. Notice how dense the vineyards are in this part of Rioja where vines are the most important crop. Small vineyard plots are common – 85 per cent of the vineyards are owned by a total of 14,000 growers.*

0 km 1 2
0 miles 1

THE SOILS OF RIOJA

Rioja has three main types of soil. The best wines come from clay with limestone soil found all over the Rioja Alavesa sub-region and in some parts of Rioja Alta. This yellowish-looking soil is densely planted with vineyards and Tempranillo flourishes here in the limestone, producing grapes with high acidity and a rich concentration of flavours. The second type, ferruginous clay, is found south of the Ebro in pockets of land on higher ground within larger areas of alluvial soil, the third Rioja soil type. Ferruginous clay produces good, sturdy wines with high levels of alcohol. Large parts of Rioja Baja and Rioja Alta are alluvial silt, much of it too fertile for good-quality grapes. Wines from this soil type tend to be high in alcohol and are used mostly for strengthening wines of lighter quality from the Alavesa and Alta.

Elevation in metres

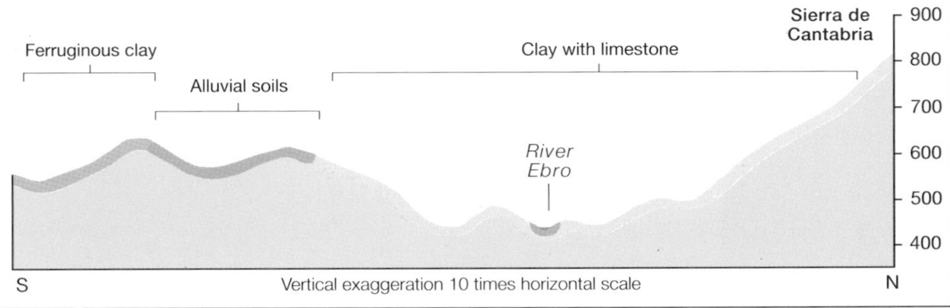

sub-regions are widely planted with Tempranillo, the great grape of red Rioja, which thrives in the relatively cool climate and on chalky and clay soils. Rioja Alta also has a little Garnacha Tinta, but the principal growing area for this variety is the third sub-region, Rioja Baja.

RIOJA BAJA

East of Logroño, the lower-lying Rioja Baja has a much warmer Mediterranean climate than the rest of Rioja and parts are even classified as semi-arid. Here vines compete with crops of artichokes, asparagus and red peppers for space on the fertile, alluvial clay soil. Garnacha Tinta grows well in the clay soil and can reach high levels of ripeness if the autumn is long and hot, leading to unsubtle, fat, alcoholic wines of up to 15 per cent alcohol. Some Tempranillo is also grown here, generally on the higher, hillier areas.

RED AND WHITE RIOJA

Just as most red wine produced in Rioja is a blend from all three sub-regions, so it is a blend of different grape varieties. Time was when over 40 different varieties were grown here, but now the DOC rules allow for just seven. Tempranillo holds sway, accounting for over half of all the vineyard area, and the local Consejo Regulador constantly encourages further planting. The grape gets its name from the word *temprano*, which means early, because it ripens well before Garnacha. Tempranillo is responsible for the graceful strawberry flavour of red Rioja and despite its pale, rather fragile appearance, it is well-suited to long aging. Garnacha Tinta is usually added to flesh out the blend, and if you're lucky, there'll be a splash of Graciano and Mazuelo too. The possibilities that the different sub-regions and varieties offer, means that the merchant bodegas can blend away happily to create a house style. Traditionally a little white Viura was added to lighten the colour and help the acid balance; this still occurs particularly in the Alavesa. Cabernet Sauvignon is not officially recommended, but the nod has been given to experimental plantings – these vines are easy to spot as they are the only ones trained on wires. White Rioja is made principally from Viura, with Malvasía Riojana and Garnacha Blanca as bedfellows.

In the vineyards the vines huddle together, planted densely and pruned in the bush shape (or gobelet style) to protect them from the elements. A few decades ago, each vineyard would have been a jumble of varieties, all grown and harvested together. Now each variety is planted and hand-picked separately, often in small plots of land that characterize the region. If the patches of low-lying bush vines tell you you're in Rioja, so will the number of coopers. There can be very few winemaking regions in the world that use so much oak – one estimate puts the number of oak casks (generally 225-litre *barricas*) in the region's bodegas at 600,000. A lot of it is American, popular for the vanilla and butter character it adds to the wine. Wine called *Rioja joven* sees no wood, and some fresh, unoaked whites are produced, but much of the red wine is either Crianza, a wine released in its third year having spent 12 months in oak casks; Reserva, released in its fourth year having spent at least 12 months in *barricas* and 24 months in bottle (or vice versa), or Gran Reserva, made only in exceptional years, and not released until its sixth year, during which time it must have spent at least 24 months in oak and 36 months in the bottle. White Crianza must have spent six months in cask.

In 1991, Rioja was granted the first DOC in Spain, a new classification reserved for the highest quality wines with stricter rules. So far Rioja stands alone in this super-category.

RIOJA ALTA AND RIOJA ALAVESA

RIOJA ALTA = RIOJA SUB-REGION

VINEYARDS

RIOJA DOC BOUNDARY

SUB-REGIONAL BOUNDARIES

TOTAL DISTANCE NORTH TO SOUTH 24KM (15 MILES)

N

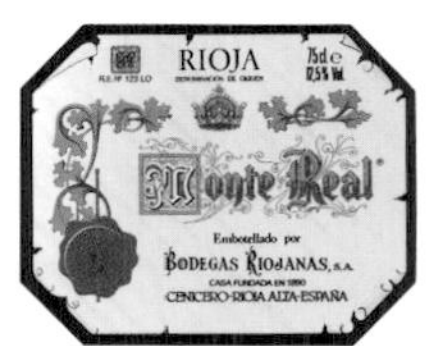

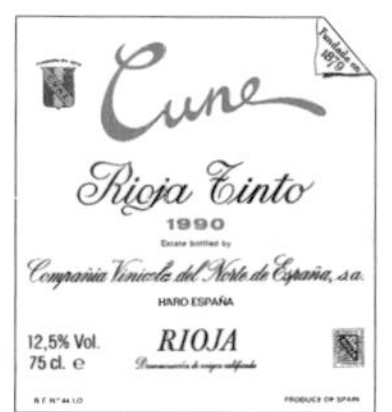

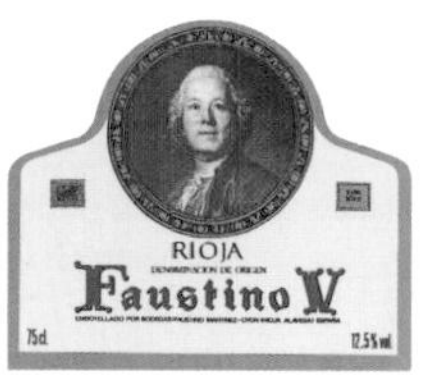

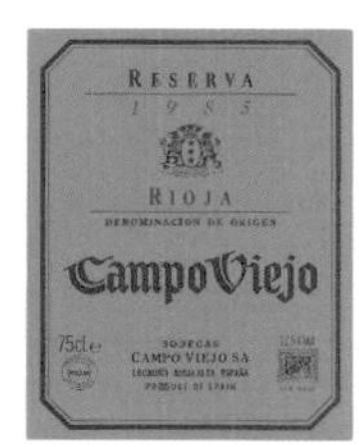

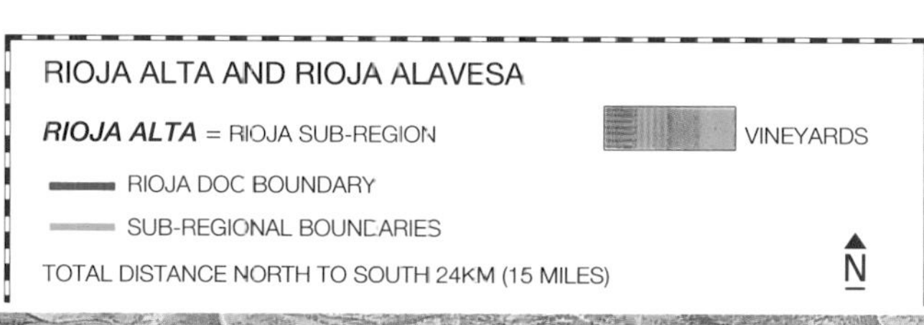

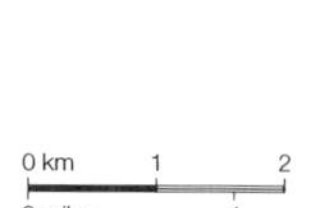

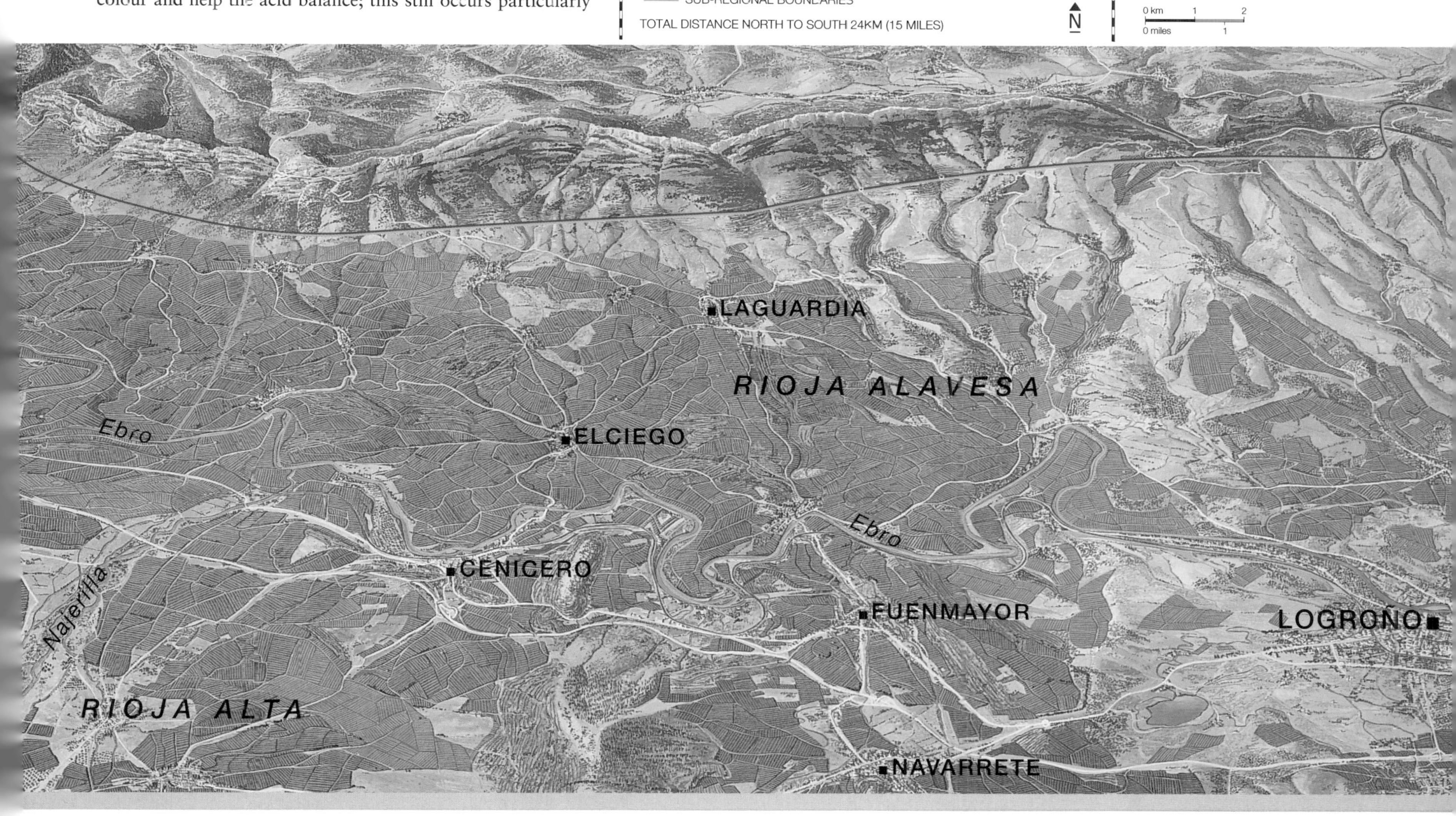

ARAGÓN & NAVARRA

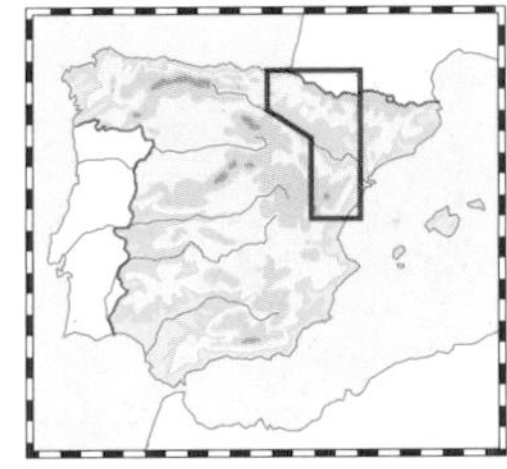

RED GRAPES
Red varieties predominate in this northern part of Spain. Garnacha Tinta is the main grape and there is some Graciano too. Increasing amounts of Tempranillo, Cabernet Sauvignon and Mazuelo are being grown for blending with Garnacha. There is even some experimental Merlot and Pinot Noir. Moristel is exclusive to Somontano.

WHITE GRAPES
Macabeo (Viura) is the most common white variety. Parellada, Malvasía, Moscatel and Chardonnay are also found.

CLIMATE
In the north the vineyards benefit from the cooling influence of the Pyrenees. The further south you go the climate becomes more continental and even semi-arid in parts.

SOIL
Both Aragón and Navarra have generally reddish-brown soil over limestone, with stony, well-drained subsoil.

ASPECT
In the north the vineyards are situated in the green valleys of the Pyrenean foothills. Further south they are mainly along rivers and tributaries.

REMEMBER THE PROUD RULERS of Aragón from history lessons at school? King Ferdinand of Aragón, who married Queen Isabella of Castilla in the fifteenth century, uniting their two kingdoms, and their daughter, poor Catherine of Aragon, who suffered so badly at the hands of her husband King Henry VIII of England. Aragón is a place heaving with ancient feuds and romances, but today it is also another of Spain's exciting wine regions, making an effort to realize its potential. Most of the traditional wines from Aragón were strong reds from Garnacha, mainly sold in bulk for blending. Garnacha ripens very easily and becomes very sweet and all that sugar in the grapes turns into head-thumping degrees of alcohol levels, as high as 17 or 18 per cent, unless the grapes are picked as soon as the grapes are ripe. Serious efforts are being made by some of the large co-operatives that dominate wine production in Aragón to cater for modern tastes by lowering the alcohol levels and selling the wines younger. Garnacha is now often blended with better varieties such as Tempranillo, Spain's best native red grape and grown all over the north of the country.

Aragón takes in a good part of the Spanish Pyrenees in the far north of Spain and reaches down south as far as Valencia and Castilla-La Mancha. You'll come away with an impression of scenery that changes as often as a kaleidoscope. In the cool Pyrenean foothills there are rivers and forests. Creep further south into a little more warmth and you'll find the verdant landscape of Somontano, followed by flatter plateau land with patches of vines, and finally the harsher, continental climate of the flat, broad Ebro Valley.

Tucked onto the southern end of the large Navarra DO along the right bank of the Ebro river is the Campo de Borja DO. It's back to historical romance here, as the area is named after the small estate or 'campo' of Borja. Borja was also the original name of a local family who emigrated to Italy in the fourteenth century and changed their name to Borgia, giving an entirely new meaning to the phrase, 'What's your poison?' when being offered a drink. Campo de Borja remained so obscure for so long, but an impressive twelfth-century monastery has survived by dint of selfless devotion and lifelong prayer. It's now the promotional centre for the DO's wines.

Campo de Borja has a harsh continental climate. During the winter temperatures can be as low as -7°C (19°F) while the summers are hot and dry, with temperatures soaring up to 40°C (104°F). That's not all the poor vines have to put up with: late spring frosts crack the ground and threaten the buds – and to cap it all there's a harsh wind that blows down from the Pyrenees which locals have named *El Cierzo* ('the north wind'). Perhaps it was in order to escape the wind that farmers used to build labyrinthine cellars under their hill villages, which are still used today for storing wine. It's not all bad news for vines here. The brown, sandy soils also have a stony character, so they are well drained – if there's any rain to drain, that is – and the mists coming off the river Ebro offer some protection against drought.

So the area is versatile enough for the vines of Borja to be farmed alongside olive trees, beans and asparagus. They love their Garnacha Tinta here and it occupies 80 per cent of the vineyards. Tempranillo is grown on slopes and higher plateaux and is on the increase. There is also some Mazuelo and Cabernet Sauvignon which, like the Tempranillo, are used for blending with Garnacha. Although the trend here (as elsewhere in Aragón) is towards wines with lower levels of alcohol and less wood aging, the DO regulations stipulate a minimum of 13 per cent for reds and *rosados*, so these will never be light wines. White wine with, happily, an alcohol level of only 10.5 per cent, has been allowed in the DO since 1989 and Macabeo and Moscatel Romano are the grapes used.

South of Campo de Borja is the Cariñena DO, a pretty name which also gave the title to the Carignan grape of southern France. (In northern Spain this grape is called Mazuelo.) Like Campo de Borja, there are fiercely hot summers and cold winters here, and the *El Cierzo* wind plays its part in making conditions seem extreme. Cariñena's vineyards stretch south of Zaragoza along the Huerva river to the Sierra de la Virgen. Most of the vineyards are on undulating plateaux with reddish-brown limestone soils.

The hilltop village of Alquézar is in the heart of the promising Somontano DO in Aragón's Pyrenean foothills.

Traditionally, Cariñena's wine has, like Campo de Borja's, been made from Garnacha, with pretty high levels of alcohol and an inky deep red colour. Although Garnacha still rules the vineyards here, recently there has been a move to plant other varieties, and it's now possible to find quite a lot of Tempranillo, as well as Cabernet Sauvignon and Mazuelo. White vines are much less important, accounting for just one-fifth of the vineyards, and are almost always Macabeo.

Just west of Cariñena, cordoned off by several mountain ranges, lies the Calatayud DO, where life is a slightly easier for the winemakers since it rains a little more here and is generally a degree or two cooler than elsewhere in Aragón. As you might expect, this is more fertile land – most of the small valleys with tributaries flowing into the Jalón river are planted with fruit trees, producing rich crops of peaches, pears and cherries, and the vineyards are found around the valley edges. The DO, only granted in 1990, limits the grapes to traditional Spanish varieties. Garnacha Tinta is the main red grape, with some Tempranillo and a little Monastrell and Mazuelo. Macabeo (known here as Viura) is the main white grape, with a little Malvasía, Moscatel and Garnacha Blanca.

The final Aragón DO is Somontano, and it is also the prettiest. Its name means 'under the mountain', and so it is, lying far over to the north-east of the region in the green foothills of the central Pyrenees, isolated on the north side of the river Ebro from the other Aragón DOs. It's a little wine paradise – relatively cool because of its altitude, with a rainfall nearly twice as high as the other Aragón wine regions, and watered by a network of tiny mountain streams that criss-cross the region. Mountains loom up to 1100m (3600ft) high, forming a dramatic backdrop to the vineyards and sheltering them from inclement weather from the north. Vines are grown on the slopes of the foothills as well as lower down in the valleys of tributaries running down to the Ebro. Almond trees and silvery olive trees colour the landscape, and perched high on a rocky hill is a striking landmark of the ancient Monasterio de Pueyo.

Enchanting indeed and, to add to its beauty, Somontano is Aragón's most promising DO, since the milder continental climate means progressive winemakers can experiment with different grape varieties. The local grape Moristel is still important for red wines with Viura and Alcañón for whites, but the regional government has encouraged experimental planting. There is now almost as much Tempranillo as Moristel and hundreds of acres are being planted with Cabernet Sauvignon, Merlot, Pinot Noir, Chardonnay and Gewürztraminer.

NAVARRA

The region of Navarra is famous for the ancient festival of San Fermin that takes place in its capital Pamplona in July, with the world-famous bull running spectacle. Fine if you like that sort of thing, but now Navarra is becoming renowned for something that interests me rather more – its progressive wine-making. Navarra's history is fascinating. Strangely enough for a region only just now realizing its potential, this was the original site of Spain's wine-making industry; archaeologists have found a second-century Roman site on the Argua river, built to make wine for the Roman soldiers located in Spain. Wine from Navarra was certainly well-known by the eleventh century, when the kingdom stretched from Bordeaux as far south as Rioja. Yet it has taken until relatively recently for Navarra's vineyards to pull themselves round from the devastation that was caused by phylloxera in the late nineteenth century.

The region sits between Aragón and the País Vasco, bounded to the north by the Pyrenees and to the south by the Ebro river that forms a boundary with La Rioja. Up in the mountains sheep trip across the grey rocks – they are kept for their milk which produces Navarra's famous Roncal cheese. In between the Pyrenean foothills are soft, green valleys covered in vineyards and fields. In the north, mountain peaks rise to over 1400m (4600ft) while in the fertile Ebro Valley in the south of the DO the land is only 275m (900ft) above sea level. Here vegetables are cultivated (especially asparagus, for which Navarra is famous) and, of course, vines.

The Señorío de Sarría bodega, with its vast vineyard holdings at Puente la Reina in the north of the Navarra DO, is just one of many innovative producers in the region.

Some of the Rioja DOC lies within Navarra (see page 190) but here we are interested in the Navarra DO. Vineyards are spread across five zones which lie south of Pamplona. The three hilly, northern zones, Baja Montaña, Valdizarbe and Tierra Estella, are influenced by the Pyrenees, so they escape drought and extremes of temperature; some of the new Chardonnay plantings here are doing well. In the two southern zones, Ribera Alta and Ribera Baja, the land flattens out towards the Ebro plain, and here the climate is hotter and more arid.

The soil is fairly uniform throughout the region, deep and fertile topsoil over gravel with a chalky bedrock – in fact, great conditions for viticulture. Vineyards are planted at between 250 and 550m (820 and 1800ft) above sea level. The southern zones produce the bulk of Navarra's grapes, which are mainly Garnacha. Although this grape plays second fiddle to Tempranillo in neighbouring Rioja, it accounts for over 80 per cent of Navarra's vineyards. Tempranillo is on the increase due to a rigorous replanting scheme organized by the local Consejo Regulador to take Navarra into the next century. You'll also find Graciano and the white Viura (Macabeo).

What do you do with all that Garnacha? Make great *rosado* that's what; Navarra is rightly famous for its robust pink wines, full of strawberry fruit. Reds and whites are now also being made in up-to-the-minute styles, and pockets of Cabernet Sauvignon and Chardonnay have started to appear in the vineyards. Navarra is a shining example to the rest of Spain for its progressive approach over the past 10 to 15 years. It's all come about thanks to the efforts of the regional government, which has instigated ambitious schemes for research and experimentation in the region. Sharing the applause is Evena, the Estación de Viticultura y Enología de Navarra, which used to be a humble local co-operative at Olite. Evena is largely responsible for the leaps and bounds the region has made. Vine nurseries, experimental vineyards, modern laboratories and state-of-the-art equipment are springing up across Navarra. And those *rosados* keep getting fresher, the whites more serious and some of the Tempranillo and Cabernet Sauvignon reds are among Spain's very best.

NORTH-WEST SPAIN

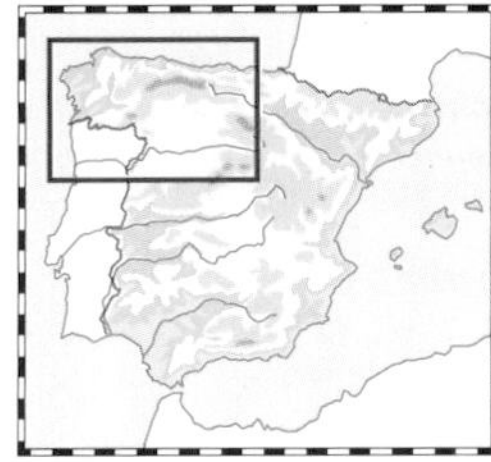

RED GRAPES

There are many varieties of varying quality but Galicia's best red is Mencía. In Castilla y León Tempranillo (Tinto Fino), Garnacha Tinta (Alicante) and Mencía do well.

WHITE GRAPES

Although there is lots of high-yielding Palomino, Albariño and Godello are Galicia's leading whites for quality wines. Rueda's Verdejo is the star of Castile and has more character than most Spanish white varieties.

CLIMATE

It is very wet and cool on the coast in Galicia and the climate becomes increasingly warm and dry as you travel inland past the mountains.

SOIL

These are very varied, from the alluvial deposits found in Galicia's Rías Baixas and Ribeiro, to Rueda's sandy and chalky soils, the ferruginous soil of Bierzo and the stony land of Cigales.

ASPECT

Because of the reliance on river valleys for viticulture in both regions, the vineyards are characterized by terracing from the river level up the hillsides, and also on plateaux in Castilla y León.

I SOMETIMES FEEL AS THOUGH I'm in Australia when I'm in the north-west of Spain. No, that's not as daft as it sounds. Australia has a precious narrow coastal strip where the rain falls and flowers bloom. But cross the Great Dividing Range and the blazing red hot heart of Australia stretches merciless and parched for thousands of miles. Spain isn't that bad, of course, but Galicia is so verdant, almost shimmering with lush plant life in the damp seaside air, that the speed with which you reach the austere, arid Spain of popular legend as you climb through the mountains is still something of a shock. And from there across to the Mediterranean, in whatever direction you aim, you'll be in the hot, harsh heart of Spain.

The regions of Galicia and Castilla y León are quite different to one another. Galicia, with Cape Finisterre at its extreme westerly point, is unlike anywhere else in Spain, and the fact that it is separated from the rest of the country by the Cantabrian mountains has helped to create a fierce spirit of independence in the region. Further inland, gentle hills start to appear, and as you approach Castilla y León, these grow more impressive and arid as the influence of the Atlantic on the climate lessens. Rivers play an important part in the landscape of both regions and their valleys are essential for crop farming.

GALICIA

No wonder it's called 'green Spain'. The rain in Spain doesn't fall mainly on the plain, as the winemakers of La Mancha know only too well, but here in Galicia it falls frequently over the craggy coastline and rolling hills covered with forest. We're right up at the top of Spain's north-west corner, surrounded by the sea on two sides and this explains why there is so much rain here – it sweeps up and drops nearly 1300mm (50in) a year on to the land, with the result that Galicia is far more verdant and forested than the rest of Spain.

Galicia is strikingly beautiful too, in a surprising way, its characteristically un-Spanish coastal landscape cut through with low, wide fjord-like inlets known as *rías*. Dotted along the coast are tiny fishing communities huddled into rocky Atlantic coves, while further inland hilltop roads plunge through thick forests and deep river valleys, past dramatically impressive fortified castles. In parts, Galicia looks and feels a little like a warmer version of Scotland, and the culture bears a similarity too, for the people of this region claim ancient Celtic origins. There's even a form of the bagpipes played here called the *gaita*. And, as in Catalonia, there is an official second language (this time a cross between Spanish and Portuguese) which tells you something about the region's independence.

Galician wine-making has only recently become even a little sophisticated. The vineyards are scattered between grain fields and plots of kiwi fruit and modern viticultural practices have taken their time to catch on. In the past visitors to the agricultural areas were more likely to notice the *hórreos*, strange stone granaries raised high on squat legs to repel hungry rats, than anything going on in the vineyard or winery.

But since the mid-1980s, and the introduction of modern technology, Galicia has made some smashing discoveries in its wines. First came the realization that its Rías Baixas DO was capable of making whites that rank among the best in the country thanks to the Albariño grape. Reds and whites are rapidly improving in Ribeiro DO, while the third official wine region, Valdeorras, although slower to improve, is making more use of the high-quality Godello grape. Galicia's progress is also marked by an increased ability to use its traditional varieties, rather than to adopt internationally fashionable grapes as is happening in some other parts of Spain.

Rías Baixas (literally, the 'lower inlets') covers three zones near the coast around Pontevedra and Vigo. It's cool here since any potentially harsh temperatures are moderated by the Atlantic. Not surprisingly, this is also one of Spain's wettest areas and fungal diseases pose a continual threat. So the vines are trained high on pergola systems, with branches pulled up on to granite posts, in order to keep them well aired.

This is how you'll see the prized Albariño grapes growing, and they are used to make the ripe, buttery, melony whites that Rías Baixas is increasingly famed for. You'll also find the white grapes Treixadura, Torrontes and the red grape Brancellao here, but it was for Albariño that Rías Baixas was awarded the DO in 1988, and this has given the area new impetus, and a programme of rapid vineyard growth.

Inland from Rías Baixas, around Ribadavia, is the DO region of Ribeiro. Less rain falls here than on the coast, but at 800 to 1000mm (31 to 40in) a year it's still a lot more than in most parts of Spain. The word *ribera* means 'riverbank', and that's exactly where the grapes grow here, in the alluvial soils

In early spring, before the onset of the long, hot summer, the Rueda vineyards are filled with wild flowers.

of three river valleys of the Miño, Avía and Arnoya, often on low terraces cut into the hillsides. Gentle winds blow from the Portuguese mountains, keeping the region relatively temperate, and flowers, especially carnations, are grown alongside the vines, which have churned out cheap and cheerful wine for centuries. The quality is improving, though, especially now that vineyards are being replanted with more aromatic whites such as Treixadura and Torrontes instead of the high-yielding Palomino, and making fresher, juicier reds from Garnacha.

Valdeorras is the third Galician DO, and the furthest inland, about 150 km (90 miles) from the coast. As you might expect, the Galician rain starts to dry up here, and temperatures are not moderated by the Atlantic – the summers can be blindingly hot, at up to 44°C (111°F). Most of Valdeorras' vineyards lie in the valley of the Sil river, where about half the grapes are the heavy-cropper Alicante, a local name for Garnacha. At their best these wines are inky and intense, but many are sold in bulk. Mencía, one of Galicia's best grape varieties and a close relation of Cabernet Franc, produces better results. Mencía was brought to Spain by pilgrims heading for the famous shrine at Santiago de Compostela in Galicia, where St James' bones are said to have lain. Whites are usually made from the aromatic Godello grape.

CASTILLA Y LEÓN

Castile, to give it its English name, was one of the original Spanish regions to unite against the Moors in the Middle Ages and thus became the north-west stronghold of the Catholics. Now, although it's the largest *autonomía* in the country, covering one-fifth of the land, it's sparsely populated. The historic towns with their castles, ancient fortifications and royal residences contrast strongly with the visually unexciting landscape – most of Castile consists of plateaux with rolling terrain used for grain and the occasional grazing flock of sheep.

The weather is much harsher in Castile than in Galicia, with hot summers and cold winters. The DO wine areas stretch west as far as Bierzo, on the Galician border, and east to Ribera del Duero in the province of Burgos, where the scenery starts to grab your attention again.

Apart from Ribera del Duero, with its worldwide reputation (see page 196), there are four DO wine regions in Castile. Bierzo in the west marks the transition from Galicia; it lies between the Cantabrian mountains and the Montes de León, sheltered by these mountain ranges from any extremes of temperature. In fact, Bierzo is altogether suitable for wine-making, with plenty of sunshine but less rain than Galicia, and an iron-rich reddish-brown soil which the vines like. Its producers have lagged behind, however, and Bierzo is only now raising the profile of its Mencía wines. About time – they're delicious.

Rueda, with its sleepy little villages scattered across flat plains and low hills, is probably the most famous Castile DO after Ribera del Duero, and rightly so, for it now produces very good whites. Around the town of Rueda are long cellars that date back to the fourteenth century – it is here that wine is traditionally made and stored. But the public can't visit them, and the whole place seems a little dull. And so it was until the 1970s when the Rioja bodega Marqués de Riscal decided to make white wine here and concentrated on the local Verdejo grape and Sauvignon Blanc grown in sandy and chalky soils, with a dash of gravel in the best vineyards. The experiments paid off and Rueda now leads the way in Castilian white wine.

The Toro DO borders Rueda to the north-west. Pilgrims who took this route to Santiago de Compostela in Galicia used to stop off in Toro and quench their thirst on the local wines. It's still a thriving wine centre, although again the fairly flat terrain, alternating with fields of corn, isn't much to write home about. Toro's best wine comes from the Tinta de Toro grape, which makes powerful blockbuster reds.

Right in the middle of Castilla y León is Cigales which follows the course of the Pisuerga river north from Valladolid. The DO, only granted in 1991, was mostly due to Cigales' pleasant *rosados*, made from Tinta del País (the local name for Tempranillo) and Garnacha blended with some white Albillo or Verdejo. Again as in Rueda, there are cellars running under the town of Cigales, with ventilators sticking up like small domes in the surrounding fields. Go over to take a look but take care not to stub your toe on one of the large stones which litter the vineyards, and which keep the soil well drained.

Many of Ribeiro's vineyards are on the verdant hillsides above the Miño river.

Ribera del Duero

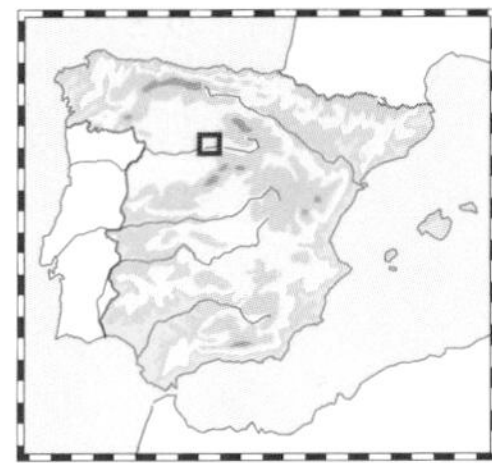

RED GRAPES
Most of the grapes are Tinto Fino or Tinta del País, a local variant of Tempranillo. There is also some Garnacha Tinta, Cabernet Sauvignon, Merlot and Malbec.

WHITE GRAPES
White wines are not included in the DO but Albillo is sometimes used in the red blend.

CLIMATE
The climate is a mixture of continental and temperate – hot, dry summers and long, cold winters with a serious risk of frost as late as May due to the high altitude.

SOIL
There is clay and alluvium near the river Duero and more limestone on higher slopes.

ASPECT
This is high-altitude viticulture, with vineyards at 700 to 850m (2300 to 2790ft). Vineyards start near the river and climb the valley slopes.

Just what is it that makes the wines of Ribera del Duero so exciting? The landscape isn't as spectacular as in some regions of Spain – apart from the flat-topped mountains and occasional striking landmark such as the imposing castle of Peñafiel, Ribera mostly stretches out in rolling plateaux and forested hills. We're in a relatively moderate climate, but because of the high altitude frosts can be a daunting threat to the vines. And until the late twentieth century there were only a couple of show estates in the region which could boast of truly magnificent wines.

Yet Ribera del Duero now ranks among the greatest of all Spain's DOs, certainly outstripping its neighbours in Castilla y León for the quality of its red wines and sheer, breathless rate of progression. The region simply buzzes with life, as more and more winemakers invest and experiment, cashing in on Ribera's rising star.

Ribera del Duero means 'the banks of the Duero', the river best known to most of us as the Douro – its name when it flows through port country across the border in northern Portugal. The region lies in the heart of Castile, 190km (120 miles) north of Madrid, in the broad river valley of the Duero, which passes through the provinces of Burgos, Valladolid and Soria. There are also some vines in the northern province of Segovia – a total of approximately 12,000 hectares (29,650 acres) under vine. The area forms part of Spain's central plateau or *meseta* and so the vineyards are high, at between 700 and 850m (2300 and 2790ft).

The altitude, which is near the upper limits for viticulture, plays a large part in Ribera's success. Although the day time temperatures in summer are hot here – it can reach as high as 40°C (104°F) – at night they drop dramatically, giving the grapes marvellous concentration and enhanced aromas. Add to this the perfect soil for viticulture (rather poor quality yet easy to work), and you'll get vines which work hard to push a great deal of intensely concentrated flavour and high levels of acidity into what little fruit they can produce. The continental climate is tempered by an Atlantic influence – rainfall is moderate and mists from the nearby Duero river provide welcome additional humidity.

Ribera's success story is typical of many modern wine regions, only more dramatic than some. Although red wine had been produced here for centuries, it was mostly sold in bulk, just like in any other second-rate Spanish wine region. No-one really understood its potential. Ribera's rise to fame began in the mid-nineteenth century when Don Eloy Lecanda Chaves set up a bodega in the west of the region just south of Valbuena de Duero. The estate was known as Pago de la Vega Santa Cecilia y Carrascul, eventually shortened to Vega Sicilia. Breaking with local tradition, the vineyards were planted with the red Bordeaux varieties, Cabernet Sauvignon, Merlot and Malbec as well as with the more traditional Tinto Fino. If not identical, this is at least a very close relation to the Tempranillo grape grown widely throughout Spain. For more than a century, Vega Sicilia was renowned as one of the best bodegas in Spain and the prices of its powerful, complex red wines vie with those of a top Bordeaux, yet it remained the sole estate with any clout in Ribera. Even the King of Spain has to stand in line to await his allocation.

Then in the late 1970s Alejandro Fernández set up a successful bodega making red wine called Pesquera from the local Ribera grape, Tinto Fino. Fernández discovered that the high altitude of the Ribera vineyards meant that this grape grew thin-skinned with high levels of acidity, and the resulting rich, aromatic red wines were a revelation. Importantly, the wines seemed to age brilliantly, something that caught the attention of international critics, with subsequent rave reviews, in the mid-1980s. In 1982 the region was awarded the DO. Ribera del Duero had arrived.

The region makes *rosado* wine too, mostly from Garnacha, but the best ones have about 50 per cent Tinto Fino. There is a little white Albillo planted, which is sometimes added to the red wine blend to make the wines more fragrant and to dilute their inky colour, as well as being used for dessert grapes. White wines are made in the region but are not allowed to be part of the DO yet. About 85 per cent of the vineyards are planted with Tinto Fino, and although some bodegas have followed Vega Sicilia's example by planting Cabernet Sauvignon and Merlot, the rules limit French varieties to districts which, in 1982, already had plantations of these grapes. Wines with the Ribera del Duero DO must be made with a minimum of 75 per cent Tinto Fino. Some experts report that, after centuries of cultivation in the valley, the grape has adapted to its

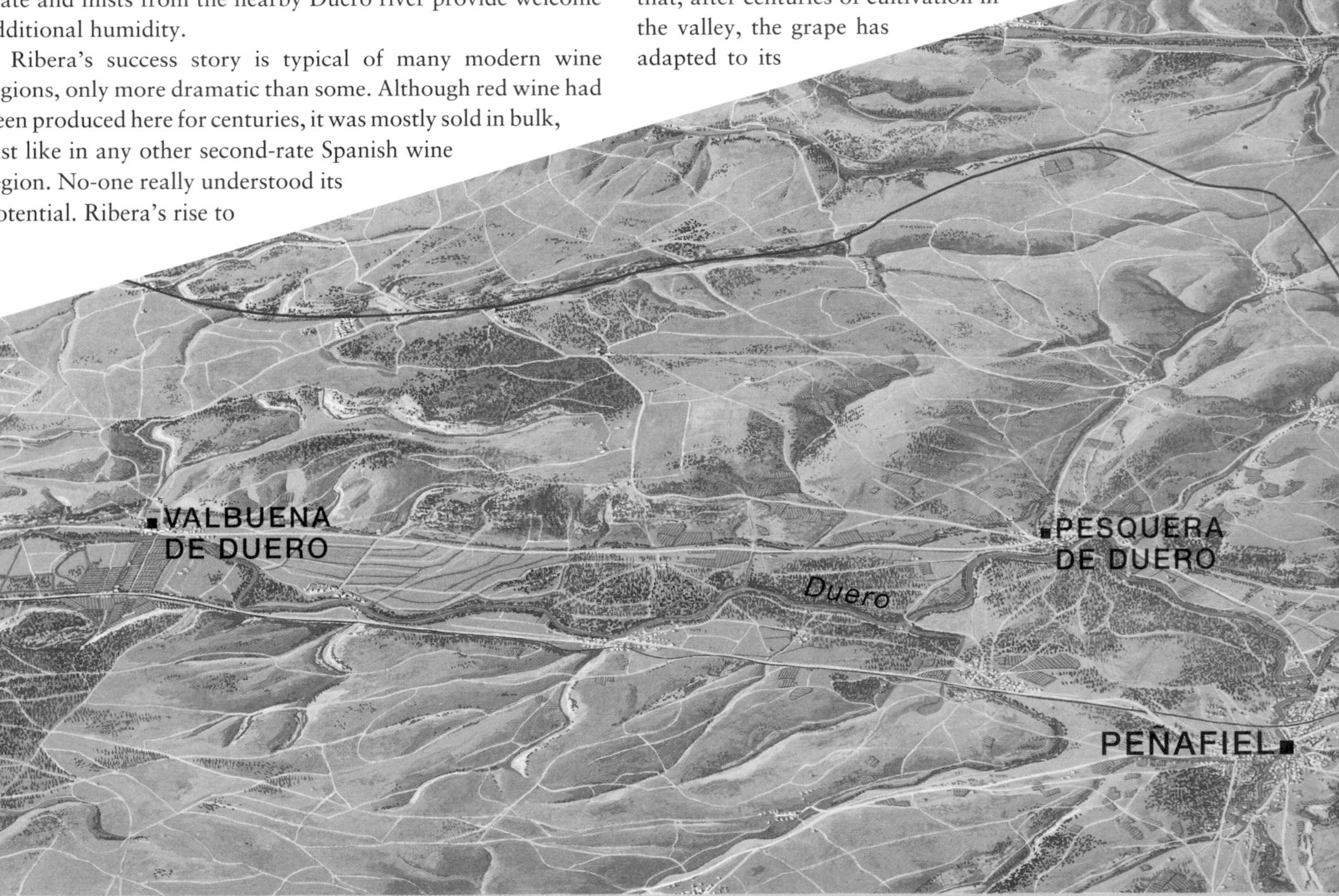

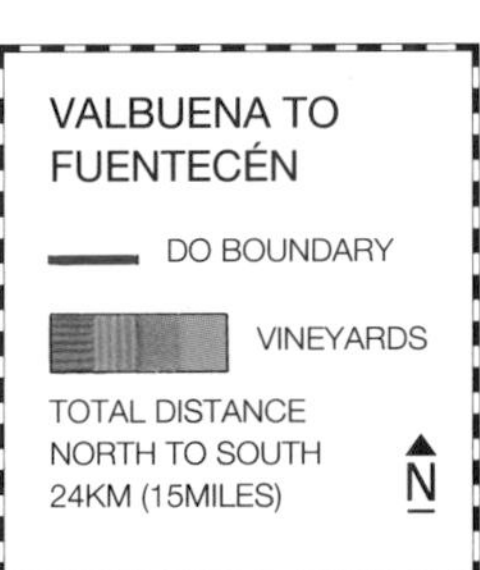

environment, developing a thicker skin and ripening a good deal earlier than it used to. Whatever the truth, it can make a fine drop of red here.

Many of these vineyards are at the upper limits of 800m (2600 feet) altitude, for the river itself is only just below this height. The character of the vineyards varies considerably the further away from the river you go, and at each stage there is a name for the type of land you reach. The lower-lying plots, on the banks of the river, are called *campinas*, and these are based on more clayey, alluvial soil with some sand. Climb a little higher, and you reach the *laderas*, or higher slopes, with more limestone in the soil. In places these vineyards are so chalky-white they start to resemble the famous *albariza* vineyards of Jerez of southern Spain. These are the best plots of land, and the local Consejo Regulador is seeing to it that much of the vineyard investment takes place here. Next come the *cuestas*, and here viticulture starts to peter out as the land gets less easy to work. The highest land, on steepest slopes and flat-topped mountain peaks, is known as *paramos*, and tends to be too exposed for anyone to want to plant vines.

The oldest Ribera vineyards are to the north-west of Peñafiel where the Vega Sicilia and Viña Pesquera vineyards are located. The west of the region was traditionally considered the best area, although much of the development today seems to be taking place in the east, around Roa de Duero and east to Aranda de Duero, with encouraging results. This part of the broad valley used to produce *rosados*, but it is rapidly becoming home to many of the most progressive producers.

Right across Ribera it's a jumble of small and large plots of land, with over 14,000 active vineyards. The smaller vineyards – those under 1 hectare (2½ acres) – are vital to the region as a whole, for they account for nearly 90 per cent of the vineyards. Inevitably this means there are several important co-operatives in Ribera and equally inevitably it means that even as quality increases, faulty wines will still occur.

The magnificent castle of Peñafiel dominates the vineyards around the town.

WHERE THE VINEYARDS ARE *The map shows the western end of the Ribera del Duero region around the little town of Peñafiel. This is the traditional heartland of the DO where two of Ribera's best-known wine estates are located – the world-famous Vega Sicilia vineyards are at Valbuena on the south bank of the Duero and Alejandro Fernández's Pesquera vineyards are just to the east of Pesquera. See how the Ribera vineyards spread out along the Duero river valley. Many of them are close by the river, on both the north and the south banks, but the wine region stretches out up to 35km (22 miles) from the Duero. A great deal of development is taking place across the region as a whole, but most interesting is the area to the east – particularly the north-east – where you can see the vineyards clustered near Roa. This part of the region used to produce basic fruit for rosado wine but is now a hive of activity, with producers experimenting with more modern techniques, sometimes using American oak barrels for aging, sometimes French. Alejandro Fernández has established his second bodega and vineyard in Roa which is fast becoming Ribera's new wine capital.*

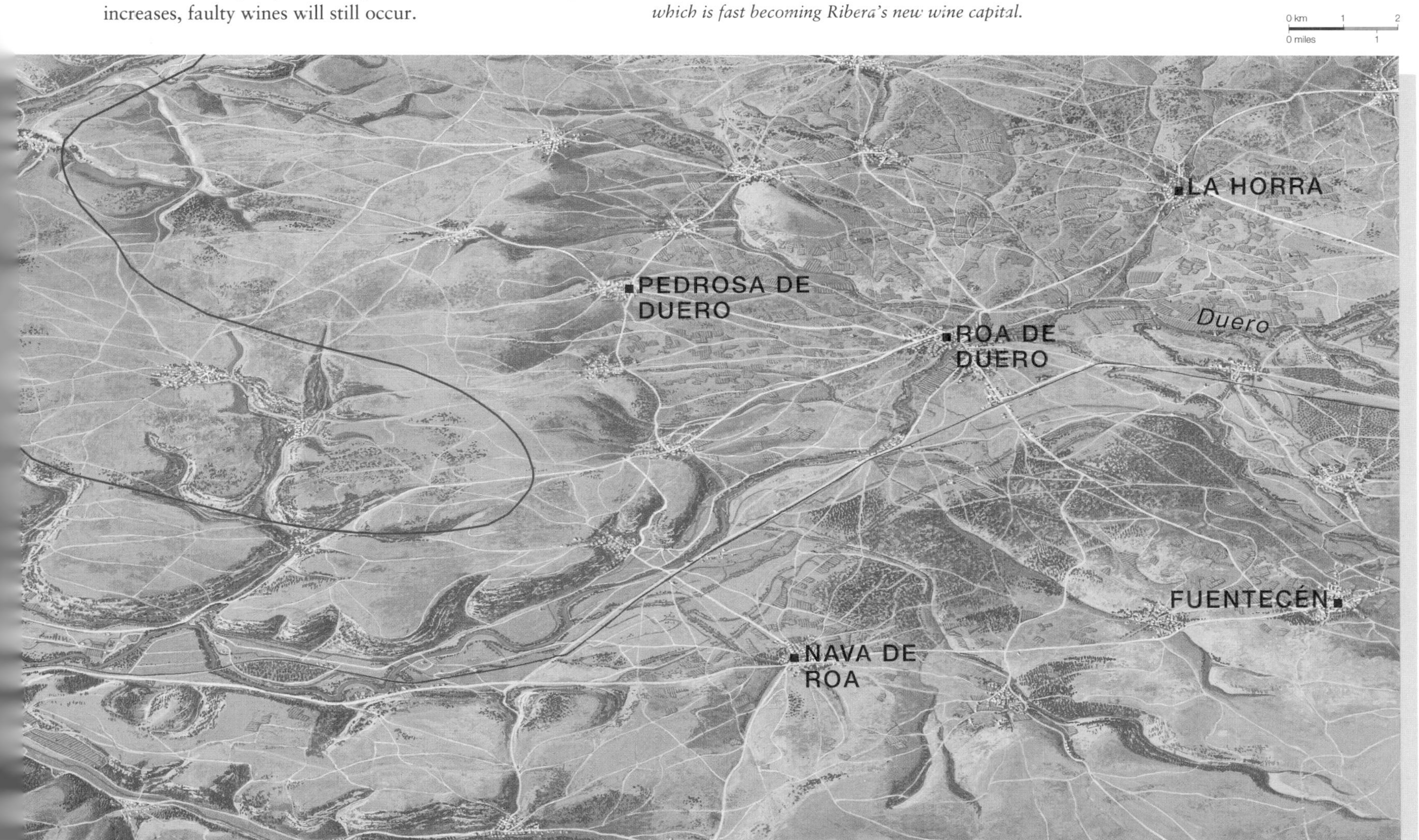

0 km 1 2
0 miles 1

LA HORRA
PEDROSA DE DUERO
ROA DE DUERO
Duero
FUENTECÉN
NAVA DE ROA

Central Spain

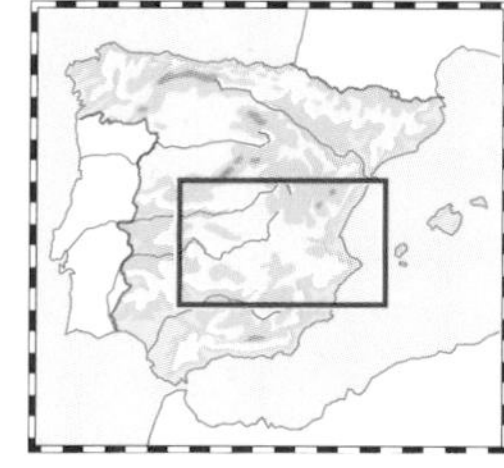

RED GRAPES
Tempranillo (locally called Cencibel) is the best quality grape. Others include Monastrell, Garnachas Tinta and Tintorera, and Bobal.

WHITE GRAPES
Airén is the dominant grape in Castilla-La Mancha and Merseguera in the Levante.

CLIMATE
The high central plain has a continental, semi-arid climate. Further east in Levante it is wetter, and less extreme.

SOIL
Varied, with sandy clay throughout, but rich in limestone in places.

ASPECT
On the high central plain the vines are planted in large plots. The vineyards are more scattered further south-east in the rolling Levante hills.

The Valdepeñas vineyards are mainly on flat open land with reddish soil.

Spain's vast landlocked central plateau, Castilla-La Mancha, and Murcia and Valencia to its east, contain the country's most important regions for table wine. Even if this part of Spain does not produce the finest Spanish wines, the sheer volume of wine that comes from here is astonishing. There is still much rough, old-style wine, mostly whites from the Airén grape, but progress is slowly taking place, especially with oak-aged reds from Cencibel (Tempranillo's local name).

CASTILLA-LA MANCHA AND MADRID

All I can see are vines, reaching right up to the horizon on every side. No, wait a minute, there's a row of windmills, their black arms stretching up out of the vast plain, the only things to punctuate the skyline. I'm in the southern half of Spain's central *meseta*, in Castilla-La Mancha, the huge flat table of land that makes up the heart of the country and supplies more than half its wine. I'm at least 500m (1640ft) above sea level and but there are no hills in sight. Castilla-La Mancha is entirely bordered by rivers and mountains and just occasionally you can see a faint, misty outline of mountain tops on the horizon across the vast plain.

I rather like it here, though it's pretty inhospitable. Despite being bordered by rivers and mountains, the region flings itself so wide that these natural defences can do nothing to protect it from freezing cold winters and scorching, relentless summers. The temperature veers wildly between extremes, from as much as 42°C (108°F) in the high summer to -22°C (-8°F) during the long winter delivered with a bitingly cold wind, and although violent electric storms occasionally bring slanting rain in the autumn and spring, the desolate plateau is generally arid; thus the Arabic name *al-Manshah* or 'dry land' was coined.

It's easy to be overwhelmed by the size of such a seemingly endless landlocked region. Here and there small groups of whitewashed homes huddle together, or a straggling flock of sheep bleats about a lone tree. The windmills, at which Cervantes' hero Don Quixote tilted stride across the plain, reminding the visitor that this was once useful grain country. But apart from the windmills and the odd castle, all you'll see to break the monotony are row after row of vines, planted in grid patterns and pruned with their canopy draped over the ground to retain as much precious moisture as possible.

Then again, you might spy shiny new wine tanks, for investment in modern wine technology is happening even here. Castilla-La Mancha used to supply Spain with most of its cheap table wine, or base wine for distillation. It still produces a lot of sub-standard stuff, especially white, and only one-tenth of the total wine produced in the region has DO status – although even that doesn't guarantee palatable quality here. Nevertheless, efforts are being made to improve the wine in some parts of the region, with EU subsidies providing an impetus. In the region's best DOs, La Mancha and Valdepeñas, vastly improved new-style wine, pale, fresh and fruity rather than yellowy-orange, flat and dull, is now being produced for export markets. It's a gradual change rather than a revolution, but Castilla-La Mancha's hot sunshine and healthy aridity means that the potential exists for a vast ocean of decent stuff if they can overcome a lack of irrigation and rainfall.

La Mancha is Castilla-La Mancha's largest DO and, indeed, Spain's, with over 400 bodegas. Its 189,511 hectares (468,275 acres) of vineyards stretch up almost as far as Madrid in the north and cover areas rich in limestone. The world's most planted grape variety, the white Airén, covers 90 per cent of La Mancha's vineyards and, with its thick skin and heavy leaf canopy, it's ideally suited to the climate. New technology and early picking mean that the wines are increasingly light, fresh and faintly aromatic rather than dark and heavy. There is also a small amount of Cencibel.

The Valdepeñas DO is a hot, dry enclave on the southern border of Castilla-La Mancha, where the central plain begins to descend towards Andalucía. A small basin surrounded by sheltering hills, there are excellent vineyard areas in its Los Llanos ('the plains') and Las Aberturas ('the open spaces') sub-regions. Airén is the main grape, some of it blended into the red wine. The amount of Cencibel for quality reds is rapidly increasing and Chardonnay and Cabernet Sauvignon are used experimentally by several progressive local winemakers.

In the north of Castilla-La Mancha, and with a few vineyards across the border in Madrid, is the large Méntrida DO,

making dull, tannic reds and heavy *rosados* mainly from Garnacha. There is still a long way to go before the region justifies its DO. The Vinos de Madrid DO covers the vineyard communes around the southern edge of the capital city; a new DO created in 1990, it offers a range of quality levels, to put it politely. The Arganda sub-region south-east of the city with vineyards on terraces of clay loam with high concentrations of limestone seems to be the most promising area so far.

Overshadowed by the better known DOs of La Mancha and Valdepeñas, the Almansa DO is right down in the south-east where the great La Mancha plain gives way to the Murcian plateau. Its easterly position means its climate is a little less extreme than the rest of Castilla-La Mancha; although most of the vineyards are on fairly flat terrain down on the plain, there are some on the rolling foothills. Thank goodness – I was beginning to think I'd never spy a bump in the landscape again... The wines are mainly dark reds, from Monastrell and Garnacha Tintorera, with some of the better ones from Cencibel.

MURCIA AND VALENCIA

Bordering Castilla-La Mancha to the east, this part of Spain is also known as Levante. The scenery is a good deal more varied, if less dramatic – its green fertility is soothing after the desolate plain, as low mountains which cut off the *meseta* give way to the *huertas* , the pleasant irrigated tiers of land covered in apple trees, apricots, olives and peaches which form a giant stairway to the coast. Here you come to the huge bays surrounding the cities of Valencia and Alicante, with the resort of Benidorm in between. I'm being thrust back into civilization, if you can call it that – there are tourists, millions of them, and the ugly industrialization around the ports.

Within Levante there are six main wine districts. Valencia, with its pretty blue ceramic tiles covering the church roofs, is more famous for orange trees than grapes. Here the *huerta* is covered in brightly-coloured citrus trees, but hilly vineyard areas grow mainly Merseguera which makes rather boring whites. There is also some red and *rosado* from Monastrell and Garnacha Tintorera. None of these are great grapes but the bodegas are some of the most modern in Spain, equipped with the latest technology. Look at wine labels and see for yourself how many Spanish 'own label' wines hail from Valencia. Valencia's most famous and exciting wine is a lusciously sweet fortified white made from Moscatel (the Spanish name for Muscat). Although in no way a sophisticated dessert wine, good ones have an appealing crunchy tablegrape character.

As you drive south-west from Valencia, along the ridge between the *meseta* and the coast, you pass through a more rocky terrain where the vines peek out from between the pine forests. This is Utiel-Requena, a promising region where the important Valencian bodegas have large holdings. The vines are likely to be the red grape Bobal, usually used for making *rosado* and which can be some of Spain's best, and there are increasing amounts of decent reds from Tempranillo and Garnacha. Macabeo is the main white variety. The wines made here are promising, but no more than that for the moment.

Further south lie Jumilla, Yecla and Alicante, forming a line of DOs marching progressively inland from the city of Alicante to the regional boundary. To find a vineyard here you have to scale the hills inland, cross the *huerta*, and emerge the other side in cooler wine country. To be fair, some dessert grapes (mostly Moscatel) are grown down by the coast, but up on the higher ground, expect Monastrell, Tempranillo and experimental Cabernet Sauvignon. Yecla and Jumilla, further inland, are hard to tell apart, their terrain marked by low hills, chalky soil and a more dramatic mountain range, the Sierra del Carche, in the distance. Monastrell and some Garnacha grows here.

Which leaves us trailing south to Bullas, a district around the historic town of Lorca, and a fruitful part of the region – literally, for here farmers effortlessly grow heaps of apples, apricots, peaches and nuts. Monastrell dominates the hilly vineyards, and at last we are in wetter territory: Bullas' higher land receives 500mm (20in) of rain per year. Most of the wine is rather basic *rosados*, but Bullas is a quietly promising region. And, after the wind-whipped plain of Castilla-La Mancha, and the sweaty tourist resorts of the Costa Blanca, it's as refreshing and relaxing a place as any to end up in.

Southern Spain

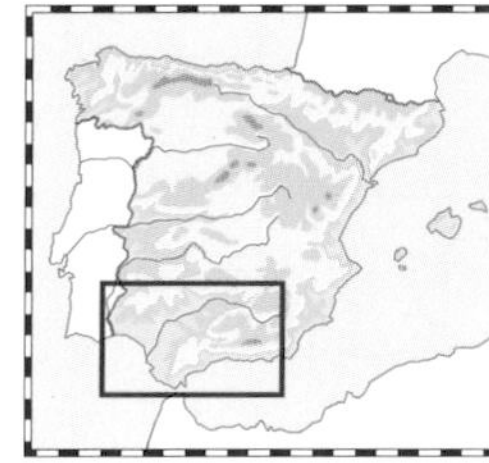

 **RED GRAPES**
There is a little experimental Cabernet Sauvignon and Tempranillo in Montilla-Moriles.

 **WHITE GRAPES**
Palomino Fino is the classic sherry grape while Pedro Ximénez is grown throughout Andalucía's wine regions.

CLIMATE
Cooling Atlantic breezes moderate the hot summer temperature in Condado and Málaga's coastal vineyards also benefit from sea breezes. Inland Montilla-Moriles has a hot continental climate.

SOIL
Jerez has its famous chalky *albariza* soil and Montilla-Moriles also benefits from limestone soils. There is reddish sandy soil in Condado and varied soils in Málaga.

ASPECT
Condado's vineyards start at just 25m (80ft) above sea level. The land rises to gentle slopes in Jerez and Málaga, and up to 300-700m (985-2300ft) in Montilla-Moriles.

THIS IS HOW EVERYONE IMAGINES Spain to be – a picture postcard image of sun-filled vistas, with proud gypsy flamenco dancers, golden beaches and white-washed villages perched on hilltops. And don't forget the Moorish influence which lasted for seven centuries: the Moors made their capital first at Córdoba, then at Seville, and for centuries these cities were the cultural focal point of southern Europe. Their influence lives on the cooking, customs and architecture of the region. Andalucía is also the home of *tapas*, light snacks of cold meat, seafood, olives, salted almonds and bread, eaten while you stand in a small, cool bar, washing down your fare with a *copita* of chilled sherry.

Andalucía is Spain's second largest region, covering the whole of the southern part of the country. It is hemmed in by the Atlantic Ocean in the south-west, and beyond the Straits of Gibraltar by the Mediterranean. In the north the Sierra Morena forms a natural boundary between Andalucía and the high plateau of Castilla-La Mancha, while to the east, the Sierra Nevada, the highest mountain range on Spain's mainland, rises in a huge swell between Granada and the coast. In fact, much of Andalucía is mountainous and the remainder of the region is dominated by the basin and delta formed by the Guadalquivir river between Seville and Cádiz.

Being so far south, the climate is hot, but not uncomfortably so, because the cooling breezes from the Atlantic act as an effective air-conditioner. In Jerez (see page 202) these wet Atlantic winds and the resulting humidity also encourage the development of the all-important yeast flor, a vital part of the sherry process. In the areas where crops are cultivated, the soil is relatively fertile, thanks to the Guadalquivir as well as to a history of ingenious water engineering started by the Moors. So where you might expect dry baked plains, with little in the way of green vegetation, what you get are rolling plains and plateaux covered in dark green olive trees, citrus groves, cornfields, almond crops and, of course, vineyards.

Wine-making has long been an important industry here. Indeed, between the seventeenth and nineteenth centuries, Andalucía's fortunes were predominantly founded on its wine trade. All eight provinces produce some wine, although the eastern ones, especially Almería, are more famous for their dessert grapes. Led by the world-famous sherries from the Jerez region, the style of wine in Andalucía traditionally has been fortified, with the wine aged in a solera system. But this is also one of the reasons why Andalucian wine-making is generally suffering a crisis of image – a worldwide fashion for light, dry table wines has led to a decline in popularity of certain southern Spanish wines. This has encouraged a rethink on the part of some of Andalucía's winemakers and, in places, a change of direction towards lighter wines.

CONDADO DE HUELVA

Situated near the border with Portugal, this is Andalucía's most westerly DO. The southern section of the DO borders the Atlantic Ocean and includes the Coto de Doñana national park, a protected strip of wetland of great ornithological interest at the southern end of the Guadalquivir estuary, and sadly under threat from the developers. At the moment, to reach the rest of the Andalucian coastline from Condado, you have to make a detour around the park and past Seville.

Most of the Condado vineyards lie around the town of Bollullos del Condado on the road between Seville and Huelva. The vineyards sit on low-lying plains, sometimes as little as 25m (80ft) above sea level. The soils are predominantly reddish sand, although the best plots also have a high lime content. The climate is almost identical to that of Jerez further south along the coast, with hot, dry summers, and relatively mild, wet winters. The sherry-style wines of this region used to be famous worldwide – they were mentioned as long ago as the fourteenth century by Chaucer in *The Pardoner's Tale*. But around the seventeenth century a decline set in, partly because Condado's wines were mostly ending up in the bodegas of Jerez. Gradually, inexorably, the area found itself living in the shadow of its more famous neighbour.

Now the sherry producers have more wine of their own than they can cope with and some of the Condado vineyard land has been turned over to strawberries, grain, sugar beet and olives. Local winemakers have attempted to diversify away from fortified wine by making light table wine or *joven afrutado* from the bland local Zalema grape, which still occupies 91 per cent of the Condado vineyards. More of the vineyards are being turned over to sherry's classic grape, Palomino Fino (locally called Listán) and Garrido Fino, two grapes not renowned for wild displays of character, but which are a little more interesting than the stultifyingly neutral Zalema. Making light white wines in this climate, where the average annual temperature is 18°C (64°F), is not easy and, despite early harvesting in August, the Zalema often oxidizes and spoils unless extreme care is taken between picking and wine-making. The traditional fortified styles of Condado Viejo (*olorosos*, ranging from dry to sweet) and Condado Pálido (aged for at least two years under a film of flor, like *fino* sherry but less fine in style) are still consumed locally.

MÁLAGA

Across the Serranía de Ronda from Jerez lies the Málaga DO, another region with a glorious past which has found itself thoroughly out of fashion in the late twentieth century. Poor Málaga. Its sweet toffee-and-nuts style of wine used to be among the most prized of southern Spain's 'sack', more famous even than the wines of Jerez, but the region became notorious towards the end of the nineteenth century as it was the first area in Spain to be attacked by the vine louse phylloxera. The devastation of the vineyards (then totalling the enormous figure of 113,000 hectares/279,000 acres) by phylloxera, the destruction of the city of Málaga during the Spanish Civil War and changing habits in wine-drinking have meant that it is now one of Spain's smallest DOs with just 1036 hectares (2560 acres) of vines.

Most of the vineyards are split between two sub-regions; one in the west of the region around Estepona on the coast, an area more famous for its Moscatel grapes destined for the table than for wine; and a second and more important one around the city of Málaga itself – there are a few vineyards in the coastal areas around Nerja and also inland along the border with the province of Granada as far north as the mountain town of Cuevas de San Marcos but most of the vines for Málaga are on the rolling Antequera plateau around the village of Mollina. Here, in this hotter inland area, about half the vineyards are planted with Pedro Ximénez ('PX') and many bodegas have their own presses for fermenting the wine.

There is a huge range of wine styles with varying degrees of sweetness – 'PX' is the main grape in traditional Málaga wine, although vineyards are also planted with what's known locally as *vidueno*, a jumble of neutral grape varieties, usually Airén, (called Lairén locally) or Doradillo. The Moscatel de Málaga grape can be used for Málaga wine too, but is usually found only in the cooler coastal vineyards. High-yielding Lairén is also used to make basic white wine.

The fortified wine has to be matured for at least two years in single barrels or a solera system in the city of Málaga down on the coast, where it is cooler than in the inland vineyards where the wines are fermented. Its distinctive burnt toffee style is due to the complex blending of different wines and grape juices, including *arrope*, a dark grape juice concentrate, and *vino tierno*, sweet wine made from grapes that have been dried in the sun. Classic Málaga is aged in wood, but the style made from Moscatel is not, and therefore tends to be lighter and more grapily fresh.

MONTILLA-MORILES

Montilla-Moriles, directly to the north of Málaga, covers the southern part of the province of Córdoba. Montilla-Moriles was classified as part of the sherry area until well into the twentieth century and was only recognized as a separate wine region in 1933. The wine is made in the same way as sherry, and in a similar range of styles from very dry to very sweet, but it is produced from 'PX', not from Palomino Fino which is the main sherry grape.

Montilla's gentle landscape consists of low hills and small plains carpeted with vines and olive and almond trees. Villages are usually built on hilltops and occasionally a ragged rock like the famous La Lengue ('the Tongue') interrupts the calm scenery. The most inland of Andalucía's wine regions, its climate is continental: at the height of summer the temperature can reach 45°C (113°F), but the winters are short and cold. The vines huddle together under the trees, in an attempt to find shade and retain some precious moisture – something hot and bothered pickers must be grateful for, come harvest time.

The vineyard areas with the best soils, called the *zonas de superior calidad*, are found east of the whitewashed town of Montilla up in the slightly cooler Sierra de Montilla, and in the sub-region called Moriles Alto around the village of Moriles. Here the off-white soils contain large amounts of limestone and resemble the best chalky soils or *albarizas* of Jerez. In summer the hot sun bakes a hard crust on the surface of the soil and this not only reflects the heat back onto the grapes from underneath but also helps prevent the winter rains from evaporating during the long hot summer. Other vineyard areas in the DO have inferior reddish sandy soil with clay and limestone, and are known as *ruedos*.

Almost 90 per cent of the grapes grown here are Pedro Ximénez, a vine that can stand up to the withering heat, unlike a more sensitive soul like Palomino Fino. As well as Pedro Ximénez, a small amount of Airén and Torrontés is grown. These grapes are used either to produce a slightly less alcoholic blend ('PX' can produce a wine of 15 per cent alcohol unaided here), or for making the new-style, light table wines or *joven afrutado* wines. Yes, it's the same story here as in Condado – old-style fortified wines aged in soleras are in decline despite the best being of stunning quality, and progressive winemakers are looking to other styles to boost their flagging fortunes.

The sad thing is, the fortified wines of Montilla-Moriles – its *finos*, *amontillados*, *olorosos* and *palo cortados* – are what it does best; dry whites are made so much better elsewhere in Spain, in Rueda and Rías Baixas in the cooler north-west of the country, for example. I love some of the fabulously strong and vibrant fortified wines of Andalucía, and not just the famous ones of Jerez either. Let's just hope the sweeping tide of fashion comes round again before we lose them forever.

The hilltop town of Montilla is surrounded by vineyards on excellent limestone soil.

JEREZ

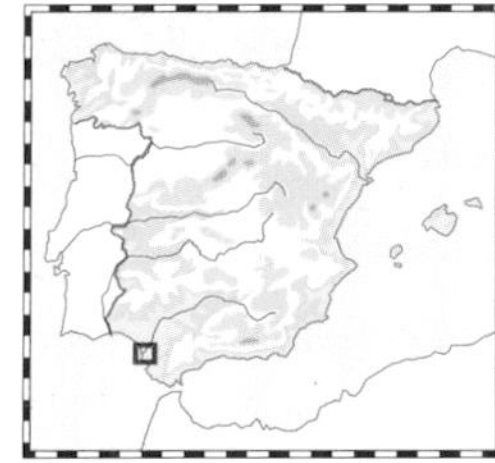

IF I VENTURE INTO SHERRY COUNTRY, I make sure I pack my sunglasses. It isn't that it's desperately hot; in August the temperature can reach 40°C (104°F), but gentle, cooling breezes from the nearby Atlantic Ocean keep things comfortable. No, it's the effect of the sun glinting off the bleached land that dazzles me and makes me screw up my eyes in pain. The vineyards of Jerez look as though someone has cut down all the trees, then taken a big pot of whitewash and splashed it over the scenery before marking out the green vines against the bright canvas. This effect is caused by the special chalky soil of region, called *albariza* – literally, 'snow white'. It's one of the keys to the special character of sherry, the fortified wine that has spawned a thousand imitations, but which only truly comes from this corner of south-west Spain, near Cádiz.

It surprises many who imagine southern Spain to be baked and arid to discover that Jerez has a relatively high rainfall – much higher, at 635mm (25in) a year, than Rioja right up in the north-east of Spain, for example. March is the wettest month, but rain falls frequently during the winter, sweeping inland from the Atlantic. And this is where *albariza* comes in handy, for it soaks up the rain and stores it away in its subsoil like an underground camel's hump. This large amount of water will see the vines through the long hot summer months. During the rainy season the vineyards are ploughed in such a way that the water is soaked up and doesn't roll away down the gentle slopes. Come summer, the sun bakes a smooth crust on the surface of the chalk, which stops too much water from evaporating. *Albariza* is also good for ripening grapes; the hot sun is reflected off the bright white soil and helps the maturing process along nicely.

Add to this the pleasant climate of Jerez, and you've got very contented, high-yielding vines. And that's true especially of the white Palomino Fino grape, a heavy cropper even in poor conditions. Palomino Fino now covers 94 per cent of the Jerez vineyards. If you were to make table wine from these grapes, it would be pretty dull, insipid stuff. But the neutral must, with its relatively low acidity, is perfect for undergoing the magical transformation that turns Jerez wine into sherry.

The creation of sherry calls for another clever performance by Mother Nature. The humidity from the nearby Atlantic encourages a yeast growth called flor to form on the surface of the new wine, though only usually when the wine has been made from quite acidic grapes and given a light fortification with *aguardiente* (grape spirit). At first the flor just looks like a sprinkling of powder, but the growth soon spreads and thickens to form a creamy protective layer, which prevents oxidation and adds its own salty, nutty character to the wine maturing in the cask. The bone-dry, pale straw sherry that emerges from this process is *fino*. *Fino* is produced in large volumes at the bodegas in the towns of Jerez de la Frontera and El Puerto de Santa María. At Sanlúcar de Barrameda, a coastal fishing town, the humid climate means that the flor layer on the casked wine grows thicker and denser than elsewhere in the region. Sanlúcar produces a particular type of *fino* known as

WHITE GRAPES
Palomino is the classic sherry grape. Palomino Fino is by far the better variety and is planted in most of the vineyards. There is also some Palomino de Jerez and Pedro Ximénez, with Moscatel grown for the sweet wines.

CLIMATE
The long hot summers (at times up to 40°C/104°F) are moderated by the influence of the Atlantic. The humidity near the coast is crucial to the development of flor and the production of sherry. In the winter there is fairly heavy rainfall in the region.

SOIL
Chalky *albariza* soil with smaller amounts of clay and sand is the best type. The less good soils contain large amounts of clay, mud or sand.

ASPECT
The vineyards lie mainly on bare, rolling hills up to 150m (500ft) high or else on flat land.

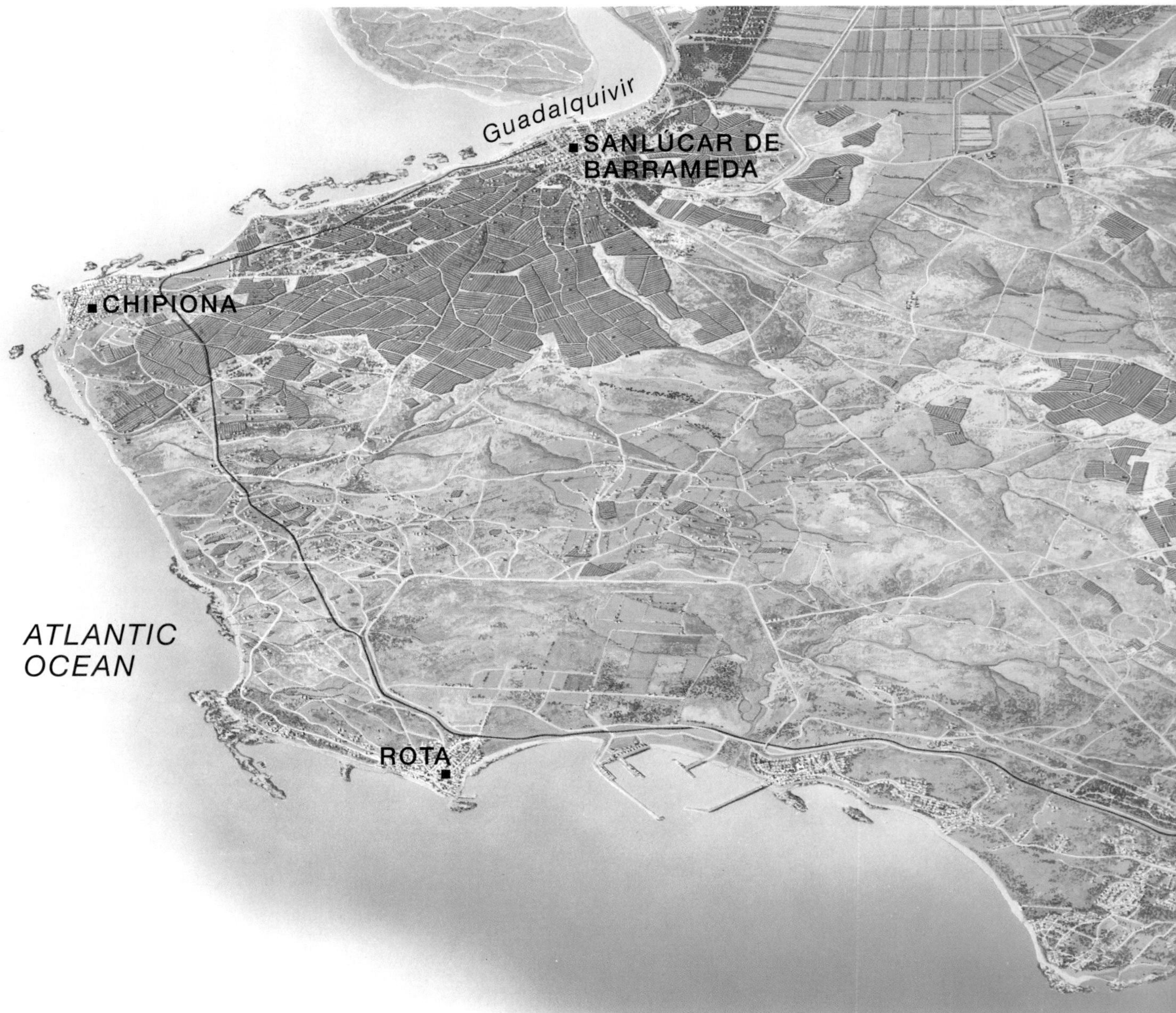

Dark oloroso *sherry matures without the aid of flor and develops rich, nutty flavours.*

manzanilla, which is saltier, lighter and more delicate than *fino*. *Amontillado* sherry is *fino* which has been allowed to mature and oxidize developing a more rounded, nutty flavour. *Oloroso* is sherry which has had no protective layer of flor, so it develops a dark colour, marked oxidized flavours and greater richness. All sherry is matured in a solera system – a stack of casks containing progessively older wines, which are continually refreshed by blending with younger wines to create greater complexity. Commercial sherry is sweetened by the addition of concentrated grape juice.

In recent years the Consejo Regulador of Jerez-Xérès-Sherry and Manzanilla de Sanlúcar (Spain's oldest *consejo*) has offered financial incentives to growers in poorer areas to persuade them to grub up their vineyards and replant in Jerez Superior. Some have done so, while others have chosen to opt out of the DO altogether and not make sherry any more. As a result, the area under vine in Jerez Superior is growing, but overall vineyard holdings are decreasing. It's all good news, since a boom in the sherry market during the 1970s had led to a doubling of vineyard area and the inevitable use of some pretty grotty patches of land. Today quality is rising as less sherry is made in volume terms, but the better, chalkier soils are encroached upon more and more to provide better quality Palomino Fino grapes.

So what does sherry country look like? If you can stop squinting in the sun, cast your eye over huge vistas of very gently sloping land with rows and rows of neatly pruned vines. They are nearly all Palomino Fino. This wouldn't have been so a hundred years ago when the area was planted with the traditional local grape, Palomino de Jerez or Palomino Basto. Both this and the grape used for sweetening sherry, Pedro Ximénez, have had to yield most of their territory as Palomino Fino takes over. Here and there a shimmering white building stands out on the soft brow of a hill. It will doubtless belong to a bodega – everything does here. You won't see much else around the major sherry centres, although further afield in the region you'll catch a glimpse of the bright yellow sunflower crops.

Sanlúcar and El Puerto de Santa María lie on lower, flatter land on the coast. Sanlúcar's vineyards are mostly on plainland, based on *albariza* soil, while Puerto's is less chalky. The grapes grown near each town are not necessarily used in that town – they may be used by bodegas all over the region. It's just that to qualify as a *manzanilla*, a sherry must have been matured in Sanlúcar. The town's seafront, with its little blue and white fishing boats pulled up on the beach and traditional bars all serving the chilled sherry straight from the cask, is one of the most delightful spots in the region. After this, drinking sherry back at home is never the same again...

The chalky soil of Jerez helps reflect the bright sun back on to the grapes.

WHERE THE VINEYARDS ARE *The three important centres for sherry production, Jerez de la Frontera, Sanlúcar de Barrameda and El Puerto de Santa María, form a rough triangle north of the Guadalete river with most of the vineyards fanning out around Jerez and Sanlúcar in rolling countryside. Jerez has always been the most important of these three towns and its Moorish name, Seris, is the origin of the English word, sherry. The shippers' headquarters and bodegas are concentrated in these towns and the wine is no longer made in the* casieros *out in the vineyards.*

Centuries ago the vineyards were sited more to the east of Jerez, but over the years they have crept gradually westwards to occupy the albariza *or chalkier soils to the west of the town. The road between Jerez and Sanlúcar takes you past some of the finest sherry vineyards. There are vineyards further afield, both to the north and the south, but the ones on the map, lying between the three sherry-producing towns, make up what is known as Jerez Superior, the best zone for sherry vines, and 80 per cent of the vineyards are found here.*

Most of the vineyards lie on huge, very gently sloping hillsides with few buildings and almost no trees to break up the landscape. As the aspect of the vineyards does not matter in such a southerly latitude, the hills are usually planted with vines on all sides. A few of the big sherry companies have large vineyard holdings but most of the vineyards are small and divided between 4500 and 5000 growers.

ALBARIZA CHALK

The finest sherry vineyards are located on *albariza* chalk soil which contains between 60 and 80% chalk. This soil can appear almost as white as snow in summer and is very high in calcium. It is finely grained and this even texture is very important in the Jerez climate where there are heavy rains in winter and early spring. The deep *albariza* soil absorbs the rain like a sponge and this then sustains the vines during the long summer drought.

Most of the *albariza* soil is found in two areas between Sanlúcar and Jerez and the more outlying vineyards are mainly the poorer, darker soils which contain less chalk – *barros rojos* or clay soils contain up to 30% chalk and *arenas* or sandy soils have about 10% chalk. In an effort to improve quality the proportion of vineyards on the *albariza* soil has grown from 50% in 1960 to 80% in 1980.

PORTUGAL

THE AGONY AND THE ECSTASY of Portuguese wine are so intertwined that I approach any attempt at unravelling the jumbled strands with some trepidation. Its very unpredictability and refusal to conform to modern international norms are what makes Portugal such a gloriously fascinating wine country and yet such an infuriating one. Until recently Portugal was such an enthusiastic consumer of her own table wines that she simply saw no need to bow to the demands of an export market. She did have some wines that were intended for export – the great fortified wines of port and Madeira were invented by traders, largely from Britain; the medium-sweet, lightly sparkling rosé wines of Mateus and Lancers were created after World War Two with the export market very much in mind – but the remainder was mostly lapped up by the domestic market and countries like Brazil and Angola with strong Portuguese connections.

This has meant that many wine producers have begun only recently to bring their methods and machinery close to accepted modern standards. But it also meant that the rush to uproot old vine varieties and replace them with the international favourites like Chardonnay and Cabernet only happened on a very small scale. For which we should give thanks because Portugal is a jewel house of ancient vine varieties, many unknown outside her borders. In a world of increased standardization, Portugal shines like a beacon of individuality and independence. The careful application of modern methods to these varieties, far from spoiling their character, will demonstrate just how good they are. Portugal has been through several Golden Ages as a fortified wine producer. Its Golden Age as a table wine producer is only just beginning.

As it is, Portugal, with the tempering influence of the Atlantic affecting all her coastal regions, already offers a fascinating array of wine styles. These range from the fiercely acidic yet fragrant Vinho Verdes of the Minho in the north, through the majestic ports and succulent soft reds of the Douro Valley, past the rudely impressive reds of Bairrada and the potentially magnificent reds and whites of Dão, and on down to the bulk wines of the broad fertile plains and gentle rolling hills of the south. All over the country, however, a new quality-conscious yet thrillingly non-conformist Portugal is being born. And the torrid hinterland up towards the Spanish border, with its indigenous grape varieties able to produce wonderful flavours despite the desert conditions, may yet prove to be the most exciting region of all.

Surrounded by its terraced vineyards for port, Malvedos is one of many beautiful white-washed traditional farmhouses or quintas high up in the Douro Valley.

THE WINE REGIONS OF PORTUGAL

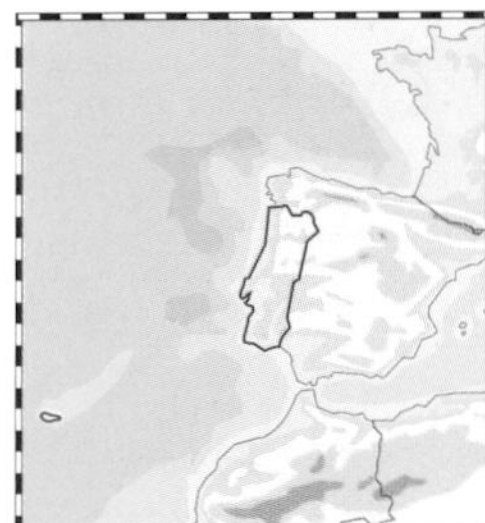

IMAGINE TWO GLASSES OF WINE standing side by side. The first, a Vinho Verde, is almost water-white with a few rather lazy bubbles clinging on the side of the glass. It smells vaguely citrusy and it knocks you sideways with its acidic rasp. Then on to the second, a port, with its deep impenetrable colour. A heady aroma of super-ripe fruit wafts from the glass and its rich, bold flavours are warming and soothing, conjuring up images of a homely winter's evening by the fireside.

It is hard to believe that the two wines, with at least ten degrees of alcohol separating them, come from the same country, let alone adjacent regions, but Vinho Verde and port live cheek by jowl alongside each other in the north of Portugal. It's not as if we're talking about a large area. Port and Vinho Verde literally cohabit in a country that is little more than 160km (100 miles) wide. You're driving along, you turn a corner and you go from one wine region to the next just like that.

That's the beauty of Portugal. For such a small country she has a strong regional feel and the climate plays a vital role in this. With its prevailing westerly winds, the Atlantic Ocean exerts a strong influence on the coastal belt but this diminishes sharply as you journey inland. As you cross a mountain range, grey rain-bearing clouds scudding inland from the sea suddenly seem to disappear. Taking a straight line across the north of the country, climate statistics illustrate this dramatic change. The Atlantic coast north of Oporto is drenched by over 1200mm (47in) of rainfall a year. This rises to 2000mm (79in) on the mountains inland, a figure comparable with Bergen on the fjord coast of Norway. Then in the rain-shadow to the east of the mountains the figure falls progressively to as low as 400mm (16in) near the frontier with Spain, drought conditions by any standard. In between these two extremes is the heart of the Douro Valley with around 700mm (28in) of rainfall, the perfect climate for ripening the grapes that produce port, Portugal's most famous wine.

As you travel across Portugal, the landscape, the architecture and the traditions change dramatically too. As mountains rise and subside, the temperate maritime climate with its lush vegetation gives way the further south and east you go to more extreme temperatures and arid scrub. Sturdy grey granite houses built to withstand wind and rain become flimsy shelters painted white to reflect the burning rays of the sun.

This regional identity is reflected in the sheer breadth of Portugal's wines. Two fortified wines, port and Madeira, are world-famous. Others like Sétubal and Carcavelos which used to be popular in the nineteenth century have virtually given in to the commercial pressures of the late twentieth century. Apart from light, spritzy Vinho Verdes, the north of the country also produces reds that are earning very different reputations for themselves. The Douro's best reds have a luscious, perfumed, soft-textured depth; Bairrada demands a sterner reaction to her aggressive but impressive wines; and Dão is at last beginning to show why it was so well regarded generations ago. Modern vinification methods are producing some increasingly attractive fresh whites. In the south ripeness is the key, with healthy red grapes that would be the envy of many a cool-climate Frenchman being turned into wines packed to the brim with ripe, berry-fruit flavours. It is perhaps here in the south that Portugal shows the most promise, having attracted the attention of a number of international winemakers.

But long-standing traditions, often deeply rooted in the rural culture, are only reluctantly cast aside. Nowhere is this better illustrated than in Portugal's rather chaotic vineyards. One grape variety may have four or five different names according to where it is planted. The red variety called Castelão Frances on the west coast is also known by the names of João de Santarém in the Ribatejo, Periquita on the Setúbal Peninsula and elsewhere in the south and sometimes by the name of Trincadeira (which, just to add to the confusion, is used elsewhere as a synonym for another Portuguese variety). Ask a farmer how much of this or that he has in his muddled vineyard and he will probably shrug his shoulders.

This is a shame because one of Portugal's greatest winemaking strengths is her wealth of native grape varieties, many of which are unique. Grapes like the deeply coloured Touriga Nacional, planted in the Douro and Dão, or the white Arinto de Bucelas, which has the wonderful asset of being able to hang on to its acidity in the heat of central southern Portugal, have the potential to be world class. There are plenty of other unfamiliar grape names besides. In Vinho Verde country there's the white triumvirate of Alvarinho, Loureiro and Trajadura, each of which are now being allowed to make their own promising varietal wines. In Bairrada there's Baga which produces solid opaque red wines and the white Maria Gomes which turns up again in the Ribatejo as Fernão Pires, where it is responsible for soft, spicy whites, some of which respond well to aging in new oak. Tinto Roriz (thought by some to be the same as Rioja's Tempranillo) is one of the top port grapes which is being planted increasingly for a new generation of unfortified red Douro wines. It turns up again in the Alentejo where it acknowledges its origins under the name of Aragonez.

THE CLASSIFICATION SYSTEM FOR PORTUGUESE WINE

Portugal's wine laws have been in a state of flux ever since the country joined the European Union in 1986. That's the polite way of describing the chaos that has resulted from bureaucrats in Brussels meeting bureaucrats in Lisbon. The new wine regions are now beginning to settle into a framework but the shenanigans of recent years rather detract from the fact that Portugal mothered the modern *appellation* system over two centuries ago. After a period of fraud and scandal in the fledgling port industry, in 1756 Portugal's autocratic but forward-thinking prime minister, the Marquis of Pombal, drew a boundary around the Douro vineyards to protect the authenticity of the wine – one of the first examples of vineyard delimitation in the world. Nothing more happened until the early twentieth century when several other Portuguese wine regions were similarly demarcated. The situation then remained static until after the 1974 Revolution when Bairrada's vineyards (which were uprooted by Pombal) were finally awarded demarcated status. On joining the European Union, Portugal's wine classification was brought into line with that of other EU countries.

QUALITY CATEGORIES

- **Denominação de Origem Controlada (DOC)** This top tier replaced the Região Demarcada (RD) category in 1990. It parallels the French *Appellation d'Origine Contrôlée* (AC, AOC) and is being expanded as newer regions make the grade.
- **Indicação de Proveniência Regulamentada (IPR)** Also known as Vinho de Qualidade Produzido em Região Determinada (or VQPRD). This intermediate category of over 30 wine regions entered the statute books in 1989/90 and is roughly similar in status to the French VDQS. In theory all IPRs are candidates for promotion to DOC but many will fade into insignificance.
- **Vinho Regional (VR)** This is a new and potentially important category, particularly in the south where wines are often made from grapes grown over a wide area. These large regions parallel the French regional Vins de Pays and allow similar flexibility, making them more popular with winemakers than the rather obscure IPRs. Vintages and grape varieties can go on the labels.
- **Vinho de Mesa** The most basic category: table wine.

The Portuguese only began to sort out their chaotic vineyards when the country joined the European Union (EU) in 1986 but since then progress has been painfully slow. Much more visible are the impressively dangerous mountain-breaching roads that have been built with EU funds to link Portugal's more remote inland regions to the coastal centres, where most of the country's population reside. The result is that landlocked wine regions like Dão which used to be a good half-day's drive from the city of Oporto can now be reached by car within a couple of hair-raising hours.

WINE REGIONS

A journey around Portugal's wine regions can hardly ever be whistle-stop. From the Minho province which marks the border with Spain in the north-west to the Algarve in the south may be just under 650km (400 miles) as the crow flies but there are nearly 50 officially recognized wine regions in between, as well as a new tier of Vinhos Regionais (VR) or Regional Wines which cover most of the country except for the highest peaks of the northern and central mountain ranges, where viticulture is not feasible. Wherever you go in Portugal it seems someone somewhere is making wine.

The largest wine region is Vinho Verde which covers the entire soggy north-west of the country, including the lower reaches of the Douro Valley. The Douro wine region itself, delimited both for port and table wine, begins 80km (50 miles) or so upstream and extends east to the Spanish border. In the granite mountains immediately to the south, the Dão region spreads over three river valleys, the vineyards climbing into the foothills of the Serra da Estrêla, Portugal's highest mountain range, which rises to a lofty 1993m (6539ft). Bairrada, with its solid, tannic red wines, occupies the flat coastal strip between the misty Aveiro lagoon and the ivory-towered university town of Coimbra.

Stretching along the rolling coastal hills to the south, Estremadura (often known as the Oeste or 'west') is a colourful region with flourishing vineyards producing large quantities of bulk wine for the thirsty local market. For many years the region was perhaps best known for its historic enclaves of Colares, with its centenarian, phylloxera-free vines growing in the sand, and Bucelas whose white wines were drunk by Wellington's army during the Peninsular War nearly two hundred years ago. More recently, the town of Alenquer has lent its name to a new vineyard enclave which is being taken seriously by a number of forward-thinking single estates.

The Tagus or Tejo river which flows into the Atlantic near Lisbon marks the clear divide between the hilly north and the great plains of the south. Inland the Ribatejo region spans the broad river valley, its fertile alluvial soils producing fat, juicy tomatoes and large crops of well-ripened grapes. The Setúbal Peninsula, south-east of Lisbon, is one of the few Portuguese regions to embrace foreign grape varieties which seem to have found a niche on the limestone slopes of the Serra da Arrábida. To the east and south the undulating Alentejo plain sweeps across to the Spanish border with vineyards concentrated around the small whitewashed wine-making towns of Portalegre, Borba, Redondo, Reguengos, Granja-Amareleja, Moura and Vidigueira, not forgetting Évora which is the regional capital. Last and probably least on the Portuguese mainland, the Serra de Monchique separates the Alentejo from the Algarve, where the warm maritime climate is ideal for sun-seeking tourists but less well suited to wine. But there's more to Portugal than the mainland, or *continente* as it is known.

The Portuguese are custodians of a number of volcanic Atlantic islands which their early navigators were the first to discover. Vines were introduced to the Azores by Portuguese settlers in the fifteenth century. Two islands in this remote archipelago, Pico and Graciosa, exported fortified wines but the industry was all but wiped out by oidium and phylloxera in the nineteenth century. Madeira, 1100km (680 miles) south-west of Lisbon, has been home to a flourishing wine industry ever since it was first discovered in the fifteenth century, and by the end of the seventeenth century there were already 30 wine shippers on the island. It too suffered oidium and phylloxera but the wine industry underwent a slow and painful recovery. Madeira wine hardly fits into a text book. The humid subtropical climate and the process of heating the wine goes against wine-making norms, but nevertheless Madeira is one of the world's most distinctive fortified wines.

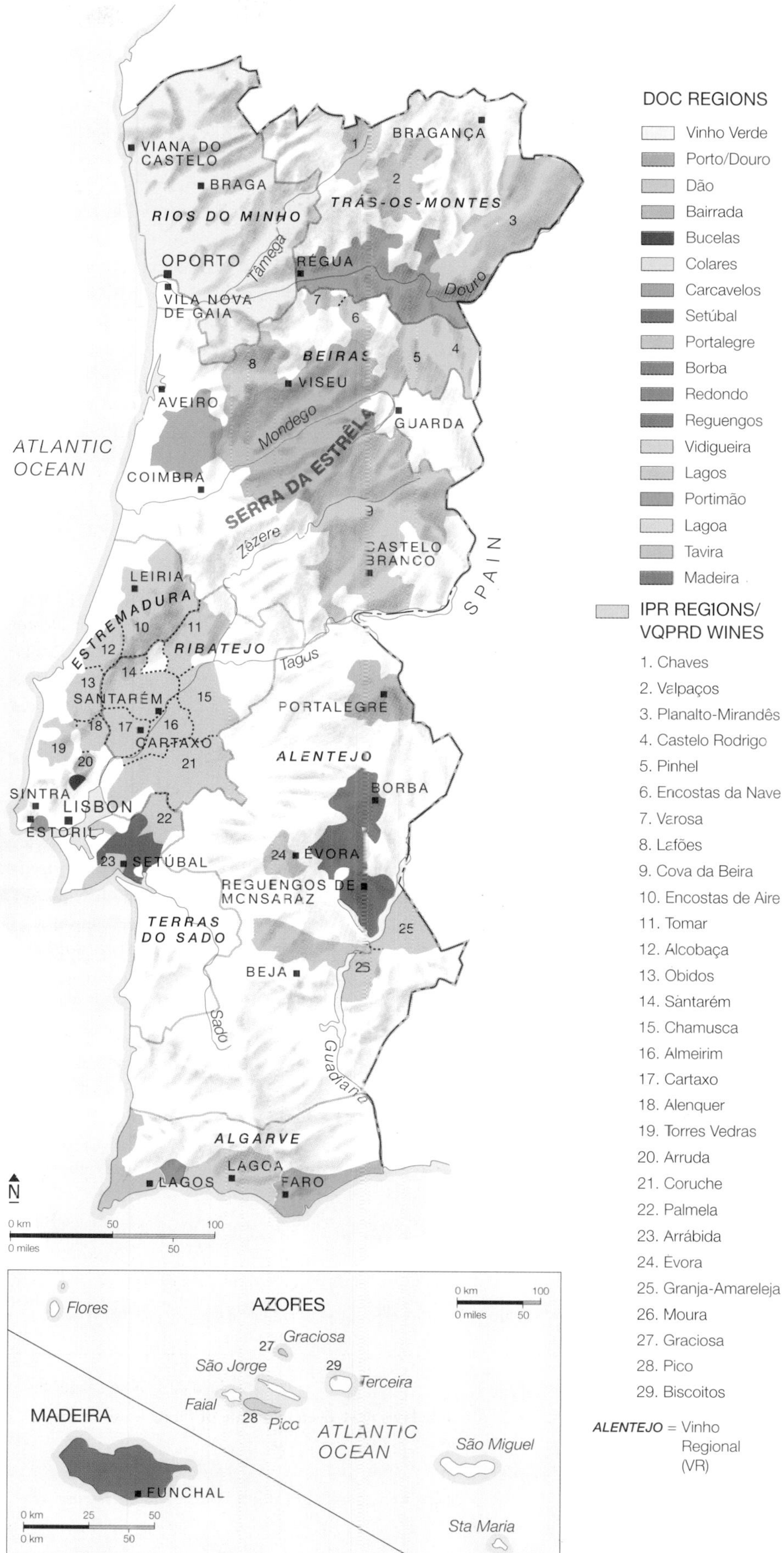

PANORAMIC MAPS
The Douro Valley *pages 210–11*
Madeira *pages 214–15*

Northern Portugal

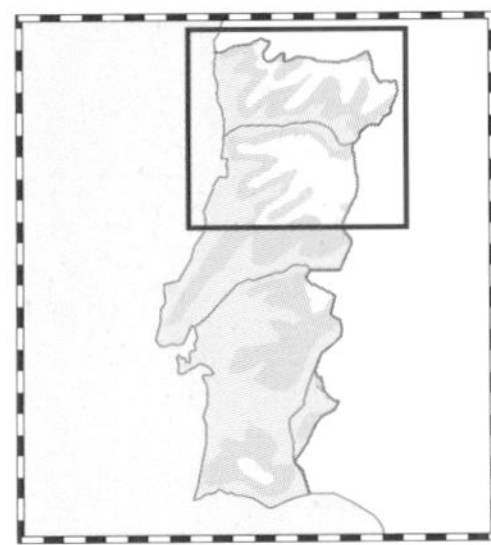

RED GRAPES
The best varieties are Bairrada's and Dão's Baga, and Touriga Francesa and Touriga Nacional used in port.

WHITE GRAPES
Alvarinho, Loureiro, Trajadura, Viosinho and Gouveio are the main grapes.

CLIMATE
Near the coast there is ample rainfall and a long warm ripening season. The inland Douro Valley has harsh winters and hot summers.

SOIL
The heavy lime-rich clay of Bairrada gives way to granite in Dão and slate in the Douro.

ASPECT
The steep Douro terraces contrast with the flat farming land of Vinho Verde.

IT'S ALL TOO EASY to lose your way in northern Portugal. On the road map there's a tempting and challenging maze of country lanes linking tiny villages but when you're driving along there are very few road signs to point you in the right direction. And there's no shortage of distractions. One minute you pass a grumbling ox cart stacked high with colourful local produce, the farmer, his wife, two children and a dog peering over the side. Then, look to the left and you spy a bacchanalian scene as a whole family and their neighbours come together to gather in the harvest. You just have to stop and pinch yourself because it's like going back in time.

But in fact what seems like a rural dream has become something of a nightmare. North-west Portugal, alongside neighbouring Galicia across the border in Spain, is one of the most densely populated parts of the Iberian Peninsula. It must have seemed like paradise to the early settlers, browned off with the barren wastes of central Iberia. Rivers and streams, filled to the brim by warm, rain-bearing Atlantic westerlies, support a riot of vegetation. But down the centuries, with successive generations staking their rightful claim, land holdings have diminished in size to such an extent that many are almost unworkable. Just imagine making a living from a plot of land smaller than a suburban back garden! As you peer from the roadside into the jungle of greenery, count the number of different crops that you can see within a stone's throw. Depending on the time of year, the chance is that you will spy a few tall cabbages growing alongside some maize, a tethered goat or a cow, and across the top of all this, trained off the ground because of the damp climate, there'll be a lush canopy of vines dripping with grapes.

VINHO VERDE

The grapes you see here are destined for Vinho Verde, Portugal's famous 'green wine'. For most people outside Portugal Vinho Verde conjures up an image of a light, slightly sparkling, medium-dry white wine, often instantly recognizable because of its dumpy, flagon-shaped bottle. But back in its country of origin, ask for a glass of Vinho Verde in one of the numerous rough and ready roadside bars and you are likely to be shocked into the truth that around half the region's production is not the widely exported white wine but a dark, rasping, fizzy red drunk only in northern Portugal. Even the authentic Vinho Verde white will taste different. The lack of any of the residual sweetness which is thought to be necessary to mollycoddle foreigners exposes the searing acidity which is the hallmark of true Vinho Verde. The climate here is so mild and wet that it takes an unusually hot summer to ripen all the grapes, and this results in low-sugar, high-acid grapes.

But Vinho Verde is moving on apace, albeit at its *own* pace. The vines that used to be grown on trellises along the border of fields or, even more primitively, trained to climb the trunks of tall poplar trees, have largely disappeared and some growers are even abandoning the picturesque but impractical pergola polyculture in favour of vines trained along low wires, a practice which actually makes them look like vineyards.

The wines are changing too. There's an encouraging trend towards varietal wines as the old muddled 'pick and mix' vineyards are uprooted and poorer grape varieties are weeded out. The Alvarinho grape growing along the river Minho in the extreme north of the region heads the varietal tree, producing a relatively full but delicate, dry white wine with an aroma and flavour akin to a freshly picked Cox's apple. Further south in the Lima and Cavado valleys around Braga, the Loureiro grape makes a lighter, crisper, more typical style of Vinho Verde which sometimes has a faint floral whiff of Muscat. Trajadura, which is often used alongside Loureiro, makes a slightly softer style of wine, while inland along the lower reaches and tributaries of the Douro river, the tangy Avesso grape ripens to produce fuller, riper flavours.

A growing band of single estates or quintas is tending to make wines with more character than those from the larger producers who have to rely on the traditional mish-mash of different grapes from farmers with their pocket-sized plots. But the quality from the co-operatives and single estates is still patchy and it is generally better to look for wines from one of the large private firms in the region who grow their own grapes and bottle their own wines. Vintages only tend to appear on the labels of single-quinta wines, very few of which have the capacity to age. Other wines are just assumed to be from the most recent harvest, hence the name Vinho Verde, so called because it should be drunk green in its first flush of youth. From time to time, appallingly wet years like 1988 and 1993 force up prices and remind us that these vineyards are at the mercy of the fickle Atlantic weather. But an ice-cold bottle of searingly dry Vinho Verde is still a great picnic wine.

DOURO VALLEY

After the Tagus, the Douro is the most important river in Portugal (and its importance continues over the border into Spain, as the Duero). The Douro Valley (see page 210) is a wild and beautiful part of Portugal and the poverty of its natural resources has driven the inhabitants to ingenious extremes in order to wrest a living out of what can only just be called soil. The vineyards here must be some of the most labour-intensive in the world. In order to grow anything on these slopes of schistous rock, terraces have to be carved out of the hillsides, sometimes to support no more than a row or two of vines. Hillside profiles like pyramids make you think that the Douro should be one of the wonders of the world. Mechanization of the vineyards was impossible until a replanting programme began in the early 1980s. Now there are there four different methods of vine cultivation cohabiting along the Douro Valley (see diagram on page 209). Mechanical pruning and harvesting, on the other hand, will always be impossible.

Demarcated for port in the eighteenth century, the Douro Valley is now recognized as a source of some increasingly good

The Quinta da Cha belongs to Luís Pato, Bairrada's best-known winemaker.

table or 'light' wines, to use the official parlance (but most are anything but light!). Made from the same varieties used for port, many of these red table wines have tended to be rather hard and unapproachable, probably not very far removed from the so-called 'blackstrap' wines that were first exported from the Douro over 300 years ago. However, a new generation of winemakers seems to be getting to grips with the tannins that lend much-needed structure to port but tend to make harsh, mouth-numbing wines when all the natural sugar has fermented to heady alcohol. Ferreira's Barca Velha, made in the upper reaches of the Douro near the Spanish border, is the best example of what can be done, with properties downstream like Quinta do Côtto, Quinta de la Rosa and Quinta de Gaivosa following suit with supple wines which capture the port-like flavours of ripe Douro grapes.

TRÁS-OS-MONTES

Mountain ranges separate the high, barren country of north-east Portugal, which certainly deserves its name of Trás-os-Montes or 'Behind the Mountains', from the heavily populated north-western coast. The climatic extremes of this high, inland area make agriculture difficult and the mountainous slopes offer more to walkers than to farmers. However, there are three IPR wine regions here which make wine from some of the same grapes as in the Douro Valley just to the south: Chaves, which is better known for its cured hams or *presunto*; hot, dry Planalto-Mirandês along the border with Spain, which only has a few scrubby vineyards; and Valpaços, whose co-operative is one of the north-east's better ones. But in general here it's the old Portuguese story of growers sending their grapes to be made into mediocre wine at the local co-operative.

DÃO

Until recently the Dão region in the heart of Portugal around Viseu has been in a time warp of its own. For over 30 years dowdy co-operatives had a stranglehold on the region's wine-making, leaving anyone with a jot of initiative standing with apoplexy on the sidelines as Dão wines went from bad to worse. The rules and regulations that enshrined this monopoly situation were blown away by Brussels when Portugal joined the EU in 1986 and Dão has been given a new lease of life. The potential is certainly there. Bottles that predate the dark ages have aged well, retaining their powerful, spicy concentration of flavour and some recent wines from the huge Sogrape company – who have taken it upon themselves to reinvigorate the region – share some of the same character. Touriga Nacional has been accepted as the best red grape variety for Dão, with the better runners-up including Bastardo and Tinta Pinheira, but most vineyards are still in a muddle.

Like so much of northern Portugal, Dão is lumbered with thousands of tiny plots in clearings among the fragrant pine and eucalyptus forests that cover the hard granite hills. Dão is almost completely surrounded by wild, forbidding mountains, with a narrow gap south of the Serra do Buçaco through which Portugal's largest home-grown river, the Mondego, drains towards the coast. The mountains tend to protect this eyrie from the unpredictable onslaught of Atlantic storms and summer months therefore tend to be warm, with winter temperatures often plunging well below freezing. Away from the new highway that slices impressively through the granite, remote villages specialize in the pungent local cheese, Queijo da Serra, which is a good foil for a glass of peppery red Dão.

The Serra do Buçaco, with its exotic pine forests surrounding the flamboyant Buçaco Palace Hotel, marks the boundary between Dão and the coastal strip of fertile clay known as Bairrada. The nineteenth-century castle hotel just outside Luso buys in grapes from Dão and Bairrada to make its own reds and whites which rank as some of Portugal's best. Sadly the wines are only available to guests who endure the hotel's archaic plumbing (and at other hotels in the same group).

In warm, damp Vinho Verde country the vines are grown mainly on trellises.

BAIRRADA

Like the Vinho Verde region, Bairrada is at the mercy of the Atlantic, with frequent sea mists and annual rainfall reaching 1000mm (40in). The countryside is mainly flat and featureless, with tall pine and eucalyptus trees sheltering small plots of land planted with cereals, beans and knotty old vines. Bairrada is unusual in Portugal in that it is very nearly a one-grape region and Baga's small, dark berries produce fiercely tannic red wines. Other varieties like Castelão Frances and even Cabernet Sauvignon are being planted to make wines that are softer and more approachable when young. However, the best wines, from traditional producers like Caves São João and Luís Pato, reward patience. A small amount of aromatic dry white wine is produced, most of which is used by the local sparkling wine industry. It's worth turning off the Lisbon-Oporto highway to sample a firm-flavoured red Bairrada with the local delicacy, *leitão* or suckling pig.

TERRACING IN THE DOURO

Since the late nineteenth century experiments have been made with different terracing systems in the Douro in an effort to minimize costs.

1 shows traditional *Socalcos*. These narrow, walled terraces built around hill contours were established mainly in the nineteenth century when labour was abundant and cheap. Since mechanization is impossible, labour costs have made this traditional method increasingly expensive.
2 shows newer-style *Socalcos*. These inclined terraces became more popular early in the twentieth century but are similarly costly to maintain.
3 shows *Patamares* or contour terraces. These unwalled terraces have well-positioned tracks for small tractors. The system, devised in the 1970s, is widely used because of lower labour costs but it is wasteful of land and unsightly.
4 shows vertical planting up-and-down the slope or *vinha ao alto*. This 1980s technique allows easier maintenance and therefore reduces costs. Although soil erosion is not as adverse as predicted, it is limited to slopes of less than 30°.

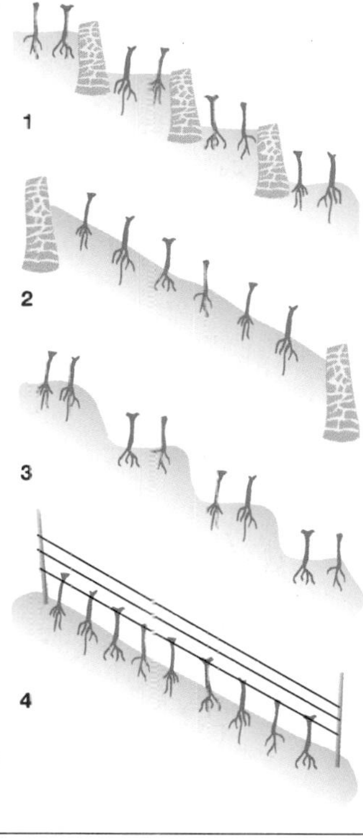

Traditional Vinho Verde wines are medium-dry to dry and positively tart.

THE DOURO VALLEY

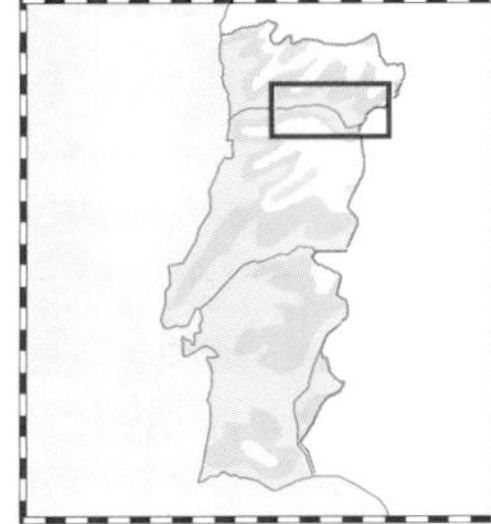

TAKE MY ADVICE and leave the car behind. I'm not suggesting it because of the port but because going by train is much the best way to see the Douro. The corkscrew roads tend to cross the deeply incised valley from side to side whereas the railway runs alongside the river affording the best possible views of the vineyards stacked up on high terraces on either side. The journey starts at Oporto's noisy São Bento railway station. Before finding the platform for the train to Pocinho take a look at the panels of blue and white tiles or *azulejos* that adorn the concourse illustrating glorious moments from Portugal's history. Built on the site of a convent, it's a railway station like no other.

The Douro vineyards are between 80 and 200km (50 and 125 miles) upstream from Oporto, the city that has given its name to 'Vinho do Porto' or port wine. The train isn't built for speed and the journey takes nearly three hours, almost exactly the same time as it does by road. As you leave the rather murky suburbs and the sea mist behind, the train passes through chaotic Vinho Verde country with its characteristic tall crops growing underneath a lush canopy of vines. About an hour into the journey the Douro comes into view and from there on to the end of the line the train snakes alongside the river. It's not uncommon for passengers to sit with the door open on the steps of the carriage and there are even places along the track where you can almost dangle your feet in the still, dark waters.

The train rounds a bend and the landscape changes. Hard grey granite gives way to flaky, silver-coloured schist. This is where the port vineyards begin, today as they did in the mid-eighteenth century when Portugal's prime minister, the forward-thinking Marquis of Pombal, first drew a boundary around the Douro Valley vineyards to protect the authenticity of port wine.

The Douro DOC divides unofficially into three sub-regions. The most westerly one, Baixo Corgo, is centred on the town of Régua. Here the climate is cooler and wetter than further upstream and the wines from here tend to be lighter and less substantial – ideal for young rubies and the light tawnies that supply the seemingly insatiable French taste for port. The train pauses at Régua but it is worth continuing upstream, at least as far as Pinhão. This is the heart of the next sub-region, the Cima Corgo, and from Pinhão's station platform, adorned with blue and ochre *azulejos* illustrating scenes from the vintage, you can see Cálem's Quinta da Foz, Ferreira's Quinta do Seixo, Dow's Quinta do Bomfim and Royal Oporto's Quinta das Carvalhas. The Pinhão Valley hides properties belonging to Taylor, Warre, Fonseca and perhaps the finest quinta of all, the immaculately maintained Quinta do Noval. As the train climbs towards Tua more famous port names come into view: Croft's Quinta da Roêda, Graham's Quinta dos Malvedos and Cockburn's Quinta do Tua. Upstream from Tua the vineyards cease for a while.

A massive outcrop of granite squeezes the river into a narrow, forbidding gorge. The railway disappears into a tunnel only to reappear once again among terraced vineyards carved from the schist. This, the most easterly of the three sub-regions, is known as the Douro Superior. It has attracted port shippers like Cockburn and Ferreira who have pioneered vineyards on the relatively flat land towards the Spanish frontier. The train crosses the river and two of the grandest of all vineyard properties can be spotted: first Taylor's Quinta de Vargellas followed by the Symington's Quinta do Vesúvio, both of which have their own railway stations. Beyond here

RED GRAPES
Over 50 grape varieties can be used in port, but the best is Touriga Nacional.

WHITE GRAPES
Varieties used for white port include Gouveio (Madeira's Verdelho) and Viosinho.

CLIMATE
The humid Atlantic climate in Oporto is ideal for aging port. Further east it is more arid.

SOIL
Port vines are only planted on schistose soils.

ASPECT
The Douro is famous for its steep terraces which follow the narrow river valleys.

FOLGOSA TO VESUVIO

VINEYARDS

TOTAL DISTANCE NORTH TO SOUTH 17 KM (11 MILES)

N

WHERE THE VINEYARDS ARE *This map of the Douro Valley shows the Cima Corgo and part of the Douro Superior sub-regions where the best port vineyards are located. The finest tawny, vintage and late bottled vintage ports are sourced from the Cima Corgo where all the major port shippers have large vineyard holdings. The little town of Pinhão is surrounded by steep terraces of vines, with some of the most famous names in port emblazoned on the high-retaining walls shoring up these terraces. Properties (known as quintas) are graded officially from A to F according to 12 different factors, among them altitude, aspect, locality and soil. Nearly all the best A and B grade quintas are within sight of the Douro or one of its tributaries, the Tedo, Távora, Torto and Pinhão. The higher vineyards around the towns of Sabrosa, Alijó and São João da Pesqueira are awarded lower grades (C, D, E and F) and a much smaller proportion of their production is made into port. The railway runs right alongside the river, stopping at tiny stations* en route *and it is a lifeline for many farmers whose vineyards are difficult to reach by road. A boat is sometimes the only other option.*

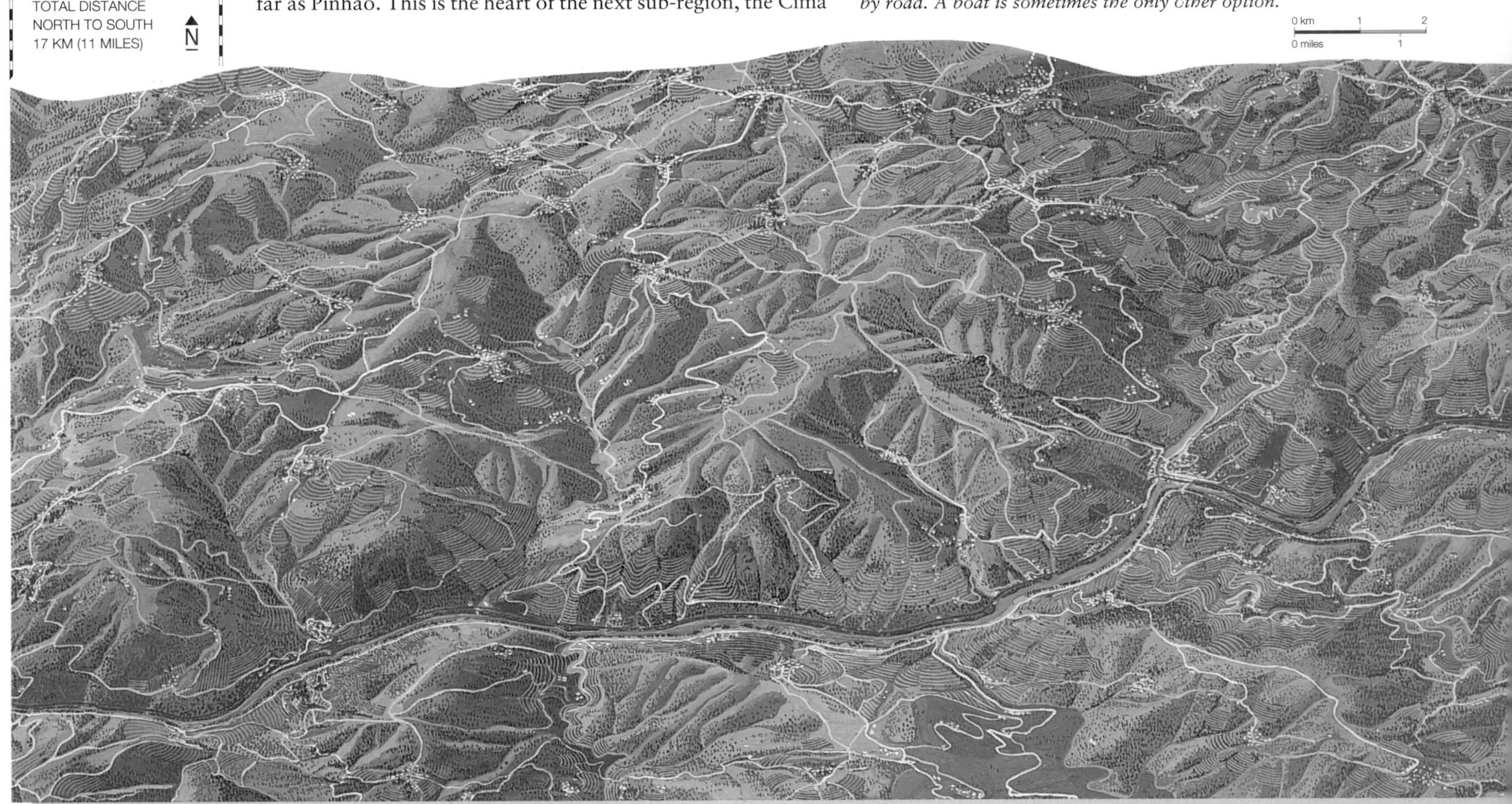

0 km 1 2
0 miles 1

the landscape begins to look increasingly arid and vineyards tend to be planted on the high land out of sight of the river. Just before the train reaches the end of the line Ferreira's Quinta do Vale do Meão appears, home of Portugal's most sought after red table wine, the now legendary Barca Velha. At Pocinho the driver shunts the engine to the other end of the carriages and the train returns to Oporto.

Throughout much of the year the Douro is a peaceful place with the train the only source of disturbance as it hoots and rattles along the valley. However, in mid- to late September the Douro comes alive as pickers chatter their way along the terraces to pick the grapes. Sleepy quintas wake up and the heady aroma of ripe, fermenting juice fills the air. At some properties they still tread the grapes by foot in stone troughs known as *lagares*. Others are equipped with the latest in modern technology and stainless steel vats gleam in the bright sunlight.

In the spring after the harvest the young wines are brought downstream to Vila Nova de Gaia which faces Oporto at the mouth of the Douro river. There the wines are put into wood where they age in the relative cool and calm of long, low buildings called lodges. Here the wines evolve into their different styles. Ruby port is the simplest wine, bottled young while it retains its spicy personality and its dark, purple-ruby colour. Vintage character is a premium ruby, left to age for five years or so before bottling. Tawny ports are left for longer until they become smooth and silky, sometimes up to 20 to 30 years. Vintage port is a wine from a single exceptional year and bottled after spending a short time in wood. The wine continues to age for 20 years or more in bottle, throwing a 'crust' or sediment as it loses colour and gains complexity with age. Late Bottled Vintage or LBV is a port from a single year, bottled ready to drink after spending between three and six years maturing in wood. Crusted port is a blend of two or three vintages bottled at between three and four years. A small amount of white port is also made from white grapes.

From the two-tier bridge that links the two cities on either side of the Douro you can look down on the black roofs of the lodges, many of them illuminated at night by garish neon signs. The road along the waterfront is lined with boats called *barcos rabelos* which used to bring the wine downstream before the river was dammed in the 1970s. Laden with precious young port it must have been an unnerving journey through the rapids. Thank goodness for the train!

Port comes in many styles, including Late Bottled Vintage or LBV, which is wine from a single vintage, bottled after four to six years maturing in wood.

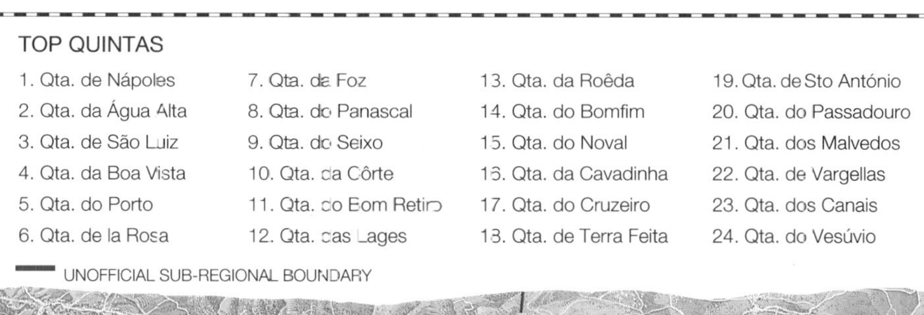

TOP QUINTAS

1. Qta. de Nápoles	7. Qta. da Foz	13. Qta. da Roêda	19. Qta. de Sto António
2. Qta. da Água Alta	8. Qta. do Panascal	14. Qta. do Bomfim	20. Qta. do Passadouro
3. Qta. de São Luiz	9. Qta. do Seixo	15. Qta. do Noval	21. Qta. dos Malvedos
4. Qta. da Boa Vista	10. Qta. da Côrte	16. Qta. da Cavadinha	22. Qta. de Vargellas
5. Qta. do Porto	11. Qta. do Bom Retiro	17. Qta. do Cruzeiro	23. Qta. dos Canais
6. Qta. de la Rosa	12. Qta. das Lages	18. Qta. de Terra Feita	24. Qta. do Vesúvio

UNOFFICIAL SUB-REGIONAL BOUNDARY

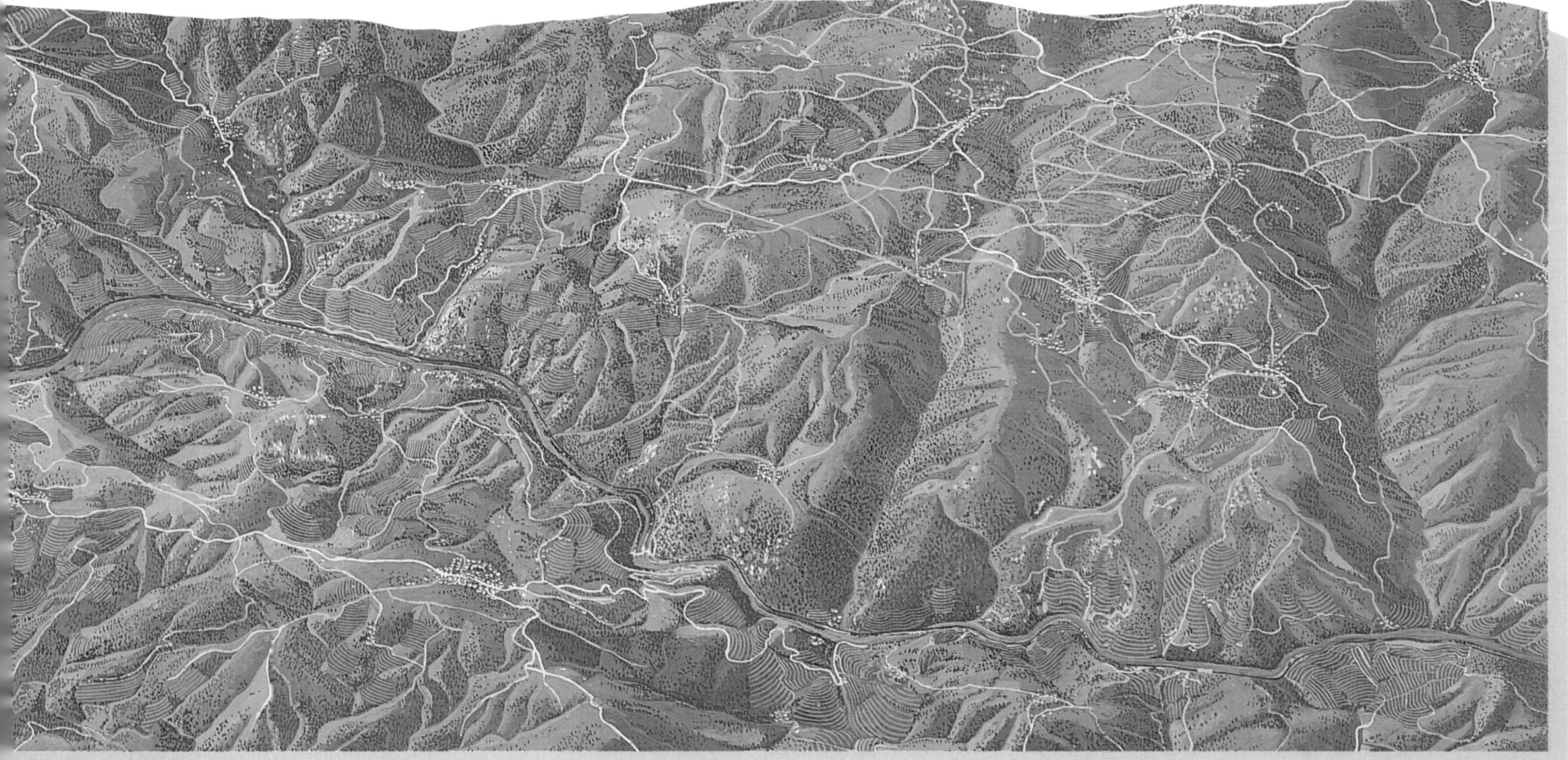

Central & Southern Portugal

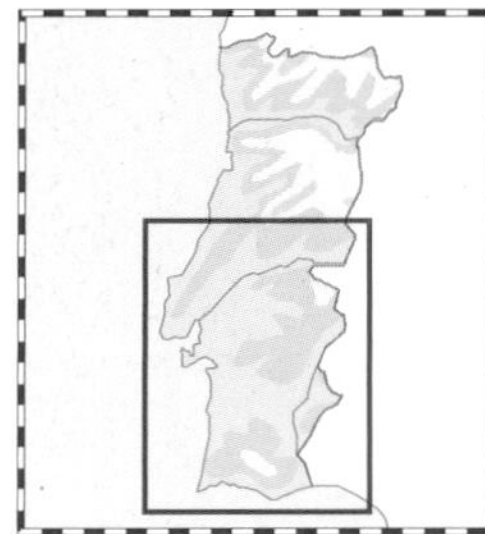

RED GRAPES
Castelão Frances is found throughout. Ramisco is in decline as Cabernet Sauvignon expands.

WHITE GRAPES
Arinto has the potential for good wines. Fernão Pires is widely planted and Malvasia is found in various guises.

CLIMATE
The influence of the Atlantic is important in the west. Inland, the arid Alentejo can be very hot in summer.

SOIL
Estremadura has calcareous clay and limestone, Ribatejo clay, sand and fertile alluvial soils and Alentejo granite, limestone and red clay.

ASPECT
The Ribatejo and Alentejo plains contrast with the hillier Torres Vedras, Alenquer and Arruda.

THE MUDDY TEJO or Tagus river flows south-west through central Portugal dividing the country into two roughly symmetrical halves. Just north of the river the mountains subside and as you drive south the roads straighten out and the patchwork of poor, intensively farmed smallholdings of the north gives way to vast estates or *latifúndios*, some of which cover thousands of acres of low-lying plain.

ESTREMADURA

This strip of rolling countryside, stretching from Lisbon's populated hinterland along the wild and windy western Atlantic coast, is known colloquially as the Oeste (pronounced 'wesht', a rather drunken-sounding version of the word 'west' which is what it means). Although Estremadura produces more wine than any other single region in Portugal, not many people have ever heard of it as there are few wines of quality. It has recently been subdivided into six smaller wine regions: Alcobaça, Encostas de Aire, Óbidos, Torres Vedras, Alenquer and Arruda. Each one is centred on a huge co-operative winery, the largest of which is at Torres Vedras, but big is not beautiful here and even now there is little to see in the way of up-to-date wine-making and consequently little memorable wine.

The towns and villages are considerably more picturesque than most of the wines. Lush, high-yielding vineyards planted with bland white grape varieties like Vital and Jampal produce anonymous wines which quickly find their way on to the undemanding local market. Ripening can be difficult in this relatively cool maritime climate and red wines made from the ubiquitous Periquita grape often taste thin and mean. But there is hope in the region.

One or two of the larger co-operatives are getting their act together and producing some fresh, sappy, bargain basement reds. The Arruda co-operative, just a few miles north of the Tagus, makes some simple, satisfying young reds from a blend of local grapes, mainly João de Santarém and Tinta Miúda. Inland around the quiet, whitewashed town of Alenquer are two of the best Estremadura estates, Quinta de Abrigada and Quinta das Pancas, making good if very different red and white wines, the latter with a proportion of Cabernet Sauvignon and Chardonnay, both of which seem to blend quite well with the local grape varieties.

Moscatel vines in a João Pires vineyard near Azeitão on the Setúbal Peninsula.

Two tiny enclaves in Estremadura are worth a special detour. The windswept, seaside vineyards of Colares just 35km (22 miles) from the centre of Lisbon grow in the sandy soil on the clifftops, their roots anchored in the clay below. This sand protected the vines from the phylloxera louse which attacked vineyards throughout Europe in the nineteenth century. Consequently, the local Ramisco vine is one of the only European varieties that has never been grafted onto phylloxera-resistant American rootstock. Cultivating vines in the sand is difficult and expensive today and the region has been in slow decline for the last 30 years. Still, the few gnarled old vines that remain are a pilgrimage for incurable wine romantics who like to sample these strangely wild, tannic reds within sight and smell of the great briny ocean.

Inland, shielded from the damp, misty Tagus estuary by a low range of hills, the Bucelas region produces dry white wines from two grape varieties, the Arinto and the aptly named Esgana Cão meaning 'dog strangler'. Both grapes, especially the latter, retain plenty of natural acidity in a relatively warm climate producing crisp, dry white wines that became popular in Britain in the nineteenth century under the title 'Portuguese Hock'. Mention the name to a Brussels legislator today and it would send him into apoplexy. Carcavelos, a rich, raisiny, fortified wine with a nutty, port-like length, enjoyed a moment of glory in the eighteenth century, but it's hard to find any vineyards today. With the relentless expansion of Lisbon along the Tagus estuary, most of the Carcavelos vineyards have disappeared under roads and blocks of apartments. Just one property, Quinta dos Pesos, remains.

RIBATEJO

Journeying inland, the broad Tagus Valley, known as the Ribatejo, serves the capital as a kitchen garden. Ripe, fat tomatoes, curly beans, maize and grapes compete for space on the fertile alluvial flood plain which is regularly irrigated by the swollen river. Like neighbouring Estremadura, it has been subdivided into a number of small wine regions: Tomar, Santarém, Chamusca, Cartaxo, Almeirim and Coruche. Wines range from rough, astringent reds and basic dry whites which find a ready market in Lisbon's noisy bars and cafés to smooth, distinguished *garrafeiras*, the cream of the crop put to one side for at least three years before being released for sale.

Carvalho, Ribeiro & Ferreira and Caves Velhas are among the *garrafeira* specialists, although until recently few bottles displayed the region's name as well as the producer's. Quinta do Casal Branco makes some spicy whites from the local Fernão Pires grape and satisfying reds, both bottled under the name of Falcoaria. Giant co-operatives at Almeirim and Benfica do Ribatejo are producing some good, sappy young reds.

SETÚBAL PENINSULA

An elegant, red-painted suspension bridge spans the Tagus linking the north bank of the river to the densely populated Setúbal Peninsula on the opposite side. After a while Lisbon's tall suburbs finally subside and you find yourself travelling through a forest of fragrant umbrella pines growing on the warm, sandy plain. Around Setúbal to the south, the rugged Arrábida hills rise out of the plain and then shelve steeply to the Atlantic. The region around Setúbal, now officially delimited as Terras do Sado after the river immediately to the south, is now home to some of Portugal's most enterprising winemakers. A touch of New World flair has crept into companies like José Maria da Fonseca Successores, with its California-trained winemaker, and J P Vinhos (formerly known as João Pires) where wines are made by a globe-trotting Australian called Peter Bright. The wines, made from a wide variety of Portuguese and foreign grape varieties, are bottled either as

The broad, fertile Tagus Valley, here at Azambujeira, is Portugal's agricultural heartland where grapes grow prolifically.

Terras do Sado or under the name of one of the smaller IPR regions, Palmela or Arrábida.

The large fishing port of Setúbal at the mouth of the Sado lends its name to an unctuous, raisiny fortified wine made mainly from Muscat grapes grown on the limestone hills behind the city. In recent years this traditional sweet Muscat has been upstaged by other wines from the region, including the light, dry, João Pires Muscat, first made in 1981 from a surplus of Moscatel grapes, and Quinta de Bacalhôa, a ripe, minty red made from a Bordeaux blend of Cabernet Sauvignon and Merlot. Chardonnay also seems to be well suited to the north-facing limestone soils of the Arrábida hills and the warm maritime climate. But foreign grape varieties still have some way to go before they oust native grapes like Castelão Frances (nicknamed 'Periquita') which thrives on the broad, sandy plain around the walled town of Palmela. José Maria da Fonseca's raspberryish red Periquita is one of Portugal's best known red wines and they also produce some excellent *garrafeiras* labelled with curious code names like 'CO' and 'TD'.

ALENTEJO

After a brief stop at Fonseca Successores' old winery in the main street at Azeitão, it's time to head east. After a few miles batting along a long straight road – what a change after the winding roads of northern Portugal – the landscape begins to change and a giant, undulating plain unfolds before our eyes. This is the Alentejo. Golden wheat fields extend for almost as far as the eye can see, flecked by deep evergreen cork oak and olive trees that provide shade for small nomadic herds of sheep, goats and black pigs. Green in spring, the landscape turns an ever deeper shade of ochre with summer temperatures that frequently soar over 40°C (104°F) and rainfall that barely reaches 600mm (24in) a year. The open vista is broken only by the occasional dazzling whitewashed town or village with the jagged outline of a ruined castle on the crest of a low hill.

At first sight vineyards don't seem all that prominent but as we approach a town rows of vines stretch out before us. Until fairly recently cork was the Alentejo's main connection with wine and cork oaks, stripped of their bark, are a common sight. Now there are eight small wine regions: Portalegre, Borba, Redondo, Évora, Reguengos Granja-Amareleja, Vidigueira and Moura, but more commonly the words 'Vinho Regional – Alentejo' are found on wine labels.

The Portuguese used to deride the Alentejo as 'the land of bad bread and bad wine'. Conventional wisdom dictated that the climate was against it. It seemed that healthy, fault-free wine was an impossibility when the summer temperatures were high enough for the indolent locals to retreat indoors out of the relentless sun. This wasn't helped in 1974 when the south was the most determined and aggressive part of the country in overthrowing the dictatorship. Having been a land primarily of absentee landlords – unlike the Douro where relationships between landowner and worker were close and the 1974 revolution was a positively gentlemanly affair – the peasants and workers took pleasure in occupying the large estates. Unfortunately they weren't interested in making them work, even on a co-operative basis. But now with a bit of gleaming stainless steel technology the Alentejo has begun to prove that it can produce good wines, especially reds from evenly ripened native grapes. Among the red grapes, Periquita, Trincadeira and Aragonez perform well and both the white Arinto and scented Roupeiro manage to hang on to good, crisp natural acidity in spite of the heat. The best Alentejo vineyards are over to the east not far from the Spanish border – Cartuxa near Évora, Quinta do Carmo at Estremoz and Esporão near Reguengos are just three Alentejo properties which deserve to be singled out for their wines. Co-operatives at Borba, Redondo, Reguengos and Granja make wine on a larger scale but are turning out some sound, full-flavoured reds.

ALGARVE

The title 'land of bad wine' should probably have passed to the Algarve where four large wine-making co-operatives bottle headaches for the thousands of tourists that flock to the region each year. Lagoa, the best of the bunch, makes an intriguing dry aperitif wine aged like *fino* sherry under a veil of flor.

MADEIRA

RED GRAPES
Tinta Negra Mole is Madeira's most widely planted variety.

WHITE GRAPES
Of the four quality varieties, Verdelho and Malvasia are the most common. Bual and Sercial are much rarer.

CLIMATE
The warm, damp subtropical climate means that oidium and botrytis can be a problem. Rainfall varies from 3000mm (118in) inland to about one-third on the coast.

SOIL
The soil is volcanic. The pebbles of basalt have often weathered red.

ASPECT
The vineyards are planted on terraces up to 1000m (3280ft) in the south of the island and lower down in the north.

IT'S DIFFICULT TO GET a really good look at Madeira. The early Portuguese navigators who observed a bank of dense black cloud billowing over the Atlantic thought that they had reached the end of the world and steered well clear. Approaching the island's precarious airport today with a view of dark, cloud-covered mountains on one side and the ocean on the other, you could be forgiven for thinking the same.

There are two ways to appreciate Madeira when you have safely reached land. First of all, clamber down to the rocky shore that passes for a beach, turn your back to the sea and stare inland. Behind the subtropical shoreline with its profusion of decorative palms and exotic flowers, tiny shelf-like terraces stack up the mountainsides until they seem to be subsumed in the clouds. Then drive up one of the tortuous roads leading from the coast to Pico de Arieiro which, at 1818m (5965ft) above sea level, is nearly the highest point on the island. On the way you will pass through a belt of dank, dispiriting mist only to emerge once again in bright sunlight before you reach the summit. From here you can see volcanic peaks poking through the cloud but on a rare clear day you might just catch a glimpse of the ocean.

On the face of it Madeira is an unlikely place to make wine. But then this humid, subtropical island 700km (435 miles) from the coast of North Africa flies in the face of wine-making lore. With long, warm winters and torrid summers and a mean annual temperature in Funchal of 19°C (66°F), the island doesn't really belong to the temperate latitudes that are supposed to produce the world's finest, most delicate, individual wines. But Madeira wine certainly has individuality and there's no lack of delicacy or finesse in a glass of venerable Malmsey.

Like so many of the best inventions, Madeira wine came about almost by accident. Soon after the island was discovered beneath its almost perpetual shroud of cloud, it became an important supply point for ships *en route* to Africa and the east. Wine was one of many products to be taken on board and a generous drop of brandy, probably distilled from the island's sugar cane, was added to prevent the wine from spoiling on its long sea voyage. The pitching and rolling across the tropics seemed to suit Madeira and it was found that the wine often tasted better when it reached its destination than at the start of the journey. The taste caught on and a fashion developed for *vinho da roda*, wine that had crossed the equator and back.

As Britain and the United States emerged as important customers for Madeira in the nineteenth century, merchants looked for ways to simulate the long but costly tropical sea voyages that had proved to be so beneficial to the wine. They constructed *estufas*, store rooms with huge vats heated by fires to produce the maderized aromas and flavours that the world had become accustomed to.

But Madeira's isolated island economy has suffered from a catastrophic cycle of boom and bust. The boom began in the eighteenth century when demand for Madeira began to outstrip supply. It lasted until the 1850s when oidium (powdery mildew) reached the island and spread rapidly through the vineyards encouraged by the warm, humid climate. Sulphur dusting of vine leaves was eventually found to be satisfactory prevention, but not before the island's monocrop economy had been devastated. Worse was to come when, 20 years later, the root-munching phylloxera struck, destroying whole vineyards in its wake.

Shippers left the island, and the wine trade, which suffered setbacks with the Russian Revolution and Prohibition in the USA, never really recovered. Bananas replaced vines as the island's most important crop and the vineyards that remained were planted with disease-resistant hybrids which produced large amounts of dreary wine. In 1913 a number of shippers merged to form the Madeira Wine Association, the precursor of the Madeira Wine Company which produces the lion's share of Madeira today, as well as controlling half the exports. Few of the shippers own any vineyards. They buy their grapes from a myriad of tiny smallholdings perched on little terraces, called *poios*, carved out of the mountainsides; with approximately 4000 growers owning only 1800 hectares (4450 acres) of vines, the average vineyard holding is only half a hectare (1 acre) and the largest single vineyard on the island is less than 4 hectares (10 acres).

Along with vines most of the farmers also grow other crops, including bananas, avocados, lemons and, especially in the east of the island, willow for baskets and other items to sell to the tourists. The warm, damp climate means that the vines have to be trained off the ground in order to lessen the risk of fungal diseases and this makes backbreaking work in the vineyards as the labourers duck in between the lattice of straggly interconnected vines to apply treatments or harvest the grapes. Agriculture is really only possible on Madeira because of the high annual rainfall on the inland mountains, more than three times the amount that falls in Funchal down on the coast. This water is diverted into a complex network of over 2000km (1200 miles) of man-made channels called *levadas* which ensure an even distribution of water to every tiny property as well as being used to generate the island's electricity.

Most of Madeira is destined for the French market and for cooking rather than for drinking. It is made from the versatile but dull red local *vinifera* grape, Tinta Negra Mole. These pale, pink-red wines are fortified with grape brandy and heated in an *estufa* to between 40 and 50°C (104 and 122°F) for a minimum of 90 days. The cheaper wines that tend to be made in this somewhat heavy-handed manner often smell and taste coarse and stewed and are a poor imitation of the real thing.

The finest Madeiras are made without any *estufagem* or artificial heating at all, which is still a controversial practice even after two centuries of continuous use. These wines are usually produced from one of four top-quality or 'noble' grapes, Sercial, Verdelho, Bual and Malvasia, and they age slowly on *canteiros* or racks under the eaves in lodges in the island's capital, Funchal. Warmed naturally by the sun in this subtropical climate, they gradually develop a unique pungency and intensity of flavour. Having been subject to this long, slow, controlled maturation, fine Madeira stands the test of time like no other wine.

Traditionally, different styles of Madeira have been distinguished from each other by the grapes from which the wines were made, and the styles range from dry to sweet. Of the four traditional 'noble' grape varieties, Verdelho and Malvasia are the most planted, and there are smaller amounts of Sercial and Bual. Sercial likes the coolest vineyards and grows on the north side of the island and at the highest altitudes in the south. With a lower accumulation of sugar it makes the driest wine with a distinctly nervy acidic tang. Verdelho is also planted on the cooler, north coast but in slightly warmer locations and it ripens more easily than Sercial, producing a wine that is softer and medium-dry. Bual is found growing on the warmer, steamy south side of the island where it produces richer, medium-sweet wines. Finally, Malvasia (better known in English as Malmsey) grows in the warmest, low-altitude locations on the south coast, like the spectacular vineyards at the foot of the island's highest cliff, Cabo Girao. The darkest and sweetest Madeira, a good Malmsey will be raisiny and unctuous, still retaining a characteristic tang of acidity which prevents the wine from cloying.

The productive American hybrid grapes which crept into the vineyards, following the destruction of the island's best vineyards by phylloxera, can no longer be used for bottled wine and most Madeira now comes from Tinta Negra Mole. Recently Madeira producers have been obliged to comply with EU legislation which states that a varietal wine must be made from at least 85 per cent of the variety named on the label. A replanting programme is currently underway in the Madeira vineyards to increase production of the four 'noble' varieties which are in short supply, but for the moment most Madeira blends are labelled with the terms *seco* (dry), *meio seco* (medium-dry), *meio doce* medium-sweet) and *doce* (sweet or rich).

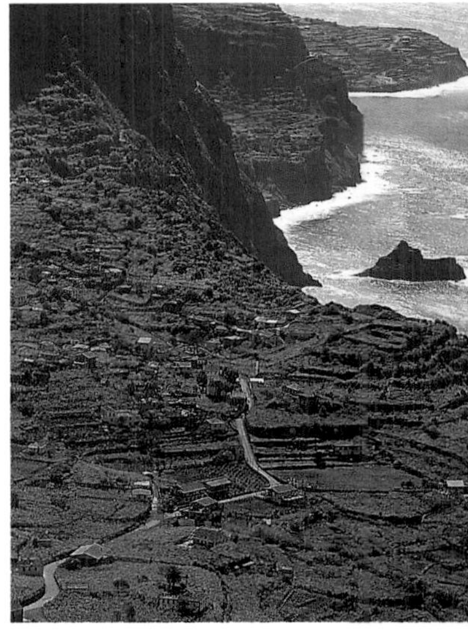

Vineyards on Madeira, here at Santana, are perched on tiny terraces or poios, *hacked out of the mountainsides.*

WHERE THE VINEYARDS ARE *Agriculture on this small, densely populated island is confined to the narrow coastal fringe where banana plants compete with vines and other crops for precious space in the tiny terraced fields. Vineyards tend to be concentrated around the capital Funchal on the warmer south side of the island where the best Malvasia and Bual vineyards are situated. Over recent years bananas have ousted vines from some of the best land above the picturesque fishing village of Câmara de Lobos. There are plots of Sercial at Jardim da Serra ('mountain garden') lying at around 900m (3000ft) above the south coast, but grapes for the drier styles of wine come mainly from the cooler vineyards clinging to the near-vertical slopes on the north side of the island. Here, the spectacular vineyards have to be protected by high bamboo and broom wind-breaks from the fierce northerly winds.*

England

English wine production is no longer the domain of retired servicemen, hobbyists and eccentrics. Those who survive must contend with apathy from the home market, a government which has seemed determined to eliminate them and the reliably unreliable weather. Many of the vineyards which set up in the 1960s and 1970s are either no longer in operation or concentrate on grape-growing, leaving the wine-making to those more adept at it. The emergence in the 1990s of outfits such as the Harvest Wine Group, in which an Australian winemaker, John Worontschak, oversees production for around a dozen vineyards, gave the industry a much-needed jolt, and showed that it was possible for English wine to be commercially viable, rather than a loss-making sideline to other activities.

While vineyards do appear as far north as Rotherham, the bulk lie south of a line drawn from the Wash to the Bristol Channel, with most of these being in Kent and Sussex. The vineyards lie at the northern extreme of wine production. This is possible only due to the tempering influence of the Gulf Stream. The maritime climate ensures the absence of heavy winter frosts, but spring frosts just as the buds begin to open pose more of a threat. Rainfall is high, particularly in the south-west, and the humidity can cause rot and mildew.

In the vineyards, the various subsoils include limestone, gravel, chalk (south Kent), clay (Essex, north Kent) and Kimmeridgian clay (Dorset). However, more important is a climate which permits the ripening of grapes. The best sites are on sheltered slopes with southern aspects at heights of less than 100m (330ft). Certain local climates permit the growing season to extend well into November.

The variety of grapes grown is limited to ones that will ripen in such a marginal climate, and these tend to be mostly German crosses specially developed for such conditions. Most controversial is Seyval Blanc, a disease-resistant hybrid variety which can produce some of England's best wines, both still and sparkling. European legislation seeks to ban all hybrid grapes from any quality wine scheme, and producers are still waiting to hear how they will be affected by such action. Müller-Thurgau is the most widespread variety, accounting for roughly a sixth of total plantings. This is followed by the early cropping but rather neutral Reichensteiner, the aromatic, almost Muscat-like Bacchus, the hardy Schönburger, almost like a light Gewürztraminer, and the reliable but boring Madeleine Angevine. Chardonnay is seldom made into a table wine, but is useful for sparklers.

WHITE WINES

The flavour of the wines varies more between wineries than between regions, and depends on factors such as the use of oak, how high the acidity was at harvest and how ripe the grapes were. They should be delicate and aromatic, with flavours of apples, grapefruit, elderflower, grapes and smoky hints, with the best having enough ripeness and depth to balance the crisp acidity. Sparkling wines, too, are improving rapidly, with Seyval Blanc, Chardonnay and Pinot Noir being particularly widely used. Both still and sparkling wines benefit from aging for at least a couple of years from vintage.

In the past extra sweetness was sometimes used to conceal poor wine-making, but that is changing. Clean, grapy fruit has replaced the clumsiness in the better wines, while those patient enough to make botrytized wines have already produced impressive, if slightly light, results.

RED WINES

Ripening red grapes can be a problem. Pinot Noir produces a few rather weedy reds and rosés (with notable exceptions such as Chiddingstone and Thames Valley Vineyard), as well as more successful sparkling wine. A sole outpost of Cabernet Sauvignon and Merlot exists at Beenleigh Manor in Devon, where the vines are grown in greenhouse conditions under plastic sheeting. Thames Valley Vineyard produces a very decent Gamay – but it's white and sparkling.

A Quality Wine Scheme was hastily brought into operation in 1992 in an attempt to circumvent certain European Union wine regulations, and the result is something which has brought plenty of headaches and seemingly no benefits to many English winemakers. There is some confusion over the rules of the scheme and its relation to threshold production limits, and some producers have opted out completely. So as with virtually every wine region, the best guarantee of quality is the name of the producer on the bottle.

MAIN VINEYARDS

●

1. Astley
2. Bodenham
3. Three Choirs
4. Wootton
5. Pilton Manor
6. Moorlynch
7. Oatley
8. Sharpham
9. Beenleigh Manor
10. Horton Estate
11. Adgestone
12. Hambledon Wines
13. Wickham
14. Meon Valley
15. Cane End
16. Chiltern Valley
17. Thames Valley
18. Denbies
19. Nutbourne Manor
20. Rock Lodge
21. Chapel Down
22. Barkham Manor
23. Breaky Bottom
24. Hidden Spring
25. Sedlescombe
26. Leeford
27. Carr Taylor
28. Tenterden
29. Biddenden
30. Lamberhurst
31. Penshurst
32. Headcorn
33. High Weald Winery
34. Staple Vineyard
35. New Hall
36. East Mersea
37. Shawgate
38. Bruisyard
39. Pulham
40. Elmham Park

Czech & Slovak Republics

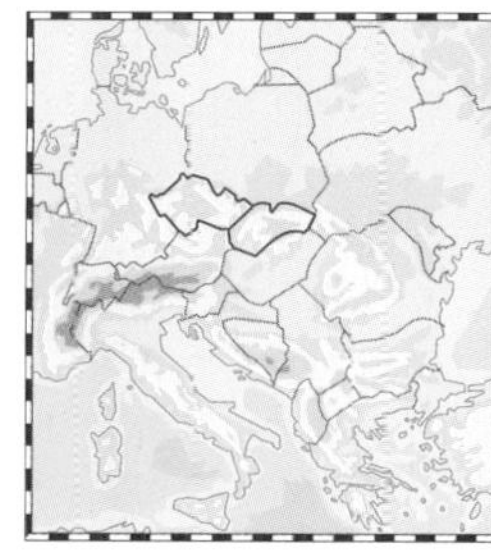

IN THE OLD DAYS of the one nation of Czechoslovakia, there was reckoned to be a pretty natural divide: Slovakia made the wine, the Czechs brewed the beer. As I write this, I'm very contentedly swigging a bottle of the great Czech Budvar beer rather than wine from either side. Yet this divide is simplistic. There's no doubt that Slovakia generally does have the better conditions for viticulture; indeed in the far east, she even has some of the original Hungarian Tokay villages within her borders. But the Czech vineyards of Moravia aren't that far off Slovakian quality. However, if I had to choose the wines from either country that have given me most pleasure so far, they would be the violet-scented, damson-juicy St-Laurent, the 'boudoir and en suite bathroom'-scented Irsay Oliver, and the crackly, peppery, celery stick Grüner Veltliner – all from Slovakia.

And, despite the irresistible gluggability of that St-Laurent – and the occasional rather green, twiggy Frankovka – both countries are basically suited to white, not red, production. But the potential for quality as the wine industry eases itself into the modern world is immense. The latitude is virtually the same as that of Alsace, and many of the best wines have the same spicy fatness. Unlike the wine industries of other countries, with their huge concerns, Czech and Slovak companies are run on a human scale, and flying winemakers report on the reasonable quality of wine-making equipment in several cellars.

Following the revolution in Czechoslovakia in 1989, and the subsequent peaceful division of the country into the Czech and Slovak Republics that existed prior to 1918, Slovakia found itself with two-thirds of the former country's 47,000 hectares (116,000 acres) of vineyards. If you talk to the café drinkers of Prague, they'll swear to you that the best *quality* wines come from the Moravia regions of Znojmo-Mikulov, Hustopeče-Hodonin and Bzenec-Strážnice on the Czech side of the border. Well, Prague cafés are very seductive places in which to drink: I'll stick with Slovakia for now, especially as the flying winemakers there are making a fair go of improving basic standards without sacrificing national individuality.

Both countries enjoy a climate in the settled continental style: warm and dry in the growing season, with cool, dry autumns and little variation between regions. Slovakia is slightly warmer than the Czech Republic, but otherwise the weather conditions are much the same.

Most of Bohemia's vineyards are clustered round the Labe (Elbe) and its tributaries. The wines are seldom seen outside the region and resemble their Sachsen counterparts across the border in the former East Germany, being dry with marked acidity. The predominant grapes are Müller-Thurgau, Rhine Riesling, Pinot Blanc and Gewürztraminer – but you begin to see why most people drink the beer.

In Moravia, vines grow in the valleys of the Svratka, Morava and Dyje rivers which flow into the Danube. The less famous varieties include Palava – a white somewhere between Riesling and Gewürztraminer in style – and the juicy, spicy, plummy, red St-Laurent. The wines from Archioni near Znojmo have a good reputation, and can age well.

Slovakia's vineyards are located mainly around the Váh, Hron and Nitra tributaries of the Danube. The vines are planted either on the foothills of the Tatra mountains or on undulating land around Bratislava, although there are several smaller vine-growing regions as you travel east along the border with Hungary, each producing perfumed whites such as Irsay Oliver, Veltliner and Riesling, and light red wines. The state winery at Nitra is Slovakia's most important producer, but better quality can be found in the smaller wineries to the south and west, such as Gbelce and Hurbanovo near the Hungarian border at Komárno. The grape varieties are virtually the same as the Czech ones, with the addition of some tasty Grüner Veltliners, the supple, fruity Frankovka red and the local Ezerjó and Leányka. At Slovakia's eastern extreme, in Tokájská, the Furmint, Muscat Ottonel and Hárslevelü varieties are said to produce wines with similar characteristics to the more famous wines of neighbouring Hungary.

It is certain that we shall see increasingly more impressive wines coming from the Czech and Slovak Republics in the future. The disappearance of the Soviet market in the late 1980s has meant that the wineries need more than ever to export to the West. However, governmental organization does not seem to have progressed as quickly in Slovakia as in the Czech Republic, and foreign companies (and indeed domestic wine producers) are waiting for the dust to settle before they invest large amounts of money.

Château Melnik on the steep banks of the River Labe (Elbe), in Bohemia.

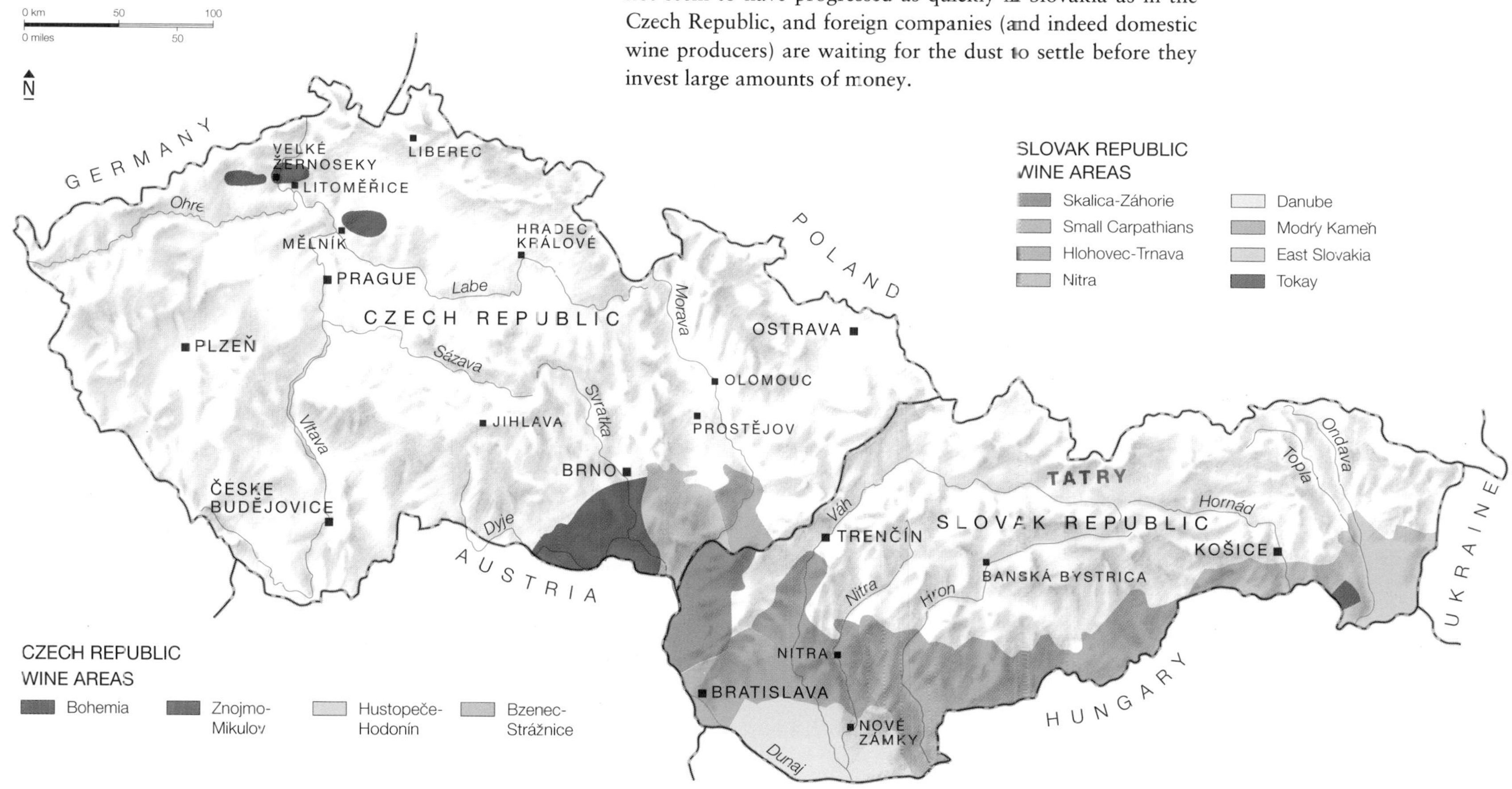

HUNGARY

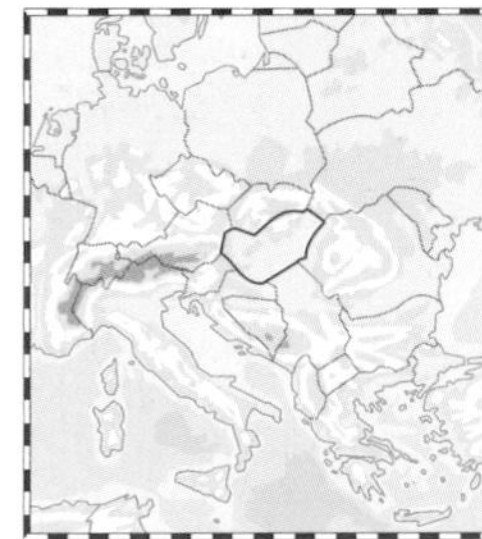

I THINK I'VE ONLY DONE IT ONCE. Given a perfect score to a wine: 20 out of 20. A 1957 from Tokajhegyalja. Somehow this bottle had escaped the process of homogenization that the Hungarian wine industry suffered after the Soviet invasion of 1956. Of all Eastern Europe's nations, Hungary's traditions were the proudest and most individual, and they died slowly under the Soviet system of state-run farms and wineries.

In the 1960s, fine reds were still being released under the Bull's Blood or Egri Bikavér label. Indeed it was international distributors clamouring for the rights to such a marketable name that encouraged the authorities to debase what was a splendid wine. At the end of the 1960s you could still find marvellous yet fiery whites, golden in colour, almost viscous lanolin in texture, with sparks of spicy perfume darting in and out of their dry but mellow fruit flavours like fireflies on your tongue. Hárslevelű from Debrő, and Szürkebarát and Kéknyelű from Badacsony – no shrinking violets with names like these – fell into a sleep a generation long through the 1970s and 1980s, before the 1990s saw a reawakening of Hungary's pride and energy.

The rebirth of Hungary as a great wine producer is taking place at breakneck speed. The initial wine export boom in the 1990s was led by the international grape varieties – in particular Chardonnay, Sauvignon, Cabernet and Merlot – and the country has welcomed the flying winemakers more enthusiastically than any other Eastern European nation. There is now a rapidly expanding band of young Hungarians determined to put their New World principles into practice, as well as to rediscover Hungary's great past, and they are set to produce gorgeous wines during the next generation. Tokajhegyalja has already attracted multinational wealth and expertise. The rest of the country, well-stocked with the necessary international grape varieties as well as a clutch of marvellous indigenous ones, is ideally placed for the twenty-first century.

The climate is similar to much of inland Europe, warm and dry, with the only variation being due to altitude. However, the vineyards around Lake Balaton enjoy the tempering effect of Central Europe's largest inland lake. Badacsony and Balatonfüred-Csopak on its north shore produce some of Hungary's best whites. They benefit from well-draining soil, a mix of sand and volcanic rock, and are also said to gain extra heat from the reflection of the sun off the lake. Badacsony can produce good to excellent Furmint, Olaszrizling, Szürkebarát (Pinot Gris) and Traminer, as well as its own grape variety, the spicy but increasingly rare Kéknyelű. East of Badacsony, Balatonfüred was a vineyard and major spa town in Roman times. The vineyards are on the south-facing lower slopes of the Bakony hills, and are 75 per cent planted with Olaszrizling, more's the pity.

DÉL-BALATON

Dél-Balaton on the southern shore of the lake is one of the country's newest regions. Labelled as Balaton or Balatonboglár, the wines are mainly whites produced from familiar varieties such as Chardonnay, Sauvignon Blanc, Rhine Riesling and Traminer as well as less well-known Irsai Olivér and Királyleányka. You may find a Chasselas-based sparkling wine, as well as the occasional red made from Pinot Noir.

EGER

The south-facing vineyards of Eger are famous for Egri Bikavér (Bull's Blood of Eger), a one-time hearty blend of Kékfrankos, Cabernet Sauvignon, Blue Oporto, Merlot and Kadarka. While vinous anaemia may have diluted much of the current output, especially when Kadarka has been replaced, good examples can still be found, particularly that of Thummerer. There are interesting white wines made from Leányka and Hárslevelű (meaning Linden Leaf), but the increasing presence of Chardonnay and Olaszrizling means that these are hard to find. Nagyréde has a reputation for reds and rosés made from Kadarka, although the whites being produced under the guidance of Kym Milne do seem more promising. The ubiquitous Hugh Ryman has been experimenting with fruit from the region, but the first wines are still to be released.

VILLÁNY-SIKLÓS

Better for reds is Villány-Siklós in the south, with its loam and limestone soil. The eastern (Villány) end of the region produces lovely, juicy, soft red wines make from Kékfrankos, Cabernet Sauvignon, Blue Oporto and Merlot, while Siklós is better for whites such as Chardonnay, Olaszrizling, Traminer and Hárslevelű. The Mecsekalja region around the city of Pécs has good Olaszrizling, while Szekszárd has its own Bikavér as well as Ovörös – old red wine – made mainly from Kékfrankos, a wine much enjoyed in Hungary but rarely seen abroad.

Vineyards on the slopes of Mount Badacsony, on the north shore of Lake Balaton.

MÓR

Speciality of the region of Mór is the Ezerjó grape (Ezerjó means 'a thousand good things'), whose wines have been described perhaps rather damningly by Jancis Robinson as 'Hungary's nearest answer to the fragile charms of Muscadet'. The majority of the country's output – easy-drinking styles made from Kadarka and Olaszrizling grapes – comes from the Great Plains between the Danube and Tisza rivers, where the sandy soil is suitable for nothing but viticulture.

TOKAY WINE

Wine from the region of Tokajhegyalja (Tokay in English) truly is the stuff of legend. A Commission for Hungarian wines was set up in St Petersburg to ensure regular supplies of it for the Tsars, and bottles of the precious nectar were kept by the bedside to revive ailing monarchs. The Communist regimes of this century succeeded in removing most traces of greatness from the region by blending the top wines with the mediocre, achieving something which, while drinkable, was hardly remarkable. However, there are hopeful signs that new ownership will restore most of the former glory.

Tokay has been produced since the middle of the seventeenth century. A hundred and fifty years before the classification of the Médoc, the Rákóczi family, one-time princes of Transylvania, did the first appraisal of the Tokaji vineyards in 1700. A subsequent classification in 1804 defined three Great Growths, followed by First, Second, Third and Unclassified Growths. The three Great Growths were all on the slopes of Mount Kopaszhegy, Bald Mountain. Of these, only Mézesmály in Tarcal remains, Tokay having been amalgamated with various other First Growth areas.

Most of the vines have been planted on south-east- to south-west-facing slopes, but what makes the great vineyards great is their soil. Tarcal, parts of Tokajhegyalja and neighbouring Mád are fast draining loess. The bulk of the other soils is stony clays. The vines on the loess ripen faster and give the richest, most aromatic wines. Those on clays tend to produce wines of higher acidity and possibly longer life.

The region is sheltered by the Carpathian mountains to the north, while warm winds off the Great Plains maintain a reasonably high temperature. Mists rising from the Bodrog river in autumn encourage the onset of noble rot in the Furmint grapes which make up around two-thirds of a typical Tokay with the balance being the sugar-rich Hárslevelű and Muskotály (Muscat Ottonel).

The botrytized grapes, known as *aszú*, spend about a week in a bucket, during which time, an unctuous juice known as Eszencia seeps out. This precious fluid is so rich in sugar that even with special strains of yeasts, it can take years to ferment. Tom Stevenson and Michael Broadbent both report tasting an Eszencia which had been fermenting for 13 years yet had achieved less than two per cent alcohol. Pure Eszencia is seldom sold, being used to bolster lesser wines. However, bottles do appear occasionally, and the current vintage – 1947 – is available for around US$750 per half litre.

After the removal of the Eszencia, the remaining grapes are mashed to a syrupy paste, and are then added to dry base wine. The quality of the wine is determined by the number of *puttonyos* (30-litre tubs) of paste added to each *gönc* (136-litre barrel) of dry wine. Two-*puttonyos* wine is never made; three, four and five are reasonably easy to find; six is only made in good years. The *aszú* Eszencia available today is about an eight-*puttonyos* wine, while *Szamorodni* (literally 'as it comes') is a wine to which no *aszú* has been added, and can come as either a sweet (*édes*) or dry (*száraz*) wine. While not as complex as Tokaji *aszú*, it is nonetheless a fine wine which can age for almost as long.

After the grapes have steeped in the grape paste for around a week, the wine is then racked off to begin its long, slow fermentation in barrel. The casks are not topped up, encouraging a degree of oxidation, although new, non-oxidized styles have been written into the regulations. In addition, a flor-like fungus attacks the wine, giving it further complexity. The resulting flavours – a perfumed, maderized cocktail of honey, burnt toffee and ripe, raisiny fruit – do take some getting used to, but they are certainly unique in the world of wine.

Of all Eastern Europe's wine regions, Tokajhegyalja is the one currently receiving the bulk of investment from outside companies. The Borkombinat (State Wine Farm) began a process of privatization in 1991, and some of the world's top wine names have taken major stakes in the region.

New stainless steel tanks on an old estate are a visible sign of recent financial investment in Tokajhegyalja.

Three-puttonyos Tokaji aszú, labelled the 'King of Wines and Wine of Kings'.

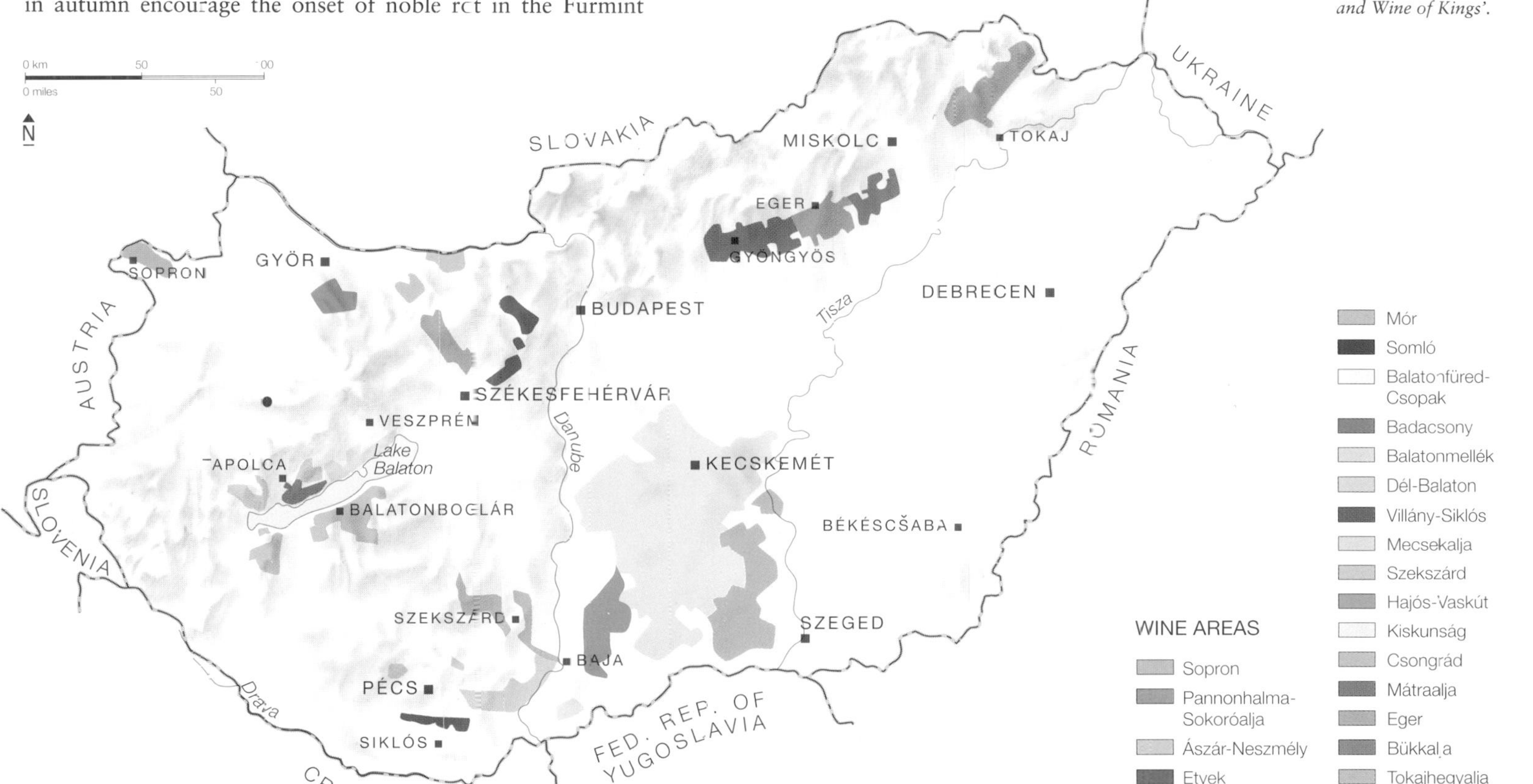

Black Sea States

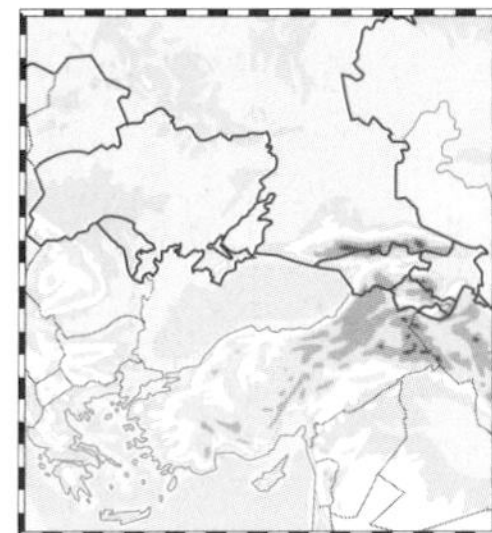

The wine-making picture following the collapse of the Soviet Union is now clearer, but it has emerged as one in need of major restoration. The industrial scale of much of the wine industry, allied with a lack of modern equipment and hard cash for investment, does little to promote the production of quality wines which are desperately needed to break into new markets. The disappearance of centralized bodies may have given winemakers freedom from bureaucracy, but a new set of problems has emerged. A cry in Moldova in 1994, for instance, was 'who used to supply our corks?'

MOLDOVA

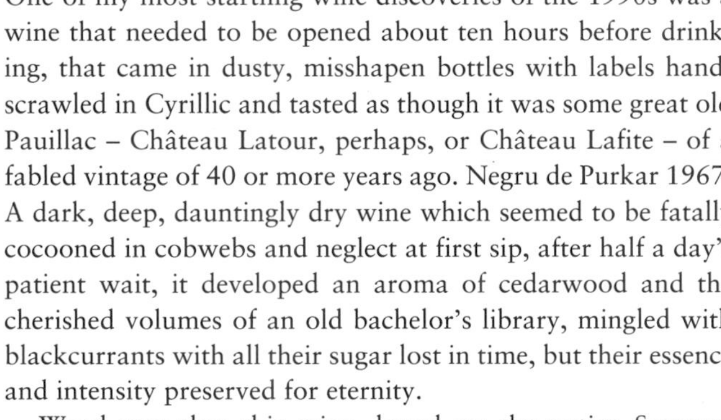

One of my most startling wine discoveries of the 1990s was a wine that needed to be opened about ten hours before drinking, that came in dusty, misshapen bottles with labels hand-scrawled in Cyrillic and tasted as though it was some great old Pauillac – Château Latour, perhaps, or Château Lafite – of a fabled vintage of 40 or more years ago. Negru de Purkar 1967. A dark, deep, dauntingly dry wine which seemed to be fatally cocooned in cobwebs and neglect at first sip, after half a day's patient wait, it developed an aroma of cedarwood and the cherished volumes of an old bachelor's library, mingled with blackcurrants with all their sugar lost in time, but their essence and intensity preserved for eternity.

Word was that this wine, based on the native Saperavi grape and mellowed with a bit of Cabernet Sauvignon and Rara Niagra, was the cream of the Moldovan crop, which were shut away for decades in slate cellars to be broached only when the local bosses went feasting. But we didn't have to rely on word of mouth: we all got the chance to see the glorious quality of these wines for ourselves. These bottles of Negru de Purkar – and several others like them – showed that Moldova really did deserve its great nineteenth-century reputation and that, with such evidence as this, the glories could be recreated.

Moldova is still suffering dreadfully in the wake of its emergence as an independent state. Flying winemakers only look forward to a Moldovan posting with considerable trepidation, and in 1992 I had two trips there cancelled because of the dangers of roving ruffians and warring armies that were ranged along the banks of the Dniester. But as the state recovers, so will the reputation of its wines. Not only will we see lots of easy-drinking 'international' styles, but Negru de Purkar and its fellows will rise again. In wine terms, the small state of Moldova, which provided one-fifth of the wine for the former Soviet Union and where one hectare in seven is planted with vines, is the CIS's most important state; its vineyard area is over twice that of Australia.

At the invitation of Tsar Alexander, French winemakers brought their grapes and expertise to the country in the early nineteenth century. The result is that there is a long history in Moldova of growing popular grapes such as Cabernet Sauvignon, Pinot Noir (here known as Pinot Franc), Merlot, Chardonnay and Sauvignon Blanc. But standards of wine-making and equipment still leave a great deal to be desired. However, the quality of the fruit is excellent, and the wines produced since independence in 1991 under the guidance of (among others) Jacques Lurton, Alain Thiénot and Hugh Ryman have been good, and are improving with each vintage. An initial attempt to develop a quality wine scheme resulted in 13 wines being given government-controlled region of origin in 1992. These are being reviewed in 1996.

Although the country has no coastline – Ukraine has snapped that up – the Black Sea still has a tempering effect on the continental climate. Summers are dry and reasonably

WINE AREAS

MOLDOVA | UKRAINE | RUSSIA | GEORGIA | ARMENIA | AZERBAIJAN

warm, although enough rain falls in the rest of the year to prevent the need for irrigation. Well-drained loess and loam soils cover three-quarters of the country, with the southern regions having more clay and more northerly areas having some limestone and marlstone.

The central zone suits varieties like Sauvignon and Chardonnay. The warmer, drier southern and south-eastern zones are better for reds. The most important white grapes are Aligoté, Rkatsiteli, Sauvignon, Feteasca, Chardonnay and Traminer. The leading reds are Merlot, Cabernet Sauvignon, Pinot Franc and Saperavi.

The vineyard area around Bălti in the north of the state is mainly white grape country. In Purcari in the south-east, Cabernet is important. Negru de Purkar, a blend of Cabernet and Saperavi plus an occasional dollop of Rara Niagra, can age remarkably well into something similar to fine old-fashioned Médoc, despite corks the size of a thimble. Romaneşti, from north of Chişinău, is another good red, and takes its name from the former owners of a vineyard here, the Romanovs. Cricova too produces excellent Cabernet, although it is better known for its sparkling wines. Made mainly from Chardonnay and Pinot Franc, these are among the best Champagne-method wines in the CIS, and they mature in vast underground cellars which have a 65km (40 mile) road network complete with road signs and traffic lights.

Some of the most encouraging whites to have appeared have come from an enterprise involving the Australian Penfolds group and the winemaker Hugh Ryman at Vitis Hincesti, 40km (25 miles) to the south-west of Chişinău. The 1993 production was only 15,000 cases, but there are plans to vastly increase this, and quality should improve each year.

UKRAINE

Ukraine's most important region is Crimea. Vineyards are mostly along the southern coast of the peninsula, since inland temperatures can be too cold in winter. The sparkling Krim is a Champagne-method wine of indifferent quality made from Chardonnay, Pinot Noir, Riesling, Aligoté and Cabernet Sauvignon. Ruby of Crimea, a hearty red blend of Saperavi, Matrassa, Aleatica, Cabernet and Malbec, is better. The best wines to have emerged from Crimea, however, are those produced at the Massandra winery near Livadia. When these amazing dessert wines, some of which date back to the nineteenth century, first appeared at auction in London in 1990, they created a sensation. The quality of current releases doesn't look to be up to the splendid level of these museum pieces, but the potential for a return to old glories clearly exists. Elsewhere in Ukraine, there are vineyards around Odessa on the Black Sea coast and Cherson on the Dnipro river. The sparkling wines of Odessa can be quite reasonable.

GEORGIA

Georgian wines come in every colour and degree of sweetness imaginable, although this is not surprising, given the hundreds of grape varieties at the disposal of the country's winemakers. The wines, many of them still destined for the Russian market, leave much to be desired. Currently, the only project with foreign input is Chalice Wines JV, in the town of Sagarejo in the Khaketi region. It is owned 50 per cent by the Georgian firm Sameba and 50 per cent by American investors, including Wente Brothers of Livermore, California and former US Secretary of State George Schultz.

Although the broad Rion Valley in the centre of the country has most of the vineyards, Khaketi, on the southern slopes of the Caucasus mountains in north-eastern Georgia, is the most important quality region. It is slightly drier and warmer here than in the humid west, although streams running down from the mountains ensure that there is no lack of water in the usually loam-based soils. The main city of the region is Telavi, also the name of a Rkatsiteli-based white and a Saperavi red. Two of Georgia's best known whites, Gurdzhaani and Tsnandali, are both Rkatsiteli/Mtsvane blends aged in oak for three years. Other important white varieties are Chinuri (particularly for sparkling wine), Tsitska, Krakhuna and Tsolikauri.

Vineyards in Crimea in the Ukraine, bounded by the Krymskiy Gory mountain range.

A peculiar Georgian tradition is that of the Marani. This is a special building for storing the grape harvest and making wine. It contains a wine press, the bottom of which is covered with a mat woven from Cornelian cherry or *gvimri* plant osiers. From here, the wine is then channelled into *kvevris*, large clay vessels dug into the floor. Fermentation takes place, then the vessels are sealed with stone slabs and covered with earth while the wine matures. A variation of this is for the vessels to be filled with whole bunches of white grapes and then sealed and the wine allowed to ferment. The vessel is reopened three weeks later revealing wines which, according to Eric P Wente, president of the Californian wine firm Wente Brothers, are remarkably stable and amber in colour with high tannin!

RUSSIA

Russia has two main vineyard regions, both in areas where the presence of a mass of water tempers the effect of the icy winters. Around Krasnodar on the Black Sea coast, Riesling, Aligoté, Sauvignon, Sémillon, Pinot Gris and Cabernet Sauvignon are used for still and sparkling wines, with the best coming from vineyards around Anapa. Further north at Rostov, where the Don river runs into the sea of Azov, sparkling wines of varying hues and sweetness levels are made from the Black Tsimlyansky grape. Stavropol north of the Caucasus has a reputation for dry Riesling and Silvaner and sweet Muscat, and there are also vineyards producing reds and dessert wines on the Caspian Sea coast around Makhachkala.

KAZAKHSTAN, AZERBAIJAN AND ARMENIA

Heading north along the same coast, Kazakhstan has a good reputation for dessert wines and for Riesling. Further south, the vineyards of Azerbaijan grow Bayan Shirey, Matrassa, Isabella and several other indigenous varieties. The Sadilly white and Matrassa red from near the city Baku on the Caspian Sea are the not-too-bright stars amid a sky of Azerbaijani dessert wines, port-like only in their alcohol levels. The simiarly alcoholic reds and fortified wines of Armenia are equally uninspiring, although the wines of the Echmiadzin region are reputed to be quite good.

ROMANIA

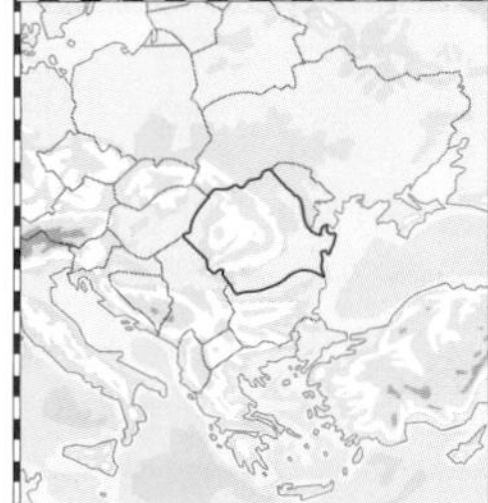

ALTHOUGH SURROUNDED ON MOST FLANKS by people of Slavic origins, the proud brown eyes of the Romanian burn with a definite Latin fire. The capital Bucharest, even after the ravages of Ceauşescu, still has much of the ambience and architecture which earned it the nickname 'Little Paris'. It comes as no surprise then to discover that grapes have been grown in the country for over 6000 years.

The country covers much the same latitudes as France but the climate is very different, being generally continental, with hot summers and cold winters. The Black Sea exerts a tempering influence, while the Carpathian mountains act as a barrier to cooler weather systems from the north. In general, the northern regions of the country, especially Moldavia and Transylvania, favour white wine production, while the best reds come from the south, from Muntenia and Dobrogea.

Major replanting programmes both at the end of the nineteenth century due to phylloxera, and in the 1960s under the Communists, have meant that Romania now produces more wine than any other Balkan state, and has the fifth-largest area under vine in Europe (after Spain, Italy, France and Portugal). The first set of plantings introduced French varieties to the country, notably Cabernet Sauvignon, Merlot and Pinot Noir. The second was mainly of the indigenous varieties. As a result, Romania now has some of the best raw materials in Eastern Europe, in the form of mature, reasonably healthy vines of a wide range of familiar and unfamiliar grape varieties. Such a state of affairs should lead to a major Romanian assault on the world wine market, but as in all the former Eastern bloc countries, the wine industry desperately needs some hard cash to invest. The formation in 1992 of Vinexport, a body owned 10 per cent by the state, 40 per cent by the wineries and 50 per cent by companies in England, Germany, Holland and Denmark to promote and market Romanian wine, augurs well for the future. However, bottles are in short supply, the quality of some of the corks leaves a lot to be desired, and although many of the wineries have some reasonable equipment, cooling facilities and other necessities of modern wine-making are something of a luxury.

Romanian wine drinkers take age as a sign of quality, and tannin as a defect in reds as well as whites. However, where temperature can be regulated and where there is some residual sugar, the whites can be certainly good, if not great. The dessert styles can be excellent, whether botrytis-affected or not. The acidity tends to be high, meaning that wines of 30 years old or more still taste remarkably fresh, although more fruit flavours would be welcome.

The same could be said for much of the red wine, where softness is the desired attribute, and there is frequently a degree of sweetness, although this is disappearing. Warm fermentations promote jammy characteristics in many, and long aging in oak does nothing to promote freshness. However, much of the fruit is of sufficient quality to mask wine-making defects, and there are some delicious examples around. The Pinot Noir is particularly good,

QUALITY WINE REGIONS AND SUB-REGIONS

BANAT
1. Teremia
2. Recaş Tirol
3. Miniş Arad

TRANSYLVANIA
4. Alba Iulia-Aiud
5. Tîrnave
6. Biştrita-Nasaud

MOLDAVIA
7. Cotnari
8. Dealurile Moldovei
9. Odobesti-Panciu-Nicoresti
10. Tecuci Galaţi

DOBROGEA
11. Sarica-Miculiţel
12. Murfatlar

MUNTENIA
13. Dealu Mare

OLTENIA
14. Argeş-Stefaneşti
15. Drăgăşani
16. Segarcea
17. Drobeta-Turnu Severin Corcova

Tămîioasă dessert wine from Pietroasele in the Dealu Mare region of Muntenia.

for example – few other countries manage to extract the essence of this temperamental grape in such an affordable way. As wine-making equipment improves, Romania will become one of Europe's leading sources of Pinot Noir.

NATIVE GRAPE VARIETIES

Of the native grape varieties, Fetească Neagră – similar to Mourvèdre – is the best red, producing deep-coloured, robust red wines which are full and fruity when young, but which can age for decades. Babeaşča Neagră and Crimpiosa produce lighter wines, while Cadarca, Hungary's Kadarka, is used for more basic fare in the west of the country. For whites, the spicy, grapefruity Fetească Albă is of better quality than the Fetească Regală, while the ubiquitous Riesling is always Riesling Italico rather than Rhine Riesling. The best sweet wines usually come from Grasă and Tămîioasă – known as the frankincense grape due to its aroma – while Traminer, Muscat Ottonel and Kékfrankos, here known as Burgund Mare, are used for wines of all degrees of sweetness and quality.

Most successful of the French varieties are Cabernet Sauvignon, Pinot Noir and Merlot for reds, and Chardonnay for whites. An increasing number of plantings which were thought to be other varieties are turning out to be Sauvignon Blanc, with an ensuing increase in price and demand.

ROMANIA'S WINE REGIONS

Dealu Mare, in the foothills of the Carpathian mountains, is one of the most important regions, where the warm climate allows the production of good, and not excessively tannic, red wines. The only white wine of note is from Pietroasele to the east, whose vines thrive in the calcareous, stony soil, and whose grapes are often affected by botrytis.

In Oltenia, Drăgăşani, on the left bank of the Olt, and Argeş, to the north-east, both produce reasonable dry, and even better sweet, wines while on the Olt's opposite bank at Simburesti, the Cabernet Sauvignon is highly thought of.

Moldavia is predominantly white wine country. At Bucium, near Iasi, whites made with Aligoté and Traminer can be especially good. Merlot is the best of the reds, demonstrating a minty, eucalyptus character, and sparkling wines are also produced. Nicoresti is known for its Babeaşča Neagră, and Pinot Noir from Cotesti has a good reputation.

More notable is Cotnari, known as the pearl of Moldavia and Romania's most famous wine. It is a sweet, botrytis-affected white which at one point enjoyed the same prestige as Hungary's Tokay. Cotnari is sheltered from the cold east winds in an amphitheatre of hills. It enjoys warmth and mist, and the harvest continues as far into the year as November. In good years, sugar levels can reach 300g per litre, and the wines, full of raisin, honey and orange peel flavours, can last almost indefinitely.

Transylvania's premium wine area is Tîrnave, surrounding the Tirnava Mare and Tirnava Mica rivers. The high altitude promotes a cool climate, although the rivers act as a tempering influence. White grapes predominate, and Traminer is particularly good at several sweetness levels.

Murfatlar in Dobrogea vies with Dealu Mare for producing Romania's best reds. The 300 days of sunshine a year are tempered by cool winds from the nearby Black Sea, enabling an extended growing season. The long, warm autumns encourage the development of noble rot in the Muscat Ottonel and Támîioăsa, though the best wines are the full, fruity reds.

At present, Romanian wine classifications are in a state of flux. The current system for quality wines follows a German-style format, with the VSO corresponding to QbA level and VSOC to QmP. However, the quality wine system is currently undergoing huge changes and, as yet, no-one knows what to expect from the new classifications.

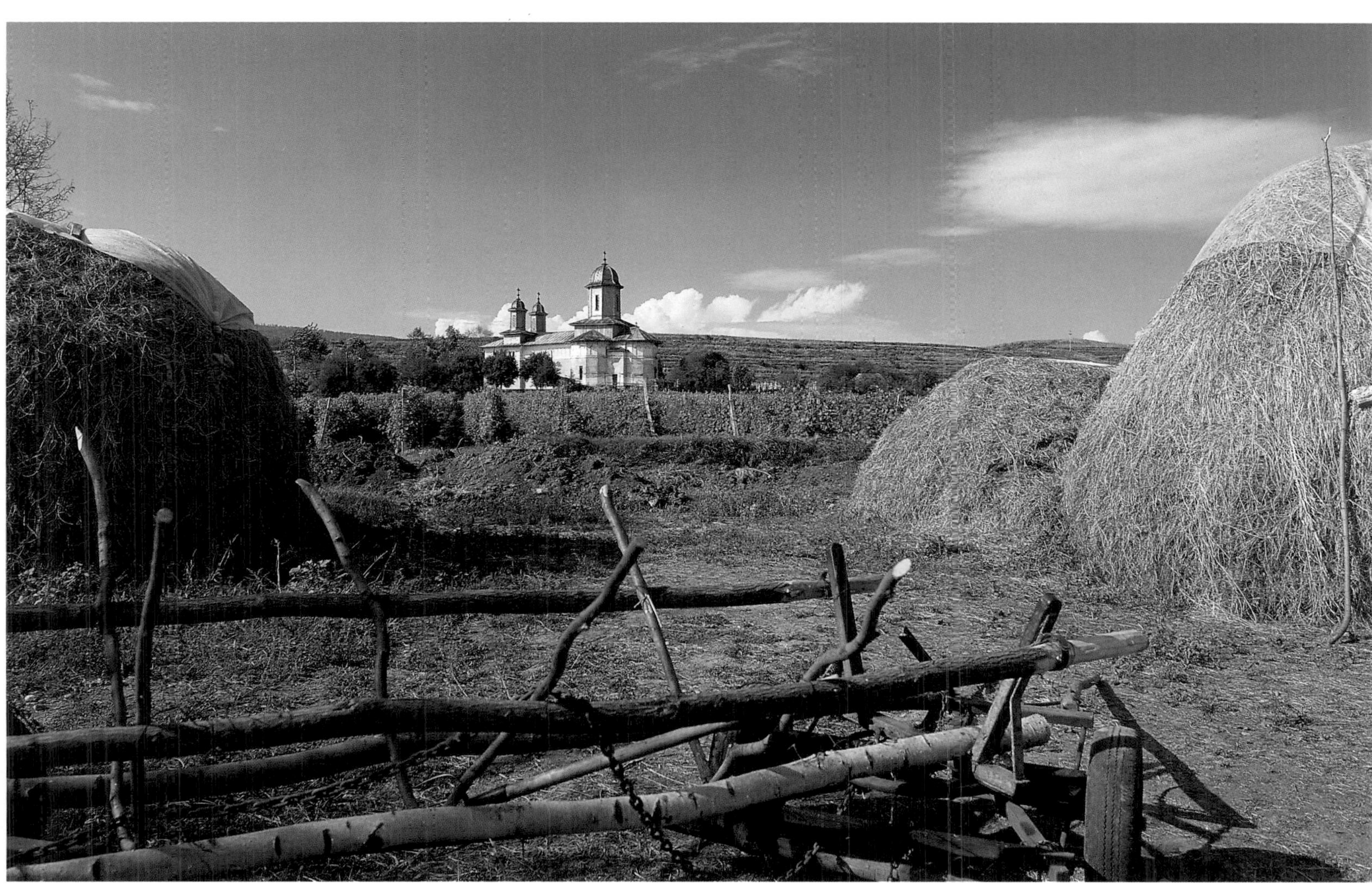

The gently hilly region of Dealu Mare produces some of Romania's best red wines.

Western Balkans

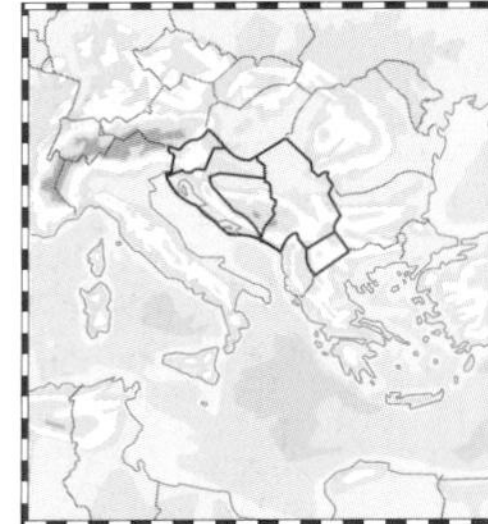

The western Balkan states – torn by civil war in the early 1990s – have emerged sufficiently from the bloodshed and upheaval to rebuild their wine industry and infrastructure. Slovenia is now established as a separate nation, and six of the other seven states are in a relatively stable condition.

The exception – Bosnia-Herzegovina – with its Muslim traditions, has never been a strong wine-producing area, though some may miss its red Blatina and the dry, unusually full-flavoured white Zilavka. However, the other states have much to offer, and the potential for even better quality.

The western Balkans lie roughly across the same latitudes as Italy, with similar viticultural conditions, and yet the two wine industries share remarkably few characteristics. Austria, with its aromatic, sometimes sweet, wines, lies due north of Slovenia and provides more of a comparison.

The vineyards of Croatia split into two distinct areas. Inland Croatia or Kontinentalna Hrvatska runs south-east along the Drava tributary as far as the Danube and is mainly white wine country, growing grapes such as Traminer, Welschriesling (here known as Graşevina), Muscat Ottonel and Pinot Blanc, often on terraced vineyards. The best wines are said to come from the slopes of Baranja, known as 'The Golden Hill' since Roman times, in the Danube Valley north of Osijek.

Along the strip of coastal Croatia – Hrvatsko Primorje – the sun, sea and rocky soil combine to produce good red wines, particularly those using the characterful and ageworthy Plavac Mali grape. The best-known wines are Postup and Dingač from the Peljeşac peninsula and Faros from the island of Hvar, although Plavac of varying quality and sweetness is produced all along the beautiful Dalmatian coast. West of Split, another native variety, Babic, is grown on the rocky terraces of Primoşten. The Istrian peninsula's best-known wine is Motovunski Teran, a dry white, fairly low in alcohol, which goes well with the local truffles. Istria also grows Malvasia, Pinot Blanc, Merlot, Gamay and Cabernet Sauvignon. Croatia is alone among the seven states in having a quality wine scheme. Controlled Origin of Wines of Croatia have existed since 1986, and wines are labelled S for select, B for premium and C for table wines.

Central Serbia, with its mild, dry climate, is the largest wine-making area. Red grapes predominate, particularly the native Prokupac, which is often blended with Pinot Noir and Gamay. The vineyards of Župa, in the Kruševac area, are some of the former Yugoslavia's oldest, and still rank among Serbia's finest. Some of the country's best Cabernet Sauvignon comes from the various Morava River regions. White grapes include the Smederevka, named after the town of Smederevo.

The cold winters and hot summers of Vojvodina in the north give the region much in common with neighbouring Hungary and Romania. Vines are grown mainly on flat or undulating plateaux, with the exception of the district of Srem where they spread out on the slopes of Mount Fruska Gora. The poor soils of Kosovo, south of Serbia, made up of barren karst with a lot of bauxite, are suitable only for viticulture. Reds predominate, and Pinot Noir, Cabernet Franc, Prokupac, Merlot and Gamay are all planted. Whites include Welschriesling, Rhine Riesling and Zilavka. Most of the Kosovo vineyards grow grapes for red and white wines sold under the Amselfelder label in Germany.

Macedonia's mild winters and dry subtropical summers are ideal for viticulture, although the high temperatures favour production of dessert grapes rather than those for wine. The best wine is red Kratosija made from Kratosija and Vranac. In Montenegro, red Vranac, with its bitter cherry flavour, predominates. The best-known vineyards are those in the sparse, pebbly soil on the southern and south-western slopes surrounding Lake Skadar. Vranac is also blended with Merlot and Cabernet and the best examples, as in those of the Agrokombinat '13 Jul', are excellent.

WINE AREAS

CROATIA

- INLAND CROATIA
  1. Plešivica
  2. Zagorje-Medimurje
  3. Prigorje
  4. Bilogora-Drava Valley
  5. Moslavina
  6. Kupa River
  7. Middle Slavonia
  8. Sava Valley
  9. Danube Valley
- CROATIAN COAST
  10. Istria
  11. Hrvatsko Primorje and Islands of Kvarner
  12. Northern Dalmatia
  13. Dalmatinska Zagora
  14. Middle and Southern Dalmatia

BOSNIA-HERZEGOVINA

- HERZEGOVINA

VOJVODINA

- SUBOTICA-HORGOS DESERT
- SREM
- BANAT

SERBIA

- POCERINA
- ŠUMADIJA-GREAT MORAVA RIVER
  15. Belgrade
  16. Mlava River
  17. Oplenac
  18. Jagodina
- TIMOK VALLEY
  19. Krajina
  20. Knjaževac
- NIŠAVA AND SOUTHERN MORAVA RIVERS
  21. Aleksinac
  22. Toplica River
  23. Nis
  24. Nisava River
  25. Leskovac
  26. Vranje
- WESTERN MORAVA RIVER
  27. Čačak
  28. Kruševac

MONTENEGRO

- MONTENEGRO

KOSOVO

- KOSOVO

F.Y.R.M. (MACEDONIA)

- PELAGONIJA-POLOG
- VARDAR VALLEY
- PČINJA OSOGOVSKE

SLOVENIA

The relative calm of the new independent nation of Slovenia established in 1991 is testimony to the common heritage of the Slovenian people. Wine has always been part of that heritage, and it comes as no surprise to discover Roman writers praising the wines from the Devin area of Karst in the first century AD. Today, Slovenia has just over 20,000 hectares (50,000 acres) planted, and a further 10,000 hectares (25,000 acres) which have been designated for vineyard development, still much less than the 50,000 hectares (125,000 acres) under vine at the end of the nineteenth century when the country was part of the Austro-Hungarian empire.

A quality wine scheme for Slovenian wines was passed in 1968. A gold sticker indicates a select wine, silver a premium wine and black a fine table wine of designated geographical origin. However, the incentive to make more than adequate wines does not exist, and a forceful drive towards quality is needed before Slovenia will be able to fulfil its potential to make some truly excellent wines.

The Primorski region of Slovenia is tucked between mountains and karst plateau.

WINE DISTRICTS

The country has three defined wine districts. The Littoral region (also known as Primorski) touches the Adriatic for a stretch of the coast around Koper and extends north along the Italian border. This is hilly country with a karst plateau, and many of the vineyards are in the valleys between the mountains and the karst. The proximity of the Alps tempers the effects of the Mediterranean climate, and the wines have much in common with those of neighbouring Friuli-Venezia Giulia in Italy (see page 168). This is particularly seen in the presence of grapes such as Refosco (also known here as Teran), Ribolla (Rebula), Tocai Friuliano (Tocay) and Picolit (Pikolit). Also grown are Malvasia, Sauvignon Blanc, Chardonnay, Pinots Blanc and Gris, Merlot, Cabernets Franc and Sauvignon and Barbera. Indigenous white specialities of Vipava are Zelen (Austria's Rotgipfler) and Pinela. The white wines from Koper can be good, but for Slovenians, the most noted wine is the red Kraski Teran, made from Refosco grapes grown around Sezana where *terra rossa* (literally, 'red earth') overlays the karst.

The Sava Valley, or Posavski, is the source of the country's best whites. This is the meeting point of three different weather systems – alpine, continental and Mediterranean. The result is a climate with showers in spring, hot summers and warm sunny autumns. High sugar levels are possible, and a recent development has been the production of Eiswein in the Metlika district. The vineyards are mainly on the steep slopes, and grow Laski Rizling, Traminer, Sauvignon Blanc, Pinot Blanc, Šipon (Hungary's Furmint) and Silvaner. Rumeni Plavac, a white relation of Dalmatia's Plavac Mali, is grown around Bizeljsko, although its lack of character often means that it is blended with grapes such as Laski Rizling. The speciality of the Dolenjska region is the light red Cviček, and other reds and rosés are made from Blaufränkisch, Zametovka (or Kîlner Dark), Blauer Portugieser and Pinot Noir.

Podravski, or the Drava Valley, has much the same climate and grape varieties, as well as wine-making practices similar to those of the Austrian Steiermark region just across the border, producing young, fresh, tangy whites. The best-known wine is the Ljutomer Laski Rizling, once the top-selling wine in the UK, although the Chardonnay, Gewürztraminer (known here as Traminec) and especially the Sauvignon Blanc are much better. The semi-sweet wine called Tiger Milk is produced from Bouvier, or Ranina as it is locally known. In Gorna Radgona, Pinot Blanc is sometimes used to make sparkling wines by the traditional method.

BULGARIA

I'VE HAD A LOVE-HATE RELATIONSHIP with Bulgarian wine right from the beginning. The first tasting I did was when Jancis Robinson asked me at zero hour minus one minute's notice to 'guest edit' a well-known monthly newsletter for her. We organized a tasting of Bulgarian wines because, well, I think I had some – simple as that. These were some of the first samples to hit British shores, at the very beginning of the 1980s. And I remember them still. There were some remarkable hefty, violent, scabrous reds – strange, soupy and thick on the tongue. But there was fruit there too. Swathed in this shroud, but not completely swamped by it, was a proud, rip-roaring essence of blackcurrant, quite unlike the delicate, lacy perfume of old Bordeaux, quite unlike the bright, keen flavours of Chilean Cabernet. This Bulgarian Cabernet fruit had been stewed in a cauldron by witches.

Which was infinitely preferable to the whites, whose blend of searing acidity, reckless sulphur and building-site dust made them so painful to the lips that I suggested – perhaps unwisely – that they would be better employed in umbrellas for poisoning people (there had just been a notorious murder of a Bulgarian dissident who was stabbed with a poisoned umbrella-tip). My first editorial commission. My first scandal.

Since then, though the red wines still easily outshine the whites in Bulgaria, the flavours have changed. The stentorian old Cabernets are no longer so impressive, but the bright young Cabernets and Merlots are infinitely better. One gets the impression that in the 1980s, Bulgarian Cabernet Sauvignon was made for an export market that was starved of new and exciting affordable flavours. A decade later Bulgaria continues to be Eastern Europe's biggest wine success story.

But Hungary, in particular, and even Romania, are closing the gap. Hungary is finding it much easier to embrace the New World concepts of modern wine styles and wine-making technology, and not lose sight of her proud past stretching back centuries. Bulgaria's past doesn't stretch back much past the end of World War Two. Although there had been hillside plantings established after the end of Turkish Islamic domination in the nineteenth century, it was the Soviet decison that Bulgaria should be a massive modern vineyard to supply the USSR that caused the planting of all the fertile flatland vineyards that now mark out Bulgaria. And it was some canny bartering with American cola companies that gained her the vast acreage of international grape varieties upon which she has made her export reputation.

The grape most readily associated with Bulgaria, and which is the country's most widely planted, is Cabernet Sauvignon. The wines first appeared in the West in the early 1980s, and they were, and still are, unassuming but tasty and affordable. Since their debut the easy, ripe, plummy wines arguably have done as much as anything from Australia or California to establish the variety as the world's most famous red grape.

Those first Bulgarian wines, rich, creamy and blackcurranty, with some oak and some bottle age were virtually identikit pictures of what

WINE REGIONS AND CONTROLIRAN WINE AREAS

NORTHERN REGION
1. Novo Selo
2. Lositza
3. Svishtov
4. Roussenski Briag
5. Pavlikeni
6. Suhindol
7. Liaskovetz

EASTERN REGION
8. Kralevo
9. Khan Krum
10. Novi Pazar
11. Varna
12. Jujen Briag

SUB-BALKAN REGION
13. Sungurlare
14. Rozova Dolina

SOUTHERN REGION
15. Oriachovitza
16. Sakar
17. Stambolovo
18. Assenovgrad
19. Brestnik

SOUTH-WESTERN REGION
20. Harsovo

wine drinkers were seeking, and we lapped them up. In a rush to provide us with more of what we were clamouring for, production increased, and quality slipped. It may just be nostalgia, but current releases still don't seem as good as those first Suhindol Cabernets from the late 1970s.

Merlot can also be good, particularly from Stambolovo. Gamza (Hungary's Kadarka) is vigorously fruity when young but can age to a meaty richness, while the similarly sturdy, plummy Mavrud also produces wines of character. Pamid is the most widely planted native variety, but generally the wines are thin and lacking in character, though modern wine-making may yet produce bright gluggers from this variety. Much better is the Shiroka Melnishka Losa, usually just called Melnik, a powerful, fruity wine which handles oak aging very well.

Native white varieties include Dimiat, which manages to maintain a fairly aromatic, creamy character even from quite high yields, and Red Misket, a musky, grapy variety which one might think had some relation to the Muscat family but it doesn't. Rkatsiteli is the most widely planted white, and there are also significant amounts of Chardonnay, Ugni Blanc, Sauvignon Blanc, Riesling, Muscat Ottonel and Aligoté.

While the reds have thrived, the whites have been, on the whole, disappointing. The reds have been developed along French lines, and have been able to cope with some pretty rudimentary winery conditions. The whites initially followed Germanic models, with Riesling and Welschriesling being prominent. But Germanic models require positively aseptic conditions to succeed. In Bulgaria, grapes were frequently unhealthy and the wineries simply not clean enough: even today, sulphurous brews outnumber attractive drinks.

Chardonnay and Sauvignon Blanc came later, but the local winemakers have so far failed to understand how to make the wines: the arrival of Australian Kym Milne in 1993 at the Lyaskovets Winery was of enormous importance. His first releases have immediately eclipsed what went before. If other wineries are prepared to learn from him, we will at last see Bulgaria fulfilling its potential, especially in areas like Varna and Khan Krum which have occasionally – just occasionally – produced Chardonnay pointing to a bright future.

The 1978 wine laws guarantee quality and origin for Bulgaria's wines. Country Wine corresponds to France's *vin de pays*, Varietal Wine is more strictly controlled and is made from a single grape variety, while Premium Wine is better still. At the top of the tree are the Controliran wines, of which there are currently less than 30. The scheme works reasonably well, though as with France's *appellation contrôlée* system, many of the Controliran wines can be nothing special, while some of the most appealing bottles are those bearing the humble Country Wine tag. In addition, those which conform to special aging requirements can claim the titles Reserve or Special Reserve. Since excessive old oak aging is one of Bulgaria's problems, these are rarely worth seeking out. A new move towards early-release Young Vatted Cabernets and Merlots is much more encouraging.

Harvesting Chardonnay grapes at Blatetz in the Sub-Balkan Region.

Cabernet Sauvignon is Bulgaria's most widely-planted grape variety.

WINE REGIONS

The Eastern Region is mostly white wine country. Around Shumen, there are important wineries at Novi Pazar, Preslav and Khan Krum, the last of which is well-known for its Chardonnay, although the Controliran wine is the Gewürztraminer. Varna Chardonnay is the best-known of the wines from the strip along the northern Black Sea coast.

Reds and whites are made in roughly equal amounts in the Northern Region, although the reds are the real gems. Suhindol's best-known wine is the Cabernet Sauvignon although the Merlot and Gamza are also good. Suhindol was the first Bulgarian area to become famous with its Cabernet Sauvignon. It would be nice to see the return of the old fire in the belly.

Ready to take the crown of Bulgaria's top wine when the quality at Suhindol slipped were the Cabernet and Merlot from the foothills around Russe in the north-east of the region. The wines come in young, fruity carbonic maceration styles, sold abroad as Young Vatted Cabernet Sauvignon and Young Vatted Merlot as well as deeper, darker oak-aged versions. Another decent Cabernet comes from the Svishtov region on the border with Romania.

Cabernet Sauvignon is also important south of the Balkans in the Southern Region, both on its own or blended with Merlot or Mavrud. That from Plovdiv is good, although nearby Assenovgrad produces a better version, as well as impressive chunky Mavrud. The vines are planted in rich black and red carbonated soils on gentle slopes chosen for their low susceptibility to frost.

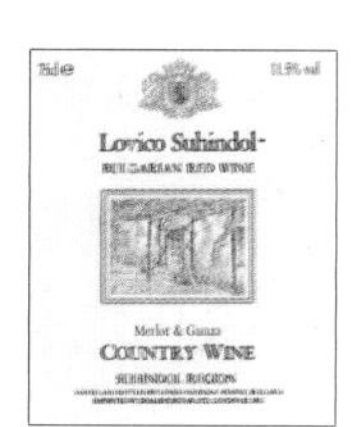

The hilly districts of Sliven, Oriachovitza and Stara Zagora on the border of the Sub-Balkan Region are also sources of good Cabernet Sauvignon. The vineyards enjoy a sheltered southerly exposure and the soils are mostly well-drained sand and clay. Sliven also produces a very drinkable Chardonnay and a fine cheap blend of Merlot and Pinot Noir. In the hilly regions of the south, Merlot from Stambolovo can be excellent, with the special Reserve releases sometimes being Bulgaria's best wines. The Merlot from Sakar is also good, as is the Cabernet Sauvignon.

The South-Western Region is the warmest area in the country. The continental climate is modified by warm air rising from the Strouma river, and has a distinctly Mediterranean feel, although the altitude prevents temperatures from rising too high for viticulture. This is the home of Melnik, a variety which thrives on the clay and sand soils around Damianitza and Harsovo. Even in such warm conditions, Melnik ripens late, and autumn rains can occasionally give rise to problems with botrytis before harvest in October.

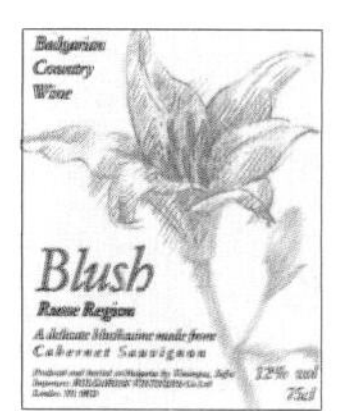

Experiments are underway, particularly with Melnik, to produce new strains of grape designed to have a growing period two to three weeks shorter than other varieties, so that it can be harvested before the rains begin, thus avoiding damage to the crop. Cabernet Sauvignon, Merlot, Rkatsiteli and Muscat Ottonel are also important. Further north, the wineries in and around Kjustendil produce small amounts of Rkatsiteli, Pamid and Cabernet Sauvignon.

EASTERN MEDITERRANEAN

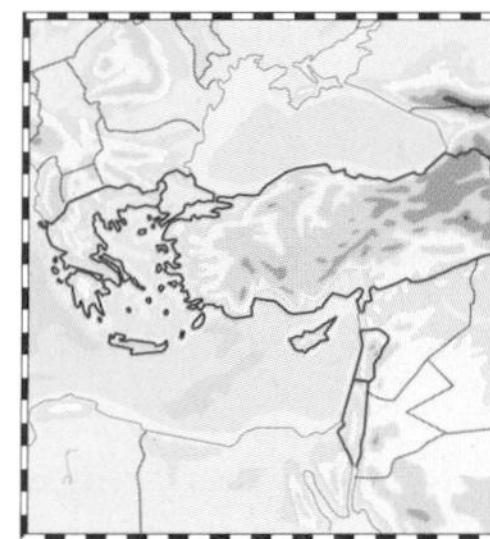

FOR A REGION WHICH HAS BEEN MAKING WINE for thousands of years, the present situation in most of the eastern Mediterranean makes a sad picture. Heavy, oxidized wines may please local drinkers, but wine-making standards need drastic improvement before there can be serious thought of establishing a presence in the rest of the world's wine cellar.

Greece, however, is currently seeing a slow but steady increase in standards from established companies such as Achaia Clauss, Kourtakis and Boutari, together with the emergence of a new band of small, quality-minded producers such as Papaioannou, Gerovasiliou, K Lazaridis, Gentilini, Hatzimichali and Strofilia. It is encouraging to see the newer estates not eschewing the native grapes in favour of more international varieties.

NORTHERN GREECE

The Xynomavro grape is responsible for Macedonia's dark, soft but spicy Naoussa and the somewhat light Goumenissa and Amindeo. The best producers of Naoussa are Boutari, Tsantalis and the Wine Co-operative of Naoussa (which also makes rosés and whites from Xynomavro).

Tsantalis Cava, made with Xynomavro plus 30 per cent Cabernet Sauvignon, is good and ages well, although, as with many Greek reds, less time in the barrel and more in the bottle would greatly improve the flavour. On the peninsula of Mount Athos in Halkidiki, Tsantalis lease vineyards from the Hourmistas monastery and produce a white from Sauvignon Blanc and a fine rosé from the two Cabernets and Limnio.

On the Sithonian peninsula to the west is Domaine Carras, the sole property in the Côtes de Meliton *appellation*. Vines are planted on terraces of sandy and schistose soils with indigenous varieties on south-facing slopes, and the French grapes facing north. A replanting programme is currently underway to move vines to higher altitudes (and thus cooler weather). Best of the whites produced is Melissanthi, a fleshy, fruity blend of Assyrtiko and Athiri. Château Carras, a blend of 80 per cent Cabernet Sauvignon plus Cabernet Franc, Merlot and Limnio, is Greece's internationally best-known red wine.

CENTRAL GREECE

Other parts of the country produce wine of equally high standard, particularly the Hatzimichali estate north-west of Athens where 14 different grape varieties are grown. The Cabernet Sauvignon, Merlot, and Chardonnay, and the Ampelon Estate white, which is 100 per cent Robola, are all good, if a little pricey. Robola plays second fiddle to the Savatiano grape further east on the island of Euboea. This is the source of the majority of retsina, which derives its particular character from the addition of Aleppo pine resin during fermentation. Love it or loathe it, retsina when fresh and young is a brilliantly individual drink.

The delicate, appley Debina grape is only found in Epirus. Here the Zitsa co-operative uses a combination of the Debina and Xynomavro grapes to produce still dry, medium and semi-sparkling wines, as well as a rosé.

THE PELOPONNESE

The best wine of the Peloponnese, and possibly of all Greece, is the dark, spicy Nemea, made from Agiorgitiko. Vineyards are found between 250 and 800m (820 and 2600ft) with the best being found on the slopes below the mountain plateau of Asprokambos. Wines from Achaia Clauss, Andrew P Cambas, Kourtakis, Kokotos, and Papaioannou, are all worth seeking out. Further west, the aromatic white Moscofilero produces Mantinia, one of Greece's most promising dry and off-dry whites; those produced by Andrew P Cambas, Achaia Clauss and Spyropoulos are especially good. Elsewhere in the Peloponnese, Patras whites are usually basic, neutral wines made from rather dull Roditis – but the Kouros brand of Kourtakis is good. There are two *vins doux naturels* – one is Muscat of Patras made from Muscat Blanc à Petit Grains, the other is Mavrodaphne of Patras made mainly from the red Mavrodaphne grape supplemented by Korinthiaki.

GREEK ISLANDS

Cephalonia also produces Muscat and Mavrodaphne, although it is better known for its dry white Robola. Most exciting are the Gentilini wines made by Nick Cosmetatos. His basic white, reminiscent of Australian Sémillon, with its crisp lemon acidity and mineral perfume, is a blend of Robola and another native Cephalonian grape, Tsaoussi, together with Moscofilero and a small amount of Sauvignon Blanc. There is an oak-aged Fumé version of the same wine which includes some Chardonnay.

In the Aegean, Crete produces an awful lot of awful wine but Kourtakis has begun to produce remarkable reds from ungrafted wines as well as crisp clean whites. Boutari also have a decent white. Better wines can found in Rhodes, particularly the Muscat, although better still is the Muscat from Samos. The unfortified Samos Nectar from the Union des Co-operatives de Samos is a truly great wine.

The white wines produced on the volcanic island of Santorini are made from the Assyrtiko and Aidani grapes. They have the minerally grip and tang of Sémillon matching an

GREEK WINE REGIONS WITH APPELLATIONS OF ORIGIN

NORTHERN GREECE
1. Goumenissa
2. Amindeo
3. Naoussa
4. Côtes de Meliton

CENTRAL GREECE
5. Rapsani
6. Zitsa
7. Ankalos
8. Cephalonia
9. Kantza

PELOPONNESE
10. Nemea
11. Mantinia
12. Patras

THE ISLANDS
13. Lemnos
14. Samos
15. Paros
16. Santorini
17. Rhodes

CRETE
18. Sitia
19. Peza
20. Dafnes
21. Arhanes

intense baked-apple fruit; a magnificent old-fashioned sweet *vin santo* is also produced. Château Vatis on the island of Syros manages to produce an excellent white from Assyrtiko and Monemvasia (believed to be Malvasia). Winter rain is collected for irrigating the vines, which face east and are protected from the violent winds by nylon wind-breaks.

TURKEY

Only three per cent of the huge acreage of Turkey under vine is used for wine production, and of this, there is little of interest. Turks who do drink – and 99 per cent of them, being Muslim, do not – do so for the effect rather than the flavour, and the oxidized, high-alcohol style of many wines find few devotees in today's wine world.

Most famous of the red wines is Buzbag from Eastern Anatolia, made from the native Öküzgözü and Bogazkere. It can be good, but is just as likely to be awful. I wouldn't go out of my way for any of the whites I've tried so far. The good producers are Diren from Tokat in Eastern Anatolia, Kavaklidere near Ankara and Doluca from Thrace.

LEBANON

Of the few wineries in Lebanon, the most important are Château Musar and Kefraya, both of whose vineyards are located on the east-facing slopes of Mount Barouk overlooking the Bekaa Valley. The high altitude, over 1000m (3300ft) above sea level, keeps temperatures low.

Kefraya's top red is 70 per cent Cabernet Sauvignon plus Mourvèdre, Syrah and Grenache, while Musar is between 50 and 80 per cent Cabernet Sauvignon, the balance being mostly Cinsaut. The result is a fascinating, exotic kasbah-scented red wine unlike any other. White wines are made with Ugni Blanc, Clairette, Bourboulenc and Sauvignon Blanc at Kefraya, while Musar's intriguing ageworthy whites are a blend of the local Obaideh (might be Chardonnay) and Merweh (could possibly be Sauvignon Blanc).

ISRAEL

Several good wines have appeared in Israel since the mid-1980s: most notable are those under the Yarden (Jordan) or the Gamla labels from the Golan Heights Winery up on the Golan Heights. The vineyards, in the shadow of Mount Hermon, are on well-drained soils over basalt and other volcanic rocks, and produce excellent Cabernet, Merlot, Muscat, Chardonnay and Sauvignon. The altitude keeps daytime temperatures below 25°C (77°F). Shomron, between the Mediterranean and the Carmel mountains, is Israel's largest viticultural region. Carmel, responsible for 70 per cent or so of the country's wine, has vineyards here, as well as another property at Rishon Le Zion in Samson. Better quality can be found at Baron Wine Cellars at Binyamina – the dry Muscat is decent. Also worth seeking out are the Musar-like reds of Askalon.

CYPRUS

The Cypriot wine industry is still recovering from the double whammy of the collapse of the Russian wine market and the banning of the name 'sherry' from the island's fortified wines. Native varieties, particularly Mavron (black) and Xynisteri (white), cover around 85 per cent of the total vineyard area, with the rest given over to Palomino and major French grapes. The most famous wine is Commandaria, made with sun-dried Mavron and Xynisteri grapes, and aged in solera systems. The best of a poor bunch of table wines are produced on the southern slopes of the Troodos mountains, where melting snow provides much-needed water in this arid region. Wines such as Keo's Othello and Aphrodite, and Etko's Semeli show what can done with a little effort.

Vineyards and almond trees in spring in the foothills of the Troodos mountains, Cyprus.

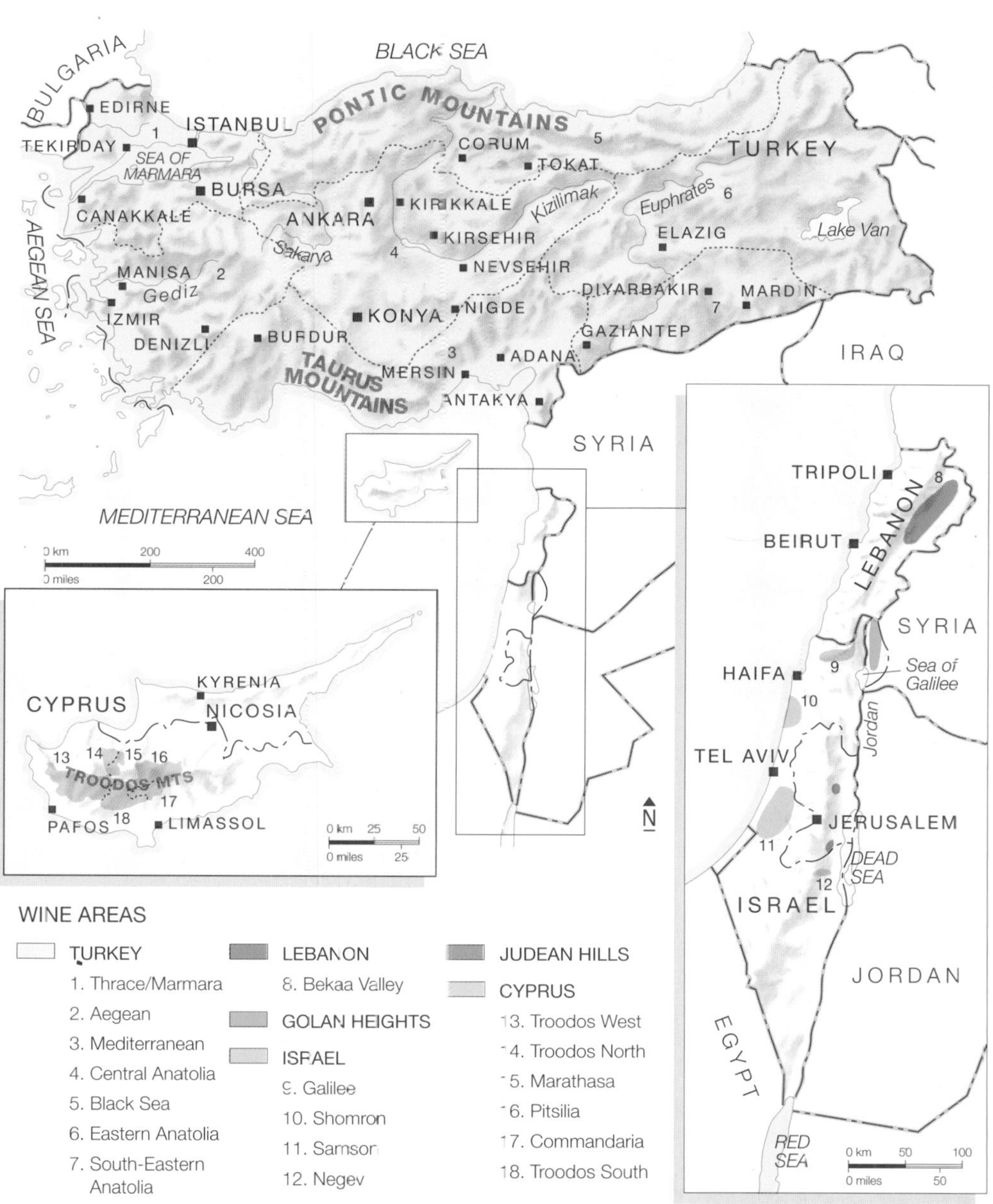

NORTH AMERICA

AN EVENT IN PARIS on 26 May 1976 proved to be a watershed in North America's wine-making history, the date with destiny the country had been heading towards since 1619 when Lord Delaware had tried to establish a vineyard of French wine grape varieties in Virginia. That sounds pretty sensationalist, I know, but that day has had a more far reaching effect on the world's perception of fine wine than any other in the modern era.

Stephen Spurrier, a young British wine merchant, held a tasting in Paris for the most finely tuned French palates of the day. Ostensibly a Bordeaux and Burgundy tasting, it also included a few Californian wines, which the French judges then proceeded to denigrate in pretty condescending terms.

Except that this was a blind tasting. The wines they were denigrating turned out to be French, some of the top names in Bordeaux and Burgundy. The wines they were praising as typical examples of great French wines...weren't. The top white was Chateau Montelena Chardonnay 1973 from California's Napa Valley, trouncing wines from vineyards in Burgundy planted a thousand years before. The top red was Stag's Leap 1973 Cabernet – only the second vintage of this Napa Valley wine, beating off the challenge of wines like Bordeaux's Château Haut-Brion and Château Latour which had the benefit of being rooted in hundreds of years of history.

Until that moment France had reigned supreme in the world of wine, and had generally behaved as though its hallowed wines had a God-given right to be the best. No more. The astonishing victory at the blind tasting gave Americans the confidence to believe that they could match the best of the Old World, but on their own terms, and it inspired the other nations of the world that now produce world class wines – ranging from Australia and New Zealand to South Africa, Chile and others – to do the same.

It also fashioned the American approach to making wine. With the exception of the bulk producers, winemakers in California, Oregon, Washington, Texas, Virginia, New York – and now Ontario and British Columbia in Canada, too – all take 'the best' as their goal, the top wine as their role model and purchase the finest equipment to achieve their aim. Sometimes sheer ambition is their downfall. But more often their efforts sing with the excitement of a new industry turning the tables on old, revered institutions, and the whole world has cause to be grateful for that.

Wild mustard blooming between rows of vines in Carneros heralds the onset of spring and is a common sight in California's North Coast vineyards.

THE WINE REGIONS OF NORTH AMERICA

THERE ARE NUMEROUS TALES about the cradle of wine-making being in the Eastern Mediterranean, in Mesopotamia, in Asia Minor or Persia – and all of them make sense. The grape grows very well there, and probably always did. More to the point, they've been writing things down there for thousands of years for archaeologists and historians to discover.

But what about the Americas? Two twelfth- and thirteenth-century Norse sagas tell of Leif Ericsson who established the colony of Vinland ('Wine Land') in north-east America, named after the wild vines which grew in profusion. Did he find bushes laden down with grapes? And would he have made these into wine? If so, surely the Indian tribes would have discovered the grape's ability to ferment many centuries – if not millenia – before, just as the Mesopotamians had. There is evidence that fermented grape juice was offered to the gods of Native American tribes such as the Seneca and Cayuga. How long had this been going on? Maybe for as long as in the courts of Cairo and Baghdad. Maybe.

But, since the Europeans arrived on the continent in force during the sixteenth and seventeenth centuries, extensive records have been kept that show a relentless determination to establish vineyards and wineries in almost every state of the Union. At the same time, the fact that American wines didn't break into the premier league until the 1970s is evidence of the succession of natural and man-made obstacles that winemakers had to overcome.

On the east coast, the combination of a difficult climate and the presence of the indigenous vine-chomping phylloxera louse baffled generations of winemakers trying to make European-style wine from European grape varieties. In the centre and the south, climatic conditions defeated all but the hardiest pioneers. On the west coast, a brighter start with European grape varieties was unceremoniously cut short by the invasion of phylloxera from the east.

To cap it all, Prohibition, like an angel of doom, overshadowed the entire nation. From 1919 to 1933 alcohol was basically an illegal drug in the States. People still drank – they probably drank more than ever before – but the whole concept of wine as a noble, uplifting beverage went out of the window. By the time the Prohibition laws were repealed, the Great Depression was stifling interest in the finer things of life, and then there was a World War to fight. By the 1950s, two generations had grown up with no experience of wine as anything other than a sweet, fortified drink to be consumed for the effect, rather than the flavour.

The picture only began to change in the late 1960s, when Robert Mondavi established his Napa Valley winery, filling what was a virtual quality vacuum. During the 1970s and 1980s, wine-making spread to every suitable nook and cranny in California and the Pacific North-West. The 1980s and 1990s saw the south-western and the eastern seaboard states at last conquer their difficult climate. And during the 1990s the Canadians of Ontario and British Columbia threw over their old mediocre wine traditions and struck out for the title of newest New World kid on the block, to startling effect.

INDIGENOUS VINE SPECIES

Back in the seventeenth and eighteenth centuries, every visitor from Europe who travelled along the east coast commented on the vines, which seemed to flourish from New England right down to Florida. But all early efforts to make decent wine from them failed, largely because the prevailing vine species – *Vitis labrusca* – simply will not make pleasant-flavoured wine, though it makes excellent grape juice and grape jelly. So generation upon generation of colonists imported the European *Vitis vinifera* varieties – but with conspicuous lack of success.

The most obvious reasons for this failure were the very cold winters and hot humid summers, which either killed off the vines or provided perfect conditions for fungal diseases. But there was another hazard – the tiny phylloxera louse, indigenous to north-east America and able to feed off the roots of the hardy *Vitis labrusca* without weakening the vine. The *Vitis vinifera* vines had no natural tolerance of phylloxera and every plantation succumbed within a few years.

THE EASTERN SEABOARD

The whole pattern of vineyards in the north-east was fixed by these sets of circumstances. Wine was and is made from *labrusca* grapes from New England down to the Carolinas and across to the Great Lakes, yet even now no-one has managed to make it taste very good. However, some natural hybrids with phylloxera resistance and a less offensive flavour did evolve and others were bred specifically.

When in the late nineteenth century the French were desperate for rootstocks and plants that were resistant to phylloxera for their own vineyards, a large number of so-called

THE CLASSIFICATION SYSTEM FOR AMERICAN WINE

Wine laws are a relatively new phenomenon in the United States, as the provenance of grapes for wine made in North America was unimportant up until the 1980s. About the most specific labels ever got was to mention the county of origin, but this didn't tell the consumer anything about quality. As US wine began to hold its own at international level it competed in export markets against wine from countries with more developed methods of quality control. The need for home-grown wine legislation led to the introduction of officially recognized American Viticultural Areas (AVAs) in 1983, roughly modelled on the French principle of Appellation Contrôlée, or the Italian Denominazione di Origine Controllata.

AVAs are administered by the US Federal Government Bureau of Alcohol, Tobacco and Firearms. Boundaries are based on topographic and climatic zones, and soil types, but unlike their European counterparts they don't yet involve restrictions on the grape varieties that may be grown, or on yields, and do not guarantee quality. Further restrictions may come in the future, as growers have the chance to observe where particular varieties do best, and can pinpoint the optimum crop yields for quality wine. There are currently over 100 AVAs in the US, more than 60 of which are in California.

MAJOR REQUIREMENTS OF THE LABELLING LAWS

- **Labelling by grape variety** American wines are most commonly labelled by the dominant grape variety used in the blend. The wine must contain at least 75% of the named variety (except in Oregon where the minimum is 90%, with an exception of 75% for Cabernet Sauvignon to allow for the Bordeaux-style of blending common with this variety). If an AVA is named, at least 85% of the grapes must come from that AVA.
- **Region of origin** The winery and the region of origin also appear on the label. At the most basic level this may be stated simply as 'America', used for a blend of wine from two or more states, or the label can be more specific and mention a state or a county name. If the wine has only the name of a state, the grapes must be 100% from that state; if only the county is named, at least 75% must be from that county, regardless of variety.
- **Health warnings** Various health warnings are mandatory on US labels. There are warnings about the dangers of alcohol on bottles destined to stay within the US (puritanical values die hard) and labels must declare the presence of sulphites (used as a preservative) and other additives.

French hybrids were developed. These now dominate plantings in the eastern and central states, although the classic *vinifera* varieties are at last succeeding on the east coast and provide the majority of the crop in such places as Virginia and New York's Long Island.

CALIFORNIA AND THE SOUTH

The southern United States is largely unsuitable for *vinifera* grapes because of the humid summers and insufficiently cold winters; the best known wine is a non-*vinifera* style called Scuppernong. But French and German immigrants did establish thriving wine businesses in Arkansas and Missouri, using a wide spectrum of grape varieties, and it was from Mexico in the early seventeenth century that *Vitis vinifera* grapes made their gradual progress north, when Franciscan missionaries planted the first Californian vines in 1779.

The Gold Rush of 1849 drew the centre of attention in California north from Los Angeles to San Francisco, and saw the establishment of the great vineyard regions of Sonoma and Napa north of San Francisco, as well as Livermore and Santa Clara to the south and east of the city, and the huge San Joaquin Valley in the interior.

By the late nineteenth century California had more than 800 wineries growing over 300 different *vinifera* varieties. Phylloxera, two World Wars, Prohibition and the Great Depression doused the bright flame of Californian wine for almost a hundred years, until progress in the last quarter of the twentieth century changed the face of North America's, and the world's wine, for good.

THE PACIFIC NORTH-WEST

Further north, in Oregon, Washington and Idaho, winemakers set out to change the face of American wine as defined by the Californians. But it was the rekindling of fires in California that sent sparks north to these states. Although there are a couple of references to nineteenth-century wineries in places like Oregon's Willamette Valley, and Washington State did have a wine industry of sorts based on hybrids and *labrusca* varieties, things only really got moving in 1966 when a couple of university professors making wine in their garage were noticed by a leading American wine critic. This coincided with the arrival of several refugees from the heart of California who were prodding about in Oregon, trying to establish a vineyard for Pinot Noir. And it wasn't until the 1970s that some Idaho fruit farmers decided to diversify into wine grapes. The wine industries of the Pacific North-West and Idaho are as recent as that.

CANADA

Far from being new to wine-making, Canada has been a producer since the nineteenth century, and in 1916 stole the march on the rest of North America by partially avoiding the Prohibition ban on alcohol. Grape growers managed to negotiate an exemption from the Act, and by 1927 when Canadian Prohibition ended, more than 50 wineries had a licence to operate. Wine is now produced in Ontario, Nova Scotia and Québec in the east and in British Columbia in the far west.

Despite harsh winter weather conditions producers have moved away from the *labrusca* varieties which used to go into sweet 'port' and 'sherry' and are having success with *vinifera* varieties ranging from Chardonnay to Pinot Noir. Robust hybrids such as Seyval Blanc, Vidal, Maréchal Foch and Baco Noir are still popular for their ability to withstand the alternate freezes and thaws of the Canadian spring. Winemakers have turned some factors to their advantage. Whereas in Europe, mainly in Germany and Austria, conditions are right only once every decade or so to leave the grapes to freeze on the vine, in Canada this happens every year, and a luscious, perfumed, sweet Icewine results.

Quality in Canada is controlled by the Vintners Quality Alliance (VQA) which was set up in 1988 and does a similar job to the AVAs south of the border in the USA, although Canadian wine laws vary slightly from province to province.

US AVA & OTHER WINE AREAS

CANADIAN VQA & OTHER WINE AREAS

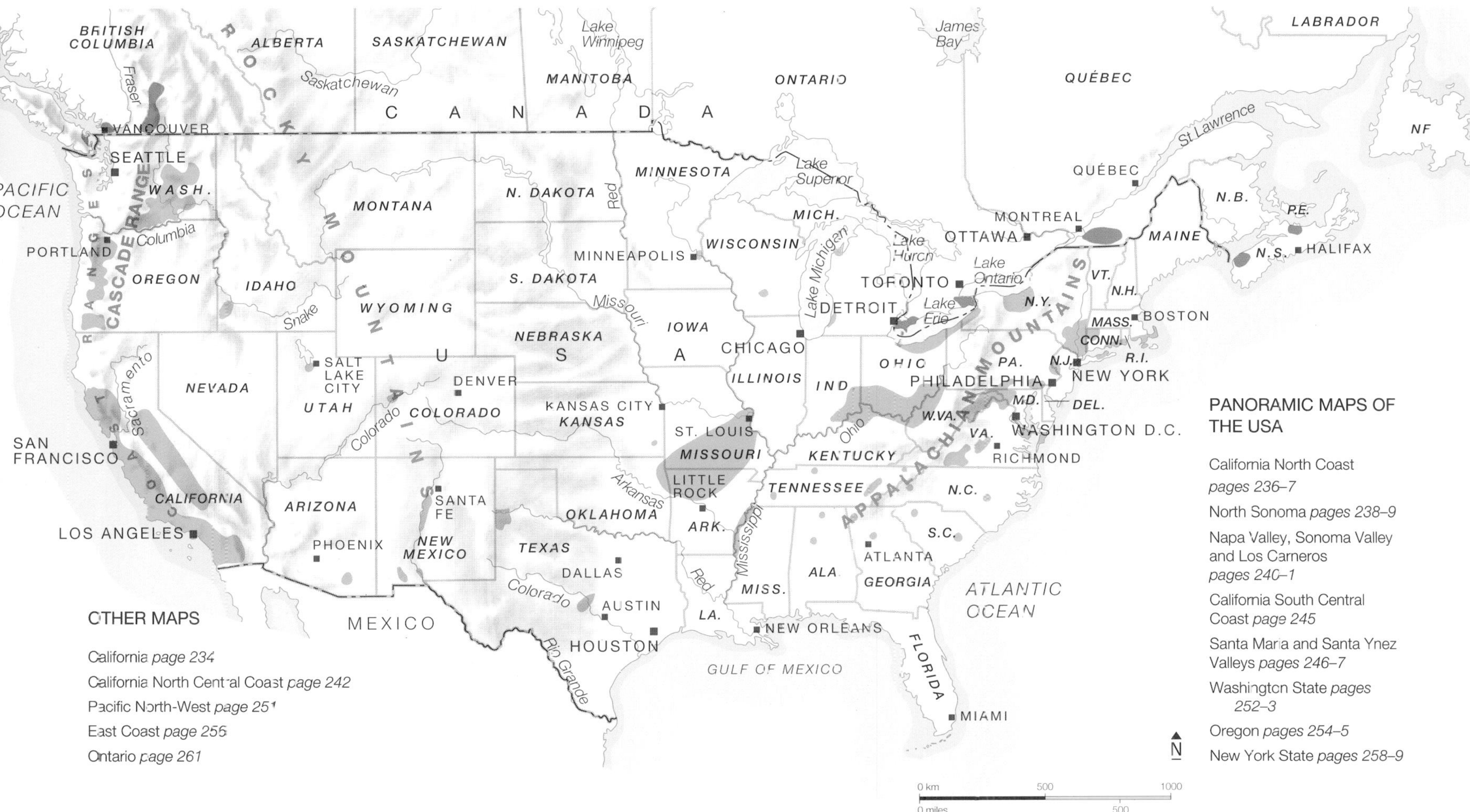

OTHER MAPS

California *page 234*

California North Central Coast *page 242*

Pacific North-West *page 251*

East Coast *page 255*

Ontario *page 261*

PANORAMIC MAPS OF THE USA

California North Coast *pages 236–7*

North Sonoma *pages 238–9*

Napa Valley, Sonoma Valley and Los Carneros *pages 240–1*

California South Central Coast *page 245*

Santa Maria and Santa Ynez Valleys *pages 246–7*

Washington State *pages 252–3*

Oregon *pages 254–5*

New York State *pages 258–9*

CALIFORNIA

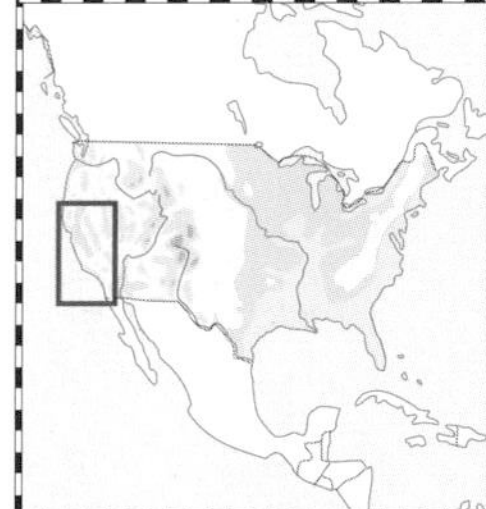

ON MY FIRST TRIP to the USA I never got anywhere near California. But as a student actor with a notable thirst – and many like-minded cronies – I did get to the very heart of Californian wine as it then was. Draining flagon after flagon of brews with such names as Hearty Burgundy and Mountain Chablis – neither in any way related to the famous wine areas of France – I got my first ever experience of good, cheap wine.

Until then, cheap for me had invariably meant filthy. But that was in Europe. In California, on the other hand, the world's first inexpensive, juicy, beverage wines were widely available. Winemakers had harnessed the vast, sun-baked desert of her Central Valley, and irrigated its parched soils with the limitless streams running off the mighty Sierra Nevada mountains to produce these enjoyable wines in bulk. They were way ahead of their competitors, for this was at a time when Australia was still stumbling out of a long period when beer and fortified wines were the national drinks, and before Argentina, southern France and Eastern Europe had even grasped the concept that people might actually want a basic table wine to taste good.

That's one half of the Californian story, the side which has influenced the producers of basic wines across the world in the last 20 years, and which will eventually make bad wine at any price obsolete. But there's another side to California that has been even more inspirational in the world of wine.

The second half of the story begins in the 1970s, around the time of my second trip to the USA, when I did get to California and I immersed myself, without realizing it, in the revolution of fine wine that had been gathering pace since the 1960s. I didn't know it then but the bottles I used to pick off the wine shop shelves with names like Mondavi, Heitz, Sterling, Freemark Abbey and Schramsberg, were in the process of changing the face of the world of wine.

These were the new wineries of the Napa Valley, north of San Francisco, that had thrown down the gauntlet to the classic French regions of Bordeaux, Burgundy and Champagne. Not only that, but they were attempting to emulate these ancient wines, not at their basic level, but at the level of the greatest Grand Cru or De Luxe Cuvée they offered. They used the same grape varieties, they used the same methods of production as far as they could, and they bought the equipment that only the very best of the French producers could afford. The wines were stunning. So clearly related to the great French models, yet so startlingly, thrillingly different. And they set the tone for this other side to California that has been avidly pursued ever since in the cooler vineyards of the state.

And there's the crux. Cooler. The Central Valley is a broad, torrid, irrigated, mass producer of grapes, making wines that never manage to achieve greatness because climatic conditions here don't bring about exciting enough fruit. You need less sun, less heat, longer ripening seasons and lower yields. Yet if you look at the map, the Central Valley stretches from above Sacramento almost to Los Angeles, and that's exactly the same latitude covered by all the other California vineyard regions that produce some of the world's most thrilling wine. The one factor they share and which the Central Valley, tucked inland between the coastal ranges and the Sierra Nevada mountains, doesn't is that they're all near to the sea. Even that wouldn't be enough by itself. But the California coastline produces unique climatic conditions, and with the co-operation of some cold Pacific currents, the coastal range

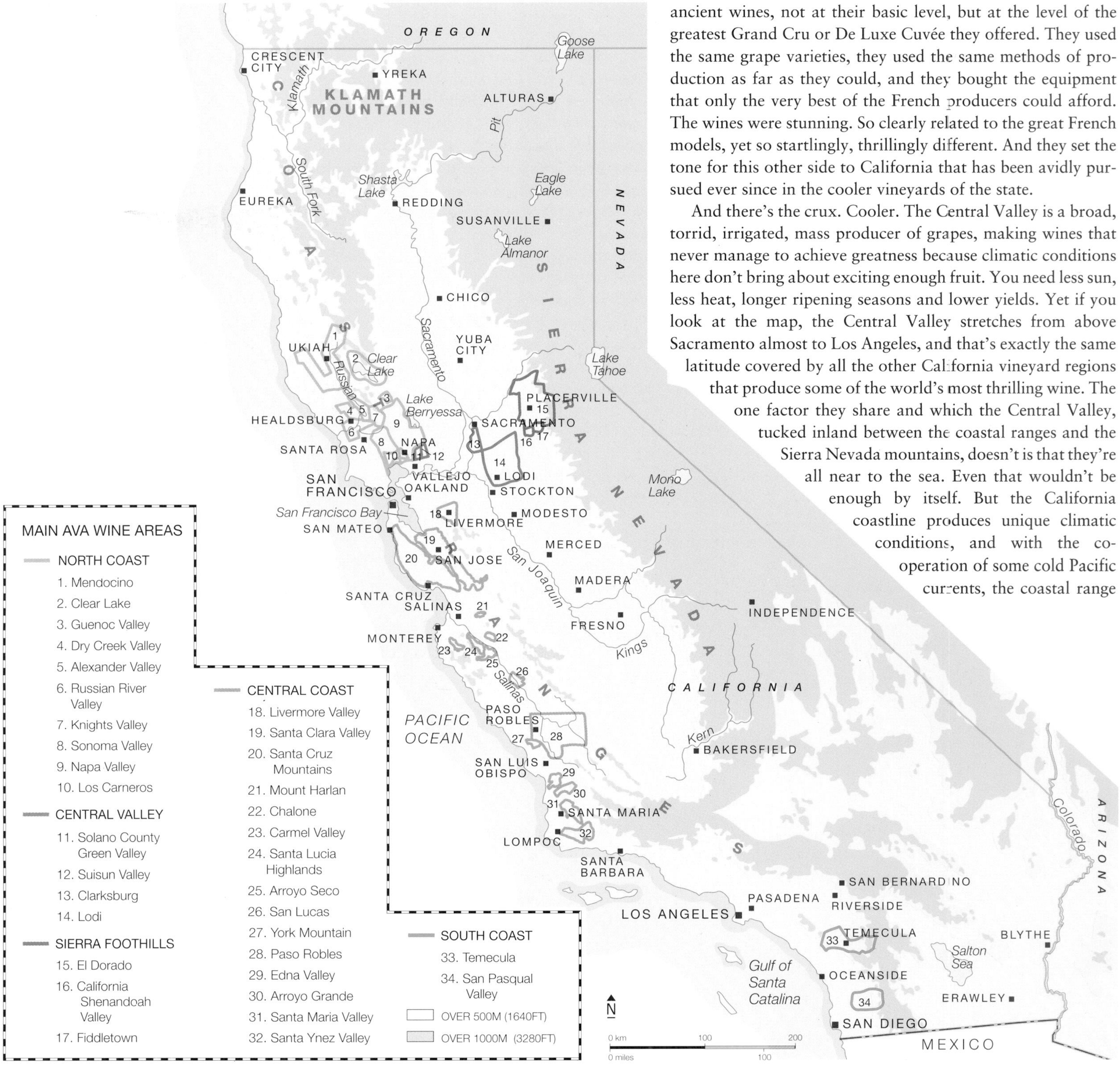

MAIN AVA WINE AREAS

NORTH COAST
1. Mendocino
2. Clear Lake
3. Guenoc Valley
4. Dry Creek Valley
5. Alexander Valley
6. Russian River Valley
7. Knights Valley
8. Sonoma Valley
9. Napa Valley
10. Los Carneros

CENTRAL VALLEY
11. Solano County Green Valley
12. Suisun Valley
13. Clarksburg
14. Lodi

SIERRA FOOTHILLS
15. El Dorado
16. California Shenandoah Valley
17. Fiddletown

CENTRAL COAST
18. Livermore Valley
19. Santa Clara Valley
20. Santa Cruz Mountains
21. Mount Harlan
22. Chalone
23. Carmel Valley
24. Santa Lucia Highlands
25. Arroyo Seco
26. San Lucas
27. York Mountain
28. Paso Robles
29. Edna Valley
30. Arroyo Grande
31. Santa Maria Valley
32. Santa Ynez Valley

SOUTH COAST
33. Temecula
34. San Pasqual Valley

OVER 500M (1640FT)
OVER 1000M (3280FT)

of mountains, and the Central Valley itself, creates every conceivable vineyard climate, from overcoat cool to sunshade hot, often in the space of a few miles.

It works like this. There's an extremely cold current from Alaska that runs down the California coast, and every summer this causes bodies of ice-cold water to well up from depths of several hundred feet. Being 7 to 9°C (12 to 16°F) colder than the surface water it replaces, the warm air above the sea condenses and cools into massive fog banks. Meanwhile, over 160km (100 miles) inland, the Central Valley is heated every summer's day by a broiling sun. The hot air rises and creates a vacuum. There's no replacement air available from the east because of the High Sierras, so it has to come from the west. At the top of the valley, the San Joaquin River creates a gap as it flows westwards into San Pablo Bay and thence out to sea through the mile-wide Golden Gate gap.

As the Central Valley heats up, cold air and fog is sucked through the Golden Gate gap and over dips in the coastal ranges. Most of the fog is drawn into the San Joaquin Valley, but some sweeps over Carneros and heads up both the Napa and Sonoma valleys. All the way down the coast south to Santa Barbara and north to Mendocino, wherever there is a dip in the hills or a river valley, creating a gap in the coastal ranges, the fogs and the cold winds sweep in.

On the coast itself it is too cold to ripen any grape. But as the fog and wind sweep inland they gradually lose their force and it is reckoned that for every mile you travel up one of the valleys, the temperature rises by 0.5°C (1°F). So Carneros, right down by the San Pablo Bay is quite cool, yet Calistoga, 50km (30 miles) up the Napa Valley is very warm. There are quirks of mesoclimate in all the valleys, and there are sites where altitude plays more of a part than fog and sea breezes, but this relationship between the cool Pacific and the warm interior is the most important influence on vineyard quality in California.

GRAPE VARIETIES

It is only recently that the relationship between different grape varieties and their suitability for the various Californian soil and climatic conditions has been fully exploited. Before the 1960s the number of acres planted with bulk varieties dwarfed those growing top-quality grapes. Since then, with the birth of California's fine wine tradition, things have changed so dramatically that Chardonnay is the most widely planted variety of all, and Cabernet Sauvignon the most common red. But there is a danger here. Because Chardonnay and Cabernet Sauvignon – and, more recently, Merlot – sell for the highest prices, they have frequently been planted in inappropriate locations in place of other varieties which would have been better suited to the local conditions.

In the late 1980s, producers had the perfect chance to re-evaluate what was planted in their vineyards and how it was grown, when phylloxera – or, as some people believe, a mutation called Biotype B phylloxera – reappeared. This led to the uprooting and replanting of almost all the vineyards in the state. It could have been the ideal time to replace inefficient vineyards and unsuitable varieties with modern systems and ideal grape varieties. If this had happened, we'd be seeing a lot more Syrah, Sangiovese, Mourvèdre, Marsanne, Roussanne and numerous others. In reality, we're seeing a lot more Chardonnay, Cabernet Sauvignon and Merlot, as market forces rather than the relationship between *terroir* and variety lead the way. That's a great pity, but even so, some areas have established themselves as having particularly suitable soils and climate for certain varieties. Carneros is good for Pinot Noir and Chardonnay, as is the Santa Maria Valley. Santa Ynez is good for Pinot Noir and Edna Valley for Chardonnay. The mountainside vineyards in Napa and Sonoma are proving themselves with Cabernet and Merlot, and Zinfandel pops up in the most surprising places in many different guises.

Robert Mondavi's Spanish Mission-style winery building is one of the Napa Valley's best-known landmarks.

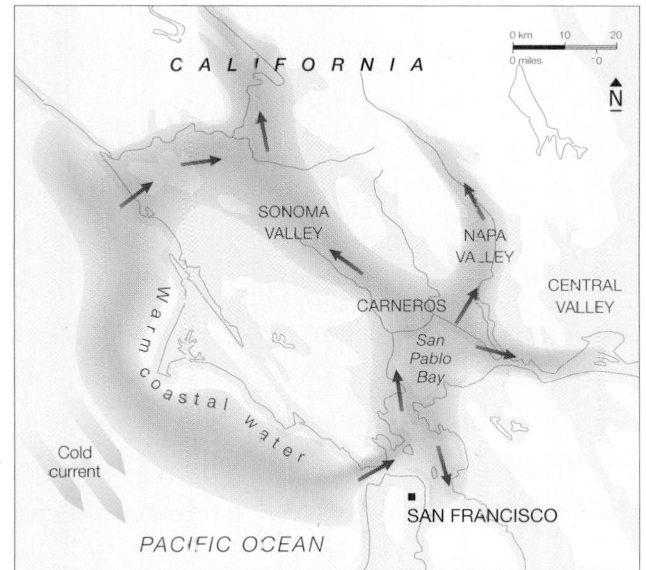

THE CALIFORNIA CLIMATE

The very cold summer water along the US west coast has a direct influence on making fine wine in coastal California. The cold ocean current running down the Pacific coast from Alaska wells up off north California, partly as a result of the strong coastal winds turning the water over. The colder water below comes to the surface and meets the warmer surface air, causing it to cool and condense into massive fog banks.

Meanwhile on the land, the broiling morning sun heats up the interior valleys, the hot air rises and pulls the cooler air and the fogs from the coast inland through any gaps in the coastal ranges to fill its space. The temperature falls, fogs roll in throughout the night and disperse the next day with the midday heat. If it weren't for this cooling influence, the coastal areas would be too hot for fine wine grapes. As it is, the influence lessens gradually as the breezes and fog banks travel inland. There is as much as a 10°C (18°F) difference in temperature on a typical summer day between cool Carneros and warmer Calistoga 48km (30 miles) up the Napa Valley.

Zinfandel is California's local grape variety and makes a wide range of reds and rosés.

North Coast

RED GRAPES
Certain districts are associated with particular varieties such as Dry Creek Valley Zinfandel, Napa Cabernet, and Carneros Pinot Noir. Merlot also features.

WHITE GRAPES
Chardonnay is most widely planted. Sauvignon Blanc shows regional variations in style. There is also Pinot Blanc, Gewürztraminer and Riesling.

CLIMATE
The two-season climate of short, mild winters and long, dry, hot summers is dramatically influenced by summer fogs coming off the Pacific.

SOIL
An extraordinary variety of soils ranges from well-drained gravel and loam to infertile gravel and rock, volcanic ash with quartz and sandy loam.

ASPECT
Hill slopes are favoured for important vineyard sites though much of Napa Valley is flat.

IT'S A GOOD IDEA to start with Mendocino way up in northern California because we're going to have to get used to the wild fluctuations in climate that afflict – or bless, depending how you look at it – every single coastal wine region down to Santa Barbara. Up in Mendocino are some of California's hottest high-quality vineyards (I'm excluding the bulk-producing San Joaquin or Central Valley), best suited to grand, old-style, rip-roaring, throaty Zinfandel reds. But there are fog-draped, drizzly, chilly sites as well that can just about coax Chardonnay and Pinot Noir to some sort of ripeness, and that make the eyes of a winemaker from the windswept Champagne region of northern France well up with tears of homesickness.

It's all to do with those cold Pacific air currents and their accompanying fogs. Most of Mendocino County doesn't feel their influence too much and broils. But the Anderson Valley, slicing north-west through the towering redwood forests, feels them right to the bone. This is fascinating backwoods country, with two very different wine cultures. Up on the ridges above the valley, way above the fog line at between 400 and 700m (1300 and 2300ft), are some great old Zinfandel vineyards, their origins dating back to the sites first planted by Italian immigrants in the 1890s. With a surfeit of sun, but cooled by their elevation above sea-level, these old vines give some thrilling flavours.

Down in the valley, things couldn't be more different. Even the early pioneers in the 1970s planted cool-climate grapes like Gewürztraminer and Riesling, and all the recent action is to do with Pinot Noir and Chardonnay destined for sparkling wine.

MENDOCINO AND LAKE COUNTY

The main north-south valley in Mendocino was carved out by the Russian River (though the Russian River Valley region doesn't appear until further south, in Sonoma County). We're at the river's source here, so that the maritime influence which affects things further downstream has been pretty well played out. The coastal range in Mendocino is between 600 and 900m (2000 and 3000ft) high, so no cooling breezes come from that direction either. The results are strong, ripe reds from the north around Ukiah; reds that are still quite hefty following the Russian River south; and the beginnings of cooler conditions giving some fair whites down by Hopland. Potter Valley, to the north of Ukiah, is even hotter, and McDowell Valley, east of Hopland, is doing tasty things with the Rhône varieties. Further east is Lake County, where vineyards around Clear Lake, mostly at sites above 400m (1300ft), experience baking days with ice-cold nights to good effect.

SONOMA

If Mendocino is relatively simple to understand, Sonoma County, directly to the south, is the most complex but also the most intriguingly satisfying of the other two main wine counties north of San Francisco Bay. Again the dominant factor in the various vineyard regions is the cooling effect of maritime fogs and breezes, both as they push inland through the Russian River Valley, and as they flow off the northern slopes of the San Pablo Bay – although, obviously, different soils, different elevations and different exposures to the sun also count.

Going over from Mendocino on Highway 101, the Alexander Valley opens out north of Cloverdale; it's warm here, and the Zinfandel and Rhône varieties ripen easily. However, the valley doesn't really begin to show its form until south of Geyserville. The broad fertile swathes of gravelly loam encourage vines to run riot, but modern methods of pruning, trellising and yield restraint now produce wonderfully soft-edged, yet mightily flavoured Cabernets that are a

WHERE THE VINEYARDS ARE *You only catch sight of a sliver of the Pacific Ocean to the west, and a tiny inlet or two of San Pablo Bay to the south, but keep a good eye on those two splashes of water: they're crucial to an understanding of the vineyards north of San Francisco. Also take note of the Coast Ranges. These are the mountains that run down to the Pacific edge. They're not particularly high but they are high enough to act as a barrier to most of the fog and icy wind that would otherwise sweep in from the ocean. On the other hand, the areas inland from the sea would be far too hot for growing good wine grapes were it not for some cooling influence. And this is provided by the sea. In Mendocino County, the Anderson Valley; in Sonoma County the Russian River Valley; and in Sonoma, Napa and other counties east, the Golden Gate gap allows fog and cold air to be sucked in to the warm interior day by day. Without this effect, there would be no fine wine industry in California. With this effect, we have cool vineyards near the sea, gradually warming as the maritime influence weakens further inland. Areas cut off from the maritime influence, like Potter Valley and Clear Lake, rely on altitude to keep their vines cool. There are also areas that rely upon altitude to moderate the heat by being well above the fog line. Howell Mountain, Atlas Peak, Spring Mountain, Mount Veeder and Sonoma Mountain are the best known.*

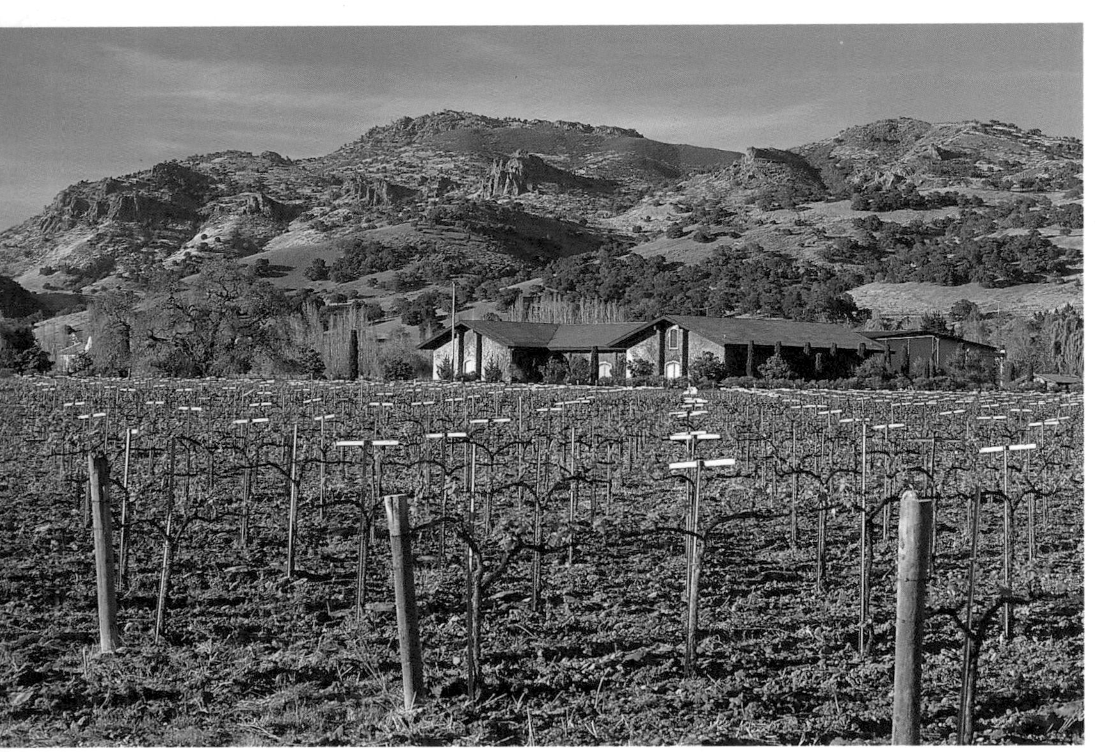

The Clos du Val winery lies in hills in Stags Leap.

joy in youth and yet age with grace. The small Knights Valley AVA further east on the road to Calistoga in the Napa Valley does a similar job.

Dry Creek Valley was planted with Zinfandel by Italian immigrants during the 1870s and it is still Zinfandel, in the breezeless, baking northern half of the valley, that makes Dry Creek special. On both sides of the river are deposits of reddish rocky, gravelly soil, well-drained but able to retain the higher than average rainfall the valley receives. Cabernet is encroaching on these sites, but it is the ruddy-hued, brawny sweetness of the Zinfandel that makes me want to shout for joy. On the valley floor, well-drained gravels produce surprisingly good Sauvignon Blanc and Chenin Blanc, and at the cooler, southern end of the valley some fine Chardonnay is grown.

It's really only south of Healdsburg in the Russian River Valley AVA that Sonoma County changes from a warm environment with a few cooling influences to a cool environment with warm patches, especially in the areas affected by the presence of the river. It really should be too cold for Zinfandel along this stretch of the Russian River, but some marvellous examples crop up, frequently in vineyards that also grow superb Pinot Noir! There's also lovely Gewürztraminer, Chardonnay and Merlot. Green Valley, south of Forestville, is even cooler, and a prime site for Chardonnay, Pinot Noir and sparkling wine.

The Sonoma creek rises south-east of Santa Rosa and the Sonoma Valley AVA stretches southwards, taking in the lower slopes of the Mayacamas mountains to the east, and bordering the Los Carneros AVA down towards San Pablo Bay. From Santa Rosa south to Kenwood, some of the cooling fog and ocean air from Russian River can still be felt, but the more powerful tempering forces are the fog banks and wind that have roared though the Golden Gate gap at San Francisco, howled across Carneros and still had enough chilly life in them

CABERNET SAUVIGNON
RESERVE
ROBERT MONDAVI WINERY

PINOT NOIR
1990
SAINTSBURY

ESTATE BOTTLED CHARDONNAY
1988
SONOMA-CUTRER
CUTRER VINEYARD

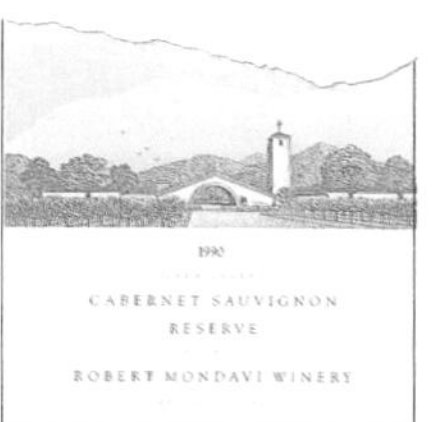

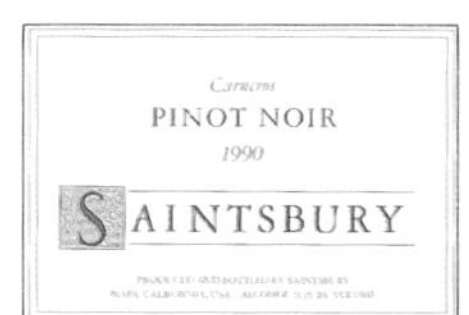

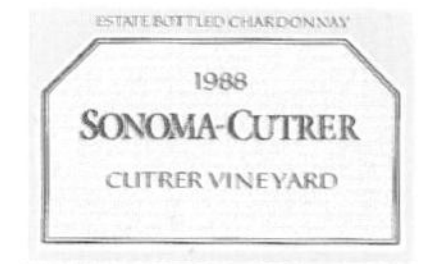

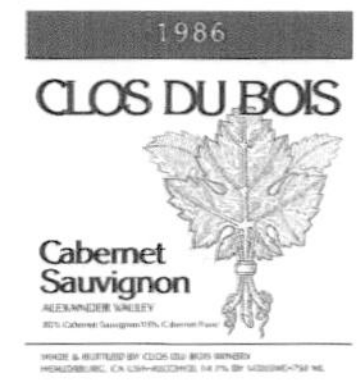
1986
CLOS DU BOIS
Cabernet
Sauvignon

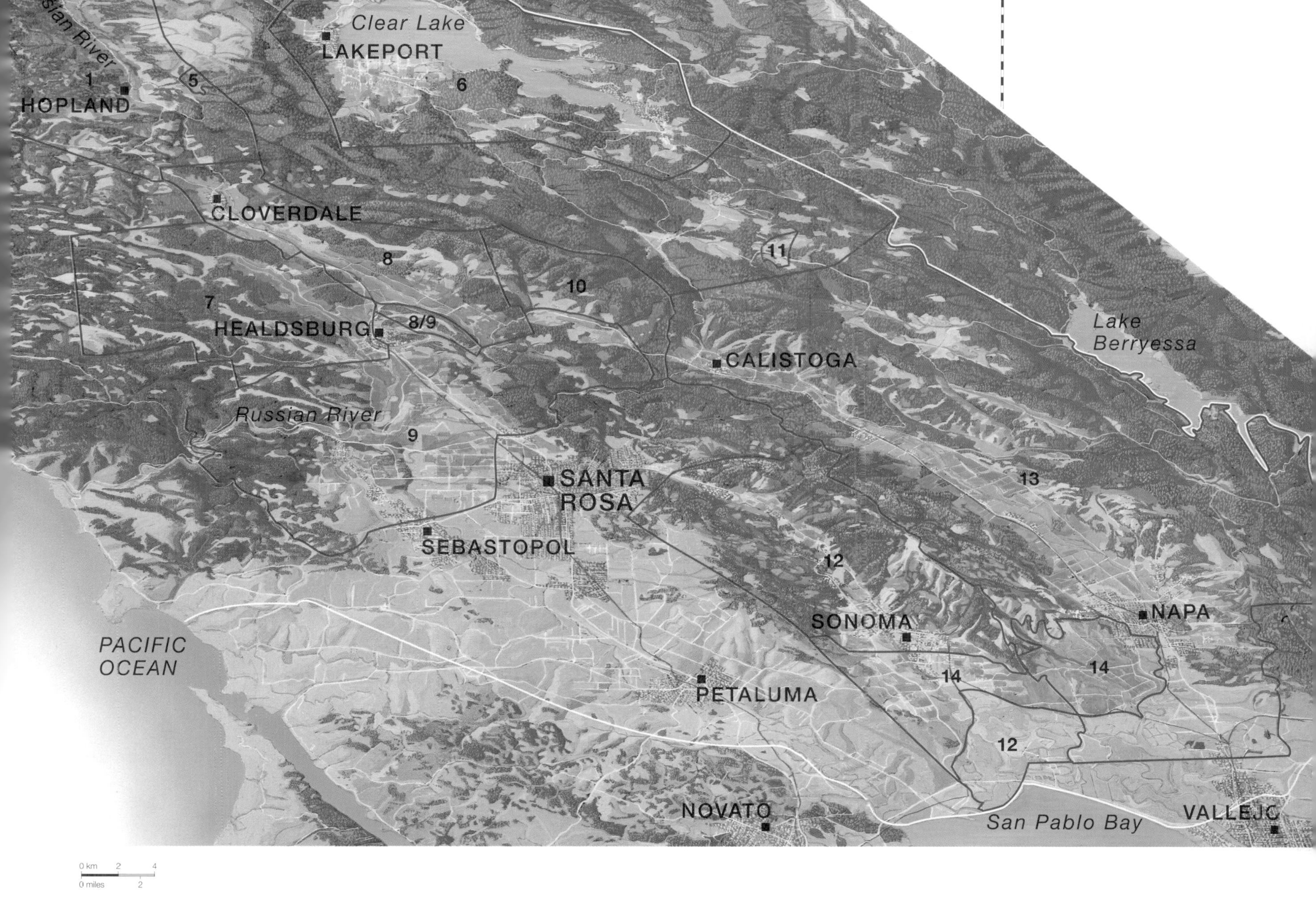
MAIN AVA WINE AREAS
1. Mendocino
2. Anderson Valley
3. Cole Ranch
4. Potter Valley
5. McDowell Valley
6. Clear Lake
7. Dry Creek Valley
8. Alexander Valley
9. Russian River Valley
10. Knights Valley
11. Guenoc Valley
12. Sonoma Valley
13. Napa Valley
14. Los Carneros
VINEYARDS
CALIFORNIA NORTH COAST AVA BOUNDARY
OTHER AVA BOUNDARIES
TOTAL DISTANCE NORTH TO SOUTH 139KM (86 MILES)
N
UKIAH
Russian River
HOPLAND
Clear Lake
LAKEPORT
CLOVERDALE
HEALDSBURG
8/9
CALISTOGA
Lake Berryessa
Russian River
SANTA ROSA
SEBASTOPOL
SONOMA
NAPA
PACIFIC OCEAN
PETALUMA
NOVATO
San Pablo Bay
VALLEJO
0 km 2 4
0 miles 2

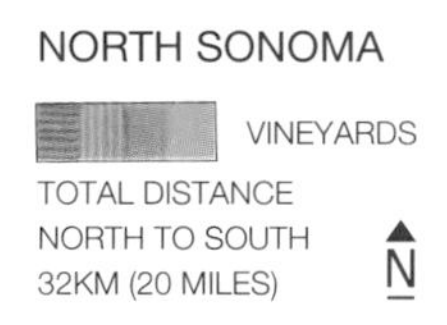

at Kenwood to see off the wispy fingers of fog from the north. But this double influence does make for unpredictable, if cool, conditions particularly south of the town of Glen Ellen, where the Mayacamas and Sonoma mountains crowd in on the valley from the east and west. Good Chardonnay, Pinot Noir and Merlot are grown in these cooler climates – as you'd expect with Carneros nudging the southern border.

Conditions change dramatically when you climb above the fog line. On the west-facing slopes of the Mayacamas, the greater intensity of afternoon sunshine produces deep-fruited, dark-hearted Cabernets and Zinfandels. Sonoma Mountain is also above the fog line, but has more vineyards angled east-to-north-east to avoid direct exposure to the midday and afternoon rays. With relatively warm nights due to the fogs on the valley floor pushing warmer air up the mountain sides, equally intense, but more thrillingly fragrant and soft-hearted Cabernets and Zinfandels are produced, as well as a famous Chardonnay at McCrea vineyard south-west of Glen Ellen.

So. That's Sonoma County – except for the section of Carneros which lies within its territory (see page 240). Now let's head back to Healdsburg, turn east through Knights Valley, and swoop down into Calistoga at the head of Napa Valley.

NAPA VALLEY

The valley is only about 48km (30 miles) long, running north-west to south-east, but the difference in conditions along this short distance is dramatic. Calistoga, at the head of the valley, has a daytime climate hot enough to ripen every known red variety, and is only saved from being a cauldron in which to bake the life out of its fruit by the ice-cold air that drains down the high mountains hemming it in on three sides. Yet down at the mouth of the valley is Carneros, continually chilled by fogs and gales, only able to ripen its cool-climate Pinot Noir and Chardonnay because of the brief bursts of sun that separate the morning fogs from the afternoon wind.

And throughout most of the valley, it is still the climatic conditions that govern what types of grape are grown and what wines excel, rather than the soils and their exposure to the sun. There are, in fact, more soil types in Napa, I'm told, than in the whole of France, and some committed growers are trying to match variety with soil conditions as they replant. But, with a few brilliant exceptions such as the well-drained fans of soil around Rutherford and Oakville, much of the soil on the Napa Valley floor is heavy, clayish, over-fertile and difficult to drain, and certainly unfit to make great wine. There's no shame in this because much of Bordeaux's great Médoc region cannot spawn a decent grape. The only shame is in pretending it isn't so.

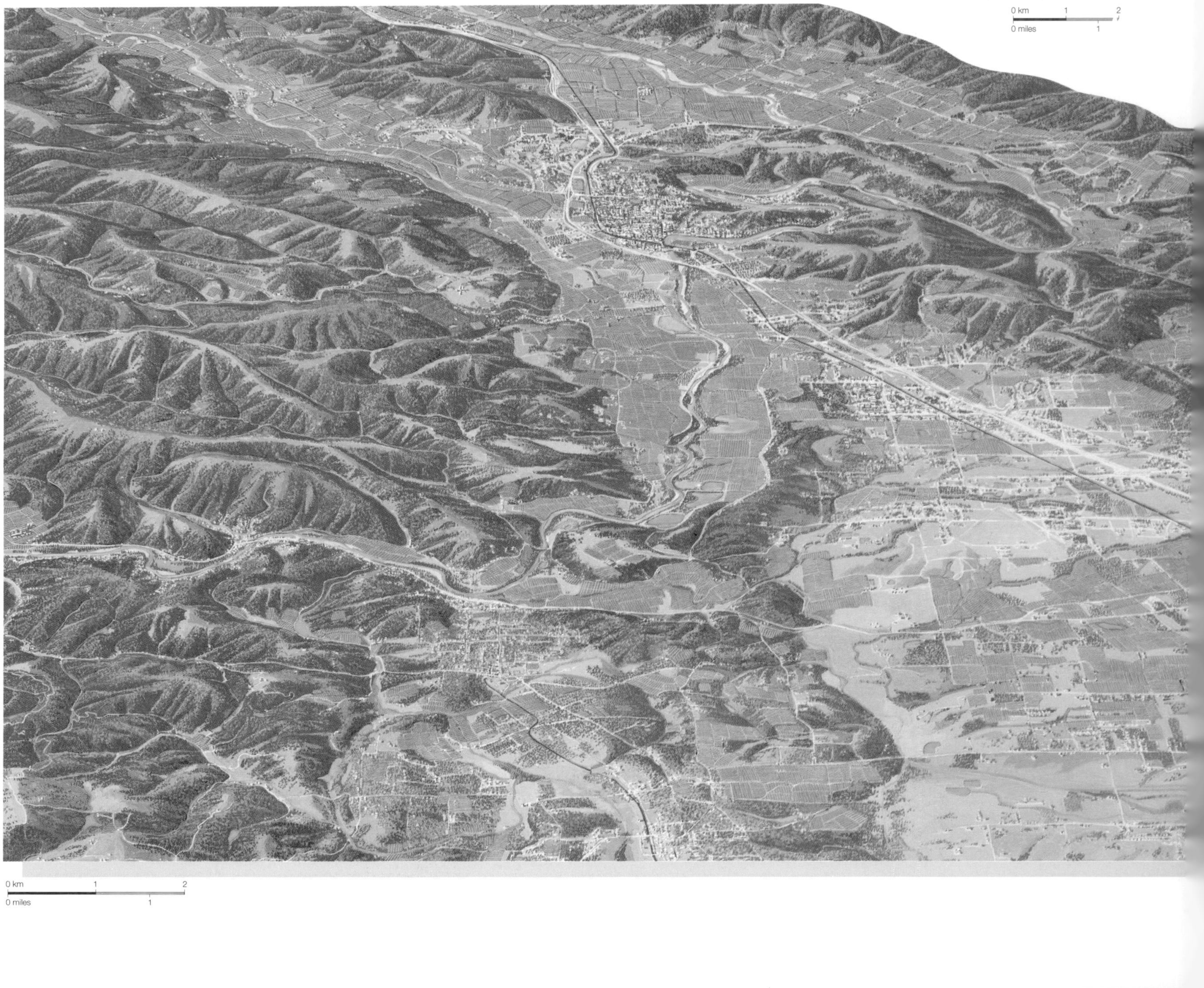

The trouble is that the wines made from the good soil have been so good that every man and his dog wanted a piece of the action. When two Napa wines, a Chardonnay and a Cabernet Sauvignon, won the famous 'Judgement of Paris' tasting in 1976 against Grand Cru white Burgundy and Premier Cru Bordeaux, Napa became a promised land – for those with ambition and money. Vineyards were planted and wineries sprang up like mushrooms after rain; a couple of dozen wineries at the end of the 1960s had become over 200 by the beginning of the 1990s. And, sadly, this traffic jam of growers and producers, many blending grapes and wines from sites all over the valley and outside it as well, has led to a blurring of personality and a dilution of recognizable flavours. Winemakers have frequently compounded the problem by applying rigid, college textbook wine-making methods rather than seeking to maximize the individuality of each batch of fruit by evolving their own. However, brilliant conditions do exist in Napa Valley, and there are committed owners and gifted winemakers at work. So let's see where they grow their fruit.

We'll work from north to south. And we'll stick to the valley floor first, and then look into the mountains where some of the most exciting fruit is grown. Calistoga at the head of the valley has a touch of the frontier town about it, with a more rough-hewn feel than the other wine towns and villages, and I always head here to try to dissolve some of the black Cabernet tannin off my teeth with draughts of tasty home-brewed ale. But it has good vineyards too. One or two mesoclimates like Storybook Mountain to the north-west of Calistoga produce startling Zinfandel; otherwise, the rocky outcrops and sandy loams produce good results with Cabernet and Merlot.

Just above St Helena the Napa Valley changes direction: instead of running east-south-east, it alters to something more like south-south-east and it keeps this orientation more or less until Carneros. As the valley begins to broaden out, vineyards stretch right across the valley floor, though the best, like Spottswoode, Grace Family and Chabot, are still tucked into the base of the mountain slopes on either side.

The only time when there seems to be a general consensus about valley floor conditions being truly excellent over one great swathe rather than just in dribs and drabs, is at Rutherford and Oakville. All the great original Cabernet Sauvignon vineyards were planted here, some over 100 years ago, mostly on the so-called Rutherford Bench. Two alluvial fans spread out at Rutherford and at Oakville, though Rutherford attached its name to the Bench first. They are well-drained in Napa terms, though also heavy enough to hold moisture during summer, and they slope just perceptibly towards Highway 29, which is crucial for drainage. Whether or not these soils go beyond the road is one of those arguments to keep lawyers and pedants happy for generations. Suffice it to say that Napa Valley Cabernet made its reputation on fruit from these Rutherford and Oakville acres.

But was it just the soil? I personally think the soil gets heavier and more cloddish east of the road, but fine Cabernets still turn up from sites not only east of the road, but east of the river too. Nevertheless, the Rutherford Bench and Oakville vineyards do seem to have struck the right balance between water-holding and drainage, between vigour and restraint, for

Young Chardonnay vines near Forestville in the Russian River Valley will help fulfill the demand for the area's Chardonnay, much of it used in sparkling wine.

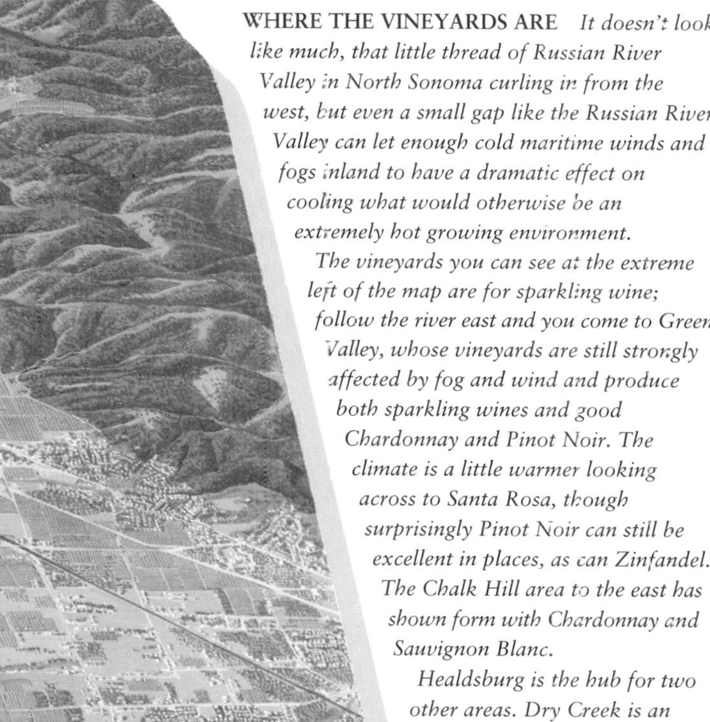

WHERE THE VINEYARDS ARE *It doesn't look like much, that little thread of Russian River Valley in North Sonoma curling in from the west, but even a small gap like the Russian River Valley can let enough cold maritime winds and fogs inland to have a dramatic effect on cooling what would otherwise be an extremely hot growing environment.*

The vineyards you can see at the extreme left of the map are for sparkling wine; follow the river east and you come to Green Valley, whose vineyards are still strongly affected by fog and wind and produce both sparkling wines and good Chardonnay and Pinot Noir. The climate is a little warmer looking across to Santa Rosa, though surprisingly Pinot Noir can still be excellent in places, as can Zinfandel. The Chalk Hill area to the east has shown form with Chardonnay and Sauvignon Blanc.

Healdsburg is the hub for two other areas. Dry Creek is an excellent warm region in a short, north-west-running valley. And north of Healdsburg, Alexander Valley provides some of California's most approachable, super-textured Cabernets.

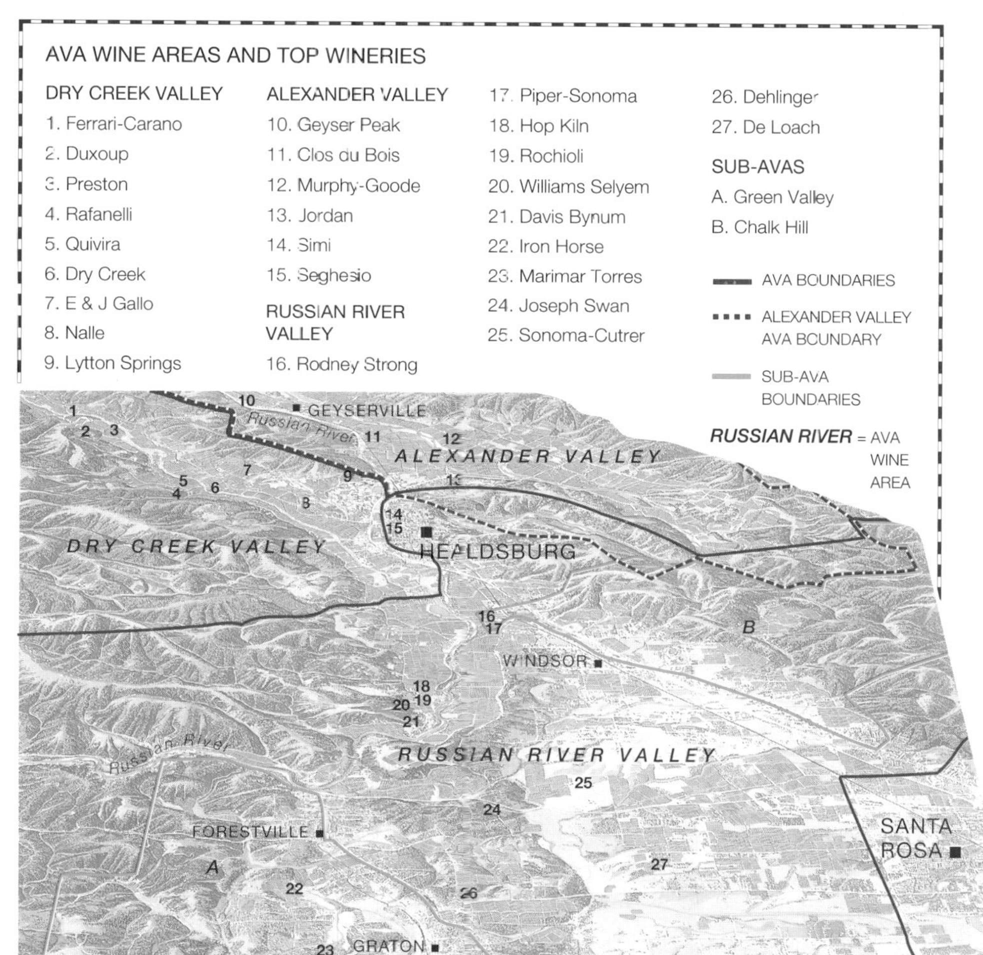

the climatic conditions of this particular part of the Napa Valley. Imprecise, sure. But there's more than a century of experience that says it's so. This imprecise but definable balance of elements affecting the grape is what the French would call *terroir*. It took them quite a while to work it out too.

Since no-one, unsurprisingly, will agree on what was Bench and what wasn't, Rutherford and Oakville have simply settled for separate AVAs. Cabernet is what they do best, but there's good Chardonnay and Sauvignon Blanc too. Yet when you drive past the bluffs in the middle of the valley, just north of Yountville, you're driving past a barrier to the fog and wind that brings about a discernible dip in temperature to their south. Yountville is decidedly cooler than Oakville and it gets even cooler down by the town of Napa. They do grow reds here, but the most impressive results are from Chardonnay.

The Mayacamas Range to the west is a collection of gaunt, thinly populated peaks, with coyotes, rattlesnakes and wild deer as likely to impede your progress as humans. But they do harbour some smashing vineyards, especially on Mount Veeder, Spring Mountain and Diamond Mountain. We're talking primarily incisive, focussed red wines from low-yielding volcanic soils at heights that can go past 600m (2000ft).

Stags Leap District spreads out onto the valley floor and up the sides of several small hillocks about a mile away from the eastern mountains proper, towards Yountville, and produces Cabernets that are rich, pinging with fruit, yet artfully balancing tannin and acidity. Many Californian wine regions acquire their fame through relentless marketing effort. Stags Leap is famous because its wines taste better. Higher up the eastern mountains are Atlas Peak, Chiles Valley, Pope Valley and above all, Howell Mountain, whose vineyards 600m (2000ft) up give deliciously scented, but sturdy, reds.

LOS CARNEROS

The final vineyard area in the North Coast, and one of the most important in California, is Carneros. In the search to make wines of a supposedly European delicacy and finesse, Carneros was singled out as long ago as 1938 by Californian wine wizard André Tchelistcheff, but had been growing vines for maybe a century before that. It was the very un-California-ness that

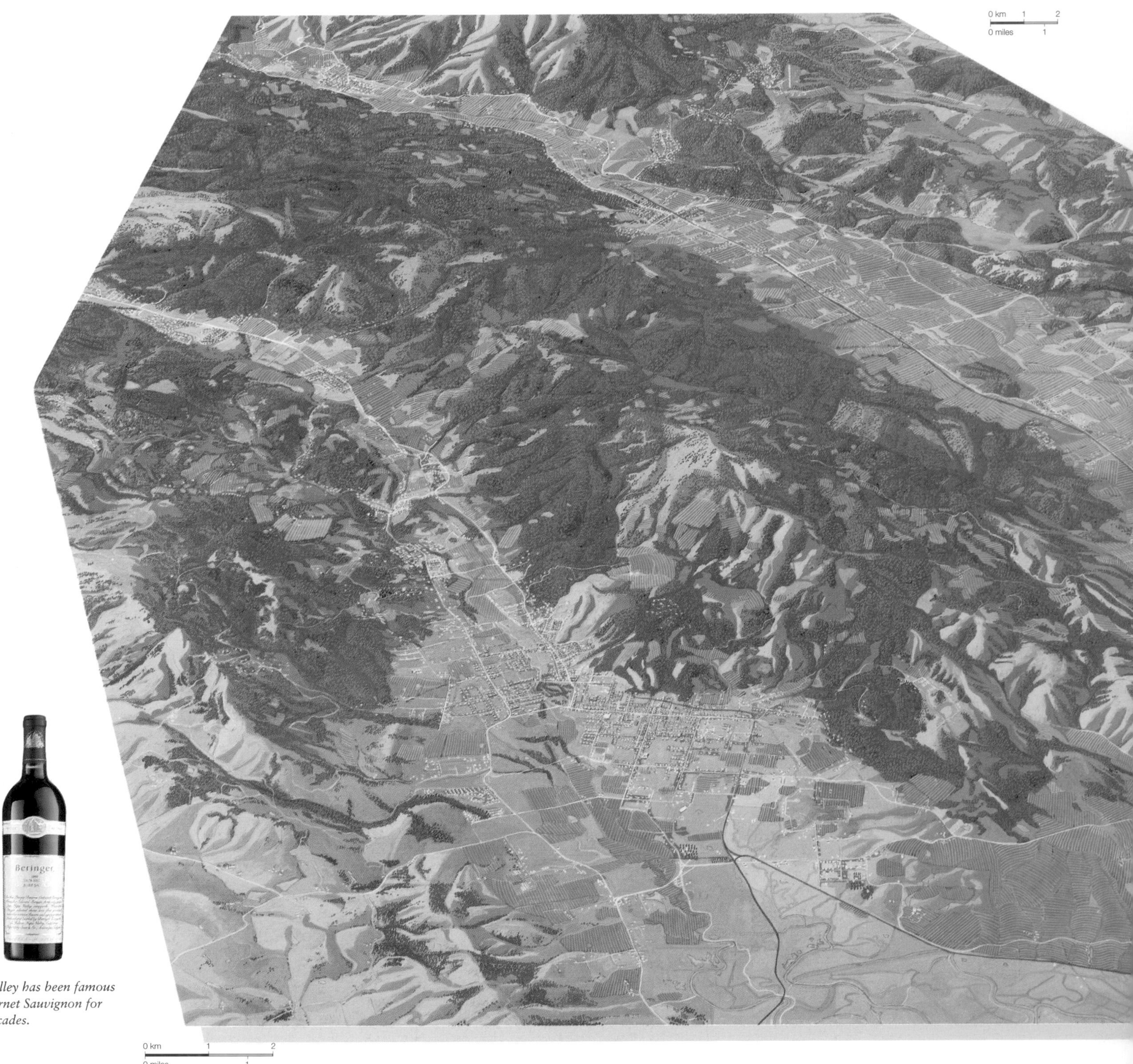

Napa Valley has been famous for Cabernet Sauvignon for many decades.

attracted Tchelistcheff – small crops and small grapes struggling manfully to survive in conditions which included difficult soil and not enough rain, and with fog and wind a virtual certainty throughout the growing season. Delicate Pinot Noirs, zingy, crisp Chardonnays and tartly refreshing sparkling wines, along with the occasional fine Merlot and decent Cabernet all bear a 'European' look, though the vineyards and the climate resemble nowhere in Europe's winelands that I know of.

The Carneros wine region slithers across the southern end of Napa and Sonoma, the Mayacamas and Sonoma mountains splaying their feet into a series of rumpled hummocks that gradually subside into the water of San Pablo Bay. Farmers have always known that this was difficult soil to grow anything on, and traditionally most of it was consigned to grazing. With an annual rainfall that is the lowest in both Napa and Sonoma counties – usually about 560mm (22in) – and a shallow, silty soil often only a couple of feet above impenetrable, dense clay, few people felt inclined to plant the area.

And then, when the search for a cool-climate vineyard began, they were converted. The Golden Gate gap at San Francisco is the only place the Pacific Ocean breaches the Coast Ranges to form the vast enclosed sea of San Francisco Bay and San Pablo Bay. And as the fogs and the winds are sucked inwards by the baking heat of the inland valleys, the first land they come to is Carneros. Fogs blanket Carneros during the summer nights; these clear by late morning, to be replaced by bright sunshine – and then up comes the afternoon breeze, merely strong or positively howling depending on the conditions that day.

The net result of this combination of hot sun and clammy fog is a very long, cool ripening period, from early March to well into October. The wind cools the vines, but its strength can also cause the vines' photosynthetic system to shut down temporarily, delaying ripening. This is almost too much for most grape varieties, but remember, even if the warmth of Carneros is not that much different from somewhere like Chablis in Burgundy, we're at latitude 38° North here. That's the equivalent of the toe of Italy in Europe. The intensity of sunshine, warm or hot, is massively greater in southern Italy than in northern France. And it's the same in Carneros.

WHERE THE VINEYARDS ARE *This magnificent map is almost too much of a good thing, because so many of California's great vineyards are packed into the flatlands of Sonoma, Carneros and Napa and up on the surrounding mountains that I hardly know where to start. But I'll try.*

Let's begin with Carneros, which extends across the bottom of the map. To the south, just off this map, are the waters of San Pablo Bay, whose roaring winds and billowing fogs affect all these vineyards, especially those nearest the Bay. The cooling influences do extend up the Sonoma and Napa valleys, lessening as they go. North-west of the town of Sonoma are the fine vineyards of Sonoma Mountain, while there are equally good sites in the Mayacamas mountains directly north of Sonoma. Crossing over to the Napa side of the Mayacamas, Diamond Mountain (west above Calistoga), Spring Mountain and Mount Veeder all have fine, high-altitude vineyards, as does Howell Mountain to the north-east of St Helena. There are also excellent sites in Stags Leap, east of Yountville, and on various patches of hillside near Napa itself. The valley floor is a carpet of vines, from cool Napa right up to warm Calistoga, and the most famous sites are at Oakville and Rutherford.

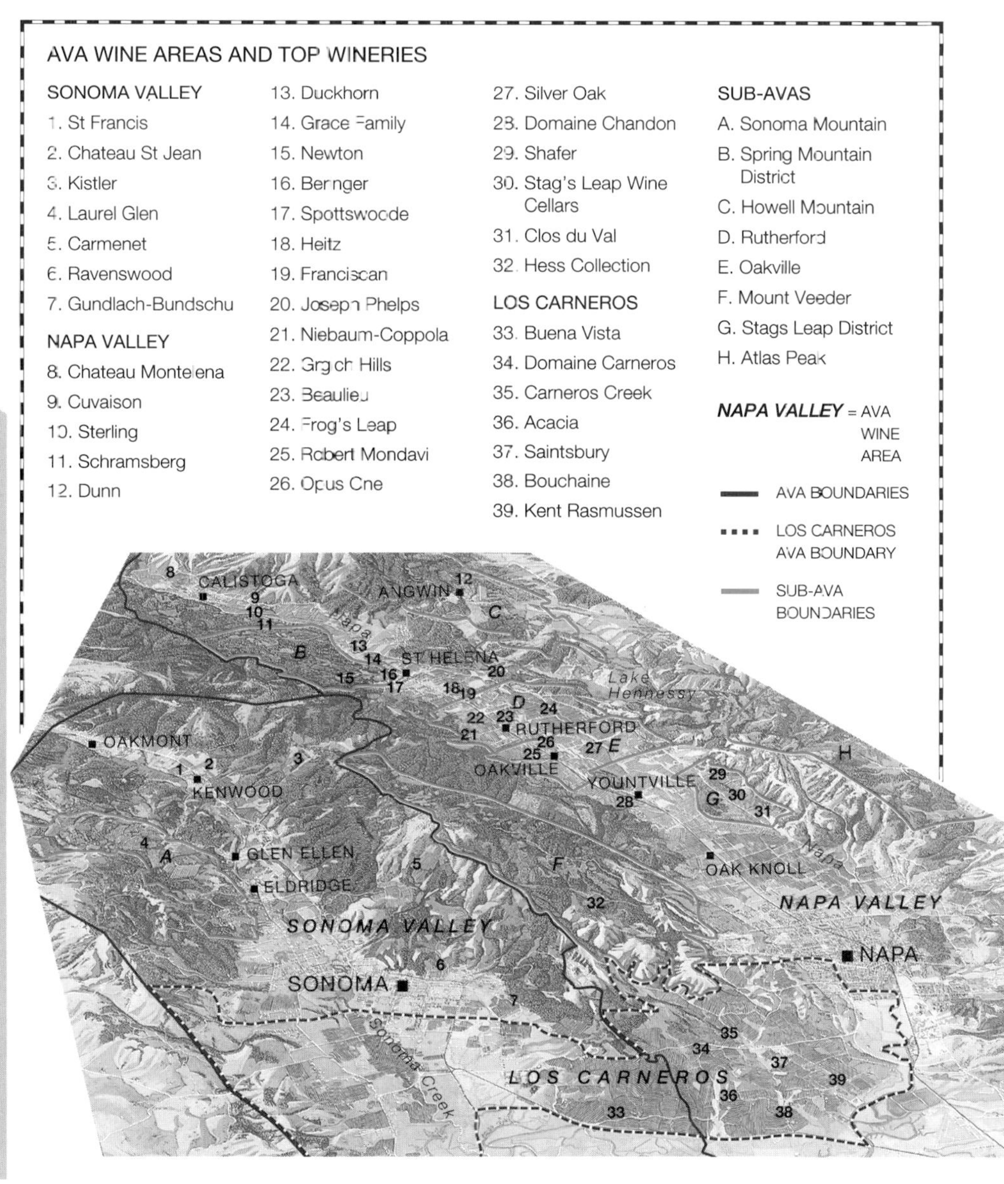

North Central Coast

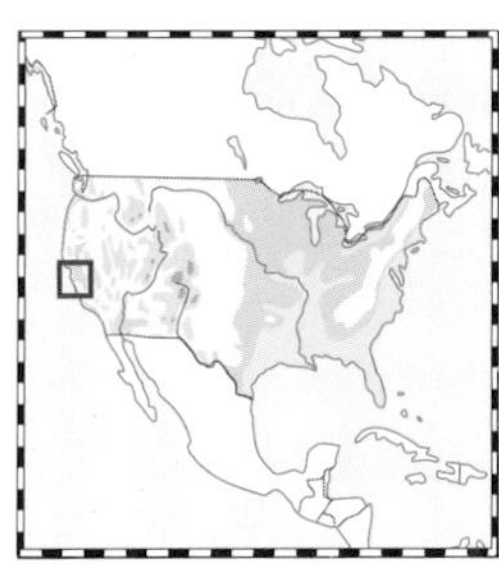

RED GRAPES
Cabernet Sauvignon, Pinot Noir and Zinfandel are widely planted. Minor varieties include Petite Sirah and Merlot.

WHITE GRAPES
Chardonnay and Sauvignon Blanc are ever-present plus Chenin Blanc, Riesling and Pinot Blanc.

CLIMATE
This ranges from cool and foggy when influenced by San Francisco and Monterey bays, to dry and very hot. Strong, incessant winds can also represent a threat to the vineyards. Rainfall is low.

SOIL
A wide variety of soils includes gravel, stones of considerable size, clay and loam, with occasional granite and limestone outcrops. These can be mixed, even within single vineyards.

ASPECT
Vineyard exposure is very important in order to ensure correct ripening of the grapes. Elevation varies widely, causing great differences in the influence of fog, sunshine and wind.

THERE AREN'T MANY OF MY FAVOURITE VINEYARDS that I can say I prefer to visit at night, but Ridge, high in the Santa Cruz Mountains, is one of them. Climb to the top of the rise above the tasting room on the night of a full moon. As the moon hangs heavy in the vast night sky, its cloak of silver stars spread-eagled across the purple blackness, the dark crags of the forested mountain peaks pierce the pale night light to the west. And to the east, 600m (2000ft) below me, lies the bustling city of San José, so far below that the brilliant city lights are just twinkling patterns on the valley floor. The sullen drone of its cars and businesses fades to silence halfway up my mountain slope, and away to the north, San Francisco Bay glows with a faint pewter sheen.

Ridge is the most famous of the wineries that are sprinkled sparsely around San Francisco Bay itself. There used to be many more, but as the Bay area's urban sprawl reaches further into the hinterland, few wineries or vineyards have been able to resist the temptation of the easier profits to be gained by selling up to housing developers. But that doesn't mean the companies have all gone out of business. They haven't. They've simply moved their vineyard interests south. This North Central Coast region divides neatly into the old regions of Livermore, Santa Clara and Santa Cruz, where wineries outnumber vineyards, and the great new tracts of land centered on Monterey County, where wineries are few and far between, but contract vineyards can stretch as far as the eye can see.

You have to use your imagination in the Livermore Valley to see it as one of the original great vineyard sites of California. Getting there either from the north or the south is a seemingly endless trek through industrial parks and housing subdivisions which don't let up till you're right in the vineyards themselves, glancing nervously at the nuclear facility to one side and the futuristic wind generator farms to the other. But Livermore is a fine vineyard site, albeit one that has its back to the wall as the late-twentieth century decides its land is more useful for houses and factories. There are still about 650 hectares (1600 acres) of vines, mostly owned by the Wente family who are staunchly leading a fight back against urbanization.

Livermore is relatively warm because hills to the west block off most of the chill Pacific winds, and its gravelly Médoc-like soils promise good results from grapes like Cabernet Sauvignon. Curiously, the reds are not that special, but the white Bordeaux specialities – Sémillon and Sauvignon Blanc – can be outstanding here.

Santa Clara County's vines have been pushed relentlessly south by San José's suburbs, and it is really only around Gilroy that you get a sense of a wine culture still hanging on. Gilroy is the self-dubbed 'garlic capital of the world' and, boy, can you smell it when you stop on Highway 101 to fill up with gas. But good fruit is grown to the east of town, and if you turn west off 101 and head up through the Hecker Pass, you'll find remnants of the old farmgate Italian wineries that used to pepper Santa Clara and Santa Cruz counties. Santa Cruz County is important for its wineries, rather than its vineyards, though locals estimate there may be 160 hectares (400 acres) or more of vines sprinkled through the majestic forested hills that rear up on this Pacific Coast between San Francisco and the resort of Santa Cruz. Some of these vines – as at Bonny Doon, Mount Eden, David Bruce and, of course, Ridge – produce stunning wines, but much fruit is bought in from other areas. It is impossible to characterize the Santa Cruz conditions, with vineyards ranging in height from over 600m (2000ft) high down to the fog level, and with aspects to the east, south, north and west, but a good deal of the soil is infertile, impoverished shale which keeps yields low and contributes to the startling flavours in many of the local wines.

Startling flavours were nearly the undoing of the other part of the North Central Coast – the vast, flat, supremely fertile, dark-soiled acres of Monterey County. The 'Monterey veggies' these flavours were called, and since, as I head down for Santa Cruz, I pass through Watsonville, Prunedale, Castroville, Salinas and so on, towns which variously proclaim themselves World Capital of the artichoke kingdom, or prunes, or broccoli, lettuces and pretty well anything else a starving vegetarian might crave – I suppose I shouldn't be too surprised.

The Salinas Valley in Monterey County does have every reason to proclaim itself the Salad Bowl of America, and most of its eerily flat valley floor is given over to intensive vegetable and fruit cultivation. However, as long ago as 1935, experts were suggesting it would be a good area for grape vines, and when the Bay area vineyards were squeezed by urban development in the late 1950s and 1960s, big companies like Masson and Mirassou upped sticks and headed south to the Salinas Valley, planting like fury as they came.

At its peak, Monterey County had 14,000 hectares (35,000 acres); one vineyard alone near King City was 18 by 8km (11 by 5 miles). The only problem was they mostly planted the wrong grapes, and in the wrong places, and in particular, too many red grapes, too near the sea.

Let me explain. The first point is, as usual in California, the influence of the Pacific Ocean. Monterey Bay is about 56km (35 miles) wide and acts as an enormous funnel at the mouth of the Salinas Valley. Its waters stay at a chilly 13°C (55°F) all year round. Looking

AVA WINE AREAS

- Livermore Valley
- Santa Cruz Mountains (sub-AVA Ben Lomond Mountain)
- Santa Clara Valley (sub-AVA San Ysidro)
- Mount Harlan
- Carmel Valley
- Santa Lucia Highlands
- Arroyo Seco
- Chalone
- San Lucas
- OVER 500M (1640FT)
- OVER 1000M (3280FT)

Bonny Doon's fancifully named Le Cigare Volant has a bizarre but distinctive label.

The Jekel Vineyard, with its well-known red barn winery, was one of the first wineries in Arroyo Seco, in the heart of the large Salinas Valley.

south-east up the valley, the Santa Lucia mountains lie between the ocean and the valley, virtually without a break along their 138-km (86-mile) length. On the inland side, the Gabilan mountains are much more broken up, with large gaps leading through into the Central Valley. The Central Valley bakes daily under the sun, its hot air rises, creating a thirsty vacuum which then sucks the cold Monterey Bay air up the valley with sometimes terrifying ferocity. The closer to the sea, the colder and more violent the wind. It's cold enough to destroy any vine's chance of ripening and violent enough to rip the branches off a tree, let alone a young vine trying to set its first crop.

As we move further up the Salinas Valley, the winds become milder and warmer. At Gonzales, you can just about ripen white grapes, you can ripen most red grapes by Soledad and Greenfield, and by King City, with the wind dropping to a pleasant breeze, you can ripen anything, although, so far, nobody's been thrilled by the result. There is very little rainfall throughout the valley – an average of 250mm (10in) a year – and with the eternal sunshine, some growers claim that the valley has the longest ripening period in the world. With budbreak as early as February due to the mild winters, and an autumn that can linger on into December, they may well be right, though you'll hear the same claim from growers in Edna Valley and Santa Maria Valley further south.

But where's the Salinas River? Right under your feet. In fact, the Salinas River is California's largest underground river and is fed by the Santa Lucia, Gabilan and Diablo ranges. Given that the soil is mostly deep, free-draining silt and sandy loam, I can see why the early pioneers saw it as a paradise for the vine. But the vine is a greedy plant, and the early plantations suffered from massive over-irrigation, leading to vigorous vines pushing out forests full of foliage – and producing grapes of a decidedly green vegetable flavour that gave wines with an equally vegetal taste. If we humans were going to gain any benefit from this paradise, we were going to have to take the vine firmly in hand.

Vineyard management in the late 1990s is now far more advanced. The cooler areas are left to white grapes, irrigation is properly controlled, and areas away from the valley floor have been developed for higher quality whites and reds – indeed, the only exciting wines have come from these sites. Facing north-east towards Gonzales and Soledad are the Santa Lucia Highland slopes; Carmel Valley and Arroyo Seco have some favoured spots; and high up in the Gabilan range, both Chalone and Calera make world class reds and whites in splendid isolation.

A gruff old Frenchman, André Noblet, the legendary winemaker at Domaine de la Romanée-Conti at Vosne-Romanée in the heart of Burgundy, would murmur 'limestone, limestone' under his breath in response to the endless requests from callow young Americans about his marvellous wines, and the magic ingredient that made them so special. This belief in the power of limestone so devotedly held by Burgundy's top winemaker provided the spur for Calera and Chalone, which are now two of California's most famous – and most individual – wines.

Limestone isn't easy to find in California, but is at the heart of the greatest sites in Burgundy – places where finesse usually wins over power. In the nineteenth century one roving Frenchman called Curtis Tamm searched along the Californian coast for years for limestone soil to make sparkling wine. He finally found what he wanted on a parched wilderness 600m (2000ft) up in the Gabilan range below the Pinnacles peaks, the site of the present-day Chalone. A dozen miles north, 670m (2200ft) up on the north-east-facing slopes of Mount Harlan, Josh Jensen established Calera on limestone soils he had to clear of virgin scrub.

This being California, neither winery manages to make wines of Burgundian delicacy, but what they do achieve is something more exhilarating – the savage, growling, unfathomable, dark beauty of the great red wines of Burgundy's Côte de Nuits. In land that deserves a desert rating for its aridity, the grape yields are tiny (as they have to be with Pinot Noir), the methods of wine-making are traditional to a fault, and as is the case of their Burgundian role models, the Chalone and Calera Pinot Noirs are of an unpredictable yet magnificent brilliance.

South Central Coast

RED GRAPES
While Cabernet Sauvignon has greater acreage in Santa Barbara, Pinot Noir is better suited to local conditions. In San Luis Obispo, Cabernet and Zinfandel are planted extensively, with increasing amounts of Pinot Noir, Syrah, Nebbiolo and Sangiovese.

WHITE GRAPES
Chardonnay is widely planted, with lesser amounts of Sauvignon Blanc, Riesling and Gewürztraminer.

CLIMATE
Differences are huge, being largely related to the influence of the Pacific sea fogs.

SOIL
Alkaline sandy and clay loams, with some rich limestone.

ASPECT
Paso Robles vineyards are on a valley floor sheltered by mountains. Santa Maria has half its vines on benchlands above the fog line.

I'M AFRAID I ONLY get to see Paso Robles, the northernmost wine region of the so-called South Central Coast, if I'm in a hurry. There it is, straddling Highway 101 right at the source of the Salinas River; it seems easy enough to get to. But there's another road southwards from Santa Cruz and Monterey. Highway 1. Hugging the coastline, dipping and diving in and out of the cliff face and soaring up above the crashing ocean waves, and – I'm a 60s boy remember – traversing Little Sur, Point Sur and Big Sur, what am I supposed to do? Hurry down boring old 101, or bask in the glory of this wild Pacific coast.

Well, I take Highway 1, don't I? Not a vine in sight, and no passing places. I once left Santa Cruz to try to make a lunch appointment in Santa Barbara County. Unwisely, but inevitably, I took Highway 1. And I got behind a band of six camper vans, laden with spaced-out hippies dawdling contentedly down the coast, drinking in every second of the majesty of Big Sur and its stuff of dreams. Lunch? I just about made dinner. Luckily my host was a dreamer, a romantic – and an ace winemaker. He understood.

Paso Robles, though, *is* a good wine area. Right next door to the rather underperforming San Lucas region, it should really be taken as the southern outpost of North Central Coast rather than the northern outpost of South Central Coast. I know, I know. Does it really matter? No. Do I care? No. Its just another example of the AVA system doggedly following political boundaries, not geological ones. Paso Robles is the highpoint in the Salinas Valley that runs north-west through Monterey County to the sea. And its hot, dry climate is the natural progression from foggy and cold at the seaward end to baking and arid at its head as the influence of Monterey Bay's chilly waters is finally dissipated under the burning sun.

But the San Luis Obispo County line crunches across the map about 14km (8½ miles) north of Paso Robles, so Paso Robles is in South Central. Never mind that a 460-m (1500-ft) high pass has to be traversed to get down to the sea level of San Luis Obispo. Nor that San Luis Obispo's reputation is for some of the coolest-climate fruit in the whole of California, as the fog and sea breezes chill Edna Valley and Arroyo Grande so successfully that some of the most Burgundian Chardonnay in the state comes from Edna Valley, and some of the best sparkling wine comes from Arroyo Grande.

Well, that's the way it is. So let's turn back up 101 as it heads away from the sea at San Luis Obispo and climbs to the hot inland gaps at Paso Robles. There are several reasons why Paso Robles makes an increasing amount of red wine. It is divided from the Pacific to the west by the 900-m (3000-ft) Santa Lucia Range. Even the California fogs and sea winds can't get over that, although a stiff breeze sometimes works its way up to Templeton along Highway 46 and even causes ripening difficulties for Cabernet in one or two spots south of Templeton. To abet the last gasps of ocean breeze puffing up the valley from Monterey or along Highway 46, you've got altitude. The vineyards are at between 180 and 300m (600 and 985ft), though the small, cool York Mountain area west of Paso Robles reaches 500m (1640ft) above sea level. And being protected from the maritime influence means that temperature plummets at night. In the broiling months of July and August, the difference between day and night temperature is over 22°C (40°F). That's great for the standard of the fruit.

And it is fruit quality that makes Paso Robles exciting. That, and a willingness to break the stranglehold of Cabernet Sauvignon. Paso Robles does have Cabernet, mostly grown on its east side, on river terraces and the rolling grassland of the Estrella Prairie to the north-east, but it has a joyous ripe quality, and minimal tannic intrusion that makes for some of California's most easily enjoyable examples.

The limestone soils to the west are home to numerous old Zinfandel plantings, and both sides of the valley are becoming more interesting for their plantings of Rhône and Italian varieties. The creation of an estate to grow Rhône varieties near Adelaida to the west of Paso Robles by the Perrin Brothers, who own Château de Beaucastel in Châteauneuf-du-Pape, is a clear indication that things are getting exciting down here. Watch this space.

EDNA VALLEY AND ARROYO GRANDE

On into the real San Luis Obispo, and the areas of Edna Valley and Arroyo Grande. Neither of these areas is big, neither is well known, but both are exceptional. And I can vividly remember the first example of each of their wines that I tried. With Edna Valley it was a Chardonnay, made by Dick Graff at Chalone. Was it a 1979, or a 1980? One or the other, it's not important. The wine was dry yet luscious, lean yet viscous with a heavenly savoury quality: butter melting on toast or hazelnuts lightly grilling above a log fire. Such wine was rare enough from Puligny-Montrachet; from California, it was a

Firestone is one of the biggest vineyard owners in Santa Ynez Valley.

WHERE THE VINEYARDS ARE *This map shows in dramatic manner the way that the sea's influence makes great vineyards possible in California. The sea may look nice and blue on the map, but more likely it will be covered with a thick blanket of fog during the summer, and wherever there is a break in the mountains for a river to force its way to the sea, this blanket would stream inland for between 16 and 32km (10 and 20 miles). But that wouldn't look so nice, so we chose a rare, totally sunny summer's day!*

Right at the top of the map, look how dry and parched the land seems to be around Paso Robles. It is parched, and the vineyards here are only slightly cooled by air currents from the Salinas Valley to the north and the odd breeze from the west that comes up from the sea through what is known as the Templeton Gap. Most of the vineyards are in the drylands, east of Paso Robles, but there are some excellent sites in the wooded hills to the west.

However, near San Luis Obispo, Edna Valley and Arroyo Grande are both strongly influenced by maritime cool, and the vineyards just east of Arroyo Grande are some of the coolest for sparkling wine in the state. It's far too cold for vines west of Santa Maria, but south and east, the conditions are perfect. Many people think this may prove to be one of California's top vineyard regions for Chardonnay and Pinot Noir – and I'm one of them. Lompoc is also too cold, but a few miles east along the Santa Ynez Valley are some of the best cool-climate vineyards in California, gradually warming up as the valley opens out at Santa Ynez and Los Olivos.

revelation. The Arroyo Grande wine was hidden in an endless line-up of Californian sparkling wines. Just as I was tiring of the unattractive malic greenness of some and the floppy over-ripe dullness of others, I suddenly came upon Maison Deutz, its foaming bubble wheedling a charmed response from my brain. The wine's acidity and fruit were in perfect balance, with a suggestion of yeast, and, just as I thought that was it, a fascinating, irresistible, lingering perfume of good Havana tobacco emerged.

Things haven't changed too much. Chardonnay is still Edna Valley's best wine, and Edna Valley Chardonnay is still one of California's best. Sparkling wine is still Arroyo Grande's strong point, and the vintage releases from Maison Deutz still shine, despite great improvements among the opposition. For once in California we really can thank the soils in Edna Valley. At last, really fine limestone made up of marine fossil deposits high in calcium and therefore ideal for producing white wines. They were left here by the sea 25 million years ago and are similar to the kind that give Chardonnay in Champagne its rare quality. It's obviously much warmer here than in Champagne, but it's cool and temperate by Californian standards, with an early February budbreak and flowering, yet a long, gentle ripening period due to ocean air and fog sucked inland from the sea. These conditions create a particularly long ripening period, and, interestingly, the morning fogs become more frequent in autumn, making the grapes susceptible to noble rot – which adds that touch of magical richness in the finished wine as harvest sometimes lingers on as late as November. Arroyo Grande also has marine deposits in its soil which improves the quality of the fruit, along with a fair bit of

CRESTON
VINEYARDS
1992 Pinot Noir
PASO ROBLES

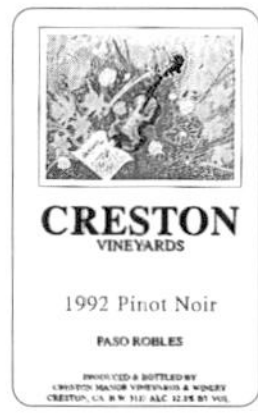

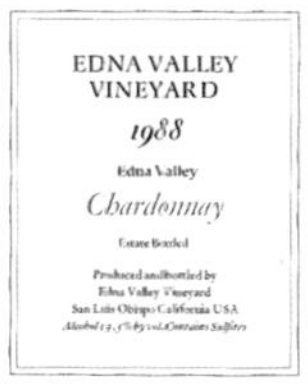
EDNA VALLEY
VINEYARD
1988
Edna Valley
Chardonnay
Estate Bottled
Produced and bottled by
Edna Valley Vineyard
San Luis Obispo California USA

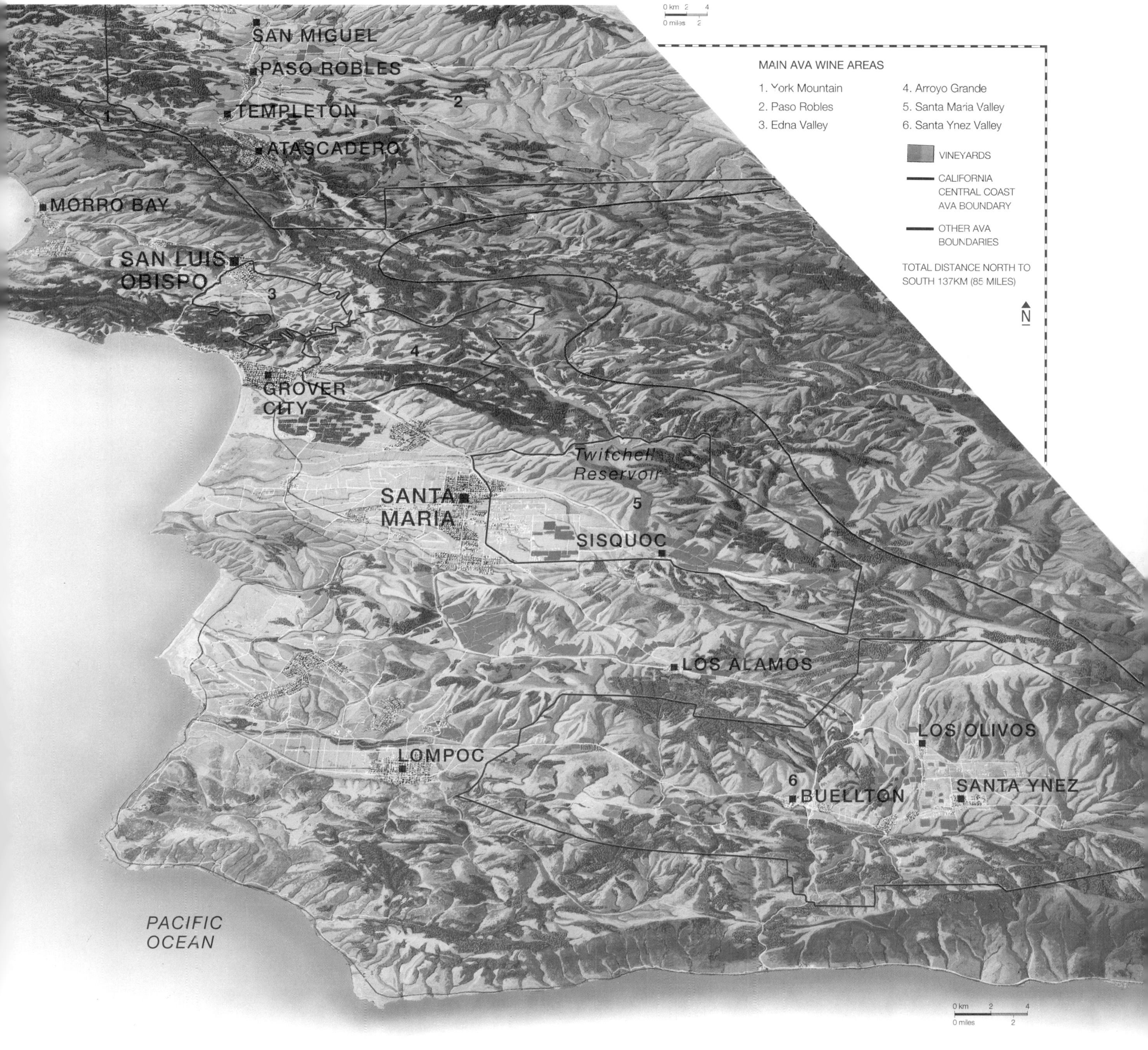
0 km 2 4
0 miles 2
MAIN AVA WINE AREAS
1. York Mountain
2. Paso Robles
3. Edna Valley
4. Arroyo Grande
5. Santa Maria Valley
6. Santa Ynez Valley
VINEYARDS
CALIFORNIA CENTRAL COAST AVA BOUNDARY
OTHER AVA BOUNDARIES
TOTAL DISTANCE NORTH TO SOUTH 137KM (85 MILES)
N
SAN MIGUEL
PASO ROBLES
TEMPLETON
ATASCADERO
MORRO BAY
SAN LUIS OBISPO
GROVER CITY
Twitchell Reservoir
SANTA MARIA
SISQUOC
LOS ALAMOS
LOMPOC
LOS OLIVOS
BUELLTON
SANTA YNEZ
PACIFIC OCEAN
0 km 2 4
0 miles 2

Pinot Noir from the Santa Maria Valley is considered to be some of the best in California.

clay loam. Deutz is down near the sea in the coldest part, and has a mix of Pinot Blanc, Pinot Noir and Chardonnay planted for its fizz, while the highest part of the valley is hot enough to ripen Zinfandel from a patch of vines planted in 1879. And in between, excellent Pinot Noir and Chardonnay is grown by Talley Vineyards. All in less than 16 km (10 miles).

SANTA MARIA VALLEY

Onward down the 101, and over another county line into Santa Barbara County, and the Santa Maria Valley region. I'm beginning to pine for Highway 1 and Big Sur again, because this is dull country. As I swoop into the wide valley, the dusty anonymous town of Santa Maria sprawls away to my right, and to the left, inland, looks like yet another sub-'East of Eden' lettuce prairie spreading gloomily away to the distant hills. OK, time to turn off the freeway. It may not look like much, but the Santa Maria Valley is one of the most important fine wine regions in California, in particular producing Chardonnay that frequently puts better-known vineyard areas north of San Francisco to shame, as well as exciting Pinot Noir and Syrah. But, I admit, it's not pretty.

There are several parallels with the development of Monterey's Salinas Valley further north. During the 1960s and 1970s as demand for wine boomed, various farmers decided to give grapes a try, and planted what rapidly became vast spreads of grapes grown almost entirely for purchase by wineries in other regions which were desperate for a decent supply of grapes. This was fine so long as the demand for grapes outstripped supply, but the 1980s saw a serious over supply situation develop just as the region was finally proving its worth and the reputation for Santa Maria Chardonnay and Pinot Noir was rocketing. With banks and insurance companies repossessing the land, but not at all keen to get into the grape-growing business, three of California's most important quality wineries – Mondavi, Beringer and Kendall-Jackson – put their money where their mouths were and snapped up vast tracts of prime vineyard land to stop any of their rivals getting their hands on it. We consumers are already reaping the benefits in greatly improved Chardonnays from the three players. So, as in the Salinas Valley, most of the vineyard land is held in large blocks, and there are very few local wineries. But as far as quality goes, Santa Maria has won hands down over the Salinas Valley so far.

Sea fogs play a part yet again. Santa Maria must be one of the least pleasant of all wine towns to live in – it gets on average 87 days a year of heavy fog, generally in the late summer to autumn period. The late summer is particularly bad when deep, cold ocean currents well up and are carried inland as the summer progresses, and are pushed southwards along the California coast. By August these cold currents are icing up the shoreline as far south as Santa Barbara County. The wet offshore winds are cooled right down and head inland to meet warm inland air head on – *et voilà* – fog. Loads of it.

But remember we're a long way south here. The sun is incredibly powerful; glance up at the hilltops on both sides of the Santa Maria Valley and they are scorched and wind-swept. So the fog may ooze in from the sea, but it is burnt off by the sun. Yet as soon as that happens, cool ocean breezes take up the slack. So there's loads of sun, but it is always being tempered by the ocean.

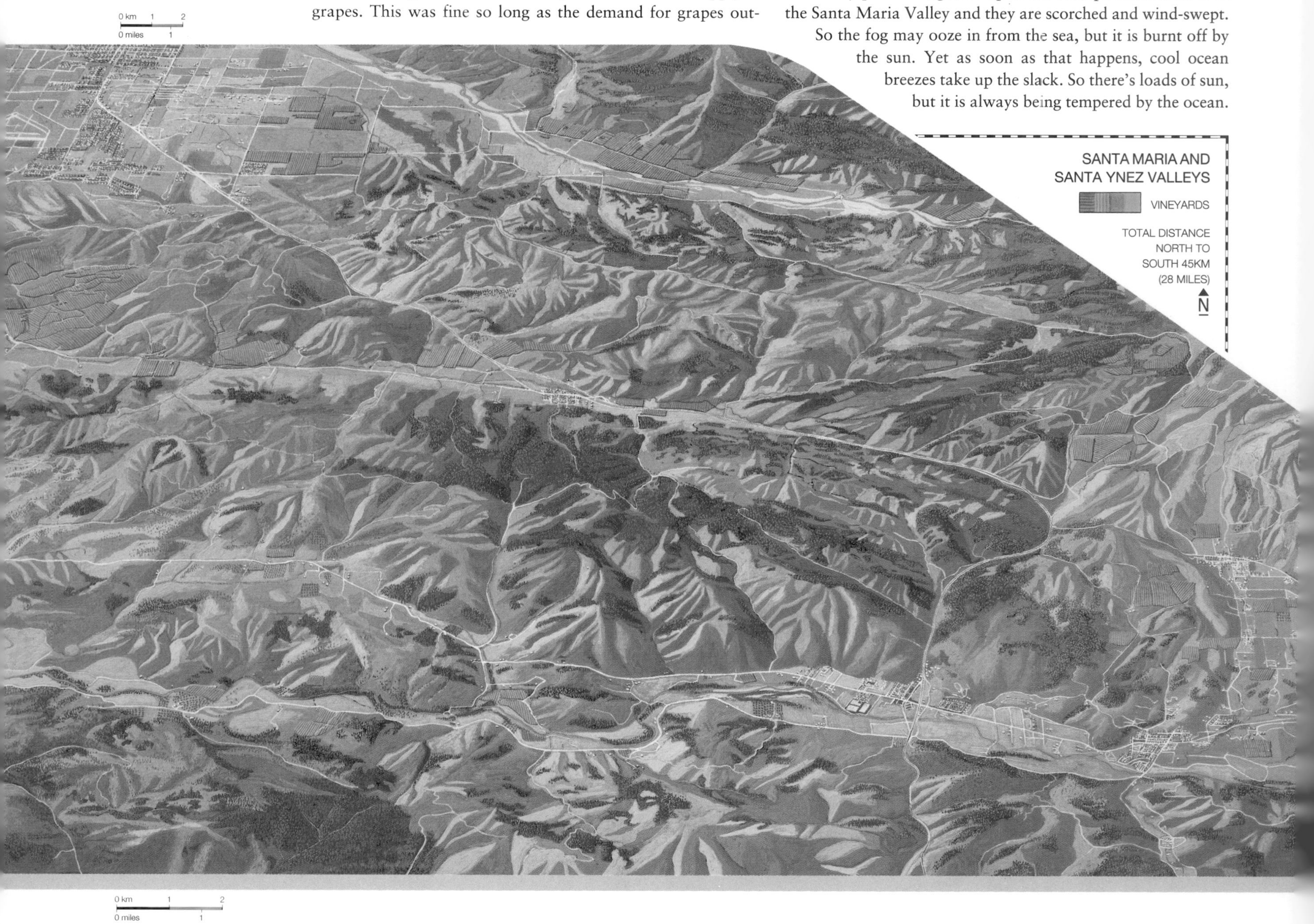

0 km 1 2
0 miles 1

SANTA MARIA AND SANTA YNEZ VALLEYS

VINEYARDS

TOTAL DISTANCE NORTH TO SOUTH 45KM (28 MILES)

N

0 km 1 2
0 miles 1

Average summer temperature is only 24°C (75°F), but the crucial thing, with the danger of the hot afternoon sun, is that the heat peak is at 1.30pm after which up come those cold ocean breezes and get to work sparing the grapes from a roasting. (North of San Francisco in the better-known areas of Sonoma and Napa counties the heat peak is often about 4pm.) Add to that an early budding and flowering in Santa Maria – and, because of the more southerly latitude, a long, reliable autumn giving the grapes extra time to hang on the vine – along with the odd touch of noble rot again, and you've got a Chardonnay nirvana if it's handled properly.

Mostly it is. The soil here is a mix of sandy loam and marine limestones which don't encourage foliage vigour, and lead to yields that can be as little as two or three tons an acre – that's low for California. Most of the vines are managed in an extremely competent manner by farmers who know that – stuck in the middle of a not very attractive nowhere as they are – quality is everything. With average rainfall only running at between 300 and 380mm (12 and 15in) a year, irrigation is essential, but so far, it hasn't been abused.

The majority of the almost 2000 hectares (5000 acres) of vines are situated on a curious ledge to the north of the river called the Santa Maria Mesa, though there are a few excellent properties quite close to Santa Maria township, on the south side of the Santa Maria River. Chardonnay is the clear favourite, but Pinot Noir can be spectacular (from Au Bon Climat and others) and the Bien Nacido ranch even has the Rhône varieties Syrah and Viognier, both of which have already produced startlingly good wines. And a few miles further south, over the Solomon Hills, there are considerable plantings – about 1200 hectares (3000 acres) in total – in Los Alamos, an area without an AVA, but with a good reputation for Chardonnay and Pinot Noir.

SANTA YNEZ VALLEY

While the Santa Maria Valley goes from ultra-cool to, well, mild at best, the Santa Ynez Valley goes from equally cool to hot, so much so that it's hot enough for Cabernet Sauvignon and Merlot to ripen easily in the upstream vineyards. But whereas the Santa Maria Valley is very broad-mouthed, rapidly narrowing as it turns from west to south, Santa Ynez is a narrow valley near the sea which opens out and fragments inland above Solvang. The whole feeling of the valley, only a short distance away from the city of Santa Barbara, couldn't be more different to that of Santa Maria. There are numerous small estates, fine homes, ancient trees and paddocks sporting handsome stallions. It's wealthy country with more than a sprinkling of Hollywood and Los Angeles glamour about it, and this can't have hindered its entry into the limelight during the 1970s as the source of California's supposedly finest Pinot Noirs.

In fact, those early Pinot Noirs were pretty weird, but underlying the maverick wine-making there was a core of exciting fruit, most of all from the mean, shaley soils of the Sanford & Benedict Vineyard 11km (7 miles) west of Buellton, and 29km (18 miles) from the coast. Located at between about 25 and 40km (15 and 25 miles) from the sea, with north-facing slopes avoiding the direct strong afternoon sun, and with the usual fog and sea breezes shrouding the vines until midday, this area is said by some to be the greatest site for Pinot Noir in the whole of California.

Vineyards in Paso Robles produce good quality fruit due to a combination of altitude, sun and low night time temperatures.

WHERE THE VINEYARDS ARE *Santa Barbara County is virtually unique on the US west coast because its river valleys run east to west. Being so far south, Santa Barbara would be too hot were it not for the influence of the cold ocean currents that run along the coast and send cooling fogs and winds inland up the valleys. The town of Santa Maria is at the top of the map and is just too cold for grapes, but as you move up the valley, the effect of fogs and breezes lessens, and vineyards appear. The most important section is the ledge of continual vineyard to the north of the river between Au Bon Climat and Rancho Sisquoc. Just to the south, vineyards along the course of the San Antonio Creek west of Los Alamos are similarly impressive, despite not having their own AVA. The Santa Ynez Valley is very cool at the western end and is a prime site for Pinot Noir. At Solvang the valley splays out and is much warmer, particularly to the east and south. However there are numerous good sites north of Solvang, still warm, but helped by altitude and the remains of the cool air systems of the Santa Maria Valley to the north-west.*

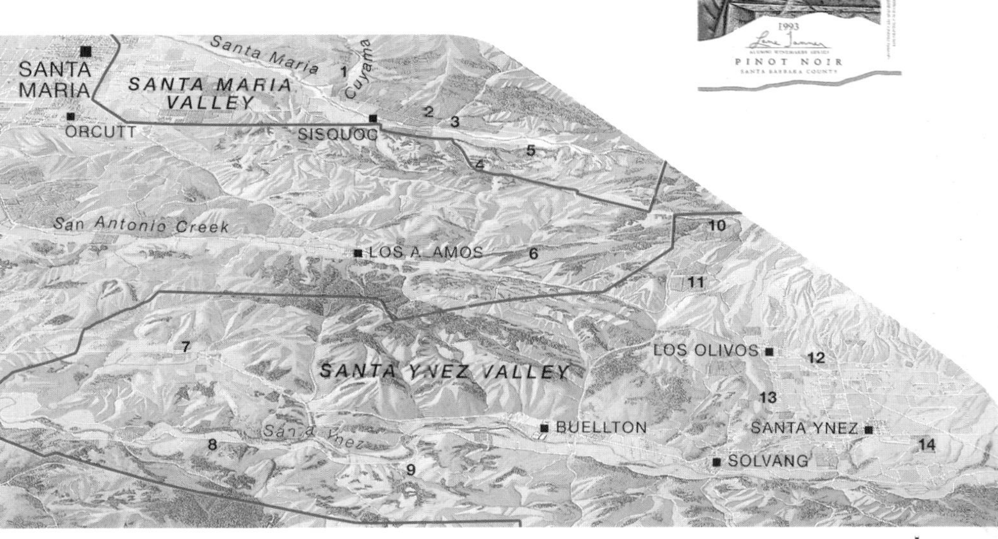

AVA WINE AREAS, TOP WINERIES AND VINEYARDS

1. Au Bon Climat/Qupé
2. Cambria
3. Byron
4. Rancho Sisquoc
5. Foxen
6. Austin
7. Babcock
8. Sanford & Benedict Vineyard
9. Sanford
10. Zaca Mesa
11. Firestone
12. Brander
13. Carey
14. Gainey

AVA BOUNDARIES

SANTA YNEZ VALLEY = AVA WINE AREA

CENTRAL & SOUTHERN CALIFORNIA

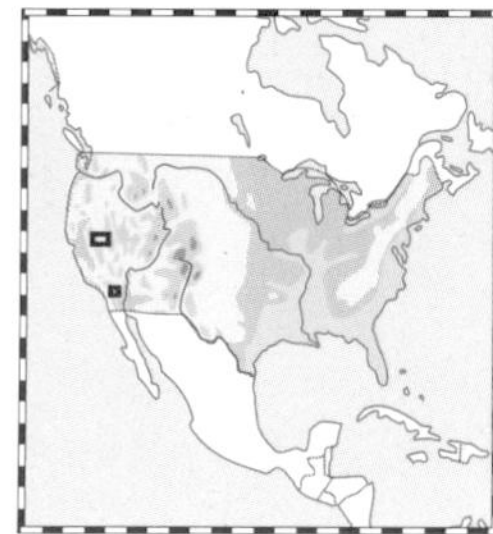

I SUPPOSE I SHOULD APOLOGIZE for allowing the region that produces four out of every five bottles of California's wine less than a full page to itself, but the trouble is, there's not a lot to say about most of the wine, and there's not a lot to say about most of the region. A minute proportion of the wine actually attempts to proclaim its provenance as California's Central Valley – or, more correctly, the San Joaquin Valley – and my chief problem in driving around the interminably flat, sun-baked and over-irrigated land is trying to stay awake.

Yet the valley is a triumph of agro-industry, even if glamour is signally absent, and indeed an air of moody secretiveness hangs over not only the massive wine complexes, but the other enormous vegetable and fruit concerns that dominate the landscape. The Central Valley is not a place to linger in; strangers don't receive too kindly an eye down here.

Technically, there are two parts to the Central Valley – the San Joaquin Valley and the Sacramento River Valley – and there is a significant difference between the two, because around Sacramento, and pushing just a little south towards Lodi, the cool maritime breezes can still make their way up through the gap the Sacramento River has forged in the Coast Ranges. At Lodi, at Clarksburg below the daunting levees of the Sacramento River delta, and in parts of Solano County just above San Pablo Bay, interesting table wines can be produced.

However, the awesome vastness of the Central Valley starts south of Lodi. This is where a substantial amount of the USA's vegetables and fruit are produced, as well as the massive majority of its wine, where wineries that would dwarf oil refineries produce more than many serious wine-producing nations. The Gallo company has four plants whose combined capacity is 330 million gallons. Chile and Australia don't produce much more than 100 million gallons apiece.

The vineyards run right down to Bakersfield, a distance of 370km (230 miles) and the deep fertile soils can spread as wide as 110km (70 miles) between the Coast Ranges and the Sierra Nevada. There is almost no moderating influence for the overpowering heat and there's precious little rain, but two reservoir and canal systems based on nineteenth-century irrigation schemes draw off all the water from the Sierra Nevada range for hundreds of miles making rain irrelevant.

Few producers have made a name for quality wine, although, given the torrid conditions, there have been some high-quality fortified wines created. Andrew Quady at Madera makes the best of these, and his imagination was fired by a batch of Zinfandel grapes from Amador County in the Sierra Foothills in the early 1980s. If the Central Valley can seem like a late twentieth-century nightmare, the attractive Sierra Foothills towns can just as easily seem like a delightful leftover from a century ago.

SIERRA FOOTHILLS

This is where the great goldrush began in 1848, and just as gold fever gripped the nation in Australia, so it did in California. Gold miners have massive thirsts and by the 1870s there were over 100 wineries, largely in El Dorado and Amador counties. Some of the ancient Zinfandel vines are still bearing fruit, and though more fashionable varieties have made their mark, dark, alcoholic, massively flavoured Zinfandels are still what the Sierra Foothills do best.

The vineyards can be as high as 900m (3000ft) high around Placerville in El Dorado but are likely to be just over 300m (985ft) high in the main Amador area of the Shenandoah Valley and between 450 and 750m (1500 and 2500ft) in Fiddletown. The highest vineyards will attract rainfall of up to 1150mm (45in) a year, the lower ones less than 760mm (30in). Differences between day and night time temperatures are similarly more extreme in the higher vineyards, helped by night time mountain breezes and the tail end of maritime breezes off San Francisco Bay. But in the ripening season, daytime temperatures usually hover between 27 and 38°C (80 and 100°F) and the resulting mix of tannin and intensity of fruit makes for some of California's most impressive and traditional wines.

SOUTHERN CALIFORNIA

South of Santa Barbara, the coast takes a long lurch eastward, and the effects of the ice-cold waters are largely lost. There is only one more vineyard region of significance along this coast – Temecula. Situated 38km (24 miles) inland to the south-east of Los Angeles, it's a strange spot. Its high elevation – 430m (1400ft) – gives it a welcome cool edge and the mild Pacific breezes also help, but even so, this far south, you'd expect red wine to be the major player. In fact, almost all Temecula's best wine is white. As in the Livermore Valley, east of San Francisco Bay, urban expansion is squeezing the vineyard areas, although local politicians and property developers do see vineyards as part of the lifestyle they are trying to promote.

The Temecula vineyards, in the hot, arid countryside south-east of Los Angeles, rely on irrigation for their regular supply of water.

Southern & Mid-West States

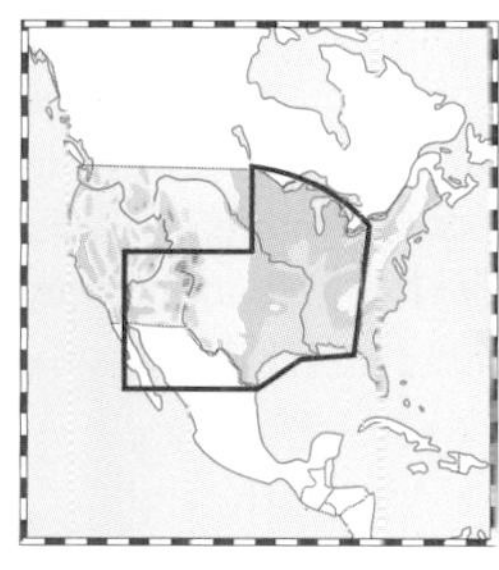

NEW MEXICO LIKES TO CLAIM that it is the original wine-making state of what is now the USA, and I must say, there's no reason why not. The *conquistadores* headed up from Mexico along the Rio Grande – it makes sense to me that they'd have planted vines to rectify the extremely haphazard supply of hooch from Spain. They'd have found it tricky, though. Rainfall is very sparse – as little as 200mm (8in) a year around Albuquerque – and the height of the Rio Grande Valley, rising to 2000m (7000ft) at Santa Fe, not only causes savage winter frosts, but also extremely cold summer nights, with the consequence of very acid grapes.

Nowadays, all these factors are considered to be advantages when trying to grow grapes with good flavours. Irrigation water is now readily available, winter frosts can be countered by piling up earth round the vines as protection, and without the high-altitude cold, it would be too hot to grow decent *vinifera* grapes. Wineries like Anderson Valley produce remarkably good Cabernet Sauvignon wine, but that ability to ripen grapes in the relentless sun yet preserve high acids has not surprisingly led to some excellent fizz being made by producers such as Domaine Cheurlin and Domaine Mont-Jallou.

The high altitude has also attracted winemakers to southern Arizona, around Tucson, and Colorado, at about 1200m (4000ft) up along the Grand Valley of the Colorado River, where a clutch of wineries make intense, rather piercing *vinifera* wines for a chic and well-heeled holiday crowd, as well as Colorado Cellars' Alpenglo – a sweetish Riesling given a sunset hue by adding a tiny amount (1.5 per cent to be precise) of red Lemberger juice.

But the slumbering giant of south-west wine is Texas. I've been tasting these wines since the boom-time days of the 1983 vintage when the volume of production was doubling every year, and you could catch vintners like Bobby Cox of Pheasant Ridge making gobsmacking assertions like 'If half the cotton fields on the high plains around Lubbock were planted to grapes, we could produce as much wine as all of France.'

I'm sure you could, Bobby, but you'd have to make sure the stuff tasted decent if you weren't going to oversee the biggest bust in viticultural history. And the trouble throughout the 1980s was that ambitious vineyard developments simply weren't matched by good wine-making skills. From the biggest vineyard to the smallest – well, relatively smallest; this is Texas after all – I didn't taste one exciting wine, and most ranged from dreary to worse.

Somehow you expect Texans to be able to conquer all their problems by money, effort and self-belief. Perhaps it is humbly reassuring to realize that establishing a wine culture is more complicated than that. There do seem to be several areas suitable for viticulture. The High Plains near Lubbock in north-west Texas, around 1200m (4000ft) above sea level, have dramatic shifts between day and night time temperatures, deep, fairly loose, limestone soil and low humidity, yet reasonable rainfall. The West Texas Mountains are surprisingly cool. And the Texas Hill Country around Austin is vaguely hilly and there's a fair amount of decent limestone and sandy loam soil here as well as some cool mesoclimates. Scattered sparsely through these vast and isolated regions and Dallas-Fort Worth in the north-east are a mere 30 or so wineries, almost all miles, if not hundreds of miles, from their nearest wine-making neighbour. From these, occasional good Cabernets, Chardonnays, Sauvignon Blancs and Rieslings emerge from time to time, but I expect Texan flavours to be brash and assertive: these aren't. What the wines are, though, are cleaner and more correct than they were before. Maybe they're in the transitional phase of correctness before daring to start expressing themselves. In which case, let's see the next phase soon.

Since the 1980s southern New Mexico has been the scene of new vineyard plantings, as here at Chateau Sassenage near Engle.

In general, the rest of the south finds it pretty difficult to grow decent grapes. But that doesn't mean that they haven't had a damn good try. Napoleon's soldiers planted Cabernet vines in Alabama when they were left at a loose end after the French defeat at the Battle of Waterloo. Mississippi, which kept Prohibition on the statute books until as recently as 1966, understandably hasn't been a hotbed of activity, and indeed many other southern states still have local by-laws restricting or even forbidding sale of alcohol. But there is still a wine industry, and in several of the states, they've made a virtue out of necessity by championing non-*vinifera* wine.

Scuppernong isn't exactly a poetic title for a grape variety, but it is the leading member of the Muscadine varieties of *Vitis rotundifolia* that manage to survive the humidity and heat on the Gulf of Mexico and round to the southern Atlantic seaboard. These are massive vines – a single wild Scuppernong vine can cover up to half a hectare (1 acre) – and the grapes, which can be 2.5cm (1in) in diameter, grow in loose clusters, so resisting the rot that is the scourge of tightly bunched *vinifera* grapes down here. The wine flavour is musky and distinctly fruity, and was the basis for Virginia Dare – for some years after Prohibition the bestselling wine in the USA.

Even so, there are *vinifera* plantings. The magnificent Chateau Biltmore in North Carolina has a 32-hectare (80-acre) vineyard. Swiss, Germans and Italians planted vines in Arkansas in the nineteenth century and, particularly around Altus in the state's north-west, vines still do well. Further north, Missouri actually had the first AVA granted, for Augusta in 1980, though most of the state's wineries grow hybrids and *labrusca* rather than *vinifera* grapes. And all the states bordering the Great Lakes in the north have some sort of wine industry. Even Minnesota and Wisconsin squeeze a few wines out of mainly hybrid vines. Indiana has a mix of hybrid and *vinifera* plantations struggling along. But Michigan and Ohio do better than that. Michigan is the USA's fifth biggest wine producer, and though a lot of it is hybrid and *labrusca*, there is a healthy clutch of wineries on the south-eastern shores of Lake Michigan, as well as some delicious Riesling from the Leelanau peninsula further north. Ohio used to grow more grapes than California in the nineteenth century, and though those days are long gone, the conditions along the south shore of Lake Erie and on the offshore islands north of Sandusky, aided by the warm waters of this shallow lake, are good enough for some excellent Chardonnay and Riesling.

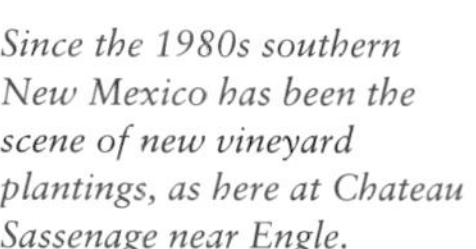

PACIFIC NORTH-WEST

IT'S HARD TO IMAGINE two more totally different wine regions than those of Washington's Columbia River Valley and of Oregon's Willamette Valley. The Willamette Valley has a gentle, long-settled rural quality, with quietly prosperous, self-contained families running back generations tending the farm. It's more like New England than the next door state to California, or more like one of the bucolic counties of Old England, like Gloucestershire or Herefordshire.

The Columbia Valley is a desperate desert of a place – wild, empty, far too savage for most people to settle in however hardy they are. And through this inhospitable desperado's backyard runs the great Columbia River, and here and there along its banks are vast spreads of green gardens sprouting in the desert. Not people, not nice friendly communities, gabled barns and paddock fences – just the raw bones of fields and crops against an eerie wilderness of bleached sagebrush ranges.

Yet both owe their existence to the same geographical phenomena. And both owe their rise from obscurity to international renown to a desire to prove that California and its particular styles of wine, based in the 1960s and 1970s upon big, ripe, assertive flavours, weren't the only valid American styles, and maybe weren't even the best.

The best place to read the geological tale is in Ted Jordan Meredith's *Northwest Wine* where the author makes the activities of the earth's plates, volcanoes and rivers over millions of years sound as fresh and immediate as a news report. I'll just précis the story – but it's a vital story since the activities of the tectonic plates in America's Pacific North-West are still visible today. Remember Mount St Helens exploding in 1980? That was the tectonic plates in action.

What has been happening for millions of years in the Pacific North-West is that the Oceanic plate has been crunching up against the Continental plate and sinking beneath it, at the same time depositing sedimentary layers on the Continental crust and pushing it upwards. This uplift has pushed the Willamette area above sea level and created the Coast Ranges, which ward off just enough of the cold Pacific influences to make the Willamette Valley an ideal cool-climate vineyard area. Meanwhile the Oceanic plate keeps on pressing inland, deeper and deeper below the Continental plate, until it melts. And about 160km (100 miles) inland the molten basalt forces itself upwards creating the series of volcanic peaks known as the Cascades. As the Mount St Helens eruption showed, this process is ongoing, and parts of the volcano are only 2000 years old. The youth of the Cascades explains the majestic soaring beauty of the major peaks and the overall height of the range – often reaching 3650m (12,000ft). Almost all the ocean influences, the breezes, the fogs and the rain get stopped by this mountain barrier. To its east is the virtual desert of the Columbia River basin – endless sunshine, almost no rain. All it took was human ingenuity in harnessing the Columbia's mighty flow for irrigation and you had one of the great *un*natural vineyards of the world.

There's a lot more to the story than this – massive floods of lava sweeping across thousands of square miles of landscape at 48km (30 miles) an hour, these enormous lava flows being buckled into ridges as the west coast itself moves northward, vast glacial floods up to 300m (985ft) deep scouring the landscape during the last ice age. If you want to get excited about geology and geography, the Pacific North-West is the place to do it. And it explains the primeval desolation of so much of the land east of the Cascades.

The Willamette Valley has been settled since the first migrants arrived along the Oregon trail, and parts of the Columbia, the Yakima and Snake River valleys have been exploited agriculturally for the best part of a century, but neither had been exploited for classic wine grapes. Western Oregon was reckoned to be too cool and damp for *vinifera*

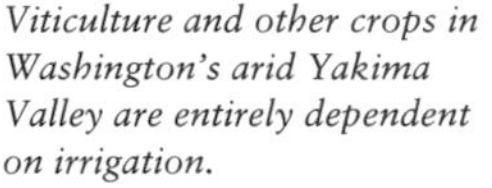

Viticulture and other crops in Washington's arid Yakima Valley are entirely dependent on irrigation.

varieties. The Columbia Valley in eastern Washington was simply too far over the Cascades from any sizeable market and, although moderating winter influences did come from the Columbia River, these weren't always able to combat periodic bouts of intense winter frost, as freezing weather from Alaska got caught in the Columbia River basin.

And yet, beginning in the 1960s and advancing through the 1970s, these two totally different wine regions grew and flourished together. Oregon's cool, wet Willamette Valley was sought out by Californians keen on cool climate grapes like Pinot Noir, Riesling and more recently Pinot Gris, and by refugees from the big, brash California way of living.

In Washington State in the early 1960s a group of university professors founded a little wine company to produce home-made wine from some *vinifera* grapes they'd located in the Yakima Valley, at a time when the state was suffering from archaic liquor laws and a wine industry based on cheap, sweet fortified wine made out of *labrusca* grapes. Within a decade their company – Associated Vintners, now called Columbia – was fashioning new vineyards out of the sagebrush along the Yakima and Columbia rivers, together with a big new operation based on a Yakima growers' co-operative called Chateau Ste Michelle, owned and generously financed by US Tobacco.

Chateau Ste Michelle came here looking for an alternative to the wine regions further to the south – land was expensive and egos were big in the California of the 1970s. Columbia and Chateau Ste Michelle studied the figures for eastern Washington and saw a healthy bottom line based not on cheap bulk, but on high-quality wine, grown in controlled conditions on a latitude similar to Bordeaux.

With slower ripening fruit, and the combinations of long sunny days and chilly nights giving higher acids than California, yet ample sugar, Washington wine producers realized that perhaps they could approach the European ideal of a balanced wine more easily than their California colleagues, and they have based their business on this argument ever since.

The European card has worked for both states. Oregon's Eyrie Vineyard's 1975 Pinot Noir equalled Burgundy's greatest reds in a 1979 'Olympiad' held in Paris, and since then Pinot Noir has been Oregon's greatest achievement. However, 30 years after the first planting of Pinot Noir in the Willamette Valley consistent success has not yet been achieved. Which is fair enough. It's a very marginal climate. It took Burgundy a thousand years to get sorted. Thirty years is early yet.

Washington's first great success came with Riesling, but since then, greater efforts have been put into the Sémillon, Sauvignon Blanc and, of course, Chardonnay grapes, as well as the red Bordeaux varieties – both Cabernets and Merlot. Yakima and Columbia flavours needed taming. Sorting out how to grow the fruit wasn't difficult, but Washington, like Oregon, is still working out how to fashion the best wine from some of America's best vineyards.

IDAHO

There is a third member of the Pacific North-West wine family – Idaho. The wine-making tradition in Idaho actually goes back to the nineteenth century when European immigrants brought wine-making ambitions with them, and an Idaho wine won a prize at the 1898 Chicago World Fair! But Idaho was a keen prohibitionist state, and during most of the twentieth century the potato has seen off the grape without too much difficulty. But there's something catching about the winebug. A guy called Bill Broich started the Ste Chapelle winery in 1975 in the Snake River Valley which was such a success that it is now the North-West's fourth biggest winery.

Even so, if it weren't for fruit farms wanting to diversify, Idaho wouldn't seem a perfect spot for a wine industry. The Snake River does allow some moderating maritime influence to flow up from the Columbia Valley, which is necessary, because the Idaho vineyards are at 600m (2000ft) above sea level. The vineyards get hot bright summer days, but intensely cold nights – and are continually at risk from frost. Many of the best wines have been made from grapes grown in Washington, but despite the hot daytime temperatures, the very cold nights and the foreshortened high-altitude growing season leave me unsure as to whether home-grown grapes can really ripen fully here. There *is* some extremely good Idaho sparkling wine however – but then, the best sparklers don't come from fully ripe grapes.

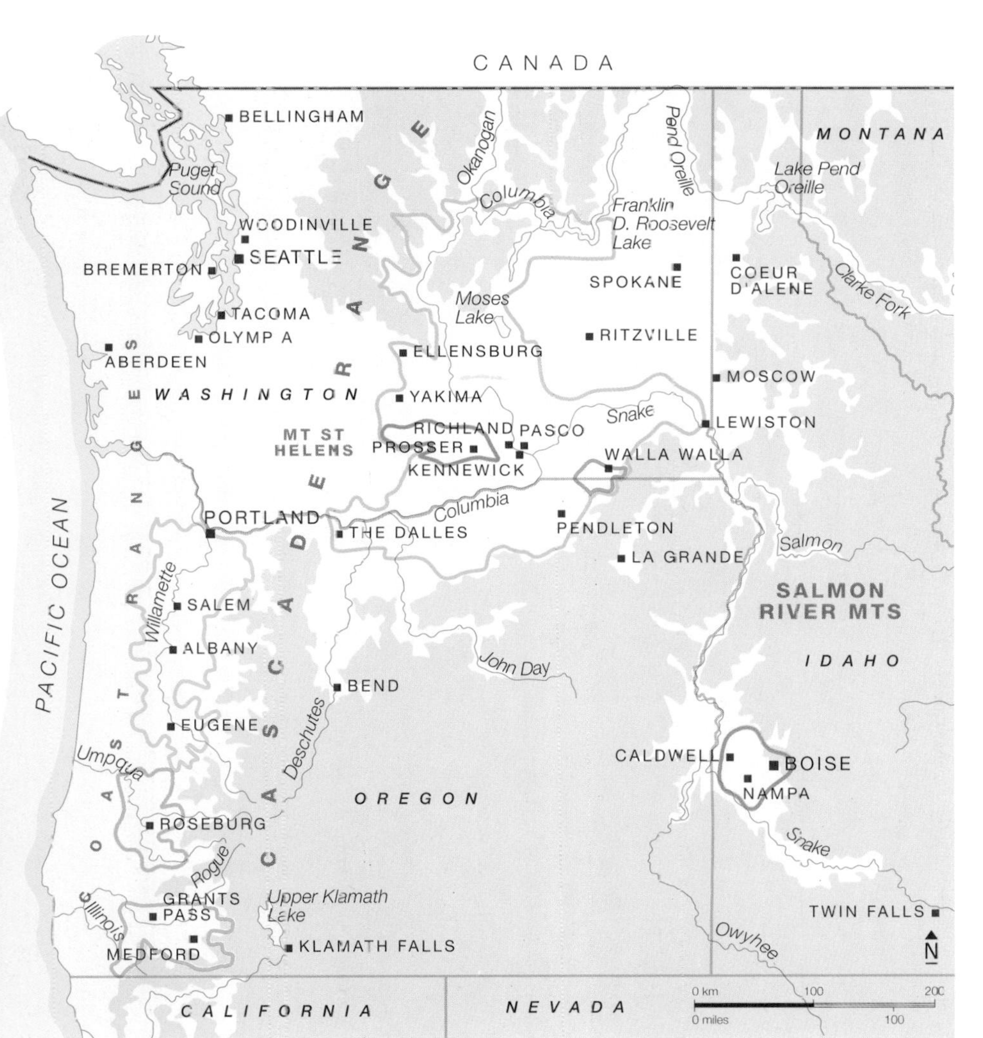

WASHINGTON STATE

 RED GRAPES
Merlot is the main grape, followed by Cabernet Sauvignon. The hardy Lemberger is popular in the Yakima Valley, and there is now some Pinot Noir. Syrah and Nebbiolo are at experimental stage.

 WHITE GRAPES
Riesling was the first success in Washington State. Sémillon and Sauvignon Blanc are now out-planted by Chardonnay but Chenin Blanc and Gewürztraminer are declining in popularity.

 CLIMATE
There can be very dramatic contrasts between summer and winter temperatures. The region west of the Olympic Mountains has a maritime climate with high rainfall. East of the Cascades the pattern is continental and some areas are semi-desert.

 SOIL
Most of the Columbia Valley is basaltic sand with some loess and occasional river gravel. The Yakima Valley has sandy soils with low water retention, making irrigation essential.

ASPECT
Vineyards are few and far between. All plantings have been made on either low ridges, the south-facing slopes of hills, or near rivers. The most important factor is avoiding damaging winter cold rather than excessive summer heat.

YOU'VE GOT A CHOICE FOR the most unlikely, inhospitable vineyard site ever. The Australian outback. Or the moon. You get both in the Columbia River Valley basin to the east of the towering Cascade Range in Washington State up in the cold, foggy Pacific North-West corner of the United States.

But there are two vastly different landscapes here. The part of Washington State where people live, make money, support football teams and go to the opera *is* cool and foggy. This lies to the west of the Cascades, and is open to all the influences of the northern Pacific Ocean that in 1579 had Sir Francis Drake reeling, beaten back by 'the most vile, thick and stinking fogges'. They're still there, around Puget Sound, Seattle and the mouth of the Columbia River.

But take Interstate 90 south-east out of Seattle, up away from the verdant leafy suburbs, through the Snoqualmie Pass and over the Cascades into the head of the Yakima Valley at Ellensburg. You'll feel that you've moved into a completely different world already as you reach the clear, dry mountain air, barren ridges and uneasy civilization. Here you have a choice. Take the Interstate 90 further east across the Columbia River, across Moses Lake way across to Ritzville. You wanted moonscape? You've got it. Windswept sagebrush ranges start out like the great hunched backs of vast animals spreading across the plain, and as the signs of habitation get less and less, the vast sky loses its charm and starts to threaten you with its emptiness, and you find yourself nervously checking your fuel gauge every quarter of an hour. Then the plains flatten and spread, lifeless, inhospitable, useless. That's eastern Washington.

But take the right turn just after Ellensburg and head south. Sure the mountain ridges are still as desolate and gaunt as you could wish them to be, but you'll suddenly see the Yakima Valley open out beneath you, a brilliant splash of dappled greens like a lush turf carpet laid on a sun-bleached earthen floor. Someone wasn't too clever with the carpet shears, though: the neatly defined edges are erratically cut, and the fertile greens come to razor-sharp edges, then nothing but parched bleached uplands, the hills like the vertebrae of some giant fossilized lizard. This is eastern Washington too.

That spread of bright green is agro-industry at its most intense, the jagged edges marking out the limits of irrigation water rights. Without human resourcefulness there'd be little more growing here than out in the empty vastness towards Ritzville and beyond.

Eastern Washington is desert. The curtain of volcanic peaks making up the Cascade Range runs north to south only 80km (50 miles) east of Seattle, and continues to rise inexorably towards the Rocky Mountains of Idaho and Montana. Pretty much nothing grows there except firs. But there's one vast bowl gouged out between the mountains and skirted by the mighty Columbia River as it hurls its mighty flow against the Cascades, turns unwillingly south until, aided by the extra volume of the Snake and Yakima rivers, its torrent forces its way back westwards and out to the ocean.

This is the Columbia River basin, all 60,000 square km (23,000 square miles) of it, one third of Washington's landmass. And among these millions of empty acres lie 4900 hectares (12,000 acres) of vines. They're not here by chance. None of the hop fields or plantations and orchards which pack the valley floor are there by chance. They're there because the Cascade Range, rising to 3650m (12,000ft), creates a virtual rain-shadow to its east, guaranteeing minimal rainfall and maximum sunshine. Not maximum heat though. The Columbia Valley can get incredibly hot, but all the vineyards

WHERE THE VINEYARDS ARE *You're looking here at one of the most remarkable landscapes in the world of wine. Without human effort, this whole vista would be nothing but a discoloured, drab, sun-parched expanse, saved from being a wilderness only by the mighty Columbia River to the right, and the Yakima River running across the map left to right. But irrigation has transformed the Yakima Valley into a prolific producer of vegetables, fruits and, nowadays, wine grapes.*

Most of the valley floor is taken up with orchards and other crops apart from grapes – but look at those watercourses that appear to be running across, rather than down, the hills. Those to the north, in the Rattlesnake Hills, are the Roza and Sunnyside canals, the one to the south running across the base of the Horse Heaven Hills is the Satus number 2 pump canal. These take off water from the Yakima and its tributaries and pump it to the hillside properties where nearly all the wine grape vineyards are.

These hills are two examples of the buckled basalt ridges that crop up in the Columbia River basin and afford protection from severe Alaskan weather patterns, as well as south-facing slopes for vines.

YAKIMA VALLEY
VINEYARDS
TOTAL DISTANCE NORTH TO SOUTH 44KM (27 MILES)
N

0 km 4 8
0 miles 4

are in mesoclimates that are warm at best. Yet being so far north – most vineyards are between 46° and 47° North – you can get up to two hours more sunlight per day than you get further south in California's Napa Valley. Crucial, since it is photosynthesis in the leaves from sunlight that ripens the grape, not blasts of midday heat. At night time, since this is a continental climate, the temperature plummets. So you get grapes full of sugar because of long, sun-filled days, yet you keep your acids high through the chilly nights. It sounds like the perfect recipe for growing wine grapes.

One more thing – there's almost no rain. So you irrigate. The Columbia is America's second river in terms of volumes of water shifted. The Yakima and Snake rivers are two other significant performers. On the Columbia and Snake rivers, the vineyards are either planted right on the banks, to reduce the very real threat of winter and spring frosts, or on low south-facing ridges close to the water. Irrigation is simply a case of obtaining water rights.

The Yakima Valley floor is more protected by hills on the north-east and the south-west and is mostly taken up with other forms of horticulture. But the low ridges are also traversed by irrigation canals and it is here, especially on south-facing patches of the Rattlesnake Hills east of the city of Yakima, that vineyards have been developed.

Traditionally, Washington's wine industry was based on orchard fruits, *labrusca* vines and a few plantations of varieties like Müller-Thurgau in the west near Seattle. Several major wine concerns are still based there, including the two biggest, Chateau Ste Michelle and Columbia near the small town of Woodinville. But 99 per cent of the state's grapes are grown east of the Cascades in the Columbia Basin. Although the whole of Washington's acreage is only one third that of the Napa Valley, Washington has the second largest planting of classic *vinifera* varieties in the USA, after California. Figures are approximate, since new plantings keep coming on line. The overall AVA is Columbia Valley. This encompasses all the vineyards east of the Cascades, though Yakima Valley and Walla Walla can use their own names if they want. Yakima has about 1800 hectares (4500 acres), Walla Walla less than 40 (100) and the rest of Columbia Valley under 2800 (7000), but counting. There are also vines way up near Spokane. West of the Cascades only adds another 64 hectares (158 acres) of *vinifera* vines, the best of these being on the Oregon border near Portland, though Yakima Valley still has big plantings of *labrusca* grapes for jam and juice manufacture.

Initially, Washington was seen as white wine country because of its relatively cool climate, but those long sunlight hours have started to produce superb Merlots as the vines mature, and the rare Lemberger makes excellent crunchy reds in Yakima Valley. But whites still dominate. Chardonnay leads in acreage, but not in quality. Both Riesling and Sémillon positively shine, while Chardonnay flares brightly in places such as Woodland Canyon but is more frequently pleasant rather than exciting.

Washington State is known for its varietal wines, including excellent Merlot.

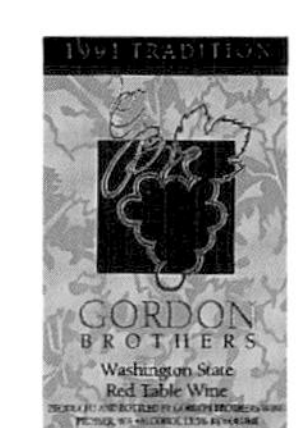

AVA WINE AREA, TOP WINERIES AND VINEYARDS

1. Staton Hills
2. Covey Run
3. Portteus
4. Stewart
5. Chateau Ste Michelle
6. Otis Vineyard (Columbia)
7. Wycoff Vineyard (Columbia)
8. Chinook
9. Hogue
10. Blackwood Canyon
11. Kiona

YAKIMA VALLEY = AVA WINE AREA

AVA BOUNDARIES

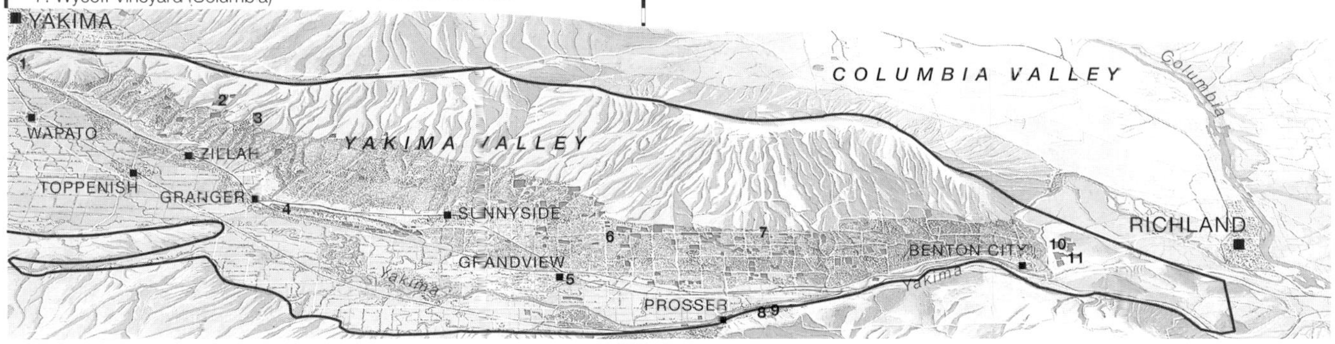

0 km 4 8
0 miles 4

Oregon

RED GRAPES
Pinot Noir rules in Oregon, especially in the Willamette Valley, but Cabernet Sauvignon is also present, as well as small amounts of Merlot and Zinfandel.

WHITE GRAPES
Chardonnay and Riesling are dominant but Sauvignon Blanc, Gewürztraminer and Müller-Thurgau have a following. Pinot Gris is the new star in Oregon.

CLIMATE
The lower Willamette Valley is cooler than the upper part which in turn is cooler than Umpqua, itself cooler than Rogue Valley. Frequent rainfall in the north declines in a similar sequence. The Rogue Valley acts as a heat trap with long hot spells, but sunshine is generally less reliable than in California.

SOIL
In the Willamette Valley, particularly the Dundee Hills, the soil is of volcanic origin and rich in iron. The Rogue Valley is more mixed with some granite.

ASPECT
Most vineyards are planted on slopes, to avoid spring frosts and to make the most of summer sun, but the Rogue Valley also has plantings on the valley floor.

Domaine Drouhin's Pinot Noir vineyards near Dundee were planted in the late 1980s.

THERE WOULDN'T HAVE BEEN an Oregon wine industry if it weren't for the bloody-mindedness of its pioneers. But by pioneers, I don't mean the settlers who followed the Oregon trail out west in the 1850s *or* the first wave of Californians who trekked north a bit later and began planting grapes just over the state line. No. I'm talking about the second wave of Californians. The 1960s wave, which has continued to this day and results in perhaps half of Oregon's wineries being owned by people who, for whatever reason, couldn't hack California any longer and decided to head north.

Nowadays, there's good reason to forsake the easy life in California for the damp, cool Oregonian hills. Thirty years of pioneering wine-making has finally proven that Oregon can make some remarkable wines quite unlike anything produced in California. Thirty years ago a betting man wouldn't even have offered odds on such a dumb proposition. But a few 1960s kids took the gamble all the same. Although California's astonishing growth didn't begin before 1966 at the earliest, when Robert Mondavi set up shop, the University of California at Davis already boasted the most important wine-making and vineyard management course in the nation. It then was – and to some extent still is – a programme more intent upon teaching how to raise huge crops of healthy grapes in warm climates and how not to foul up, rather than encouraging students to strive for something difficult and unique.

But a few of the students didn't simply want to head off to warm fertile valleys and effortlessly produce copious amounts of adequate wines. Above all they had visions based on two great European wine styles that California had never mastered: the great Rieslings of the Rhine and Mosel valleys in Germany, and the great Pinot Noir red wines of Burgundy. One of the Davis professors is said to have told David Lett, a young student passionate about Pinot Noir, 'You'll be frosted out in the spring and fall, rained on all summer and you'll get athlete's foot up to your knees'. Given that Oregon's own State University was warning that quality *vinifera* wine varieties would not ripen, you did have to be pig-headed to give Oregon a go. Richard Sommer of Hillcrest and David Lett of Eyrie were just that. First Sommer established a Riesling vineyard in the Umpqua Valley in southern Oregon, then David Lett headed further north – cooler, more unpredictable weather, more like Burgundy. That's exactly what Lett wanted and what he got.

WHERE THE VINEYARDS ARE *This map shows less than half of the Willamette Valley, but the northern half of the valley does include nearly all the important quality vineyard sites. Only the Eola Hills just to the south of McMinnville have any claim, on quality grounds, to be included with the vineyard sites shown here. If you think the Willamette landscape looks a bit cool and green to be a major wine region, you'd not be far wrong – it is chilly and damp here. That's why there are no grand swathes of vines; the growers here have to search out the few little pockets of land that will manage to ripen their grapes.*

Virtually all of the vineyards are on low hillsides, facing south-east to south-west. It's a marginal climate in the Willamette Valley. The Coast Ranges to the west of the valley cuts off most of the foggy, wet Pacific influence, but can't exclude it completely. The Cascades to the east cut off the worst of the continental winters that could otherwise kill the vines.

The most important grouping of vineyards is on the Dundee Hills just to the south-west of Newberg. Here are many of the original plantings, as well as recent additions like Domaine Drouhin, established by Robert Drouhin from Burgundy in the late 1980s. North-west of Newberg the Chehalem Mountains have good, well-protected sites. There are some vineyards right up next to Portland, but the other important area on the map is in the north-west, where the Coast Ranges offer good protected sites. At the top-left corner is Montinore, Oregon's largest vineyard development.

The reputation of Oregon has been made on Pinot Noir. Lacking local expertise, many grape growers did turn to the University at Davis, and in general they got advice on methods of cultivation and ground preparation, choice of clones, especially in the case of Chardonnay, that might have suited California but weren't relevant to Oregon's situation. The big winery mentality didn't suit Oregon because, of all the American wine regions, Oregon is based on small family units. Five acres, ten acres, maybe 25 is typical, anything much bigger is rare. The whole state production is less than that of the Robert Mondavi Winery in California, and there is a homespun air even to the most successful wineries.

The parallels with Burgundy don't end there. The sun often doesn't shine, and rain frequently falls before the grapes are ripe. And in Oregon, as in Burgundy, mesoclimate is everything in the battle to ripen grapes. Uniquely, among the great red varieties, Pinot Noir needs cool spots rather than hot ones.

Let's look at the Willamette Valley first, since almost all the well-known Oregon wines come from here. The long valley stretches from north-west of Portland to just below Eugene, with the Coast Ranges to the west and the Cascades to the east. The rather haphazard Coast Range crests allow a fair amount of maritime influence, usually in the form of cloud cover and damp, cool air. With a latitude similar to that of Bordeaux, the daytime summer temperatures are actually slightly warmer on average but the nights here are considerably cooler.

Though its wine history is still very short, a surprising number

of sub-regions are already staking a quality claim. Almost all of these are based on small ridges of hills running down the west side of the Willamette Valley which afford protected south- and south-east-facing slopes. The Tualatin Valley has a group of good, primarily white, vineyards in the north, and there are good vineyards almost within Portland's suburbs. Heading south the Chehalem Mountains look promising; the Dundee Hills with their red volcanic soil are the most heavily planted, while the Eola Hills towards Salem are also looking good. The climate slowly warms as you head south, and so, though there are vineyards right down to Eugene, the real cool-climate action is between the Eola Hills and the Tualatin River.

The Umpqua Valley, squeezed between the Coast Ranges and the Cascades, is warm enough to grow fair Cabernet Sauvignon alongside Pinot Noir. On the California border the Rogue Valley sites, though higher than 300m (985ft), are still fairly warm. Illinois Valley, cooled by Pacific influences, can take even longer than Willamette to ripen its fruit. In the north-east, bordering Washington State along the Columbia River, there are now irrigated plantings of a similar character to the Washington vineyards on the far bank of the Columbia.

TOP WINERIES

1. Montinore	4. Fonzi	7. Knudsen-Erath	10. Cameron
2. Elk Cove	5. Adelsheim	8. Domaine Drouhin	11. Argyle
3. Oak Knoll	6. Fox Hill	9. Sokol Blosser	12. Eyrie

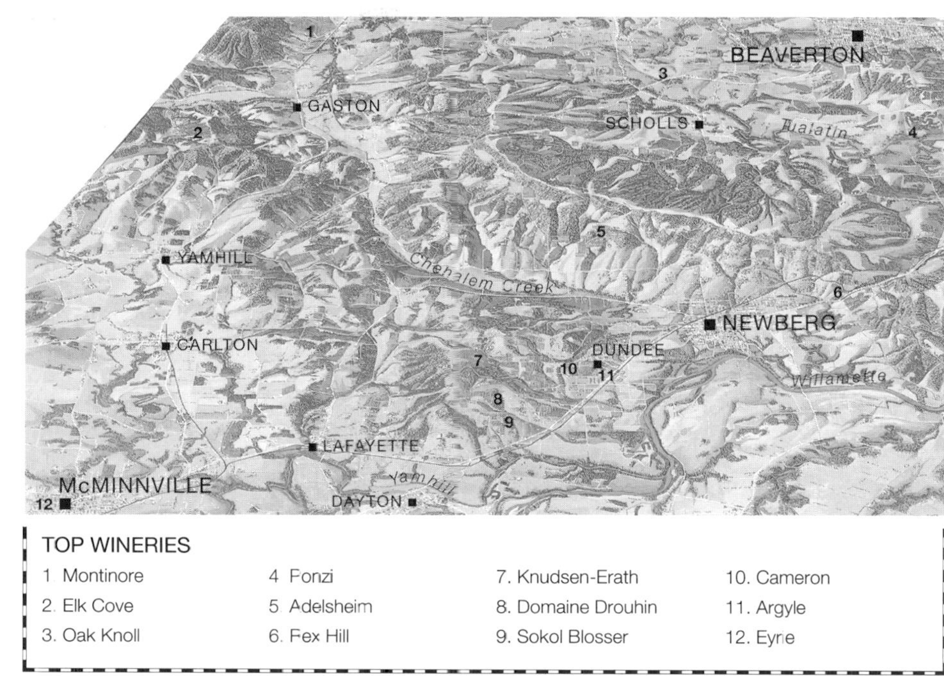

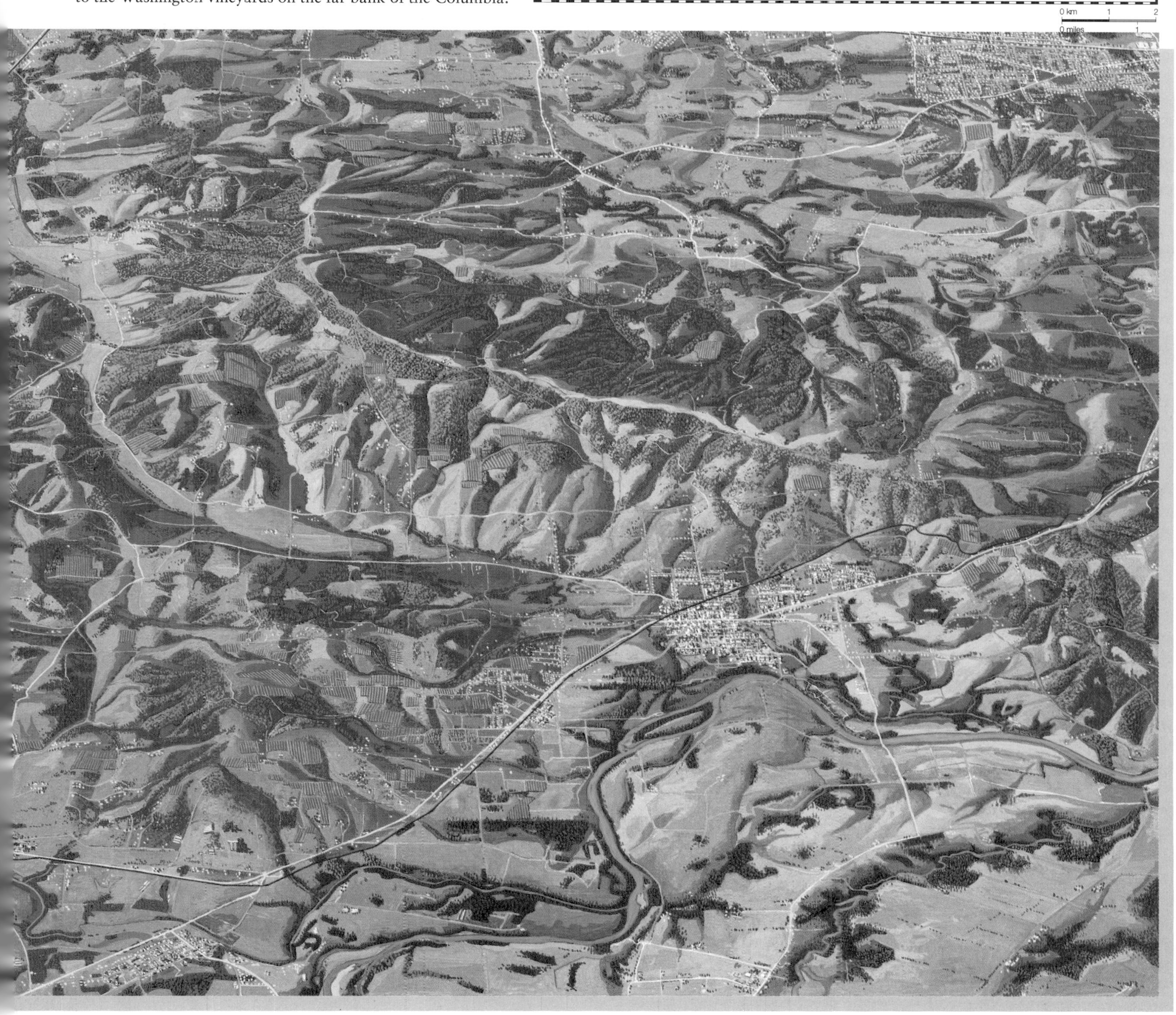

East Coast

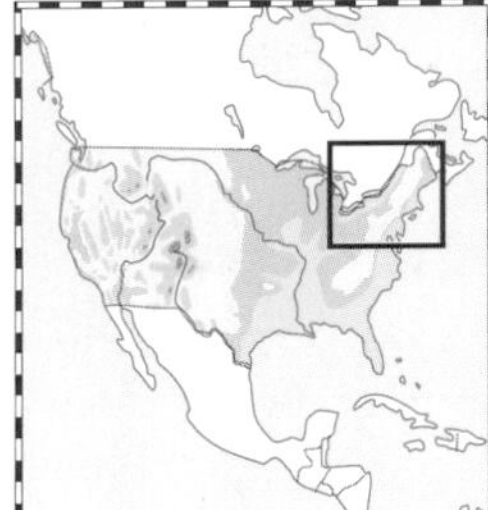

The East Coast is where the American wine industry started, but it took a long time to work out how to make anything half-decent. America must have seemed to be a winemaker's paradise when the first settlers arrived to find fat, juicy grapes hanging off the trees at every turn in New England and Virginia. But as early as 1606 a certain Captain Smith was complaining that while they might be good to eat, these native varieties made horrendous wines.

In 1619 Lord Delaware brought over French vine cuttings and French *vignerons* to try to emulate French wines. No go. The vines died in droves, and the *vignerons* weren't any more successful with making drinkable wine out of the native vines than the original guys. Moses 'the Frenchman' Fournier was having a go on Long Island and Peter Stuyvesant, governor of what was then called New Amsterdam, was planting vines on Manhattan. His successor helped French Huguenot settlers to plant vineyards up the Hudson River Valley. Nothing worked.

The chief problem was phylloxera. This is a tiny aphid that preys on the roots of vines, sucking out their sap and killing the vine. It is endemic in North America, and so domestic varieties of vines evolved that could thrive even in soils seething with phylloxera. The imported European vines had no such tolerance, and immediately succumbed. The only legacy they left is that some of these doomed vines may have cross-bred with native vines. These so-called hybrids gained an immunity to phylloxera's depredations, and at the same time ameliorated the strange, sickly, sweet-scented yet sour-edged fruit of local varieties, in particular those of the *Vitis labrusca*.

This is probably how the first well-known American hybrid – the Alexander or Cape – came about, and this led to such varieties as Isabella, Catawba and Concord in the early nineteenth century. These hybrids gave good crops, could cope with the fierce north-eastern winters without rotting in the humid, sticky summers and produced wine that was, well, barely drinkable at worst – the sickly *labrusca* parentage still showed – but if made into 'sherry', 'port' or sparkling wine, it was really quite palatable.

Throughout the nineteenth and twentieth centuries a reasonably thriving wine industry grew up on the East Coast, dominated by New York State, and dominated by grapes like Concord. During Prohibition, this reliance on Concord served the industry well. The grapes and their juice could be sold for eating or drinking as they were. If you had to print such helpful instructions on what were called 'grape bricks' (blocks of pressed grapes) as 'To prevent fermentation add one-tenth per cent Benzoate of Soda' – well, sometimes you just forgot, and the damned thing fermented. It seemed such a waste to throw it away, so you drank it. It may not have tasted good, but in the era of bathtub gin, who cared what it tasted like? The fact that business in the Finger Lakes and along the shores of Lake Erie is still flourishing means that someone must like it.

It wasn't until a few tentative moves in the 1960s, followed by a slow push first towards quality hybrids and then towards classic European *vinifera* grapes grafted onto American rootstock, that things began to hum. New York has been the leader in this movement, but a surprising number of other states have managed to produce attractive *vinifera* wines before the fading sunlight and icy air of Maine kill off the grape's chance of ripening in the north, or the humid climes of South Carolina and Florida rot it on the vine to the south.

New Hampshire does grow a few vines, and Massachusetts grows rather more, with the most attractive efforts so far being those wines made from vines grown on the island of Martha's Vineyard – proving that the sea's

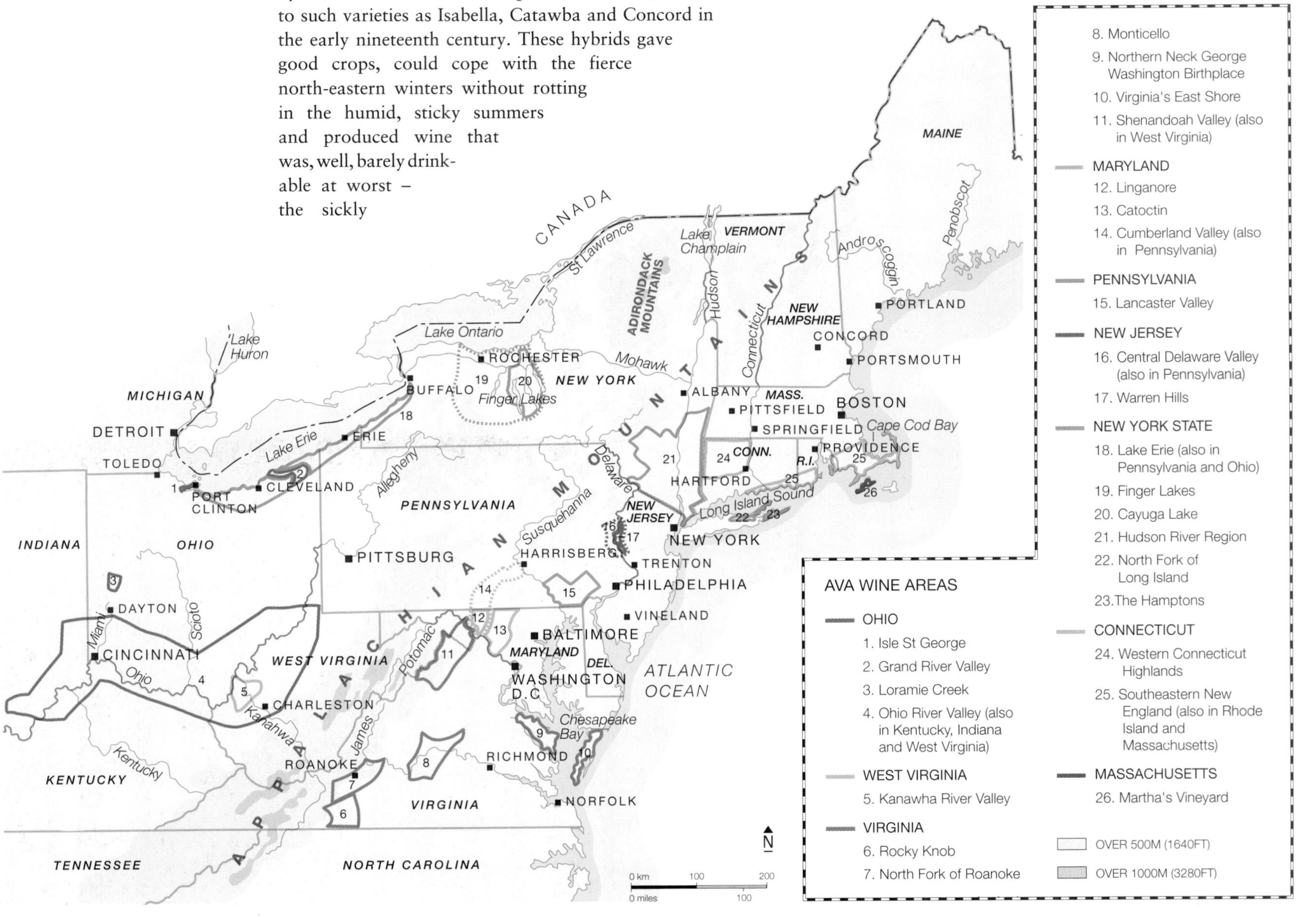

AVA WINE AREAS

OHIO
1. Isle St George
2. Grand River Valley
3. Loramie Creek
4. Ohio River Valley (also in Kentucky, Indiana and West Virginia)

WEST VIRGINIA
5. Kanawha River Valley

VIRGINIA
6. Rocky Knob
7. North Fork of Roanoke
8. Monticello
9. Northern Neck George Washington Birthplace
10. Virginia's East Shore
11. Shenandoah Valley (also in West Virginia)

MARYLAND
12. Linganore
13. Catoctin
14. Cumberland Valley (also in Pennsylvania)

PENNSYLVANIA
15. Lancaster Valley

NEW JERSEY
16. Central Delaware Valley (also in Pennsylvania)
17. Warren Hills

NEW YORK STATE
18. Lake Erie (also in Pennsylvania and Ohio)
19. Finger Lakes
20. Cayuga Lake
21. Hudson River Region
22. North Fork of Long Island
23. The Hamptons

CONNECTICUT
24. Western Connecticut Highlands
25. Southeastern New England (also in Rhode Island and Massachusetts)

MASSACHUSETTS
26. Martha's Vineyard

OVER 500M (1640FT)
OVER 1000M (3280FT)

tempering influence does allow *vinifera* vines to survive at such a northern latitude.

Rhode Island claims a similar climate to Bordeaux – an awful lot of maritime vineyard regions do. I wouldn't go that far, but good mesoclimates do abound, the sea does help, and certainly Sakonnet Vineyards has produced some pretty fair Chardonnay. Connecticut benefits from the mild influence of Long Island Sound. There are wines made upstate, but the climate gets pretty continental away from the maritime influence, and all the best ones I've had, like Chamard Chardonnay, have come from vines grown down near the Sound.

Skirting round New York, New Jersey is struggling to put her past as a *labrusca* producer behind her, and West Virginia produces some wine up in her north-east corner, but the important players are Pennsylvania, Virginia and Maryland. Maryland's chief claim to fame is Boordy Vineyards where Philip Wagner planted America's first French-American hybrids – just as resistant to the cold winters, the scorching summers and the phylloxera as the American versions but with a much more European flavour. Until recently most of the best East Coast wines came from these hybrids like Vidal and Chambourcin, and though there are an increasing number of *vinifera* success stories, like Byrd, Catoctin and Montbray, growers such as these generally keep their share of hybrids.

Pennsylvania divides its vineyards between the shores of Lake Erie in the north-west where long but cool days suit some of the northern European varieties like Riesling and Pinot Noir, and the south-east, in the Lancaster and Cumberland valleys, where a new generation of winemakers are having particular success with Chardonnay, though the hybrid Chambourcin from wineries like Chaddsford and Naylor is also surprisingly good.

Some winemakers say south-east Pennsylvania reminds them of Burgundy, but Virginia which shares the same sweep of mountain slopes that run down to the west of Washington DC actually provides a more realistic comparison. This was where Captain Smith tried and failed in the seventeenth century, and where Thomas Jefferson suffered the same fate in the eighteenth. Things got so bad that in 1960 Virginia boasted only 6.5 hectares (16 acres) of vines – all for dessert grapes. Now around 600 hectares (1500 acres) sport vines; over two-thirds of them are *vinifera* varieties, with Chardonnay leading the way. That almost goes without saying, since to build up a cellar door trade you have to offer a Chardonnay and Virginia is perfectly placed not only for Washington D.C. but also for a thriving tourist trade – even colonial Williamsburg has its own winery now. Luckily Chardonnay has taken well to Virginia. But that hasn't stopped people experimenting not only with obvious choices like Riesling, Merlot or Cabernet Franc, but also with such long shots as Viognier and Barbera.

Things still aren't easy, however. Phylloxera may be conquered, but the climate is a continual battle, and one wonders if, without the nearby market of the capital, Washington D.C., many wineries would continue the struggle. With most of the vineyards planted inland on the eastern slopes of the Blue Ridge Mountains, away from the tempering effects of Chesapeake Bay, and with a latitude similar to southern Italy and southern Spain, the winemakers have got the classic problems of a continental climate – cold winters, spring frosts and tremendous heat and possible excess humidity and rainfall in summer. Even the soils are by no means perfect, being largely fertile red clays and clay loams.

But they do it. By planting the vineyards mostly between 335 and 460m (1100 and 1500ft) up on slopes, the grape growers can provide drainage for excess water and good air circulation. This is vital in order to combat spring frosts and to reduce the incidence of grape rot when the humidity climbs. Wide spacing of vines and an open trellis canopy also help to minimize rot. Some of the more cold-sensitive *vinifera* varieties find the winters too hard in Virginia, but the Rieslings, Sauvignon Blancs, Chardonnays, Cabernets and Merlots, from wineries like Barboursville, Linden, Tarara, Montdomaine, Meredyth, Misty Mountain and even Williamsburg, down on sandy soils near the coast, point the way to Virginia challenging New York for East Coast quality in the not-too-distant future.

Vineyards in upper New York State, here at Lake Canandaigua in the Finger Lakes, have to contend with long, severe winters.

NEW YORK STATE

RED GRAPES
Native American and hybrid varieties continue to dominate the east coast, with Concord accounting for 75% of total plantings, plus Baco Noir and De Chaunac. *Vinifera* vines include Cabernet Sauvignon, Merlot, Cabernet Franc and Pinot Noir.

WHITE GRAPES
Chardonnay is the leading *vinifera* variety, followed by Riesling, Gewürztraminer and Sauvignon Blanc. However, these are overshadowed in volume by such hybrids as Aurora, Seyval Blanc, Cayuga and Vidal Blanc.

CLIMATE
The Finger Lakes have a short, humid growing season followed by severe winters. The Hudson River is milder while Long Island benefits from the moderating influence of the Atlantic Ocean.

SOIL
Soils are varied. By Lake Erie there is gravelly loam and around the Finger Lakes calcareous shale. The Hudson River has shale, slate, schist and limestone. Long Island is sandy with silt and loam.

ASPECT
The Allegheny plateau traps the warmth of Lake Erie. Finger Lakes vineyards are on slopes to avoid frost and the steep Hudson River Valley is an efficient conduit for warm Atlantic air.

Long Island is now producing some wonderful Chardonnay.

I KNOW THEY SAY THAT LONG ISLAND is the closest vineyard area to New York City, but it depends on when you decide to visit. Don't do it in June, or July, or August, or any time when it's sunny, or weekends – and don't drive. If you do, you'll need to leap out of bed before dawn, slam the hire car into 'drive', hare through the Midtown Tunnel, out through Queens on Interstate 495 and in no time – well, even obeying the speed limit, in about an hour and a half – you should be at Riverhead, with time for some leisurely vineyard visits. Except for me it didn't work out like that: I visited in summer. Four hours to Riverhead, every appointment missed, and then the long drive home. Too much sea and sand. Too popular.

Well, that's Long Island for you. It's the reason everyone rushes out there as soon as the sun comes out and tries to forget the chaos of the City. It's also the reason that it is seen increasingly as America's answer to the continuing quest for a genuine Bordeaux look-alike wine region. It's got similarities, I'll grant you, and it is making a good stab at Cabernet and Merlot, although most of its best wines so far come from Chardonnay, as is the case so frequently on the East Coast. And the vineyards that are laying claim to a slice of Bordeaux's glory are virtually all on the North Fork. The South Fork has the Hamptons: they throw better parties down there, the houses are bigger, the limos longer, but in wine terms the soil is rather heavy, leading to waterlogging when summer and autumn rains get excessive. Here, the spring frosts can strike as late as May, the prevailing winds are cooler and the ripening period is two or three weeks shorter than on the North Fork. Makes you wonder why the socialites didn't choose the North Fork. Luckily the winemakers did.

Long Island is New York's newest vineyard area. There were a few vines planted in the seventeenth and eighteenth centuries but nothing of note occurred until 1973 when Alex and Luisa Hargraves uprooted a patch of potatoes and cauliflowers at Cutchogue, a couple of miles up the North Fork from Riverhead, and planted vines. So? So the vines they planted were the French classics of Bordeaux and Burgundy, together with Riesling. The rest of New York's reputation, such as it was, had until then been based on native American vines and French hybrids: a few plantations of classic *vinifera* grapes existed upstate. Everyone said they couldn't survive the bitter cold winters and short, fiery summers.

This didn't bother the Hargraves. They had realized that the waters of Long Island provided a moderating effect on the North Fork, cooling the summer heat and warding off the worst of the north-east winter cold. They'd also found that the sandy loam and gravel soils of the gently undulating farmland around Cutchogue – sitting on deep sand and gravel subsoils – were ideal for marrying decent drainage with reasonable water retention. And their thoughts turned to Bordeaux, to the Médoc especially, which juts out into the Bay of Biscay on its tongue of low-lying land. They checked the growing season temperatures and found that, though the season starts a little later than in Bordeaux, slightly warmer summer temperatures bring both areas' grapes to ripen at much the same time in mid-September to mid-October. Given the prevalence of sandy soil, a slightly higher rainfall isn't that much of a problem, and the good drainage reduces the chance of late season rot.

But it hasn't been an easy ride. Effective fungicide sprays are crucial to control the rot caused by the humid atmosphere. The soils are more fertile than those of Bordeaux's best properties and pruning and trellising must be adapted accordingly. And New York City has been slow to take Long Island's wines to its heart. I remember in 1982 trying to persuade the city's gastronomic glitterati of Long Island's brilliant potential. I might as well have been extolling the friendly nature of the Great White Shark to a group of scuba divers. At last, in the 1990s, the rare quality of Long Island Chardonnay, the increasingly fine Merlots, Cabernets, and, occasionally, Sauvignon Blancs and late-harvest Rieslings, have become a hot item in the Big Apple.

WHERE THE VINEYARDS ARE *We're looking at a tiny sliver of land here. Riverhead to Southold is a mere 19km (12 miles), and Jamesport north to Long Island Sound is only 5km (3 miles). But dotted about among the flat, scarcely undulating fields full of lush market produce for New York's dinner tables are about 400 hectares (1000 acres) of vineyards that many experts think will prove to be some of the best in the USA. Indeed you can narrow things down even more to the area around Cutchogue where the majority of the best vineyards are and which people have begun whispering about as the Médoc of America.*

There are some vines on the South Fork of Long Island, but the North Fork clearly has better potential; the South Fork's soils are heavier, the climate a little cooler and the risk of spring frosts catching you unawares lasts a little longer. Long Island's soils were formed by the retreating Wisconsin glaciation, about 10,000 years ago, but the North Fork's thin claw has grabbed the freest draining, more gravelly and sandy soils. It has also grabbed the better climate.

Stretching north-east into Long Island Sound, with Peconic Bay to its south, the North Fork is surrounded on three sides by relatively warm water. The prevailing westerlies reach the North Fork after blowing across the Sound. This helps create a mild growing period of up to 230 days length, although the relative air humidity does require fairly strict anti-fungal spray regimes as does a likelihood of late season rain. The climate during September and October mirrors that of Bordeaux, and winemakers in the North Fork can experience the same heartbreak that a sudden downpour in the middle of harvest causes as their French counterparts.

But if they want to be thought of as this transatlantic Médoc they're going to have to get used to dreams of 'Vintage of the Century' turning to ashes far more frequently than they become glorious reality.

NORTH FORK OF LONG ISLAND

VINEYARDS

TOTAL DISTANCE NORTH TO SOUTH 23KM (14 MILES)

N

0 km 1 2

0 miles 1

But the other areas of New York have a longer grape-growing tradition and contribute the vast majority of the volume that makes New York the number two state for grapes after California. Long Island only boasts about 445 hectares (1100 acres) out of a state total of 12,000 (30,000), yet has the higher reputation. The Lake Erie region boasts 8000 hectares (20,000 acres), yet no one has ever heard of it. There is a 5-km (3-mile) band of gravelly loam soil running between Lake Erie and the Allegheny Plateau that traps the maritime influences of the lake, giving a long ripening period and protection against spring and autumn frosts. It probably will produce good table wines in time, but for now the reason we don't know its name is that almost all the vineyards are planted with Concord, which makes excellent grape juice but pretty duff wine.

The Finger Lakes region also relies upon the critical effects of water in tempering a climate that would otherwise be far too harsh for conventional wine grapes. Lake Ontario is just to the north of these eleven thin, deep lakes running north to south, gouged out of the rock by glaciers during the last Ice Age. The three biggest – Keuka, Seneca and Cayuga – have most of the vineyard plantings out of the region's total of 5300 hectares (13,000 acres), and Cayuga now has its own separate AVA designation. Initially seen as only suitable for native varieties and hybrids, a visionary called Konstantin Frank reckoned he knew better. Coming from Russia, where wine grape varieties survive in sub-zero conditions, he believed that varieties such as Riesling and Chardonnay could survive the icy winters if grafted on to sufficiently hardy rootstocks. He eventually proved his point with rootstock he acquired from a convent in Quebec, and there are now an increasing number of delicate but delicious white wines being produced on the shale-dominated soils. The lower altitude and greater depth of the Seneca and Cayuga lakes, allowing a slightly longer protection from frost, are now seen as the best sites.

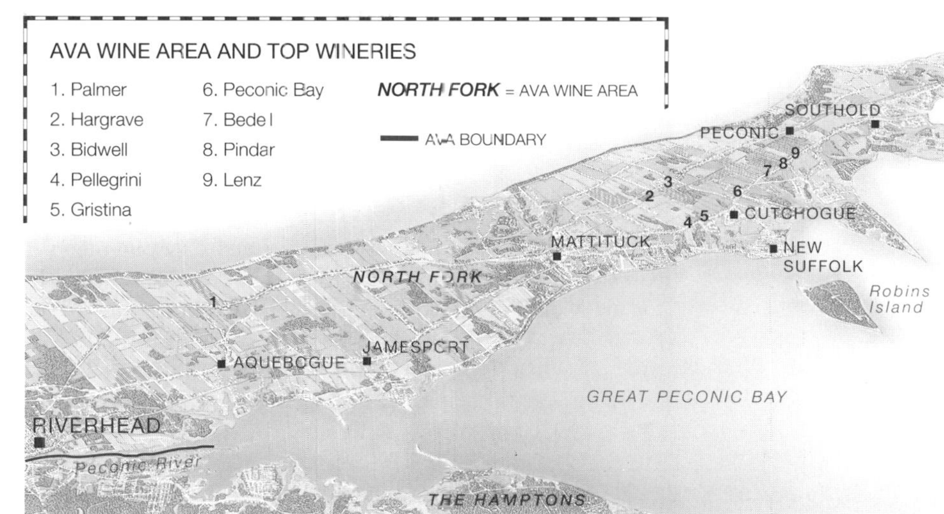

The Hudson River Valley, directly north of New York City, has the longest unbroken grape-growing tradition in the USA. Only recently have the 400 hectares (1000 acres) of slate, shale and schist soils begun producing rather good *vinifera* wines as growers realized that the steep Pallisades through which the Hudson flows south act as a potent conduit for the warming maritime influences from the nearby Atlantic Ocean.

CANADA

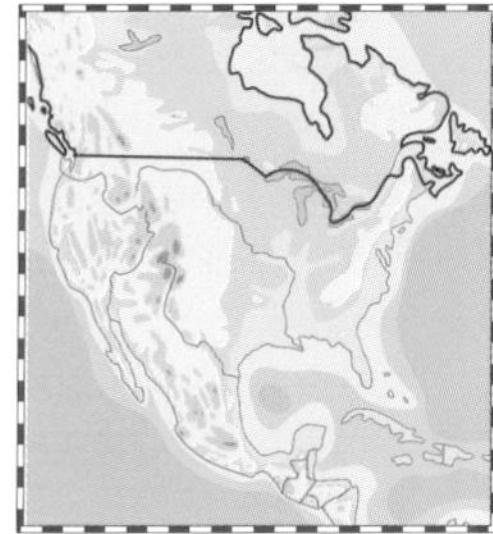

I MUST ADMIT, I'D NEVER GIVEN IT a second thought. The first vineyards I visited were those of Bordeaux when I was a student. But I wonder, I wonder. Before I went to university I trailed across Canada, hanging out and playing the guitar. Tired of thumbing lifts I snuggled down one late afternoon in a sun-bathed orchard just north of Peachland in British Columbia's Okanagan Valley, and drifted off to sleep. It wasn't a vineyard then but, looking at the map, could it be the site of what is now Château Ste Claire or Hainle? It just could.

And a little later when I visited my parents in Ontario I drove down to Vineland, and tramped through the rows of vines below the Niagara Escarpment before getting my first samplings of Maréchal Foch, De Chaunac and Vidal Blanc while gazing out over the sullen grey waters of Lake Ontario. I was warmed and cheered up by a smashing 'port' made from *labrusca* grapes and I concluded, upon this evidence alone, that perhaps Ontario was fortified wine country at best. Had I been to Bordeaux yet? Or was Ontario first?

I don't really know but there's no doubt that Bordeaux captured my imagination more than the Niagara Peninsula or the Okanagan Valley for the next decade or two. Which is fair enough. The New Age of wine was scarcely drawing its first breath in the Canada of the early 1970s. By the mid-1990s, however, Canada was, albeit timidly, knocking on the door and asking to be regarded as the newest wine nation.

To be taken seriously, any new country has to have a product that other people are not already doing better. Australia without Chardonnay, or New Zealand without Sauvignon Blanc, would have had a far greater struggle for recognition. For Canada, it wasn't the grape variety that mattered – it was the type of wine. One of the rarest, most difficult styles of wine to achieve in the world can be made every single year in Canada – and all because of her terrible Arctic winter weather. Every winter, the temperatures in the vineyards of Ontario and British Columbia drop way below freezing and frequently stay there for weeks, if not months, on end. If your grapes are still on the vine in late November and December, they freeze.

Above: Canada is the world's largest producer of lusciously sweet Icewine. Below: Vineyards on the Niagara Peninsula benefit from the warming influence of nearby Lake Ontario.

This doesn't sound good. But if you gather these grapes, frozen, and take them, still frozen, to the winery, and delicately press them – *still* frozen – you'll discover that the water which constitutes more than 80 per cent of the grape juice has turned into ice crystals, and the sugar has separated out into a thick, gooey, sludgy syrup that is ridiculously sweet. Remove the ice from the syrup and you've got the basis for one of the most distinctive flavours in the wine world – the phenomenally rich Icewine. Once or twice a decade a few German vineyards attempt this wine style and sell their minute production at astronomical prices. In Canada, they can make it every year, and most Canadian Icewine comes from Ontario, with small amounts made in British Columbia.

If the numbing winter weather makes Icewine possible, the rapid onset of winter and the late arrival of spring make life perennially difficult for anyone attempting to make any other sort of decent wine. For a long time it was thought to be virtually impossible to ripen *vinifera* grapes satisfactorily in Canada, and to prevent them being killed during the worst of the cold spells. Until the 1990s, vineyards were dominated by native *labrusca* varieties and early-ripening hardy hybrids

The change in the 1990s has been dramatic. The Canada-US Free Trade Agreement removed tariff protection for Canadian wines and, faced with competition from better-tasting Californian wines, most of the *labrusca* hybrid growers threw in the towel. Vineyard acreage declined by two-thirds in British Columbia and by almost a third in Ontario. Those who remained in business were the quality-conscious producers who increasingly grow the international noble grape varieties.

There are vineyards in Québec, mostly about 80km (50 miles) south-east of Montreal around the town of Dunham, and, scarcely believably, in the Annapolis Valley in Nova Scotia. In both places, chance local climates make it just about possible to ripen hybrids like Seyval and there's circumstantial evidence that when Leif Ericsson established his colony of Vinland for one brief winter a thousand years ago, it just may have been at L'Anse aux Meadows in Newfoundland. He certainly found grapes growing, though whether he made them into wine is a matter for conjecture. In modern times, however, Ontario and British Columbia make most of the wine.

ONTARIO

Ontario's 7300 hectares (18,000 acres) of vineyards lie on the shores of Lake Ontario and Lake Erie between 41° and 44° North – a band equivalent to central Italy and southern France. That sounds extremely promising for some fairly gutsy flavours, but it isn't as simple as that. Those European vineyards are strongly influenced by the perenially warm Mediterranean sea. In the middle of winter you can still jump

VINTNERS QUALITY ALLIANCE

I really like the description the Ontario and British Columbia wine producers have given to their Vintners Quality Alliance (VQA) scheme. They call it 'a contract between the vintners and the consumer'. If only the *appellation* systems of Europe and elsewhere in North America held dear to such a contract. I am, in general, critical of *appellation* schemes, since they rapidly become catch-all descriptions with the unintentional result both of inhibiting the talented winemakers as well as protecting the mediocre. But in marginal climates like Canada's, where the classic grape varieties will only ripen in the best mesoclimates, a proactive scheme like the VQA, which lays down guidelines on geographical designations, minimum ripeness levels and grape types, makes sense.

- Each potential VQA wine is subjected to a tasting panel – judging takes place blind and a VQA medallion marks out the best of the bunch.
- The majority of wines in the VQA scheme are from *vinifera* grapes (though Icewine often uses hybrids like Vidal).
- Table wines labelled with one of the three Ontario Designated Viticultural Areas – Pelee Island, Lake Erie North Shore or Niagara Peninsula – must be made entirely from *vinifera* grapes.

Harvesting grapes for Icewine, here at the Henry of Pelham Estate in Ontario, is a torturous business usually resulting in numb fingers and raw cheeks.

into the sea at Nice or Portofino and experience, at worst, a mildly bracing immersion. Jump into the sea off Canada's 44th parallel in midwinter and you'll be nursing some extremely nasty cold bruises from the icebergs. And that's only half the story. Proximity to the sea tempers any region's extremes, but Ontario's vineyards are hundreds of miles inland. Long, numbing winters and short searing summers would rule out any chance of wine-making – if it weren't for the lakes. It's the lakes that make viticulture possible, storing up summer heat to release it slowly though the winter, yet providing maritime breezes to cool the fierce, if short-lived, summer sun. We end up with summer temperatures that are hotter than both Bordeaux and Burgundy, a crucial point because, until the end of May, Ontario is appreciably cooler, and by September her temperature drops below that of Bordeaux once again. In the south, Pelee Island, 18km (11 miles) out in Lake Erie, has a ripening period 30 days longer than the Canadian mainland, helped by the southerly latitude and the warming effect of the shallow Lake Erie. Lake Erie North Shore, near Windsor, also benefits from the water's warm surface temperature.

However, the heart of Ontario viticulture is on the Niagara Peninsula. The vineyards are either on the lakeshore plain, or on benchland below the Niagara Escarpment. Again the lake moderates winter and summer temperatures – the escarpment creates a through draught of lake breezes that is vital in keeping vines rot-free during autumn and frost-free in the spring. Year by year, the wines get better, and so far the whites have taken most of the honours, with Chardonnay leading the way for dry whites, and Riesling and Vidal for Icewine. But both Merlot and Cabernet Franc show some form, even if the flavours are still a bit on the reedy side. Pinot Noir seems to find the frequent humidity a bit difficult to cope with.

BRITISH COLUMBIA

The Okanagan Valley in British Columbia doesn't have a humidity problem. Although it is on a more northerly latitude than Niagara, corresponding to Champagne and the Rhine Valley, it is a virtual desert, some areas getting only 150mm (6in) of rain a year. During the short summer, the days are hot, but the nights can be ice-cold. The result is grapes with high levels of sugar and acidity, but only from the best sites, where the Okanagan Lake's stored warmth helps temper the icy nights, and where the ripening process isn't too brutally arrested by October frosts. The original Canadian Icewine was made here, at Hainle; and recent showings of Chardonnay and Pinot Blanc have been impressive, especially from wineries like Mission Hill who have employed wine-making talent from that world leader in making the best of a cool climate – New Zealand. Red *vinifera* wines are proving tricky, but there are some good, gently perfumed reds from hybrid varieties. Vancouver Island is also trying to establish a vineyard region amid the forest of the Cowichan Valley.

KINGSTON
St Lawrence
Moira
TRENTON
Lake Scugog
OSHAWA
TORONTO
Lake Ontario
Grand
Nith
CANADA
ONTARIO
HAMILTON
BRANTFORD
ST CATHARINES
NIAGARA FALLS
NEW YORK STATE
Lake Huron
SARNIA
MICHIGAN
LONDON
ST THOMAS
Long Point Bay
Thames
USA
DETROIT
Lake St Clair
CHATHAM
WINDSOR
Lake Erie
LEMINGTON
Pigeon Bay
Pelee Is.
PENN
OHIO
0 km 50 100
0 miles 50

ONTARIO VQA WINE AREAS
Niagara Peninsula
Lake Erie North Shore
Pelee Island

SOUTH AMERICA & MEXICO

THE PAN AMERICAN HIGHWAY makes for the geographical ride of a lifetime: this great, long road which runs south from the US-Mexican border takes you through a political, cultural and economic landscape of incredible diversity. Mad drivers and the impressive mountainous spine of the Andes are almost the only constants on a road which connects the heat of Mexico with the chill blasts of Patagonia.

Apart from football, one of the major forces that provides any cohesion or unity on this southward trek is religion. Early missionaries propagated Christianity in the mid-sixteenth century, beginning their journey in Mexico and spreading throughout South America. With them came the *vinifera* vine from Europe, and the traditional view is that they made their own supply of wine in order to celebrate the Eucharist.

Wine was also made by many of the conquistadores for normal consumption – importing wine from back home in Iberia was far too risky an enterprise. Few wines reacted well to the long sea voyage across the Atlantic, even less to the hot, bumpy overland journey to the Pacific coast followed by yet another stage by sea down to Chile and Peru. The subsequent dispersal of settlers and missionaries took wine-making from the mile-high plateau of Mexico to the Rio Negro in Argentina.

Since the first plantings, various waves of largely European immigrants have had their effect on the development of both the wine industry and the culture that supports it, in particular the influence of the French in Chile and the Italians in Brazil and Argentina. These days knowledge and wine-making techniques arrive in the form of visiting winemakers from overseas – known as 'flying winemakers'. Their expertise should bring out some of the unbeatable quality that could exist, particularly in the parts of Chile and Argentina which enjoy a maritime or Mediterranean climate, well away from the influence of the tropics.

TOPOGRAPHY AND CLIMATE

Latitude and climate are the most obvious restrictions on wine-making in South America and Mexico. From the Tropic of Cancer which bisects Mexico, to the Tropic of Capricorn which cuts across Argentina's northern border, the humidity and high temperatures alternately rot the grapes or bake them, making it difficult in many places to produce quality wine. A clever use of altitude, together with stubborn persistence do, however, create exceptions to the rule. French winemaker Michel Rolland has exploited the benefits of being 1800m (6000ft) above sea level to make an award-winning white wine in the Argentine region of Salta, barely 150km (90 miles) from the tropics. And Venezuela, too, has made a substantial investment in tropical wine experiments.

The massive Andean chain and cooling breezes off the Pacific Ocean are the most important physical influences on viticulture. These maritime breezes help regulate excessive temperatures the length of the coast, from Baja California, down through the Ica region of Peru and on into Chile's Central Valley. In the case of Chile, the cold Humboldt Current creates an additional chilling factor which is beneficial for white wine areas such as Casablanca. On the eastern side of the continent, vineyards in Uruguay and parts of southern Brazil are influenced by the problematic combination of warm, wet oceanic weather off the Atlantic, and regular blasts from the cold *Pampero* wind that originates in the Argentine pampas.

The effect of the Andean mountain chain is most evident in South America's two most important wine regions: Chile's Central Valley and the Mendoza region of Argentina. Just 150km (90 miles) separate the two, yet, because the Andes lie between them, shielding Argentina from the moist Pacific breezes, the differences in temperature and rainfall are enormous. Mendoza gets virtually no rain and would be a virtual desert were it not for abundant irrigation from rivers fed by mountain run-off. The presence of the Andes has had a dramatic effect on soil, too. Over millenia, silt washed down onto the alluvial plains has created rich, fertile soils, which as Chile demonstrates, creates ideal conditions for most kinds of horticulture, but not necessarily for growing top-quality vines.

MEXICO

With the exception of the excellent Domecq Cabernet and L A Cetto Petite Sirah from the Baja California area, quality in Mexico is closely linked with altitude. Areas with the most potential include the Parras Valley and the 2000-m (7000-ft) high vineyards of Zacatecas, although even at this altitude high temperatures tend to lead to over-jammy reds and sparkling wines without any real bite. Mexico's main hope of success is with brandy grapes and, spurred by the boom induced by the North American Free Trade Agreement, the country has attracted investment from foreign companies such as González Byass, Suntory and Seagram.

CHILE

In South America, Chile continues to lead the way. Since the mid-1980s, Chilean winemakers have been returning from California, France, Australia and New Zealand bringing with them knowledge, ideas and technology for use in their own wine industry. Foreign investors have been attracted by the political and economic stability with the result that Chile's portfolio numbers more than 35 wineries, whose total annual export earnings are now worth over US$140 million, compared with US$23 million in 1988.

WINE AREAS
Mexico
Venezuela
Peru
Bolivia
Brazil
Uruguay
Argentina
Chile

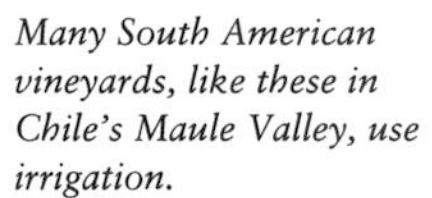

Many South American vineyards, like these in Chile's Maule Valley, use irrigation.

Planted on the flat valley floor and protected by the coastal ranges, the Casablanca Valley vineyards provide the grapes for some of Chile's finest white wines.

Like the country itself, the wine industry is squeezed into a narrow, long north-to-south strip either side of the capital, Santiago, with vineyards never further than 100km (60 miles) from either the coast or the Andes, and with no huge variations in climate. By matching grape varieties with subtle differences in soils and mesoclimates, winemakers have been able to produce a good range of wine styles.

ARGENTINA

Over to the east a sleeping giant is at last starting to wake. Who would have thought the world's fifth largest producer of wine, with over 1200 wineries in the Mendoza area alone, could have remained so quiet on the international scene for so long? The reason for this is a thirsty Argentine population ready to consume most of what's produced and triple figure inflation that makes any kind of economic activity problematic. However, stability arrived in the late-1980s, when the banks found new ways to deal with the country's huge debt crisis. Fixing their internal communications was next on the agenda – a popular joke in Chile was that, if the Argentinians made a good wine, they wouldn't have been able to tell you because the phones didn't work. Torrontes, Syrah, Malbec and Barbera – these are the grape names making Chilean winemakers nervous, and the world should soon start hearing more about what this vast country has to offer.

BRAZIL

The name Marcus James may not have a Latin ring, but it does come from the rolling hills of Rio Grande do Sul, the heartland of Brazilian wine production. It's also one of the top-selling imported brands in the USA, and has helped push Brazil's wine exports past those of Argentina. The quality of the Chardonnay, White Zinfandel, Riesling and Cabernet Sauvignon available under this label hint at huge potential and, as if to prove the point, the first flying winemakers have started to arrive in the country. One wonders if their optimism survives, once they've landed in humid São Paulo – but, if Cinzano can harvest grapes near Recife, less than 1000km (600 miles) from the Equator, then anything is possible!

URUGUAY

Uruguay's wine culture was developed at the end of the nineteenth century, predominantly by Basque settlers, and it is now the fourth biggest producer of wine in South America. Although most of the vineyards are located on the low hillsides west of the capital city of Montevideo, the most progressive spot for *vinifera* grapes is the Rivera region, bordering the Caxias do Sul region of Brazil. Newly imported varieties such as Pinot Blanc, Chardonnay, Cabernet Sauvignon and Merlot are replacing the traditional hybrids producing sweet rosés. Results from this replanting, however, are difficult to gauge as the few exported examples have been of mixed quality. Interestingly, the rare red Tannat grape is effective here.

PERU

Next on the list of relative unknowns is Peru. In the dry heat of the Ica valley, 300km (200 miles) south of Lima, local grape varieties such as Quebranta, Moscatel and Torontel are grown for the Peruvian national drink, an aromatic brandy known as Soldeica Pisco. Quality table wines are produced as well, but in much smaller quantities: producers to look out for are Ocucaje, Vista Alegre and Tacama Wines.

Vineyards can be found between Pativilca, north-west of Lima, down to Tacna on the Chilean border, and in all cases the most important factor is the cooling influence of the Pacific. Annual rainfall in this coastal zone is often as little as 2mm (0.08in), making irrigation essential if the motley crew of grape varieties is to survive. These include Cabernet Sauvignon, Malbec, Grenache and Chenin

OTHER COUNTRIES

Wine is made in Paraguay, Ecuador, Colombia and Bolivia but with a taste and style that hasn't caught on in the international market. Some of the more palatable efforts come from Bolivia's southern region of Tarija. On a high, gently rolling plateau not unlike parts of the Spanish *meseta*, Muscat of Alexandria is the predominant variety grown for both table wine and the sweet, aromatic brandy known as Singani. The latter is lower in alcohol but stronger in flavour than Pisco.

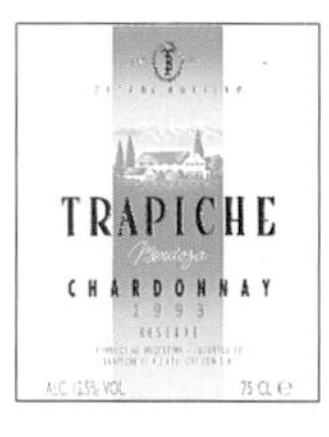

CHILE

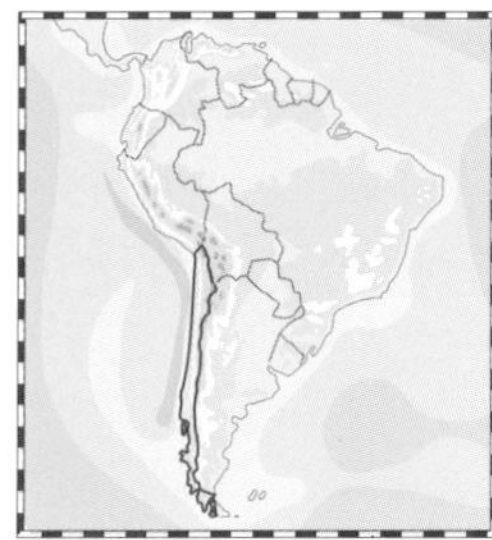

DAWN IN CHILE'S CENTRAL VALLEY is spectacularly slow. The silhouette of the Andes appears like some giant frozen wave of water, gradually swelling in colour and shape as the sun struggles over the ridge. As more light filters through, the older but lower coastal range comes into view to the west and you realize you're caught in a lush, green trough between two immense walls of stone. Shielding your eyes from the brilliant Chilean light, there's nothing but fruit and vines as far as the eye can see. If wines were judged only on the beauty of the vineyards, this country would be hard to beat.

Pedro de Valdivia, founder of the capital Santiago, arrived in 1541 and in his day, before the region was shrouded in smog, it must have been a near-perfect place in which to live. Cool winters and long dry summers make it climatically similar to California, but with a more spectacular backdrop of snow-covered mountains. A perfect place to live, and an excellent place to grow grapes.

For the first three hundred years of its colonized life, the valley grew only the País grape, an unremarkable black variety identical to the Mission of California. Modern wine-making began as recently as the 1850s, when wealthy landowners around Santiago imported French winemakers, out of work after phylloxera had destroyed the European vineyards, and employed them to tend new *Vitis vinifera* rootstocks, partly as an experiment in improving the quality of their own vineyards, partly as a status symbol.

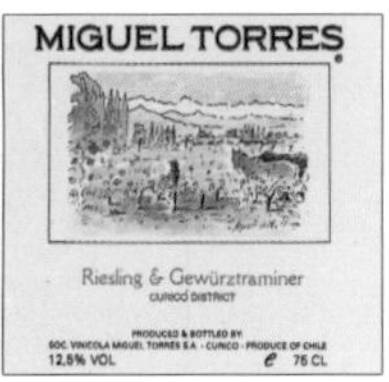

Chile has managed to stay phylloxera-free because of its geographical isolation, with the Atacama desert, the Andes and the Pacific Ocean all forming natural barriers against the pest. In fact, when France and the rest of Europe were ready to replant their vineyards, Chile supplied many of the scions to be grafted onto phylloxera-resistant American rootstock.

Today there are five recognized wine regions in Chile. Atacama and Coquimbo, off our map, produce the grape spirit Pisco. The wine regions are Aconcagua with the sub-region of Casablanca; the Central Valley; and the Southern Region.

CLIMATE

The Andean range is one of the most influential forces affecting Chile's viticultural zones that now extend from Copiapó, 700km (435 miles) north of Santiago, down to the Bío Bío river, 400km (250 miles) south of the capital. From the singeing heat bouncing off the Elqui Valley north in the province of Coquimbo, to the glacial chill slipping down from the Maipo Canyon south-east of Santiago, these mountains make their presence felt in every Chilean vineyard and wine.

Although the vineyards extend for more than 1000km (600 miles) north to south, the most important climatic disparities are in the opposite direction, east to west across Chile's meagre breadth. The explanation for this is the presence of the Andean and the Coastal ranges which, together with the maritime climate, have a critical effect on temperature and rainfall on each vineyard area. The extent of this influence depends very much on where the vineyards are located.

Those on the eastern slopes of the Coastal Range are in a rain-shadow and receive lower rainfall and warmer temperatures than vines situated closer to the Andes. Vineyards in the Andean foothills benefit from big variations between night- and daytime temperatures, with great downdrafts of cold night air producing high levels of grape acidity and a good concentration of fruit. Just north of Rancagua the Coastal Range and the Andes squeeze together and then diverge, and gaps appear in the lower coastal ranges, allowing the cooling effect of Pacific Ocean breezes to influence most vineyards further inland.

Plentiful Andean run-off provides water for irrigation, young fertile soils make grape-growing child's play, and dry conditions help prevent most pests and diseases. Add the fact that this is the only country without phylloxera and you realize that a struggling Chilean vine is an exception, not the rule.

Maybe Chilean winemakers could do with less complacency and a few challenges in the vineyard, because this would force change, which could lift Chilean wines to far greater recognition than they currently enjoy. The use of irrigation should certainly be examined, as the all-too-common sound of gurgling water as you walk through most Chilean vineyards, indicates the overuse of this readily available resource.

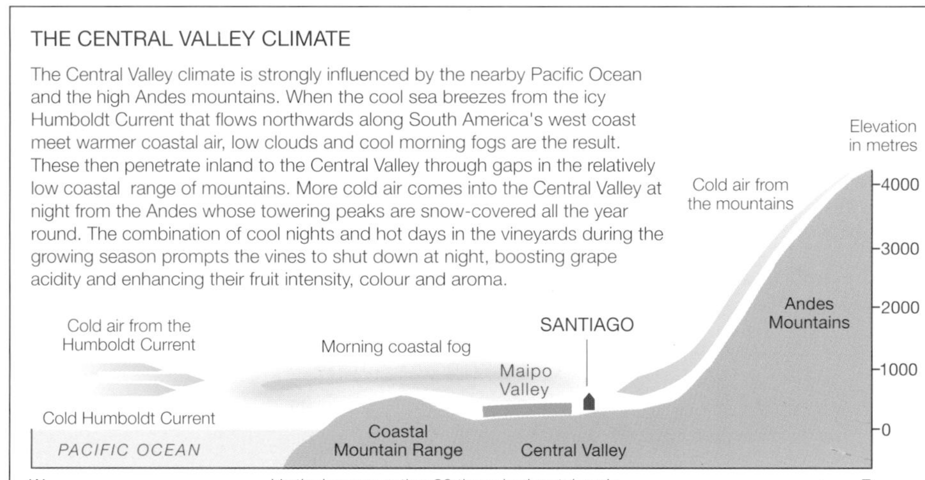

WINE REGIONS

Chile's viticultural areas are often divided into the Irrigated zone, whose rivers have traditionally created the regionalization of Chile's wines, and the Unirrigated zone. The latter involves areas to the west of the coastal range, and in the wetter regions of Chillán and Bío Bío, where results from low-yield vines are changing the perception that Chile's fine wine region stops at Talca. But a statute created by the Chilean government in 1995 has created regions and sub-regions based on the huge river valleys which slice the country, and these are the ones shown on our map.

Experimental plots of Syrah, Mourvèdre and Cabernet Franc in the commune of Cauquenes have drawn the attention of the Californian giant Kendall-Jackson, and Concha y Toro has even dared to make a Gewürztraminer from Mulchén, barely a bottle's throw from the lush green Lake District in the

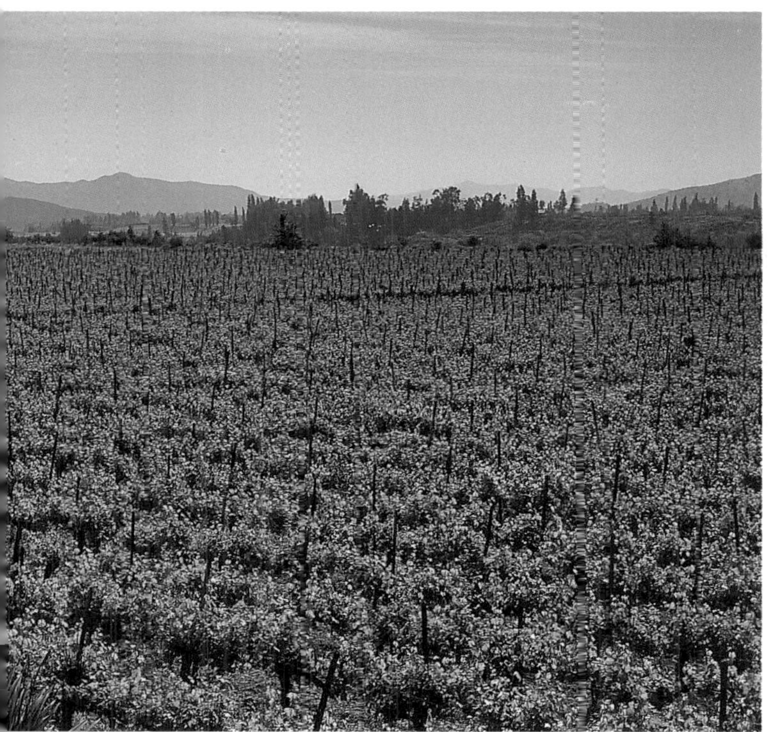

Vineyards of Concha y Toro at Pirque in the Maipo Valley, near Santiago.

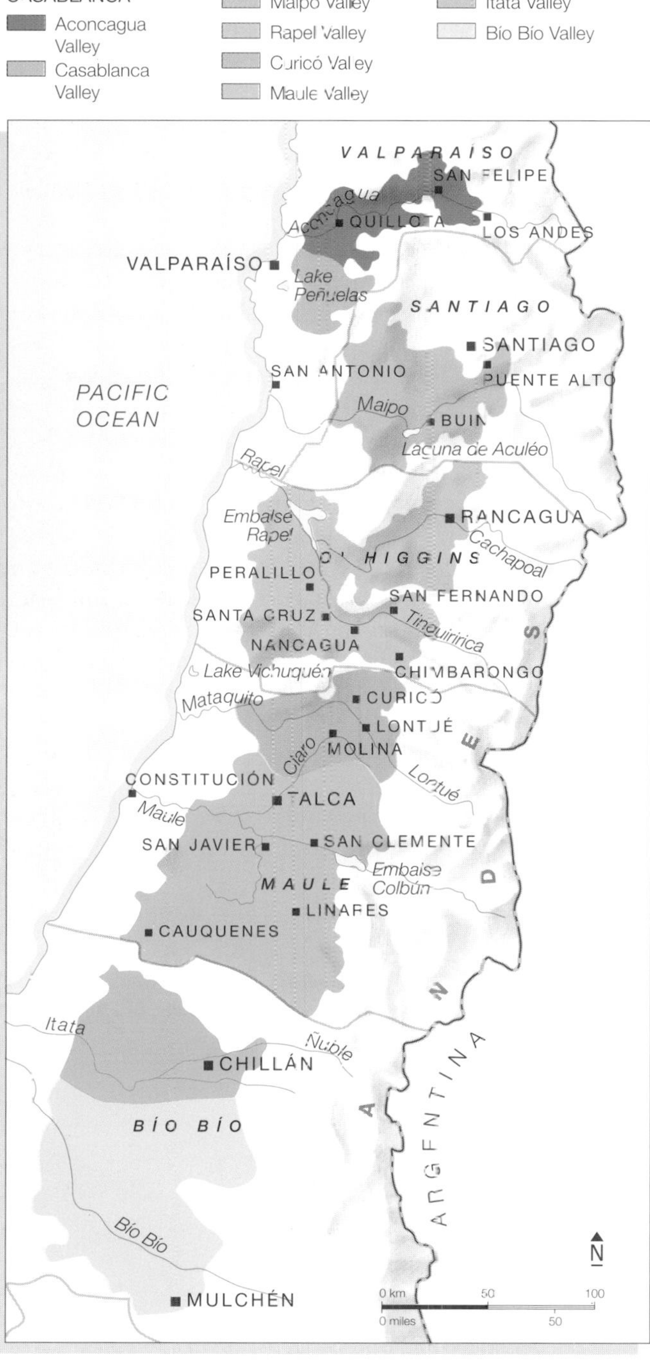

far south. The landscape of wine is spreading out its fingers, and despite an impression of being in a thin strip, there are still plenty of mesoclimatic nooks and crannies yet to be explored. The large US wine companies, Mondavi and Gallo have been down to Chile for a look, and there are even rumours that Australia's giant wine producer, Penfolds, have considered gate-crashing the party.

The international connections don't stop there; in the early 1990s, Chile became a destination popular with flying winemakers. Whether they will fuse the unique Chilean character with an 'international style' is not yet known, but what the New Zealanders, Californians and French *are* doing is raising the overall quality of the Chilean portfolio. And it is a portfolio that now includes a large number of boutique wineries, formed by grape growers deciding to bottle their own product rather than just sell to the big companies. The latter, in turn, have been forced to become self-sufficient and the result has been some spectacularly large single-estate vineyards.

RED AND WHITE WINES

At their best, Chilean wines are packed with exhilarating, youthful fruit that almost kicks its way out of the bottle; at their worst, they are stringy, dilute efforts from grapes such as País and Sauvignonasse, which often masquerades as the superior Sauvignon Blanc.

País, still Chile's most widely planted grape, rarely finds its way into export wines these days, and the more classic, international varieties are now beginning to dominate. Cabernet Sauvignon from the Maipo Valley launched the country's reputation in the nineteenth century, but the varieties creating more excitement among reds today are Merlot, full of capsicum and soft, black cherry fruit flavours; highly aromatic red-berry-and-spice Pinot Noir; and a Malbec that is softer and less weighty than its Argentine counterpart.

The white wine revolution has happened more recently, with the discovery of cool climates such as Casablanca and the implementation of up-to-the-minute wine-making techniques. The results with the rich, tropically laced Chardonnays – greener and firmer in acidity when they from are from Casablanca – have been more positive than with Sauvignon Blanc, which is still the most widely planted white *vinifera* grape. The most underrated and underplanted varieties are the crisp, apple-packed Chenin Blanc and Gewürztraminer, whose lychee-spiced personality has shone in Casablanca and, more recently, in the southern area around of Mulchén.

However, to make a Casablanca Valley Chardonnay costs four times that of any other Chilean white wine. The reason is simple: there's no water, no labour, and for seven weeks every year, the valley is on frost alert. Take a night time stroll through the Casablanca vineyards between mid-September and November and, chances are, you'll witness helicopters overhead, burners on, sprinklers running and agronomists nervously clutching thermometers.

Shaped like a giant cul-de-sac, the valley collects the cold night air of spring, which seems to have an uncanny ability to afflict the vines with frost just after budbreak. Agronomists are experimenting with late pruning and different soil surfaces which may affect the exchange of heat between the warm soil, and the cold night air just above ground level. So as well as being one of the New World's most exciting white wine regions, Casablanca is also an important research centre for anti-frost techniques.

A dark cherry Merlot from Viña Carmen, now based in the Maipo Valley.

ACONCAGUA & CENTRAL VALLEY

RED GRAPES
The most important varieties are Cabernet Sauvignon, Merlot, Pinot Noir and Malbec.

WHITE GRAPES
Sémillon and Sauvignon Blanc are widely planted, followed by Chardonnay, Moscatel and Riesling.

CLIMATE
Summers are hot and dry and winters cool, with most rain between May and September.

SOIL
The fertile soil, with a limestone-clay mix or alluvial silt nearer the rivers, is good for drainage, but not ideal for vine stress.

ASPECT
Only in the foothills of the Andes and Coastal ranges will you find vineyards on a significant incline. The east–west orientated river valleys tend to be broad, with gently sloping sides.

THERE IS NO EASY EXPLANATION of the landscape of the Central Valley; no simple division of hot and cool areas, nor coherent pattern of white grapes here, red there. The confusion is caused by a myriad of local climates that are the essence of the geography of this wine industry, and whose many parts make up a fascinating whole. Once you've stood in the chill fog of a Chimbarongo morning and been blasted by the dry heat of a Talca afternoon you begin to appreciate the complexities of what on paper is just a long north-to-south strip of vineyards.

Imagine you're standing on a dry crumbly ledge overlooking the Don Maximiano estate near Panquehue. Looking east, a panorama of positively humbling beauty spreads out to a horizon dominated by the 6960-m (22,835-ft) high Aconcagua mountain. Below you, neat rows of drip-irrigated Cabernet Sauvignon stand in defiance of the surrounding parched land. Although only 80km (50 miles) north of Santiago, it feels as though the Atacama desert is just around the corner, and only the daily Pacific breezes keep the vines and Errázuriz's New Zealand winemaker from expiring through heat exhaustion.

To the west, and barely 40km (25 miles) from the port of Valparaíso, the same afternoon winds sweep down the Casablanca Valley. You'll struggle to find more than two rows of Cabernet in this valley, which used to be devoted to dairy farming, and which has been transformed over the last five years into Chile's premium white wine region. This east-to-west finger of infertile sandy soil now supports over 1400 hectares (3500 acres) of vineyards, 80 per cent of which is Chardonnay. The strong maritime influence means that in summer the valley suffers only one hour a day of excessive temperatures, and so the harvest is delayed by up to a month after the Central Valley.

The definitions of Central Valley vary enormously, but the government has now decided that, for viticultural purposes, it signifies all vineyards from the Maipo to the Maule catchment areas. The Maipo Valley is close enough to the outskirts of Santiago for the smog, which in winter half-hides the Andes with its haze, to finger its way into the most northern vineyards. Little is known about this pollutant's effect on vines, but one wonders when exorbitant real estate values will encourage wineries like Cousiño Macul to move to cleaner air.

Drive around the vineyards of the Maipo with the window down, and you can almost smell the history and money in the air. The beautiful private homes and gardens of Santa Rita, Concha y Toro and Undurraga take you back to the founding era of Chilean wine in the nineteenth century, when having your own wine on the table was proof of your wealth.

Today, it's families such as the Claros and Guilisastis who maintain this tradition, while taking their wineries into an era of modern technology. The contrast between old and new is particularly marked in the Upper Maipo, where the old Estancia buildings of Santa Rita stand alongside the steel gleam of Carmen's state of the art winery. Thirty-year-old Cabernet vines which produce Santa Rita's powerful, mint-and-tobacco Casa Real rub shoulders with experimental plots of Sangiovese, Barolo and Syrah, while in another corner an area has been cleared for Chile's first organic vineyard. This valley was and still is the pioneering wine region of Chile.

Back on the Pan American highway, the journey south takes you past a seemingly continuous line of fruit factories, to the Rapel region. Centred around the towns of Rancagua and San Fernando, a clutch of small wineries are exploiting the various local climates of the Cachapoal and Colchagua valleys.

Cono Sur has made a home for Pinot Noir, crammed with fresh raspberries and vanilla flavours, on the sandy soils and fog-bound vineyards of Chimbarongo; Rothschilds is making deep, austere Cabernets further east near Peralillo; and Santa Carolina is turning out some of the country's most vibrant, rich damson

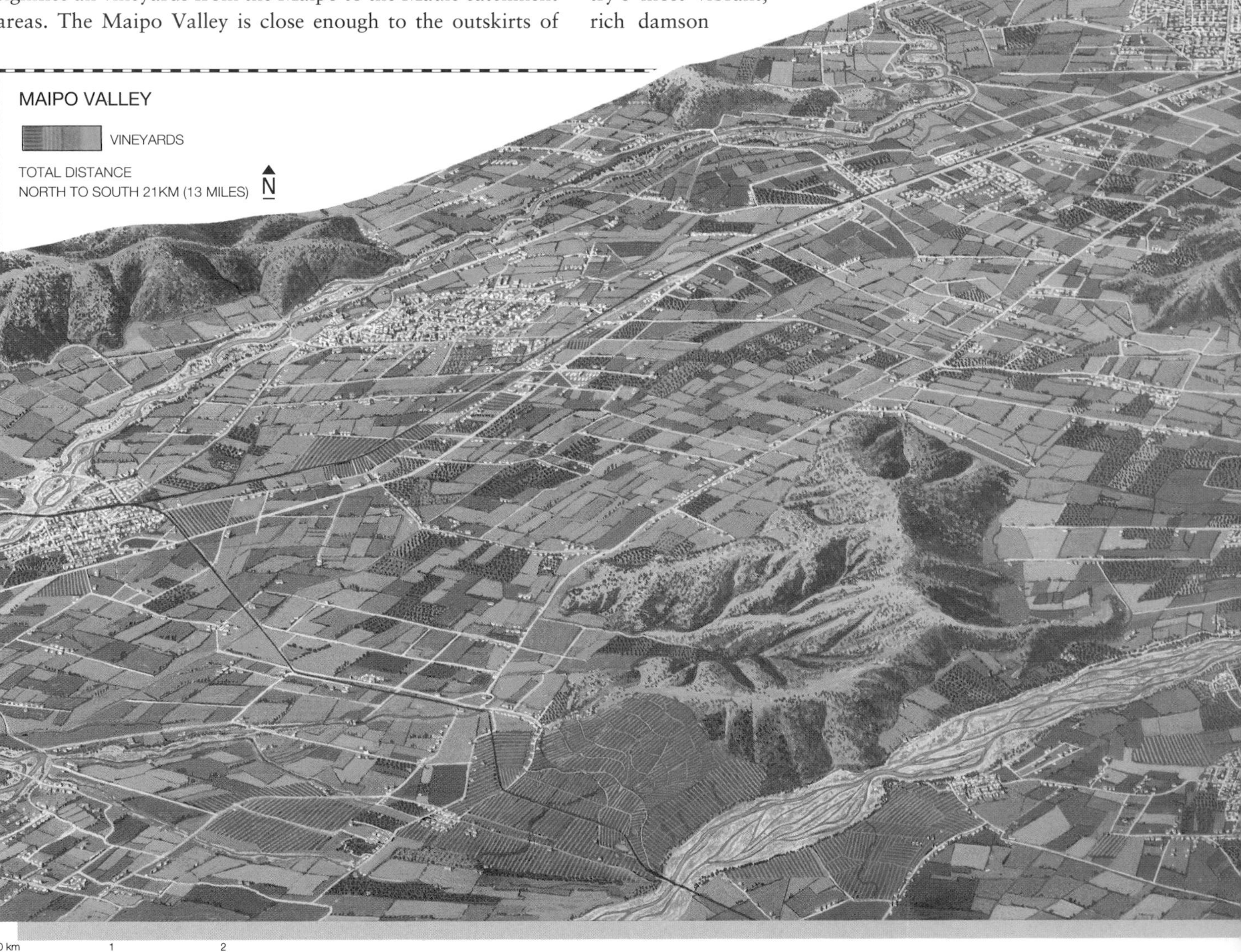

Merlots close to San Fernando. The quality of the air becomes noticably clearer with each mile south, making the Andes seem somehow closer and more imposing. On the journey to Curicó you cross river after river like the rungs of a ladder, while to your right gaps in the Coastal Range allow cool sea breezes to seep through. Miguel Torres arrived here in 1979, and became one of the most innovative figures in the Chilean wine industry, implementing the sort of techniques and equipment that are now widespread throughout the Central Valley.

Although Curicó's average summer temperatures vary little from those in Rapel and Maipo, the region experiences huge daily temperature fluctuations: it can be 23°C (73°F) during the day, dropping to 5°C (41°F) at night. This is ideal for white wine-making, since the grapes ripen slowly, keeping their balancing acidity. The Chardonnays, with their distinctive pineapple and smoky flavours, and grassy Sauvignons from Curicó, have been at the forefront of the Chilean wine revolution.

Another 100km (60 miles) south and you come to the agricultural boom town of Talca in the Maule Valley. This predominantly white wine region is being tipped as Chile's second Casablanca, despite being presently over-endowed with the País grape. Cauquenes, close to the fragmented Coastal Range, has already been likened to northern Sonoma in California.

Soils are more volcanic in substance and rainfall is higher here in the Maule Valley, although summer temperatures can often be hotter than in Maipo. The potential for whites, particularly Sauvignon, has been enough to attract Touraine wizard Henri Marionnet to set up camp. My prediction, however, is that he'll be wishing he drove down the Pan American a bit further – keep an eye out for the name Mulchén.

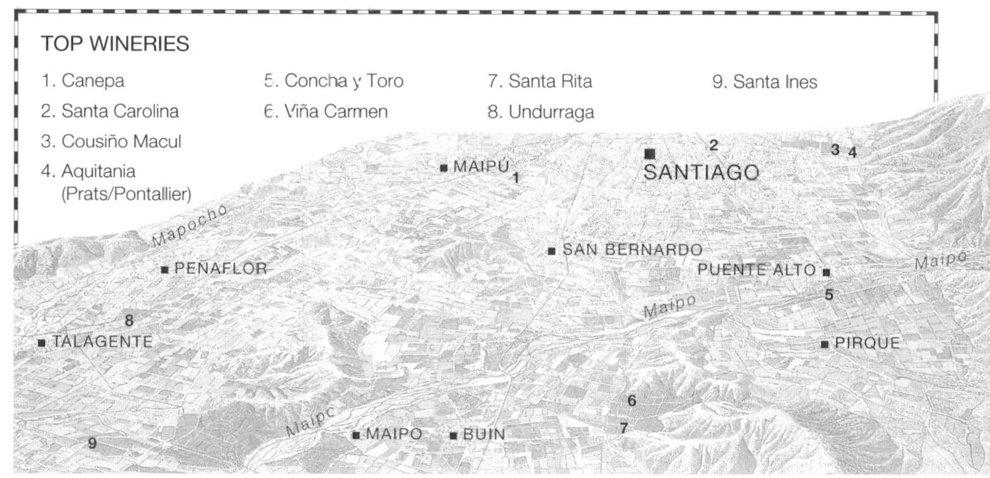

WHERE THE VINEYARDS ARE *This is the Maipo Valley, the most famous wine valley in Chile, which relies for irrigation on the Maipo river which tumbles off the foothills of the Andes. The Maipo skirts the southern suburbs of Santiago, watering the vineyards which flank its banks, before wending its way to the Pacific Ocean (off the map to the left). Without this thread of glacial water the whole area would be a dustbowl.*

Below all the lush green of the vineyards are rich alluvial soils and thick bunches of Cabernet Sauvignon grapes, and a tour of this landscape reads like a who's who of Chilean Cabernet. Towards the centre bottom of the map are the 30-year-old Santa Rita vines for Casa Real. A glance up to the river and right brings you to the source of Concha y Toro's great Don Melchor reds; and over in the right-hand corner, almost surrounded by the city, are the vineyards for Cousiño Macul's Antiguas Reservas.

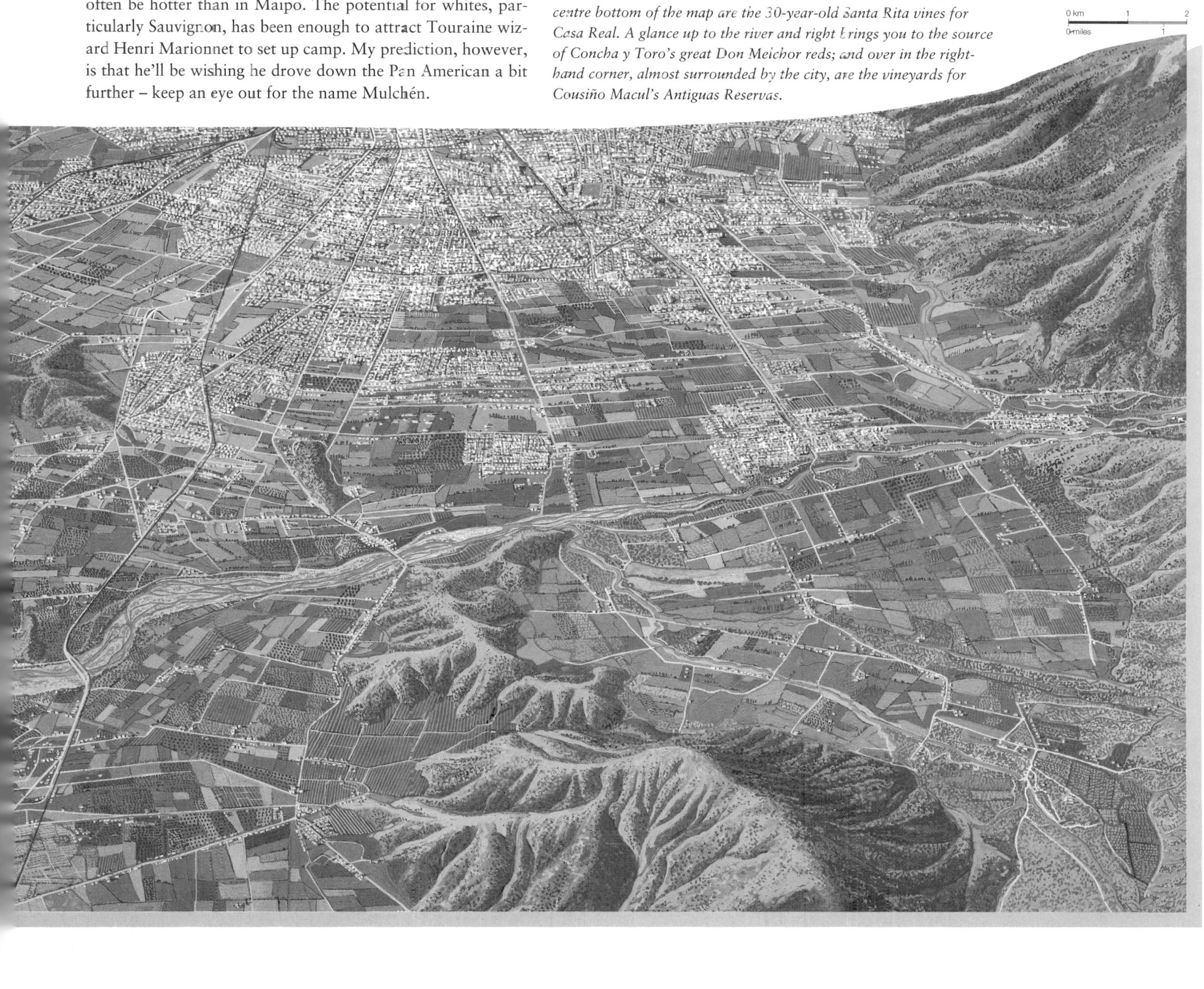

0 km 1 2
0 miles 1

ARGENTINA

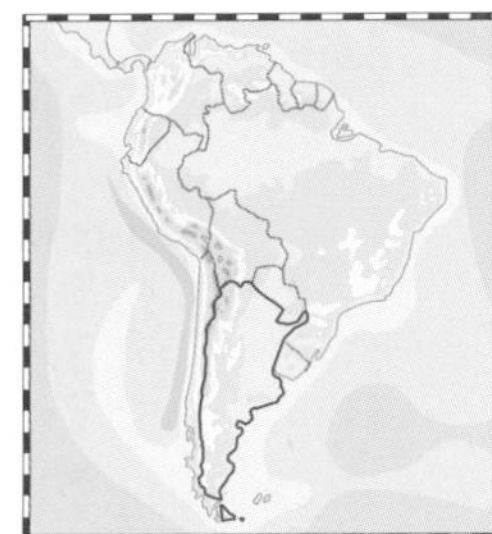

IN ARGENTINA, EVERYTHING SEEMS to come in extra large size – distances, hailstones and steaks all give the impression that you've arrived in the land of the giants. The wine industry is equally gargantuan in proportion: Argentina is the fifth-largest producer of wine in the world, with annual per capita consumption totalling an impressive 90 litres a head, though only a little wine ever crosses its borders.

For a long time this enthusiastic domestic consumption, the uncertain economy and inflation of 5000 per cent a year kept Argentine wines locked away from the rest of the world. Until recently, that is. After some major restructuring of the economy in the late 1980s, Argentine wine producers can now finally set an export price for their wines, and begin to invest in the future. And this has meant that people have begun talking about the wines, and of the wine-making potential that exists on the eastern side of the Andes.

GRAPE VARIETIES

The Spanish started planting Criolla, the pink-skinned grape used to make huge quantities of deep-coloured, oxidized white wine, in 1557. Since then, the vine has spread out over a distance of 1700km (1050 miles), from the Río Negro to the south, up to the Calchaqui Valley, close to the far northern town of Salta. Most of the 14 million hectolitres of wine produced each year is still made from varieties such as Criolla, Torrontes and Palomino. Walk into any wine shop in Argentina, and you'll see lines of bottles labelled Borgoña or Chablis; both are comprised of unknown blends and require little in the way of tasting notes.

Of the European varieties, the intense black, liquorice-lined Malbecs and ripe, spicy Syrahs show the most potential for red wines. Italian immigration has brought in varieties such as Sangiovese and Barbera, but their flavours traditionally have been fused together in blends. Malbec is undoubtedly the grape best suited to the hot continental climate, producing wines which are packed with blackcurrants, damsons and spice – nothing like the French counterpart.

Of the white grape varieties, Sémillon, Chenin Blanc, Ugni Blanc and Chardonnay are widely planted these days and the latter seems most at home in the hot climate. Many Argentine whites are distinguishable for their overripe fruit and lack of acidity, but there are exceptions to this rule from Salta, the Tupungato Valley and Luján de Cuyo.

The Andes form the most important physical influence on Argentine vineyards. This barrier removes all moisture from Pacific winds, thus creating bone-dry conditions and 320 days of sunshine every year, but also providing plentiful water for irrigation. A more negative role played by the mountains helps explain why nets are strung over many vines in the Mendoza region. High-altitude thunderstorms formed over the Andes regularly drop golfball-sized hailstones just before the harvest, and this is more of a hazard than frost.

Unlike Chile, Argentina does not have the natural barriers to protect it against phylloxera which is now widespread in the country, but which appears to cause little concern among winemakers. Most argue that the poor soils and the use of flood irrigation methods keep the louse at bay. In general terms, soils are arid and stony with very little humus, creating stressful conditions for the vines.

Although Mendoza is climatically more suited to reds, cooler temperatures can be found in the southern Río Negro region, making white wine production possible – the other notable white wine-making region at the same latitude in the southern hemisphere is Gisborne in New Zealand. The stark contrast between the green vines and orchards on the north bank of the Río Negro, with the dry scrub on the south, illustrates the total dependence on irrigation. The best producer is Humberto Canale who makes a wonderfully fresh Sémillon, and who is speculatively eyeing the Colondrino Valley, 200km (125 miles) further south.

The snow-covered Andes make a dramatic backdrop to vineyards in the Tupungato Valley in Mendoza.

MENDOZA

A seven-hour, hair-raising trip by car over the Andes from Santiago delivers you into the piercing heat of Mendoza, a city full of old Citroëns, Peugeots and street cafés; a place where a maze of irrigation channels brings green into what should be desert, and where a Frenchman is making wines in old railway storage tanks. Jacques Lurton, a flying winemaker working on both sides of the Andes, may be frustrated by the quality of equipment at Bodega Escorihuela, but he knows the raw material is there in abundance.

Mendoza is Argentina's most important wine region, producing 90 per cent of the country's exportable fine wine. It enjoys summer temperatures of up to 40°C (104°F), plenty of run-off from the mountains for irrigation, and produces grapes with ideal sugar levels, and fruit-filled wines. So far, only two regions in Argentina have been given denominated appellation status: Luján de Cuyo and San Rafael. The latter, 200km (125 miles) south of Mendoza city, is more suited to reds, the best of which is Goyenechea's rich, jammy Aberdeen Angus Cabernet. It matches the meat from the same animal perfectly.

Luján de Cuyo, with an altitude of 1000m (3280ft) and clay soils, has sufficiently cool night time temperatures to allow white wines to flourish. Firm evidence comes from Leoncio Arizu whose Sauvignon, Chardonnay and Riesling have enough fresh acidity to lift them above their often flabby competitors. The same winery also makes a Syrah, whose peppery wallop could give many an Aussie Shiraz a run for its money. The next area due to be given appellation status will be Maipú, which at 700m (2300ft), doesn't have the chill of Luján, but is making big, powerful Cabernets and Malbecs.

Most recent vineyard expansion has been targeted on the Tupungato Valley, whose lofty slopes lie in the shadow of Mount Tupungato, South America's second highest mountain. The cold Andean downdrafts and poor sandy soils are helping produce some of the first Argentine whites with true varietal character. The best of the new bunch is the Sauvignon from Trapiche, the fine wine arm of Bodegas Peñaflor.

Only a fraction of Mendoza's 1200 wineries have made the necessary investments for producing export-quality wines, but the few in question which have seem to be dividing the money equally between winery and vineyards. Argentine agronomists are now modifying the vine canopy to take into account the very high levels of ultraviolet light in this part of the world which affects the speed of photosynthesis. This is a crucial factor in the vine-growing process which has not been addressed in any other South American country.

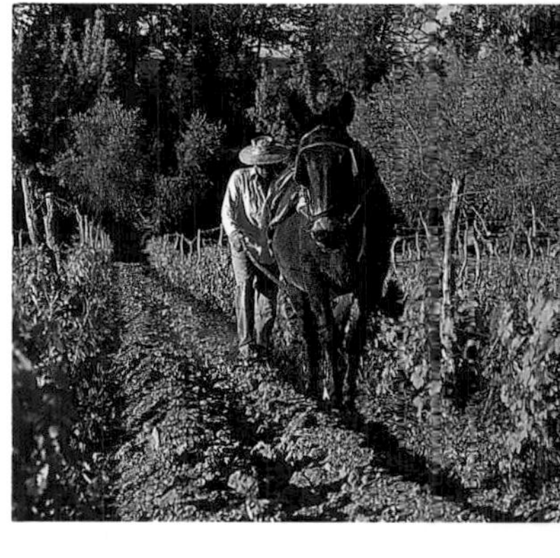

Keeping irrigation channels open in vineyards in Luján de Cuyo, Mendoza, is an important task.

OTHER REGIONS

North of Mendoza are the hotter regions of San Juan, La Rioja, Catamarca and Salta. Most of the production is for concentrated must and wines for sherry production, but surprisingly, Salta is home to Argentina's best white wine. At 1800m (6000ft), its vineyards are some of the highest and most beautiful in the world, and the soft, highly aromatic wine made from the indigenous Torrontes grape variety has already won many international awards.

As far as the wine industry as a whole is concerned, changes are happening slowly. Democratization is only just being realized; decision-making is still top heavy and people at lower levels are afraid to suggest vital changes. If this constraint can be removed, the giant will truly wake up, flex its muscles and begin to roar.

AUSTRALIA

Australia didn't have many advantages when it came to establishing a wine industry. There was no history of wine among the aboriginal people because there weren't any native vines. None of Australia's trading partners in South-East Asia had ever had wine as part of their culture. And it didn't seem propitious that the nation which decided to colonize the vast continent was Britain. Now, if the French, or the Italians, or the Spanish...

We forget one thing. The British weren't much good at growing grapes at home, but they were the world's greatest connoisseurs when it came to appreciating the wine of other European countries, in particular the table wines of France and the fortified wines of Portugal and Spain. Since Australia was initially settled as a penal colony, the authorities were keen to establish a temperate wine-drinking culture rather than one based on the more savage rum. And at the end of the eighteenth century, when New South Wales was gradually establishing itself, Europe was embroiled in war. The idea of a British Imperial vineyard not hostage to the recurrent political crises in Europe must have seemed enticing.

Well, it almost did work out like that. For considerable portions of the nineteenth and twentieth centuries, Australia provided a steady stream of unchallenging wines that were lapped up by Britain. But by the last quarter of this century the country had embarked on a remarkable voyage of wine discovery that has placed her at the forefront of all that is best in the New Age of wine – despite having a vineyard area that is dwarfed by the major European nations.

This position has been achieved without Australia enjoying many of the perceived benefits of Europe's classic regions. The general rule in Europe is too much rain and not enough sunshine. The general rule in Australia is more than enough sunshine and not nearly enough rain. Australia's winemakers have turned this to their advantage, highlighting the ripeness of the grapes in a succession of sun-filled, richly textured reds and whites. These may initially have been inspired by the best of Europe, but they have now created such a forceful identity of their own that it is Europe which is now attempting to ape the styles of these Down Under Wonders. In the meantime, improvements in the understanding of how to bring grapes to optimum ripeness – not over- or underripe, but just so – have led to an explosion of cool-climate wine regions in the fringes of this parched continent that challenge, but in no way imitate, the old classic regions of Europe.

Poplar trees act as a windbreak in the Mildara vineyards in the cool-climate region of Coonawarra, South Australia.

The Wine Regions of Australia

WATER, WATER, WATER. That's the story of Australia. On this vast, parched continent, finding meagre supplies of moisture is an ever-present factor of life, not just of grape-growing. The actual population of the nation, let alone the development of vineyards, is limited by the availability of water and little of the rain that does fall arrives when it is most needed – during the long, hot summers. And yet the Australians show astonishing resourcefulness: new vineyards constantly appear, and entire new regions emerge where no-one had suspected the vine could flourish. At the beginning of the 1980s, when its thoughts turned winewards, the country was known abroad for little more than the odd bottle of Kanga Rouge red (there was a white sister wine that I rather disrespectfully dubbed 'Bondi Bleach'), and as the butt of the Monty Python team's humour. Since then Australia has established a reputation for approachable yet high quality, characterful wines of every possible style that is nothing short of astonishing.

All the major states manage to find a mixture of cool, warm and positively broiling conditions in which to grow their wines. All the major players, that is. The Northern Territory's Chateau Hornsby near Alice Springs probably qualifies as the hottest – and maddest – winery in the universe. Queensland is pretty torrid too, though some high-altitude vineyards down on the New South Wales border like to think of themselves as coolish. Tasmania endlessly seeks patches of land warm enough to ripen grapes in a climate once condemned by its own government as too cool for grapes and about right for apples. Most of the main vineyards, based in the north of the island, don't find it easy, though odd strips of land in the east and south somehow do ripen even varieties like Cabernet Sauvignon. How? When they work it out, I'll let you know.

WESTERN AUSTRALIA

Western Australia is a vast state, virtual desert except for its south-western coastal strip. Its wine industry was one of the first to be established in Australia, but the isolation of Perth from the rest of Australia kept it focussed on supplying the local market. The Swan Valley was the exception to the rule, its Houghton White Burgundy being highly successful in the eastern states. This old-fashioned, sun-baked vineyard region used to be best suited to throaty reds and fortified wine. But Australian winery and vineyard expertise is so sophisticated that remarkably good dry whites are now appearing. Even so, the most exciting wines come from the secluded vales of the Margaret River and the Lower Great Southern regions, where the continent's south-western tip turns away from the Indian Ocean towards the cold depths of the Southern Ocean.

SOUTH AUSTRALIA

South Australia was the last of the major wine states to be established, but has more than made up for lost time. It now dominates the Australian wine scene, not only growing the greatest tonnage of grapes, but also making the greatest volume of wine, and harbouring the majority of the nation's biggest wine companies within its borders. The bulk of these grapes will have been grown in the impressive vineyards along the banks of the Murray River where mechanization, bountiful sunshine and a plentiful supply of water from the river have created some of the most efficient vineyards in the world.

But South Australia has more to offer than oceans of attractive, undemanding gluggable wine. In the north, the verdant outpost of the Clare Valley, scooped out of the parched grazing land that stretches away on all sides, is an unexpected but excellent producer of 'cool-climate' table wines. Not *that* cool, however, because, as so often in Australia, local climates within an area provide a far broader spectrum of styles than one would find in Europe. Clare Shiraz and Clare 'port' are just as good as delicate Clare Riesling.

The Barossa Valley is South Australia's traditional heartland, where most of the big companies are based. However, they don't process much Barossa fruit – most of their wine is based on Riverland grapes. Luckily there are some stubborn, talented, wild men left in the valley who are preserving what is left of the ancient vineyards and redefining Barossa wines in their own, rip-roaring style.

The hills to the east of the Barossa Valley are home to vineyards providing a spectrum of styles, from great Shiraz to delicate sparkling wine. Chronic water shortage is the only inhibitor for these outstanding vineyards. Just south of Adelaide are the Southern Vales, the first area to be developed in South Australia, once famous for 'ferruginous' reds and fortified wines shipped to England in vast quantities. Despite incursions from the expanding city, the area is now a major producer of high quality reds and whites.

Population explosion has never been a problem at Padthaway and Coonawarra – hardly anyone lives down in this damp, forlorn corner of the state, but this has allowed the development of tracts of superb vineyard land, producing

THE CLASSIFICATION SYSTEM FOR AUSTRALIAN WINE

Australia's system for classifying wines is, at the time of writing, undergoing some changes. Under a 1994 agreement with the EU, the wine-producing states are being divided into new zones, regions and sub-regions. The complete extent of each one is yet to be agreed and the boundaries are unlikely to be enshrined in law before 1997.

The new system, currently being thrashed out all over Australia (but not yet appearing on labels), has to encompass certain peculiarities. The main one is the widespread system of regional blending in Australia: that is, trucking grapes from several different regions, possibly in different states, for blending together. Four major wine companies (Penfolds, BRL Hardy, Orlando and Mildara Blass) make 80 per cent of Australia's wine and they rely a lot on blending varieties and wines from different regions for their big-selling brand wines. Brand names such as Koonunga Hill and Jacob's Creek will continue to be an important part of the Australian wine scene, and will not legally have to disclose origin or variety of grapes. Small wineries may opt to advertise grape variety and region on the label. If they do so, 85 per cent of grapes must be the named variety, and the same percentage must come from the area specified.

QUALITY CATEGORIES AND GEOGRAPHICAL INDICATIONS

- **The Label Integrity Program** This system (also called LIP) was introduced in 1990 and guarantees all claims made on the label, for example, the vintage, variety and region, by making annual checks and audits on specific regions, varieties and wineries.
- **Produce of Australia** This is the most general geographical designation. Any wine sold solely under this category will not be able to have a grape variety or a vintage on its label.
- **South-Eastern Australia** This is the next level, a category which covers, in fact, most of the wine-producing areas of Australia and is already widely seen.
- **State of Origin** This is the next most specific category.
- **Zones** Many of Australia's traditional wine areas are being incorporated into these new zones which are in the process of being delimited. For example, the new zone of Central South Australia will incorporate Adelaide, Adelaide Hills, Barossa and Clare.
- **Regions** These are the next level, for example, Barossa.
- **Sub-regions** Some regions are being divided into sub-regions, for example, Barossa Valley within the region of Barossa.

thrilling wines, and the lack of a local population has forced these areas to become world leaders in the science of totally mechanized vineyard operation.

VICTORIA

If South Australia's vineyard regions seem reasonably compact and organized, Victoria's often seem as though they've been hurled into position with all the precision of a scatter-gun. Partly this is because the vineyards followed the Gold Rush, and when the gold was exhausted odd areas of vineyard were left all over the state. Those that still survive, however, can produce some of the most exhilarating and distinctive wines in Australia, albeit in tiny quantities.

Victoria was Australia's major producer for most of the nineteenth century until the phylloxera louse devastated her vineyards, while sparing those of South Australia. It is only in recent years that Victoria has reassumed her position as provider of the most startling array of wine styles in Australia. Substantial volumes are produced in the Murray River vineyards, but it is the stunning liqueur Muscats of Rutherglen and Glenrowan, the thrilling dark reds of Central Victoria, the urbane Yarra Valley and Mornington Peninsula reds and whites, the off-the-wall, intense Gippsland Chardonnay and the hauntingly perfumed Delatite Pinot Noir that imprint their flavours on my mind.

NEW SOUTH WALES

Colonial Australia began in New South Wales. The revolution in wine that has propelled Australia to the front of the world stage began here too. Although the Hunter is now less important than it once was, and the irrigated vineyards of the hinterland dominate production, the unashamed exuberance of the Hunter Valley and its Sydney supporters set Australian wine on course for where it is today.

PANORAMIC MAPS OF AUSTRALIA

Barossa Valley *pages 276–7*
Coonawarra *page 279*
Clare Valley *page 281*
Yarra Valley *pages 284–5*
Hunter Valley *pages 288–9*
Margaret River *page 292*

OTHER MAPS

South Australia *page 275*
Victoria *page 282*
New South Wales *page 287*
Western Australia *page 291*
Tasmania *page 294*
Queensland and Northern Territory *page 295*

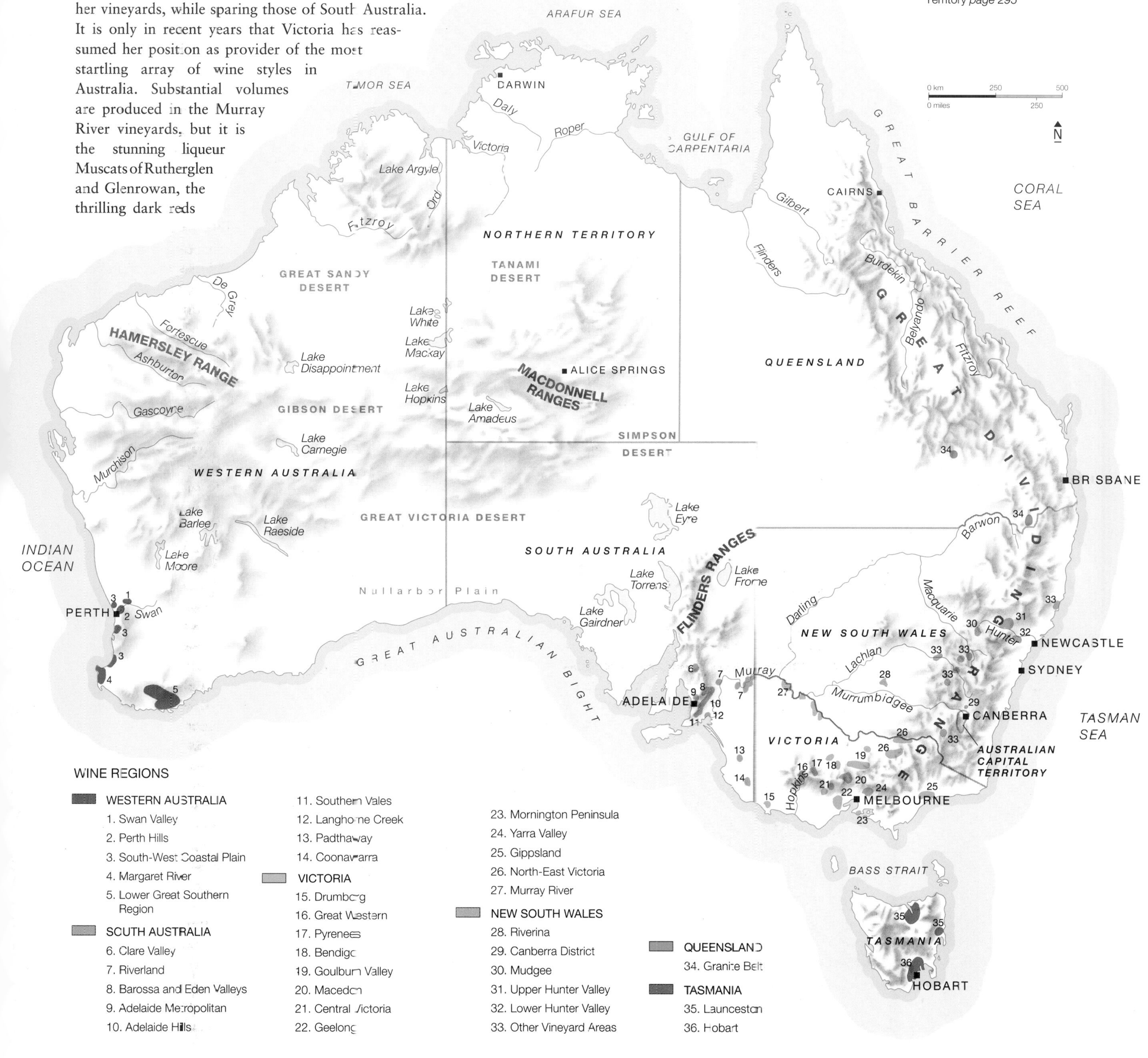

WINE REGIONS

WESTERN AUSTRALIA
1. Swan Valley
2. Perth Hills
3. South-West Coastal Plain
4. Margaret River
5. Lower Great Southern Region

SOUTH AUSTRALIA
6. Clare Valley
7. Riverland
8. Barossa and Eden Valleys
9. Adelaide Metropolitan
10. Adelaide Hills
11. Southern Vales
12. Langhorne Creek
13. Padthaway
14. Coonawarra

VICTORIA
15. Drumborg
16. Great Western
17. Pyrenees
18. Bendigo
19. Goulburn Valley
20. Macedon
21. Central Victoria
22. Geelong
23. Mornington Peninsula
24. Yarra Valley
25. Gippsland
26. North-East Victoria
27. Murray River

NEW SOUTH WALES
28. Riverina
29. Canberra District
30. Mudgee
31. Upper Hunter Valley
32. Lower Hunter Valley
33. Other Vineyard Areas

QUEENSLAND
34. Granite Belt

TASMANIA
35. Launceston
36. Hobart

SOUTH AUSTRALIA

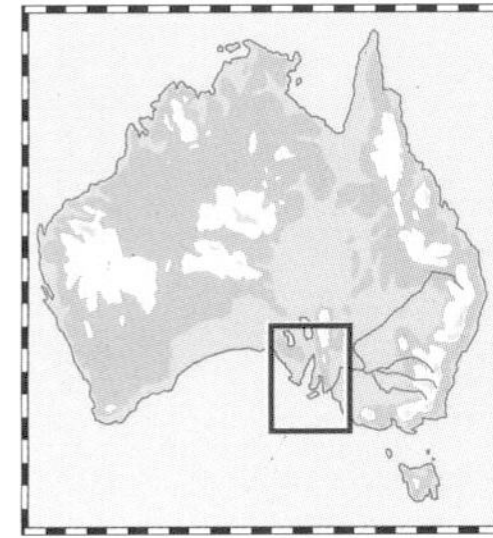

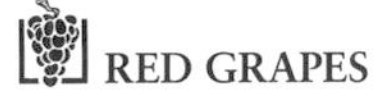

RED GRAPES
Shiraz, Cabernet Sauvignon and Grenache predominate.

WHITE GRAPES
Rhine Riesling, Chardonnay, Gewürztraminer, Sauvignon Blanc and Sémillon are widely planted, with some Palomino and Pedro Ximénez.

CLIMATE
This ranges from 'cool climate' areas like the Adelaide Hills and Coonawarra, to hot, dry areas like Barossa.

SOIL
The soil is a mix of sandy loam, red loam, various clays and fertile volcanic earth. Coonawarra has an area of *terra rossa* over a limestone subsoil.

ASPECT
This varies widely, from the flat vineyards of Coonawarra to vines on the slopes of the East Barossa ranges.

THEY RECKON ADELAIDE'S DRINKING WATER is some of the worst in the civilized world. I do too. Luckily the beer is excellent, so, apart from brushing my teeth, I don't have a lot to do with Adelaide's water. However, throughout the state, water – or lack of it – is a hot topic. The only part of South Australia that has enough water is the southern tip where Coonawarra almost drowns in the stuff. In the rest of the state every drop of water counts. Luckily South Australia has one massive zillion gallon water resource – the Murray River, which follows a tortuous route for nearly 2600km (1615 miles) along the border between New South Wales and Victoria before executing a final arc through South Australia and trickling out into the ocean at Lake Alexandrina.

The exploitation of the Murray River's waters for irrigating hundreds of thousands of otherwise uncultivable barren acres in the heart of Australia is one of the great agro-industrial feats of the twentieth century. Even more impressive is South Australia's historic position at the forefront of quality wine production. In the early 1950s, Max Schubert, winemaker at Penfolds near Adelaide, produced his first, experimental barrels of Grange based on a combination of scientific principle, ingenuity and sheer determination.

He was the first winemaker – not just in Australia, but in the New World – to make a concerted, scientifically-inspired effort to produce a top-quality red wine. This approach is not approved of by the traditionalists of Europe, who maintain, through their systems of controlled *appellation* of origin, that great wines only come from special, rare patches of land, pinpointed after centuries of trial and error. They've had a thousand or two years to fine-tune this principle of *terroir,* which lays all the emphasis for specialness on the place, and regards the men or women merely as transient guardians of the flame. But they're missing half the trick.

Australia hasn't had hundreds of years to gradually pick and choose her favourite spots. She hasn't had a hundred generations of inhabitants whose lives revolved around the vine, developing a fine wine tradition across the ages.

Max Schubert's success at creating a great wine is proof of Australia's greatest gift to the world of wine – the belief that everything is possible. And you can do it from scratch, with whatever materials suit your purpose. Of course, you can't guarantee what the end result will be like, but if you follow your vision with courage and determination – you can do it.

The Barossa Valley is home to Australia's biggest wine producers, but also has substantial quality vineyards.

ADELAIDE'S FIRST VINEYARDS

As with the other states, vines were planted within a year of the first settlement in 1836, and as with Sydney and Melbourne, these first vineyards have long since disappeared under the tarmac and brick of modern Adelaide, although a small patch of the original Penfold vineyard at Magill is still producing grapes, hemmed in by suburbia. Vineyards were fairly quickly established in the northern reaches of the city, and the influx of German settlers to the Barossa Valley created a vineyard and winery community that has played a dominant role in Australian wine ever since.

But the first moves out of Adelaide were in fact to the south: to Morphett Vale, Reynella, McLaren Vale and Langhorne Creek. Areas like Morphett Vale and most of Reynella have now largely disappeared under the creeping tide of urban sprawl, but Adelaide is not only much smaller than Melbourne and Sydney, it is also more aware of the importance of wine production to the state. Consequently the attractive neighbourhood of McLaren Vale has largely been able to resist the offers of property developers and to enjoy a burgeoning number of vineyards and wineries, both large and small.

THE RIVERLAND

Australia has two Californians to thank for much of the wine they drink today. The Chaffey brothers arrived in Australia at the end of the 1880s, having successfully established irrigation schemes in Californian desert conditions. They had the foresight and determination to utilize their experience to transform the annual flooding of the Murray River into the most important resource in Australian viticulture.

The headwaters of the Murray River are numerous streams fed by the melting snowfields of the Great Dividing Range. Every year the river used to bulge and burst with the thaw. The waters flooded vast expanses of empty, arid land that gratefully lapped up the moisture – but to no avail, since no-one knew how to exploit this annual bounty.

Initially at Renmark in South Australia, and then at Mildura further upstream in north-west Victoria, the Chaffeys built pumping stations, dams, locks and irrigation channels to harness the Murray River. As a result verdant market gardens and vineyards were planted where nothing but saltbush desert had existed before.

Both Renmark and Mildura went through tricky times, but the Murray Valley regions of South Australia and Victoria flourished, and so did the Riverina region which lies on a Murrumbidgee River tributary in New South Wales. Today, the grapes for all the low-priced, but attractively fruity, red and white Australian wines will have come from these mechanized, irrigated vineyards.

This large-scale irrigation has helped Australia transform the quality of budget wine worldwide, but it is a relatively recent phenomenon. The heart and soul of the South Australian wine industry is still in the water-starved, sun-soaked fields and vales to the north and south of Adelaide.

GRANGE

It was near Adelaide that Australia's fine wine tradition began when Max Schubert, Penfolds chief winemaker, began work in 1951 on what was to become one of the greatest wines in the world – known first as Grange Hermitage, now as Grange.

Schubert had returned from a trip to Europe's vineyards the year before, fired up most of all by the great red wines of Bordeaux's Médoc – a fine wine area with a lot of rain, barely enough sunshine, and a predominance of the Cabernet Sauvignon grape. The region produced wine that was aged in new French oak barrels and could mature for half a century. He was determined to make the same style of wine in South

Australia – where there was tons of sunshine, hardly any rain, about one shopping basket full of Cabernet Sauvignon in the entire state, and not a new French oak barrel to be found, not for ready money nor cucumber sandwiches. And until his visit to Bordeaux he had had no idea that a red wine could hope to age for more than ten years at the outside.

No worries. Schubert had the vision. He decided the Shiraz grapes – the same variety as Syrah in France's Rhône Valley – were the best South Australia could offer. So he'd use these. Different flavour to Cabernet, but if he picked them early from low-yielding vines and treated them with kid gloves from the moment of picking to the moment of bottling, he reckoned he could get the result he wanted. He managed to secure a few American rather than the more usual French oak barrels, and decided they were in any case more suitable for his Shiraz.

Ah yes, the vineyards. Well, Schubert began with some vines at Morphett Vale, south of Adelaide, and some at Magill in the foothills above Adelaide. They weren't famous vineyards, but he knew them, he knew their soils, their ripening patterns, and the flavour of their fruit. They served him well for the first Grange. Later he added Kalimna, in the Barossa Valley, and when Morphett Vale was sold for housing he expanded into the Clare Valley too. These days, with Penfolds controlling a massive amount of South Australia's top vineyards, Coonawarra fruit joins McClaren Vale, Barossa, Clare, indeed *any* fruit that is good enough. Simple as that. If the fruit is good enough – regardless of where it is grown – it will be considered for Grange.

Whenever someone starts to lecture me about the necessity of colonizing the world with self-serving, protectionist *appellations* that stifle so much of Europe's creativity, I triumphantly raise the case of Grange. All it claims on the Grange label is 'Wine made in Australia'. That's a proud enough statement for me. I hope it never has to change.

SOUTHERN VALES

The region directly south of Adelaide is called the Southern Vales, with McLaren Vale at its centre. Its success right up to the 1950s was based on its ability to ripen black grapes sufficiently to create fortified 'ports' of high quality, or strapping great red table wines that used to boast of their 'ferruginous' character as being of medicinal quality. Generations of respectable British ladies supped happily on Tintara and Emu Burgundy, convinced they were imbibing for their health's sake. Well, perhaps they were.

In fact Southern Vales has proved a highly adaptable wine region. Although it is sunny, and McLaren Vale and further north is genuinely hot, most of the vineyards benefit from afternoon sea breezes, cooling down the vines. Langhorne Creek on the Fleurieu Peninsula is positively cool and is also fairly heavily irrigated. Water is short in McLaren Vale and the Cabernet, Shiraz and even Grenache are rich and heady, but there are also surprisingly good Chardonnays and Sauvignons.

CENTRAL SOUTH AUSTRALIA

Just inland from McLaren Vale you can see the southern tip of the Adelaide Hills. These head north, skirting Adelaide, to become part of the Mount Lofty Range, continuing up east of the Barossa Valley. Here boundaries between the Barossa Range, Eden Valley and Adelaide Hills are blurred. Opinions are divided, but a general rule of thumb is that vineyards over 400m (1300ft) in height are categorized as Adelaide Hills.

The hills more or less directly east of Adelaide, around Piccadilly, are high and cool, and even slightly damp and they produce some exceptional 'cool-climate' whites and exciting sparkling wines. Lenswood, a little to the north, can also produce gorgeous reds. It's an area which has attracted some of

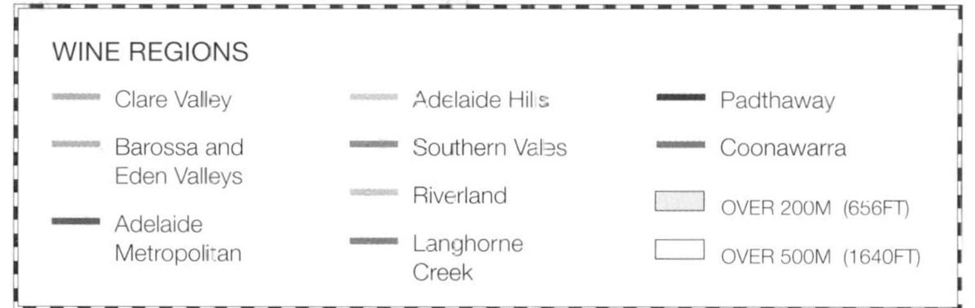

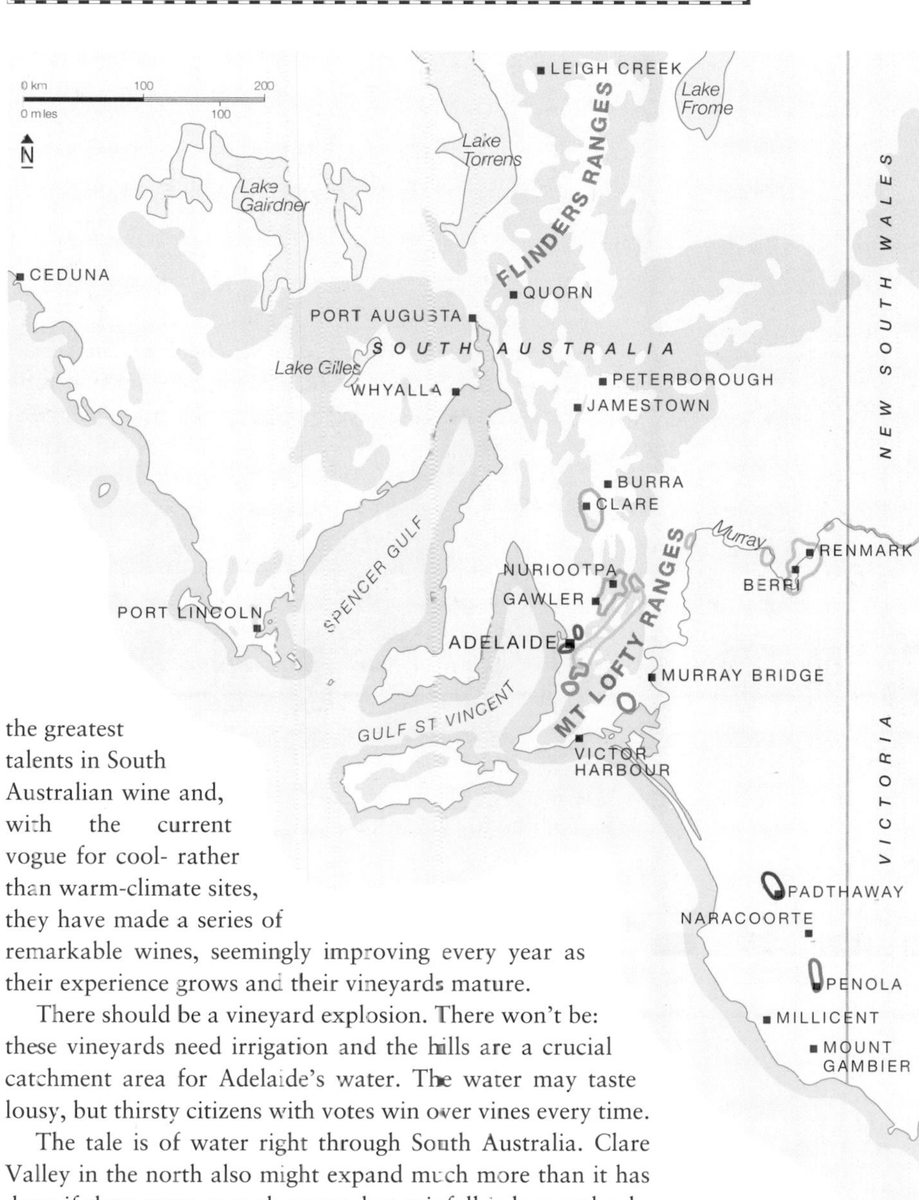

the greatest talents in South Australian wine and, with the current vogue for cool- rather than warm-climate sites, they have made a series of remarkable wines, seemingly improving every year as their experience grows and their vineyards mature.

There should be a vineyard explosion. There won't be: these vineyards need irrigation and the hills are a crucial catchment area for Adelaide's water. The water may taste lousy, but thirsty citizens with votes win over vines every time.

The tale is of water right through South Australia. Clare Valley in the north also might expand much more than it has done if there were enough water, but rainfall is low and subterranean water hard to come by.

SOUTH-EASTERN SOUTH AUSTRALIA

Water dominates the cool far south of the state as well, but in a different way. The Great Artesian Basin stretches across the south towards the sea. The water table is so high that most of the land is far too swampy for viticulture. But there are a series of limestone ridges in the south-east of the state that offer brilliant conditions for vines. Coonawarra's exceptional qualities have been known about since the end of the nineteenth century and it is now perhaps Australia's most sought after locality for vineyard land. Padthaway, 65km (40 miles) to the north of Coonawarra, has proved brilliant for white wines, notably Chardonnay, Riesling and Sauvignon.

Other sites are now being developed all over the area. But the politics of a thirsty population rears its head once more. To preserve supplies of drinking water to Victoria in the east, South Australia has had to accept strict limitations on how much water she extracts on her side of the state border. Even when there's water, water everywhere, someone is going to stop you doing what you want with it.

Barossa Valley

RED GRAPES
Shiraz is the star red, with Cabernet Sauvignon close behind. The latter is often best when blended with grapes from other areas.

WHITE GRAPES
Rhine Riesling predominates, with a small amount of Sémillon, Chardonnay, Palomino and Pedro Ximénez.

CLIMATE
The Barossa Valley is hot, with a drip irrigation system to counteract the arid summers. The Eden Valley and the East Barossa Ranges are cooler with more rain, but at the wrong time for the vines, so irrigation is necessary.

SOIL
Topsoils are varied, ranging from heavy loam with clay, to light sand; some soils need the addition of lime to counteract acidity. Subsoils are limestone, quartz-sand and clay, and red-brown loams.

ASPECT
Traditional valley floor estates are best at producing big reds; estates at 300 to 400m (985 to 1300ft) in the East Barossa Ranges are excellent for cooler climate styles.

Just listen to these names – Kaiser Stuhl, Siegersdorf, Bernkastel, Gnadenfrei – names of wineries and vineyards in the Barossa. And listen to these names – Johann Gramp, Johann Henschke, Peter Lehmann, Leo Buring – names of Barossa winemakers, ancient and modern. Add to these a delightful assembly of old Lutheran bluestone churches, bakeries offering *Strudels* and *Torten* rather than buns and cakes, delicatessens displaying *Sauerbraten* (braised beef) and *Leberwurst* (liver sausage), and the strains of lusty-lunged choirs and the oompah of brass bands at practice cutting through the still warm air of a summer's evening – and you know the Barossa Valley is different. It's in a time warp, from the early days when Lutheran settlers from Silesia (now part of Poland) travelled halfway round the world to spread themselves across this valley just to the north of Adelaide, intent upon creating a new homeland.

Scratch the surface, though, and you find a different story. These days Kaiser Stuhl and Leo Buring are now mere brand names for the giant Penfolds group. Many of Australia's largest-scale and most efficient wineries now cluster round the old settler towns of Nuriootpa, Tanunda and Angaston. Indeed, today over 50 per cent of all Australia's wine is made by these big Barossa-based companies. But hardly any of the grapes for it are *grown* in the Barossa by the descendants of Silesian settlers who used to provide the fruit.

One of the biggest crises for Australian wine in the late twentieth century was when, one by one, the famous old Barossa wine concerns grew into nationally important operations, and two things dawned on the accountants in charge of their finances. First, that Barossa vineyards might produce good grapes, but the yields were low and prices were high. Second, that the reverse was true of the vast irrigated vineyards which were springing up along the banks of the Murray River. These might not produce exciting grapes but their yields were *high* and their prices low.

Depending upon your level of cynicism, these large companies realized that talented corporate winemakers could make perfectly good wines out of these inferior grapes, so why use expensive local fruit? Maybe they said, even if the Barossa grapes are better, what's a bunch of inbred, antediluvian grape growers to us? Then maybe they had to stop right there. The Barossa is a proud place where passions are easily aroused. The old Barossa and the new went through a traumatic standoff in the 1980s when financial pragmatism was pitched against tradition. The scars are still visible. But the two must learn to co-exist and I believe they can. Both of them are simply too important to the wealth of Australian wine to founder.

The Barossa Valley was settled by a mixture of German and British pioneers in the 1840s and 1850s. George Angas, a Scot, was one of South Australia's most important frontiersmen. To counteract the chronic shortage of labour to work his estate north of Adelaide, he paid for three shiploads of German Lutherans to emigrate from Silesia. They arrived in the Barossa Valley in 1842 and, though Anglo-Saxon families like the Smiths of Yalumba have thrived since settling at Angaston in 1849, it was the Germans – or Barossa Deutsch – who moulded the character of the valley. Vineyards and wine companies were established, which by the beginning of twentieth century were already dominating South Australian production. With the abolition of interstate tariffs and the decimation of rival Victoria's vineyards by phylloxera, South Australia rapidly assumed the dominant position in Australian wine, and the efficient Barossa companies were the natural leaders.

BAROSSA AND EAST BAROSSA VINEYARDS

Vineyards were established in two main areas, the gently undulating valley floor following the amblings of the North Para River from round Lyndoch to north of Nuriootpa, and the hillside to the east. The valley floor is hot, often very hot, and dry, often very dry, and the soils veer between distinctly infertile

0 km 1 2
0 miles 1

0 km 1 2
0 miles 1

yellow clays to deep red soils ideally suited to the production of dark, burly red wines or ports. But there isn't much rainfall, and there isn't much suitable subterranean water for irrigation either. Indeed many grape growers, even in the 1990s, stick to ancient bush-pruning techniques simply to give the vines the best chance of surviving drought conditions at the height of most summers. Add to this a sudden swing in public taste towards fruity white wines in the 1970s and you can see why the big Barossa companies decided to give up using Barossa grapes, and began to develop massive, easily irrigated, mechanized vineyards to the north-east on the Murray River.

Once supplies to the big companies were severed, it was possible that Barossa Valley as a grape-growing region might virtually disappear during the late 1970s and 1980s. Luckily there was a local hero – Peter Lehmann – awaiting his hour. He established a wine company with the sole objective of saving vineyards from the plough. Now, a new wave of committed small-scale producers, and companies like Penfolds and Yalumba, have joined him. As a new generation of wine drinkers embrace the dark, intense flavours of low-yield Barossa Shiraz one can only be thankful there was someone around to protect one of Australia's greatest wine heritages.

EDEN VALLEY

Up in the hills it was very different. Though companies like Henschke grow brilliant Shiraz north of Eden Valley, and Mountadam has produced remarkable Pinot Noir on the outcrops to the west, the greater height provides much cooler conditions. This has made Eden Valley and the surrounding hills one of Australia's top white wine producers: the Eden Valley Rieslings, in particular, with their marvellous lime-acid attack and floral fragrance are frequently Australia's best. And though the big companies do use Eden Valley fruit for their top wines, it is the old families like Henschke and the newcomers like Adam Wynn at Mountadam who bear the brightly burning torch for this exciting region.

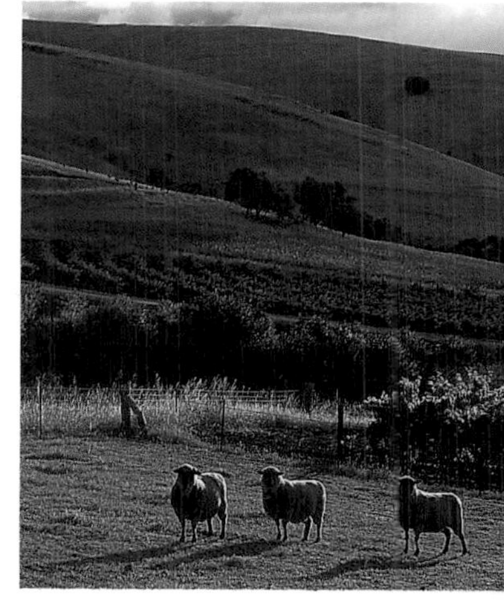

German settlers brought sheep and vines to the open spaces of the Barossa Valley.

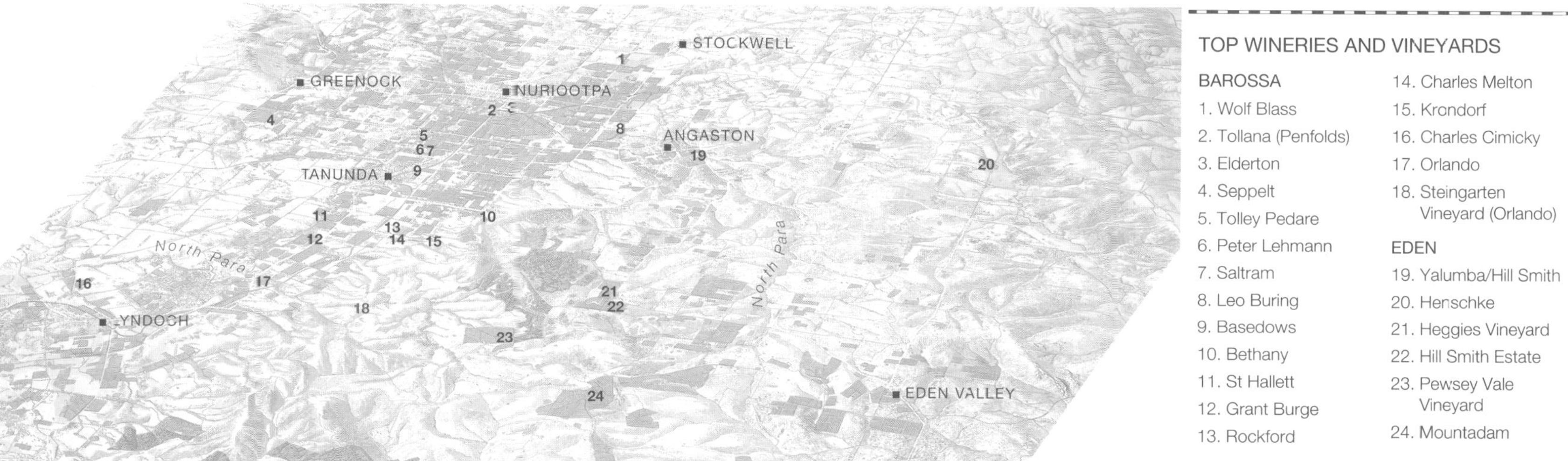

TOP WINERIES AND VINEYARDS

BAROSSA
1. Wolf Blass
2. Tollana (Penfolds)
3. Elderton
4. Seppelt
5. Tolley Pedare
6. Peter Lehmann
7. Saltram
8. Leo Buring
9. Basedows
10. Bethany
11. St Hallett
12. Grant Burge
13. Rockford
14. Charles Melton
15. Krondorf
16. Charles Cimicky
17. Orlando
18. Steingarten Vineyard (Orlando)

EDEN
19. Yalumba/Hill Smith
20. Henschke
21. Heggies Vineyard
22. Hill Smith Estate
23. Pewsey Vale Vineyard
24. Mountadam

N

BAROSSA AND EDEN VALLEYS

VINEYARDS

TOTAL DISTANCE NORTH TO SOUTH 31KM (19 MILES)

WHERE THE VINEYARDS ARE *This map is a marvellous panorama of the whole Barossa grape-growing region. One of the things that always strikes me in South Australia is how seemingly insignificant the mountains are. The inaptly named Mount Lofty Range stretches up the right of the map, yet these ancient hills have been worn away through the millennia into mere hummocks of storm-smoothed rock. Yet they are a crucial couple of hundred yards above the valley floor. This creates cooler, windier conditions for viticulture, and since they are some of the first obstacles the westerly winds have encountered since coming in from the Indian Ocean, whatever moisture there is will drop predominantly in these hills.*

As you can see, all the vineyards have lakes next to them. These are to catch winter rains for irrigation in the dry summers when each vine may need 5 litres (9 pints) of moisture per day. Mountadam, for instance, at the bottom of the map, is an estate of 1000 hectares (2500 acres), yet only 48 (119) are planted with vines. The rest of the land is largely used as a catchment area for the 86cm (34in) of rain that fall each winter. Their lakes hold 900 million litres (250 million gallons) of water – enough to irrigate the vines for six years.

The valley floor doesn't get nearly so much winter rain and very little summer rain. Not only that, but the subterranean water to the west of the North Para River is too salty to be much use for irrigation. Consequently, most of the vineyards are established to the east of the river. However, the dry country to the north and around Nuriootpa and Greenock can produce stunning reds from old, low-yielding vines. Grange produced by Penfolds is based on Kalimna fruit from north of Nuriootpa. Further south, wineries such as St Hallett and Rockford are building a similar reputation.

In the Eden Valley hills water is less of a problem – so long as you are prepared to build large catchment dams to hold the winter rains, because precious little falls in summer. Distinctly cooler conditions prevail here, due to the height of the hills themselves: most vineyards are at between 400 and 500m high (1300 and 1640ft), producing some of Australia's top white wines.

Shiraz (Syrah) is the most widely planted grape variety in Australia.

COONAWARRA

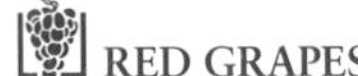

RED GRAPES
Successes with Cabernet Sauvignon make this the predominant variety now, though Coonawarra was first known for its Shiraz.

WHITE GRAPES
Riesling is the most widely planted variety, with Chardonnay on the increase.

CLIMATE
These are the southernmost, and therefore coolest of South Australian vineyards. The easily accessible water table gives high yields of good quality. Vintage can take place from April to as late as June.

SOIL
An area of *terra rossa* (literally 'red soil'), or crumbly red loam, covers the low ridges, with both black cracking clay and sandy soils over a clay base on lower ground.

ASPECT
It is flat here – uniformly so, and with its long growing season, high light intensity and unique soil structure, ideal for vines.

MOST OF THE GREAT VINEYARDS of the world owe their presence to a river which at some point has carved its path towards the sea and created a mixture of valley slopes and river plains that provide unique conditions for grapes to ripen. Coonawarra owes its uniqueness to the fact that there aren't any rivers anywhere near. There are mountains to the east. There's sea to the west. But there are no rivers to connect one to the other.

There's a lot of water, though, falling in the mountains every winter. And it seeps, inch by inch, just below the surface across the bleak, barren swathe of bogland that makes up the southern tip of South Australia. They call this the rump end of the Great Artesian Basin – at least, that's how *I* interpret their vernacular. Depending on which experts you talk to this water has seeped from neighbouring Victoria or all the way from Queensland. And depending on how far the water has come it could be thousands of years old or merely hundreds. But however old it is, it is so pure you almost need actually to add salts to it to make it suitable for irrigating vines. And there's lots of it, just below the surface.

That's all very well. But what about what happens above ground? What about the climate; and, for that matter, what about the soil? So far this sounds like a graphic description of one of the world's all-time squelchy hell-holes. What's it to do with wine? Let's go back a bit. About 600,000 years.

Coonawarra was underwater then, with the shoreline being marked by the Comaum Range east of Coonawarra. But two things happened. First, there was a reversal in the earth's magnetic field, followed by a slow but continual upheaval in the land that has by now raised Coonawarra 60m (200ft) above sea level. Second, about every 50,000 years, there has been an ice age and the seas have retreated. With each consequent warm period, the seas have crept back to find the land sufficiently raised that a new beach is established, and a new ridge is built up of limestone over sandstone. There have been 12 ice ages in the last 600,000 years. There are 12 ridges between the Comaum Range and the sea – one for each ice age – running north to south, parallel to the shore. Between each ridge the land is a sullen mix of sandy soil over a clay subsoil, or black cracking clay. On the barely perceptible ridges, a thin sprinkling of fertile reddish soil sits above a tough limestone cap. Break through that cap and the limestone becomes so damp and crumbly you can poke your finger into it and waggle it about. And a yard or two further down, the pure mountain waters from the east seep slowly towards the sea.

The limestone ridges topped with *terra rossa* soil provide perfectly drained sites for vines, islands in a vast expanse of waterlogged land. And the underground water provides one of the best natural resources for irrigation that any wine area in the world possesses – that is, if the vines need it: many of the older vines' roots tap directly into the water. Given that Australia is a hot country, this should be a recipe for the efficient production of vast amounts of reliable, low cost wine.

CHILLY VINEYARDS

But there's one other thing. It's *not* hot in the south of South Australia. Coonawarra, 400km (250 miles) south of Adelaide, is surrounded by the chill Southern Ocean. The winters are cold and damp, with the majority of the rain dumping uselessly on the area during the winter months, often waterlogging all but the scattered limestone ridges. Springtime is squally, and often frosty too. Summer starts out mild but dry, yet in February and March there are often hot spells that scorch and exhaust the vines and cause the bore holes to pump day and night, providing life-saving irrigation for the vines. And as the grapes slowly ripen into April the weather can break into sour, joyless early winter before the harvest is in and stay unfriendly and raw until the following spring.

Cabernet Sauvignon from the Bowen Estate, one of Coonawarra's top vineyards

RED WINES

And yet some of Australia's greatest red wines are made on this thin strip of perfect vineyard land, where the climate makes the vine struggle all year round, but the famous red soil and subsoil cosset and spoil it, and more than compensate for its effort. Indeed Coonawarra has been called the 'Médoc' of Australia, and its cooler and drier than usual conditions do resemble those of Bordeaux, with irrigation easily making up for Bordeaux's higher summer rainfall.

Since its foundation as a vine-growing area in 1891, 'French-style' reds, primarily from Shiraz and Cabernet, have constituted the majority of production. However, it is only since the 1960s that the world's wine drinkers have begun to appreciate the remarkable, relatively light yet intensely flavoured qualities of Coonawarra reds. By the early 1990s, Coonawarra's *terra rossa* acres had become among the most sought after vineyard land in Australia.

This has led to problems. On both sides of the *terra rossa* limestone ridges there are heavy clay plains. Hundreds of acres of these have been planted with vines. Although some decent white wine and sparkling base has been produced, such damp cold soils cannot ripen Cabernet or Shiraz. Should their wines be allowed the name Coonawarra? I rather think not. The quality potential is so good on the *terra rossa* soils, however, that some producers grossly overcrop, and wines get sent to market that are unworthy of the Coonawarra label they bear.

TERRA ROSSA

The diagram shows a vine root growing in the Coonawarra red earth, commonly known as *terra rossa*. It is one of the best soils for growing vines in Australia, and covers a north-south strip 15km (9 miles) long and 2km (1 mile) wide. Although both the limestone and the red topsoil have excellent drainage, it is not fully understood why this soil produces such fine grapes.

1 is the rich, red-brown topsoil, a freely drained earth between 2 and 50cm (¾ and 20in) deep.

2 is a band of hard calcrete of up to 15cm (6in), a result of calcium carbonate being leached out of the topsoil and redeposited above the limestone. This layer needs to be broken up before planting to provide access for vine roots and passage through for water.

3 is a thick, free-draining limestone, an ideal environment for root nourishment.

4 is where the rock becomes saturated with ground water. The water table is unusually high in Coonawarra, at a depth of only 2 to 4m (6½ to 13ft) and the vine roots that extend deep enough can benefit from year-round water.

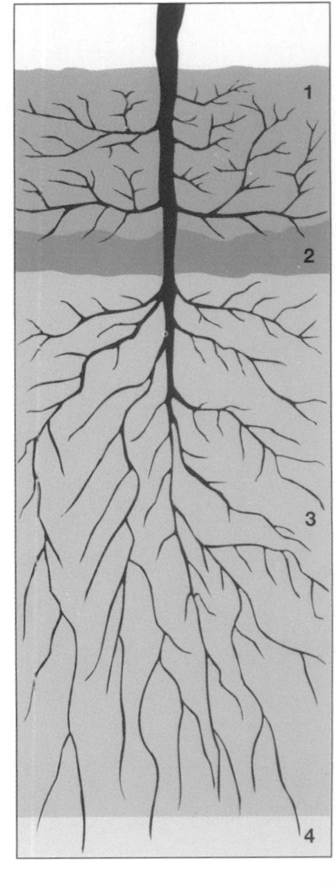

OTHER VINEYARD AREAS

Of course, Coonawarra is only one ridge. There are similarly good conditions on the other ridges. St Marys, 15km (9 miles) west of Coonawarra, Mount Benson on the coast and various sites around Naracoorte, to the north of Coonawarra, are being exploited with high hopes of superb quality. And Padthaway, 65km (40 miles) north of Coonawarra, is already producing fantastic whites.

Padthaway was never developed with superb quality in mind. In the early 1960s industry analysts forecast that Australian wine consumption would triple during the 30 years that followed. So the big companies began to look for large tracts of land that they could buy and operate cheaply. Seppelt, Hardy and Lindemans have developed such efficient mechanized vineyards that they reckon to need only one human per 40 hectares (100 acres). Although planted with all kinds of varieties at first, the astonishing quality of top-line whites has propelled this featureless prairie to deserved star status.

TOP WINERIES AND VINEYARDS

1. Sharefarmers Vineyard (Petaluma)
2. The Ridge
3. Rymill
4. Evans Vineyard (Petaluma)
5. Penley
6. Brand's Laira
7. Redman's Redbank
8. Wynns Coonawarra Estate
9. Rouge Homme (Lindemans)
10. Zema
11. Penfolds Vineyard
12. Mildara
13. Katnook
14. Leconfield
15. Bowen Estate
16. James Haselgrove
17. Hollick
18. St Hugo Vineyard (Orlando)
19. Parker
20. Ladbroke Grove
21. Kirri Bill Vineyard (Rosemount)

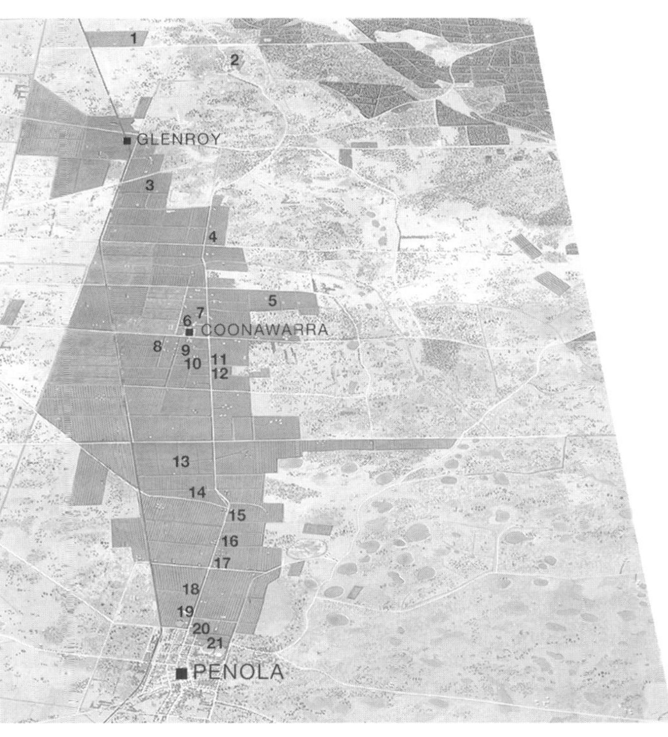

0 km 1 2
0 miles 1

WHERE THE VINEYARDS ARE *Well, here it is – Australia's most famous vineyard area in all its glory. It is a spectacular place to grow vines, but it just so happens to be dumped in the middle of what is virtually a swamp. When the rain starts, you keep to the roads or take a pair of water-wings. Penola – the little town at the bottom of the map – is aboriginal for 'big swamp'.*

But if you take the main road north out of Penola, for about 15km (9 miles) you travel along the low limestone ridge of Coonawarra. This slight increase in altitude raises the road and a thin strip of land either side a crucial few feet above the surrounding waterlogged clay soils, and provides brilliant conditions for growing an abundance of healthy vines.

The best land has a thin covering of red-brown topsoil which lies directly over a layer of calcrete and then limestone. This terra rossa *topsoil is extremely fertile so the best results come from thin coverings of as little as an inch or two on top of barely perceptible rises in the land.*

However, those vines you can see west of the railway are on black clay soils, and some of the vines stretching east are on white clay, part of which is little more than partially reclaimed swamp. Neither is capable of ripening Cabernet or Shiraz grapes.

The underground water that nourishes the Coonawarra vines is remarkably pure, but as more and more water is drawn out of the Great Artesian Basin, damaging salts are likely to be leached out from further inland. A water-sharing agreement between South Australia and Victoria, only 20km (12½ miles) to the east of here, is aimed at limiting any water extraction in the future.

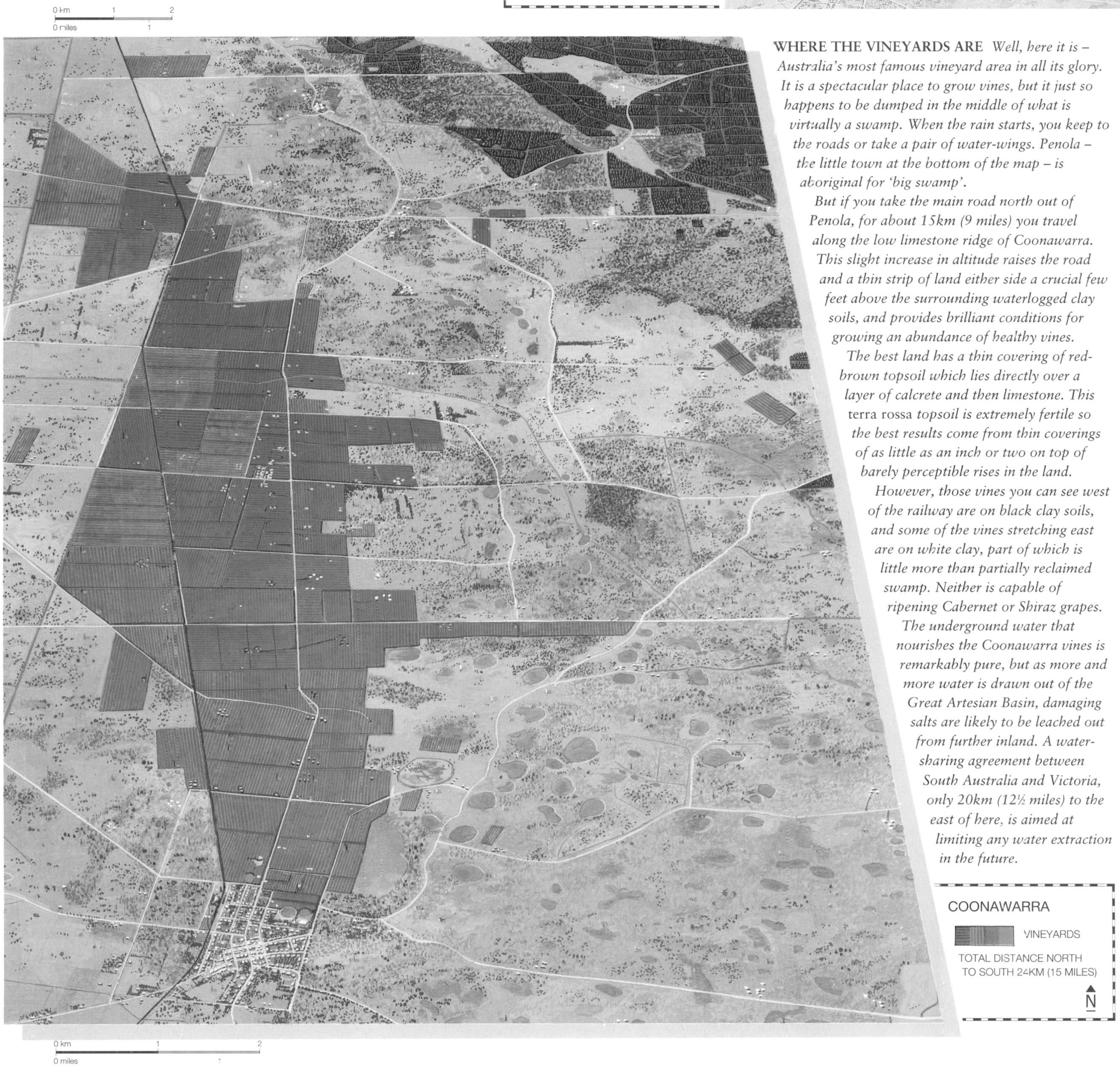

COONAWARRA

VINEYARDS

TOTAL DISTANCE NORTH TO SOUTH 24KM (15 MILES)

N

0 km 1 2
0 miles 1

Clare Valley

RED GRAPES
The main plantings are Cabernet Sauvignon and Shiraz, with some Grenache.

WHITE GRAPES
Rhine Riesling is the principal variety, with some Palomino and Pedro Ximénez, Crouchen, Sauvignon Blanc, Sémillon and Chardonnay.

CLIMATE
The heat should lower acidity and send sugars soaring, but instead produces light wines, especially Rhine Rieslings, with an unexpected natural acidity and delicacy.

SOIL
The main subsoil is of calcareous clay. In the north, there's a sandy loam topsoil, in the centre, red loam, and in the south, red clay.

ASPECT
Vineyards are planted at 400 to 500m (1300 to 1640ft) above sea level, in the narrow valleys running from north to south, and in the foothills to the west. Aspects vary, with twisting contours.

IT DOESN'T MAKE SENSE. Here I am, heading out of Adelaide in South Australia, the hottest and driest of Australia's major wine-making states. And I'm heading north – towards the torrid, parched centre of the continent. Yet I'm looking for a famous cool-climate vineyard area – the Clare Valley. It might make a little more sense if I were heading up into the Adelaide Hills I can see to the east, since a climb of a few hundred yards dramatically cools the air, and the craggy hills also attract whatever rainfall there might be.

But I'm driving along the flat northern highway out past Gawler and Tarlee, through the arid, dun-coloured cereal fields interrupted by occasional grain silos. The vista of broad, bone-dry acres peppered with doughty gums makes my tongue stick to the roof of my mouth as I ache for an ice-cold beer. And suddenly, in a dip in the land just north of Auburn, there's a field full of shocking green. There are vines – the first vines of the Clare Valley – healthy, vigorous, their leaves waving gently in the breeze.

The breeze? There wasn't any breeze when I stopped back at Tarlee for a beer. There is one now, unmistakably taking the harshness out of the hot afternoon sun. And the air feels fresh, hillside fresh. Without once realizing that I was climbing at all, I've reached over 400m (1300ft) above sea level. At last some of the possible reasons for Clare's reputation as one of Australia's great cool-climate vineyard regions are now beginning to fall into place.

TOP WINERIES AND VINEYARDS

1. Jim Barry
2. Tim Knappstein
3. Leasingham
4. Tim Adams
5. Wendouree
6. Petaluma Vineyard
7. The Clare Estate Vineyard (Penfolds)
8. Sevenhill
9. Wilson Vineyard
10. Pikes Polish Hill River Estate
11. Pauletts
12. Skillogalee
13. Mitchell
14. Crabtree Watervale
15. Eaglehawk
16. Mount Horrocks
17. Wakefield
18. Jeffrey Grosset

Don't worry. They'll fall out of place again. Clare may have a great reputation for elegant, balanced Riesling, but it also produces some of the most startlingly concentrated, brawny Shiraz in South Australia. Its 'ports' and Liqueur Tokays are pretty exceptional too, for that matter. In one vineyard Riesling struggles to ripen by late April. A couple of miles north-east, another vineyard is harvesting the port variety Touriga Nacional in February. I'll try to explain.

I've seen Clare described as a frontier town and as the 'hub of the north' in its early days. I'll buy that. After the long trek up from Adelaide, nearly 130km (80 miles) away, Clare promises to offer the last relief before the endless parched plains that stretch away to the north towards Jamestown and Port Pirie. Since the town of Clare's establishment in 1846, it has always been a focal point both for trading and for the refreshment of tired limbs and parched throats for the whole area. It's been a boom town several times. Copper was discovered nearby in 1845. Clare serviced that boom. There were massive wheat plantations established during the 1870s. Clare serviced these too. World-class slate reserves were discovered at neighbouring Mintaro, and there was a silver rush leading to the formation of the Broken Hill Propriety Co – currently Australia's largest company – in 1855. Once again, this small town reaped its share of the benefits.

What is left now is a traditional, well-worn market town, still quietly prosperous long after those early frenzied years – and vines. Vineyards throughout much of Australia were established to slake the thirsts of wealth-crazed pioneers in the nineteenth century. Clare was no exception, though one distinct novelty, for Australia, was the establishment of Sevenhill Jesuit monastery in 1851. Naturally they planted vines. Just as naturally, they are still making wine.

Clare was luckier than many areas in that there was a genuine effort made to plant only the better varieties – and particularly Cabernet Sauvignon, Malbec and Shiraz. As elsewhere in Australia, these were largely supplanted by varieties planted for cheap fortified wine and brandy in the early twentieth century, but the re-establishment of Clare Valley as a quality region during the 1950s and 1960s saw the better varieties, as well as Rhine Riesling and (more recently) Chardonnay, dominate new vineyard plantings.

VINEYARD AREAS

The trick was to have planted the vines in the right place. Clare Valley isn't really an accurate description of the region. There are really three valley systems, stretching both south and north with a watershed plateau in the middle at Penwortham. Incorporated into this are five sub-regions with differing soils at different heights above sea level – and differing mesoclimates too. Yes, confusing, especially since Clare seems to get about as much heat and even less rain in the growing season as the broiling Liqueur Muscat centre of Rutherglen in Victoria. Well, it does and it doesn't. Except in the valley bottom it would be impossible to establish vineyards without irrigation. Storage dams to collect winter rain are the most effective source of water. And the tumbling landscape allows a wide variety of aspects to the sun, while nights are generally chilly and breezes arise to cool the vines during the day.

There is some disagreement about these cooling breezes because they have a fair way to travel inland from the sea 50km (30 miles) to the west and south-west. It seems likely that they only arise in the late afternoon, thereby cooling the vines in the evening and at night, yet not affecting the most intense heat of the early afternoon. So ripening is not hindered, but acid levels remain high in the fruit. Some locals say that it is the daily fade-out at around 4pm of the hot, northerly winds

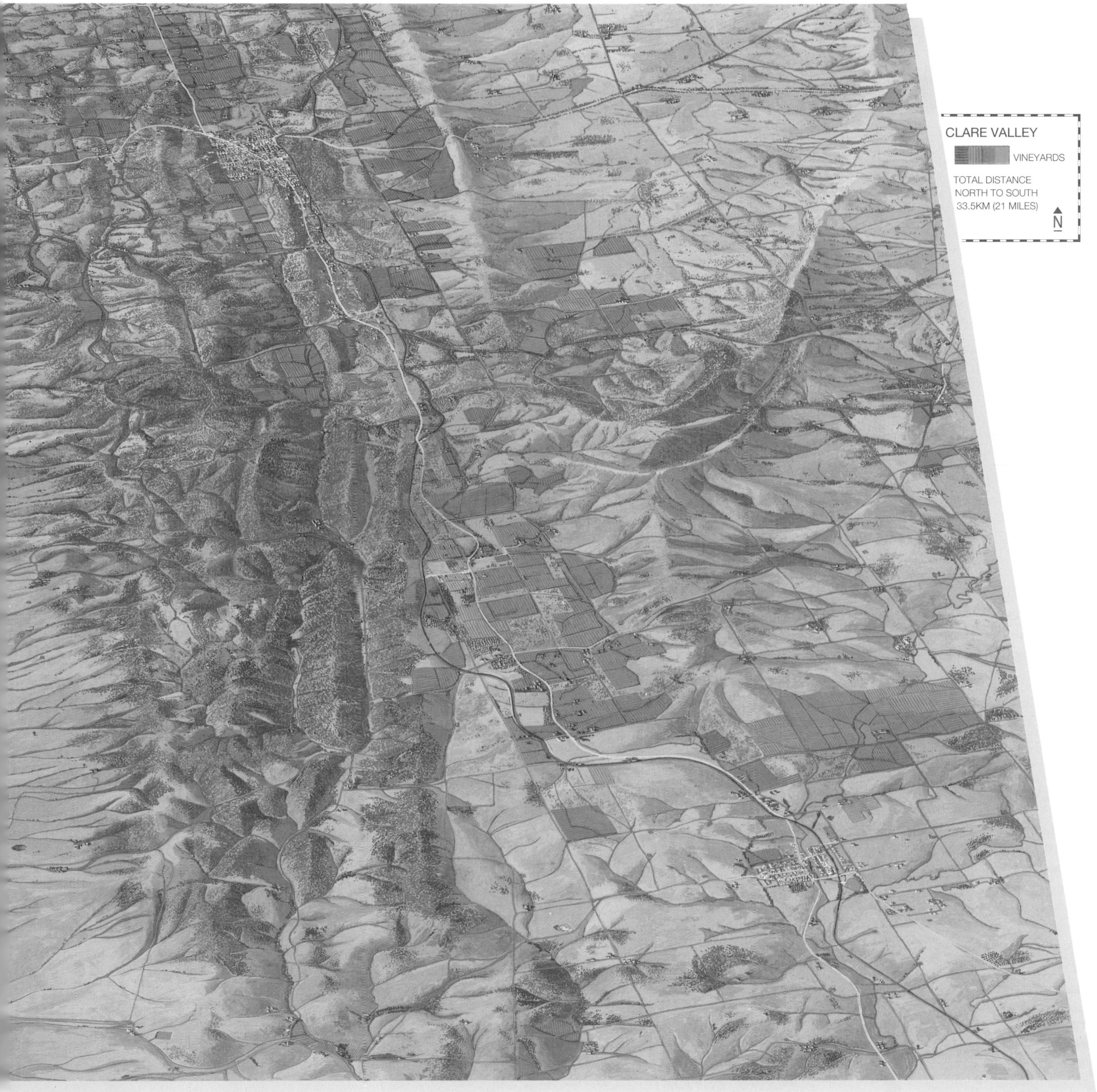

0 km 1 2
0 miles 1

CLARE VALLEY
VINEYARDS
TOTAL DISTANCE NORTH TO SOUTH 33.5KM (21 MILES)
N

0 km 1 2
0 miles 1

that is the most significant factor in cooling the vineyards, particularly in the north-facing valleys above Penwortham.

Altitude certainly seems to help. The excellent Enterprise and Petaluma vineyards, both giving outstanding Riesling wine, are over 500m (1640ft) high, facing west over the town of Clare. The vineyards of the Skillogalee Valley south-west of Sevenhill are approaching 500m (1640ft) and protected from the north. The fruit flavours are particularly fine and focussed.

Soil also plays a major role. The deep dark loams below Watervale produce ripe, fat reds and whites, yet the ridge of limestone north of Watervale provides white wines with an acid bite that such a warm climate should deny. In Polish Hill River east of Sevenhill an acidic slaty soil seems to retard ripening by as much as two weeks and the results are surprisingly delicate structured whites and reds. A paradoxical place, the Clare Valley? It sure is, thank goodness.

WHERE THE VINEYARDS ARE *The Clare Valley is only 25km (15 miles) long, but a surprising number of different growing conditions exist for the near 2000 hectares (5000 acres) of vines. To call it a valley isn't actually accurate, because the watershed at Penwortham forms a plateau from which three river systems run, two north – including the Clare – and one south. However, the whole area together with its remarkably crisp, fragrant whites and elegant (for Australia) reds, is baffling. Conditions seem too hot and dry for such wines. Certainly height above sea level is of the utmost importance. None of the vineyards you can see here are at less than 400m (1300ft), and those east of the town of Clare exceed 500m (1640ft). The ridge of hills to the west are a mixed blessing. They protect the vineyards from cool, damp westerly winds. However, Clare has one of the lowest summer rainfalls of any of Australia's quality wine regions and could do with a bit more. And Clare relies crucially on sea breezes from the west and south-west to cool the vines down and would prefer to have an uninterrupted flow.*

Sémillon from the Mitchell Estate, bottled after being aged in new oak barriques.

Victoria

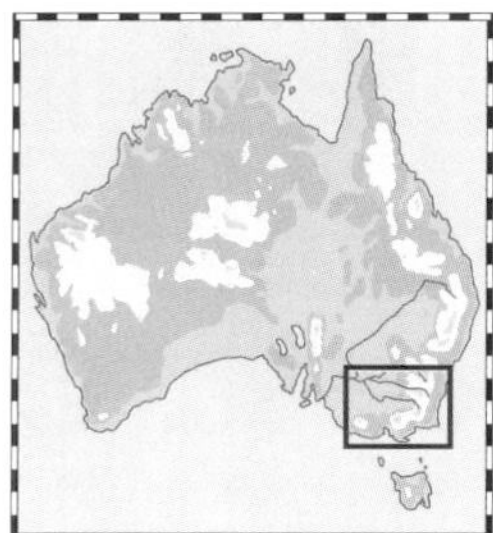

RED GRAPES
Shiraz, Cabernet Sauvignon and Pinot Noir predominate.

WHITE GRAPES
The main varieties are Chardonnay, Rhine Riesling, Gewürztraminer, Marsanne, Sauvignon Blanc, Muscat Blanc à Petits Grains and Muscadelle.

CLIMATE
Coastal areas have a maritime climate. The north-east, producing fortified wines, is hot.

SOIL
There is red loam in the north, quartzose alluvial soils in the Goulburn Valley, crumbly black volcanic soil at Geelong.

ASPECT
Steep, sloping, north-facing vineyards in cool-climate areas allow extended ripening.

ROLL UP! ROLL UP to the Great Victorian Wine Show! All of human life is here, with its triumphs and its tragedies, its noblest qualities and its greed. Especially greed. Swiss settlers were the first to make their mark, with toil and honest endeavour. Later, Gold Fever hit Victoria, bringing speculators with a mighty yet indiscriminate thirst. Soon after came the first attempts to harness the Murray River and turn a desert into orchards and vineyards. Then the vineyards of the State were laid waste by phylloxera, the world's most feared vine predator. The Great Bank Crash, bankruptcies and ruin followed on. A proud vineland was laid waste until just a few outposts remained, struggling for survival against a nation's disinterest.

And then the new Victoria emerged. All the old vineyard areas have now been re-established so long as no-one has built a housing estate or an airport there in the meantime. New vineyard areas have flared into life, offering a wealth of styles more diverse than any in Australia, ranging from some of the richest, most succulent fortified wines in the world made at Glenrowan and Rutherglen in the torrid north-east, down to damp, windy Drumborg in the south-west tip, where the grape struggles to ripen enough even for sparkling wine. The greatest problem is that the quantity of many of these remarkable wines is pitifully small, and with few exceptions the wineries are spread thinly across the State rather than bunched together in comprehensible regional groups. But that just makes the effort to find them all the more rewarding.

FIRST PLANTINGS

Let's have a quick look at the history first. The vine arrived in 1834 from Tasmania, of all places. Melbourne itself, at the north of Port Phillip Bay, proved ideally suited to vine-growing: not too hot, with an attractive maritime climate easing the grape towards ripeness. But the city's expansion was obviously always going to push out the vineyards, and the two areas that thrived were at Geelong and the Yarra Valley.

Geelong is to the west of Port Phillip Bay, and is challenging vineyard land. The best sites are on outcrops of deep, crumbly, black volcanic soil, and are water-retentive but not prone to waterlogging. Although it isn't that wet, it's rarely that hot either and the cold Antarctic gales haven't crossed any landmass to reduce their chilly force when they hit Geelong. The reason Geelong did well – by 1861 it was the most important vineyard area in the State – was largely due to the settlement of Swiss *vignerons* who knew how to coax good flavour out of cool surroundings. They did the same in the Yarra Valley and we look at that in more depth later (see page 284).

The next wave of vineyards was established not because the land was thought suitable, but because gold was discovered there in 1851. From all over the world men flocked to the heartland of Victoria, their minds giddy with dreams of untold wealth from these extensive, easily dug lodes of precious metal. And they were thirsty too. Avoca established vineyards in 1848, Bendigo followed suit in 1855, Great Western in 1858 and Ballarat in 1859. North-East Victoria already had vines near Rutherglen but was equally boosted by the madhouse prosperity brought by gold. Wine could be sold for as much as £5 a gallon in the goldfields – 20 times the price it would fetch in New South Wales, southern Victoria or South Australia.

Eventually the Gold Rush died, and with it most, though not all, of the vines. But far worse was to come. Phylloxera, the rapacious aphid that destroyed Europe's vineyards in the nineteenth century, arrived in Australia via Geelong in 1875. Geelong's vines were uprooted by Government order, and so were those of Bendigo, but to no avail. Phylloxera spread through most of Victoria and by 1910 the state that was once the jewel in Australia's crown had seen her wine industry reduced to a withered rump centred on North-East Victoria, the Murray vineyards, whose founders, the Chaffey brothers, were paupered by the combination of the Great Bank Crash of 1893 and the Murray River inexplicably drying up – plus a few vines at Tahbilk in the Goulburn Valley and at Great Western.

RED AND WHITE WINES

The rebirth of Victoria as a key wine region began with the re-establishment of vines at Geelong in 1966, but really only began to accelerate in the 1980s. The result has been dramatic

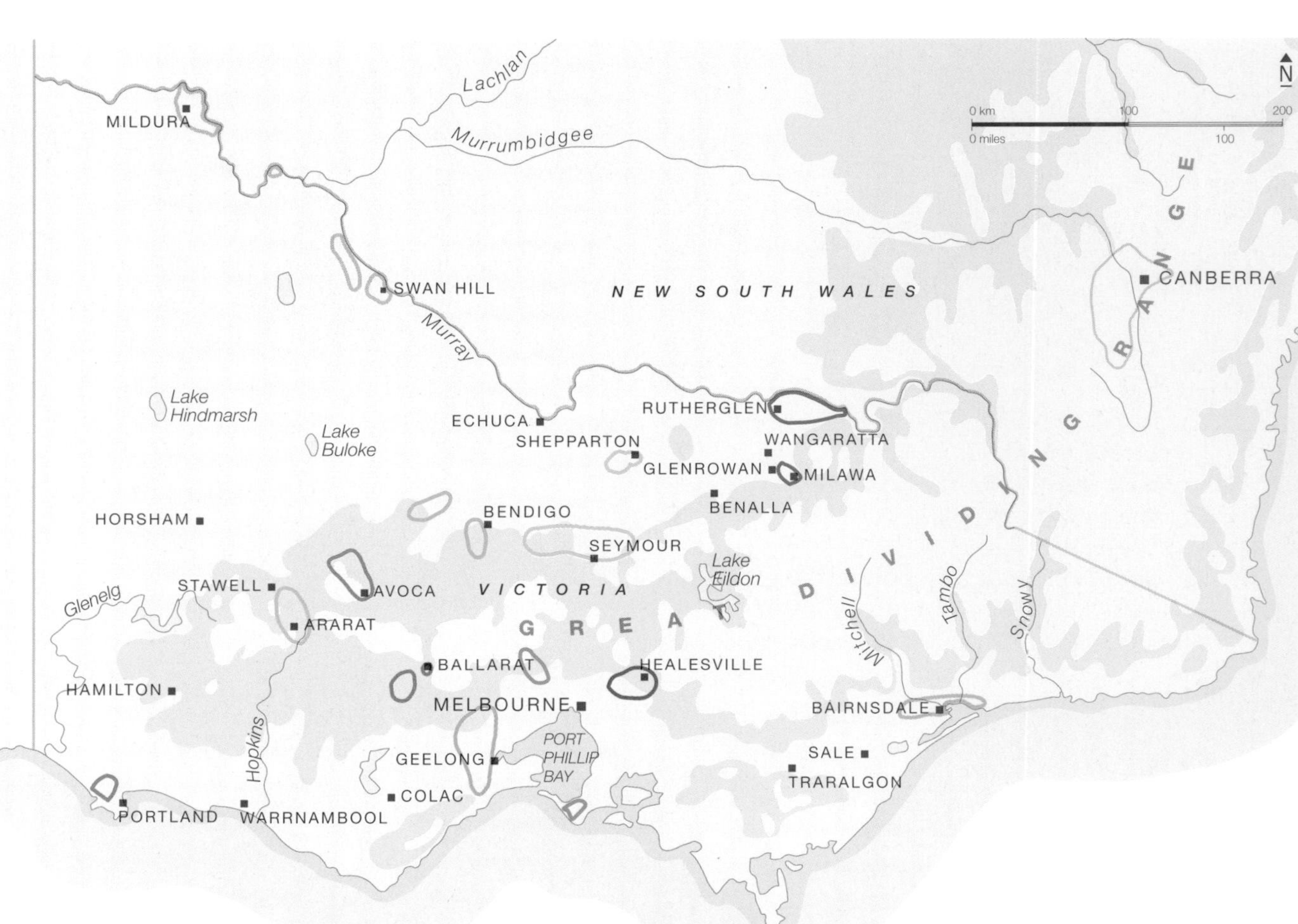

and triumphant. Among the wine areas to have enjoyed a resurgence, Geelong is no easier a place to grow vines than it was 150 years ago, but manages to produce brilliantly focussed, dark-hearted reds and attractive whites when the sun stays out long enough. The Mornington Peninsula, on the eastern claw of Port Phillip Bay, is still windy, but its position provides more maritime stability than Geelong, and any harsh north and north-east winds are cooled and dampened by their journey across the waters of the bay. The wines, especially the Chardonnays, Pinot Noirs and Rieslings, are light in texture but magnificently piercing in fruit intensity.

There are further cool-climate vineyards whose fruit intensity is remarkable, near Portland in the south west and at Gippsland in the south-east. Macedon, barely further north of Melbourne than its airport, combines fine sparkling wine with stunning lean but concentrated reds and whites. The Central Goulburn Valley north of Melbourne is warmer and principally famous for Chateau Tahbilk whose ancient vines provide palate-crunching reds and heady but approachable whites. At Mansfield north-east of Melbourne, Delatite make beautiful wines under the baleful eye of the snowfields of Mount Buller.

CENTRAL VICTORIA

Scattered sparsely across the Central Victoria region are the remnants of the great goldfield vineyards. The soils are mostly poor, producing a low yield of fruit, and rainfall is generally meagre. Although there is a good amount of sunshine, high altitudes, at places like Ballarat, the Pyrenees and much of Great Western, moderate the heat and produce remarkable results from Shiraz, Cabernet Sauvignon, Chardonnay and even Riesling. If you think you spot a fascinating streak of eucalyptus and mint in these reds, you're not wrong – they were commenting on its presence 150 years ago.

MURRAY RIVER

The Murray River marks the northern border of Victoria. The majority of Victoria's wine comes from the vast, irrigated fields on either side, with an increasing amount made to a remarkably high standard. Lindemans' Karadoc, the biggest winery in Australia, processes much of the fruit, and the giant Mildara company at Merbein, just north of the small town of Mildura, does a similar job.

NORTH-EAST VICTORIAN 'STICKIES'

There are three main sub-regions in North-East Victoria – Milawa, where Brown Brothers make good fortified and table wines in significant quantities, and have established one of Australia's highest vineyards, Whitlands, at 800m (2600ft) above sea level; Glenrowan, where Baileys make startling reds and sensational sweet fortified 'stickies'; and Rutherglen. Here a host of winemakers, young and old, make a hotchpotch of wine styles but, above all, magnificent sweet 'stickies' that leave your lips smeared and stained, your palate shocked and seduced, and your soul uplifted by their unashamed richness.

Red soils often crop up at the site of Australia's best vineyards, and it's the same in North-East Victoria. At Rutherglen all the finest wines come from a bank of red loam soil. At Glenrowan, Baileys grow their Muscat and Muscadelle (often called Tokay) on a deep seam of pulverized red granite soil. Both of these are friable, but do hold water and allow the vines to develop a deep, massive root structure. Each vine is reckoned to want up to 5 litres (9 pints) per day, and Baileys, with their access to water from Lake Mohoan and the Broken River, prefer to irrigate than leave things to nature.

North-East Victoria gets no maritime breezes to cool its sunshine so the grapes really do bake in the heat (though cold nights help preserve acid). Muscat and Muscadelle often reach a strength of 20 to 22 per cent potential alcohol as they droop and shrivel in long warm autumns. When they are picked, the grapes ooze richness and the thick juice is hardly fermented before being whacked with spirit to kill the yeasts; it's then left for anywhere between one year and two hundred years. The best examples, from makers like Chambers, Morris, Baileys, and Stanton and Killeen, blend the bright floral grapiness of young Muscat with small amounts of deep, staggeringly thick and viscous ancient wines to produce a uniquely 'sticky' experience.

Intensely flavoured, but relatively light, fortified wine from Stanton and Killeen in North-East Victoria.

Early morning mists hang over the Coldstream Hills, in the cool-climate region of the Yarra Valley.

YARRA VALLEY

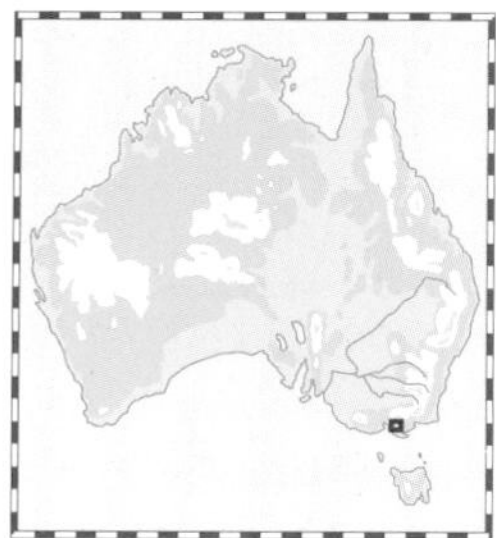

I CAN SEE IT NOW. William Ryrie breasting the hills above Healesville in the blazing afternoon sun. He'd trekked over mountain and prairie all the way down from Cooma in New South Wales. He must have been parched and exhausted. Spreading out below him was a valley, packed with greenery and trees, with a glistening, if sluggish, river curling its way down the centre. As the sweet air drifted up to him from the valley way below, he must have thought – yes, this'll do.

That was in 1837. Ryrie did settle in the Yarra Valley, and he laid the foundations both of its wine industry and its importance as a cattle-rearing centre. These two interests have been at odds with each other ever since. But the beauty and the serenity that must have filled his heart with exultant joy in 1837 are still there. Eagles still soar overhead, kingfishers race like arrows near the river, and gum trees rear majestically over the flat parkland and way up the mountain slopes too.

All very romantic, to be sure. It's easy to forget that the tranquillity of this peerless rural landscape has been earned and created by its inhabitants. The first people to thank are the Swiss. Ryrie employed a Swiss assistant to prune the vines he planted and to help make the wine. In 1845 he managed to produce a red resembling Burgundy and a white resembling Sauternes. This sounds an improbable combination, but it may say something about the Yarra's climate that has been proven time and again in the late twentieth century. The valley is not at all hot by Australian standards, providing rare suitable conditions for the finicky, cool-climate Pinot Noir of Burgundy. And it *is* relatively humid for Australia – thus encouraging the noble rot which has produced a string of brilliant sweet Yarra wines in recent times.

The Swiss rapidly assumed the dominant position in the Yarra Valley, and their expertise quickly created a reputation for delicacy and balance in its wines that was uncommon in Australia. Their success garnered such accolades as a Grand Prix – the only one for a southern hemisphere wine – at the 1889 Paris International Exhibition.

And yet 30 years later, phylloxera and a series of financial and natural disasters put an end to all this. It wasn't until the 1960s that vine leaves rustled once more in the valley breezes, and it was the 1980s before the big hitters of Australian wine remembered the Yarra's former reputation and wondered whether the valley could do it all again.

RED AND WHITE WINES

It could and it has. And the remarkable thing is that the Yarra Valley has shown an ability to produce virtually every type of classic cool-climate wine within its small boundaries in a way that would make French traditionalists, hemmed in with restrictive *appellations contrôlées*, wring their hands in horror. Marvellous champagne-method sparkling wines are made by Domaine Chandon, and superb Burgundian-style reds and whites are made by such outfits as Coldstream Hills, De Bortoli and Yarra Ridge. The latter also manage excellent Bordeaux styles, though these are surpassed by Yarra Yering, which also excels in Rhône styles, while wonderful sweet wines are made by producers such as Seville Estate and St Huberts.

Yet none of these wines actually taste like their European role models. They are, in general, softer in texture, fuller of fruit, equally well-structured but easy to appreciate at every stage of their lives. This is because increasingly the Yarra is attracting very talented winemakers, but they couldn't do it without Mother Nature's help.

Certainly the Yarra Valley is cool – in Australian terms. But it neatly dissects the conditions that might pertain for good vintages in Bordeaux and Burgundy: generally not quite so warm as Bordeaux, but warmer than Burgundy. Yarra's temperature during the ripening season is more consistent than either of the two. Rainfall, though it can disrupt flowering in late spring, almost always stops around the end of December, and, except for the odd welcome shower, doesn't usually return until autumn, after the harvest has been completed. So you can let the fruit ripen gently on the vine, the prerequisite for delicate, perfumed wine.

But all this depends on exactly where your vineyards are. Up in the hills it is often too cold for vines. The valley floor is a broad flood plain and its flat, boggy soil wouldn't have a chance of ripening a crop of grapes, even if such a vineyard did avoid inundation and spring frosts. Some sites face north, some face south; the difference in ripening dates according to sun exposure can be two weeks, even at the same altitude.

YARRA VALLEY SOILS

The two main soil types in the Yarra Valley are very different. The southern side of the valley, to the east and south of the Warramate Hills, is primarily deep, fertile red soil. Vines are extremely vigorous here, and whites and dessert wines are the speciality. The classic Yarra soils, spreading across the centre and north of the valley, are grey sandy clays and clay loams, often directly above a heavy clay pan. Vigour is restricted, vines struggle to establish themselves and often need help from irrigation during the summer, but it's these soils that first gave Yarra vines their reputation, and most of the greatest reds and whites still come off these sites.

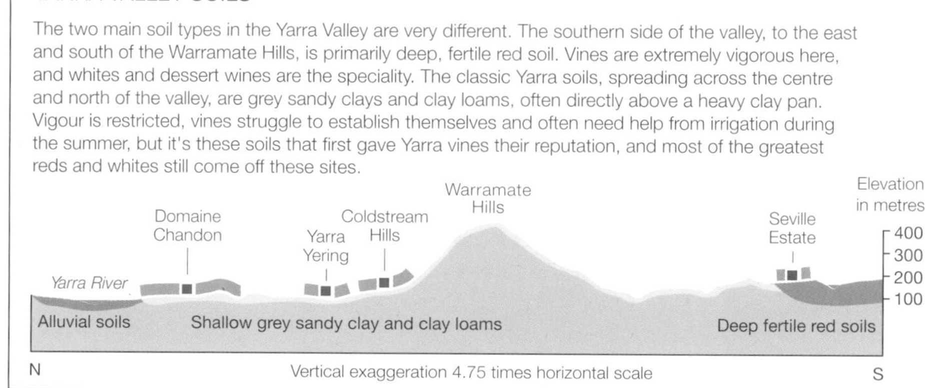

Vertical exaggeration 4.75 times horizontal scale

RED GRAPES
Pinot Noir comprises one quarter of vineyard area, with some Cabernet Sauvignon and tiny amounts of Shiraz, Merlot and Cabernet Franc.

WHITE GRAPES
One third of vineyards are planted with Chardonnay, with small amounts of other varieties.

CLIMATE
The cool climate allows extended ripening. Wind and rain can interfere with flowering and fruit-set in December and January.

SOIL
There are two main types of soil: grey, sandy clays or clay loams and deep, fertile, red volcanic soil.

ASPECT
The angle of slope and height above sea level vary enormously with vineyards planted at between 50 and 400m (165 and 1300ft).

YARRA VALLEY

VINEYARDS

TOTAL DISTANCE NORTH TO SOUTH 27.5KM (17 MILES) N

WHERE THE VINEYARDS ARE *That's the outskirts of Melbourne in the lower lefthand corner, and the Great Dividing Range of mountains is over on the right. The Yarra Valley is beautiful, and it's only a short journey via electric train from Lilydale to the city centre. The pressure from property development is the biggest threat to face the Yarra Valley, and a flourishing wine industry is one of the best ways to combat it. Luckily, vineyards here are expanding rapidly.*

The vineyards originally stretched north-east of Coldstream on grey loam soils at St Huberts and Yeringberg, and a little further west towards Yarra Glen at Yering Station. Only well-drained banks are suitable on the valley floor. There has been a lot of development around Dixons Creek in the north of the valley, again only on the raised ground. The land around the Warramate Hills is high enough, and as in Coldstream Hills' case, steep enough for drainage not to be a problem. East and south of the Warramate Hills, away from the flood plain, the soil changes to a highly fertile, deep red terra rossa. This continues into the wooded hills to the south (off the map) where large developments at locations like Hoddles Creek, are producing high-quality grapes, primarily for sparkling wine.

TOP WINERIES

1. Diamond Valley
2. Yarra Yarra
3. De Bortoli
4. Long Gully
5. Yarra Ridge
6. Tarrawarra
7. Yering Station
8. Domaine Chandon
9. Yeringberg
10. St Huberts
11. Mount Mary
12. Bianchet
13. Warramate
14. Coldstream Hills
15. Yarra Yering
16. Lillydale Vineyards
17. Seville Estate
18. Oakridge

New South Wales

RED GRAPES
Shiraz, Cabernet Sauvignon and Pinot Noir are widely planted.

WHITE GRAPES
The main varieties are Sémillon, Chardonnay, Rhine Riesling and Traminer. In Riverina, there are also plantings of Trebbiano, Muscat Gordo Blanco and Colombard.

CLIMATE
It is hot, even by Australian standards, particularly in the Hunter Valley and Riverina. Wet, humid autumns encourage rot.

SOIL
Sandy, clay loams, along with red-brown volcanic loams, granite and alluvial soils predominate.

ASPECT
Vines are planted on the gently undulating valley floors (Cowra, Riverina and Upper Hunter Valley), or in the foothills of the Brokenback and Great Dividing ranges (Lower Hunter Valley and Mudgee).

New South Wales is where I started my Australian wine odyssey. It's where Australian wine started its journey too. The very first vines to reach Australia sailed into Sydney Harbour with the First Fleet in 1788. They'd been picked up in Rio de Janeiro and the Cape of Good Hope on the long voyage out from England, and in no time the settlers had cleared some scrub by the harbour and planted vines. They weren't a great success – the humid atmosphere encouraged 'black spot' disease knocking out any grapes before they had a chance to ripen – but the scene had been set. All the main Australian settlements took the same line, establishing vineyards at the same time as establishing a community. And the reason usually given was to encourage sobriety! In a new, savage country, where rough men became more savage and wild under the influence of fiery high-strength spirits, wine was seen as a moderating influence, a weapon against drunkenness and disorder.

And I have to admit my first Australian hangover was in New South Wales, though it was the result of beer, not wine; but I wouldn't vouch for the genesis of numerous subsequent ones. Attempts in New South Wales to promote a benevolent, rosy-cheeked, wine-sipping society didn't work out too well, because there were very few places near Sydney suitable for vines. Close to the sea, the climate is too subtropical and vines routinely rotted. Further inland, around Bathurst, the cooler, high-altitude terrain looked promising, but harsh spring frosts simply made vine-growing economically unviable.

Although a couple of vineyards did survive until modern times near Sydney at Camden Park, Rooty Hill and Smithfield, the story of New South Wales wine is one of establishing vineyards well away from the main consumer market-place, with quality acting as the magnet drawing Sydney's attention. This movement is still continuing today.

The crucial factors in New South Wales are excessive heat from the relatively northerly latitude; the presence of the sea close by; and the Great Dividing Range of mountains which separates the humid, populated seaboard from the parched, empty interior. The Great Dividing Range provides cool vineyard sites in some of its high hill passes, as well as the springs from which flow enough rivers to irrigate some of the largest agro-industrial vineyards in Australia. Proximity to the sea brings with it advantages and disadvantages: the priceless bounty of cooling breezes but also the seasonal curse of anticyclonic cloudbursts, frequently at around vintage time.

HUNTER VALLEY

The first real success came with the Hunter Valley, about 130km (80 miles) north of Sydney and just inland from the major industrial city of Newcastle. Vineyards were being planted there as early as the 1820s, but it wasn't until the 1860s that the areas now thought of as best – those around the mining town of Cessnock – were planted. I cover the Hunter Valley more fully on page 288.

MUDGEE

At about the same time, explorers pushed up into the mountains to the west of the Hunter and founded the community of Mudgee. Helped by an influx of German settlers and by a minor goldrush, vineyards were well-established by the end of the nineteenth century but, as with the other New South Wales regions, Federation in 1901, with the lowering of trade barriers between States and the flood of cheap wines from South Australia – virtually did for the region. It wasn't until the 1960s that Mudgee began to get up on its feet again.

Now, its qualities are being realized. Hunter Valley wineries often used to rely on Mudgee wine for blending in the past, because the acid soils produce fat, strongly flavoured reds and whites. In addition, Mudgee's position at over 450m (1500ft) above sea level on the western slopes of the Great Dividing Range gives easily enough heat to ripen any grape variety, yet protects the vines from late summer rains. The growers are sufficiently proud of their individuality that they have organized one of Australia's first *appellation* systems. I find the flavours solid and imposing, rather than enthralling. The Chardonnays are full and sturdy, sometimes with an earthy streak lurking behind the fruit. This earthy, stony quality seems to play a more natural role in the Cabernet and Shiraz reds, whose flavours, particularly when made by Australia's organic pioneer, Gil Walquist at Botobolar, can be massive.

COWRA

Heading down off the mountains towards the interior, we come to the great irrigated vineyards of the State. The highest quality wine so far has come from Cowra on the Lachlan River, which has long been recognized as a prime source of fruit. The first Petaluma Chardonnays, beginning with the 1977, were made from Cowra fruit and immediately exhibited a fat, lush style quite unlike the modern Petaluma

Rosemount's famous Roxburgh vineyard in the Upper Hunter is planted with Chardonnay.

Chardonnays, whose fruit is sourced in the ultra-cool Adelaide Hills. Even so, they lasted well, and their quality persuaded Len Evans of Rothbury to make the leap into Chardonnay when 40 hectares (100 acres) came up for sale in 1981. Rothbury Cowra Chardonnay, with its rich, creamy style, has been one of the winery's most successful wines ever since.

Certainly, Cowra produces some of my favourite New South Wales Chardonnay, and one of the area's great virtues is its relentless reliability. The soil is sandy and free-draining, the sun shines throughout the summer, with almost no interruption from rain, and the Lachlan River provides an abundant source of irrigation water. Total reliability. But there's more. The large irrigated vineyards along the Murray River, which provide the bulk of Australia's wine grapes, are generally owned by thousands of smallholders. Their sole objective is to produce as large a crop of reasonably healthy grapes as possible, get them picked as early as they can – regardless of whether or not the grapes are truly ripe – to minimize the risk of disease and bad weather, and bank the money. Much of the region's potential is thus never realized.

But Cowra has been developed largely by major wine companies like Rothbury, or quality-orientated, large-scale growers. With the winemakers having full control over the ripeness of crop, Cowra fruit, and Chardonnay in particular, has created what is still not that common in Australia – a totally recognizable style of its own.

RIVERINA

Riverina, centred on the town of Griffith, way down in the scorched flatlands, is the most significant wine region in New South Wales in terms of the volume of wine it produces. Also known as the Murrumbidgee Irrigation Area, it taps into the river system of the Murrumbidgee to produce approaching 100,000 tons of grapes from about 5000 hectares (12,350 acres) of featureless land. The quality is getting better every vintage, with regard in particular to Sémillon and Chardonnay. One special feature is the remarkable botrytis-affected sweet Sémillon which the De Bortoli winery produces. The grapes are left to hang on the vines for up to two months after the normal vintage date, and the quality easily matches that of a top Sauternes from Bordeaux.

CANBERRA

Vineyards have always developed in Australia in tandem with the major cities, to slake the thirsts of their growing populations. In the nineteenth century, sites as close as possible to the cities were used until disease (Sydney) or urban expansion (Melbourne and Adelaide) pushed the vineyard sites further out into the country. But down towards the Victorian border, Australia's newest city is its capital – Canberra. With the transport efficiency of the late twentieth century, Canberra didn't need its own vineyards unlike the cities developed in the nineteenth century, but that hasn't stopped a few impassioned inhabitants developing some.

Because you can't buy land freehold within the Australian Capital Territory (A.C.T.), the vineyards have been developed just outside the A.C.T. in New South Wales – mostly to the north-east near Lake George and to the north around Murrumbateman. Luckily, few of these winemakers rely upon their wines for their living, because conditions are difficult and results patchy. The summer days are hot and dry, and not tempered by sea breezes, yet the nights are cold. The autumn, however, is cool and frequently wet. The soils and subsoils are not water retentive so irrigation is crucial. Because of the cold night air moving north from the Australian Alps snowfields, sites have to be selected with care to avoid spring frosts that can occur as late as November. If this all sounds a bit negative,

I'd have to say – if Canberra weren't there, these vineyards wouldn't be there either, but wineries like Lark Hill and Doonkuna Estate have had success with Riesling, Chardonnay and, surprisingly, with Cabernet Sauvignon.

OTHER VINEYARD AREAS

Although there are irrigated vineyards along the Murray Valley, most of the action is not in New South Wales but across the state border in Victoria, on the left bank of the river. The other developments in New South Wales are more concerned with trying to locate high-quality sites, despite challenging climatic conditions. In particular, the state's winemakers hanker after a source of cool-climate fruit and successful attempts are being made in two areas.

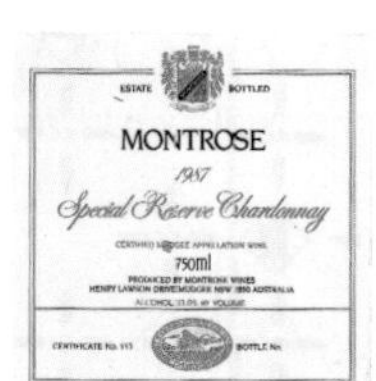

Tumbarumba in the Snowy Mountains, way down south near the border with Victoria, is considered to be on-line for producing some outstanding sparkling wine and red Pinot Noir. It has red volcanic soils planted at over 750m (2500ft), and granite soils in slightly warmer, yet still cool, sites at around 550m (1800ft).

The Hilltops region near Young is better established. It is warm enough for most of the New South Wales varieties, but the higher altitude and the well-drained soils encourage a slow, regular ripening season with consequently intensified fruit flavours. There are also vineyards around Orange, but here we're getting back into the spring frost problems that deterred settlers in the nineteenth century.

The most bizarre vineyard development is in the Hastings Valley near Port Macquarie, north of Newcastle. Here one of Australia's hottest vineyard sites combines with the highest recorded rainfall – most of it during the ripening season – but somehow Cassegrain manages to make interesting wine.

Classic bottle-aged Sémillon from McWilliam's Mount Pleasant in the Hunter Valley.

HUNTER VALLEY

RED GRAPES
Mainly Cabernet Sauvignon and Shiraz are grown, with some Pinot Noir and Merlot.

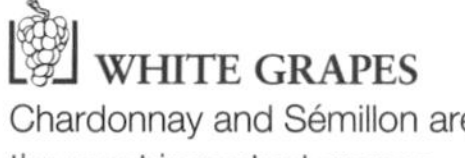

WHITE GRAPES
Chardonnay and Sémillon are the most important grapes.

CLIMATE
The summer heat is tempered by cloudy skies. The Upper Hunter Valley needs irrigation.

SOIL
The rich, red volcanic loams and the alluvial soils near the Goulburn River are the best. The poor-draining, heavy clay subsoils are less suitable.

ASPECT
Vines are planted next to the Goulburn River in the Upper Hunter Valley. Lower Hunter vineyards are on the lower slopes of the Brokenback Range, or on the valley floor.

I STILL HAVE VIVID MEMORIES of the first time I realized just how special the Hunter Valley could be. Some roaming wine gypsy I knew had strayed far from his usual European pastures and ended up in Sydney. Eventually escaping with liver and limb more or less intact, he'd brought some wine back to London and decided to try it out on a group of us young whipper-snappers. Tyrrell's Vat 47 1973. A Chardonnay – well, mostly Chardonnay, with a little Sémillon too, I shouldn't wonder. I can still see the astonishing day-glo, green-gold colour, all fiery-eyed and demanding attention, and the sensual viscous texture of the wine that swirled lazily round the glass like a courtesan interrupted during her siesta.

And the flavour. I'd been brought up on French Chardonnay from Burgundy. I knew and understood the generally austere but fascinating, if intellectual, pleasure of those pale, oatmeal- and mineral-scented whites from the centre of France. And then there was my first mouthful of Vat 47. The explosion of peaches and honey, hazelnuts, wood smoke and lime sent stars bursting across my palate. In that single split second I foresaw the greatness that Australia could bring to Chardonnay and that Chardonnay could bring to Australia.

Yet what I was tasting was not some classic wine style, carefully honed over the generations. This was only the third vintage of the Hunter Valley's very first varietal Chardonnay. And its brilliance was even more astounding because you shouldn't really be able to create exciting wine in the Hunter at all. Ask any modern vineyard consultant about establishing a vineyard in the Hunter Valley and he'd say you must be barmy even to consider it. So what's going on? Have all the great Hunter wines of the last 150 years been made by madmen? Or do they know something we don't? For a start, you've got the heat against you, the rainfall patterns against you, and, except in a few charmed sites, the soils against you too. But, as Hunter winemakers have shown, if you're stubborn and obsessive – and, well, yes, slightly mad – you can sometimes produce wines of quite shocking individuality and quality.

UPPER HUNTER VALLEY

The Hunter Valley divides wine-wise into two parts as it snakes inland from Newcastle. The Upper Hunter (not shown on this map) is to the north around Denman and, although initially planted in the nineteenth century, only achieved any kind of prominence in the 1980s and still only has one famous winery – Rosemount. The area was heavily planted in the wine boom of the 1960s and 1970s, mostly on rich, alluvial soil with irrigation enthusiastically applied. You *can* make pleasant whites under these conditions, but the grape most frequently planted was the black Shiraz whose reaction to such fertile, high-yielding conditions was to produce limp, lifeless wine only half-way to red. White wines fare better under these conditions and fleshy Chardonnays and Sémillons are commonplace in the Upper Hunter. There is so far only one world-class vineyard – Rosemount's Roxburgh – a weathered limestone and basalt outcrop in the middle of pastureland between Denman and Muswellbrook that produces sensational Chardonnay and Sémillon.

LOWER HUNTER VALLEY

The Lower Hunter is now centred around Cessnock, a town more dominated by coal-mining than wine during most of its existence. Spread out to the west and north-west are numerous blocks of vines, the healthiest-looking being those that run up to the slopes of the Brokenback Range to the west and north-west, and odd volcanic 'pimples' – ridges of weathered basalt typified by Lake's Folly and Evans Family vineyards. These red soils are fertile, well-drained and deep, and capable of producing good crops of high-quality red grapes.

The volcanic outcrops are marvellous soils, but they still have to combat the heat and the rain. Lake's Folly and Evans Family face south, away from the sun, and the best sites on the Brokenback slopes are those rising up as high as 400m (1300ft) at Mount Pleasant and the properties set back on the slopes of Mount View directly west of Cessnock. These escape the warm westerlies, get a little more rain and often ripen up to two weeks later than the vines on the valley floor.

FORMER VINEYARD AREAS

There are also some alluvial flats with sturdy-looking vines, but then you notice fields full of weary, stunted vines and great patches of barren land where you think – funny, I could have sworn there was a vineyard there. There was. But the problem is that most of the good topsoil has been washed away over the generations. The notoriously thick, impermeable pug clays that remain are very difficult to work and can hardly support any crop, let alone a vine. Yet thousands of acres were planted in the mad Vine Rush of the 1960s on this yellow-orange hopeless clay. Rothbury Estate used to have a Home vineyard of 180 hectares (450 acres) – which Len Evans, the Rothbury chief, freely admits was 'a total cowpat' anyway. It now totals a mere 15 hectares (40 acres) of vines and even those vines are left in the ground only because Evans says you can't have a winery without any vines.

HUNTER VALLEY CLIMATE

Because the Hunter is relatively far to the north and close to the hotter, inland zones, the climate does at first sight seem oppressive. Yet the quality of wine made here means there must be some compensating factors. There are. Though Cessnock would appear to get appreciably more heat than Montpellier in the broiling south of France, warm spring and autumn temperatures that don't affect the grapes' ripening distort the figures. Heat does build up fast until early afternoon, but the Great Dividing Range dips to the north and west of Cessnock, allowing the warm interior to suck in cold air up the Hunter Valley. Most summer afternoons there's cloud cover over the Hunter, and in any case, being closer than Montpellier to the Equator means relatively shorter summer days. The humidity is also important in reducing vine stress.

But water is a problem in the Hunter Valley. There is not enough when you want it and too much when you don't. The annual rainfall of 700mm (27in) would be fine if it fell at the right time, but it tends to get dumped at the end of summer, often just before the Shiraz grapes are ripe. You also need good winter rains to fill the irrigation dams, since borehole water in the Hunter is far too saline, but the Hunter Valley suffers from frequent winter droughts.

When the rain does arrive in January and February, cyclones come in off the Coral Sea and bang up against the mountains of the Great Dividing Range. When they hit Queensland, winemakers know they've got two or three days to harvest, regardless of ripeness, before the rains reach the Hunter Valley. You can make great Sémillon from underripe grapes, fair Chardonnay, even passable Cabernet, but you just can't transform a rain-bloated Shiraz into a classy red, and you'll only break your heart, however hard you try.

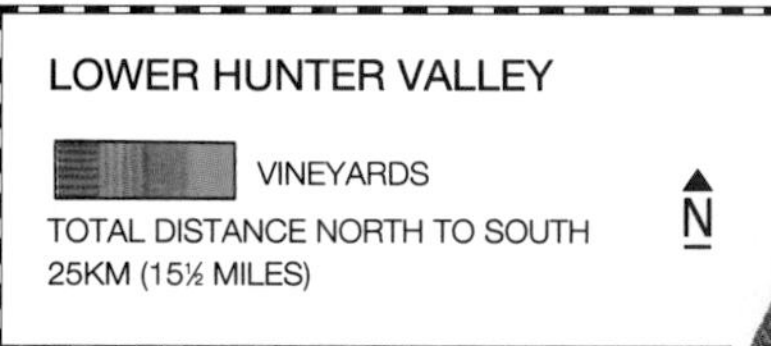

0 km 1 2
0 miles 1

WHERE THE VINEYARDS ARE *The Hunter River is just visible on the map snaking briefly in and out of the top righthand corner. It continues to run from the west just above the top of the map. All the original important vineyards were established on these fertile river flats. You can just see one remaining example on the bend of the river at Wyndham Estate. However, from the 1860s onwards, plantings shifted southwards and westwards, towards the slopes of the Brokenback Range, an isolated ridge to the west of Cessnock. The best Hunter vineyards are almost all on these slopes, where rich red volcanic loams provide that unusual combination – high quality and high volume. The most famous of these are McWilliam's Mount Pleasant and Lindemans' Ben Ean.*

The little Mount View Range directly west of Cessnock is also particularly suited to vines, and if you look at the centre of the map just past Cessnock airfield, you'll see a clump of vineyards round Lake's Folly, and another patch at Evans Family, which also share this red volcanic soil. Interestingly, they both face south away from the sun to slow down the ripening of the grapes.

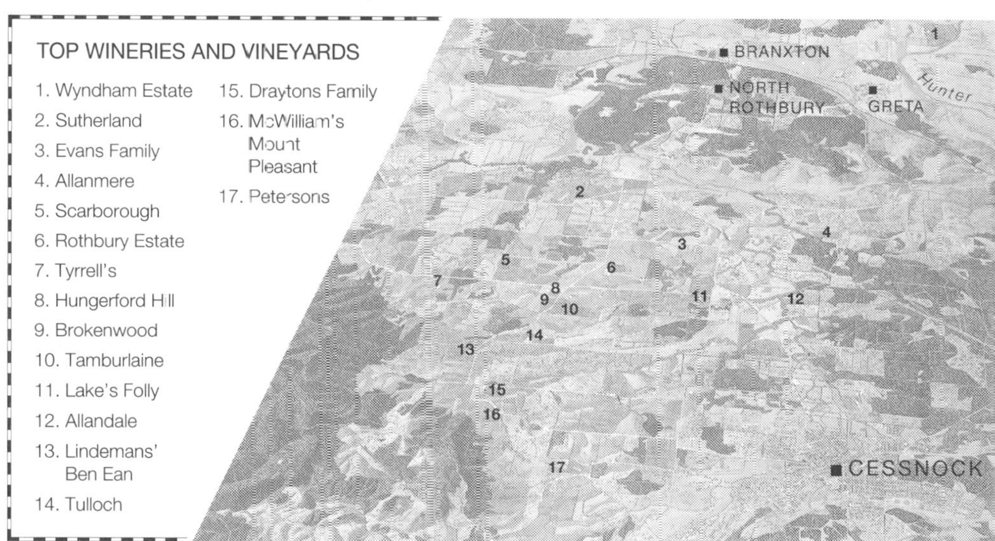

0 km 1 2
0 miles 1

Western Australia

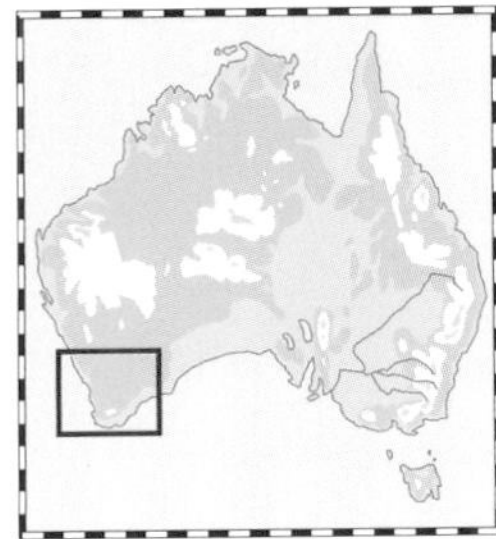

RED GRAPES
Cabernet Sauvignon, Merlot, Shiraz, Pinot Noir and Malbec are the main varieties.

WHITE GRAPES
Rhine Riesling, Chardonnay, Sauvignon Blanc, Sémillon and Chenin Blanc are used for white wines. In addition, the Swan Valley grows Muscat Gordo Blanco, Verdelho and Muscadelle.

CLIMATE
The coastal regions have a maritime climate. Regions further inland and to the north are hotter and drier.

SOIL
Mainly brown or grey-brown alluvial topsoil, frequently fairly sandy with some gravel.

ASPECT
Vineyards are concentrated on the valley floors and along the coast, although there are some vines in more hilly areas around Albany.

'Wines should be resplendent with generosity; unless a wine can be diluted with an equal volume of water, it wasn't worth making in the first place.' This wonderful remark was made by Jack Mann, the greatest of Western Australia's old-time winemakers. He made wines in the Swan Valley, the hottest serious vineyard area in Australia and one of the hottest in the world. He admitted he never picked his grapes until the sun-baked vine simply had nothing more to offer them, and I've tasted some of the old Houghton White Burgundy wines with which he made his reputation – deep, thick, viscous golden wines, oozing with over-ripeness but aging with all the sequined majesty of a dowager in love with a chorus boy.

SWAN VALLEY

Until the 1970s, Houghton White Burgundy was the only Western Australian wine to make any impact across the state line. It was originally based on Chenin Blanc and Muscadelle (nowadays aided by a little Chardonnay) and was, at one time, Australia's most popular white wine.

Well, it was about the only shooting star Western Australia had in wine between 1829, when the Memerlia landed to establish the colony, and the late 1970s, when the pioneers of Margaret River began making waves. Yet in the nineteenth century the Swan Valley had more wineries than any other viticultural area of Australia. Phylloxera hadn't hit Western Australia so there was a great boom in plantings during the 1890s as Victoria's vineyards fell to the rapacious aphid. And as usual the discovery of gold and the attendant influx of wealth-crazed, sun-parched prospectors in need of a bit of rest and recuperation didn't do any harm either.

After World War One a large number of Yugoslavs took refuge in Perth, much as they did in the North Island of New Zealand. They proved to be doughty winemakers and loyal consumers of their competitors' wares, dominating the local wine scene. Until the late 1960s, that local wine scene was almost entirely centred on the broiling Swan Valley.

We *are* talking broiling here, by the way. The Swan has January and February temperatures that can soar to 45°C (113°F) – hotter than any other serious Australian wine region. Air humidity is extremely low, further stressing the vines, and the summer rainfall is the lowest of any Australian wine district – though the bulk of this does occasionally fall in February bang in the middle of vintage. And you won't be surprised when I tell you that the Swan also gets the most sunshine hours per day as well.

People bake; grapes bake. It would all be too much if it weren't for the afternoon breezes that come belting across the bay from Fremantle, swoop into the Swan Estuary at Perth and then funnel north-east up the valley, sucked across the riverside vineyards by the heat of Australia's hot desert heart. The best of the Swan vineyards are on river terraces of deep, well-drained young alluvial soils, often with a sandy clay subsoil to conserve winter rains for high summer use, although few vineyards nowadays get by without irrigation.

All of this, despite the efforts of the sea breeze, still sounds a lot more like fortified wine than table wine conditions. And many experts have predicted that the future of the Swan *is* in fortifieds. Yet fortifieds belong to the past, not the future of Australian wine, and as Jack Mann proved with his Houghton White Burgundy, something pretty spectacular can be achieved with table wines too.

The most surprising point is that whites perform better here than reds. Many of the reds get a rather cooked flavour, though the Shiraz can be good – Evans and Tate's Gnangara shows how tasty it can be. Remarkably, Cabernet vinified as a rosé is frequently better than the red version, as Houghton Cabernet Rosé shows.

The reason whites are better becomes clearer when we look at the varieties planted. Chenin Blanc has the largest acreage, and Verdelho and Sémillon easily outstrip such varieties as Riesling and Chardonnay. Chenin's great ability is to retain acidity under virtually any conditions. Indeed, it positively courts the heat that it so rarely gets in its homeland of the Loire Valley in France. Verdelho is used to make Madeira in Portugal, where it retains its attractive honeyed character despite high temperatures. Sémillon is the best variety in New South Wales' near subtropical Hunter Valley.

Houghton makes good use of all of these and is still the major Swan producer, but, just as in the other states, as the national and export palate has shifted away from overripe or fortified wine styles, so the hotter areas go out of fashion. As the Barossa and McLaren Vale in South Australia show, they can, with a few adjustments to wine style, come back into fashion again. Houghton now sources many of the grapes for their excellent whites from the slightly cooler Moondah Brook about 60km (37 miles) north of the Swan Valley at Gingin, as

Evans and Tate's Redbrook Estate at Wilyabrup, in the Margaret River region.

well as from the considerably cooler Margaret River and Lower Great Southern areas way to the south.

These latter two are the areas now making the running for Western Australia. Both had been considered suitable for grape-growing before. The Lower Great Southern had impressed Jack Mann himself between the wars, and earlier still the Western Australian government had tried to get Penfolds to establish a vineyard at Mount Barker. But Western Australia is a very sparsely populated state. Until recently in Australia, unless there was a decent centre of population nearby, you couldn't establish a wine industry. Perth, with its Swan Valley, was really the only sizeable city in the state.

But the Swan was having trouble in the 1950s. The vineyards were decaying, yields were falling and in 1955 the government called in Professor Olmo of California to find the cause. He did (it was nematodes, a root-nibbling worm, and poor drainage), and he also remarked in passing that he thought the Swan was too hot anyway and that someone should plant the area around Mount Barker and Frankland, north of the port of Albany – sites now at the heart of the Lower Great Southern. This was easier said than done.

LOWER GREAT SOUTHERN

We're talking about a big area here – the largest recognized agricultural area in Australia – and we're talking about some fairly diverse conditions, as well as taming a wild landscape of jarrah and red gum trees and scrub. Progress was slow, the first vines not going in at Forest Hill near Mount Barker until 1966, and progress hasn't exactly been quicksilver since then. Small vineyards established themselves east of Mount Barker beneath the rounded granite Porongurup Hills, west around Frankland, and even further west near Manjimup, and down near the coast far inland from Denmark and Albany.

Most of these are on gravelly sandy loams though these may well be underpinned by impermeable clay subsoils, inhibiting drainage. The temperatures around Mount Barker and Frankland are fairly similar to those of the Médoc in Bordeaux – which is as cool as Western Australia gets – and this results in good, dark but lean Cabernet styles and, interestingly, lovely lean Rieslings as well.

The Porongurup vineyards are cooler because the slopes are planted up to 350m (1150ft) and this can slow ripening by a good week, which merely serves to intensify the fruit of the Cabernets and Rieslings. The coastal vineyards between Albany and just west of Denmark benefit from cooler days and warmer nights because of the ocean's influence, though some good vineyards near Denmark face north and are sheltered from the sea. The vines also get more rain, but this is a plus in a dry state, since the extra rain usually falls outside the March to April harvest period. Piercing cool flavours are once more the order of the day, with even some good Pinot Noir rearing its head north-east of Albany.

There are now some signs of large-scale activity by wineries in the Lower Great Southern Region – Houghton relies upon the 100 hectares (250 acres) of Frankland River's vineyards for a lot of top quality white grapes, and Goundrey are rapidly expanding. However, the wine industry is still fragmented and remote, very much like the region.

A honeyed, Gold Reserve Verdelho from Houghton in the Swan Valley.

MARGARET RIVER

More crowded, more inhabited and organized is the Margaret River region on the south-western tip of Australia. The Southern Ocean influences meet those of the Indian Ocean, and the natural potential which results has already been exploited by brilliant winemakers and self-publicists alike. Since this is now undoubtedly Western Australia's highest profile and most successful area, I talk about it separately over the page.

SOUTH-WEST COASTAL PLAIN

However, there are two other wine regions in the state – rather straggly and indistinct as yet, but both producing interesting wines. There is a group of wineries loosely bound together as the South-West Coastal Plain for want of a better name. This unpromising title hides some good producers strung over almost 200km (125 miles) from north of Perth to south of Bunbury. As you can imagine, there are major differences in climate over this distance, with the Bunbury vineyards enjoying similar temperatures to the cool Margaret River. But the Indian Ocean tempers any extremes of climate, and in the north, the south-western sea breezes usually chill things down by noon. The unifying factor is that the vineyards all share the same fine-grained grey soil called Tuart Sand, named after the local Tuart gum trees. With almost all the rain coming in the winter and spring, irrigation is essential, but the free-draining sands allow the producers wide flexibility and good tasty whites are coming on stream, as well as one of Australia's only Zinfandels – spicy, rich and red.

PERTH HILLS

The other small area is the Perth Hills which are, in effect, the Darling Range. These overlook Perth from about 20 to 30km (12 to 18 miles) inland, and the wooded valleys have vineyards established at between 150 and 400m (500 and 1300ft) above sea-level. Sea breezes blowing in across the range's western escarpment reduce daytime temperatures; by contrast, warm sea air stops the temperature dropping too much at night. The hilly, irregular nature of the valleys creates widely differing mesoclimates that, at their coolest, ripen grapes two to three weeks later than those in vineyards in the nearby Swan Valley flats. Soils are good, with a fair amount of gravelly loam, and rainfall is high – but almost all of it is in the winter. If you've got storage dams for spring and summer irrigation, that's no problem; but if you haven't, those gravelly soils will be too free-draining to raise a crop.

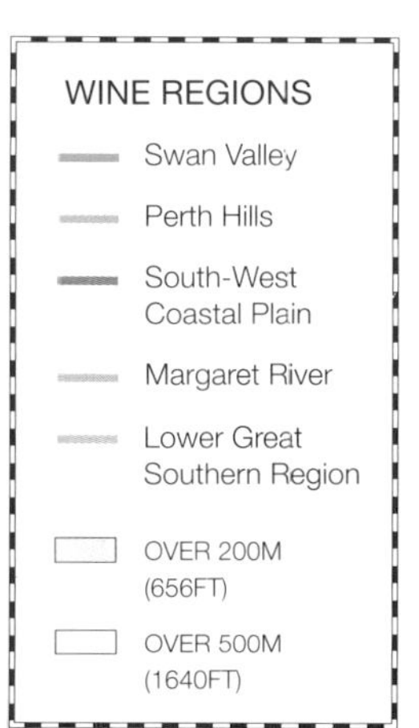

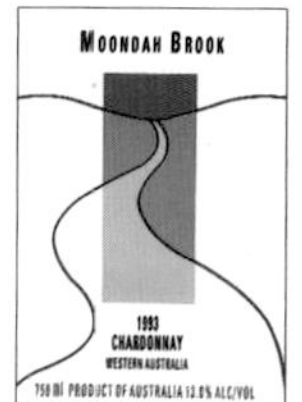

Margaret River

The Margaret River might never have been discovered as a fine wine vineyard area had it not been for a clutch of beady-eyed local doctors. They saw a couple of reports in 1965-6 by a certain Dr John Gladstones that the Margaret River had unusually close climatic analogies with Bordeaux during the vine-growing season, but with less spring frost, more reliable summer sunshine, and less risk of hail or excessive rain during ripening. For some reason, Australian doctors right across the nation have never been able to resist such pronouncements. First Dr Tom Cullity at Vasse Felix, then fellow doctors Bill Pannell at Moss Wood and Kevin Cullen of Cullens at Wilyabrup, planted vineyards that were to form the heart of the Margaret River region right from the start. Indeed, Margaret River went on to establish itself as a remarkably versatile, if capricious, cool-climate region which was good as any in Australia. But Bordeaux? Well, yes and no.

In fact Dr Gladstones was supposed to be doing research on lupins – rather the same as Cullity and Co were supposed to be keeping the locals hale and hearty – but his good luck was that the legendary Jack Mann at Houghton vineyard in the Swan Valley let him use a spare couple of acres of land next to the winery cellars for his lupin experiments. Lupins are all very well, but the ever-open cellar door at his neighbour's winery began to weave its magic on the doctor and distract him from his original research. The nascent possibilities in Western Australia for fine wine, as yet barely touched upon by winemakers in the torrid Swan Valley, began to take up more and more of Dr Gladstones' attention.

A visiting Californian, Professor Olmo, had already suggested in 1956 that the far south of the state near Albany would make a more suitable high-quality vineyard site. Gladstones thought the area on the south-west coast, between the Margaret River and Cape Naturaliste almost 50km (30 miles) further north, would be warmer, much more predictable in weather and more flexible in the varieties of grapes that could be grown. He felt the Lower Great Southern Region, with its cooler, southerly maritime influence could indeed match Bordeaux's cooler regions, but that the Margaret River, influenced by the Indian Ocean to the west, could match the warmer Bordeaux regions of Pomerol and St-Émilion. The added advantage for Margaret River was that it was an area which was free of the risk of frost and rain at vintage that so often spoiled things in Bordeaux. It was these thoughts that galvanized the local wine-making doctors into action.

Yet there are problems, and the most intractable is wind. Sea breezes are crucial for cooling down vines in many areas of Australia, but these are gales we're talking about – especially in the springtime – when salt-laden winds power in off the Indian Ocean and can crucially affect the vine as it attempts to flower and set a crop. Given the fact that the winters are some of the mildest in Australia, vines are likely to wake up early and the early-budding Chardonnay and Merlot often get into trouble.

And then there's the wildlife. Those lovely mysterious stands of tall Karri gums are home to legions of kangaroos. Delightful, shy little roos; how we Europeans wish they were less timid so that we could feed them lettuce leaves from the palms of our hands. Try giving that sentimental tosh to a grape grower in springtime when the little fellas have nipped out overnight and chewed all the emerging buds off his vines. And don't talk to him about how divine those lime

NORTHERN MARGARET RIVER

VINEYARDS

TOTAL DISTANCE NORTH TO SOUTH 39.5KM (24½ MILES)

N

0 km 1 2
0 miles 1

0 km 1 2
0 miles 1

green parrots are fluttering and cawing among the vines. They are rapacious pests that munch away at the grapes for nourishment and then, replete with his best Cabernet Sauvignon, chew through the vine branches for recreation. And don't mention silver-eyes either, sweet little migratory birds that actually find the vineyards' protective netting rather good for nesting in – and in any case they're tiny enough to wriggle through and devour the crop *under* the nets.

These kinds of problems rarely occur in Europe – or even in the traditional wine areas of Australia. But where new vineyards are being carved out of virgin land that has developed its own rhythms of natural life over the centuries, there are bound to be upsets. In such thinly populated areas as Margaret River the relatively few cultivated acres of vines and grapes make easy targets for hungry animals and birds.

Interestingly, the only effective defence against the annual invasion of silver-eyes is one that occurs naturally. Their traditional refuelling food is the nectar of the red gum's blossom. When the gums flower on time, the silver-eyes prefer this feast. If the flowering is late, they turn their feeding frenzy onto the sugar-sweet grapes.

But it does seem to be worth it. Across a remarkable spectrum of wines, the quality of the Margaret River fruit sings out loud and clear. These range from mighty, gum-scented Pinot Noirs, to classically structured Cabernets and Chardonnays, from unnervingly French, yet tantalizingly individual Sémillons and Sauvignons, to positively un-Australian Shiraz and Zinfandel, even to vintage 'port'.

VINEYARD AREAS

There were intermittent attempts in the nineteenth century to plant the area, but Doctors Cullity, Pannell and Cullen really showed the way when they planted small vineyards in the late 1960s and early 1970s. They chose an area approximately 15km (9 miles) north of Margaret River itself, around Wilyabrup, an area which still boasts the majority of the flagship estates. However, two of the highest profile estates – Cape Mentelle and Leeuwin – are actually south of the Margaret River. There is also a third group of estates north of the town of Wilyabrup, led by Amberley and Cape Clairault. The average temperatures are significantly, but not appreciably, higher the further north you go.

When the red gum trees flower at harvest time, they provide food for the local population of silver-eyes, so sparing the grapes.

CLIMATE AND SOIL

Soils do differ but the majority of the good vineyard sites in Margaret River are either gravels or sands over clay. They mostly drain well – which is fine so long as you've built some dams to store your irrigation water. Of the average 1160mm (46in) of rainwater per year, only 200mm (8in) falls between October and April, the time in the vine's growing season when it needs most nourishment. Except for estates like Leeuwin that are content to harvest small crops – and to sell the wines at high prices – efficient irrigation is a necessity. The intensity of the fruit, and the acid and tannin structure in the wines are the best rebuttal I can think of when people start complaining that you can't make great wine using irrigation. With the exception of the Leeuwin Estate, in the Margaret River region you can't make great wine without it.

RED GRAPES

The main varieties are Cabernet Sauvignon, Shiraz, Pinot Noir, Zinfandel and Merlot.

WHITE GRAPES

Sémillon and Sauvignon Blanc are often blended together and with Chenin Blanc. Chardonnay is also commonly grown.

CLIMATE

This is a maritime climate, with a coolish growing season and a mild, wet winter. Cold Antarctic currents flowing beneath the land mass, and westerly winds from the Indian Ocean cool this region and make it more temperate than Perth to the north. Sea breezes are good for preventing overheating, but bad for drying out the soil, sometimes making irrigation necessary. In spring the breezes may reach gale force, damaging early bud break.

SOIL

The topsoil tends to be sand or gravel, the subsoil is often clay loam. These subsoils have the capacity to retain water, but irrigation is often necessary.

ASPECT

Vines are planted on low, gentle slopes, at around 40m (130ft) above sea level.

WHERE THE VINEYARDS ARE *You shouldn't have too much trouble getting casual labour around vintage time in the Margaret River. But be warned – it may be very casual, depending on the size of the waves rather than the ripeness of the grapes, because that long, inviting coastline that you see on the left of the map is one of the greatest surfing beaches in the world. So don't expect the pickers to stay bent over the vines when the waves get up.*

The sea influence, though, is one of the crucial points about Margaret River. That's the Indian Ocean there, a warm sea, and the difference between summer and winter temperatures is smaller here than anywhere else in Australia. But this isn't always a benefit: early-flowering varieties like Chardonnay often get lashed by westerly gales just when they are trying to set a crop, and the winds can carry salt miles inland; grapes and salt don't get on. On the other hand, those long, baking, sun-soaked autumns ripen most varieties to perfection.

The first group of vineyards established by the local doctors mentioned on page 292 are those in the middle of the map. They are still the most important group. It becomes cooler as you head south below the Margaret River itself, but some of the most famous vineyards are those right at the bottom of the map. At the top, inland from Cape Clairault, are the latest wave of new wineries and vineyards.

TOP WINERIES AND VINEYARDS

1. Amberley Estate
2. Cape Clairault
3. Chapman's Creek Vineyard
4. Moss Wood
5. Evans & Tate
6. Sandalford
7. Brookland Valley
8. Pierro
9. Willespie
10. Hay Shed Hill
11. Cullens
12. Vasse Felix
13. Cape Mentelle
14. Redgate
15. Leeuwin Estate

TASMANIA

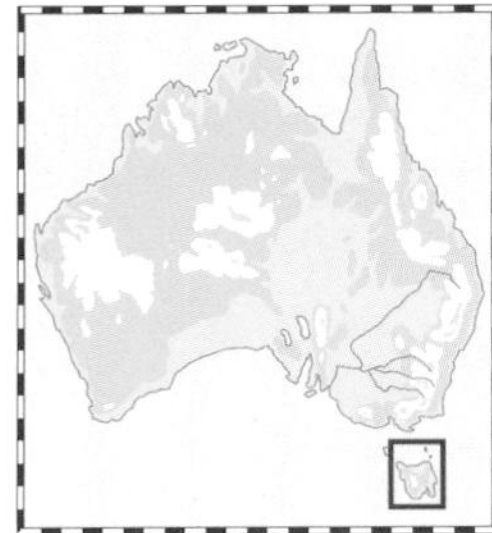

RED GRAPES
Cabernet Sauvignon and Pinot Noir are grown, with some Merlot.

WHITE GRAPES
Chardonnay is the most popular white, followed by Rhine Riesling.

CLIMATE
Temperatures are lower and humidy levels higher than most other Australian wine regions. Wind-breaks protect vines from sea winds on seaward slopes.

SOIL
In the north rich, moisture-retentive clays predominate, and in the south there are peaty, alluvial soils.

ASPECT
Strong westerly winds increasingly restrict vineyards to east-facing slopes.

For as long as Australians have dreamt of a promised land of cool-climate grape-growing along the lines of the classic cool areas of northern Europe, Tasmania has featured high on the list of possibilities. But throughout the 1970s, 1980s and early 1990s, a vintage that would fulfil that promise remained resolutely elusive. There were some good wines, certainly, but far more bad ones, and several of the best came from areas like the east and the south of Tasmania – areas that were supposedly not so naturally blessed as the rest of the island.

The Tasmanian Department of Agriculture's view until recently was that Tasmania was unsuitable for grapes and more effort should be put into apples. Dr Andrew Pirie's view, which gained him the first viticultural Ph.D. awarded by the University of Sydney, was that certain areas around the Pipers and Tamar rivers were the nearest thing Australia could find to Burgundy. The truth lies somewhere in between.

One of the most difficult facts to accept is that irregularity of vintage quality, ranging from sensational to dismal, has been the norm in the great French vineyards for centuries. No one in the New World can set up a commercial venture with such a haphazard likelihood of harvesting good fruit. Such a scenario affects red grapes more than white in France, and so it does in Tasmania; particularly in the north, the red grape crop frequently just doesn't get ripe enough to make good table wine. Good base for sparkling wine, however, needs to be acidic and the biggest recent plantings have been by companies expanding their top-quality sparkling production.

VINEYARD AREAS

Vineyards were established in Tasmania in 1823, before either Victoria or South Australia, but they were short-lived and weren't revived until the 1950s. It was in 1974 that the modern era really began with Pirie's establishment of Pipers Brook on iron-rich but relatively exposed soils to the north-east of Launceston. The annual heat summation is generally similar to that of Burgundy's Côte de Nuits, but aggressive winds off the Bass Strait mean that only the best sites will really ripen grapes well. Within a few miles, temperatures as cool as the Mosel Valley can be found. This would explain why the area is most successful at Riesling and sparkling wine base. The Tamar River running north of Launceston is protected from the winds and warmed by the estuary. This, along with lower rainfall, allows red grapes to ripen reasonably well and even Cabernet Sauvignon can be good.

However, the only places to ripen Cabernet and Pinot Noir satisfactorily, even excitingly, on a regular basis, are on the east coast and the Coal River to the south. The eastern vineyards near Bicheno, in particular Freycinet, are squeezed behind a bluff that deflects the coastal winds and allows the long sunshine hours maximum effect. The Coal River is in a rain-shadow north of Hobart and the long sunshine hours balanced by cool nights bring about full-coloured, ripe-flavoured reds and intense whites. With its own Tasmanian Appellation of Origin scheme, the growers are determined to promote their regional individuality, but their best bet for fame is still as a world-class producer of sparkling wine grapes.

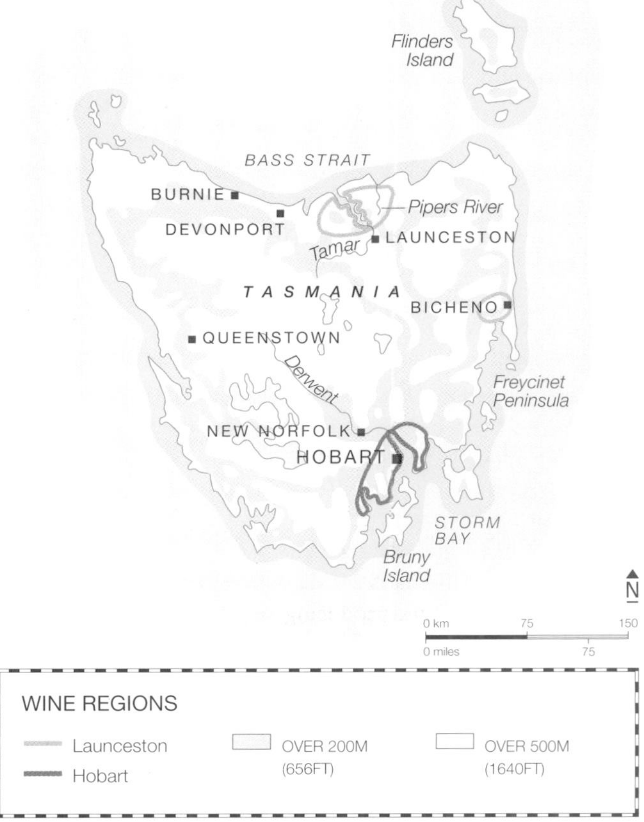

Some of Tasmania's best vineyards are in the Tamar Valley, north of Launceston.

Queensland & Northern Territory

There was a time when Queensland produced more than twice as much wine as Western Australia and even a quarter as much as volume leader South Australia. I don't know what it was like, but since most of this wine came from Roma, north-west of Brisbane, where the temperature would make a Sahara camel gasp for water, I suspect it was pretty fierce stuff.

They do still make some wine there today, but the centre of Queensland wine-making has now settled on the high valleys of the Granite Belt, south of Stanthorpe, right on the New South Wales border, which actually regards itself as a cool-climate area!

Well, there's cool and there's cool. If you look at the amount of heat the area generally gets, it's hotter than Rutherglen in North-East Victoria whose torrid conditions are turned to good account, producing sweet fortified wines. The Granite Belt likes to be seen as a table wine region, and just about manages this because of the height of the vineyards – between 750 and 900m (2500 and 3000ft).

They also have a fairly late vintage, often mid-March to mid-April, which is something of an advantage since the same cyclonic storms that drench the Hunter Valley further south in New South Wales often sweep in here too. The rains can arrive late, in March, in which case they'll cause vintage rain dilution and disruption. But they are just as likely to be earlier, in February or even January, when they cause havoc in the Hunter Valley. In any case, the rolling landscape of the Granite Belt allows winemakers to choose mesoclimates on slopes facing away from the sun, and where these are of the prevalent decomposed granite, they are sufficiently free-draining to cope.

Despite all this, the Granite Belt produces some good, rather four-square wines. It may sound fanciful, but I do find a stony, mineral quality, in particular in the Cabernet Sauvignons. However, the Shiraz, which was the first classic variety planted here, seems to be more successful, giving quite a rich, beefy performance at its best. Interestingly, the white Sémillon also does well – shades of the more famous Hunter Valley, some 400km (250 miles) to the south.

Vines at Chateau Hornsby, Alice Springs, have some respite from the heat during the cold desert nights.

NORTHERN TERRITORY

I don't blame you if you execute a massive double-take about this inclusion of Northern Territory in a wine atlas. When some intrepid friend told me they'd just sampled the local brew at Alice Springs on the way back from a visit to Ayers Rock I presumed they were taking the mickey. I mean, the centre of Australia is just this great baking red desert, isn't it? It has certainly looked like that whenever I've flown over it. Golden Rule time. Never underestimate the ingenuity of an Australian winemaker when it comes to turning a quid.

Yes, the centre of Australia is an arid, fly-blown desert. And yes, there *is* a vineyard there, Chateau Hornsby. If you get the plane to fly low enough on its approach to Alice Springs, you can see the name stencilled in white on the corrugated iron roof. And there are vines, too. I suppose the thing is that Alice Springs, with at least a notional supply of water available, is the only place for thousands of miles around that a vineyard would have the slightest chance of survival. The wines are unashamedly labelled with pictures of Alice Springs, Ayers Rock and the rest, but the vineyard – about 11km (7 miles) south of Alice Springs – does produce grapes. Drip irrigation is hard at it right through the growing season, fed by a couple of 100-m (330-ft) deep boreholes, and the winery itself is underground to try to keep things cool. Vintage is usually underway in the first few days of January and the owner is always eager to proclaim the first vintage in Australia. Indeed his top seller is Early Red, a Shiraz he starts to pick as the clock strikes midnight each New Year's Eve. I'm surprised that anyone in Australia is sober enough at that time to tell a grape from a coconut, but there you go.

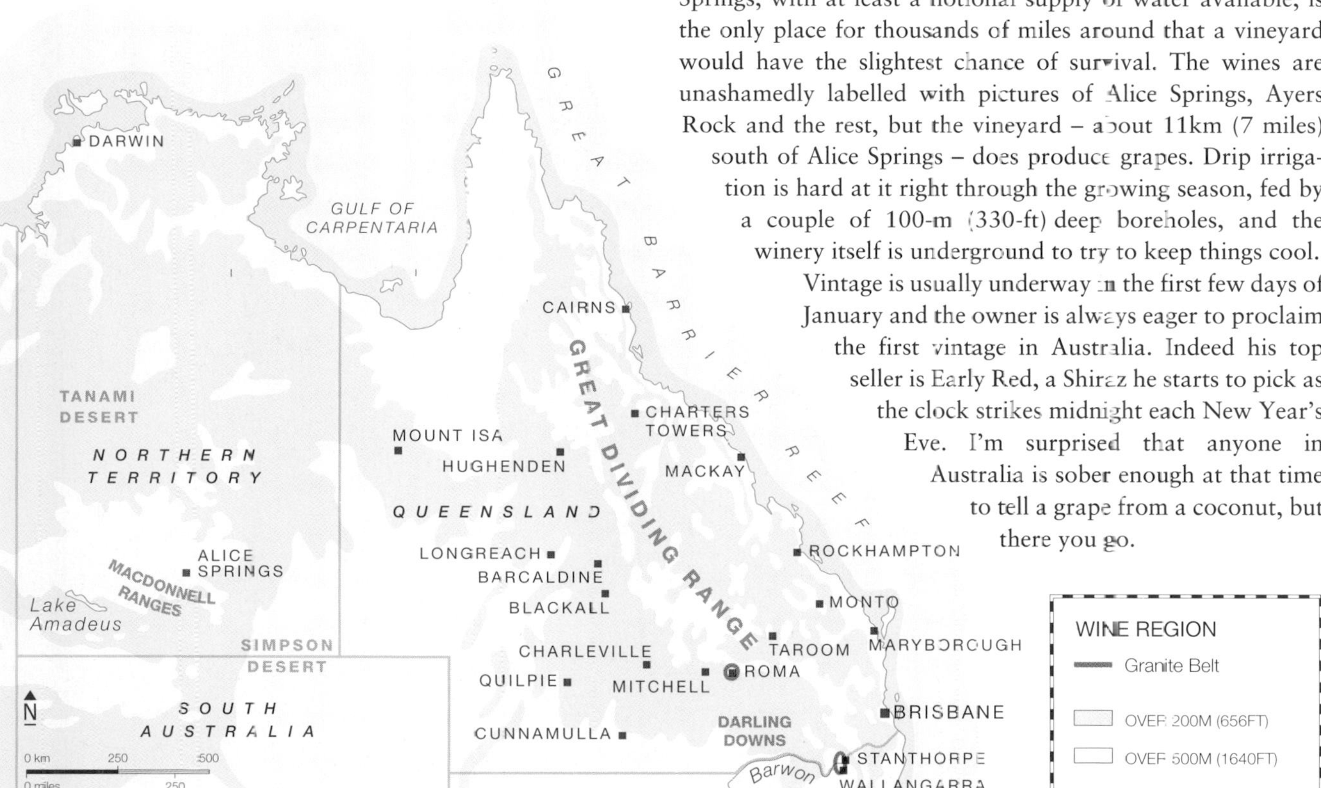

RED GRAPES
Shiraz is the principal red grape, with small plantings of Cabernet Sauvignon and Pinot Noir in Queensland.

WHITE GRAPES
Almost half the Granite Belt is planted with Chardonnay.

CLIMATE
It is relatively hot in Queensland and very hot in Alice Springs; the latter uses drip irrigation fed by local boreholes. Queensland's late vintage avoids the worst of the rains but frost and hail can damage the crop.

SOIL
Queensland's soils are generally slightly acid. They can be granitic and sandy grey or brown-grey soil over a subsoil of white sand and clay. Around Roma, the soil is a rich, sandy, alluvial loam.

ASPECT
The Granite Belt vineyards are at 750–900m (2500–3000ft) in the hilly area around Stanthorpe. Chateau Hornsby is at 600m (1969ft).

NEW ZEALAND

THE DRAMATIC TRANSFORMATION of New Zealand during the 1990s is nothing short of astonishing. From being thought of as a rather quaint, introverted nation at the far side of nowhere down towards the South Pole, New Zealand has become a vibrant, self-confident, exciting place to be. Yes, *exciting*. Has anyone but a sheep farmer ever called New Zealand *exciting* before? *Has* New Zealand ever been exciting before? I can't vouch for what the early settlers thought two hundred years ago, but even the most venerable of my present-day New Zealand acquaintances don't admit to ever having been excited by their homeland.

And the same goes for its wine industry. Strangely, it seems to have started off well enough. A visiting Frenchman in 1840 enjoyed the local product – which he described as a 'light, white wine, very sparkling, and delicious to taste' (not bad praise from a Frenchman) – an early hint that light whites and sparklers were the most likely styles to succeed. During the nineteenth century, other good reports of vines and their wine surfaced from time to time, but by the 1860s, temperance societies were lobbying for laws that hedged the wine producer round with more and more restrictions, with the ultimate aim of prohibiting alcohol altogether.

There was a brief period in the 1890s when Hawke's Bay produced some supposedly good quality wines, but districts were already starting to vote for local prohibition. Indeed, the whole country voted for prohibition in 1919, only for the result to be overturned by the thinnest of majorities by the votes of servicemen returning from World War One.

Clearly New Zealand society had little regard for its wine industry, so how on earth could it flourish? It didn't. Vine diseases like oidium (powdery mildew) were already making life hell in the warmer, more humid areas, and phylloxera was laying waste to vineyards on all sides. Replanting, when it occurred, was either with *Vitis labrusca* – Albany Surprise was the most widely planted variety until the 1960s – or with French hybrids, and the production was mostly of thoroughly mediocre fortified wines.

Good fortified wines all come from very hot vineyard conditions. Nowhere in New Zealand gets remotely hot enough to produce them. When a Royal Commission after World War Two stated that a 'considerable quantity of wine made in New Zealand would be classified as unfit for human consumption in other wine-producing countries', it was a reflection on how low the quality of New Zealand wine had sunk.

But look at the way society treated drinking: there were restrictions on every side. You couldn't drink on trains until 1968, in theatres until 1969, at airports until 1970, or at cabaret shows until 1971. It wasn't until 1976 that caterers were allowed to serve drink, or wineries themselves could sell a glass of wine. The first wine bar licence was granted in 1979, and, good grief, sports clubs couldn't sell drink until 1980!

Although legislation against the 'demon drink' gradually eased, a whiff of disapproval still lingered over the New Zealand wine industry well into the 1980s. Close economic relations with Australia in the late 1980s finally forced New Zealand to liberalize its drinking rules at much the same time as a new wave of free-market politics was sweeping through the country and galvanizing society in general. In 1990, 'dry' areas were abolished, licensing laws were relaxed so that anyone could start a wine business if they wanted, and supermarkets were given permission to sell wine: they now sell something like 40 per cent of all wine consumed in New Zealand. At last the past is being left behind – a wine past with nothing of value to cherish, a prim colonial legacy with a sell-by date which has long expired.

If ever there was a wine nation which should look forward and not back, it is New Zealand. Having a past that you are ashamed of can be a marvellously liberating experience. No fusty old traditions which you have to try to drag into the modern world; no cobwebby wine styles stubbornly clung to by faithful consumers. But if you are going to make a fresh start, you have to take care choosing where and how you're going to do it. New Zealand didn't quite get it right the first couple of times round.

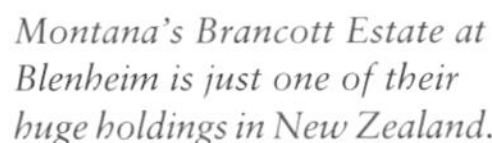

Montana's Brancott Estate at Blenheim is just one of their huge holdings in New Zealand.

PANORAMIC MAPS
Hawke's Bay *pages 300–1*
Marlborough *pages 304–5*

They got the idea right – a cool climate – well, a lot cooler than their near, or rather only neighbour Australia, in any case. And they realized that no-one in the dispirited industry itself seemed to have much idea about what to do – so they'd better call in a foreign expert. In 1895 an Italian-trained Dalmatian called Romeo Bragato arrived. He gave lots of good advice over the next few years, little of which seems to have been taken.

In the 1960s they decided to go for top advice, and this time to act upon it. Not unreasonably, they looked to Germany as their model. The German influence had been important in teaching Australia how to make delicious, dry Riesling wines under difficult conditions. German wine was highly thought of at the time and it seemed that a Southern Ocean Rheingau or Mosel was a feasible objective.

Dr Helmut Becker, their chosen adviser, was an excellent fellow, and a first-rate scientist. But his life's work was to prove that cross-bred grape varieties could be produced which gave the quality of Riesling without any of its drawbacks. He might have recommended wholesale plantings of Riesling, which probably would have led to many outstanding wines. But he didn't. But he chose Müller-Thurgau. So the brave new dawn for New Zealand wine which could have concentrated on creating a new Bernkasteler Doctor instead set about creating a better Liebfraumilch.

Well, they succeeded there. New Zealand Müller-Thurgau pretty quickly became the best in the world – and I wouldn't be surprised if it still is. But the advice to go for light, Germanic white wines can be seen, in retrospect, to have been shallow in the extreme. It is possible superficially to equate cool South Island regions like Central Otago and Canterbury, maybe even parts of Marlborough, with some parts of Germany. But no grapes were planted in these South Island regions in the 1960s. Instead, all the plantings took place in the North Island, whose climate goes from pleasantly Burgundian in the south to subtropical in the north. Of course you can grow the Müller-Thurgau in these conditions – and get massive crops of simply flavoured wine from it – but it is never going to create a drink fit for heroes.

New Zealand's heroes were late in coming. The country's social revolution was a tortuously slow affair, and long after Australian and Californian winemakers were touring the world, drinking up every wine experience they could learn from, New Zealanders were still poking about at home. It wasn't until the 1970s that visionaries like John Buck of Te Mata, or the Spence Brothers of Matua Valley began to establish vineyards, and when they did, it wasn't Müller-Thurgau they had in their sights – it was the classics of Burgundy and Bordeaux.

It soon became clear that Chardonnay and Pinot Noir could ripen easily, indeed, that the North Island was mostly too hot for Pinot Noir. Buck was convinced that he could find ways to ripen Cabernet Sauvignon and Merlot in Hawke's Bay. The Spences hit lucky straight away with Sauvignon Blanc. And by 1973, the new era of New Zealand wine was finally ushered in with the planting of the first vines at Marlborough.

By 1986, there was such a glut of grapes that the Government paid growers NZ$6,175 per hectare to rip up vines. Too many people had rushed into the grape-growing market and had mostly chosen to plant the high-yielding bulk varieties in fertile soils. As many as 507 hectares (1253 acres) of Müller-Thurgau alone were grubbed up. Gisborne, Hawke's Bay, Auckland, even the brand new plantations in the South Island, lost substantial areas; all in all, 25 per cent of the total national vineyard area – 1517 hectares (3748 acres) – was pulled out.

After the vinepull, the wine industry regrouped and licked its wounds. By the end of the 1980s New Zealand was becoming known worldwide for the quality of its wines, in particular its Sauvignon Blancs and Chardonnays, although Riesling, Pinot Noir, Cabernet and Merlot were also making their mark.

Despite the success of other varieties it is undoubtedly the Sauvignon Blancs from those early Marlborough vines which have taken the world by storm and created a new classic wine style so thrillingly different that it has been the standard bearer for New Zealand ever since. No New Zealand wine had ever tasted like those Sauvignon Blancs from the South Island. But then, no wine anywhere in the world had ever tasted like them. No previous wine had shocked, thrilled, offended, entranced the world before with such brash, unexpected flavours of gooseberries, passion fruit and lime, or crunchy green capsicum and asparagus spears. They catapulted New Zealand into the front rank of New World wine producers, and the gift she brought to the party was something that even California and Australia had been unable to achieve – an entirely new, brilliantly successful, wine style that the rest of the world has been attempting to copy ever since. New Zealanders now often prefer to talk of their Chardonnays, Rieslings, Cabernets or Pinot Noirs, but the world is still thanking them for their Sauvignon Blanc.

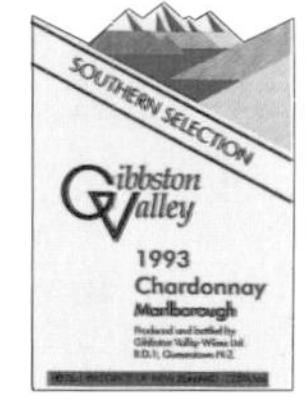

THE CLASSIFICATION OF NEW ZEALAND WINE

Wine labelling legislation in New Zealand has remained relatively relaxed until now. This is set to change in the near future with the introduction of a system of Certified Origin to ensure international confidence by guaranteeing all the claims on a wine label.

- **Certified Origin system** This system will guarantee that 85 per cent of the grapes in a particular wine will come from the geographical area, the vintage and the variety stated on the label.
- **Geographical denominations** The broadest designation is New Zealand, followed by North Island or South Island. These will cover regional blends. Next come 16 regions, such as Canterbury, followed by specific localities, and finally individual vineyards.

North Island

RED GRAPES
Cabernet Sauvignon and Pinot Noir are most popular, followed by Merlot. There is also a small amount of Cabernet Franc and Pinotage.

WHITE GRAPES
Even though New Zealand established its reputation with Sauvignon Blanc, this variety comes third in planting behind Chardonnay and Müller-Thurgau. Riesling is growing in importance. Other varieties include Muscat, Gewürztraminer, Chenin Blanc and Palomino.

CLIMATE
The North Island is generally warmer than the South Island, but overall the climate in both is maritime. Rainfall is plentiful and is often a problem during the ripening season when it can lead to rot.

SOIL
Soils range from glacial and alluvial at Hawke's Bay, to loam and clay in the north, and friable gravelly silt around Martinborough.

ASPECT
Vineyard site selection is carefully considered after a boom period when poor varieties were planted in many unsuitable places. Most vines are found on flatlands or gently rolling hills where too high yields are controlled by skilled management of the vine canopy.

Coleraine Cabernet/Merlot from the prestigious Te Mata estate in Hawke's Bay

WHAT'S ALL THIS about New Zealand being a cool-climate wine region? That's a bit like saying France is a cool-climate wine region. Some bits are, to be sure, but some bits are as hot as Hades. And it's the same with New Zealand. Way down in the South or Central Otago it's as cool as in the Mosel Valley of Germany. But that's 1000km (620 miles) south of the vineyards north of Auckland. And don't try to draw any conclusion from latitude. Central Otago's latitude is 44° South, about the same as some of the warmer parts of that not-particularly-cold-area Bordeaux in the northern hemisphere.

As for the furthest vineyards of the Northland, above Auckland, they're at about latitude 34° South. In the northern hemisphere 34° slices across the top of Tunisia and Algeria. Now, it isn't like Tunisia north of Auckland, but there are a fair few vineyards that struggle under warm, humid conditions that can verge on the subtropical, so I think I'm going to leave most of this cool-climate chat until we get to the South Island.

Now, if you want to suggest that New Zealand is a wet-climate wine region – I'll go for that. With the exception of the tiny Wairarapa area near Wellington, which behaves as though it were a virtual extension of Marlborough on the other side of the Cook Strait, the North Island is a wet place to grow grapes. And if you want to suggest that it is a wonderfully fertile landscape ideally suited to growing vines, I'll say, yes – fertile soils, lots of sun, lots of rain: you can grow vines the size of peach trees in no time at all. But don't expect a decent crop of grapes fit for making fine wine. The best wines come from vines grown in dry areas with just the right amount of sun, giving small crops off infertile, impoverished, free-draining soil. That's not too much of a problem in the South Island, but in the North, such conditions are few and far between. And the story of how to locate such sites – and if you can't, what to do instead – is very much the story of the North Island's wine industry.

Many producers actually started out in the nineteenth century by growing their grapes in greenhouses. That seems a bit extreme, and could explain why hardly any wineries grew to any size during the nineteenth century! But the early growers may not have been so dumb. Most of the vines in the North Island do suffer from the weather, in particular around Auckland where most of the early plantings were located.

Though the latitudes should imply hot to very hot conditions, things aren't as simple as that. In Europe, the main maritime influences are the warm Gulf Stream and the warm Mediterranean. New Zealand is set alone among seas strongly influenced by the icy Antarctic currents. Strong prevailing westerly winds continually pummel the west coast. Until you get to the central mountain ranges that protect Gisborne and Hawke's Bay on the east coast, there is no protection from the westerlies, and the rain clouds happily deposit their loads on the vineyards around Auckland and Northland.

You might get away with this if you were guaranteed a dry autumn. But that's one thing you're not guaranteed in the North Island. If the westerlies don't keep drizzling down on you, you've got the cyclonic depressions of the Pacific to think about. These are likely to move in from the east in the early autumn. Some years you'll have picked your crop, some years you won't have. These cyclonic rainstorms are a particular problem over to the east in Gisborne and Hawke's Bay, which are otherwise well-protected from westerly rain.

Lots of rain, lots of sun – all you need is fertile soil for the vines to grow like jungle. Well, with a couple of exceptions in parts of Hawke's Bay and Wairarapa, North Island soil goes from fertile to supremely fertile and that makes it very difficult indeed for quality-minded grape growers. Fertile soils rarely drain well, and they encourage large crops of grapes. Large crops take longer to ripen.

North Island has a history of autumn downpours, so you have to pick early even though the crop isn't really ripe. For all the negative aspects of having Müller-Thurgau as your major grape variety, at least it will provide you with adequate, mildly fruity wine at low alcohol levels from high crops. Not very ambitious, I admit, but until the 1980s it was the mainstay of North Island vineyards.

CANOPY MANAGEMENT

Fertile soils also encourage vigorous leaf growth, and this is a serious problem if you want to progress from hybrids and Müller-Thurgau on to the classic grape varieties. Excessive leaf growth shades your fruit, retarding physical maturity in the grapes and causing a lean, green streak to dominate red wine flavours even when the alcohol levels seem acceptable. Heavy foliage also reduces air movement. In the frequently damp North Island climates, this causes outbursts of bunch rot (botrytis) which can ruin the harvest. The desire to compete in international markets with acceptable styles of wines, allied to an increasingly demanding domestic market, forced New Zealand's wine industry to attempt to find solutions to these problems. Led by Dr Richard Smart, New Zealand has become the world leader in developing trellising and pruning systems for fertile, warm-air vineyard conditions.

The results have been dramatic. For almost the first time we are seeing red wines of a fully ripe, yet memorably individual, style coming from all parts of the North Island – Auckland, Hawke's Bay, Wairarapa, and even in a few cases, from Gisborne. White wines are achieving far better ripeness without the accompanying botrytis flavours that used to be a mark of much New Zealand Chardonnay and Müller-Thurgau, and the prevailing acidity of the fruit is far better integrated in the wine. Even in cool years like 1992 and 1993, which, throughout most of New Zealand, were about as bad as vintages can get, the vineyards using modern vineyards techniques still produced fair fruit. With the wholesale replanting made necessary by phylloxera infestation, we're seeing more and more vineyards adapting to the challenging conditions of New Zealand's North Island.

AUCKLAND AND WAIKATO

Nowhere are the conditions more challenging than around Auckland. There are now very few plantings left in Northland, where subtropical conditions make it virtually impossible to ripen *vinifera* grapes before they rot on the vine. Matakana over on the Hauraki Gulf is an exception. However, the Dalmatians who came to New Zealand to work the Kauri gumfields were good old-fashioned thirsty Europeans, and many, having saved a bit of money, migrated nearer to Auckland and set up as winemakers. Almost all the traditional wine companies in Northland, as well as several of the newer ones, were founded by families of Dalmatian origin.

The hot, humid weather and the mostly heavy clay soils didn't matter too much when the chief product was fortified sherries and ports. But the swing to fine table wine production has found most of the go-ahead Auckland area wineries sourcing the majority of their grapes from elsewhere – Gisborne, Hawke's Bay and Marlborough. Even so, there are some vineyards over by the airport to the south, rather more at Henderson just to the north, and a good deal more further up the road at Huapai and Kumeu. The soils are largely heavy clay, the weather warm, and with the Tasman Sea on one side and the Pacific on the other, humidity is high, but at least that gives cloud cover against the harsh effects of the sun. There are some inspired home-grown wines from estates like Kumeu River and Matua Valley, but most of the best are from brought-in grapes. Indeed the best estate-grown wines may well come from offshore on Waiheke Island, which usually avoids the mainland rains and whose summer and autumn warmth brings Cabernet to impressive ripeness. There's even a vineyard out on Great Barrier Island at Okupu Beach. Some guys have all the luck.

The Waikato region south of Auckland is one of the North Island's historic regions, but this rather damp, humid spot is probably better suited to dairy farming. Though there are some large vineyards there, there are few wineries, and much of the crop is actually made into grape juice. Even so, de Redcliffe has made some good, dry wines, and Rongopai has used the warm, clammy conditions to make some superb botrytis-affected sweet wines.

GISBORNE

Heading east below the Bay of Plenty, there are several wineries – most importantly Morton Estate – but few vineyards, though there is a small vineyard on the pumice soils of Galatea to the south. But it is Gisborne, on Poverty Bay, that concerns us. Most of the vineyards are sprawled across the Gisborne plains where a deep bed of alluvial silt supplies such fertile soil conditions that varieties like Müller-Thurgau can easily produce 30 tonnes per hectare of acceptable fruit. But the excessive fertility isn't as suitable for higher quality varieties, since it encourages dense foliage and hefty crops and retards ripening. Chardonnay has still managed to produce high yields of decent fruit due to plenty of sunshine hours and protection from wet westerlies by the Huturau Mountains. That protection counts for nothing, however, when cyclonic depressions form to the east in the autumn. Gisborne has unacceptably high rainfall in the vintage period of February to April, a fact that has deterred most growers from trying red grapes. However, state of the art vineyard management, replacement of phylloxera-infected vines with better clones, and a move into the less fertile hillside sites is turning round Gisborne's reputation. People have begun to talk of Gisborne as New Zealand's Chardonnay capital; the soft, gentle, ripe quality of many recent releases shows that they may well be right.

WAIRARAPA

Hawke's Bay is far down the coast from Gisborne, and I cover it more fully over the page. But there is one more booming area – Wairarapa just north of Wellington. This is centred on the little town of Martinborough, though vineyards are now appearing further north towards Masterson as well.

If the North Island's weak points are too much rain and excessively fertile soil, Martinborough has the answer. Surrounded by mountains to the south-west, west and north-east, the region is protected from both summer and autumn rains. And although the land down by the river flats is heavy clay, a series of flat-topped river terraces to the north-east round the town of Martinborough are shallow gravelly silt over deep, free-draining, virtually pure gravel.

Add to this relatively cool and windy, but rainless, summers and autumns, and a bit of drip irrigation and you have positively Burgundian conditions for great Chardonnay and Pinot Noir. That, plus a splash of Pinot Gris, Riesling, Sauvignon and what-have-you, is increasingly exactly what you get.

Cooks' Longridge vines in Hawke's Bay are planted on flat land for ease of cultivation.

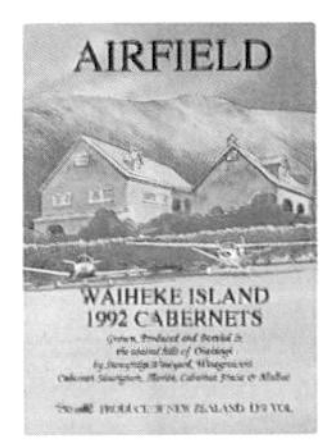

HAWKE'S BAY

RED GRAPES
Cabernet Sauvignon is the most widely planted red variety. Merlot is also grown but is usually blended with Cabernet rather than sold as a varietal, and there is some Pinot Noir.

WHITE GRAPES
Chardonnay is the most important variety of all in Hawke's Bay. Müller-Thurgau comes second in volume terms. Sauvignon Blanc and Chenin Blanc also do well here.

CLIMATE
This is ideal for high-quality wine production. Regular sunshine ensures full ripening of the grapes and there's optimum rainfall.

SOIL
Almost all the vineyards are planted on alluvial plains but soil types still vary from well-drained gravel and sandy loam, to fertile, heavier silty loam.

ASPECT
The best vineyards are on free-draining soils of low fertility. Most Hawke's Bay plantings hitherto have been made on flat land, but nearby limestone hills may be found superior in the future.

'WELCOME TO SUNNY HAWKE'S BAY' the sign says, and they're not kidding. I last arrived here in March – straight from the heartland of Australia where I'd been broiled and bullied by the merciless sun day after day, but where the Factor 30 cream had kept my face, neck and hands a pleasant hue lying somewhere between blancmange pink and butterscotch orange. Quite fetching I thought, and not a blister. Until I got to Hawke's Bay. I had wondered, well, New Zealand is so much cooler than Australia, do I really need sun lotion in March? But I'd slapped some on anyway and gone off to my first meeting. By late morning I was decidedly uncomfortable. By lunchtime I was hurting. I didn't feel hot, really, but I was burning. By evening my hands were a welter of bright red blisters, so sore I could neither bear the sunlight on them nor soothe them with anything but cool water. Sunny Hawke's Bay? They should post a health warning at the airport.

But it's a serious point I'm making here. The sun may not feel hot, but it does shine relentlessly at Hawke's Bay. New Zealand is known as the Land of the Long White Cloud, and you can watch the clouds piling up near Gisborne to the north. You can watch them follow the coastline down towards Napier, yet a mile or two before the Bay, the clouds seem to head inland, and stay hugging the mountain range until, south of Havelock North and Te Mata, they return to the coastline.

But, more importantly, the ozone layer at the moment is extremely thin over the southern Pacific and several growers told me that ultraviolet penetration round Hawke's Bay is higher than in any other populated area in the Southern Hemisphere. Opinions are divided as to what effect this has on grape ripening, whether it aids or impedes photosynthesis, the development of pigment, and the physical maturing of the grapes. My hands are here to tell you it must have some effect.

And long before ozone layers were even discovered, Hawke's Bay's blend of long sunshine hours, reasonable rainfall that usually, but not always, fell at precisely the right times, and easy availability of large tracts of suitable vineyard land, had made the area New Zealand's most exciting vineyard region. That was at the end of the nineteenth century. Various vineyards were established, mostly on good, infertile land, and mostly with classic grape varieties, and by 1913 Hawke's Bay was producing 30 per cent of New Zealand's wine. Bernard Chambers' Te Mata vineyard in Hawke's Bay was the largest in New Zealand. As elsewhere in New Zealand, phylloxera, prohibition and disinterest took their toll, vineyards were turned over to *Vitis labrusca* and hybrid varieties, and the heavy Heretaunga river flats were planted in preference to the low-yielding gravel beds. One man, Tom McDonald kept the flame of Chardonnay and Cabernet Sauvignon flickering, but despite heavy plantings in the 1960s and 1970s, this was mostly still in the high-yielding, unsuitable black soils of the plain.

But when John Buck visited Tom McDonald in the 1960s, Tom had pointed over to the Te Mata peak and said, 'That's the best Cabernet land you'll get in Hawke's Bay – frost-free, facing north, and free-draining.' John bought the old Te Mata property in 1974, and released a Cabernet in 1980 that sparked the revival of Hawke's Bay as a great vineyard area, rather than a bulk provider of grapes like Müller-Thurgau, Chasselas and Seibel. At last Hawke's Bay could enter the contest again to be New Zealand's premier wine region.

It isn't really a battle that can ever be won though, because other large areas like Marlborough produce such completely different styles, and tip-top areas like Nelson, Wairarapa or Waiheke Island are a fraction of its size, and so don't bear comparison. Hawke's Bay's reputation relies increasingly on its ability to ripen the red Bordeaux varieties fully – not easy in New Zealand – backed up by an impressive performance in the less challenging arena of Chardonnay and Sauvignon Blanc. With the welcome decline of vineyards on the Heretaunga river flats, this reputation will be built upon three different areas.

The warmest of these areas is Bay View and the Esk Valley. It is also the least planted, so far. Nevertheless, the conditions are excellent. The bay swoops inwards north of Napier and presses up against the hills. There's not much land, but it's warm – apricot trees are all around – and bud-burst comes as much as two weeks ahead of the rest of the Bay. On the terraces cut into the hillside the grapes can really fry, and the Bordeaux red varieties romp to ripeness. The Esk Valley joins the sea just north of Bay View and offers well-protected, sandy alluvial soils over gravel that welcome the sea breeze which appears every day. There's a lot of Müller-Thurgau still

TOP WINERIES

1. Esk Valley
2. Brownlie
3. Sacred Hill
4. Mission
5. Church Road (Montana)
6. Brookfield
7. Ngatarawa
8. Stonecroft
9. C.J. Pask
10. Vidal
11. Te Mata
12. Akarangi
13. Waimarama

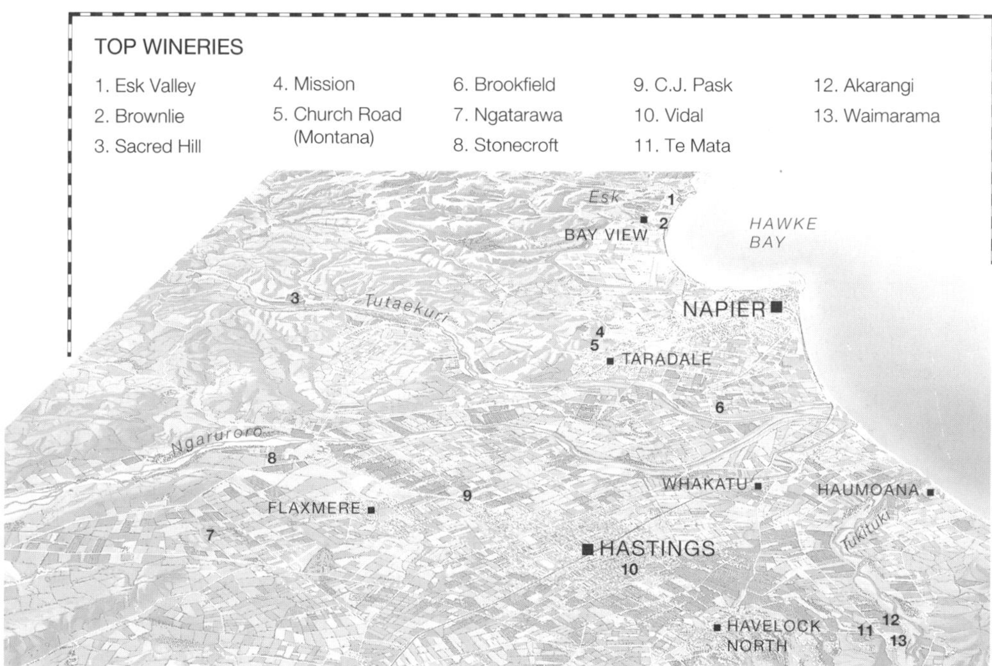

WHERE THE VINEYARDS ARE *The centre of the valley, between Hastings and Napier, is where most of the vineyards used to be, but with fertile soils and a high water table, quality was never good and most of the land has reverted to fruit and vegetables. One of the commonest sights now is the long line of poplars acting as a windbreak for kiwi fruit orchards. North of the airport, Bay View and the Esk Valley don't have that many vines, but Bay View is a sun-trap, and the sandy alluvial soils over gravel in the sheltered Esk Valley are excellent for grapes.*

The real action is happening along the Tutaekuri and Ngaruroro rivers. Their rushing waters have scoured parts of the valley floor clean of soil and silt until there's almost nothing but gravel left, and the rivers have also changed paths in the past, leaving great swathes of gravel ripe for vineyards. This is particularly obvious with the Ngaruroro near Stonecroft, and each year, more of those vacant plots will be filled with vines as the planting fever runs its course.

The best southern sites are east of Havelock North below the Te Mata peak, where several of the vineyards for Te Mata's outstanding wines are situated, but there are also good, largely unexploited sites in the Tukituki Valley, where once again, the river has scoured the land of its topsoil, leaving bare gravel beds.

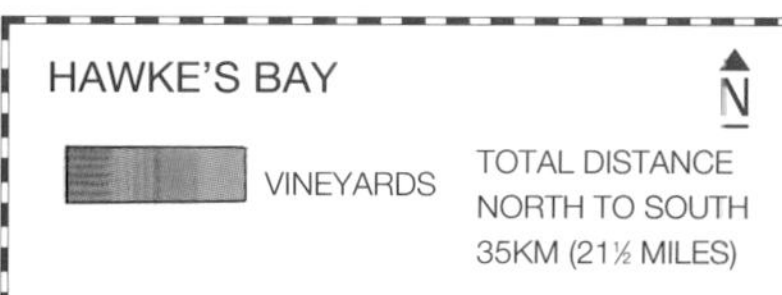

0 km 1 2
0 miles 1

planted, but it looks like a top Chardonnay site of the future.

The heart of the Hawke's Bay revival lies in the gravel beds left behind by the various rivers flowing into the Bay. Most important of these rivers are the Tutaekuri and especially the Ngaruroro. It's worth driving along and across these rivers to gaze on some of the purest gravel beds you are ever likely to see. Only the centre of Margaux in Bordeaux gets anywhere near them and yet here they stretch for mile upon mile westwards up into the hills. You get out of the car and tramp through the vineyards next to Highway 50 and the Gimblett Road and you're walking along the old river-bed itself. Half the time there's no soil at all – just this grey, ashen gravel everywhere, with an aquifer running beneath to provide you with as much irrigation water as you could want. There's an air of feverish activity along the Ngaruroro at the moment as all the major players in New Zealand are planting like mad to make sure they all get their share of what they rightly see as Kiwi red wine heaven. In the tracts of land not yet planted, the land is so poor it can't even support sheep. It's virtually hydroponic in places and nothing survives without irrigation. Indeed, the gravel is so pure it lacks nutrients and these sometimes have to be added back in to avoid the vines turning out with all the right technical figures, but tasting dull.

The crucial thing about such free-draining soil is that it hands control back to the winemaker. The crop can be regulated and the vines trellised in such a way as to maximize the sun. But the weather does still come into it. The normal weather patterns at Hawke's Bay are similar to those of Bordeaux in a good year, with slightly lower maximum temperatures but a larger spread of sunny days and less rain. You can almost always rely upon a dry warm autumn, though cyclones in 1979 and 1988 deluged the vineyards at vintage time. The real heat cauldron is around Fernhill where even Syrah ripens. As you head up the valley past Ngtarawa, the cooling influence of the mountains means delays in budding and ripening of a good week up at Riverview, but increasingly good conditions for Pinot Noir and Riesling.

The Tutaekuri river cuts its way through the hills north of the Ngaruroro and for much of its course is protected from maritime winds by the ridge of hills. The same supremely gravelly conditions exist but the extra heat can ripen grapes up to two weeks earlier than in the broader Ngaruroro Valley. The great Matua Valley Arararimu Cabernet frequently comes from the centre of the Dartmoor-Smith vineyard, where the river has been redirected behind a levee and all that is left is pure gravel.

Gravel also features in the Tukituki Valley to the south-east and certain outcrops near Havelock North and the Te Mata peak. However, the southern side of Hawke's Bay is more marked by shallow alluvial topsoils over impenetrable pug clays. These conditions are more difficult to control than pure gravel, but they restrict vigour and yields, and can produce fine wines. Te Mata's best vineyards are either on tan-coloured, gravelly terraces ('red metal'), or loess over limestone and sandstone. The flavours of the various blocks are markedly different but uniformly outstanding.

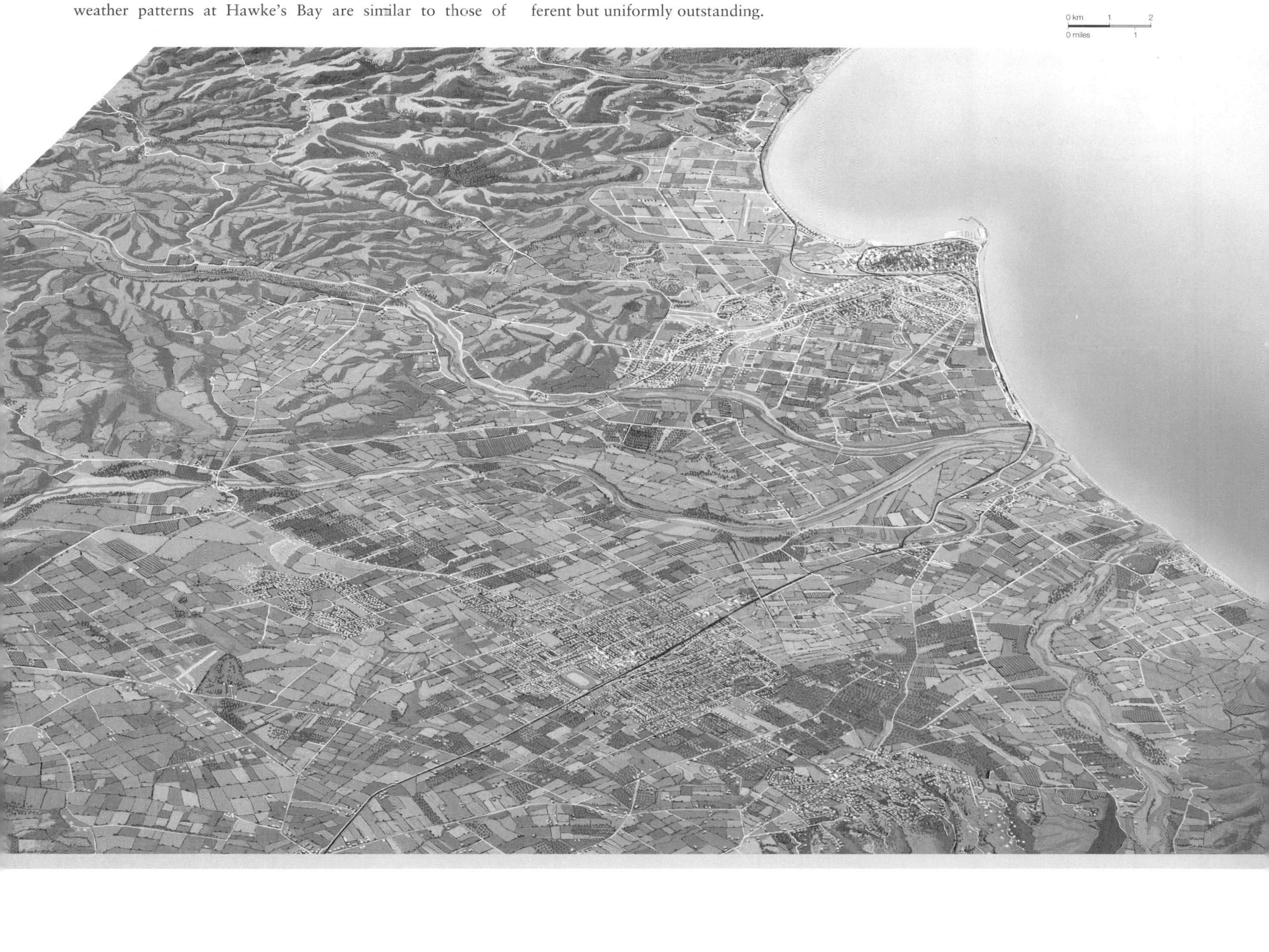

0 km 1 2
0 miles 1

South Island

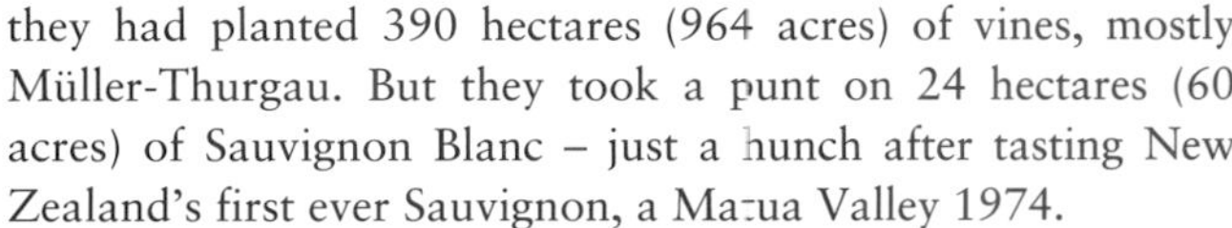

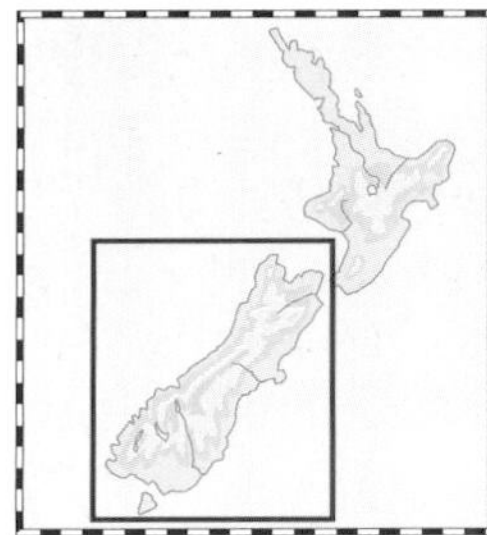

RED GRAPES
Pinot Noir is best suited to the cool conditions but Cabernet Sauvignon, Cabernet Franc and Merlot are also grown.

WHITE GRAPES
Müller-Thurgau is still widely planted but Sauvignon Blanc and Chardonnay are more highly regarded. Riesling, Gewürztraminer and Pinot Gris also feature.

CLIMATE
The climate is cool with abundant sunshine to help the ripening process. Autumn rainfall is low, but wind and frosts can be troublesome.

SOIL
Soil types are variable. Alluvial gravel, or alluvial silt loams over gravel subsoils, are well draining. In addition there are areas of chalky, limestone-rich loams and patches of loess.

ASPECT
Much of the vineyard land is flat and quite low-lying. Nelson is more hilly with some sheltered, well-exposed sites.

Neudorf, whose vineyards are shown here, is one of South Island's leading producers.

WINE-MAKING IN THE SOUTH ISLAND is a lot older than you might think. It's perfectly true that when the large-scale producer Montana began planting in Marlborough in 1973 it was generally seen as the beginning of the modern industry there – the modern industry, yes, but of the centres of wine-making now spread across the island, Marlborough was the only place that hadn't had a proper wine industry before.

Well, perhaps wine industry is stretching the point, since none of the original wine producers survived very long. But Nelson, to the north-west of Marlborough, was visited in 1843 by boat-loads of Germans who, looking at the steep hills covered in virgin bush, thought the place looked too tough for them, and sailed on to Australia. Standing on the low hills running down to the sparkling waters of Tasman Bay while a long white cloud, piled high with meringue fluff and with a base as flat as a smoothing iron, hangs motionless in the warm sky, I find it inconceivable anyone could ever want to leave this paradise. But there you go; maybe it didn't look tough *enough* for the Germans. Eventually some sort of wine-making got going there in 1868 and continued fitfully until 1939.

The French showed a bit more nerve in 1840 when they landed at Akaroa, south of Canterbury, and planted vines on a small scale around their dwellings on the mountainous Banks Peninsula. But there are no records of them trying to do anything except make enough wine for their own consumption, and when they died off, so did their vineyards.

Further south, in Central Otago, was born that perennial fair-weather friend of the winemaker – a Gold Rush. It didn't spawn vineyards on the same scale as the Australian or Californian gold fevers, but there's no doubt that a Frenchman called Jean Desiré Feraud was doing good business in 1870 selling his wine and liqueurs to speculators. Yet this, too, waned as the lustre of precious metal faded, and the whole island reverted back to sheep, cattle, and fruit – to a quiet, unobtrusive, unpolluted prosperity, lost in the southern seas.

Until 1973, that is. That's when Marlborough, now New Zealand's leading wine region, was born out of nothing. At the time Montana, New Zealand's biggest wine company, was looking to expand and wanted cheap, easy land. Hawke's Bay was NZ$2000 an acre. Marlborough was between NZ$250 and $500 an acre, depending on whether it was good for nothing but pasture or good for *almost* nothing but pasture. They bought 14 farms, 1600 hectares (4000 acres), and by 1975, before the locals had even woken up to what was happening, they had planted 390 hectares (964 acres) of vines, mostly Müller-Thurgau. But they took a punt on 24 hectares (60 acres) of Sauvignon Blanc – just a hunch after tasting New Zealand's first ever Sauvignon, a Matua Valley 1974.

What a hunch to follow. Without Marlborough Sauvignon Blanc, New Zealand might still be struggling for acceptance in the World Premier League of wine. With Marlborough Sauvignon Blanc, they created a classic flavour that no-one had ever dreamed of before, and set a standard for tangy, incisive, mouth-watering dry wines as crunchy as iceberg lettuce, and as aggressive as gooseberries and lime, that the rest of the world has been trying to copy ever since.

SOUTH ISLAND GROWTH SPURT

Startling changes in the South Island wine industry have happened over the last generation, not least in the development of new wine regions such as Marlborough. Back in 1960 the total vineyard area for the whole of New Zealand was 388 hectares (959 acres). The South Island didn't have a single vine, and the most widely planted was the *labrusca* variety, Albany Surprise, followed by a clutch of hybrids like Baco 22A and Seibel 5455.

By 1975, when there was massive vineyard expansion in the North Island, with six times the number of acres under vine than there had been in 1960, the first South Island vines were only just being planted. The hybrids had increased their acreage in the North Island, but the German influence was evident with Müller-Thurgau, nationally the most widely planted variety, with 649 hectares (1604 acres) yielding fruit.

Expansion continued at a breakneck pace, and although North Island led the way, Marlborough on South Island was rapidly proving its worth. By 1982, New Zealand's total vineyard area stood at 5901 hectares (14,581 acres); Auckland and Waikato still had the same area of vineyard as before, but the leaders now were Gisborne with 1922 hectares (4749 acres), Hawke's Bay with 1891 (4672 acres), and Marlborough with a remarkable 1175 hectares (2903 acres). Small areas like Nelson and Canterbury in South Island, and Wairarapa in North Island, had now begun planting grapes too.

The dramatic vinepull of the mid-1980s led to a sea-change in the industry and the significant growth since then has been entirely in quality areas. By 1995, hectares in production totalled 6107 (15,090 acres), with Marlborough the most important at 2095 hectares (5177 acres), Hawke's Bay with 1642 hectares (4057 acres) and Gisborne with 1427 hectares (3526 acres). And new areas of high-quality vines are bursting out. On South Island, Nelson has 92 hectares (227 acres), but Canterbury has burgeoned to 208 (514 acres), while Central Otago, invisible in 1982, has 48 hectares (119 acres).

That's not the whole story. New Zealand's booming economy and urgent export drive has meant that in 1995 the total vineyard area, including vines not yet bearing or in the process of being planted, stood at 8039 hectares (19,864 acres). Hawke's Bay shows another 626 hectares (1547 acres), Canterbury adds 52 hectares (128 acres), Central Otago has a remarkable 189 hectares (467 acres) extra, but Marlborough beats them all with 905 hectares (2236 acres) more.

It's interesting to look at grape varieties too. In 1970, the hybrid Baco 22A was the top variety with 217 hectares (536 acres). It is now officially extinct. Müller-Thurgau had 194 hectares (479 acres) in 1970, but by 1983 was easily the leader with ten times this amount. However, by 1995 this had dropped to 1014 hectares (2505 acres). There was *no* Sauvignon Blanc in 1970, but in 1995 1061 hectares (2622 acres) were planted, along with 626 hectares (1547 acres) of Cabernet Sauvignon, and 1439 hectares (3556 acres) of Chardonnay.

But there's one more fascinating figure. There are 1358 hectares (3355 acres) of non-bearing vines in 1995 listed as 'other' varieties. Some will be lesser varieties, but the majority will turn out to be Chardonnay, Sauvignon Blanc, Cabernet, Merlot and Pinot Noir when they yield their first crop.

NELSON

Back in the South Island's early days, one of the first regions to stir was Nelson, 75km (45 miles) north-west of Marlborough. The tiny Victory Grape Wines vineyard at Stoke, a mile or so south-west of the city of Nelson, produced its first vintage in 1973, and in 1974 Hermann Seifried established what is Nelson's largest vineyard; others have since joined.

Yet development has been relatively small scale. The Waimea Plains, on flat but well-drained land running across to Rabbit Island and Tasman Bay, could have become another Marlborough except that land prices and start-up costs are significantly higher. So much of the development has been in the beautiful Upper Moutere hills, just a few miles further to the north-west. The soils are mostly clay loam, but well-drained on these slopes, as they need to be, because Nelson is cooler than Marlborough and gets more concentrated periods of rain in autumn. Yet overall it has more rain-free days and long hours of sunshine, with the west coast taking the brunt of the westerlies. Despite the grapes ripening a week later than in Marlborough, and with the attendant risk of rain during vintage, some of the South Island's best Pinot Noir, Riesling and Chardonnay come from here.

CANTERBURY

Three hours' drive to the south from Marlborough, Christchurch sits at the heart of the Canterbury region on the shores of Pegasus Bay. The local Lincoln University began grape trials in 1973 despite the fact that all the traditional indicators said the area had to be too cold for grapes. There appears to be less heat here than in Champagne in France, hardly as much as on the Rhine in Germany, and yet, and yet... One of my most vivid 'road to Damascus' tasting experiences ever was the St Helena Pinot Noir 1982, grown on an old potato field 20 minutes' drive north of Christchurch, and only its second vintage. Startling, intense, brimming with passionate fruit and heady perfume, it could have held its own with any of the Côte de Nuits' Grands Crus.

From a standing start, Canterbury suddenly became New Zealand's Pinot Noir promised land. But it's not as simple as that – Wairarapa on North Island would dispute this claim for a start, and Canterbury does have several different mesoclimates. The most regularly exciting Pinot Noirs and Chardonnays are now coming from Waipara, 40km (25 miles) north of Christchurch, where a range of hills protects the vines from the sea breezes and reminds me of the Freycinet area of Tasmania – another area that should be too cold for viticulture, but isn't. The wines have a similar lush, warm richness to them. Vines near Christchurch are battered by wind, none more so than Giesen's, which nonetheless manages to produce fabulously concentrated Rieslings. And to the south, French Farm is giving the Banks Peninsula another go.

The overriding influence allowing grapes to ripen is low rainfall and free-draining soils. Long, dry summer days lead to a dry, mild autumn that allows grapes to hang on the vine until May, providing April frosts don't strike. But of course, long, slow ripening is what brings flavour intensity – just like in northern Europe, without the vintage rains.

CENTRAL OTAGO

Even so, you do have to have a reasonable amount of heat for flavour intensity. Won't Central Otago, the world's most southerly wine region, way down near Queenstown in the heart of New Zealand's skiing region, be just too cold? On paper, yes. But this is the one Continental climate among South Island's wine regions. After all, Latitude 44° South lies on the same parallel as the heart of the Rhône Valley as well as Bordeaux in the northern hemisphere. And there are hot spots here and there – on the shores of lakes, beneath sheer rock faces that reflect heat and retain it in the chilly summer nights – where heat readings rocket upwards.

This far south, the summer days are very long with very low rainfall, and between December and February, the number of cloudless days with temperatures hour upon hour over 15°C (59°F) – or indeed 20°C (68°F) – is exceptional, temperatures often peaking at over 30°C (86°F). Obviously the Germanic varieties like Riesling, Gewürztraminer and Müller-Thurgau are widely planted but I've had some pretty nice Pinot Noir too, and the Chardonnays, though a bit out of balance as yet with high acidity, are still fairly tasty.

It still isn't easy to make a success of it, but with experts like Dr Richard Smart excited by the region and keen to develop vine systems suited to local conditions, and with a tourist trade already in place that other regions would die for, I can quite see why Central Otago is now the country's fastest growing vineyard area. I just hope there are enough sheltered mesoclimates to go round, because I'm sure there will be enough thirsty tourists prepared to stash a few bottles in the backs of their cars, and plenty of skiers pining for liquid refreshment after a hard day on the slopes.

The gleaming tanks of Montana's top Riverlands Winery in Marlborough stand in startling contrast with the arid hills behind.

MARLBOROUGH AND NELSON CLIMATES

Protected from the strong sea winds, Marlborough is one of the few South Island regions warm enough for large-scale viticulture. The Southern Alps dissipate the prevailing westerly winds and help to create a rain shadow in the region, reducing rainfall over the vineyards as well as cloud cover, which, in turn, increases the amount of valuable sunshine. The southern tip of North Island protects the vineyards from the cyclonic autumn storms that come in from the Pacific Ocean. The only winds that affect the Marlborough vineyards down on the flat Wairau River Valley are warm and dry and they help to boost grape ripening. Like Marlborough, Nelson also has warm summers and promisingly high sunshine hours but as the harvest approaches there is a strong risk of damaging autumn rains.

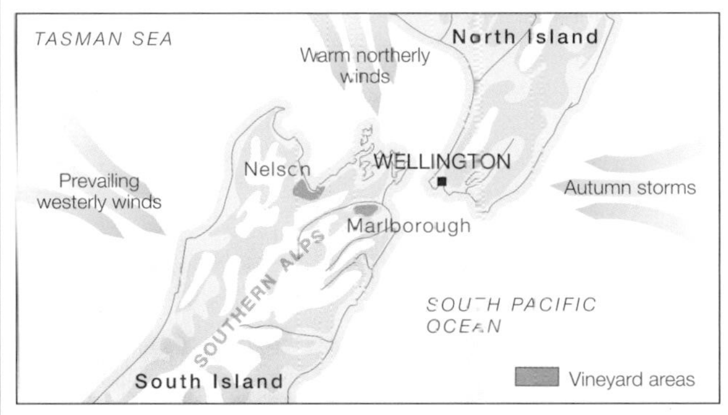

Daniel le Brun fizz from Marlborough is made by the Champagne method.

MARLBOROUGH

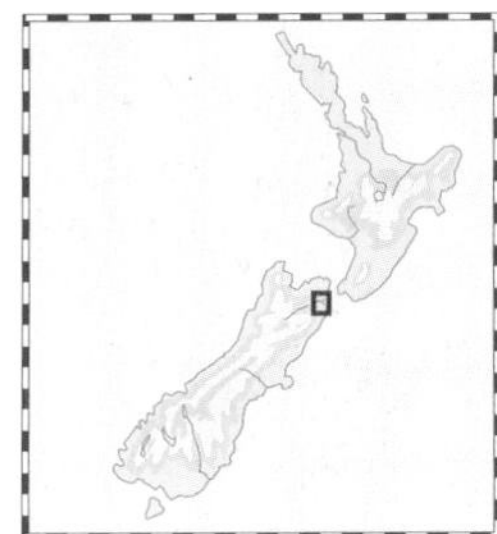

RED GRAPES
Although best-known for white wines, Marlborough also produces Cabernet Sauvignon, Cabernet Franc and Merlot. Pinot Noir is often used for sparkling wines.

WHITE GRAPES
Müller-Thurgau is declining as Sauvignon Blanc becomes increasingly important in Marlborough. Chardonnay also thrives and contributes to sparkling wine production. Rhine Riesling is very successful in botrytized wines.

CLIMATE
The climate is cool but sunshine is abundant. Rainfall is scarce between October and April, and frost and wind can be problems.

SOIL
Soil varies from clay to stony gravel. Very stony districts are so well-drained that irrigation is essential.

ASPECT
Generally low and flat, but the Awatere Valley benefits from protected terraces allowing maximum exposure.

I DON'T HAVE MANY REGRETS IN LIFE, but one thing I would like to have done is to have seen the Marlborough region in New Zealand's South Island at the beginning of the 1970s. What would I have seen? Drab pastureland, sheep, garlic, cherry trees, sheep, a dozy market town – and maybe some more sheep. Sort of… nothing much really. But I would like to have seen it precisely because it was so ordinary, so unmemorable, so dull. And because it didn't boast one single vine.

Now, in the mid-1990s, it grows more vines than any other area of New Zealand and is expanding at an exhilarating but scary rate that gives the entire region a real Klondike feel. For every vast field of vines, their lush foliage glistening in the summer sunshine, there seems to be another vast field of raw earth being straddled and stretched by posts and wires as the land is prepared for yet another carpet of vines. And there's only one reason for all this: Marlborough is such a damned good place to grow vines. In fact, I'll go further than that. It's one of the greatest places on earth to grow them, producing some of the world's most remarkable wines. And I would love to have been in on it right from the start.

But why is it so good? And is Marlborough just about Sauvignon Blanc? First – no, Marlborough isn't just about Sauvignon and it isn't just about Montana either, though they own, or control through contracts, between a third and half of Marlborough's grapes. There are now other higher-profile labels, led by the brilliant Cloudy Bay – one of the world's most sought after wines, whose first vintage was as recent as 1985.

The whole spectrum of grapes has been planted, as people have prodded and poked to see precisely what limits there are to Marlborough's abilities. Well, there are limits. Like any other great vineyard area, Marlborough is not an all-purpose producer, because then you'd have to trade memorable brilliance for overall reliability. Most of Marlborough can't do much with Cabernet Sauvignon, though where the soil is rocky and well-drained and yields are kept low, warm years will ripen it; Merlot does give good results, though. People thought the cool conditions were tailor-made for Pinot Noir, but few convincing examples have yet been made, and most ends up as fizz. Chardonnay, too, was expected to be uniformly brilliant. It isn't. Again, much of it ends up as fizz but, that said, there are already some stunning examples of luscious, full, buttery intense Chardonnays, as producers work out how to make it perform better, and we will see top-quality wines in due course.

Sauvignon Blanc was world class virtually from its first vintage and every year more new examples appear. I love Marlborough Sauvignon. You may hate it. It's that sort of wine: it demands a reaction. It would be nice if Riesling one day demanded a reaction again, as opposed to the apathy with which it is normally greeted, because Marlborough makes superb Riesling too, usually dry, occasionally lusciously sweet.

Right. So where does all this flavour intensity come from? A long, slow ripening season is the key. Blenheim, the main town, often gets more sunshine hours than any other town in New Zealand. Over a ripening season, Marlborough gets about the same amount of heat as Burgundy, and slightly less than Bordeaux. But the average daily temperature is lower than either as the sunny ripening season spreads into April, or even into May, with cold nights helping to preserve acidity.

This is fine if you can guarantee a dry autumn. Almost always, you can. Most of New Zealand's bad autumn weather comes in from the Pacific in the east and is soaked up by the North Island. The southerlies get headed off by the Southern Alps, and the wet westerlies during the growing season are headed off by the mountains to the west. Rainfall from February to April is lower than in any other New Zealand wine region, while March is Marlborough's driest month.

Given that it is relatively cool, it is vital that the growers have the confidence to let their fruit hang, and the dry autumns provide them with that, though occasionally an autumn frost may wreak havoc. A lack of rain also allows growers to minimize anti-disease programmes, with substantial cost savings.

But lack of rain means irrigation is essential. The north side of the valley has as much water as it needs from the Wairau River and its aquifers. The south side is more barren and water

In the Stoneleigh vineyard, heat radiates from the stony soil long after the sun has gone.

WHERE THE VINEYARDS ARE *Well, here it is. The world's newest fine wine region in all its glory. Every vine you see here has been planted since 1973. And a lot more of those wide open spaces that gaze out so invitingly from the map will be filled with vines in the next few years.*

But not all of Marlborough is suitable for vines. Much of the land towards the sea at the right of the map is too silty, and despite the odd gravelly patch, most of these low-lying parts are too prone to frost for successful viticulture. Indeed, spring and autumn frosts can strike right the way up the valley.

Conditions are quite different on the two sides of the Wairau plains. In the north, near the river itself, the ground is mostly very stony and well-drained with ample water supplies for irrigation. The land is generally flat, but there are dips which hold more fertile soil. Vines in the dips ripen more slowly than vines on the stony ridges.

The south side of the valley has more fertile, water-retentive soils, but not much water availability, and vines ripen up to two weeks after those near the Wairau River. The Awatere Valley is just off the bottom right-hand corner of the map, and its marginally warmer climate allied with extremely stony, low-yielding soil, offer the region's best conditions for ripening red grapes successfully.

MARLBOROUGH

VINEYARDS

TOTAL DISTANCE NORTH TO SOUTH 33KM (20½ MILES)

N

0 km 1 2

0 miles 1

often needs to be pumped from the north. However, the south needs less water, having more fertile, water-retentive soils. The vineyards in the north are mostly shallow silt over virtual free-draining gravel. In some vineyards you can't even see the soil for the stones. Add to this a drying northerly wind aiding transpiration from the leaves, and you need irrigation alright.

Just south-east of Blenheim on Highway One, the Awatere Valley has a series of incredibly stony, flat-topped river terraces. The vineyards there are some of the stoniest I have ever visited. These flat, round stones reflect heat on to the vines and then continue to radiate heat after the sun has gone. With low yields and good protection from north-westerly winds, though exposure to the occasional southerlies, Vavasour has already produced the region's best Cabernets and excellent whites too.

Marlborough is still in a quandary as it tries to decide what its role should be. Already it is acknowledged for great Sauvignon and Riesling, and excellent sparkling wine and Chardonnay. That's not bad, I'd have thought. Yet people kept asking me what the next fad flavour in Britain was going to be, and I'm sure they wanted me to say, oh, Viognier, Marsanne, Malvasia – anything they hadn't yet got so that they could fret like mad. But Marlborough must build on what it has already achieved. As my friend Auberon Waugh said, 'It's very difficult to be best in the world at anything, but New Zealand has achieved that distinction with Sauvignon Blanc. You should simply get on with the job of making more of it.' I'll drink to that.

Cloudy Bay Sauvignon Blanc has been a success since its first vintage in 1985.

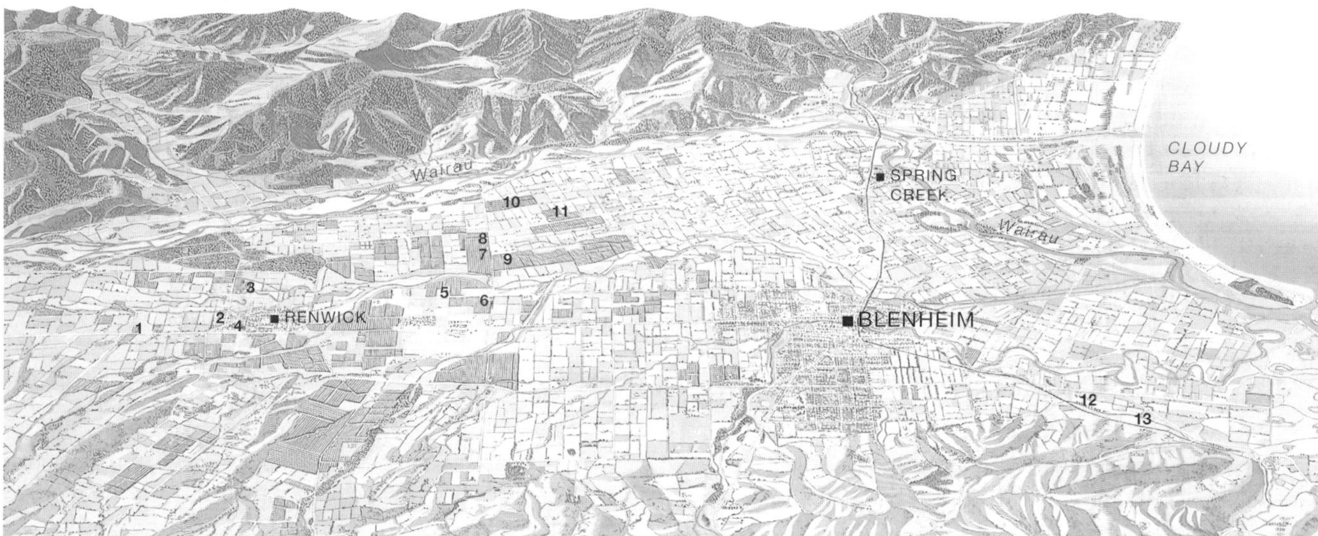

TOP WINERIES

1. Grove Mill
2. Cellier le Brun
3. Forrest
4. Te Whare Ra
5. Merlen
6. Jackson Estate
7. Allan Scott
8. Corbans Stoneleigh Cellars
9. Cloudy Bay
10. Wairau River
11. Hunters
12. Lawson's Dry Hills
13. Montana

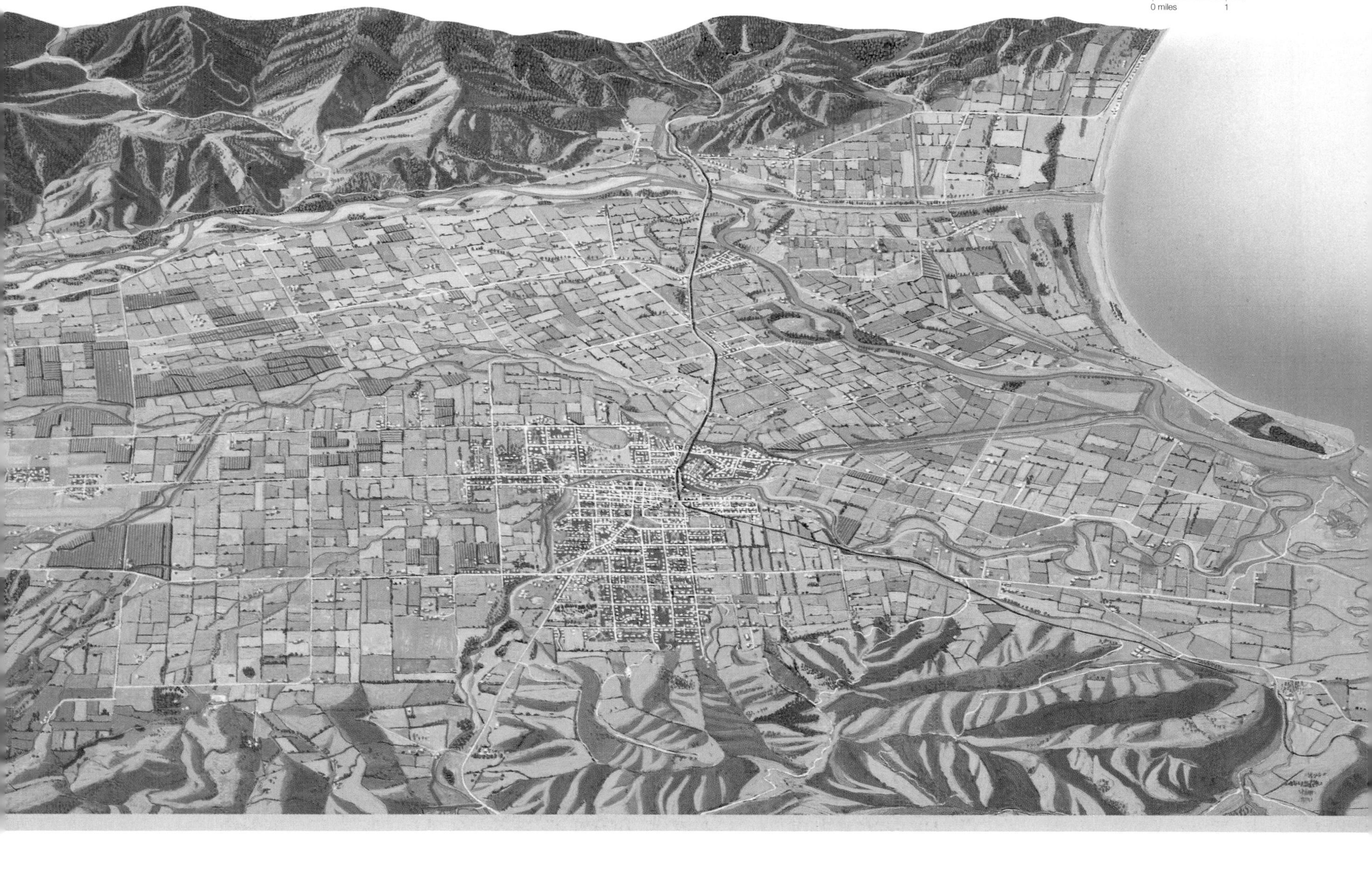

0 km 1 2
0 miles 1

SOUTH AFRICA

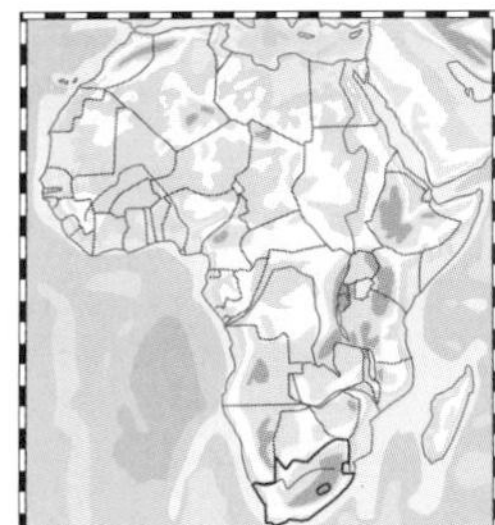

SOUTH AFRICA HAS BEEN on the brink of great things for so long that it hurts to dwell on it. I suppose I may have made my first value judgements about South Africa's wine before I pronounced on any other. My declarations were not of a particularly intelligible kind: in fact my mother had a devil of a job getting the mark out of the carpet. It was my sister's christening, you see. She's three years younger than me. My father had poured out the Paarl 'sherry' that he swore was better than the real thing from Spain before the service, so that the other guests would have a drink as soon as they got back home from the church. Yes, he should have known better. So should my brother and I. We both were punished severely.

Years later I agreed with my father. Paarl sherry was excellent. The 'ports' and fortified Muscats I then got hold of were excellent too. South Africa could clearly make good, mass volume table wines too. Through the 1970s into the 1980s in Britain, when the New World-led wine revolution was still a tiny flicker in the future, KWV Chenin Blanc white and KWV Roodeberg red did the business – full of flavour, relentlessly reliable, keen in price. There wasn't a single European brand that could match them.

And then, just occasionally, but with tantalizing infrequency, something wonderful and rare would appear from the Cape, something brimming with personality and promise. A Pinot Noir from the fledgling cold-climate Hamilton Russell Vineyards would whisper 'Burgundy' from the glass; an early Cabernet Sauvignon from Meerlust would taste uncannily similar to a St-Julien Bordeaux from the mid-1970s. But they were teasers, tiny strands of brilliance floating up from the bottom of Africa. And as rigorous anti-apartheid sanctions pushed South Africa into isolation during the 1980s, the Cape, whose wines should have been as well placed as any to lead the New World wine revolution, slithered and flailed in the wake of California, New Zealand and Australia.

This enforced isolation from the worldwide trends in wine couldn't have come at a worse time. The 1980s saw more progress in technology and winery knowledge and increased flexibility among a new wine-wise generation of drinkers unfettered by tradition than any other previous decade. Yet South Africa's only solace was to look inward and reassure herself that the wine styles she was producing were as good as any from the rest of the world. But they weren't. Her vineyards were full of diseased vines; the clones of important varieties like Cabernet, Pinot Noir and Chardonnay were inferior; there was an obsession with risk elimination and 'control' among many of her winemakers that was positively Germanic, and an unwillingness to experiment in this the most experimental decade of the century. The wine world was becoming a global village. South Africa was still the hermit on the hill.

The moment when President de Klerk released Nelson Mandela in 1990 was a signal for change. The winemakers heard the starting cannon louder than anybody. International contacts were made and remade, ideas and opinions were at last exchanged, and by the time the 1994 vintage was being celebrated with the country's first ever multiracial elections, South Africa was tumbling over herself in its rush to present a modern front, without forgetting the traditions it had already built.

Yet such traditions as there were could often be seen as shortcomings, not advantages. The use of new oak barrels to soften and deepen red and white wines is a recent phenomenon, as is the general employment of air conditioning in winemaking and storage areas. Vast tracts of the nations's vineyards were hopelessly virus-infected, leading to grapes being unable to achieve full ripeness, and the unbalanced flavour characteristics were frequently offered in a defensive tone of voice as the 'national' style. And there was, and still is a serious shortage of the top international grape varieties, as well as private estates.

South Africa is the world's eighth-largest wine producer, though its position of only twentieth in actual vineyard area shows you how high some of the vineyard yields are – as much as 350 hectolitres per hectare in the most irrigated regions like Olifantsrivier and Orange River. The vines of Stellenbosch or Paarl,

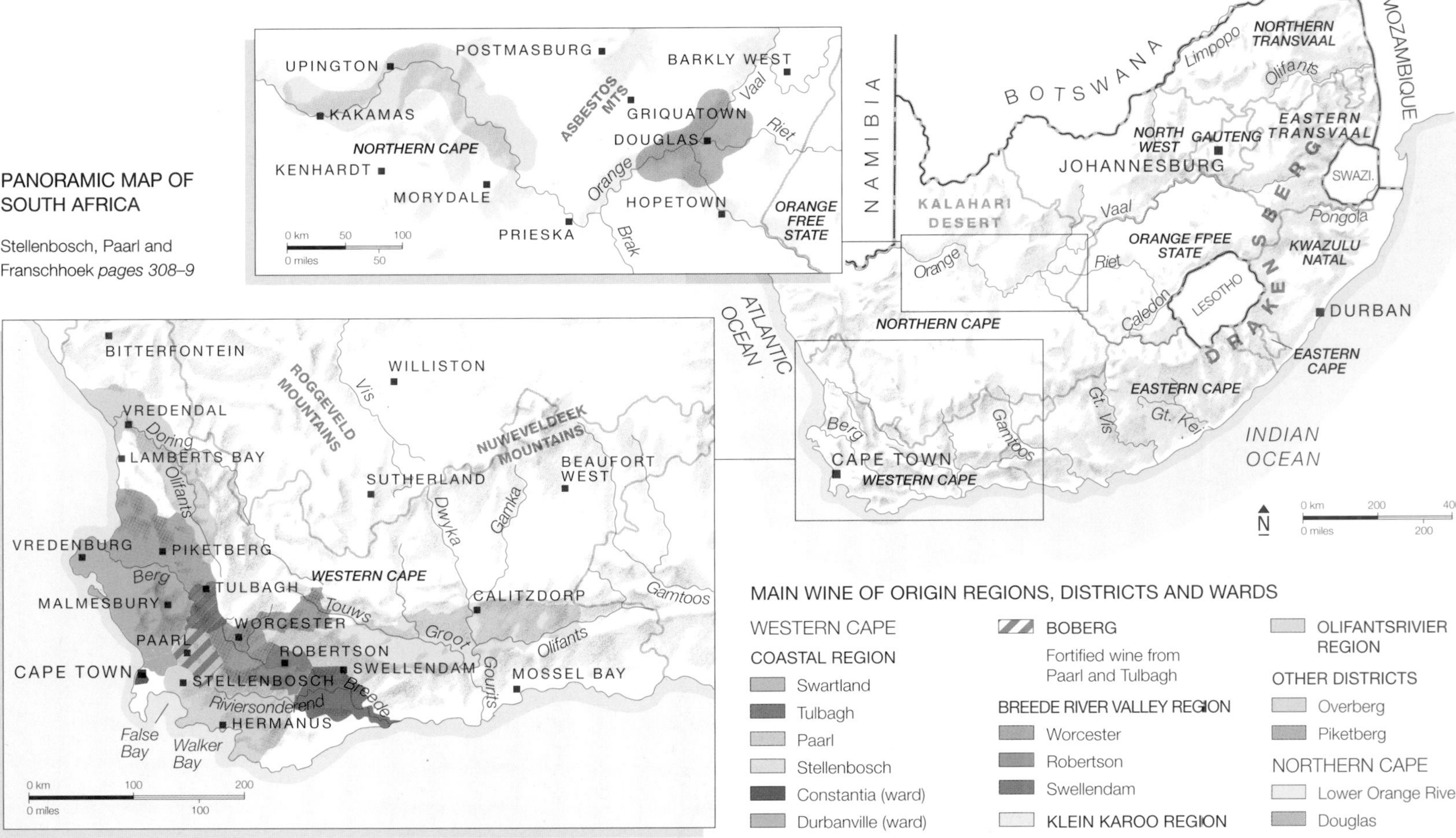

PANORAMIC MAP OF SOUTH AFRICA

Stellenbosch, Paarl and Franschhoek *pages 308–9*

however, can yield as little as 20 hectolitres per hectare. Five thousand grape growers farm these 102,000 hectares (252,000 acres), yet only about 100 produce their own wine. This number will increase every year from now, but at the moment a good 85 per cent of the crop is processed in co-operatives, dominated by the national co-operative body, the KWV. Of the annual crush less than 25 per cent ends up as table wine, and of that which does, seven out of eight bottles are white, with Chenin Blanc (here known as Steen) the dominant variety, followed by Palomino, Colombard and various Muscats. These are all quite useful for simple fruity whites and they form the bulk of South African wine exports. Cinsaut is the chief red variety, often blended with a gutsy local variety Pinotage, and both of these can make good wine. Yet none of these, red or white, are the mainstream classics that have fuelled other New World success stories. It could be, of course, that the world already has enough Cabernet, Merlot, Sauvignon and Chardonnay – but I doubt it, and so do the growers here who are planting madly.

WINE REGIONS

The first vineyards were established down by Cape Town in 1655, and virtually the whole industry has since confined itself to the south-western Cape area of South Africa from about 32° to just over 34° South since this is the only area that can at least partially boast a Mediterranean climate. There's good rainfall in the cold wet winters, and the long hot summers stretching out from November right through to May would actually be too hot for really fine wines were it not for the Benguela current of chilly water that surges up from the Antarctic and sends cooling breezes inland up the river valleys. Some of the best wines are from growers who have also planted high up the slopes of the ever-present mountain ranges to further reduce temperatures. Soils also tend to be more suitable there because, although there are numerous soil types – Stellenbosch alone has more than 50 – many of them, especially in the lower, heavily planted sites, are acidic with consequent difficulties for the vine in achieving full ripeness.

Traditionally the best table wines have all come from vineyards close to False Bay with its cooling winds. Earliest and most famous are the wines of Constantia, just south of Cape Town. Spectacular sweet wines are supposed to have been made here in the eighteenth and nineteenth centuries, comparing favourably with the greatest in the world. In the 1990s, after a long gap, its reputation is being revived.

The vast majority of the top wines always have come from Paarl and Stellenbosch and its side valleys like Franschhoek, and they still do (see page 308). But the conditions there are still relatively warm, so some pioneers have headed south-east through the Hottentots-Holland mountains to the decidedly cooler regions of hilly Elgin and coastal Walker Bay. Tim Hamilton-Russell, Walker Bay's leading grower, says he wishes South Africa extended another 200km (125 miles) into the South Atlantic so that he could really emulate cool central French conditions, but he doesn't do badly as it is.

The largest volume of wine comes from much warmer inland areas, where most grapes were used for fortified wine or concentrate. However, regions like Worcester and Olifantsrivier have been transformed into producers of high-yield, light, fruity, easy-priced whites. Robertson already has taken advantage of some rare limestone soils, high temperatures and good irrigation to produce a series of top-quality whites.

THE CLASSIFICATION OF SOUTH AFRICAN WINE

The Wine of Origin system, with its certificate or seal on a wine bottle, was first introduced in 1973 and underwent a major change in 1993. From the seal's number, the entire history of the wine can be traced back to its source but quality is not guaranteed. Like many other New World wine countries, South Africa's labelling laws emphasize the grape variety, rather than the vineyard origin or wine style. Varietal wines can be made from 100 per cent of the named grape, with up to 25 per cent (15 per cent for export) of other varieties in the blend. To qualify as an 'estate', a producer must vinify his wine from grapes grown only on his property.

Mountain ranges, here the Simonsberg at the eastern end of the Stellenbosch district, form a dramatic backdrop to many of the Cape vineyards.

Stellenbosch & Paarl

RED GRAPES
The best red wines come from the classic grape varieties, Cabernets Sauvignon and Franc, Merlot and Pinot Noir. Shiraz and Pinotage also prosper here.

WHITE GRAPES
Internationally popular Chardonnay and Sauvignon Blanc are widely planted. Sémillon is a speciality of Franschhoek. Chenin Blanc and Riesling produce good sweet wines.

CLIMATE
The climate is Mediterranean in character, with most rainfall in winter and fairly hot, dry summers. The much-needed cooling winds of summer, known as the 'Cape Doctor' blow across the land from False Bay.

SOIL
The eastern mountain slopes of granite favour red wine production. The sandier soils in the west are better suited to white wines.

ASPECT
Historically the vineyards were planted in low-lying river valleys but quality producers are now planting up on the mountain slopes which benefit from cooler altitude, cooling sea breezes and less direct exposure to the sun.

Pinotage is South Africa's most famous home-bred grape variety.

The most enduring memory of my arrival in the Cape will soon be nothing more than that – just a memory, and despite its beauty, it will disappear into legend unlamented by the winemakers of South Africa. As I drove from the airport out towards Somerset West, then turned north towards Stellenbosch along the banks of the Eerste river, a great carpet of purply crimson vines stretched away on both sides of the road glinting in the evening sun and casting a glorious rose glow onto the slopes of the Helderberg rearing up like giants' teeth to the east. The dark red vine leaves seemed like the perfect harbinger of succulent red wines stuffed with the ripeness of the southern sun.

Far from it. This memorable sight was nothing more than that of an entire vineyard region suffering from virus infection. It looked wonderful, but these leaves had turned red and curled up before the grapes were ripe. It used to happen every year, halting photosynthesis, arresting the build up of sugars, leaving acids too high and tannins too raw to make balanced wine. If you ever wondered why even the finest traditional Cape reds seemed acid and harsh, the reason lay in that gorgeous autumn spread of blood-red, wine-dark foliage gladdening the eye and killing the chance of great wine.

Nowadays an autumn drive around Stellenbosch and Paarl will still reveal pockets of virused vines, but enormous efforts are being made to replant the vineyards with high-quality clones of virus-free stock which will sprout bright green leaves until every grape has been ripened and picked. And it can't happen fast enough, because ranged beneath the towering peaks of the Helderberg, the Stellenbosch, the Simonsberg and the Drakensteinberg mountains are some stunning vineyard sites, few of which have even yet begun to show what they can do. All of these sites are relatively warm and relatively dry. If you want vineyards a little bit cooler and wetter, those of the Constantia Valley within the confines of Cape Town itself would suit your purpose. If you want conditions a good deal cooler and damper, then the areas of Elgin and Walker Bay, to the east of the Helderberg range, are just beginning to be exploited and Mossel Bay, about 300km (200 miles) to the east, is new and exciting. All of these have to take the full blast of the southern winds cooled by the Benguela Current from Antarctica and are eager to do so. But the heart of South Africa's quality wine tradition lies in Stellenbosch and Paarl.

And it is a relatively warm-climate tradition. Though Stellenbosch would like to claim for itself a cool-climate description, the growers have to fight quite hard, searching out cooler mesoclimates that are angled away from the sun, and exposed to the maritime breezes that regularly blow off False Bay directly to the south. The most imaginative and most successful are those who have pushed their vineyards up the mountain slopes in places as high as 600m (1970ft), cooling their vines through altitude and less direct exposure to the sun. Paarl has never claimed to be a cool area, receiving only the tail end of the False Bay breezes as well as some Atlantic winds from the west, and yet it has produced many of the most successful wines, both from supposedly cool-climate varieties like Chardonnay as well as warmer varieties like Shiraz and Cabernet. But then Australia would be the first to tell South Africa that there's nothing wrong with a warm climate so long as you learn how to handle it. Indeed, Paarl's initial reputation was for fortified wine and, in particular, 'sherry'. Paarl 'sherry', produced by the solera system, is remarkably good, and flor yeast grows as naturally here as it does in Spain's Jerez. The fortified wine regions of South Australia are at about 34° South, Paarl is at 33.45° South. They also make

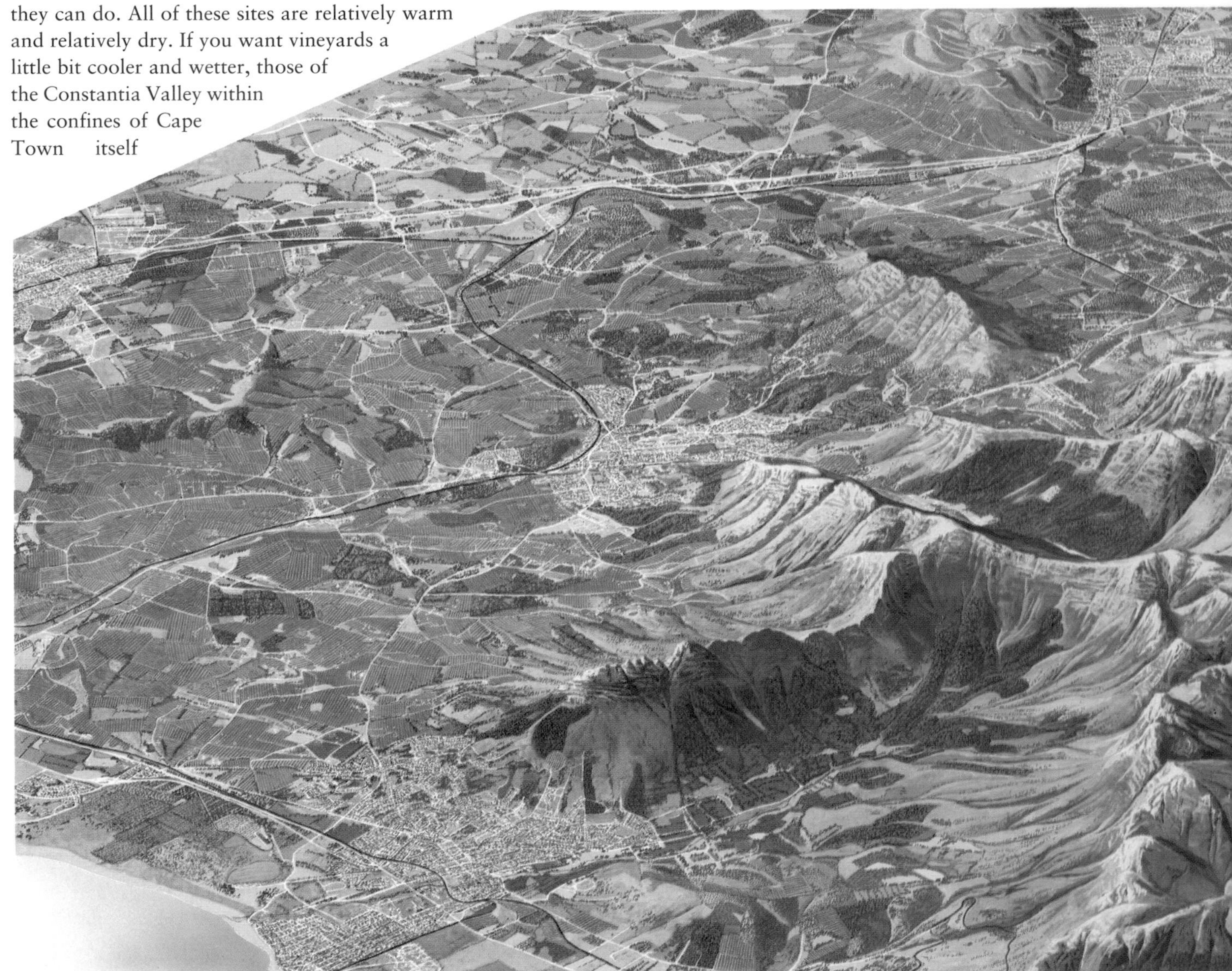

wonderful flor 'sherry' and use the solera system. And they, just like Paarl, have been able to convert to table wines with enormous success. South Australia's Barossa Valley and Riverland vineyards produce big, ripe Shiraz, Cabernet and Chardonnay. Paarl Shiraz and Chardonnay are big, gutsy styles too, and both Merlot and, amazingly, Sauvignon Blanc show excellent form.

The current 'head for the hills' philosophy is effective for more than just temperature. Rainfall, though not great, is more plentiful up there on the hills, and the soils are in general decomposed granites, well-drained and not too fertile. One of the biggest problems of the flatter, valley floor vineyards which still dominate the region is that the soils are high in clay content and extremely acid, restricting the development of a healthy vine root system. A criticism frequently levelled at South African white wines is that acidity levels are too aggressive, yet when the winemakers have been forced to adjust the acidity levels for generations just to make a decent drink, the national palate can easily get to like a level of acidity that other nationalities find excessive.

Though excellent white wines, in particular, have come from further inland at Worcester and especially at Robertson, where limestone outcrops help growers defy the hot, arid climates and produce wines of great finesse, the most exciting wines of the near future are still likely to come from Paarl and Stellenbosch and the various side valleys, only one of which, Franschhoek, has so far been exploited extensively. Vineyard areas need a ready market to flourish, and although the main national marketplace of Johannesburg at about 1600km (1000 miles) is equally far from most of the Cape vineyards, Stellenbosch is only an easy 45-km (28-mile) drive from Cape Town, with Paarl in the next valley. Stellenbosch in particular is a gorgeous university town, full of Cape Dutch and Cape Georgian buildings and surrounded by independent wine estates eager to sell to the legions of visitors. In a country only just beginning to find its modern wine identity, and with the vast majority of its production still dominated by co-operatives, this concentration of characterful private estates will provide the variety and the healthy competition needed to see just how good South Africa can be.

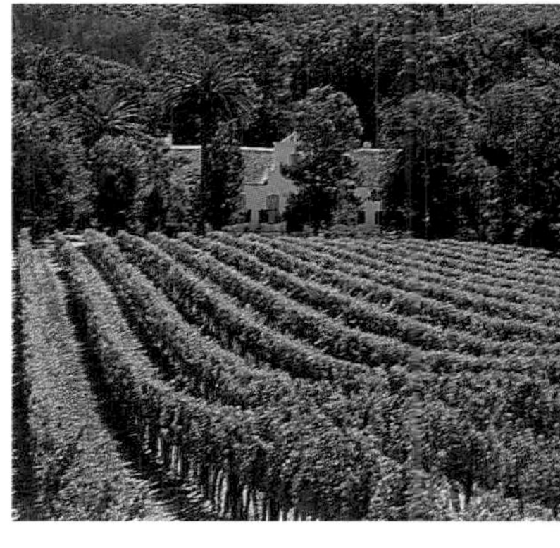

The Buitenverwachtung vineyards in the hills behind Cape Town were part of the famous Constantia estate, founded by Simon van der Stel in 1685.

WHERE THE VINEYARDS ARE *The most important feature in this map is down in the bottom left-hand corner – the chilly water of False Bay. With the Stellenbosch and Paarl vineyards lying around 34° South, the sun would simply be too strong for fragrant, subtle wines to be produced. But the Benguela Current swoops up from the Antarctic and bathes the Cape in icy water. Every day as the sun warms the vines at Stellenbosch and Paarl, cold breezes are drawn inland from False Bay, keeping the vines cool enough to produce fine quality fruit. The next most important feature on the map are the mountains. They really are spectacular and the contrast between cosy verdant valley farms with their delightful Cape Dutch whitewashed homesteads and these towering peaks is worth the trip for that alone. But the mountains have a more important role to play than mere tourist fodder. They provide excellent, sloping vineyard sites, up to about 600m (1970ft) high at which point the slopes generally become too steep for cultivation and the soil gives way to bare rock, and mostly facing away from the direct sunlight. But of course these sites are much more difficult to work than the vineyards on the river flats, and yields are lower, if of far higher quality. So if you look at the map and think, well, most of the vineyards are not on the mountain slopes, they're on the valley floor: quite right – for now. But every year will see more intrepid wine enthusiasts trekking up those slopes, clearing the soil, and planting vines.*

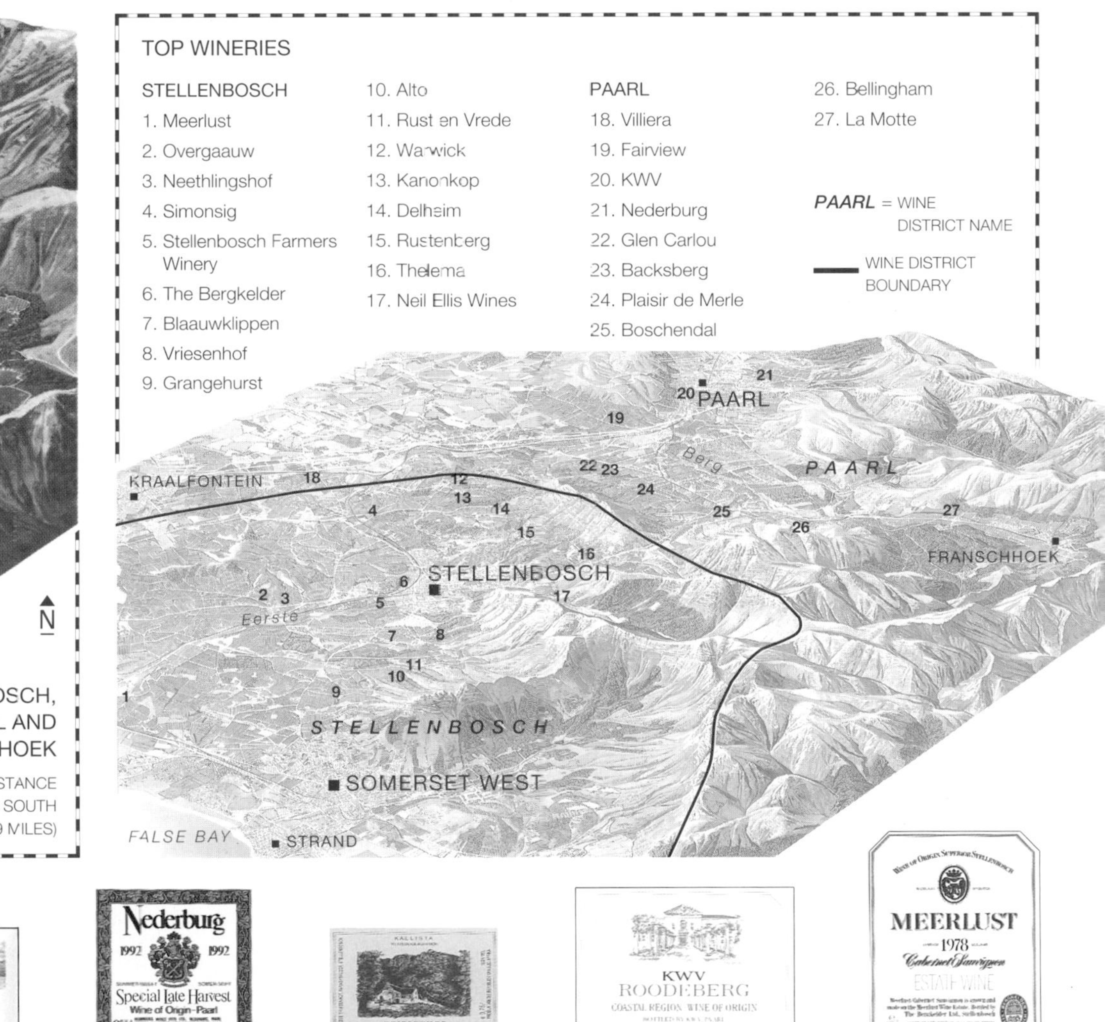

NORTH AFRICA

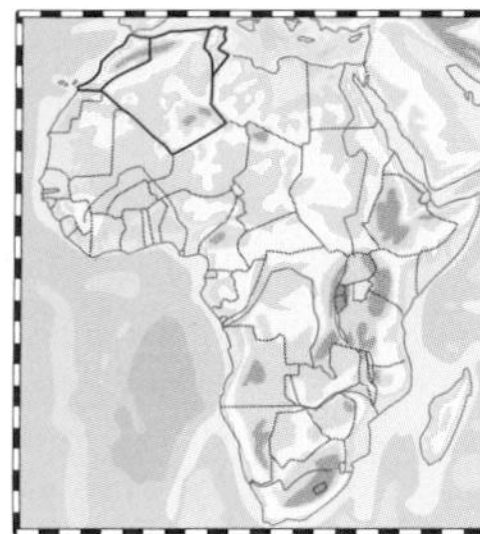

IT'S THE WASTED POTENTIAL that makes me want to cry. There are so many good vineyards here – or at least, vineyards that could be good, if anybody bothered, if anybody cared. Eighty per cent of the vines in Algeria are over 40 years old. Anywhere else – for example, in Australia or Burgundy – they'd be jumping up and down with resources like that. They'd be making incredibly concentrated, earthy, spicy red wines and they'd have buyers queuing down the street. What happens here? Nothing. They just go on making rough, fruitless, baked wines without flavour or acidity. Yet you can't blame the growers or the winemakers. There simply hasn't been a market for these wines since the French left in the 1950s and early 1960s. And as the French quit their colonies, the best winemakers left too, heading for France's Midi, where they're currently engaged in the renaissance of that region.

France was North Africa's biggest market for wine from the early 1900s onwards, and in the 1950s between one half and two-thirds of the entire international wine trade was in North African wines. When the wine arrived in France it was mostly blended, in a way that would be illegal now. As the market fell away, so did the area under vine: Algeria, always the biggest producer of the three North African wine countries, boasted 400,000 hectares (990,000 acres) in 1938, and just 102,000 hectares (252,000 acres) in 1990, with only 40 per cent of those grapes destined for the winery rather than the table.

When the French left Morocco in 1956, the area in the country under wine vines was about 55,000 hectares (136,000 acres); this had fallen to about 13,000 hectares (32,100 acres) by 1990. Tunisia's vineyards have also shrunk to 29,000 hectares (71,500 acres), of which around half produce wine grapes.

CLIMATE

And yet it's not all doom and gloom – or it needn't be. The vineyards that have been uprooted are those on the hot plains: those that remain are on the cooler coastal ranges, where they are planted at up to 1200m (4000 ft) above sea level. This relatively high altitude for viticulture also helps in the search for cooler temperatures. Morocco, in particular, unlike Algeria and Tunisia, benefits from an Atlantic coastline with its cooling breezes. However, wind can be a problem here: imagine being a vine in a near-desert country, with winds sweeping in from the Atlantic at 65km (40 miles) per hour. In Tunisia it's the hot, dry Scirocco wind that reduces the yields. What all these countries badly need is specialist advice on the sort of trellising and planting that could provide protection from the wind. Because there's no reason why they couldn't be making brilliant wines – if they took the right advice. Sure, it's hot and dry. In Algeria the vineyards only get between 400 and 600mm (16 and 24in) of rain each year, with the more westerly vineyard areas like Coteaux de Mascara getting the lower figure. But parts of Spain are drier than that.

GRAPE VARIETIES

Most of the grape varieties planted in North Africa's vineyards are frankly not exciting. Carignan is king, and shows over and over again just what reliably fruitless, tough red wine it can produce. Alicante Bouschet, Aramon and Cinsaut are equally uninspiring, though Cinsaut can do better if it's handled well. But there is also some Cabernet Sauvignon, Syrah and Mourvèdre: the growers should concentrate on these last three varieties and forget trying to grow cool-climate vines like Pinot Noir. Because sometimes when you taste the better reds, you get a glimpse – just a glimpse – of what sort of wines they could achieve. Earthy, dusty, rather rustic (I'm not asking for miracles here), but with some sweetly ripe raspberry fruit. A bit of carbonic maceration could help no end in getting some juiciness and freshness into the wines.

As for whites, there's a fair bit of Clairette and Ugni Blanc, both of which could make reasonable fresh wines if the investment were available, which it is not. Tunisia's sweet and dry Muscats are probably the best whites. They're generally pretty hefty, but at least they have perfume and fruit. Clairette and Ugni Blanc, both contenders for the world's dullest wine grape, are never going to be thrilling, and here they always tend to lack acidity.

But investment is the crucial problem. No market equals no spare cash. North Africans aren't great wine drinkers, and the growth of Islamic fundamentalism means that attitudes to wine are increasingly ambiguous. On the one hand, the Koran forbids the drinking of alcohol, but on the other, the hard currency earned from wine exports is an overwhelming attraction. So wine continues to be made and exported, and it is in this trend that one can find a tiny ray of hope for the future, since if they want to export more, they'll have to make it better. But don't hold your breath.

ASIA

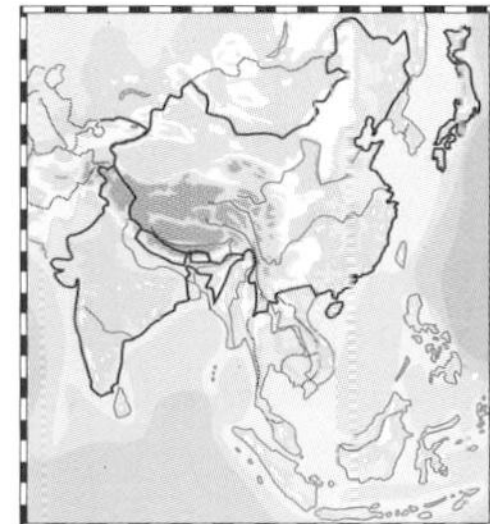

OH, THE WONDERS of the East. Replete with exotic scents and spices, Asia has forever bewitched us with its charms. This has always been a place of travellers' tales, of things so strange that nobody has quite believed them. And even in our prosaic century, when we thought there were no more wonders left, here they are. Go to the magical East and you'll find grape varieties called Cow's Nipple and Cock's Heart. You'll find vineyards planted 150m (500ft) below sea level. You'll find Siberian cold and tropical heat. And you'll find a history of wine-making that goes back over 2000 years. In none of these Asian countries, though, has wine proved as overwhelmingly popular as it has in Western Europe; and so they are, inevitably, on the fringes of the wine-making world, dependent on Western advice if they wish to export. Some Asian countries have already made use of Western expertise – most noticeable among them are China and India.

Irrigation canals flood the vines with much-needed water in India's Maharashtra hills above Bombay.

CHINA

In China, where roughly one-fifth of the total grape crop is turned into wine from some 65,000 hectares (160,000 acres) of vineyards, the inland regions, with their extreme climate, are best for dessert grapes or raisins – that, indeed, is the destination of those below-sea-level grapes, grown in Xinjiang province in the north-west. In the north-east, a maritime climate, moderate but for the occasional typhoon, produces the best wines, particularly in the coastal provinces of Shandong, Hebei and Tianjin. Many of the grape varieties are German or Russian, but joint ventures with the French companies Rémy Martin and Pernod Ricard have led to increased plantings of Chardonnay, on south-east- and south-west-facing slopes. This Western involvement has led to a major change of style. The Chinese taste in wine (really the Chinese taste is for rice wine, or better still, brandy, or better still, Cognac) is for something sweetish and probably oxidized. But there's no point in planting Chardonnay to make that sort of thing, and in any case, it is Western wallets these wines are aimed at. So, just like everywhere else in the world, the newest Chinese wines seem to imitate classic European styles. So far they show promise.

INDIA

India's fame as a wine-producing country is due entirely to Omar Khayyam, a Champagne-method sparkler launched in 1985, made in collaboration with Piper-Heidsieck of Champagne. The grapes for it are grown in the Maharashtra hills above Bombay, and it is these highland areas that come nearest to escaping India's heat. Even so, huge amounts of irrigation are necessary. Omar Khayyam is a blend of Chardonnay, Ugni Blanc, Pinot Noir, Pinot Blanc and Thompson Seedless: clean, perfectly drinkable, but frankly not up to the excitement with which it was greeted at its launch. Other wines are also produced by the same company called Indage: a sweeter fizz called Marquise de Pompadour, and a red and white still wine optimistically called Riviera. But *vinifera* vines must be grafted in India because phylloxera reached the subcontinent in the 1890s, and wreaked as much havoc with the local wine industry as it did everywhere else. The state of Maharashtra produces around 40 per cent of India's grapes, the rest coming from Karnataka, Andhra Pradesh and the Punjab, although less than one per cent of the total are made into wine.

JAPAN

In Japan the problem is not drought, as in India, but too much rain. There are monsoons in spring and autumn, typhoons in summer, and winters are icy. The land is either mountainous or flat and waterlogged; there's not much of the gently sloping terrain beloved of vine growers. Nevertheless, a vine-trellising system called *tana-zukuri* has been devised which spreads the vine out along wires and allows it to dry, and the Mount Fuji area, west of Tokyo, is proving the best so far. On the east coast it becomes more extreme. In all, wine is produced in 46 out of 47 Japanese provinces, with tropical Okinawa being the odd one out. Japanese varieties and hybrids account for most of the vineyards, and only about ten per cent of the grapes are used to make wine anyway. The favourite *vinifera* vine is Koshu which produces big, juicy dessert grapes and light white wines. The quantity of rain, and the high yields given by the vines tend to make most Japanese wines light in body. Suntory make some exceptions to the rule, from Bordeaux varieties.

INDEX

Note: D = Diagram, K = Map Key, M = Map

D

E

F

G

N

O

Picture Credits

The publishers would like to thank the following for supplying photographs for the Wine Atlas.

Page 1 Mick Rock/Cephas Picture Library; 5 Mick Rock/Cephas Picture Library; 6 Mick Rock/Cephas Picture Library; 7 Mick Rock/Cephas Picture Library; 8 (above) Mick Rock/Cephas Picture Library; (below) Mick Rock/Cephas Picture Library; 9 Rick England/Cephas Picture Library; 10 Mick Rock/Cephas Picture Library; 12 (above) Mick Rock/Cephas Picture Library; (below) Mick Rock/Cephas Picture Library; 13 Mick Rock/Cephas Picture Library; 14 Andy Christodolo/Cephas Picture Library; 16 (above) Mick Rock/Cephas Picture Library; (below left) Mick Rock/Cephas Picture Library; (below right) Ted Stefanski/Cephas Picture Library; 17 (left) Nigel Blythe/Cephas Picture Library; (right) Kevin Judd/Cephas Picture Library; 18 (above) Mick Rock/Cephas Picture Library; (centre left) Mick Rock/Cephas Picture Library; (centre right) Mick Rock/Cephas Picture Library; (below left) Mick Rock/Cephas Picture Library; (below right) Mick Rock/Cephas Picture Library; 20 (above left) Mick Rock/Cephas Picture Library; (above right) Mick Rock/Cephas Picture Library; (centre above) Jerry Alexander/Cephas Picture Library; (centre below) Mick Rock/Cephas Picture Library; (far below) Mick Rock/Cephas Picture Library; 21 (top row left) Alain Proust/Cephas Picture Library; (top row centre) Mick Rock/Cephas Picture Library; (top row right) Mick Rock/Cephas Picture Library; (second row left) Mick Rock/Cephas Picture Library; (second row centre) Mick Rock/Cephas Picture Library; (second row right) Mick Rock/Cephas Picture Library; (third row left) Mick Rock/Cephas Picture Library; (third row centre) Mick Rock/Cephas Picture Library; (third row right) Mick Rock/Cephas Picture Library; (bottom row left) Mick Rock/Cephas Picture Library; (bottom row centre) Mick Rock/Cephas Picture Library; (bottom row right) Nigel Blythe/Cephas Picture Library; 22 Mick Rock/Cephas Picture Library; 25 (above) Kevin Argue; (below) Mick Rock/Cephas Picture Library; 26 Mick Rock/Cephas Picture Library; 30-1 Mick Rock/Cephas Picture Library; 36 (above) Mick Rock/Cephas Picture Library; (below) Mick Rock/Cephas Picture Library; 37 Philippe Roy; 38-9 Mick Rock/Cephas Picture Library; 43 Michel Guillard/Scope; 46 Michel Guillard/Scope; 49 Mick Rock/Cephas Picture Library; 52 (above) Philippe Roy; (below) Michael Busselle; 53 Philippe Roy; 56 Mick Rock/Cephas Picture Library; 57 Jean-Luc Bard/Scope; 59 M. Plassart/Explorer; 61 Jean-Luc Bard/Scope; 62 Michael Busselle; 64 P. Wysocki/Explorer; 66 Jean-Luc Bard/Scope; 68 Francis Jalain/Explorer; 72 Jean-Daniel Sudres/Scope; 74 Mick Rock/Cephas Picture Library; 75 Michael Busselle; 76 Michael Busselle; 83 Michael Busselle; 84 Stuart Boreham/Cephas Picture Library; 87 Daniel Valla/Cephas Picture Library; 88 Mick Rock/Cephas Picture Library; 92 Mick Rock/Cephas Picture Library; 93 Michael Busselle; 95 Jacques Guillard/Scope; 96 Jacques Guillard/Scope; 100 Mick Rock/Cephas Picture Library; 103 Michael Busselle; 105 Michael Busselle; 106 Michael Busselle; 109 Jean-Daniel Sudres/Scope; 110 Michael Busselle; 112-13 Zefa Pictures; 119 Jacques Guillard/Scope; 120 Jacques Guillard/Scope; 122 Werner Otto; 125 Mick Rock/Cephas Picture Library; 129 Janet Price; 131 Janet Price; 132 Werner Otto; 136 Nigel Blythe/Cephas Picture Library; 138 Zefa Pictures; 140 Janet Price; 141 Hans-Joachim Boldt/NBL; 143 Hans-Peter Siffert/Fotos der Weinwelt; 145 Mick Rock/Cephas Picture Library; 147 Milan Horacek/Bilderberg; 149 Mick Rock/Cephas; 152-3 Mick Rock/Cephas Picture Library; 156 Mick Rock/Cephas Picture Library; 157 Mick Rock/Cephas Picture Library; 158 Mick Rock/Cephas Picture Library; 159 Hans-Peter Siffert/ Fotos der Weinwelt; 162 Mick Rock/Cephas Picture Library; 165 Hans-Peter Siffert/Fotos der Weinwelt; 169 Mick Rock/Cephas Picture Library; 170 Mick Rock/Cephas Picture Library; 172-3 Jan Traylen/Patrick Eagar; 176 Jan Traylen/Patrick Eagar; 179 Mick Rock/Cephas Picture Library; 182-3 Mick Rock/Cephas Picture Library; 186 Mick Rock/Cephas Picture Library; 189 Mick Rock/Cephas Picture Library; 192 Mick Rock/Cephas Picture Library; 193 Mick Rock/Cephas Picture Library; 195 (above) Mick Rock/Cephas Picture Library; (below) Mick Rock/Cephas Picture Library; 197 Mick Rock/Cephas Picture Library; 198 Michael Busselle; 201 Mick Rock/Cephas Picture Library; 203 Michael Busselle; 204-5 Mick Rock/Cephas Picture Library; 208 Mick Rock/Cephas Picture Library; 209 Mick Rock/Cephas Picture Library; 212 Mick Rock/Cephas Picture Library; 213 Mick Rock/Cephas Picture Library; 215 David Copeman/Cephas Picture Library; 217 M. J. Kielty/Cephas Picture Library; 218 Mick Rock/Cephas Picture Library; 219 Janet Price; 221 M Barlow/Trip; 223 Mick Rock/Cephas Picture Library; 225 Joco Znidarsic/Delo; 227 Mick Rock/Cephas Picture Library; 229 Helen Stylianou/Cephas Picture Library; 230-1 Ted Stefanski/Cephas Picture Library; 235 R&K Muschenetz/Cephas Picture Library; 236 Mick Rock/Cephas Picture Library; 239 Mick Rock/Cephas Picture Library; 243 Mick Rock/Cephas Picture Library; 244 Mick Rock/Cephas Picture Library; 247 Zefa Pictures; 248 Bryan Pearce/Cephas Picture Library; 249 Fred Lyon; 250 Mick Rock/Cephas Picture Library; 254 Mick Rock/Cephas Picture Library; 257 Fred R. Palmer/Cephas Picture Library; 260 Mick Rock/Cephas Picture Library; 261 Kevin Argue; 262 Andy Christodolo/Cephas Picture Library; 263 Andy Christodolo/Cephas Picture Library; 264-5 Andy Christodolo/Cephas Picture Library; 268-9 Andy Christodolo/Cephas Picture Library; 269 Andy Christodolo/Cephas Picture Library; 270-1 Patrick Eagar; 274 Patrick Eagar; 277 Patrick Eagar; 278 Patrick Eagar; 283 Mick Rock/Cephas Picture Library; 286 Patrick Eagar; 290 Mick Rock/Cephas Picture Library; 293 Mick Rock/Cephas Picture Library; 294 H. Shearing/Cephas Picture Library; 295 Chris Davis/Cephas Picture Library; 296 Mick Rock/Cephas Picture Library; 299 Mick Rock/Cephas Picture Library; 302 Mick Rock/Cephas Picture Library; 303 Mick Rock/Cephas Picture Library; 304 G. R. Roberts/Documentary Photographs; 307 Patrick Eagar; 309 Patrick Eagar; 311 Janet Price

Acknowledgments

The publishers would like to thank the countless people all over the world who have given invaluable help and advice in preparing the maps and diagrams in this Atlas, and especially the following:

FRANCE

Jean-Claude Audebert, Bourgueil
Jean Baumard, Domaine Baumard
Christine Behey Molines, FIAL, Languedoc
Daniel Brissot, Cave de Tain l'Hermitage
Yves Chidaine, Montlouis
CIVCR, Rhône
Joël Deniau, Maison du Vin, Saumur
Mme Denoune, CIVA, Alsace
M. d'Espinay, INAO, Paris
Franck Duboeuf, Georges Duboeuf
M. Fribourg, INAO, Valence
GETEVAY, Chablis
Oliver Humbrecht, Domaine Zind-Humbrecht
Institut Technique du Vin
M. Lescaillon, INAO Centre d'Épernay
Anne Marbot, Fiona Morrison MW, CIVB, Bordeaux
Catherine Manac'h, Sopexa, London
Jean-Michel Masson, Syndicat Viticole de Pouilly
A.F. Milo, CIVCP, Provence
Office International de la Vigne et du Vin (OIV), Paris
Alain Paret, St Pierre-de-Boeuf
Rapet Père et Fils, Pernand-Vergelesses
René Renou, Domaine de Terrebrune
Jean-Max Roger, Sancerre
Professor G. Seguin, Bordeaux University
Jean-Charles Servant, BIVB, Bourgogne
Syndicat Viticole d'Aloxe-Corton
Syndicat Viticole de St-Émilion
Various Syndicats Viticoles in Bordeaux

GERMANY

Peter Anheuser, Weingut Paul Anheuser
Matthew Boucher, Barbara Tysome, German Wine Information Service, London
Bernhard Breuer, Weingut Georg Breuer
Deinhard and Co, London and Germany
Hessisches Landesamt für Bodenforschung
Karl-Heinz Johner, Baden
Carl Koenen
Horst Kolesch, Weingut Juliusspital
Rainer Lingenfelder, Weingut Lingenfelder
Egon Müller, Egon Müller Jr, Weingut Egon Müller-Scharzhof
Weingut Rudolf Müller
Margaret Rand
Dirk Richter, Weingut Max Ferd. Richter
Dr Thanisch, Weingut Dr Thanisch
Verband Deutscher Prädikats und Qualitätsweingüter
Peter von Weymarn, Weingut Heyl von Herrnsheim

SWITZERLAND

Provins, Valais
Margaret Rand

AUSTRIA

Ferdinand Auersperg, Österreichische Weinmarketingservice
Geoffrey Kelly, Austrian Wine Information Service, London
Margaret Rand

ITALY

Dr Maurizio Castelli, Progetto Agricoltura SRL
Emilio Fasoletti, Consorzio Valpolicella
David Gleave MW
Dr Giacchina La Franca, Italian Trade Centre, London
Alois Lageder, Azienda Vitivinicola Alois Lageder
Paul Merritt
Pietro Ratti, Cantine Renato Ratti
Dr Vanni Tavagnacco, Servizio della Vitivinicoltura, ERSA
Aldo Vacca, Produttori del Barbaresco

SPAIN

Susy Atkins
Berta Bartolomé, Consejo Regulador de la DOC Rioja
Raül Bobet, Miguel Torres SA
Iñigo Cañedo, Rioja Wine Exporters Group
Joachin Galvez, Madrid
Josep Ribas, Consejo Regulador DO Penedés
Juan Ruiz, INDO
Bartolome Vergara, ACES, Jerez de la Frontera
Blanca Villalba, Consejo Regulador de la DO Jerez
Jeremy Watson, Wines from Spain, London
Javier Zaccagnini, Consejo Regulador DO Ribera del Duero

PORTUGAL

Joanna Delaforce
Direcção Regional de Agricultura, Região Autónoma da Madeira
Jacques Faro da Silva, Madeira Wine Company
Bruce Guimaraens, Fonseca Guimaraens
Richard Mayson

ENGLAND, EASTERN EUROPE AND EASTERN MEDITERREAN

Adam Montefiore, Golan Heights Winery
Angela Vitkovitch, Vitkovitch Brothers, London
Janez Vrečer, Poslovna Skupnost za Vinogradništvo in Vinarstvo Slovenije
Simon Woods
John Worontschak, Thames Valley Vineyard

USA

Steve Burns, Pat McKelvey, Wine Institute of California, San Francisco
Carneros Quality Alliance
Stan Clarke, Viticultural Consultant, Grandview, Washington State
Larry Challacombe, Oregon Wine Advisory Board
Carla Chambers, Yamhill County Vineyards Association
John Clewes, Konocti Winery
David Crippen, Mitch Timko, Covey Run
Sally Gordon, Gary Lipp, Chalone Wine Group
Tim Hanni MW, Wine World Estates
Dan Kleck, Palmer Vineyards
McDowell Valley Vineyards
Richard Sanford, Sanford
Paul Sheffer, Sonoma Valley Vintners and Growers Alliance
Simon Siegl, Washington Wine Commission
Don Talley, Talley Vineyards
Rick Theis, Sonoma County Grape Growers Association
University of California at Davis
US Government Bureau of Alcohol, Tobacco and Firearms (BATF)
Steve Vuylsteke, Oak Knoll
Larry Walker
Dick Ward, Saintsbury/Napa Valley Vintners Association
Wade Wolfe, Hogue Wine Cellars

SOUTH AMERICA

David Murray, Canepa
Richard Neill
Sue Pike, Wines of Chile, London
Asociación de Exportadores y Embotelladores de Vinos A.G.

AUSTRALIA

Chris and Angus Barnes, Blaxlands, Hunter Valley Vineyard Association
Tony Brady, Wendouree
Peter Douglas, Wynn's Coonawarra
Ralph Fowler, Richard Hamilton Wines
Dr Tony Jordan, Domaine Chandon
Tony Keys
Tim Knappstein, Tim Knappstein Wines
Max and Stephen Lake, Lake's Folly Vineyards
The producers of the Lower Hunter Valley
Joan McGuren, Wine Industry of Western Australia
Bob McLean, St Hallett
Liz Morrison, Hay Shed Hill Vineyard
Hazel Murphy, Wine of Australia, London
Southcorp Wines, Coonawarra
Chris Rogers, Adam Wynn, Eden Valley Winemakers Association
The Viticultural Council of the South East of South Australia

NEW ZEALAND

Vicky Bishop, The New Zealand Wine Guild, London
John Buck, Philip Gregan, Wine Institute of New Zealand
Alwyn Corban, Ngatarawa
David Jordan, Horticultural and Food Research Institute of New Zealand

SOUTH AFRICA

Dave Hughes
Dave Johnson, Cape Bay Wines

GENERAL

The Royal Geographic Society Map Room
Thanks are also due to many other wine producers worldwide and their UK importers, Sandy Carr and Douglas Wilson